ENCYCLOPEDIA OF HOME DESIGNS

500 HOUSE PLANS

HOME PLANNERS, LLC
Wholly owned by Hanley-Wood, Inc.
TUCSON, ARIZONA

Published by Home Planners, LLC
Wholly owned by Hanley-Wood, Inc.

Editorial and Corporate Offices:
3275 West Ina Road, Suite 110
Tucson, Arizona 85741

Distribution Center:
29333 Lorie Lane
Wixom, Michigan 48393

Rickard D. Bailey, CEO and Publisher
Stephen Williams, Director of Sales & Marketing
Cindy Coatsworth Lewis, Director of Publications
Jan Prideaux, Senior Editor
Paulette Mulvin, Project Editor
Sara Lisa Rappaport, Manufacturing Coordinator
Paul Fitzgerald, Senior Graphic Designer

Hanley-Wood, Inc.:
Michael J. Hanley, Chairman
Michael M. Wood, Chief Executive Officer
Frank Anton, President
Michael J. Tucker, President/Magazine Division
John M. Brannigan, Senior Vice President
James D. Zielinski, Chief Financial Officer
Paul Kitzke, Corporate Editorial Director/Vice President
Ann Seltz, Vice President/Marketing
Maxx MacConnachie, Vice President/Circulation
Joanne Harap, Vice President/Production
Cynthia Gordon-Nicks, Vice President/Finance
Leslie Elsner, Vice President/Human Relations
Adriaan Bouten, Vice President/Information Technology

Photo Credits
Front Cover: Main image—John Griebsch (Design C120)
Inset photos—Andrew D. Lautman (Design 2774 on right; Design 2973 on left)

Back Cover: Main image—Bizzo Photography (Design Q457)
Inset photo—Raef Grohne Photographer (Design Q305)

First Printing: November 1998

10 9 8 7 6 5 4 3 2

Printed in the United States of America

Library of Congress Catalog Card Number: 98-73742

ISBN: 1-881955-50-8

On the front cover: Covering the gamut of sizes and styles, the homes in Encyclopedia of Home Designs offer infinite variety. For additional information and to view floor plans for the cover homes see page 5 for Design C120 (top), page 19 for Design 2774 (right), and page 362 for Design 2973 (left).

On the back cover: Picture-perfect plans lead to a one-of-a-kind home for your family. For additional information and to view floor plans for the homes on the back cover see page 7 for Design Q457 (main image) and page 4 for Design Q305 (inset photo).

Table of Contents

Design Q385, page 133

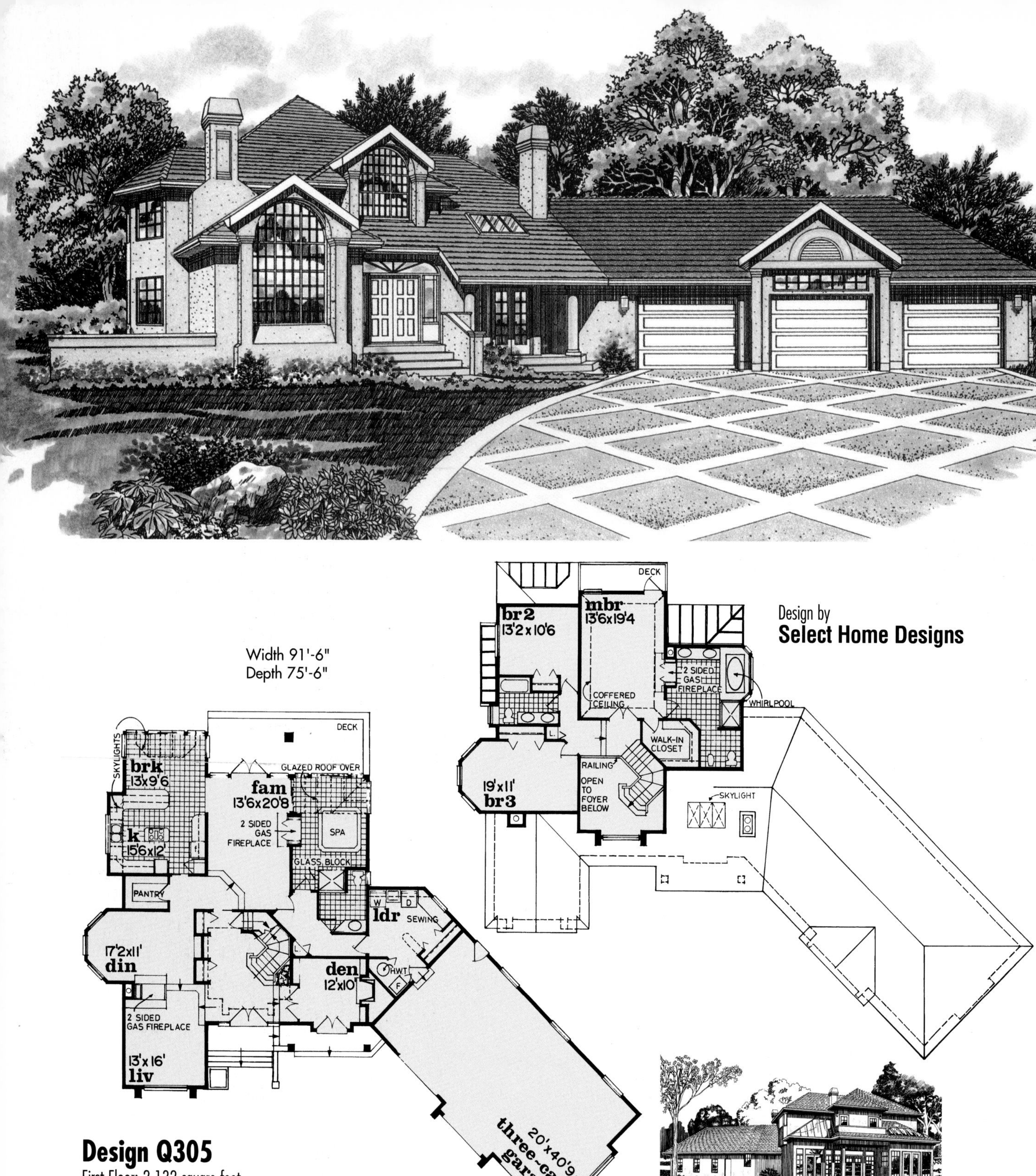
Width 91'-6"
Depth 75'-6"
Design by
Select Home Designs
DECK
SKYLIGHTS
brk 13x9'6
GLAZED ROOF OVER
fam 13'6x20'8
2 SIDED GAS FIREPLACE
SPA
k 15'6x12
GLASS BLOCK
PANTRY
W D
ldr SEWING
17'2x11' din
den 12'x10'
HWT
F
2 SIDED GAS FIREPLACE
13'x 16' liv
20'x40'9 three-car garage
br2 13'2x10'6
mbr 13'6x19'4
2 SIDED GAS FIREPLACE
WHIRLPOOL
COFFERED CEILING
WALK-IN CLOSET
RAILING
OPEN TO FOYER BELOW
19'x11' br3
SKYLIGHT

Design Q305

First Floor: 2,132 square feet
Second Floor: 1,295 square feet
Total: 3,427 square feet

Rear Elevation

■ Sand-finished stucco, distinctive columns and oversized circle-top windows grace this luxurious three-bedroom home. The circle-head window over the entry brightens the grand two-story foyer and its curved stair to the second level. A sunken living room features a two-sided gas fireplace that it shares with the formal dining room. The casual living area—the family room—is also sunken and has a two-sided fireplace through to an indoor spa with glazed roof overhead. The family room also has double doors to the deck in the back. Separating the formal and informal living areas are the U-shaped kitchen with walk-in pantry and the breakfast room. Both have sunny skylights. A den to the right of the foyer features a fireplace and foyer access, plus double-door access to a covered front patio. Bedrooms are on the second floor and include a master suite that has a through-fireplace between the bath and the bedroom. Two additional bedrooms share a full bath. Plans include details for both a basement and a crawlspace foundation.

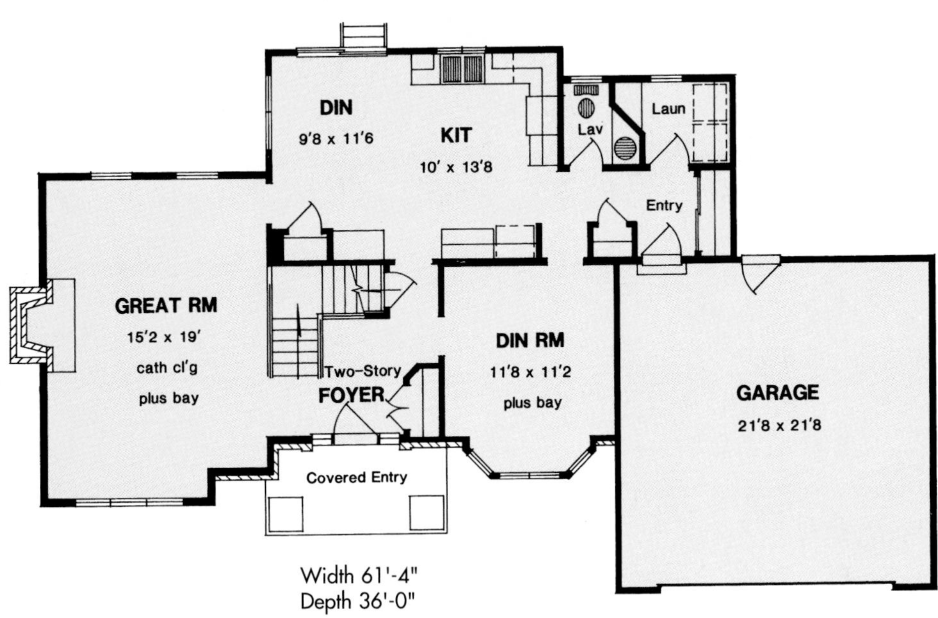
DIN
9'8 x 11'6
KIT
10' x 13'8
Lav
Laun
Entry
GREAT RM
15'2 x 19'
cath cl'g
plus bay
Two-Story
FOYER
DIN RM
11'8 x 11'2
plus bay
GARAGE
21'8 x 21'8
Covered Entry
Width 61'-4"
Depth 36'-0"

Design by
James Fahy Design

Design C120

First Floor: 1,070 square feet
Second Floor: 789 square feet
Total: 1,859 square feet

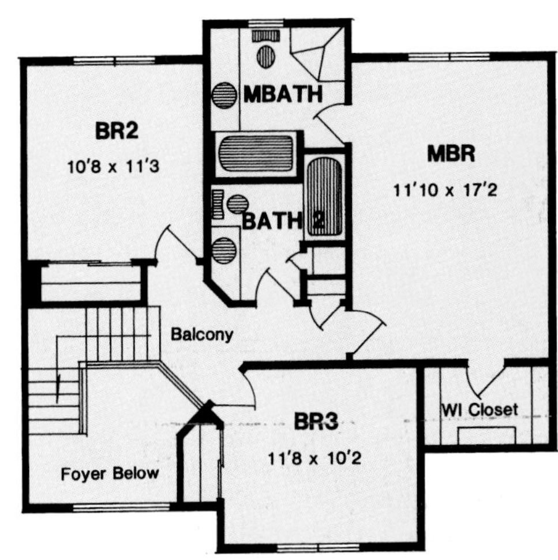
MBATH
BR2
10'8 x 11'3
MBR
11'10 x 17'2
BATH 2
Balcony
WI Closet
BR3
11'8 x 10'2
Foyer Below

■ Exterior appeal with elegant tradition is created by a detailed arched entry porch with Palladian window which brightens the two-story foyer interior. The great room has an open and spacious atmosphere with its ten-foot walls and cathedral ceiling. Both the kitchen and dinette areas are filled with abundant natural light. The L-shaped stairs lead to a three-bedroom second floor with an angled balcony overlooking the foyer and great room. The master bedroom has a large walk-in closet and a master bath featuring a corner glass shower and separate soaking tub.

This home, as shown in the photograph, may differ from the actual blueprints.
For more detailed information, please check the floor plans carefully.

Photo by John Griebsch

Design Q467

Square Footage: 1,215

■ The main entry to this home is well protected by a columned front porch. The living room is vaulted and has a warming fireplace. The vaulted ceiling carries over to the country-style kitchen which features a work island and generously sized eating area. A deck just beyond is the perfect spot for outdoor dining. The bedrooms are up a few stairs and include a master suite with walk-in closet and full bath. Two additional bedrooms have wall closets and share the use of a main bath in the hallway. Space on the lower level may be developed later as needs grow. It features area for a family room, and two bedrooms or one bedroom and a den. The laundry room and a full bath are also on this level.

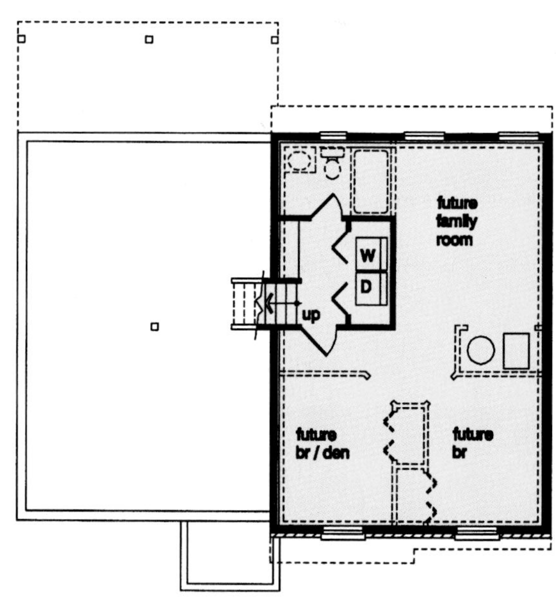
future family room
W
D
up
future br / den
future br

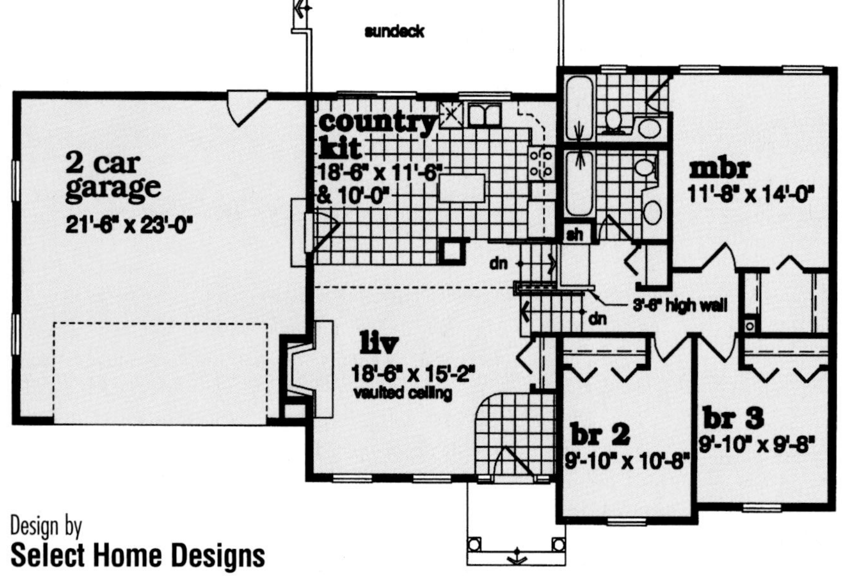
sundeck
country kit
18'-6" x 11'-6" & 10'-0"
2 car garage
21'-6" x 23'-0"
dn
liv
18'-6" x 15'-2"
vaulted ceiling
sh
3'-6" high wall
dn
mbr
11'-8" x 14'-0"
br 2
9'-10" x 10'-8"
br 3
9'-10" x 9'-8"

Width 62'-0"
Depth 34'-2"

Design by
Select Home Designs

This home, as shown in the photograph, may differ from the actual blueprints.
For more detailed information, please check the floor plans carefully.

Photo by Bizzo Photography

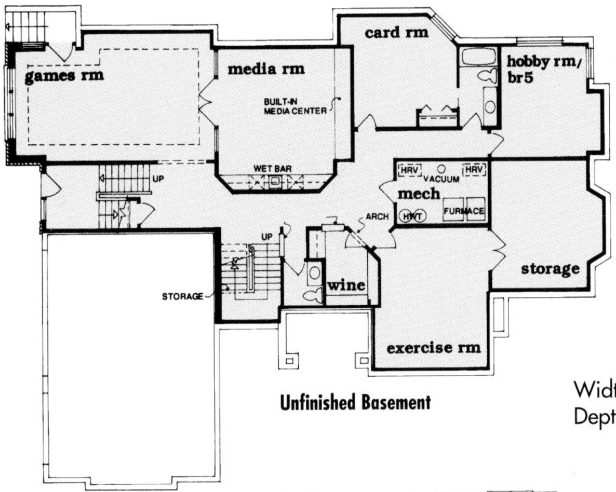

games rm
media rm
BUILT-IN MEDIA CENTER
card rm
hobby rm/ br5
WET BAR
mech
storage
wine
exercise rm
STORAGE
Unfinished Basement

Width 81'-0"
Depth 61'-0"

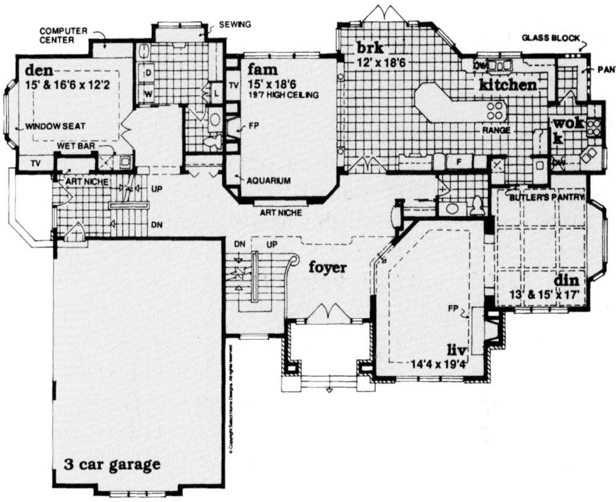

COMPUTER CENTER
SEWING
den 15' & 16'6 x 12'2
WINDOW SEAT
WET BAR
fam 15' x 18'6 19'7 HIGH CEILING
AQUARIUM
ART NICHE
brk 12' x 18'6
GLASS BLOCK
PANTRY
kitchen
RANGE
wok k
BUTLER'S PANTRY
foyer
din 13' & 15' x 17'
liv 14'4 x 19'4
3 car garage

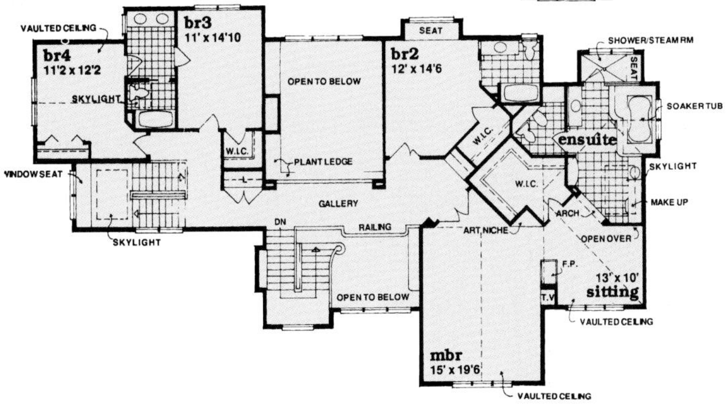

VAULTED CEILING
br4 11'2 x 12'2
SKYLIGHT
br3 11' x 14'10
OPEN TO BELOW
br2 12' x 14'6
SEAT
PLANT LEDGE
WINDOW SEAT
GALLERY
RAILING
SKYLIGHT
SHOWER/STEAM RM
SOAKER TUB
ensuite
W.I.C.
MAKE UP
ART NICHE
OPEN OVER
13' x 10' sitting
VAULTED CEILING
OPEN TO BELOW
mbr 15' x 19'6
VAULTED CEILING

Design Q457

First Floor: 2,596 square feet
Second Floor: 2,233 square feet
Total: 4,829 square feet

Design by
Select Home Designs

This grand, two-story European is adorned with a facade of stucco and brick, meticulously appointed with details for gracious living. Guests enter through a portico to find a stately, two-story foyer. The formal living room features a tray ceiling and fireplace and is joined by a charming dining room with large bay window. A butler's pantry joins the dining room to the gourmet kitchen that holds a separate wok kitchen, an island work center and a breakfast room with double doors leading to a rear patio. The family room is nearby and has a built-in aquarium, a media center and fireplace. A den with tray ceiling, window seat and built-in computer center is tucked in a corner for privacy. The laundry is large enough to accommodate a sewing center. Served by two separate staircases, the second floor features a spectacular master suite with separate sitting room, oversized closet and bath with shower/steam room and spa tub. Three additional bedrooms—one with a private bath—share the second floor. If you choose, you may develop the lower level to include an exercise room, a hobby room, a card room, a game room, a media room, a wine cellar and large storage space.

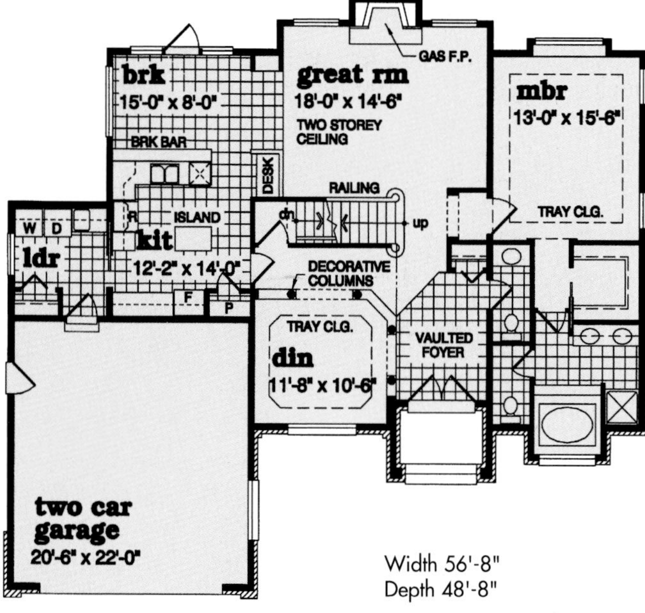
brk
15'-0" x 8'-0"
BRK BAR
great rm
18'-0" x 14'-6"
TWO STOREY CEILING
GAS F.P.
mbr
13'-0" x 15'-6"
TRAY CLG.
DESK
RAILING
dn
up
W D
ldr
ISLAND
kit
12'-2" x 14'-0"
DECORATIVE COLUMNS
F
P
TRAY CLG.
din
11'-8" x 10'-6"
VAULTED FOYER
two car garage
20'-6" x 22'-0"

Width 56'-8"
Depth 48'-8"

Design by
Select Home Designs

Design Q479

First Floor: 1,542 square feet
Second Floor: 739 square feet
Total: 2,281 square feet

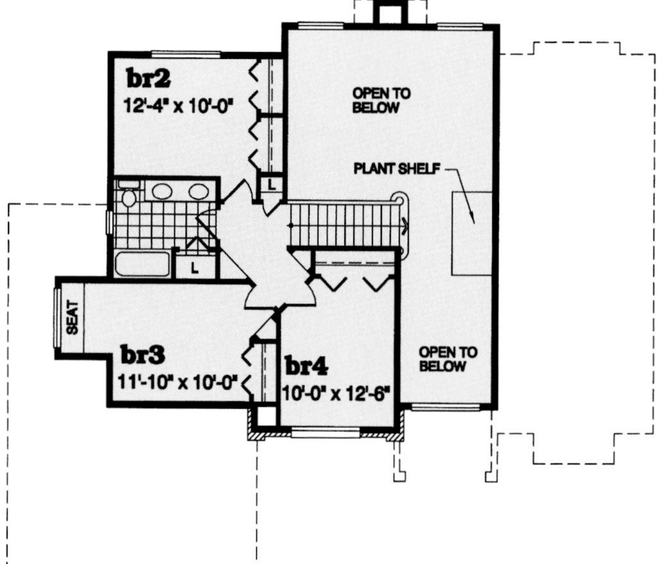
br2
12'-4" x 10'-0"
OPEN TO BELOW
PLANT SHELF
L
L
SEAT
br3
11'-10" x 10'-0"
br4
10'-0" x 12'-6"
OPEN TO BELOW

■ A traditional brick facade, with soaring rooflines, gives this two-story family home an air of distinction. The impressive vaulted entry is flanked by an elegant formal dining room with a tray ceiling and decorative columns to the left, and the master suite to the right. The gourmet kitchen with center island and spacious eating area leads to a great room with an imposing fireplace and impressive eighteen-foot ceiling. The elegant main-floor master suite features a large walk-in closet and bath with whirlpool and separate shower. Family bedrooms are on the second floor—one is appointed with a window seat. All three of these bedrooms share the use of a full bath. Plans include details for both a basement and a crawlspace foundation.

Design 5554

First Floor: 1,356 square feet
Second Floor: 1,162 square feet
Total: 2,518 square feet

■ A bright, circle-head window bathes the foyer of this two-story traditional with warmth and light, introducing the comfortable feeling that the floor plan offers throughout. To the left of the foyer, the large combination living and dining room leads to an open kitchen, breakfast nook and family room with rear-yard access and a welcoming fireplace. All are conveniently located near a powder room and a laundry room with access to the two-car garage. A quiet study (or, with the walk-in closet, a secluded guest room) completes the first floor. On the second floor, three family bedrooms share a full bath with a separate tub and toilet area. The master bedroom includes a walk-in closet and a private master bath.

Design by
Home Planners

PATIO
DW
RANGE
REF
SNACK BAR
SHLVS
KIT
10^2 x 14^4
NOOK
8^{10} x 14^4
FAMILY RM
14^4 x 12^0
DINING
13^0 x 9^0
PANTRY
SHELF
DESK
DN
W
D
LAUNDRY
RAILING
PDR RM
WALK-IN CLOSET
LIVING
13^0 x 14^2
UP
FOYER
STUDY
12^4 x 10^2
GARAGE
22^0 x 22^6
COVERED PORCH
CURB
DESK
BEDRM
10^6 x 10^6
BATH
OPEN TO BELOW
SLOPING CEILING
BEDRM
10^8 x 10^2
LINEN
RAILING
WALK-IN CLOSET
DN
RAILING
OPEN TO BELOW
PLANT SHELF
BEDRM
13^0 x 10^2
MASTER BEDRM
14^6 x 12^6
VANITY
SLOPING CEILING
SHWR
SEAT
MASTER BATH
GARDEN TUB
Width 58'-8"
Depth 44'-6"

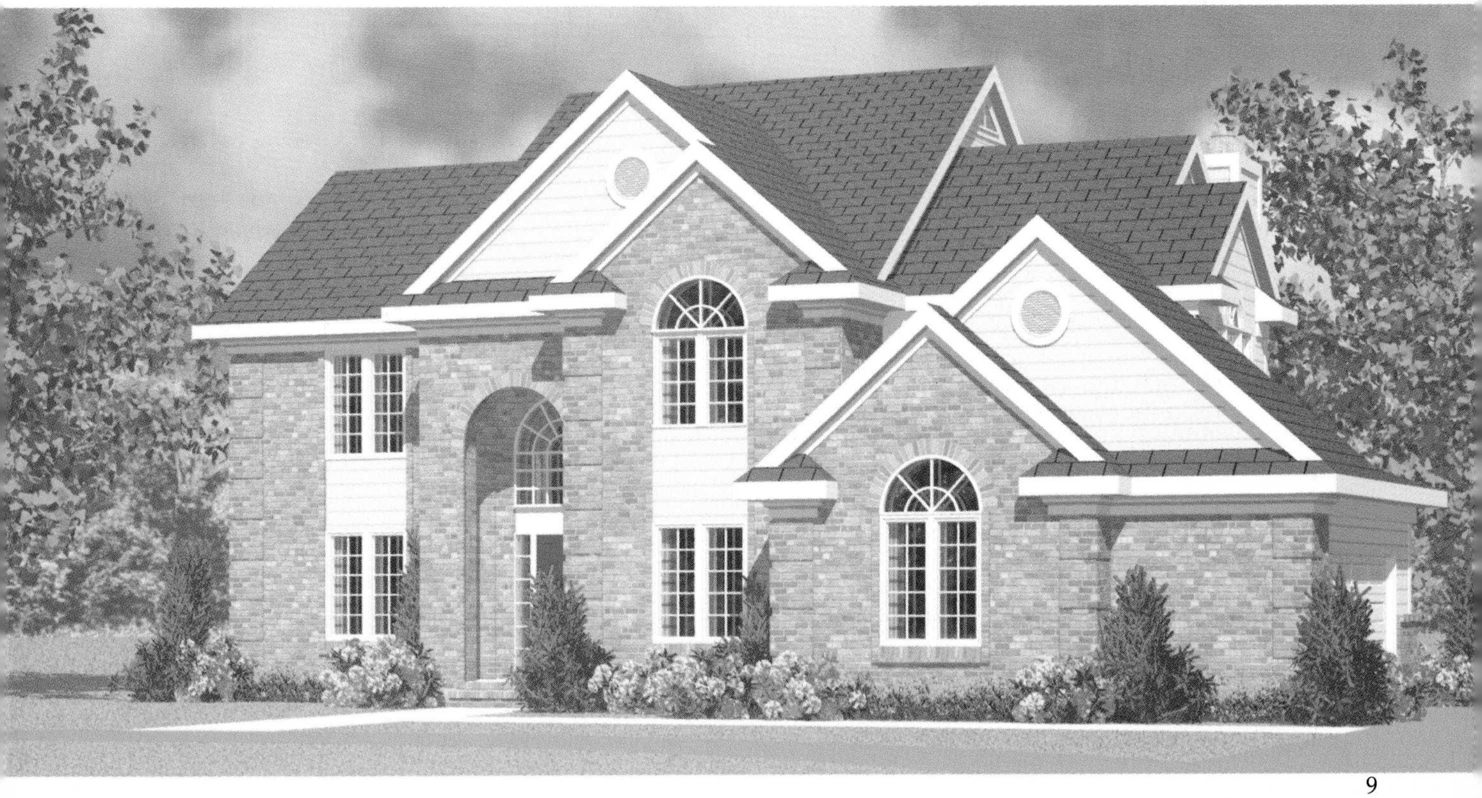

Design Q376

First Floor: 1,040 square feet
Second Floor: 840 square feet
Total: 1,880 square feet

■ A covered veranda, prominent bay windows and decorative woodwork adorn this three-bedroom home. The vaulted foyer is brightened by a second-level window and holds a stair to the second floor. The living room and dining room are on the left. The living room has a cozy fireplace. The gourmet kitchen features an angled sink, corner windows with a plant shelf, an island preparation area and a bay-windowed breakfast nook. The nearby family room has sliding glass doors to the rear and another fireplace. The vaulted master suite, on the second floor, contains a walk-in closet with plant ledge and a bay-window sitting area. Its attendant bath is lit by a skylight. Bedroom 2 also has a bay sitting area. Bedroom 3 features a window seat in a box-bay. Plans include details for both a basement and a crawlspace foundation.

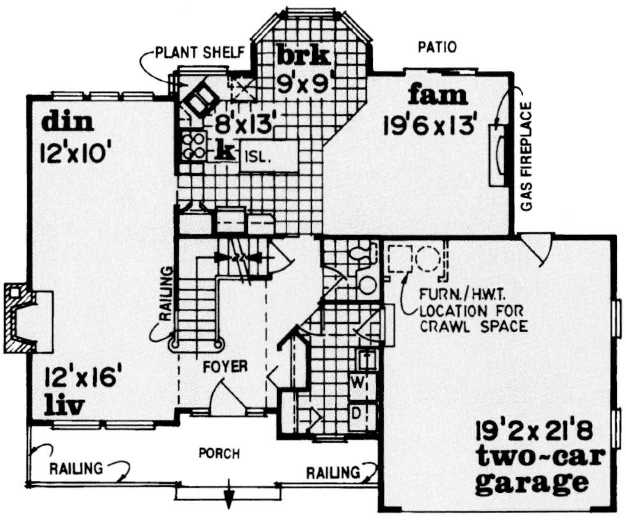
PLANT SHELF
brk
9'x9'
PATIO
fam
19'6 x 13'
din
12'x10'
8'x13'
k
ISL.
GAS FIREPLACE
RAILING
FURN./HWT.
LOCATION FOR
CRAWL SPACE
FOYER
12'x16'
liv
W
D
19'2 x 21'8
two-car
garage
PORCH
RAILING
RAILING

Width 49'-6"
Depth 41'-0"

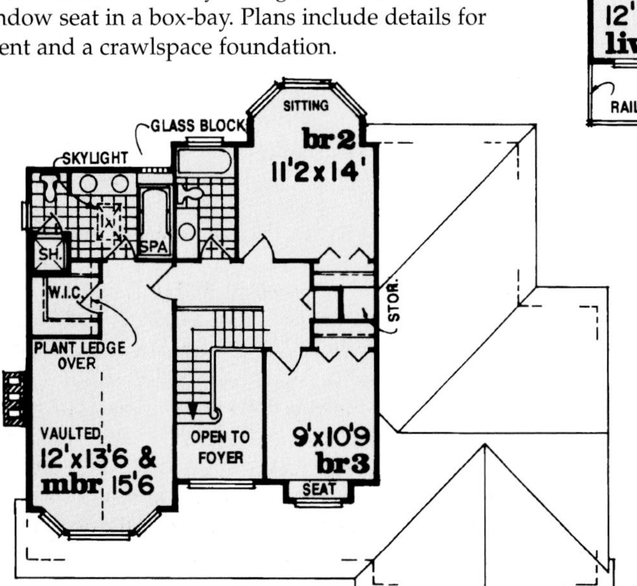
GLASS BLOCK
SITTING
br2
11'2 x 14'
SKYLIGHT
SPA
SH.
W.I.C.
STOR.
PLANT LEDGE
OVER
VAULTED
12'x13'6 &
mbr 15'6
OPEN TO
FOYER
9'x10'9
br3
SEAT

Design by
Select Home Designs

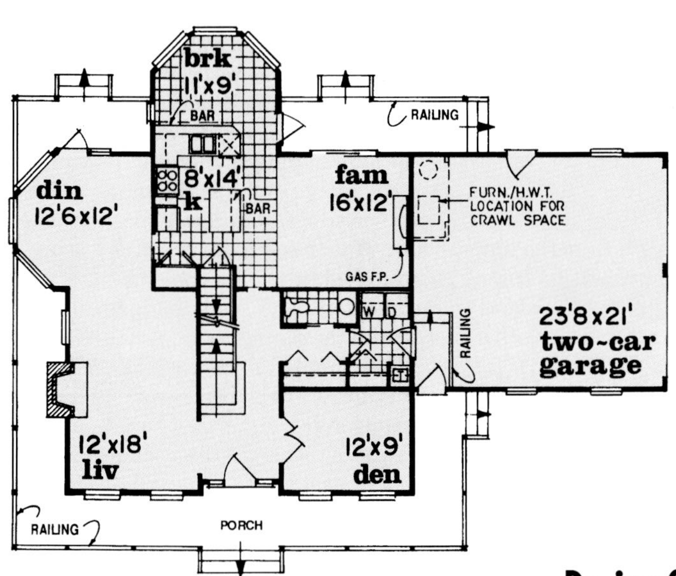
brk
11'x9'
BAR
RAILING
din
12'6x12'
8'x14'
k
BAR
fam
16'x12'
FURN./H.W.T.
LOCATION FOR
CRAWL SPACE
GAS F.P.
RAILING
23'8x21'
two-car
garage
12'x18'
liv
12'x9'
den
RAILING
PORCH

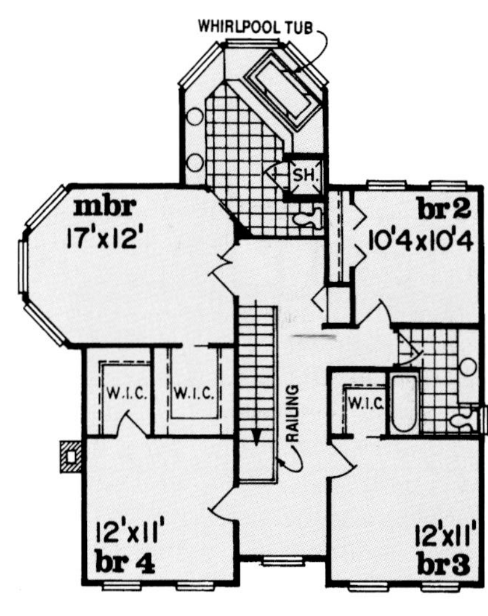
WHIRLPOOL TUB
SH.
mbr
17'x12'
br2
10'4x10'4
W.I.C.
W.I.C.
RAILING
W.I.C.
12'x11'
br 4
12'x11'
br3

Width 62'-0"
Depth 47'-0"

Design Q400

First Floor: 1,193 square feet
Second Floor: 1,188 square feet
Total: 2,381 square feet

Design by
Select Home Designs

■ Graced by a wraparound veranda, multi-paned shutters and decorative wood trim, this four-bedroom design is as attractive as it is comfortable. Large bay windows and high ceilings throughout the first level further enhance the charm. The living room, with masonry fireplace, extends to the bay-windowed dining area. Eating or serving bars on the counter and a center preparation island make easy work of mealtimes. The sunny bayed breakfast room opens to a rear railed veranda as does the family room with fireplace. Bedrooms on the second floor include a master suite with bayed sitting area, walk-in closet and bath with whirlpool spa and double vanity. Two of the three family bedrooms have walk-in closets, as well. All three share a full bath in the main hallway. Plans include details for both a basement and a crawlspace foundation.

Rear Elevation

Design Q473

First Floor: 852 square feet
Second Floor: 829 square feet
Total: 1,681 square feet
Bonus Room: 374 square feet

Rear Elevation

■ Options abound in this three-bedroom home. Choose one of two elevations—both are included in the floor plans. There is also an optional two-car garage, which you may build if you choose. The bonus room, which sits over the garage, may be finished at the initial building stages or left for future development. And the plan includes specs for both a basement and a crawlspace foundation. The main entry opens to a great room with nine-foot ceiling, corner gas fireplace and media-center alcove. The country kitchen features an abundance of cabinets and counterspace. It is adjacent to the bayed dining area and to the family room. A covered porch and sundeck in the rear are reached through a French door in the family room. The upper hall is skylit and features three bedrooms and the large bonus area. The master suite has a private bath and walk-in closet. Family bedrooms share a full hall bath.

Design by
Select Home Designs

Alternate Elevation

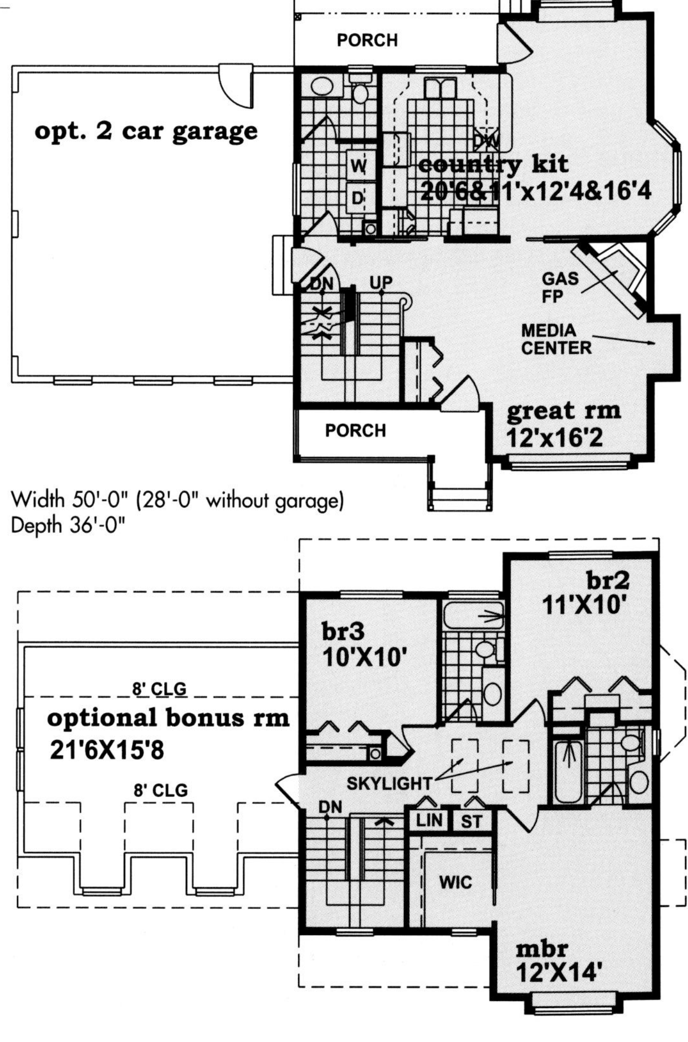
SUNDECK
PORCH
opt. 2 car garage
W
D
DW
country kit
20'6&11'x12'4&16'4
DN
UP
GAS
FP
MEDIA
CENTER
PORCH
great rm
12'x16'2
br2
11'X10'
br3
10'X10'
8' CLG
optional bonus rm
21'6X15'8
8' CLG
SKYLIGHT
DN
LIN
ST
WIC
mbr
12'X14'

Width 50'-0" (28'-0" without garage)
Depth 36'-0"

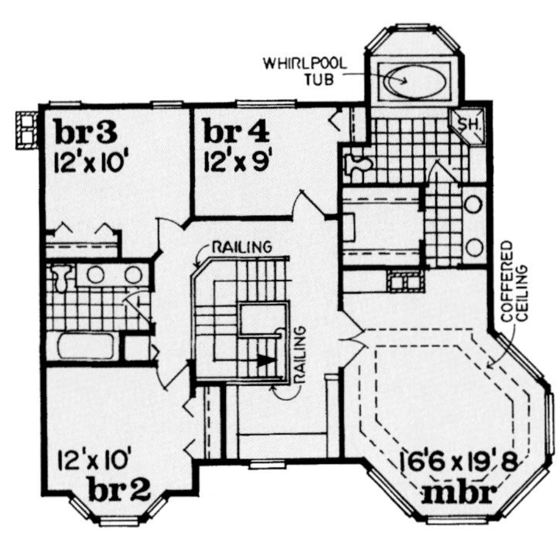
WHIRLPOOL TUB
SH
br3
12'x10'
br 4
12'x9'
RAILING
RAILING
COFFERED CEILING
12'x10'
br2
16'6x19'8
mbr

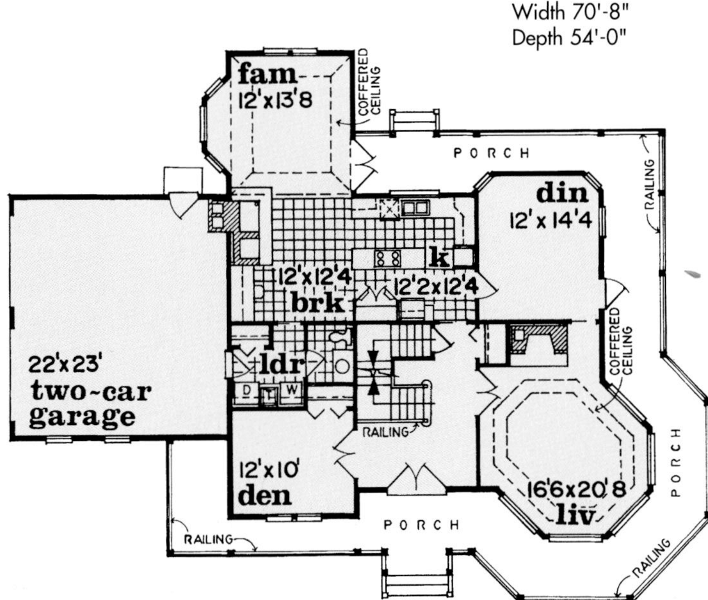
Width 70'-8"
Depth 54'-0"
fam
12'x13'8
COFFERED CEILING
PORCH
din
12'x 14'4
RAILING
k
12'x12'4
brk
12'2x12'4
22'x23'
two-car
garage
ldr
D
W
COFFERED CEILING
RAILING
12'x10'
den
16'6x20'8
liv
PORCH
PORCH
RAILING
RAILING

Design Q300

First Floor: 1,462 square feet
Second Floor: 1,288 square feet
Total: 2,750 square feet

A touch of Victoria enhances the facade of this home: a turret roof over a covered railed porch (note the turned wood spindles). The porch wraps around three sides of the home and is accessed from the foyer, the dining room and the family room. Special attractions on the first floor include a tray ceiling in the octagonal living room, fireplaces in the country kitchen and the living room, a coffered ceiling in the family room and double-door access to the cozy den. The master suite sits on the second floor and boasts a coffered ceiling, walk-in closet and bath with whirlpool tub, double vanities and separate shower. Three family bedrooms share a full bath with double vanities. Plans include details for both a basement and a crawlspace foundation.

Design by
Select Home Designs

Rear Elevation

Design Q328

First Floor: 1,098 square feet
Second Floor: 996 square feet
Total: 2,094 square feet

■ This farmhouse deluxe is decorated with a covered railed veranda and shuttered windows on the outside and a comfortable floor plan on the inside. Flanking the foyer are a den with double-door entry and the living room/dining room combination with fireplace. The L-shaped kitchen can be reached from either the central hall or from an entry at the dining room. An island work counter and planning desk add to the kitchen's efficiency. A light-filled breakfast room serves casual meals. Open to this area is the family room with corner fireplace and access to a covered porch. The second floor holds four bedrooms. Three are for the family and share a full bath. The master suite has a bayed sitting area, double wall closets and a bath with whirlpool tub. Plans include details for both a basement and a crawlspace foundation.

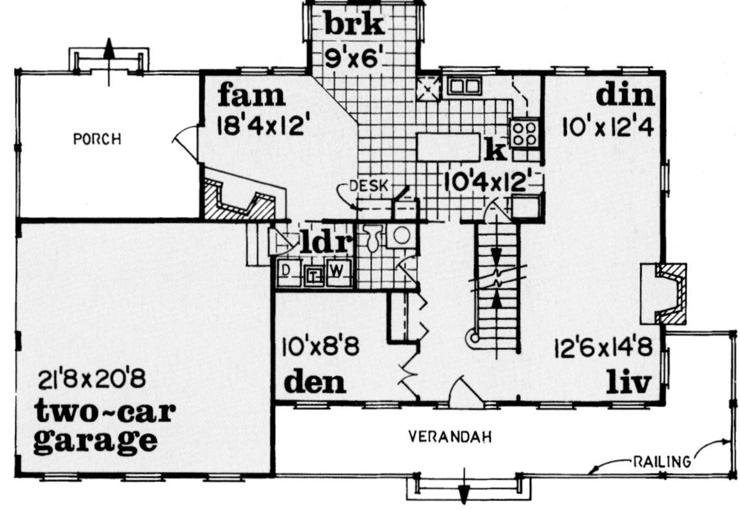
brk
9'x6'
fam
18'4x12'
din
10'x12'4
PORCH
k
10'4x12'
DESK
ldr
D
W
10'x8'8
den
12'6x14'8
liv
21'8x20'8
two-car
garage
VERANDAH
RAILING

Width 62'-6"
Depth 40'-0"

Design by
Select Home Designs

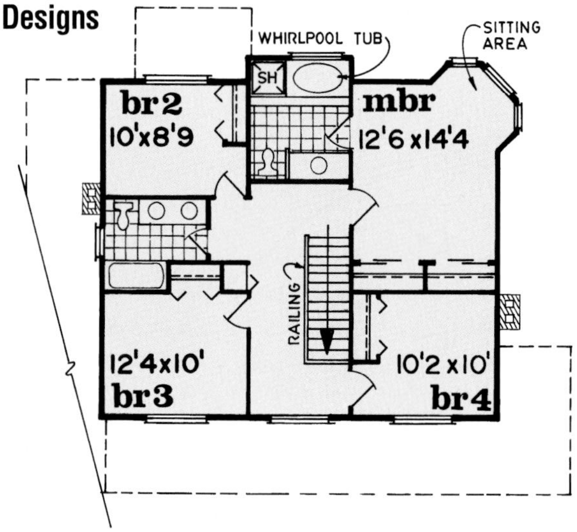

WHIRLPOOL TUB
SITTING AREA
SH
br2
10'x8'9
mbr
12'6x14'4
RAILING
12'4x10'
br3
10'2x10'
br4

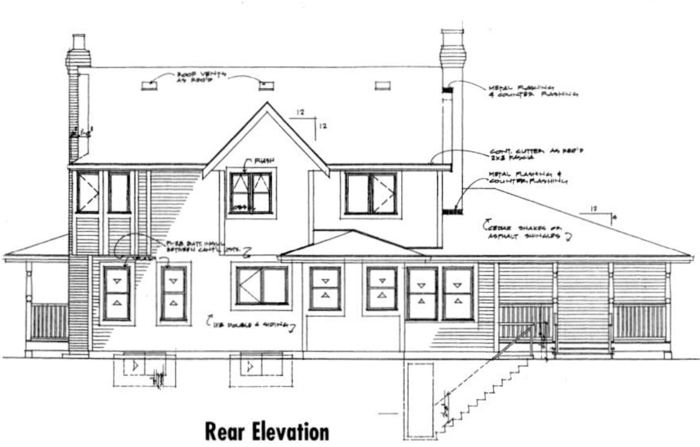

Rear Elevation

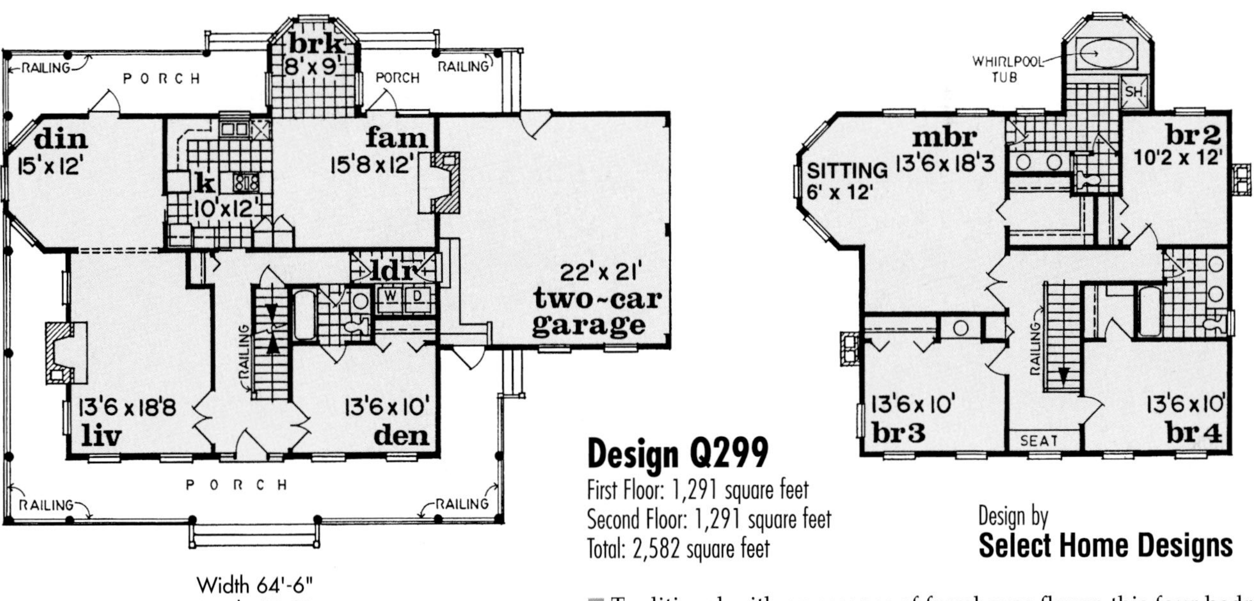
RAILING
PORCH
brk
8'x9'
PORCH
RAILING
din
15'x12'
k
10'x12'
fam
15'8x12'
ldr
W D
22'x21'
two-car
garage
RAILING
13'6x18'8
liv
13'6x10'
den
PORCH
RAILING
RAILING
WHIRLPOOL TUB
SH.
mbr
13'6x18'3
SITTING
6' x 12'
br2
10'2 x 12'
RAILING
13'6x10'
br3
SEAT
13'6x10'
br4

Width 64'-6"
Depth 47'-0"

Design Q299

First Floor: 1,291 square feet
Second Floor: 1,291 square feet
Total: 2,582 square feet

Design by
Select Home Designs

■ Traditional with an essence of farmhouse flavor, this four-bedroom home begins with a wraparound covered porch. The floor plan revolves around a central hall with a formal living room and dining room on the left and private den on the right. The casual family room sits to the rear and is open to a bayed breakfast room and the L-shaped kitchen with island work center. Both the family room and the living room are warmed by hearths. Two rear porches are reached through doors in the family room and the bayed dining room. The master suite on the second level has a bayed sitting room and bath with whirlpool tub and separate shower. Three family bedrooms share a full bath. Plans include details for both a basement and a crawlspace foundation.

Rear Elevation

Photo by Andrew D. Lautman

This home, as shown in the photograph, may differ from the actual blueprints. For more detailed information, please check the floor plans carefully.

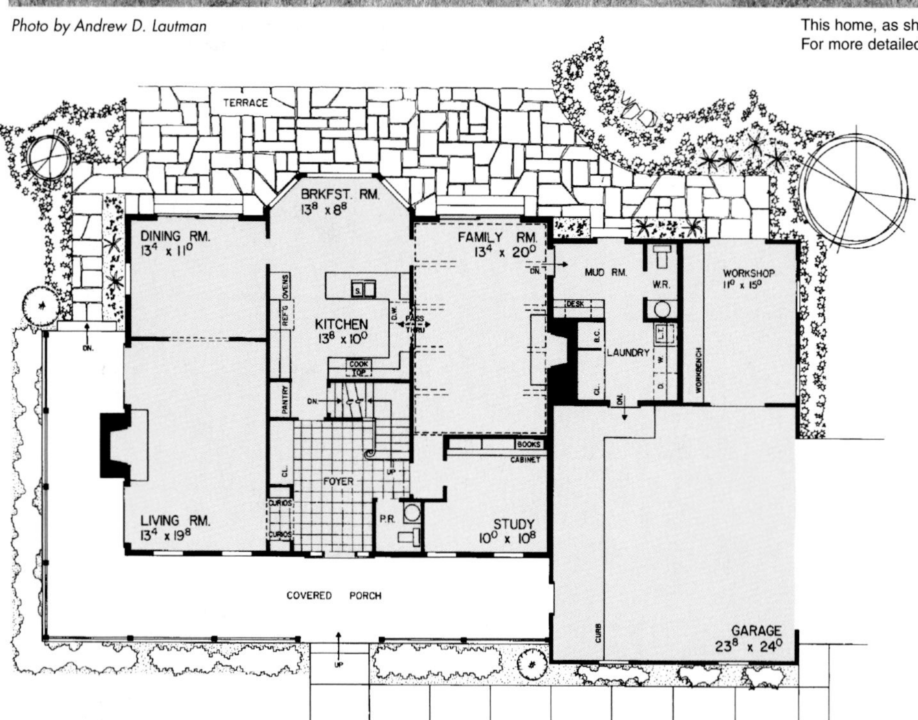

TERRACE
BRKFST. RM.
13⁸ x 8⁸
DINING RM.
13⁴ x 11⁰
FAMILY RM.
13⁴ x 20⁰
MUD RM.
W.R.
WORKSHOP
11⁰ x 15⁰
KITCHEN
13⁸ x 10⁰
COOK TOP
PANTRY
DESK
LAUNDRY
WORKBENCH
FOYER
BOOKS
CABINET
CURIOS
P.R.
STUDY
10⁰ x 10⁸
LIVING RM.
13⁴ x 19⁸
COVERED PORCH
CURB
GARAGE
23⁸ x 24⁰

Width 74'-0"
Depth 46'-0"

QUOTE ONE®

Cost to build? See page 516 to order complete cost estimate to build this house in your area!

Design 2946

First Floor: 1,581 square feet
Second Floor: 1,344 square feet
Total: 2,925 square feet

L D

Design by
Home Planners

■ Here's a traditional farmhouse design that's made for down-home hospitality and the good grace of pleasant company. Star attractions are the large covered porch and the entertainment terrace. The hard-working interior offers separate living and family rooms, each with its own fireplace, and a formal dining room with separate access to the terrace. The U-shaped kitchen shares natural light from a bayed breakfast nook and offers a sizable pantry and lots of counter space. The mud room and laundry offer access from the garage and from the rear terrace, while the adjoining workshop enjoys its own entries.

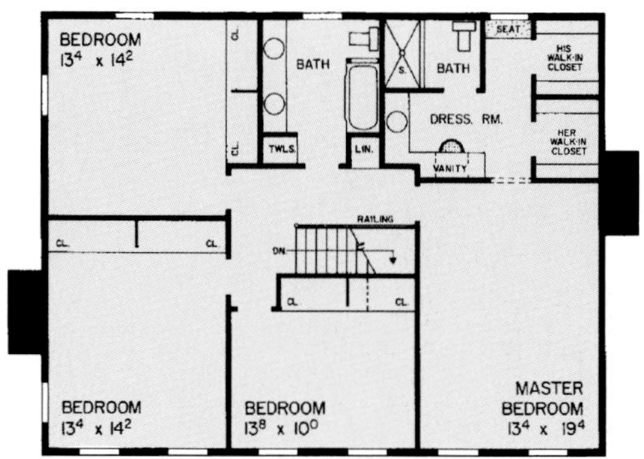

BEDROOM
13⁴ x 14²
BATH
BATH
SEAT
HIS WALK-IN CLOSET
DRESS. RM.
HER WALK-IN CLOSET
TWLS.
LIN.
VANITY
RAILING
BEDROOM
13⁴ x 14²
BEDROOM
13⁸ x 10⁰
MASTER BEDROOM
13⁴ x 19⁴

Photo by Carl Socolow

This home, as shown in the photograph, may differ from the actual blueprints. For more detailed information, please check the floor plans carefully.

Design 2774

First Floor: 1,366 square feet
Second Floor: 969 square feet
Total: 2,335 square feet

L **D**

■ Here's a best-selling farmhouse adaptation with deluxe amenities. The quiet corner living room opens to a sizable dining room with bumped-out bay, while the U-shaped kitchen offers built-ins and a pass-through to the breakfast room, which features a rustic beam ceiling. Sliding glass doors open to outdoor areas from the family room and breakfast area, and let in natural light. The service entrance to the garage offers a coat closet and a walk-in pantry. Second-floor sleeping quarters include a master suite with a private dressing room and bath, and three family bedrooms—or make one a study—and a hall bath.

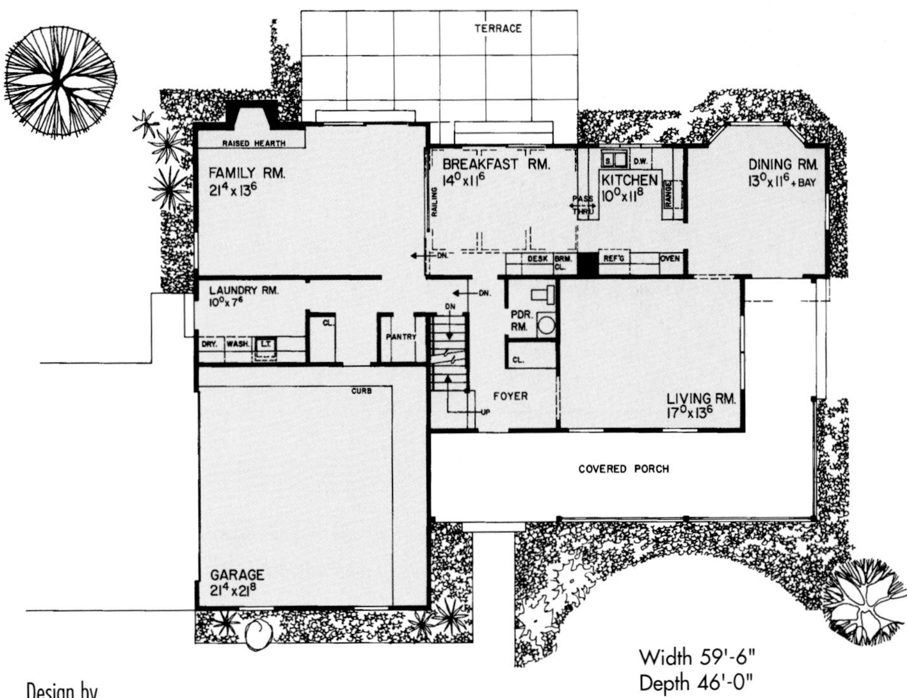
TERRACE
RAISED HEARTH
FAMILY RM.
$21^4 \times 13^6$
BREAKFAST RM.
$14^0 \times 11^6$
KITCHEN
$10^0 \times 11^8$
DINING RM.
$13^0 \times 11^6$ + BAY
LAUNDRY RM.
$10^0 \times 7^6$
DRY. WASH.
PANTRY
PDR. RM.
FOYER
LIVING RM.
$17^0 \times 13^6$
COVERED PORCH
GARAGE
$21^4 \times 21^8$

Width 59'-6"
Depth 46'-0"

Design by
Home Planners

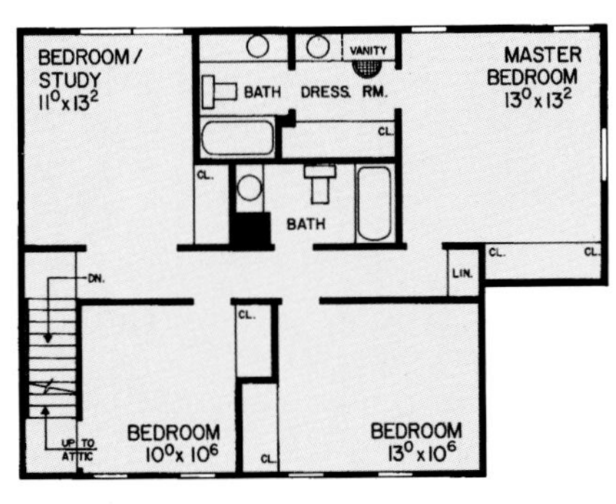
BEDROOM / STUDY
$11^0 \times 13^2$
BATH
DRESS. RM.
MASTER BEDROOM
$13^0 \times 13^2$
BATH
BEDROOM
$10^0 \times 10^6$
BEDROOM
$13^0 \times 10^6$

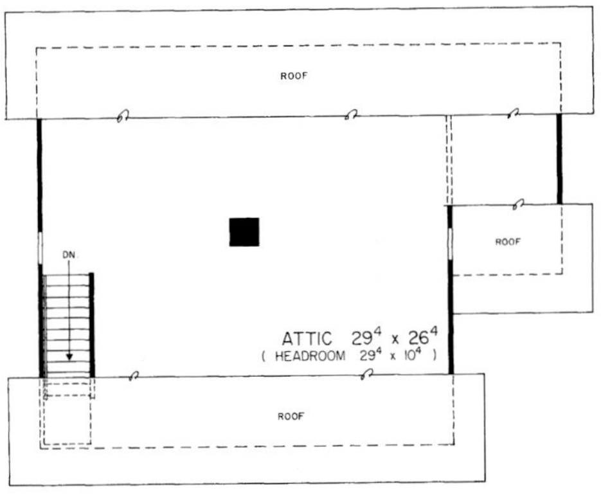
ROOF
ROOF
ATTIC $29^4 \times 26^4$
(HEADROOM $29^4 \times 10^4$)
ROOF

QUOTE ONE®

Cost to build? See page 516 to order complete cost estimate to build this house in your area!

Design Q406

First Floor: 1,205 square feet
Second Floor: 1,254 square feet
Total: 2,459 square feet

■ With details reminiscent of Victorian design, this home is graced by a covered veranda wrapping on three sides and an elegant bay window. The vaulted foyer introduces an octagonal staircase and an archway to the living room. Details in the living room include a tray ceiling and adjoining dining room with beam ceiling. French doors in the dining room open to the porch. A country kitchen offers a spacious walk-in pantry, a center prep island and a breakfast bay with porch access. The nearby family room has its own fireplace. The upstairs master bedroom is graced by a bayed sitting area and bath with private deck. Bedrooms 2, 3 and 4 share the use of a full hall bath. Plans include details for both a basement and a crawlspace foundation.

Design by
Select Home Designs

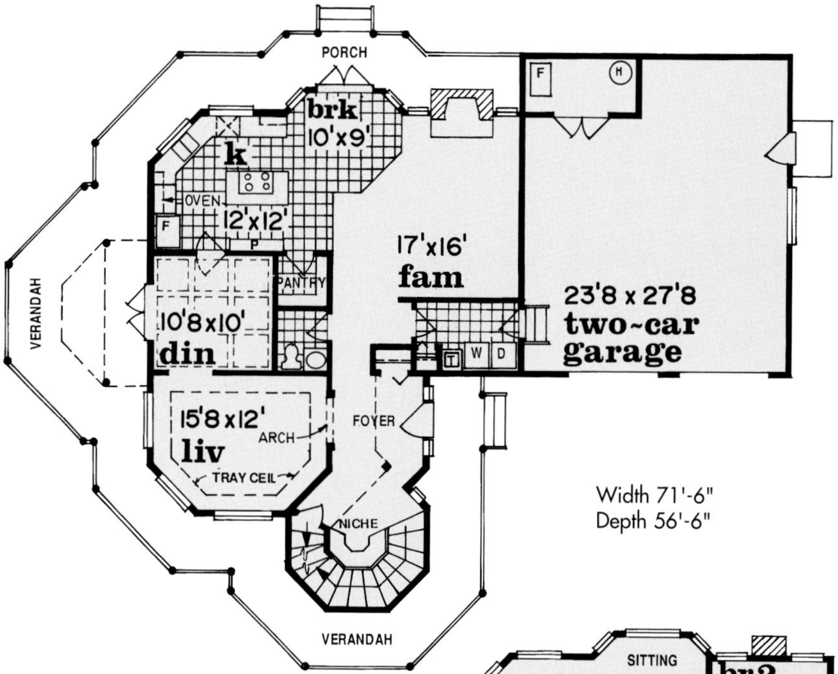

PORCH
brk 10'x9'
k 12'x12'
OVEN
F
P
PANTRY
17'x16' fam
23'8 x 27'8 two-car garage
F
M
W D
VERANDAH
10'8x10' din
15'8x12' liv
ARCH
TRAY CEIL
FOYER
NICHE
VERANDAH

Width 71'-6"
Depth 56'-6"

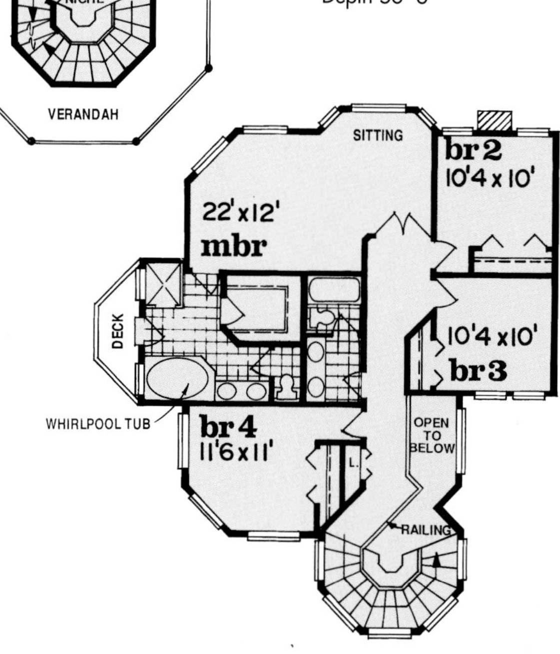

SITTING
br2 10'4 x 10'
22'x12' mbr
DECK
10'4 x10' br3
WHIRLPOOL TUB
br4 11'6 x 11'
OPEN TO BELOW
L.
RAILING

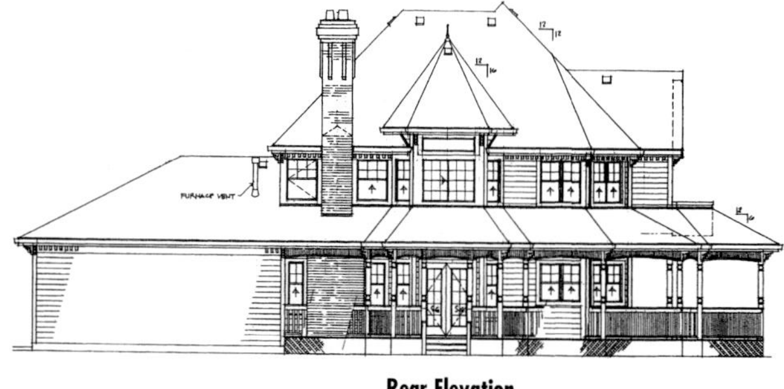

Rear Elevation

Design 3309

First Floor: 1,375 square feet
Second Floor: 1,016 square feet
Total: 2,391 square feet

L

■ Covered porches, front and back, are a fine preview to the livable nature of this Victorian. Living areas are defined in a family room with a fireplace, formal living and dining rooms and a kitchen with a breakfast room. An ample laundry room, a garage with storage area, and a powder room round out the first floor. Three second-floor bedrooms are joined by a study and two full baths. The master suite on this floor has two closets, including an ample walk-in, as well as a relaxing bath with a tile-rimmed whirlpool tub and a separate shower with a seat.

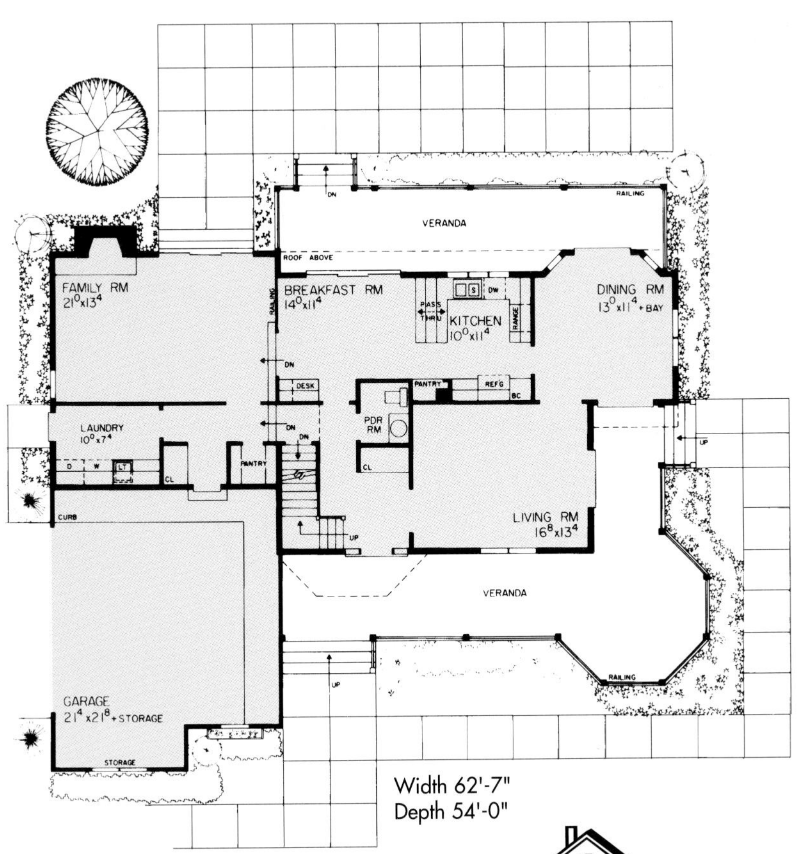
VERANDA
ROOF ABOVE
RAILING
FAMILY RM $21^0 x 13^4$
BREAKFAST RM $14^0 x 11^4$
KITCHEN $10^0 x 11^4$
DINING RM $13^0 x 11^4$ + BAY
PASS THRU
DW
RANGE
DESK
PANTRY
REFG
BC
PDR RM
CL
LAUNDRY $10^0 x 7^4$
D
W
LT
DN
UP
LIVING RM $16^8 x 13^4$
VERANDA
RAILING
CURB
GARAGE $21^4 x 21^8$ + STORAGE
STORAGE

Width 62'-7"
Depth 54'-0"

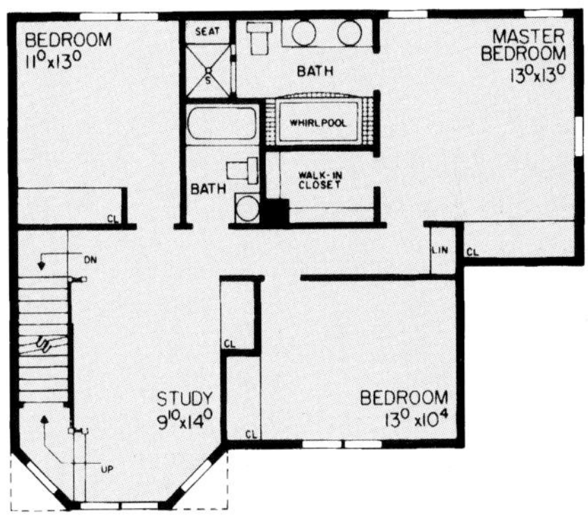
BEDROOM $11^0 x 13^0$
SEAT
BATH
MASTER BEDROOM $13^0 x 13^0$
WHIRLPOOL
BATH
WALK-IN CLOSET
CL
LIN
CL
DN
STUDY $9^{10} x 14^0$
CL
BEDROOM $13^0 x 10^4$
CL
UP

QUOTE ONE®
Cost to build? See page 516 to order complete cost estimate to build this house in your area!

Design by
Home Planners

Photo by Andrew D. Lautman

This home, as shown in the photograph, may differ from the actual blueprints. For more detailed information, please check the floor plans carefully.

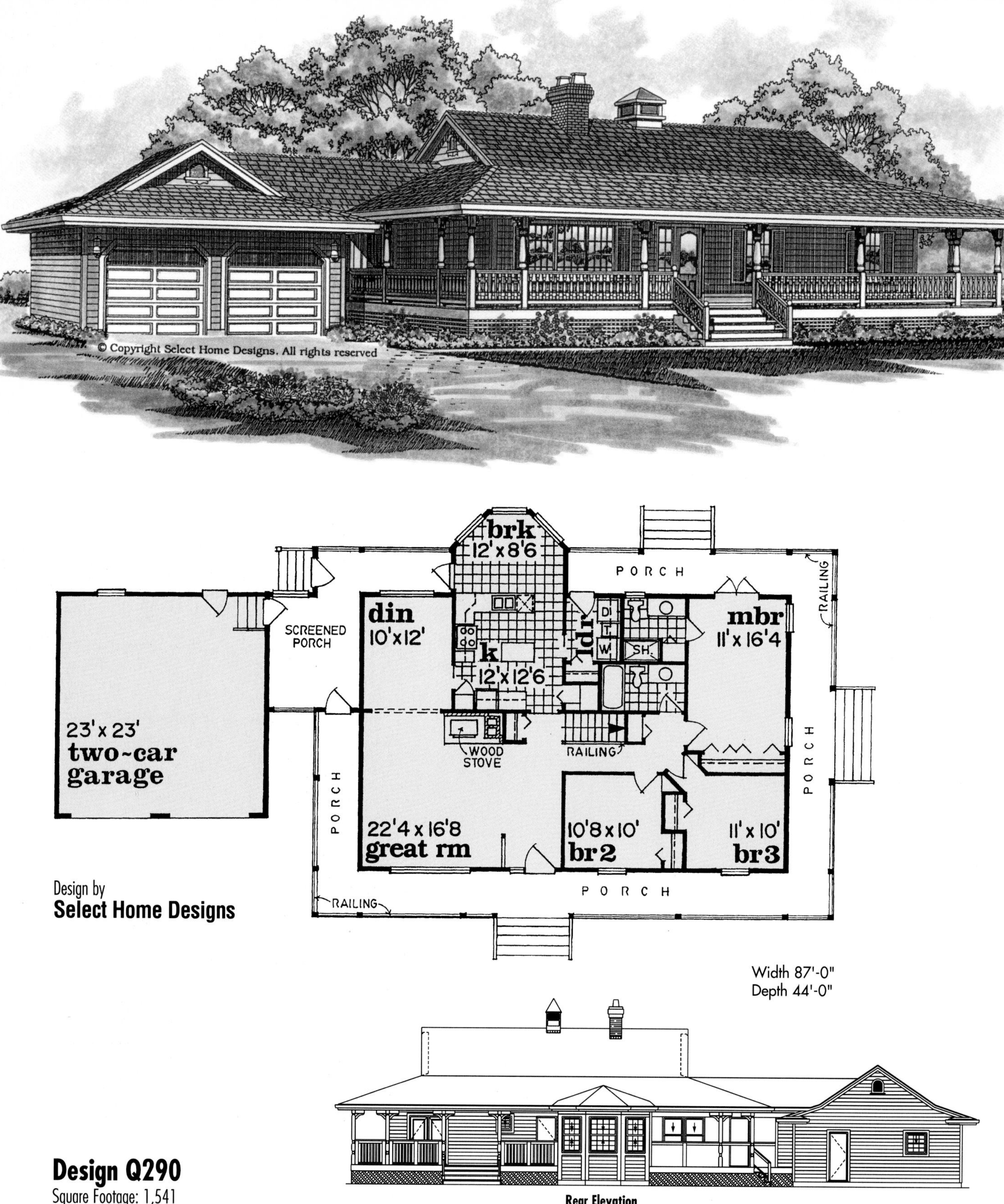

© Copyright Select Home Designs. All rights reserved
brk
12'x8'6
PORCH
RAILING
din
10'x12'
SCREENED PORCH
k
12'x12'6
ldr
DI
T
W
SH
mbr
11'x16'4
23'x23'
two-car garage
WOOD STOVE
RAILING
PORCH
22'4 x 16'8
great rm
10'8x10'
br2
11'x10'
br3
PORCH
RAILING

Design by
Select Home Designs

Width 87'-0"
Depth 44'-0"

Rear Elevation

Design Q290

Square Footage: 1,541

Because this home has such special detailing, it has become one of our most popular designs. It begins with a covered porch with turned wood spindles wrapping the home almost all the way around. The entry opens directly into the great room, which is warmed by a wood stove and open to the adjoining dining room, which has a screened porch for outdoor dining. The country kitchen features a center island and a bayed breakfast area for casual meals. A master bedroom and two family bedrooms are found to the right of the plan. The master has double doors to the porch and a full bath with shower. Family bedrooms share a full bath with soaking tub. A two-car garage connects to the plan via the screened porch. Plans include details for both a basement and a crawlspace foundation—the choice is yours.

Photos by Allen Maertz

Design 3471

First Floor: 3,166 square feet
Second Floor: 950 square feet
Guest Living Area: 680 square feet
Total: 4,796 square feet
L

Design by
Home Planners

This home, as shown in the photographs, may differ from the actual blueprints. For more detailed information, please check the floor plans carefully.

■ A long, low-pitched roof distinguishes this Southwestern-style farmhouse design. The tiled entrance leads to a grand dining room and opens to a formal parlor secluded by half-walls. A country kitchen with cooktop island overlooks the two-story gathering room with its full wall of glass, fireplace and built-in media shelves. The master suite satisfies the most discerning tastes with a raised hearth, an adjoining study or exercise room, access to the wraparound porch, and a bath with corner whirlpool tub. Rooms upstairs can serve as secondary bedrooms for family members, or can be converted to home office space.

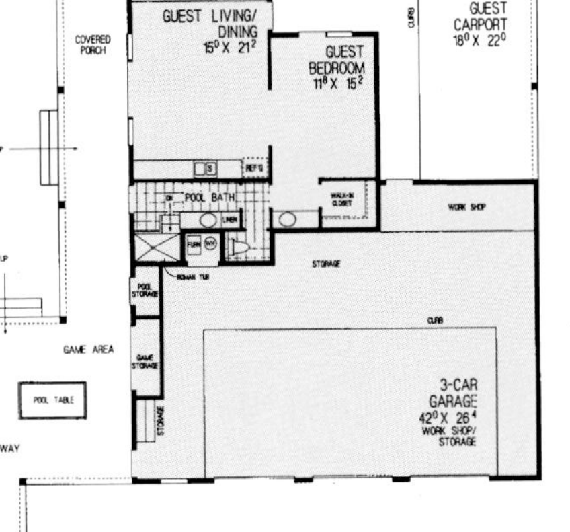

GUEST LIVING/ DINING 15^0 X 21^2
GUEST BEDROOM 11^6 X 15^2
GUEST CARPORT 18^0 X 22^0
COVERED PORCH
POOL BATH
WORK SHOP
STORAGE
GAME AREA
POOL TABLE
BREEZEWAY
3-CAR GARAGE 42^0 X 26^4 WORK SHOP/ STORAGE

Width 154'-0"
Depth 94'-8"

QUOTE ONE®

Cost to build? See page 516 to order complete cost estimate to build this house in your area!

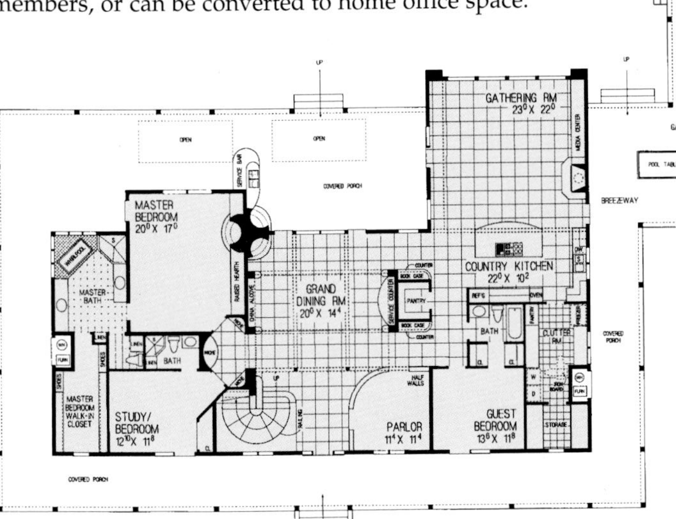

GATHERING RM 23^0 X 22^0
COVERED PORCH
MASTER BEDROOM 20^0 X 17^0
MASTER BATH
GRAND DINING RM 20^0 X 14^4
COUNTRY KITCHEN 22^0 X 10^2
PANTRY
BATH
STUDY/ BEDROOM 12^{10} X 11^8
MASTER BEDROOM WALK-IN CLOSET
PARLOR 11^4 X 11^4
GUEST BEDROOM 13^6 X 11^8
HALF WALLS
COVERED PORCH

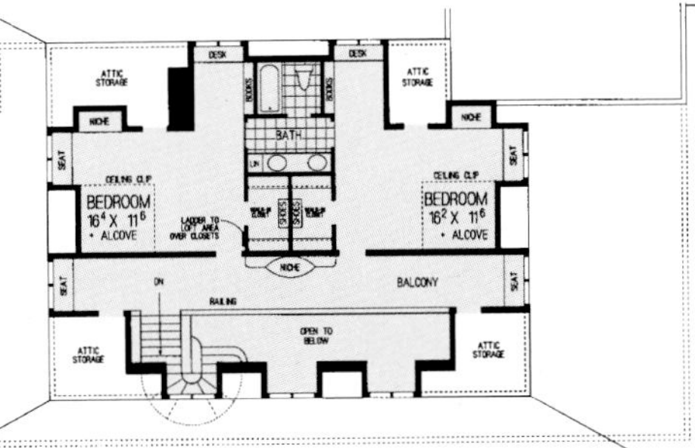

ATTIC STORAGE
BATH
BEDROOM 16^4 X 11^6 + ALCOVE
BEDROOM 16^2 X 11^6 + ALCOVE
BALCONY
OPEN TO BELOW

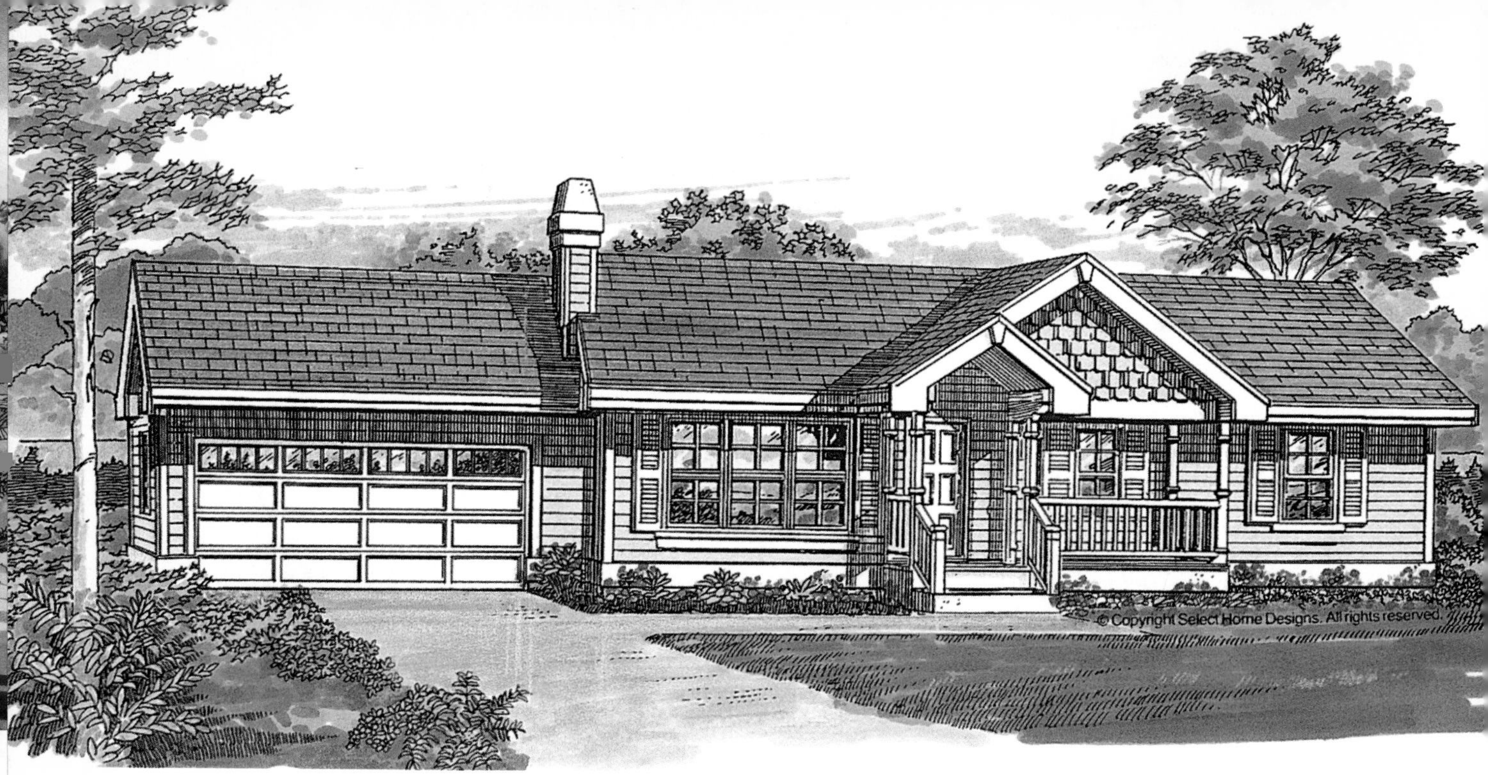

Design by
Select Home Designs

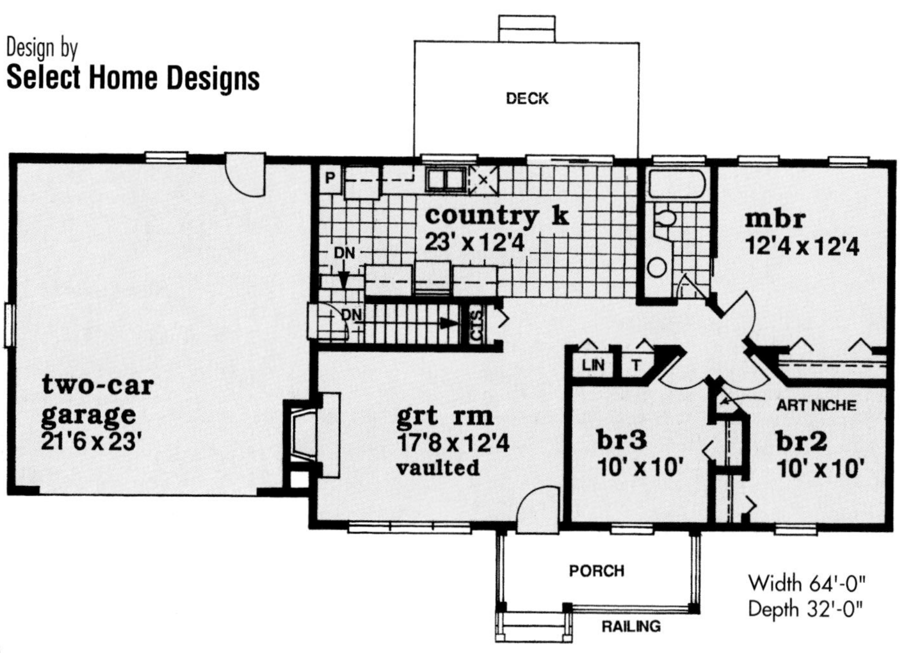
DECK
P
country k
23' x 12'4
DN
DN
CLS
mbr
12'4 x 12'4
LIN
T
ART NICHE
two-car
garage
21'6 x 23'
grt rm
17'8 x 12'4
vaulted
br3
10' x 10'
br2
10' x 10'
PORCH
RAILING
Width 64'-0"
Depth 32'-0"

Design Q440

Square Footage: 1,092

■ Compact, yet efficient, this one-story home opens with a quaint covered porch to a convenient floor plan. The great room has a vaulted ceiling and warming hearth for cozy winter blazes. The step-saving galley kitchen is pure country with space for a family-sized dining area and sliding glass doors to the rear deck. The master bedroom has an angled entry and windows overlooking the rear yard. It shares a full bath that has a split entry with two family bedrooms (note the art niche at the entry to Bedroom 2). If you choose the crawlspace option, you'll gain space for a washer and dryer and a spot for a built-in media center. The two-car garage is reached through a side door in the kitchen.

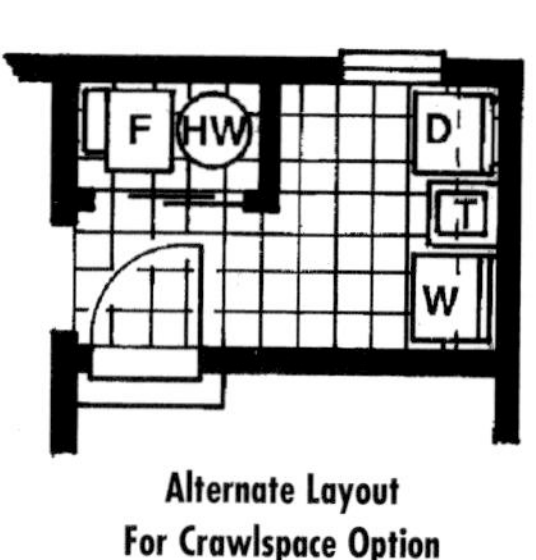
F
HW
D
T
W

Alternate Layout
For Crawlspace Option

Design by
Select Home Designs

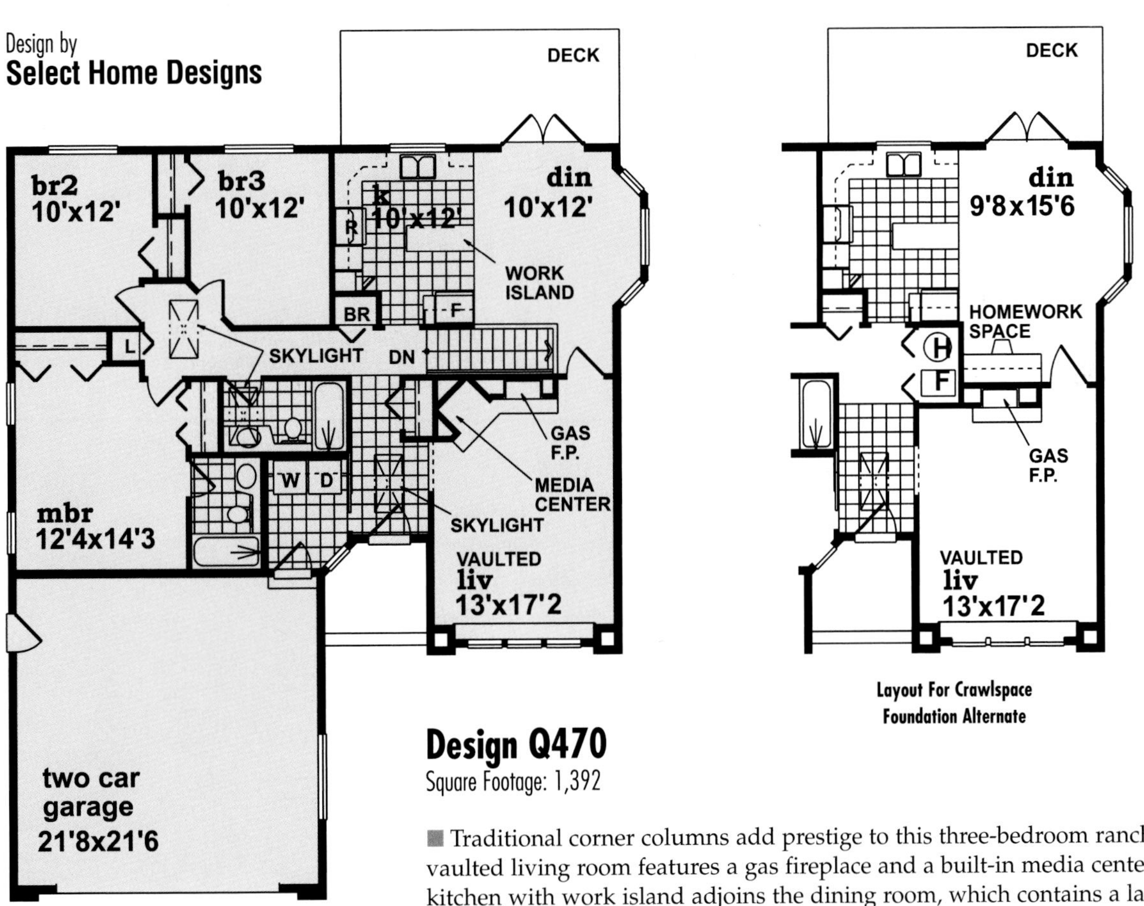
DECK
br2
10'x12'
br3
10'x12'
k
10'x12'
R
din
10'x12'
WORK ISLAND
BR
F
L
SKYLIGHT
DN
GAS F.P.
MEDIA CENTER
SKYLIGHT
W
D
mbr
12'4x14'3
VAULTED
liv
13'x17'2
two car garage
21'8x21'6
Width 44'-0"
Depth 52'-6"
DECK
din
9'8x15'6
HOMEWORK SPACE
H
F
GAS F.P.
VAULTED
liv
13'x17'2

Layout For Crawlspace Foundation Alternate

Design Q470

Square Footage: 1,392

■ Traditional corner columns add prestige to this three-bedroom ranch. The vaulted living room features a gas fireplace and a built-in media center. An open kitchen with work island adjoins the dining room, which contains a large bay window and double French doors leading to the rear deck. An abundance of natural light from the skylights in the main hallways add dramatic effects. The master suite is appointed with His and Hers wall closets and a private bath. Family bedrooms share a full hall bath. The laundry room has space for a full-sized washer and dryer with cabinets overhead. The crawlspace option allows for a convenient homework-space between the dining room and living room.

Photos by Bob Greenspan

Design 3405

Square Footage: 3,144

QUOTE ONE®

Cost to build? See page 516 to order complete cost estimate to build this house in your area!

■ In classic Santa Fe style, this home strikes a beautiful combination of historic exterior detailing and open floor planning on the inside. A covered porch running the width of the facade leads to an entry foyer that connects to a huge gathering room with a fireplace and a formal dining room. The family kitchen allows special space for casual gatherings. The right wing of the home holds two family bedrooms and a full bath. The left wing is devoted to the master suite and a guest room or a study.

This home, as shown in the photographs, may differ from the actual blueprints. For more detailed information, please check the floor plans carefully.

Design by
Home Planners

Width 139'-10"
Depth 63'-8"

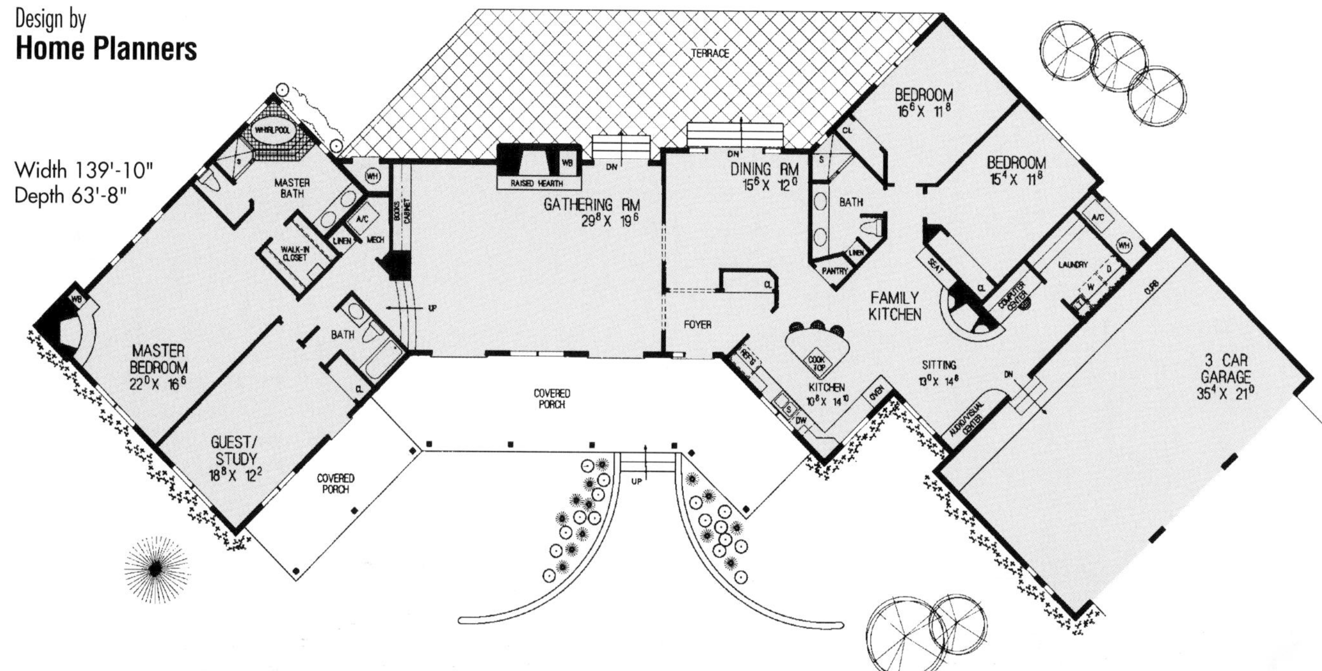
TERRACE
BEDROOM
16^6 X 11^8
BEDROOM
15^4 X 11^8
DINING RM
15^6 X 12^0
BATH
GATHERING RM
29^8 X 19^6
RAISED HEARTH
MASTER BATH
WHIRLPOOL
WALK-IN CLOSET
FAMILY KITCHEN
LAUNDRY
COMPUTER CENTER
FOYER
SITTING
13^0 X 14^8
KITCHEN
10^8 X 14^{10}
COOK TOP
3 CAR GARAGE
35^4 X 21^0
MASTER BEDROOM
22^0 X 16^6
BATH
GUEST/ STUDY
18^8 X 12^2
COVERED PORCH
COVERED PORCH
AUDIO/VISUAL CENTER

QUOTE ONE®

Cost to build? See page 516 to order complete cost estimate to build this house in your area!

Design 3433

Square Footage: 2,350

L

Width 92'-7"
Depth 79'-0"

COURTYARD
COVERED PORCH
BEDROOM 11⁰ X 11⁰
BATH
BEDROOM 10⁶ X 11⁶
BRKFST 9⁸ X 11⁰
KITCHEN 10⁶ X 14⁰
FAMILY RM 11⁰ X 10⁴
DINING RM 11⁴ X 9⁰
3 CAR GARAGE 29⁸ X 21⁶
SKYLIGHT
FOYER
ENTRY COURTYARD
LIVING RM 12⁰ X 17⁰
COVERED PORCH
STUDY 11² X 11⁰
MASTER BEDROOM 14⁰ X 13⁰
WALK-IN CLOSET
MASTER BATH

■ Santa Fe styling creates interesting angles in this one-story home. A grand entrance leads through a courtyard into the foyer with a circular skylight, closet space, niches and a convenient powder room. Fireplaces in the living room, dining room and on the covered porch create a warming heart of the home. Make note of the island range in the kitchen and the cozy breakfast room adjacent. The master suite has a privacy wall on the covered porch, a deluxe bath and a study close at hand. Two more family bedrooms are placed quietly in the far wing of the house near an open family room. The three-car garage offers extra storage.

Design by
Home Planners

This home, as shown in the photograph, may differ from the actual blueprints. For more detailed information, please check the floor plans carefully.

Photo by Bob Greenspan

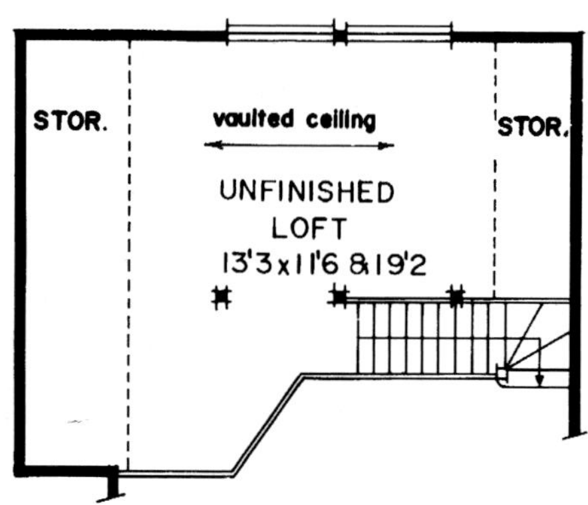
STOR.
vaulted ceiling
STOR.
UNFINISHED
LOFT
13'3x11'6 & 19'2

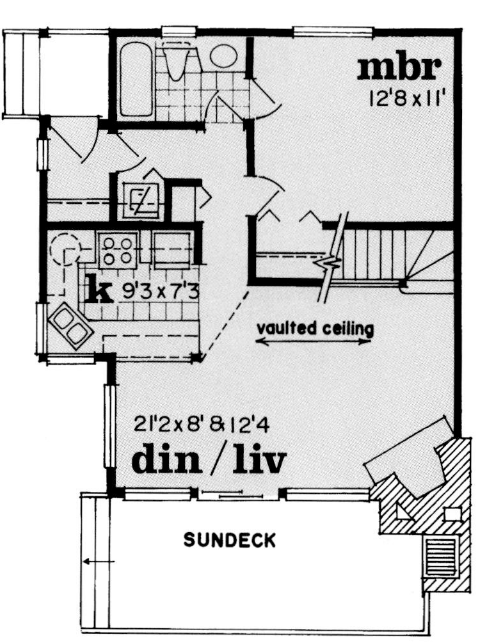
mbr
12'8x11'
k 9'3x7'3
vaulted ceiling
21'2x8' & 12'4
din/liv
SUNDECK

Design Q202

Square Footage: 680
Unfinished Loft: 419 square feet

Design by
Select Home Designs

■ Full window walls flood the living room and the dining room of this rustic vacation home with natural light. A full sundeck with built-in barbecue sits just outside the living area and is accessed by sliding glass doors. The entire large living space has a vaulted ceiling to gain spaciousness and to allow for the full-height windows. The efficient U-shaped kitchen has a pass-through counter to the dining area and a corner sink with windows over. A master bedroom is on the first floor and has the use of a full bath. A loft on the second floor overlooks the living room. It provides an additional 419 square feet not included in the above total. Use it for an additional bedroom or as a studio. It has a vaulted ceiling.

Width 26'-6"
Depth 28'-0"

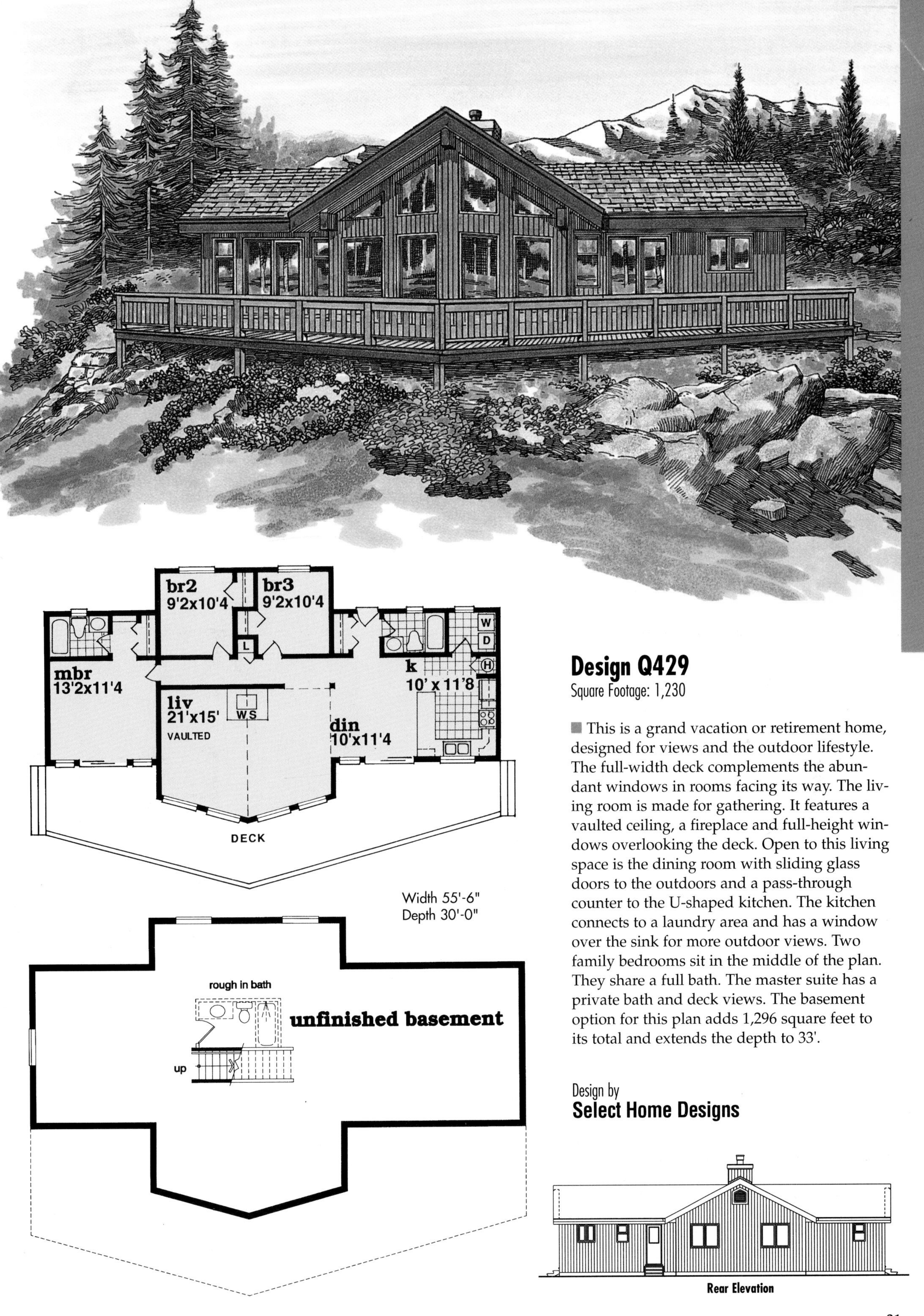
br2
9'2x10'4
br3
9'2x10'4
W
D
L
H
mbr
13'2x11'4
k
10' x 11'8
liv
21'x15'
VAULTED
WS
din
10'x11'4
DECK
Width 55'-6"
Depth 30'-0"
rough in bath
unfinished basement
up
Rear Elevation

Design Q429

Square Footage: 1,230

This is a grand vacation or retirement home, designed for views and the outdoor lifestyle. The full-width deck complements the abundant windows in rooms facing its way. The living room is made for gathering. It features a vaulted ceiling, a fireplace and full-height windows overlooking the deck. Open to this living space is the dining room with sliding glass doors to the outdoors and a pass-through counter to the U-shaped kitchen. The kitchen connects to a laundry area and has a window over the sink for more outdoor views. Two family bedrooms sit in the middle of the plan. They share a full bath. The master suite has a private bath and deck views. The basement option for this plan adds 1,296 square feet to its total and extends the depth to 33'.

Design by
Select Home Designs

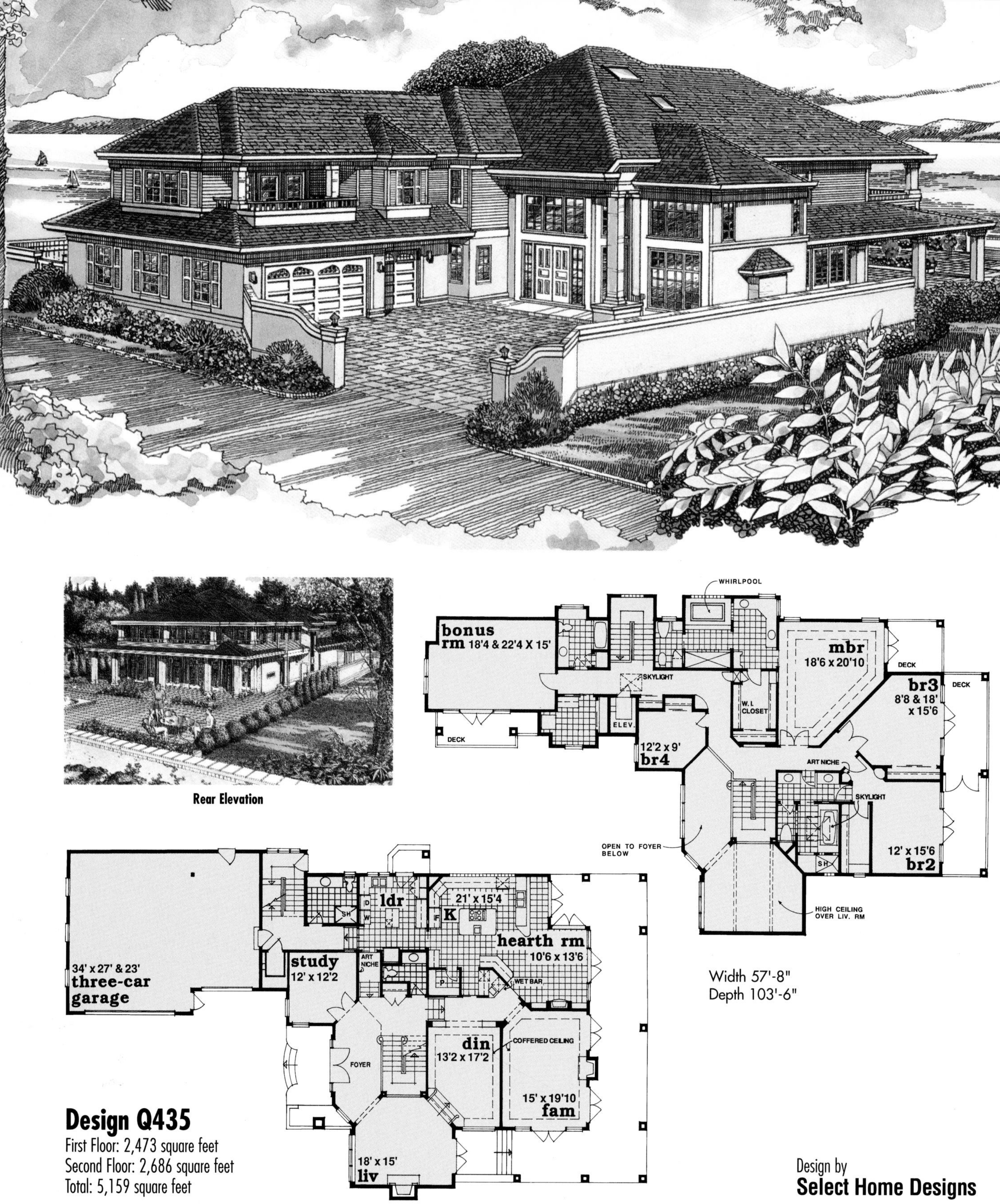
Rear Elevation
bonus rm 18'4 & 22'4 X 15'
WHIRLPOOL
SKYLIGHT
mbr 18'6 x 20'10
DECK
br3 8'8 & 18' x 15'6
W.I. CLOSET
ELEV.
12'2 x 9' br4
ART NICHE
SKYLIGHT
OPEN TO FOYER BELOW
12' x 15'6 br2
HIGH CEILING OVER LIV. RM
34' x 27' & 23' three-car garage
ldr
21' x 15'4
K
hearth rm 10'6 x 13'6
study 12' x 12'2
WET BAR
FOYER
din 13'2 x 17'2
COFFERED CEILING
15' x 19'10 fam
18' x 15' liv
Width 57'-8"
Depth 103'-6"

Design Q435

First Floor: 2,473 square feet
Second Floor: 2,686 square feet
Total: 5,159 square feet

Design by
Select Home Designs

■ This unusual stucco-and-siding design opens with a grand portico to a foyer containing a volume ceiling that extends to the living room. A multi-paned transom lights the foyer and the open staircase beyond. The living room has a fireplace and then proceeds up a few steps to the dining room with coffered ceiling and butler's pantry which connects it to the gourmet kitchen. Cooks will love the wet bar in the butler's pantry, the walk-in food pantry, a wine cooler, a built-in desk and the center island with cooktop and salad sink. The attached hearth room has the requisite fireplace and three sets of French doors to the covered porch. The family room sports a coffered ceiling and fireplace flanked by French doors. The second floor boasts four bedrooms, including a master suite with tray ceiling, covered deck and lavish bath. Two full baths serve the family bedrooms and a bonus room that might be used as an additional bedroom or hobby space.

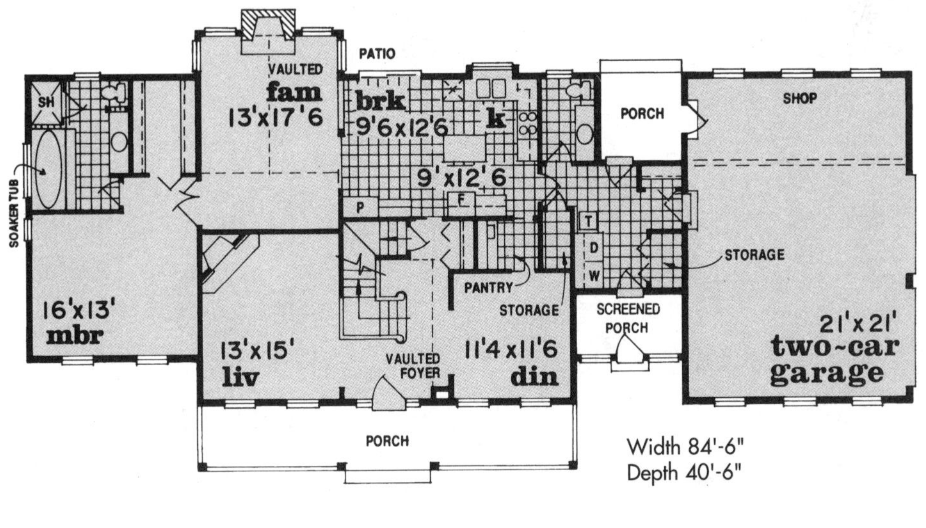
PATIO
VAULTED
fam
13'x17'6
brk
9'6x12'6
k
9'x12'6
PORCH
SHOP
SH
SOAKER TUB
P
T
D
W
16'x13'
mbr
13'x15'
liv
VAULTED
FOYER
PANTRY
STORAGE
11'4x11'6
din
SCREENED
PORCH
STORAGE
21'x21'
two-car
garage
PORCH
Width 84'-6"
Depth 40'-6"

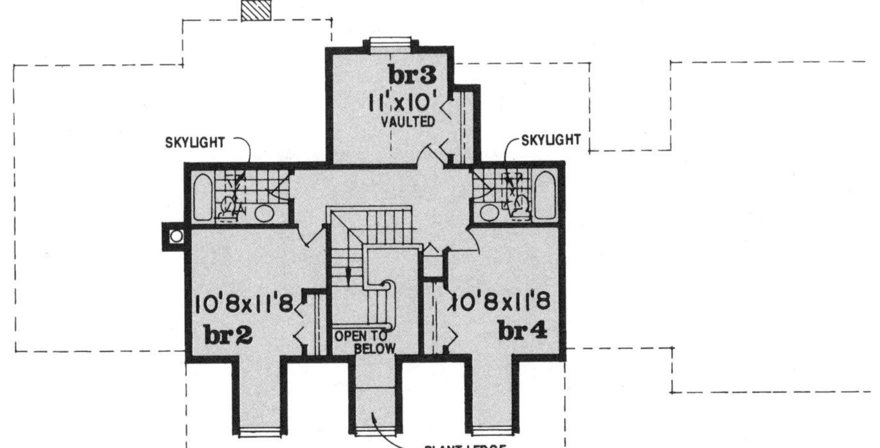
br3
11'x10'
VAULTED
SKYLIGHT
SKYLIGHT
10'8x11'8
br2
OPEN TO
BELOW
10'8x11'8
br4
PLANT LEDGE

Design Q411

First Floor: 1,722 square feet
Second Floor: 812 square feet
Total: 2,534 square feet

■ A home in the country, this design offers delightful details on its exterior: a trio of dormers, shuttered windows and a covered front porch. The vaulted foyer is brightened by a second-story dormer and is flanked by the living and dining rooms. A corner fireplace warms the living room. The gourmet kitchen offers a center prep island, a convenient butler's pantry and an attached breakfast room with sliding glass door access to the rear garden. A vaulted family room with fireplace is separated from the breakfast room by a half wall. The master bedroom remains on the first floor for privacy. It features a large walk-in closet and bath with whirlpool tub. Three family bedrooms share two baths with skylights on the second floor. Bedroom 3 has a vaulted ceiling.

Design by
Select Home Designs

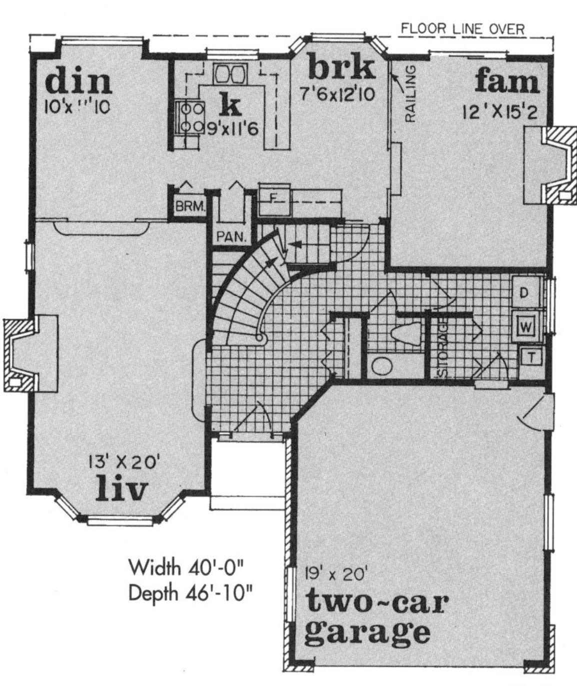

FLOOR LINE OVER
din
10'x11'10
k
9'x11'6
brk
7'6x12'10
RAILING
fam
12'X15'2
BRM.
F
PAN.
D
W
T
STORAGE
13' X 20'
liv
Width 40'-0"
Depth 46'-10"
19' x 20'
two-car
garage

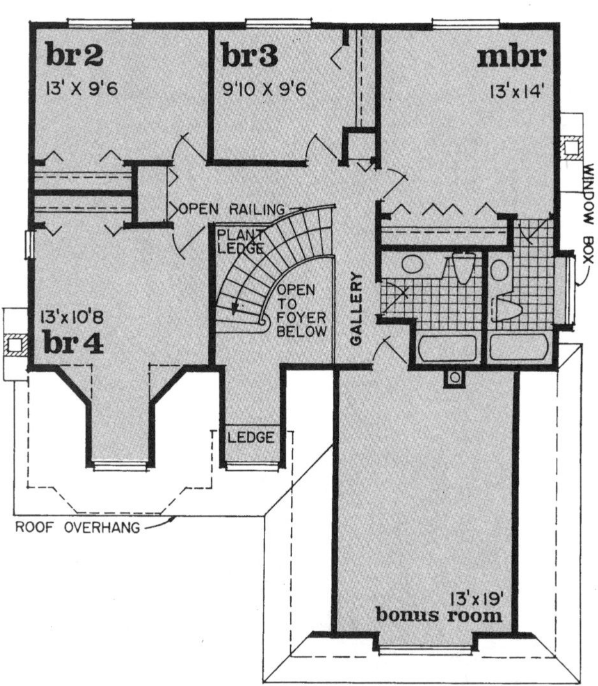

br2
13' X 9'6
br3
9'10 X 9'6
mbr
13'x14'
WINDOW BOX
OPEN RAILING
PLANT LEDGE
OPEN TO FOYER BELOW
GALLERY
13'x10'8
br4
LEDGE
ROOF OVERHANG
13'x19'
bonus room

Design Q258

First Floor: 1,167 square feet
Second Floor: 1,095 square feet
Total: 2,262 square feet
Bonus Room: 260 square feet

Design by
Select Home Designs

■ Dormer windows, a Palladian over the garage and a bayed bump-out add to this home's quaint appeal. Inside, a sweeping, curved staircase dominates the two-story foyer. The spacious sunken living room has a front-view bay and a fireplace. The attached dining room has a box-bay overlooking the rear yard. The U-shaped kitchen is appointed with a walk-in pantry and a broom closet. The attached breakfast nook overlooks the sunken family room. On the second level are three family bedrooms and a master suite. The master bedroom has a private bath, while family bedrooms share a full bath. A bonus room adds 260 square feet of space that can be developed at a later time, if desired. Plans include details for both a basement and a crawlspace foundation.

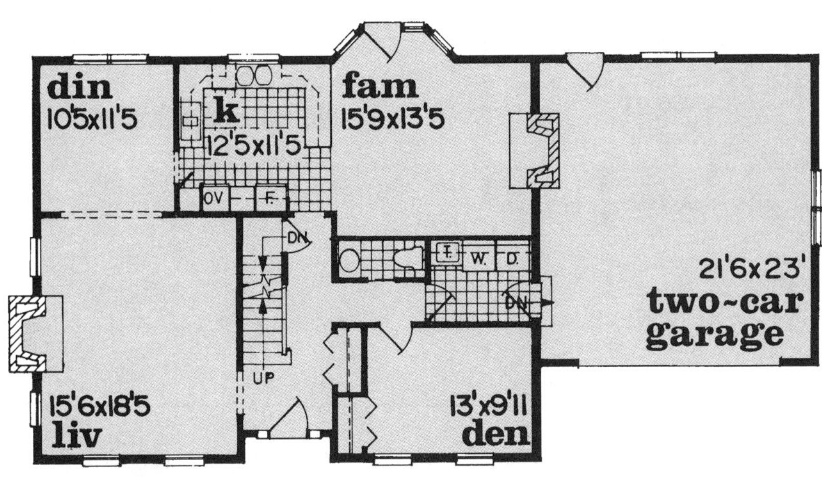

din
10'5x11'5
k
12'5x11'5
fam
15'9x13'5
OV
F
DN
W
D
DN
21'6x23'
two~car
garage
UP
15'6x18'5
liv
13'x9'11
den

Width 62'-0"
Depth 33'-10"

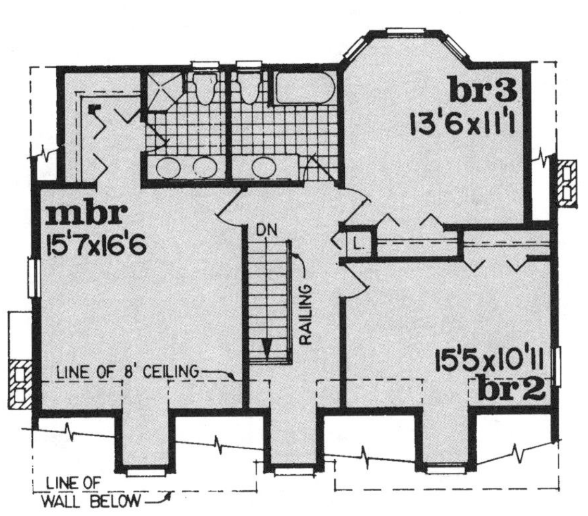

br3
13'6x11'1
mbr
15'7x16'6
DN
L
RAILING
LINE OF 8' CEILING
15'5x10'11
br2
LINE OF
WALL BELOW

Design Q259

First Floor; 1,260 square feet
Second Floor: 1,064 square feet
Total: 2,324 square feet

■ With overtones of Cape-Cod styling, this lovely design has dormer windows and shutters. The foyer opens to a spacious living room and dining room on the left and a den on the right. Because the den has an adjacent powder room, it might make a fine guest room. The fireplace is warmed by a fireplace, as is the family room with bay window and backyard access. Between the two living spaces is a U-shaped kitchen with abundant counterspace. An open-railed stair leads to a gallery on the second floor. On the right are two family bedrooms sharing a full bath. On the left is the master suite with private bath and walk-in closet. Note the dormer in the two front bedrooms and the bay window in Bedroom 3.

Design by
Select Home Designs

Design Q267

First Floor: 672 square feet
Second Floor: 571 square feet
Total: 1,243 square feet

■ This affordable starter or retirement home is charming with an exterior finished in beveled siding and shutters. The combination living room-dining room sits on the right of the foyer and offers a fireplace and double-door access to the rear yard. A den or third bedroom is on the left of the foyer and has a walk-in closet. The kitchen features an L-shaped work counter, plus space for a breakfast table and leads to the single-car garage through the laundry room and half-bath. Two bedrooms are found on the second floor; each has a dormer window. A full hall bath includes a soaking tub. Note the extra storage space in the garage and the built-in shelves in each of the bedrooms.

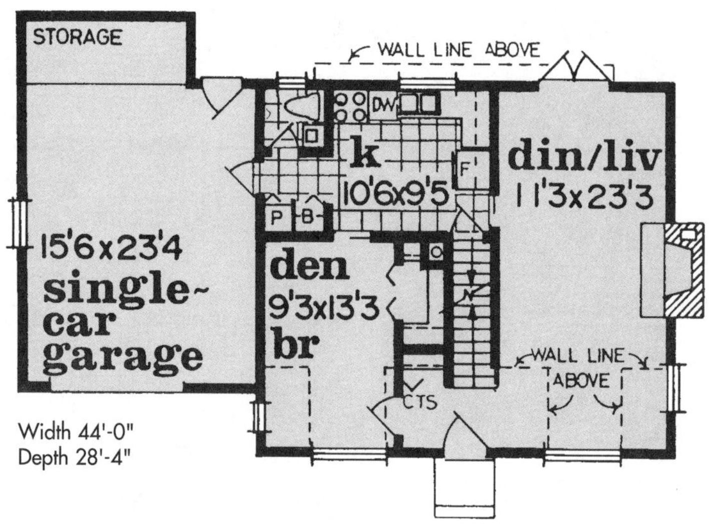
STORAGE
WALL LINE ABOVE
DW
k
10'6x9'5
F
din/liv
11'3x23'3
P
B
15'6x23'4
single-car garage
den
9'3x13'3
br
WALL LINE ABOVE
CTS
Width 44'-0"
Depth 28'-4"

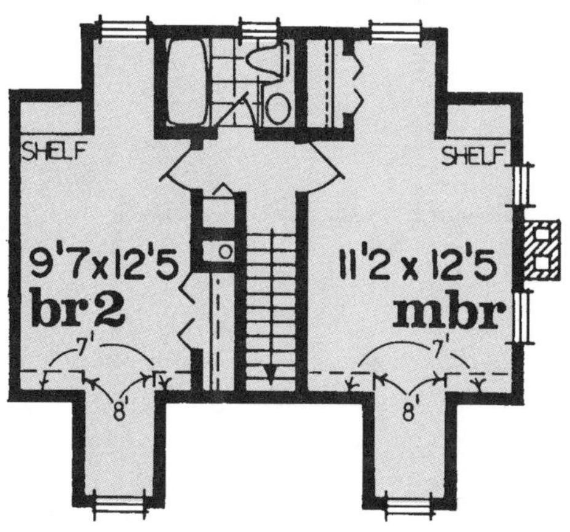
SHELF
SHELF
9'7x12'5
br2
11'2 x 12'5
mbr
7'
8'
7'
8'

Design by
Select Home Designs

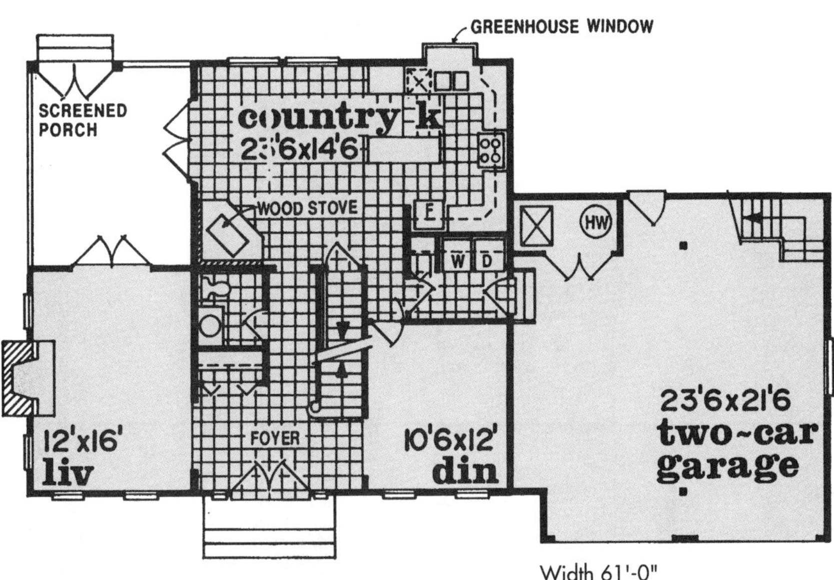
GREENHOUSE WINDOW
SCREENED PORCH
country k
23'6x14'6
WOOD STOVE
E
HW
W D
12'x16'
liv
FOYER
10'6x12'
din
23'6x21'6
two-car
garage

Width 61'-0"
Depth 35'-6"

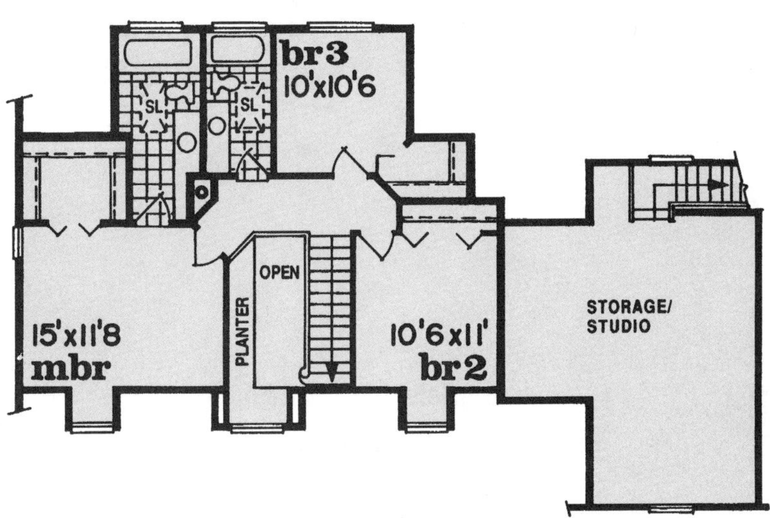
br3
10'x10'6
SL
SL
OPEN
PLANTER
15'x11'8
mbr
10'6x11'
br2
STORAGE/
STUDIO

Design Q375

First Floor: 996 square feet
Second Floor: 831 square feet
Total: 1,827 square feet
Storage/Studio: 356 square feet

■ A richly gabled roofline defines this fine three-bedroom home. Double doors open to a wide foyer flanked by the formal living and dining rooms. The living room features a fireplace and double-door access to a screened porch. The country kitchen also has access to the screened porch and boasts a center work island, a wood stove, a greenhouse window and space for a breakfast table. The two-car garage is reached via the service entrance through the laundry alcove. Three bedrooms on the second floor include a master suite with walk-in closet and private skylit bath. Bedroom 3 also has a walk-in closet. Both family bedrooms share the use of a full hall bath with skylight. Plans include details for both a basement and a crawlspace foundation.

Design by
Select Home Designs

Design Q253

First Floor: 895 square feet
Second Floor: 660 square feet
Total: 1,555 square feet

■ A covered veranda and gabled roofline combine with an efficient use of space in this compact home. Formal living areas are on the right side of the plan. The living room has a vaulted ceiling and fireplace; a full wall of windows overlook the veranda. A half-wall separates the living and dining rooms. Near the dining room, a U-shaped kitchen has a breakfast bar and laundry alcove. The attached breakfast room/family room features sliding glass doors to the patio at the rear. A two-car garage rounds out the main level—reached through a service entrance with half-bath. Three bedrooms on the second floor include a master suite with private bath and a large wall closet. Family bedrooms share a full hall bath. Plans include details for both a basement and a crawlspace foundation.

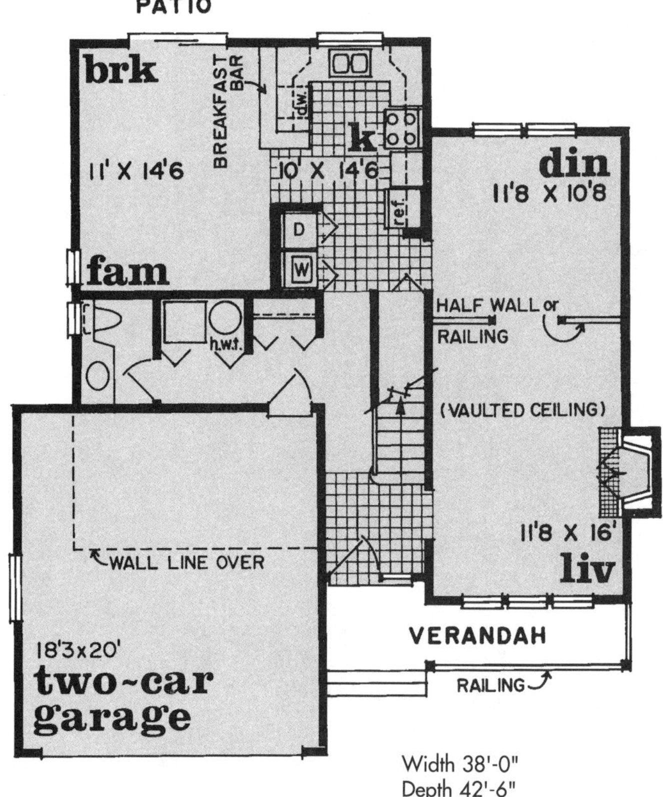

PATIO
brk
11' X 14'6
fam
BREAKFAST BAR
d.w.
k
10' X 14'6
ref.
D
W
din
11'8 X 10'8
HALF WALL or RAILING
h.w.t.
(VAULTED CEILING)
11'8 X 16'
liv
WALL LINE OVER
18'3x20'
two-car garage
VERANDAH
RAILING

Width 38'-0"
Depth 42'-6"

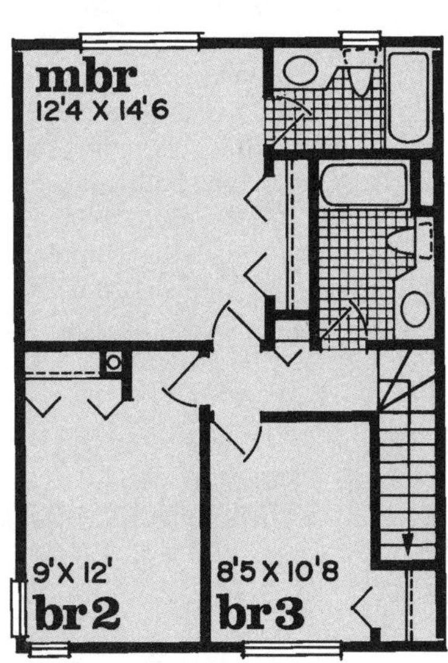

mbr
12'4 X 14'6
9'X 12'
br2
8'5 X 10'8
br3

Design by
Select Home Designs

Design Q234

First Floor: 879 square feet
Second Floor: 869 square feet
Total: 1,748 square feet

■ Special exterior details—a railed veranda, multi-paned windows and a dormer—lend a country flavor to this three-bedroom home. A central hall at the entry holds a half-bath and a stair to the second floor and also allows passage to the formal living and dining rooms. The living room contains a fireplace; the dining room features a private veranda. The country kitchen is also warmed by a fireplace and features sliding glass doors to the rear patio (note the built-in barbecue). An L-shaped work counter is convenient and is complemented by a large pantry. The two-car garage is reached through the laundry area. On the second floor are three bedrooms. The master has a grand bath with separate shower and tub. Family bedrooms share a full hall bath. Plans include details for both a basement and a crawlspace foundation.

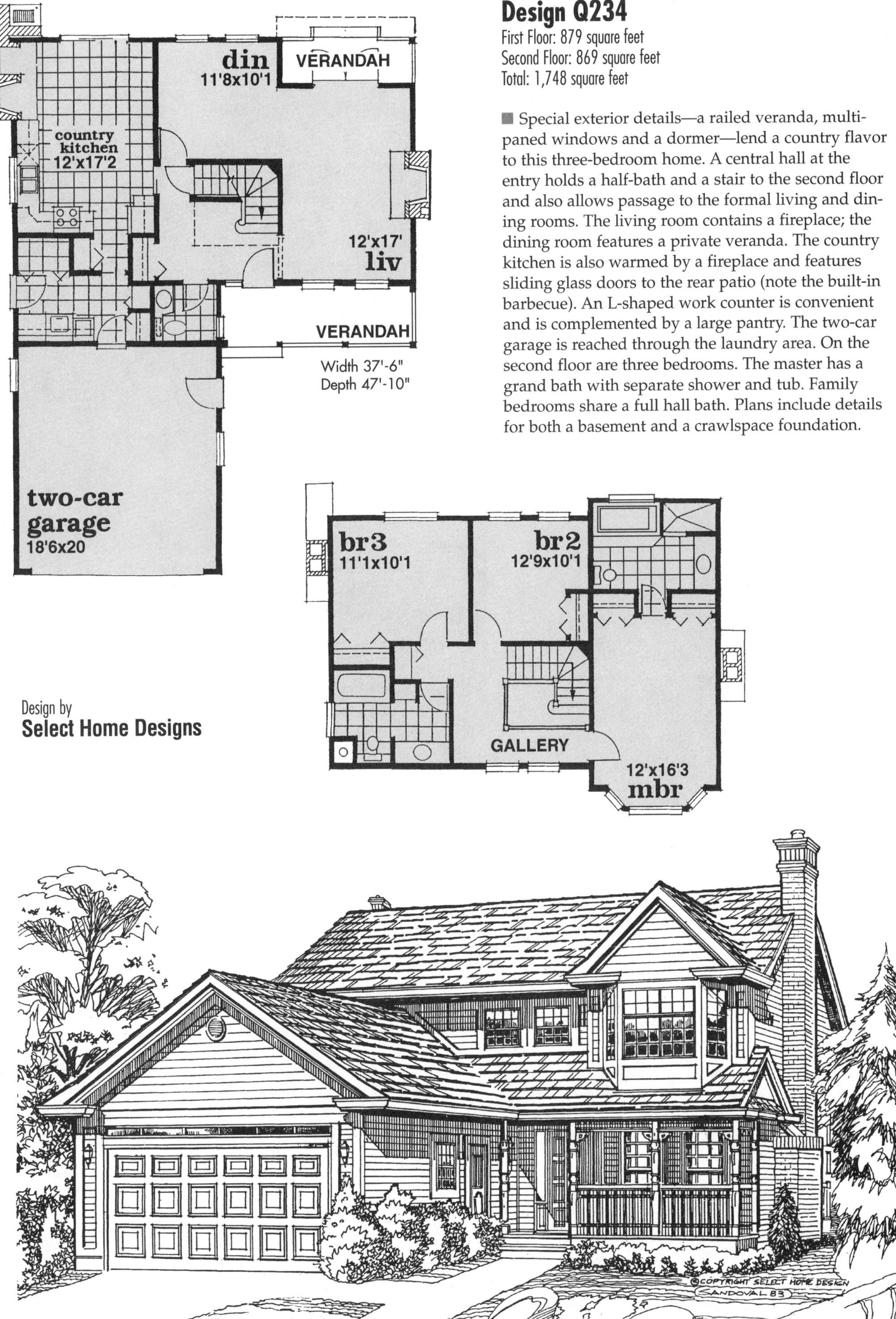
din
11'8x10'1
VERANDAH
country
kitchen
12'x17'2
12'x17'
liv
VERANDAH
Width 37'-6"
Depth 47'-10"
two-car
garage
18'6x20
br3
11'1x10'1
br2
12'9x10'1
GALLERY
12'x16'3
mbr
©COPYRIGHT SELECT HOME DESIGN
SANDOVAL 83

Design by
Select Home Designs

Design Q332

First Floor: 1,324 square feet
Second Floor: 1,206 square feet
Total: 2,530 square feet

■ This design may be finished in brick or horizontal siding with a wrapping veranda. Details for both options are included in the plans. The same, roomy floor plan serves both exteriors. From the wide foyer, the plan stretches to a living/dining room combination with tray ceiling, fireplace and French doors to the covered porch at the back. On the opposite side of the foyer is a den with bay window. A half-bath nearby allows the den to double as a guest room. The family room has a fireplace and access to a private deck. The octagonal breakfast room and kitchen are nearby. Amenities in the kitchen include a spacious angled counter and work island. Four bedrooms are situated on the second floor. The master bedroom is vaulted and has a vaulted bath with whirlpool tub and double sinks. The three family bedrooms share a bath with compartmented tub and vanity. Plans include details for both a basement and a crawlspace foundation.

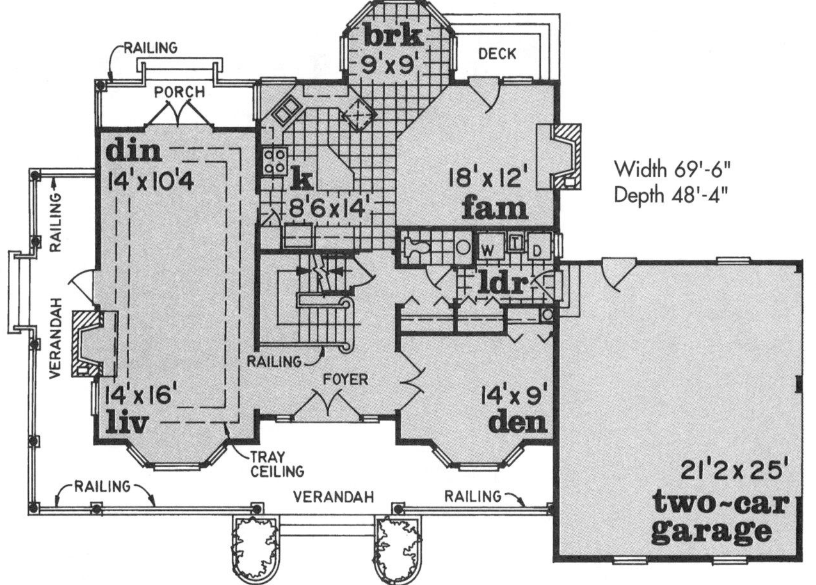
RAILING
brk
9'x9'
DECK
PORCH
din
14'x10'4
k
8'6x14'
18'x12'
fam
Width 69'-6"
Depth 48'-4"
RAILING
VERANDAH
W
D
ldr
RAILING
FOYER
14'x16'
liv
14'x9'
den
TRAY CEILING
RAILING
VERANDAH
RAILING
21'2x25'
two-car garage

Design by
Select Home Designs

Alternate Elevation

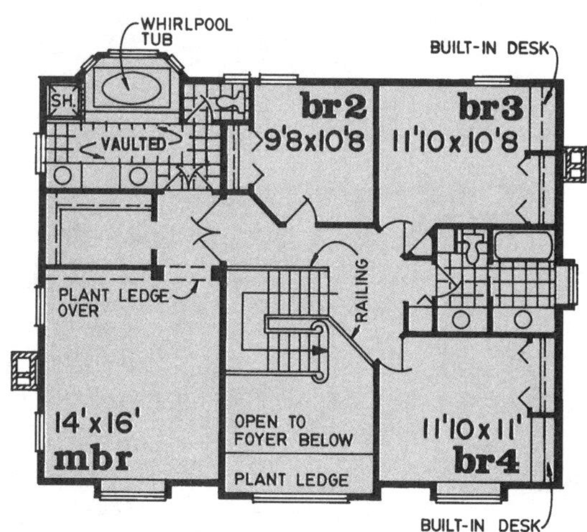
WHIRLPOOL TUB
BUILT-IN DESK
SH.
VAULTED
br2
9'8x10'8
br3
11'10x10'8
PLANT LEDGE OVER
RAILING
14'x16'
mbr
OPEN TO FOYER BELOW
PLANT LEDGE
11'10x11'
br4
BUILT-IN DESK

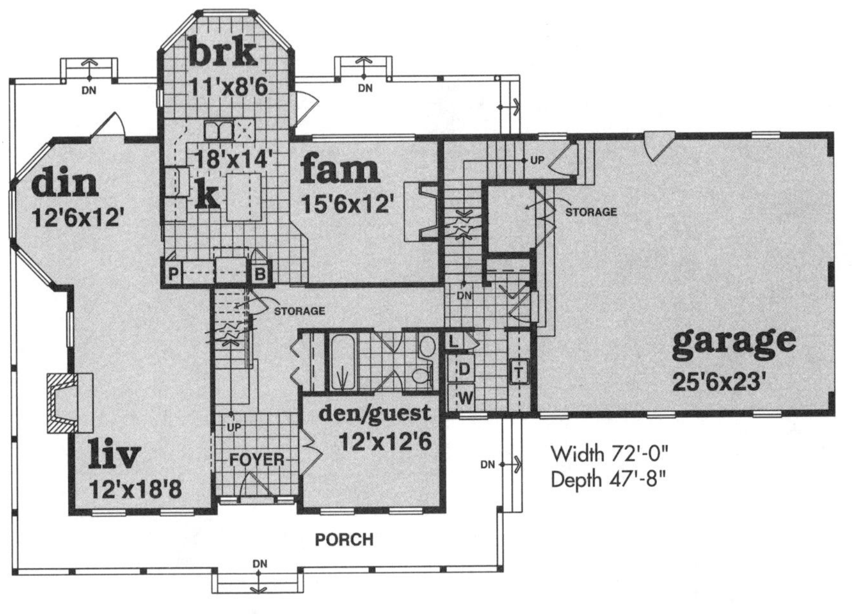
brk
11'x8'6
DN
DN
din
12'6x12'
18'x14'
k
fam
15'6x12'
UP
STORAGE
P
B
STORAGE
DN
L
D
W
T
garage
25'6x23'
den/guest
12'x12'6
UP
FOYER
liv
12'x18'8
DN
Width 72'-0"
Depth 47'-8"
PORCH
DN

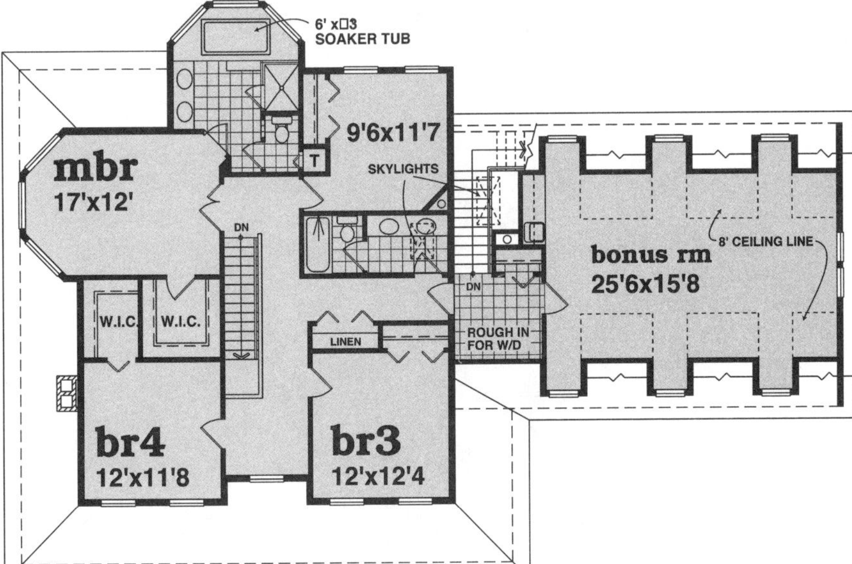
6' x□3
SOAKER TUB
9'6x11'7
mbr
17'x12'
T
SKYLIGHTS
DN
bonus rm
25'6x15'8
8' CEILING LINE
DN
W.I.C.
W.I.C.
LINEN
ROUGH IN
FOR W/D
br4
12'x11'8
br3
12'x12'4

Design Q510

First Floor: 1,422 square feet
Second Floor: 1,273 square feet
Total: 2,695 square feet
Bonus Room: 640 square feet

■ With a veranda that almost completely surrounds the first floor, this house is made for indoor/outdoor living. The veranda can be accessed at three different points in the plan: the main entry, the octagonal dining room and the bayed breakfast room. Both the living room and the family room are warmed by hearths; the den has access to a full bath so it can easily double as a guest room. The main stairway in the center is complemented by an additional stairway near the laundry that leads up to the bedrooms or to a handy bonus room that can be developed later. Four bedrooms are found on the second floor—one a master suite with lavish bath. Both the master bedroom and Bedroom 4 have walk-in closets. The two-car garage contains a large storage area. Plans include details for both a basement and a crawlspace foundation.

Design by
Select Home Designs

Design Q246

Square Footage: 1,107
Unfinished Lower Level: 819 square feet

■ This unusually designed home is planned with the bulk of the living space on the second floor. For areas with spectacular views, this is a real bonus. The entry foyer, occupying 95 square feet of finished floor space, leads up to a living and dining room with a fireplace and sliding glass door access to a beautiful sundeck. The nearby kitchen is U-shaped for convenience and has a box window over the sink. The adjoining breakfast area is perfect for casual meals. Three bedrooms line the rear of the plan. The master bedroom has a private half-bath and dual wall closets. Family bedrooms share a full bath with soaking tub. Space on the lower level will add two bedrooms, a full bath and a family room—819 square feet—when completed.

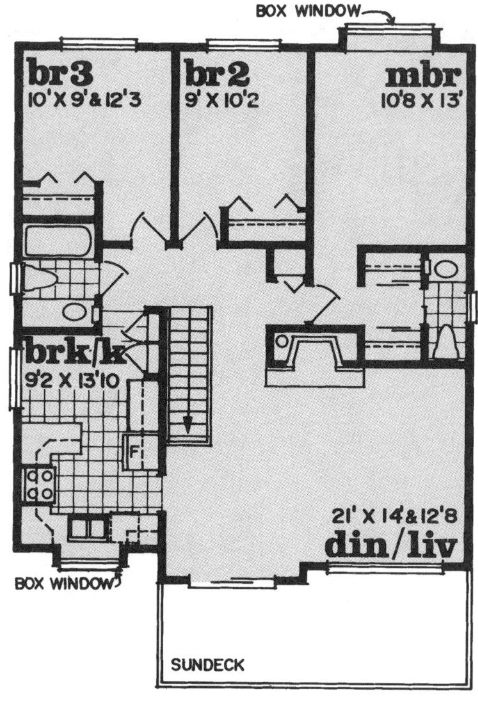
BOX WINDOW
br3
10'X 9'& 12'3
br2
9' X 10'2
mbr
10'8 X 13'
brk/k
9'2 X 13'10
F
21' X 14'& 12'8
din/liv
BOX WINDOW
SUNDECK

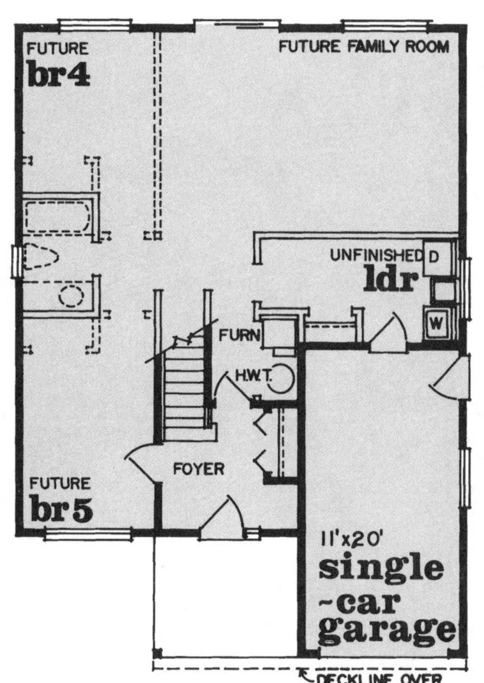
FUTURE
br4
FUTURE FAMILY ROOM
UNFINISHED
ldr
D
W
FURN
H.W.T.
FOYER
FUTURE
br5
11'x20'
single
-car
garage
DECKLINE OVER

Width 31'-6"
Depth 43'-0"

Design by
Select Home Designs

Design Q409

First Floor: 1,323 square feet
Second Floor: 1,243 square feet
Total: 2,566 square feet

■ Choose a classic design in brick or horizontal siding with a covered veranda for the facade of this home. Details for both options are included when you purchase the plans. The central foyer is flanked by a formal living room, with corner fireplace, and dining room, with butler's pantry to the kitchen. A dual access stairway begins in two places—in the foyer and in the kitchen—to lead to a common landing up to the skylit second floor. The family room is sunken and has another corner fireplace and sliding glass doors to an optional sunroom. The breakfast room opens to a patio at the back. Four bedrooms grace the second floor. The master suite has a walk-in closet and private bath. Family bedrooms share a full bath. A quiet study area near the master bedroom entry has built-in shelves. Plans include details for both a basement and a crawlspace foundation.

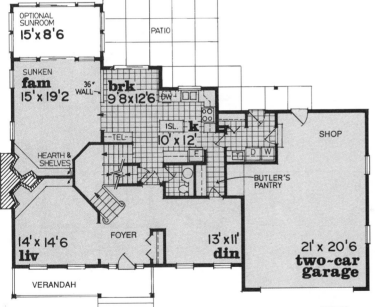

OPTIONAL SUNROOM
15'x8'6
PATIO
SUNKEN
fam
15'x 19'2
36" WALL
brk
9'8x12'6
DW
ISL.
k
10'x 12'
TEL
HEARTH & SHELVES
F
T D W
SHOP
BUTLER'S PANTRY
FOYER
14'x 14'6
liv
13'x11'
din
21' x 20'6
two-car garage
VERANDAH

Width 61'-6"
Depth 40'-0"

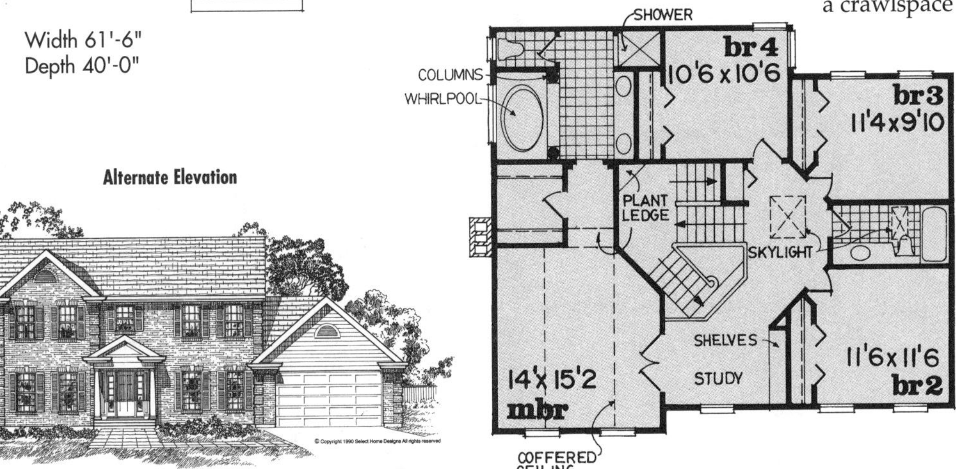
SHOWER
br4
10'6 x 10'6
COLUMNS
WHIRLPOOL
br3
11'4x9'10
PLANT LEDGE
SKYLIGHT
SHELVES
STUDY
11'6x11'6
br2
14'x 15'2
mbr
COFFERED CEILING

Alternate Elevation

Design by
Select Home Designs

Design 5514

First Floor: 718 square feet
Second Floor: 691 square feet
Total: 1,409 square feet
Bonus Room: 268 square feet

■ Built for regular or corner lots, this floor plan offers plenty of flexibility and room for growth. Adding to this home's appeal, the front covered porch provides enough space for a cozy swing or a rocking chair or two. Inside, the sunny foyer accesses both the kitchen and breakfast nook, and the formal living room with its warming fireplace. A rear corner dining room and a convenient powder room complete the first floor. Upstairs, two bedrooms share a full bath while the master bedroom features a bay window and a private bath. Additional space is available in the attic for storage, a quiet studio or an another bedroom. A bonus room over the garage provides more opportunity for expansion.

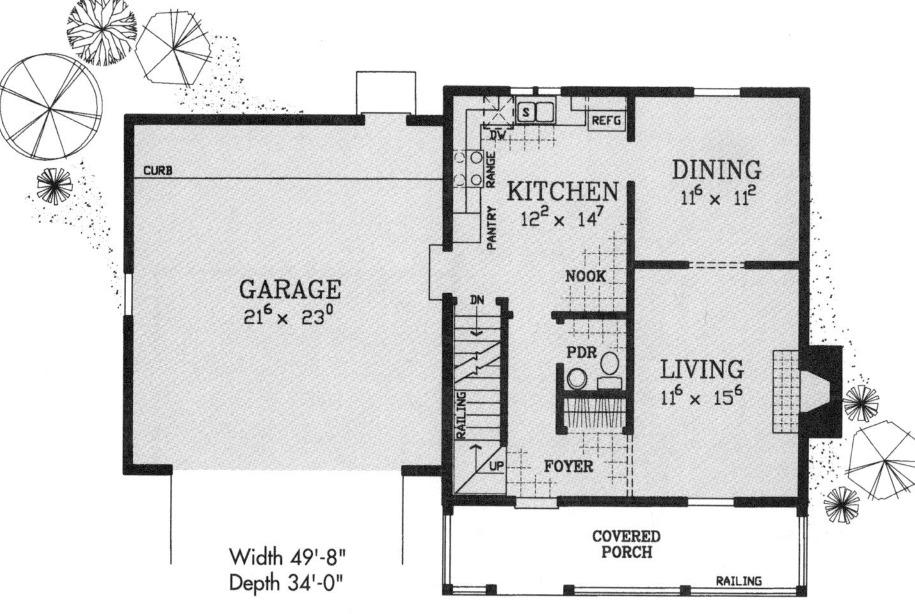

CURB
GARAGE
21⁶ x 23⁰
KITCHEN
12² x 14⁷
DINING
11⁶ x 11²
REFG
DW
RANGE
PANTRY
NOOK
DN
PDR
LIVING
11⁶ x 15⁶
RAILING
UP
FOYER
COVERED PORCH
RAILING
Width 49'-8"
Depth 34'-0"

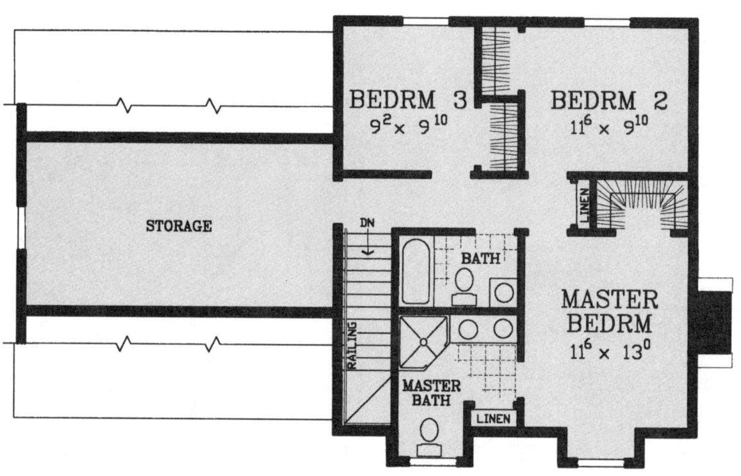

BEDRM 3
9² x 9¹⁰
BEDRM 2
11⁶ x 9¹⁰
STORAGE
LINEN
DN
BATH
MASTER BEDRM
11⁶ x 13⁰
RAILING
MASTER BATH
LINEN

Design by
Home Planners

QUOTE ONE®

Cost to build? See page 516 to order complete cost estimate to build this house in your area!

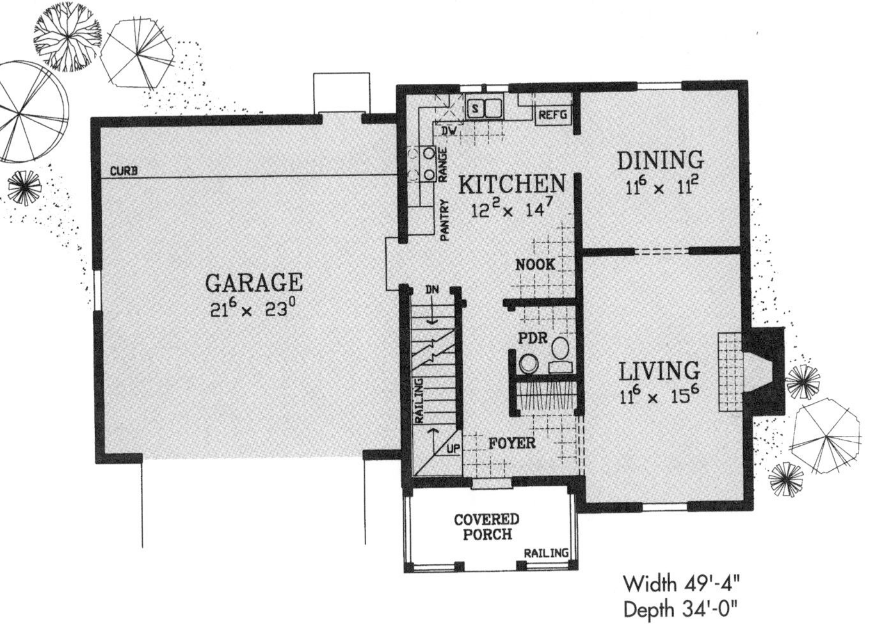
GARAGE
21⁶ x 23⁰
CURB
KITCHEN
12² x 14⁷
DINING
11⁶ x 11²
REFG
DW
RANGE
PANTRY
NOOK
DN
PDR
LIVING
11⁶ x 15⁶
RAILING
UP
FOYER
COVERED PORCH
RAILING
Width 49'-4"
Depth 34'-0"

Design 5516

First Floor: 743 square feet
Second Floor: 707 square feet
Total: 1,450 square feet
Bonus Room: 268 square feet

■ Within this compact design lies a wealth of livability. The foyer includes a handy powder room and a coat closet and leads to both the living room, with its central fireplace, and the comfortable kitchen and breakfast nook. The dining area accesses not only the kitchen and living room, but the rear yard as well. Three bedrooms are located upstairs. The family bedrooms share a full bath while the master bedroom features a private bath and a walk-in closet. Additional space is available in the third-floor attic area and can be made into another bedroom, an office, a studio or used for storage space. The bonus room above the garage also provides additional space as it is needed.

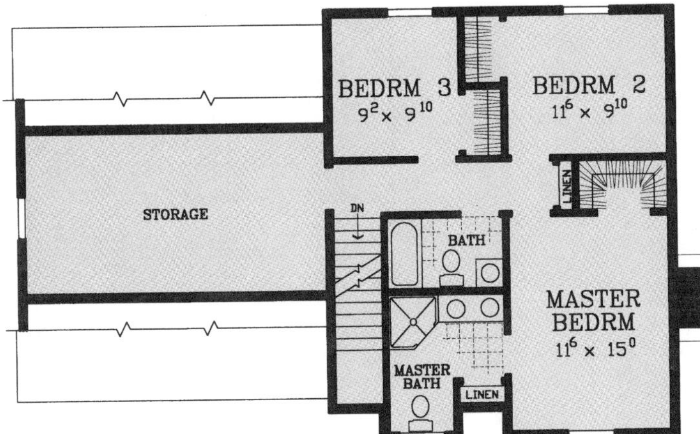
BEDRM 3
9² x 9¹⁰
BEDRM 2
11⁶ x 9¹⁰
LINEN
STORAGE
DN
BATH
MASTER BEDRM
11⁶ x 15⁰
MASTER BATH
LINEN

Design by
Home Planners

QUOTE ONE®

Cost to build? See page 516 to order complete cost estimate to build this house in your area!

Design 1957

First Floor: 1,042 square feet
Second Floor: 780 square feet
Total: 1,822 square feet

L **D**

Design by
Home Planners

■ When you order blueprints for this design you will receive details for the construction of each of the three charming exteriors pictured. Whichever exterior you finally decide to build, the floor plan will be essentially the same except for the location of the windows. The layout is classic center-hall design. The entry foyer holds a stairway to the second floor and leads to a large living room with connecting dining room. Sliding glass doors in the dining room allow access to a rear dining terrace. The U-shaped kitchen has a window sink and attached breakfast area with window overlooking the rear yard. The family room is sunken and adorned with a beam ceiling. A focal point fireplace is flanked by built-in bookshelves. Access to the play terrace is through sliding glass doors in the family room. There are four bedrooms and two full baths (one with a stall shower) upstairs. All bedrooms have ample closet space.

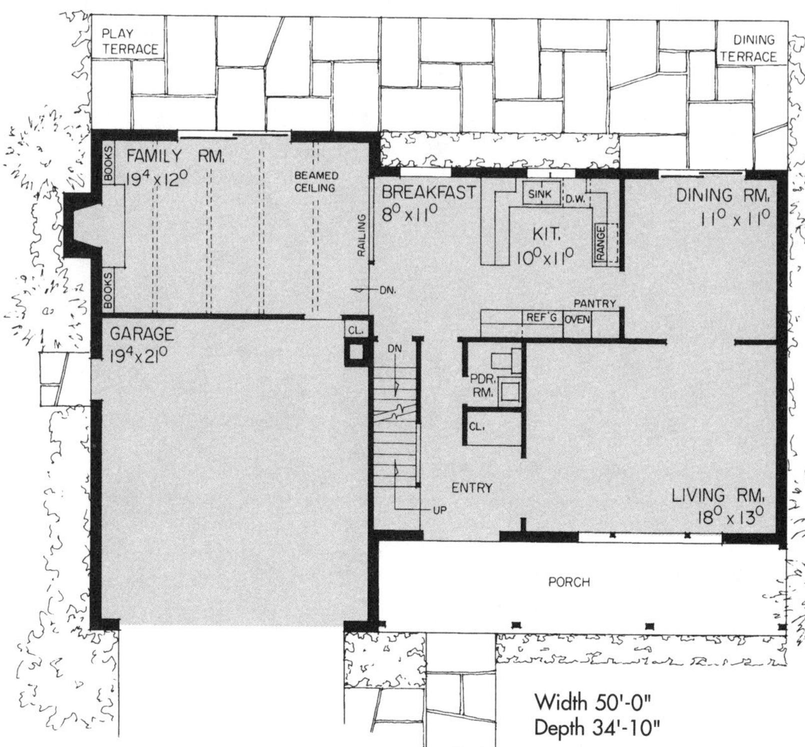
PLAY TERRACE
DINING TERRACE
BOOKS
FAMILY RM. 19^4 x 12^0
BEAMED CEILING
RAILING
BREAKFAST 8^0 x 11^0
SINK
D.W.
KIT. 10^0 x 11^0
RANGE
DINING RM. 11^0 x 11^0
DN.
PANTRY
REF'G
OVEN
CL.
GARAGE 19^4 x 21^0
DN
PDR. RM.
CL.
ENTRY
UP
LIVING RM. 18^0 x 13^0
PORCH
Width 50'-0"
Depth 34'-10"

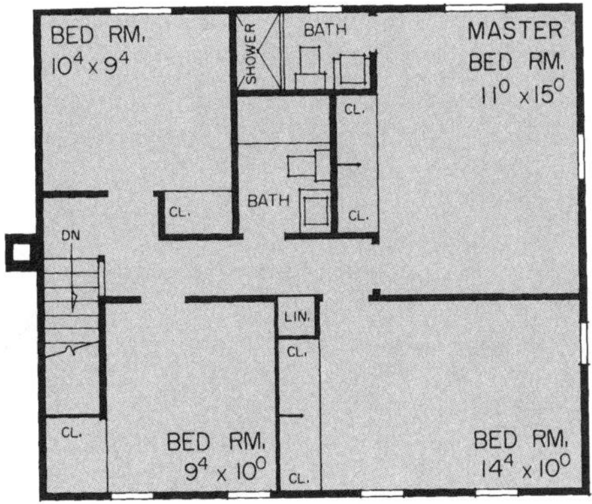
BED RM.
10^4 x 9^4
SHOWER
BATH
MASTER
BED RM.
11^0 x 15^0
CL.
BATH
CL.
CL.
DN
LIN.
CL.
CL.
BED RM.
9^4 x 10^0
CL.
BED RM.
14^4 x 10^0

QUOTE ONE®

Cost to build? See page 516 to order complete cost estimate to build this house in your area!

Design Q357

Square Footage: 1,391
Unfinished Lower Level: 932 square feet

■ Build this interesting design where second-floor living space can take advantage of a great view. The lower level can remain unfinished until needed. The foyer contains 132 square feet of finished space and leads up to the living areas and bedrooms on the second floor. Living areas here are comprised of a living room/dining room combination with wide windows overlooking the front, plus a cozy fireplace. A smaller family room is to the rear with sliding glass doors to a deck. The breakfast room also has sliding glass doors, which open to the front deck. The kitchen nestles in between the formal and informal living areas. Three bedrooms sit quietly to the rear of the plan. The master suite features a walk-in closet and a private bath. A box-bay window lights the master bedroom. Two family bedrooms share a full bath.

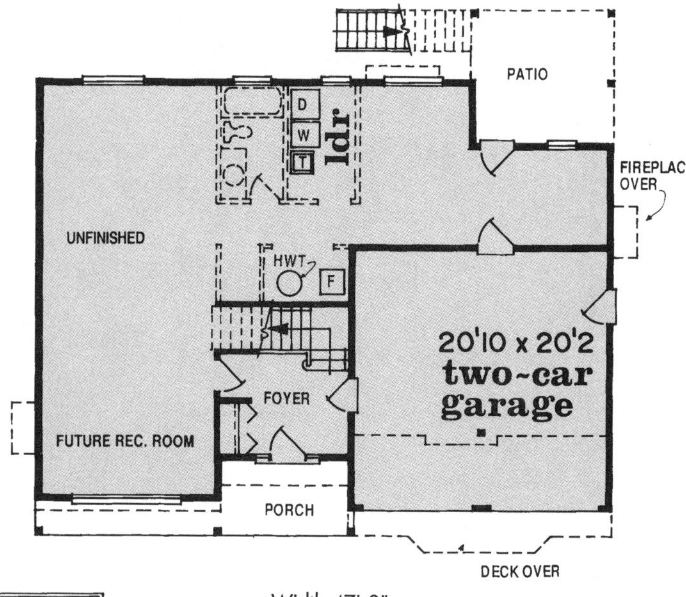

PATIO
D
W
T
ldr
FIREPLACE OVER
UNFINISHED
HWT
F
20'10 x 20'2
two-car
garage
FOYER
FUTURE REC. ROOM
PORCH
DECK OVER

Width 47'-0"
Depth 36'-0"

DECK
br2
11'6 x 9'2
mbr
11'2 x 13'8
fam
11'4 x 14'2
10'2 x 9'
br3
k
10'8 x 13'8
10'2 x 8'2
brk
11'2 x 10'2
din
14'4 x 12'2
liv
DECK
ROOF BELOW

Design by
Select Home Designs

Design 5547

First Floor: 1,239 square feet
Second Floor: 1,120 square feet
Total: 2,359 square feet
Optional Rec Room: 406 square feet

■ From the covered front porch to the rear yard, this two-story home serves up enough space to meet the versatile and growing needs of any family. The front foyer offers entry into any area on the first floor. To the right lies a quiet media room with access to a sunny breakfast nook and to either the mud room and garage, or to the backyard via glass doors. Nearby is the U-shaped kitchen. The kitchen also easily serves the great room. Upstairs, three family bedrooms share a full bath with dual basins and a conveniently located washer/dryer area. The luxurious master bedroom features a walk-in closet and a private master bath with a corner whirlpool tub. A bonus room with a half-bath is located above the garage. It can be used for an office, a quiet guest room or a games room.

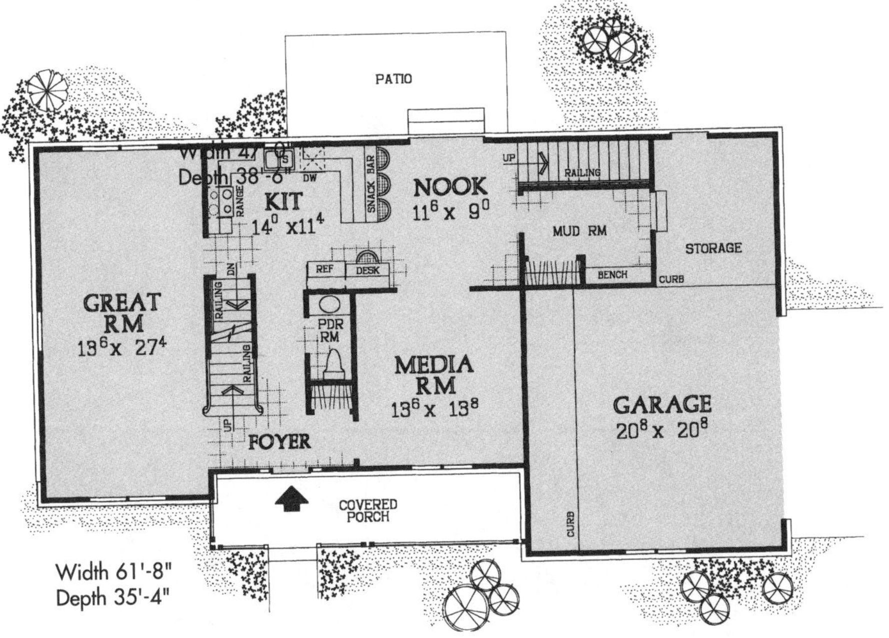
PATIO
KIT
14^{0} x11^{4}
NOOK
11^{6} x 9^{0}
UP
RAILING
MUD RM
STORAGE
BENCH
CURB
REF
DESK
GREAT
RM
13^{6}x 27^{4}
PDR
RM
MEDIA
RM
13^{6} x 13^{8}
GARAGE
20^{8} x 20^{8}
FOYER
COVERED
PORCH
Width 61'-8"
Depth 35'-4"

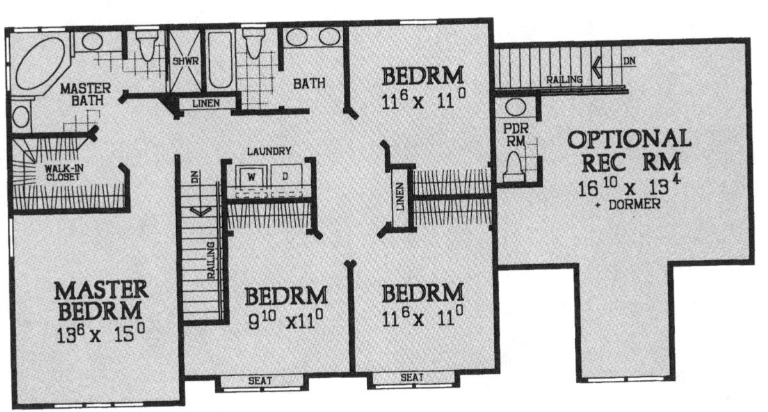
MASTER
BATH
SHWR
LINEN
BATH
BEDRM
11^{6}x 11^{0}
RAILING
DN
PDR
RM
OPTIONAL
REC RM
16^{10} x 13^{4}
+ DORMER
LAUNDRY
W
D
WALK-IN
CLOSET
LINEN
MASTER
BEDRM
13^{6}x 15^{0}
BEDRM
9^{10} x11^{0}
BEDRM
11^{6}x 11^{0}
SEAT
SEAT

Design by
Home Planners

QUOTE ONE®

Cost to build? See page 516 to order complete cost estimate to build this house in your area!

Design 5548

First Floor: 1,239 square feet
Second Floor: 1,120 square feet
Total: 2,359 square feet
Optional Rec Room: 415 square feet

■ A long covered porch with room for rocking chairs offers a hearty welcome to this two-story home. To the left of the foyer is a spacious great room with plenty of space for furniture placement. The U-shaped kitchen offers plenty of counter space and a snack bar pass-through to the breakfast nook. The nook provides access to the rear yard, the mud room and garage and the second-floor bonus room. A media room or den, and a powder room complete the first floor. On the second floor, the master bedroom features a large walk-in closet and a luxurious master bath. Three additional bedrooms share a full hall bath with an individual sink area. The bonus room and half-bath above the garage might be the perfect space for an office, a guest or for the teenager who wants to get a feel for a place of his own.

Design by
Home Planners

QUOTE ONE®

Cost to build? See page 516 to order complete cost estimate to build this house in your area!

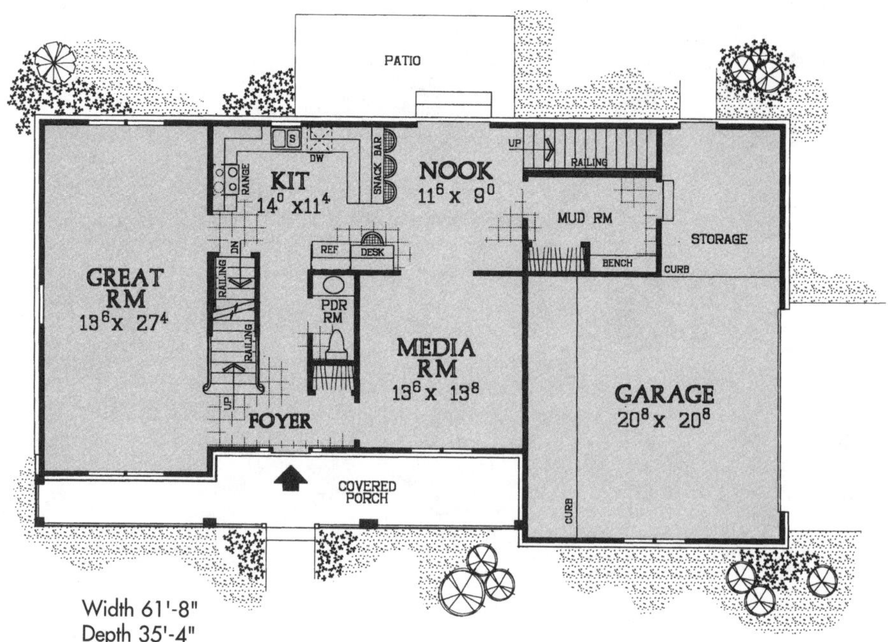
PATIO
KIT
14^0 x 11^4
NOOK
11^6 x 9^0
SNACK BAR
RANGE
DW
UP
RAILING
MUD RM
STORAGE
BENCH
CURB
GREAT RM
13^6 x 27^4
REF
DESK
PDR RM
DN
RAILING
UP
MEDIA RM
13^6 x 13^8
FOYER
GARAGE
20^8 x 20^8
COVERED PORCH
CURB

Width 61'-8"
Depth 35'-4"

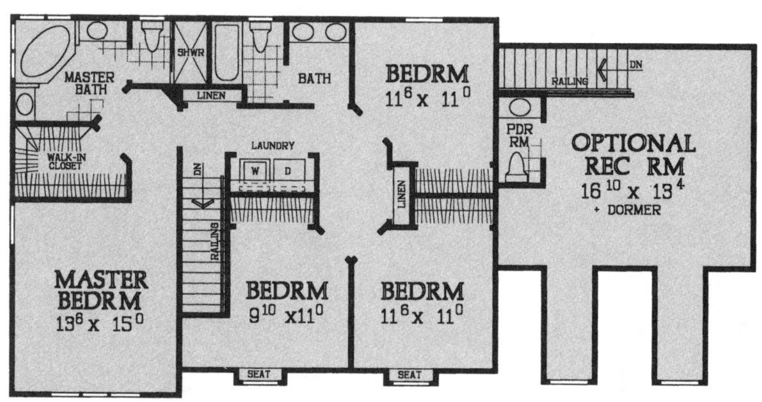
MASTER BATH
SHWR
LINEN
BATH
BEDRM
11^6 x 11^0
DN
RAILING
WALK-IN CLOSET
LAUNDRY
W
D
LINEN
PDR RM
OPTIONAL REC RM
16^{10} x 13^4
+ DORMER
MASTER BEDRM
13^6 x 15^0
BEDRM
9^{10} x 11^0
BEDRM
11^6 x 11^0
SEAT
SEAT

Design 5538

First Floor: 802 square feet
Second Floor: 757 square feet
Total: 1,559 square feet
Storage Room: 268 square feet

■ With an appealing facade and lots of room for growth or storage, this comfortable home would be the perfect plan for a young family starting out or for empty-nesters looking to retire in style. The first floor features a combination living and dining room with outdoor access and a warming fireplace. The connecting U-shaped kitchen includes a snack bar and a bayed breakfast nook with views to the front yard. With two family bedrooms, a master bedroom and plenty of storage space, the upstairs sleeping zone provides a perfect opportunity for the young family to grow or for empty-nesters to offer plenty of sleeping room for visiting friends and family, while still having space for hobbies. While the two family bedrooms share a full hall bath, the master bedroom features a private bath. An additional half-bath is conveniently located downstairs.

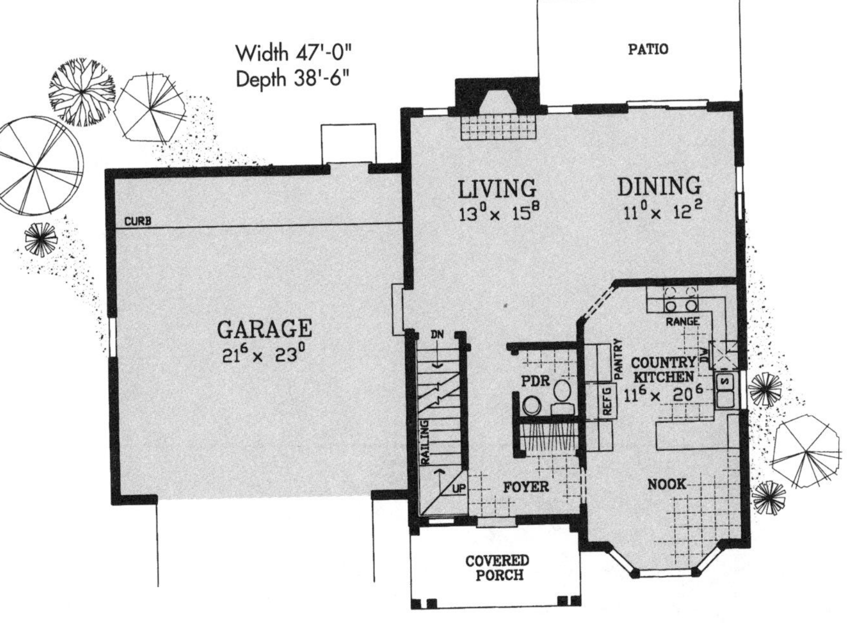
Width 47'-0"
Depth 38'-6"
PATIO
LIVING
$13^0 \times 15^8$
DINING
$11^0 \times 12^2$
CURB
GARAGE
$21^6 \times 23^0$
DN
RANGE
COUNTRY KITCHEN
$11^6 \times 20^6$
PANTRY
DW
S
REFG
PDR
RAILING
UP
FOYER
NOOK
COVERED PORCH

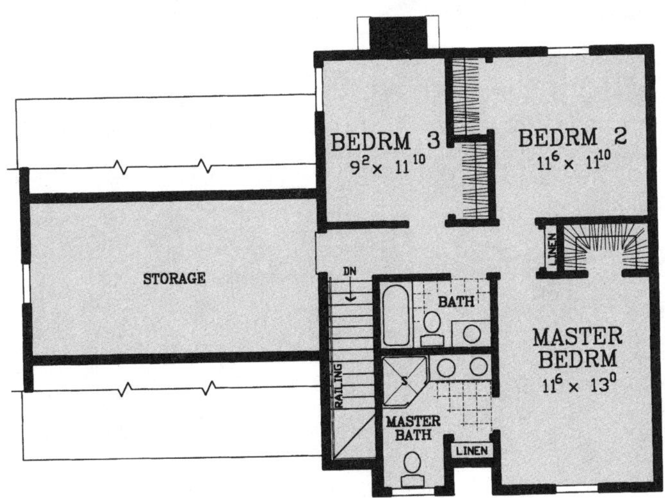
BEDRM 3
$9^2 \times 11^{10}$
BEDRM 2
$11^6 \times 11^{10}$
LINEN
STORAGE
DN
BATH
MASTER BEDRM
$11^6 \times 13^0$
RAILING
MASTER BATH
LINEN

Design by
Home Planners

QUOTE ONE®

Cost to build? See page 516 to order complete cost estimate to build this house in your area!

This two-level plan has a bonus—a roof deck with hot tub! A variety of additional outdoor spaces makes this one wonderful plan. The living spaces are on the second floor and include a living/dining room combination with deck and fireplace. The dining room has buffet space. The family room also has a fireplace, plus a built-in entertainment center, and is open to the breakfast room and skylit kitchen. Sliding glass doors in the breakfast room open to another deck. The master bedroom is on this level and features a private bath with whirlpool and two-person shower, walk-in closet and access to still another deck. Family bedrooms, a full bath and a cozy den are on the first level, along with a two-car garage.

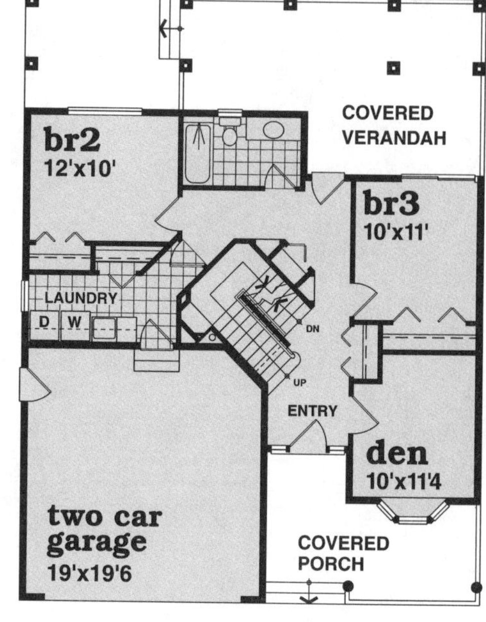

COVERED VERANDAH
br2
12'x10'
br3
10'x11'
LAUNDRY
D W
DN
UP
ENTRY
den
10'x11'4
two car garage
19'x19'6
COVERED PORCH

Width 37'-6"
Depth 48'-4"

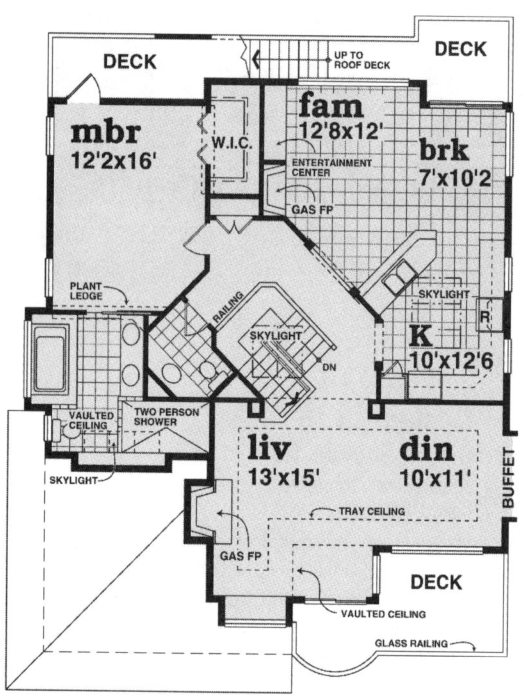

DECK
UP TO ROOF DECK
DECK
fam
12'8x12'
mbr
12'2x16'
W.I.C.
ENTERTAINMENT CENTER
brk
7'x10'2
GAS FP
PLANT LEDGE
RAILING
SKYLIGHT
SKYLIGHT
R
K
10'x12'6
DN
VAULTED CEILING
TWO PERSON SHOWER
liv
13'x15'
din
10'x11'
BUFFET
SKYLIGHT
TRAY CEILING
GAS FP
DECK
VAULTED CEILING
GLASS RAILING

Design Q482

First Floor: 832 square feet
Second Floor: 1,331 square feet
Total: 2,163 square feet

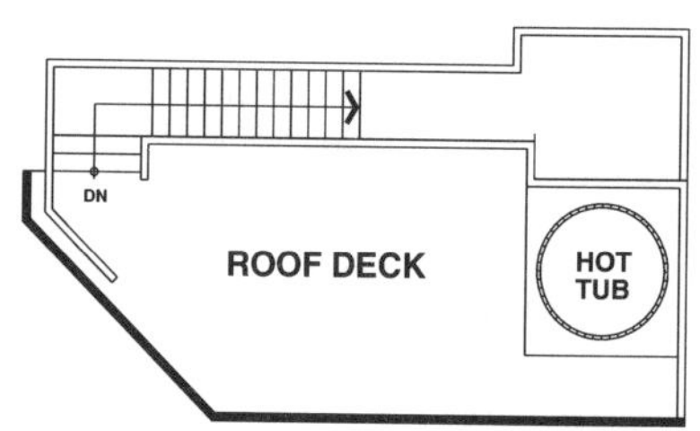

DN
ROOF DECK
HOT TUB

Design by
Select Home Designs

Design 5523

First Floor: 1,432 square feet
Second Floor: 912 square feet
Total: 2,344 square feet

■ Amenities abound in this two-story design, making it a pleasure to come home to. The formal living room features a decorative entry and a bay window. The formal dining room accesses the backyard and shares a fireplace with the angled family room. The gourmet kitchen allows the cook to converse with guests via the snack bar. It also includes a walk-in pantry, plenty of counter space and entry to the two-car garage. Additional space is available in the garage for a workshop or extra storage. Built on the first floor for privacy, the master bedroom features a pampering bath with a separate tub and shower, a separate toilet room, individual sinks and a walk-in closet. The second floor contains a multi-media loft, an ample laundry area and three bedrooms that share a full bath.

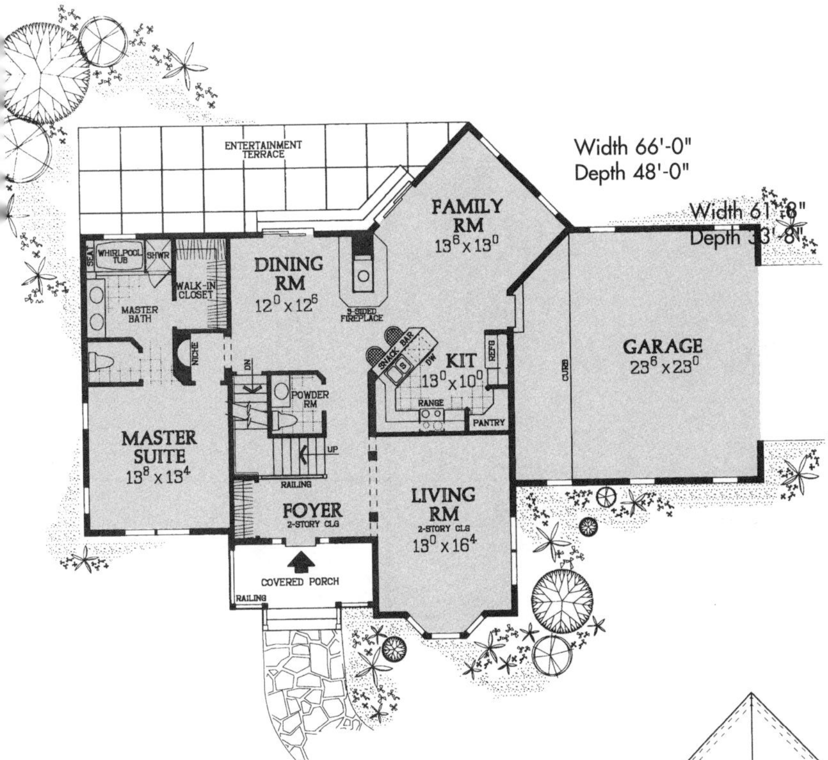

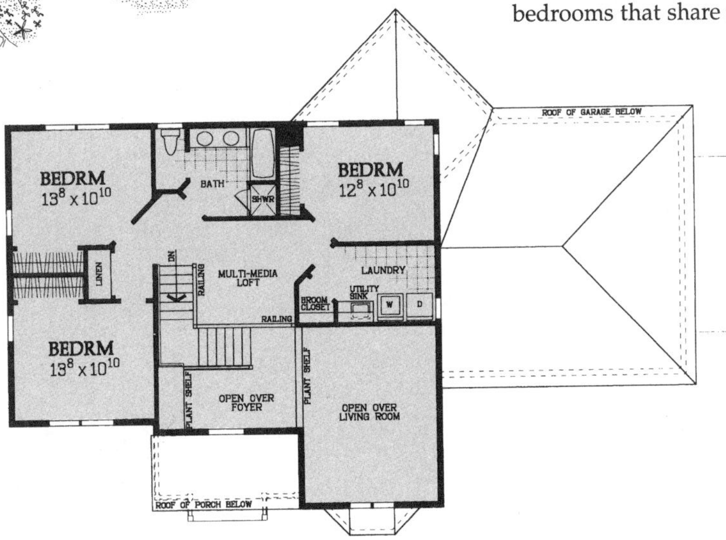

Width 66'-0"
Depth 48'-0"

Width 61'-8"
Depth 33'-8"

Design by
Home Planners

QUOTE ONE®

Cost to build? See page 516 to order complete cost estimate to build this house in your area!

QUOTE ONE®

Cost to build? See page 516 to order complete cost estimate to build this house in your area!

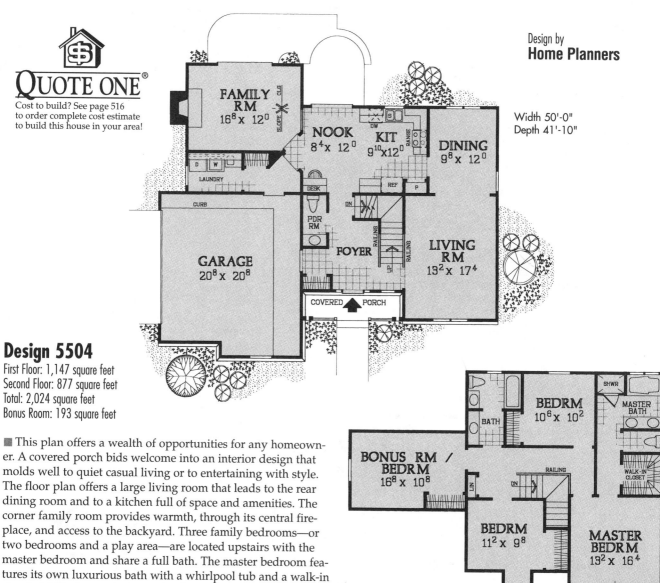

Design by
Home Planners

Width 50'-0"
Depth 41'-10"

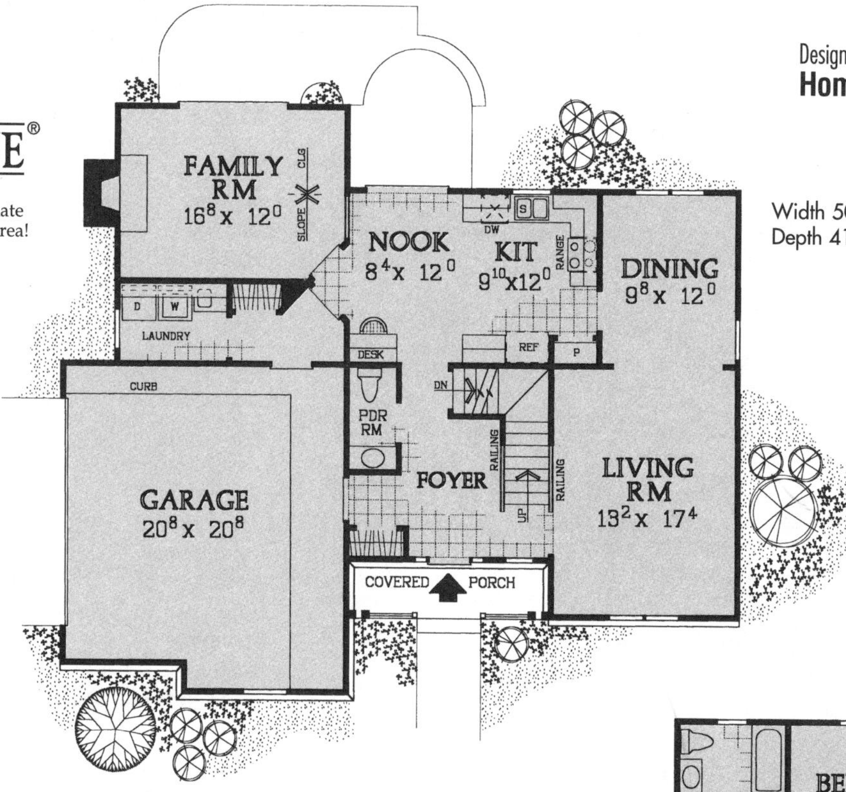

FAMILY RM
16^{8} x 12^{0}
SLOPE CLG

NOOK
8^{4}x 12^{0}

KIT
9^{10}x12^{0}

DW
RANGE
REF
P

DINING
9^{8}x 12^{0}

D W
LAUNDRY
DESK
CURB
DN
PDR RM
RAILING
RAILING
UP

GARAGE
20^{8}x 20^{8}

FOYER

LIVING RM
13^{2}x 17^{4}

COVERED PORCH

Design 5504

First Floor: 1,147 square feet
Second Floor: 877 square feet
Total: 2,024 square feet
Bonus Room: 193 square feet

■ This plan offers a wealth of opportunities for any homeowner. A covered porch bids welcome into an interior design that molds well to quiet casual living or to entertaining with style. The floor plan offers a large living room that leads to the rear dining room and to a kitchen full of space and amenities. The corner family room provides warmth, through its central fireplace, and access to the backyard. Three family bedrooms—or two bedrooms and a play area—are located upstairs with the master bedroom and share a full bath. The master bedroom features its own luxurious bath with a whirlpool tub and a walk-in closet. A large bonus room can be developed into additional bedroom space if needed.

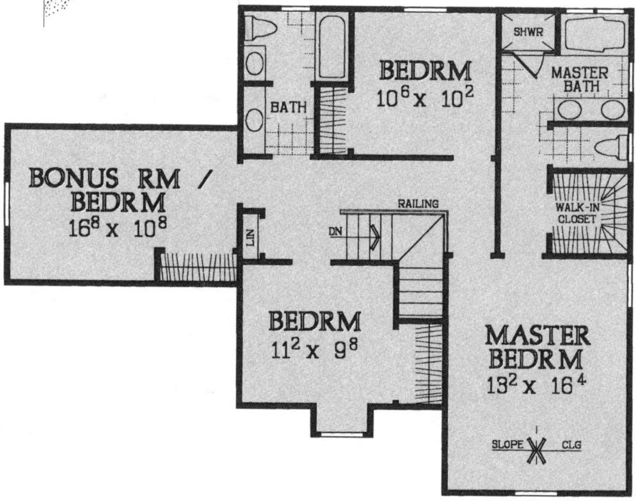

BATH

BEDRM
10^{6}x 10^{2}

SHWR
MASTER BATH

BONUS RM / BEDRM
16^{8}x 10^{8}

LIN
RAILING
DN

WALK-IN CLOSET

BEDRM
11^{2}x 9^{8}

MASTER BEDRM
13^{2}x 16^{4}
SLOPE CLG

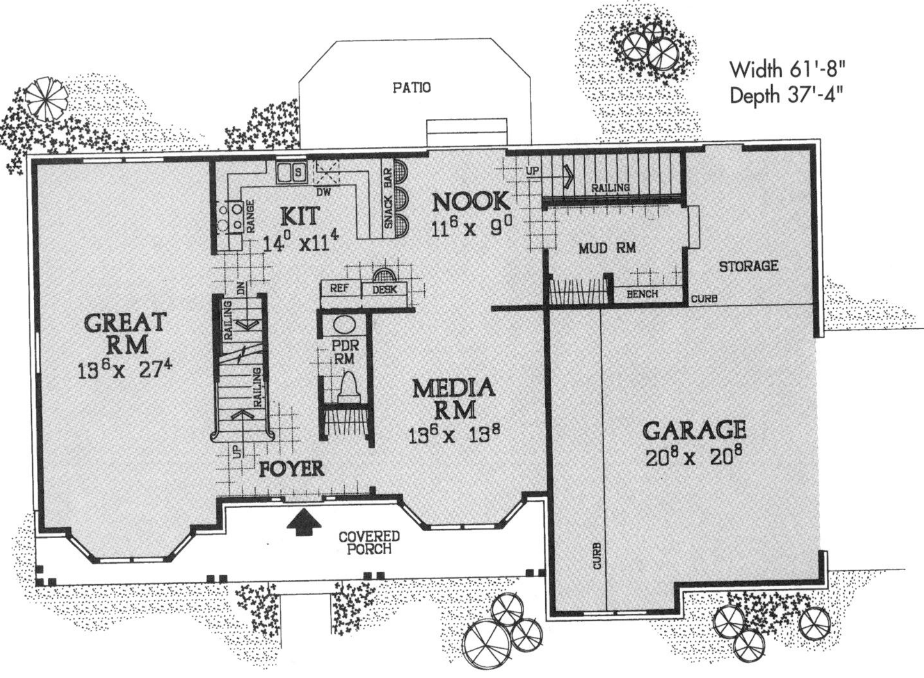
PATIO
Width 61'-8"
Depth 37'-4"
KIT
14^{0} x 11^{4}
NOOK
11^{6} x 9^{0}
SNACK BAR
RANGE
DW
UP
RAILING
MUD RM
STORAGE
BENCH
CURB
REF
DESK
GREAT RM
13^{6} x 27^{4}
PDR RM
MEDIA RM
13^{6} x 13^{8}
GARAGE
20^{8} x 20^{8}
FOYER
DN
UP
COVERED PORCH
CURB

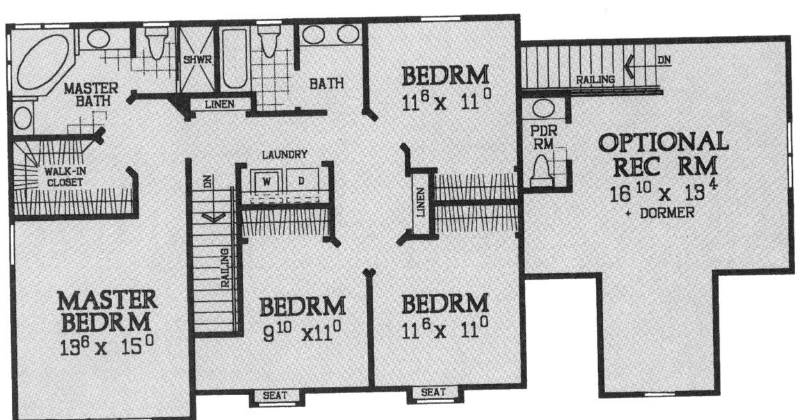
MASTER BATH
SHWR
BATH
LINEN
BEDRM
11^{6} x 11^{0}
RAILING
DN
PDR RM
OPTIONAL REC RM
16^{10} x 13^{4}
+ DORMER
WALK-IN CLOSET
LAUNDRY
W
D
LINEN
DN
RAILING
MASTER BEDRM
13^{6} x 15^{0}
BEDRM
9^{10} x 11^{0}
BEDRM
11^{6} x 11^{0}
SEAT
SEAT

Design 5549

First Floor: 1,271 square feet
Second Floor: 1,120 square feet
Total: 2,391 square feet
Optional Rec Room: 418 square feet

■ Bay windows add a special sense of romanticism to any home and, combined with the special roof and window treatment on this home's facade, make it more appealing. The bay window in the media room provides the perfect spot for relaxing, while the bay in the great room will become a favorite conversation niche. The U-shaped kitchen is conveniently located to serve both the dining area and the breakfast nook, with its access to the rear yard, the two-car garage and the second-floor bonus room. Upstairs, three family bedrooms share a full hall bath with a door separating the sinks and the shower—perfect when more than one party needs to get ready on busy mornings. A washer and dryer area is conveniently located to serve all rooms. The master bedroom includes a massive walk-in closet and a master bath with dual sinks separated by a soothing whirlpool tub.

Design by
Home Planners

QUOTE ONE®
Cost to build? See page 516
to order complete cost estimate
to build this house in your area!

Design Q276

First Floor: 957 square feet
Second Floor: 930 square feet
Total: 1,887 square feet
Bonus Room: 221 square feet

■ Decorated with two circle-head windows, this traditional design is both comfortable and appealing. The covered veranda leads to an entry foyer that is located in the center of the plan. To the left are the formal living areas—a living room with fireplace and dining room with buffet space. The stairway to the second floor is at the entry; behind it is the U-shaped kitchen and octagonal breakfast room. The family room is sunken and has its own fireplace, plus sliding glass doors to the rear patio. A half-bath in the hall is provided for convenience. Three bedrooms upstairs are separated by a railed gallery—master suite on one side and family bedrooms on the other. The master has a walk-in closet and private bath with whirlpool tub. A large bonus room can be finished in the future for additional sleeping space or for a home office. Plans include details for both a basement and a crawlspace foundation.

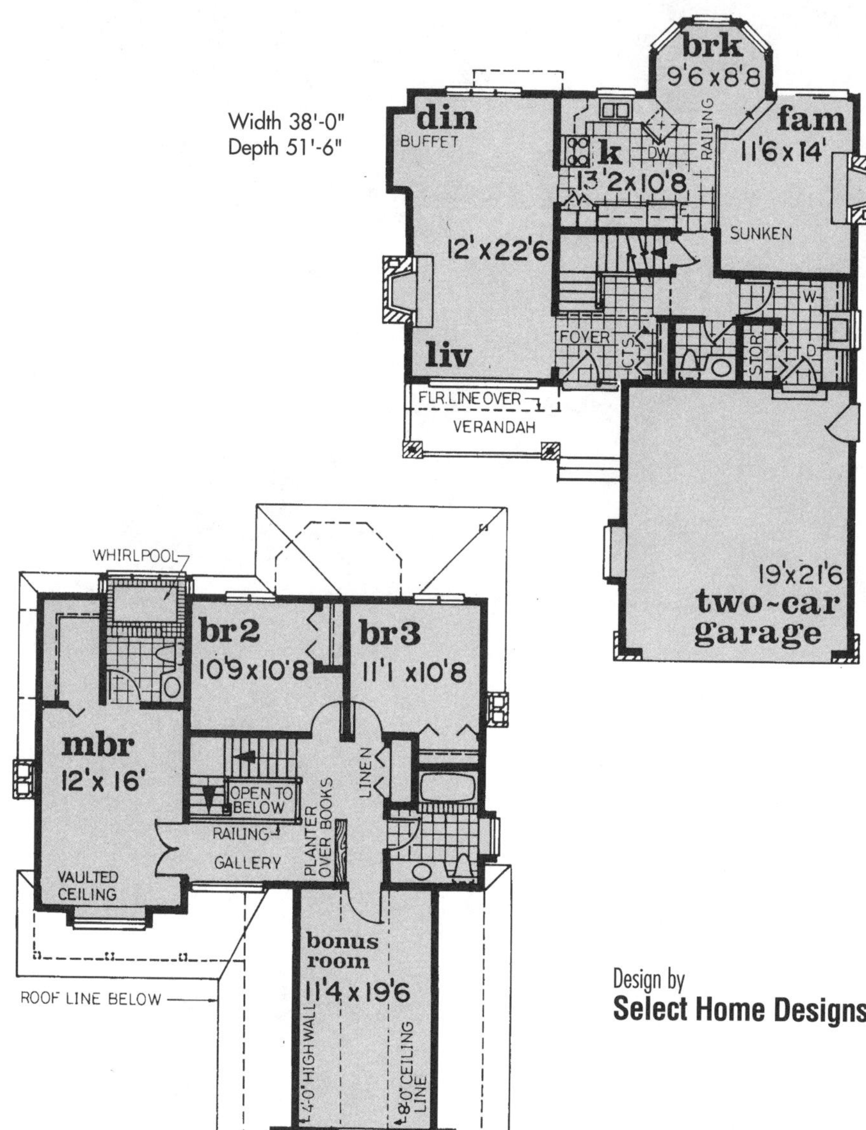

Width 38'-0"
Depth 51'-6"
PATIO
brk
9'6 x 8'8
din
BUFFET
k
13'2x10'8
DW
RAILING
fam
11'6 x 14'
SUNKEN
12' x 22'6
liv
FOYER
CTS.
STOR
W
D
FLR. LINE OVER
VERANDAH
19'x21'6
two-car garage
WHIRLPOOL
br2
10'9x10'8
br3
11'1 x10'8
mbr
12'x 16'
OPEN TO BELOW
LINEN
RAILING
GALLERY
PLANTER OVER BOOKS
VAULTED CEILING
bonus room
11'4 x 19'6
4'-0" HIGH WALL
8'-0" CEILING LINE
ROOF LINE BELOW

Design by
Select Home Designs

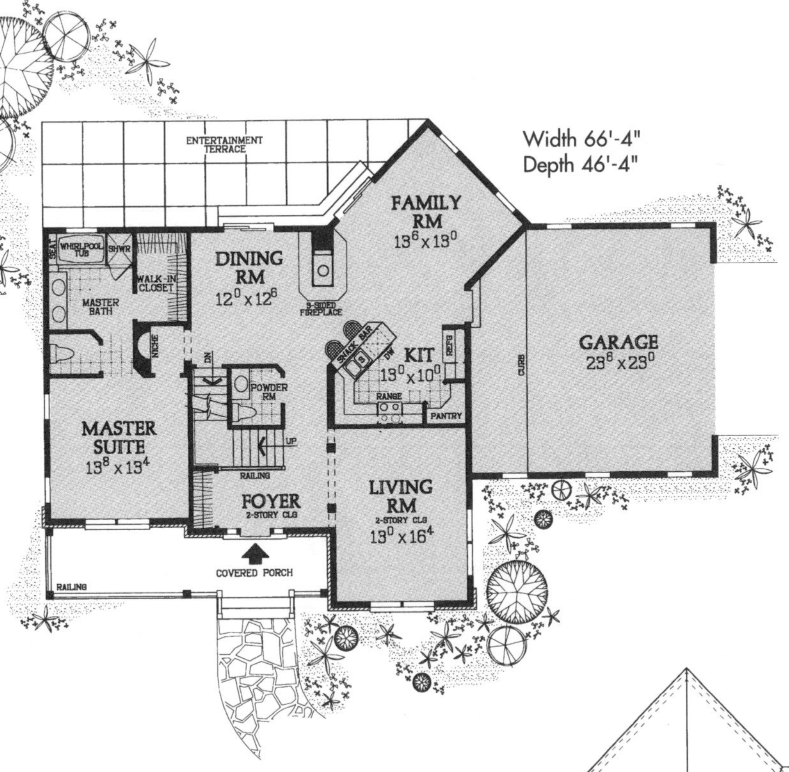
ENTERTAINMENT TERRACE
Width 66'-4"
Depth 46'-4"
FAMILY RM
$13^{6} \times 13^{0}$
DINING RM
$12^{0} \times 12^{6}$
3-SIDED FIREPLACE
WHIRLPOOL TUB
SHWR
WALK-IN CLOSET
MASTER BATH
NICHE
SNACK BAR
KIT
$13^{0} \times 10^{0}$
REFG
RANGE
PANTRY
POWDER RM
GARAGE
$23^{6} \times 23^{0}$
CURB
MASTER SUITE
$13^{8} \times 13^{4}$
UP
RAILING
FOYER
2-STORY CLG
LIVING RM
2-STORY CLG
$13^{0} \times 16^{4}$
COVERED PORCH
RAILING

Design 5522

First Floor: 1,441 square feet
Second Floor: 918 square feet
Total: 2,359 square feet

■ Corner quoins, louver vents and arches add a special touch of elegance to the brick facade of this traditional home. The two-story foyer leads to a corner living room decorated with columns and plant shelves. Beyond the convenient powder room is a formal dining room, spacious family room and amenity-filled kitchen. The dining room offers backyard access and shares a three-sided fireplace with the angled family room. The kitchen features a snack bar and a counter-laden kitchen with a walk-in pantry. A decoratively arched curios niche provides entry to the first-floor master bedroom, which features a master bath with a separate toilet area and a walk-in closet. Three additional bedrooms with ample closet space are available on the second floor. They share a full bath, a multi-media loft and a large, conveniently located utility room.

ROOF OF GARAGE BELOW
BEDRM
$13^{8} \times 10^{10}$
BATH
SHWR
BEDRM
$12^{8} \times 10^{10}$
LINEN
DN
RAILING
MULTI-MEDIA LOFT
LAUNDRY
UTILITY SINK
BROOM CLOSET
RAILING
BEDRM
$13^{8} \times 10^{10}$
PLANT SHELF
OPEN OVER FOYER
PLANT SHELF
OPEN OVER LIVING ROOM
ROOF OF PORCH BELOW

Design by
Home Planners

QUOTE ONE®

Cost to build? See page 516 to order complete cost estimate to build this house in your area!

Design 5528

First Floor: 1,228 square feet
Second Floor: 1,285 square feet
Total: 2,513 square feet

Width 36'-8"
Depth 66'-2"

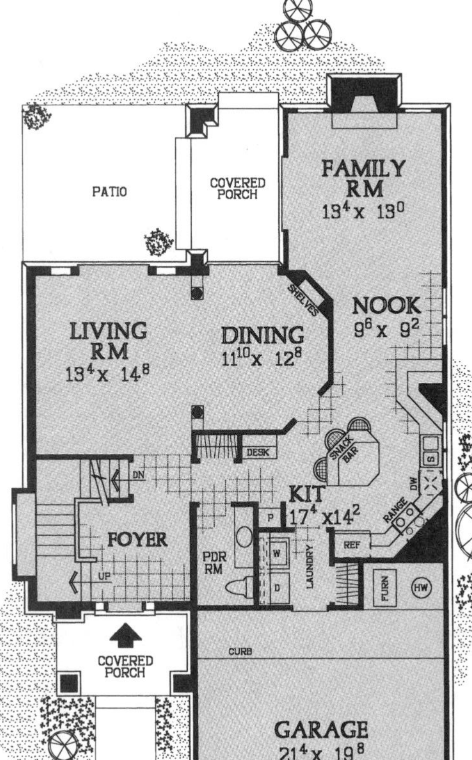

PATIO
COVERED PORCH
FAMILY RM 13⁴ x 13⁰
LIVING RM 13⁴ x 14⁸
DINING 11¹⁰ x 12⁸
SHELVES
NOOK 9⁶ x 9²
DESK
SNACK BAR
KIT 17⁴ x 14²
DN
UP
FOYER
PDR RM
LAUNDRY
RANGE
DW
REF
FURN
HW
COVERED PORCH
CURB
GARAGE 21⁴ x 19⁸

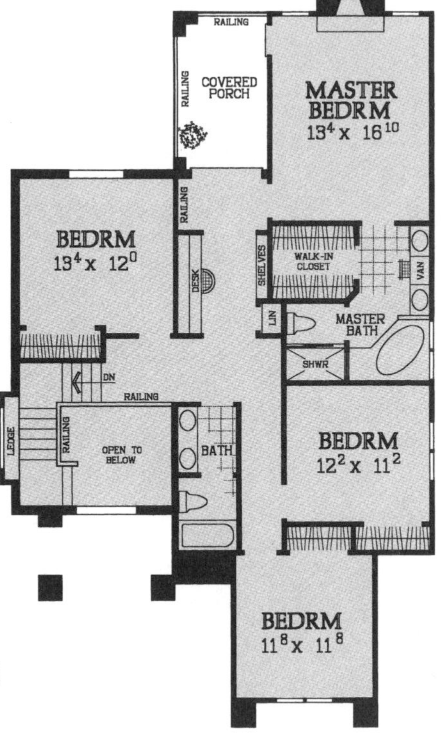

Design by
Home Planners

QUOTE ONE®
Cost to build? See page 516
to order complete cost estimate
to build this house in your area!

■ Charm is just the beginning of what this design has to offer. Inside, a sun-lit foyer leads to a combination living and dining room that lets the outdoors in through large glass doors to the rear patio. A corner shelf unit in the dining room offers a perfect home for family treasures. It accesses a uniquely shaped kitchen with an island worktop, a writing desk, a large breakfast nook and entry to the utility room and the two-car garage. The corner family room features a cozy fireplace, backyard access and plenty of room for furniture placement. Three family bedrooms and a master suite are located on the second floor, along with a full bath, a study desk and a sizable porch. The master bedroom features a well-equipped private bath with a corner tub, a vanity area and a walk-in closet.

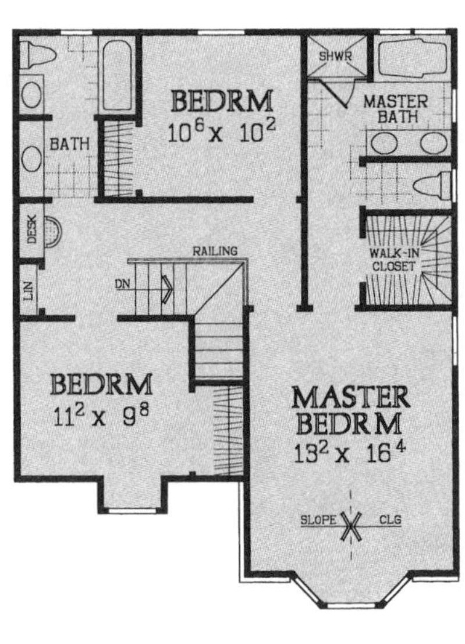
BATH
BEDRM
10^{6} x 10^{2}
SHWR
MASTER BATH
DESK
LIN
DN
RAILING
WALK-IN CLOSET
BEDRM
11^{2} x 9^{8}
MASTER BEDRM
13^{2} x 16^{4}
SLOPE
CLG

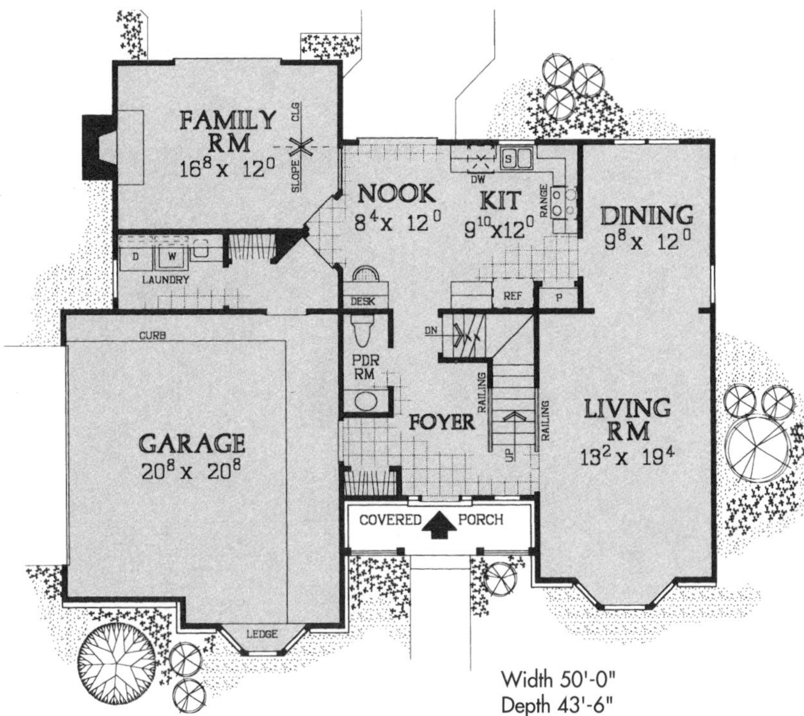
FAMILY RM
16^{8} x 12^{0}
SLOPE
CLG
NOOK
8^{4}x 12^{0}
KIT
9^{10}x12^{0}
DW
RANGE
DINING
9^{8} x 12^{0}
D
W
LAUNDRY
DESK
REF
P
DN
PDR RM
FOYER
RAILING
UP
RAILING
LIVING RM
13^{2} x 19^{4}
CURB
GARAGE
20^{8} x 20^{8}
COVERED PORCH
LEDGE

Width 50'-0"
Depth 43'-6"

Design 5503

First Floor: 1,185 square feet
Second Floor: 880 square feet
Total: 2,065 square feet

■ A stately exterior, accented with brick, interesting rooflines and classic window treatment—including a two-story bay window—will set this traditional home apart from the other homes in your neighborhood. Inside, amenities fill the plan, beginning with a half-bath and coat closet conveniently located in the front foyer. This open space leads to either the corner living room with the first of three bay windows, to the two-car garage with another bay window or to the gourmet kitchen with a pantry, a desk, a breakfast nook and plenty of counter space. The family room at the rear of the home, with its cozy fireplace and backyard access, is the perfect place to relax after dinner. Upstairs, two secondary bedrooms share a full bath with dual sinks, and a writing desk and a linen closet. The master bedroom showcases the third bay window and a sumptuous master bath with a walk-in closet, a separate toilet area, dual basins and a garden whirlpool tub.

Design by
Home Planners

QUOTE ONE®

Cost to build? See page 516 to order complete cost estimate to build this house in your area!

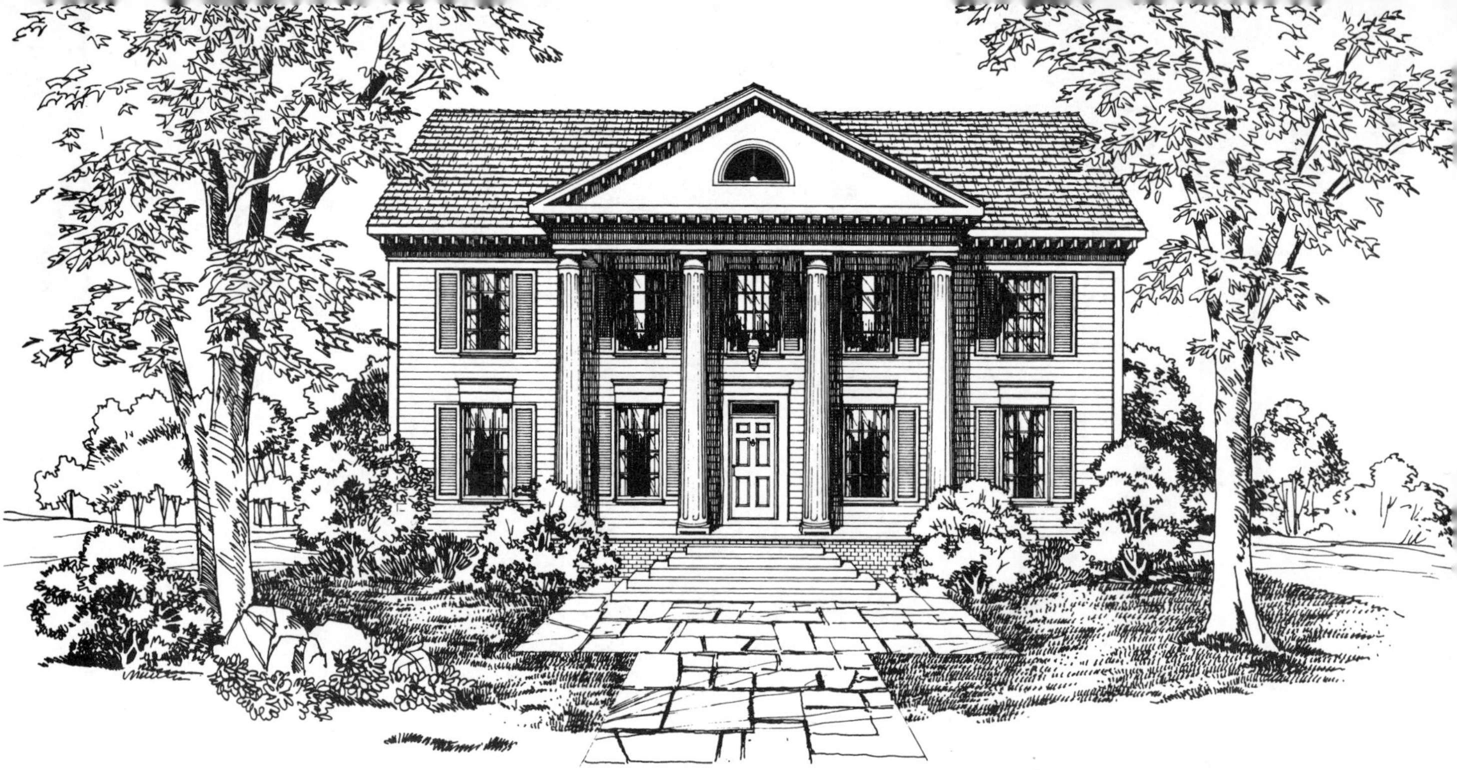

Design 2668

First Floor: 1,206 square feet
Second Floor: 1,254 square feet
Total: 2,460 square feet

L

■ This elegant Southern Colonial home is just as livable inside as the facade is grand outside, with every bit of space put to good use focusing on family living. The front country kitchen is efficiently planned with an island cooktop and pass-through to the dining room. The impressive great room is highlighted with a full two stories of pane windows—it will definitely be the center of all family activities. A secluded library in the front of the plan provides a relaxing retreat. A balcony lounge overlooks the grand windows of the great room from the second-floor landing. Three family bedrooms share a full hall bath. The master suite has a lush bath and features a balcony open to the two-story foyer below.

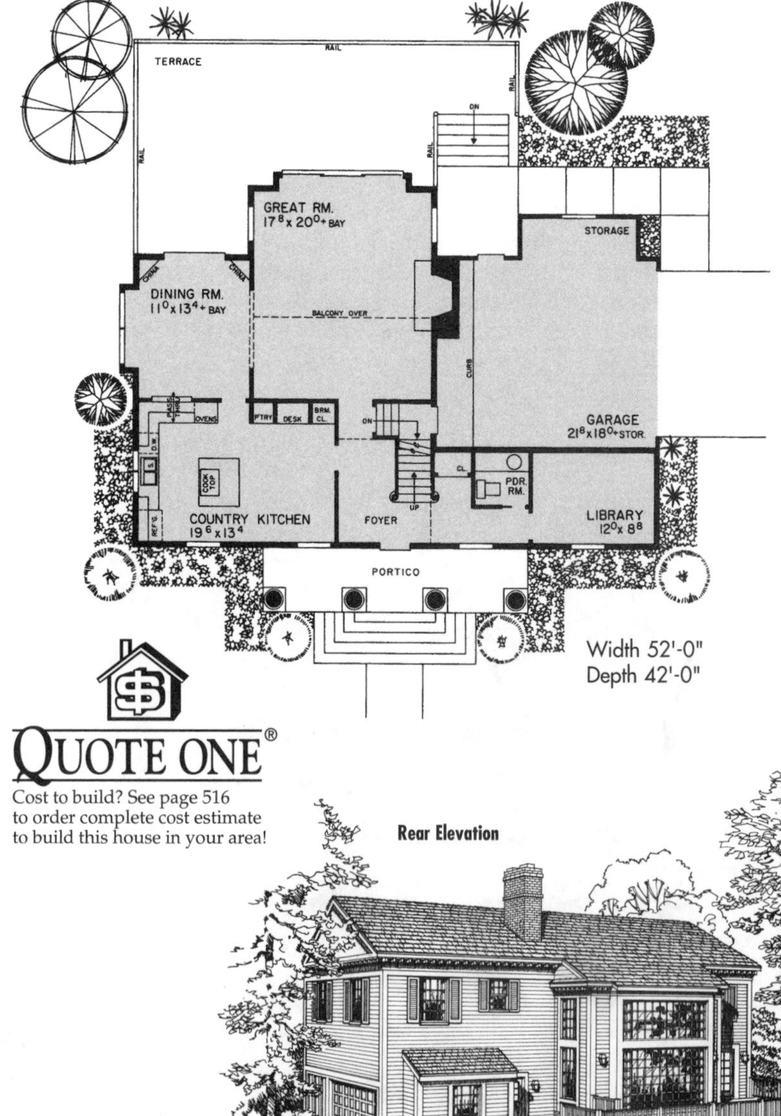
TERRACE
RAIL
GREAT RM.
17⁸ x 20⁰+ BAY
DINING RM.
11⁰x13⁴+ BAY
BALCONY OVER
STORAGE
GARAGE
21⁸x18⁰+ STOR.
COUNTRY KITCHEN
19⁶x13⁴
FOYER
PDR. RM.
LIBRARY
12⁰x 8⁸
PORTICO
Width 52'-0"
Depth 42'-0"
Rear Elevation

QUOTE ONE®
Cost to build? See page 516 to order complete cost estimate to build this house in your area!

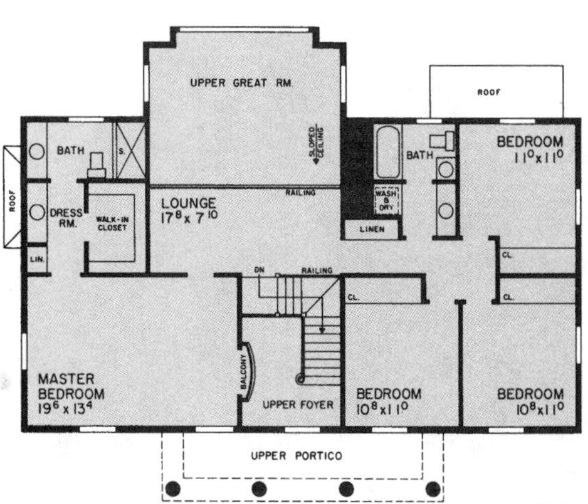
UPPER GREAT RM.
ROOF
BATH
BEDROOM
11⁰x11⁰
DRESS RM.
WALK-IN CLOSET
LOUNGE
17⁸x 7¹⁰
RAILING
LINEN
MASTER BEDROOM
19⁶ x 13⁴
BALCONY
UPPER FOYER
BEDROOM
10⁸x11⁰
BEDROOM
10⁸x11⁰
UPPER PORTICO

Design by
Home Planners

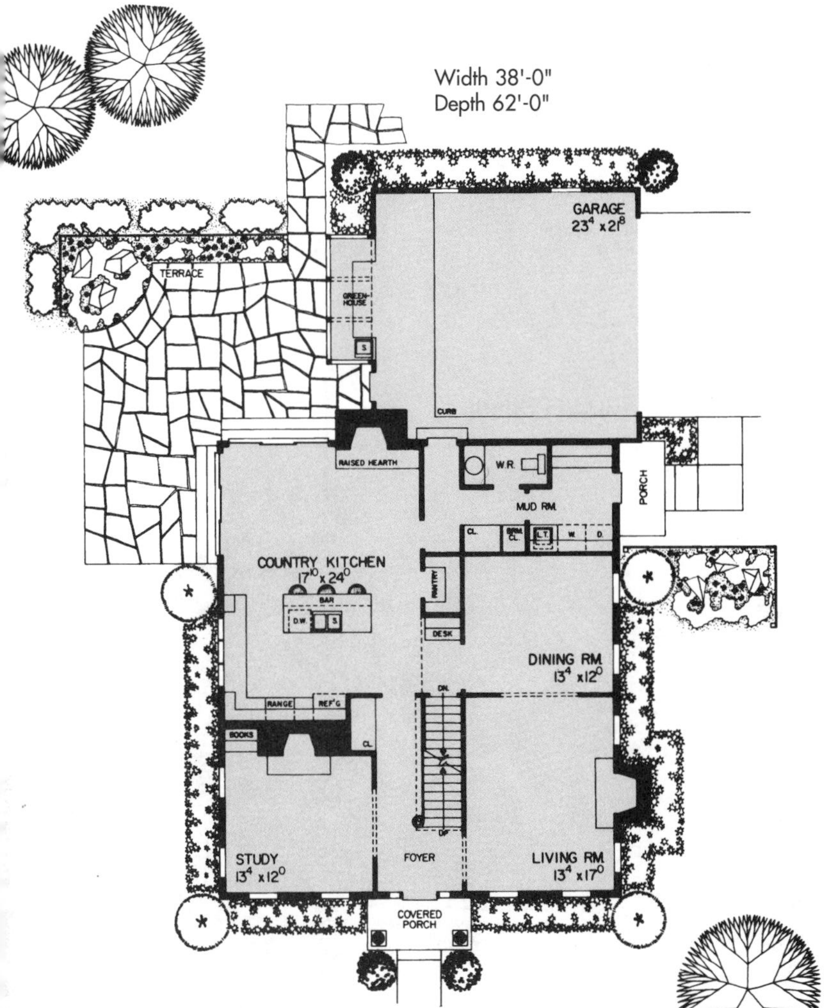

Width 38'-0"
Depth 62'-0"

Design 2979

First Floor: 1,440 square feet
Second Floor: 1,394 square feet
Total: 2,834 square feet

■ The memory of Noah Webster's house, built in 1823 in New Hampshire, is recalled in this Greek Revival adaptation. A picture home for a narrow site, it features big-house livability. In addition to the formal living and dining rooms, there is a huge country kitchen with hearth and handy mudroom. The study has a fireplace and built-in bookcases. Upstairs, four bedrooms and three full baths include a master suite with balcony, walk-in closet, make-up vanity and whirlpool tub. One of the family bedrooms has a private bath also. The two-car garage is situated to the rear of the plan. Don't miss the delightful greenhouse with utility sink attached to the garage and viewed from the terrace.

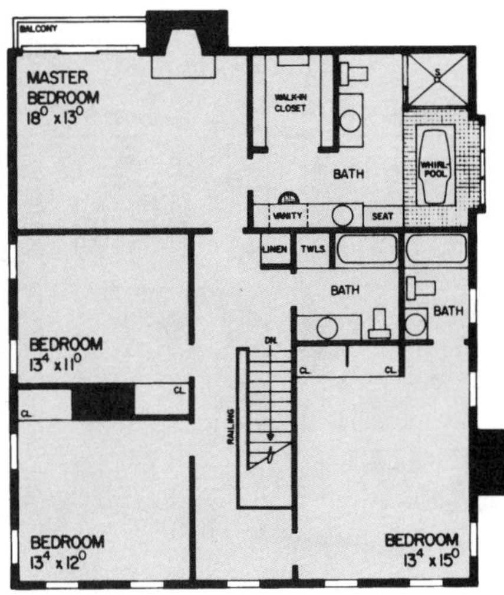
BALCONY
MASTER BEDROOM 18⁰ x 13⁰
WALK-IN CLOSET
BATH
WHIRLPOOL
VANITY
SEAT
LINEN
TWLS
BATH
BATH
BEDROOM 13⁴ x 11⁰
CL
CL
CL
CL
DN.
RAILING
BEDROOM 13⁴ x 12⁰
BEDROOM 13⁴ x 15⁰

Design by
Home Planners

Design 3333

First Floor: 1,584 square feet
Second Floor: 1,344 square feet
Total: 2,928 square feet

L

■ This Southern Colonial adaptation boasts an up-to-date floor plan which caters to the needs of today's families. The entrance hall is flanked by formal and informal living areas: to the left a spacious living room and connecting dining room, to the right a cozy study and family room. A large kitchen with a bay-windowed morning room is convenient to both the dining and family rooms. The upstairs sleeping arrangements include three family bedrooms and a sumptuous master suite complete with a deluxe bath and an exercise room.

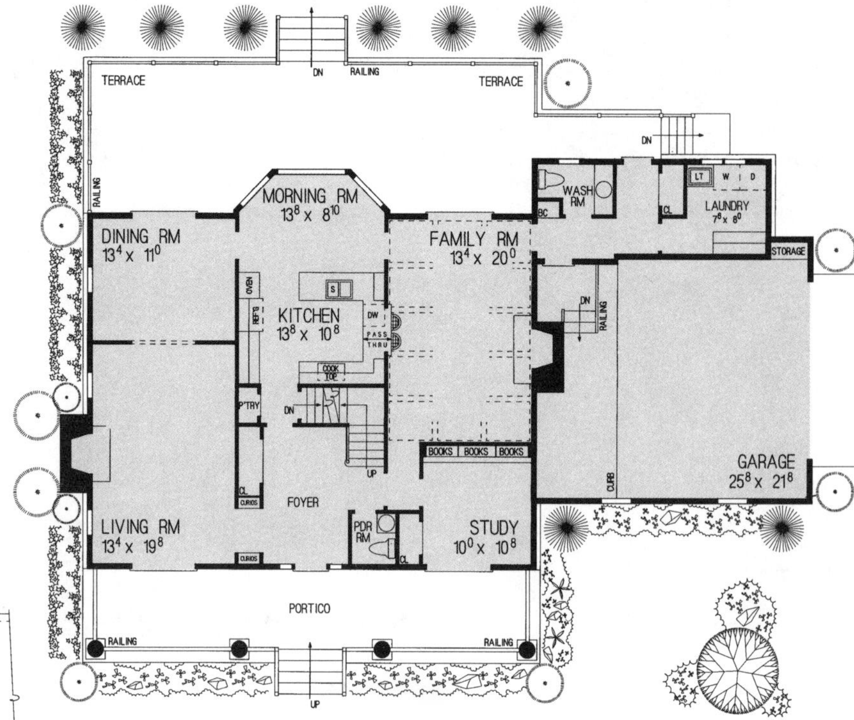
TERRACE
RAILING
TERRACE
DN
MORNING RM 13^{8} x 8^{10}
DINING RM 13^{4} x 11^{0}
FAMILY RM 13^{4} x 20^{0}
WASH RM
LAUNDRY 7^{6} x 8^{0}
STORAGE
KITCHEN 13^{8} x 10^{8}
OVEN
REF'G
DW
PASS THRU
COOK TOP
P'TRY
DN
UP
BOOKS BOOKS BOOKS
GARAGE 25^{8} x 21^{8}
CURB
FOYER
CL
CURIOS
LIVING RM 13^{4} x 19^{8}
PDR RM
STUDY 10^{0} x 10^{8}
PORTICO
RAILING
RAILING
UP

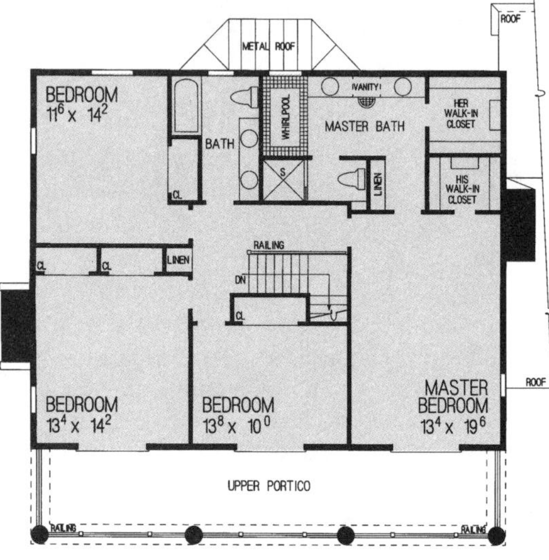
METAL ROOF
ROOF
BEDROOM 11^{6} x 14^{2}
BATH
WHIRLPOOL
VANITY
MASTER BATH
HER WALK-IN CLOSET
HIS WALK-IN CLOSET
LINEN
CL
RAILING
DN
BEDROOM 13^{4} x 14^{2}
BEDROOM 13^{8} x 10^{0}
MASTER BEDROOM 13^{4} x 19^{6}
ROOF
UPPER PORTICO
RAILING
RAILING

Width 70'-6"
Depth 54'-5"

QUOTE ONE®

Cost to build? See page 516 to order complete cost estimate to build this house in your area!

Design by
Home Planners

Design 3508

First Floor: 2,098 square feet
Second Floor: 1,735 square feet
Total: 3,833 square feet

L

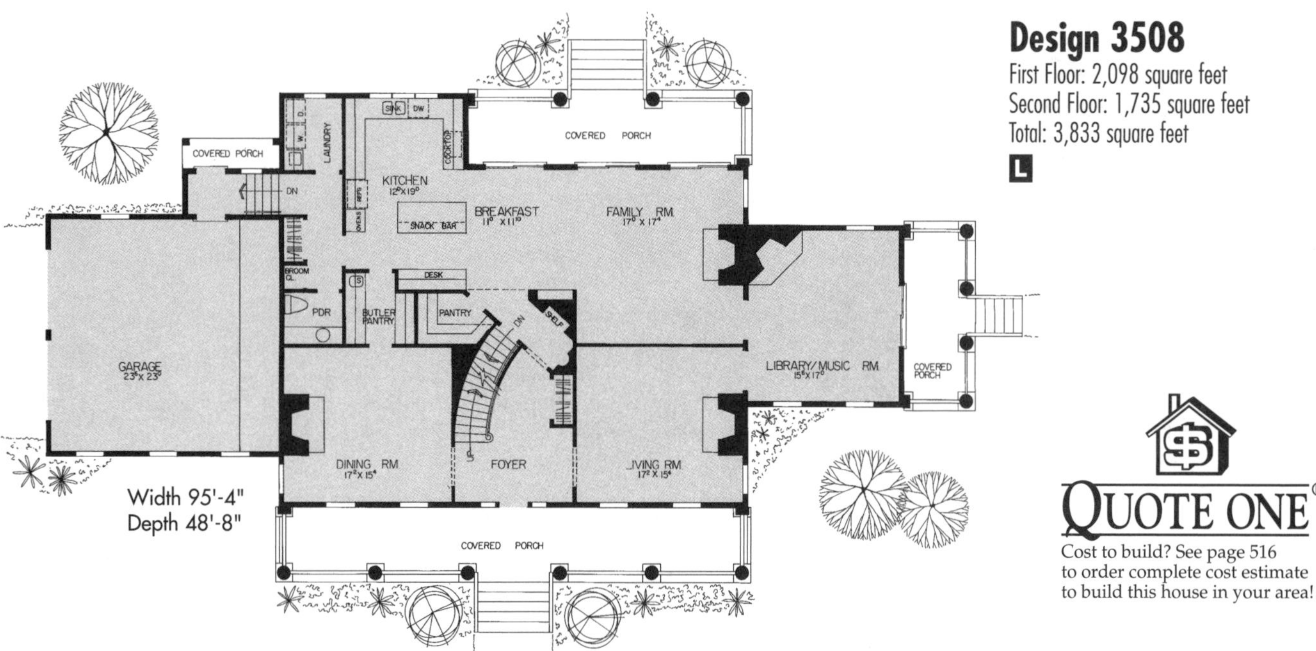
COVERED PORCH
COVERED PORCH
LAUNDRY
KITCHEN
BREAKFAST
SNACK BAR
FAMILY RM
DN
BROOM CL
PDR
BUTLER PANTRY
PANTRY
DESK
SHELF
GARAGE
LIBRARY/MUSIC RM
COVERED PORCH
DINING RM
FOYER
LIVING RM
COVERED PORCH

Width 95'-4"
Depth 48'-8"

QUOTE ONE®
Cost to build? See page 516 to order complete cost estimate to build this house in your area!

Design by
Home Planners

■ Like its predecessor—built in the 1800s—this modern version of Louisiana's "Rosedown House" exhibits splendid Southern styling, but with today's most sought-after amenities. The formal zone of the house is introduced by a foyer with a graceful, curved staircase. The dining and living rooms flank the foyer, and each is highlighted by a fireplace. Off the living room, a library or music room offers comfort with a corner fireplace and a covered porch. Adjacent to the family room is a breakfast area, an expansive kitchen and a rear covered porch. Upstairs, two secondary bedrooms—one with its own bath—and a study, which may be converted to an additional bedroom, join a gracious master suite that has its own fireplace. A large dressing room with walk-in closets leads to the luxurious bath. Two covered balconies complete the superb livability found in this plan.

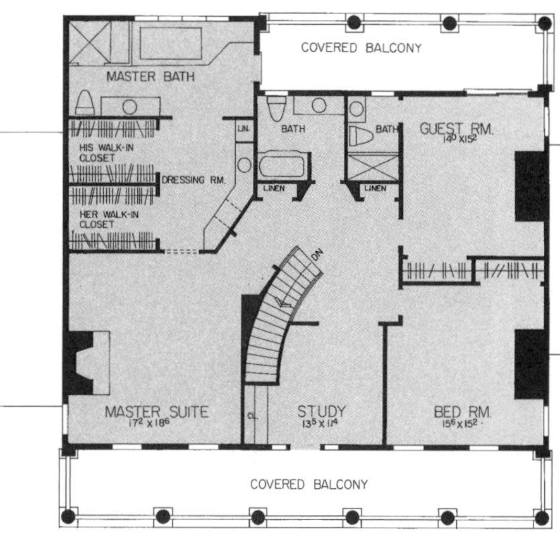
COVERED BALCONY
MASTER BATH
LIN
BATH
BATH
GUEST RM
HIS WALK-IN CLOSET
DRESSING RM
LINEN
LINEN
HER WALK-IN CLOSET
DN
MASTER SUITE
STUDY
BED RM
COVERED BALCONY

Design 2665

First Floor: 1,152 square feet
Second Floor: 1,152 square feet
Total: 2,394 square feet (excludes guest suites and galleries)

Design by
Home Planners

■ The origin of this house dates back to 1787 and George Washington's Mount Vernon. A keeping room with a pass-through to the kitchen and a fireplace with a built-in wood box, a formal dining room, a breakfast room and a formal living room with a fireplace on the first floor allow plenty of social possibilities. Separate guest quarters with a full bath, a lounge area and an upstairs studio which is connected to the main house by a gallery further enhance this home's livability. A complementary gallery is located on the other side of the house and leads to the garage with a storage room or hobby room situated above. Four bedrooms with two full baths are found on the second floor, including the master suite with a fireplace. In the left wing, the guest bedroom/lounge with its upstairs study can be optionally designed as a game room with a spiral staircase and a loft area.

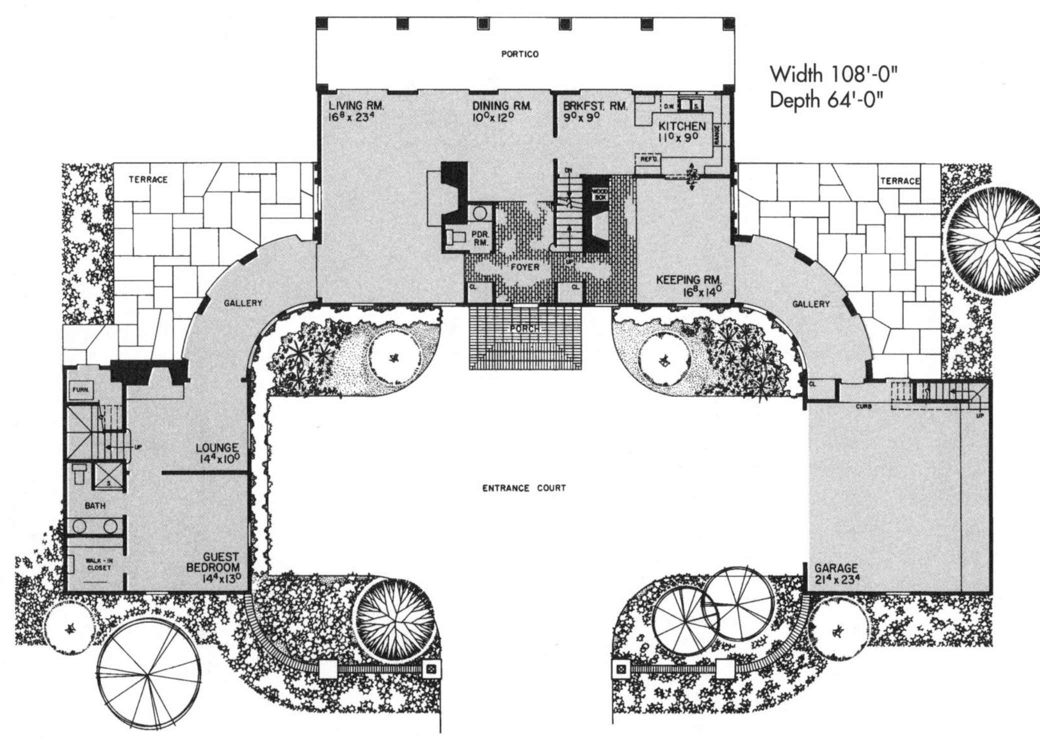

PORTICO
LIVING RM. 16⁸ x 23⁴
DINING RM. 10⁰x 12⁰
BRKFST. RM. 9⁰x 9⁰
KITCHEN 11⁰x 9⁰
TERRACE
TERRACE
PDR. RM.
FOYER
KEEPING RM. 16⁸x 14⁰
GALLERY
GALLERY
PORCH
LOUNGE 14⁴x 10⁰
BATH
GUEST BEDROOM 14⁴x 13⁰
ENTRANCE COURT
GARAGE 21⁴x 23⁴
Width 108'-0"
Depth 64'-0"

UPPER PORTICO
BEDROOM 10⁴x10⁰
BATH
SEAT
LINEN
MASTER BEDROOM 16⁸x15⁰
CL
DN
BEDROOM 16⁸x10⁸
BEDROOM 10⁰x11⁴
BATH
DRESSING RM.
LINEN
SEAT
ROOF
STUDIO 12⁰x23⁴
STORAGE / HOBBIES
RAIL
VOID
UPPER GAMES RM
LOFT 12⁰x11⁸
TERRACE
GALLERY
FURN
LOFT ABOVE
GAMES RM 21⁴x21⁴-23⁴

Option to Guest Suite Wing

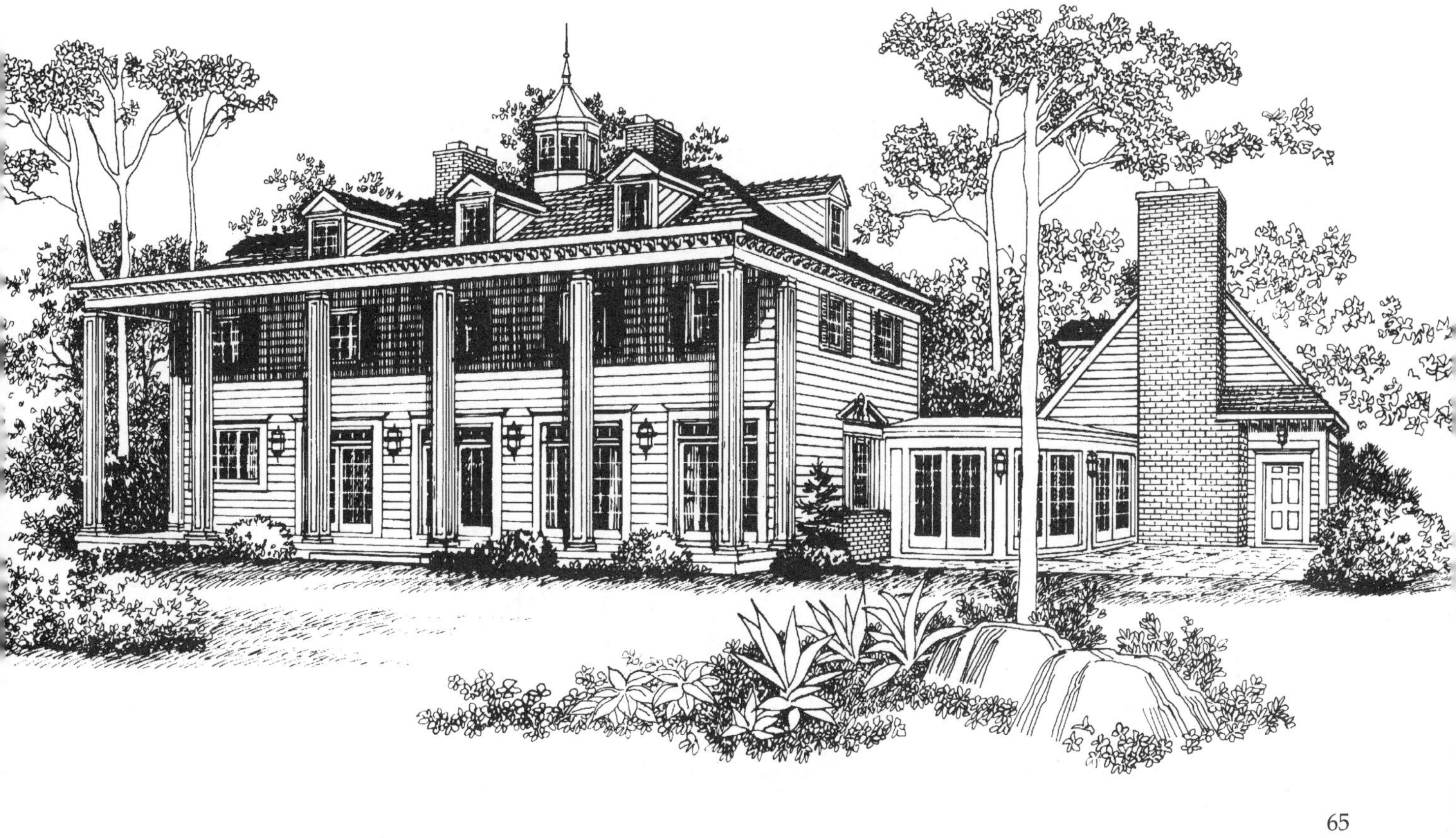

Design 1858

First Floor: 1,794 square feet
Second Floor: 1,474 square feet
Studio: 424 square feet
Total: 3,692 square feet

D

■ The stately facade of this Georgian design seems to foretell all of the exceptional features to be found inside. From the delightful entry hall, to the studio or maid's room over the garage, this home has a treasure at every turn. Both the family and formal living room feature a fireplace with a built-in wood box, while the quiet library is warmed by a raised corner hearth beneath a built-in bookshelf. The formal dining room is central in the plan and offers easy passage to the large, gourmet kitchen. The kitchen's adjoining breakfast room stairs rise to the studio apartment over the garage. The grand stairway from the entry foyer leads to three family bedrooms that share a dual-vanity hall bath. The master suite features a bookshelf hearth with plenty of room for a sitting area. A large vanity and dressing area precede the compartmented bath.

QUIET TERRACE
LIVING TERRACE
DINING RM. $13^0 \times 14^0$
LIBRARY $11^0 \times 13^6$
CL.
PDR. RM.
RAISED HEARTH
BOOKS OVER
BOOKS
WOOD BOX
D.W.
S.
REF'G
PANTRY
KIT. $12^0 \times 13^6$
BREAKFAST $9^0 \times 11^0$
UP
BRICK WALL COOK CENTER
LAUNDRY
WOOD BOX
RAISED HEARTH
DN.
ENTRY HALL
UP
SLD'G DR.
VEST.
CL.
CL.
LIVING RM. $15^6 \times 19^6$
FAMILY RM. $15^6 \times 19^6$
W.R.
STOR.
GARAGE $21^8 \times 23^4$
P.
P.
Width 76'-10"
Depth 38'-10"

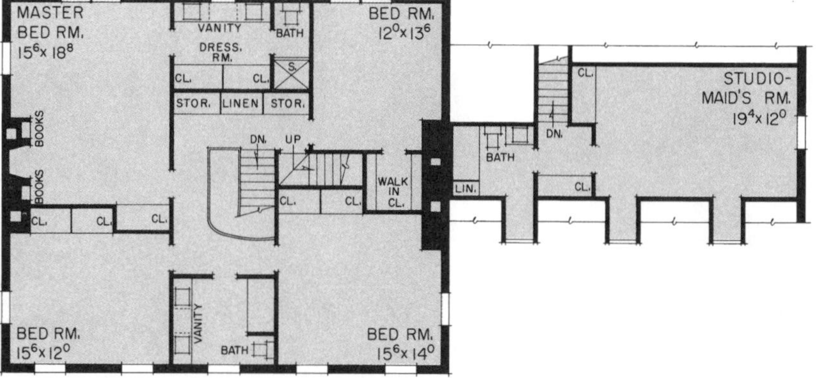
MASTER BED RM. $15^6 \times 18^8$
VANITY
BATH
DRESS. RM.
CL.
CL.
S.
STOR.
LINEN
STOR.
BED RM. $12^0 \times 13^6$
BOOKS
BOOKS
DN.
UP
CL.
CL.
CL.
CL.
CL.
WALK IN CL.
LIN.
BATH
DN.
CL.
CL.
STUDIO-MAID'S RM. $19^4 \times 12^0$
VANITY
BATH
BED RM. $15^6 \times 12^0$
BED RM. $15^6 \times 14^0$

Design by
Home Planners

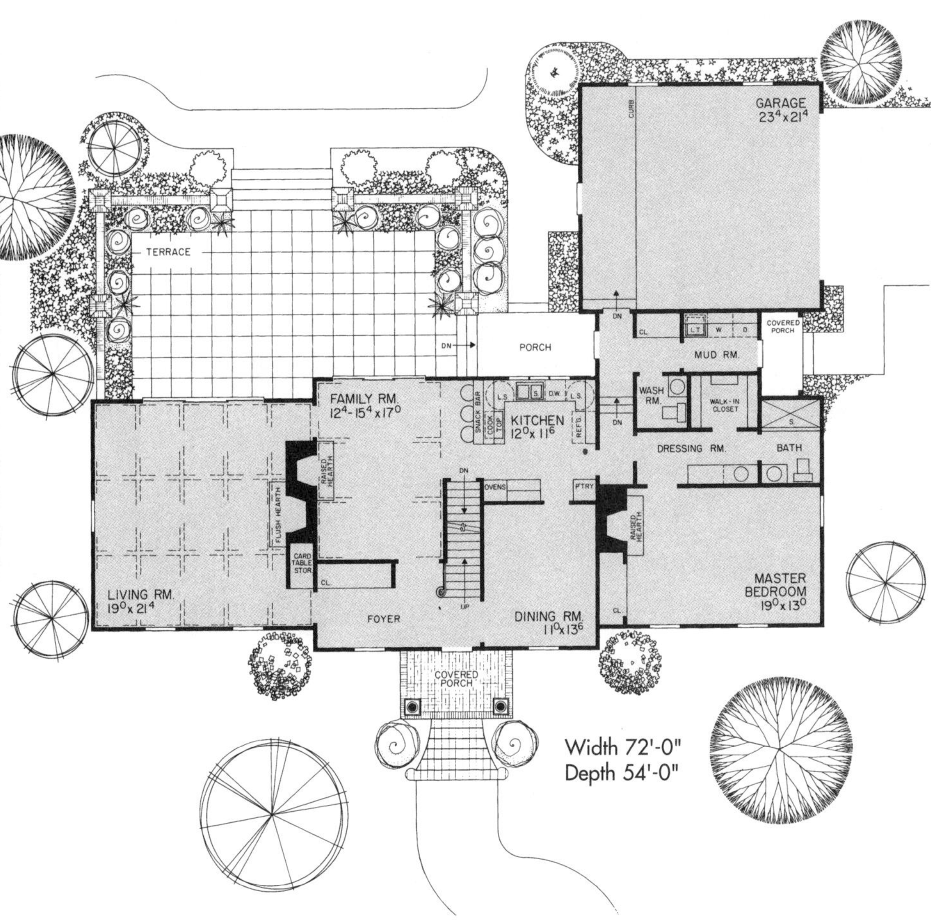

GARAGE $23^4 \times 21^4$
CURB
TERRACE
PORCH
DN
COVERED PORCH
CL.
MUD RM.
WASH RM.
WALK-IN CLOSET
FAMILY RM. 12^4-$15^4 \times 17^0$
SNACK BAR
COOK TOP
KITCHEN $12^0 \times 11^6$
REF'G.
OVENS
PTRY
RAISED HEARTH
FLUSH HEARTH
CARD TABLE STOR.
DRESSING RM.
BATH
LIVING RM. $19^0 \times 21^4$
FOYER
UP
DINING RM. $11^0 \times 13^6$
MASTER BEDROOM $19^0 \times 13^0$
COVERED PORCH
Width 72'-0"
Depth 54'-0"

Design 2667

First Floor: 1,827 square feet
Second Floor: 697 square feet
Total: 2,524 square feet

L

■ Two one-story wings flank the two-story center section of this design which echoes the architectural forms of 18th-Century Tidewater Virginia. The left wing is a huge living room; the right, the master bedroom suite, service area and garage. Kitchen, dining room and family room are centrally located. Upstairs, three family bedrooms share a full hall bath with twin vanities.

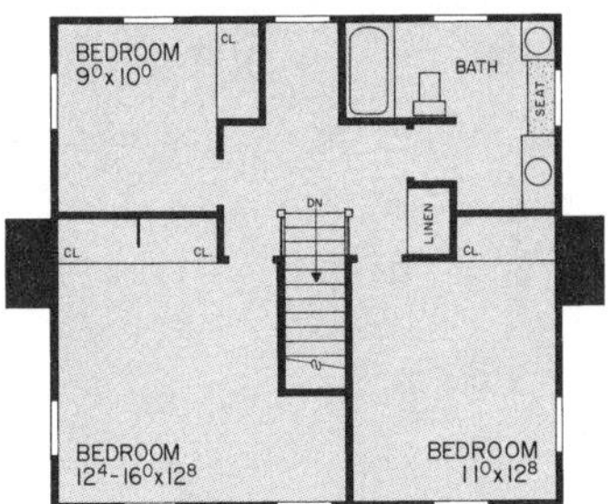

BEDROOM $9^0 \times 10^0$
CL
BATH
SEAT
DN
LINEN
CL.
BEDROOM 12^4-$16^0 \times 12^8$
BEDROOM $11^0 \times 12^8$

Design by
Home Planners

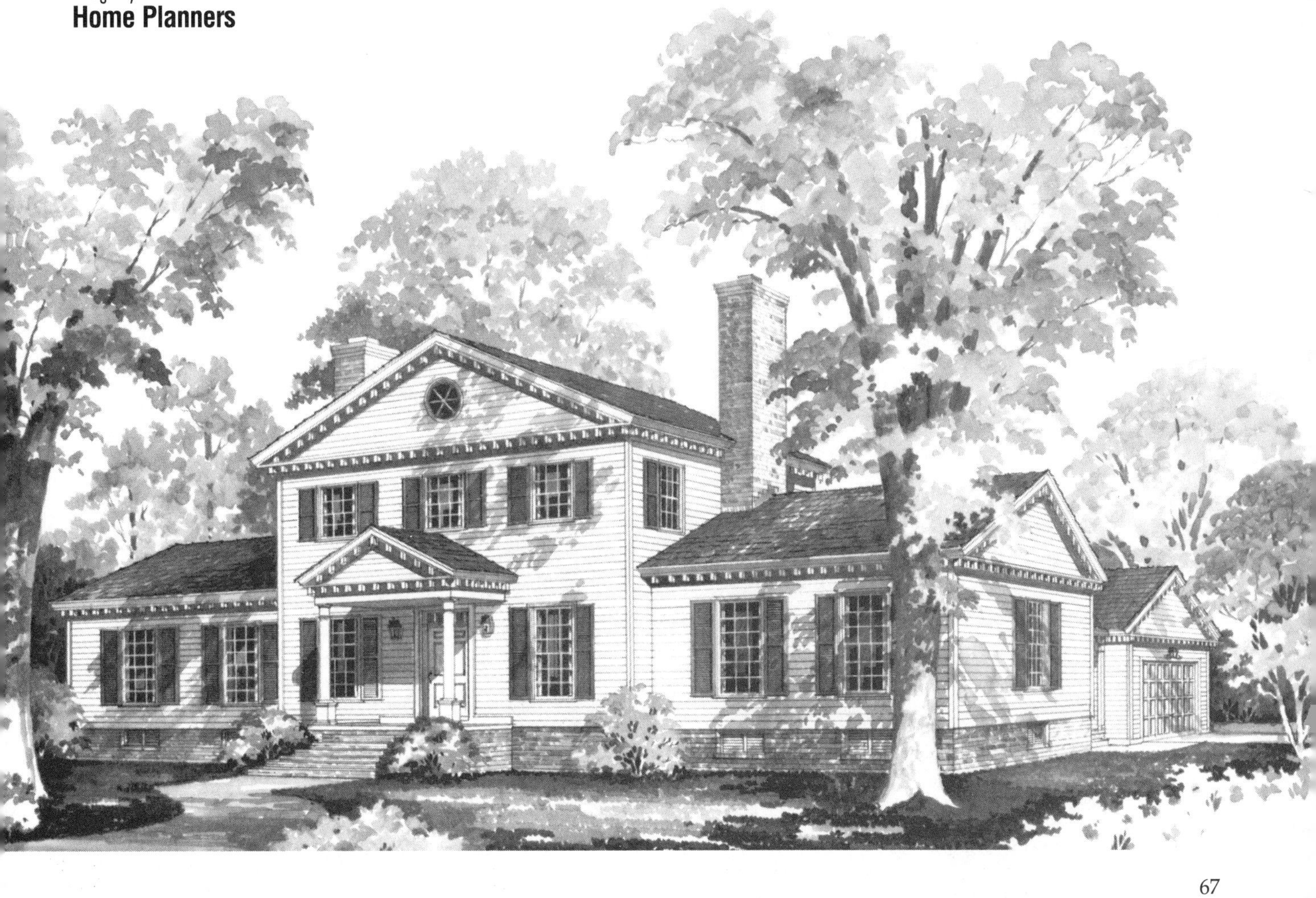

Design 2540

First Floor: 1,306 square feet
Second Floor: 1,360 square feet
Total: 2,666 square feet

L D

■ This comfortable Colonial home puts a good foot forward in family living. The entry hall is wide and gracious to receive guests (and comes complete with a powder room for convenience). Flanking it are the family room with fireplace and the formal living room. A dining room has sliding glass doors to a rear terrace and leads directly to the L-shaped kitchen with island range. A handy utility area features washer/dryer space and storage and has an exterior door to the two-car garage. Upstairs are four bedrooms with two full baths. The master bedroom has a sitting room, dressing area, walk-in closet and bath with dual vanities.

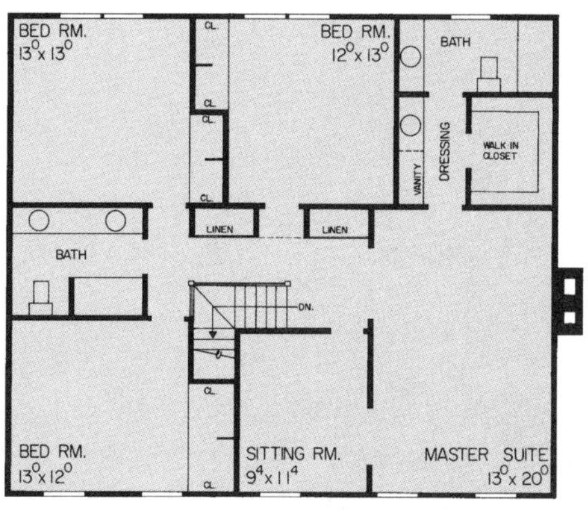

BED RM. $13^0 x 13^0$
BED RM. $12^0 x 13^0$
BATH
CL.
DRESSING
VANITY
WALK IN CLOSET
LINEN
LINEN
BATH
DN.
BED RM. $13^0 x 12^0$
SITTING RM. $9^4 x 11^4$
MASTER SUITE $13^0 x 20^0$

Design by
Home Planners

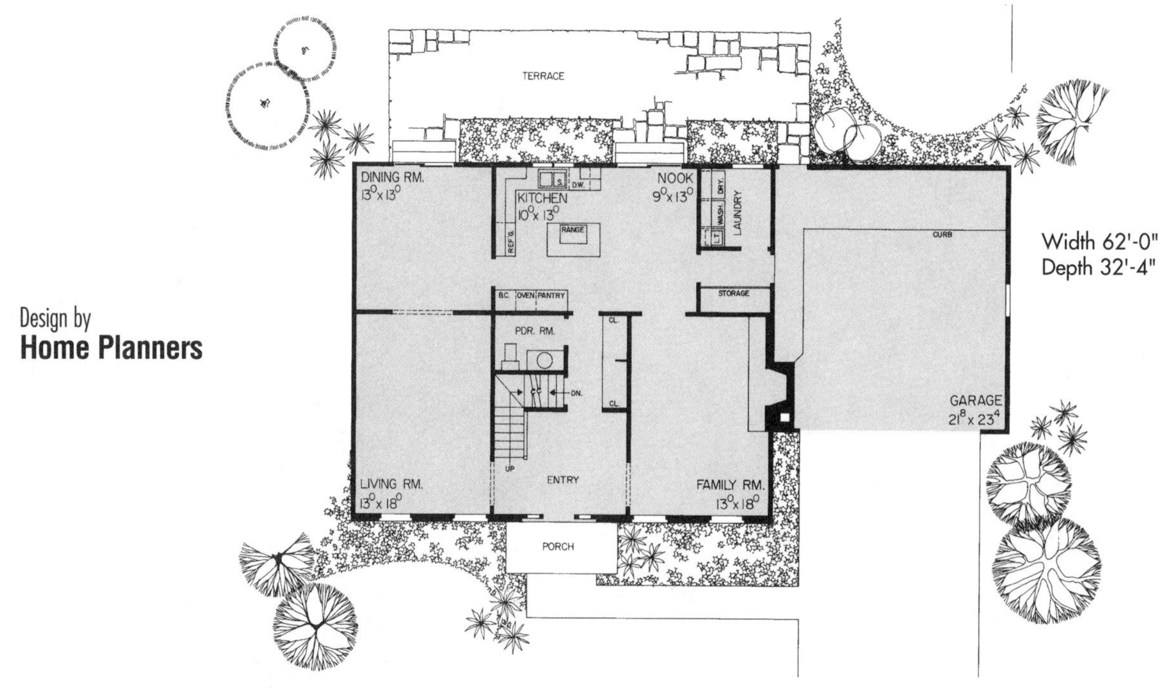

TERRACE
DINING RM. $13^0 x 13^0$
KITCHEN $10^0 x 13^0$
S.
DW.
REF'G
RANGE
NOOK $9^0 x 13^0$
WASH.
DRY.
LT.
LAUNDRY
CURB
B.C.
OVEN
PANTRY
STORAGE
PDR. RM.
CL.
DN.
UP
ENTRY
LIVING RM. $13^0 x 18^0$
FAMILY RM. $13^0 x 18^0$
GARAGE $21^8 x 23^4$
PORCH
Width 62'-0"
Depth 32'-4"

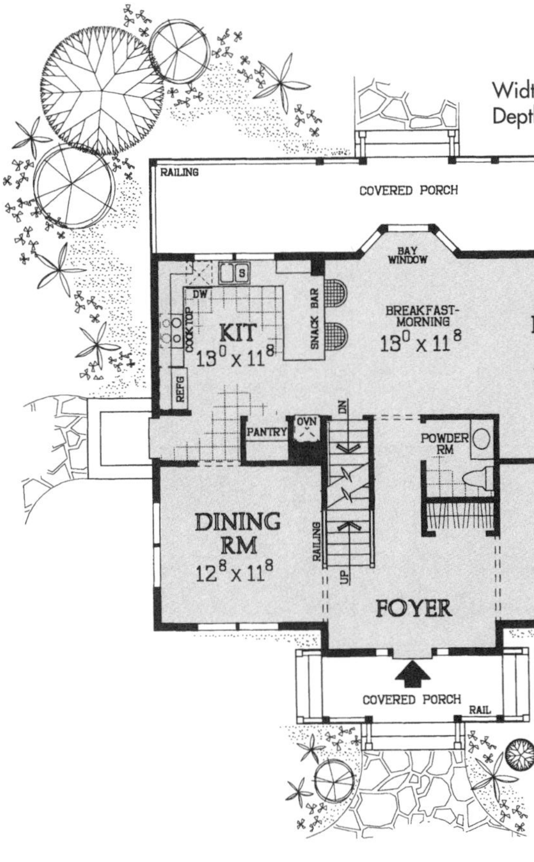

Width 42'-0"
Depth 42'-0"

COVERED PORCH
RAILING
BAY WINDOW
DW
KIT $13^0 \times 11^8$
COOKTOP
SNACK BAR
BREAKFAST-MORNING $13^0 \times 11^8$
FAMILY RM $13^0 \times 15^0$
REFG
PANTRY
OVN
DN
POWDER RM
DINING RM $12^8 \times 11^8$
RAILING
UP
LIVING RM $12^8 \times 11^8$
FOYER
COVERED PORCH
RAIL

Design 5512

First Floor: 1,160 square feet
Second Floor: 1,111 square feet
Total: 2,271 square feet

ROOF OF PORCH BELOW
LOW WALL
MASTER BATH
LINEN
WALK-IN CLOSET
BATH
LINEN
BEDRM $12^4 \times 11^2$
DN
LAUNDRY
W D
LINEN
MASTER SUITE $12^8 \times 18^8$
BEDRM $10^0 \times 11^2$
BEDRM $12^8 \times 10^6$
ROOF OF PORCH BELOW

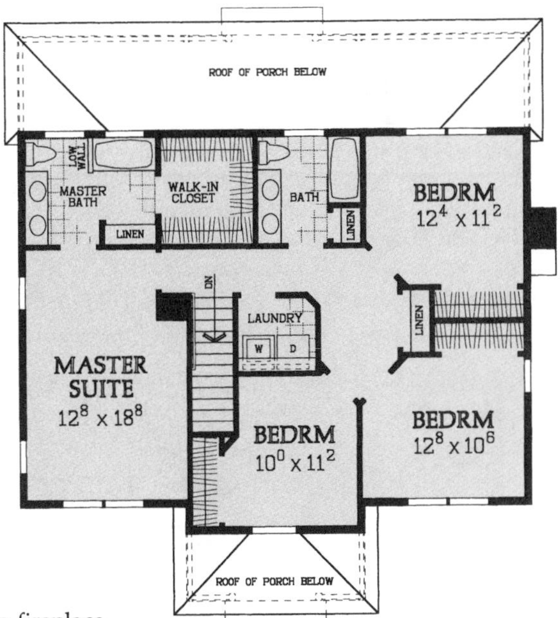

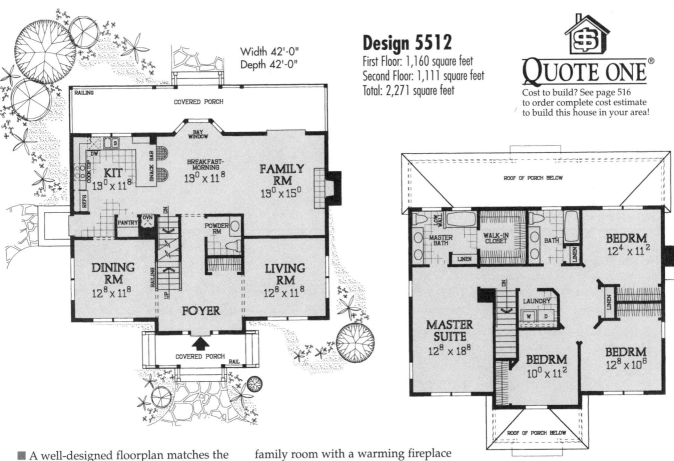

■ A well-designed floorplan matches the elegant curb appeal of this traditional two-story home. As you enter via the pleasing front porch, you are greeted by a large foyer with a formal living room on the right and a formal dining room on the left. The foyer also leads to an open area that includes a gourmet kitchen with a walk-in pantry and a snack bar, a bayed breakfast or morning room and a family room with a warming fireplace and access to the covered rear porch. A handy half-bath completes the first-floor. Upstairs, three family bedrooms share a large full bath with dual sinks, two linen closets and a convenient laundry room. The master bedroom offers plenty of space for furniture placement and a well-rounded private bath with separate sinks and a walk-in closet.

Design by
Home Planners

Design 2731

First Floor: 1,039 square feet
Second Floor: 973 square feet
Total: 2,012 square feet

L **D**

■ Affordable style is the hallmark of this Colonial design. The U-shaped kitchen with large pantry and adjacent breakfast nook is the very heart of the plan. Placed conveniently nearby is a formal dining room. The living room with fireplace, first-floor study and efficient service area round out the ground level. The second floor features a sizable master suite complete with twin vanities and a roomy walk-in closet.

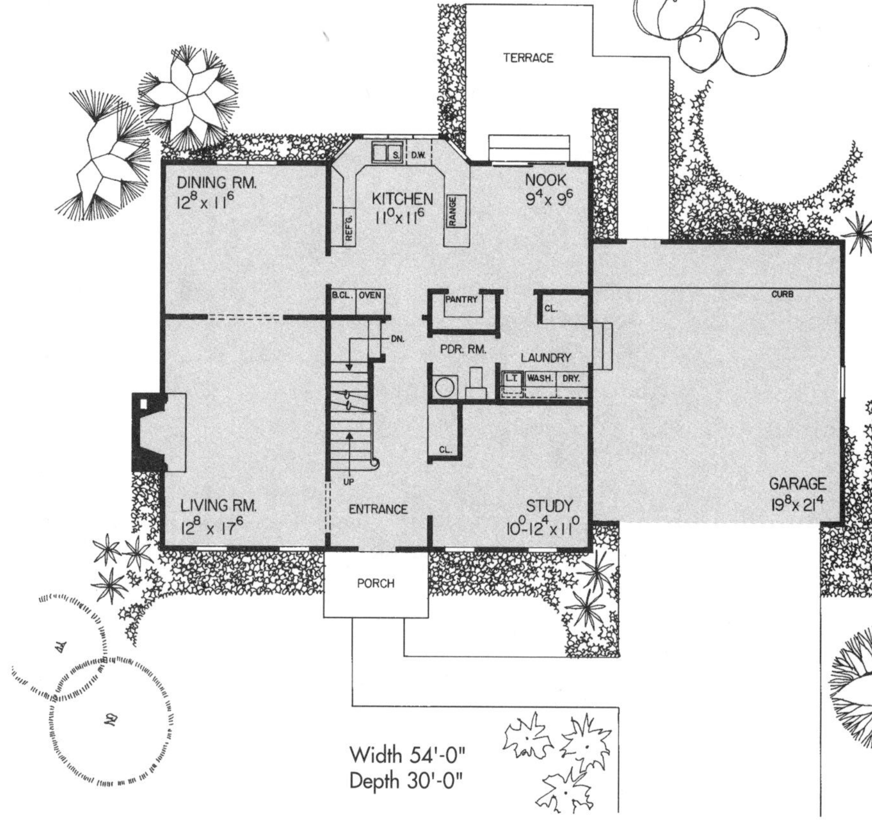
TERRACE
DINING RM.
12^{8} x 11^{6}
S.
D.W.
KITCHEN
11^{0}x11^{6}
REFG.
RANGE
NOOK
9^{4}x 9^{6}
B.CL.
OVEN
PANTRY
CL.
CURB
DN.
PDR. RM.
LAUNDRY
L.T.
WASH.
DRY.
CL.
UP
LIVING RM.
12^{8} x 17^{6}
ENTRANCE
STUDY
10^{0}-12^{4}x11^{0}
GARAGE
19^{8}x 21^{4}
PORCH
Width 54'-0"
Depth 30'-0"

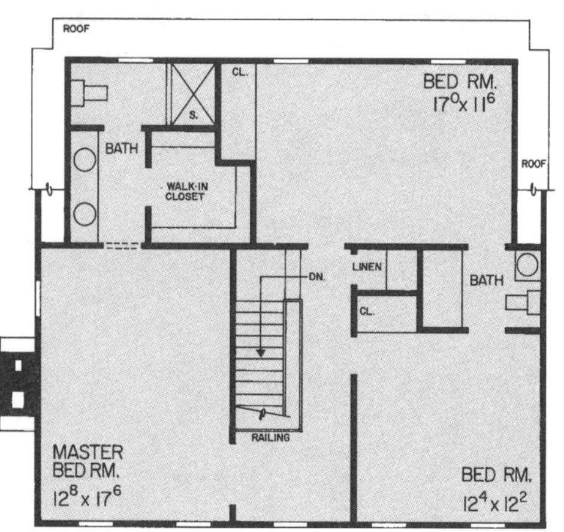
ROOF
CL.
BED RM.
17^{0}x 11^{6}
BATH
S.
WALK-IN CLOSET
ROOF
DN.
LINEN
BATH
CL.
RAILING
MASTER BED RM.
12^{8} x 17^{6}
BED RM.
12^{4} x 12^{2}

Design by
Home Planners

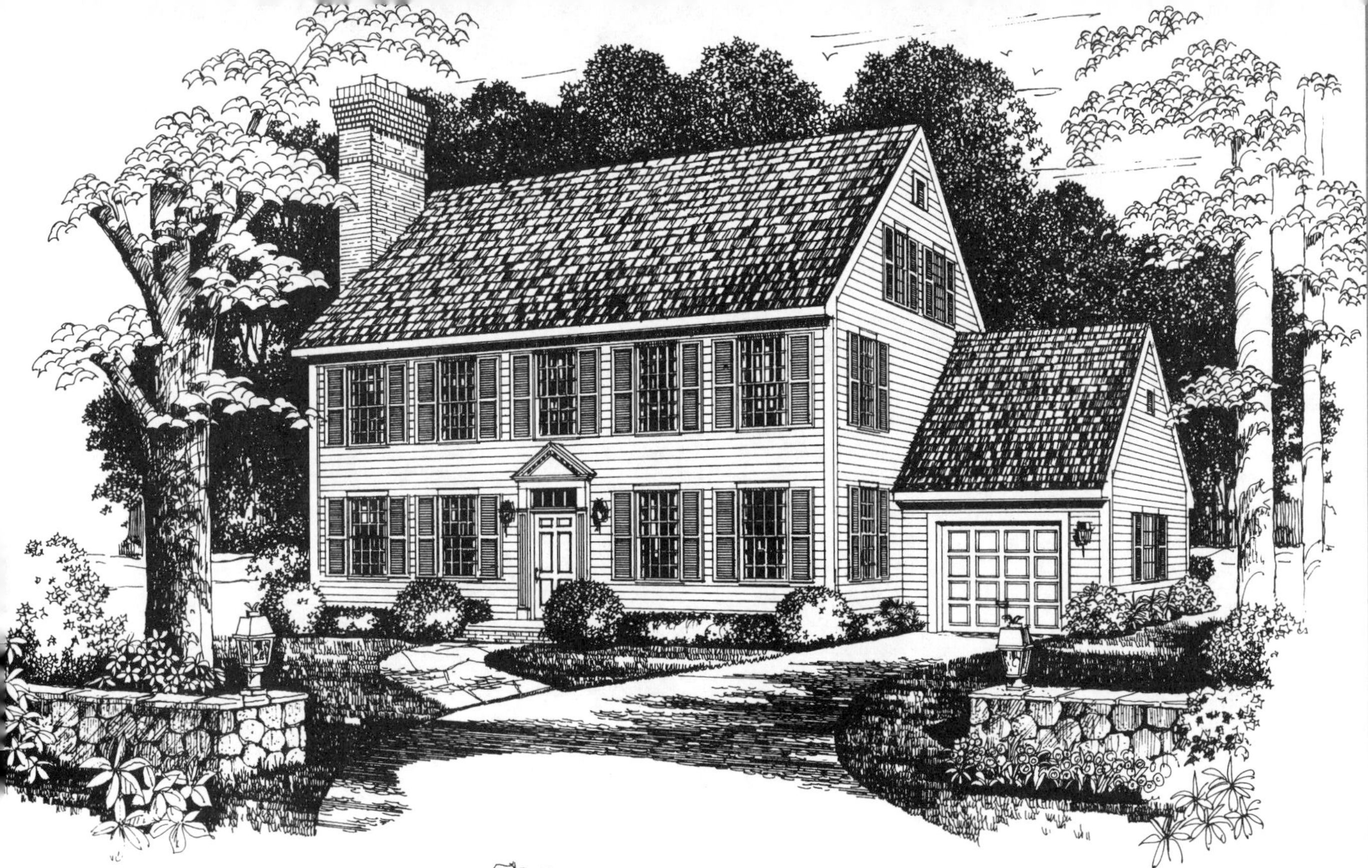

Design 2659

First Floor: 1,023 square feet
Second Floor: 1,008 square feet
Third Floor: 476 square feet
Total: 2,507 square feet

L D

■ The facade of this three-story, pitch-roofed house has a symmetrical placement of windows and a restrained but elegant central entrance. The central hall, or foyer, expands midway through the house to a family kitchen. Off the foyer are two rooms—a living room with a fireplace and a study. The windowed third floor attic can be used as a study and a studio. Three bedrooms are housed on the second floor, including a deluxe master suite with a pampering bath.

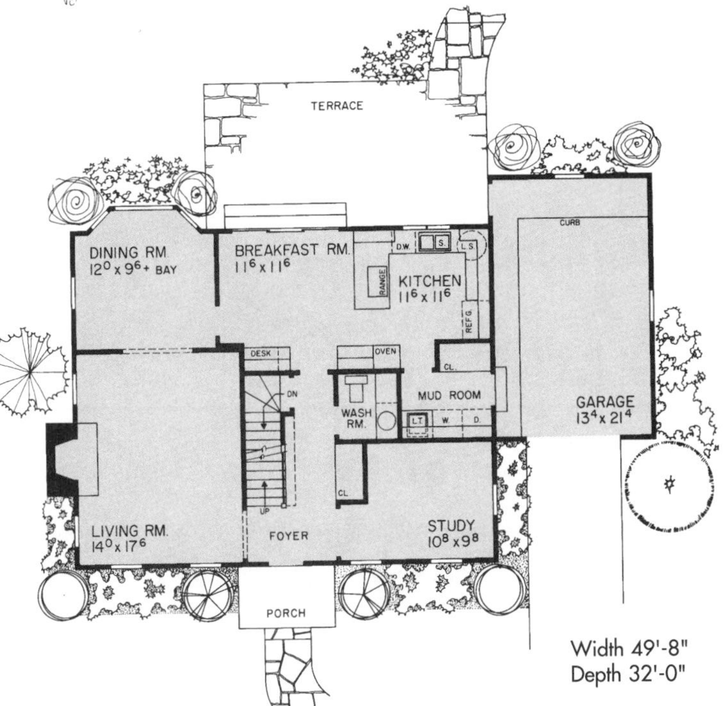
TERRACE
DINING RM
$12^{0} \times 9^{6}$ + BAY
BREAKFAST RM.
$11^{6} \times 11^{6}$
KITCHEN
$11^{6} \times 11^{6}$
CURB
GARAGE
$13^{4} \times 21^{4}$
MUD ROOM
WASH RM.
LIVING RM.
$14^{0} \times 17^{6}$
FOYER
STUDY
$10^{8} \times 9^{8}$
PORCH

Width 49'-8"
Depth 32'-0"

Design by
Home Planners

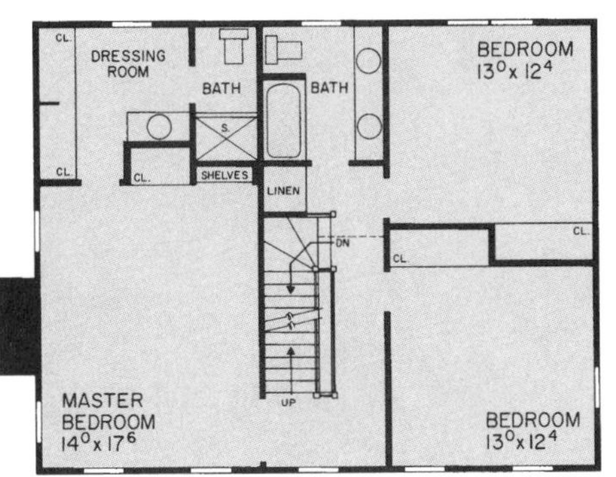
DRESSING ROOM
BATH
BATH
BEDROOM
$13^{0} \times 12^{4}$
SHELVES
LINEN
MASTER BEDROOM
$14^{0} \times 17^{6}$
BEDROOM
$13^{0} \times 12^{4}$

QUOTE ONE®

Cost to build? See page 516 to order complete cost estimate to build this house in your area!

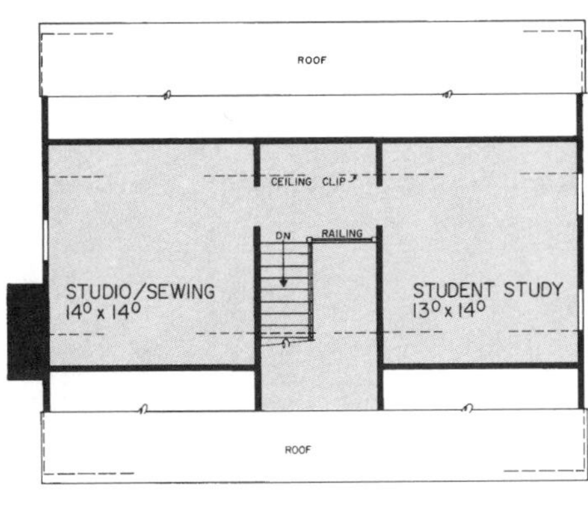
ROOF
CEILING CLIP
RAILING
STUDIO/SEWING
$14^{0} \times 14^{0}$
STUDENT STUDY
$13^{0} \times 14^{0}$
ROOF

Design 2733

First Floor: 1,177 square feet
Second Floor: 1,003 square feet
Total: 2,180 square feet

L D

■ This four-bedroom Colonial is both charming and livable. The first floor holds living and working areas—both formal and informal. The kitchen features an island range and other built-ins. All will enjoy the sunken family room with its fireplace and sliding glass doors leading to the terrace. A basement provides room for recreational activities while the laundry remains on the first floor for extra convenience. Upstairs bedrooms include a master suite with double-bowl vanity, and three family bedrooms which share a full bath.

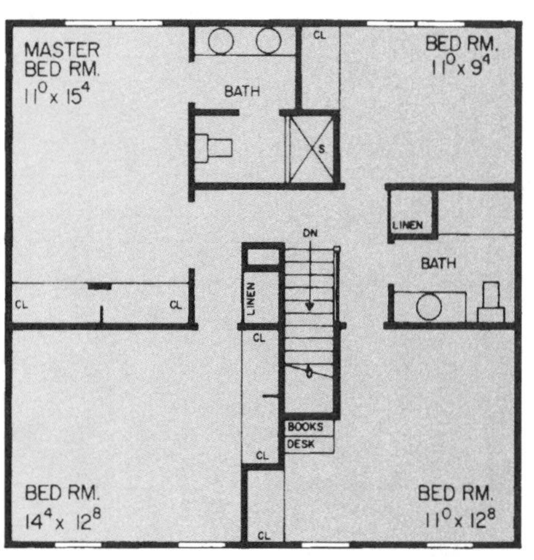
MASTER BED RM.
11⁰ x 15⁴
BATH
CL
BED RM.
11⁰ x 9⁴
LINEN
BATH
DN
CL
CL
LINEN
CL
BOOKS
DESK
CL
CL
BED RM.
14⁴ x 12⁸
BED RM.
11⁰ x 12⁸

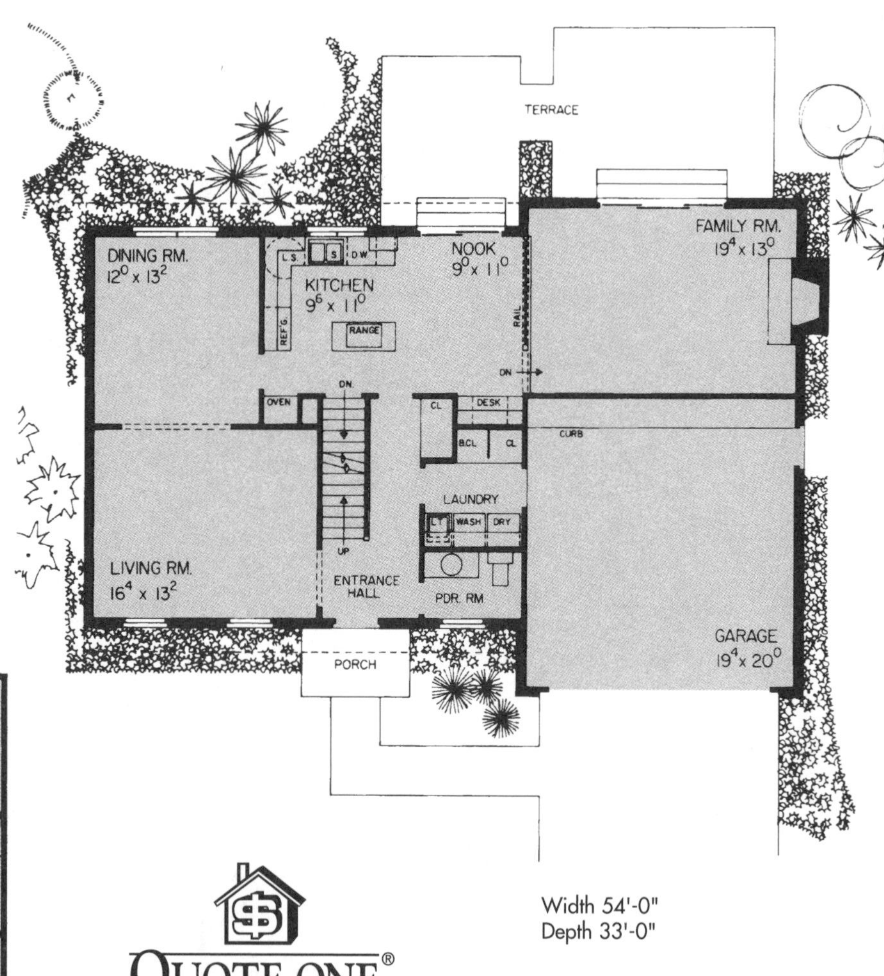
TERRACE
DINING RM.
12⁰ x 13²
KITCHEN
9⁶ x 11⁰
NOOK
9⁰ x 11⁰
FAMILY RM.
19⁴ x 13⁰
L.S.
DW
REF'G.
RANGE
RAIL
DN
OVEN
DN
CL
DESK
B.CL
CL
CURB
LAUNDRY
WASH
DRY
UP
LIVING RM.
16⁴ x 13²
ENTRANCE HALL
PDR. RM
GARAGE
19⁴ x 20⁰
PORCH

QUOTE ONE®

Cost to build? See page 516 to order complete cost estimate to build this house in your area!

Width 54'-0"
Depth 33'-0"

Design by
Home Planners

Design 2622

First Floor: 700 square feet
Second Floor: 700 square feet
Total: 1,400 square feet
Bonus Room: 268 square feet

L D

■ This Colonial adaptation provides a functional design that allows for expansion in the future. A cozy fireplace in the living room adds warmth to this space as well as the adjacent dining area. The roomy L-shaped kitchen features a breakfast nook and an over-the-sink window. Upstairs, two secondary bedrooms share a full bath with a double vanity. The master bedroom is on this floor as well. Its private bath contains access to attic storage. An additional storage area over the garage furnishes options for future development that may include a bedroom, an office, a study or an exercise room.

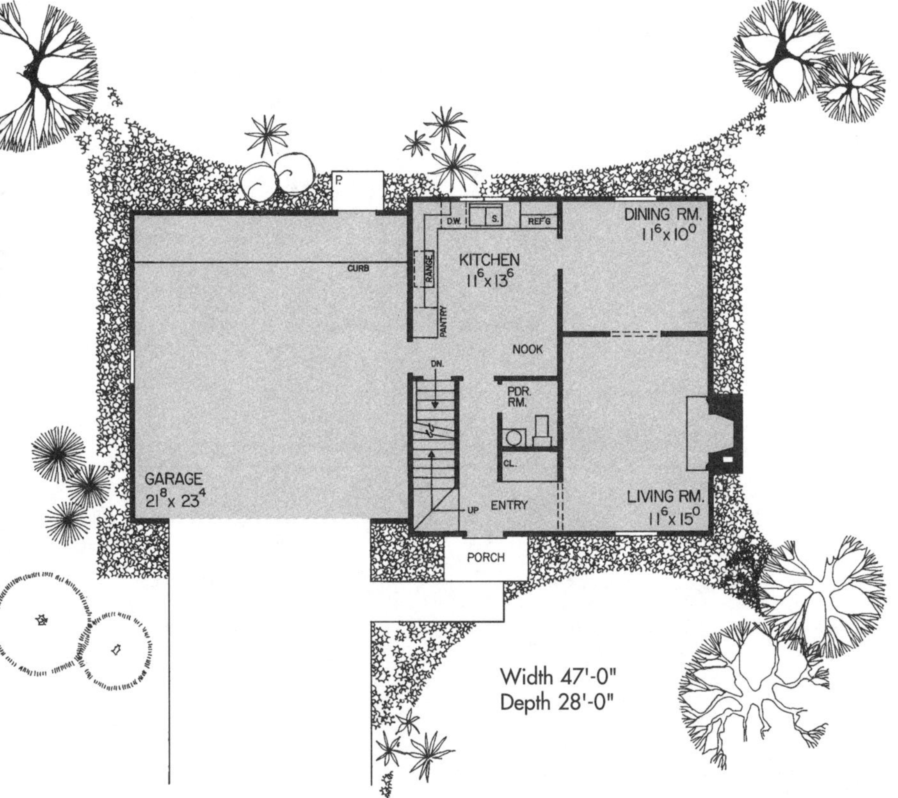
P.
D.W.
S.
REF'G
DINING RM.
$11^6 x 10^0$
KITCHEN
$11^6 x 13^6$
CURB
RANGE
PANTRY
NOOK
DN.
PDR. RM.
CL.
GARAGE
$21^8 x 23^4$
UP
ENTRY
LIVING RM.
$11^6 x 15^0$
PORCH
Width 47'-0"
Depth 28'-0"

Design by
Home Planners

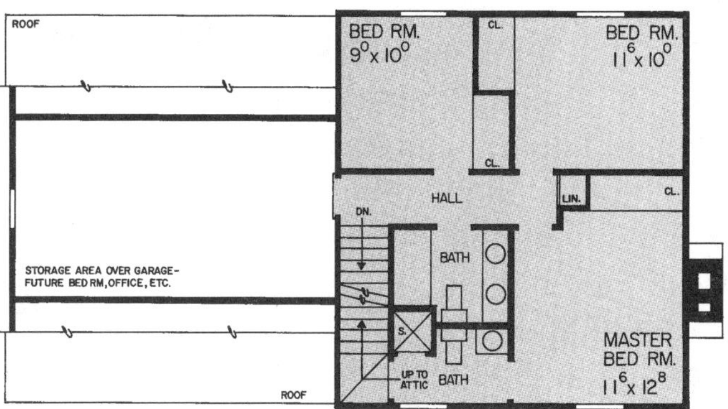
ROOF
BED RM.
$9^0 x 10^0$
CL.
BED RM.
$11^6 x 10^0$
CL.
HALL
LIN.
CL.
DN.
BATH
STORAGE AREA OVER GARAGE-
FUTURE BED RM,OFFICE,ETC.
S.
UP TO ATTIC
BATH
MASTER
BED RM.
$11^6 x 12^8$
ROOF

QUOTE ONE®

Cost to build? See page 516 to order complete cost estimate to build this house in your area!

Design 5515

First Floor: 718 square feet
Second Floor: 700 square feet
Total: 1,418 square feet
Storage Room: 268 square feet

■ Accessibility is the key word for this two-story traditional design. Each room on the first floor accesses the other for entertaining ease as well as for comfort. The front foyer leads to both the formal living room, with its cozy fireplace, and the L-shaped kitchen with breakfast nook. Both the living room and the kitchen are accessible from the rear corner dining room. Upstairs, two family bedrooms share a full hall bath while the master bedroom features its own bath. Bonus space over the garage can be used for future development. Additional space is also available in the third-floor attic area and can be used for storage, a studio, a study space, a sewing room, etc.

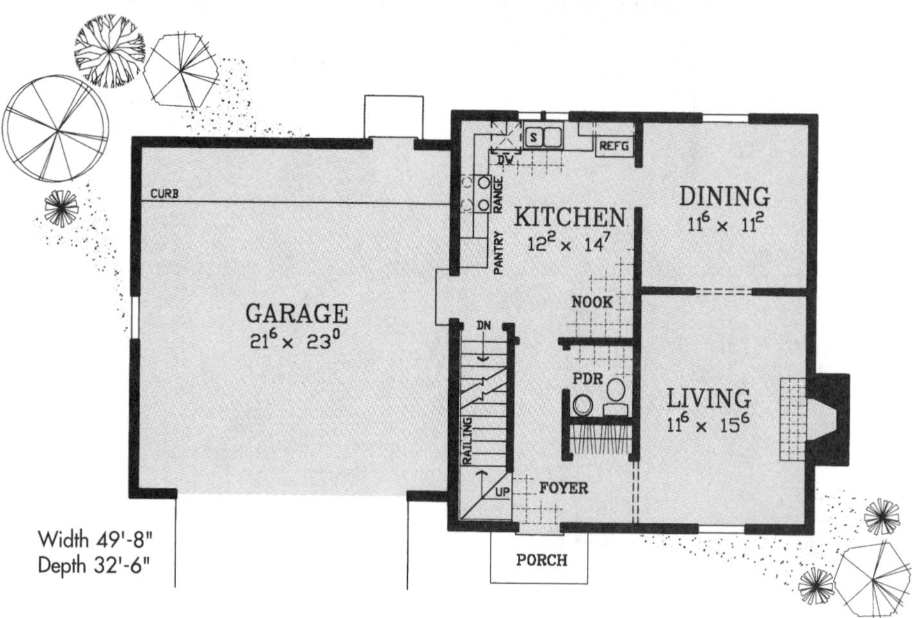

CURB
GARAGE
21⁶ x 23⁰
S
REFG
DW
RANGE
PANTRY
KITCHEN
12² x 14⁷
DINING
11⁶ x 11²
NOOK
DN
PDR
RAILING
LIVING
11⁶ x 15⁶
UP
FOYER
PORCH

Width 49'-8"
Depth 32'-6"

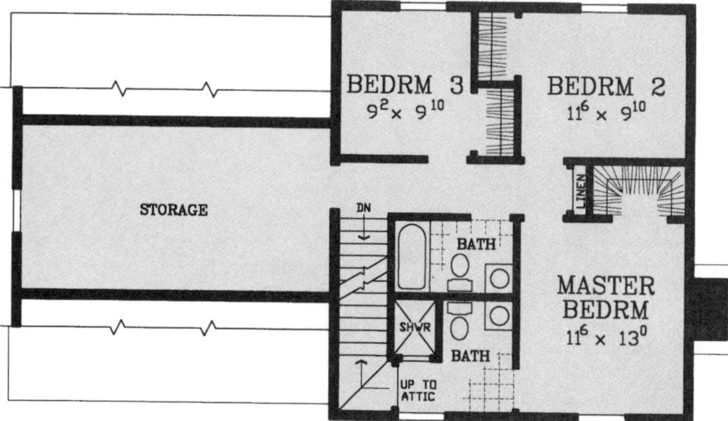

BEDRM 3
9² x 9¹⁰
BEDRM 2
11⁶ x 9¹⁰
LINEN
STORAGE
DN
BATH
MASTER
BEDRM
11⁶ x 13⁰
SHWR
BATH
UP TO
ATTIC

Design by
Home Planners

QUOTE ONE®

Cost to build? See page 516 to order complete cost estimate to build this house in your area!

Design 5537

First Floor: 777 square feet
Second Floor: 720 square feet
Total: 1,497 square feet

■ Offering spaciousness within a smaller space while still providing today's necessary amenities, this two-story traditional would be ideal for smaller or corner lots. Inside, the foyer leads to all the living areas available on the first floor. The combination living and dining room features a large fireplace and access to the rear patio. The corner kitchen includes plenty of counter space and a pass-through to a breakfast nook with a sunny bay window. Upstairs, two family bedrooms share a full hall bath while the master bedroom features its own bath with dual sinks. A large storage area on the second floor and a half-bath on the first floor complete this versatile plan.

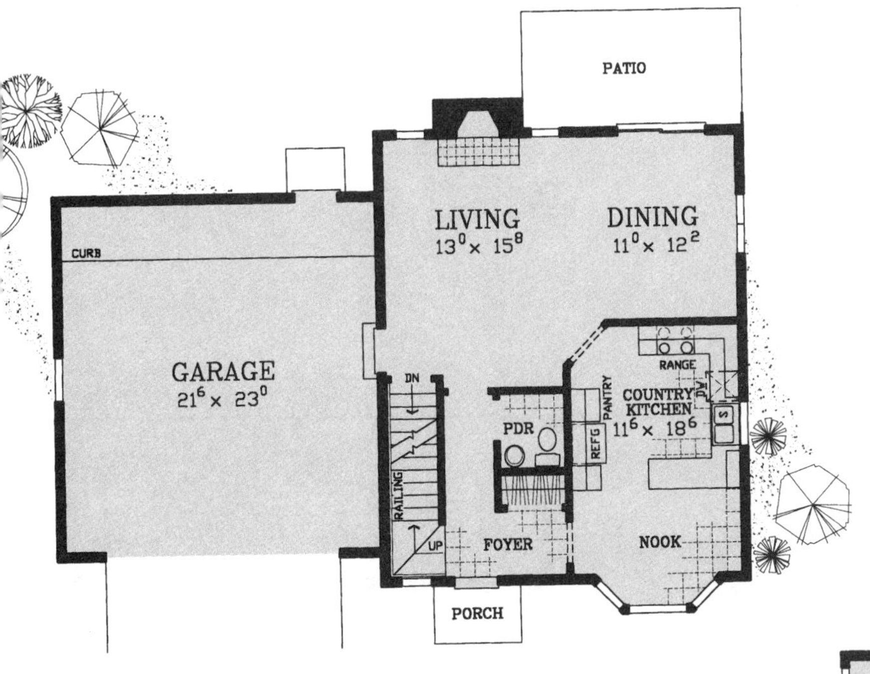
PATIO
LIVING
$13^0 \times 15^8$
DINING
$11^0 \times 12^2$
CURB
GARAGE
$21^6 \times 23^0$
RANGE
DW
DN
PANTRY
COUNTRY KITCHEN
$11^6 \times 18^6$
S
PDR
REFG
RAILING
UP
FOYER
NOOK
PORCH

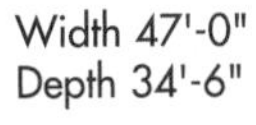
Width 47'-0"
Depth 34'-6"

Design by
Home Planners

QUOTE ONE®

Cost to build? See page 516 to order complete cost estimate to build this house in your area!

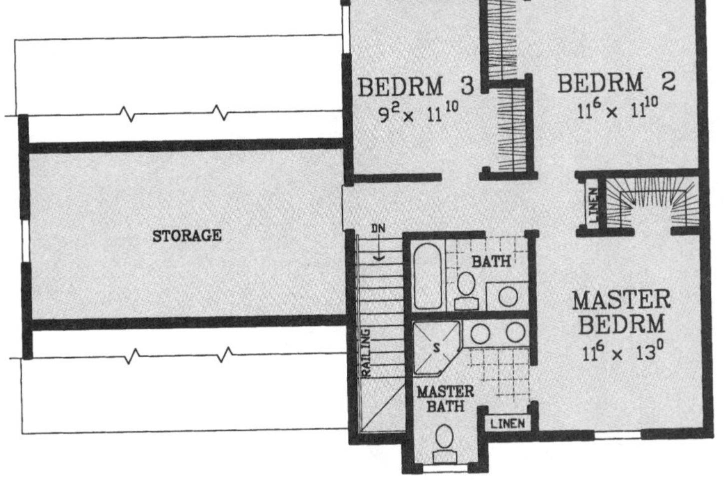
BEDRM 3
$9^2 \times 11^{10}$
BEDRM 2
$11^6 \times 11^{10}$
LINEN
STORAGE
DN
BATH
MASTER BEDRM
$11^6 \times 13^0$
S
RAILING
MASTER BATH
LINEN

Design 1719

First Floor: 864 square feet
Second Floor: 896 square feet
Total: 1,760 square feet

L **D**

■ This appealing low-cost Colonial has most of the amenities found in the largest of homes. The foyer opens to the living room, which has a cozy fireplace, or to the family room which opens to the rear terrace. A powder room located off the foyer is an added convenience. The U-shaped kitchen is positioned between the dining room and the family room, where a pass-through adds a feeling of spaciousness. Four bedrooms (two with walk-in closets) are located on the second floor. Note the built-in storage space in the garage.

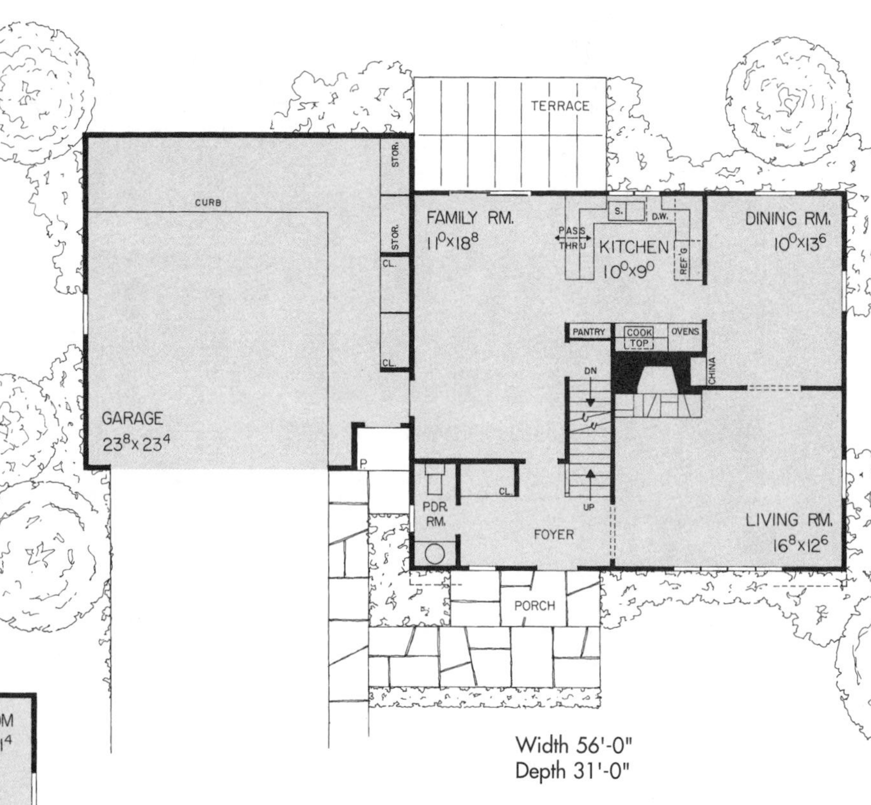
TERRACE
STOR.
STOR.
CL.
CL.
CURB
FAMILY RM.
11^{0}x18^{8}
PASS THRU
S.
D.W.
KITCHEN
10^{0}x9^{0}
REF'G
DINING RM.
10^{0}x13^{6}
PANTRY
COOK TOP
OVENS
CHINA
DN
UP
GARAGE
23^{8}x23^{4}
P
PDR. RM.
CL.
FOYER
LIVING RM.
16^{8}x12^{6}
PORCH
Width 56'-0"
Depth 31'-0"

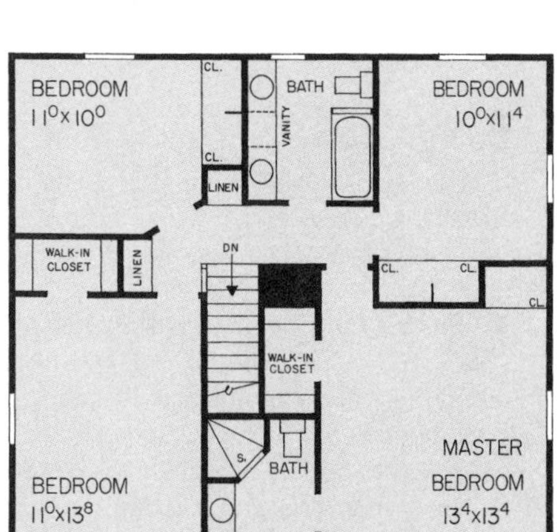
BEDROOM
11^{0}x10^{0}
CL.
CL.
LINEN
BATH
VANITY
BEDROOM
10^{0}x11^{4}
WALK-IN CLOSET
LINEN
DN
CL.
CL.
CL.
WALK-IN CLOSET
S.
BATH
BEDROOM
11^{0}x13^{8}
MASTER BEDROOM
13^{4}x13^{4}

Design by
Home Planners

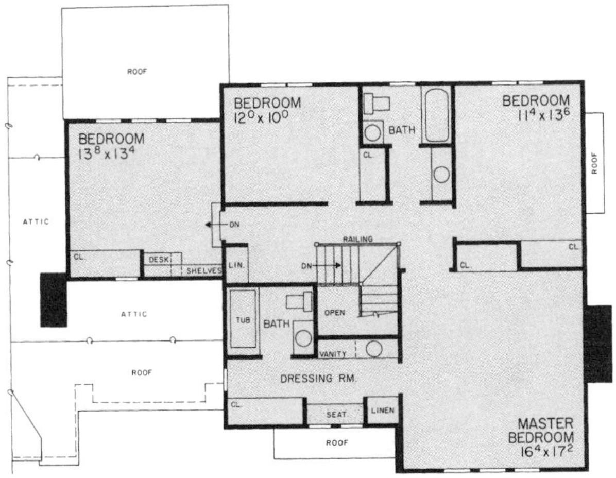

Design 2855

First Floor: 1,372 square feet
Second Floor: 1,245 square feet
Total: 2,617 square feet

L D

■ This elegant Tudor house is perfect for the family who wants to move-up in living area, style and luxury. As you enter this home you will find a large living room with a fireplace on your right. Adjacent, the formal dining room has easy access to both the living room and the kitchen. The kitchen/breakfast room has an open plan and access to the rear terrace. Sunken a few steps, the spacious family room is highlighted with a fireplace and access to the rear covered porch. Note the optional planning of the garage storage area. Plan this area according to the needs of your family. Upstairs, your family will enjoy three bedrooms and a full bath, along with a spacious master bedroom suite, complete with a window seat, two closets and a lavish bath.

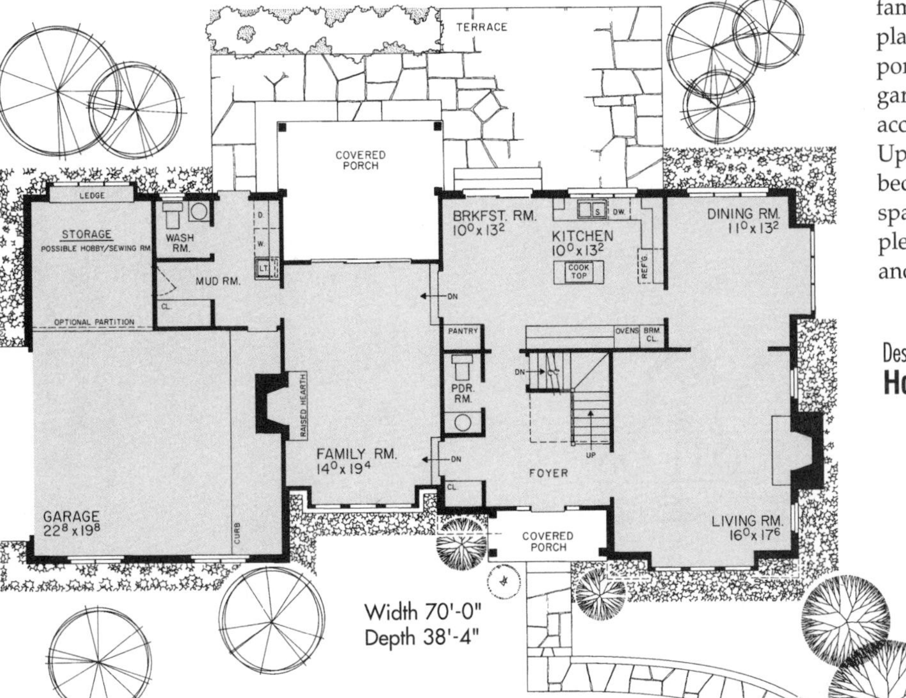
TERRACE
COVERED PORCH
LEDGE
STORAGE
POSSIBLE HOBBY/SEWING RM.
WASH RM.
MUD RM.
OPTIONAL PARTITION
BRKFST. RM. 10⁰x13²
KITCHEN 10⁰x13²
COOK TOP
DINING RM. 11⁰x13²
PANTRY
OVENS
PDR. RM.
RAISED HEARTH
FAMILY RM. 14⁰x19⁴
FOYER
GARAGE 22⁸x19⁸
CURB
COVERED PORCH
LIVING RM. 16⁰x17⁶
Width 70'-0"
Depth 38'-4"

Design by
Home Planners

QUOTE ONE®

Cost to build? See page 516 to order complete cost estimate to build this house in your area!

Design 2959

First Floor: 1,003 square feet
Second Floor: 1,056 square feet
Total: 2,059 square feet

■ Tudor styling is captured in a design suited for a narrow building site. This relatively low-budget two-story delivers all the livability found in much larger homes. Imagine—a 31-foot living-dining area that stretches across the entire rear of the house and has access to the rear terrace. The U-shaped kitchen boasts a snack-bar pass-through to the dining room. A cozy study with walk-in storage completes the first floor. On the second floor are three nicely proportioned bedrooms. The master suite contains a dressing area with vanity and walk-in closet, plus a private balcony.

Design by
Home Planners

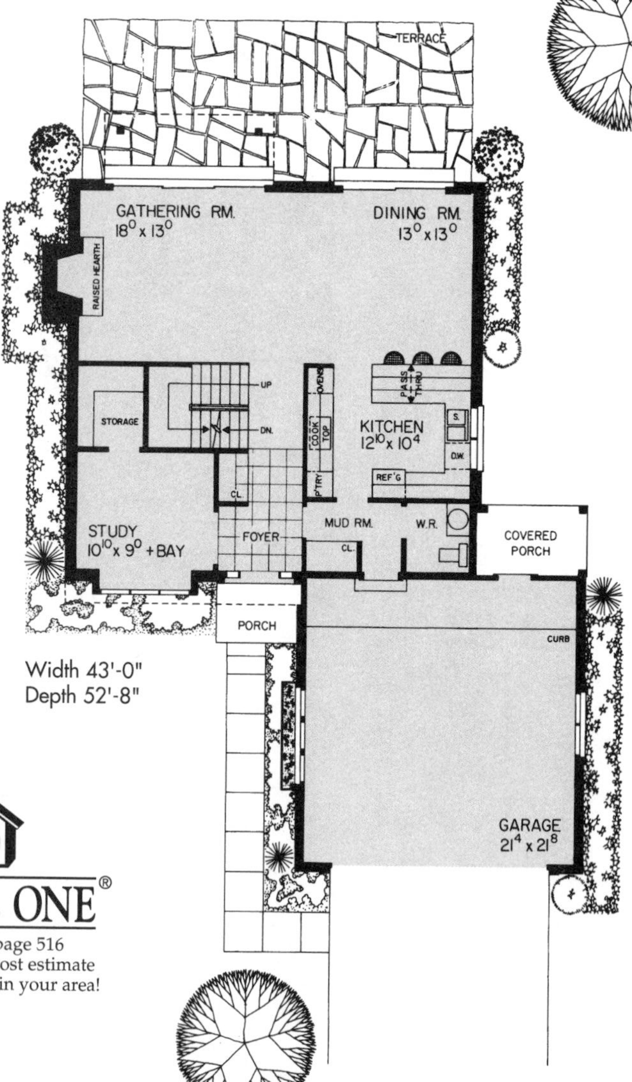

TERRACE
GATHERING RM.
18⁰ x 13⁰
DINING RM.
13⁰ x 13⁰
RAISED HEARTH
UP
DN.
STORAGE
KITCHEN
12¹⁰ x 10⁴
PASS THRU
OVEN
COOK TOP
P'TRY
REF'G
D.W.
S.
CL.
STUDY
10¹⁰ x 9⁰ + BAY
FOYER
MUD RM.
W.R.
COVERED PORCH
PORCH
CURB
GARAGE
21⁴ x 21⁸

Width 43'-0"
Depth 52'-8"

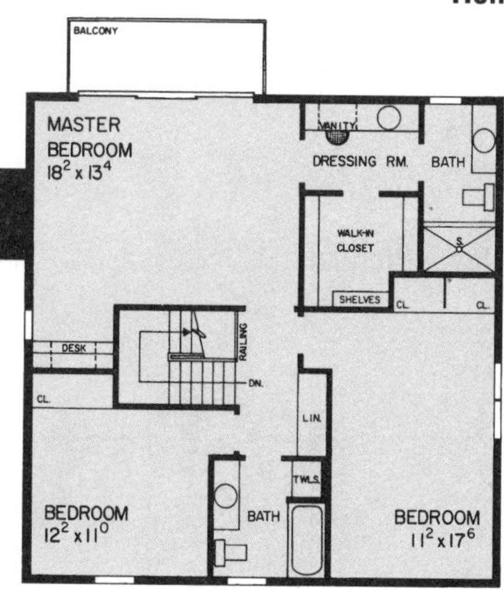

BALCONY
MASTER BEDROOM
18² x 13⁴
VANITY
DRESSING RM.
BATH
WALK-IN CLOSET
SHELVES
CL.
CL.
DESK
RAILING
DN.
CL.
LIN.
TWLS.
BEDROOM
12² x 11⁰
BATH
BEDROOM
11² x 17⁶

QUOTE ONE®

Cost to build? See page 516 to order complete cost estimate to build this house in your area!

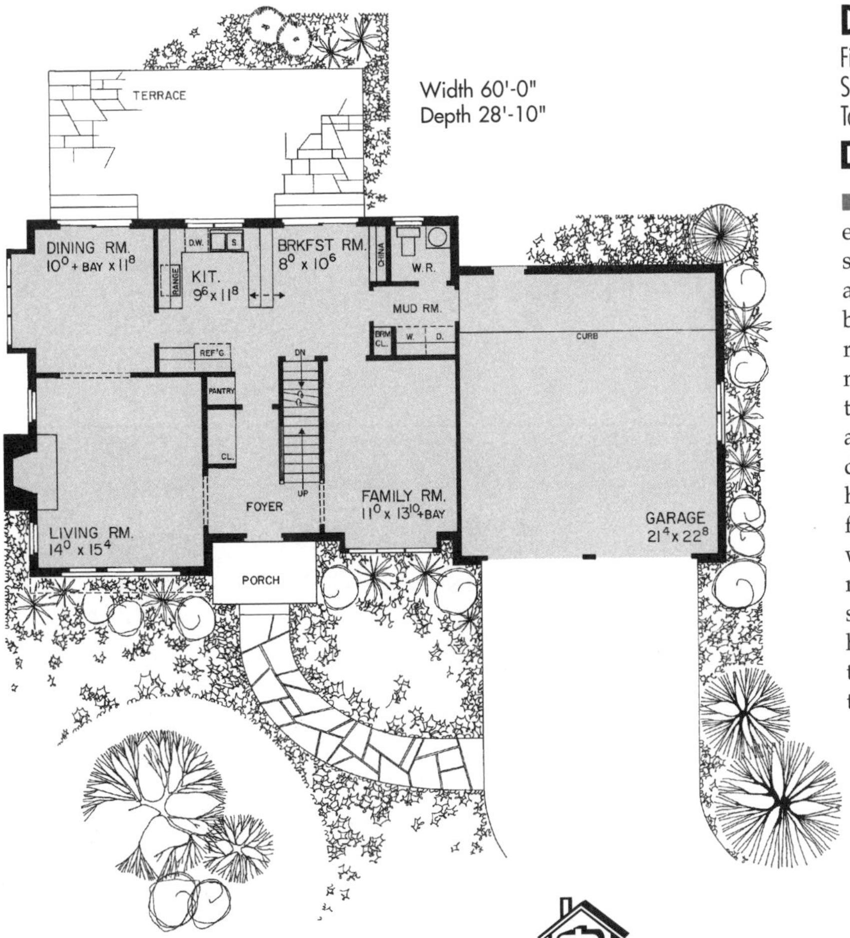

Width 60'-0"
Depth 28'-10"

Design 2800

First Floor: 999 square feet
Second Floor: 997 square feet
Total: 1,996 square feet

L D

■ Fine Tudor detailing is enhanced by other exterior details to make this facade worth considering. Besides half-timbering, and stone-and-brick work, there are box-bay windows both at the front and the side in the family room and the dining room. Inside, there is a modern, efficient floor plan in modest proportions. Flanking the entry foyer is a comfortable living room and the cozy family room. A dining room connects to the living room and has sliding glass doors to the rear terrace. The family room opens to the breakfast room, which also has sliding glass doors to the terrace and is separated from the kitchen by a snack counter. A mud room with wash room has a door to the two-car garage. Upstairs, three bedrooms include two family suites and the master suite with study or nursery.

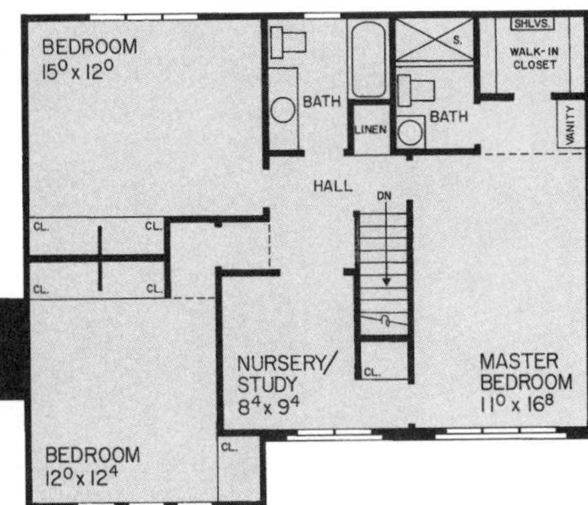
BEDROOM
15^0 x 12^0
BATH
LINEN
BATH
SHLVS.
WALK-IN CLOSET
VANITY
HALL
DN
CL.
CL.
CL.
CL.
CL.
CL.
NURSERY/ STUDY
8^4 x 9^4
MASTER BEDROOM
11^0 x 16^8
BEDROOM
12^0 x 12^4

Design by
Home Planners

Design 5501

First Floor: 1,147 square feet
Second Floor: 870 square feet
Total: 2,017 square feet

■ This comfortable two-story offers a traditional exterior and enough amenities to make any homeowner smile. A covered porch bids welcome as you enter the central foyer. To your right, the corner living room and adjoining dining room are open for entertaining. The dining room connects to a large kitchen with a desk, a breakfast nook, plenty of counter space and views to the backyard. A half-bath, a two-car garage, a convenient utility room and a quiet family room with a fireplace complete the first floor. Two family bedrooms with a shared bath and a sumptuous master bedroom make up the second-floor sleeping area. The luxurious master bath features a walk-in closet and a corner garden tub.

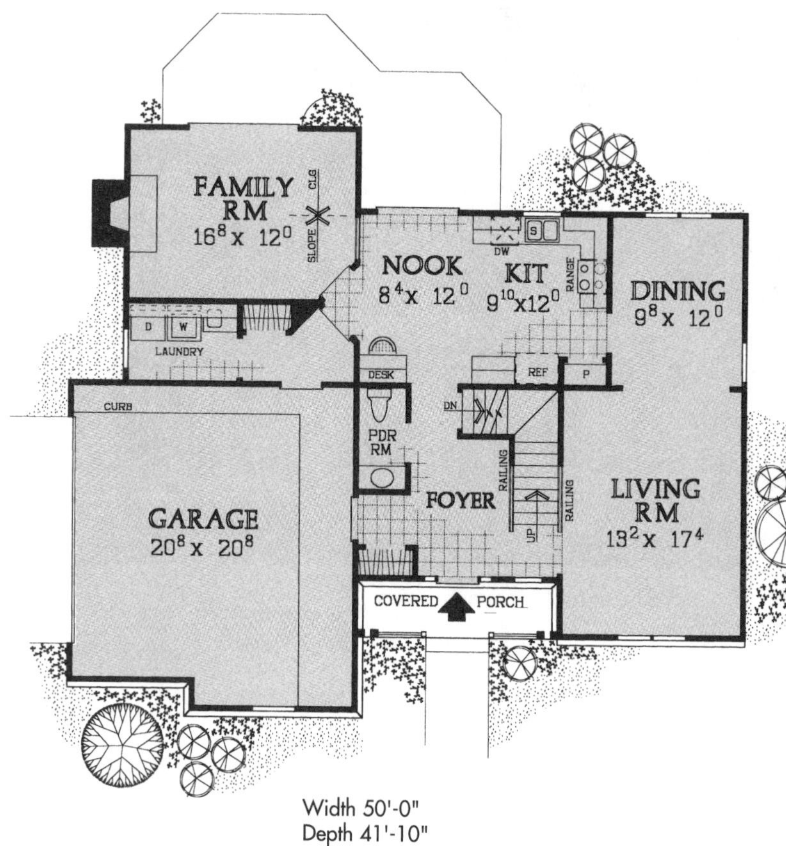
FAMILY RM
16^{8} x 12^{0}
SLOPE CLG
NOOK
8^{4} x 12^{0}
KIT
9^{10}x12^{0}
DW
RANGE
DINING
9^{8} x 12^{0}
D
W
LAUNDRY
DESK
REF
P
DN
CURB
PDR RM
GARAGE
20^{8} x 20^{8}
FOYER
RAILING
UP
RAILING
LIVING RM
13^{2} x 17^{4}
COVERED PORCH
Width 50'-0"
Depth 41'-10"

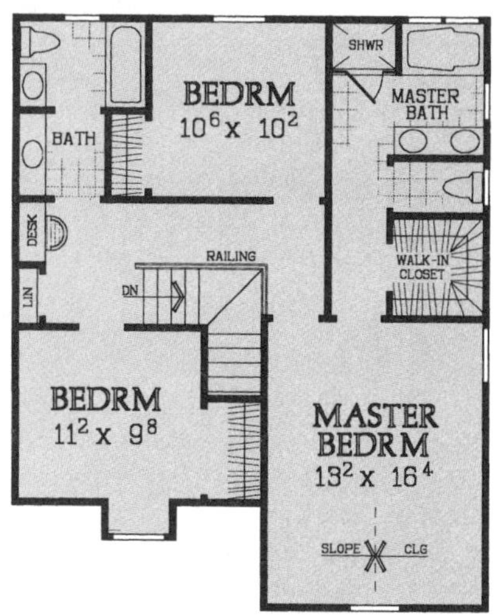
SHWR
BEDRM
10^{6} x 10^{2}
MASTER BATH
BATH
DESK
RAILING
LIN
DN
WALK-IN CLOSET
BEDRM
11^{2} x 9^{8}
MASTER BEDRM
13^{2} x 16^{4}
SLOPE CLG

Design by
Home Planners

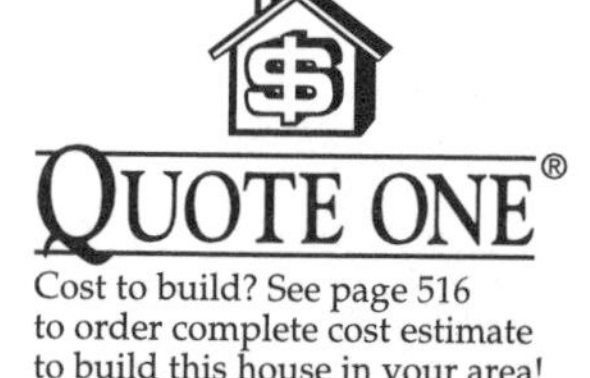
QUOTE ONE®

Cost to build? See page 516 to order complete cost estimate to build this house in your area!

Design 5502

First Floor: 1,160 square feet
Second Floor: 870 square feet
Total: 2,030 square feet

Design by
Home Planners

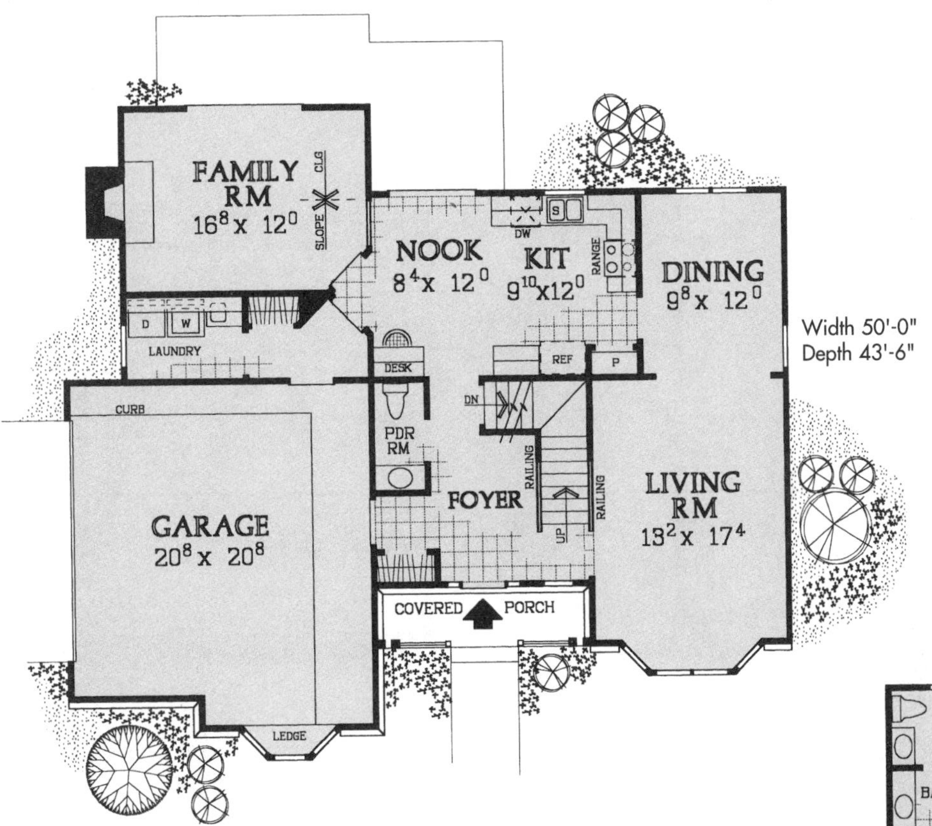
FAMILY RM
16^{8} x 12^{0}
SLOPE CLG
NOOK
8^{4} x 12^{0}
KIT
9^{10} x 12^{0}
DW
RANGE
DINING
9^{8} x 12^{0}
D
W
LAUNDRY
DESK
REF
P
CURB
DN
PDR RM
RAILING
FOYER
UP
LIVING RM
13^{2} x 17^{4}
GARAGE
20^{8} x 20^{8}
COVERED PORCH
LEDGE

Width 50'-0"
Depth 43'-6"

QUOTE ONE®

Cost to build? See page 516 to order complete cost estimate to build this house in your area!

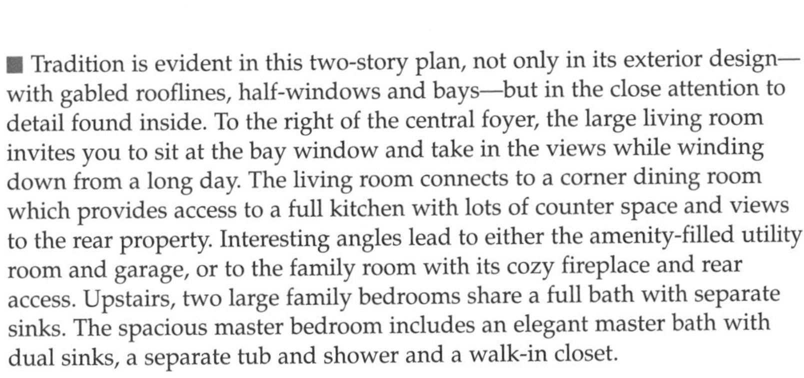

■ Tradition is evident in this two-story plan, not only in its exterior design—with gabled rooflines, half-windows and bays—but in the close attention to detail found inside. To the right of the central foyer, the large living room invites you to sit at the bay window and take in the views while winding down from a long day. The living room connects to a corner dining room which provides access to a full kitchen with lots of counter space and views to the rear property. Interesting angles lead to either the amenity-filled utility room and garage, or to the family room with its cozy fireplace and rear access. Upstairs, two large family bedrooms share a full bath with separate sinks. The spacious master bedroom includes an elegant master bath with dual sinks, a separate tub and shower and a walk-in closet.

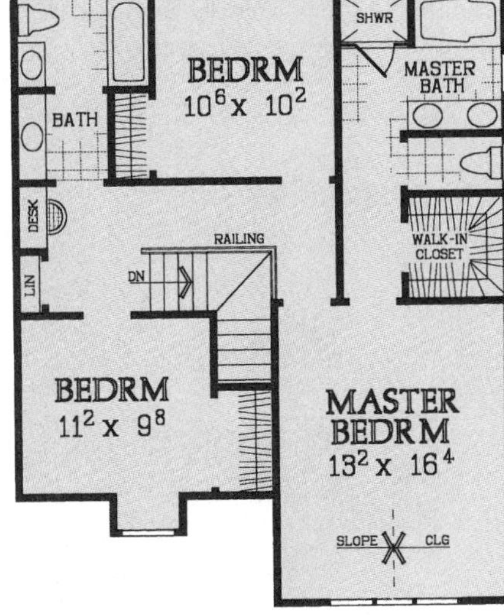
BATH
BEDRM
10^{6} x 10^{2}
SHWR
MASTER BATH
DESK
RAILING
WALK-IN CLOSET
LIN
DN
BEDRM
11^{2} x 9^{8}
MASTER BEDRM
13^{2} x 16^{4}
SLOPE CLG

Design 1956

First Floor: 990 square feet
Second Floor: 728 square feet
Total: 1,718 square feet

D

■ Simple, functional and loaded with Colonial appeal, this versatile two-story plan features the finest in family floor plans. The entry foyer offers a powder room for guests and a staircase to the second floor. A large formal living room connects to the dining room, allowing adequate space for entertaining in style. The U-shaped kitchen features a pass-through counter to the breakfast room. The family room is sunken slightly from the main body of the house and is enhanced by a beam ceiling, a raised-hearth fireplace and built-in bookshelves. Two plans are available for the second floor: one with three bedrooms and one with four. Either option allows for a master bedroom with a private bath. Other highlights of the plan include a full-length rear terrace and extra storage space.

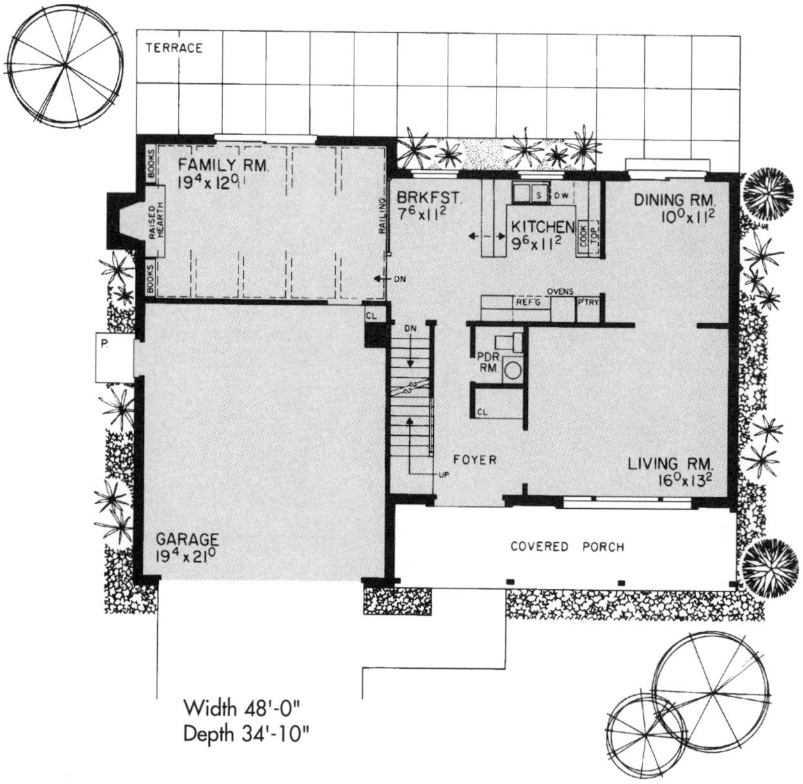

Width 48'-0"
Depth 34'-10"

Design by
Home Planners

QUOTE ONE®

Cost to build? See page 516 to order complete cost estimate to build this house in your area!

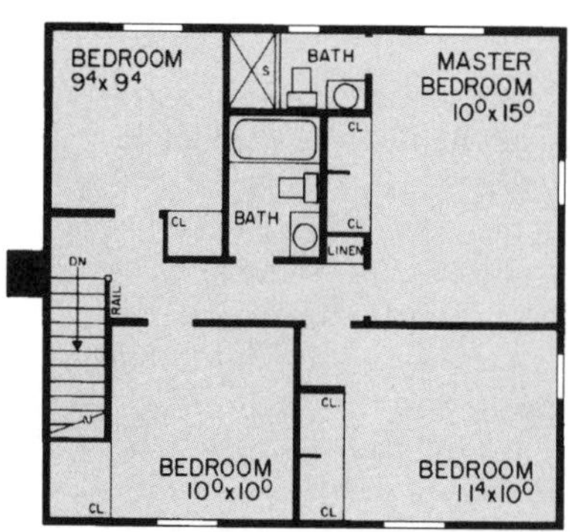
BEDROOM
9^{4} x 9^{4}
BATH
MASTER BEDROOM
10^{0} x 15^{0}
CL
BATH
CL
LINEN
DN
RAIL
CL
BEDROOM
10^{0} x 10^{0}
BEDROOM
11^{4} x 10^{0}
CL
CL

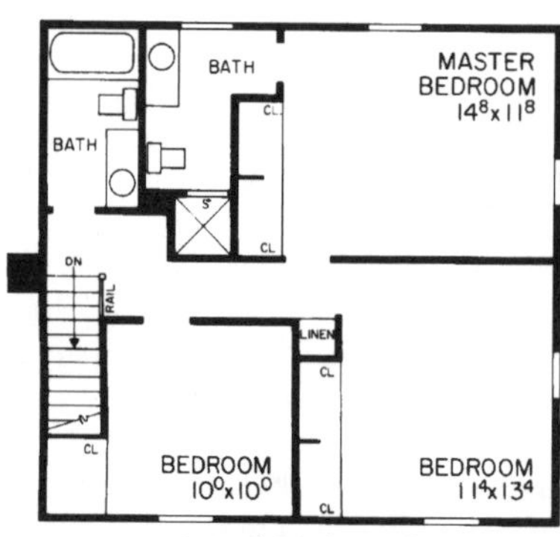
BATH
MASTER BEDROOM
14^{8} x 11^{8}
BATH
CL
CL
DN
RAIL
LINEN
CL
CL
BEDROOM
10^{0} x 10^{0}
BEDROOM
11^{4} x 13^{4}
CL

Optional 3-Bedroom Plan

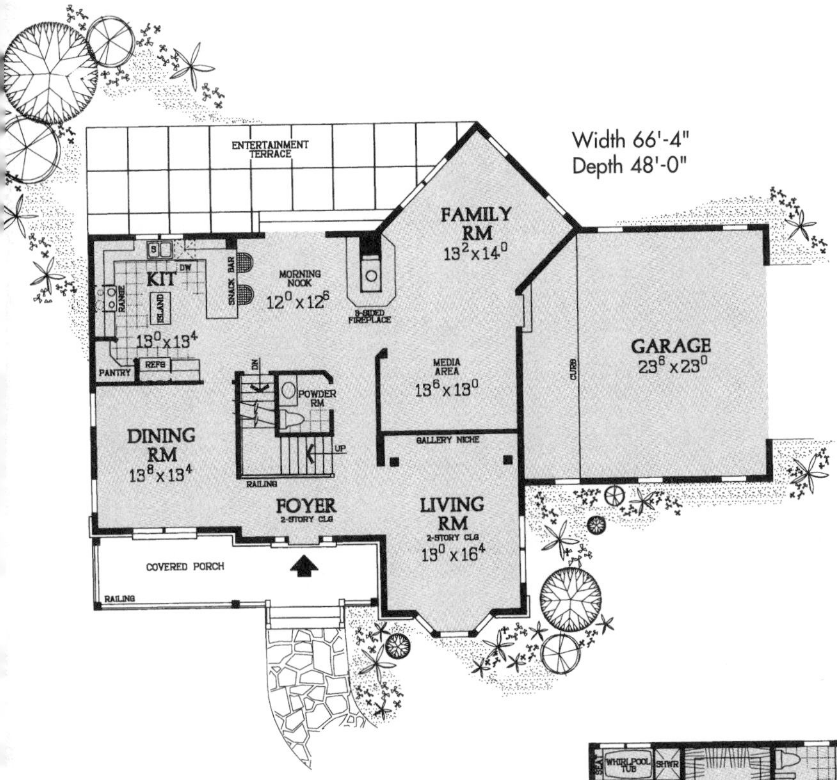

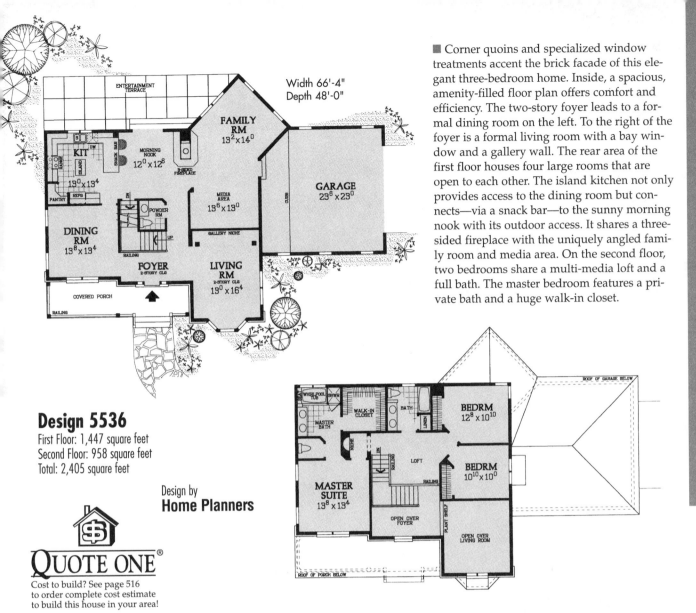

ENTERTAINMENT TERRACE
FAMILY RM 13²x14⁰
KIT 13⁰x13⁴
MORNING NOOK 12⁰x12⁶
3-SIDED FIREPLACE
PANTRY
REFRIG
SNACK BAR
ISLAND
RANGE
DW
MEDIA AREA 13⁶x13⁰
POWDER RM
GARAGE 23⁶x23⁰
CURB
DINING RM 13⁸x13⁴
GALLERY NICHE
RAILING
FOYER 2-STORY CLG
LIVING RM 2-STORY CLG 13⁰x16⁴
COVERED PORCH
RAILING
UP
DN

Width 66'-4"
Depth 48'-0"

Corner quoins and specialized window treatments accent the brick facade of this elegant three-bedroom home. Inside, a spacious, amenity-filled floor plan offers comfort and efficiency. The two-story foyer leads to a formal dining room on the left. To the right of the foyer is a formal living room with a bay window and a gallery wall. The rear area of the first floor houses four large rooms that are open to each other. The island kitchen not only provides access to the dining room but connects—via a snack bar—to the sunny morning nook with its outdoor access. It shares a three-sided fireplace with the uniquely angled family room and media area. On the second floor, two bedrooms share a multi-media loft and a full bath. The master bedroom features a private bath and a huge walk-in closet.

WHIRLPOOL TUB
SHWR
SEAT
WALK-IN CLOSET
MASTER BATH
NICHE
BATH
LINEN
BEDRM 12⁸x10¹⁰
LOFT
BEDRM 10¹⁰x10⁰
RAILING
DN
MASTER SUITE 13⁸x13⁴
OPEN OVER FOYER
PLANT SHELF
OPEN OVER LIVING ROOM
ROOF OF GARAGE BELOW
ROOF OF PORCH BELOW

Design 5536

First Floor: 1,447 square feet
Second Floor: 958 square feet
Total: 2,405 square feet

Design by
Home Planners

QUOTE ONE®
Cost to build? See page 516 to order complete cost estimate to build this house in your area!

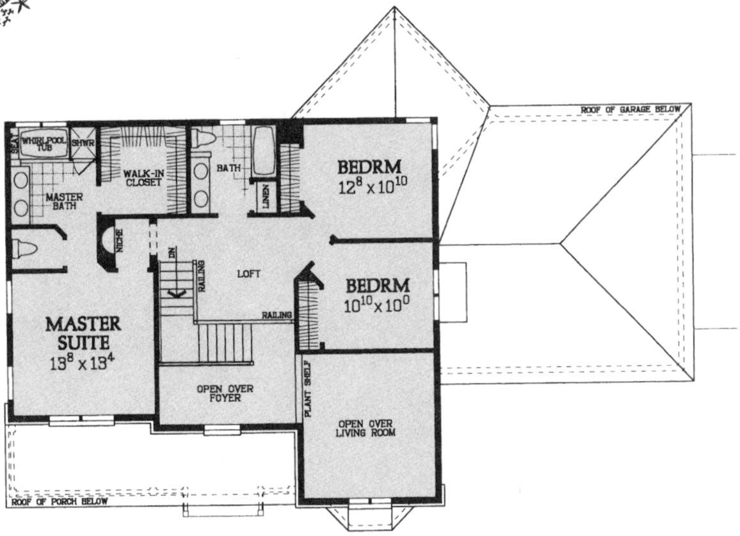

Design 2283

First Floor: 1,559 square feet
Second Floor: 1,404 square feet
Total: 2,963 square feet

L **D**

■ Reminiscent of the stately character of Federal architecture during an earlier period in our history, this two-story is replete with exquisite detailing. The cornice work, the pediment gable, the dentils, the brick quoins at the corners, the beautifully proportioned columns, the front door detailing, the window treatment and the massive twin chimneys are among the features which make this design so unique and appealing. Livability is great as well. Notice the quiet study, the beamed-ceiling family room and the large formal living room.

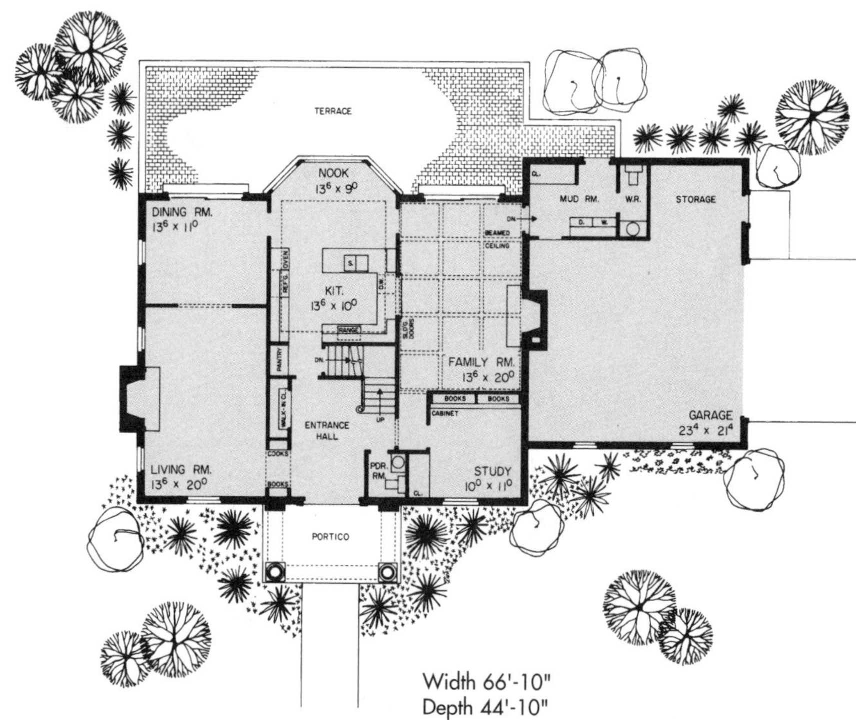
TERRACE
NOOK
13^{6} x 9^{0}
DINING RM.
13^{6} x 11^{0}
KIT.
13^{6} x 10^{0}
RANGE
PANTRY
MUD RM.
W.R.
STORAGE
BEAMED CEILING
FAMILY RM.
13^{6} x 20^{0}
BOOKS
CABINET
GARAGE
23^{4} x 21^{4}
ENTRANCE HALL
LIVING RM.
13^{6} x 20^{0}
PDR. RM.
STUDY
10^{0} x 11^{0}
PORTICO

Width 66'-10"
Depth 44'-10"

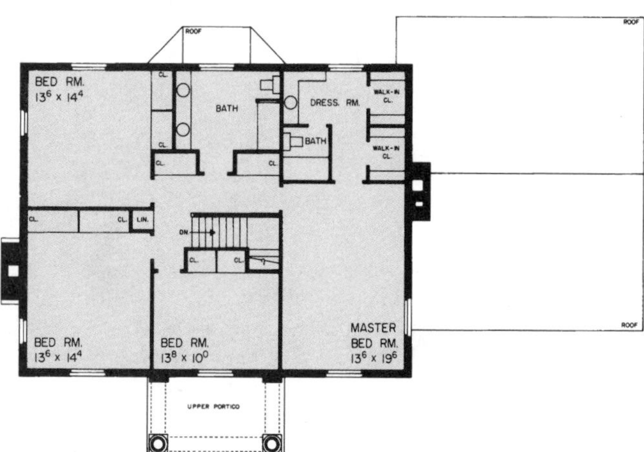
ROOF
BED RM.
13^{6} x 14^{4}
BATH
DRESS. RM.
WALK-IN CL.
BATH
BED RM.
13^{6} x 14^{4}
BED RM.
13^{8} x 10^{0}
MASTER BED RM.
13^{6} x 19^{6}
UPPER PORTICO

Design by
Home Planners

Design by
Home Planners

Design 2211

First Floor: 1,214 square feet
Second Floor: 1,146 square feet
Total: 2,360 square feet

L D

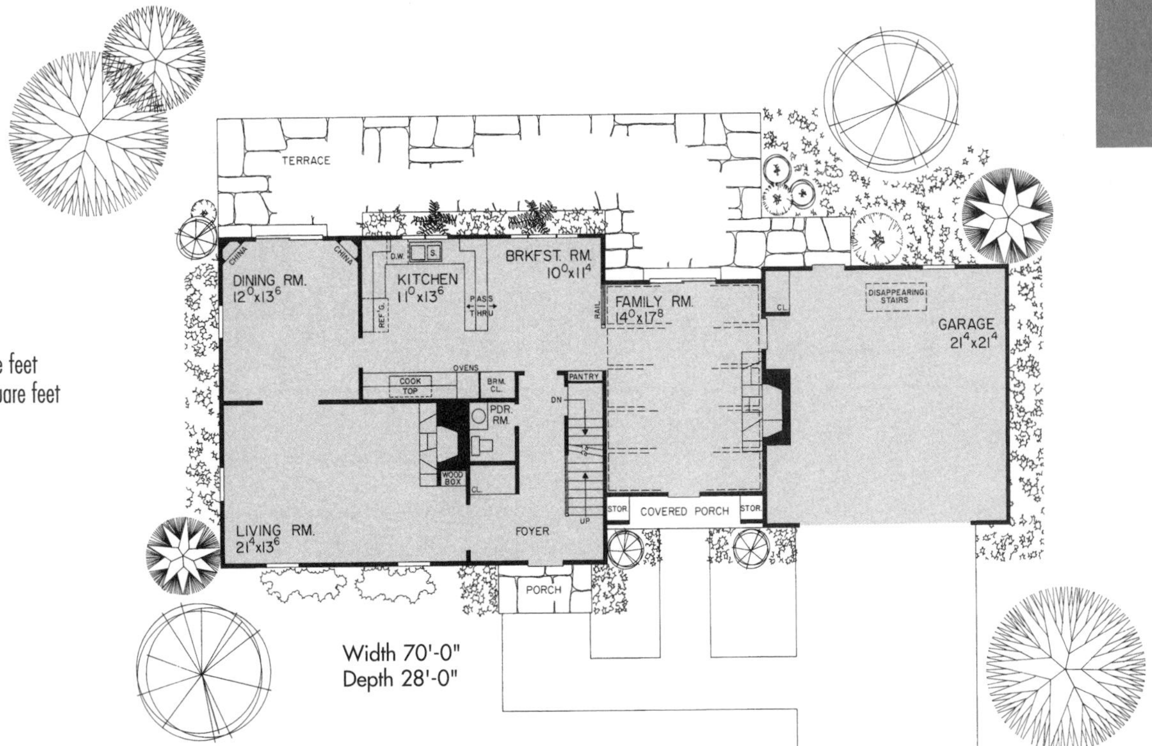

Width 70'-0"
Depth 28'-0"

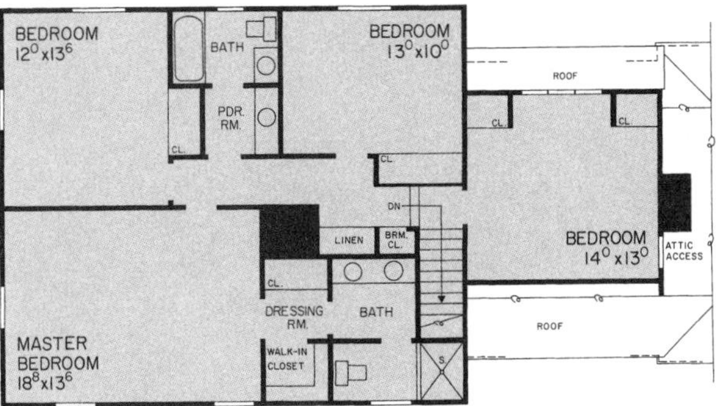
BEDROOM 12^0x13^6
BATH
BEDROOM 13^0x10^0
ROOF
PDR. RM.
CL.
DN
LINEN
BRM. CL.
BEDROOM 14^0x13^0
ATTIC ACCESS
DRESSING RM.
BATH
MASTER BEDROOM 18^8x13^6
WALK-IN CLOSET

■ The appeal of this Colonial home will be virtually everlasting. Entertaining will take place in the front living room, which is spacious and has an end fireplace. When dinner is ready, guests can flow to the adjacent dining room with built-in china cabinets. Sliding glass doors in the dining room and family room lead to a rear terrace. The powder room is convenient to all first-floor areas. Four generous-sized bedrooms occupy the second floor. The master suite has a large dressing area, a walk-in closet and dual lavatories.

Design Q231

First Floor: 1,087 square feet
Second Floor: 850 square feet
Total: 1,937 square feet

■ The choice is yours—a brick finish with architrave over the entry or horizontal siding with shutters. Details for both exterior options are included in the plans. Inside, the floor plan is commodious. Formal living reigns on the right side of the plan with a living room and dining room with bay window. A more private den is to the left, near a half-bath in the hallway. The U-shaped kitchen serves a breakfast room and the family room with fireplace beyond. The family room is sunken and has sliding glass doors to the rear yard. Four corner bedrooms are found on the second floor. The master suite has a large wall closet and private bath. Three family bedrooms share a full bath. Plans include details for both a basement and a crawlspace foundation.

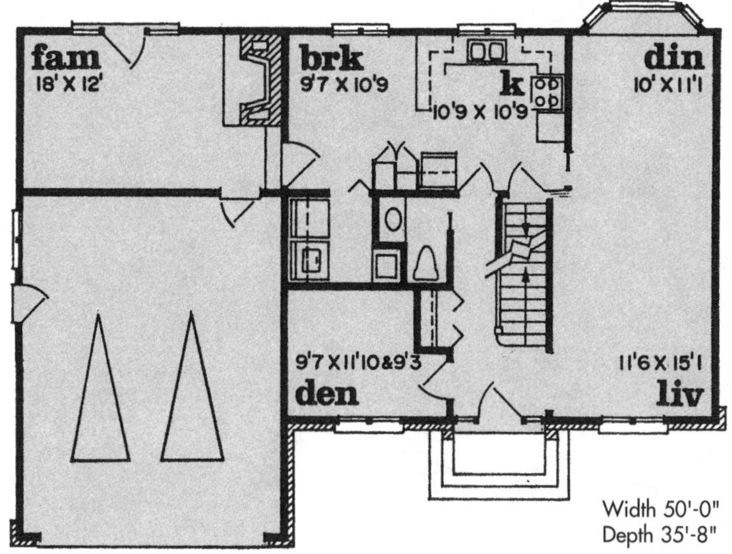
fam
18' X 12'
brk
9'7 X 10'9
k
10'9 X 10'9
din
10' X 11'1
9'7 X 11'10 & 9'3
den
11'6 X 15'1
liv
Width 50'-0"
Depth 35'-8"

Design by
Select Home Designs

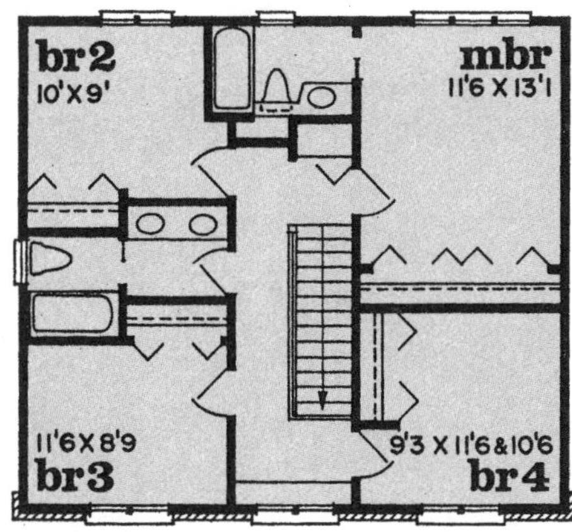
br2
10' X 9'
mbr
11'6 X 13'1
11'6 X 8'9
br3
9'3 X 11'6 & 10'6
br4

Alternate Elevation

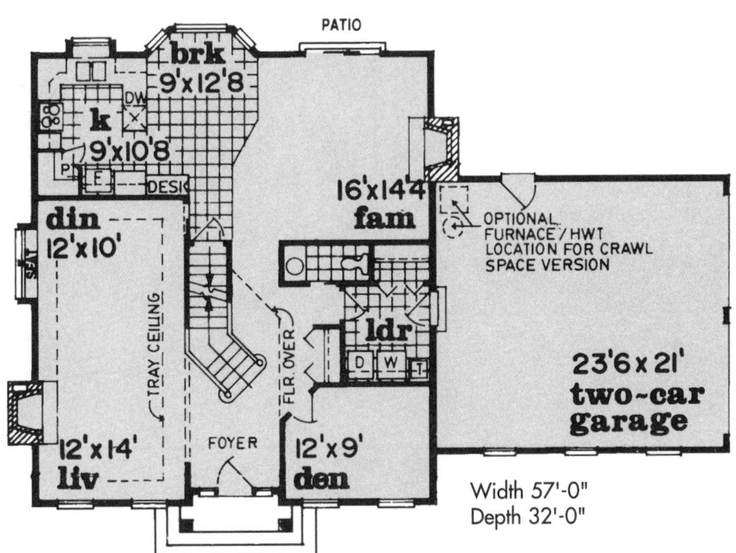
PATIO
brk
9'x12'8
k
9'x10'8
DW
P
DESK
din
12'x10'
SEAT
TRAY CEILING
12'x14'
liv
FOYER
FLR. OVER
16'x14'4
fam
OPTIONAL
FURNACE / HWT
LOCATION FOR CRAWL
SPACE VERSION
ldr
D W T
23'6 x 21'
two-car
garage
12'x9'
den
Width 57'-0"
Depth 32'-0"

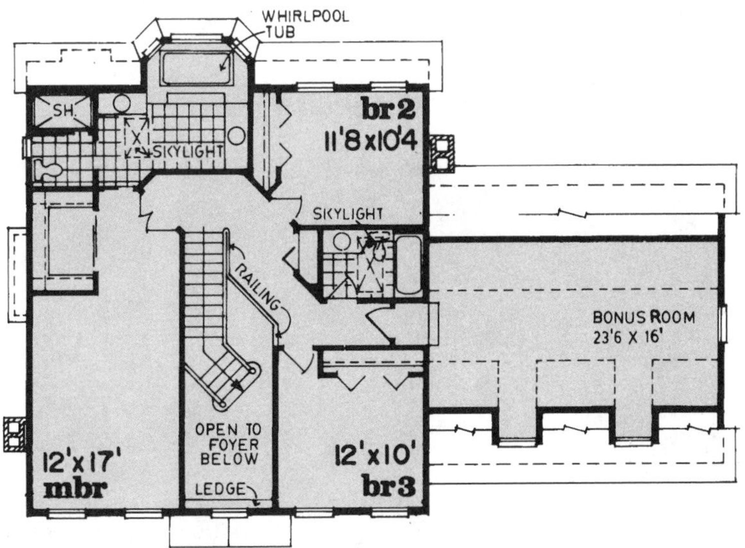
WHIRLPOOL
TUB
SH.
SKYLIGHT
br2
11'8x10'4
SKYLIGHT
RAILING
BONUS ROOM
23'6 X 16'
OPEN TO
FOYER
BELOW
LEDGE
12'x17'
mbr
12'x10'
br3

Design Q397

First Floor: 1,196 square feet
Second Floor: 1,069 square feet
Total: 2,265 square feet
Bonus Room: 430 square feet

■ Classic in its timeless style, this home offers shuttered windows and a covered porch on the outside and an up-to-date floor plan on the inside. The center foyer is brightened by a second-story window and opens to a tray ceiling in both the living room and dining room. The dining room also offers a window seat in a box window; the living room has a fireplace. Across the foyer, a cozy den offers space for quiet study. The family room is to the rear and has another fireplace and sliding glass doors to the rear patio. The kitchen and bayed breakfast room are close by. Upstairs are three bedrooms and two skylit baths. The master bedroom has a walk-in closet. A bonus room offers an additional 430 square feet of finish-later space. Plans include details for both a basement and a crawlspace foundation.

Design by
Select Home Designs

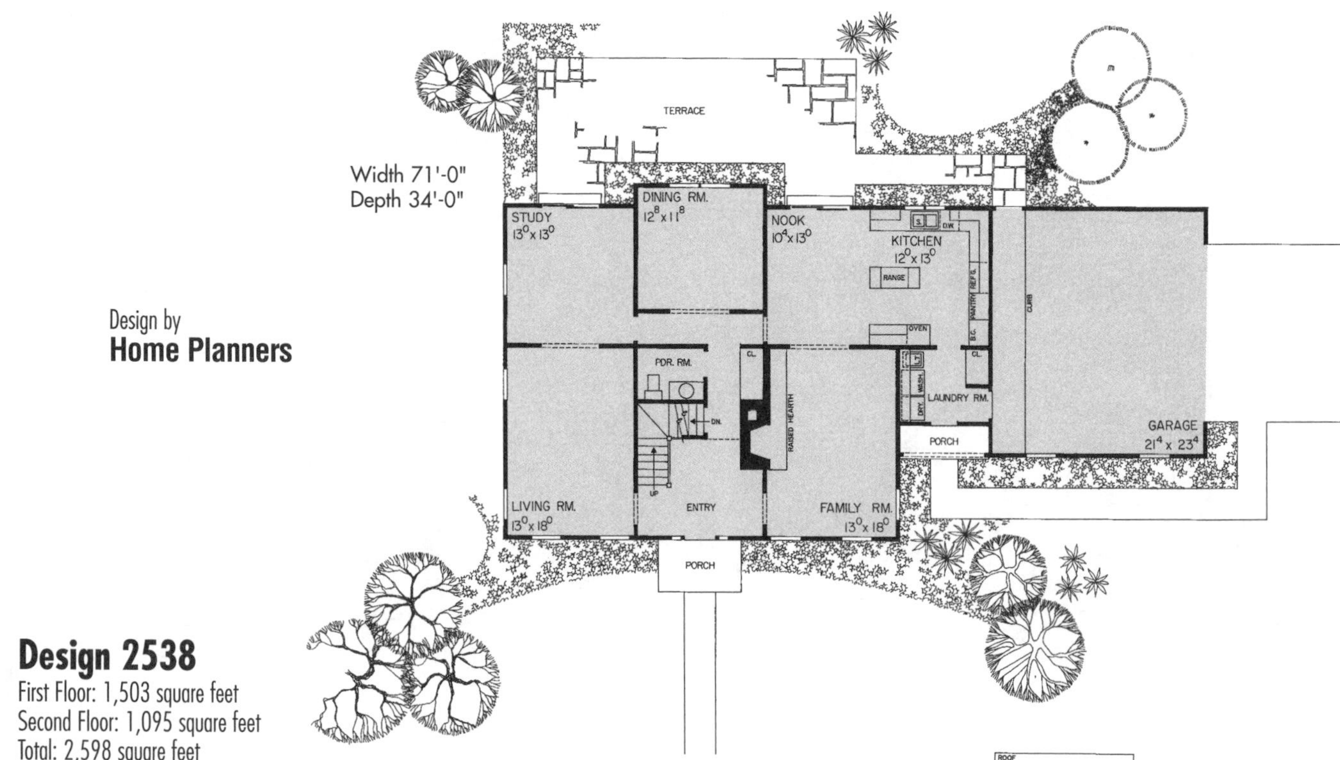
TERRACE
Width 71'-0"
Depth 34'-0"
STUDY
$13^0 \times 13^0$
DINING RM.
$12^8 \times 11^8$
NOOK
$10^4 \times 13^0$
KITCHEN
$12^0 \times 13^0$
RANGE
OVEN
PANTRY
LAUNDRY RM.
PDR. RM.
RAISED HEARTH
PORCH
GARAGE
$21^4 \times 23^4$
LIVING RM.
$13^0 \times 18^0$
ENTRY
FAMILY RM.
$13^0 \times 18^0$
PORCH

Design by
Home Planners

Design 2538

First Floor: 1,503 square feet
Second Floor: 1,095 square feet
Total: 2,598 square feet

L **D**

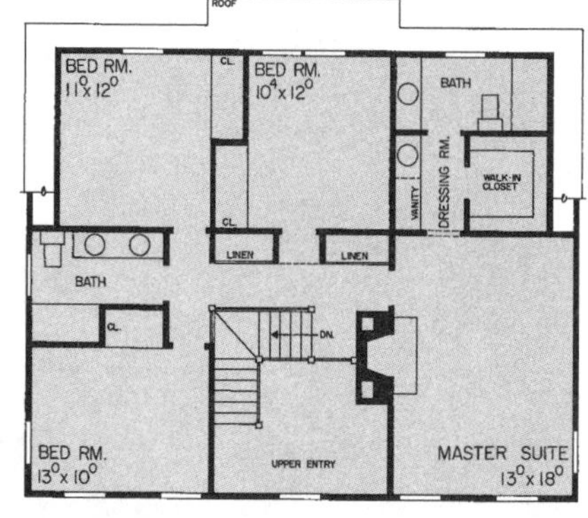
ROOF
BED RM.
$11^0 \times 12^0$
BED RM.
$10^4 \times 12^0$
BATH
DRESSING RM.
WALK-IN CLOSET
VANITY
LINEN
LINEN
BATH
BED RM.
$13^0 \times 10^0$
UPPER ENTRY
MASTER SUITE
$13^0 \times 18^0$

■ This Saltbox provides great livability for the growing family. The entry is spacious and open to the second-floor balcony. Living areas include a formal living room and dining room, a private study and family room with raised-hearth fireplace. The grand kitchen offers an island range and attached nook with sliding glass doors to the terrace. The master suite on the second floor contains its own fireplace and a large walk-in closet in the dressing area. Three more bedrooms share a full bath.

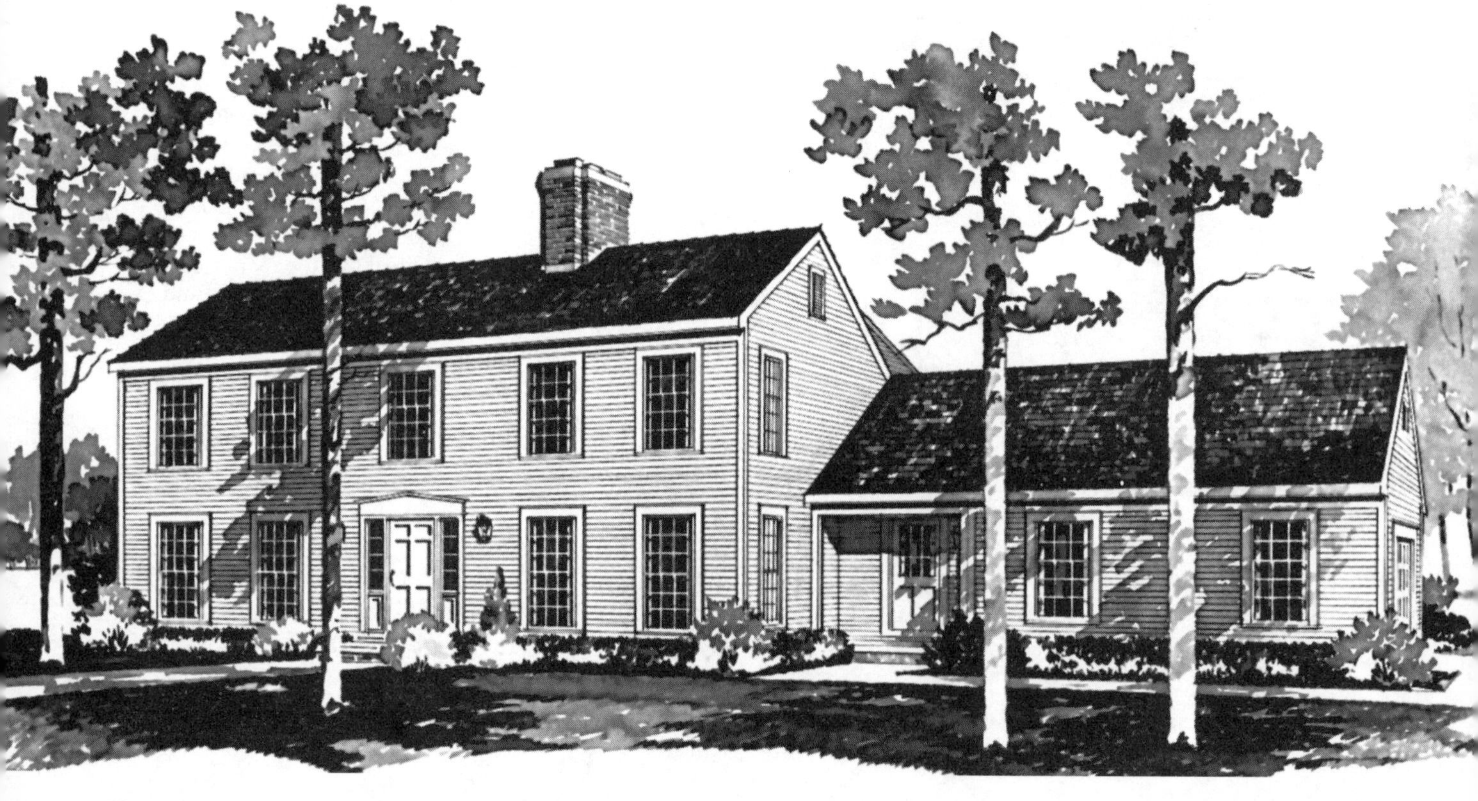

QUOTE ONE®

Cost to build? See page 516 to order complete cost estimate to build this house in your area!

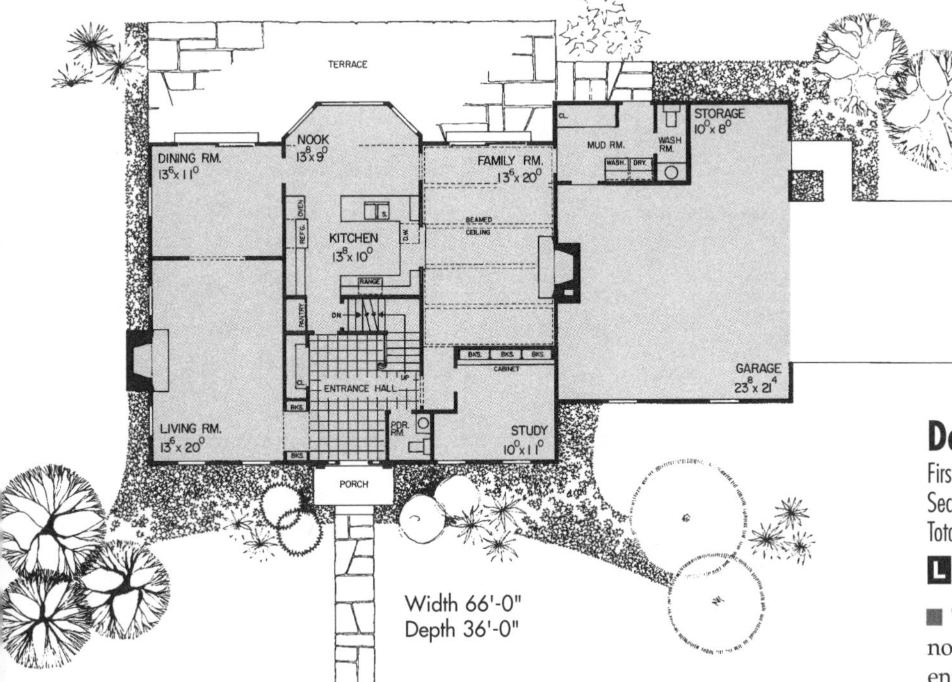
TERRACE
NOOK 13⁶x9⁰
DINING RM. 13⁶x11⁰
FAMILY RM. 13⁶x20⁰
MUD RM.
WASH RM.
STORAGE 10⁰x8⁰
KITCHEN 13⁸x10⁰
BEAMED CEILING
RANGE
PANTRY
DN
UP
ENTRANCE HALL
CABINET
BKS
GARAGE 23⁸x21⁴
LIVING RM. 13⁶x20⁰
PDR. RM.
STUDY 10⁰x11⁰
PORCH
Width 66'-0"
Depth 36'-0"

Design 2610

First Floor: 1,505 square feet
Second Floor: 1,344 square feet
Total: 2,849 square feet

L **D**

■ This full two-story traditional will be noteworthy wherever it is built. The front entrance detail is inviting. The narrow horizontal siding and the corner boards are appealing as are the two massive chimneys. The center entrance hall is large with a handy powder room nearby. The study has built-in bookshelves and offers a full measure of privacy. The interior kitchen has a pass-through to the family room and enjoys all that natural light from the bay window of the nook. A beam ceiling, a fireplace and sliding glass doors are features of the family room. The mud room highlights a closet, laundry equipment and an extra washroom. Study the upstairs with those four bedrooms, two baths and plenty of closets.

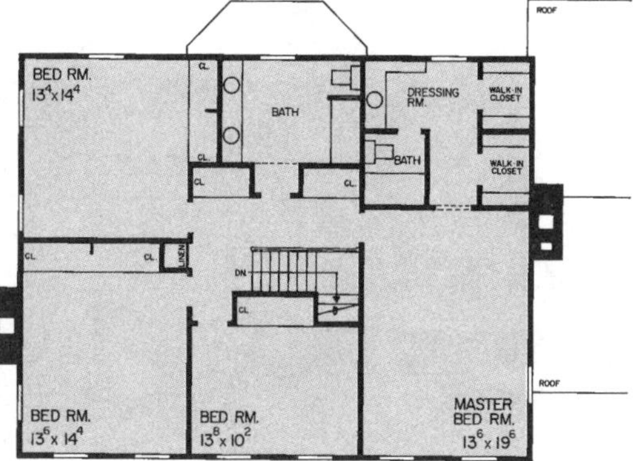
ROOF
BED RM. 13⁴x14⁴
BATH
DRESSING RM.
WALK-IN CLOSET
BATH
WALK-IN CLOSET
CL
DN
BED RM. 13⁶x14⁴
BED RM. 13⁸x10²
MASTER BED RM. 13⁶x19⁶
ROOF

Design by
Home Planners

Design Q279

First Floor: 1,584 square feet
Second Floor: 1,277 square feet
Total: 2,861 square feet

■ A double-door entry is the perfect introduction to the imposing two-story foyer of this traditional design. Flanking the foyer are a sunken living room with vaulted ceiling and fireplace and a formal dining room with bay window. A cozy den is tucked behind the living room, near a full bath, allowing it to double as a guest room if needed. The vaulted family room is open to the gallery above and has its own fireplace and double access to the rear yard. The nearby kitchen and octagonal breakfast room feature access to a private covered porch for casual dining. The master bedroom, on the second floor, has a sitting room, a dressing room and a bath with whirlpool tub. Two family bedrooms share a full bath. Note the workbench space in the two-car garage. Plans include details for both a basement and a crawlspace foundation.

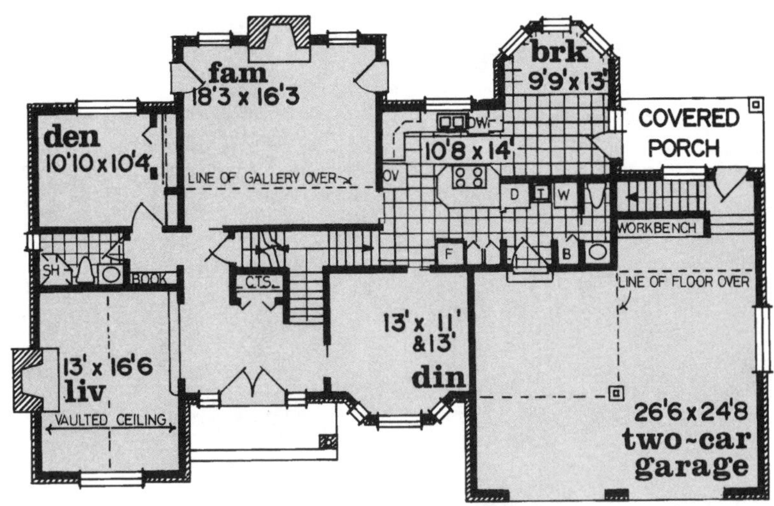
fam
18'3 x 16'3
brk
9'9'x13'
COVERED PORCH
den
10'10x10'4
LINE OF GALLERY OVER
10'8 x 14'
DW
OV
D
T
W
WORKBENCH
SH
BOOK
CTS.
F
B
LINE OF FLOOR OVER
13'x 16'6
liv
VAULTED CEILING
13'x 11' &13'
din
26'6x24'8
two-car garage

Width 68'-8"
Depth 43'-2"

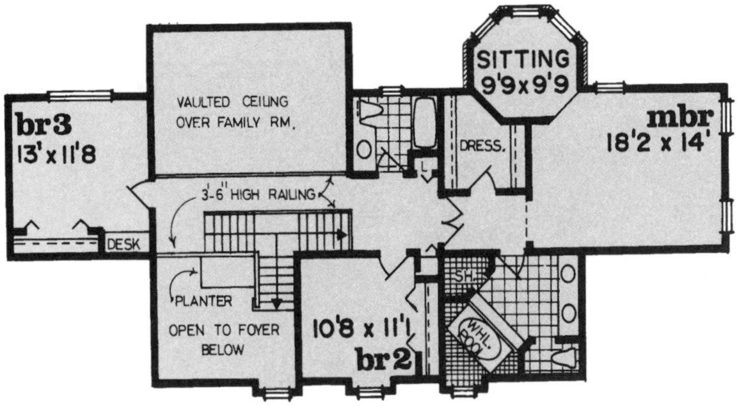

Design by
Select Home Designs

Rear Elevation

A. J. YOUNG
FUQUAY VARINA, N.C.

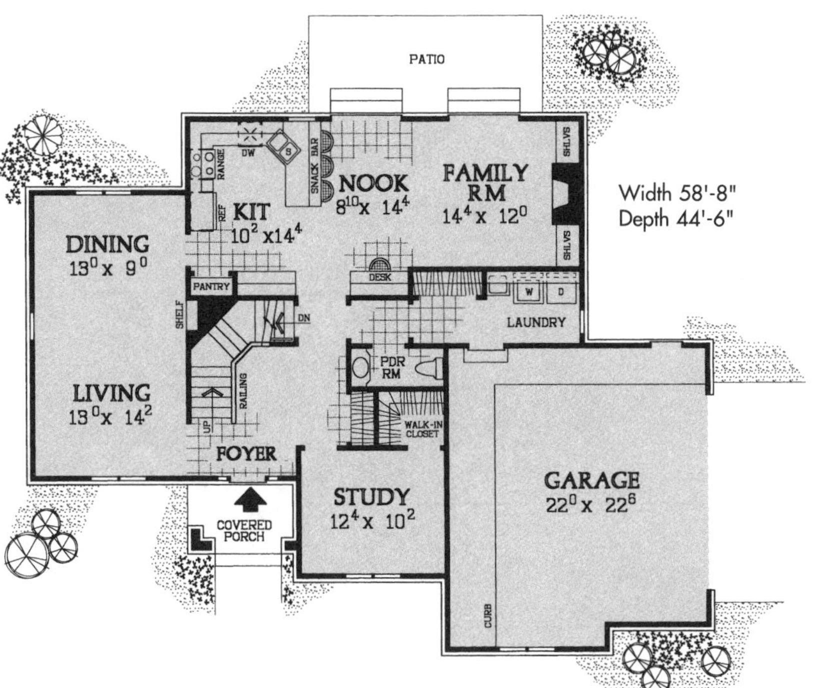
PATIO
NOOK
8^{10} x 14^{4}
FAMILY RM
14^{4} x 12^{0}
SHLVS
SNACK BAR
DW
RANGE
REF
KIT
10^{2} x 14^{4}
DINING
13^{0} x 9^{0}
PANTRY
SHELF
DN
DESK
W
D
LAUNDRY
PDR RM
WALK-IN CLOSET
LIVING
13^{0} x 14^{2}
RAILING
UP
FOYER
COVERED PORCH
STUDY
12^{4} x 10^{2}
GARAGE
22^{0} x 22^{6}
CURB
Width 58'-8"
Depth 44'-6"

Design 5555

First Floor: 1,356 square feet
Second Floor: 1,162 square feet
Total: 2,518 square feet

Design by
Home Planners

QUOTE ONE®

Cost to build? See page 516 to order complete cost estimate to build this house in your area!

■ Curb appeal is a given with this two-story brick traditional home. Four gables provide the facade with elegant symmetry, while decorative segmental arches complement the three arched windows that fill each room with sunlight. The entry foyer leads to all rooms on both the first and second floors. While a quiet study, or possible guest room, is tucked away at the front of the home, the remaining first-floor rooms—combination living/dining rooms, open kitchen, breakfast nook and family room—flow from one to the other for easy living. The U-shaped kitchen offers plenty of counter space, while the family room features French doors to the rear yard and a warming fireplace. On the upper level, the master bedroom includes an large walk-in closet and a secluded master bath. Three family bedrooms share a full hall bath.

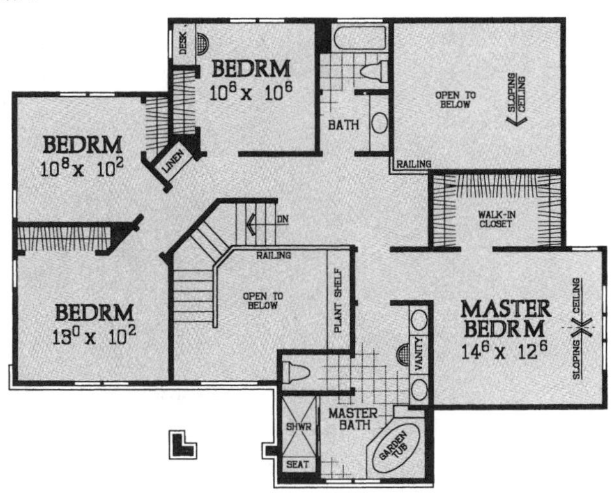
DESK
BEDRM
10^{6} x 10^{6}
BATH
OPEN TO BELOW
SLOPING CEILING
BEDRM
10^{8} x 10^{2}
LINEN
RAILING
WALK-IN CLOSET
DN
RAILING
OPEN TO BELOW
PLANT SHELF
BEDRM
13^{0} x 10^{2}
VANITY
MASTER BEDRM
14^{6} x 12^{6}
SLOPING CEILING
SHWR
SEAT
MASTER BATH
GARDEN TUB

Design 5513

First Floor: 1,192 square feet
Second Floor: 1,127 square feet
Total: 2,319 square feet

■ The heart of this stately brick two-story is found at the rear of the home, where a large area made up of the kitchen, breakfast or morning area and the family room provide the perfect atmosphere for casual living or for entertaining family and friends. The U-shaped kitchen features a double sink with views to the covered rear porch, a walk-in pantry and snack-bar and access to the bay-windowed breakfast area. The family room accesses the covered porch via French doors and includes a warming fireplace with a tile hearth. A formal dining room, conveniently accessible to the kitchen, and a formal living room, both with sunny bay windows, are located at the front of the home. On the second floor, the master bedroom features an impressive master bath with dual sinks, a linen closet and a walk-in closet. Three additional bedrooms share two additional linen closets, a full bath and a convenient laundry area.

RAILING
COVERED PORCH
BAY WINDOW
DW
KIT
13⁰ x 11⁸
SNACK BAR
BREAKFAST-MORNING
13⁰ x 11⁸
FAMILY RM
13⁰ x 15⁰
COOKTOP
REF'G
PANTRY
OVN
DN
POWDER RM
DINING RM
12⁸ x 11⁸
RAILING
UP
FOYER
LIVING RM
12⁸ x 11⁸
ROOF OF PORCH BELOW
MASTER BATH
WALK-IN CLOSET
BATH
LINEN
BEDRM
12⁴ x 11²
DN
LAUNDRY
W
D
MASTER SUITE
12⁸ x 18⁸
BEDRM
10⁰ x 11²
BEDRM
12⁸ x 10⁶

Width 42'-8"
Depth 37'-4"

Design by
Home Planners

QUOTE ONE®
Cost to build? See page 516 to order complete cost estimate to build this house in your area!

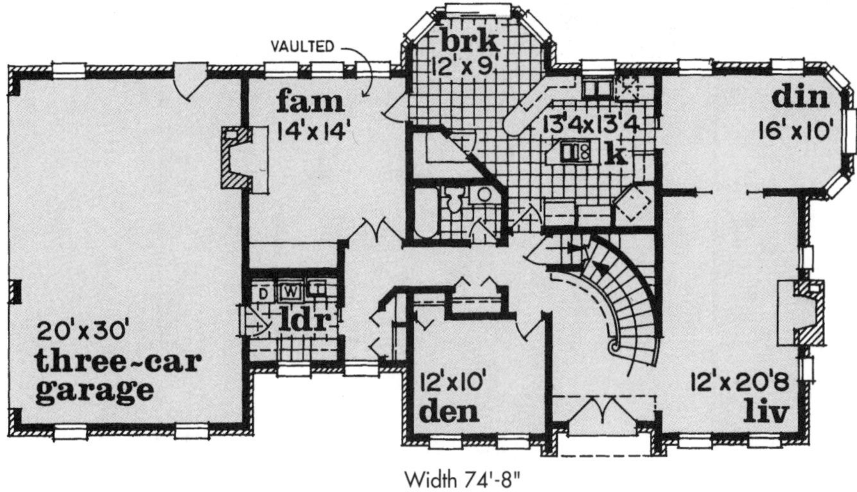
VAULTED
brk
12'x9'
fam
14'x14'
13'4x13'4
k
din
16'x10'
ldr
20'x30'
three-car
garage
12'x10'
den
12'x20'8
liv
Width 74'-8"
Depth 38'-8"

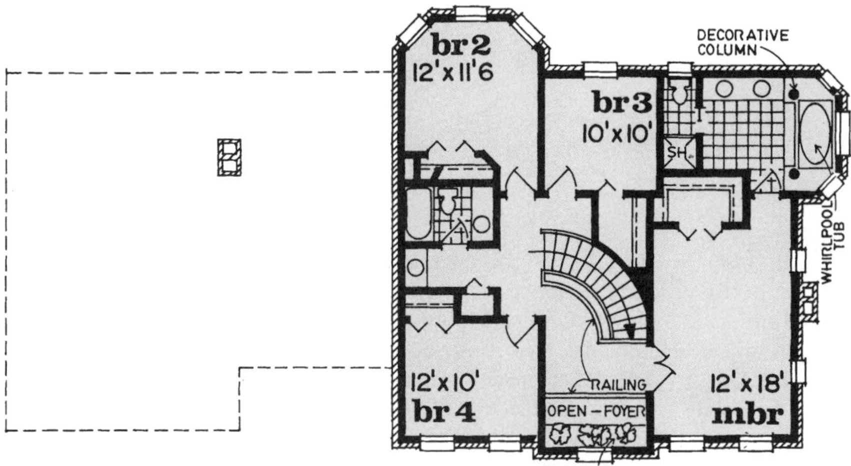
br2
12'x11'6
DECORATIVE
COLUMN
br3
10'x10'
SH
WHIRLPOOL
TUB
12'x10'
br4
RAILING
OPEN – FOYER
12'x18'
mbr
PLANTER

Design Q301

First Floor: 1,580 square feet
Second Floor: 1,232 square feet
Total: 2,812 square feet

■ This stately design features classic exterior details: circle-head windows, jack-arch detailing over the entry, shutters, corner quoins and brick veneer. The foyer is vaulted with a dominating curved staircase to the second floor. The living room is to the right and contains a fireplace and pocket doors that lead to the formal dining room. A cozy den is to the left. The family room is vaulted and has its own fireplace and audio-visual center. The kitchen is styled for gourmets with thoughtful appointments: a walk-in pantry, a center cooking island and a peninsular counter. The bayed breakfast nook is close by. Four bedrooms are on the second floor, including three family bedrooms with a shared full bath. The master suite has a walk-in closet and bath with whirlpool tub decorated with columns, a separate shower and a double vanity. Plans include details for both a basement and a crawlspace foundation.

Design by
Select Home Designs

Design 5519

First Floor: 1,228 square feet
Second Floor: 1,080 square feet
Total: 2,308 square feet

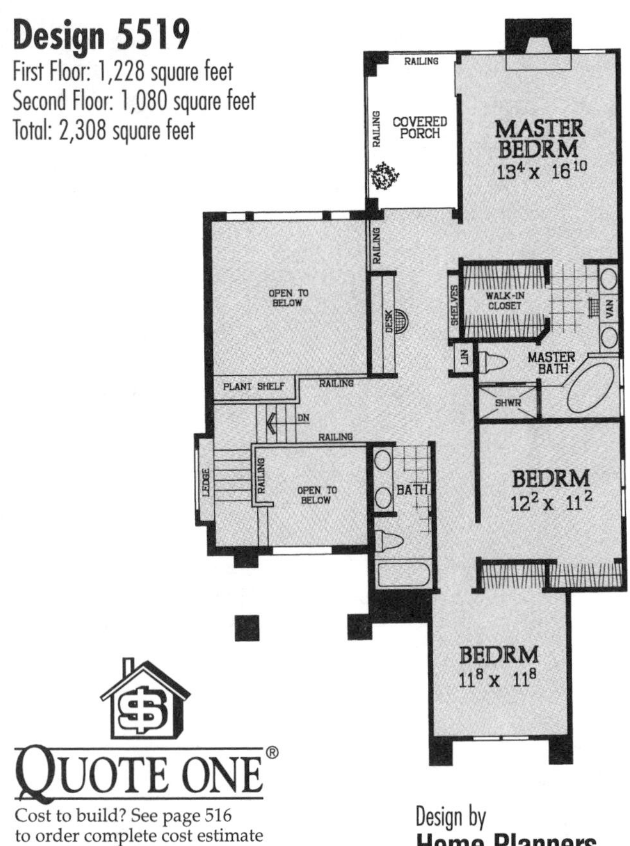

RAILING
COVERED PORCH
MASTER BEDRM
13⁴ x 16¹⁰
OPEN TO BELOW
DESK
SHELVES
WALK-IN CLOSET
VAN
LIN
MASTER BATH
SHWR
PLANT SHELF
DN
LEDGE
BATH
BEDRM
12² x 11²
BEDRM
11⁸ x 11⁸

QUOTE ONE®

Cost to build? See page 516 to order complete cost estimate to build this house in your area!

Design by
Home Planners

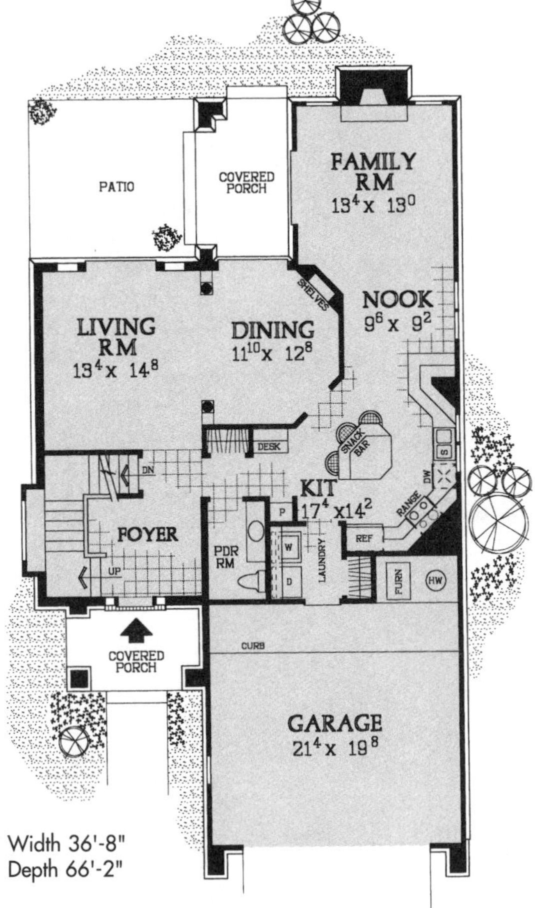

PATIO
COVERED PORCH
FAMILY RM
13⁴ x 13⁰
SHELVES
NOOK
9⁶ x 9²
LIVING RM
13⁴ x 14⁸
DINING
11¹⁰x 12⁸
SNACK BAR
DESK
DN
KIT
17⁴ x14²
DW
RANGE
REF
FOYER
UP
PDR RM
LAUNDRY
FURN
HW
COVERED PORCH
CURB
GARAGE
21⁴ x 19⁸

Width 36'-8"
Depth 66'-2"

■ Spacious rooms and a flowing floor plan in this two-story traditional home create a perfect opportunity for entertaining family and friends. The sun-lit foyer opens to a combination living/dining room separated by columns. Two glass doors let the outside in via the backyard and patio. Corner curio shelves in the dining area offer an excellent space for family heirlooms and/or conversation pieces. The spacious island kitchen features a pantry, a writing desk, access to the utility room and two-car garage. Space between the kitchen and family room provides a great spot for the breakfast nook. Upstairs, two family bedrooms share a full hall bath with dual sinks. The master bedroom features a central fireplace and a luxurious master bath with a corner whirlpool tub, separate basins and a walk-in closet. A deck provides unobstructed views and completes the second floor.

© Copyright 1990 Select Home Designs. All rights reserved

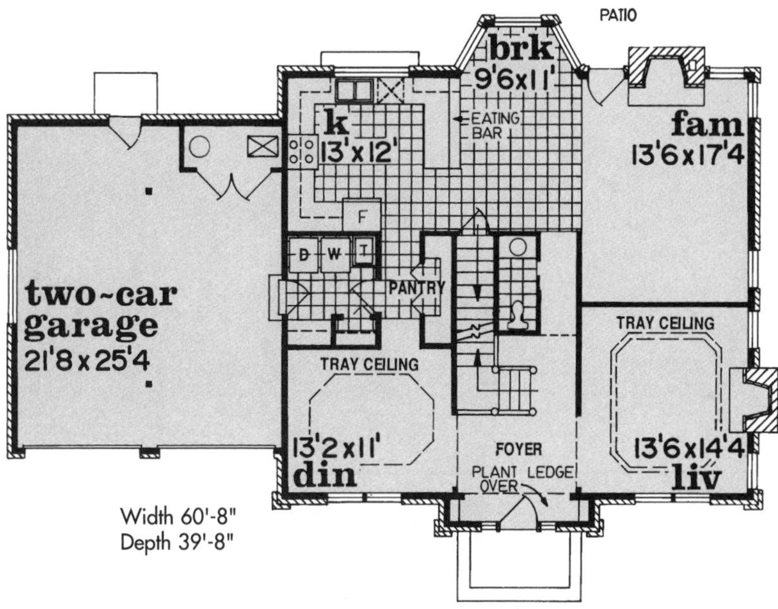
PATIO
brk
9'6x11'
EATING BAR
k
13'x12'
fam
13'6x17'4
F
D
W
T
PANTRY
two-car garage
21'8x25'4
TRAY CEILING
TRAY CEILING
13'2x11'
din
FOYER
PLANT LEDGE OVER
13'6x14'4
liv
Width 60'-8"
Depth 39'-8"

Design Q410

First Floor: 1,308 square feet
Second Floor: 1,187 square feet
Total: 2,495 square feet
Bonus Room: 366 square feet

■ This traditional three-bedroom estate clearly defines formal and informal living areas. Tray ceilings add architectural interest to the dining and living rooms. The living room also has a fireplace, as does the family room. The open kitchen design contains a U-shaped kitchen with snack bar and a bayed breakfast nook overlooking a rear patio. On the second floor, a gallery offers access to the bedrooms and a bonus room with vaulted ceiling. Develop the bonus space later, if you wish, to feature more bedrooms or a private office. The master suite is filled with natural light from the full wall of glass, broken only by a wood-burning fireplace. Glass-block detailing in the master bath adds light to the master bath at the whirlpool tub. The family bedrooms share a bath and have large wall closets.

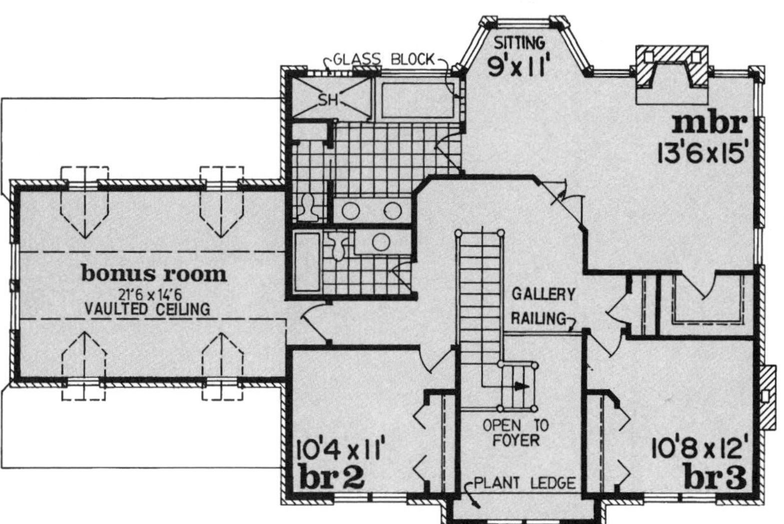
GLASS BLOCK
SITTING
9'x11'
SH
mbr
13'6x15'
bonus room
21'6x14'6
VAULTED CEILING
GALLERY
RAILING
OPEN TO FOYER
PLANT LEDGE
10'4x11'
br2
10'8x12'
br3

Design by
Select Home Designs

Design 5517

First Floor: 1,228 square feet
Second Floor: 1,080 square feet
Total: 2,308 square feet

■ Palladian windows, exterior arches and corner quoins give this two-bedroom home its distinctive curb appeal. Inside, the well-lit foyer opens to a combination living room and dining room with corner shelves for knick-knacks and curios. Glass doors in both rooms access the backyard. The dining room leads to a unique kitchen with a central work island, a corner pantry, a desk and entry to the utility room and the two-car garage. A half-bath, and a family room with a warming fireplace and patio access complete the first floor. The second floor includes a deck, two family bedrooms that share a full hall bath and a master bedroom with a fireplace and a private bath featuring a corner whirlpool tub and a walk-in closet.

Width 36'-8"
Depth 66'-2"

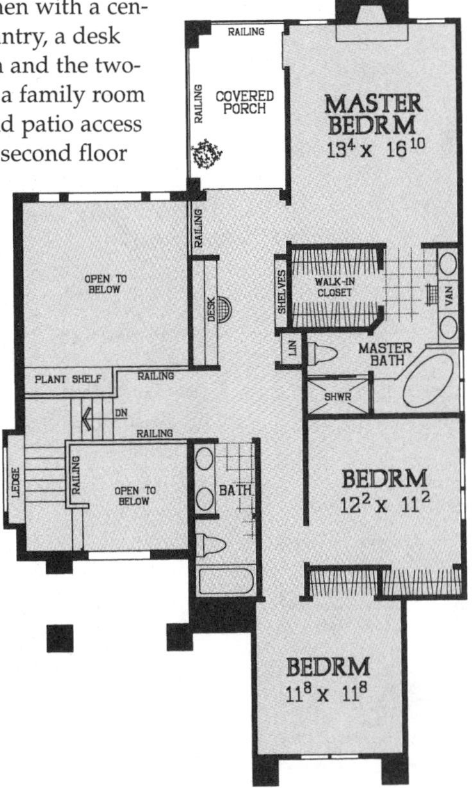
RAILING
COVERED PORCH
MASTER BEDRM
13⁴ x 16¹⁰
OPEN TO BELOW
DESK
SHELVES
WALK-IN CLOSET
VAN
LIN
MASTER BATH
SHWR
PLANT SHELF
RAILING
DN
LEDGE
OPEN TO BELOW
BATH
BEDRM
12² x 11²
BEDRM
11⁸ x 11⁸

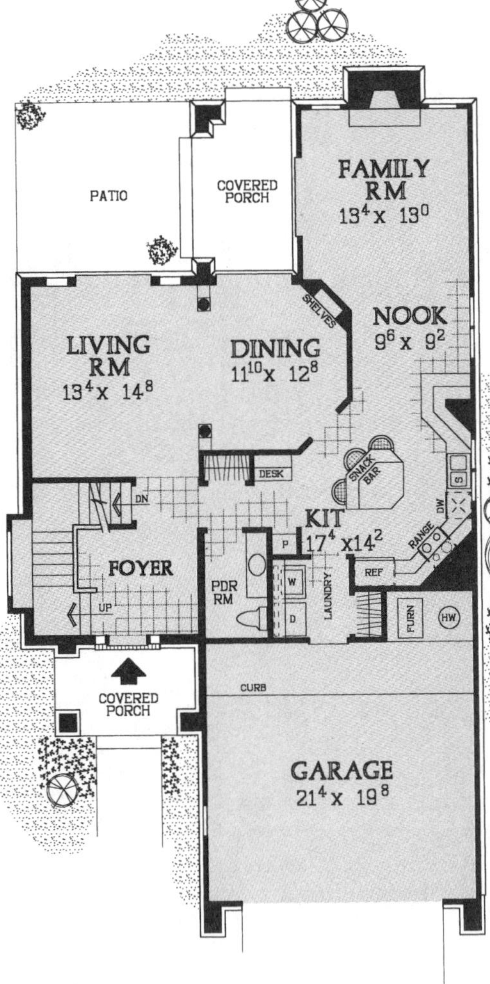
PATIO
COVERED PORCH
FAMILY RM
13⁴ x 13⁰
SHELVES
NOOK
9⁶ x 9²
LIVING RM
13⁴ x 14⁸
DINING
11¹⁰ x 12⁸
DESK
SNACK BAR
DN
KIT
17⁴ x14²
RANGE
DW
P
REF
FOYER
PDR RM
W
D
LAUNDRY
FURN
HW
UP
COVERED PORCH
CURB
GARAGE
21⁴ x 19⁸

QUOTE ONE®
Cost to build? See page 516 to order complete cost estimate to build this house in your area!

Design by
Home Planners

© Copyright 1990 Select Home Designs All rights reserved

Design Q413

First Floor: 1,464 square feet
Second Floor: 1,154 square feet
Total: 2,618 square feet

■ High vaulted ceilings and floor-to-ceiling windows enhance the spaciousness of this home. Decorative columns separate the living room from the tray-ceilinged dining room. French doors beyond open to the rear deck. A gourmet kitchen offers a center preparation island, a pantry pass-through to the family room and a breakfast bay. The family room is spacious and boasts a fireplace and vaulted ceiling open to the second-level hallway. The den has a wall closet and private access to a full bath. Use as extra guest space if needed. The master suite is on the second floor and holds a bay-window sitting area, a walk-in closet and bath with whirlpool tub and separate shower. Family bedrooms are at the other end of the hall and share a full bath. Plans include details for both a basement and a crawlspace foundation.

DECK
brk 9'x10'
fam 17'6x14'6
VOLUME CEILING
k 14'6x14'6
din 10'2x13'
FOYER
VAULTED
10'6x11'6 den
12'6x16' liv
22'6x20'2 two-car garage

Width 56'-0"
Depth 50'-0"

Design by
Select Home Designs

Rear Elevation

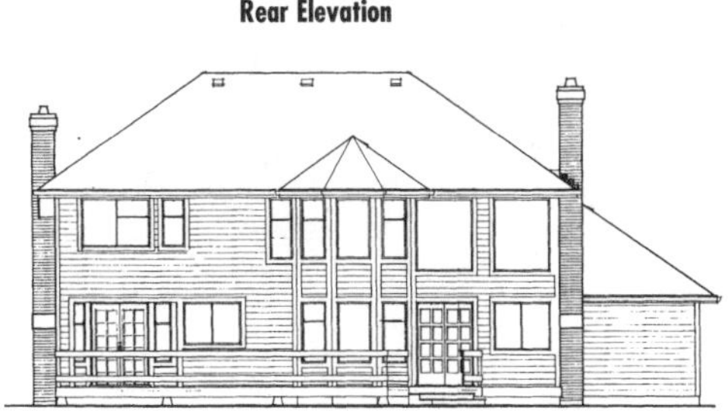

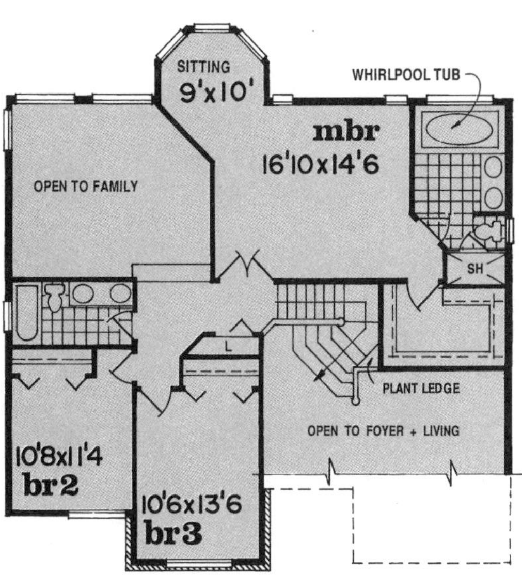
SITTING
9'x10'
WHIRLPOOL TUB
mbr
16'10x14'6
OPEN TO FAMILY
SH
L
PLANT LEDGE
OPEN TO FOYER + LIVING
10'8x11'4
br2
10'6x13'6
br3

Design 5506

First Floor: 1,185 square feet
Second Floor: 1,086 square feet
Total: 2,271 square feet
Bonus Room: 193 square feet

Design by
Home Planners

■ Bay windows on this brick two-story design offer symmetry and elegance to the first-floor living areas. The bay window in the living room adds just the right touch to this spacious room, which connects to the dining room and the kitchen beyond. The kitchen will please any gourmet with its abundant counter space, large pantry and corner nook. A convenient utility room and a family room with an optional fireplace and backyard access are located nearby. Upstairs, a bonus room can be made into a fourth bedroom or a guest room, kids' play room or game room. While the family bedrooms share a full bath with two sinks, the master bedroom features its own luxury bath, complete with a garden whirlpool tub, a walk-in closet and dual sinks. A bay window in the master bedroom provides a welcome spot to sit and relax with a good book.

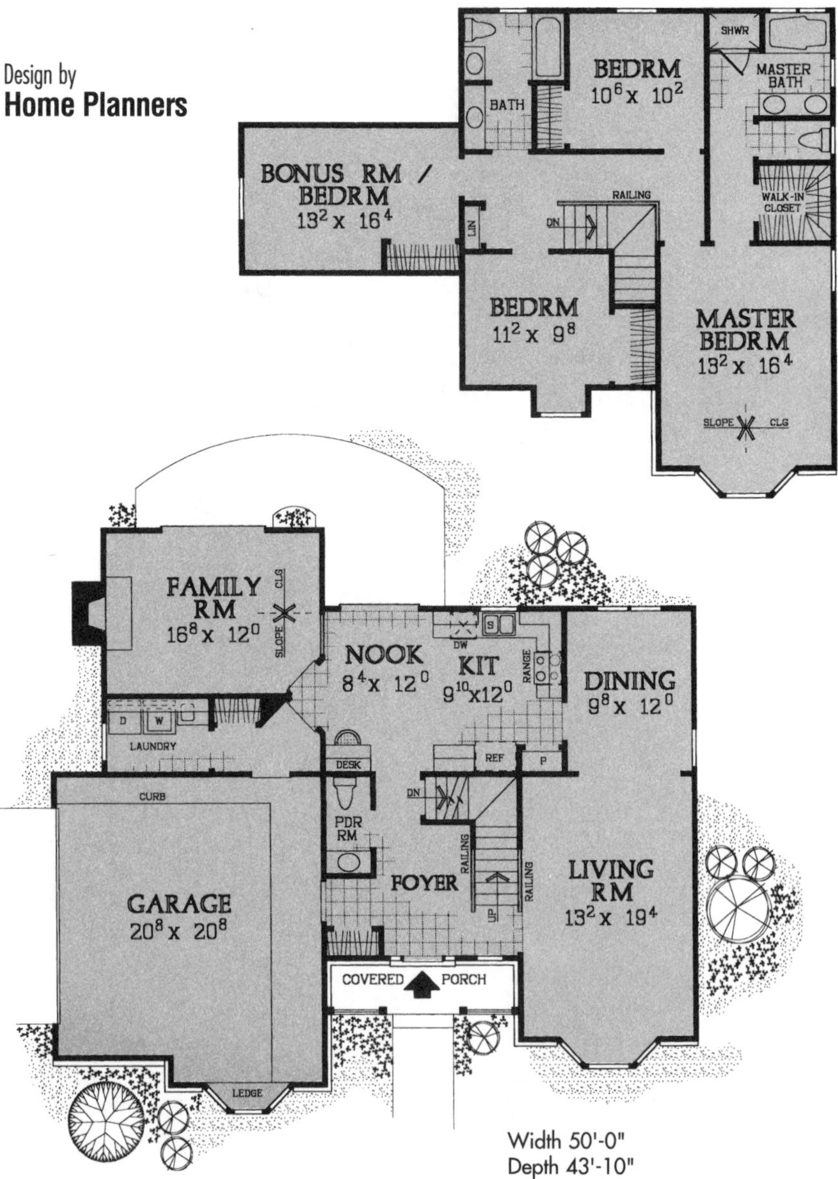

BATH
BEDRM
10^6x 10^2
SHWR
MASTER BATH
BONUS RM / BEDRM
13^2 x 16^4
LIN
DN
RAILING
WALK-IN CLOSET
BEDRM
11^2 x 9^8
MASTER BEDRM
13^2 x 16^4
SLOPE CLG
FAMILY RM
16^8 x 12^0
SLOPE CLG
NOOK
8^4x 12^0
KIT
9^{10}x12^0
DW
RANGE
DINING
9^8 x 12^0
D W
LAUNDRY
DESK
REF
P
CURB
DN
PDR RM
RAILING
FOYER
UP
RAILING
LIVING RM
13^2x 19^4
GARAGE
20^8 x 20^8
COVERED PORCH
LEDGE
Width 50'-0"
Depth 43'-10"

QUOTE ONE®

Cost to build? See page 516 to order complete cost estimate to build this house in your area!

Design 5526

First Floor: 1,228 square feet
Second Floor: 924 square feet
Total: 2,152 square feet

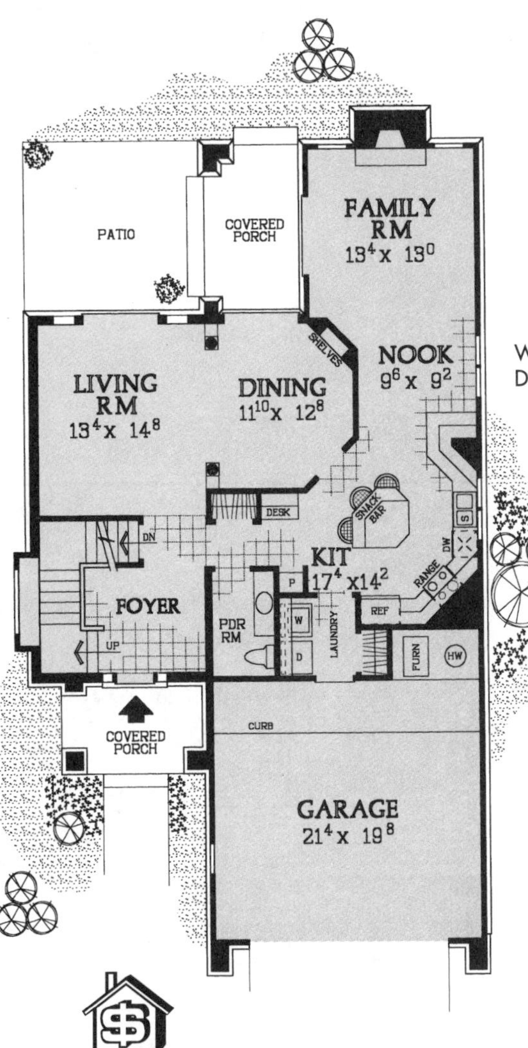
PATIO
COVERED PORCH
FAMILY RM
13^4 x 13^0
SHELVES
NOOK
9^6 x 9^2
LIVING RM
13^4 x 14^8
DINING
11^10 x 12^8
DESK
SNACK BAR
KIT
17^4 x 14^2
RANGE
DW
REF
P
W
D
LAUNDRY
FURN
HW
DN
UP
FOYER
PDR RM
CURB
COVERED PORCH
GARAGE
21^4 x 19^8

Width 36'-8"
Depth 66'-2"

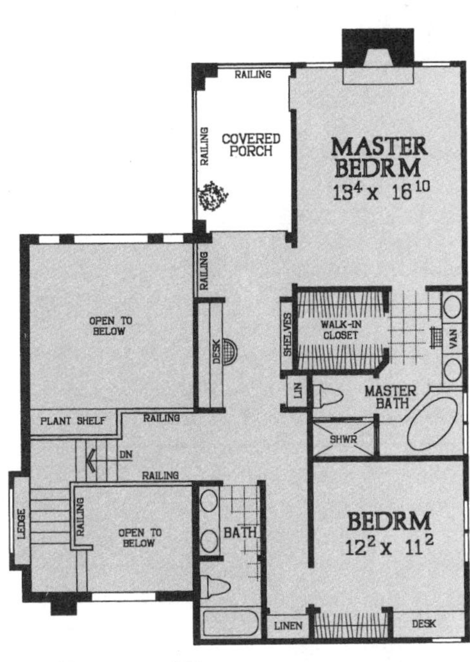
RAILING
COVERED PORCH
MASTER BEDRM
13^4 x 16^10
OPEN TO BELOW
DESK
WALK-IN CLOSET
SHELVES
VAN
LIN
MASTER BATH
PLANT SHELF
RAILING
DN
SHWR
LEDGE
OPEN TO BELOW
BATH
BEDRM
12^2 x 11^2
LINEN
DESK

Design by
Home Planners

QUOTE ONE®

Cost to build? See page 516 to order complete cost estimate to build this house in your area!

■ Whether you're a young family starting out or empty nesters with a need for a guest room or office space, this home will satisfy your needs. The expansiveness of the first floor provides a perfect layout for visiting relatives or friends. The flowing floor plan allows guests to mingle in any room with ease, whether it be in the combination living/dining room with backyard access, in the amenity-filled kitchen and breakfast nook or in the family room with its warming fireplace. The upstairs sleeping zone promotes privacy. The master bedroom, with its cozy fireplace, will become a favorite haven. The master bath separates the bedrooms and features a walk-in closet, a vanity sink, a separate shower and a corner whirlpool tub. The second bedroom can be used as either a child's room, a guest room or a corner office. It includes a built-in writing desk and easy access to a full hall bath with dual basins.

Design 5527

First Floor: 1,228 square feet
Second Floor: 1,285 square feet
Total: 2,513 square feet

■ Sunlight and warmth envelope this two-story traditional home, beginning with a Palladian window above the foyer. Separated by decorative columns, the living and dining rooms are also bathed in light via glass-door entry to the backyard. An island kitchen with a writing desk, a pantry and ample counter space leads to both the dining area, the breakfast nook and the family room with its central fireplace. Upstairs, the master bedroom features a fireplace and a massive bath with a walk-in closet. Three family bedrooms share a full bath with dual sinks that are separate from the tub and toilet area, allowing room for more than one child to get ready on busy mornings. A porch completes the second floor.

Width 36'-8"
Depth 66'-2"

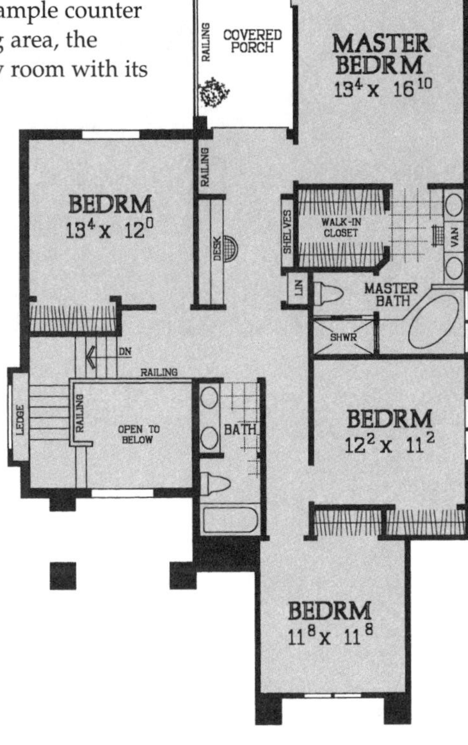

RAILING
COVERED PORCH
MASTER BEDRM
13^{4} x 16^{10}
BEDRM
13^{4} x 12^{0}
DESK
SHELVES
WALK-IN CLOSET
VAN
LIN
MASTER BATH
SHWR
DN
RAILING
LEDGE
OPEN TO BELOW
BATH
BEDRM
12^{2} x 11^{2}
BEDRM
11^{8} x 11^{8}

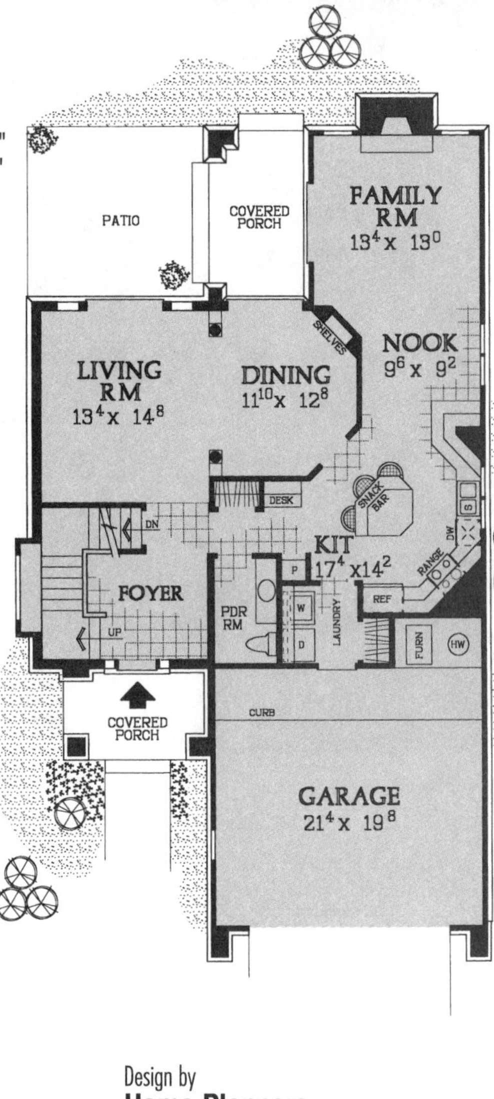

PATIO
COVERED PORCH
FAMILY RM
13^{4} x 13^{0}
SHELVES
NOOK
9^{6} x 9^{2}
LIVING RM
13^{4} x 14^{8}
DINING
11^{10} x 12^{8}
DESK
SNACK BAR
DN
KIT
17^{4} x 14^{2}
RANGE
DW
P
REF
FOYER
UP
PDR RM
W
D
LAUNDRY
FURN
HW
CURB
COVERED PORCH
GARAGE
21^{4} x 19^{8}

QUOTE ONE®
Cost to build? See page 516 to order complete cost estimate to build this house in your area!

Design by
Home Planners

Design by
Home Planners

Design 5505

First Floor: 1,160 square feet
Second Floor: 870 square feet
Total: 2,230 square feet
Bonus Room: 193 square feet

■ A Palladian window bathes the foyer of this two-story traditional with natural light and sets the tone for the warmth and comfort found throughout. In the living room, a bay window offers romantic views to the street beyond. The adjacent dining room leads to the spacious kitchen with its corner pantry, writing desk and breakfast nook. A large family room with a cozy fireplace and a convenient utility room are found nearby. On the second floor, the master bedroom provides ample room for furniture placement and features an amenity-filled master bath with a separate shower and tub, dual sinks and a walk-in closet. Three family bedrooms, or two bedrooms and a game room, share a full bath with separate sinks.

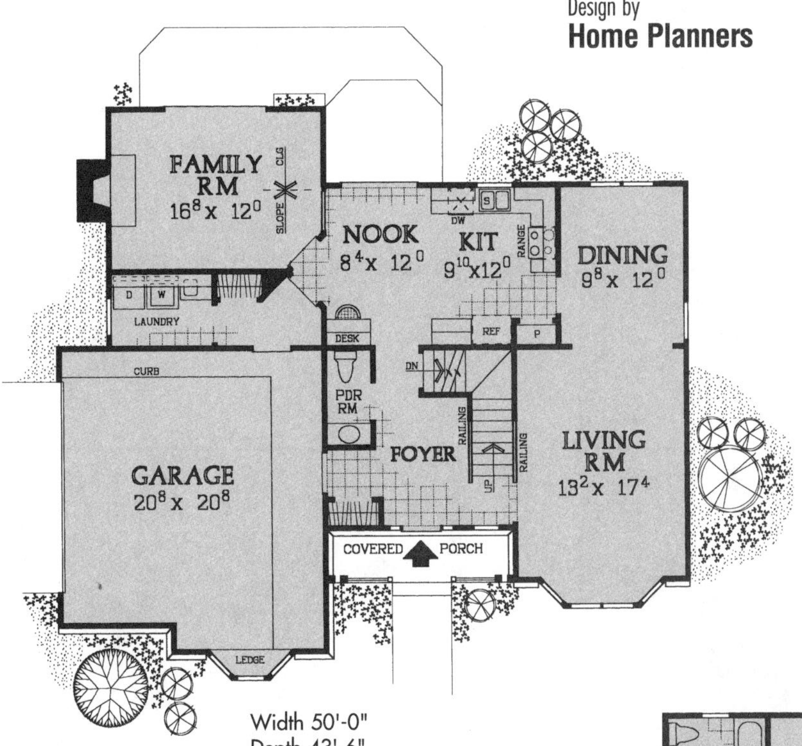
FAMILY RM
16⁸ x 12⁰
SLOPE CLG
NOOK
8⁴x 12⁰
KIT
9¹⁰x12⁰
DW
RANGE
DINING
9⁸x 12⁰
LAUNDRY
DESK
REF
P
CURB
DN
PDR RM
FOYER
RAILING
LIVING RM
13²x 17⁴
GARAGE
20⁸ x 20⁸
UP
COVERED PORCH
LEDGE

Width 50'-0"
Depth 43'-6"

QUOTE ONE®

Cost to build? See page 516 to order complete cost estimate to build this house in your area!

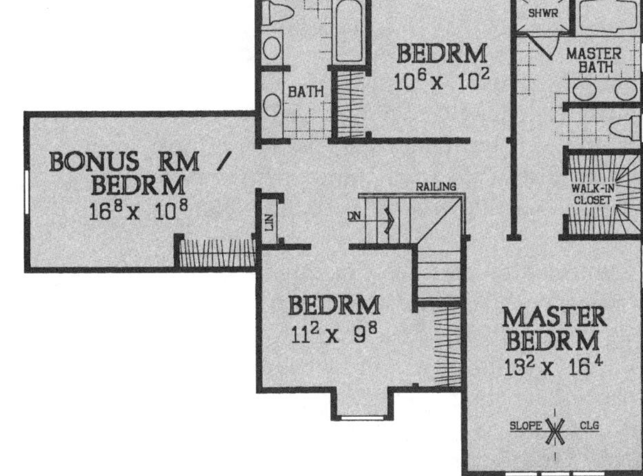
BATH
BEDRM
10⁶x 10²
SHWR
MASTER BATH
BONUS RM / BEDRM
16⁸x 10⁸
RAILING
LIN
DN
WALK-IN CLOSET
BEDRM
11² x 9⁸
MASTER BEDRM
13² x 16⁴
SLOPE CLG

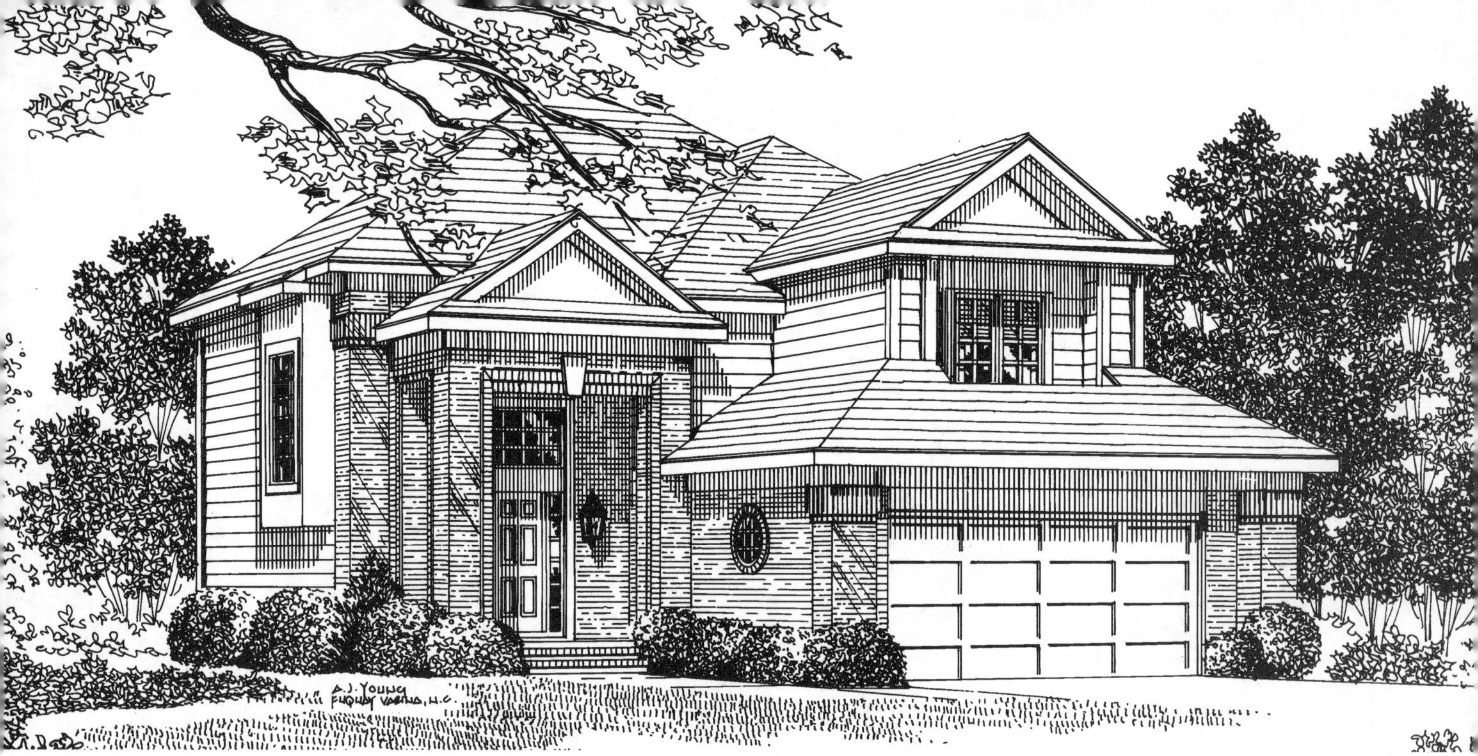

Design 5529

First Floor: 1,228 square feet
Second Floor: 1,285 square feet
Total: 2,513 square feet

Design by
Home Planners

RAILING
COVERED PORCH
MASTER BEDRM
13^4 x 16^{10}
RAILING
BEDRM
13^4 x 12^0
DESK
SHELVES
WALK-IN CLOSET
VAN
LIN
MASTER BATH
SHWR
DN
RAILING
LEDGE
OPEN TO BELOW
BATH
BEDRM
12^2 x 11^2
BEDRM
11^8 x 11^8

QUOTE ONE®

Cost to build? See page 516 to order complete cost estimate to build this house in your area!

Width 36'-8"
Depth 66'-2"

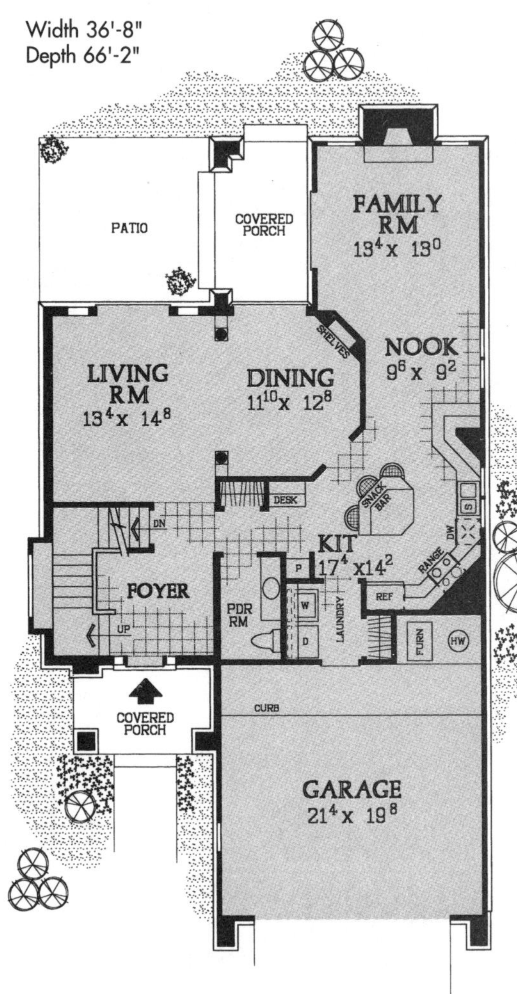

PATIO
COVERED PORCH
FAMILY RM
13^4 x 13^0
SHELVES
NOOK
9^6 x 9^2
LIVING RM
13^4 x 14^8
DINING
11^{10} x 12^8
DESK
SNACK BAR
DN
KIT
17^4 x 14^2
RANGE
DW
S
REF
P
W
D
LAUNDRY
FURN
HW
FOYER
UP
PDR RM
COVERED PORCH
CURB
GARAGE
21^4 x 19^8

■ Every home has a heart—a place where family and friends gather, that leads to other rooms and other activities. This home's heart lies in its large, circular kitchen, where an island worktop is the focal point. A corner pantry, a writing desk and ample counter space will please the cook. The kitchen blends easily with the breakfast nook, the family room—with its outdoor access and fireplace—and the living and dining areas. The dining room features corner shelves for your special family treasures and is separated from the formal living room by decorative pillars. The living room has access to the backyard via sliding glass doors. Upstairs, three family bedrooms share a full bath and a handy writing desk—big enough for a computer. Also located on the second floor is the master bedroom, which features a fireplace and a splendid bath. A porch with room to relax completes this floor.

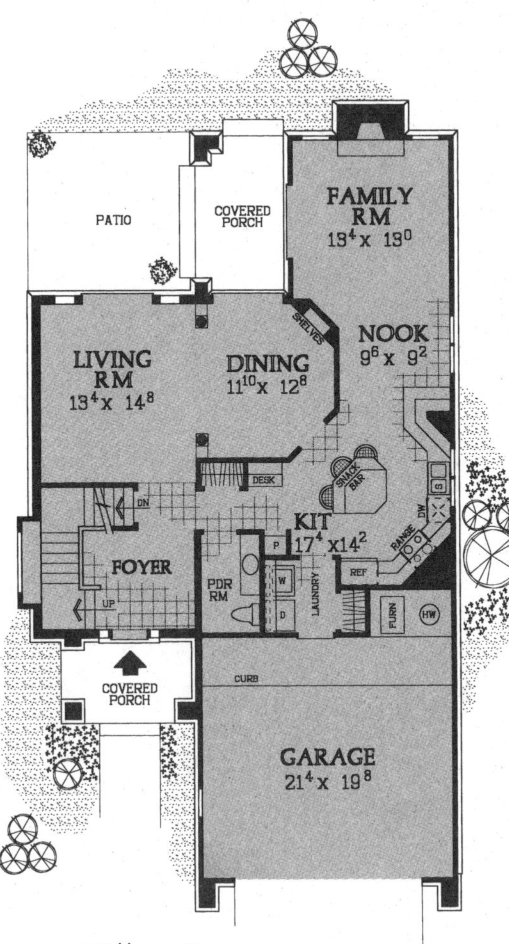
PATIO
COVERED PORCH
FAMILY RM 13⁴ x 13⁰
LIVING RM 13⁴ x 14⁸
DINING 11¹⁰ x 12⁸
NOOK 9⁶ x 9²
SHELVES
SNACK BAR
DESK
KIT 17⁴ x 14²
RANGE
DW
REF
FOYER
DN
UP
PDR RM
LAUNDRY
W
D
P
FURN
HW
COVERED PORCH
CURB
GARAGE 21⁴ x 19⁸

Width 36'-8"
Depth 66'-2"

Design 5524

First Floor: 1,228 square feet
Second Floor: 924 square feet
Total: 2,152 square feet

■ A Palladian window, an arched entry and corner quoins add to the majestic curb appeal of this two-bedroom home, ideal for empty-nesters. Inside, the foyer leads to a combination living and dining room with backyard access. Corner shelving in the dining area provides the perfect space for your special treasures. The large kitchen, complete with a worktop island, a writing desk and easy entry from the laundry room and the garage, opens to a breakfast nook and then on to the family room with its outdoor access and central fireplace. The master bedroom, on the upper level, features a large master bath with a corner tub and a walk-in closet. The second bedroom includes its own built-in writing desk. A full hall bath with dual sinks and a large desk outside both bedrooms complete this well-utilized plan.

Design by
Home Planners

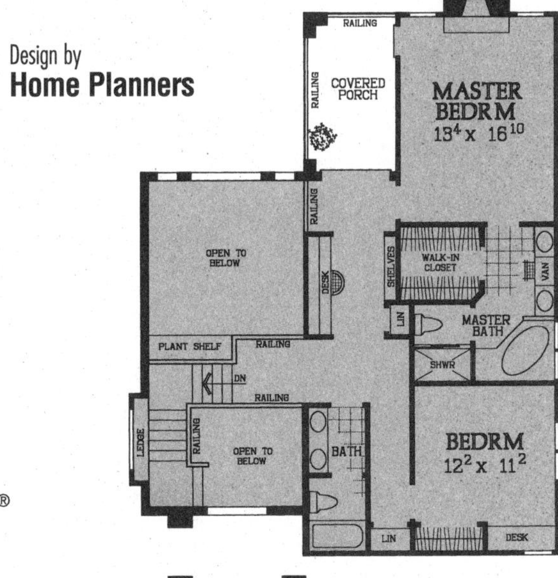
RAILING
COVERED PORCH
MASTER BEDRM 13⁴ x 16¹⁰
OPEN TO BELOW
DESK
SHELVES
WALK-IN CLOSET
VAN
LIN
MASTER BATH
PLANT SHELF
RAILING
DN
SHWR
LEDGE
OPEN TO BELOW
BATH
BEDRM 12² x 11²
LIN
DESK

Cost to build? See page 516 to order complete cost estimate to build this house in your area!

Design 5518

First Floor: 1,228 square feet
Second Floor: 1,080 square feet
Total: 2,308 square feet

■ This traditional design offers a unique sense of drama throughout both the exterior and the interior. Interesting window treatments not only give this home a dramatic facade, but bathe the foyer and the main living areas in warmth and light. From the foyer, enter an equally dramatic living room and dining room with a cathedral ceiling, backyard access and corner-shelf space for your prized possessions. An open kitchen with a convenient island worktop, a corner pantry and a writing desk, as well as access to the utility room and the garage, leads to a family room with a central fireplace and glass doors leading to the rear patio. Upstairs, the master bedroom will become a favorite getaway spot with its cozy fireplace and master bathroom. Two additional bedrooms that share a full hall bath, and a porch complete the second floor.

Design by
Home Planners

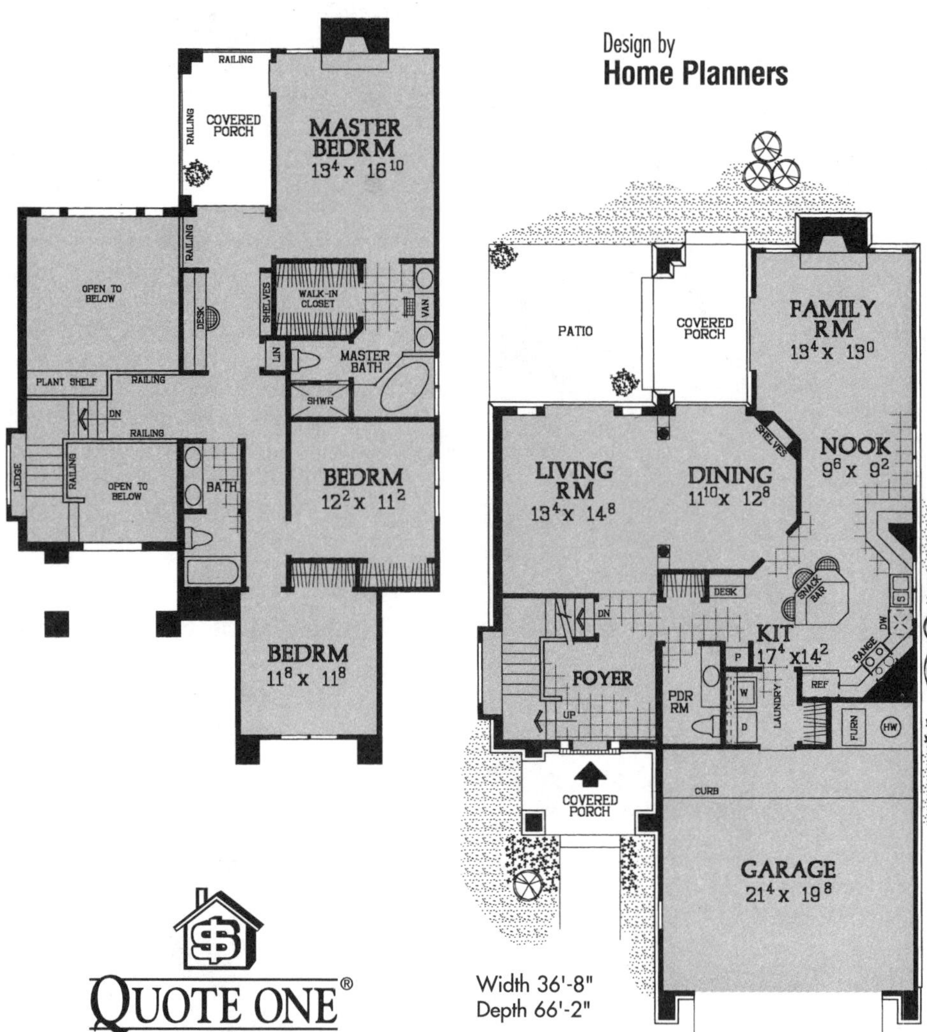

RAILING
COVERED PORCH
MASTER BEDRM 13^4 x 16^{10}
OPEN TO BELOW
DESK
SHELVES
WALK-IN CLOSET
VAN
LIN
MASTER BATH
SHWR
PLANT SHELF
RAILING
DN
LEDGE
OPEN TO BELOW
BATH
BEDRM 12^2 x 11^2
BEDRM 11^8 x 11^8
PATIO
COVERED PORCH
FAMILY RM 13^4 x 13^0
SHELVES
NOOK 9^6 x 9^2
LIVING RM 13^4 x 14^8
DINING 11^{10}x 12^8
DESK
SNACK BAR
DN
KIT 17^4 x14^2
P
RANGE
DW
REF
FOYER
UP
PDR RM
W
D
LAUNDRY
FURN
HW
COVERED PORCH
CURB
GARAGE 21^4x 19^8
Width 36'-8"
Depth 66'-2"

QUOTE ONE®
Cost to build? See page 516 to order complete cost estimate to build this house in your area!

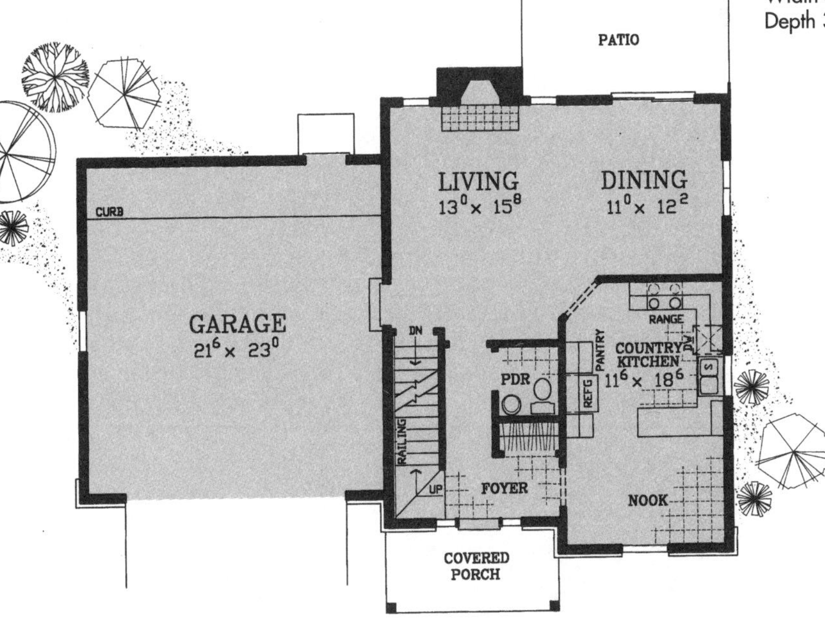
PATIO
LIVING
$13^0 \times 15^8$
DINING
$11^0 \times 12^2$
CURB
GARAGE
$21^6 \times 23^0$
DN
RANGE
PANTRY
COUNTRY KITCHEN
$11^6 \times 18^6$
PDR
REFG
RAILING
UP
FOYER
NOOK
COVERED PORCH

Width 47'-4"
Depth 38'-10"

Design by
Home Planners

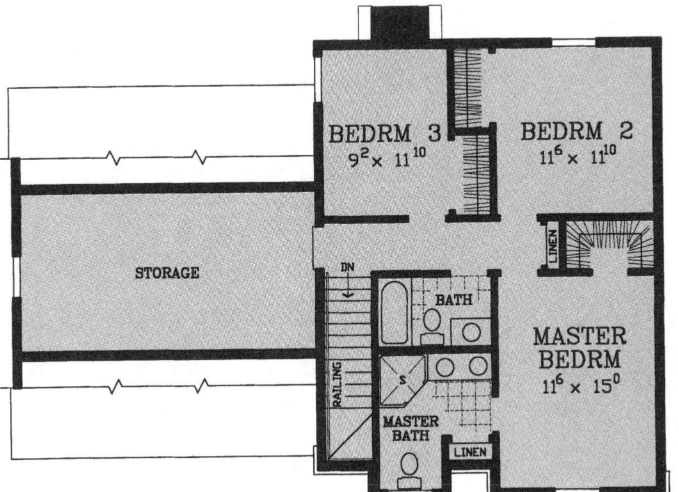
BEDRM 3
$9^2 \times 11^{10}$
BEDRM 2
$11^6 \times 11^{10}$
LINEN
STORAGE
DN
BATH
MASTER BEDRM
$11^6 \times 15^0$
RAILING
MASTER BATH
LINEN

Design 5539

First Floor: 798 square feet
Second Floor: 765 square feet
Total: 1,563 square feet
Storage Room: 268 square feet

■ Corner quoins and a covered porch add a special touch to this two-story traditional home. Inside, a tiled foyer leads either to the corner kitchen or past a convenient half-bath to the spacious combination living and dining room. The main living area features a tiled fireplace and access to the rear patio. The U-shaped kitchen features a pantry, a snack bar and a tiled breakfast nook. On the second floor, the master bedroom includes a private bath with dual sinks and a separate linen closet. Two family bedrooms share a full bath. Additional storage space can be turned into a games room, if preferred.

QUOTE ONE®

Cost to build? See page 516 to order complete cost estimate to build this house in your area!

Interesting arches and angles will set this starter home apart from its neighbors while the design's layout will make it a welcome haven for the working couple in need of a comfortable two-bedroom plan. The spacious combination living room and dining room is separated only by decorative columns, but both provide windowed access to the rear patio and yard. The open kitchen and family room, with such features as an island work table, a connecting nook and a large fireplace, will make this area a favorite meeting spot during parties and family gatherings. A powder room, a two-car garage and a laundry room complete the first floor. On the second floor, the family or guest bedroom includes a convenient writing desk and easy access to the full hall bath with its separate sink area. The master bedroom features a master bath with a walk-in closet, a vanity area between two sinks and a separate shower and tub. A cozy fireplace in the bedroom adds just a touch of luxury and comfort.

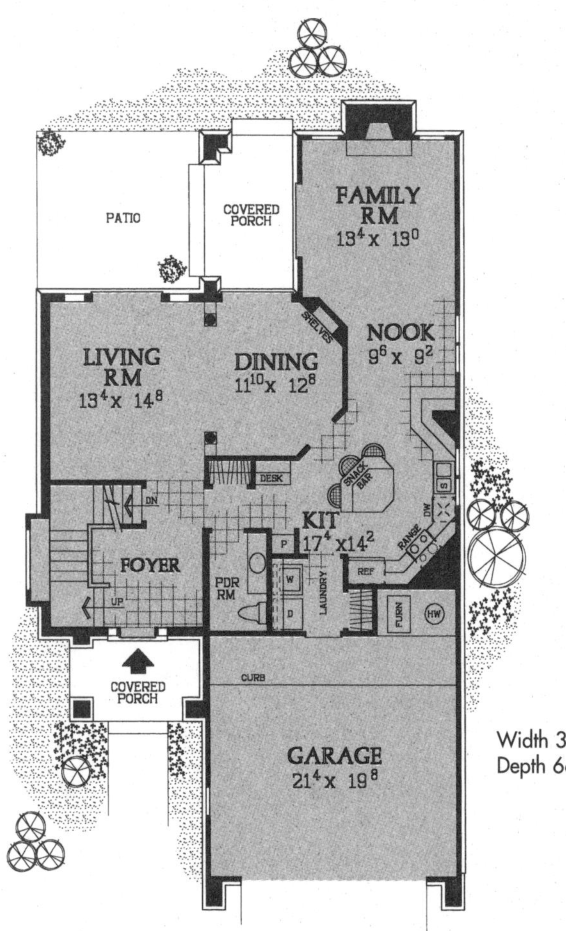
PATIO
COVERED PORCH
FAMILY RM
13^{4} x 13^{0}
NOOK
9^{6} x 9^{2}
LIVING RM
13^{4} x 14^{8}
DINING
11^{10} x 12^{8}
SHELVES
SNACK BAR
DESK
DN
KIT
17^{4} x 14^{2}
FOYER
UP
PDR RM
P
W
D
LAUNDRY
REF
RANGE
DW
S
FURN
HW
COVERED PORCH
CURB
GARAGE
21^{4} x 19^{8}

Width 36'-8"
Depth 66'-2"

Design by
Home Planners

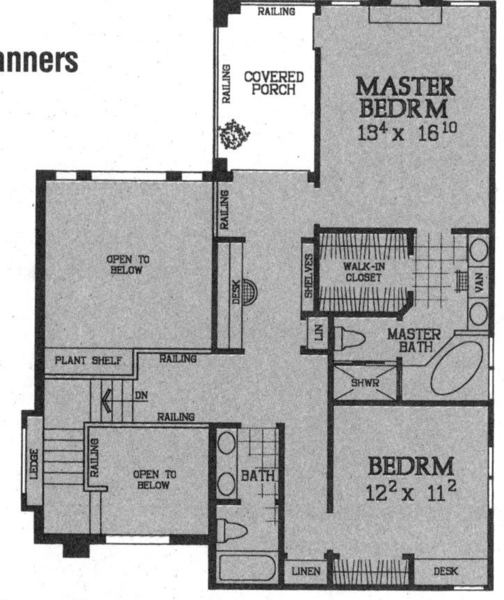
RAILING
COVERED PORCH
MASTER BEDRM
13^{4} x 16^{10}
OPEN TO BELOW
RAILING
DESK
SHELVES
WALK-IN CLOSET
VAN
LIN
MASTER BATH
PLANT SHELF
RAILING
DN
SHWR
RAILING
LEDGE
OPEN TO BELOW
BATH
BEDRM
12^{2} x 11^{2}
LINEN
DESK

Design 5525

First Floor: 1,228 square feet
Second Floor: 924 square feet
Total: 2,152 square feet

QUOTE ONE®

Cost to build? See page 516 to order complete cost estimate to build this house in your area!

Design 3310

First Floor: 1,668 square feet
Second Floor: 905 square feet
Total: 2,573 square feet

L D

■ If you're looking for a different angle on a new home, try this enchanting transitional house. The open foyer creates a rich atmosphere, framed with a second story mezzanine lounge. To the left you'll find a two-story great room with a raised brick hearth and sliding glass doors that lead out onto a wraparound deck. The formal dining room with built-in china cabinet is open to the oversized, gourmet kitchen complete with a snack bar and an abundance of cabinet space. The master bedroom is secluded on the first floor for privacy and features a master bath with whirlpool and walk-in closet. Upstairs, two family bedrooms, both with balconies and walk-in closets, share a full bath. Quiet time will be enjoyed in the lounge that's accented with a dramatic elliptical window and balcony views of the great room.

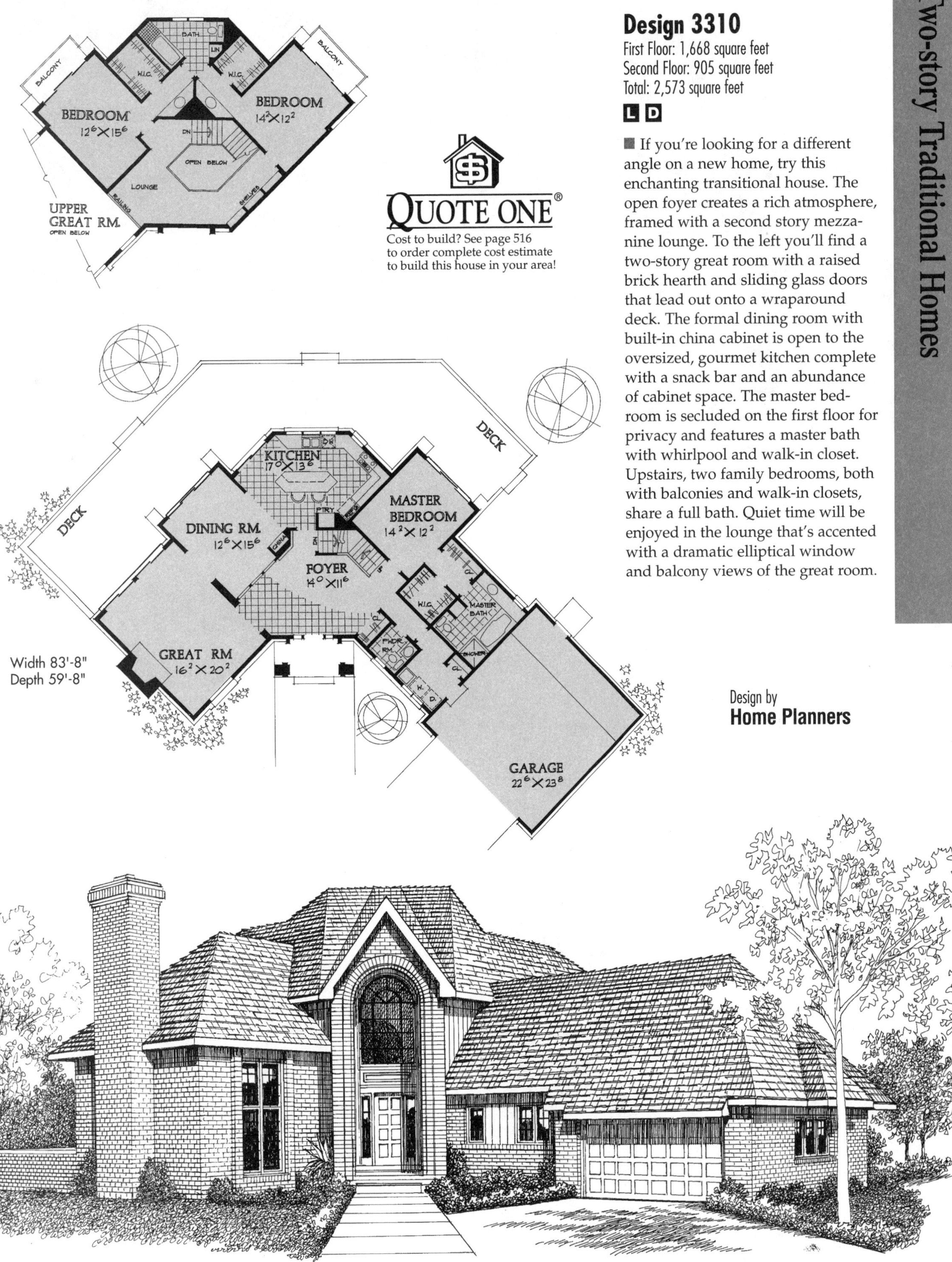
BALCONY
BATH
LIN
W.I.C.
W.I.C.
BALCONY
BEDROOM
$12^6 \times 15^6$
BEDROOM
$14^2 \times 12^2$
DN
OPEN BELOW
LOUNGE
RAILING
SHELVES
UPPER
GREAT RM.
OPEN BELOW
QUOTE ONE®
Cost to build? See page 516
to order complete cost estimate
to build this house in your area!
DECK
KITCHEN
$17^0 \times 13^6$
DECK
PTRY
DINING RM.
$12^6 \times 15^6$
CHINA
MASTER
BEDROOM
$14^2 \times 12^2$
FOYER
$14^0 \times 11^6$
W.I.C.
MASTER BATH
SHOWER
PWDR. RM.
W.
D.
GREAT RM
$16^2 \times 20^2$
GARAGE
$22^6 \times 23^8$
Width 83'-8"
Depth 59'-8"

Design by
Home Planners

Design 5546

First Floor: 728 square feet
Second Floor: 687 square feet
Total: 1,415 square feet

■ A brick facade and special exterior detailing add an air of elegance to the front of this two-story traditional home, perfect for the small family on the go. Inside, an open and comfortable floor plan awaits. The combination great room and dining room accesses a convenient side deck and leads to a U-shaped kitchen and a utility area with a powder room. On the second floor, two family bedrooms share a full hall bath. The master bedroom features a walk-in closet and a separate bath with double sinks. The sun-filled bay window in the master bedroom will become a favorite spot in which to lounge and enjoy quiet times.

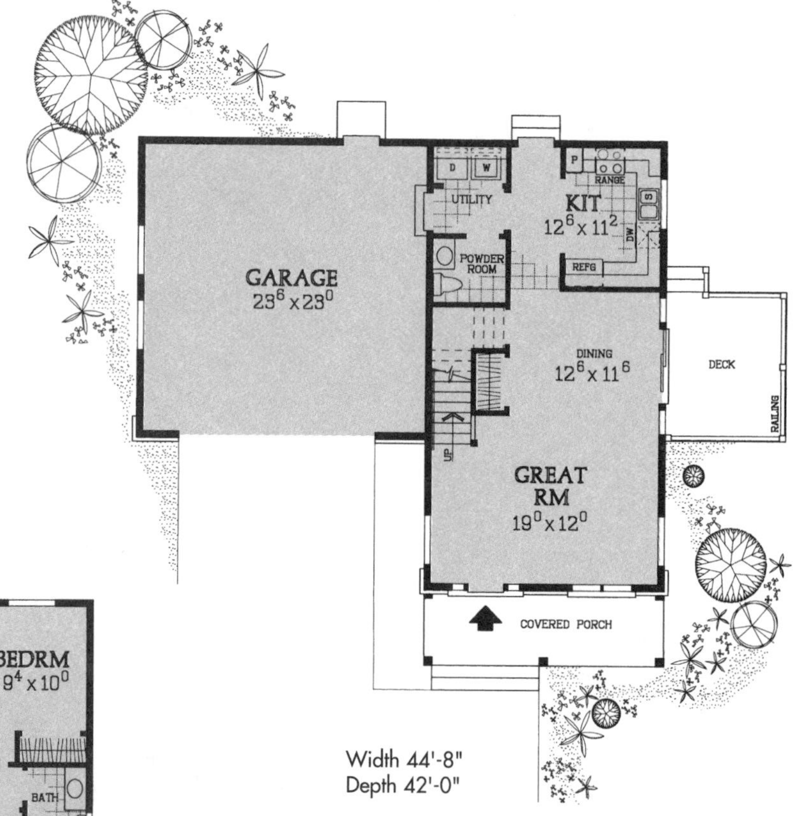
GARAGE
23^{6} x 23^{0}
UTILITY
D
W
POWDER ROOM
KIT
12^{6} x 11^{2}
RANGE
REFG
DW
DINING
12^{6} x 11^{6}
DECK
RAILING
UP
GREAT RM
19^{0} x 12^{0}
COVERED PORCH
Width 44'-8"
Depth 42'-0"

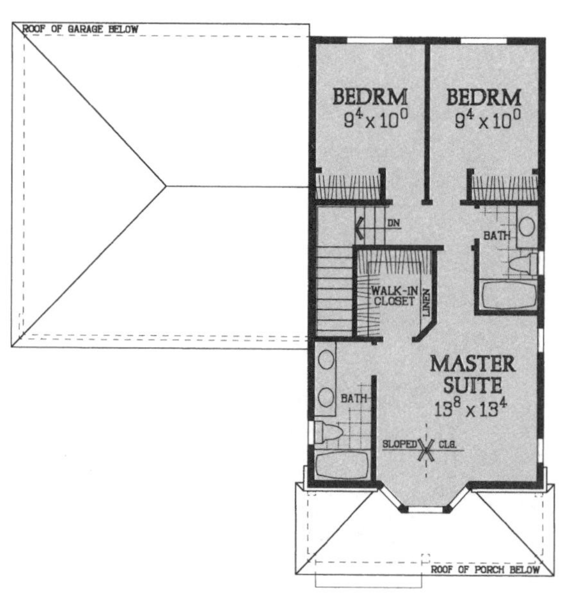
ROOF OF GARAGE BELOW
BEDRM
9^{4} x 10^{0}
BEDRM
9^{4} x 10^{0}
DN
BATH
WALK-IN CLOSET
LINEN
MASTER SUITE
13^{8} x 13^{4}
BATH
SLOPED CLG.
ROOF OF PORCH BELOW

Design by
Home Planners

QUOTE ONE®

Cost to build? See page 516
to order complete cost estimate
to build this house in your area!

Width 44'-8"
Depth 42'-4"

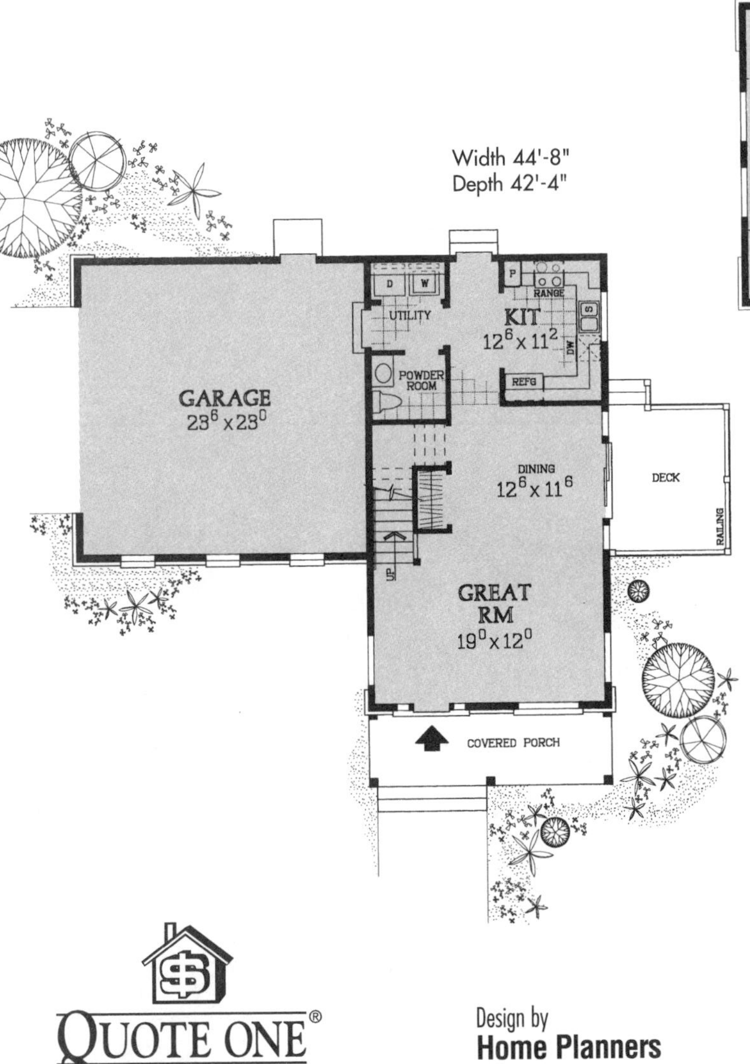
GARAGE
$23^6 \times 23^0$
UTILITY
D
W
POWDER ROOM
KIT
$12^6 \times 11^2$
RANGE
REFG
DW
DINING
$12^6 \times 11^6$
DECK
RAILING
UP
GREAT RM
$19^0 \times 12^0$
COVERED PORCH

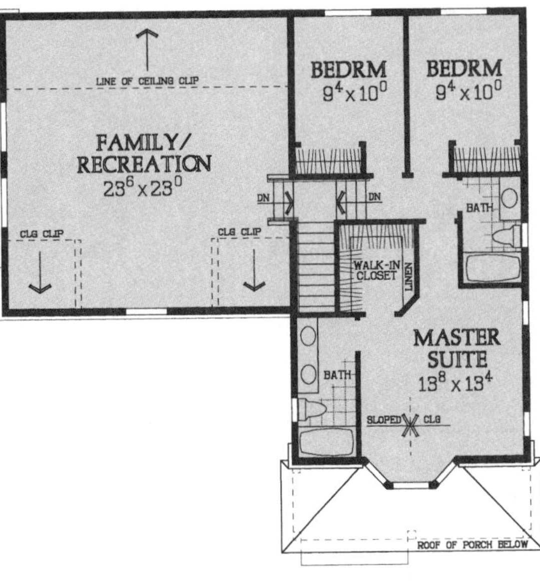
LINE OF CEILING CLIP
FAMILY/
RECREATION
$23^6 \times 23^0$
CLG CLIP
CLG CLIP
DN
DN
BEDRM
$9^4 \times 10^0$
BEDRM
$9^4 \times 10^0$
BATH
WALK-IN CLOSET
LINEN
MASTER SUITE
$13^8 \times 13^4$
BATH
SLOPED CLG
ROOF OF PORCH BELOW

Design 5551

First Floor: 728 square feet
Second Floor: 1,268 square feet
Total: 1,996 square feet

■ Built for corner or narrow lots, this two-story traditional home offers a lot of amenities within its compacted space. The covered porch entry leads to an open combination great and dining room with access to a side deck. The efficient kitchen offers plenty of counter space. A handy utility room and a powder room complete the first floor. On the second floor, the master bedroom features a bay window, a walk-in closet and a private bath with dual sinks. Two family bedrooms and a spacious family/recreation room—big enough for your computer and games or for a pool table—share a full hall bath.

QUOTE ONE®
Cost to build? See page 516 to order complete cost estimate to build this house in your area!

Design by
Home Planners

Design 5544

First Floor: 720 square feet
Second Floor: 682 square feet
Total: 1,402 square feet

■ Ideal as a vacation or second home, this narrow-lot design features not only a front covered porch, but a great side deck that accesses the dining room. Both the front entry and the dining area combine with the great room to create an large area for family gatherings and entertaining. An amenity-filled kitchen and a utility room with a half-bath complete the first floor. On the second floor, two family bedrooms share a full hall bath. The master bedroom features a sun-filled bay window with views to the front yard, a walk-in closet and a private bath with dual basins.

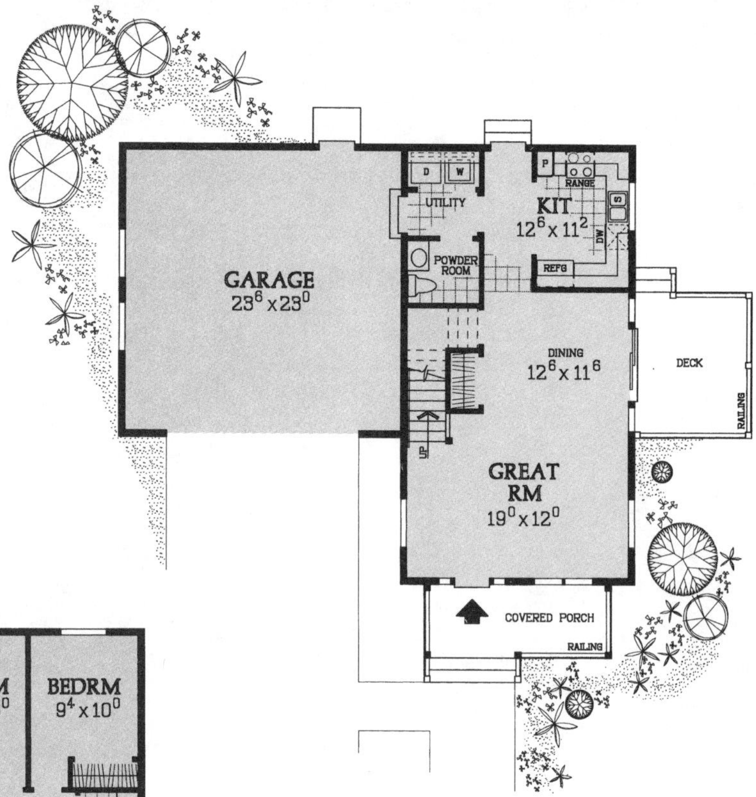

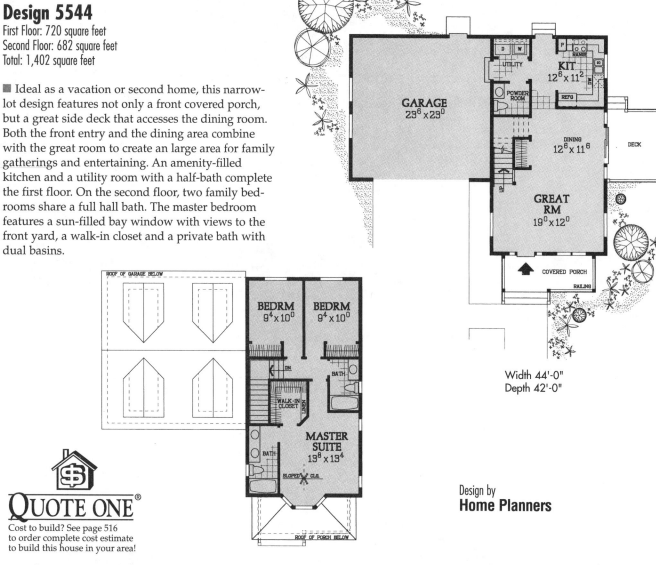

GARAGE $23^6 \times 23^0$
UTILITY
POWDER ROOM
KIT $12^6 \times 11^2$
RANGE
REFG
DW
DINING $12^6 \times 11^6$
DECK
RAILING
UP
GREAT RM $19^0 \times 12^0$
COVERED PORCH
RAILING

ROOF OF GARAGE BELOW
BEDRM $9^4 \times 10^0$
BEDRM $9^4 \times 10^0$
DN
BATH
WALK-IN CLOSET
LINEN
MASTER SUITE $13^8 \times 13^4$
BATH
SLOPED CLG.
ROOF OF PORCH BELOW

Width 44'-0"
Depth 42'-0"

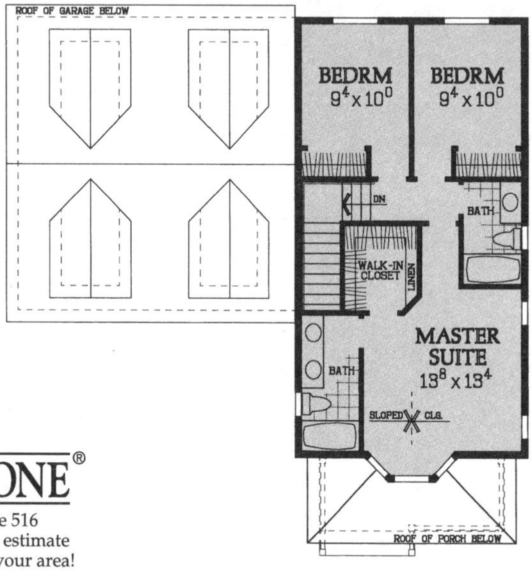

QUOTE ONE®
Cost to build? See page 516 to order complete cost estimate to build this house in your area!

Design by
Home Planners

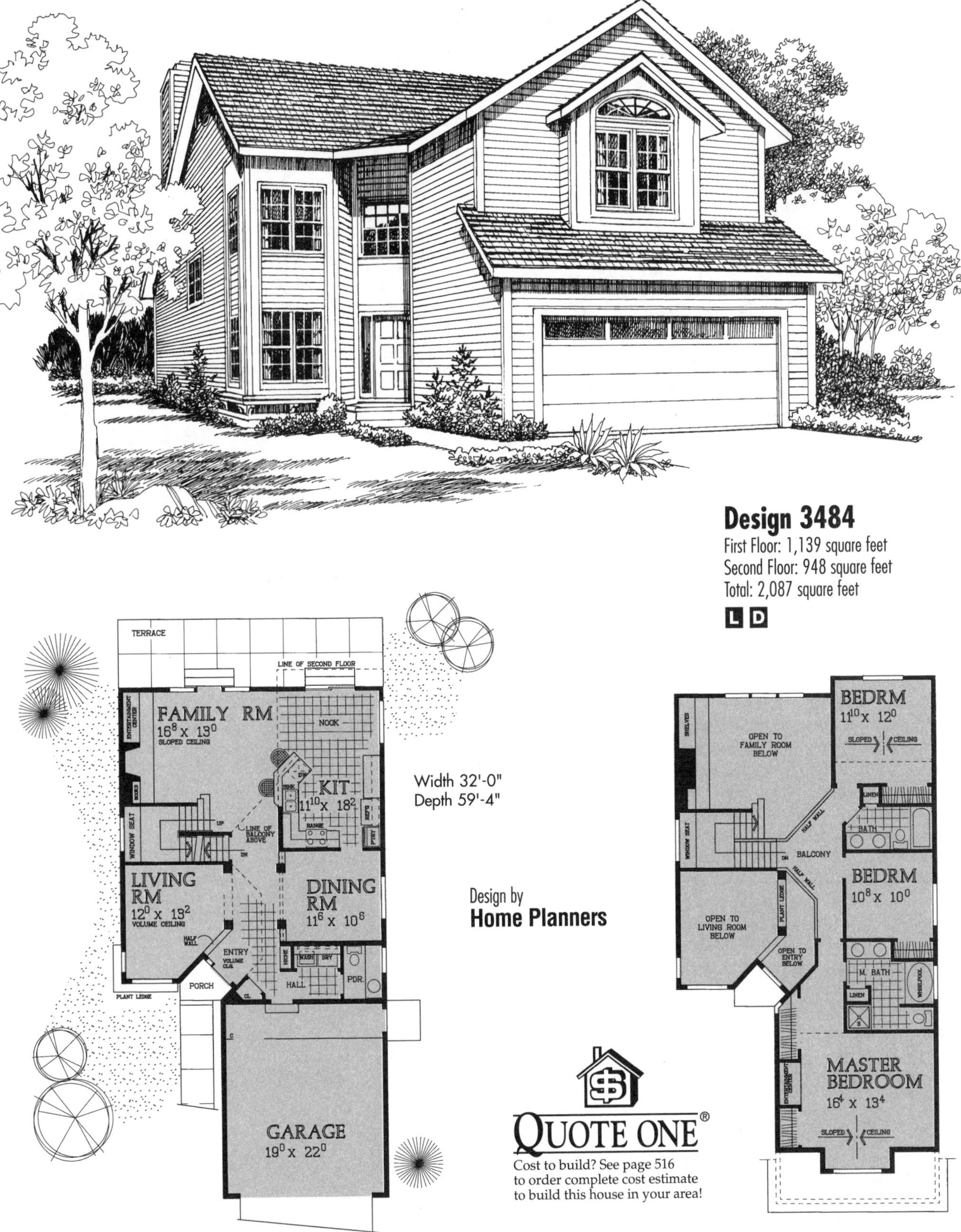
TERRACE
LINE OF SECOND FLOOR
FAMILY RM
16⁸ x 13⁰
SLOPED CEILING
NOOK
KIT
11¹⁰ x 18²
RANGE
LINE OF BALCONY ABOVE
UP
DN
LIVING RM
12⁰ x 13²
VOLUME CEILING
HALF WALL
DINING RM
11⁶ x 10⁶
ENTRY
VOLUME CLG.
WASH
DRY
HALL
PDR.
PORCH
PLANT LEDGE
GARAGE
19⁰ x 22⁰
OPEN TO FAMILY ROOM BELOW
BEDRM
11¹⁰ x 12⁰
SLOPED
CEILING
LINEN
BATH
HALF WALL
BALCONY
BEDRM
10⁸ x 10⁰
OPEN TO LIVING ROOM BELOW
OPEN TO ENTRY BELOW
M. BATH
MASTER BEDROOM
16⁴ x 13⁴
SLOPED
CEILING

Design 3484

First Floor: 1,139 square feet
Second Floor: 948 square feet
Total: 2,087 square feet

L D

Width 32'-0"
Depth 59'-4"

Design by
Home Planners

QUOTE ONE®
Cost to build? See page 516 to order complete cost estimate to build this house in your area!

■ An angled entry offers a new perspective on the formal areas of this house: living room on the left; dining room on the right. Both rooms exchange views through a columned hallway; a potshelf and a niche add custom touches to this already attention-getting arrangement. At the back of the first floor, a family room with built-in bookshelves and an entertainment-center niche opens to the kitchen and nook where both cooking and dining become a delight. The second floor provides interest with its balcony open to the living and family rooms. Three bedrooms include a master suite with a sloped ceiling, separate closets and a private bath. The two-car garage has direct access to the house.

Design 2826

First Floor: 1,112 square feet
Second Floor: 881 square feet
Total: 1,993 square feet

D

■ The classic American homestead is all dressed up with contemporary character and country spirit. Well-defined rooms, flowing spaces and the latest amenities blend the best of traditional and modern elements. The spacious gathering room offers terrace access and shares a through-fireplace with a secluded study. The second-floor master suite shares a balcony hallway, which overlooks the gathering room, with two family bedrooms. Dual vanities, built-in cabinets and shelves, and triple-window views highlight the master bedroom. In an alternate plan, the formal dining room and the breakfast room are switched, placing the dining room to the front of the plan.

Width 49'-0"
Depth 54'-4"

Design by
Home Planners

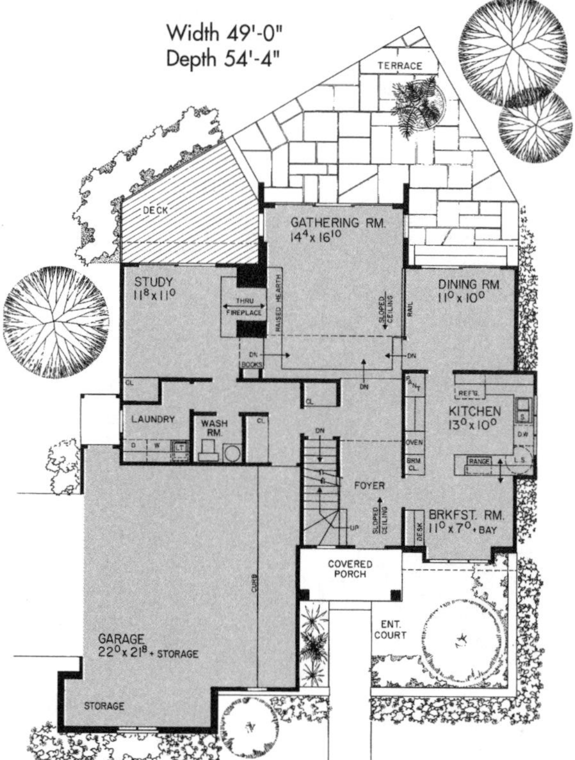
TERRACE
DECK
GATHERING RM.
STUDY
DINING RM.
KITCHEN
LAUNDRY
WASH RM.
FOYER
BRKFST. RM.
COVERED PORCH
ENT. COURT
GARAGE
STORAGE

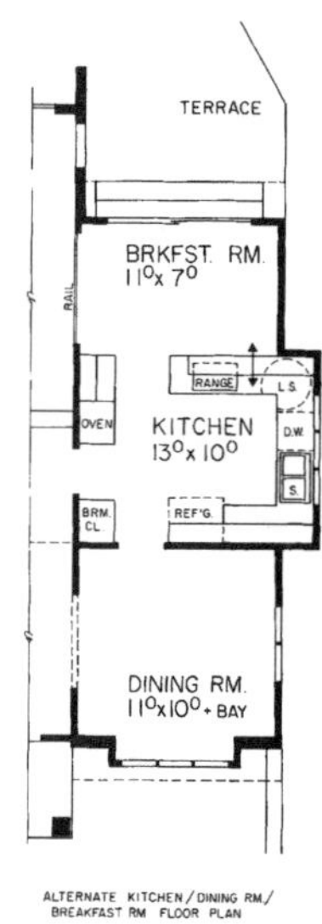
TERRACE
BRKFST. RM.
KITCHEN
DINING RM.

ALTERNATE KITCHEN / DINING RM./ BREAKFAST RM FLOOR PLAN

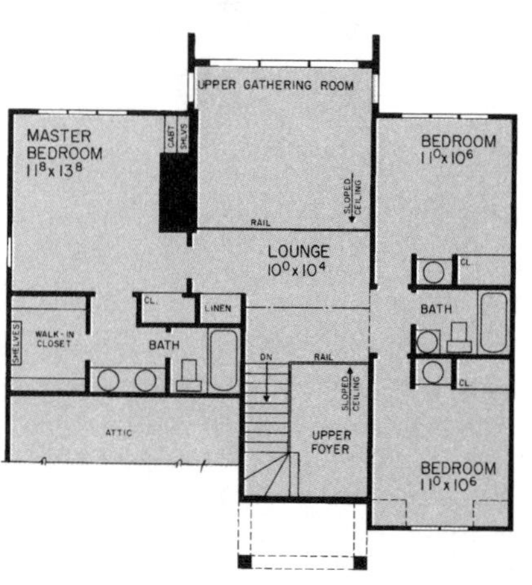
UPPER GATHERING ROOM
MASTER BEDROOM
BEDROOM
LOUNGE
WALK-IN CLOSET
BATH
ATTIC
UPPER FOYER
BEDROOM

QUOTE ONE®

Cost to build? See page 516 to order complete cost estimate to build this house in your area!

Rear Elevation

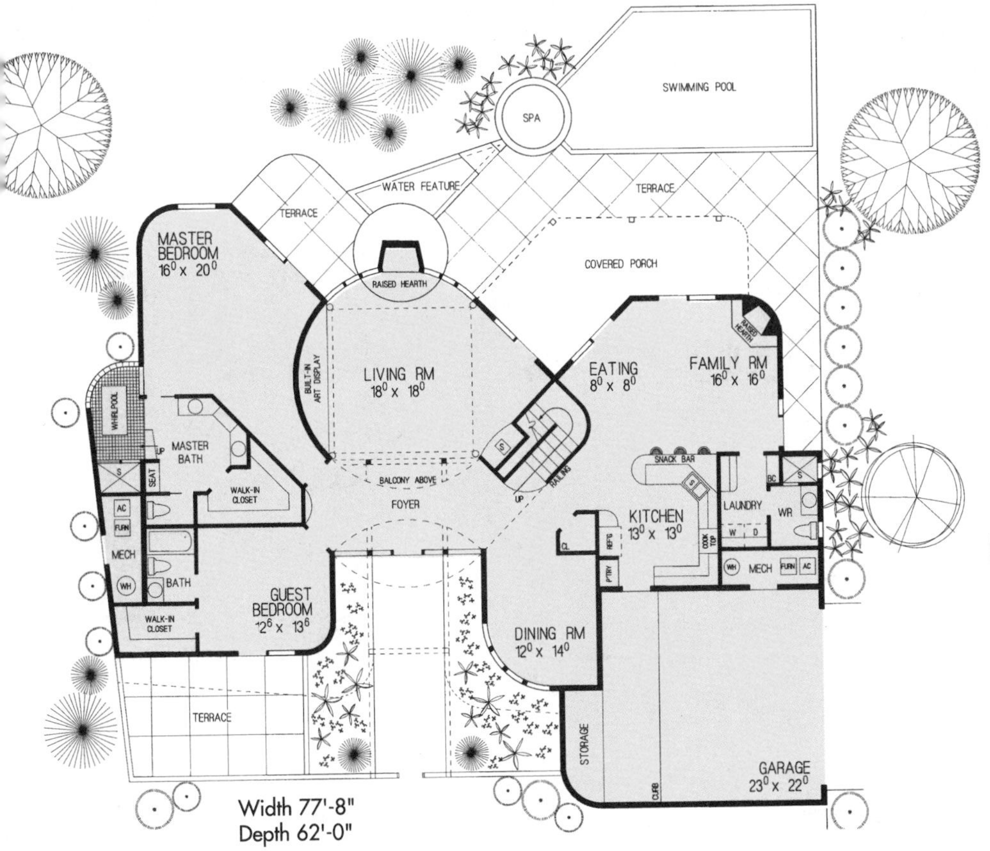

QUOTE ONE®
Cost to build? See page 516
to order complete cost estimate
to build this house in your area!

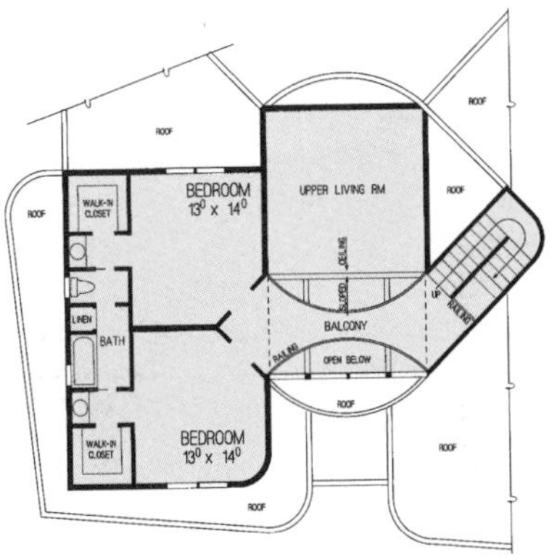

Width 77'-8"
Depth 62'-0"

Design by
Home Planners

Rear Elevation

Design 3403

First Floor: 2,422 square feet
Second Floor: 714 square feet
Total: 3,136 square feet

L

■ There is no end to the distinctive features in this Southwestern contemporary. Formal living areas are concentrated in the center of the plan, while the kitchen and family room function well together as an informal living area. The optional guest bedroom or den and the master bedroom are located to the left of the plan. The second floor holds two bedrooms that share a compartmented full bath.

Design 3456

First Floor: 1,130 square feet
Second Floor: 1,189 square feet
Total: 2,319 square feet

L

QUOTE ONE®

Cost to build? See page 516 to order complete cost estimate to build this house in your area!

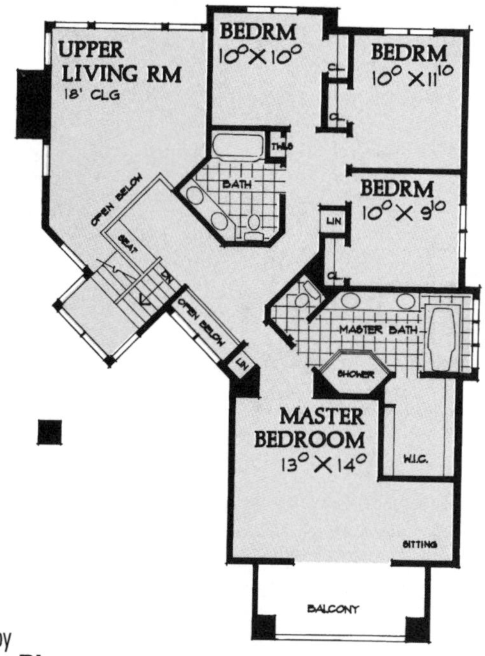

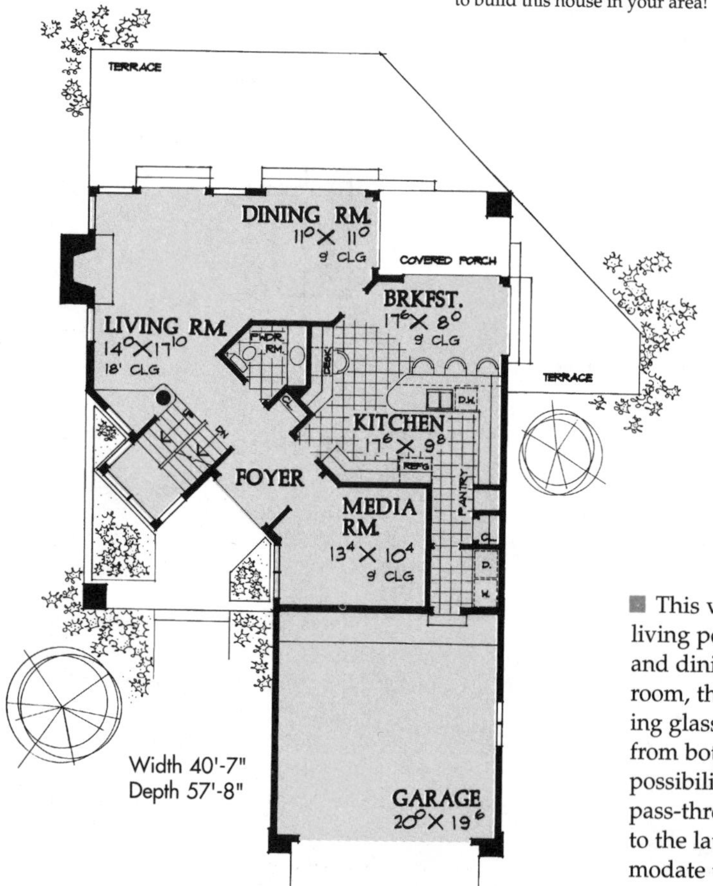

UPPER LIVING RM 18' CLG
BEDRM $10^0 \times 10^0$
BEDRM $10^0 \times 11^{10}$
BEDRM $10^0 \times 9^{10}$
BATH
MASTER BATH
SHOWER
MASTER BEDROOM $13^0 \times 14^0$
W.I.C.
SITTING
BALCONY
OPEN BELOW
SEAT
DN
LIN
CL

TERRACE
DINING RM. $11^0 \times 11^0$ 9' CLG
COVERED PORCH
BRKFST. $17^6 \times 8^0$ 9' CLG
LIVING RM. $14^0 \times 17^{10}$ 18' CLG
PWDR. RM.
DESK
KITCHEN $17^6 \times 9^8$
D.W.
REFG.
PANTRY
FOYER
MEDIA RM. $13^4 \times 10^4$ 9' CLG
CL
D.
W.
GARAGE $20^0 \times 19^6$

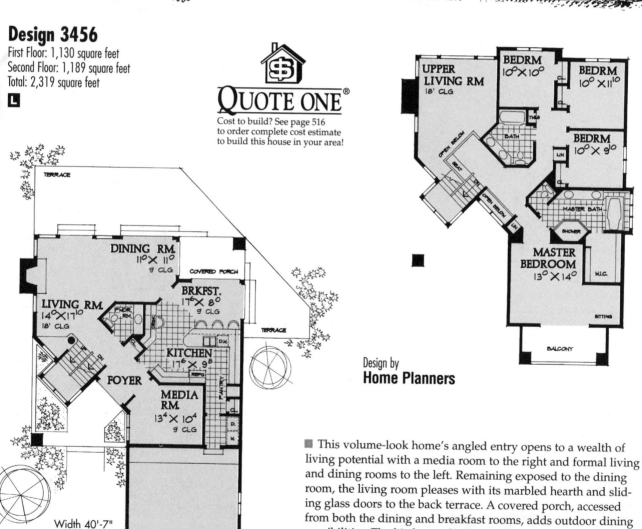

Width 40'-7"
Depth 57'-8"

Design by
Home Planners

This volume-look home's angled entry opens to a wealth of living potential with a media room to the right and formal living and dining rooms to the left. Remaining exposed to the dining room, the living room pleases with its marbled hearth and sliding glass doors to the back terrace. A covered porch, accessed from both the dining and breakfast rooms, adds outdoor dining possibilities. The kitchen utilizes a built-in desk and a snack bar pass-through to the breakfast area. A large pantry and closet lead to the laundry near the garage. Upstairs, four bedrooms accommodate the large family well. In the master suite, amenities such as a sitting area and a balcony add definition. The master bath sports a whirlpool and a walk-in closet.

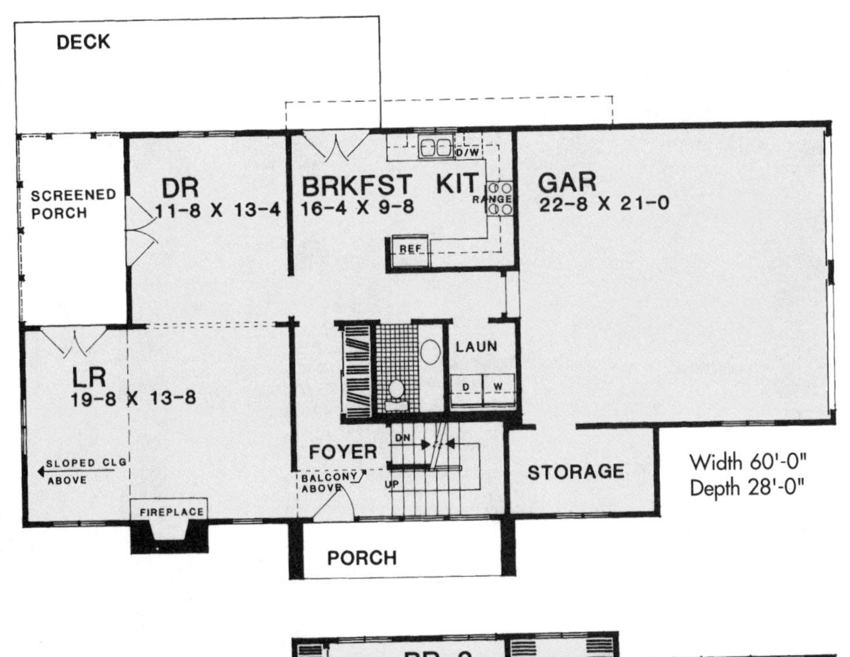
DECK
SCREENED PORCH
DR
11-8 X 13-4
BRKFST
16-4 X 9-8
KIT
D/W
RANGE
REF
GAR
22-8 X 21-0
LAUN
D
W
LR
19-8 X 13-8
SLOPED CLG ABOVE
FIREPLACE
FOYER
DN
UP
BALCONY ABOVE
STORAGE
PORCH
Width 60'-0"
Depth 28'-0"

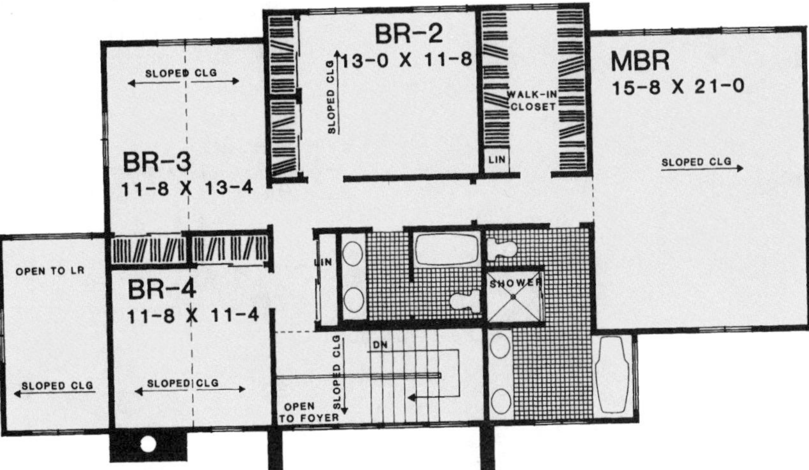
BR-2
13-0 X 11-8
SLOPED CLG
WALK-IN CLOSET
LIN
MBR
15-8 X 21-0
SLOPED CLG
BR-3
11-8 X 13-4
OPEN TO LR
BR-4
11-8 X 11-4
LIN
SHOWER
DN
OPEN TO FOYER

Design 4287

First Floor: 930 square feet
Second Floor: 1,362 square feet
Total: 2,292 square feet

L D

■ This contemporary home is perfect as a vacation getaway spot, as it uses windows as a major part of its elegant design, but it is also a grand primary residence. Consider the views that would be possible by siting this home properly. The interior is spacious without being overbearing. Living areas are to the left of the entry and include a living room with sloped ceiling and fireplace and dining room. Both of these spaces have double-door access to a screened porch with a deck beyond. The breakfast room accesses the deck directly and is attached to the U-shaped kitchen. A laundry room and half-bath round out the first floor. Upstairs, there are four bedrooms, three for the family and guests and one reserved just for the owners. A luxurious bath and walk-in closet enhance the master suite. Don't miss the large storage area in the two-car garage.

Design by
Home Planners

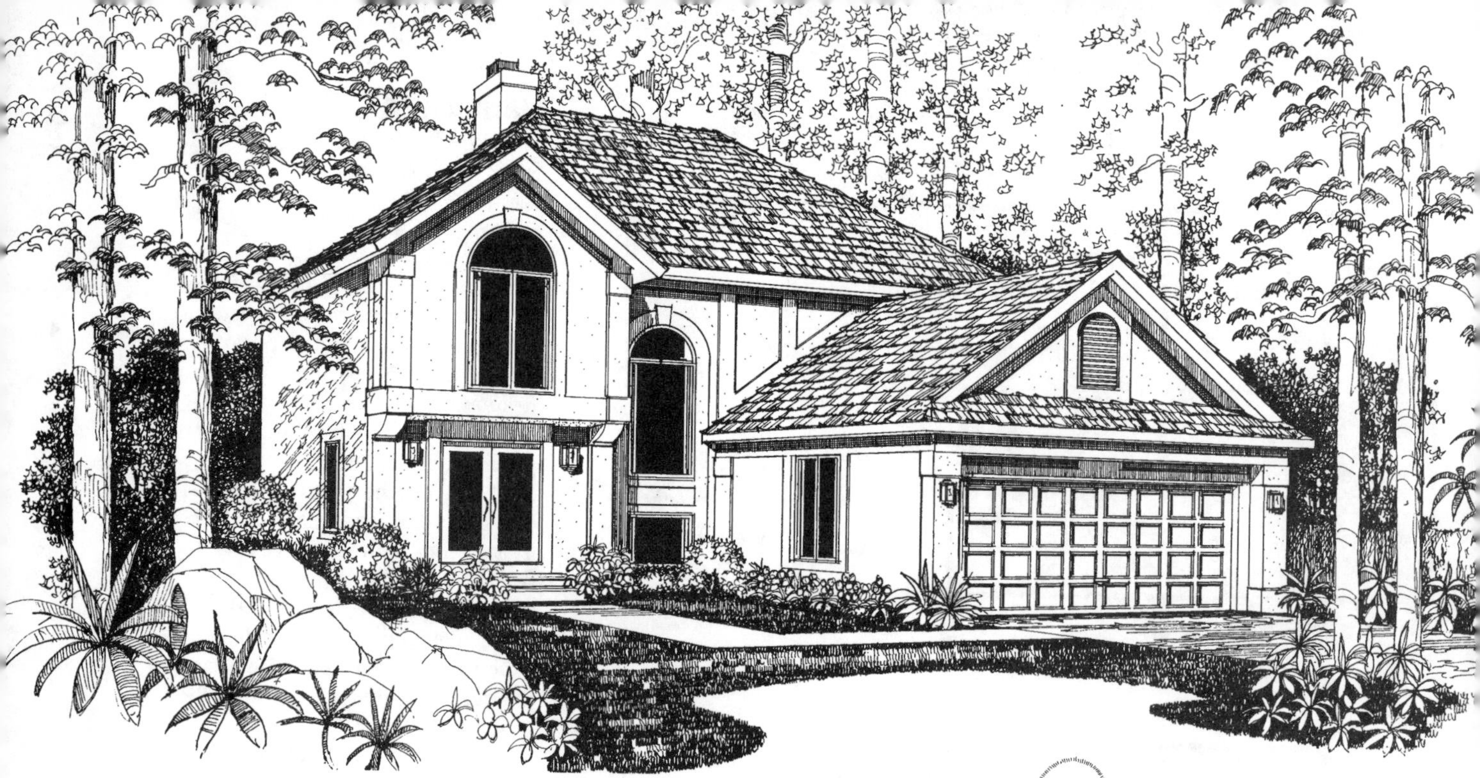

Design 3562

First Floor: 1,182 square feet
Second Floor: 927 square feet
Total: 2,109 square feet

L D

Design by
Home Planners

■ Interesting detailing marks the exterior of this home as a beauty. Its interior makes it a livable option for any family. Entry occurs through double doors to the left side of the plan. A powder room with a curved wall is handy to the entry. Living areas of the home are open and well-planned. The formal living room shares a through-fireplace with the large family room. The dining room is adjoining and has a pass-through counter to the L-shaped kitchen. Special details on this floor include a wealth of sliding glass doors to the rear terrace and built-ins throughout. Upstairs are three bedrooms with two full baths.

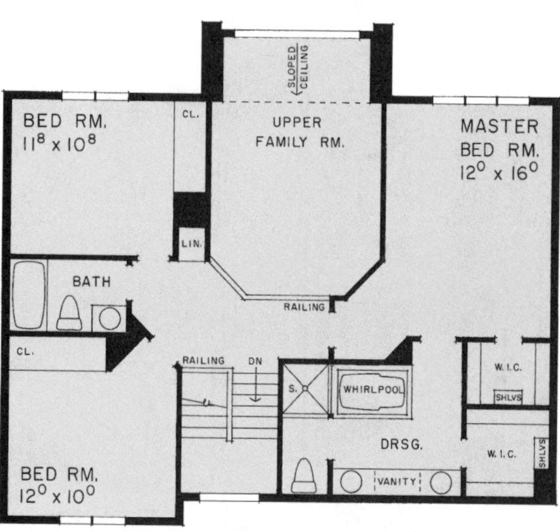

BED RM.
11^8 x 10^8
CL.
SLOPED CEILING
UPPER FAMILY RM.
MASTER BED RM.
12^0 x 16^0
LIN.
BATH
RAILING
CL.
RAILING
DN
S.
WHIRLPOOL
W.I.C.
SHLVS
DRSG.
W.I.C.
SHLVS
BED RM.
12^0 x 10^0
VANITY

Width 40'-0"
Depth 54'-0"

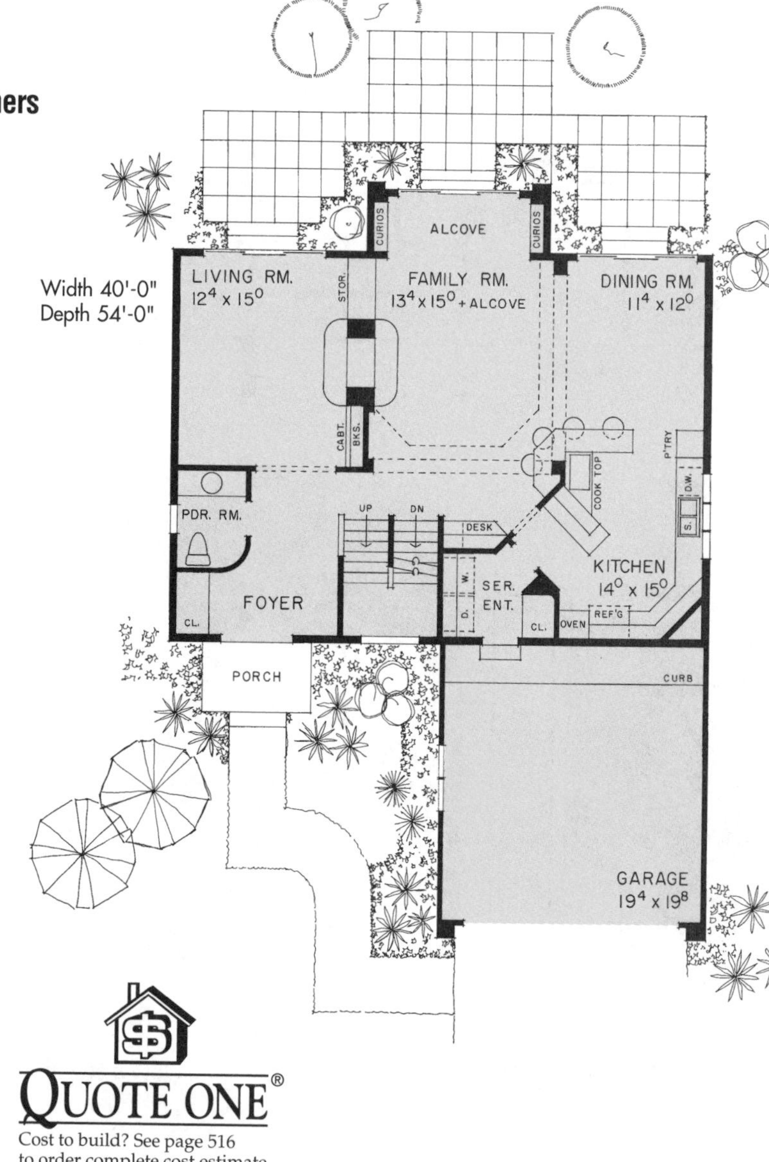

ALCOVE
CURIOS
CURIOS
LIVING RM.
12^4 x 15^0
STOR.
FAMILY RM.
13^4 x 15^0 + ALCOVE
DINING RM.
11^4 x 12^0
CABT.
BKS.
P'TRY
COOK TOP
D.W.
S.
PDR. RM.
UP
DN
DESK
KITCHEN
14^0 x 15^0
W.
D.
SER. ENT.
FOYER
CL.
CL.
OVEN
REF'G
PORCH
CURB
GARAGE
19^4 x 19^8

Design 3563

First Floor: 1,023 square feet
Second Floor: 866 square feet
Total: 1,889 square feet

L D

■ Practical to build, this wonderful transitional plan combines the best of contemporary and traditional styling. Its stucco exterior is enhanced by arched windows and a recessed arched entry plus a lovely balcony off the second-floor master bedroom. A walled entry court extends the living room on the outside. The double front doors open to a foyer with hall closet and powder room. The service entrance is just to the right and accesses the two-car garage. The large living room adjoins directly to the dining room. The family room is set off behind the garage and features a sloped ceiling and fireplace. Sleeping quarters consist of two secondary bedrooms with a shared bath and a generous master suite.

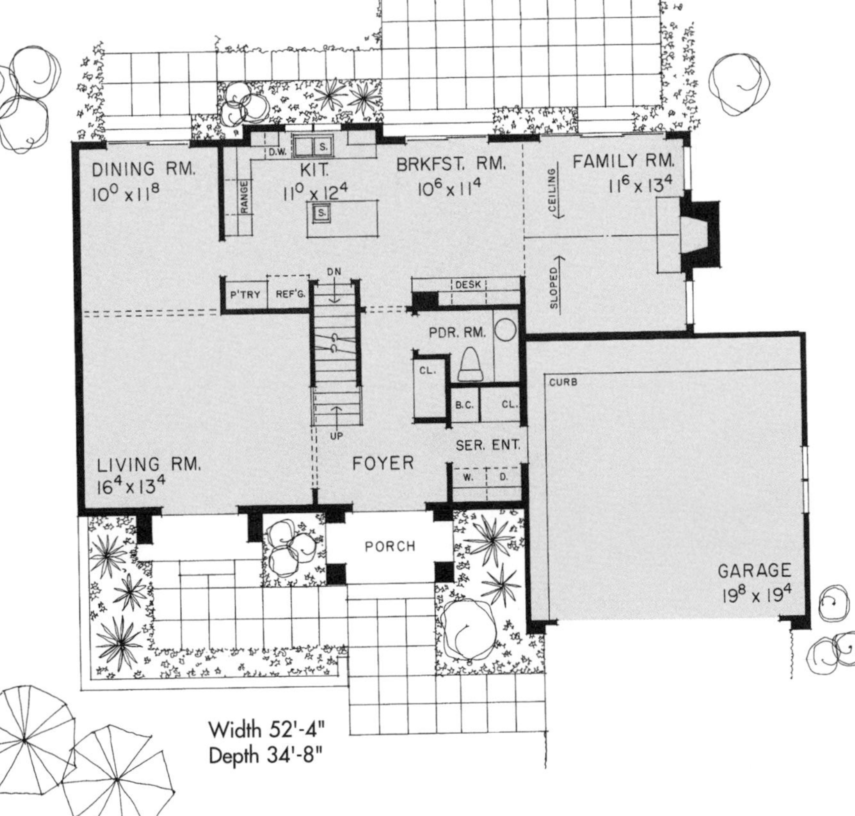
DINING RM.
$10^0 \times 11^8$
D.W.
S.
KIT.
$11^0 \times 12^4$
RANGE
S.
BRKFST. RM.
$10^6 \times 11^4$
CEILING
SLOPED
FAMILY RM.
$11^6 \times 13^4$
DN
P'TRY
REF'G.
DESK
PDR. RM.
CL.
B.C.
CL.
CURB
UP
SER. ENT.
W.
D.
LIVING RM.
$16^4 \times 13^4$
FOYER
PORCH
GARAGE
$19^8 \times 19^4$
Width 52'-4"
Depth 34'-8"

QUOTE ONE®

Cost to build? See page 516 to order complete cost estimate to build this house in your area!

Design by
Home Planners

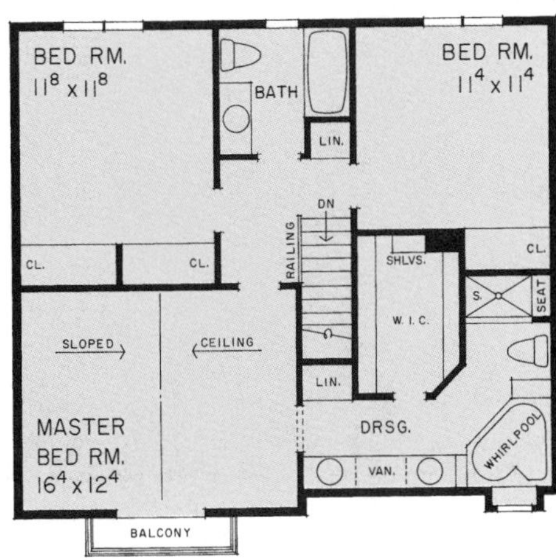
BED RM.
$11^8 \times 11^8$
BATH
LIN.
BED RM.
$11^4 \times 11^4$
DN
RAILING
CL.
CL.
SHLVS.
CL.
W. I. C.
S.
SEAT
SLOPED
CEILING
LIN.
MASTER
BED RM.
$16^4 \times 12^4$
DRSG.
VAN.
WHIRLPOOL
BALCONY

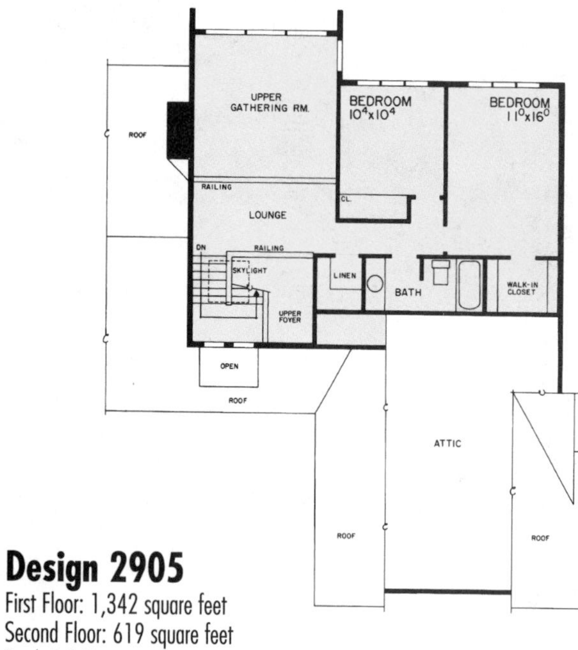
UPPER GATHERING RM.
BEDROOM
10^4x10^4
BEDROOM
11^0x16^0
ROOF
RAILING
LOUNGE
CL.
DN
RAILING
SKYLIGHT
LINEN
BATH
WALK-IN CLOSET
UPPER FOYER
OPEN
ROOF
ATTIC
ROOF
ROOF

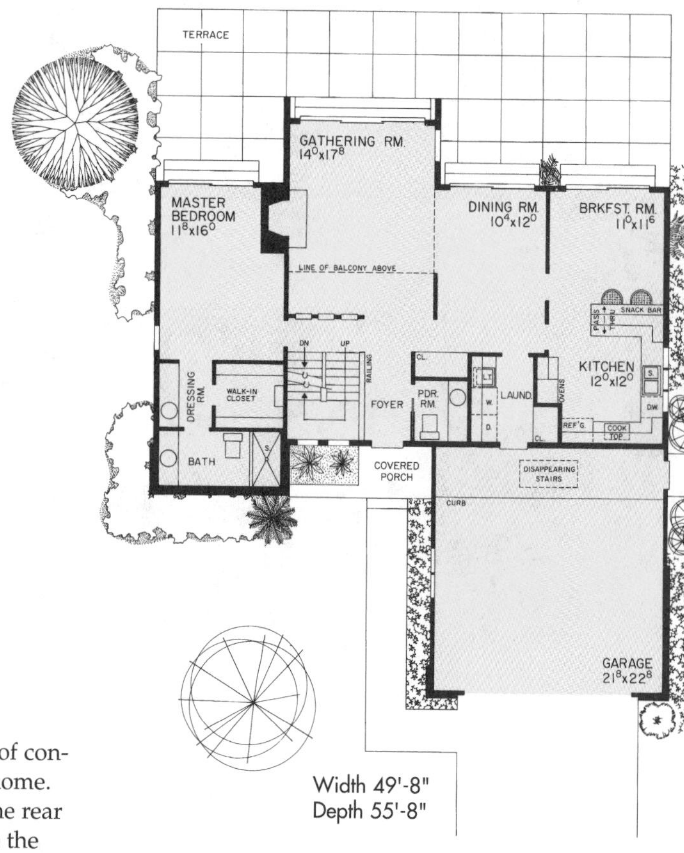
TERRACE
GATHERING RM.
14^0x17^8
MASTER BEDROOM
11^8x16^0
DINING RM.
10^4x12^0
BRKFST. RM.
11^0x11^6
LINE OF BALCONY ABOVE
SNACK BAR
DN
UP
CL.
DRESSING RM.
WALK-IN CLOSET
RAILING
FOYER
PDR. RM.
LAUND.
KITCHEN
12^0x12^0
OVENS
REF'G.
COOK TOP
DW
BATH
COVERED PORCH
DISAPPEARING STAIRS
CURB
GARAGE
21^8x22^8

Width 49'-8"
Depth 55'-8"

Design 2905

First Floor: 1,342 square feet
Second Floor: 619 square feet
Total: 1,961 square feet

L **D**

All of the livability in this plan is in the back! With this sort of configuration, this home makes a perfect lakefront or beachfront home. Each first-floor room, except the kitchen, maintains access to the rear terrace via sliding glass doors. However, the kitchen is open to the breakfast room and thus takes advantage of the view. The master bedroom delights with its private bath and walk-in closet. Two secondary bedrooms comprise the second floor. One utilizes a walk-in closet while both make use of a full hall bath. A lounge overlooks the foyer as well as the gathering room below.

QUOTE ONE®

Cost to build? See page 516 to order complete cost estimate to build this house in your area!

Design by
Home Planners

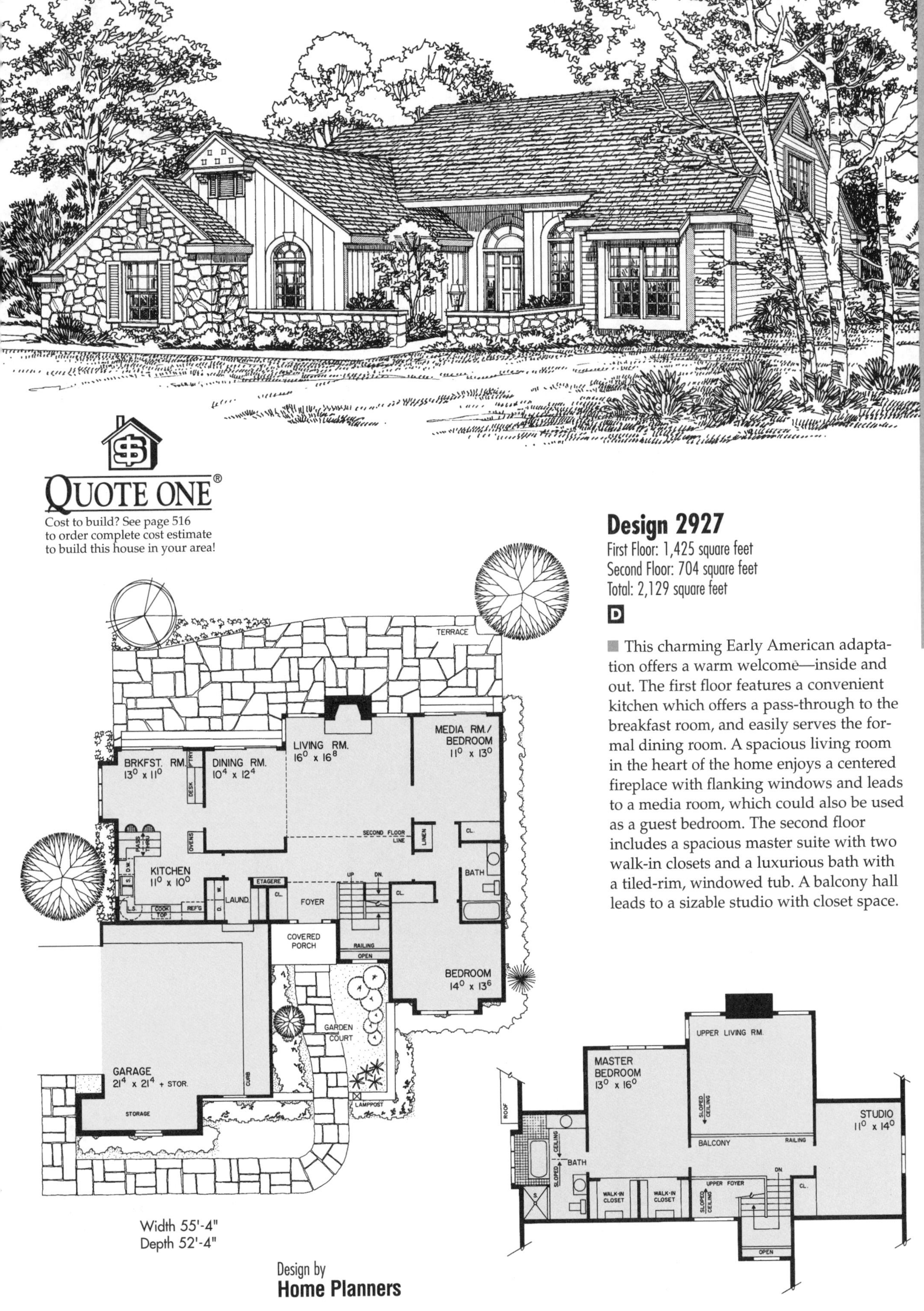
TERRACE
LIVING RM.
16⁰ x 16⁸
MEDIA RM./
BEDROOM
11⁰ x 13⁰
BRKFST. RM.
13⁰ x 11⁰
DINING RM.
10⁴ x 12⁴
PTRY
DESK
OVENS
PASS THRU
KITCHEN
11⁰ x 10⁰
COOK TOP
REF'G
LAUND.
ETAGERE
CL.
FOYER
UP
DN.
SECOND FLOOR LINE
LINEN
BATH
COVERED PORCH
RAILING
OPEN
BEDROOM
14⁰ x 13⁶
GARDEN COURT
GARAGE
21⁴ x 21⁴ + STOR.
STORAGE
CURB
LAMPPOST
Width 55'-4"
Depth 52'-4"
UPPER LIVING RM.
MASTER
BEDROOM
13⁰ x 16⁰
SLOPED CEILING
STUDIO
11⁰ x 14⁰
BALCONY
RAILING
ROOF
BATH
WALK-IN CLOSET
WALK-IN CLOSET
UPPER FOYER
OPEN

QUOTE ONE®

Cost to build? See page 516 to order complete cost estimate to build this house in your area!

Design 2927

First Floor: 1,425 square feet
Second Floor: 704 square feet
Total: 2,129 square feet

D

This charming Early American adaptation offers a warm welcome—inside and out. The first floor features a convenient kitchen which offers a pass-through to the breakfast room, and easily serves the formal dining room. A spacious living room in the heart of the home enjoys a centered fireplace with flanking windows and leads to a media room, which could also be used as a guest bedroom. The second floor includes a spacious master suite with two walk-in closets and a luxurious bath with a tiled-rim, windowed tub. A balcony hall leads to a sizable studio with closet space.

Design by
Home Planners

QUOTE ONE®
Cost to build? See page 516
to order complete cost estimate
to build this house in your area!

Design 2822

First Floor: 1,363 square feet
Second Floor: 351 square feet
Total: 1,714 square feet

L

Tailor-made for small families, this is a one-level design with second floor possibilities. The bonus room upstairs (please see alternate layout) can be nearly anything you want it to be: lounge, guest room, playroom for the kids—partitioned or open. Downstairs, a little space goes a long way: an extensive great room with extended hearth, a formal dining room with private covered porch and a master wing which includes a study, spacious bath with dressing area, walk-in closet and access to a hot tub/spa.

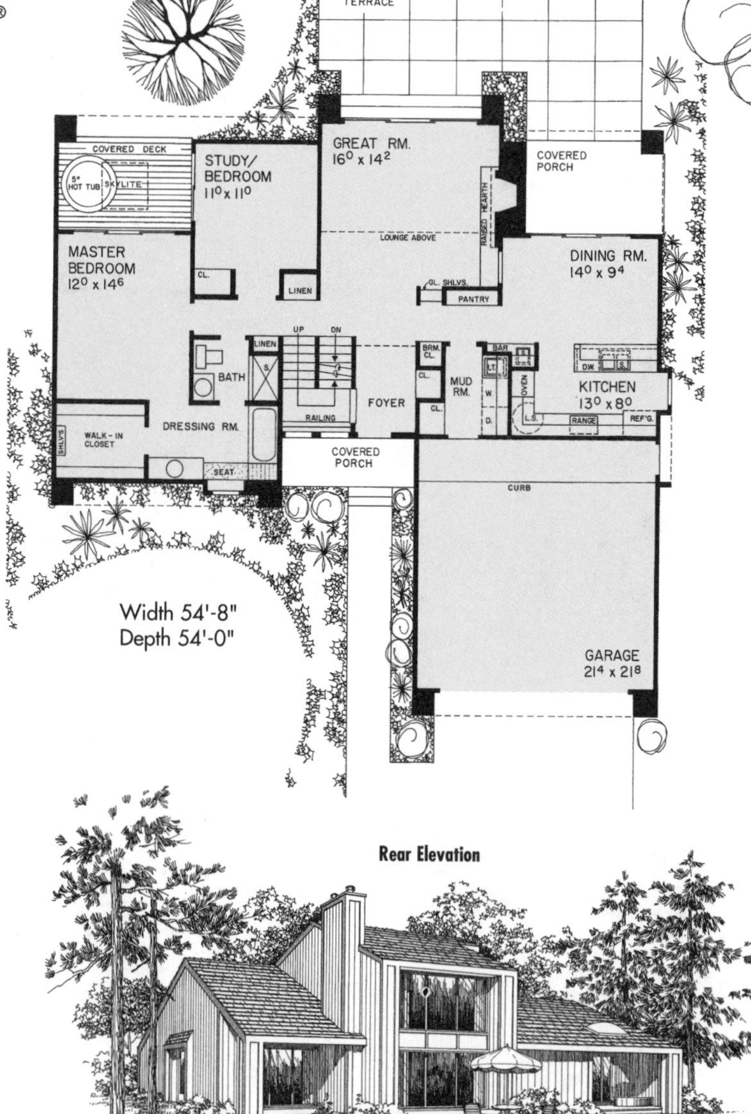
TERRACE
COVERED DECK
5' HOT TUB
SKYLITE
STUDY/ BEDROOM 11⁰ x 11⁰
GREAT RM. 16⁰ x 14²
COVERED PORCH
LOUNGE ABOVE
RAISED HEARTH
MASTER BEDROOM 12⁰ x 14⁶
CL.
LINEN
GL. SHLVS.
PANTRY
DINING RM. 14⁰ x 9⁴
UP
DN
LINEN
BATH
FOYER
BRM. CL.
CL.
MUD RM.
CL.
BAR
OVEN
D.W.
KITCHEN 13⁰ x 8⁰
RANGE
REF'G.
RAILING
WALK-IN CLOSET
SHLVS.
DRESSING RM.
SEAT
COVERED PORCH
CURB
Width 54'-8"
Depth 54'-0"
GARAGE 21⁴ x 21⁸
Rear Elevation

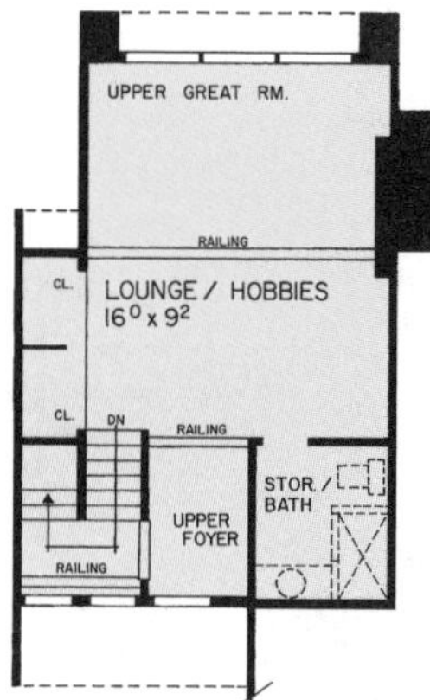
UPPER GREAT RM.
RAILING
LOUNGE / HOBBIES 16⁰ x 9²
CL.
CL.
DN
RAILING
STOR. / BATH
UPPER FOYER
RAILING

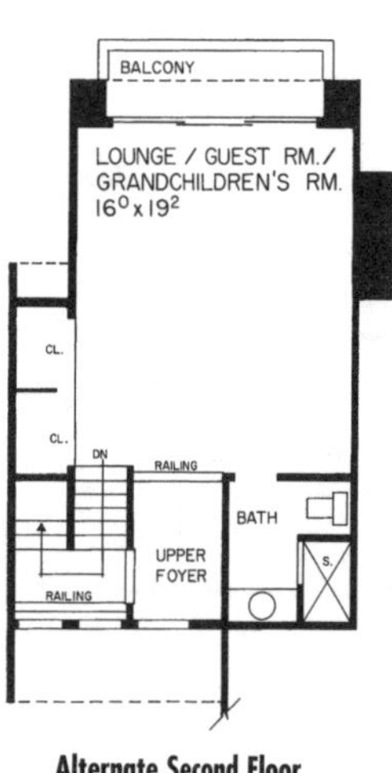
BALCONY
LOUNGE / GUEST RM. / GRANDCHILDREN'S RM. 16⁰ x 19²
CL.
CL.
DN
RAILING
BATH
UPPER FOYER
RAILING

Alternate Second Floor

Design by
Home Planners

Design Q488

Square Footage: 1,115
Unfinished Lower Level: 626 square feet

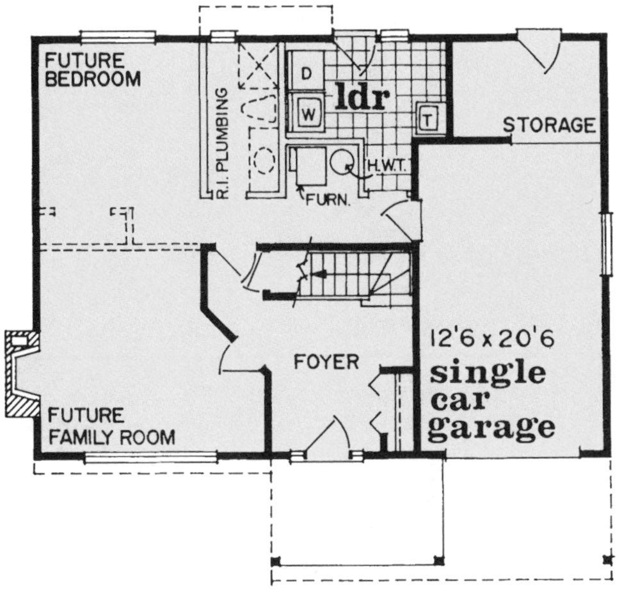

■ With the main living areas on the second floor, this plan makes a grand vacation retreat. The covered entry opens to a foyer of 175 square feet. An open rail staircase leads to the living/dining room combination with fireplace and box window. Sliding glass doors in the dining room open to the wide sundeck that shades the patio below. The kitchen and breakfast nook are nearby. The kitchen has a U-shaped workcenter and a window over the sink. Three bedrooms are found across the back of the plan. The master has a full bath and large wall closet. Family bedrooms have walk-in closets and share a full bath. The central hallway has skylights to keep it bright. If you choose to finish the lower level, you'll add 626 square feet of space for a bedroom, a full bath and a family room. Note the large storage area in the garage.

FUTURE BEDROOM
R.I. PLUMBING
ldr
FURN.
H.W.T.
STORAGE
FOYER
12'6 x 20'6
single car garage
FUTURE FAMILY ROOM

Width 39'-0"
Depth 34'-6"

Design by
Select Home Designs

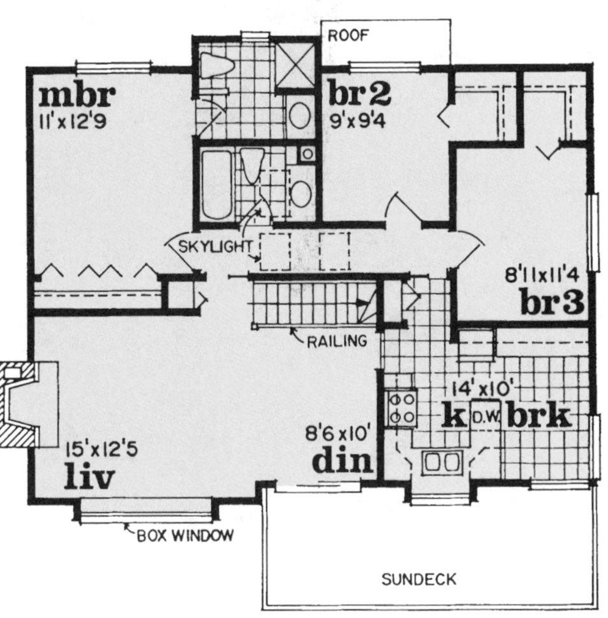
ROOF
mbr
11'x12'9
br2
9'x9'4
SKYLIGHT
8'11x11'4
br3
RAILING
14'x10'
k
D.W.
brk
15'x12'5
liv
8'6x10'
din
BOX WINDOW
SUNDECK

Design Q241

First Floor: 1,016 square feet
Second Floor: 766 square feet
Total: 1,782 square feet

This delightful contemporary design features vertical wood siding and large windows in the living room and dining room. Both the living room and family room have warming fireplaces. The family room also features sliding glass doors to the rear patio. The U-shaped kitchen and the breakfast nook combine their space to provide an open casual working and eating area. A railed gallery overlooks the foyer from the second floor. It leads to a master suite with walk-in closet and full bath and two family bedrooms with wall closets. Of special note in this design: the powder room in the entry hall, a large laundry room and a two-car garage. Plans include details for both a basement and a crawlspace foundation.

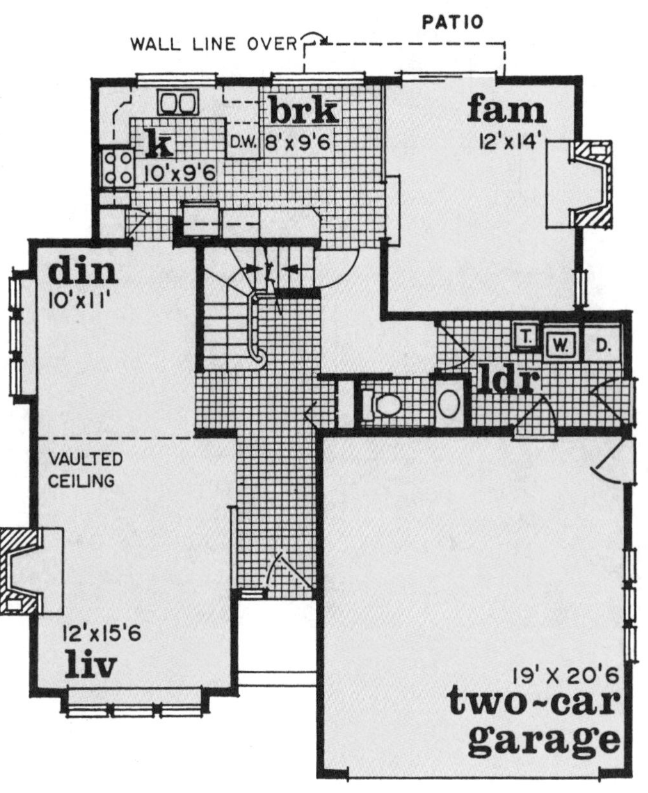

PATIO
WALL LINE OVER
brk
8'x9'6
D.W.
k
10'x9'6
fam
12'x14'
din
10'x11'
T.
W.
D.
ldr
VAULTED
CEILING
12'x15'6
liv
19' X 20'6
two-car
garage

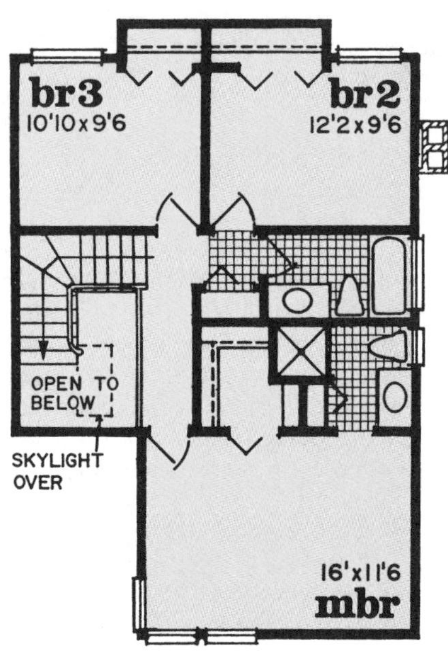

br3
10'10x9'6
br2
12'2x9'6
OPEN TO
BELOW
SKYLIGHT
OVER
16'x11'6
mbr

Width 38'-0"
Depth 43'-0"

Design by
Select Home Designs

© Copyright Select Home Designs. All rights reserved

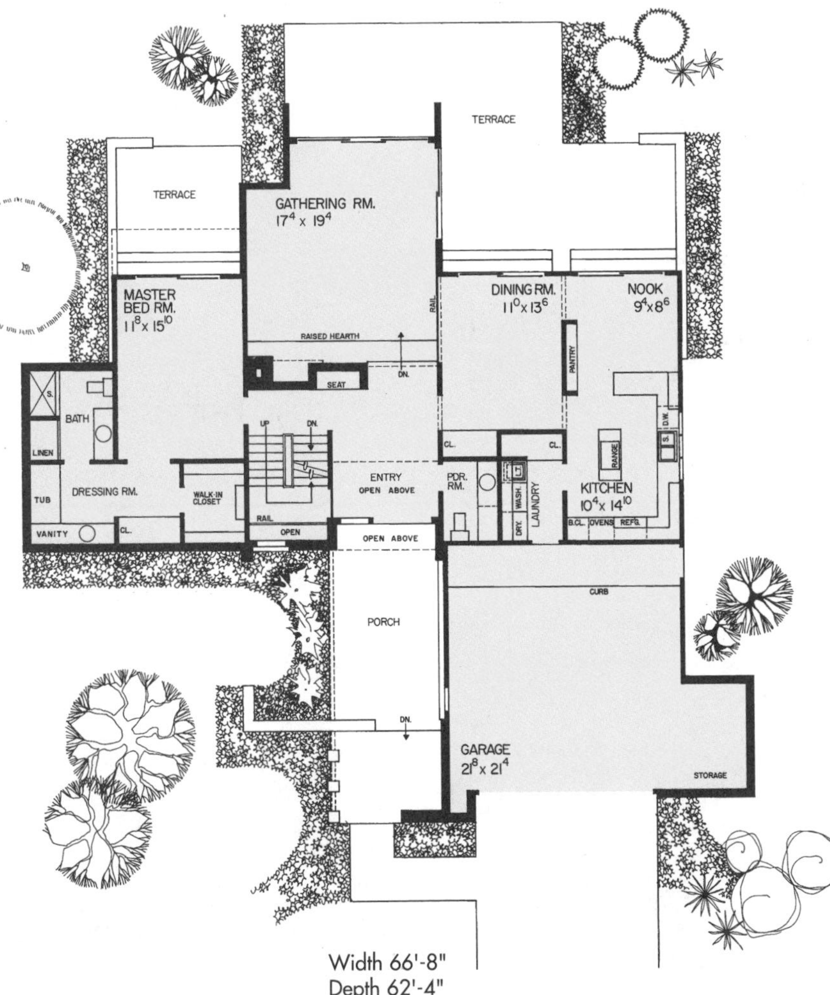

TERRACE
TERRACE
GATHERING RM.
17^{4} x 19^{4}
MASTER BED RM.
11^{8} x 15^{0}
DINING RM.
11^{0} x 13^{6}
NOOK
9^{4} x 8^{6}
RAISED HEARTH
SEAT
PANTRY
RAIL
DN.
BATH
LINEN
TUB
DRESSING RM.
WALK-IN CLOSET
VANITY
CL.
UP
DN.
ENTRY
OPEN ABOVE
PDR. RM.
LAUNDRY
WASH
DRY
KITCHEN
10^{4} x 14^{0}
RANGE
D.W.
B.CL.
OVENS
REFG.
RAIL
OPEN
OPEN ABOVE
PORCH
CURB
DN.
GARAGE
21^{8} x 21^{4}
STORAGE
Width 66'-8"
Depth 62'-4"

Design 2729

First Floor: 1,590 square feet
Second Floor: 756 square feet
Total: 2,346 square feet

L

■ Entering this home will be a pleasure through the sheltered walkway to the double front doors. And the pleasure and beauty does not stop there. The entry hall and sunken gathering room are open to the upstairs for added dimension. Three bedrooms include a lavish master suite. There are fine indoor/outdoor living relationships in this design. Note the private terrace, a living terrace, plus the balcony.

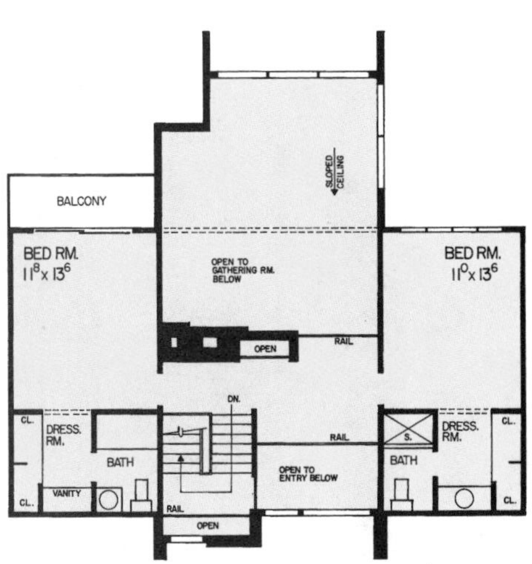

BALCONY
SLOPED CEILING
BED RM.
11^{8} x 13^{6}
OPEN TO GATHERING RM. BELOW
BED RM.
11^{0} x 13^{6}
OPEN
RAIL
DN.
CL.
DRESS. RM.
BATH
VANITY
RAIL
OPEN TO ENTRY BELOW
BATH
DRESS. RM.
OPEN

Design by
Home Planners

Design 2925

First Floor: 1,128 square feet
Second Floor: 844 square feet
Total: 1,972 square feet

■ This two-story contemporary design features expansive overhanging roofs that make a distinctive design statement. The front entry is noteworthy for its panelled double doors below the large radial head window. This window and the narrow fixed windows to the right of the doors flood the foyer with natural light. The dining room is the center of the plan. To either side are the kitchen and breakfast room and the grand gathering room. A through-fireplace connects the dining room and gathering room. A cozy media room has built-ins and a nearby powder room that make it a handy guest room. Upstairs are two bedrooms—one a master suite with fireplace and whirlpool tub.

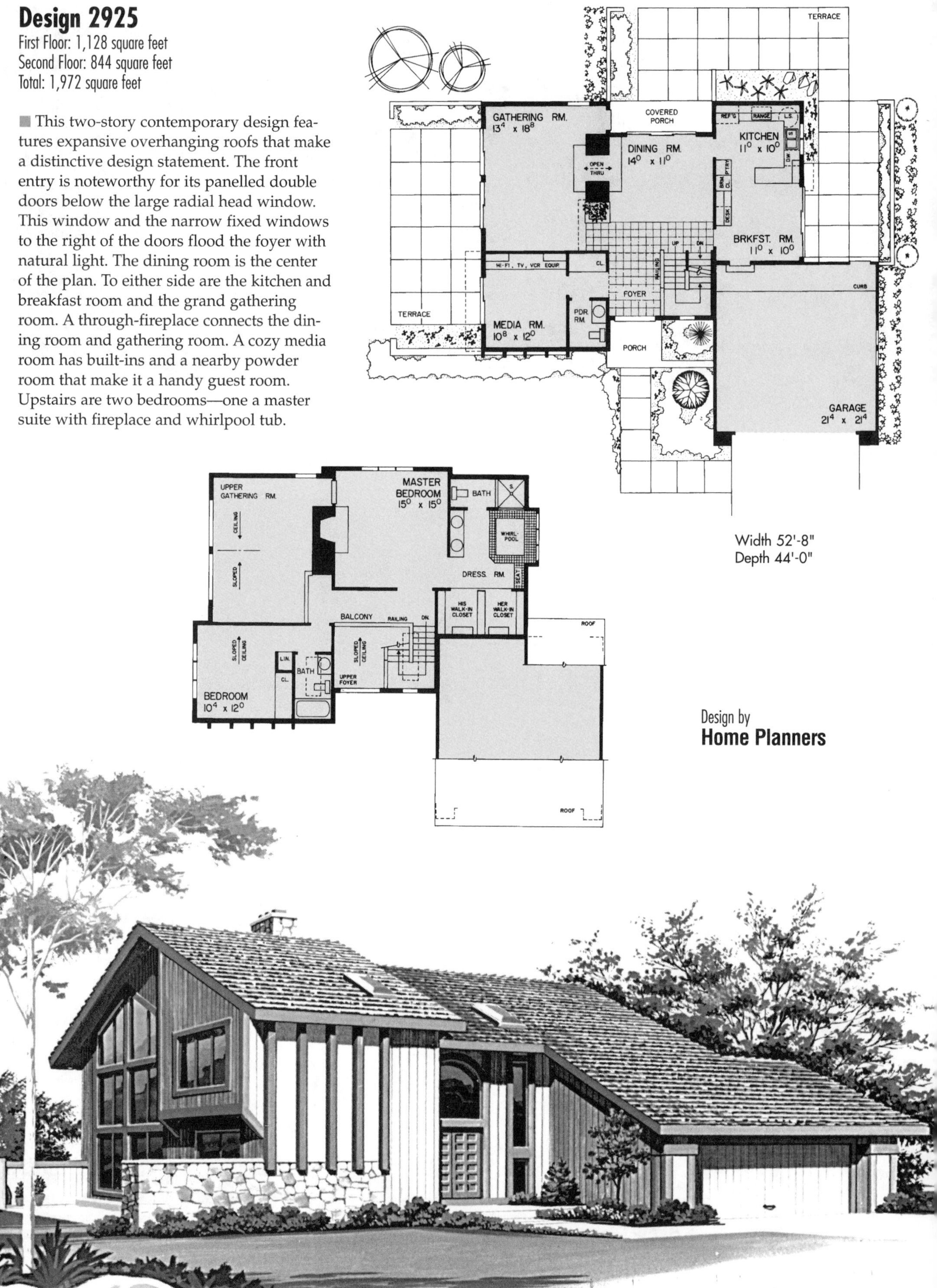

TERRACE
GATHERING RM. 13^4 x 18^8
COVERED PORCH
DINING RM. 14^0 x 11^0
OPEN THRU
KITCHEN 11^0 x 10^0
REF'G
RANGE
BRKFST. RM. 11^0 x 10^0
HI-FI, TV, VCR EQUIP.
CL.
FOYER
RAILING
UP
DN
TERRACE
MEDIA RM. 10^8 x 12^0
PDR RM.
PORCH
CURB
GARAGE 21^4 x 21^4
UPPER GATHERING RM.
CEILING
SLOPED
MASTER BEDROOM 15^0 x 15^0
BATH
WHIRL-POOL
DRESS. RM.
SEAT
HIS WALK-IN CLOSET
HER WALK-IN CLOSET
BALCONY
RAILING
DN.
ROOF
SLOPED CEILING
LIN.
CL.
BATH
UPPER FOYER
BEDROOM 10^4 x 12^0
ROOF

Width 52'-8"
Depth 44'-0"

Design by
Home Planners

Design by
Home Planners

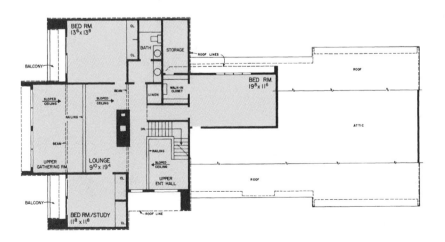

QUOTE ONE®

Cost to build? See page 516
to order complete cost estimate
to build this house in your area!

Width 90'-0"
Depth 46'-0"

Design 2781

First Floor: 2,132 square feet
Second Floor: 1,156 square feet
Total: 3,288 square feet

L D

This beautifully designed two-story provides an eye-catching exterior. The floor plan is a perfect complement. The front kitchen features an island range, adjacent breakfast nook and pass-through to a formal dining room. The master suite offers a spacious walk-in closet and dressing room. The side terrace can be reached from the master suite, the gathering room and the study. The second floor contains three bedrooms and storage space galore. The center lounge offers a sloped ceiling and skylight.

Design 2711

First Floor: 975 square feet
Second Floor: 1,024 square feet
Total: 1,999 square feet

L **D**

■ Sleek, modern lines define this two-story contemporary home. Open planning in the living areas create a spaciousness found in much larger plans. The formal dining area and informal eating counter, both easily served by the U-shaped kitchen, share the cozy warmth of the centered fireplace and generous views to the rear grounds offered by the gathering room. Amenities abound in the second-floor master suite with a private balcony, walk-in closet, separate dressing area and knee-space vanity. Two secondary bedrooms and a full bath complete this floor, perfect for guests or visiting relatives—or make one room a study or hobby room.

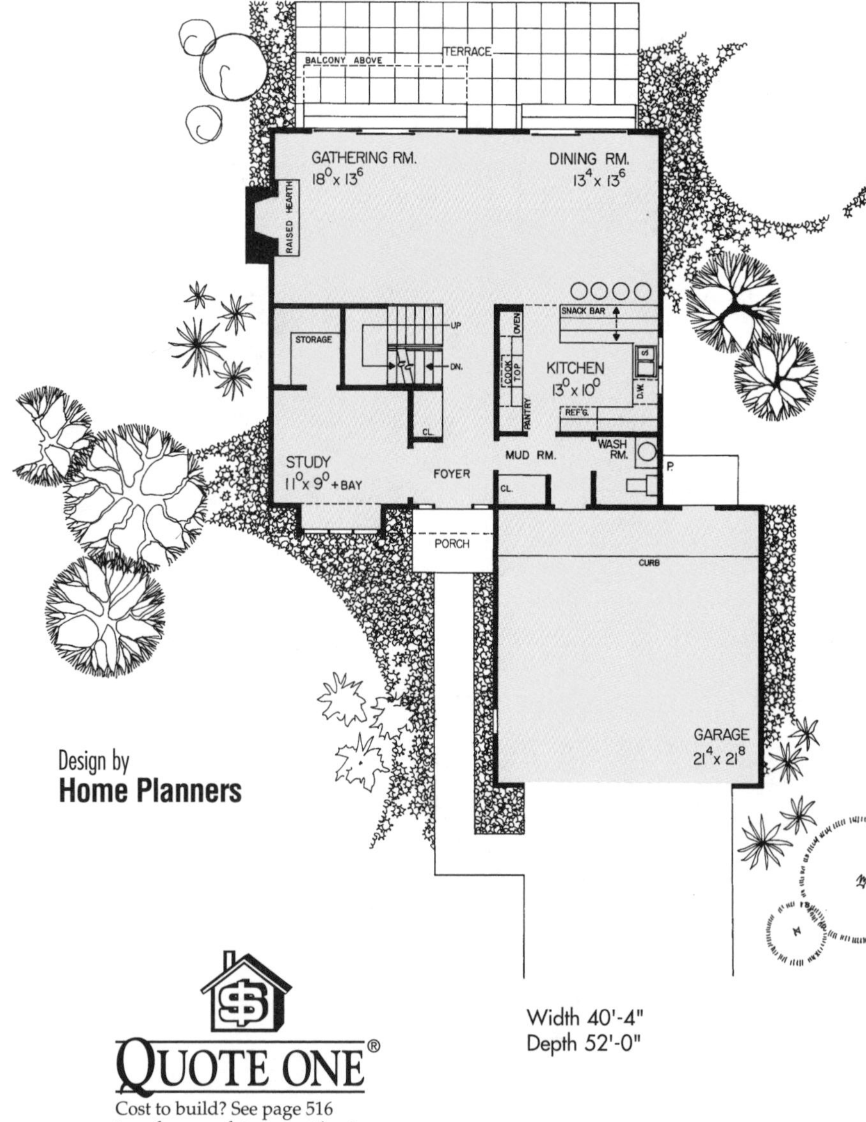

BALCONY ABOVE
TERRACE
GATHERING RM.
$18^{0} \times 13^{6}$
DINING RM.
$13^{4} \times 13^{6}$
RAISED HEARTH
SNACK BAR
STORAGE
UP
DN.
OVEN
COOK TOP
KITCHEN
$13^{0} \times 10^{0}$
D.W.
REF'G.
PANTRY
CL.
STUDY
$11^{0} \times 9^{0}$ + BAY
FOYER
MUD RM.
WASH RM.
CL.
P.
PORCH
CURB
GARAGE
$21^{4} \times 21^{8}$

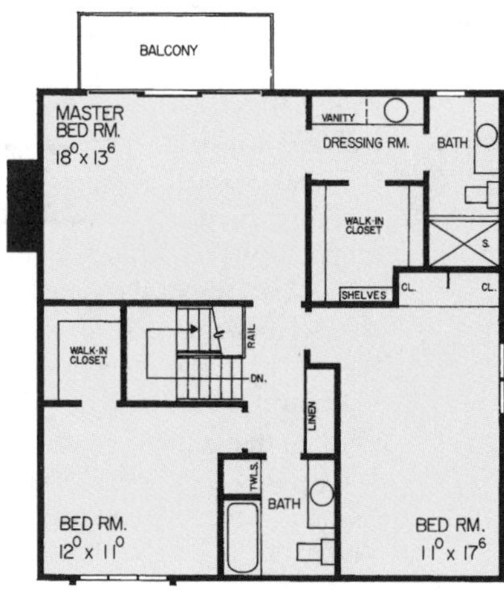

BALCONY
MASTER BED RM.
$18^{0} \times 13^{6}$
VANITY
DRESSING RM.
BATH
WALK-IN CLOSET
S.
SHELVES
CL.
CL.
WALK-IN CLOSET
RAIL
DN.
LINEN
TWLS.
BATH
BED RM.
$12^{0} \times 11^{0}$
BED RM.
$11^{0} \times 17^{6}$

Design by
Home Planners

Width 40'-4"
Depth 52'-0"

QUOTE ONE®

Cost to build? See page 516 to order complete cost estimate to build this house in your area!

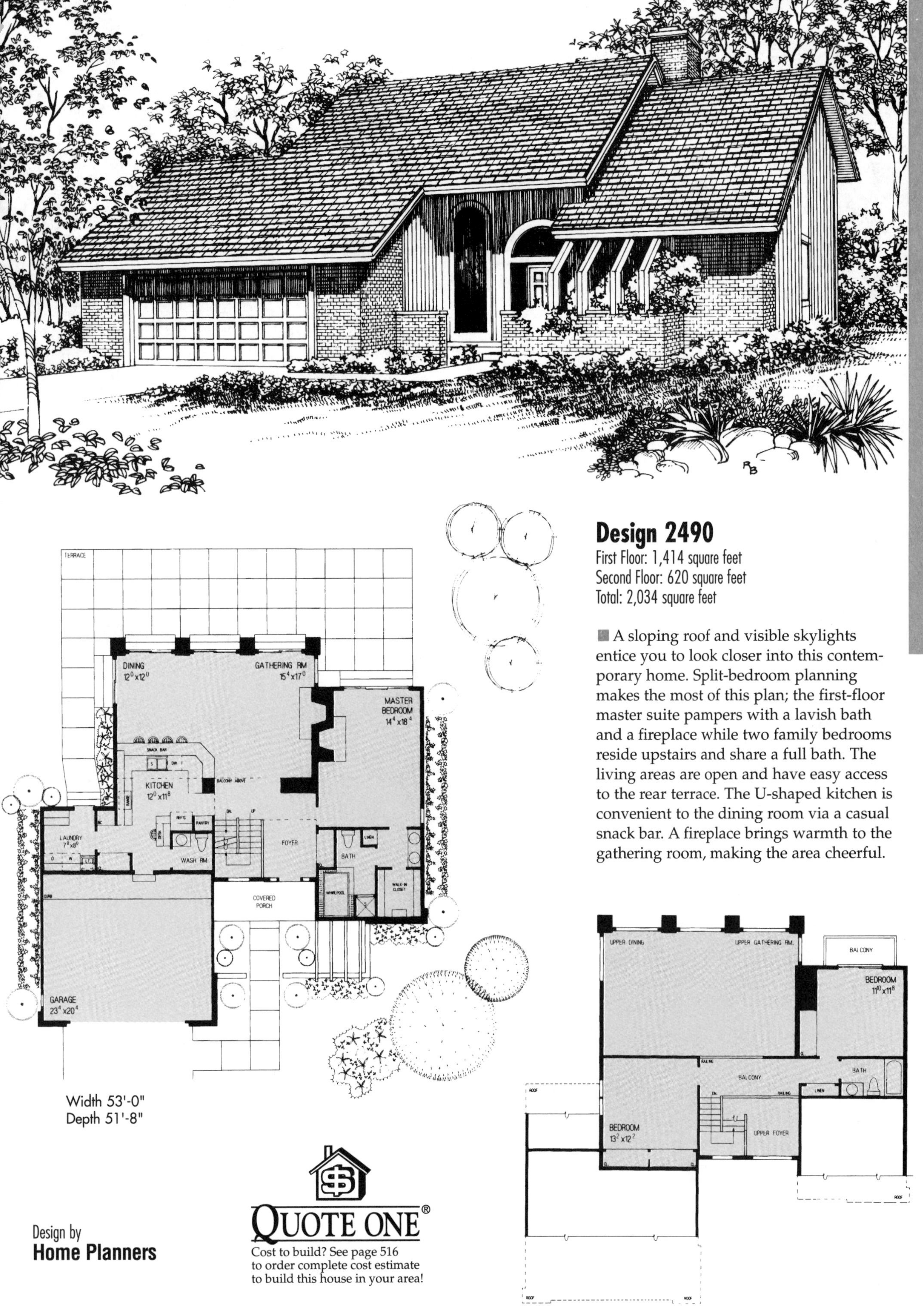
TERRACE
DINING
12⁰x12⁰
GATHERING RM
15⁴x17⁰
MASTER
BEDROOM
14⁴x18⁴
SNACK BAR
KITCHEN
12⁰x11⁸
BALCONY ABOVE
LAUNDRY
7⁸x8⁰
PANTRY
WASH RM
FOYER
BATH
WALK-IN CLOSET
COVERED PORCH
GARAGE
23⁴x20⁴
UPPER DINING
UPPER GATHERING RM.
BALCONY
BEDROOM
11¹⁰x11⁸
BATH
BALCONY
BEDROOM
13²x12²
UPPER FOYER

Design 2490

First Floor: 1,414 square feet
Second Floor: 620 square feet
Total: 2,034 square feet

A sloping roof and visible skylights entice you to look closer into this contemporary home. Split-bedroom planning makes the most of this plan; the first-floor master suite pampers with a lavish bath and a fireplace while two family bedrooms reside upstairs and share a full bath. The living areas are open and have easy access to the rear terrace. The U-shaped kitchen is convenient to the dining room via a casual snack bar. A fireplace brings warmth to the gathering room, making the area cheerful.

Width 53'-0"
Depth 51'-8"

Design by
Home Planners

QUOTE ONE®
Cost to build? See page 516 to order complete cost estimate to build this house in your area!

Design 2920

First Floor: 3,067 square feet
Second Floor: 648 square feet
Total: 3,715 square feet
Sun Room: 296 square feet

L **D**

This contemporary design has a great deal to offer. A fireplace opens up to both the living room and country kitchen. The kitchen is a gourmet's delight, with a huge walk-in pantry, a deluxe work island which includes a snack bar, and easy access to the formal dining room. A media room has plenty of storage and offers access to the rear terrace. Privacy is the key word when describing the sleeping areas. The first-floor master bedroom is away from the traffic of the house and features a dressing/exercise room, a whirlpool tub and shower and a spacious walk-in closet. Two more bedrooms and a full bath are on the second floor. The three-car garage is arranged so that the owners have use of a double-garage with an attached single on reserve for guests. The cheerful sunroom adds 296 square feet to the total.

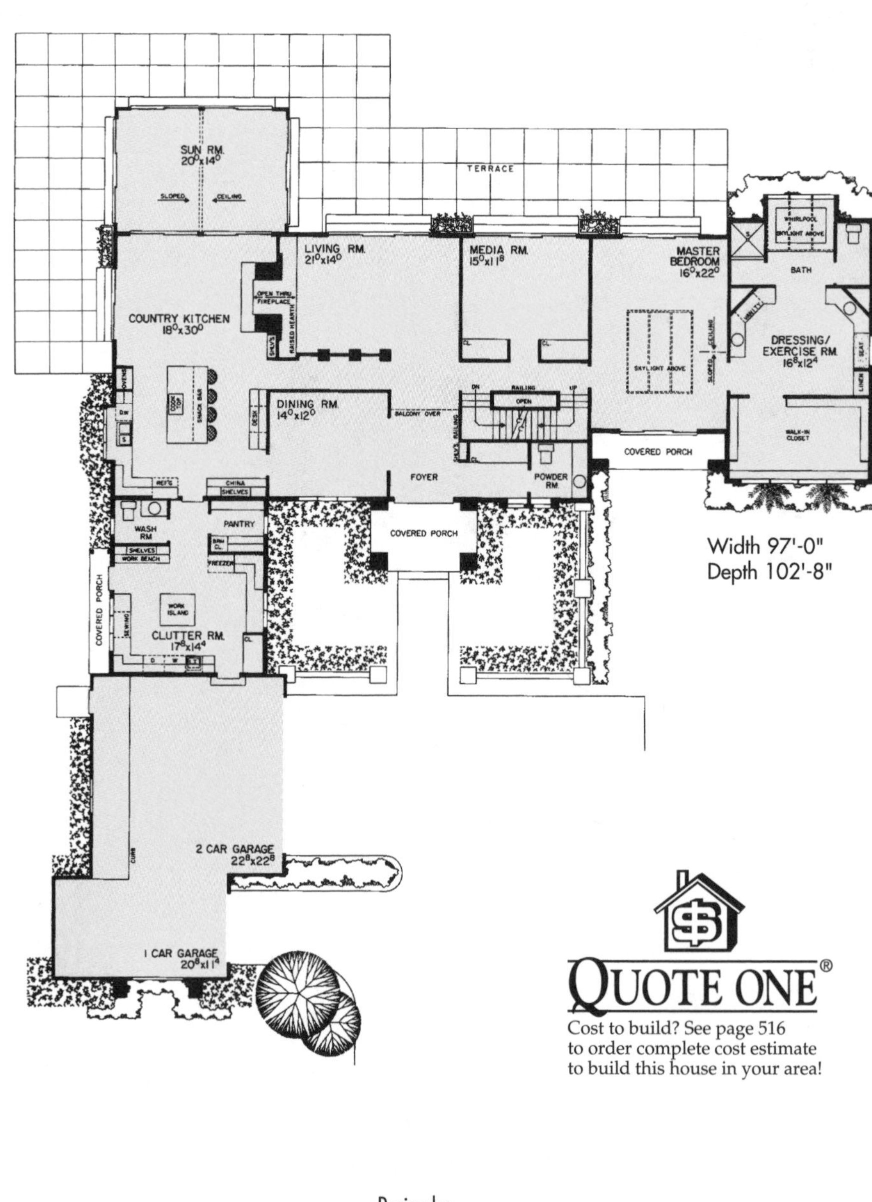

SUN RM. 20⁰x14⁰
TERRACE
LIVING RM. 21⁰x14⁰
MEDIA RM. 15⁰x11⁸
MASTER BEDROOM 16⁰x22⁰
WHIRLPOOL
BATH
DRESSING/ EXERCISE RM. 16⁸x12⁴
WALK-IN CLOSET
COUNTRY KITCHEN 18⁰x30⁰
OPEN THRU FIREPLACE
DINING RM. 14⁰x12⁰
FOYER
POWDER RM.
COVERED PORCH
COVERED PORCH
WASH RM
PANTRY
CLUTTER RM. 17⁶x14⁴
WORK ISLAND
COVERED PORCH
2 CAR GARAGE 22⁸x22⁸
1 CAR GARAGE 20⁸x11⁴

Width 97'-0"
Depth 102'-8"

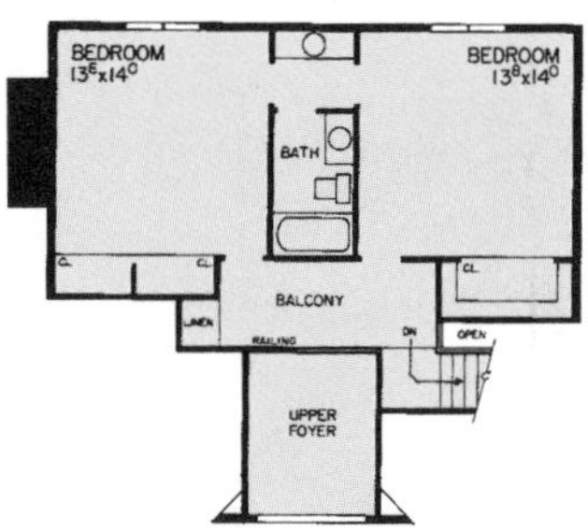

BEDROOM 13⁶x14⁰
BEDROOM 13⁶x14⁰
BATH
BALCONY
UPPER FOYER

QUOTE ONE®

Cost to build? See page 516 to order complete cost estimate to build this house in your area!

Design by
Home Planners

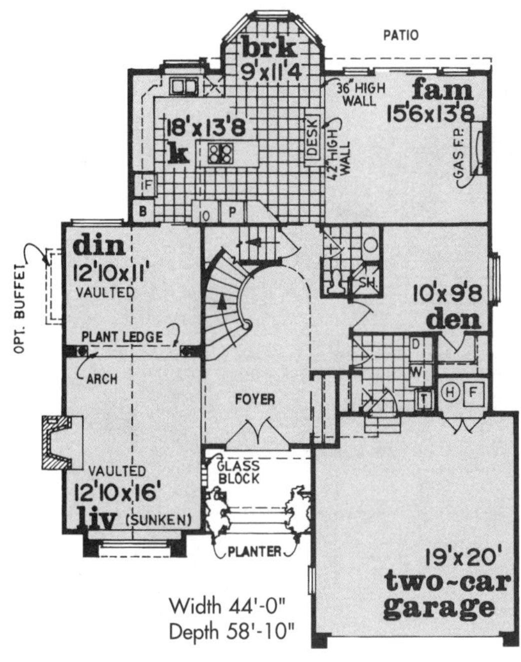
PATIO
brk
9'x11'4
36" HIGH WALL
fam
15'6x13'8
18'x13'8
k
DESK
42" HIGH WALL
GAS F.P.
F
B
P
din
12'10x11'
VAULTED
OPT. BUFFET
SH
10'x9'8
den
PLANT LEDGE
ARCH
FOYER
D
W
T
H
F
VAULTED
12'10x16'
liv (SUNKEN)
GLASS BLOCK
PLANTER
19'x20'
two-car garage
Width 44'-0"
Depth 58'-10"

Design Q396

First Floor: 1,463 square feet
Second Floor: 872 square feet
Total: 2,335 square feet

Design by
Select Home Designs

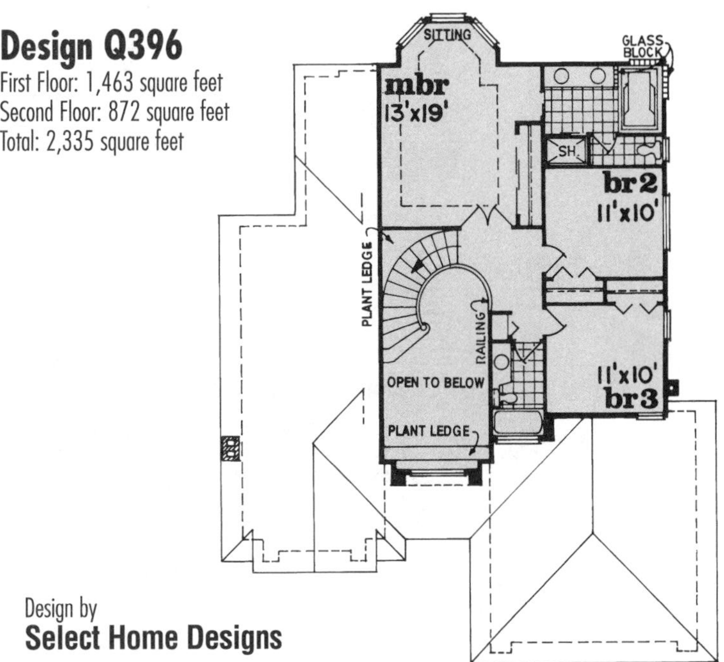
SITTING
GLASS BLOCK
mbr
13'x19'
SH
br2
11'x10'
PLANT LEDGE
RAILING
OPEN TO BELOW
11'x10'
br3
PLANT LEDGE

Alternate Front Elevation

■ Two different facades are available for this home: a California stucco or a traditional brick and siding version. Details for both options are included in the plans. The interior plan begins with a vaulted foyer hosting a sweeping curved staircase, and then spilling into a sunken living room with masonry fireplace, vaulted ceiling and a full, floor-to-ceiling half-round window. If you choose, you can include buffet space in the dining room. The kitchen features a pantry, center cooking island, built-in desk and sunny breakfast bay. A half-wall separates this area from the family room where you'll find a gas fireplace and sliding glass doors to the patio. A den with walk-in closet and nearby bath can easily double as guest space. The master suite on the second floor boasts a drop ceiling, a bay-windowed sitting area, a spacious wall closet and lavish master bath. Family bedrooms share a full bath. Plans include details for both a basement and a crawlspace foundation.

Design Q322

First Floor: 1,019 square feet
Second Floor: 750 square feet
Total: 1,769 square feet

■ This design may be finished in either horizontal siding or stucco with different window treatments. Plans include details for both exteriors. Inside, a fine floor plan reigns. A floor-to-ceiling window wall accentuates the vaulted ceiling in the living room and carries light into the open dining room nearby. The living room is further graced by a fireplace; the dining room has buffet space and a box-bay window. The step-saving U-shaped kitchen has an attached light-filled breakfast bay. Both are open to the family room, where a fireplace keeps things cozy—note the built-in audio-visual center. Sliding glass doors lead to a rear patio. A laundry rounds out the second floor. It leads to the two-car garage at the side. Second-floor bedrooms include a master suite with large wall closet, window seats in the bedroom and the bath, and a whirlpool tub. Family bedrooms share a full bath. Plans include details for both a basement and a crawlspace foundation.

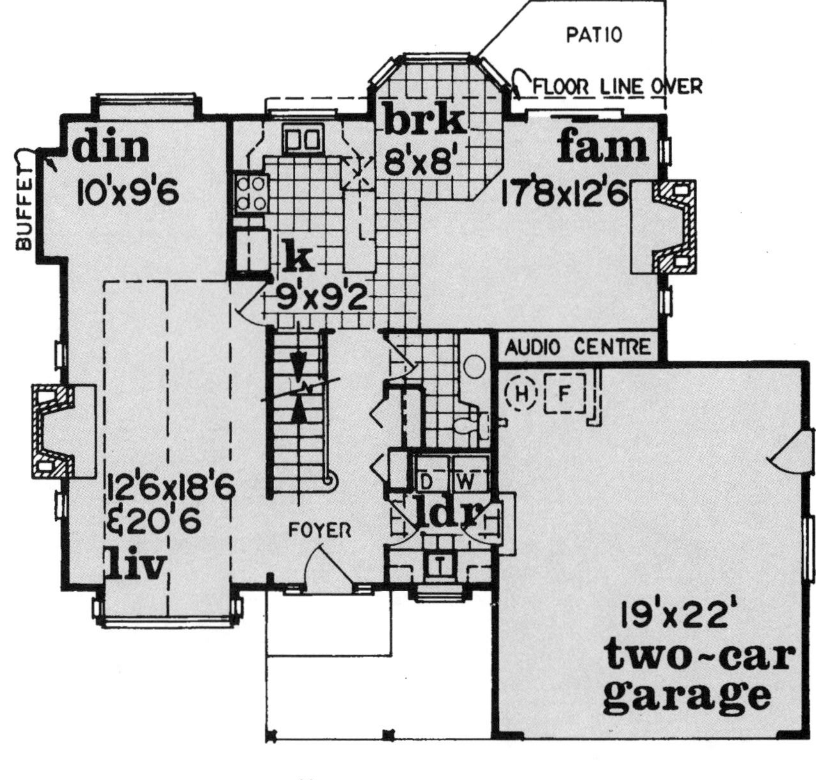
PATIO
FLOOR LINE OVER
din
10'x9'6
BUFFET
brk
8'x8'
fam
17'8x12'6
k
9'x9'2
AUDIO CENTRE
H
F
D
W
ldr
T
12'6x18'6
&20'6
liv
FOYER
19'x22'
two-car
garage

Width 47'-0"
Depth 41'-6"

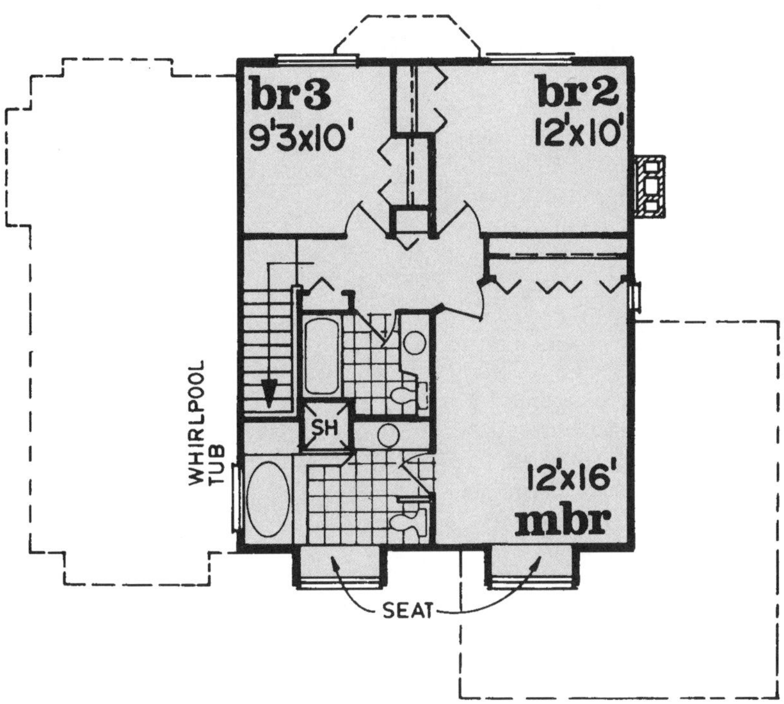
br3
9'3x10'
br2
12'x10'
WHIRLPOOL TUB
SH
12'x16'
mbr
SEAT

Design by
Select Home Designs

Design Q390

First Floor: 1,353 square feet
Second Floor: 899 square feet
Total: 2,252 square feet
Bonus Room: 183 square feet

Design by
Select Home Designs

■ This three-bedroom plan has bonus space and offers two attractive exterior finishes: horizontal siding with brick detailing or California stucco. Plans include details for both. Interior details make the floor plan unique. A plant ledge visually separates the vaulted foyer from the sunken living room. Note the fireplace and window seat here. A coffered ceiling, optional buffet recess and elegant archway distinguish the dining room. The nearby L-shaped kitchen, with center cooking island, adjoins a sunny breakfast room and large family room. A private den could serve as guest space if needed. On the second floor are three bedrooms and bonus space to develop into a fourth bedroom if needed, adding 183 square feet to the total. The master suite has a coffered ceiling and bath with raised tub and shower. Family bedrooms share a full bath. If you find that a two-car garage is not sufficient, plans include options for a triple garage. Plans include details for both a basement and a crawlspace foundation.

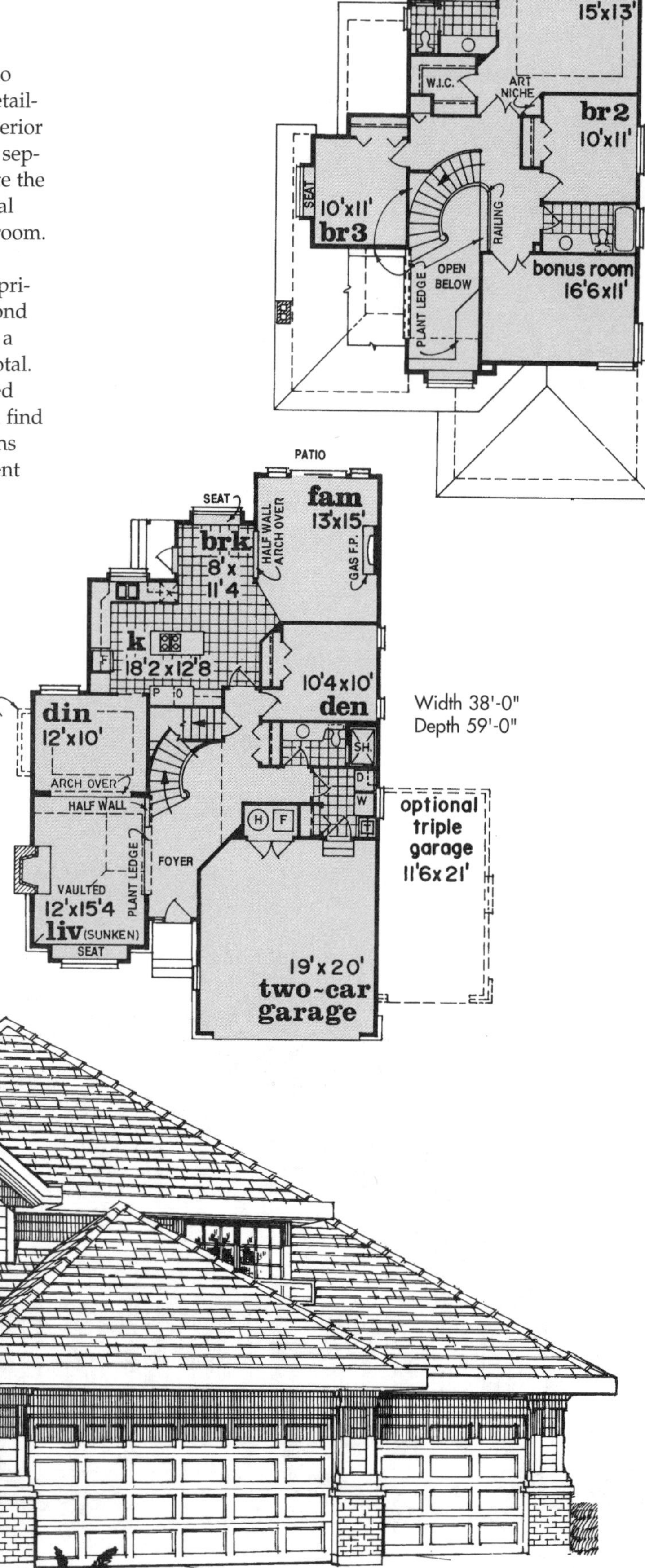
SH
mbr
15'x13'
W.I.C.
ART NICHE
br2
10'x11'
SEAT
10'x11'
br3
RAILING
OPEN BELOW
PLANT LEDGE
bonus room
16'6x11'
PATIO
SEAT
fam
13'x15'
brk
8'x 11'4
HALF WALL ARCH OVER
GAS F.P.
k
18'2x12'8
10'4x10'
den
OPT BUFFET
din
12'x10'
ARCH OVER
HALF WALL
SH.
D
W
H
F
optional triple garage 11'6x21'
FOYER
VAULTED
12'x15'4
liv (SUNKEN)
PLANT LEDGE
SEAT
19'x20'
two-car garage
Width 38'-0"
Depth 59'-0"

Alternate Elevation

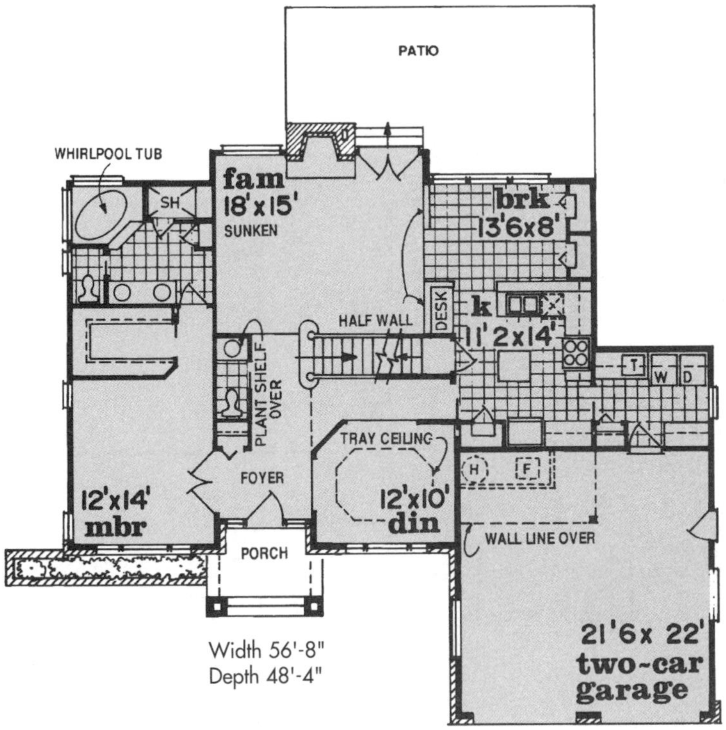

Design Q385

First Floor: 1,445 square feet
Second Floor: 652 square feet
Total: 2,097 square feet

■ A portico entry, graceful arches and brick detailing provide appeal and a low-maintenance exterior for this design. A half-circle transom over the entry lights the two-story foyer while a plant shelf lines the hallway to the sunken family room. This living space holds a vaulted ceiling, masonry fireplace and French-door access to the railed patio. The nearby kitchen has a center prep island, built-in desk overlooking the family room and extensive pantries in the breakfast area. The formal dining room has a tray ceiling and access to the foyer and the central hall. The master suite is on the first level for privacy and convenience. It features a walk-in closet and lavish bath with twin vanities, whirlpool tub and separate shower. Family bedrooms are on the second floor. Bedroom 4 and Bedroom 2 boast built-in desks. Plans include details for both a basement and a crawlspace foundation.

Width 56'-8"
Depth 48'-4"

Design by
Select Home Designs

Rear Elevation

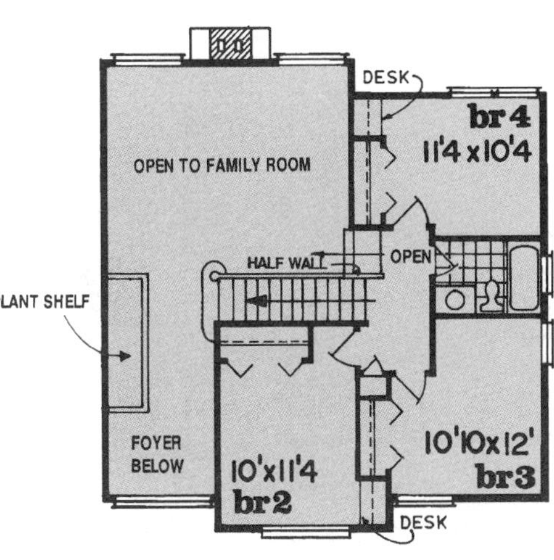
DESK
br4
11'4 x10'4
OPEN TO FAMILY ROOM
HALF WALL
OPEN
PLANT SHELF
FOYER BELOW
10'x11'4
br2
10'10x12'
br3
DESK

Design 3458

First Floor: 1,617 square feet
Second Floor: 725 square feet
Total: 2,342 square feet

L **D**

■ Brick veneer and horizontal siding blend beautifully with radial head windows and five gables to create this transitional exterior. The interior plan offers generous second-floor bedroom space for "visiting" family members and guests. Informal and formal living areas are perfectly blended in the first-floor plan, with living and dining rooms just off the foyer, and the two-story family room directly ahead, offering a dramatic view of the rear grounds. This is a comfortable area, open to the breakfast room, with built-in bookcases flanking the centered fireplace with tile hearth, and rear terrace access. In the U-shaped kitchen, a snack bar caters to on-the-run meals. The upstairs balcony hall offers an overlook to the family room below. Bonus space is available in the basement, should the development of a recreational or hobby area be desired.

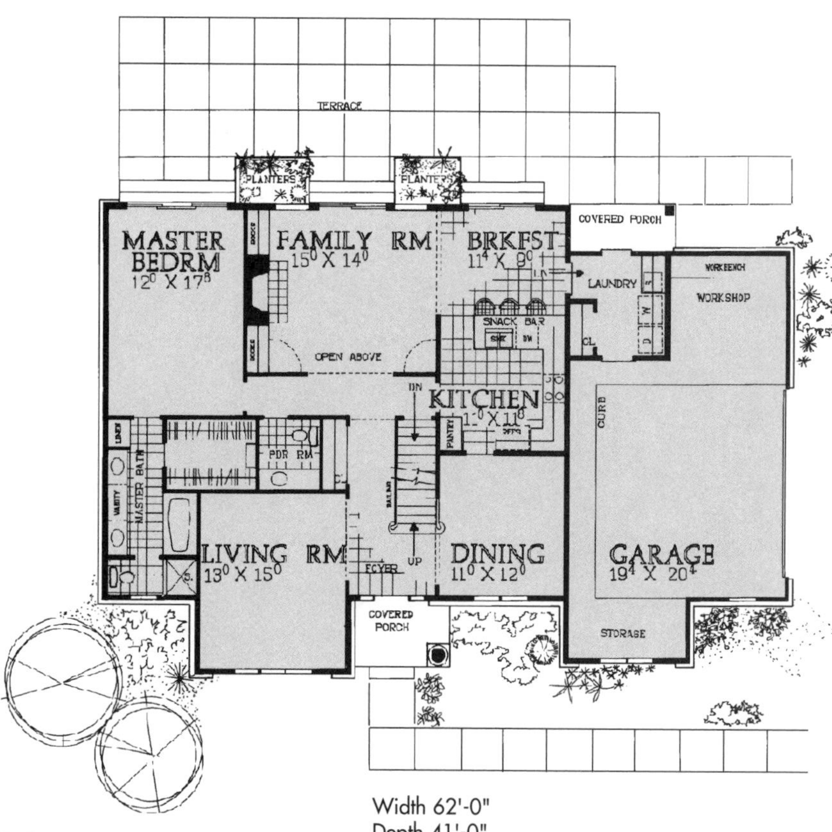
TERRACE
PLANTERS
PLANTERS
MASTER BEDRM 12^{0} X 17^{8}
FAMILY RM 15^{0} X 14^{0}
BRKFST 11^{4} X 9^{0}
COVERED PORCH
LAUNDRY
WORKBENCH
WORKSHOP
SNACK BAR
OPEN ABOVE
KITCHEN
PDR RM
MASTER BATH
LIVING RM 13^{0} X 15^{0}
FOYER
DINING 11^{0} X 12^{0}
GARAGE 19^{4} X 20^{4}
COVERED PORCH
STORAGE

Width 62'-0"
Depth 41'-0"

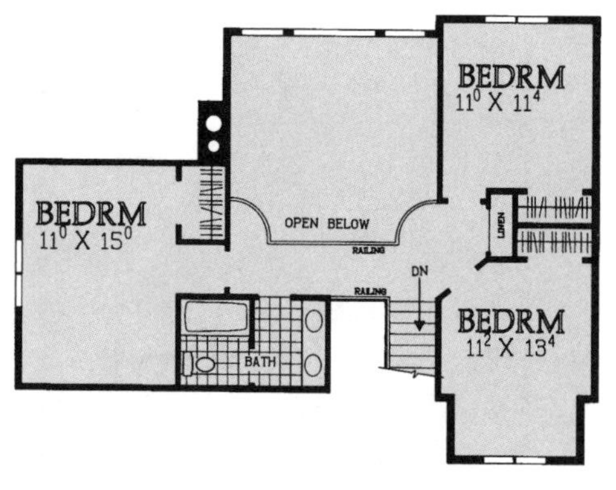
BEDRM 11^{0} X 11^{4}
BEDRM 11^{0} X 15^{0}
OPEN BELOW
RAILING
DN
BEDRM 11^{2} X 13^{4}
BATH

Design by
Home Planners

QUOTE ONE®

Cost to build? See page 516 to order complete cost estimate to build this house in your area!

Design by
Home Planners

Design 3342

First Floor: 1,467 square feet
Second Floor: 715 square feet
Total: 2,182 square feet

L

■ Just the right amount of living space is contained in this charming traditional Tudor house and it is arranged in a great floor plan. The split-bedroom configuration, with two bedrooms (or optional study) on the first floor and the master suite on the second floor with its own studio, assures complete privacy. The master suite also contains His and Hers walk-in closets and a bath with whirlpool tub and separate shower. The living room has a second-floor balcony overlook and a warming fireplace. The nearby dining room serves formal meals, while a breakfast room with box-bay window handles casual occasions. The full-width terrace in back is reached through sliding glass doors in each room at the rear of the house.

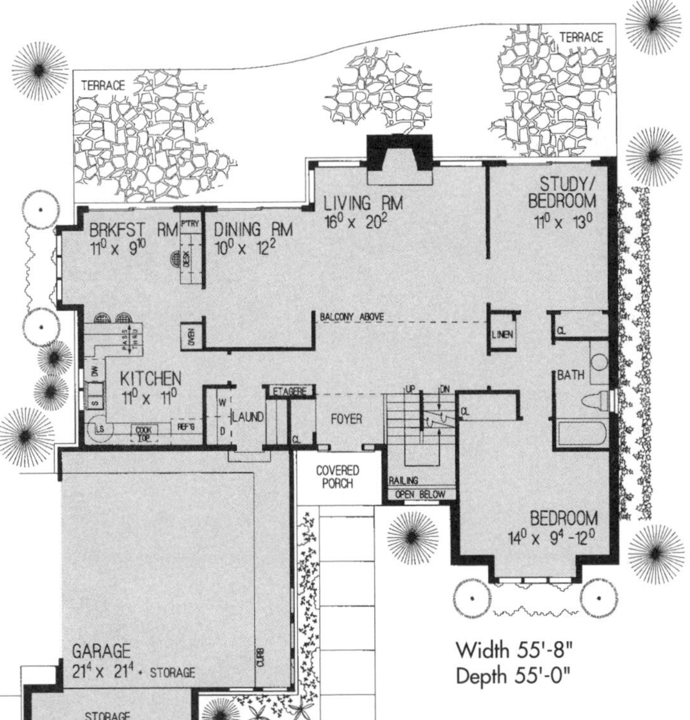
TERRACE
TERRACE
LIVING RM
16^0 x 20^2
STUDY/
BEDROOM
11^0 x 13^0
BRKFST RM
11^0 x 9^{10}
DINING RM
10^0 x 12^2
BALCONY ABOVE
LINEN
CL
BATH
KITCHEN
11^0 x 11^0
OVEN
ETAGERE
LAUND
FOYER
UP
DN
CL
COOK TOP
REF'S
COVERED
PORCH
RAILING
OPEN BELOW
BEDROOM
14^0 x 9^4 -12^0
GARAGE
21^4 x 21^4 + STORAGE
CURB
STORAGE

Width 55'-8"
Depth 55'-0"

QUOTE ONE®

Cost to build? See page 516 to order complete cost estimate to build this house in your area!

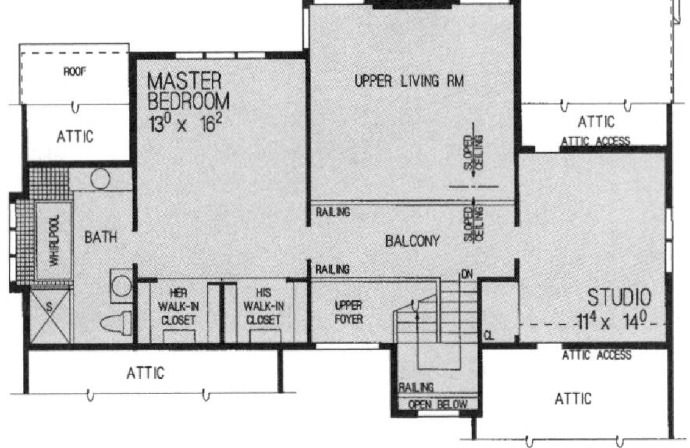
ROOF
ATTIC
MASTER
BEDROOM
13^0 x 16^2
UPPER LIVING RM
ROOF
ATTIC
ATTIC ACCESS
SLOPED CEILING
BATH
WHIRLPOOL
RAILING
BALCONY
RAILING
DN
HER
WALK-IN
CLOSET
HIS
WALK-IN
CLOSET
UPPER
FOYER
CL
STUDIO
11^4 x 14^0
ATTIC ACCESS
ATTIC
RAILING
OPEN BELOW
ATTIC

Design 2967

First Floor: 1,877 square feet
Second Floor: 467 square feet
Total: 2,344 square feet

L

■ Special interior amenities abound in this unique 1½-story Tudor. Living areas include an open gathering room/dining room area with fireplace and pass-through to the breakfast room. Quiet time can be spent in a sloped-ceiling study. Look for plenty of workspace in the island kitchen. Sleeping areas are separated for utmost privacy: an elegant master suite on the first floor, two bedrooms and a full bath on the second. Note the unusual curved balcony seat in the stairwell and the second floor ledge—a perfect spot for displaying plants or collectibles.

TERRACE
PORCH
WORKSHOP/ STORAGE 12⁸ x 14⁰
LAUND 8⁰ x 7⁸
KITCHEN 11⁶ x 13⁴
BRKFST. RM. 10⁰ x 13⁴
DINING RM. 13⁶ x 9⁰
GATHERING RM. 21⁰ x 18⁴
STUDY 12⁰ x 14⁰
FOYER
PDR. RM.
WALK-IN CLOSET
BALCONY SEAT
GARAGE 20⁸ x 23⁴
STORAGE CABINETS
MASTER BEDROOM 13⁰ x 17⁰
BATH
WHIRLPOOL
BEDROOM 10⁶ x 12⁴
BEDROOM 10⁶ x 12⁴
BATH
LINEN
UPPER GATHERING RM.
UPPER STUDY
UPPER FOYER
LEDGE
ATTIC
ROOF
Width 67'-4"
Depth 49'-8"
Design by
Home Planners
QUOTE ONE®
Cost to build? See page 516
to order complete cost estimate
to build this house in your area!

Design by
Home Planners

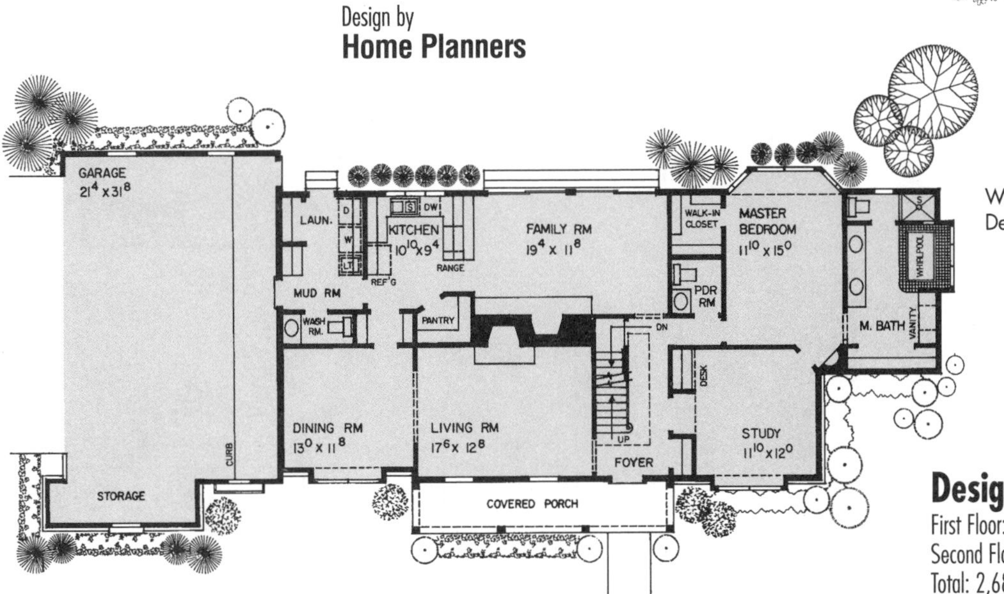
GARAGE
21⁴ x 31⁸
LAUN.
KITCHEN
10¹⁰x 9⁴
FAMILY RM
19⁴ x 11⁸
WALK-IN CLOSET
MASTER BEDROOM
11¹⁰ x 15⁰
MUD RM
PANTRY
RANGE
REF'G
WASH RM.
PDR RM
M. BATH
WHIRLPOOL
VANITY
DN
DESK
DINING RM
13⁰ x 11⁸
LIVING RM
17⁶ x 12⁸
UP
FOYER
STUDY
11¹⁰ x 12⁰
CURB
STORAGE
COVERED PORCH

Width 90'-0"
Depth 37'-4"

Design 3351

First Floor: 1,794 square feet
Second Floor: 887 square feet
Total: 2,681 square feet

L D

QUOTE ONE®
Cost to build? See page 516 to order complete cost estimate to build this house in your area!

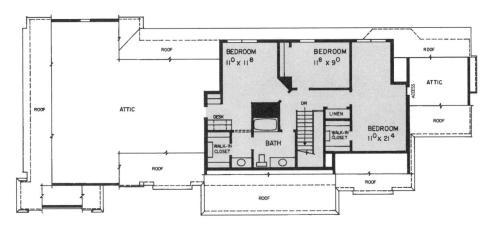

ROOF
ATTIC
ROOF
BEDROOM
11⁰ x 11⁸
BEDROOM
11⁸ x 9⁰
ROOF
ATTIC
ACCESS
DN
DESK
LINEN
BEDROOM
11⁰ x 21⁴
WALK-IN CLOSET
BATH
WALK-IN CLOSET
ROOF
ROOF
ROOF

■ Home-grown comfort is the key to the appeal of this traditionally Tudor-styled home. From the kitchen with attached family room to the living room with a fireplace and attached formal dining room, this plan has it all. The U-shaped kitchen has a huge walk-in pantry and adjacent mud room/laundry area with access to the garage. Notice the first-floor master bedroom with a whirlpool tub and an adjacent study. Further amenities in the master suite include a bay window, a walk-in closet and a corner art niche. A nearby powder room turns the study into a convenient guest room. On the second floor are three more bedrooms with ample closet space and a full bath. The two-car garage has a large storage area.

Design 2964

First Floor: 1,441 square feet
Second Floor: 621 square feet
Total: 2,062 square feet

■ Tudor houses offer their own unique exterior design features—gable roofs, simulated beam work, diamond-lite windows, muntins, panelled doors, varying roof planes and hefty cornices. This exquisite two-story home boasts a sensational first-floor master bedroom as well as generous guest quarters with a hallway balcony and lounge above. The master suite affords privacy in style with a whirlpool tub, knee-space vanity, walk-in closet and its own access to the rear terrace. The grand, two-story foyer leads to a spacious living room with sloped ceiling, warming fireplace and stunning views as well as access to the rear grounds. The formal dining area, breakfast room and U-shaped kitchen, conveniently clustered nearby, offer two additional glass doors to the rear terrace, which further enhance the bright, cheerful atmosphere of this area. Bonus space is available in the basement for development if desired.

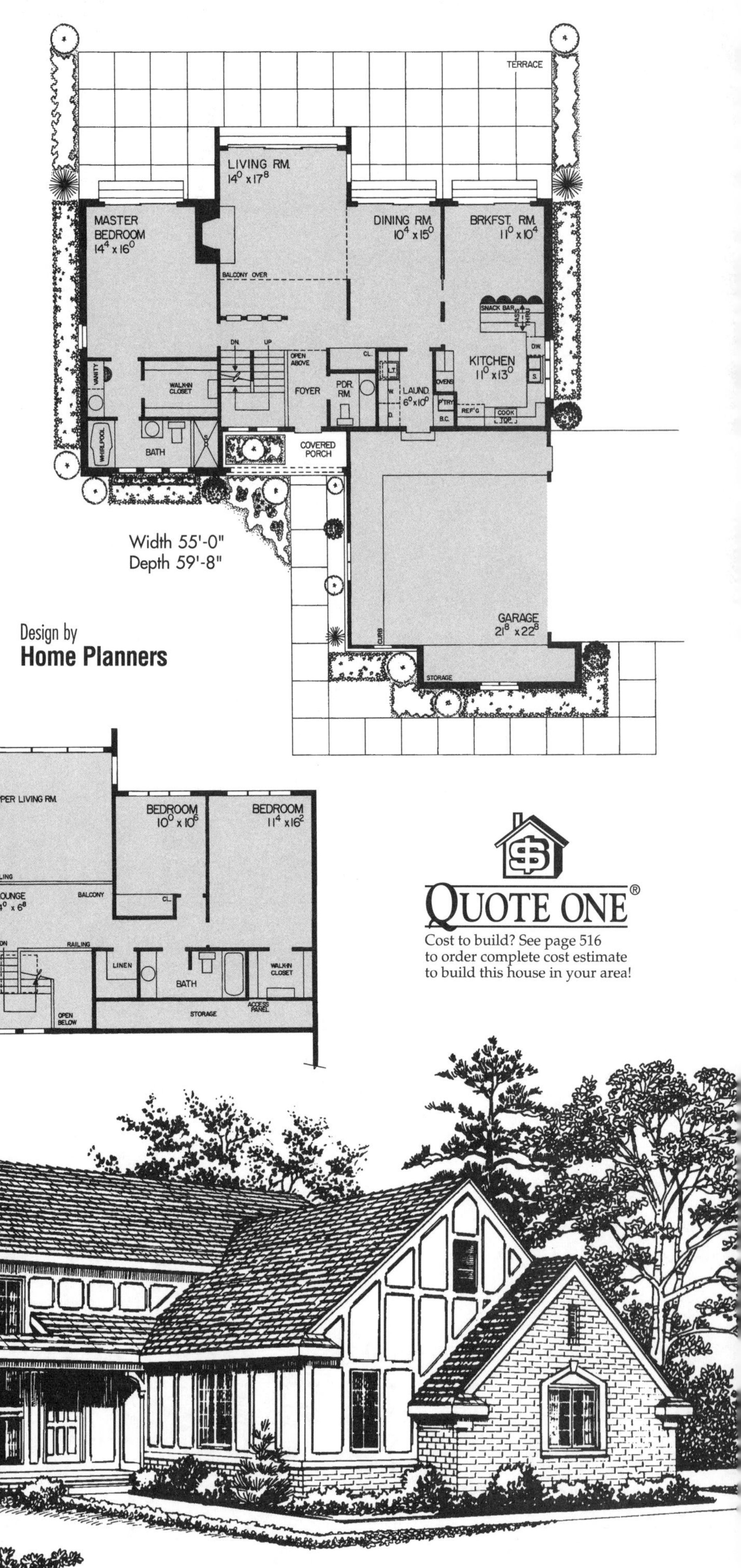

TERRACE
LIVING RM. 14⁰ x 17⁸
MASTER BEDROOM 14⁴ x 16⁰
DINING RM. 10⁴ x 15⁰
BRKFST. RM. 11⁰ x 10⁴
BALCONY OVER
SNACK BAR
PASS THRU
KITCHEN 11⁰ x 13⁰
VANITY
WALK-IN CLOSET
DN.
UP
OPEN ABOVE
CL.
FOYER
PDR. RM.
LAUND. 6⁰ x 10⁰
OVENS
P'TRY
REF'G
COOK TOP
WHIRLPOOL
BATH
COVERED PORCH
Width 55'-0"
Depth 59'-8"
GARAGE 21⁸ x 22⁸
STORAGE
Design by
Home Planners
UPPER LIVING RM.
BEDROOM 10⁰ x 10⁶
BEDROOM 11⁴ x 16²
RAILING
LOUNGE 14⁰ x 6⁸
BALCONY
CL.
RAILING
LINEN
BATH
WALK-IN CLOSET
ACCESS PANEL
STORAGE
OPEN BELOW
QUOTE ONE®
Cost to build? See page 516 to order complete cost estimate to build this house in your area!

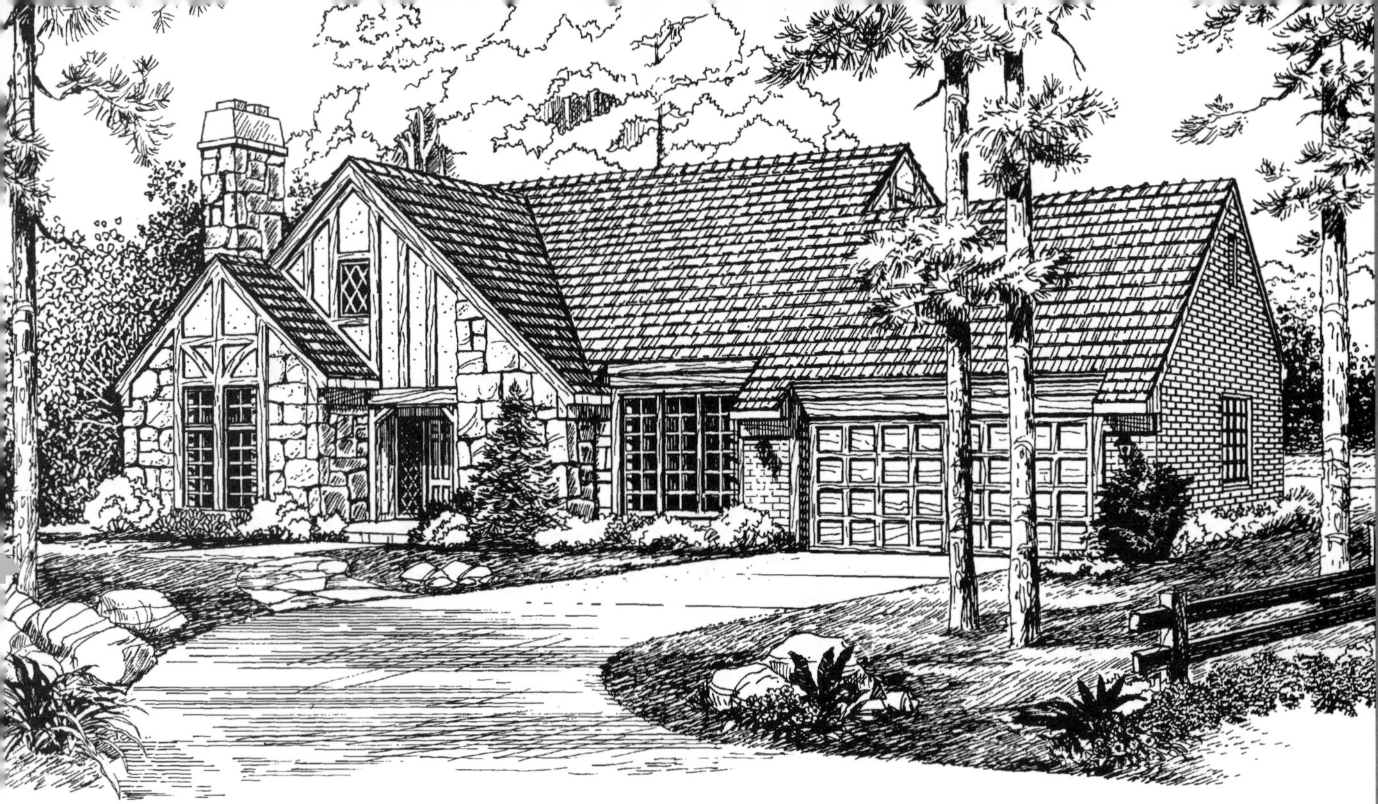

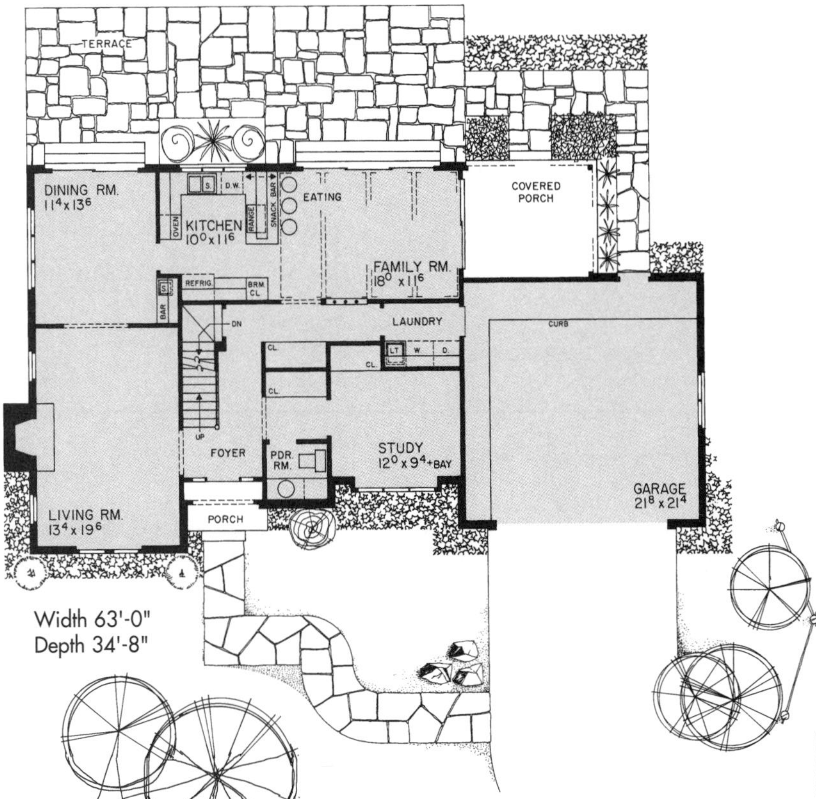

Design 2854

First Floor: 1,261 square feet
Second Floor: 950 square feet
Total: 2,211 square feet

L D

■ This charming Tudor-style home truly demonstrates a person's home is their castle. Though technically a story and a half, the second floor offers so much livability, it's more like a two-story plan. The first floor is solidly designed for efficiency and contains a living room with a fireplace, a large formal dining room, a beam-ceilinged family room, an efficient U-shaped kitchen, a study with a sunny bay window and a covered porch. In addition to a large master suite, two kids' rooms and a second full bath, the second floor includes a cozy spot that could serve as a home office, a nursery or a play area.

Width 63'-0"
Depth 34'-8"

Design by
Home Planners

QUOTE ONE®

Cost to build? See page 516 to order complete cost estimate to build this house in your area!

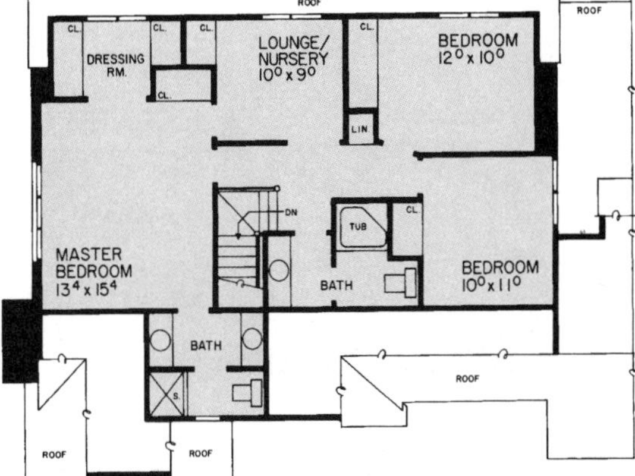
ROOF
DRESSING RM.
LOUNGE/ NURSERY 10⁰ x 9⁰
BEDROOM 12⁰ x 10⁰
LIN
MASTER BEDROOM 13⁴ x 15⁴
BATH
BEDROOM 10⁰ x 11⁰
TUB
DN

Design 3331

First Floor: 1,115 square feet
Second Floor: 690 square feet
Total: 1,805 square feet

L

■ This quaint tudor cottage has an open floor plan that is designed for easy living. The gathering room is accented with a cathedral ceiling and a full Palladian window. The dining room is joined to the efficient kitchen with extra entertaining space available on the deck. The first-floor master suite has a large compartmented bath and bumped-out windows. Upstairs, a lounge overlooks the gathering room. Two additional bedrooms and a full hall bath complete the second floor.

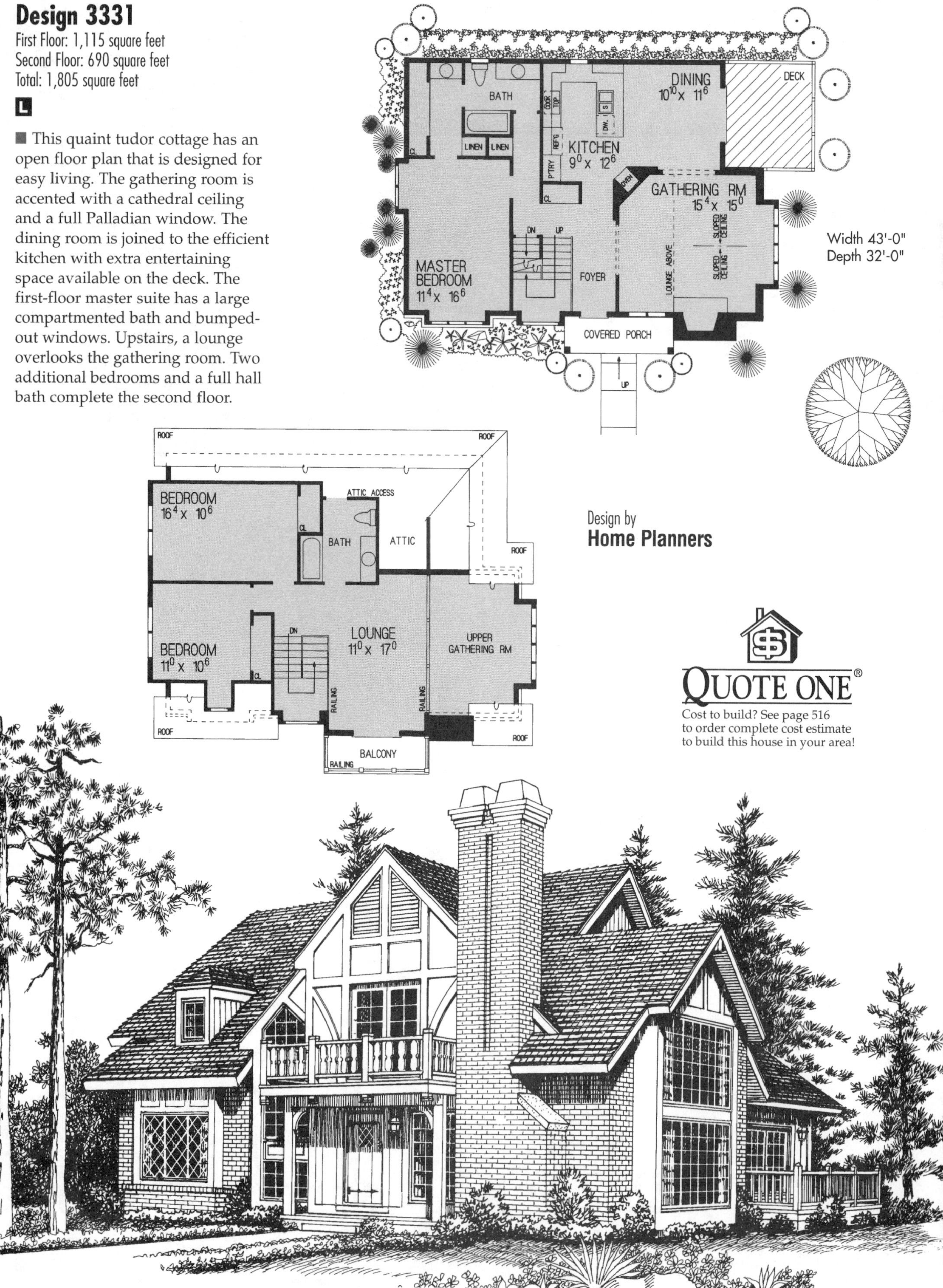
BATH
DINING
10^{10} x 11^{6}
DECK
COOK TOP
REF'G
PTRY
LINEN
LINEN
CL
KITCHEN
9^{0} x 12^{6}
OVEN
GATHERING RM
15^{4} x 15^{0}
SLOPED CEILING
LOUNGE ABOVE
DN
UP
MASTER BEDROOM
11^{4} x 16^{6}
FOYER
COVERED PORCH
UP
Width 43'-0"
Depth 32'-0"
ROOF
ATTIC ACCESS
BEDROOM
16^{4} x 10^{6}
BATH
ATTIC
BEDROOM
11^{0} x 10^{6}
LOUNGE
11^{0} x 17^{0}
UPPER GATHERING RM
RAILING
BALCONY

Design by
Home Planners

QUOTE ONE®
Cost to build? See page 516 to order complete cost estimate to build this house in your area!

Design by
Select Home Designs

Design Q395

First Floor: 1,584 square feet
Second Floor: 680 square feet
Total: 2,264 square feet

DESK
PLANT SHELF
12'x14'
br2
RAILING
OPEN TO BELOW
12'x14'
br3
SEAT
SEAT
PLANT SHELF

■ This traditional country exterior features all the modern amenities inside. Formal areas are to the front: a large living room and dining room with box-bay window. Informal living areas stretch across the rear, from the efficient kitchen, through the breakfast room to the family room with wood-burning fireplace. Columns and an arch separate the family room from center hall. A wonderful covered porch leads to a deck in the back. The first-level master suite provides privacy and includes a spacious bath with whirlpool tub, double vanity and walk-in closet. The second floor foyer is filled with natural light from the center dormer and crowned by a gallery with built-in desk. Family bedrooms on this floor share a full bath and have window seats. Plans include details for both a basement and a crawlspace foundation.

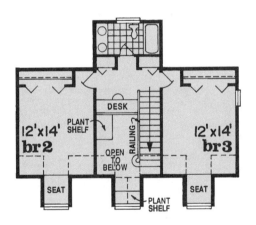

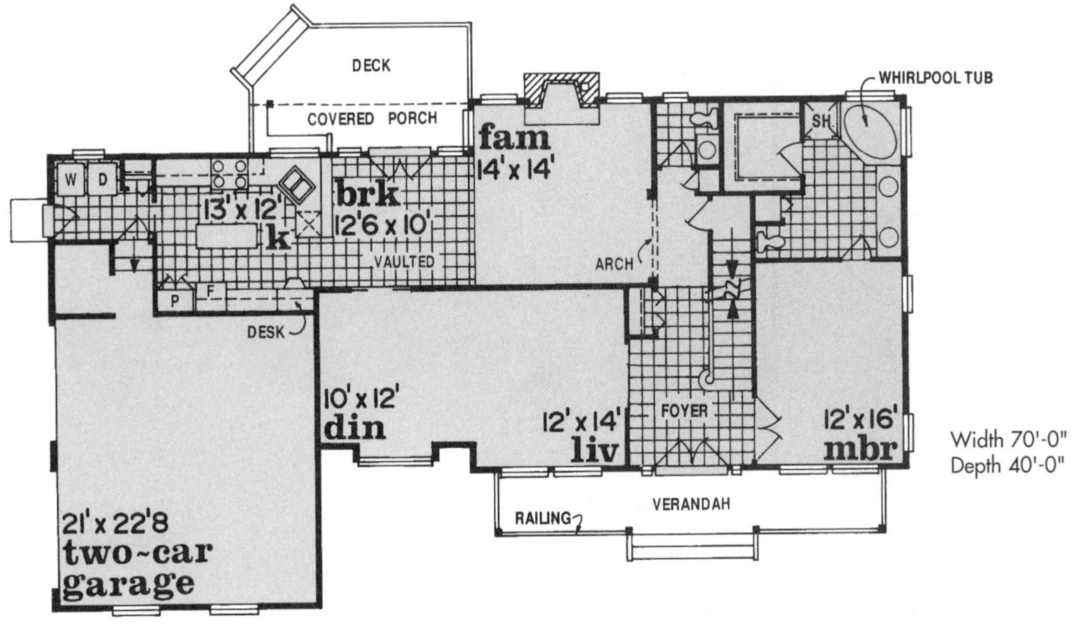
DECK
COVERED PORCH
WHIRLPOOL TUB
SH
fam
14'x14'
W
D
13'x12'
k
brk
12'6 x 10'
VAULTED
ARCH
P
F
DESK
10'x12'
din
12'x14'
liv
FOYER
12'x16'
mbr
VERANDAH
RAILING
21'x22'8
two-car
garage
Width 70'-0"
Depth 40'-0"

Design 3316

First Floor: 1,111 square feet
Second Floor: 886 square feet
Total: 1,997 square feet

L

■ Don't be fooled by a small-looking exterior. This plan offers three bedrooms and plenty of living space. Notice that the screened porch leads to a rear terrace with access to the breakfast room. A living room/dining room combination adds spaciousness to the floor plan. Other welcome amenities include: boxed windows in the breakfast room and dining room, fireplace in the living room, planning desk and pass-through snack bar in the kitchen, whirlpool tub in the master bath, an open two-story foyer. The thoughtfully placed flower box, beyond the kitchen window above the sink, adds a homespun touch to this already comfortable design.

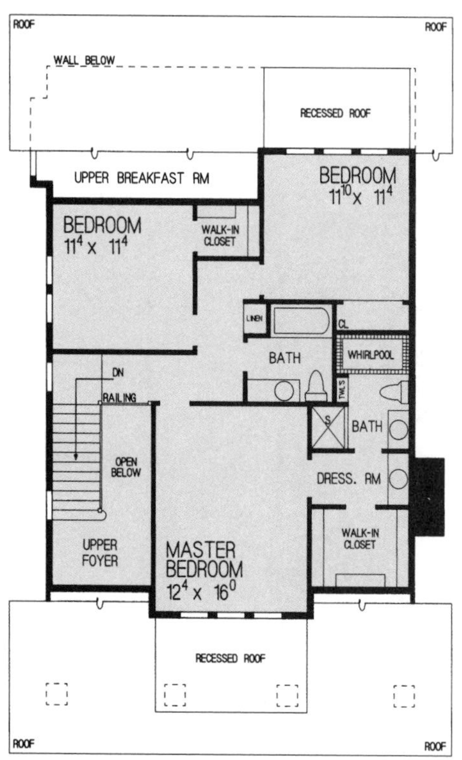

ROOF
ROOF
WALL BELOW
RECESSED ROOF
UPPER BREAKFAST RM
BEDROOM 11^{10} x 11^{4}
BEDROOM 11^{4} x 11^{4}
WALK-IN CLOSET
LINEN
CL
BATH
WHIRLPOOL
DN
RAILING
OPEN BELOW
BATH
DRESS. RM
WALK-IN CLOSET
UPPER FOYER
MASTER BEDROOM 12^{4} x 16^{0}
RECESSED ROOF
ROOF
ROOF

Width 34'-1"
Depth 50'-0"

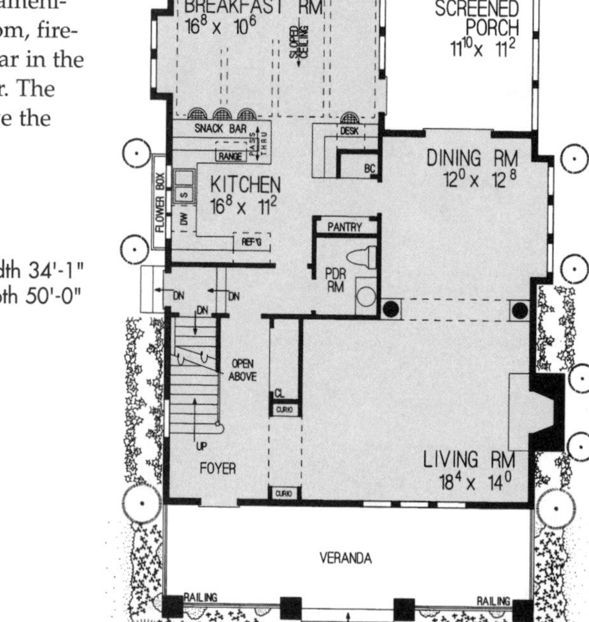

TERRACE
UP
UP
BREAKFAST RM 16^{8} x 10^{6}
SLOPED CEILING
SCREENED PORCH 11^{10} x 11^{2}
SNACK BAR
PASS THRU
DESK
RANGE
KITCHEN 16^{8} x 11^{2}
FLOWER BOX
DW
S
BC
DINING RM 12^{0} x 12^{8}
PANTRY
REF'G
PDR RM
DN
DN
DN
OPEN ABOVE
CL
CURIO
UP
FOYER
CURIO
LIVING RM 18^{4} x 14^{0}
VERANDA
RAILING
RAILING
UP

QUOTE ONE®
Cost to build? See page 516 to order complete cost estimate to build this house in your area!

Design by
Home Planners

Design 3318

First Floor: 1,557 square feet
Second Floor: 540 square feet
Total: 2,097 square feet

L D

■ Details make the difference in this darling two-bedroom (or three bedroom if you choose) bungalow. From covered front porch to covered rear porch, there's a fine floor plan. Living areas are to the rear: a gathering room with through-fireplace and pass-through counter to the kitchen and a formal dining room with porch access. To the front of the plan are a family bedroom and bath and a study. The study can also be planned as a guest bedroom with bath. Upstairs is the master bedroom with a through-fireplace to the bath and a gigantic walk-in closet.

Width 48'-0"
Depth 43'-8"

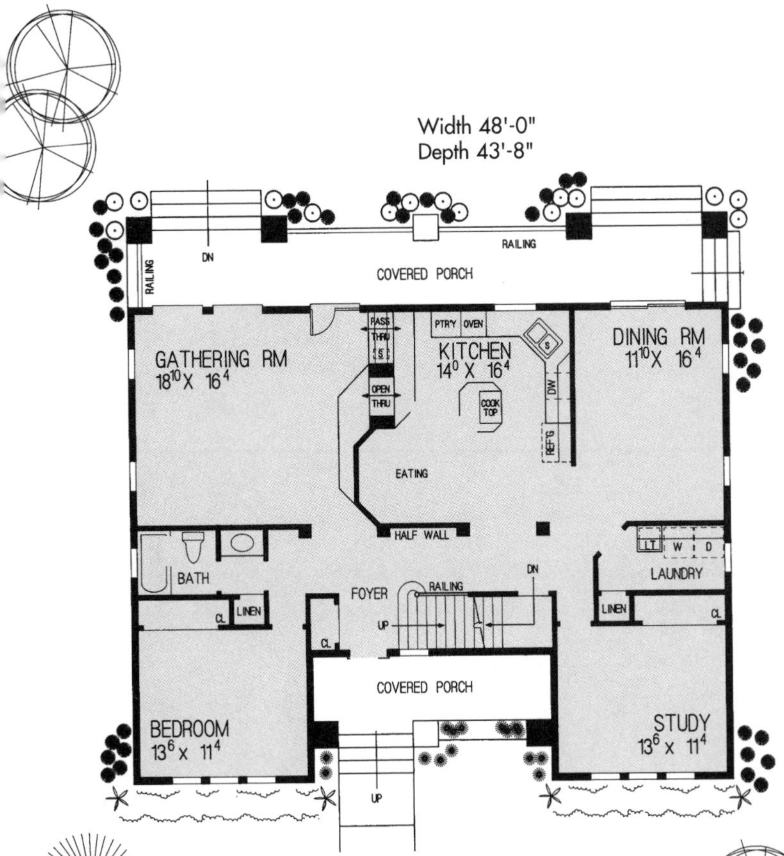

Alternate 1st Floor Plan

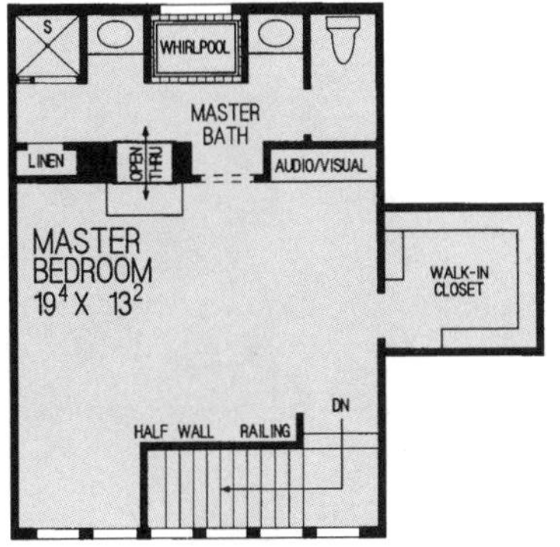
WHIRLPOOL
MASTER BATH
LINEN
AUDIO/VISUAL
MASTER BEDROOM
19⁴ X 13²
WALK-IN CLOSET
HALF WALL
RAILING
DN

Design by
Home Planners

QUOTE ONE®
Cost to build? See page 516 to order complete cost estimate to build this house in your area!

Design 2559

First Floor: 1,388 square feet
Second Floor: 809 square feet
Total: 2,197 square feet

D

Design by
Home Planners

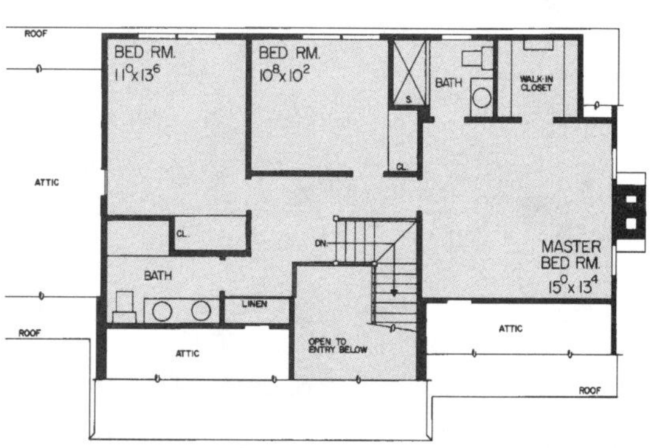

ROOF
BED RM.
11^{0}x13^{6}
BED RM.
10^{8}x10^{2}
BATH
WALK-IN CLOSET
ATTIC
CL.
DN.
MASTER BED RM.
15^{0}x13^{4}
BATH
LINEN
OPEN TO ENTRY BELOW
ATTIC
ATTIC
ROOF
ROOF

■ Imagine, a 26-foot living room with fireplace, excellent dining facilities and a quiet study with built-in bookshelves. All this, plus much more, is within an appealing, traditional exterior. The terrace is accessible from the living room, dining room and breakfast nook. A fireplace warms the living room. The U-shaped kitchen is made even more convenient with a center work island. A laundry room is nearby. The cozy study has built-ins and resides near the front entry. Upstairs, the master bedroom offers a private bath, a walk-in closet and access to attic storage. Two family bedrooms share a bath that has a double-bowl vanity. More attic storage is located above the garage.

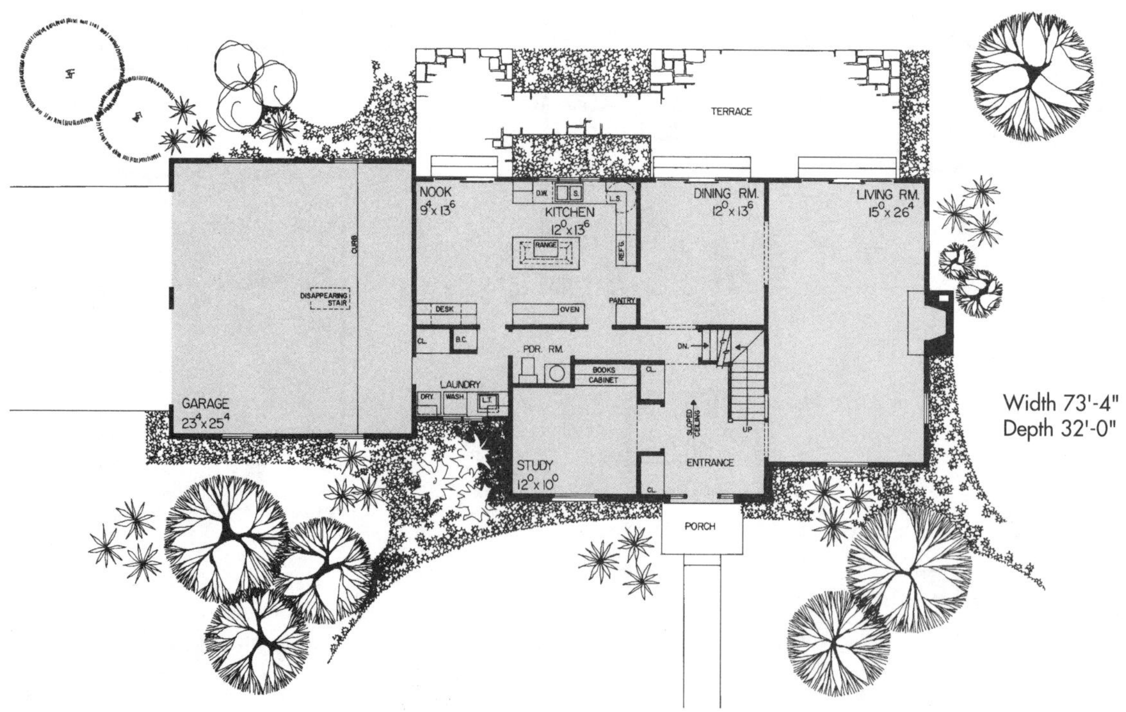

TERRACE
NOOK
9^{4}x13^{6}
KITCHEN
12^{0}x13^{6}
RANGE
REFG.
DINING RM.
12^{0}x13^{6}
LIVING RM.
15^{0}x26^{4}
DISAPPEARING STAIR
CURB
DESK
OVEN
PANTRY
CL.
B.C.
PDR. RM.
BOOKS CABINET
DN.
LAUNDRY
DRY.
WASH
GARAGE
23^{4}x25^{4}
SLOPED CEILING
UP
STUDY
12^{0}x10^{0}
ENTRANCE
CL.
PORCH
Width 73'-4"
Depth 32'-0"

Design by
Home Planners

Design 2684

First Floor: 1,600 square feet
Second Floor: 1,145 square feeet
Studio/Office: 353 square feet
Total: 3,098 square feet

L D

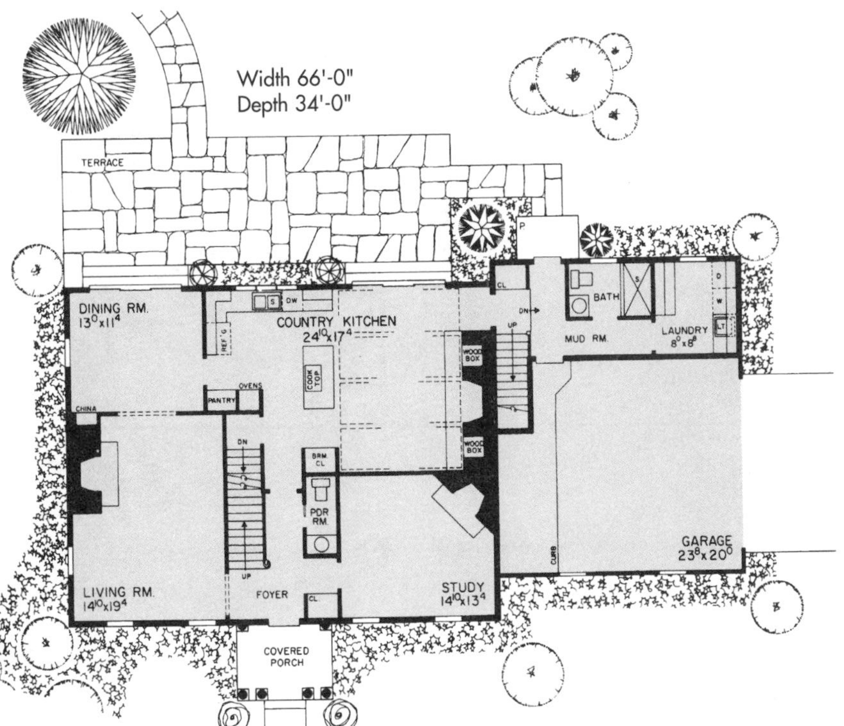

Width 66'-0"
Depth 34'-0"
TERRACE
DINING RM.
13⁰x11⁴
COUNTRY KITCHEN
24¹⁰x17⁴
COOK TOP
OVENS
PANTRY
CHINA
WOOD BOX
BRM CL
PDR RM.
DN
UP
MUD RM.
BATH
LAUNDRY
8⁰x8⁶
GARAGE
23⁸x20⁰
LIVING RM.
14¹⁰x19⁴
FOYER
CL.
STUDY
14¹⁰x13⁴
COVERED PORCH

■ Dormers and a columned entry are nicely offset by multi-paned shuttered windows on the outside of this delightful home. Highlighting this plan on the inside is the spacious, country kitchen. It features an island cooktop and casual living/dining space with sliding glass doors and a fireplace with double wood boxes. It complements the formal living and dining rooms (note the fireplace in the living room) and a study (with another fireplace!). Bedrooms are on the second floor and include a master suite with dressing area and full bath. Family bedrooms share a full hall bath. Also worth a special note is the second-floor studio/office. It is accessible by way of a staircase in the back of the plan. It features a built-in bookcase.

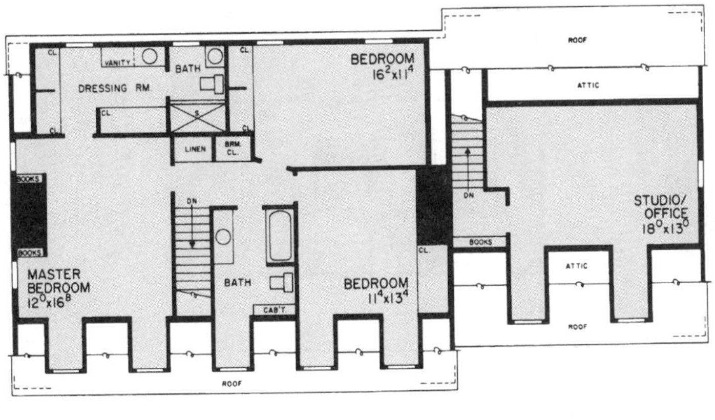

DRESSING RM.
VANITY
BATH
LINEN
BRM. CL.
BEDROOM
16²x11⁴
BOOKS
MASTER BEDROOM
12⁰x16⁸
BATH
CAB'T
BEDROOM
11⁴x13⁴
ROOF
ATTIC
STUDIO/OFFICE
18⁰x13⁰
BOOKS

Rear Elevation

Design 2682

Design by
Home Planners

First Floor (Basic Plan): 1,016 square feet
First Floor (Expanded Plan): 1,230 square feet
Second Floor: 766 square feet
Total (Basic Plan): 1,782 square feet
Total (Expanded Plan): 1,996 square feet

L D

■ Here's an expandable Colonial with a full measure of Cape Cod charm. A spider beam ceiling dresses up the country kitchen, which offers a gourmet island counter and a sitting area with a hearth. Upstairs, a spacious master suite shares a gallery hall which leads to two family bedrooms and sizable storage space. The expanded version (shown on opposite page) of the basic plan adds a study wing as well as an attached garage with a service entrance to the kitchen.

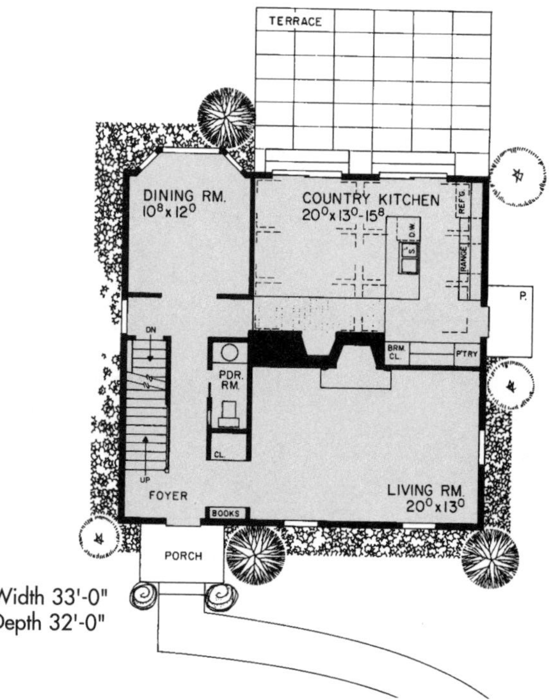

TERRACE
DINING RM.
$10^8 \times 12^0$
COUNTRY KITCHEN
$20^0 \times 13^0 - 15^8$
REF'G.
RANGE
P.
BRM. CL.
PTRY
DN
PDR. RM.
CL.
UP
FOYER
BOOKS
LIVING RM.
$20^0 \times 13^0$
PORCH

Width 33'-0"
Depth 32'-0"

Rear Elevation

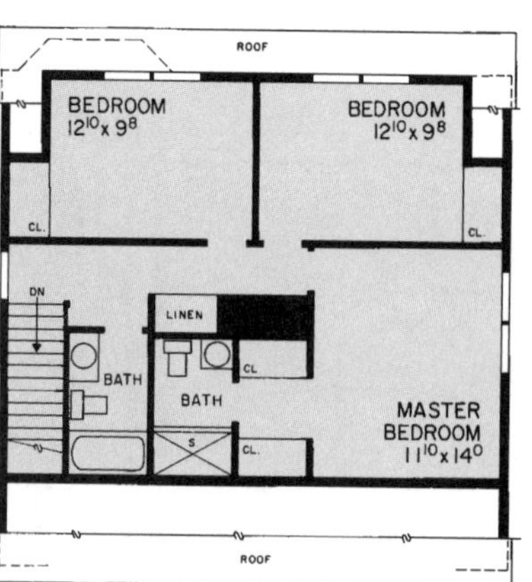

ROOF
BEDROOM
$12^{10} \times 9^8$
BEDROOM
$12^{10} \times 9^8$
CL.
CL.
DN
LINEN
CL.
BATH
BATH
S
CL.
MASTER BEDROOM
$11^{10} \times 14^0$
ROOF

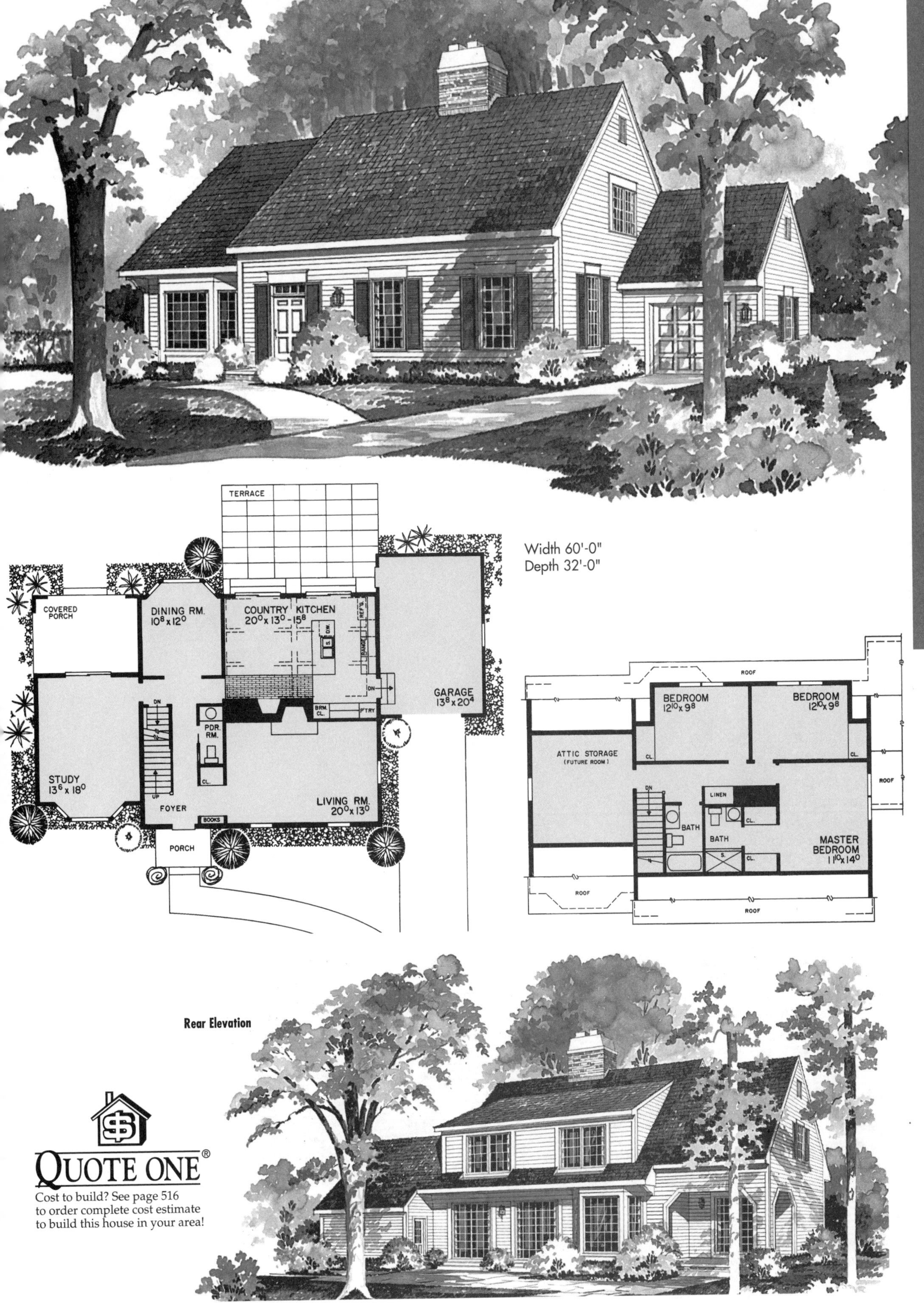

TERRACE
COVERED PORCH
DINING RM.
10⁸ x 12⁰
COUNTRY KITCHEN
20⁰ x 13⁰ - 15⁸
GARAGE
13⁸ x 20⁴
STUDY
13⁶ x 18⁰
PDR. RM.
CL.
BRM. CL.
P'TRY
FOYER
BOOKS
LIVING RM.
20⁰ x 13⁰
PORCH
Width 60'-0"
Depth 32'-0"
ROOF
BEDROOM
12¹⁰ x 9⁸
BEDROOM
12¹⁰ x 9⁸
ATTIC STORAGE
(FUTURE ROOM)
LINEN
BATH
BATH
MASTER BEDROOM
11¹⁰ x 14⁰
Rear Elevation
QUOTE ONE®
Cost to build? See page 516
to order complete cost estimate
to build this house in your area!

Design 1791

First Floor: 1,157 square feet
Second Floor: 875 square feet
Total: 2,032 square feet

L D

■ Cape Cods are among the most popular designs of all time. This moderately sized 1½-story plan is symmetrically beautiful. The traditional central foyer leads to a formal living area on the left and a study (or additional bedroom) on the right. A bay-windowed dining room is located between the spacious kitchen and the living room. A family room with a beam ceiling and raised-hearth fireplace offers access to the rear terrace through sliding glass doors. Dormer windows grace two of the three bedrooms on the second floor. The family bedrooms share a full bath. The master bedroom contains a private bath with a dressing area.

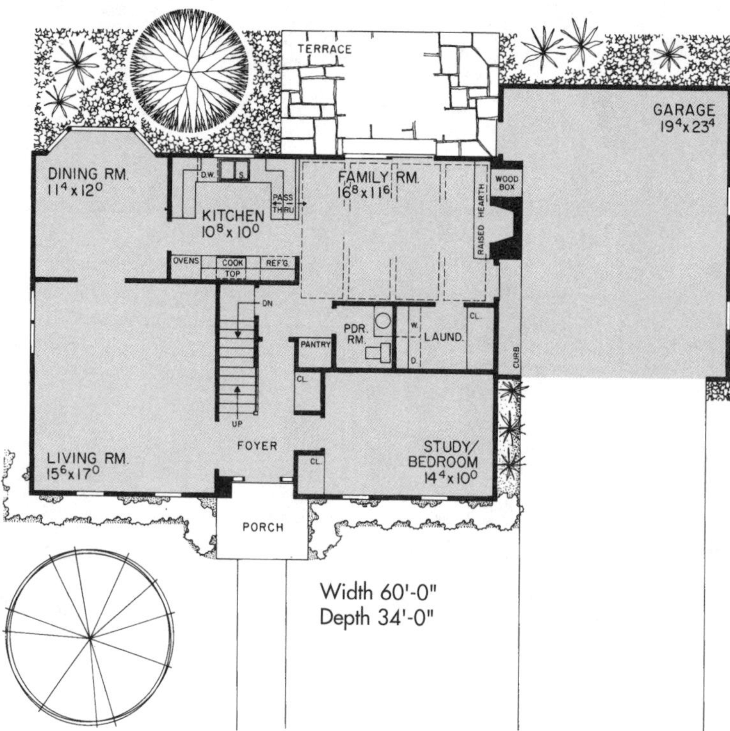
TERRACE
GARAGE
19^4 x 23^4
DINING RM.
11^4 x 12^0
D.W.
PASS THRU
KITCHEN
10^8 x 10^0
FAMILY RM.
16^8 x 11^6
WOOD BOX
RAISED HEARTH
OVENS
COOK TOP
REF'G.
DN
PDR. RM.
PANTRY
W.
D.
LAUND.
CL.
CURB
UP
FOYER
LIVING RM.
15^6 x 17^0
STUDY/ BEDROOM
14^4 x 10^0
PORCH

Width 60'-0"
Depth 34'-0"

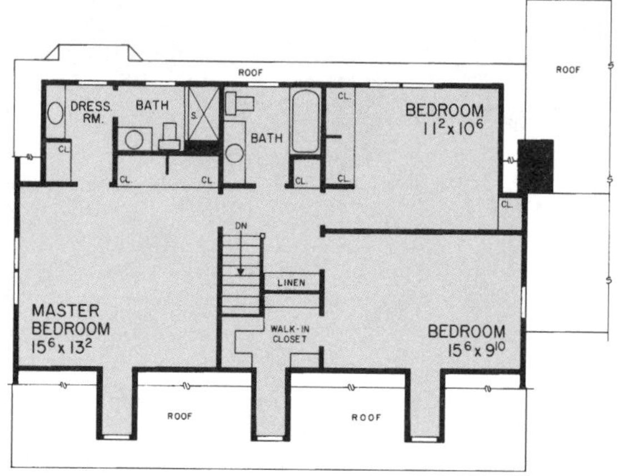
ROOF
DRESS. RM.
BATH
BATH
CL.
BEDROOM
11^2 x 10^6
DN
LINEN
MASTER BEDROOM
15^6 x 13^2
WALK-IN CLOSET
BEDROOM
15^6 x 9^{10}
ROOF
ROOF

QUOTE ONE®

Cost to build? See page 516 to order complete cost estimate to build this house in your area!

Design by
Home Planners

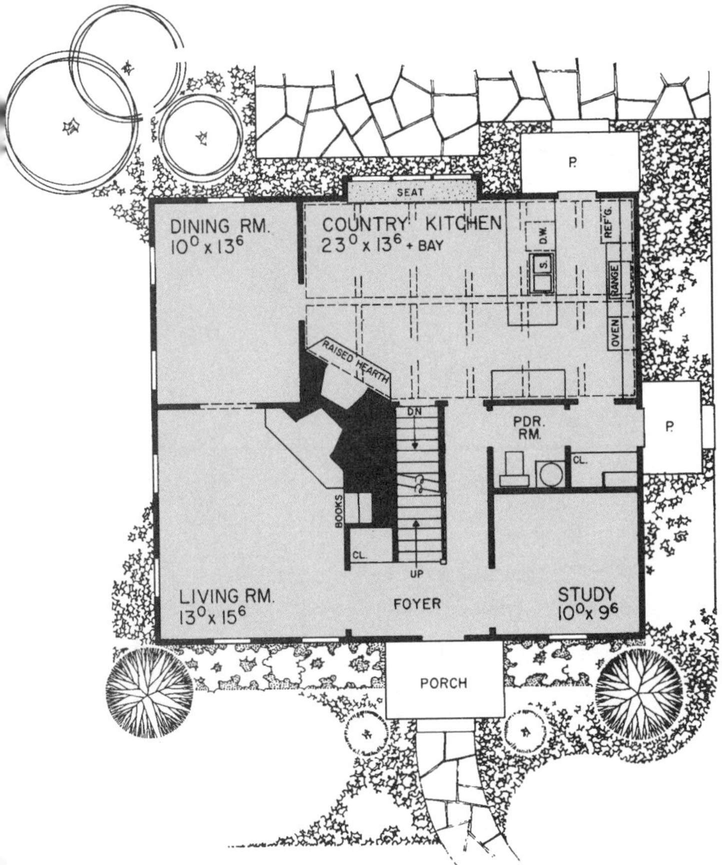

Design 2661

First Floor: 1,100 square feet
Second Floor: 808 square feet
Total: 1,908 square feet

■ This charming plan is designed to be the perfect starter or retirement home thanks to its ideal blend of comfort and easy style. Inside, it contains a very livable floor plan. An outstanding first floor centers around the huge country kitchen which includes a beam ceiling, a raised-hearth fireplace, a window seat and rear-yard access. The living room with its warming corner fireplace and private study are to the front of the plan. Upstairs are three bedrooms and two full baths. Built-in shelves and a linen closet in the upstairs hallway provide excellent storage.

Width 34'-0"
Depth 32'-0"

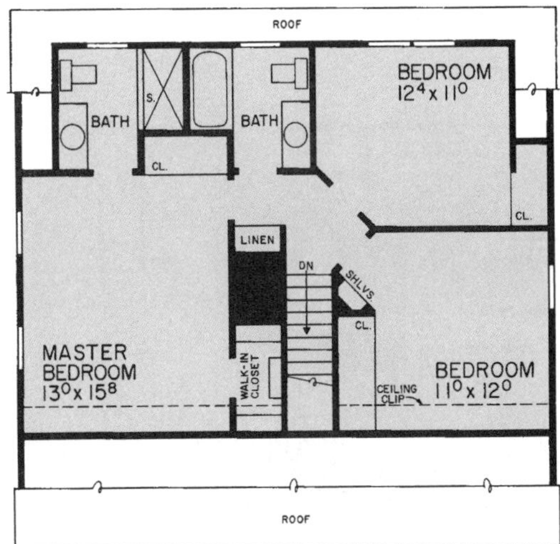
ROOF
BATH
S.
BATH
CL.
BEDROOM
$12^{4} \times 11^{0}$
CL.
LINEN
DN
SHLVS
CL.
MASTER
BEDROOM
$13^{0} \times 15^{8}$
WALK-IN CLOSET
CEILING CLIP
BEDROOM
$11^{0} \times 12^{0}$
ROOF

Design by
Home Planners

QUOTE ONE®

Cost to build? See page 516 to order complete cost estimate to build this house in your area!

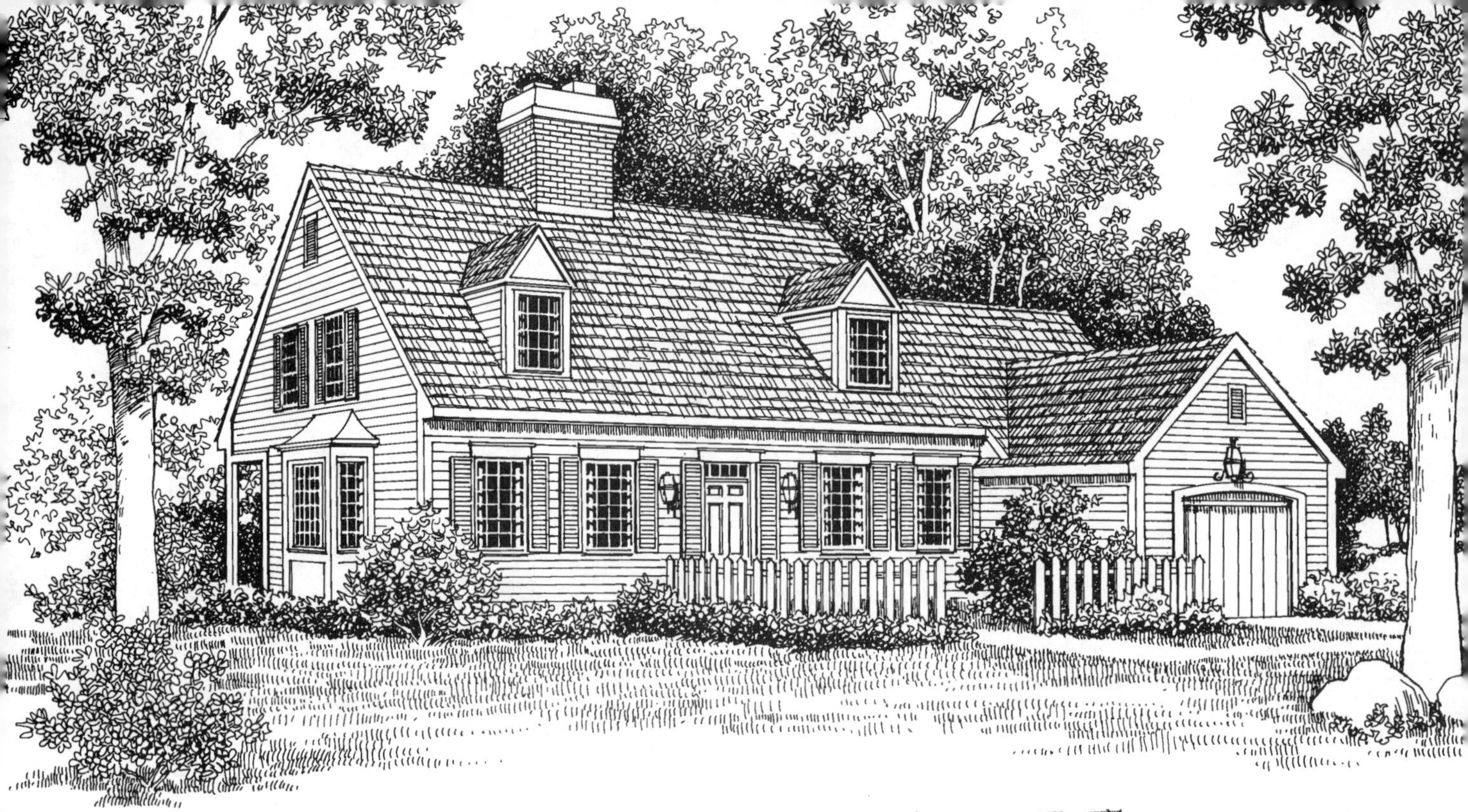

Design 2657

Design by
Home Planners

First Floor: 1,217 square feet
Second Floor: 868 square feet
Total: 2,085 square feet

L

■ This home is packed with all-American charm and no small number of features. On either side of the large entry foyer are a formal dining room and a living room with a gigantic bay window, a fireplace and access to a covered porch overlooking the backyard. Dominating the back of the first floor is an enormous country kitchen. The efficient U-shaped work area here is complemented by a number of amenities: an exposed-beam ceiling, a raised-hearth fireplace, a bay window and built-in shelves. A washroom and a laundry are close by. The cozy second floor holds three bedrooms and two full baths. Cleverly designed window seats in the dormer windows hide small storage areas.

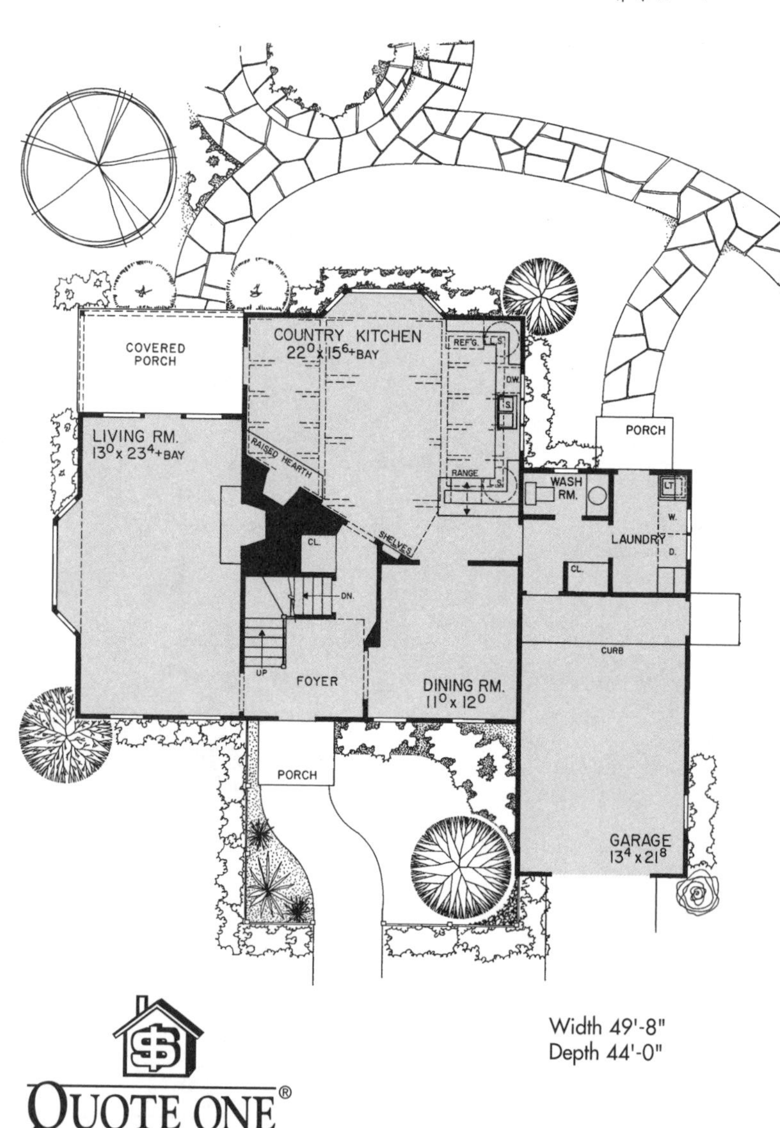
COVERED PORCH
COUNTRY KITCHEN
$22^{0} \times 15^{6}$+BAY
REF'G.
DW
RANGE
PORCH
LIVING RM.
$13^{0} \times 23^{4}$+BAY
RAISED HEARTH
SHELVES
CL.
DN.
WASH RM.
LAUNDRY
W.
D.
CL.
UP
FOYER
DINING RM.
$11^{0} \times 12^{0}$
CURB
PORCH
GARAGE
$13^{4} \times 21^{8}$

Width 49'-8"
Depth 44'-0"

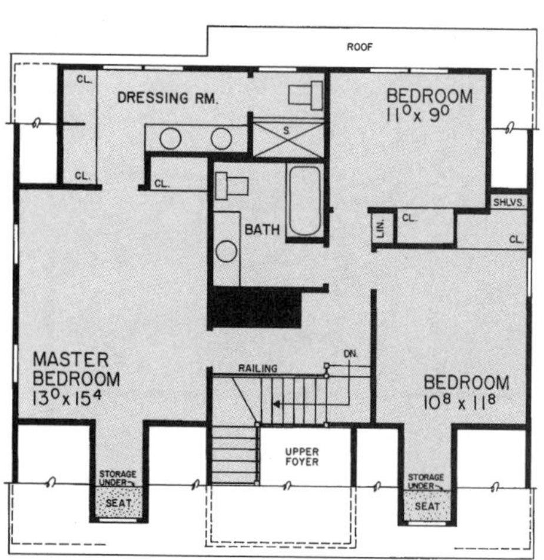
ROOF
CL.
DRESSING RM.
BEDROOM
$11^{0} \times 9^{0}$
CL.
CL.
BATH
LIN.
CL.
SHLVS.
CL.
MASTER BEDROOM
$13^{0} \times 15^{4}$
RAILING
DN.
BEDROOM
$10^{8} \times 11^{8}$
STORAGE UNDER SEAT
UPPER FOYER
STORAGE UNDER SEAT

Enhanced Plan

Design 3715

First Floor: 1,312 square feet
Second Floor: 795 square feet
Total: 2,107 square feet

■ The design of this expandable Cape Cod provides plenty of room for all your family's needs. The kitchen extends as one large room over the snack bar into an expansive family room. Both the family room and the living room open from the center hall, which also leads to the dining room at the back of the house. The downstairs study could be converted into a fourth bedroom with an adjacent full bath. The upstairs bedrooms include a master suite with a walk-in closet and a private bath. The house may be enhanced by the addition of a fireplace, a bay window, a two-car garage, a laundry room and a rear deck. The blueprints show how to build both the basic and the enhanced versions of this home.

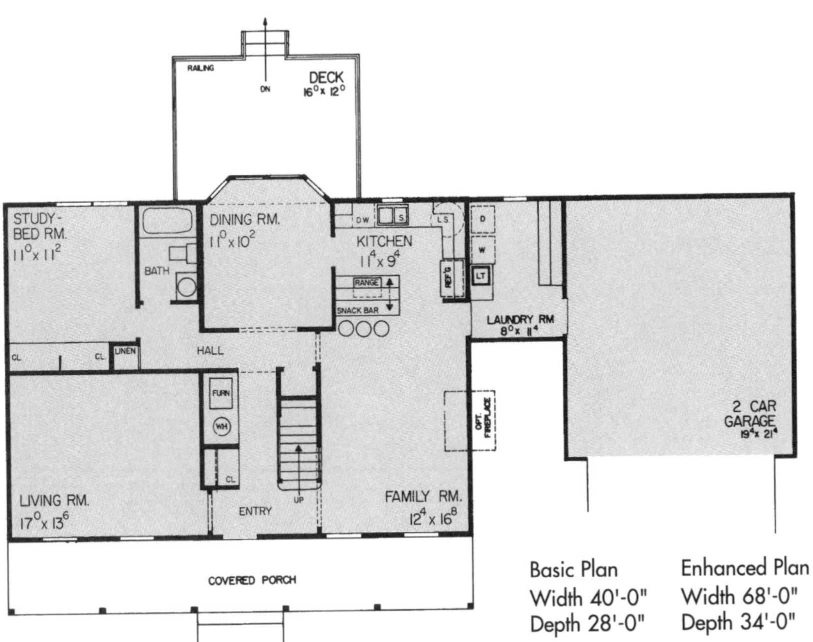
RAILING
DN
DECK 16⁰ x 12⁰
STUDY-BED RM. 11⁰ x 11²
BATH
DINING RM. 11⁰ x 10²
KITCHEN 11⁴ x 9⁴
DW
S
LS
RANGE
SNACK BAR
REF'G
D
W
LT
LAUNDRY RM 8⁰ x 11⁴
CL.
CL.
LINEN
HALL
FURN
WH
CL
OPT. FIREPLACE
2 CAR GARAGE 19⁴ x 21⁴
LIVING RM. 17⁰ x 13⁶
ENTRY
UP
FAMILY RM. 12⁴ x 16⁸
COVERED PORCH
Basic Plan
Width 40'-0"
Depth 28'-0"
Enhanced Plan
Width 68'-0"
Depth 34'-0"

Design by
Home Planners

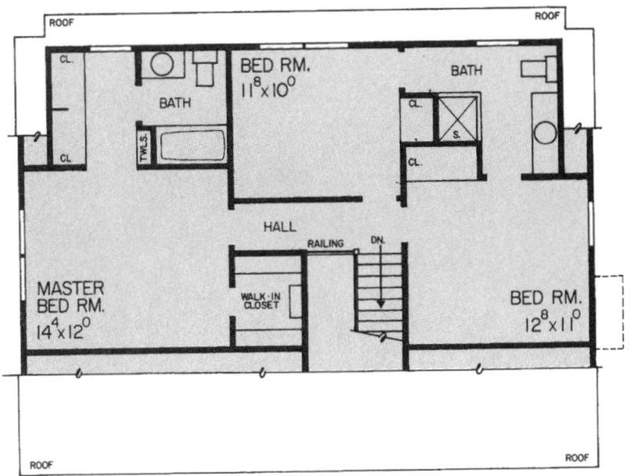
ROOF
ROOF
CL.
CL.
BATH
TWLS.
BED RM. 11⁸ x 10⁰
BATH
CL.
S.
CL.
HALL
RAILING
DN.
MASTER BED RM. 14⁴ x 12⁰
WALK-IN CLOSET
BED RM. 12⁸ x 11⁰
ROOF
ROOF

Basic Plan

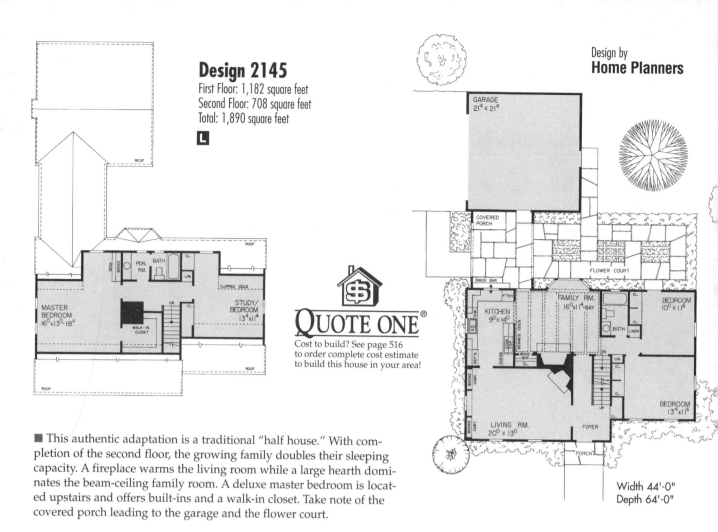

Design 2145

First Floor: 1,182 square feet
Second Floor: 708 square feet
Total: 1,890 square feet

L

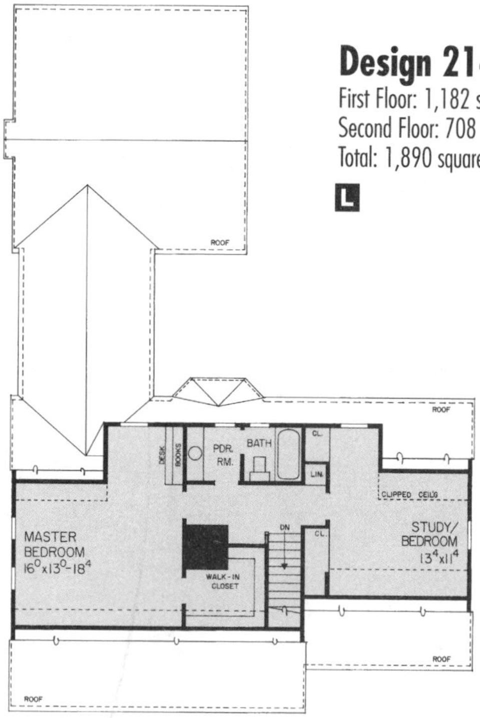

Design by
Home Planners

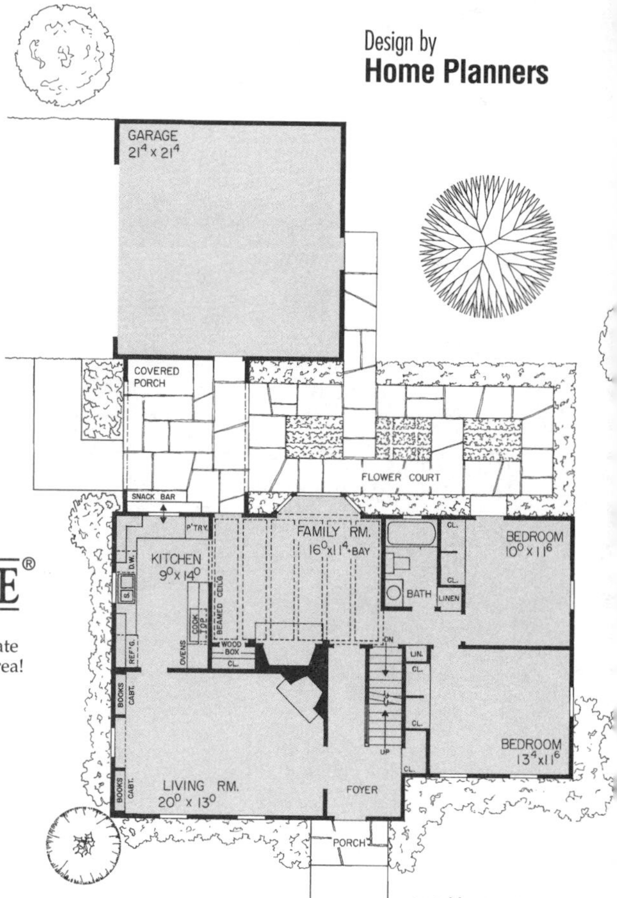

MASTER BEDROOM 16⁰x13⁰-18⁴
PDR. RM.
BATH
CL.
LIN.
CLIPPED CEILG
STUDY/ BEDROOM 13⁴x11⁴
WALK-IN CLOSET
DN
ROOF

QUOTE ONE®

Cost to build? See page 516 to order complete cost estimate to build this house in your area!

GARAGE 21⁴ x 21⁴
COVERED PORCH
FLOWER COURT
SNACK BAR
P'TRY
KITCHEN 9⁰x 14⁰
FAMILY RM. 16⁰x11⁴-BAY
BEAMED CEILG
WOOD BOX
BATH
LINEN
BEDROOM 10⁰ x 11⁶
BEDROOM 13⁴x11⁶
LIVING RM. 20⁰ x 13⁰
FOYER
PORCH

Width 44'-0"
Depth 64'-0"

■ This authentic adaptation is a traditional "half house." With completion of the second floor, the growing family doubles their sleeping capacity. A fireplace warms the living room while a large hearth dominates the beam-ceiling family room. A deluxe master bedroom is located upstairs and offers built-ins and a walk-in closet. Take note of the covered porch leading to the garage and the flower court.

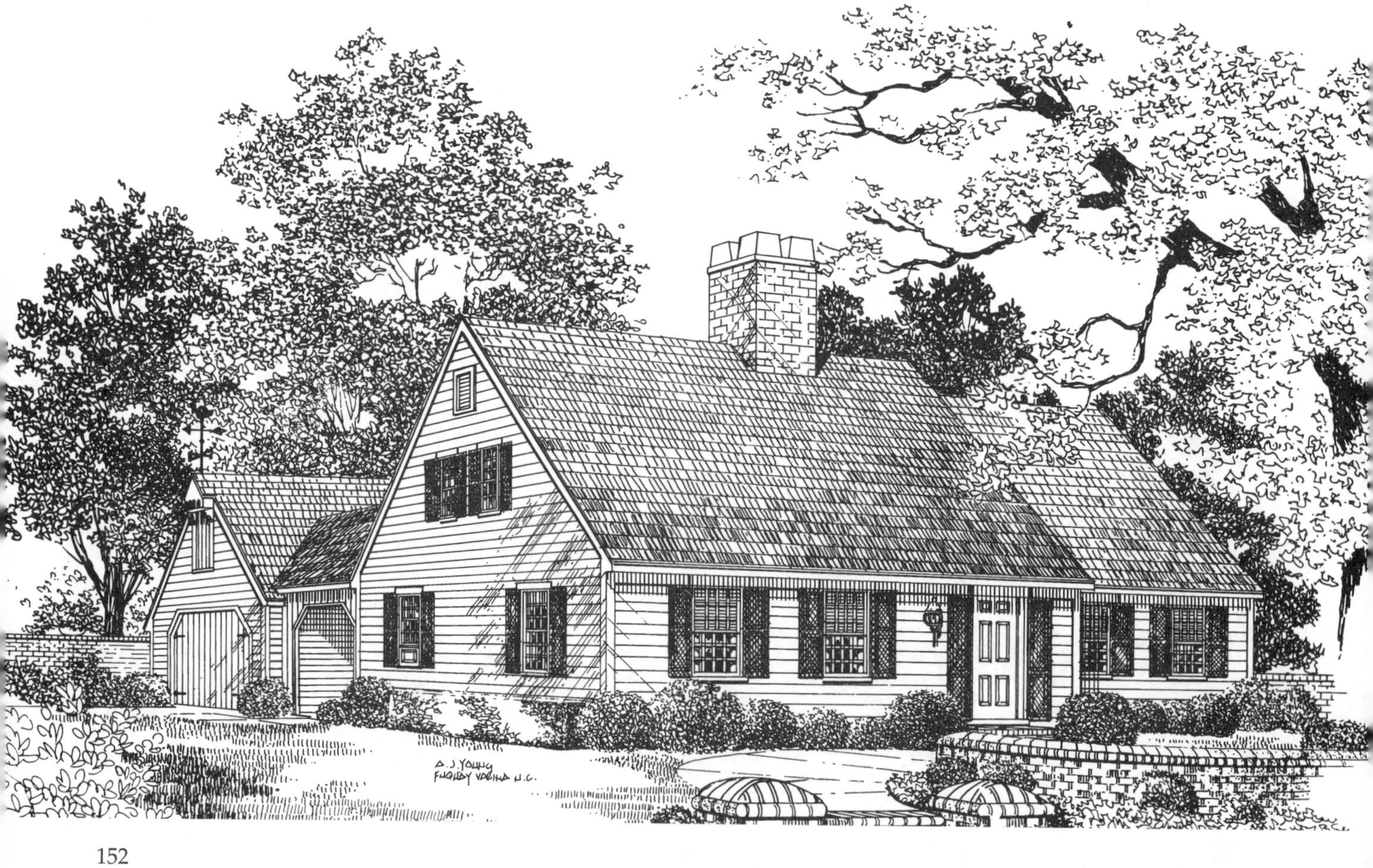

Design by
Home Planners

■ Captivating as a New England village! From the weathervane atop the garage to the roofed side entry and multi-lite windows, this home is perfectly detailed. Inside, there is a lot of living space. An exceptionally large family room, which is more than 29' by 13' including a dining area, features a raised-hearth fireplace. The adjoining kitchen has a laundry just steps away. The formal living and dining rooms are in the front and complemented by a half-bath in the center hall. Upstairs, the master bedroom offers a roomy bath with a walk-in closet and a dressing area. Two family bedrooms share a compartmented bath. Note the convenient service entrance, where the laundry is found, which also offers access to the two-car garage.

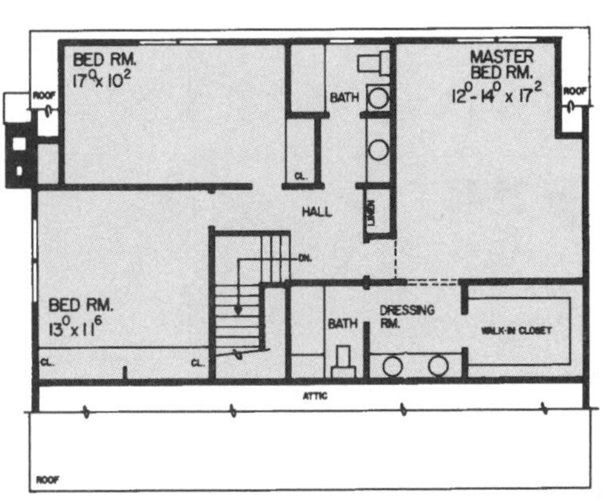
BED RM.
17⁰ x 10²
BATH
MASTER BED RM.
12⁰-14⁰ x 17²
ROOF
HALL
BED RM.
13⁰ x 11⁶
BATH
DRESSING RM.
WALK-IN CLOSET
ATTIC
ROOF

Width 76'-0"
Depth 32'-0"

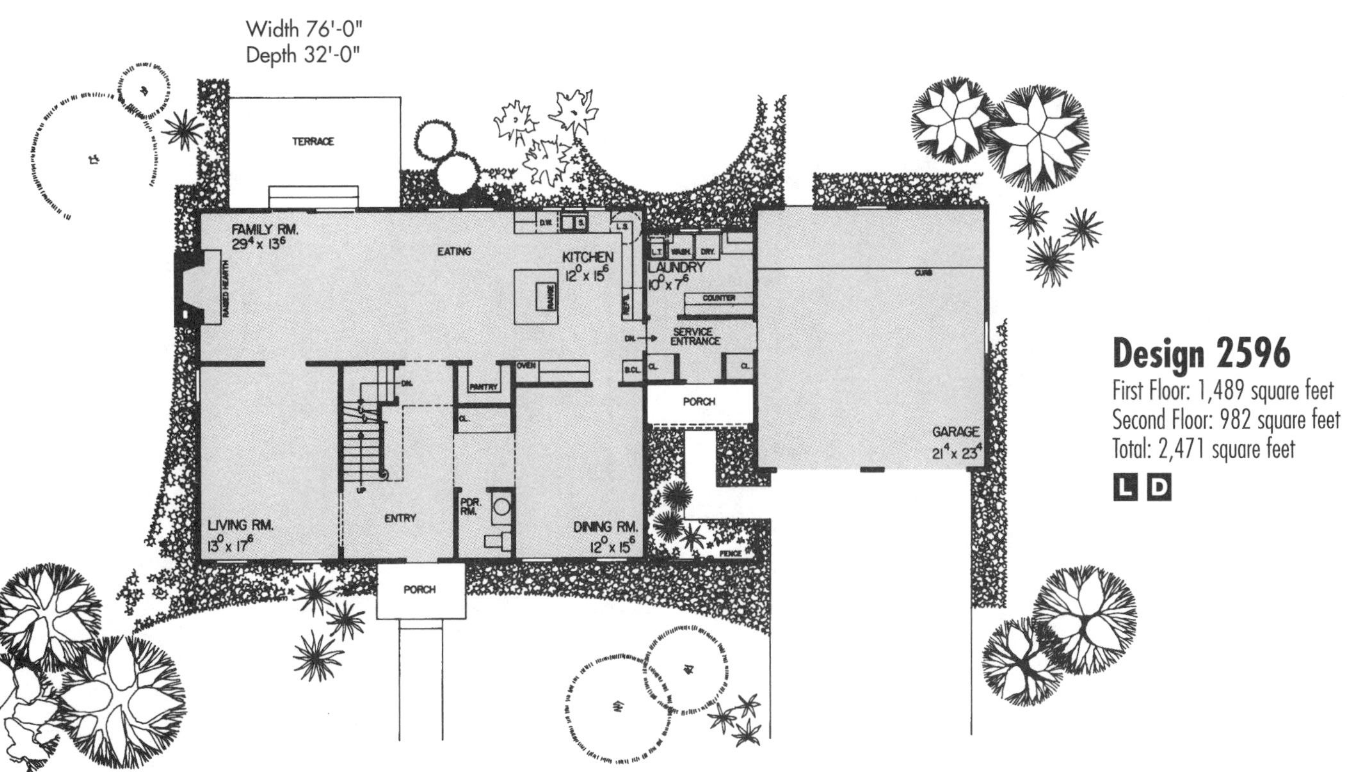
TERRACE
FAMILY RM.
29⁴ x 13⁶
RAISED HEARTH
EATING
KITCHEN
12⁰ x 15⁶
LAUNDRY
10⁰ x 7⁶
COUNTER
SERVICE ENTRANCE
PANTRY
OVEN
PORCH
GARAGE
21⁴ x 23⁴
LIVING RM.
13⁰ x 17⁶
ENTRY
PDR. RM.
DINING RM.
12⁰ x 15⁶
PORCH
FENCE

Design 2596

First Floor: 1,489 square feet
Second Floor: 982 square feet
Total: 2,471 square feet

L D

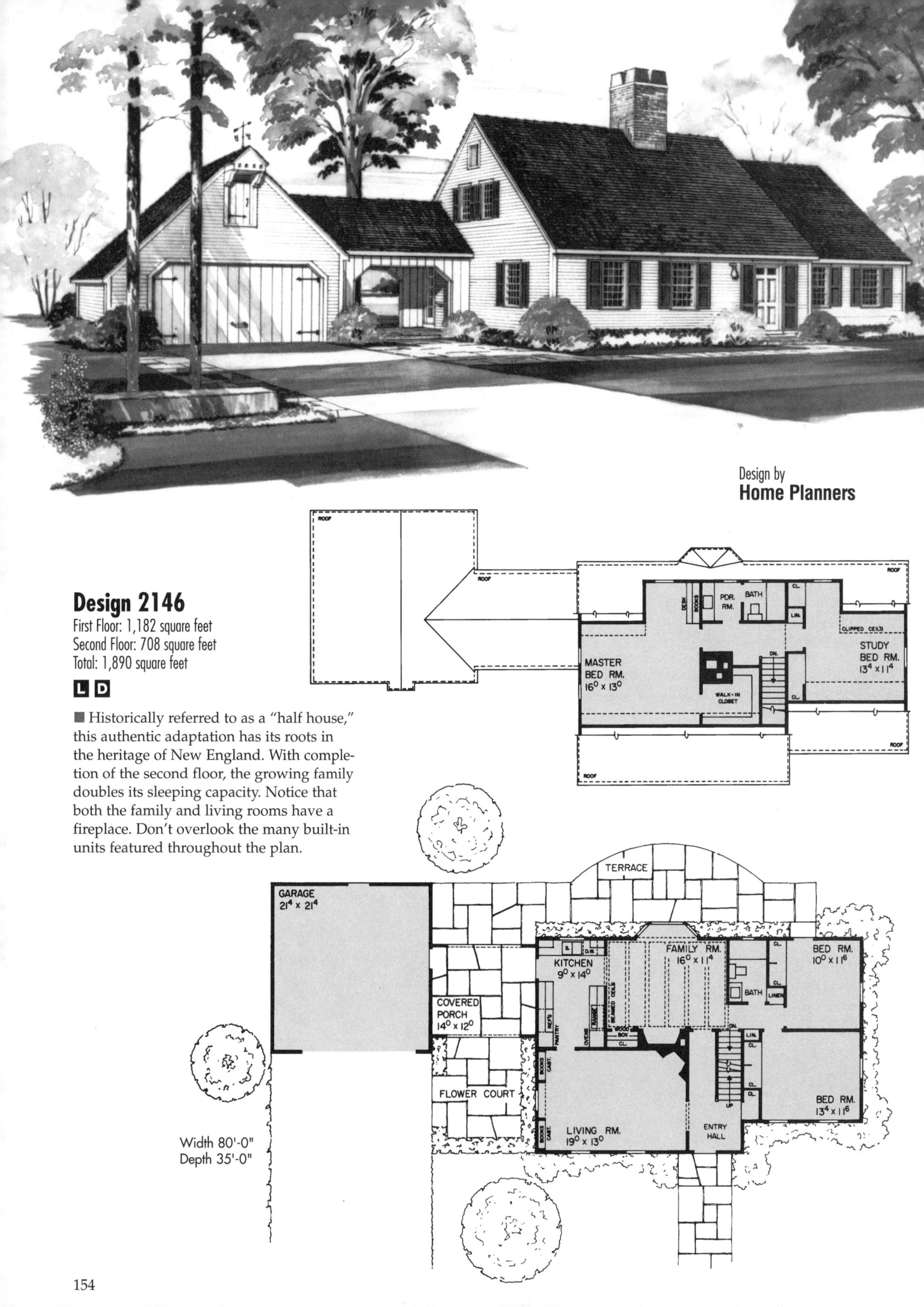
Design by
Home Planners
ROOF
ROOF
ROOF
ROOF
ROOF
DESK
BOOKS
PDR. RM.
BATH
CL.
LIN.
CLIPPED CEIL'G
STUDY
BED RM.
13⁴ x 11⁴
MASTER
BED RM.
16⁰ x 13⁰
DN.
WALK-IN CLOSET
CL.
TERRACE
GARAGE
21⁴ x 21⁴
KITCHEN
9⁰ x 14⁰
FAMILY RM.
16⁰ x 11⁴
BED RM.
10⁰ x 11⁶
CL.
CL.
BATH
LINEN
COVERED
PORCH
14⁰ x 12⁰
REF'G
PANTRY
OVENS
RANGE
BEAMED CEIL'G
WOOD BOX
CL.
DN.
LIN.
CL.
BOOKS
CAB'T.
FLOWER COURT
CL.
CL.
UP
BED RM.
13⁴ x 11⁶
BOOKS
CAB'T.
LIVING RM.
19⁰ x 13⁰
ENTRY
HALL
Width 80'-0"
Depth 35'-0"

Design 2146

First Floor: 1,182 square feet
Second Floor: 708 square feet
Total: 1,890 square feet

L D

■ Historically referred to as a "half house," this authentic adaptation has its roots in the heritage of New England. With completion of the second floor, the growing family doubles its sleeping capacity. Notice that both the family and living rooms have a fireplace. Don't overlook the many built-in units featured throughout the plan.

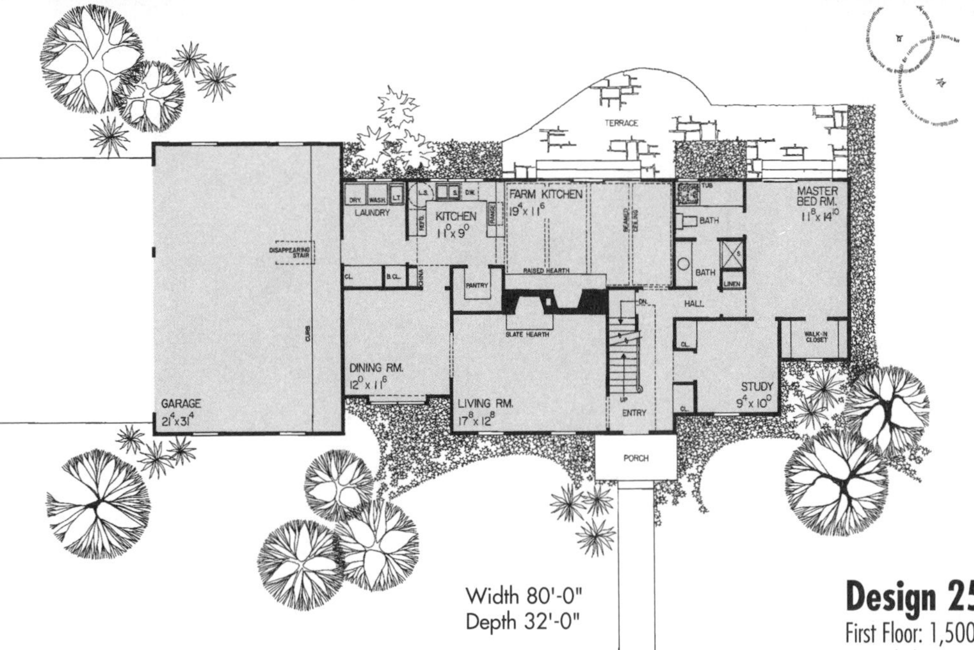
TERRACE
LAUNDRY
KITCHEN $11^{0} x 9^{0}$
FARM KITCHEN $19^{4} x 11^{6}$
MASTER BED RM. $11^{8} x 14^{10}$
BATH
PANTRY
RAISED HEARTH
SLATE HEARTH
HALL
WALK-IN CLOSET
DINING RM. $12^{0} x 11^{6}$
LIVING RM. $17^{8} x 12^{8}$
STUDY $9^{4} x 10^{0}$
GARAGE $21^{4} x 31^{4}$
ENTRY
PORCH

QUOTE ONE®

Cost to build? See page 516 to order complete cost estimate to build this house in your area!

Width 80'-0"
Depth 32'-0"

Design 2563

First Floor: 1,500 square feet
Second Floor: 690 square feet
Total: 2,190 square feet

L D

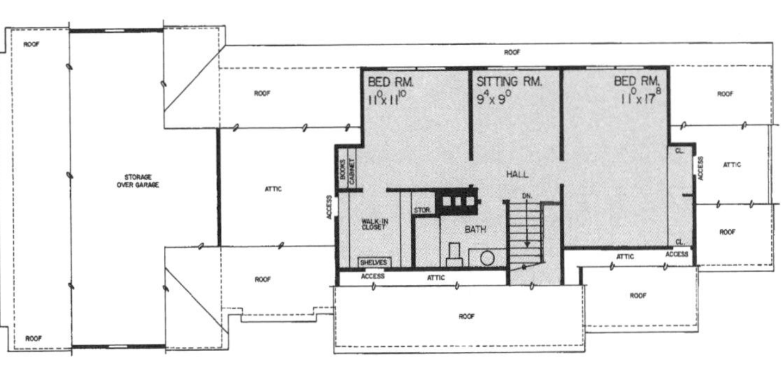
BED RM. $11^{6} x 11^{10}$
SITTING RM. $9^{4} x 9^{0}$
BED RM. $11^{0} x 17^{8}$
HALL
BATH
WALK-IN CLOSET
STORAGE OVER GARAGE
ATTIC
ROOF

■ This charming Cape Cod will capture your heart with its warm appeal. From the large living room with fireplace and the adjacent dining room to the farm kitchen with an additional fireplace, the plan works toward livability. The first-floor laundry and walk-in pantry further aid in the efficiency of this plan. The master bedroom is located on this level for privacy and is highlighted by a luxurious bath and sliding glass doors to the rear terrace. A front study might be used as a guest bedroom or a library. Upstairs there are two bedrooms and a sitting room plus a full bath to accommodate the needs of family members. Both bedrooms have access to the attic. A three-car garage allows plenty of room for vehicles and storage space.

Design by
Home Planners

Design 3126

First Floor: 1,141 square feet
Second Floor: 630 square feet
Total: 1,771 square feet

L D

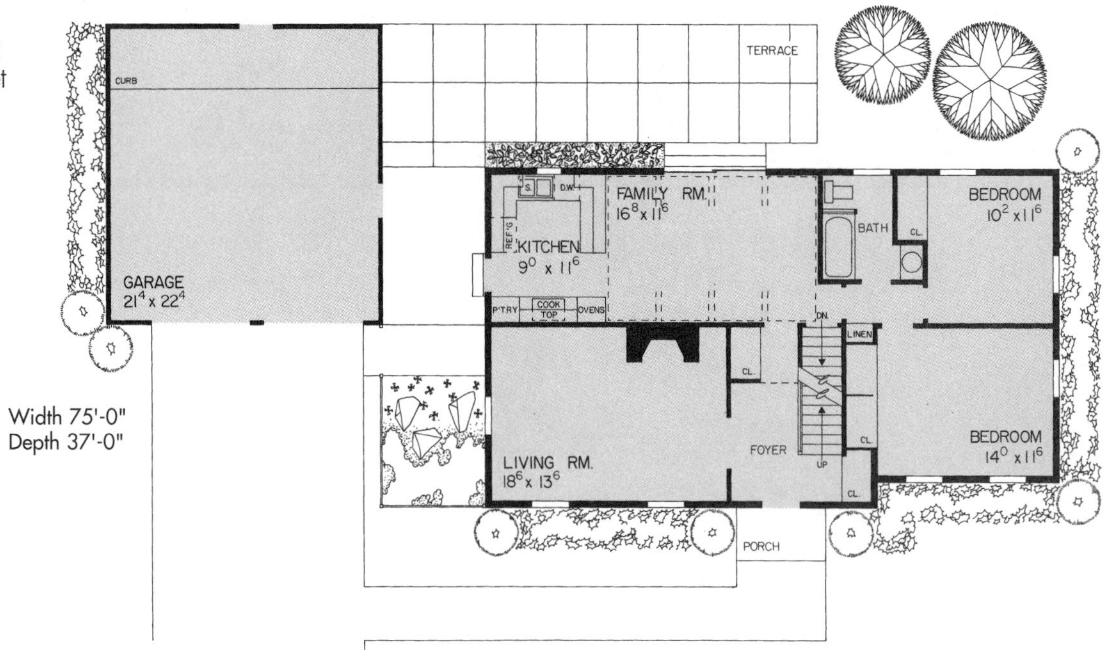

TERRACE
CURB
GARAGE
21^4 x 22^4
S.
D.W.
REF'G
KITCHEN
9^0 x 11^6
P'TRY
COOK TOP
OVENS
FAMILY RM.
16^8 x 11^6
BATH
CL.
BEDROOM
10^2 x 11^6
DN.
LINEN
CL.
LIVING RM.
18^6 x 13^6
FOYER
UP
CL.
CL.
BEDROOM
14^0 x 11^6
PORCH
Width 75'-0"
Depth 37'-0"

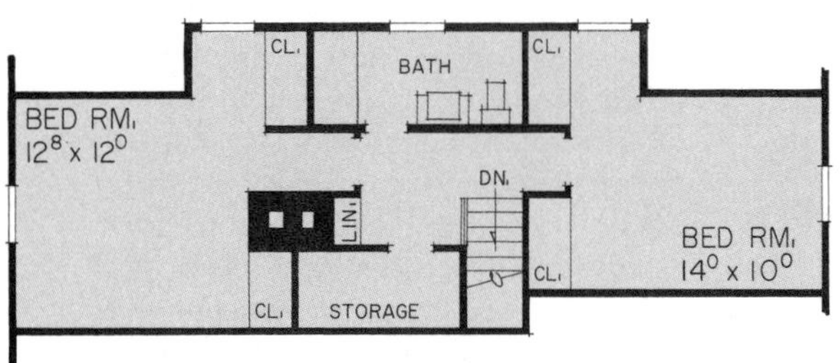

BED RM.
12^8 x 12^0
CL.
BATH
CL.
DN.
LIN.
CL.
STORAGE
CL.
BED RM.
14^0 x 10^0

■ This New England adaptation has a lot more to offer than just a beautiful facade. The interior is classic floor planning with a center hall and split-bedroom design. A U-shaped kitchen adjoins an open family/dining room, which has sliding glass doors to the rear terrace. A formal living room with a fireplace is to the left of the entry. Two bedrooms and a full bath are on the first floor, while an additional two bedrooms and full bath are found on the second floor. One of the first-floor bedrooms might make a handy den or home office. A large storage area is also on the second floor. Connecting the main house to a two-car garage, the side covered porch is as useful as it is appealing.

Design by
Home Planners

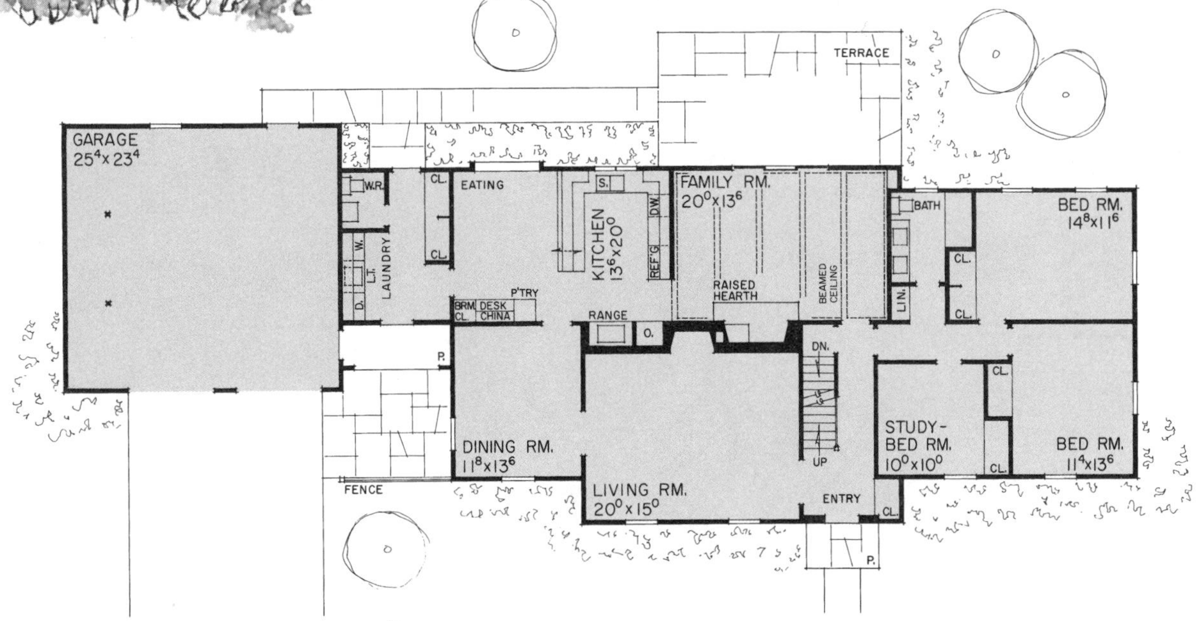

Width 100'-0"
Depth 32'-0"

Design 1718

First Floor: 2,012 square feet
Second Floor: 586 square feet
Total: 2,598 square feet

L D

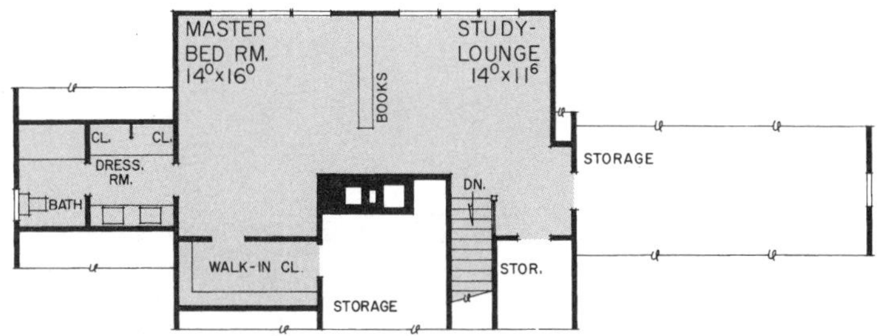
MASTER
BED RM.
14⁰x16⁰
STUDY-
LOUNGE
14⁰x11⁶
BOOKS
CL.
CL.
DRESS.
RM.
BATH
STORAGE
DN.
WALK-IN CL.
STOR.
STORAGE

■ Cape Cod styling on the outside leads to a gracious and livable floor plan on the inside of this 1½-story design. Besides a large living room with fireplace and dining room, there is a family room with beam ceiling, fireplace and sliding glass doors to a rear terrace. The U-shaped kitchen is nearby and has an adjoining casual dining area with pantry and built-in desk. Beyond that is a laundry area and half-bath. Three family bedrooms—or two and a study—remain on the first floor. They share a full bath with linen closet. The second floor is devoted to the master suite. It features a study/lounge, walk-in closet and bath with dressing area. Two large storage areas are also found on the second floor.

Design by
Home Planners

QUOTE ONE®

Cost to build? See page 516 to order complete cost estimate to build this house in your area!

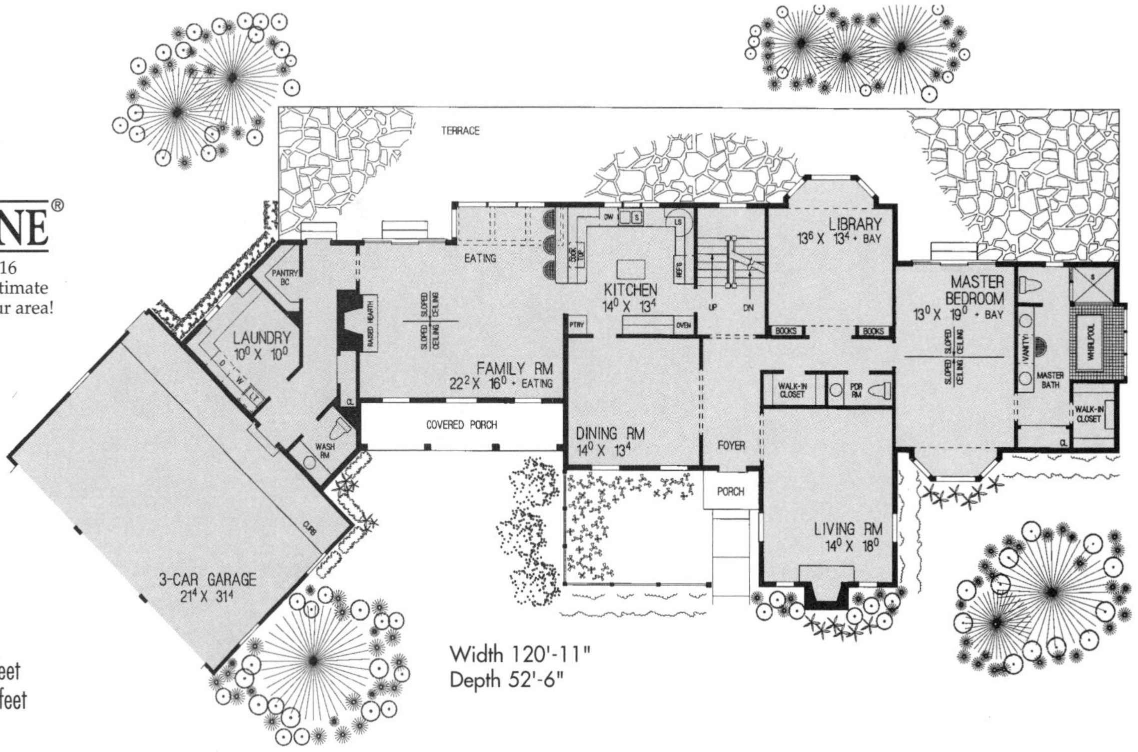

Width 120'-11"
Depth 52'-6"

Design 2995

First Floor: 2,465 square feet
Second Floor: 617 square feet
Total: 3,082 square feet

L **D**

■ This New England Colonial delivers beautiful proportions and great livability on 1½ levels. The main area of the house, the first floor, holds a living room, a library, a family room, a dining room and a gourmet kitchen. The master bedroom, also on this floor, features a sumptuous master bath with a whirlpool tub and a sloped ceiling. A long rear terrace stretches the full width of the house. Two bedrooms on the second floor share a full bath; each has a built-in desk.

Design by
Home Planners

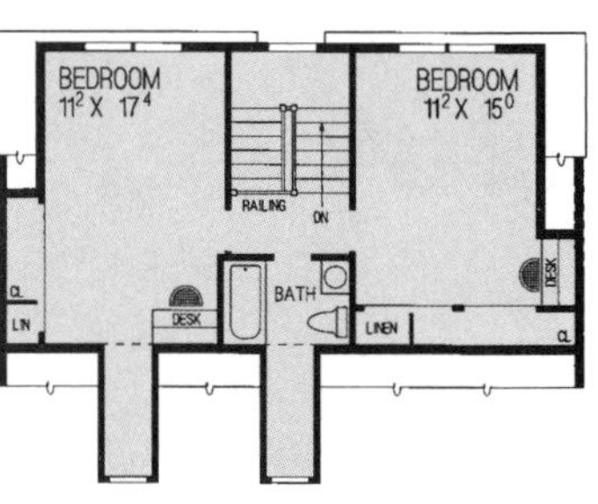
BEDROOM
11^{2} X 17^{4}
BEDROOM
11^{2} X 15^{0}
RAILING
DN
BATH
DESK
LINEN
CL
LIN

This home, as shown in the photograph, may differ from the actual blueprints. For more detailed information, please check the floor plans carefully.

Photo by Laszlo Regos

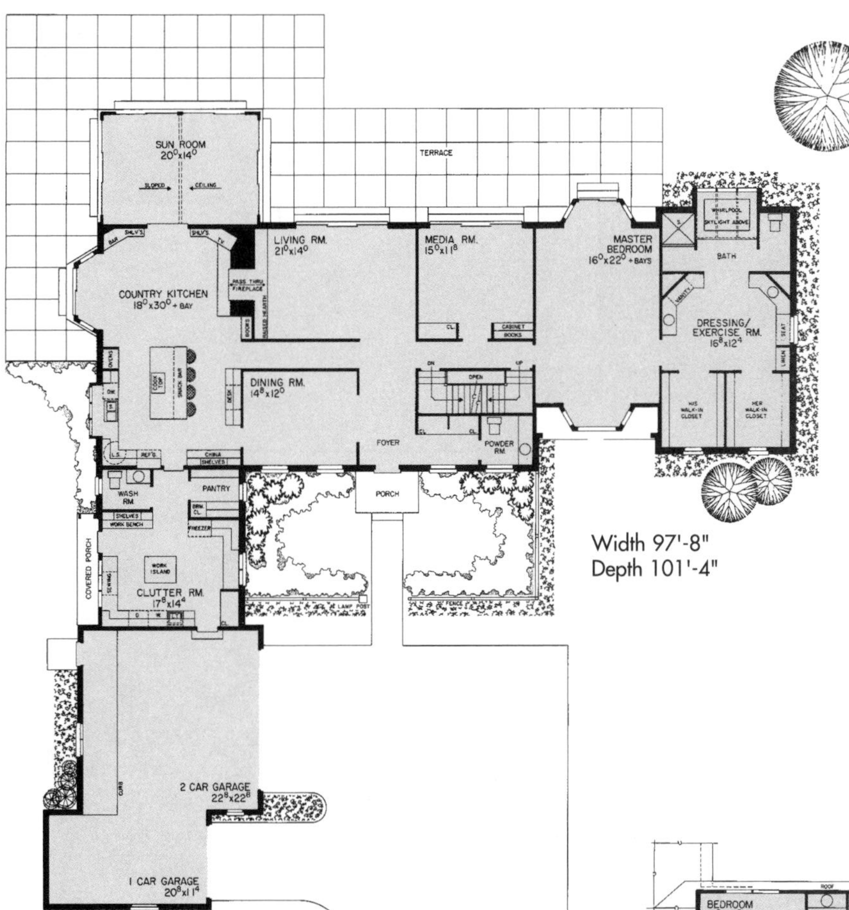

SUN ROOM
TERRACE
LIVING RM.
MEDIA RM.
MASTER BEDROOM
BATH
COUNTRY KITCHEN
DRESSING/ EXERCISE RM.
DINING RM.
FOYER
POWDER RM
PORCH
PANTRY
WASH RM
CLUTTER RM.
COVERED PORCH
2 CAR GARAGE
1 CAR GARAGE
Width 97'-8"
Depth 101'-4"

Design 2921

First Floor: 3,215 square feet
Second Floor: 711 square feet
Total: 3,926 square feet
Sun Room: 296 square feet

L **D**

■ Organized zoning makes this traditional design a comfortable home for living. A central foyer facilitates flexible traffic patterns. Quiet areas of the house include a media room and luxurious master bedroom suite with fitness area, spacious closet space and bath, as well as a lounge or writing area. Informal living areas of the house include a sunroom, large country kitchen and an efficient food preparation area with an island. Formal living areas include a living area and formal dining room. The second floor holds two bedrooms and a lounge. Service areas include a room just off the garage for laundry, sewing or hobbies.

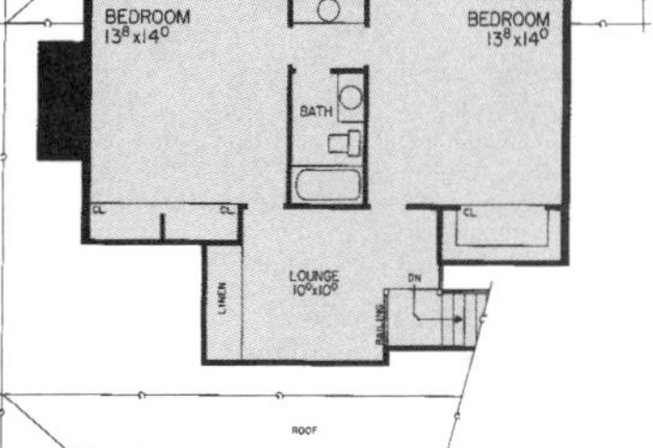

BEDROOM
BEDROOM
BATH
LOUNGE

Design by
Home Planners

QUOTE ONE®

Cost to build? See page 516 to order complete cost estimate to build this house in your area!

Design 3606

First Floor: 1,969 square feet
Second Floor: 660 square feet
Total: 2,629 square feet
Bonus Room: 360 square feet

L **D**

Design by
Home Planners

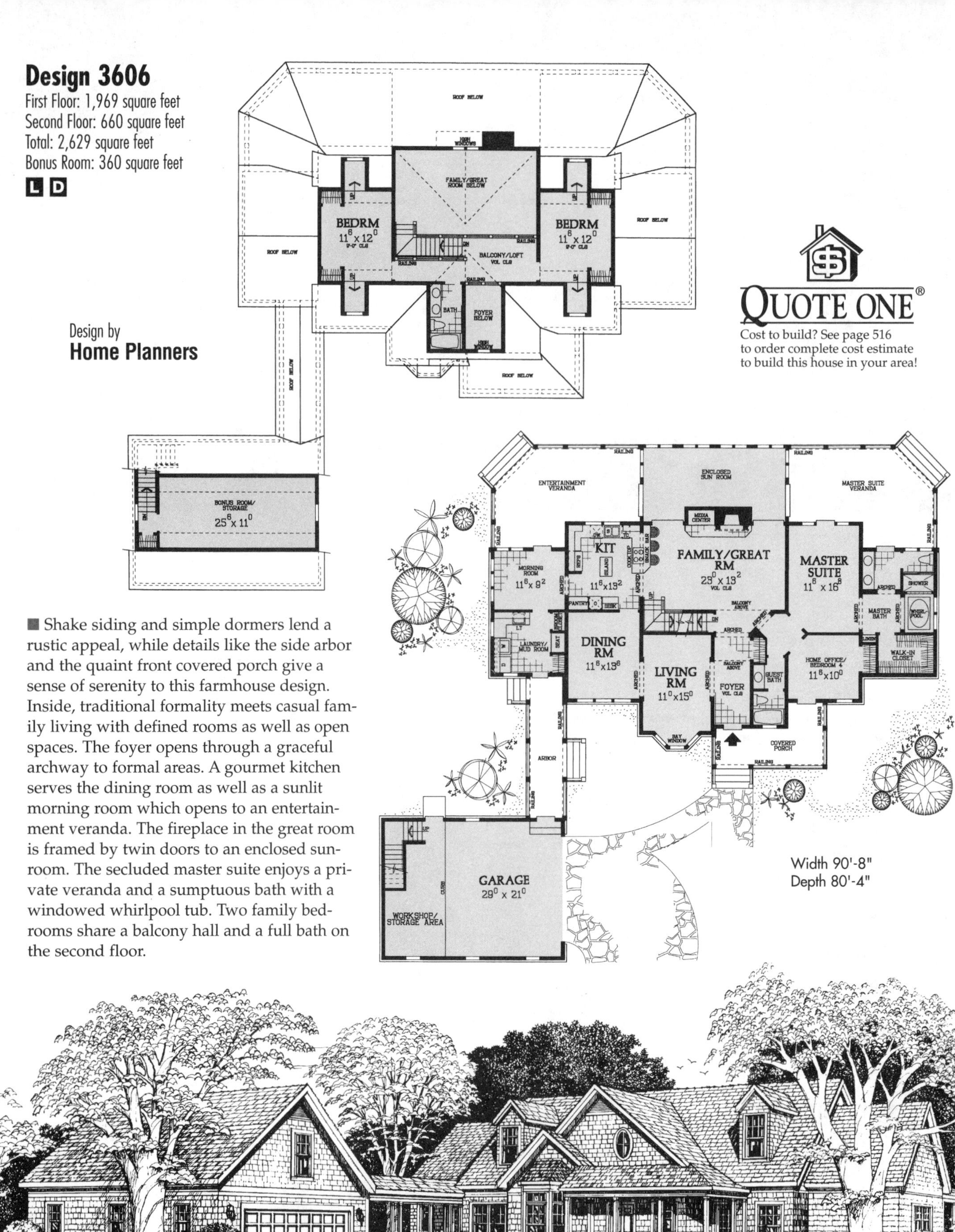

ROOF BELOW
HIGH WINDOWS
FAMILY/GREAT ROOM BELOW
BEDRM
11⁶ x 12⁰
BEDRM
11⁶ x 12⁰
BALCONY/LOFT
RAILING
BATH
FOYER BELOW
BONUS ROOM/ STORAGE
25⁶ x 11⁰
ENTERTAINMENT VERANDA
ENCLOSED SUN ROOM
MASTER SUITE VERANDA
MEDIA CENTER
KIT
11⁶x13²
FAMILY/GREAT RM
23⁰ x 13²
MASTER SUITE
11⁶ x 16⁸
MORNING ROOM
11⁶x 9²
PANTRY
DESK
DINING RM
11⁶x13⁶
LIVING RM
11⁰x15⁰
FOYER
GUEST BATH
HOME OFFICE/ BEDROOM 4
11⁸x10⁰
MASTER BATH
WALK-IN CLOSET
LAUNDRY/ MUD ROOM
BAY WINDOW
COVERED PORCH
ARBOR
GARAGE
29⁰ x 21⁰
WORKSHOP/ STORAGE AREA

QUOTE ONE®

Cost to build? See page 516 to order complete cost estimate to build this house in your area!

■ Shake siding and simple dormers lend a rustic appeal, while details like the side arbor and the quaint front covered porch give a sense of serenity to this farmhouse design. Inside, traditional formality meets casual family living with defined rooms as well as open spaces. The foyer opens through a graceful archway to formal areas. A gourmet kitchen serves the dining room as well as a sunlit morning room which opens to an entertainment veranda. The fireplace in the great room is framed by twin doors to an enclosed sunroom. The secluded master suite enjoys a private veranda and a sumptuous bath with a windowed whirlpool tub. Two family bedrooms share a balcony hall and a full bath on the second floor.

Width 90'-8"
Depth 80'-4"

This home, as shown in the photograph, may differ from the actual blueprints. For more detailed information, please check the floor plans carefully.

Photo by Andrew D. Lautman

Design 2947

Square Footage: 1,830

L D

This charming, one-story traditional home greets visitors with a covered porch, decked out with columns and balusters. Inside, a galley-style kitchen shares a snack counter with the gathering room, which offers a fireplace and opens to the formal dining room. The lavish master suite nestles to the rear of the plan and boasts a sloped ceiling, a dressing room and a relaxing bath with a whirlpool tub and a separate shower. Two additional bedrooms—one could double as a study—enjoy views of the front property.

Design by
Home Planners

Width 75'-0"
Depth 43'-5"

TERRACE
MASTER BEDROOM $11^{10} \times 17^{8}$
GATHERING RM $15^{0} \times 17^{8}$
DINING RM $12^{0} \times 9^{8}$
WHIRLPOOL
BATH
DRESS RM
PANTRY
KITCHEN $14^{2} \times 12^{0}$
GARAGE $21^{4} \times 22^{4}$ + STOR
LINEN
BATH
FOYER
BRKFST RM $8^{8} \times 10^{4}$
BOOKS CAB'T
COVERED PORCH
RAILING
BEDROOM $10^{6} \times 11^{6}$
STUDY/ BEDROOM $11^{2} \times 11^{6}$
STORAGE

QUOTE ONE®

Cost to build? See page 516 to order complete cost estimate to build this house in your area!

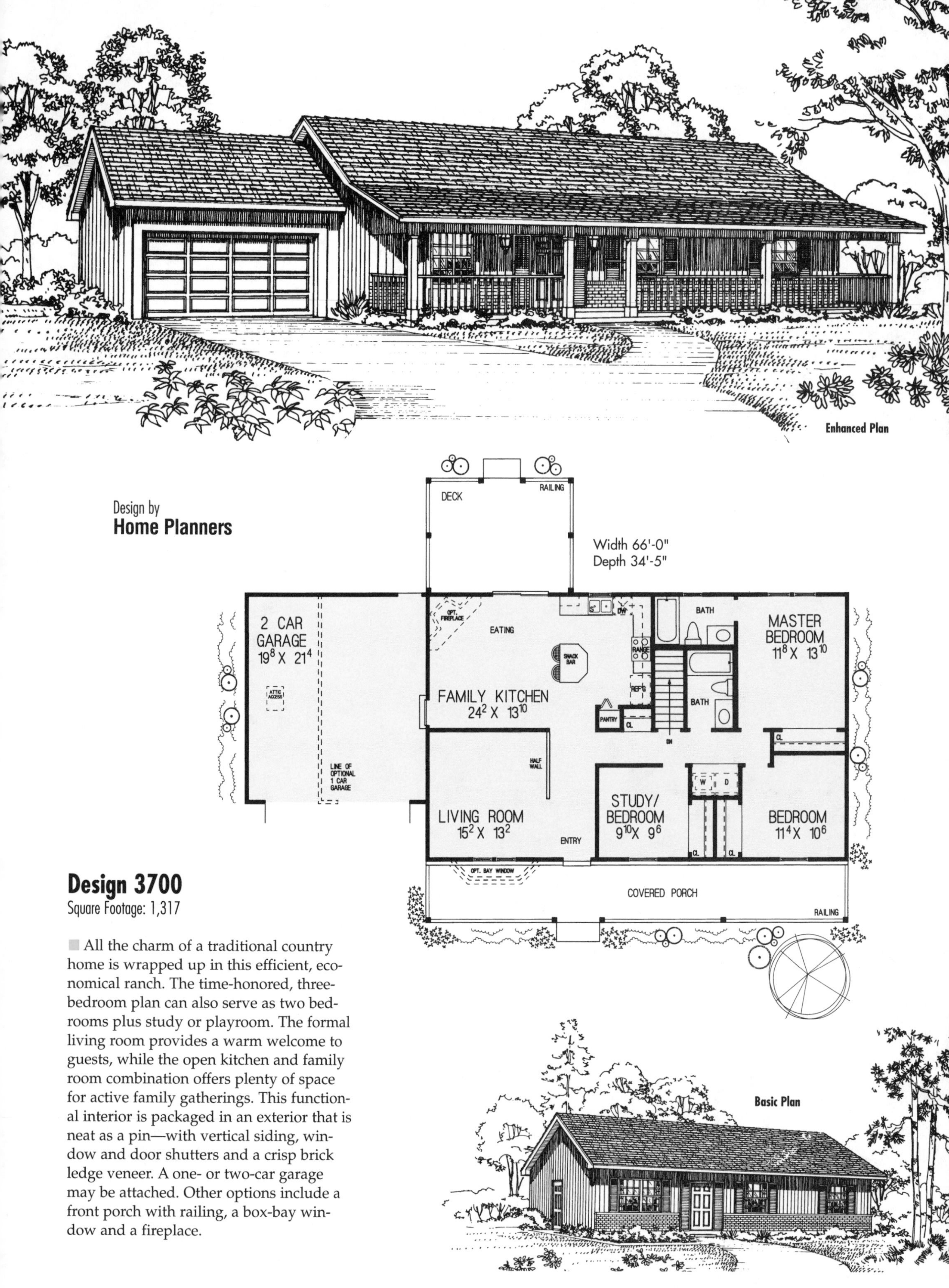

Enhanced Plan
DECK
RAILING
Width 66'-0"
Depth 34'-5"
2 CAR GARAGE
19^8 X 21^4
ATTIC ACCESS
LINE OF OPTIONAL 1 CAR GARAGE
OPT. FIREPLACE
EATING
SNACK BAR
FAMILY KITCHEN
24^2 X 13^{10}
PANTRY
CL
REF'G
RANGE
DW
BATH
MASTER BEDROOM
11^8 X 13^{10}
BATH
DN
CL
HALF WALL
LIVING ROOM
15^2 X 13^2
ENTRY
STUDY/ BEDROOM
9^{10}X 9^6
W
D
CL
CL
BEDROOM
11^4X 10^6
OPT. BAY WINDOW
COVERED PORCH
RAILING
Basic Plan

Design by
Home Planners

Design 3700

Square Footage: 1,317

All the charm of a traditional country home is wrapped up in this efficient, economical ranch. The time-honored, three-bedroom plan can also serve as two bedrooms plus study or playroom. The formal living room provides a warm welcome to guests, while the open kitchen and family room combination offers plenty of space for active family gatherings. This functional interior is packaged in an exterior that is neat as a pin—with vertical siding, window and door shutters and a crisp brick ledge veneer. A one- or two-car garage may be attached. Other options include a front porch with railing, a box-bay window and a fireplace.

Design Q221

Square Footage: 1,360

■ This economical-to-build family home features a low-maintenance exterior with stone and horizontal wood siding. A covered front veranda spans the full-width of the home and protects an entry leading to a center hall with living areas on the left and sleeping quarters on the right. The living room is enhanced by a fireplace and the dining room opens to the L-shaped kitchen with breakfast nook. Stairs to the basement are near the foyer; additional stairs offer a landing entry to the single-car garage. The master bedroom is one of three to the right of the plan. It holds separate entry to the bath shared with family bedrooms. Note the double sinks in this bath. One of the family bedrooms could serve as a den or home office.

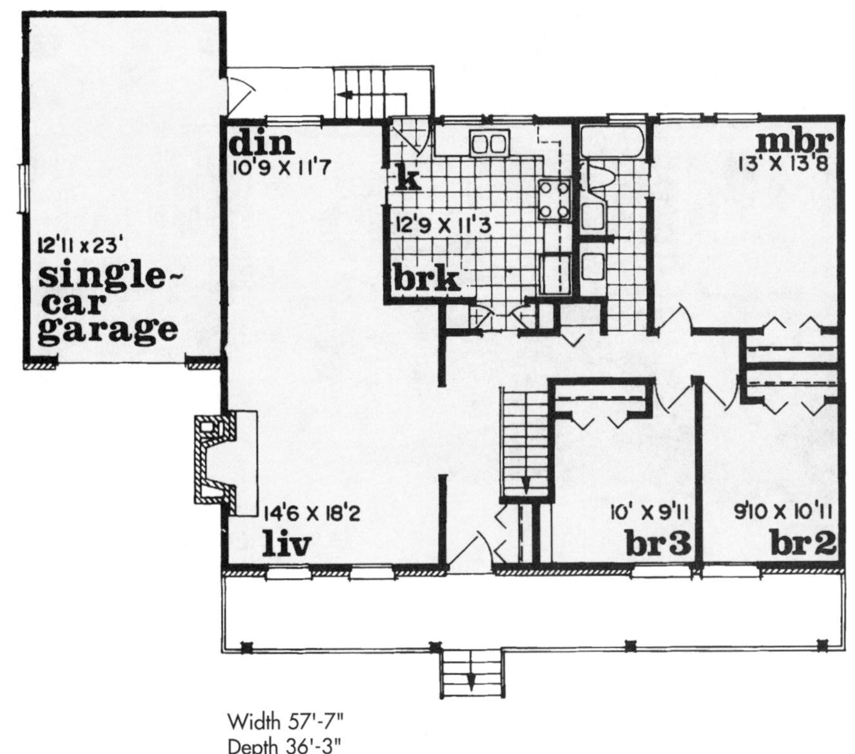
12'11 x 23'
single-car garage
din
10'9 X 11'7
k
12'9 X 11'3
brk
mbr
13' X 13'8
14'6 X 18'2
liv
10' X 9'11
br3
9'10 X 10'11
br2

Width 57'-7"
Depth 36'-3"

Design by
Select Home Designs

Design by
Home Planners

Design 1920

Square Footage: 1,600

L

This home offers a charming exterior with a truly great floor plan. The covered front porch at the entrance heralds outstanding features inside. The sleeping zone consists of three bedrooms and two full baths. Each of the bedrooms enjoys its own walk-in closet. You'll relish the efficient, U-shaped kitchen with the family room and the dining room to each side. There is also a laundry room with a wash room just off the garage.

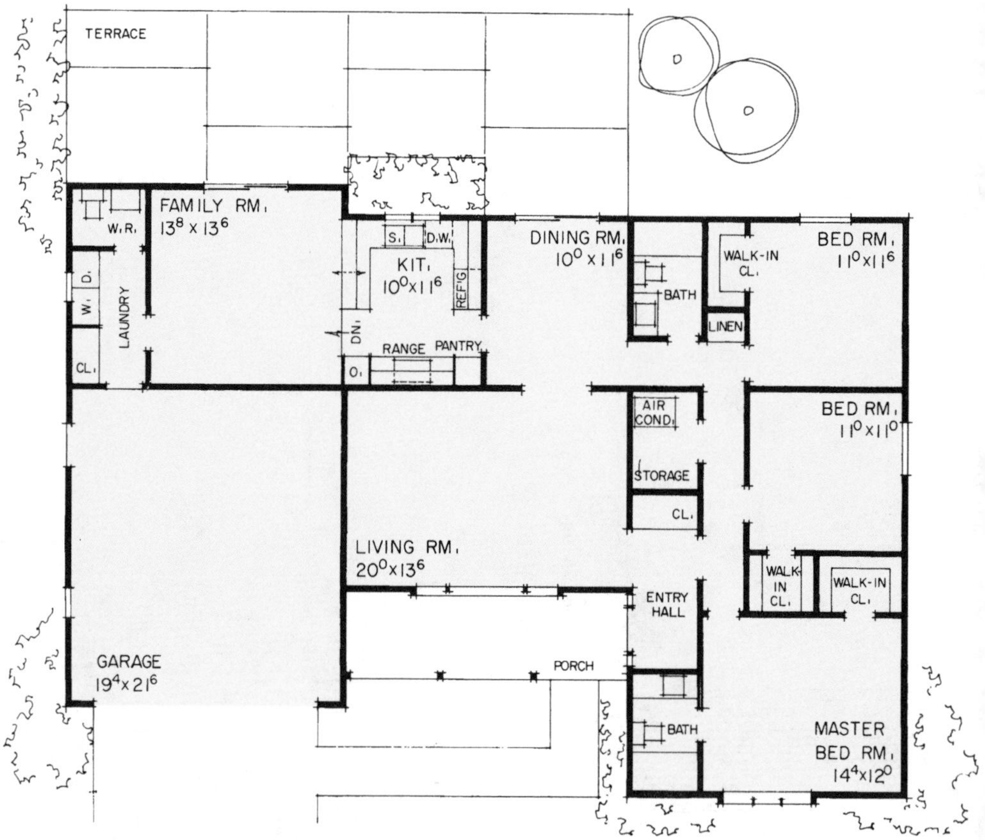

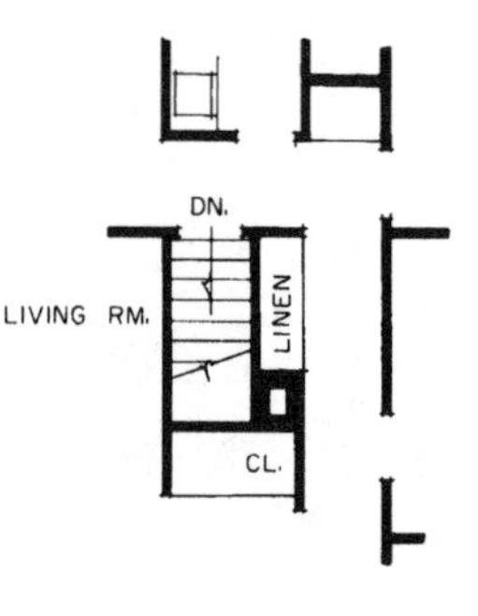
DN.
LIVING RM.
LINEN
CL.

OPTIONAL BASEMENT

Width 60'-0"
Depth 42'-0"

Design by
Home Planners

QUOTE ONE®
Cost to build? See page 516 to order complete cost estimate to build this house in your area!

Design 1323

Square Footage: 1,344

L D

Incorporated into the set of blueprints for this design are details for building each of the three charming, traditional exteriors. Each of the three alternate exteriors is distinguished in its own way. A study of the floor plan reveals fine livability. There are two full baths, a fine family room, an efficient work center, a formal dining area, bulk storage facilities and sliding glass doors to the quiet and living terraces. The laundry room is strategically located near the kitchen. Three bedrooms include a master bedroom with double closets and a full, private bath. The two secondary bedrooms share a full hall bath.

QUIET TERRACE
SCREEN
LIVING TERRACE
MASTER BED RM. 13⁰ x 13⁶
BATH
CL.
BATH
CL.
FAMILY RM 10⁶ x 13⁶
KIT. 10⁶ x 8⁰
S. D.W. W. D.
RANGE
REF'G.
LAUNDRY
CL.
DINING
AIR COND.
CHINA
STORAGE 16⁰ x 8⁰
CARPORT-GARAGE 20⁰ x 20⁰
CL.
CL.
LIN.
CL.
ENTRY
BED RM. 10⁰ x 13⁶
CL.
BED RM. 10⁸ x 10⁰
LIVING RM. 18⁰ x 19⁶
R
FENCE

Width 68'-0"
Depth 28'-0"

Design Q321

Square Footage: 1,666

A courtyard with planter box leads up a few steps to the double-door entry of this ranch home. Open-plan design minimizes hallways. For instance, the bright, skylit entry opens directly to the living room which features a corner fireplace and sliding glass doors to the rear yard. The breakfast area has a bay window and is convenient to the U-shaped kitchen with island work center. A service entry with mud/laundry room and half bath connect the kitchen to the two-car garage. The master bedroom at the other end of the plan features His and Hers wall closets and a private bath with soaking tub. Two additional bedrooms—one can serve as a den—share a main bath. Choose the crawlspace option if you prefer.

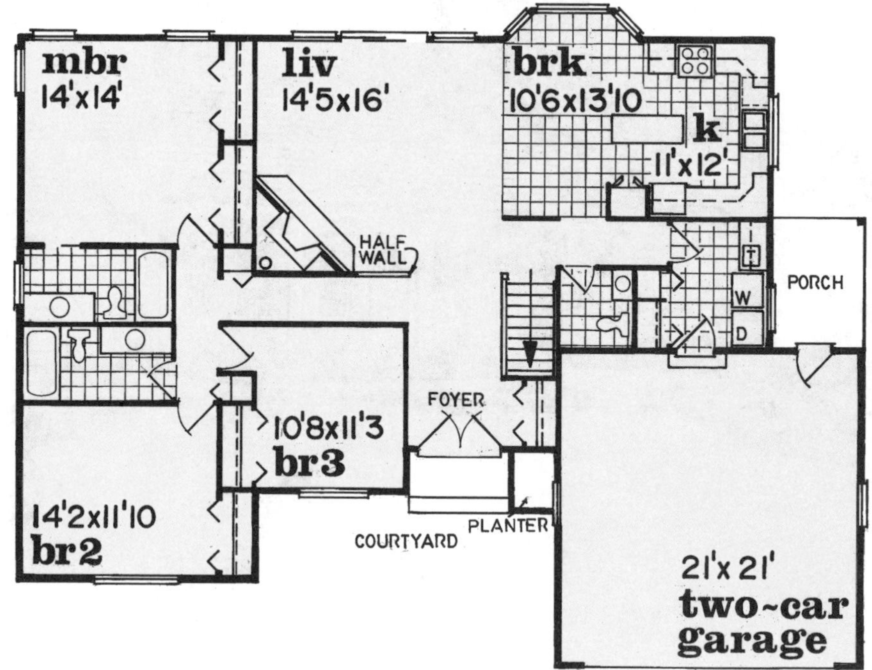
mbr
14'x14'
liv
14'5x16'
brk
10'6x13'10
k
11'x12'
HALF WALL
PORCH
W
D
FOYER
10'8x11'3
br3
14'2x11'10
br2
COURTYARD
PLANTER
21'x 21'
two-car garage

Width 60'-6"
Depth 44'-4"

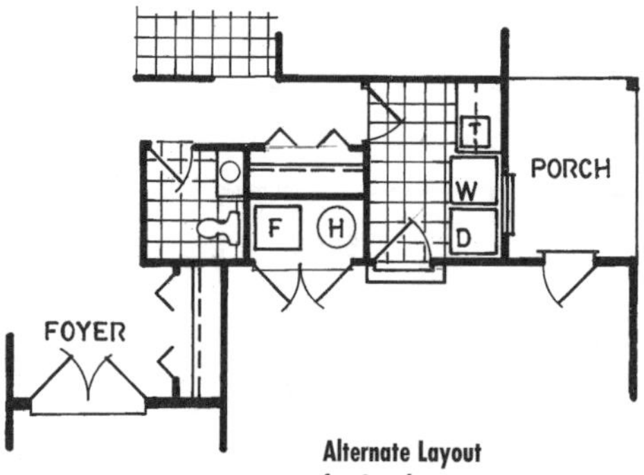

FOYER
PORCH

Alternate Layout for Crawlspace

Design by
Select Home Designs

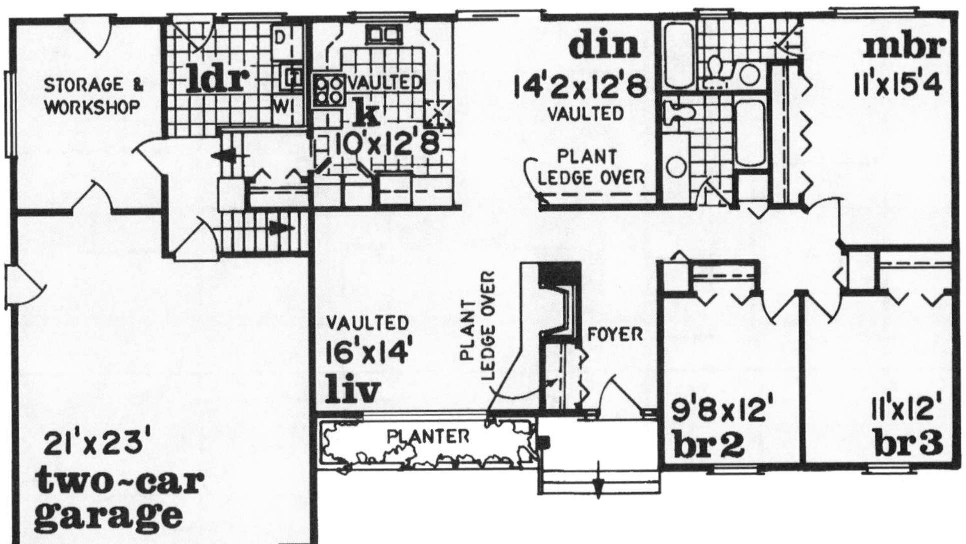
STORAGE & WORKSHOP
ldr
WI
VAULTED
k
10'x12'8
din
14'2x12'8
VAULTED
PLANT LEDGE OVER
mbr
11'x15'4
VAULTED
16'x14'
liv
PLANT LEDGE OVER
FOYER
PLANTER
9'8x12'
br2
11'x12'
br3
21'x23'
two-car garage

Width 68'-0"
Depth 37'-0"

Design Q320

Square Footage: 1,566
Storage/Workshop: 149 square feet

This simple country one-story has decorative touches at its entry including a planter box and columned front porch. The foyer introduces additional touches such as a coat closet with plant ledge above and a plant ledge in the hall. The living room is vaulted and contains a warming fireplace. Both the kitchen and dining area are also vaulted—the dining room has sliding glass doors to the rear yard. Note the U-shape of the kitchen for efficiency. The main-floor laundry room has three-way access from the workshop, the backyard and the two-car garage. The stairway to the basement is also found here. A roomy wall closet appoints the master bedroom, which also boasts a private bath. Family bedrooms share a bath with linen closet.

Design by
Select Home Designs

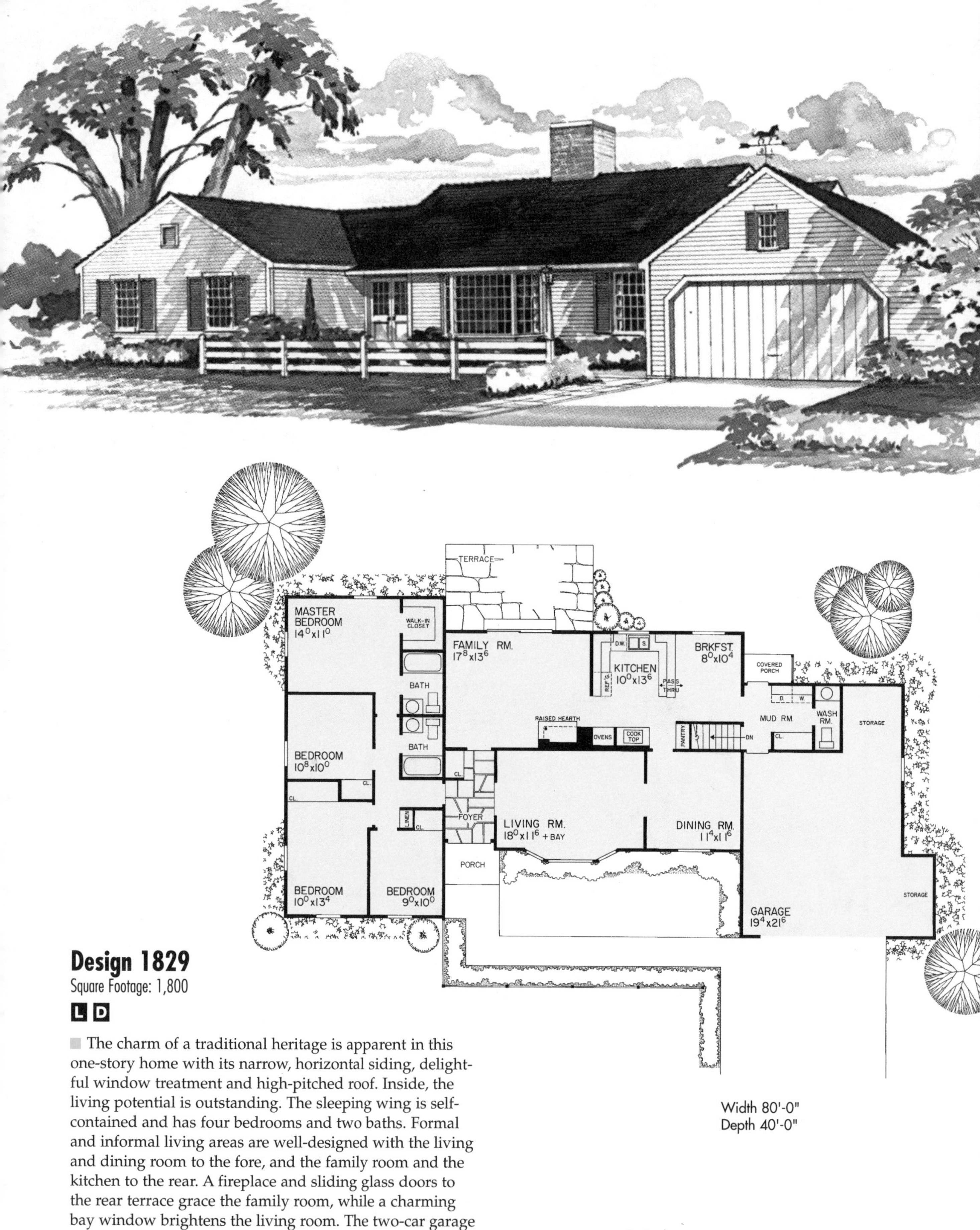
TERRACE
MASTER BEDROOM 14^{0}x11^0
WALK-IN CLOSET
BATH
BATH
BEDROOM 10^{8}x10^0
CL.
CL.
LINEN
CL.
BEDROOM 10^{0}x13^4
BEDROOM 9^{0}x10^0
FAMILY RM. 17^{8}x13^6
RAISED HEARTH
OVENS
COOK TOP
D.W.
S.
KITCHEN 10^{0}x13^6
REF'G.
PASS THRU
BRKFST. 8^{0}x10^4
COVERED PORCH
D.
W.
MUD RM.
WASH RM.
CL.
PANTRY
DN
STORAGE
CL.
FOYER
LIVING RM. 18^{0}x11^6 + BAY
DINING RM. 11^{4}x11^6
PORCH
STORAGE
GARAGE 19^{4}x21^6

Design 1829

Square Footage: 1,800

L D

The charm of a traditional heritage is apparent in this one-story home with its narrow, horizontal siding, delightful window treatment and high-pitched roof. Inside, the living potential is outstanding. The sleeping wing is self-contained and has four bedrooms and two baths. Formal and informal living areas are well-designed with the living and dining room to the fore, and the family room and the kitchen to the rear. A fireplace and sliding glass doors to the rear terrace grace the family room, while a charming bay window brightens the living room. The two-car garage is connected to the main house by a handy mud room with half-bath. Note the storage areas in the garage.

Width 80'-0"
Depth 40'-0"

Design by
Home Planners

Design 2672

Square Footage: 1,717

L **D**

QUOTE ONE®

Cost to build? See page 516 to order complete cost estimate to build this house in your area!

■ The traditional nature of this home is emphasized by a covered porch, multi-pane windows, narrow clapboard siding and vertical wood trim. Complementing this charming exterior is an interior plan that is efficient and accommodating. The front U-shaped kitchen works with a breakfast room and handy mud room (with garage access) as work space. A formal dining room has sliding glass doors to the rear terrace and to a covered dining porch. The adjoining living room also has terrace access. A fireplace and built-in cabinet further enhance the living room. Three bedrooms sit to the left of the plan. The master suite has a private bath and dressing room, plus sliding glass doors to the terrace. Family bedrooms share a full bath.

Width 76'-0"
Depth 42'-0"

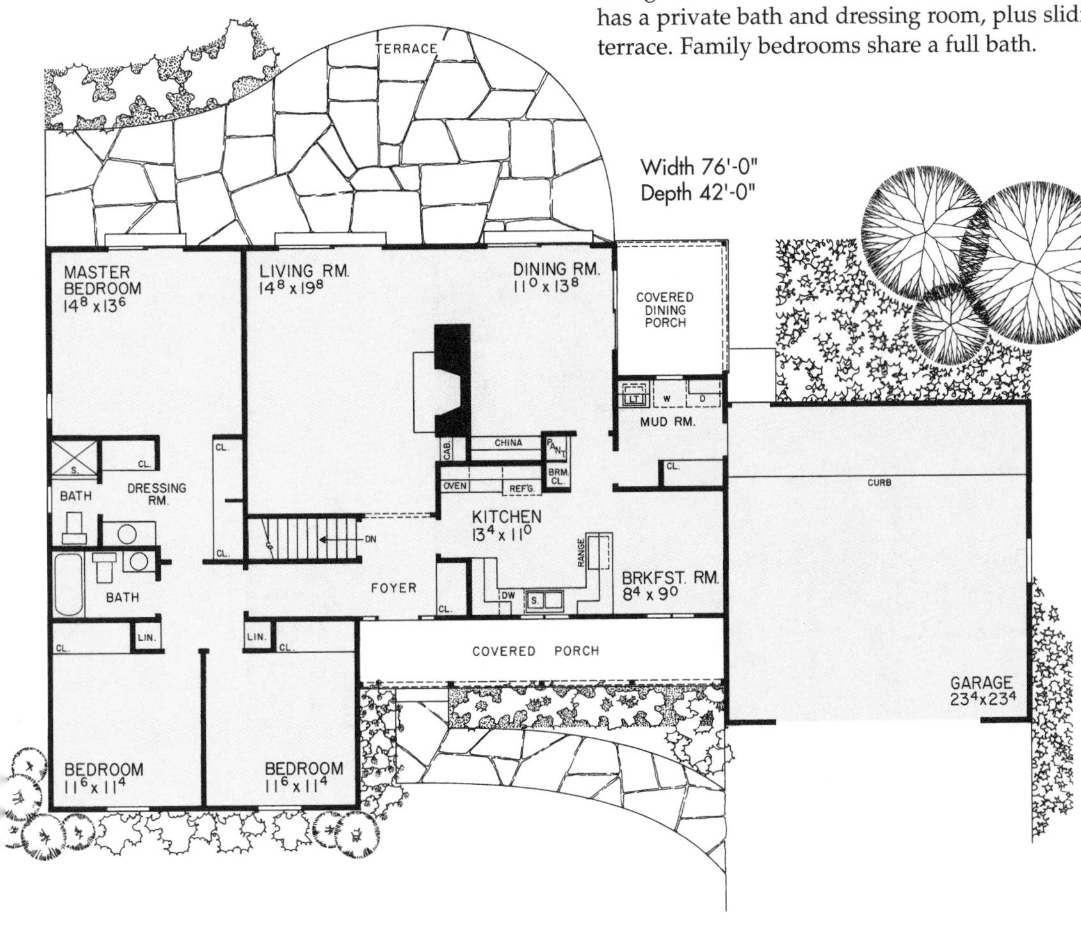

TERRACE
MASTER BEDROOM $14^8 \times 13^6$
LIVING RM. $14^8 \times 19^8$
DINING RM. $11^0 \times 13^8$
COVERED DINING PORCH
MUD RM.
CL.
CHINA
CAB.
PAN.
BRM. CL.
OVEN
REF'G.
KITCHEN $13^4 \times 11^0$
RANGE
BRKFST. RM. $8^4 \times 9^0$
DW
S.
DN
FOYER
DRESSING RM.
BATH
BATH
LIN.
COVERED PORCH
CURB
GARAGE $23^4 \times 23^4$
BEDROOM $11^6 \times 11^4$
BEDROOM $11^6 \times 11^4$

Design by
Home Planners

Design Q251

Square Footage: 1,471

A gable/cottage roof combination, with horizontal siding and multi-pane windows, lend charm to this affordable family home. The covered entry opens directly to an expansive living room featuring a corner fireplace. The kitchen, dining room and family room are warmed by a rustic wood stove. Sliding glass doors in the family room area lead out back to a patio and the rear yard beyond. The dining room rests in a bay-windowed area and provides a view to the back. Lovely skylights brighten the hallway and the staircase to the basement (finish the basement later as the family grows). Three bedrooms include a master suite with private, full bath and a walk-in closet. Family bedrooms share a full bath. The laundry alcove is nearby for convenience.

Design by
Select Home Designs

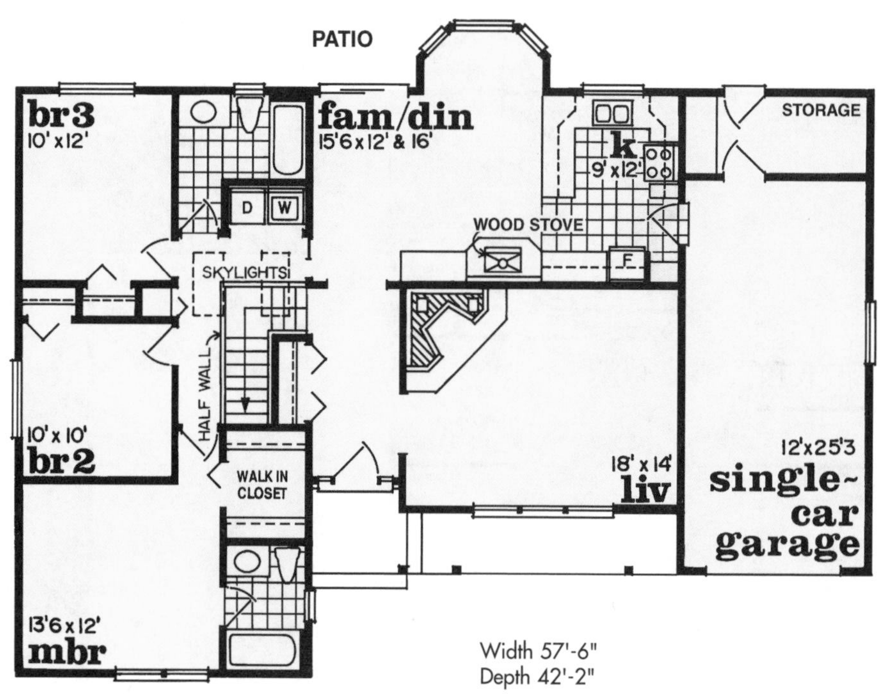

PATIO
br3
10'x12'
fam/din
15'6x12' & 16'
k
9'x12'
STORAGE
D
W
WOOD STOVE
F
SKYLIGHTS
HALF WALL
10'x10'
br2
WALK IN CLOSET
18' x 14'
liv
12'x25'3
single-car garage
13'6x12'
mbr
Width 57'-6"
Depth 42'-2"

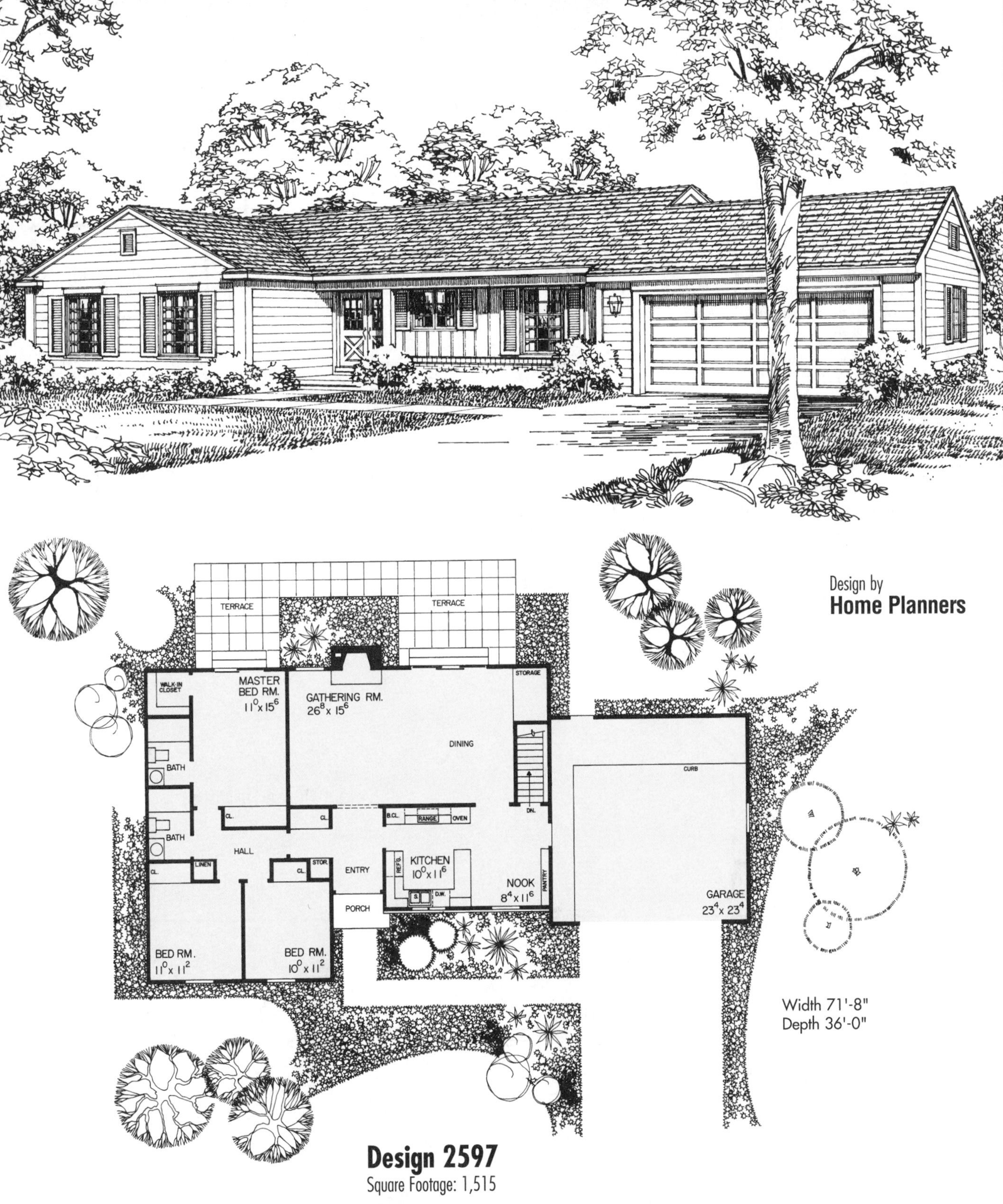
TERRACE
TERRACE
WALK IN CLOSET
MASTER BED RM. 11^0x15^6
GATHERING RM. 26^8x 15^6
STORAGE
DINING
BATH
CL.
BATH
B.CL.
RANGE
OVEN
DN.
CURB
HALL
LINEN
CL.
CL.
STOR.
ENTRY
REFG.
KITCHEN 10^0x11^6
PANTRY
NOOK 8^4x11^6
S.
D.W.
PORCH
GARAGE 23^4x 23^4
BED RM. 11^0x 11^2
BED RM. 10^0x 11^2

Design by
Home Planners

Width 71'-8"
Depth 36'-0"

Design 2597

Square Footage: 1,515

L D

Whether it's a starter house you are after, or one in which to spend your retirement years, this pleasing farmhouse will provide a full measure of pride in ownership. The contrast of vertical and horizontal lines, the double front doors and the coach lamppost at the garage create an inviting exterior. The floor plan functions in an orderly and efficient manner. The spacious gathering room and dining room have a delightful view of the rear yard and make entertaining both family and friends a joy. The master bedroom has a private bath and a walk-in closet. Two additional bedrooms share a full hall bath. Extra amenities include plenty of storage facilities, two sets of glass doors to the terraces, a fireplace in the gathering room, a basement and an attached two-car garage.

QUOTE ONE®

Cost to build? See page 516 to order complete cost estimate to build this house in your area!

Design Q367

Square Footage: 1,647

This floor plan is designed for a home that captures a view to the rear of the lot. French doors in the dining room, living room, master bedroom and breakfast room all lead out to the patio in the back. In the front, a skylit patio is visually zoned from the living room by a plant shelf. Both the living room and dining room have vaulted ceilings and enjoy a warming fireplace set between them. A U-shaped kitchen has a breakfast bar to serve the sunny breakfast room; nearby is the laundry room with access to the two-car garage. The bedrooms are to the right and include two family bedrooms sharing a full bath. The master suite is vaulted and has a walk-in closet and private bath with separate tub and shower. Plans include details for both a basement and a crawlspace foundation.

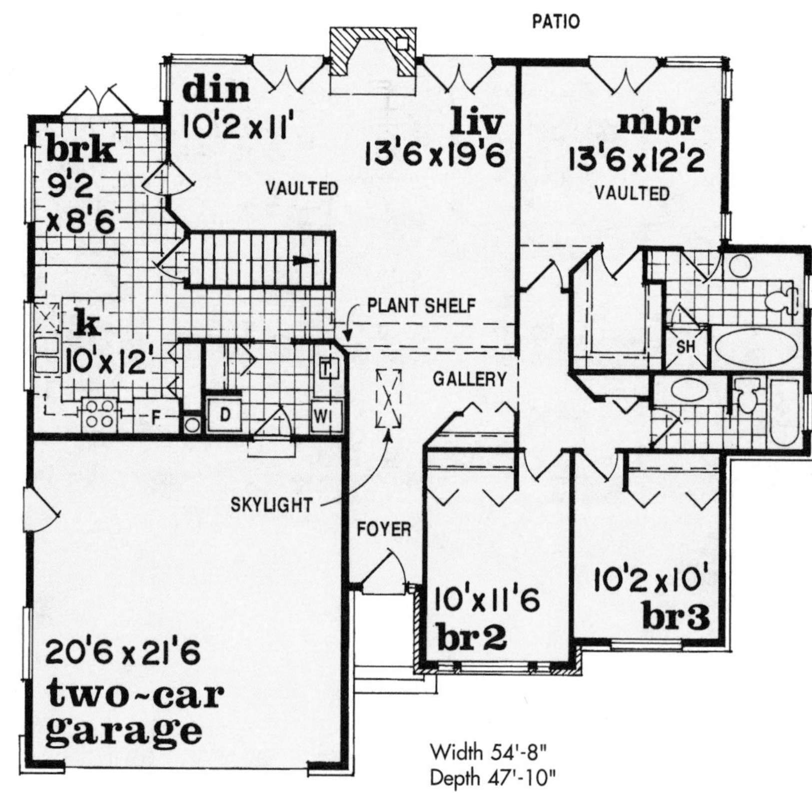

PATIO
din
10'2 x 11'
liv
13'6 x 19'6
mbr
13'6 x 12'2
VAULTED
VAULTED
brk
9'2
x 8'6
k
10' x 12'
PLANT SHELF
GALLERY
SH
F
D
WI
SKYLIGHT
FOYER
10' x 11'6
br2
10'2 x 10'
br3
20'6 x 21'6
two-car
garage

Width 54'-8"
Depth 47'-10"

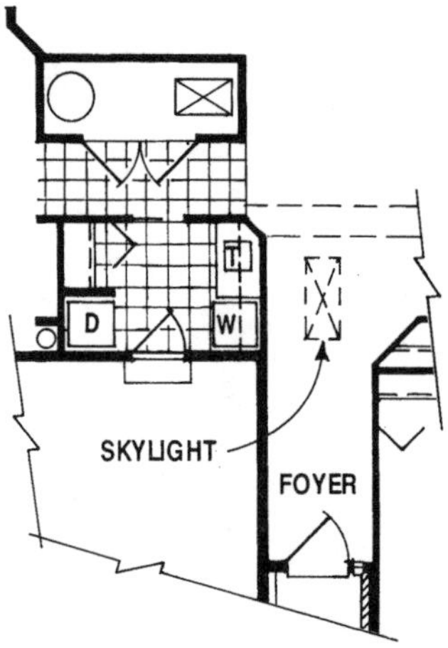

Alternate Layout for Crawlspace

Design by
Select Home Designs

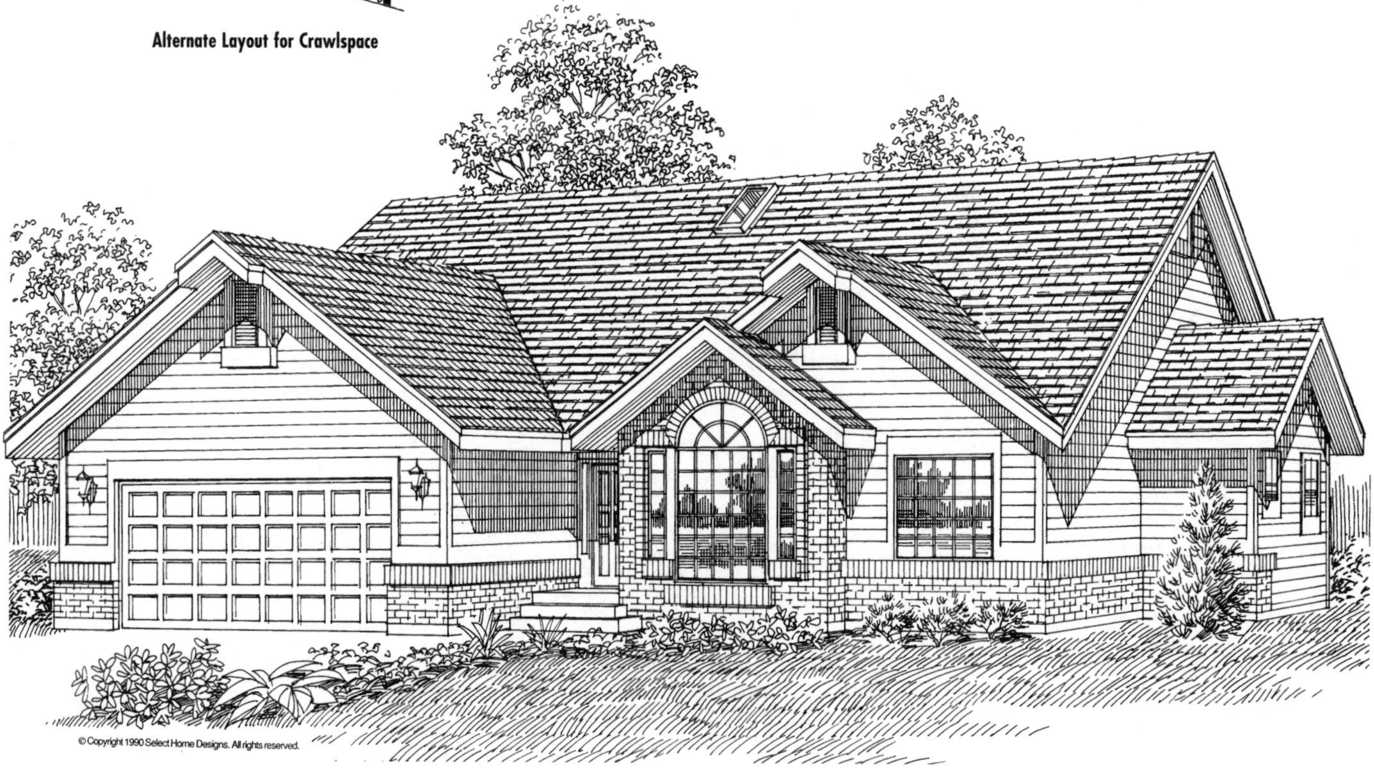

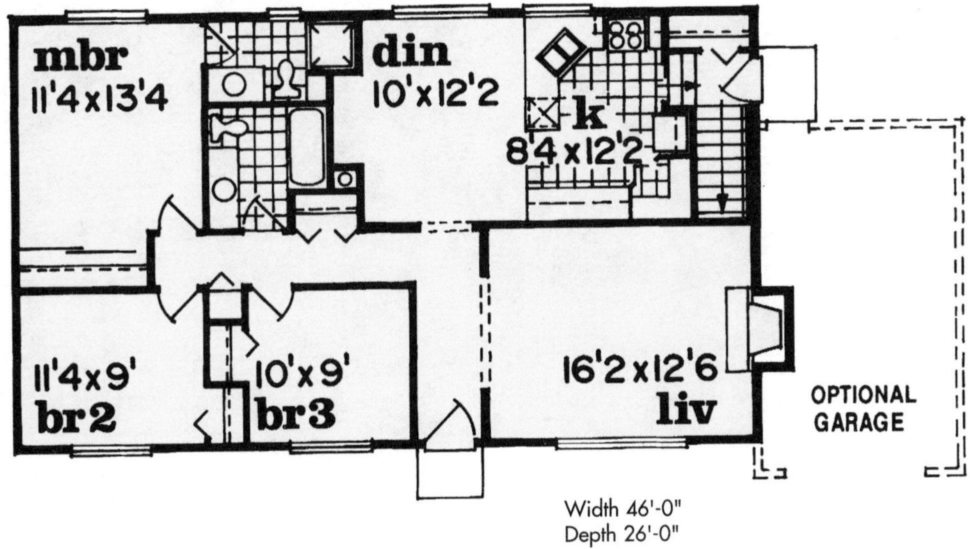
mbr
11'4x13'4
din
10'x12'2
k
8'4x12'2
11'4x9'
br2
10'x9'
br3
16'2x12'6
liv
OPTIONAL
GARAGE

Width 46'-0"
Depth 26'-0"

Design Q343

Square Footage: 1,196

Offering unique design features, this cozy bungalow is charming with horizontal siding, shuttered windows and multi-pane glass. The foyer leads to a spacious living room with warming fireplace and huge picture window. The dining room has a buffet alcove, providing extra space for entertaining. The kitchen is nearby and is well appointed with an angled sink and walk-in pantry. A short flight of stairs leads to a landing with side-door access and then on to the basement. If you wish, you may build a single-car garage for which plans are included. The master bedroom includes a full wall closet and private bath. Two additional bedrooms share the main bathroom with soaking tub.

Design by
Select Home Designs

Design 3442

Square Footage: 1,273

L D

For those just starting out or the empty-nester, this unique one-story plan is sure to delight. A covered porch introduces a dining room with a coffered ceiling and views out two sides of the house. The kitchen is just off this room and is most efficient with a double sink, dishwasher and pantry. The living room gains attention with a volume ceiling, fireplace and access to a covered patio. The master bedroom also features a volume ceiling while enjoying the luxury of a private bath. In it, a walk-in closet, washer/dryer, double-bowl vanity, garden tub, separate shower and compartmented toilet comprise the amenities. Not to be overlooked, a second bedroom may easily convert to a media room and study—the choice is yours.

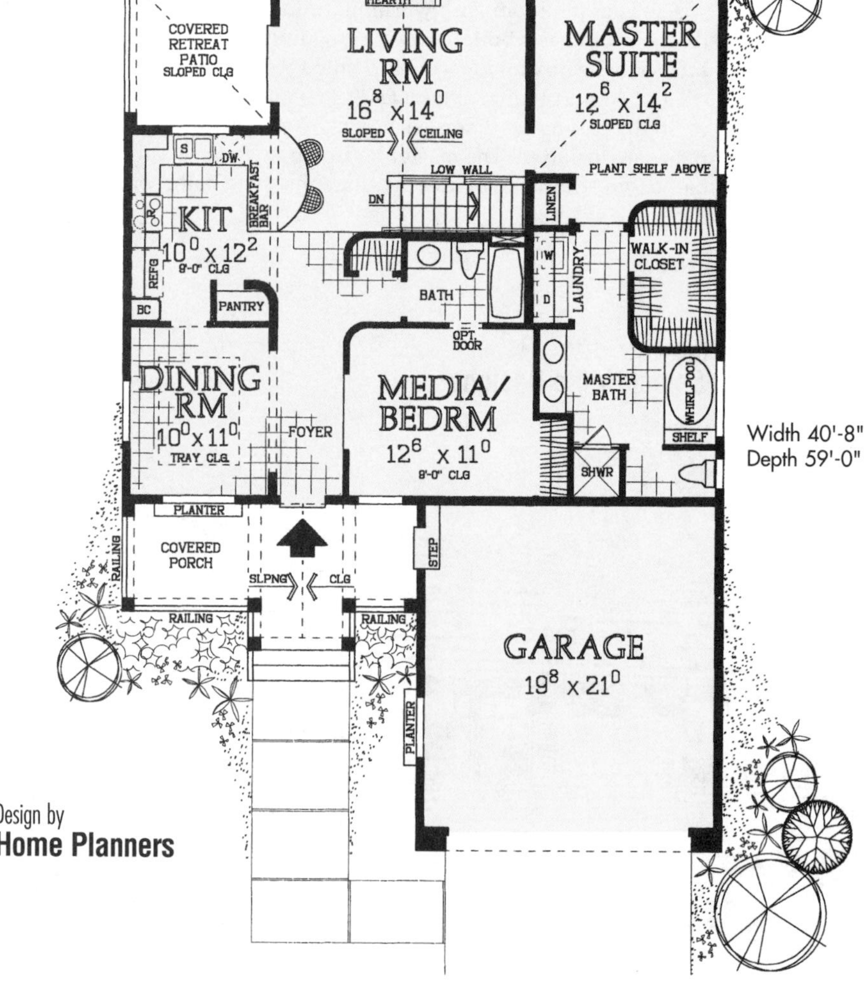

RAILING
COVERED RETREAT PATIO SLOPED CLG
TILE HEARTH
LIVING RM
16⁸ x 14⁰
SLOPED CEILING
MASTER SUITE
12⁶ x 14²
SLOPED CLG
PLANT SHELF ABOVE
LOW WALL
DN
S
DW
BREAKFAST BAR
KIT
10⁰ x 12²
9'-0" CLG
REFG
BC
PANTRY
LINEN
W
D
LAUNDRY
WALK-IN CLOSET
BATH
OPT. DOOR
DINING RM
10⁰ x 11⁰
TRAY CLG
FOYER
MEDIA/ BEDRM
12⁶ x 11⁰
9'-0" CLG
MASTER BATH
WHIRLPOOL
SHELF
SHWR
PLANTER
COVERED PORCH
RAILING
SLPNG CLG
STEP
GARAGE
19⁸ x 21⁰
PLANTER

Width 40'-8"
Depth 59'-0"

Design by
Home Planners

QUOTE ONE®

Cost to build? See page 516 to order complete cost estimate to build this house in your area!

Design by
Select Home Designs

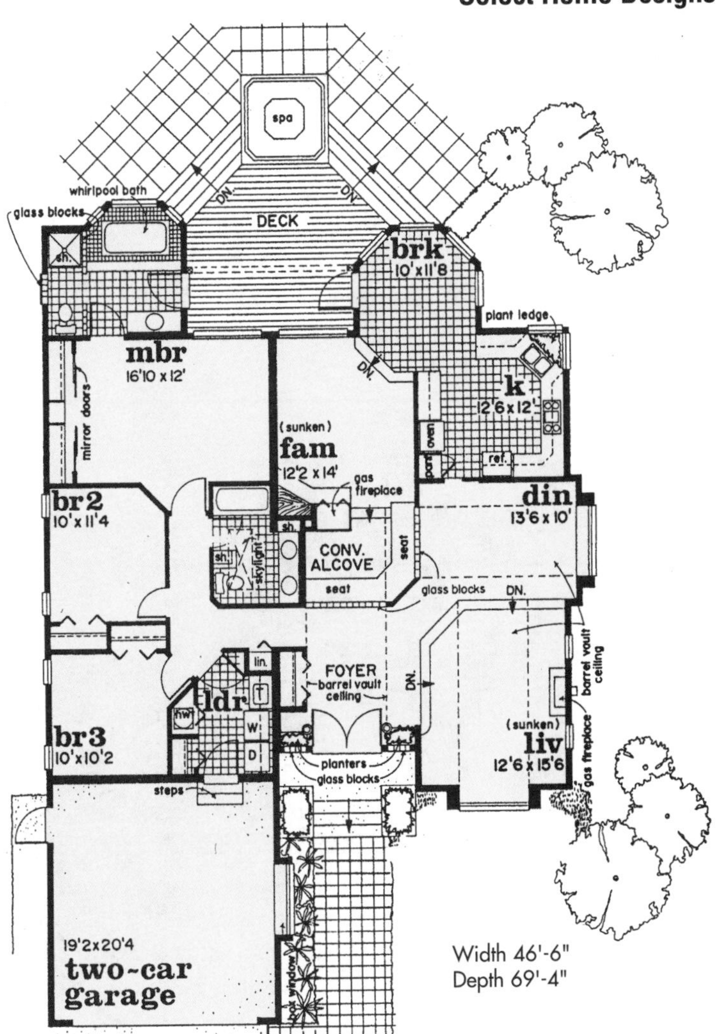
spa
whirlpool bath
glass blocks
sh.
DN.
DN.
DECK
brk
10'x11'8
plant ledge
mbr
16'10 x 12'
mirror doors
DN.
k
12'6x12'
(sunken)
fam
12'2 x 14'
oven
pant
ref.
gas fireplace
br2
10'x11'4
din
13'6 x 10'
sh
skylight
CONV. ALCOVE
seat
seat
glass blocks
DN.
lin.
FOYER
barrel vault ceiling
DN.
barrel vault ceiling
ldr
hw
W
D
br3
10'x10'2
(sunken)
liv
12'6 x 15'6
gas fireplace
planters
glass blocks
steps
19'2x20'4
two-car garage
box window
Width 46'-6"
Depth 69'-4"

Design Q296

Square Footage: 1,939

This unique design begins with a double door-entry into a barrel-vaulted foyer accented by two round-top windows and an arched glass block wall. Curved ceilings and open-plan design enhance both the living and dining rooms. The living room is sunken and features a fireplace and box-bay window. The dining room also has a box-bay. Beyond is the U-shaped kitchen, connecting directly to an octagonal breakfast nook. The nook has access to the rear deck and spa beyond. The family room is up just a step or two and is graced by a gas fireplace and conversation alcove with built-in seats. The master bedroom also has access to the rear deck via a luxurious bath with spa tub, separate shower and compartmented toilet. Two additional bedrooms share the use of a full bath with twin vanities. Plans include details for both a basement and a crawlspace foundation.

Rear Elevation

Design 3454

Square Footage: 1,699

L **D**

An efficient, spacious interior comes through in this compact floor plan. Through a pair of columns, an open living and dining room area creates a warm space for all styles of living. Sliding glass doors guarantee a bright, cheerful interior while providing easy access to outdoor spaces. The L-shaped kitchen has an island work surface, a practical planning desk and an informal eating space. The breakfast area has access to the terrace—perfect for enjoying a cup of morning coffee. Sleeping arrangements include a master bedroom with tray ceiling and access to the rear yard. Family bedrooms (one opens to the entry foyer and could be used as a study) share the use of a full bath with double sinks.

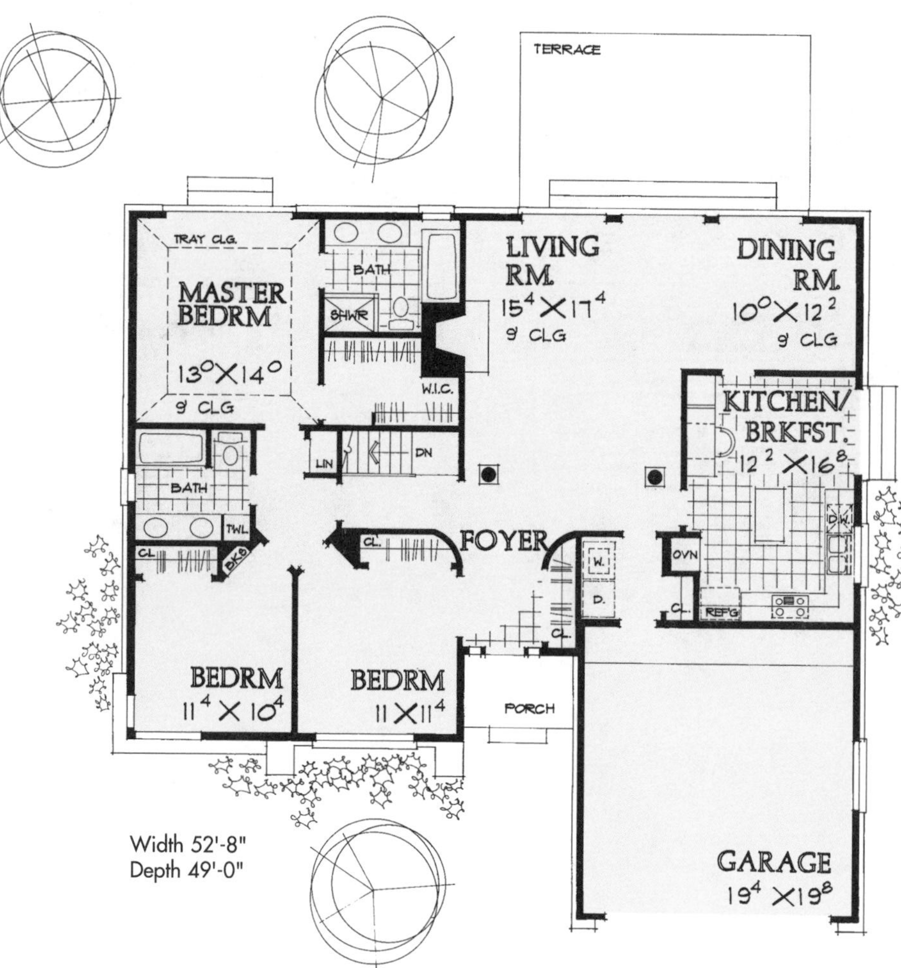

TERRACE
TRAY CLG.
MASTER BEDRM
13⁰X14⁰
9' CLG
BATH
SHWR
W.I.C.
LIVING RM.
15⁴X17⁴
9' CLG
DINING RM.
10⁰X12²
9' CLG
KITCHEN/ BRKFST.
12²X16⁸
LIN
DN
BATH
TWL
CL.
FOYER
OVN
W.
D.
REFG
DW
BEDRM
11⁴X10⁴
BEDRM
11X11⁴
PORCH
GARAGE
19⁴X19⁸
Width 52'-8"
Depth 49'-0"

QUOTE ONE®

Cost to build? See page 516 to order complete cost estimate to build this house in your area!

Design by
Home Planners

© Copyright Select Home Designs. All rights reserved.

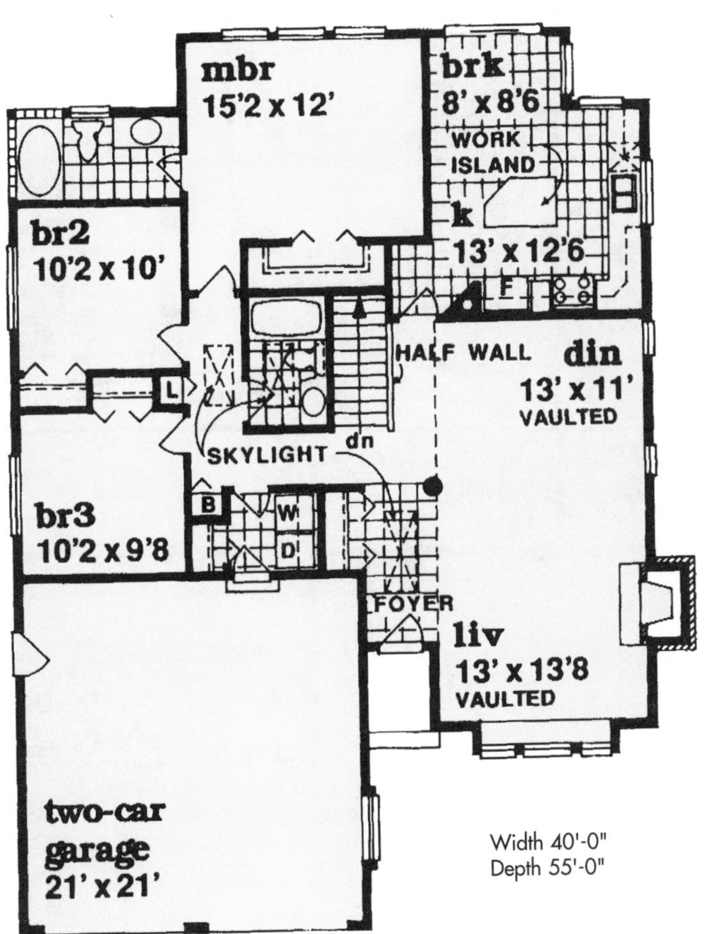
mbr
15'2 x 12'
brk
8' x 8'6
WORK
ISLAND
k
13' x 12'6
F
br2
10'2 x 10'
HALF WALL
din
13' x 11'
VAULTED
L
SKYLIGHT
dn
B
W
D
br3
10'2 x 9'8
FOYER
liv
13' x 13'8
VAULTED
two-car
garage
21' x 21'
Width 40'-0"
Depth 55'-0"

Design Q427

Square Footage: 1,424

This affordable three-bedroom starter or empty-nester home offers an efficient floor plan and maximizes square footage. The skylit foyer spills into a vaulted living room, warmed by a hearth and graced with a box-bay window. Just beyond is a vaulted dining room, near the country kitchen. The gourmet will delight in the appointments in the kitchen: a center work island, abundant counter space and a sunny breakfast area with sliding glass doors to the rear garden. The master bedroom boasts a walk-in closet and bath with whirlpool spa. Two additional bedrooms share a bath with skylight. The two-car garage can be reached through a service entrance at the laundry alcove. Plans include details for both a basement and a crawlspace foundation.

Design by
Select Home Designs

Design Q365

Square Footage: 1,624

This affordable ranch home offers a choice of exteriors—a contemporary California stucco or a traditional version with horizontal siding and brick detailing. The entry is graced by light-giving transom windows—perfect for the plant ledge over decorative columns leading to the living room. The living room has a vaulted ceiling, a fireplace and rear-yard access. The formal dining room is also vaulted with tall, arched windows at the front and has entry from the foyer and from the central hall to access the kitchen more conveniently. An attached breakfast room features a planning desk and allows space for casual dining. The master bedroom boasts French-door access to the patio and features a walk-in closet and bath with whirlpool tub. Two additional bedrooms share a main bath with soaking tub. A large laundry area leads to a two-car garage. Note the storage space in the hall near the service entrance. Plans include details for both a basement and a crawlspace foundation.

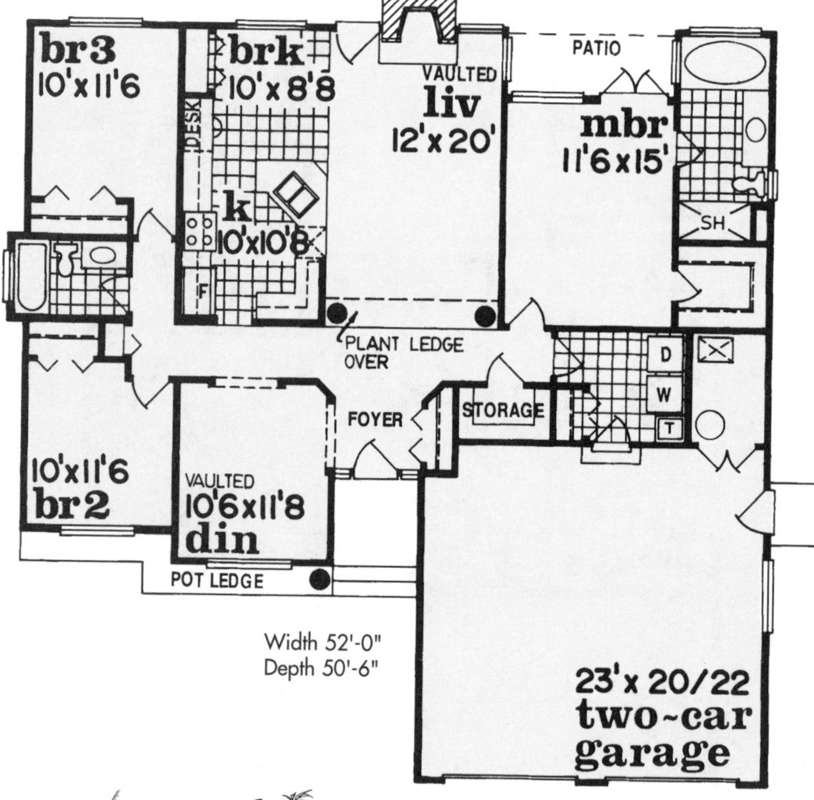
br3
10'x11'6
brk
10'x8'8
DESK
k
10'x10'8
F
VAULTED
liv
12'x20'
PATIO
mbr
11'6x15'
SH
PLANT LEDGE
OVER
D
W
T
STORAGE
FOYER
10'x11'6
br2
VAULTED
10'6x11'8
din
POT LEDGE
23'x 20/22
two~car
garage

Width 52'-0"
Depth 50'-6"

Alternate Elevation

Design by
Select Home Designs

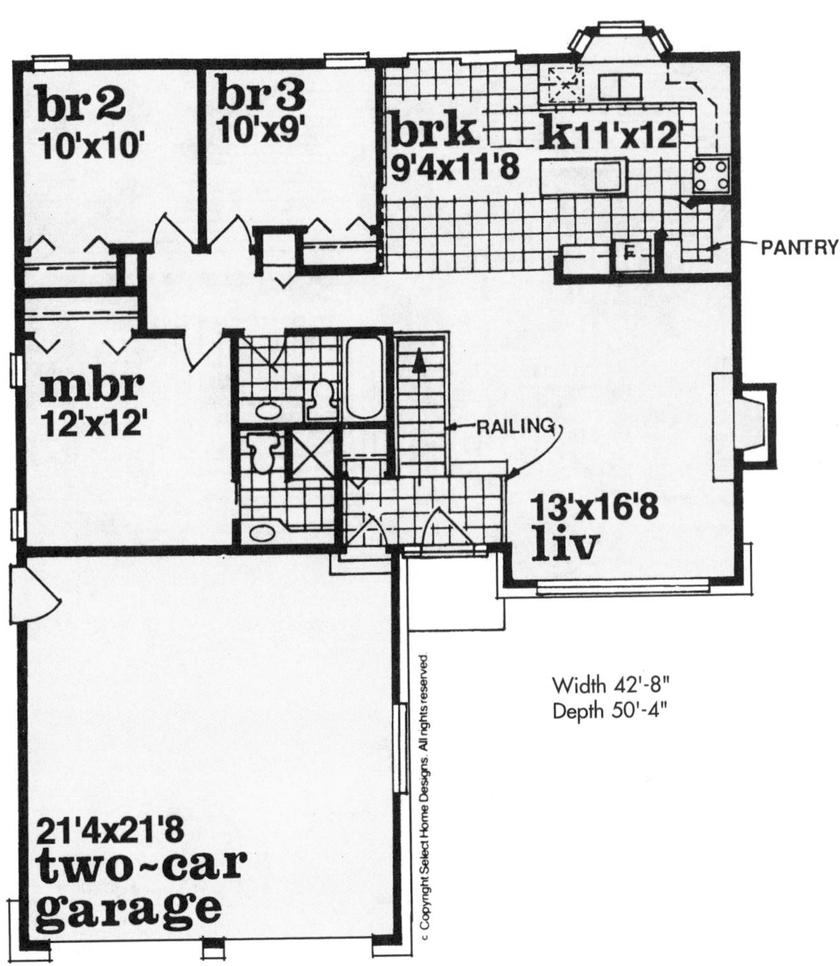
br2
10'x10'
br3
10'x9'
brk
9'4x11'8
k11'x12'
PANTRY
mbr
12'x12'
RAILING
13'x16'8
liv
21'4x21'8
two~car
garage
c Copyright Select Home Designs. All rights reserved
Width 42'-8"
Depth 50'-4"

Design Q345

Square Footage: 1,204

This attractive siding-and-brick home is not only beautiful, but economical to build. The sunken entry steps up to the living room, warmed by a fireplace. An open railing defines the stairway to the basement, enhancing spaciousness and giving this area a feeling of being much larger. A gourmet kitchen offers a walk-in pantry, a center preparation island with salad sink and greenhouse windows. Sliding glass doors in the breakfast nook lead to a rear patio. The master bedroom has a roomy wall closet and separate bath with shower. Two secondary bedrooms share a bath with soaking tub. A two-car garage sits to the front of the plan, creating privacy and quiet for the bedrooms.

Design by
Select Home Designs

© Copyright 1990 Select Home Designs. All rights reserved.

Design Q371

Square Footage: 1,794

Details make the difference in this exquisite one-story home. A bold portico entry opens to a sunken foyer which boasts a multi-paned transom window over the high tray ceiling. High tray ceilings throughout the design add distinction and increase the sense of spaciousness. Stately decorative columns adorn the sunken living room and provide visual separation between the living room and dining room. A warming fireplace acts as a focal point in the living room. The family room features a corner fireplace and French doors to the garden patio. It is also opens to the efficient kitchen and sunny breakfast room with bay window. The master suite is filled with amenities: a cozy window seat, a walk-in closet and a bath with raised whirlpool spa and separate shower. Two family bedrooms share the use of a main bath in the hall. A laundry alcove leads the way to the service entrance to the two-car garage. Plans include details for both a basement and a crawlspace foundation.

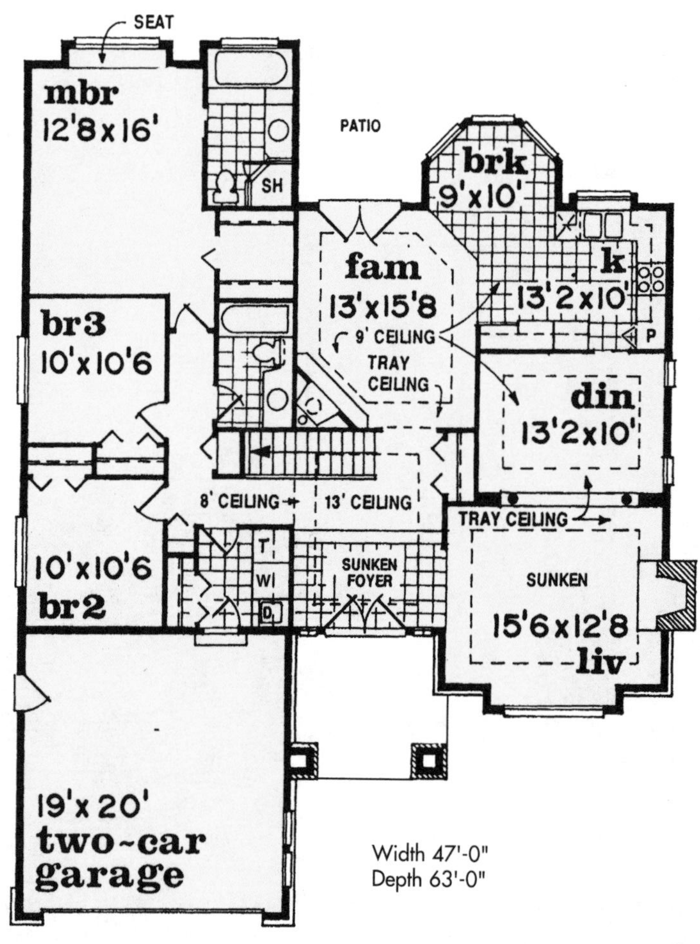
SEAT
mbr
12'8x16'
SH
PATIO
brk
9'x10'
fam
13'x15'8
9' CEILING
TRAY
CEILING
k
13'2x10'
P
br3
10'x10'6
din
13'2x10'
8' CEILING
13' CEILING
TRAY CEILING
T
WI
D
SUNKEN
FOYER
SUNKEN
10'x10'6
br2
15'6x12'8
liv
19'x 20'
two-car
garage

Width 47'-0"
Depth 63'-0"

Rear Elevation

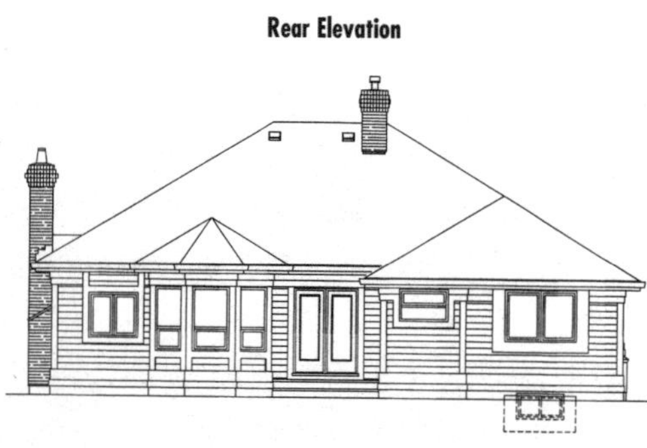

Design by
Select Home Designs

Design Q323

Square Footage: 1,936

Choose from one of two exteriors for this lovely home—details for both are included in the blueprints. The traditional version has brick veneer with horizontal wood siding as accents. The stucco version has the same general style but rendered completely in cool white. Both surround a livable, light-filled floor plan. A transom window over the entry and the living room accentuates the vaulted ceiling which stretches throughout the home. Entry to the living room has a pair of fluted columns crowned with a bridging plant shelf. Opposite are double doors to the covered deck and the patio. A glass-walled fireplace shares space with both the living room and the breakfast room, and is easily enjoyed even in the family room. Note the lovely coffered ceiling in this casual living area. The kitchen is L-shaped and features a large pantry and island cooktop. Nearby is the service area with laundry and access to the two-car garage. Bedrooms are in-line at the left of the plan and include a lovely master suite with coffered ceiling, bay-windowed sitting area, deck access, walk-in closet and very thoughtfully appointed bath. Two family bedrooms and a full bath are to the front of the home.

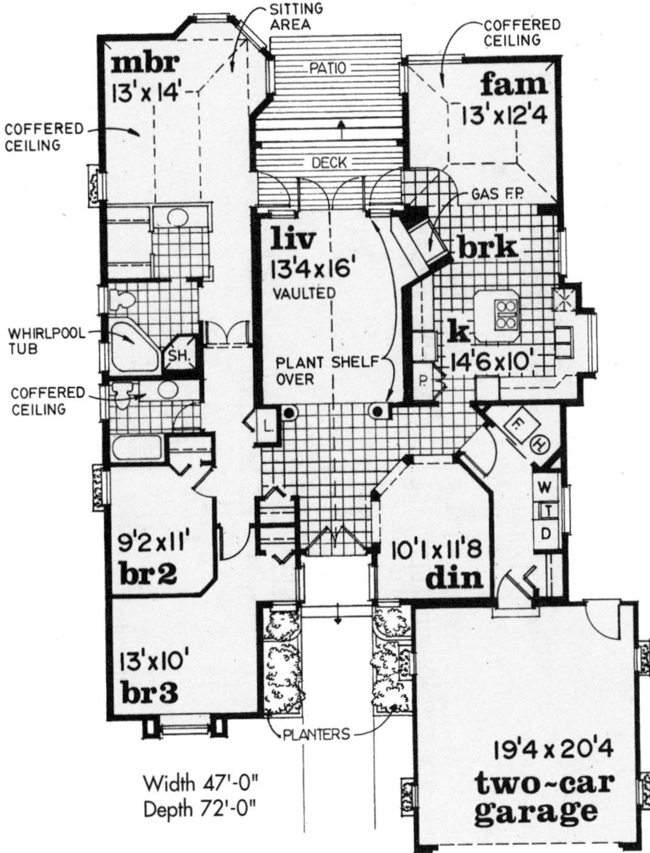
SITTING AREA
COFFERED CEILING
PATIO
mbr 13'x14'
fam 13'x12'4
COFFERED CEILING
DECK
GAS F.P.
liv 13'4x16' VAULTED
brk
WHIRLPOOL TUB
SH.
k 14'6x10'
PLANT SHELF OVER
COFFERED CEILING
P
L
F
H
W
T
D
9'2x11' br2
10'1x11'8 din
13'x10' br3
PLANTERS
19'4x20'4 two-car garage
Width 47'-0"
Depth 72'-0"

Design by
Select Home Designs

Alternate Front Elevation

Rear Elevation

Design by
Home Planners

Design 2902

Square Footage: 1,632

L

A sun space highlights this passive solar design. It features access from the kitchen, the dining room and the garage. It will be a great place to enjoy meals because of its location. Three skylights highlight the interior—in the kitchen, laundry and master bath. An air-locked vestibule helps this design's energy efficiency. Interior livability is excellent. The living/dining room rises with a sloped ceiling and enjoys a fireplace and two sets of sliding glass doors to the terrace. Three bedrooms are in the sleeping wing. The master bedroom will delight with its private bath with a luxurious whirlpool tub.

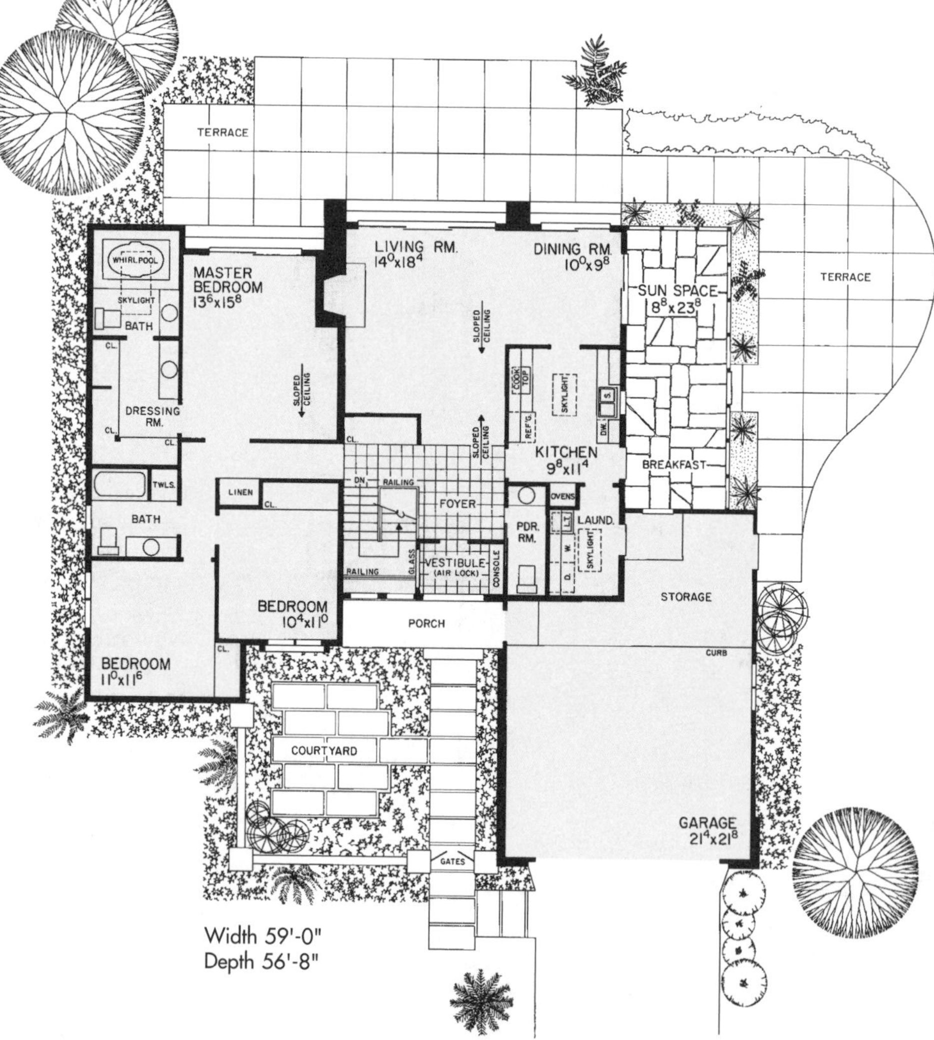

TERRACE
LIVING RM.
14⁰x18⁴
DINING RM.
10⁰x9⁸
MASTER BEDROOM
13⁶x15⁸
WHIRLPOOL
SKYLIGHT
BATH
DRESSING RM.
SLOPED CEILING
SUN SPACE
8⁸x23⁸
TERRACE
KITCHEN
9⁸x11⁴
BREAKFAST
FOYER
VESTIBULE (AIR LOCK)
PDR. RM.
LAUND.
STORAGE
LINEN
TWLS.
BATH
BEDROOM
10⁴x11⁰
BEDROOM
11⁰x11⁶
PORCH
COURTYARD
GATES
GARAGE
21⁴x21⁸
CURB
Width 59'-0"
Depth 56'-8"

QUOTE ONE®

Cost to build? See page 516 to order complete cost estimate to build this house in your area!

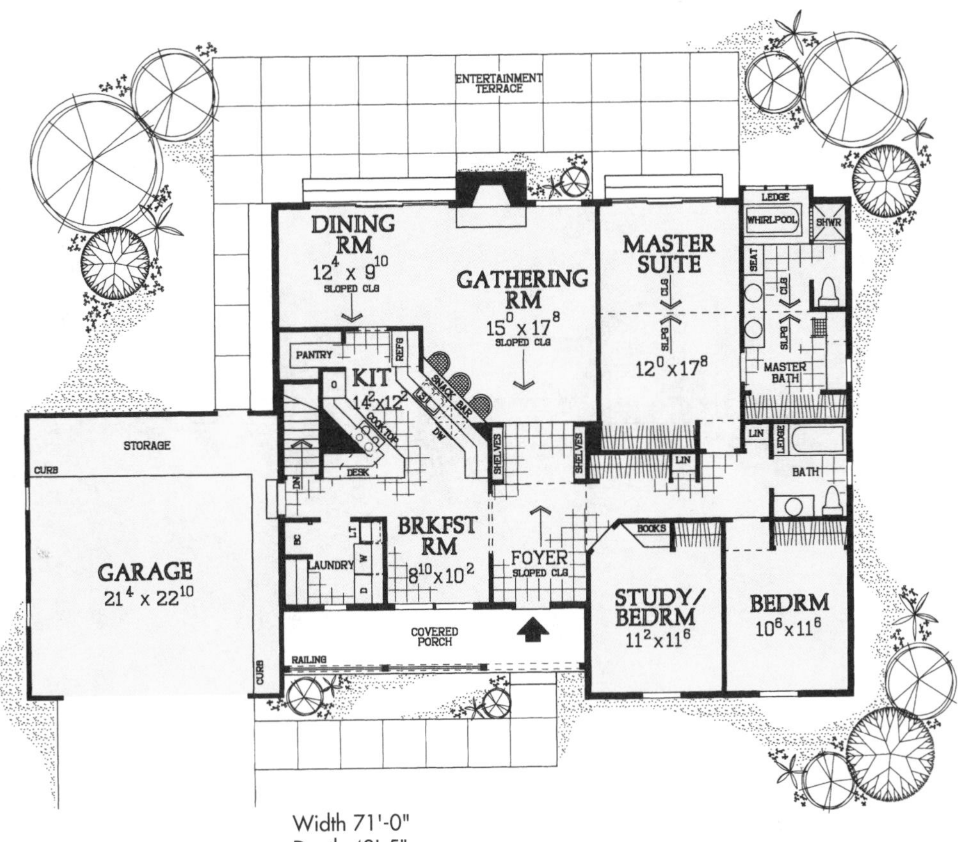
ENTERTAINMENT TERRACE
DINING RM
12⁴ x 9¹⁰
SLOPED CLG
GATHERING RM
15⁰ x 17⁸
SLOPED CLG
MASTER SUITE
12⁰x17⁸
LEDGE
WHIRLPOOL
SHWR
SEAT
MASTER BATH
PANTRY
REF'G
KIT
14²x12²
SNACK BAR
COOKTOP
DESK
SHELVES
LIN
LEDGE
BATH
STORAGE
CURB
GARAGE
21⁴ x 22¹⁰
LAUNDRY
BRKFST RM
8¹⁰x10²
FOYER
SLOPED CLG
BOOKS
STUDY/ BEDRM
11²x11⁶
BEDRM
10⁶x11⁶
COVERED PORCH
RAILING
CURB

Width 71'-0"
Depth 43'-5"

Design 3487

Square Footage: 1,835

L

Country comfort is the focus of this charming plan, ready for any region. A cozy covered porch offers a warm introduction to the tiled foyer, which leads to the living areas and opens to the breakfast room and kitchen. The expansive gathering room features an extended-hearth fireplace and adjoins the formal dining room, served by the kitchen. The entertainment terrace enjoys access from the dining room as well as the master suite. A sumptuous master bath provides a relaxing retreat for the homeowner, with a windowed whirlpool tub, a separate shower, two vanities and a sloped ceiling. A study at the front of the plan could be used as a bedroom.

QUOTE ONE®

Cost to build? See page 516 to order complete cost estimate to build this house in your area!

Design by
Home Planners

Design 2911

Square Footage: 1,233

A low-budget home can be a showplace, too. Exquisite site proportion, fine detailing, projected wings and interesting rooflines help provide the appeal of this modest one-story plan. Both bedrooms have excellent wall space and wardrobe storage. The master bath features a vanity, twin lavatories, a stall shower and a whirlpool tub. Another full bath is strategically located to service the second bedroom as well as other areas of the house. Open planning results in a spacious gathering room with fireplace and access to the outdoor terraces. Two kitchen layouts make the plan versatile. One has an angled snack bar pass-through to the gathering room; the other is more classically configured with an L-shaped work center.

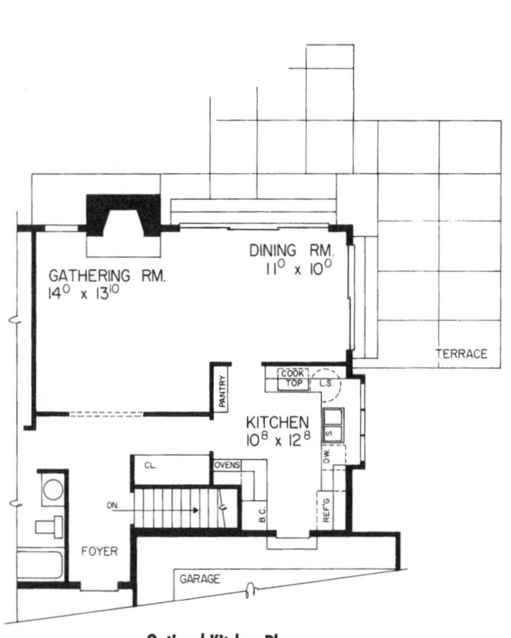
DINING RM.
11^{0} x 10^{0}
GATHERING RM.
14^{0} x 13^{10}
TERRACE
COOK TOP
L.S.
PANTRY
KITCHEN
10^{8} x 12^{8}
S.
CL.
OVENS
DW.
DN.
B.C.
REF'G
FOYER
GARAGE

Optional Kitchen Plan

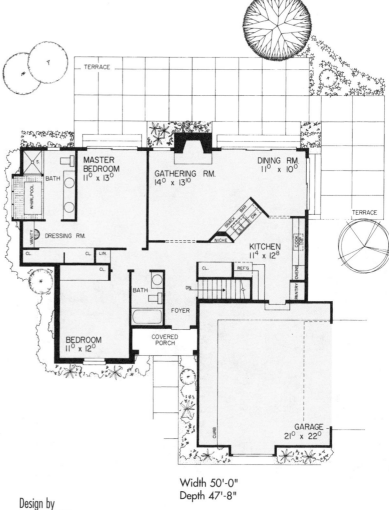

Width 50'-0"
Depth 47'-8"

Design by
Home Planners

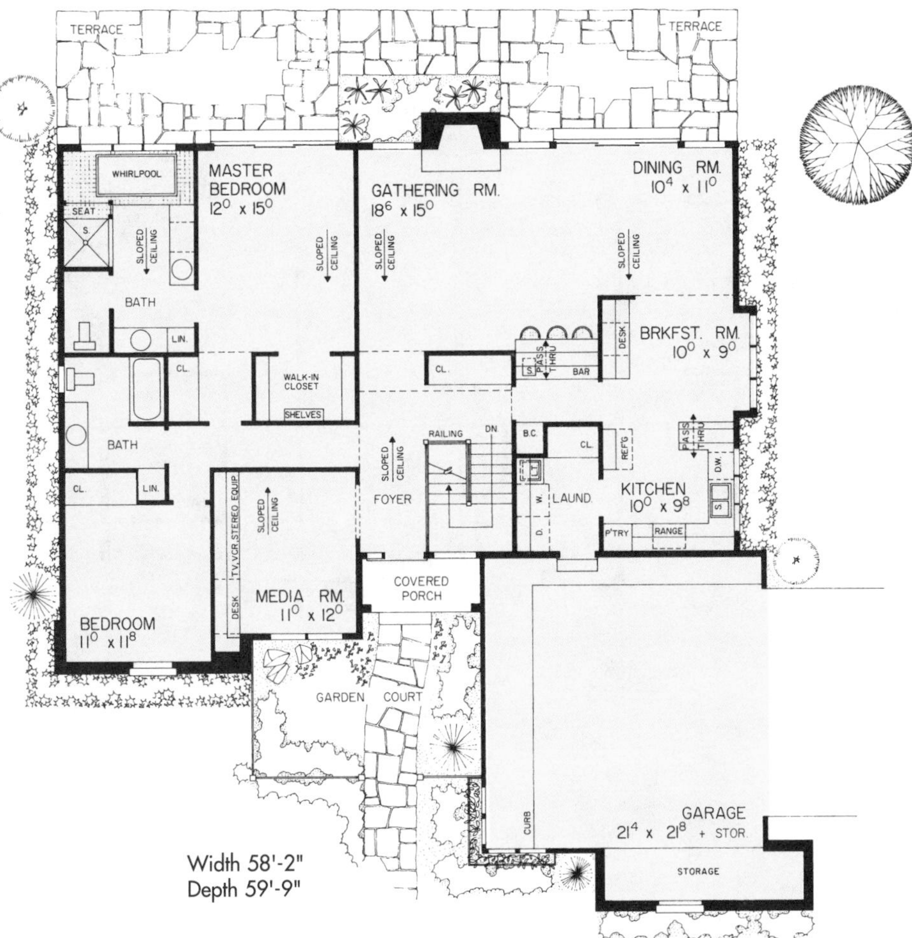
TERRACE
TERRACE
WHIRLPOOL
MASTER BEDROOM 12⁰ x 15⁰
GATHERING RM. 18⁶ x 15⁰
DINING RM. 10⁴ x 11⁰
SEAT
SLOPED CEILING
BATH
LIN.
CL.
BRKFST. RM. 10⁰ x 9⁰
DESK
PASS THRU
BAR
WALK-IN CLOSET
SHELVES
RAILING
DN
B.C.
REF'G
BATH
FOYER
LAUND.
KITCHEN 10⁰ x 9⁸
D.W.
CL.
LIN.
TV, VCR, STEREO EQUIP.
P'TRY
RANGE
COVERED PORCH
DESK
MEDIA RM. 11⁰ x 12⁰
BEDROOM 11⁰ x 11⁸
GARDEN COURT
CURB
GARAGE 21⁴ x 21⁸ + STOR.
STORAGE
Width 58'-2"
Depth 59'-9"

Design 2941

Square Footage: 1,842

D

This Early American exterior is charming with its horizontal siding, stone accents and window boxes. A dovecote, a picket fence and a garden court enhance its appeal. The covered entrance opens to a spacious foyer with a dramatic open staircase to the basement recreation area. Further on is a large gathering room with sloped ceiling and fireplace and an attached dining room, which also features a sloped ceiling. Sliding glass doors lead to a rear terrace. The L-shaped kitchen has a pass-through counter to the breakfast room, which is brightened by a box-bay window. The laundry area leads to a two-car garage with storage. A cozy media room features built-ins and also has a sloped ceiling. Nothing is left out in the master suite: sloped ceiling, terrace access, private bath with sloped ceiling and whirlpool tub and a walk-in closet with built-in shelves. An additional bedroom has the use of a hall bath.

Design by
Home Planners

Design 2565

Square Footage: 1,540

L D

This modest-sized design has much to offer in livability. It may function as either a three-bedroom home or a two-bedroom home with a study. The spacious living room features a raised-hearth fireplace, sliding doors to the terrace and a beam ceiling. The L-shaped kitchen has an island work center and adjoining nook with sliding glass doors to the rear terrace. The master bedroom also has sliding glass doors to the rear yard. A laundry area with half-bath has access to the two-car garage to the front of the plan. The stairway to the basement leads to a possible future recreation area. Blueprints for this design show details for three elevations: the Tudor, the Colonial and the contemporary.

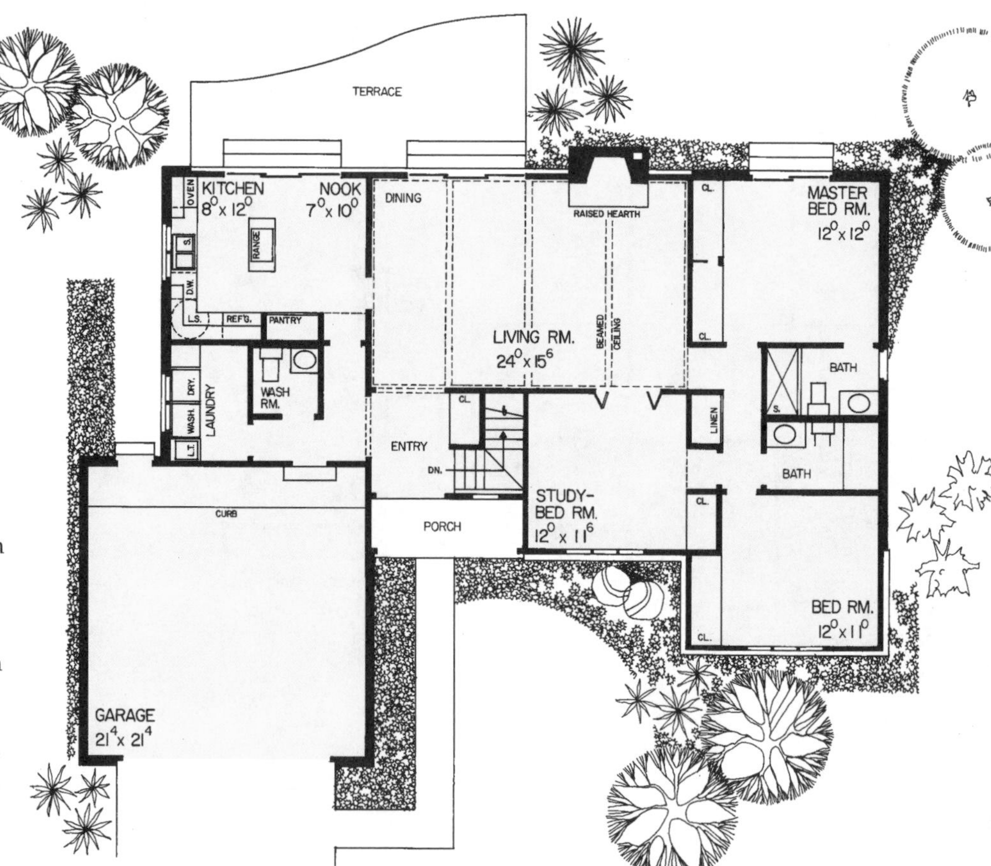
TERRACE
KITCHEN $8^0 \times 12^0$
NOOK $7^0 \times 10^0$
DINING
RAISED HEARTH
MASTER BED RM. $12^0 \times 12^0$
OVEN
RANGE
D.W.
L.S.
REF'G.
PANTRY
LIVING RM. $24^0 \times 15^6$
BEAMED CEILING
CL.
BATH
DRY.
WASH.
LT.
LAUNDRY
WASH RM.
ENTRY
DN.
LINEN
BATH
CURB
PORCH
STUDY-BED RM. $12^0 \times 11^6$
BED RM. $12^0 \times 11^0$
GARAGE $21^4 \times 21^4$

Width 61'-8"
Depth 44'-0"

QUOTE ONE®

Cost to build? See page 516
to order complete cost estimate
to build this house in your area!

Design by
Home Planners

Design by
Home Planners

Design 2802

Square Footage: 1,729

L **D**

■ This attractive plan displays an effective use of half-timbered stucco and brick as well as an authentic bay window to create an elegant Tudor elevation. The covered porch serves as a fitting introduction to all the inside amenities. The gathering room will be a favorite place for friends and family with its rustic appeal and rear terrace doors. A full-sized kitchen with snack bar and breakfast room is well suited for the gourmet. The master bedroom has a large walk-in closet, private bath and doors to the terrace. Two additional bedrooms share a hall bath. A large storage area or shop space is available in the two-car garage.

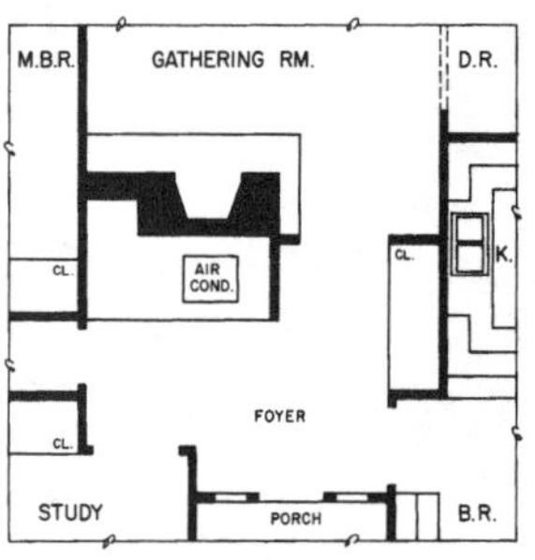
M.B.R.
GATHERING RM.
D.R.
CL.
AIR COND.
CL.
K.
FOYER
CL.
STUDY
PORCH
B.R.

Optional Non-basement

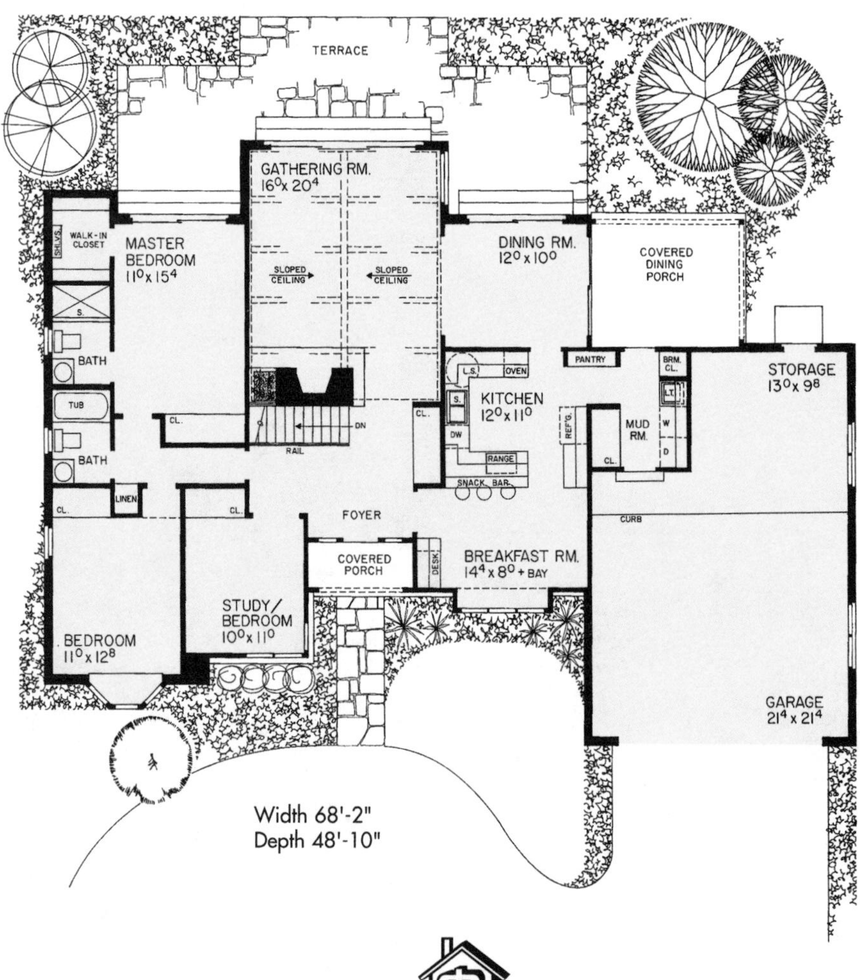
TERRACE
GATHERING RM.
16⁰x 20⁴
SLOPED CEILING
SLOPED CEILING
WALK-IN CLOSET
SHLVS.
MASTER BEDROOM
11⁰x 15⁴
S.
BATH
TUB
BATH
CL.
LINEN
CL.
CL.
RAIL
DN
DINING RM.
12⁰ x 10⁰
COVERED DINING PORCH
L.S.
OVEN
S.
KITCHEN
12⁰ x 11⁰
DW
REF'G.
RANGE
SNACK BAR
CL.
PANTRY
BRM. CL.
MUD RM.
L.T.
W
D
CL.
STORAGE
13⁰x 9⁸
CURB
FOYER
COVERED PORCH
DESK
BREAKFAST RM.
14⁴ x 8⁰ + BAY
STUDY/ BEDROOM
10⁰x 11⁰
BEDROOM
11⁰ x 12⁸
GARAGE
21⁴ x 21⁴
Width 68'-2"
Depth 48'-10"

QUOTE ONE®

Cost to build? See page 516 to order complete cost estimate to build this house in your area!

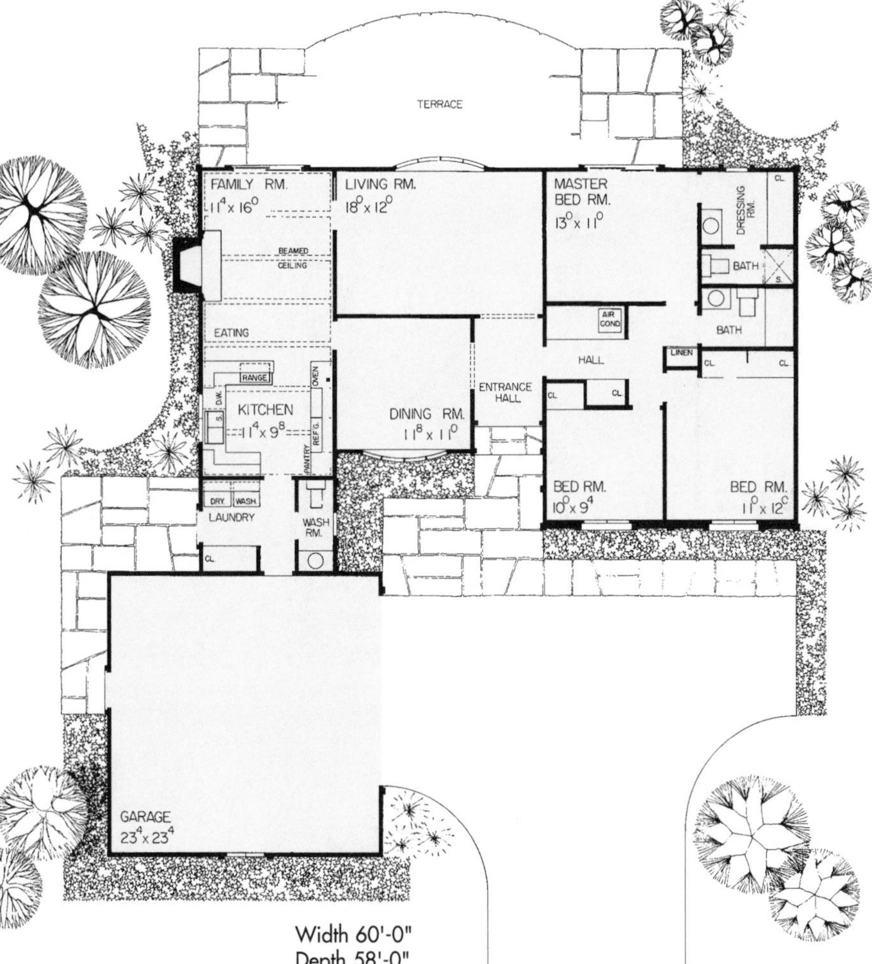
TERRACE
FAMILY RM.
$11^{4} \times 16^{0}$
BEAMED CEILING
EATING
LIVING RM.
$18^{0} \times 12^{0}$
MASTER BED RM.
$13^{0} \times 11^{0}$
DRESSING RM.
CL
BATH
BATH
AIR COND.
HALL
LINEN
CL.
CL.
RANGE
OVEN
D.W.
KITCHEN
$11^{4} \times 9^{8}$
REF'G.
PANTRY
DINING RM.
$11^{8} \times 11^{0}$
ENTRANCE HALL
CL
CL
BED RM.
$10^{0} \times 9^{4}$
BED RM.
$11^{0} \times 12^{0}$
DRY
WASH
LAUNDRY
WASH RM.
CL
GARAGE
$23^{4} \times 23^{4}$

Width 60'-0"
Depth 58'-0"

Design 2606

Square Footage: 1,499

This modest-sized house with its 1,499 square feet could hardly offer more in the way of exterior charm and interior livability. Measuring only 60 feet in width means it will not require a huge, expensive piece of property. The orientation of the garage and the front drive court are features that promote an economical use of property. In addition to the formal, separate living and dining rooms, there is the informal kitchen/family room area. Note the beamed ceiling, the fireplace, the sliding glass doors and the eating area in the family room.

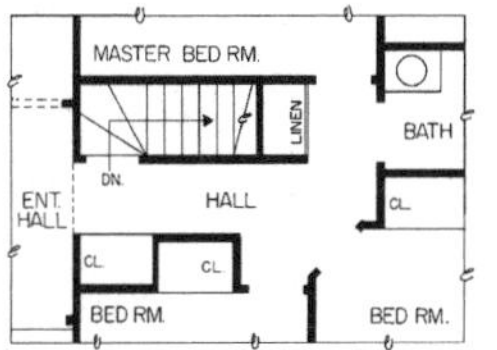
MASTER BED RM.
LINEN
BATH
DN.
ENT. HALL
HALL
CL.
CL.
CL.
BED RM.
BED RM.

Optional Basement

QUOTE ONE®

Cost to build? See page 516
to order complete cost estimate
to build this house in your area!

Design by
Home Planners

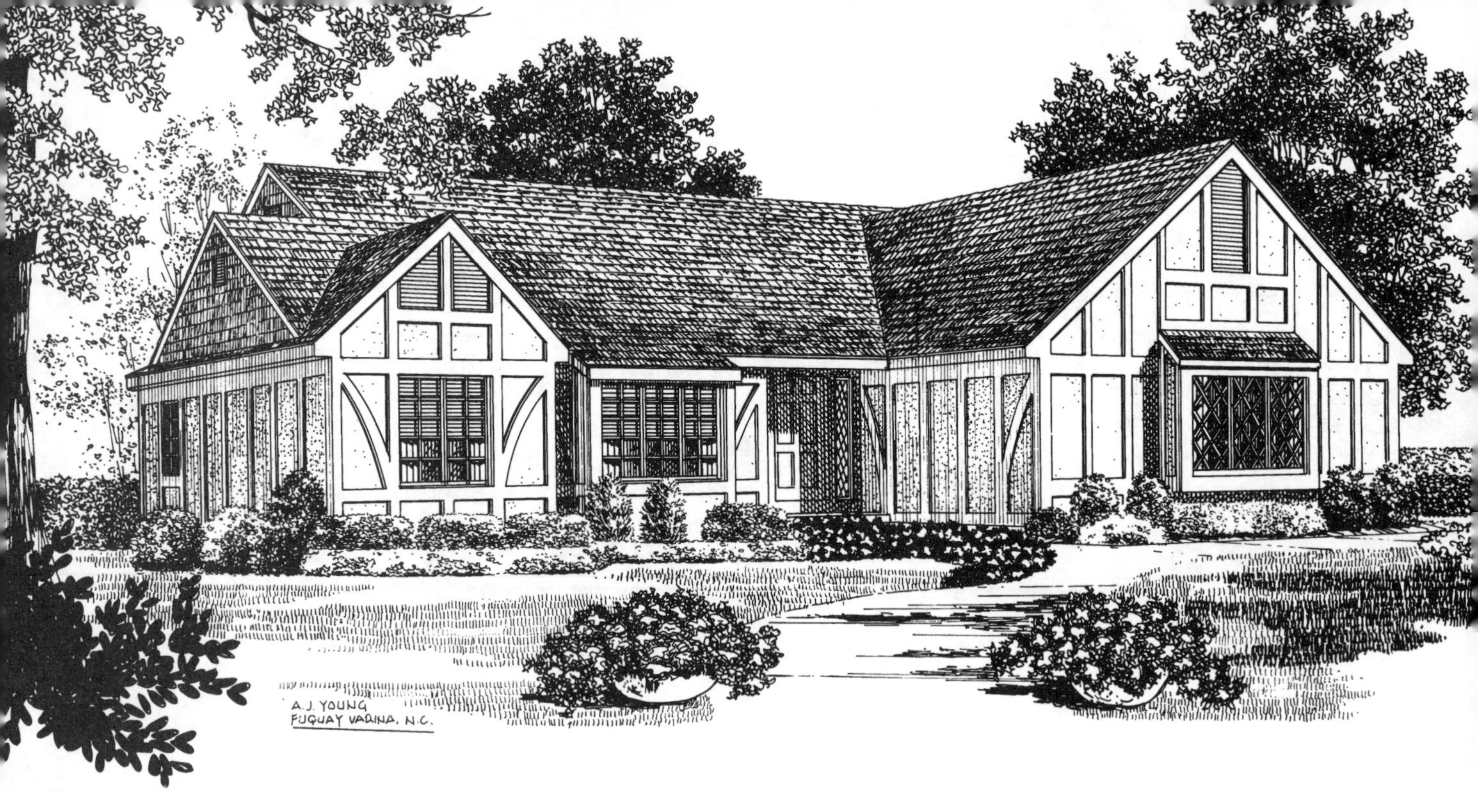

Design by
Home Planners

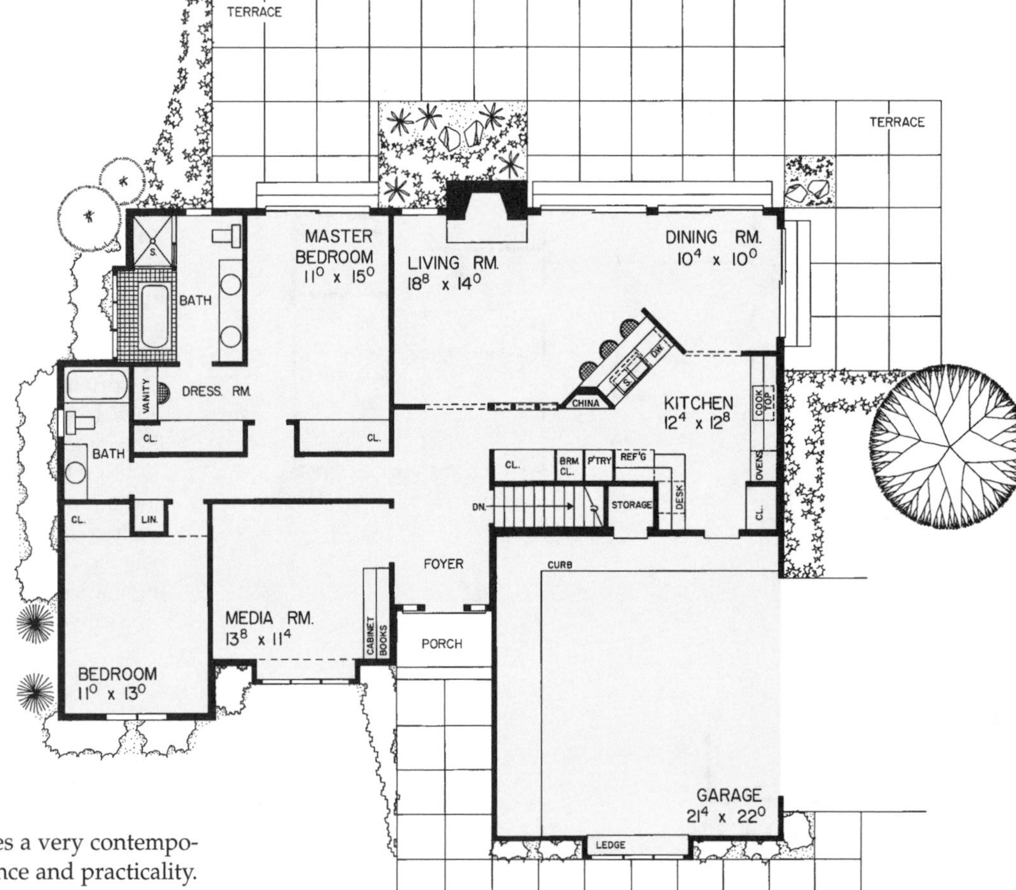
TERRACE
TERRACE
MASTER BEDROOM 11⁰ x 15⁰
LIVING RM. 18⁸ x 14⁰
DINING RM. 10⁴ x 10⁰
BATH
DRESS. RM.
VANITY
CL.
CL.
BATH
CL.
LIN.
CHINA
KITCHEN 12⁴ x 12⁸
COOK TOP
OVENS
CL.
BRM. CL.
P'TRY
REF'G
DESK
STORAGE
DN.
CL.
FOYER
CURB
MEDIA RM. 13⁸ x 11⁴
CABINET BOOKS
PORCH
BEDROOM 11⁰ x 13⁰
GARAGE 21⁴ x 22⁰
LEDGE

Width 55'-4"
Depth 46'-4"

Design 2929

Square Footage: 1,608

This cozy Tudor features a very contemporary interior for convenience and practicality. The floor plan features a strategically located kitchen handy to the garage, dining room and dining terrace. The spacious living area has a dramatic fireplace that functions with the rear terrace. A favorite spot is the media room with space for a TV, VCR and stereo system. The master bedroom is large and has plenty of wardrobe storage. The extra guest room, or nursery, has a full bath.

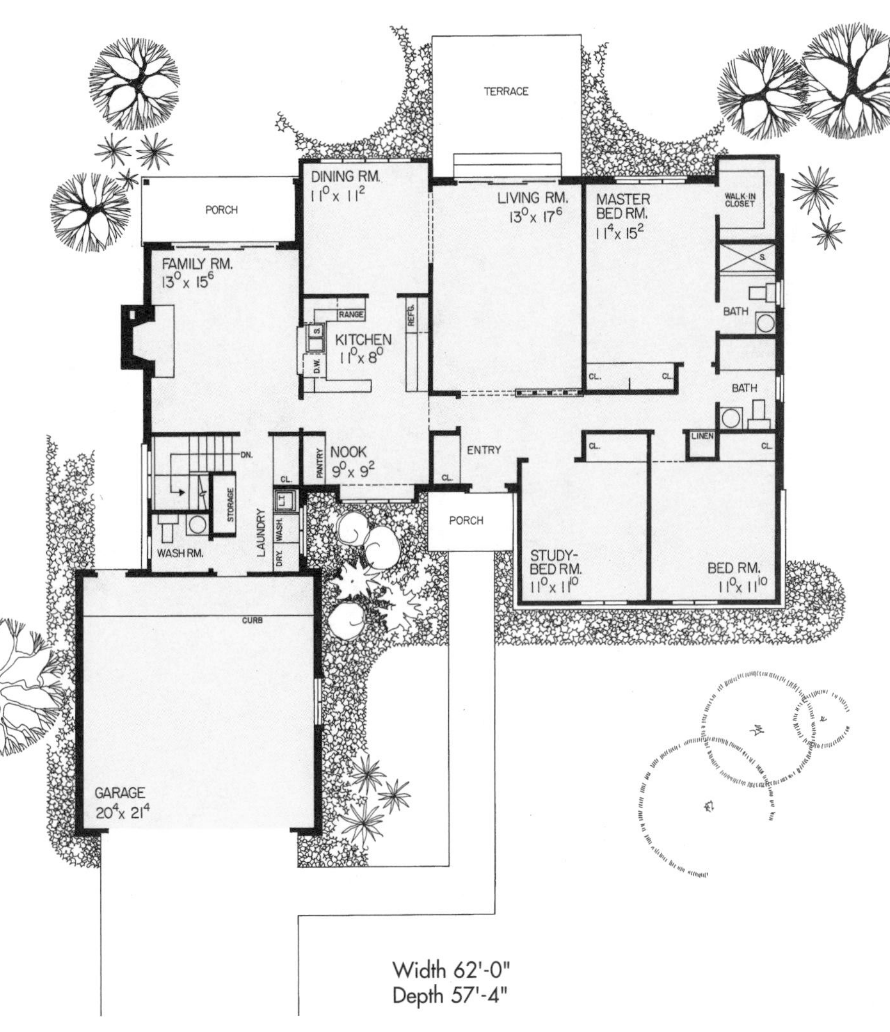
TERRACE
DINING RM. 11^0 x 11^2
PORCH
LIVING RM. 13^0 x 17^6
MASTER BED RM. 11^4 x 15^2
WALK-IN CLOSET
FAMILY RM. 13^0 x 15^6
RANGE
REFG.
KITCHEN 11^0 x 8^0
D.W.
BATH
CL.
BATH
DN.
NOOK 9^0 x 9^2
PANTRY
CL.
ENTRY
LINEN
STORAGE
LAUNDRY
PORCH
WASH RM.
DRY.
WASH
STUDY-BED RM. 11^0 x 11^0
BED RM. 11^0 x 11^{10}
CURB
GARAGE 20^4 x 21^4

Width 62'-0"
Depth 57'-4"

Design 2737

Square Footage: 1,796

L

Tudor accents add distinction to this wonderful home. Inside, livability takes priority. The step-saving U-shaped kitchen serves the formal dining room, the family room and the nook. Sliding glass doors in the family room provide access to the covered porch and backyard, while the living room opens onto a rear terrace. A fireplace warms the family room. Three bedrooms and two baths highlight the sleeping zone. Or if you prefer, use one bedroom as a study. The master suite features a walk-in closet, plus a double wall closet. Family bedrooms share a full bath with soaking tub. With the help of your builder, you may locate the garage to the side of the plan if your building site allows.

Design by
Home Planners

Design 2728

Square Footage: 1,825

L D

The curving front driveway produces an impressive approach to this delightful Tudor adaptation. A covered front porch shelters the centered entry hall which effectively routes traffic to all areas. The fireplace is the focal point of the spacious, formal living and dining areas. An efficient kitchen is conveniently located adjacent to the formal dining room and the informal family room. In addition to the two full baths in the sleeping zone, there is a handy washroom near the garage. Sliding glass doors opening from the dining room and family room provide easy access to the terrace and side porch.

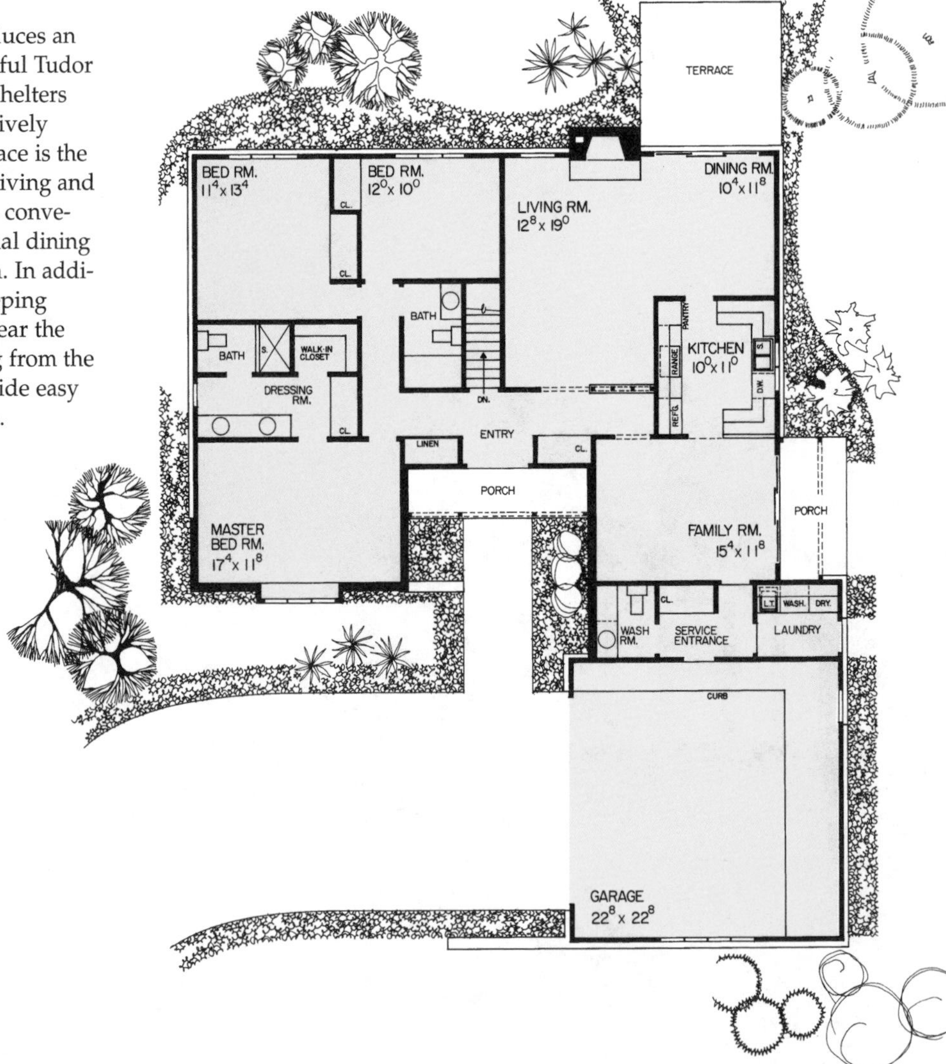

Width 56'-0"
Depth 65'-8"
TERRACE
BED RM. 11^4x13^4
BED RM. 12^0x10^0
LIVING RM. 12^8x19^0
DINING RM. 10^4x11^8
CL.
CL.
BATH
BATH
S.
WALK-IN CLOSET
DRESSING RM.
CL.
KITCHEN 10^0x11^0
PANTRY
RANGE
REFG.
D/W
DN.
ENTRY
LINEN
CL.
PORCH
MASTER BED RM. 17^4x11^8
FAMILY RM. 15^4x11^8
PORCH
CL.
WASH RM.
SERVICE ENTRANCE
L.T.
WASH.
DRY.
LAUNDRY
CURB
GARAGE 22^8x22^8

Design by
Home Planners

Design 2170

Square Footage: 1,646

L

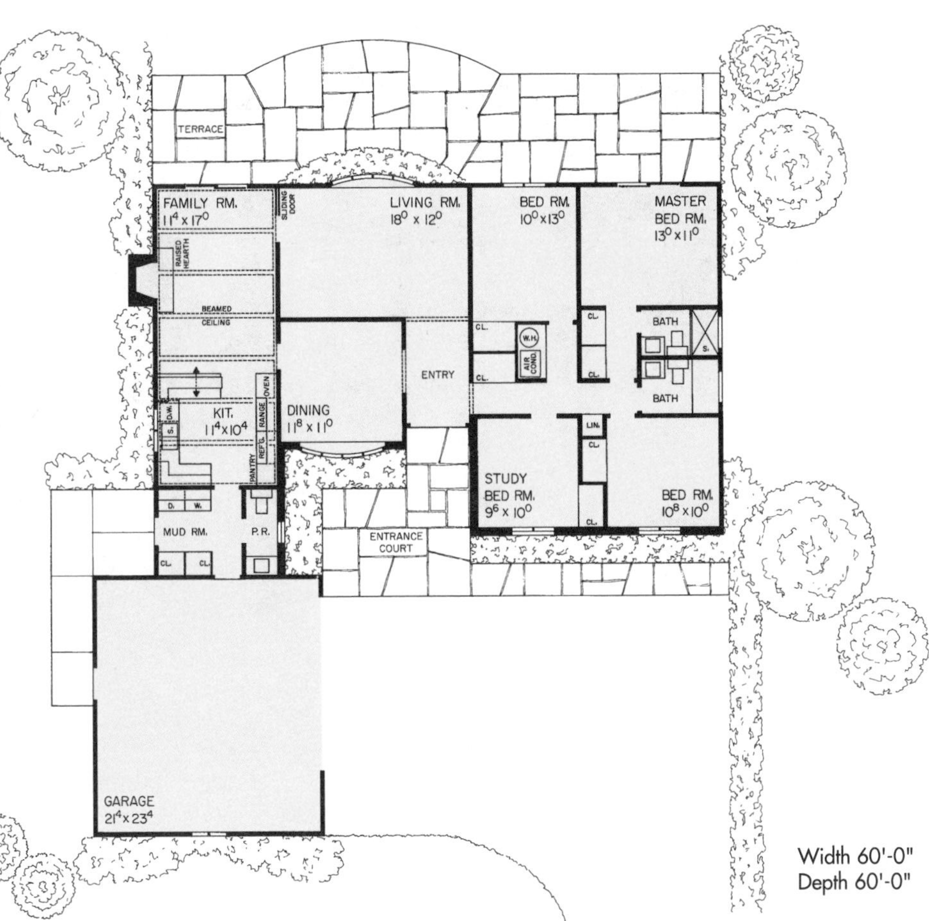
TERRACE
FAMILY RM.
11^{4} x 17^{0}
SLIDING DOOR
LIVING RM.
18^{0} x 12^{0}
BED RM.
10^{0}x13^{0}
MASTER
BED RM.
13^{0}x11^{0}
RAISED HEARTH
BEAMED CEILING
CL.
W.H.
AIR COND.
CL.
CL.
BATH
S.
BATH
CL.
ENTRY
KIT.
11^{4}x10^{4}
D.W.
S.
RANGE
OVEN
REF'G.
PANTRY
DINING
11^{8} x 11^{0}
LIN.
CL.
STUDY
BED RM.
9^{6} x 10^{0}
CL.
BED RM.
10^{8} x 10^{0}
D.
W.
MUD RM.
P.R.
CL.
CL.
ENTRANCE
COURT
GARAGE
21^{4}x 23^{4}
Width 60'-0"
Depth 60'-0"

This L-shaped home is graced with an enchanting Olde English styling. The wavy-edged siding, the simulated beams, the diamond-lite windows, the unusual brick pattern and the interesting rooflines are all elements which set the character of authenticity. The center entry routes traffic directly to the formal living and the sleeping zones of the house. Between the kitchen/family room area and the attached two-car garage is the mud room. The family room is highlighted by the beam ceiling, a raised-hearth fireplace and the sliding glass doors to a rear terrace. Four bedrooms, two full baths and good closet space are features of the sleeping area. The master has its own private bath with a shower.

Design by
Home Planners

Design 2206

Square Footage: 1,769

Old World styling, New World convenience! The Tudor character adds a unique touch to any neighborhood. The covered front porch leads to the formal front entry. The outstanding plan features a separate dining room, a beam ceiling and fireplace in the living room, an efficient U-shaped kitchen and an informal family room with pass-through counter to the kitchen and sliding glass doors to the rear terrace. Three bedrooms, each with a walk-in closet, are to the left of the plan. The master suite has a private bath, hidden by pocket doors. To reach the two-car garage, use a service entrance in the laundry room, which also features a half-bath. An optional basement plan is included in the blueprints.

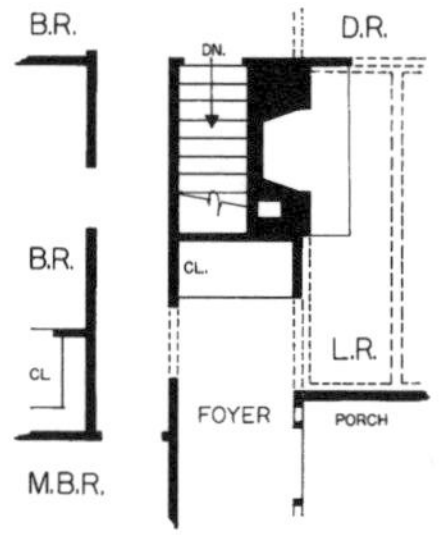

Design by
Home Planners

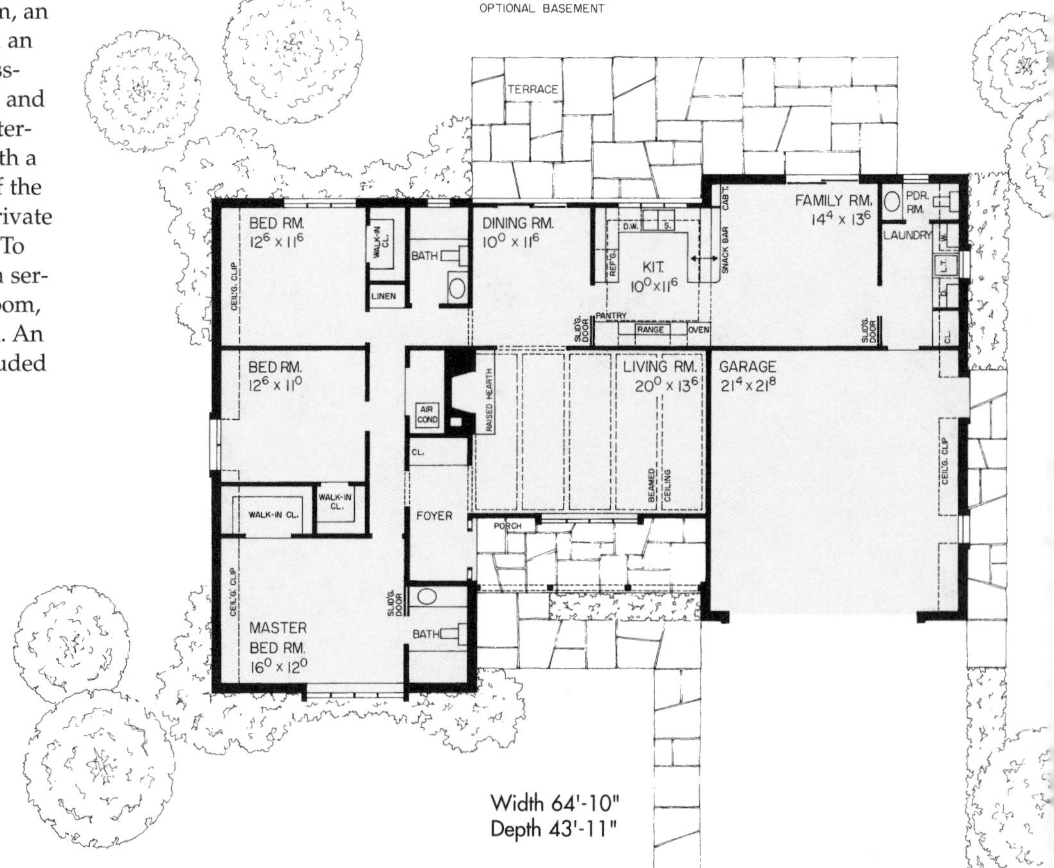

OPTIONAL BASEMENT

Width 64'-10"
Depth 43'-11"

QUOTE ONE®

Cost to build? See page 516 to order complete cost estimate to build this house in your area!

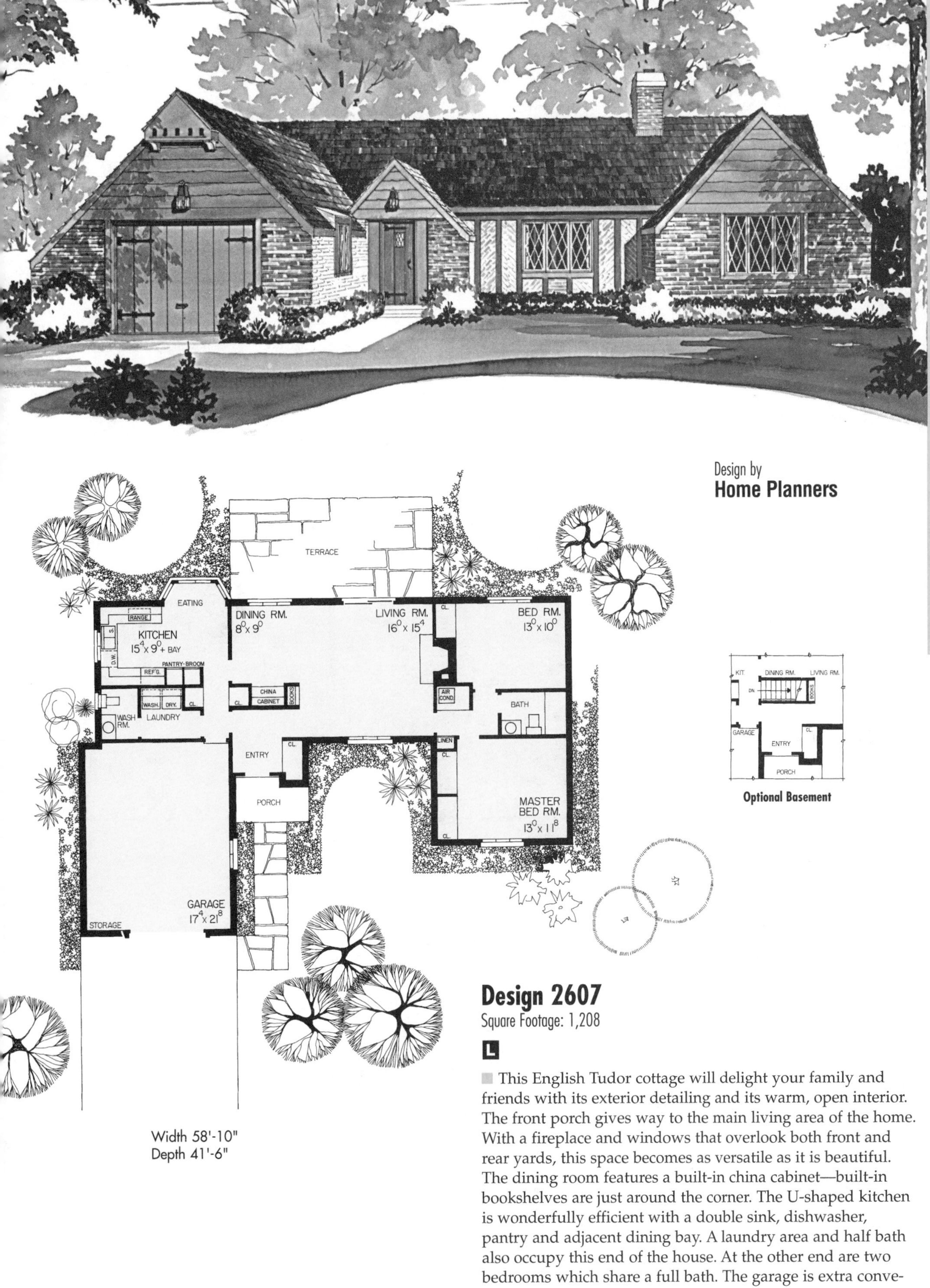
TERRACE
EATING
KITCHEN
15⁴ x 9⁰ + BAY
RANGE
D.W.
REF'G.
PANTRY-BROOM
DINING RM.
8⁰ x 9⁰
LIVING RM.
16⁰ x 15⁴
BED RM.
13⁰ x 10⁰
CHINA CABINET
BOOKS
AIR COND.
WASH. DRY.
LAUNDRY
WASH RM.
BATH
LINEN
ENTRY
PORCH
MASTER BED RM.
13⁰ x 11⁸
GARAGE
17⁴ x 21⁸
STORAGE
Width 58'-10"
Depth 41'-6"
KIT.
DINING RM.
LIVING RM.
GARAGE
ENTRY
PORCH
Optional Basement

Design by
Home Planners

Design 2607

Square Footage: 1,208

L

This English Tudor cottage will delight your family and friends with its exterior detailing and its warm, open interior. The front porch gives way to the main living area of the home. With a fireplace and windows that overlook both front and rear yards, this space becomes as versatile as it is beautiful. The dining room features a built-in china cabinet—built-in bookshelves are just around the corner. The U-shaped kitchen is wonderfully efficient with a double sink, dishwasher, pantry and adjacent dining bay. A laundry area and half bath also occupy this end of the house. At the other end are two bedrooms which share a full bath. The garage is extra convenient with storage space or room for a workshop.

Design Q448

Square Footage: 1,577

Circle-head windows lend character to the exterior of this country-style three-bedroom home. Inside, it is well designed and well appointed. The entry foyer is skylit and leads to a vaulted great room with a centrally located fireplace open to the kitchen and breakfast nook. The formal dining room is also vaulted and has sliding glass doors to the rear deck and to a side screened porch. Both entries to the kitchen/breakfast area are accented—one by an arch; one with a plant ledge. The laundry is located in a service entrance to the two-car garage. The master bedroom is all you might want with three wall closets and a private bath with separate tub and shower and double vanities. Family bedrooms have the use of a full bath with skylight. Choose the crawlspace option if you wish.

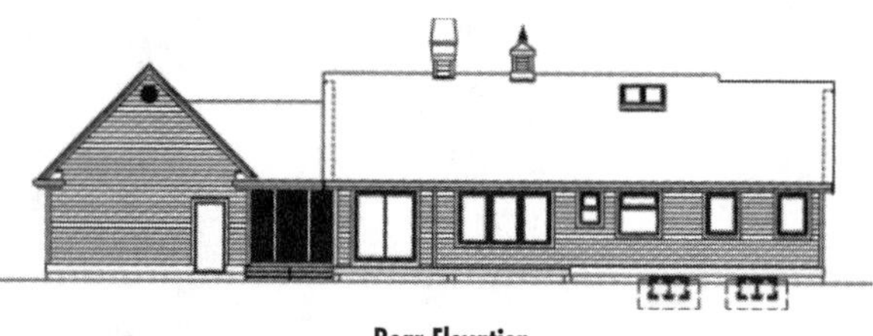

Rear Elevation

Design by
Select Home Designs

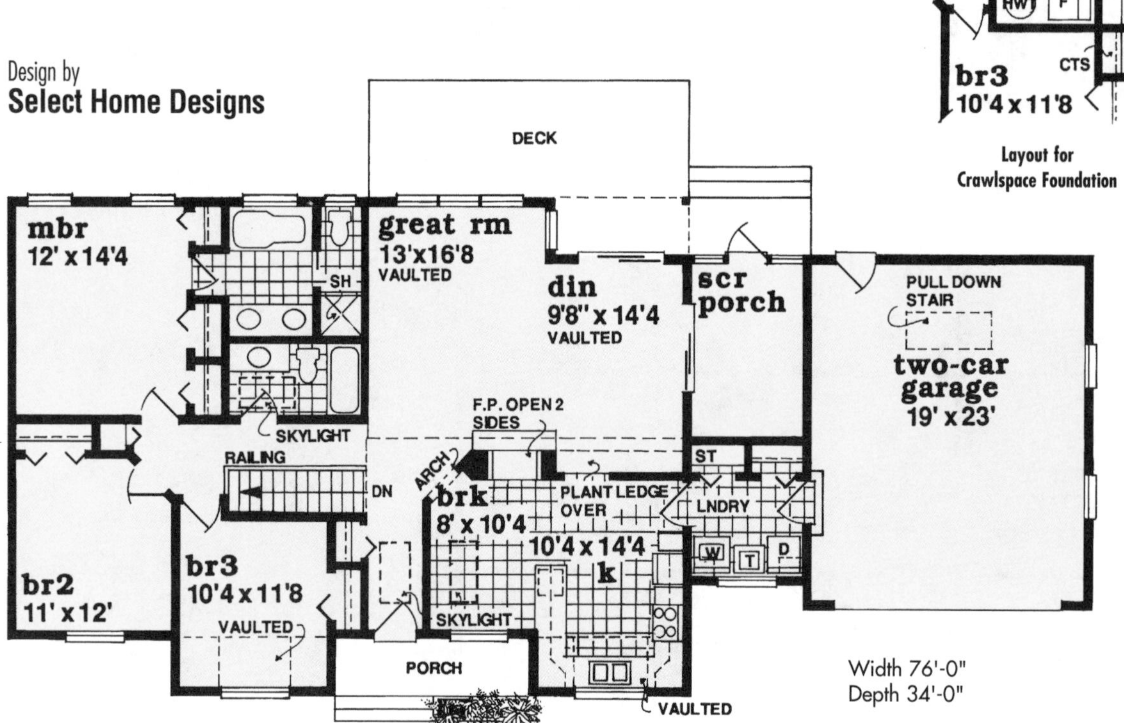

HWT
F
br3
10'4 x 11'8
CTS
DECK
mbr
12' x 14'4
great rm
13'x16'8
VAULTED
SH
din
9'8" x 14'4
VAULTED
scr porch
PULL DOWN STAIR
two-car garage
19' x 23'
F.P. OPEN 2 SIDES
SKYLIGHT
RAILING
ARCH
DN
brk
8' x 10'4
PLANT LEDGE OVER
ST
LNDRY
10'4 x 14'4
k
W
T
D
br2
11' x 12'
br3
10'4 x 11'8
VAULTED
SKYLIGHT
PORCH
VAULTED

Layout for Crawlspace Foundation

Width 76'-0"
Depth 34'-0"

Design by
Home Planners

Design 2678

Square Footage: 1,971

L D

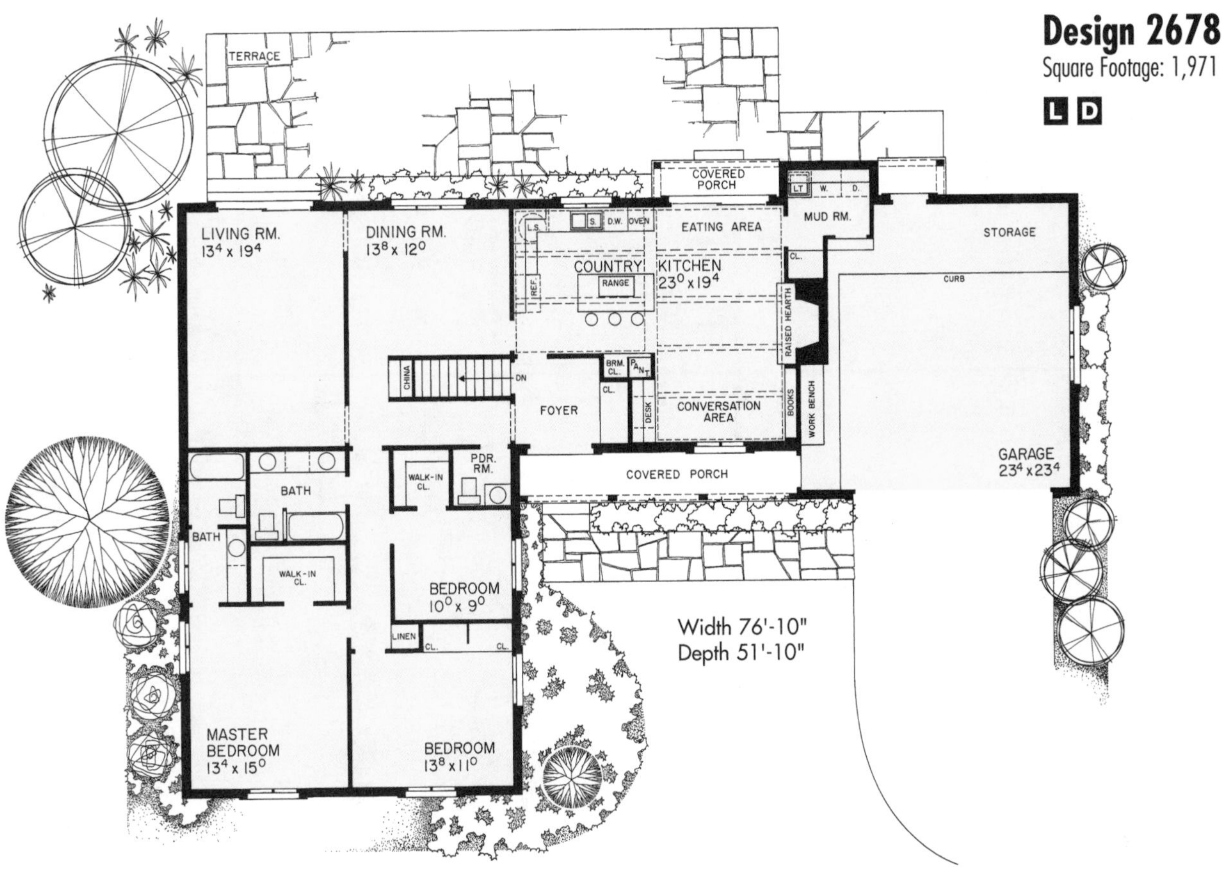
TERRACE
COVERED PORCH
LT. W. D.
MUD RM.
STORAGE
LIVING RM.
13⁴ x 19⁴
DINING RM.
13⁸ x 12⁰
L.S.
S. D.W. OVEN
EATING AREA
COUNTRY KITCHEN
23⁰ x 19⁴
RANGE
REF.
CL.
RAISED HEARTH
CURB
CHINA
DN
BRM. CL.
PANT.
FOYER
DESK
CONVERSATION AREA
BOOKS
WORK BENCH
PDR. RM.
WALK-IN CL.
BATH
COVERED PORCH
GARAGE
23⁴ x 23⁴
BATH
WALK-IN CL.
BEDROOM
10⁰ x 9⁰
LINEN
CL.
Width 76'-10"
Depth 51'-10"
MASTER BEDROOM
13⁴ x 15⁰
BEDROOM
13⁸ x 11⁰

If you've ever dreamed of having a large country kitchen in your home then this is the design for you. The features of this room are many: an island range with snack bar, pantry and broom closets, eating area with sliding glass doors leading to a covered porch, adjacent mud room with laundry facilities and access to the garage, raised-hearth fireplace and conversation area with built-in desk on one side and shelves on the other. There are also formal living and dining rooms. The living room has sliding glass doors to the terrace. Three bedrooms include two family bedrooms sharing a full bath—one bedroom has a walk-in closet. The master suite has a private bath and walk-in closet.

Design by
Home Planners

Design 2707

Square Footage: 1,347

L **D**

Here is a charming Early American adaptation that will serve as a picturesque and practical home. The living area, highlighted by the raised-hearth fireplace, is spacious and comfortable. The efficient kitchen features an eating nook, convenient passage to the formal dining room and an easy service entrance. The bedroom wing offers three bedrooms and two full baths. The front-facing secondary bedroom would make an ideal study or media room.

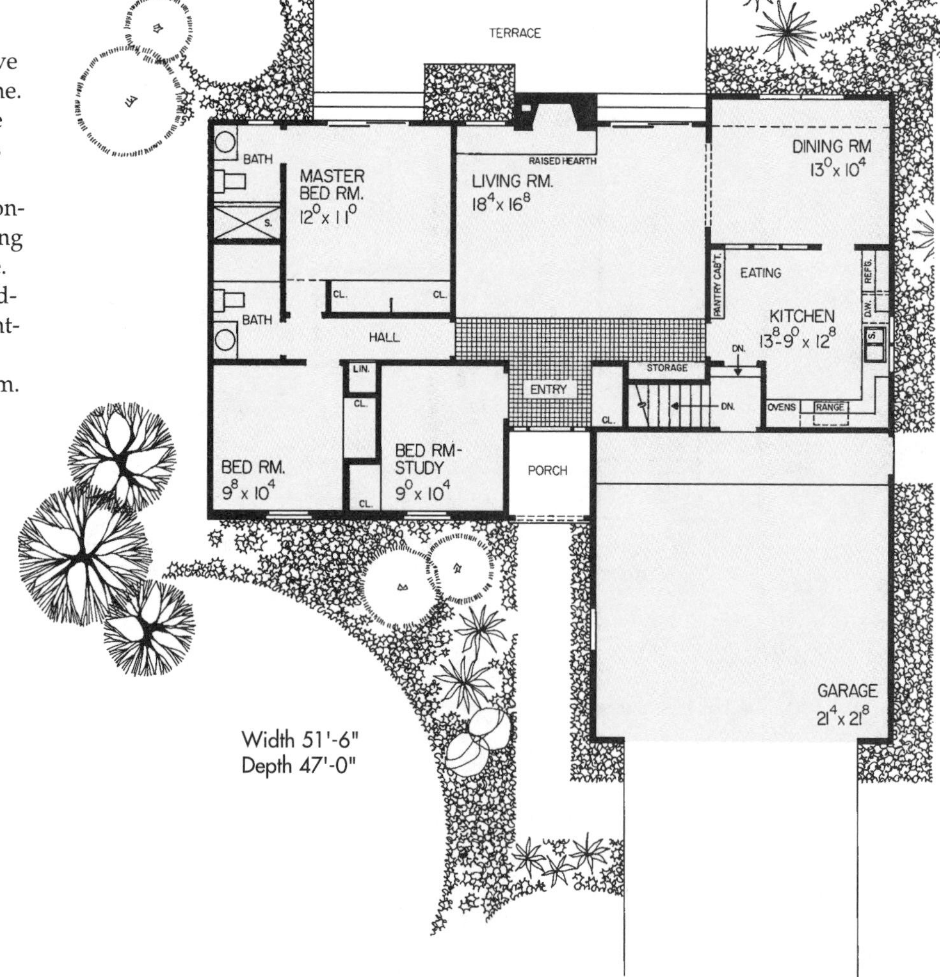
TERRACE
RAISED HEARTH
BATH
MASTER BED RM. 12^{0} x 11^{0}
S.
LIVING RM. 18^{4} x 16^{8}
DINING RM 13^{0} x 10^{4}
CL.
CL.
BATH
HALL
PANTRY CAB'T.
EATING
REFG.
D.W.
KITCHEN 13^{8}-9^{0} x 12^{8}
DN.
STORAGE
LIN.
ENTRY
CL.
CL.
DN.
OVENS
RANGE
BED RM. 9^{8} x 10^{4}
BED RM- STUDY 9^{0} x 10^{4}
CL.
PORCH
GARAGE 21^{4} x 21^{8}

Width 51'-6"
Depth 47'-0"

QUOTE ONE®

Cost to build? See page 516 to order complete cost estimate to build this house in your area!

Width 58'-0"
Depth 51'-5"

Design 2805

Square Footage: 1,547

L D

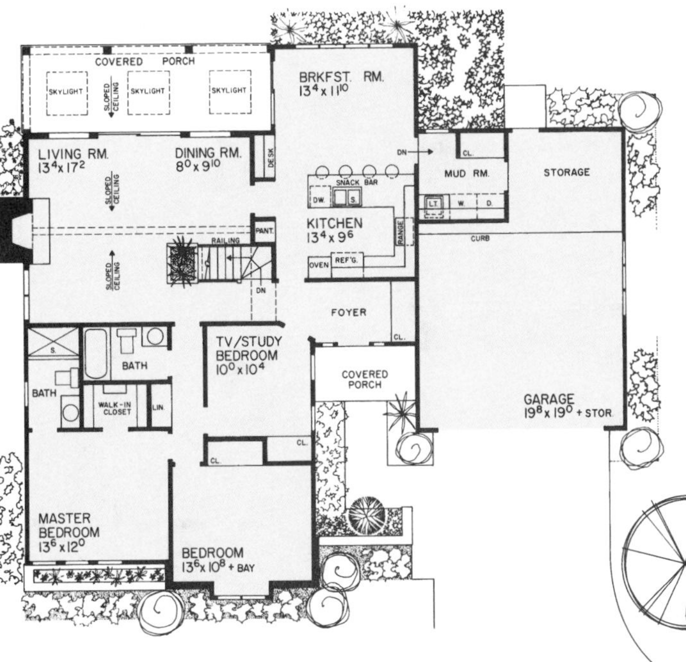
COVERED PORCH
SKYLIGHT
SLOPED CEILING
SKYLIGHT
SKYLIGHT
BRKFST. RM.
13⁴x 11¹⁰
LIVING RM.
13⁴x 17²
DINING RM.
8⁰x 9¹⁰
DESK
DN
CL.
SNACK BAR
MUD RM.
STORAGE
DW.
S.
LT.
W.
D.
SLOPED CEILING
PANT.
KITCHEN
13⁴x 9⁶
RANGE
CURB
RAILING
OVEN
REF'G.
SLOPED CEILING
DN
FOYER
CL.
S.
BATH
TV/STUDY
BEDROOM
10⁰x 10⁴
COVERED
PORCH
BATH
WALK-IN CLOSET
LIN
GARAGE
19⁸x 19⁰ + STOR.
CL.
CL.
MASTER
BEDROOM
13⁶x 12⁰
BEDROOM
13⁶x 10⁸ + BAY

This appealing home offers a practical and economical floor plan with a choice of two lovely exterior. Choose a traditional version, sided in stone or a Tudor version with half-timbering and stone. Inside, the floor plan is the same. The living/dining room at the rear of the plan has direct access to the covered porch. Notice the built-in planter adjacent to the open staircase leading to the basement. A breakfast room overlooks the covered porch. A desk, snack bar and mud room with laundry facilities are near the U-shaped kitchen. The master bedroom features a private bath and a walk-in closet. The large front bedroom has a bay window, while a third bedroom may serve as a study.

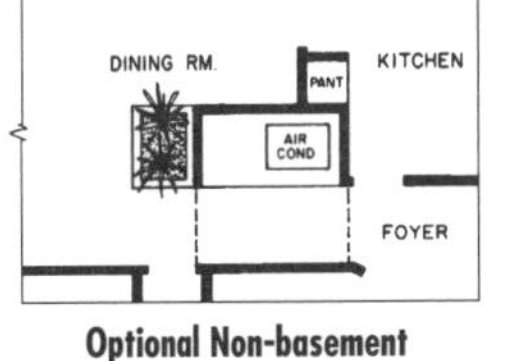
DINING RM.
KITCHEN
PANT
AIR COND
FOYER

Optional Non-basement

Design by
Home Planners

Design 2806

Square Footage: 1,584

L D

QUOTE ONE®
Cost to build? See page 516 to order complete cost estimate to build this house in your area!

(Available for Design 2805 only)

Width 58'-10"
Depth 50'-10"

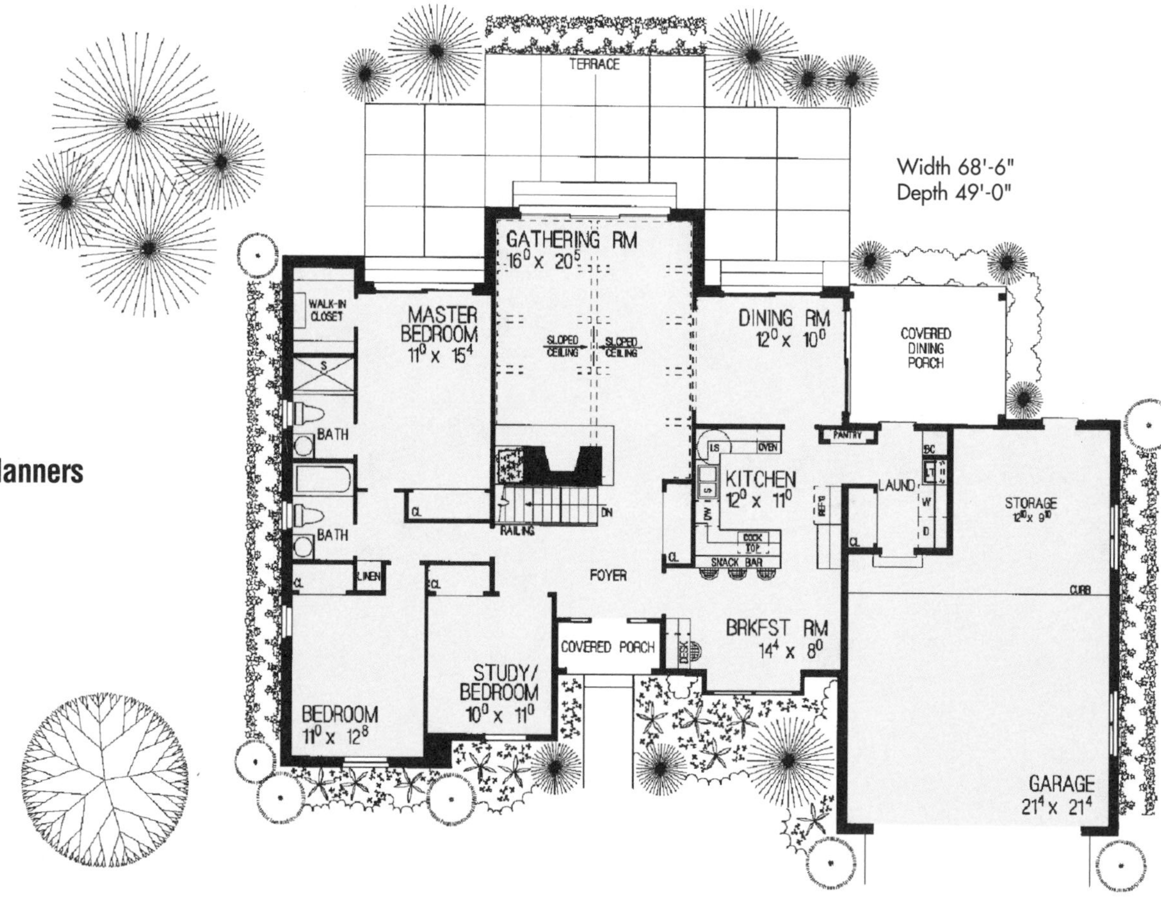

Width 68'-6"
Depth 49'-0"

Design by
Home Planners

Design 3345

Square Footage: 1,738

L

This quaint shingled cottage offers an unexpected amount of living space in just over 1,700 square feet. The large gathering room with fireplace and sloped ceiling, the dining room with covered porch and the U-shaped kitchen with breakfast room all handle formal parties as easily as they do casual family get-togethers. Three bedrooms—one that could also serve as a study—are found in a separate wing of the house. The master bedroom features sliding glass doors to the rear terrace, plus a private bath and walk-in closet. Both the gathering room and dining room have sliding glass doors to the rear terrace as well. The two-car garage includes an enormous storage area.

QUOTE ONE®

Cost to build? See page 516
to order complete cost estimate
to build this house in your area!

COVERED PATIO
SKYLIGHT
SKYLIGHT
SKYLIGHT
BREAKFAST $13^{2} \times 11^{8}$
LIVING ROOM $12^{10} \times 17^{6}$
DINING ROOM $9^{8} \times 10^{6}$
DESK
SNACK BAR
DW
S
MUD ROOM $8^{4} \times 7^{10}$
LT
W
D
STORAGE
CURB
SLOPED CEILING
SLOPED CEILING
PANTRY
KITCHEN $13^{2} \times 10^{0}$
COOKTOP
RAILING
MICRO OVEN
REFG
DN
FOYER
GARAGE $19^{6} \times 20^{6}$
WALK-IN CLOSET
BATH
LIN
BEDRM 3 $10^{0} \times 10^{6}$
PORCH
BATH
LINEN
SLOPED CEILING
SLOPED CEILING
MASTER SUITE $14^{4} \times 13^{0}$
BEDRM 2 $13^{6} \times 10^{8}$
SEAT
Width 58'-0"
Depth 52'-6"

QUOTE ONE®

Cost to build? See page 516 to order complete cost estimate to build this house in your area!

Design 3340

Square Footage: 1,689

L

Design by
Home Planners

A charming cupola over the garage and delightful fan windows set the tone for this cozy cottage. A central fireplace and a sloped ceiling highlight the living room's comfortable design, complete with sliding patio doors and an adjoining dining room. The large eat-in kitchen has a snack bar, planning desk and patio doors from the breakfast room. An angular hallway leads to the master bedroom featuring a large walk-in closet, twin-sink vanity and a compartmented bath. A secondary bedroom features a lovely window seat. A third bedroom is perfectly situated to be a study. The two-car garage has a separate storage area with a utility entrance.

Design by
Home Planners

Design 2810

Square Footage: 1,536

L **D**

A sheltering covered porch furnishes a delightful introduction to this traditional one-story home. The vestibule opens to a spacious living room graced by a built-in planter. Straight ahead is a beam-ceilinged family room with sliding glass doors to the terrace. An adjacent kitchen supplies a snack bar for quick meals and an eating nook for casual dining. Two family bedrooms are found at the front of the plan and share a hall bath. The master bedroom is located nearby and features its own private bath. Plans for an alternate garage are included for those who prefer a front-loading garage instead of the side-loading garage shown. Choose a basement or crawl-space foundation—plans include details for both.

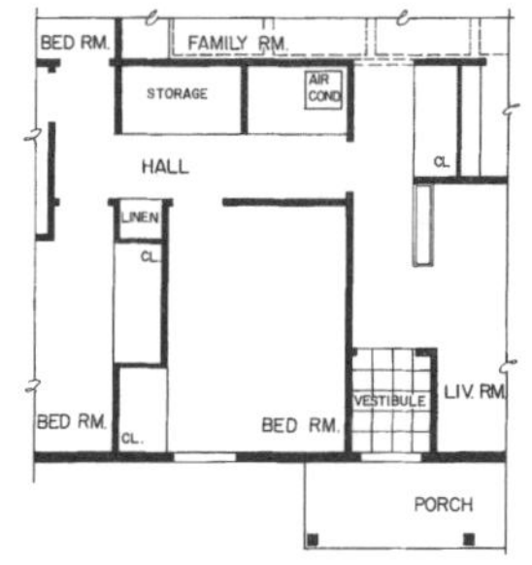
BED RM.
FAMILY RM.
STORAGE
AIR COND
HALL
LINEN
CL.
BED RM.
BED RM.
VESTIBULE
LIV. RM
PORCH

OPTIONAL CRAWL SPACE PLAN

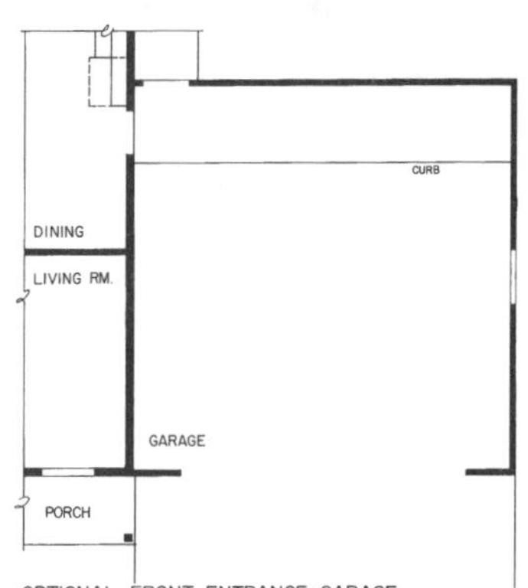
DINING
LIVING RM.
CURB
GARAGE
PORCH

OPTIONAL FRONT ENTRANCE GARAGE

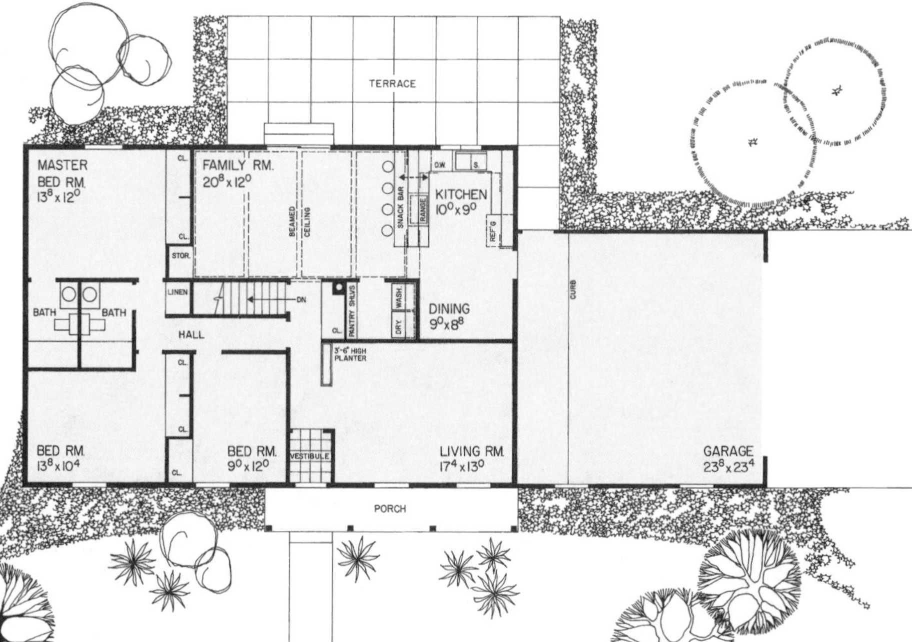
TERRACE
MASTER BED RM. 13⁸ x 12⁰
FAMILY RM. 20⁸ x 12⁰
BEAMED CEILING
SNACK BAR
RANGE
DW
KITCHEN 10⁰ x 9⁰
REFG
STOR.
LINEN
DN
BATH
BATH
HALL
PANTRY SHELVES
WASH.
DRY.
DINING 9⁰ x 8⁸
3'-6" HIGH PLANTER
CURB
BED RM. 13⁸ x 10⁴
BED RM. 9⁰ x 12⁰
VESTIBULE
LIVING RM. 17⁴ x 13⁰
GARAGE 23⁸ x 23⁴
PORCH

Width 72'-0"
Depth 36'-0"

QUOTE ONE®

Cost to build? See page 516 to order complete cost estimate to build this house in your area!

Design by
Home Planners

QUOTE ONE®

Cost to build? See page 516
to order complete cost estimate
to build this house in your area!

Design 2603

Square Footage: 1,949

L D

It would be difficult to beat the appeal of this traditional one-story home. Its slightly modified U-shape with the two front-facing gables, the bay window, the covered front porch and the interesting use of exterior materials all add to the exterior charm. Besides, there are three large bedrooms served by two full baths and three walk-in closets. The kitchen is flanked by a formal dining room and informal family room. Don't miss the pantry, the built-in oven and the pass-through to the snack bar. The handy main-floor laundry is strategically located to act as a mud room. The extra wash room is a few steps away. The sizable living room is highlighted by a fireplace and picture window. Note the convenient location of the basement stairs.

TERRACE
BED RM. 14^2x11^6
DINING RM. 12^0x11^6
KITCHEN 10^0x11^6
FAMILY RM. 16^4x13^6
WASH RM.
LAUNDRY
BED RM. 14^2x11^0
LIVING RM. 22^0x13^6
GARAGE 23^4x21^8
FOYER
COVERED PORCH
MASTER BED RM. 18^0x12^0
STORAGE

Width 74'-10"
Depth 42'-10"

Design 1325

Square Footage: 1,942

L D

Design by
Home Planners

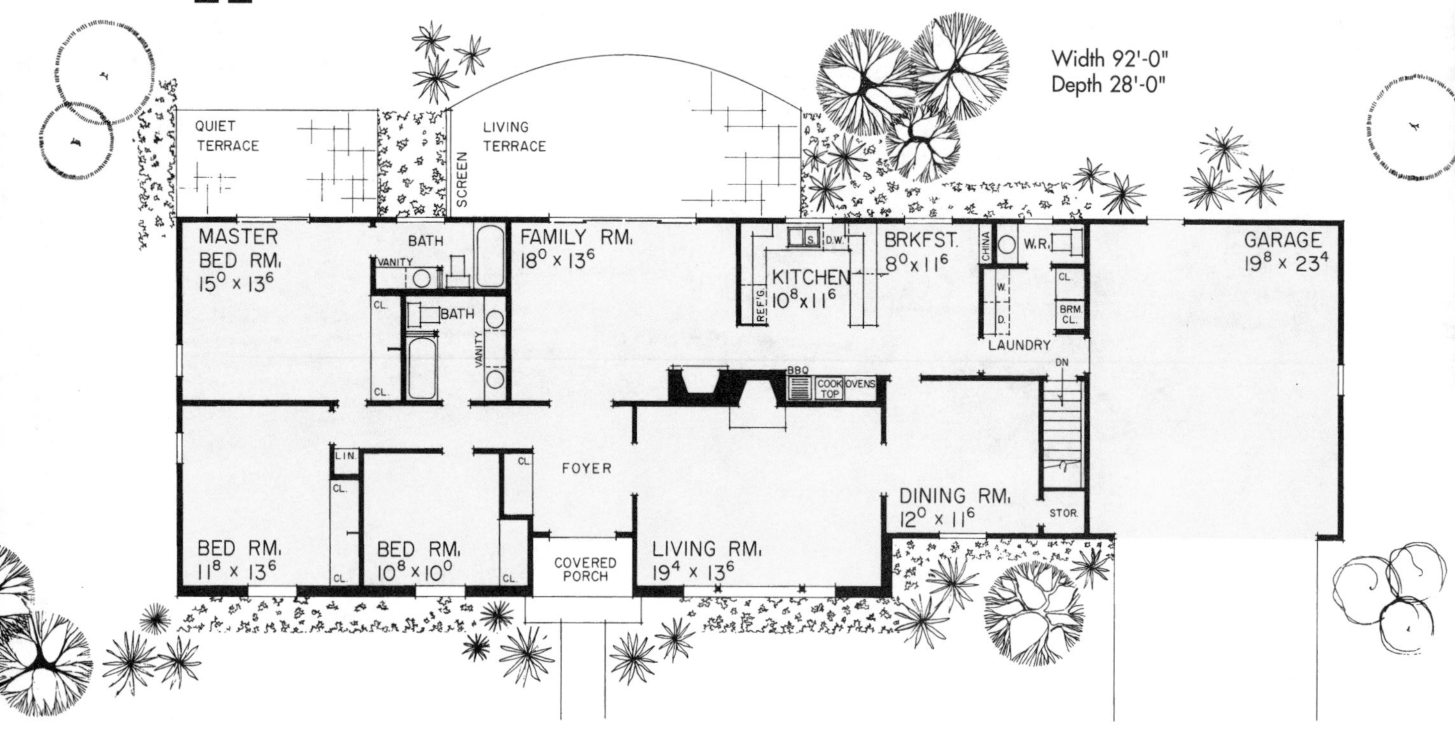

Width 92'-0"
Depth 28'-0"
QUIET TERRACE
LIVING TERRACE
SCREEN
MASTER BED RM. 15⁰ x 13⁶
BATH
VANITY
CL.
BATH
VANITY
CL.
FAMILY RM. 18⁰ x 13⁶
KITCHEN 10⁸x11⁶
REF'G.
S.
D.W.
BRKFST. 8⁰x11⁶
CHINA
W.R.
CL.
BRM. CL.
W.
D.
LAUNDRY
DN
GARAGE 19⁸ x 23⁴
BBQ
COOK TOP
OVENS
FOYER
LIN.
CL.
CL.
DINING RM. 12⁰ x 11⁶
STOR.
BED RM. 11⁸ x 13⁶
CL.
BED RM. 10⁸ x 10⁰
CL.
COVERED PORCH
LIVING RM. 19⁴ x 13⁶

Long, sleek lines grace the facade of this brick one-story—making it look as grand as it lives. The large front entry hall allows access to the formal living room and beyond to the family room with sliding glass doors to the living terrace at the back. Fireplaces enhance both of these living spaces. A formal dining room attaches to the living room, but is also directly across the hall from the U-shaped kitchen for convenience. A laundry with wash room is found at the service entrance to the garage. Three bedrooms sit at the left side of the plan: a master suite and two family bedrooms. The master suite enjoys a private "quiet" terrace and a separate bath with make-up vanity. The family bedrooms share the use of a full hall bath.

Width 78'-10"
Depth 28'-10"

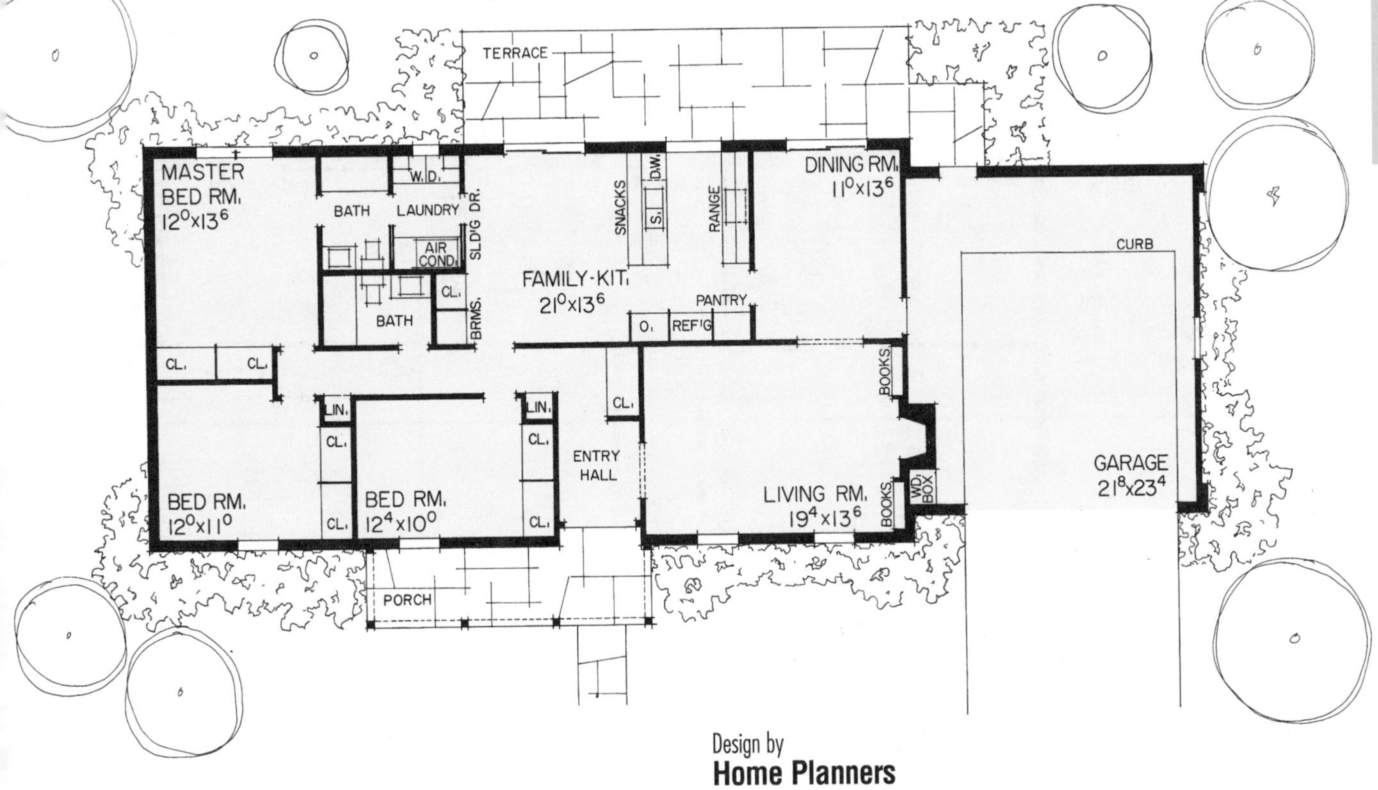

TERRACE
MASTER BED RM. $12^0 \times 13^6$
BATH
LAUNDRY
W.D.
SLD'G DR.
AIR COND.
CL.
BATH
BRMS.
SNACKS
D.W.
S.
RANGE
FAMILY-KIT. $21^0 \times 13^6$
PANTRY
O.
REF'G
DINING RM. $11^0 \times 13^6$
CURB
CL.
CL.
LIN.
CL.
CL.
LIN.
CL.
CL.
CL.
ENTRY HALL
BOOKS
WD. BOX
BOOKS
LIVING RM. $19^4 \times 13^6$
GARAGE $21^8 \times 23^4$
BED RM. $12^0 \times 11^0$
BED RM. $12^4 \times 10^0$
PORCH

Design by
Home Planners

Design 1890

Square Footage: 1,628

The pediment gable and columns increase the charm of this modestly sized home. On the inside is the kind of graciousness associated with plans twice its dimensions. The covered porch conceals a double-door entrance, opening to an entry hall with coat closet. Formal rooms include a living room with built-in bookcases and a warming hearth. Nearby is the formal dining room with sliding glass doors to the rear terrace. The casual family room is attached to a galley-style kitchen and features a snack bar and its own access to the rear terrace. A pocket door opens to the laundry room and a full bath beyond that is shared with the master bedroom. Two family bedrooms are at the front of the plan. Each has a linen closet for convenience. A two-car garage completes the plan (note the built-in wood box).

Width 62'-10"
Depth 36'-10"

TERRACE

MASTER BED RM. $13^4 x 12^0$

BATH

S.

DINING RM. $10^0 x 12^0$

KITCHEN $10^0 x 8^0$

S

REF'G

RANGE

FAMILY RM. $17^4 x 11^4$

CL.

D

W

CL.

CL.

BATH

CL.

LIN.

CL.

CL.

AIR COND.

DN.

OPTIONAL BASMENT STAIRWAY

CL.

CL.

BED RM. $10^0 x 13^0$

CL.

BED RM. $10^0 x 9^8$

ENTRY

LIVING RM. $13^0 x 17^0$

PORCH

GARAGE $19^4 x 23^8$

Design 1305

Square Footage: 1,382

D

In less than 1,400 square feet you'll find three bedrooms, two full baths, a separate dining room, a formal living room, a kitchen overlooking the rear yard and an informal family room. In addition, there is the attached two-car garage. Note the location of the stairs when this plan is built with a basement. Special features include sliding glass doors in the family room leading to the rear terrace, a private bath in the master suite and a linen closet serving the main bath in the hall. The exterior is predominantly brick—the front features both stone and vertical boards and battens, with brick on the other three sides. Multi-pane windows and shutters add to the charm.

Design by
Home Planners

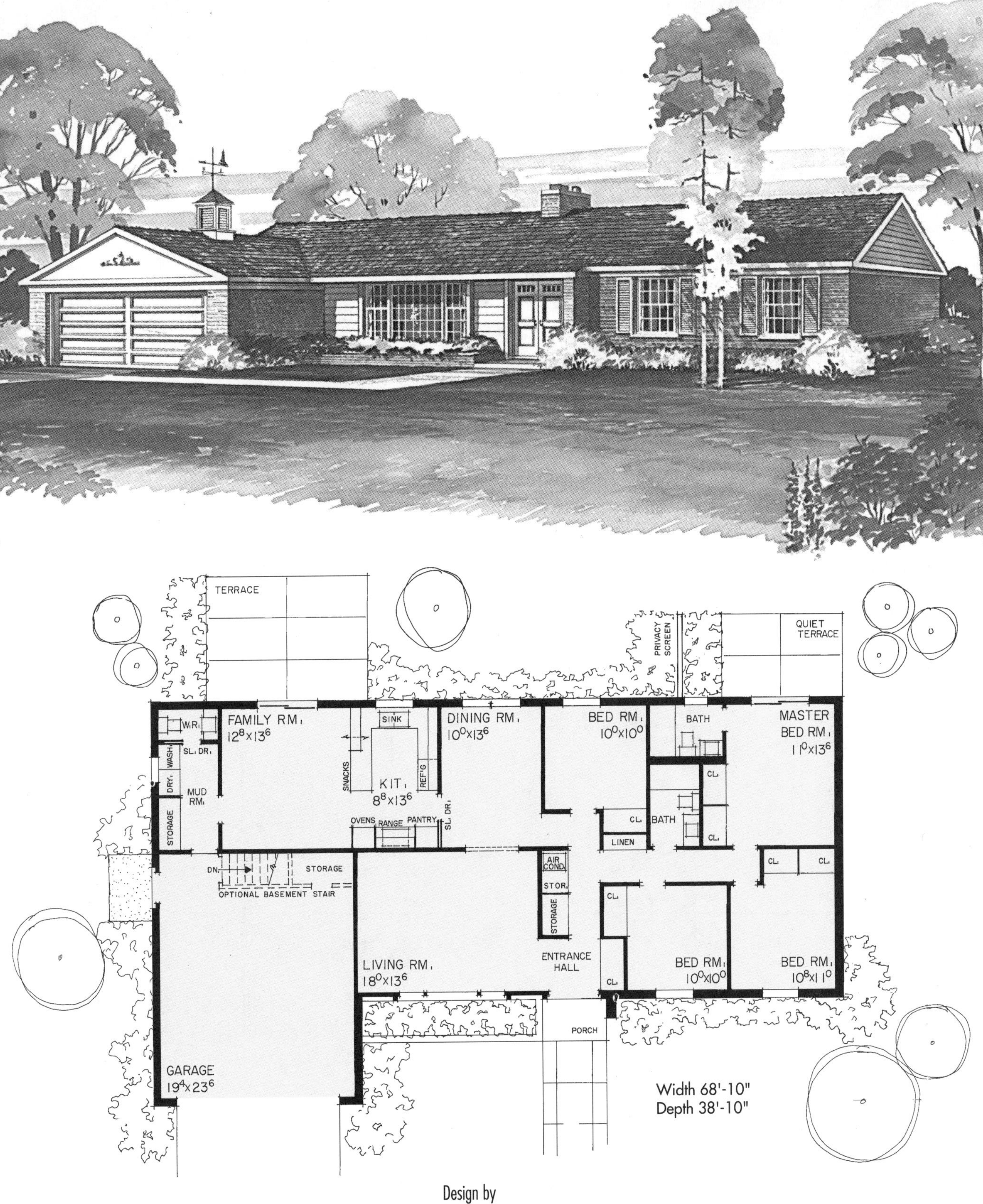
TERRACE
QUIET TERRACE
PRIVACY SCREEN
W.R.
FAMILY RM.
$12^{8} \times 13^{6}$
SL. DR.
WASH.
DRY.
MUD RM.
STORAGE
SINK
SNACKS
KIT.
$8^{8} \times 13^{6}$
REF'G
OVENS
RANGE
PANTRY
SL. DR.
DINING RM.
$10^{0} \times 13^{6}$
BED RM.
$10^{0} \times 10^{0}$
BATH
MASTER BED RM.
$11^{0} \times 13^{6}$
CL.
BATH
LINEN
DN.
STORAGE
OPTIONAL BASEMENT STAIR
AIR COND.
STOR.
STORAGE
ENTRANCE HALL
LIVING RM.
$18^{0} \times 13^{6}$
BED RM.
$10^{0} \times 10^{0}$
BED RM.
$10^{8} \times 11^{0}$
PORCH
GARAGE
$19^{4} \times 23^{6}$
Width 68'-10"
Depth 38'-10"

Design by
Home Planners

Design 1896

Square Footage: 1,690

Complete family livability is provided by this exceptional floor plan. Further, this design has a truly delightful traditional exterior. The fine layout features a center entrance hall with a storage closet in addition to the coat closet. Then, there is the formal, front living room and the adjacent, separate dining room. The U-shaped kitchen has plenty of counter and cupboard space. There is even a pantry. The family room functions with the kitchen and is but a step away from the outdoor terrace. The mud room has space for storage and laundry equipment. An extra wash room is nearby. The large family will find those four bedrooms and two full baths just the answer for sleeping and bath accommodations.

Design by
Home Planners

Design 2871

Square Footage: 1,824
Greenhouse: 81 square feet

D

A greenhouse area off the dining room and living room provides a cheerful focal point for this comfortable three-bedroom home. The spacious living room features a cozy fireplace and a sloped ceiling. In addition to the dining room, there's a less formal breakfast room just off the modern kitchen. Both kitchen and breakfast areas look out onto a front terrace. Stairs just off the foyer lead down to a basement recreation room. The master bedroom suite opens to a terrace. A mud room and a wash room off the garage allow rear entry to the house during inclement weather.

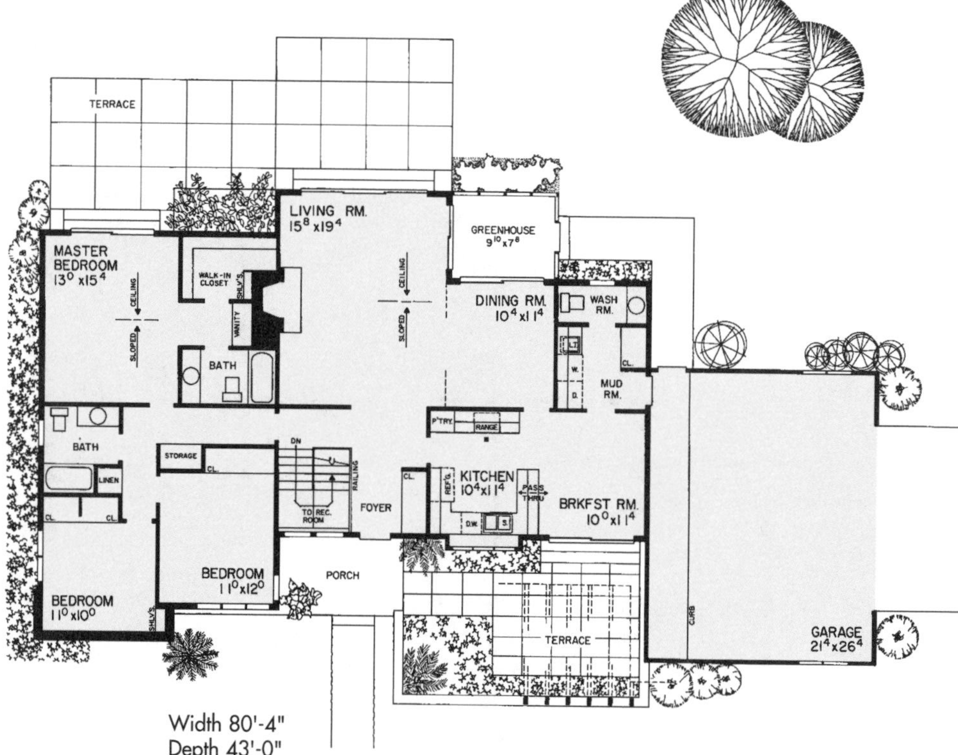

TERRACE
LIVING RM.
15⁸ x19⁴
GREENHOUSE
9¹⁰x7⁸
MASTER
BEDROOM
13⁰ x15⁴
WALK-IN CLOSET
VANITY
BATH
DINING RM.
10⁴x11⁴
WASH RM.
MUD RM.
BATH
LINEN
STORAGE
DN
FOYER
KITCHEN
10⁴x11⁴
BRKFST RM.
10⁰x11⁴
BEDROOM
11⁰x12⁰
PORCH
BEDROOM
11⁰x10⁰
TERRACE
GARAGE
21⁴x26⁴

Width 80'-4"
Depth 43'-0"

Rear Elevation

QUOTE ONE®

Cost to build? See page 516 to order complete cost estimate to build this house in your area!

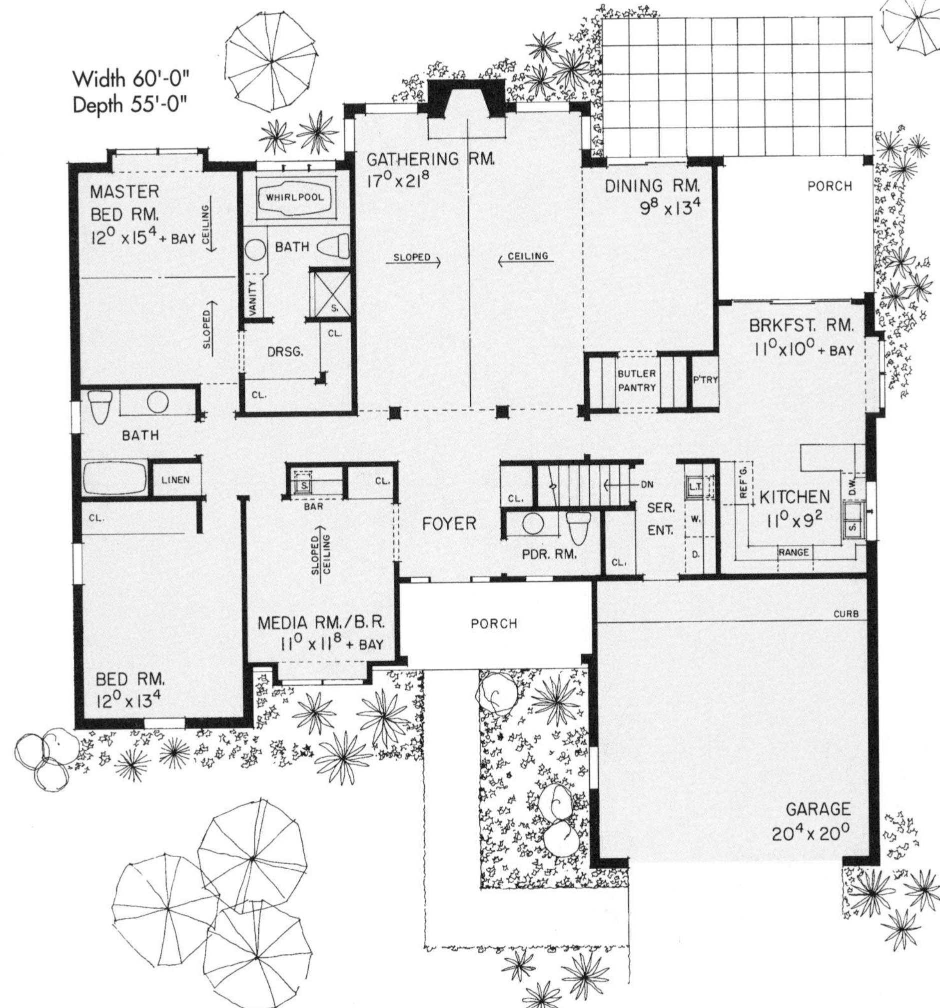
Width 60'-0"
Depth 55'-0"
MASTER BED RM. $12^{0} \times 15^{4}$ + BAY
SLOPED CEILING
WHIRLPOOL
BATH
VANITY
S.
CL.
DRSG.
CL.
GATHERING RM. $17^{0} \times 21^{8}$
SLOPED CEILING
DINING RM. $9^{8} \times 13^{4}$
PORCH
BRKFST. RM. $11^{0} \times 10^{0}$ + BAY
BUTLER PANTRY
P'TRY
BATH
LINEN
CL.
S
BAR
CL.
SLOPED CEILING
CL.
DN
SER. ENT.
L.T.
W.
D.
REF'G.
KITCHEN $11^{0} \times 9^{2}$
D.W.
S.
RANGE
FOYER
PDR. RM.
CL.
MEDIA RM./B.R. $11^{0} \times 11^{8}$ + BAY
PORCH
CURB
BED RM. $12^{0} \times 13^{4}$
GARAGE $20^{4} \times 20^{0}$

Design 3376

Square Footage: 1,999

L D

Small families will appreciate the layout of this traditional ranch. The foyer opens to the gathering room with fireplace and sloped ceiling. The dining room opens to the gathering room for entertaining ease and offers sliding glass doors to a rear terrace. The breakfast room also provides access to a covered porch for dining outdoors. The media room to the left of the home offers a bay window and a wet bar, or it can double as a third bedroom.

QUOTE ONE®

Cost to build? See page 516 to order complete cost estimate to build this house in your area!

Design by
Home Planners

Design 2671

Square Footage: 1,589

L **D**

The rustic exterior of this one-story home features vertical wood siding. The entry foyer is floored with flagstone and leads to the three areas of the plan: the sleeping, living and work center. The sleeping area features three bedrooms. The master bedroom utilizes sliding glass doors to the rear terrace. The living area, consisting of gathering and dining rooms, also enjoys access to the terrace. The work center is efficiently planned. It houses the kitchen with a snack bar, the breakfast room with a built-in china cabinet and stairs to the basement. This is a very livable plan. Special amenities include a raised-hearth fireplace and a walk-in closet in the master bedroom.

QUOTE ONE®
Cost to build? See page 516
to order complete cost estimate
to build this house in your area!

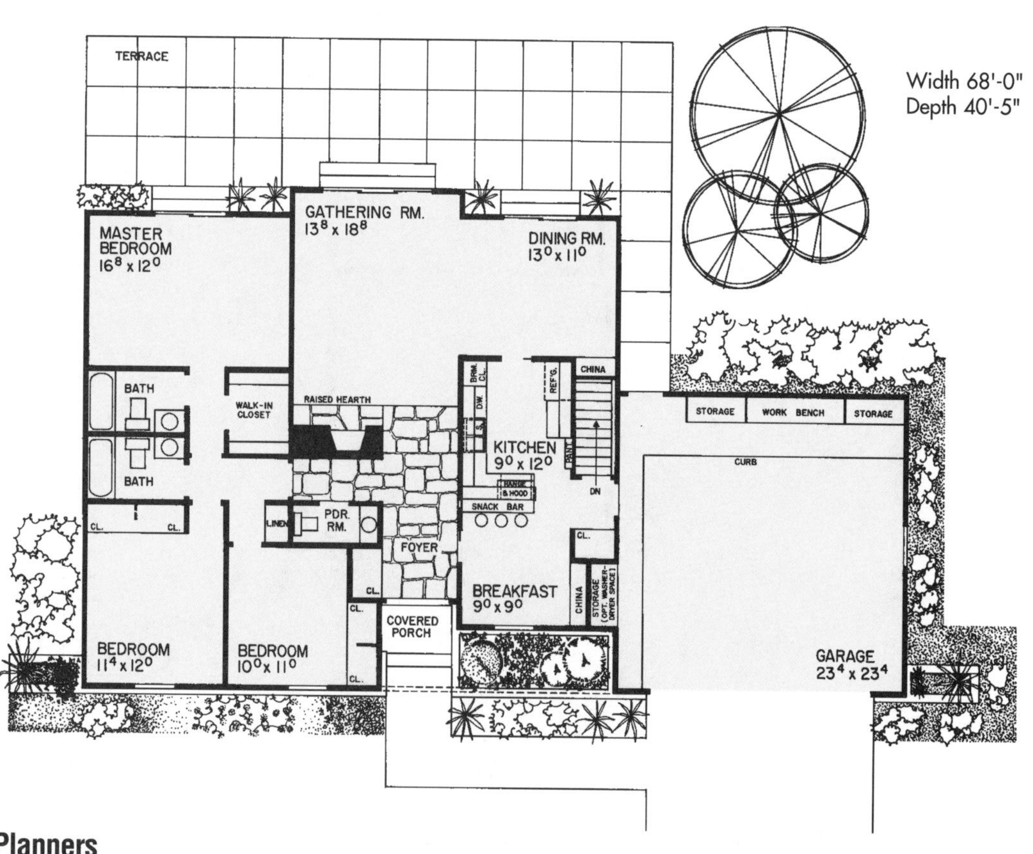
TERRACE
Width 68'-0"
Depth 40'-5"
GATHERING RM.
13^8 x 18^8
DINING RM.
13^0 x 11^0
MASTER BEDROOM
16^8 x 12^0
BATH
BATH
WALK-IN CLOSET
RAISED HEARTH
CHINA
KITCHEN
9^0 x 12^0
SNACK BAR
DN
STORAGE
WORK BENCH
STORAGE
CURB
CL.
CL.
LINEN
PDR. RM.
FOYER
CL.
CL.
CL.
CL.
BREAKFAST
9^0 x 9^0
CHINA
COVERED PORCH
BEDROOM
11^4 x 12^0
BEDROOM
10^0 x 11^0
GARAGE
23^4 x 23^4

Design by
Home Planners

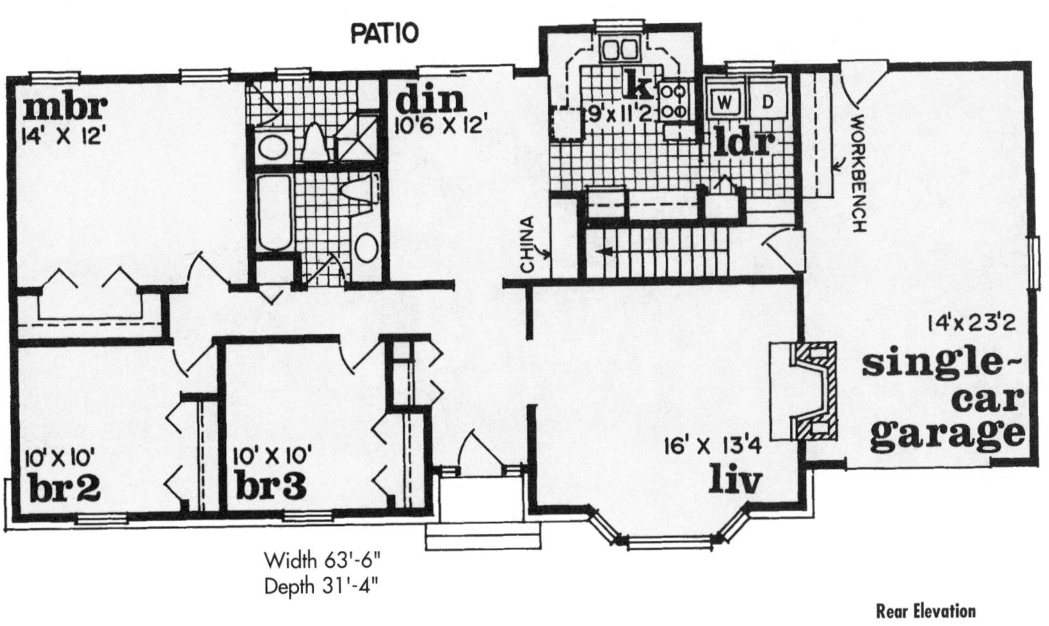
PATIO
mbr
14' X 12'
din
10'6 X 12'
k
9'x 11'2
W
D
ldr
WORKBENCH
CHINA
14'x 23'2
single-car garage
10' X 10'
br2
10' X 10'
br3
16' X 13'4
liv
Width 63'-6"
Depth 31'-4"

Rear Elevation

Design by
Select Home Designs

Design Q495

Square Footage: 1,332

Brick veneer and siding provide an attractive, low-maintenance option for this ranch home. A weather-protected entry opens to a spacious foyer with a living room on the right and the dining room straight ahead. The living room sports a fireplace and bay window, while the dining room has built-in china cabinet space. The kitchen easily serves the dining room and is U-shaped with ample counters. Sliding glass doors in the dining room lead to a rear patio and the yard beyond. The master bedroom has a walk-in closet and private bath with corner shower. Two additional bedrooms share a hall bath. The single-car garage allows room for a work bench. Note the laundry area that connects the garage to the main house.

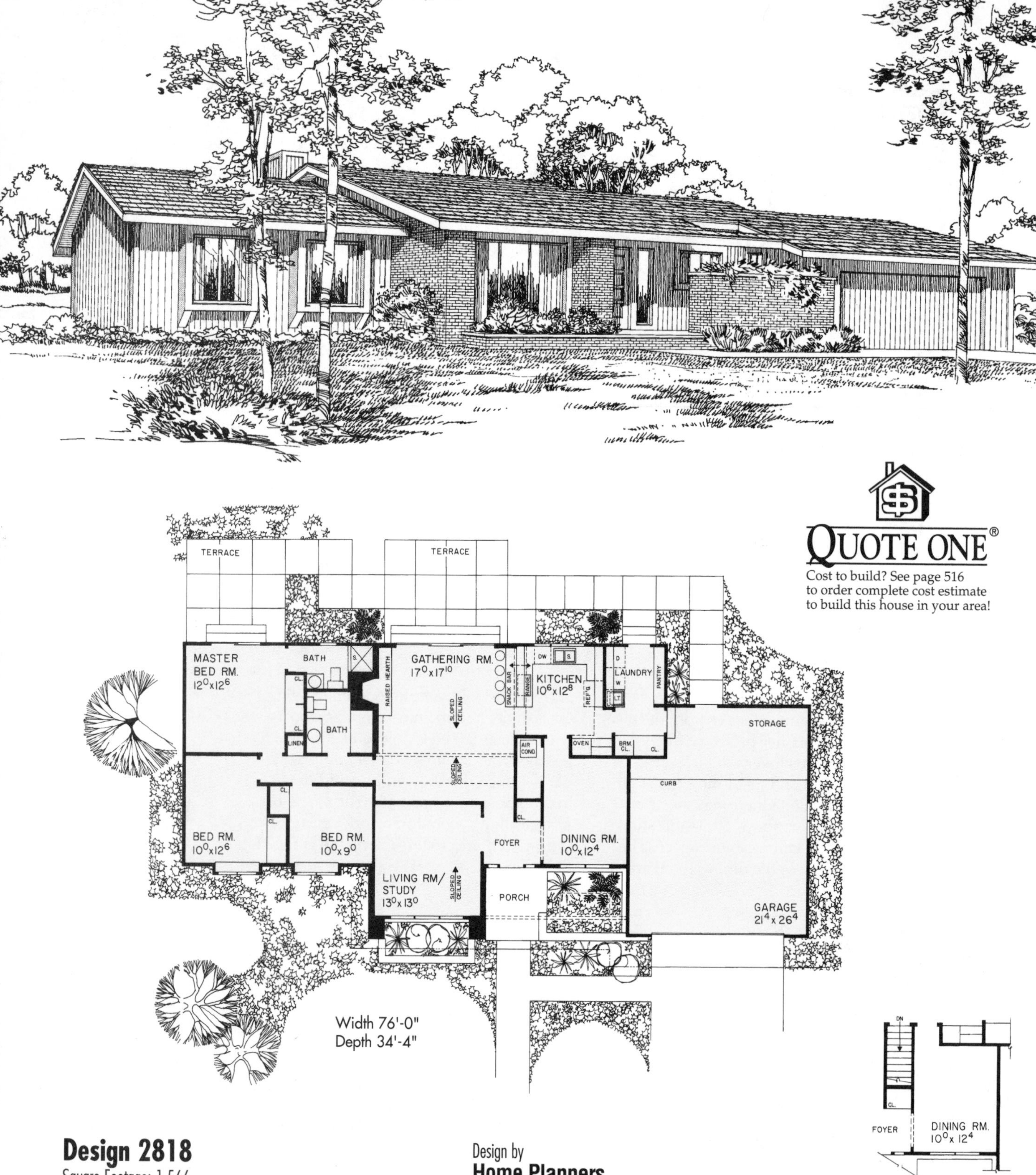
TERRACE
TERRACE
MASTER BED RM. 12⁰x12⁶
BATH
GATHERING RM. 17⁰x17¹⁰
KITCHEN 10⁶x12⁸
LAUNDRY
PANTRY
RAISED HEARTH
SNACK BAR
RANGE
REF'G
SLOPED CEILING
BATH
LINEN
CL.
STORAGE
OVEN
BRM. CL.
AIR COND.
CURB
BED RM. 10⁰x12⁶
BED RM. 10⁰x9⁰
FOYER
DINING RM. 10⁰x12⁴
LIVING RM/ STUDY 13⁰x13⁰
PORCH
GARAGE 21⁴x26⁴
Width 76'-0"
Depth 34'-4"
QUOTE ONE®
Cost to build? See page 516 to order complete cost estimate to build this house in your area!
FOYER
DINING RM. 10⁰x12⁴
CL.
DN
Optional Basement Plan

Design 2818

Square Footage: 1,566

L **D**

Design by
Home Planners

Contemporary styling demanded the clean and unique lines of this home's exterior. It boasts vertical siding, large glass areas and brick detailing. The front entry is recessed to create a covered porch with garden area. An outstanding floor plan sits beyond. The rear gathering room has a sloped ceiling, raised-hearth fireplace and sliding glass doors to the terrace. A pass-through counter separates the living space from the U-shaped kitchen. A formal living room (or study) has a sloped ceiling and opens directly off the foyer. On the opposite side of the foyer is a formal dining room with entry to the kitchen for convenience. The three bedrooms include a master suite with sliding glass doors to a private terrace, and two family bedrooms sharing a full bath. The two-car garage has a large storage area. Build this home with a basement foundation if you choose.

Design 2913

Square footage: 1,835

D

Design by
Home Planners

This smart design features a multi-gabled roof and vertical windows. It also offers efficient zoning by room functions and plenty of modern comforts for contemporary family living. A covered porch leads through a foyer to a large, central gathering room with a fireplace, a sloped ceiling, and its own special view of the rear terrace. A modern kitchen with a snack bar features a pass-through to the breakfast room with a view of the terrace. There's also an adjacent dining room. A media room is privately situated along with the bedrooms from the rest of the house to offer a quiet, private area for enjoying music or surfing-the-net. A master bedroom suite includes its own dressing area with a whirlpool tub in the bath. A large garage includes an extra storage room.

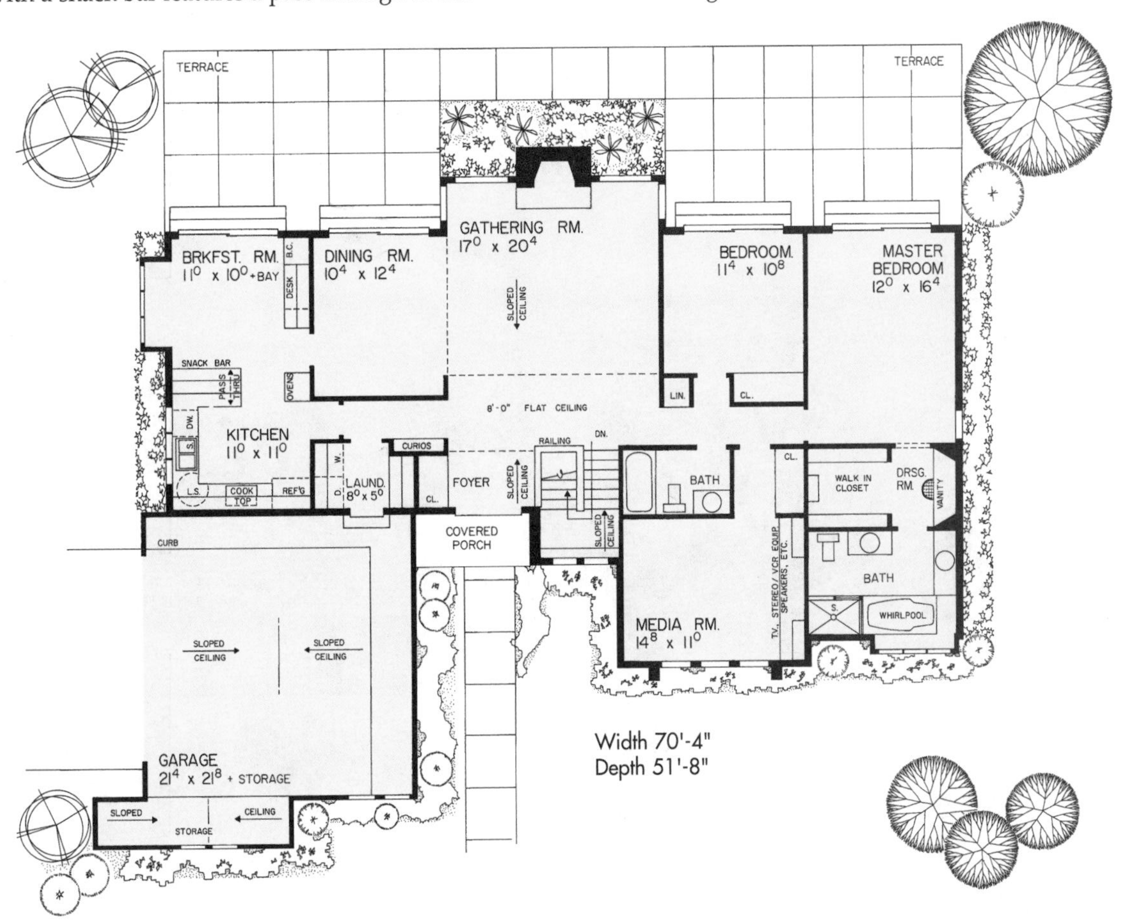
TERRACE
TERRACE
BRKFST. RM.
11^0 x 10^0 + BAY
B.C.
DESK
DINING RM.
10^4 x 12^4
GATHERING RM.
17^0 x 20^4
SLOPED CEILING
BEDROOM
11^4 x 10^8
MASTER BEDROOM
12^0 x 16^4
SNACK BAR
PASS THRU
OVENS
8'-0" FLAT CEILING
LIN.
CL.
DW.
S
KITCHEN
11^0 x 11^0
L.S.
COOK TOP
REF'G
W.
D.
LAUND.
8^0 x 5^0
CURIOS
CL.
FOYER
SLOPED CEILING
RAILING
DN.
BATH
CL.
WALK IN CLOSET
DRSG. RM.
VANITY
COVERED PORCH
SLOPED CEILING
TV, STEREO/VCR EQUIP. SPEAKERS, ETC.
BATH
S.
WHIRLPOOL
MEDIA RM.
14^8 x 11^0
CURB
SLOPED CEILING
SLOPED CEILING
GARAGE
21^4 x 21^8 + STORAGE
SLOPED
CEILING
STORAGE
Width 70'-4"
Depth 51'-8"

Design 2864

Square Footage: 1,387

L D

Many characteristics of this contemporary home deserve mention. For instance, the entrance court and covered porch are a delightful introduction to the well-appointed plan inside. The foyer leads to an interior kitchen with breakfast room and a snack bar on the gathering room side. A study with wet bar is adjacent—use the study as an extra bedroom, if you choose. Sliding glass doors in the master bedroom open to the terrace. There is also terrace access in the gathering room, the formal dining room and the study. Sloped ceilings are found in the gathering room, the formal dining room and the master bedroom. Both the hall bath and the master suite bath have large skylights over the tub area.

QUOTE ONE®

Cost to build? See page 516 to order complete cost estimate to build this house in your area!

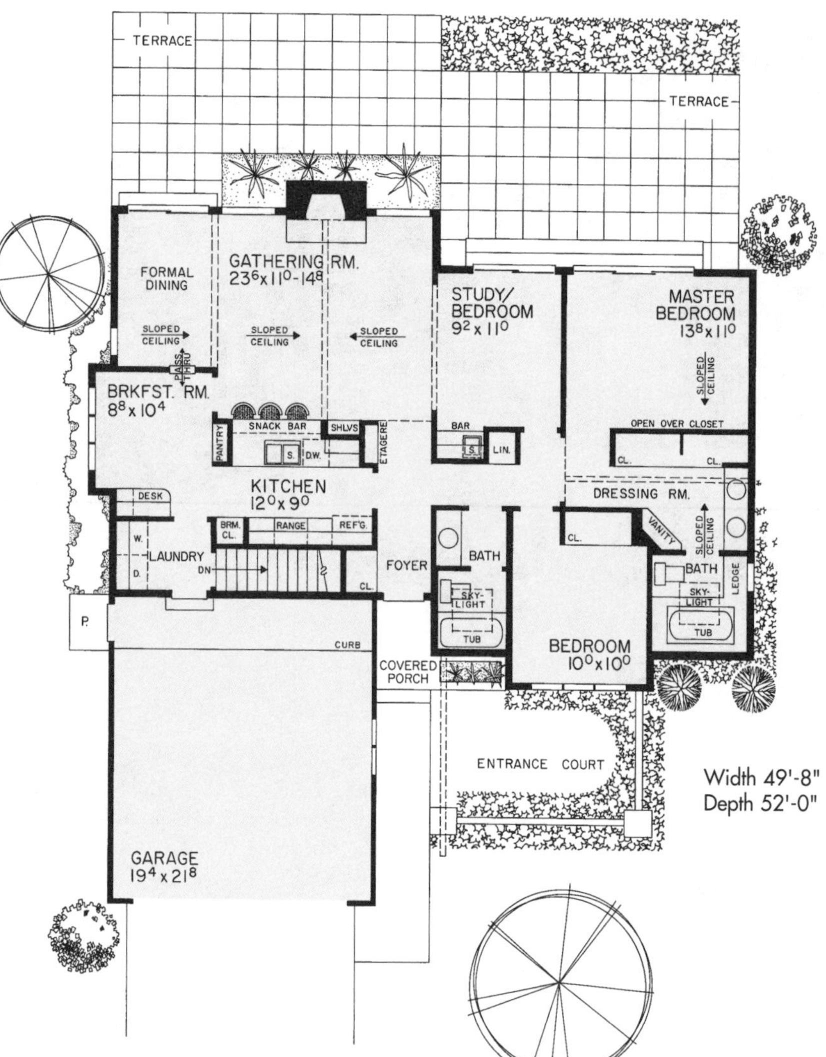
TERRACE
TERRACE
FORMAL DINING
GATHERING RM.
23⁶x11⁰-14⁸
SLOPED CEILING
SLOPED CEILING
SLOPED CEILING
STUDY/ BEDROOM
9²x11⁰
MASTER BEDROOM
13⁸x11⁰
SLOPED CEILING
BRKFST. RM.
8⁸x10⁴
SNACK BAR
SHLVS
PANTRY
ETAGERE
BAR
LIN.
OPEN OVER CLOSET
CL.
CL.
KITCHEN
12⁰x9⁰
DESK
DRESSING RM.
BRM. CL.
RANGE
REF'G.
VANITY
SLOPED CEILING
LAUNDRY
DN
FOYER
BATH
BATH
SKY-LIGHT
TUB
SKY-LIGHT
TUB
LEDGE
CL.
CL.
P.
CURB
COVERED PORCH
BEDROOM
10⁰x10⁰
ENTRANCE COURT
GARAGE
19⁴x21⁸

Width 49'-8"
Depth 52'-0"

Design by
Home Planners

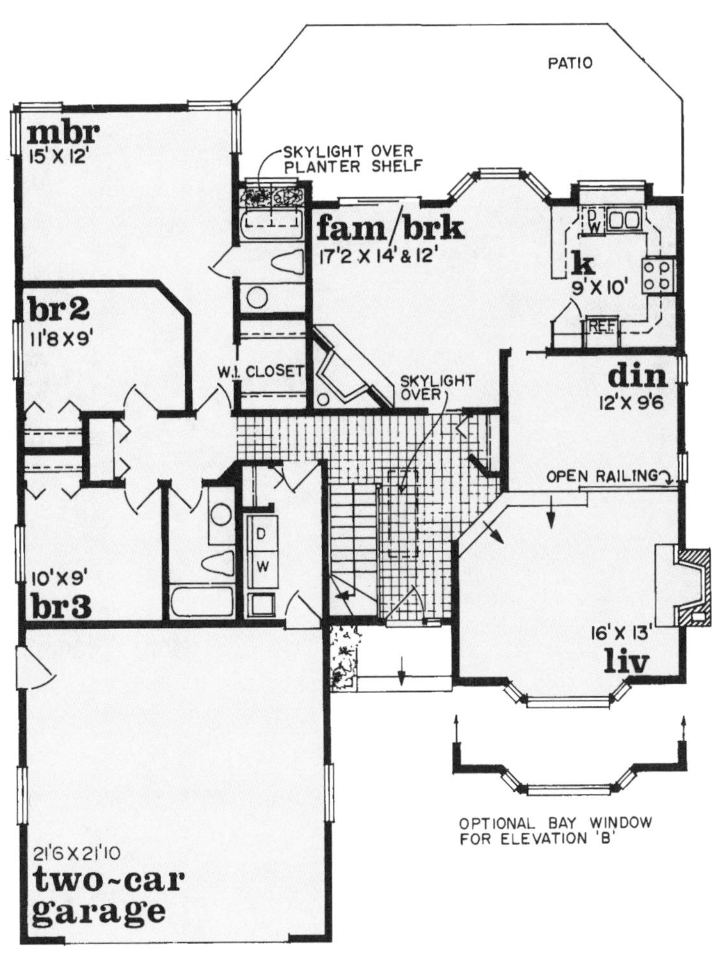
PATIO
mbr
15'X12'
SKYLIGHT OVER
PLANTER SHELF
fam/brk
17'2 X 14' & 12'
D W
k
9'X10'
REF
br2
11'8X9'
W.I. CLOSET
SKYLIGHT OVER
din
12'X9'6
OPEN RAILING
D
W
10'X9'
br3
16'X13'
liv
OPTIONAL BAY WINDOW
FOR ELEVATION 'B'
21'6X21'10
two-car
garage

Width 48'-0"
Depth 58'-10"

Design Q240

Square Footage: 1,608

The plans for this cute bungalow offer choices of exterior finishes. The recessed entry is weather-protected and opens to a skylit, tiled foyer. The living room is sunken a few steps and enjoys a bay window and focal-point fireplace. Adjoining is the formal dining room, separated from the living room by an open railing. The kitchen takes on a modified U-shape and has a bright window box over the sink. The connecting breakfast bay and family room has a corner fireplace and sliding glass door to the patio. Bedrooms are positioned away from noisy traffic areas and include a master suite with full bath (note the plant shelf and skylight). Two family bedrooms and a shared bath are nearby. The laundry room connects the main house to the two-car garage. Plans include details for both a basement and a crawlspace foundation.

Design by
Select Home Designs

Design 2505

Square Footage: 1,366

L D

Design by
Home Planners

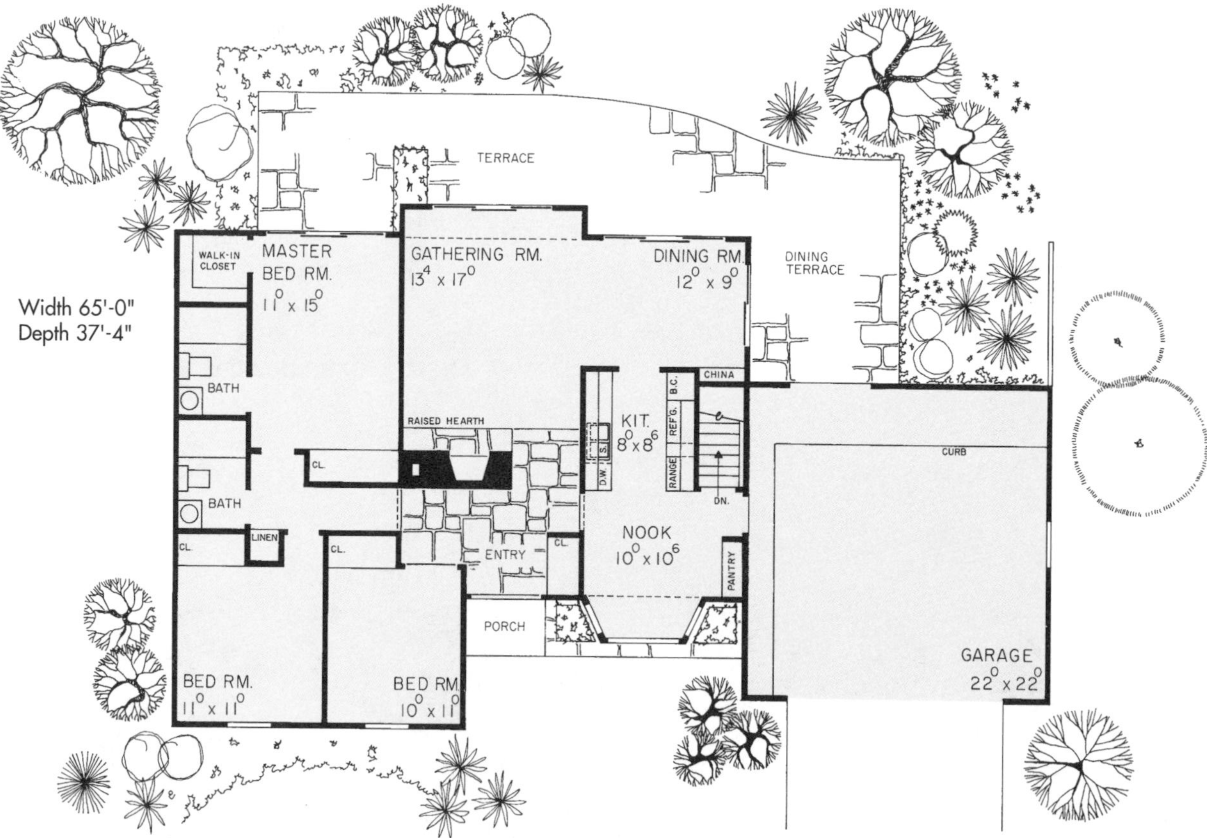

TERRACE
WALK-IN CLOSET
MASTER BED RM. 11^0 x 15^0
GATHERING RM. 13^4 x 17^0
DINING RM. 12^0 x 9^0
DINING TERRACE
Width 65'-0"
Depth 37'-4"
BATH
BATH
RAISED HEARTH
CL.
KIT. 8^0x8^6
CHINA
B.C.
REF'G.
RANGE
D.W.
S.
DN.
CURB
LINEN
CL.
CL.
ENTRY
CL.
NOOK 10^0 x 10^6
PANTRY
PORCH
GARAGE 22^0 x 22^0
BED RM. 11^0 x 11^0
BED RM. 10^0 x 11^0

This design offers you a choice of three distinctively different exteriors. Blueprints show details for all three optional elevations. A study of the floor plan reveals a fine measure of livability. In less than 1,400 square feet there are features galore. In addition to the two eating areas and the open planning of the gathering room, the indoor-outdoor relationships are of great interest. Three bedrooms include a master suite with walk-in closet and private bath. A fireplace graces the gathering room. The basement may be developed at a later date for recreational activities. Be sure to note the storage potential, particularly the linen closet, the pantry, the china cabinet and the broom closet.

QUOTE ONE®
Cost to build? See page 516
to order complete cost estimate
to build this house in your area!

Design Q366

Square Footage: 1,538

This compact three-bedroom offers a wealth of amenities—and you can make one of the bedrooms into a den or home office, if you choose! A skylit foyer spills into a vaulted living room with a bay-window seat and corner fireplace. The dining room is open to the living room and connects directly to the kitchen where there is another bay-window seat. An angled snack bar separates the kitchen from the family room; double doors open onto the patio at the back of the house. The master bedroom offers still another bay window with window seat and has a walk-in closet and private bath. The family bedrooms—one with walk-in closet—share a full bath. Note the laundry room space in the service entrance to the two-car garage. Plans include details for both a basement and a crawlspace foundation.

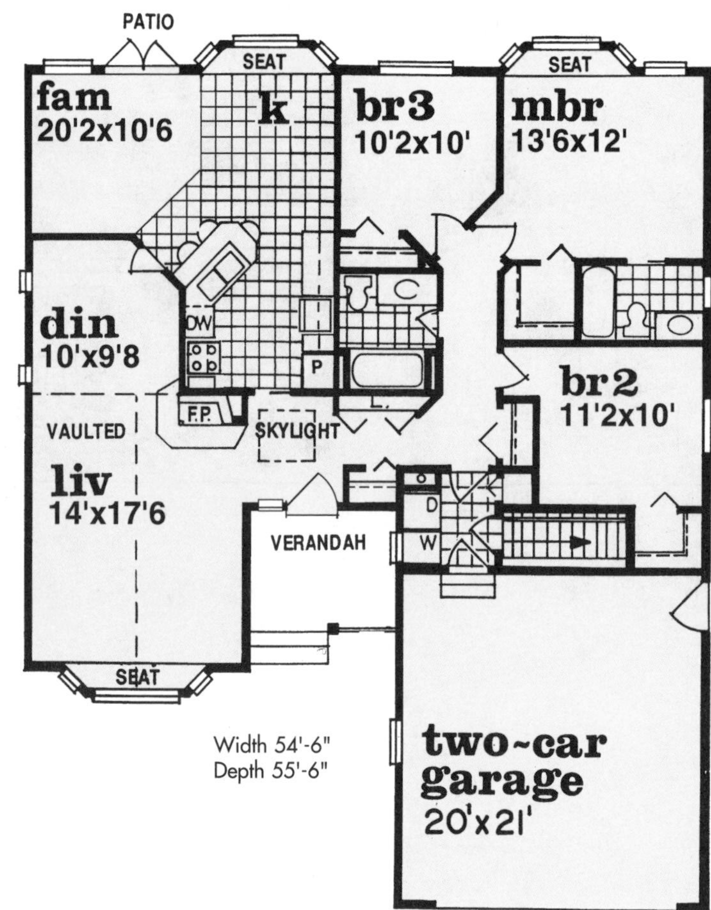

PATIO
SEAT
fam
20'2x10'6
k
br3
10'2x10'
SEAT
mbr
13'6x12'
DW
din
10'x9'8
P
br2
11'2x10'
F.P.
VAULTED
SKYLIGHT
liv
14'x17'6
D
W
VERANDAH
SEAT
Width 54'-6"
Depth 55'-6"
two-car
garage
20'x21'

Rear Elevation

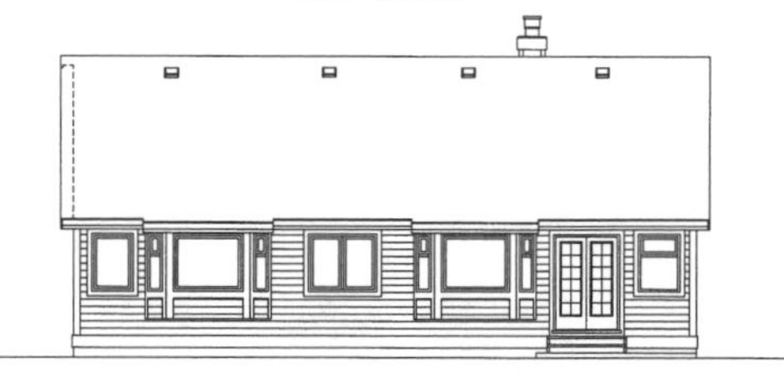

Design by
Select Home Designs

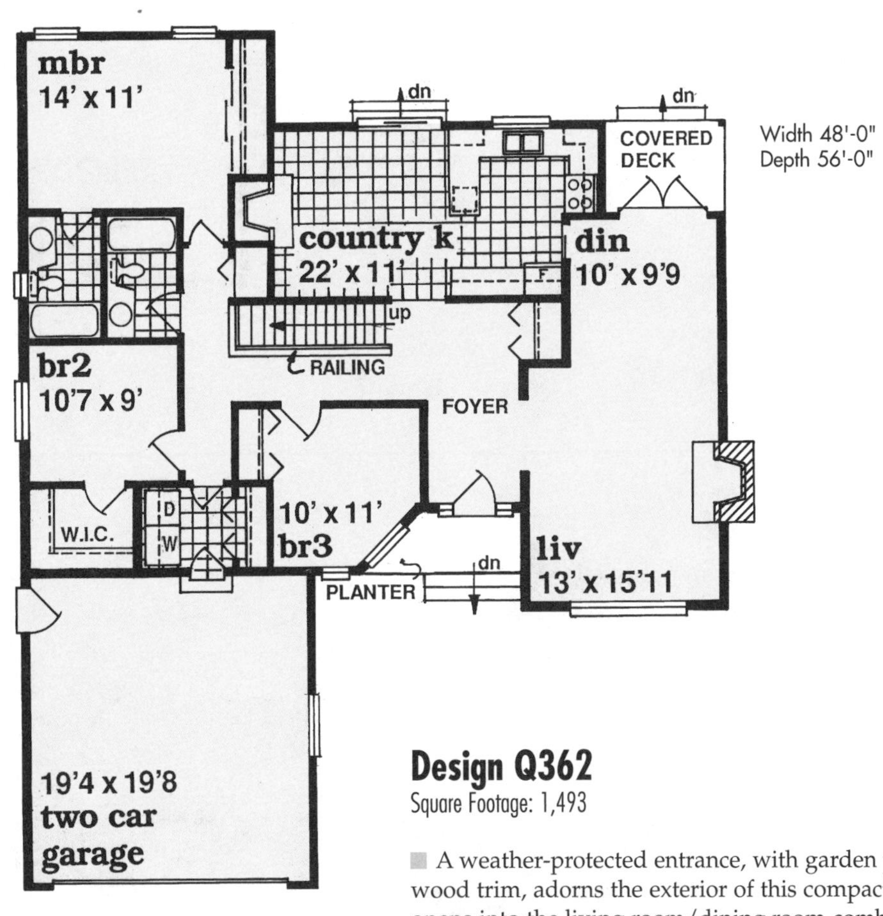
mbr
14' x 11'
dn
dn
COVERED DECK
Width 48'-0"
Depth 56'-0"
country k
22' x 11'
din
10' x 9'9
up
RAILING
br2
10'7 x 9'
FOYER
W.I.C.
D
W
10' x 11'
br3
PLANTER
dn
liv
13' x 15'11
19'4 x 19'8
two car
garage

Design Q362

Square Footage: 1,493

A weather-protected entrance, with garden planter and decorative wood trim, adorns the exterior of this compact family home. The foyer opens into the living room/dining room combination on the right. Special features here include a fireplace and double doors to a covered deck at the back. A step-saving, U-shaped country kitchen, with sliding glass door to the garden, is warmed by a masonry fireplace—a cozy gathering spot for the family. The master suite boasts a full wall closet and private bath while two family bedrooms share a hall bath. The third bedroom could easily double as a guest room, office or den. A two-car garage connects to the main house at a laundry room with washer/dryer space.

Design by
Select Home Designs

Design Q364

Square Footage: 1,495

This affordable, three-bedroom starter home has a practical layout and an appealing facade, which makes it an attractive choice in a smaller home. A bay window, horizontal siding and a covered entry with turned post and wood railings are the first details you'll notice. Inside, the floor plan minimizes hallways and maximizes floor area to encourage a sense of space. The living room/dining room combination features a window seat in the bay window and a warming fireplace. The kitchen has a breakfast bar, a bay-windowed eating area and attaches to a family room with sliding glass doors to the rear patio. Three bedrooms include two family bedrooms sharing a full bath and a master suite with walk-in closet and private bath. The two-car garage connects to the main house via a laundry area where stairs to the basement are also found.

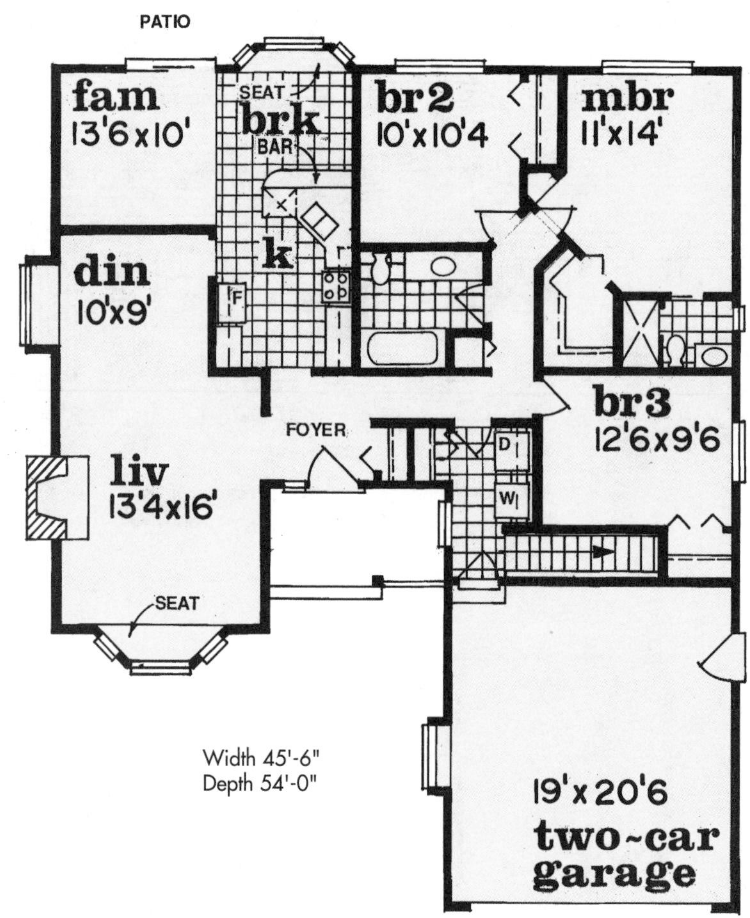

PATIO
fam
13'6x10'
SEAT
brk
BAR
k
F
br2
10'x10'4
mbr
11'x14'
din
10'x9'
FOYER
D
W
br3
12'6x9'6
liv
13'4x16'
SEAT
19'x20'6
two~car garage

Width 45'-6"
Depth 54'-0"

Design by
Select Home Designs

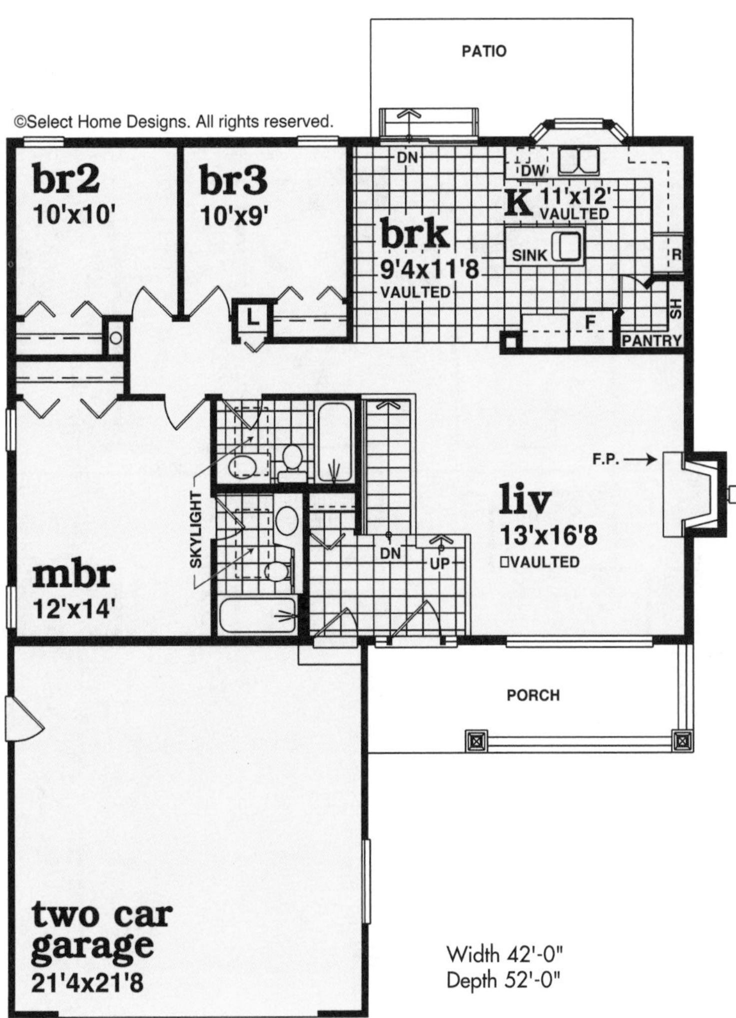

PATIO
©Select Home Designs. All rights reserved.
br2
10'x10'
br3
10'x9'
brk
9'4x11'8
VAULTED
K 11'x12'
VAULTED
DN
DW
SINK
R
F
SH
PANTRY
L
SKYLIGHT
F.P.
liv
13'x16'8
VAULTED
DN
UP
mbr
12'x14'
PORCH
two car
garage
21'4x21'8
Width 42'-0"
Depth 52'-0"

Design Q505

Square Footage: 1,260

This economical-to-build bungalow works well as a small family home or a retirement cottage. It is available with a basement foundation but could easily be converted to a slab or crawlspace foundation. The covered porch leads to a vaulted living room with fireplace. Behind this living space is the U-shaped kitchen with walk-in pantry and island with utility sink. An attached breakfast nook has sliding glass doors to a rear patio. There are three bedrooms, each with roomy wall closet. The master bedroom has a private full bath, while the family bedrooms share a main bath. Both baths have bright skylights. A two-car garage sits to the front of the plan to protect the bedrooms from street noise.

Design by
Select Home Designs

Design by
Home Planners

Design 2878

Square Footage: 1,530

L D

■ This charming, compact design combines traditional styling with sensational commodities and modern livability. Thoughtful zoning places sleeping areas to one side, apart from household activity. The plan includes a spacious gathering room with sloped ceiling and centered fireplace, and a formal dining room overlooking a rear terrace. A handy pass-through connects the breakfast room and an efficient kitchen. The laundry is strategically positioned nearby for handy access. An impressive master suite enjoys access to a private rear terrace and offers a separate dressing area with walk-in closet. Two family bedrooms, or one and a study, are nearby and share a full bath.

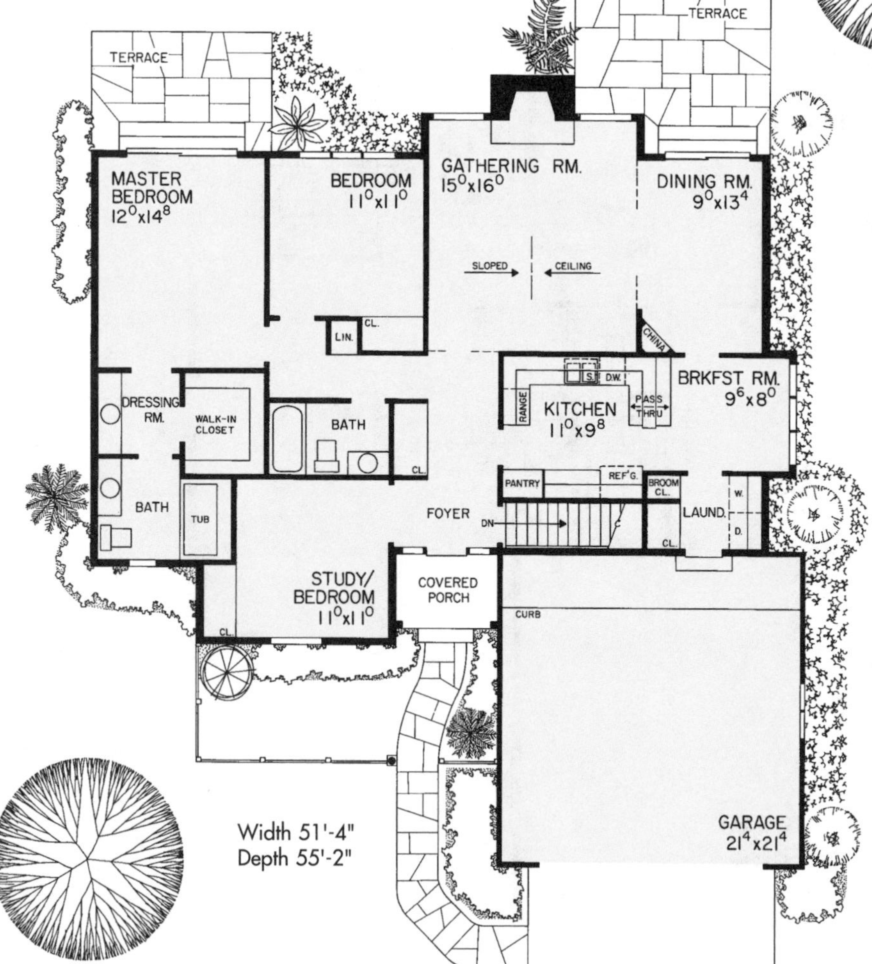
TERRACE
TERRACE
MASTER BEDROOM 12^0x14^8
BEDROOM 11^0x11^0
GATHERING RM. 15^0x16^0
DINING RM. 9^0x13^4
SLOPED
CEILING
CHINA
LIN.
CL.
DRESSING RM.
WALK-IN CLOSET
BATH
RANGE
S. DW.
KITCHEN 11^0x9^8
PASS THRU
BRKFST RM. 9^6x8^0
CL.
PANTRY
REF'G.
BROOM CL.
W.
D.
LAUND.
BATH
TUB
FOYER
DN
CL.
STUDY/ BEDROOM 11^0x11^0
COVERED PORCH
CL.
CURB
GARAGE 21^4x21^4
Width 51'-4"
Depth 55'-2"

QUOTE ONE®

Cost to build? See page 516 to order complete cost estimate to build this house in your area!

Design by
Home Planners

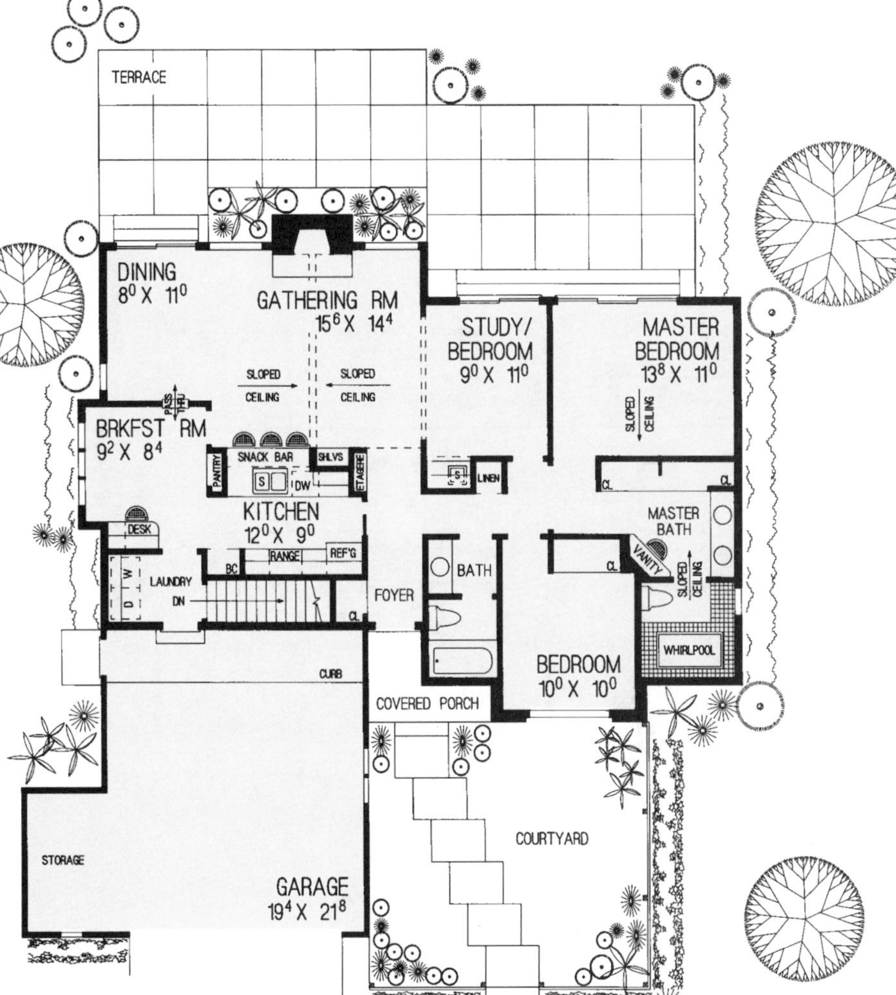
TERRACE
DINING
8⁰ X 11⁰
GATHERING RM
15⁶ X 14⁴
SLOPED CEILING
SLOPED CEILING
STUDY/ BEDROOM
9⁰ X 11⁰
MASTER BEDROOM
13⁸ X 11⁰
SLOPED CEILING
BRKFST RM
9² X 8⁴
PASS THRU
SNACK BAR
SHLVS
PANTRY
DW
ETAGERE
LINEN
CL
KITCHEN
12⁰ X 9⁰
DESK
RANGE
REF'G
MASTER BATH
VANITY
SLOPED CEILING
BC
BATH
LAUNDRY
DN
FOYER
CL
WHIRLPOOL
CURB
BEDROOM
10⁰ X 10⁰
COVERED PORCH
COURTYARD
STORAGE
GARAGE
19⁴ X 21⁸

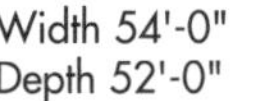
Width 54'-0"
Depth 52'-0"

QUOTE ONE®

Cost to build? See page 516 to order complete cost estimate to build this house in your area!

Design 3355

Square Footage: 1,387

L D

Though modest in size, this fetching one-story home offers a great deal of livability with three bedrooms (or two with study) and a spacious gathering room with a fireplace and a sloped ceiling. The galley kitchen, designed to save steps, provides a pass-through snack bar and has a planning desk and attached breakfast room. In addition to two secondary bedrooms with a full bath, there's a private master bedroom that enjoys views and access to the backyard. The master bath features a large dressing area, a corner vanity and a raised whirlpool tub. Indoor/outdoor living relationships are strengthened by easy access from the dining room, study/bedroom and master bedroom to the rear terrace.

Design 3314

Square Footage: 1,959

L

■ This bountiful bungalow is an owner's paradise with a luxurious master suite that far exceeds its Craftsman-style roots. The large gathering room is joined to the dining room and is accented with a large brick fireplace. The galley kitchen has an abundance of cabinet space, a walk-in pantry and a full-sized snack bar from the sunny breakfast room. A lovely screened porch that is accessed from both the dining room and the breakfast room adds an extra measure of charm to casual living. Two secondary bedrooms include one that can double as a den with a foyer entrance and another that is romanced with an expanse of corner windows and a wrap-around flower box.

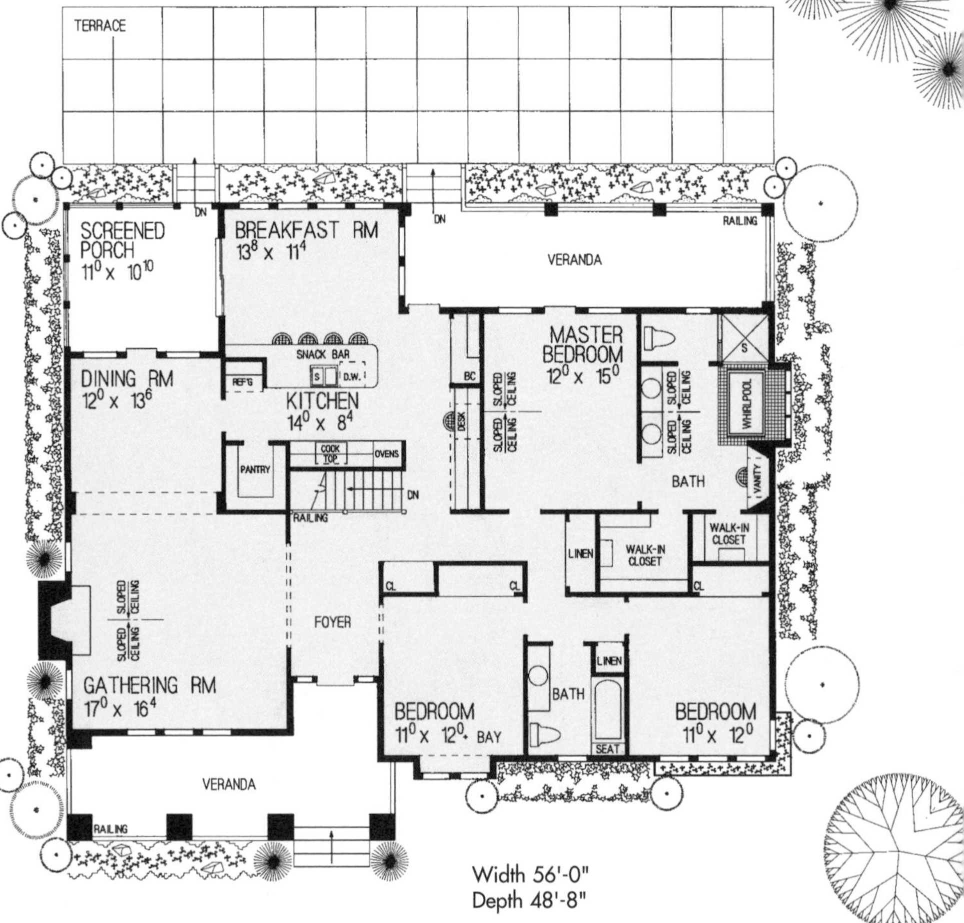
TERRACE
SCREENED PORCH 11^0 x 10^{10}
BREAKFAST RM 13^8 x 11^4
DN
VERANDA
RAILING
MASTER BEDROOM 12^0 x 15^0
DINING RM 12^0 x 13^6
SNACK BAR
S
D.W.
REF'G
KITCHEN 14^0 x 8^4
PANTRY
COOK TOP
OVENS
BC
DESK
SLOPED CEILING
WHIRLPOOL
BATH
VANITY
WALK-IN CLOSET
LINEN
CL
FOYER
GATHERING RM 17^0 x 16^4
BEDROOM 11^0 x 12^0 BAY
BATH
LINEN
SEAT
BEDROOM 11^0 x 12^0
VERANDA
RAILING
Width 56'-0"
Depth 48'-8"

QUOTE ONE®

Cost to build? See page 516 to order complete cost estimate to build this house in your area!

Design by
Home Planners

Design by
Home Planners

Design 3465

Square footage: 1,410

L

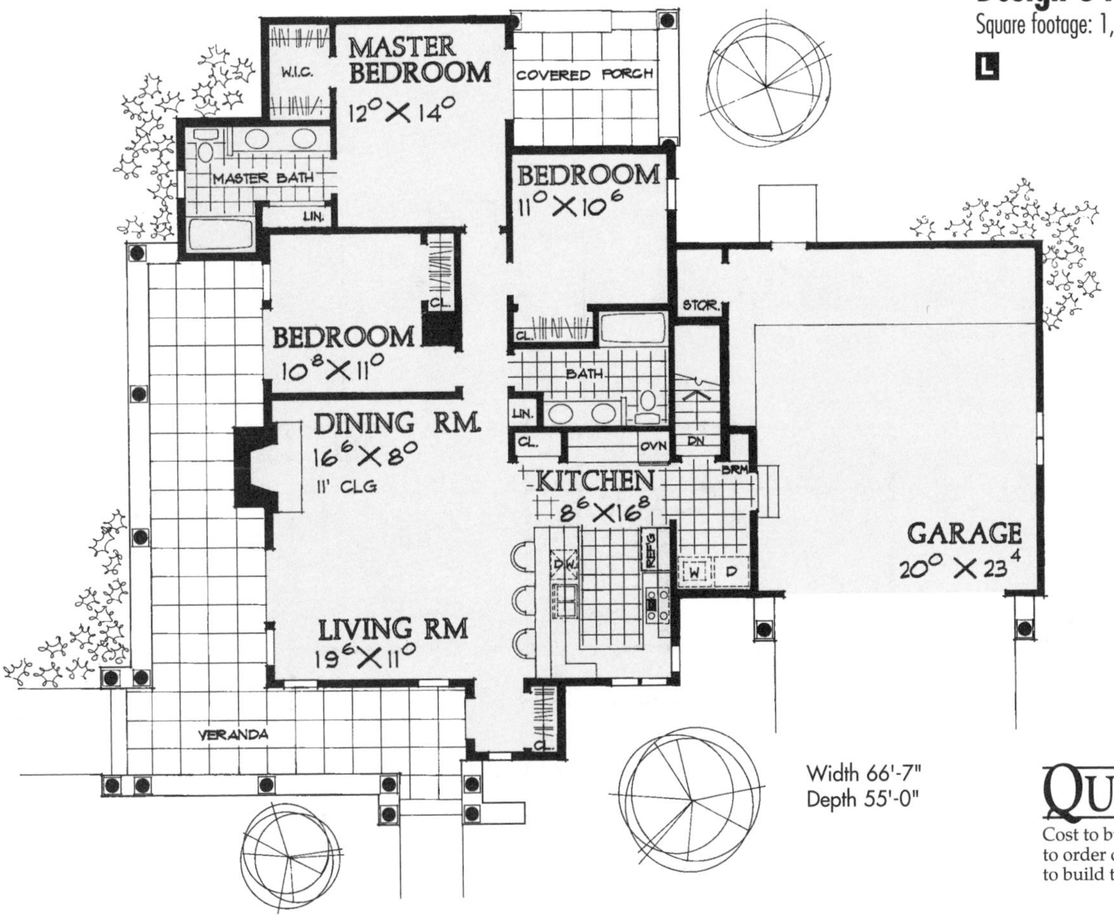

MASTER BEDROOM $12^0 \times 14^0$
W.I.C.
COVERED PORCH
MASTER BATH
LIN.
BEDROOM $11^0 \times 10^6$
BEDROOM $10^8 \times 11^0$
CL.
STOR.
BATH
LIN.
CL.
DINING RM. $16^6 \times 8^0$
11' CLG
OVN
DN
KITCHEN $8^6 \times 16^8$
BRM
REFG
DW
W D
GARAGE $20^0 \times 23^4$
LIVING RM $19^6 \times 11^0$
CL.
VERANDA

Width 66'-7"
Depth 55'-0"

QUOTE ONE®
Cost to build? See page 516 to order complete cost estimate to build this house in your area!

An L-shaped veranda employs tapered columns to support a standing-seam metal roof. Horizontal siding with brick accents and multi-pane windows all enhance the exterior of this home. Most notable, however, is the metal roof with its various planes. Complementing this is a massive stucco chimney that captures the ambience of the West. A hard-working interior will delight those building within a modest budget. The spacious front room provides plenty of space for both living and family dining activities. A fireplace makes a delightful focal point. The kitchen, set aside, has a handy snack bar and passageway to the garage. To one side is the laundry area, to the other, the stairs to the basement. The centrally located main bath has twin sinks and a nearby linen closet. One of the two secondary bedrooms has direct access to the veranda. The master bedroom is flanked by the master bath and its own private covered porch.

Extended Plan

Design 3701

Square Footage: 1,130

Traditional charm is an apt description of this economical ranch home. The master bedroom offers a full bath plus ample closet space. A full-sized bath adjoins the other two bedrooms. The kitchen is designed to serve as an eat-in kitchen for this efficient home. It features an L-shaped work counter and a walk-in pantry. A full basement is available for future development , if you choose. Other options include a one- or two-car garage, a front porch, a rear deck with a railing, a box-bay window and a fireplace. The blueprints for this house show how to build both a basic, low-cost version and an enhanced, upgraded version.

Width 60'-0"
Depth 28'-0"

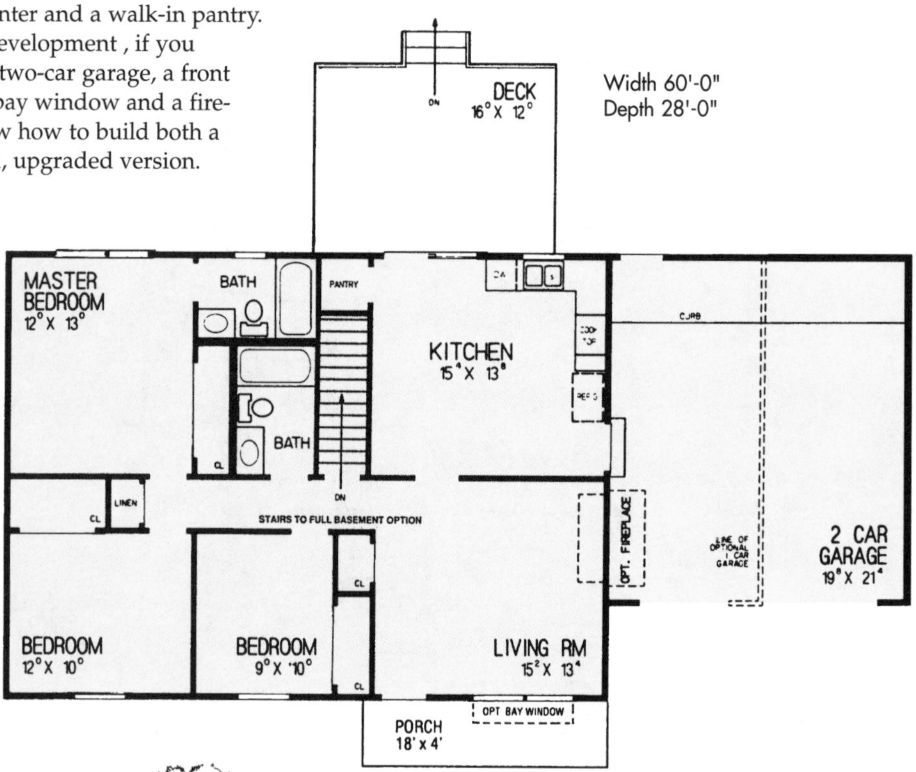

Design by
Home Planners

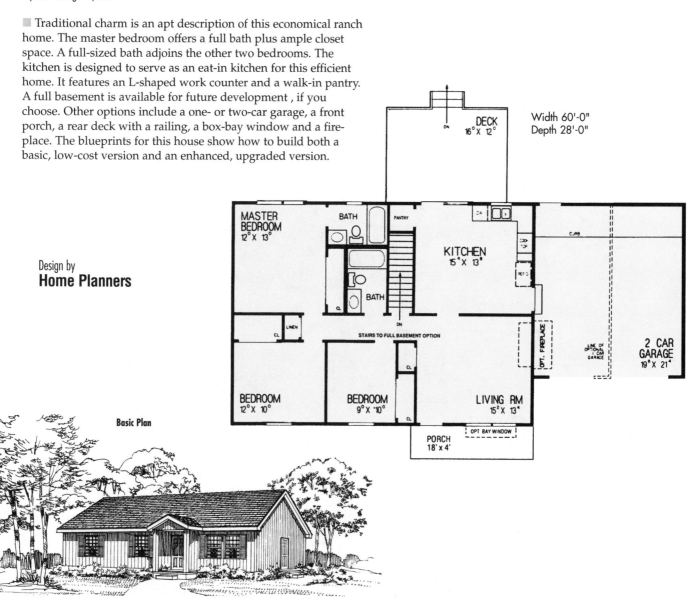

DECK 16° X 12°
MASTER BEDROOM 12° X 13°
BATH
PANTRY
KITCHEN 15⁴ X 13⁸
BATH
LINEN
CL
STAIRS TO FULL BASEMENT OPTION
OPT. FIREPLACE
LINE OF OPTIONAL 1 CAR GARAGE
2 CAR GARAGE 19⁸ X 21⁴
BEDROOM 12° X 10°
BEDROOM 9° X 10°
LIVING RM 15² X 13⁴
OPT BAY WINDOW
PORCH 18' x 4'

Basic Plan

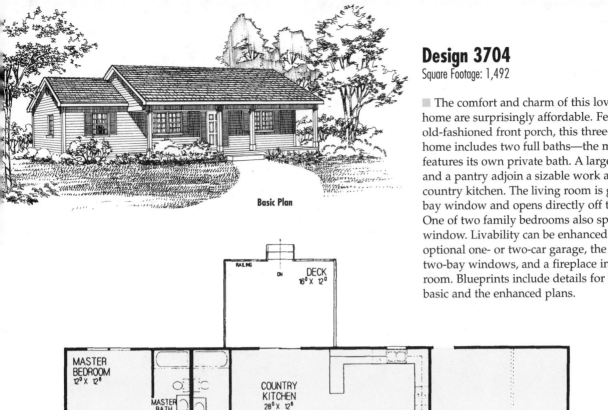

Design 3704

Square Footage: 1,492

The comfort and charm of this lovely ranch home are surprisingly affordable. Featuring an old-fashioned front porch, this three-bedroom home includes two full baths—the master suite features its own private bath. A large dining area and a pantry adjoin a sizable work area to form a country kitchen. The living room is graced by a bay window and opens directly off the foyer. One of two family bedrooms also sports a bay window. Livability can be enhanced with the optional one- or two-car garage, the rear deck, two-bay windows, and a fireplace in the living room. Blueprints include details for both the basic and the enhanced plans.

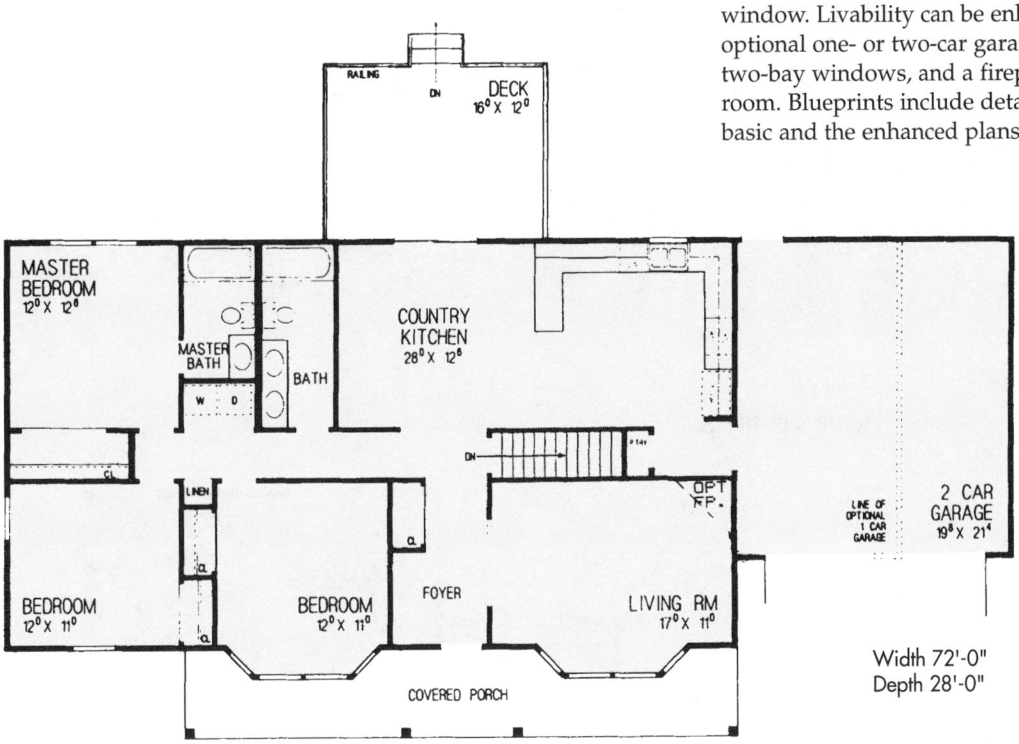

Basic Plan

RAILING
DN
DECK 16^0 X 12^0
MASTER BEDROOM 12^0 X 12^8
MASTER BATH
W D
BATH
COUNTRY KITCHEN 28^0 X 12^8
DN
CL
LINEN
CL
CL
CL
OPT FP.
LINE OF OPTIONAL 1 CAR GARAGE
2 CAR GARAGE 19^8 X 21^4
BEDROOM 12^0 X 11^0
BEDROOM 12^0 X 11^0
FOYER
LIVING RM 17^0 X 11^0
COVERED PORCH

Width 72'-0"
Depth 28'-0"

Design by
Home Planners

Enhanced Plan

Design by
Home Planners

Design 5507

Square Footage: 1,676

A wrapping covered porch sets the tone for this expansive one-story home. Set primarily along the side of the home, the porch conjures images of country life, where children play tag among the railed floor boards and grown-ups relax on swings or rocking chairs. Inside, bayed windows in the living/dining room combination and the family room offer great views to the porch beyond. Between these two rooms is a U-shaped kitchen with a large pantry and an adjacent utility room. The master bedroom features a large bath with a corner whirlpool tub, a separate shower and dual lavs, and an equally large walk-in closet. Two additional bedrooms share a full bath. The two-car garage, built to protect the bedroom areas from street noise, completes this well-rounded plan.

Width 45'-0"
Depth 64'-0"

RAILING
COVERED PORCH RETREAT
MASTER SUITE
$13^8 \times 16^2$
SLOPED CLG
PLANT SHELF ABOVE
MASTER BATH
GARDEN TUB
LIN
SHWR
WALK-IN CLOSET
FAMILY RM
$12^6 \times 13^0$
SLOPED CLG
BAY WINDOW
W
D
LAUNDRY
UTILITY SINK
LINEN
BEDRM
$10^0 \times 12^2$
SLOPED CLG
SNACK BAR
PANTRY
COVERED PORCH
DW
KITCHEN
$12^6 \times 10^0$
S
RANGE
REFG
BATH
BEDRM
$10^0 \times 10^6$
SLOPED CLG
BAY WINDOW
DINING
PLANT SHELF ABOVE
HVAC
WH
LIVING RM
$15^{10} \times 19^0$
SLOPED CLG
CURB
HALF WALL
ENTRY
GARAGE
$21^8 \times 23^0$
COVERED PORCH
RAILING

QUOTE ONE®

Cost to build? See page 516 to order complete cost estimate to build this house in your area!

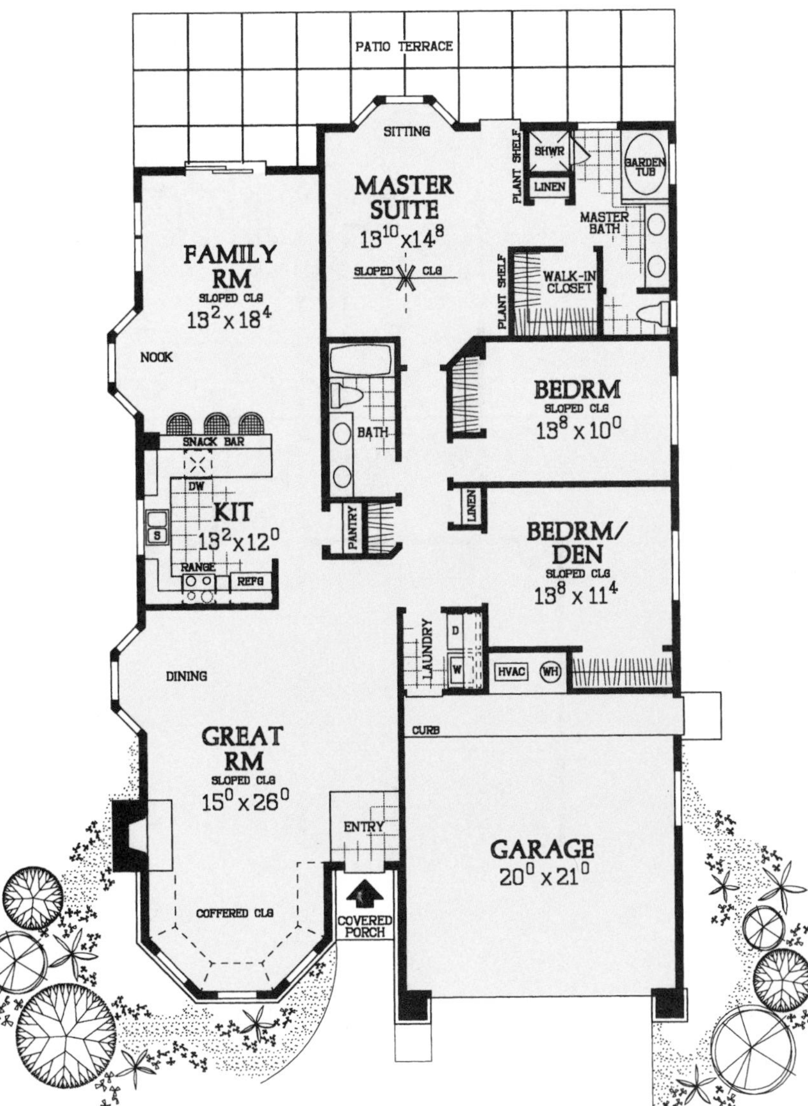
PATIO TERRACE
SITTING
MASTER SUITE
13¹⁰x14⁸
SLOPED CLG
PLANT SHELF
SHWR
LINEN
GARDEN TUB
MASTER BATH
WALK-IN CLOSET
FAMILY RM
SLOPED CLG
13²x18⁴
NOOK
BATH
BEDRM
SLOPED CLG
13⁸x10⁰
SNACK BAR
DW
KIT
13²x12⁰
RANGE
REFG
PANTRY
LINEN
BEDRM/ DEN
SLOPED CLG
13⁸x11⁴
LAUNDRY
D
W
HVAC
WH
DINING
CURB
GREAT RM
SLOPED CLG
15⁰x26⁰
ENTRY
GARAGE
20⁰x21⁰
COFFERED CLG
COVERED PORCH

Design 5532

Square Footage: 1,968

■ The four bay windows placed throughout this three-bedroom design fill it with warmth and light. The large bay in the great room will be a favorite spot during parties and family gatherings. It is accented by a warming fireplace and a smaller bay in the adjoining dining area. The efficient kitchen provides easy access to both the dining room and the large family room with its rear patio access and bay-windowed breakfast nook. The master bedroom offers another bay window, sure to be a special spot to relax at the end of the day, as well as a separate door to the patio. It also features a master bath with a corner whirlpool tub, a separate shower and a large walk-in closet. Two additional bedrooms share a full hall bath with dual sinks. The third bedroom can be used as either a bedroom, a den or an office.

Width 42'-4"
Depth 65'-10"

Design by
Home Planners

QUOTE ONE®

Cost to build? See page 516 to order complete cost estimate to build this house in your area!

Design Q352

Square Footage: 1,322
Unfinished Basement: 1,031 square feet

This handsome starter or retirement home offers a wealth of features in a smaller square footage. It also has space in the basement for future development when needed. The vaulted living room, with fireplace and bay window, shares a level with the skylit foyer. Up a few steps is the railed dining room which overlooks the living room. The nearby efficient kitchen has a breakfast carousel and access to the rear yard. Bedrooms line the left side of the plan and include a master suite with private bath and two family bedrooms sharing a full bath. The lower level has space for a recreation room, a bedroom or home office, a full bath, plus a large storage area and laundry-room alcove. Plans for a crawlspace foundation are also included.

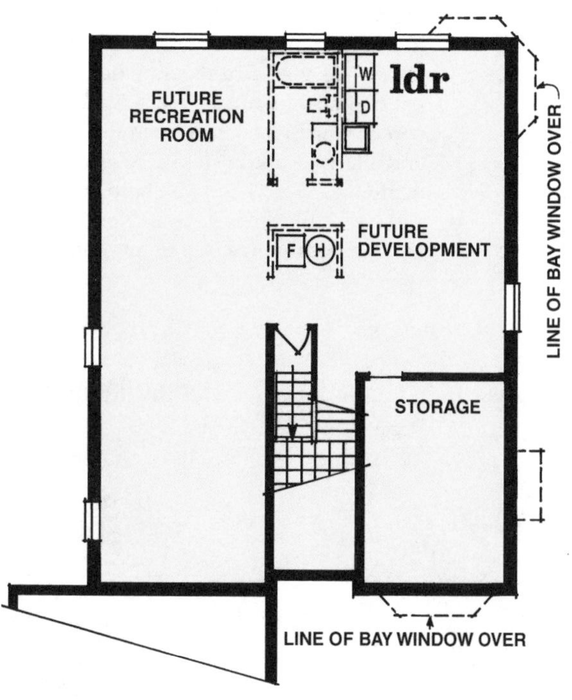

FUTURE RECREATION ROOM
ldr
W
D
F
H
FUTURE DEVELOPMENT
LINE OF BAY WINDOW OVER
STORAGE
LINE OF BAY WINDOW OVER

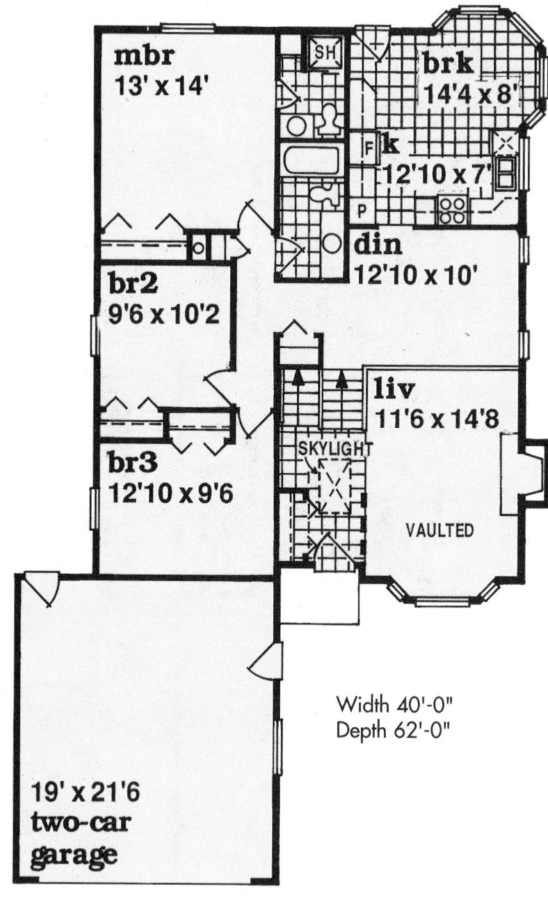

mbr 13' x 14'
SH
brk 14'4 x 8'
F
k 12'10 x 7'
P
din 12'10 x 10'
br2 9'6 x 10'2
liv 11'6 x 14'8
SKYLIGHT
br3 12'10 x 9'6
VAULTED
19' x 21'6 two-car garage

Width 40'-0"
Depth 62'-0"

Design by
Select Home Designs

Design Q513

Square Footage: 1,293

Meeting the needs of first-time homebuilders, this design is, nonetheless, economical to build. Craftsman detailing and a quaint covered porch go a long way to create the charming exterior on the design. Open planning filled with amenities add to the livability on the interior. The foyer opens to a hearth-warmed great room. Vaulted ceilings and a half wall separating the stairs to the basement and the foyer add to the spaciousness. An open island kitchen has an adjoining dining room with sliding glass doors to the deck and box-bay buffet space. The master bedroom adjoins two family bedrooms down the hall. It boasts His and Hers wall closets and a full bath with soaking tub. Family bedrooms—or make one a den—share a full bath. Plans include details for both a basement and a crawlspace foundation.

Width 42'-0"
Depth 54'-4"

Design by
Select Home Designs

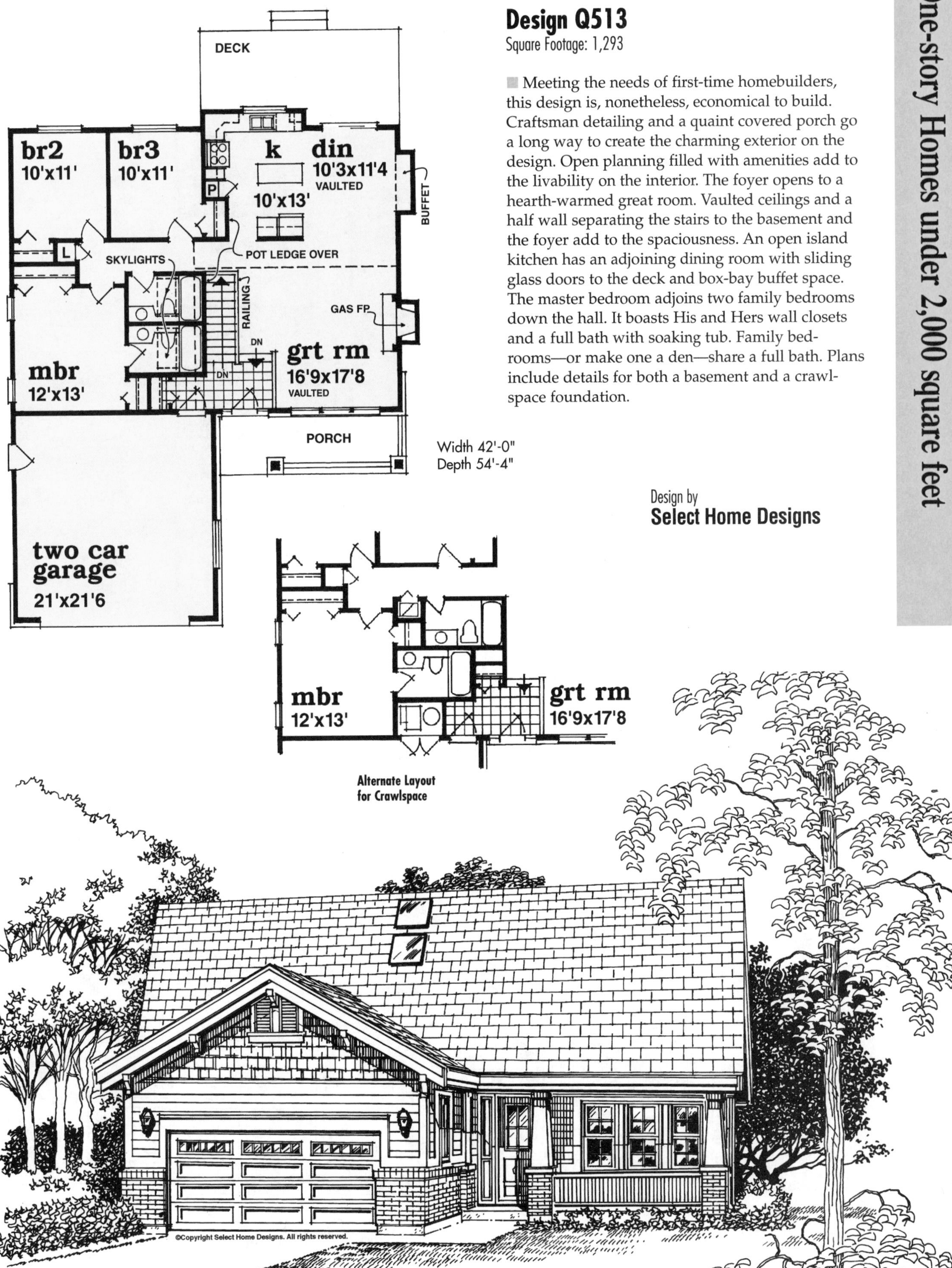
DECK
br2
10'x11'
br3
10'x11'
k
10'x13'
din
10'3x11'4
VAULTED
BUFFET
P
L
SKYLIGHTS
POT LEDGE OVER
RAILING
GAS FP
DN
grt rm
16'9x17'8
VAULTED
mbr
12'x13'
PORCH
two car garage
21'x21'6
mbr
12'x13'
grt rm
16'9x17'8
Alternate Layout for Crawlspace
©Copyright Select Home Designs. All rights reserved.

Design 5531

Square Footage: 1,952

Every inch of space in this one-story home is designed to provide the ultimate in comfort and enjoyment. The front-facing great room offers a sloped ceiling, a box-bay window, an inviting fireplace and access to a formal dining area with a bay window. The U-shaped kitchen maximizes counter space and provides entry to both the dining area and the family room with its bayed breakfast area and rear-patio access. The master bedroom features another bay window—the perfect spot to wind down with a good book—and a master bath with a windowed whirlpool tub, dual sinks and a walk-in closet. Two additional bedrooms share a full hall bath with dual basins. Bedroom 3 can be used as either a bedroom or a private den. A two-car garage and a convenient laundry room complete this amenity-filled plan.

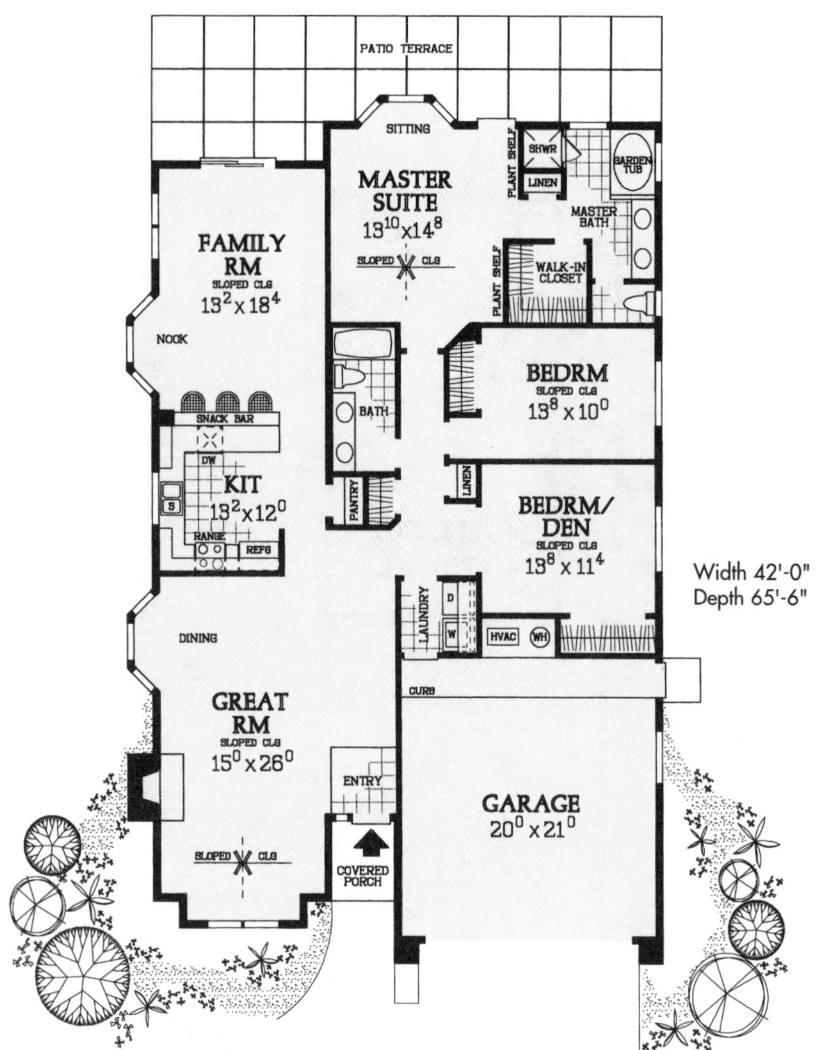

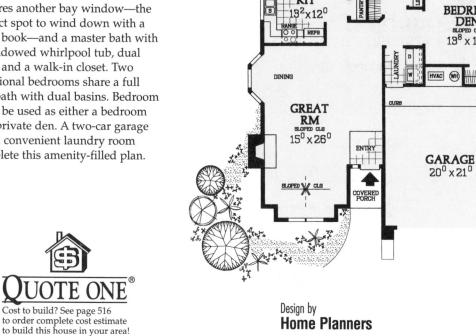

PATIO TERRACE
SITTING
MASTER SUITE
13^10 x 14^8
SLOPED CLG
SHWR
LINEN
GARDEN TUB
PLANT SHELF
MASTER BATH
WALK-IN CLOSET
PLANT SHELF
FAMILY RM
SLOPED CLG
13^2 x 18^4
NOOK
BATH
BEDRM
SLOPED CLG
13^8 x 10^0
SNACK BAR
DW
KIT
13^2 x 12^0
RANGE
REFG
PANTRY
LINEN
BEDRM/ DEN
SLOPED CLG
13^8 x 11^4
Width 42'-0"
Depth 65'-6"
LAUNDRY
D
W
HVAC
WH
DINING
CURB
GREAT RM
SLOPED CLG
15^0 x 26^0
ENTRY
GARAGE
20^0 x 21^0
SLOPED CLG
COVERED PORCH

QUOTE ONE®

Cost to build? See page 516 to order complete cost estimate to build this house in your area!

Design by
Home Planners

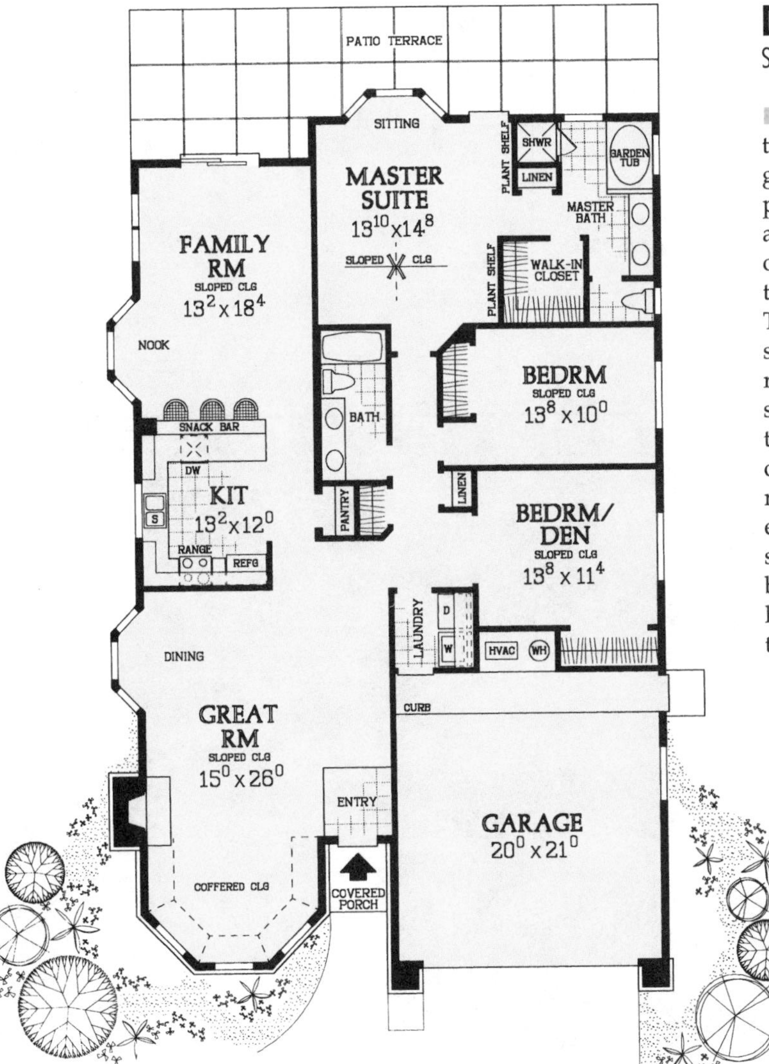

PATIO TERRACE
SITTING
MASTER SUITE
$13^{10} \times 14^{8}$
SLOPED CLG
SHWR
LINEN
GARDEN TUB
MASTER BATH
PLANT SHELF
WALK-IN CLOSET
PLANT SHELF
FAMILY RM
SLOPED CLG
$13^{2} \times 18^{4}$
NOOK
BATH
BEDRM
SLOPED CLG
$13^{8} \times 10^{0}$
SNACK BAR
DW
KIT
$13^{2} \times 12^{0}$
S
RANGE
REFG
PANTRY
LINEN
BEDRM/ DEN
SLOPED CLG
$13^{8} \times 11^{4}$
LAUNDRY
D
W
HVAC
WH
DINING
CURB
GREAT RM
SLOPED CLG
$15^{0} \times 26^{0}$
ENTRY
GARAGE
$20^{0} \times 21^{0}$
COFFERED CLG
COVERED PORCH

Design 5533

Square Footage: 1,971

A large bay window and corner quoins add to the brick facade of this spacious one-story plan, giving it a unique curb appeal. Inside, the floor plan not only invites you in, but bids you to stay and enjoy the many luxuries that each room offers. The large great room features not one, but two bay windows and a fireplace with a hearth. The U-shaped kitchen, with its abundant counter space, will satisfy any cook. The quiet family room and bayed breakfast nook are awash in sunlight and offer access to the rear patio through sliding glass doors. Located at the rear of the home for privacy, the elegant master bedroom features another bay window, backyard entry and a master bath with a linen closet, a separate shower and a whirlpool tub. Two family bedrooms, or one bedroom and a den, share a hall full bath and are conveniently located near the laundry room.

Width 42'-8"
Depth 65'-10"

Design by
Home Planners

QUOTE ONE®

Cost to build? See page 516 to order complete cost estimate to build this house in your area!

Design 5509

Square Footage: 1,676

A wraparound porch enhances the entrance to this country-style home. Inside, guests will be welcomed into a large living room and dining room combination with a tile-hearth fireplace and a bay window. The U-shaped kitchen allows the cook to converse, via a handy snack bar, with family and guests in the rear bay-windowed family room. Two family bedrooms are conveniently located near a full bath and a large utility area. The master bedroom features access to the covered rear porch retreat and a private master bath with a corner whirlpool tub, a separate shower, dual basins and a spacious walk-in closet. A two-car garage with plenty of space for storage completes this amenity-filled design.

Design by
Home Planners

QUOTE ONE®

Cost to build? See page 516 to order complete cost estimate to build this house in your area!

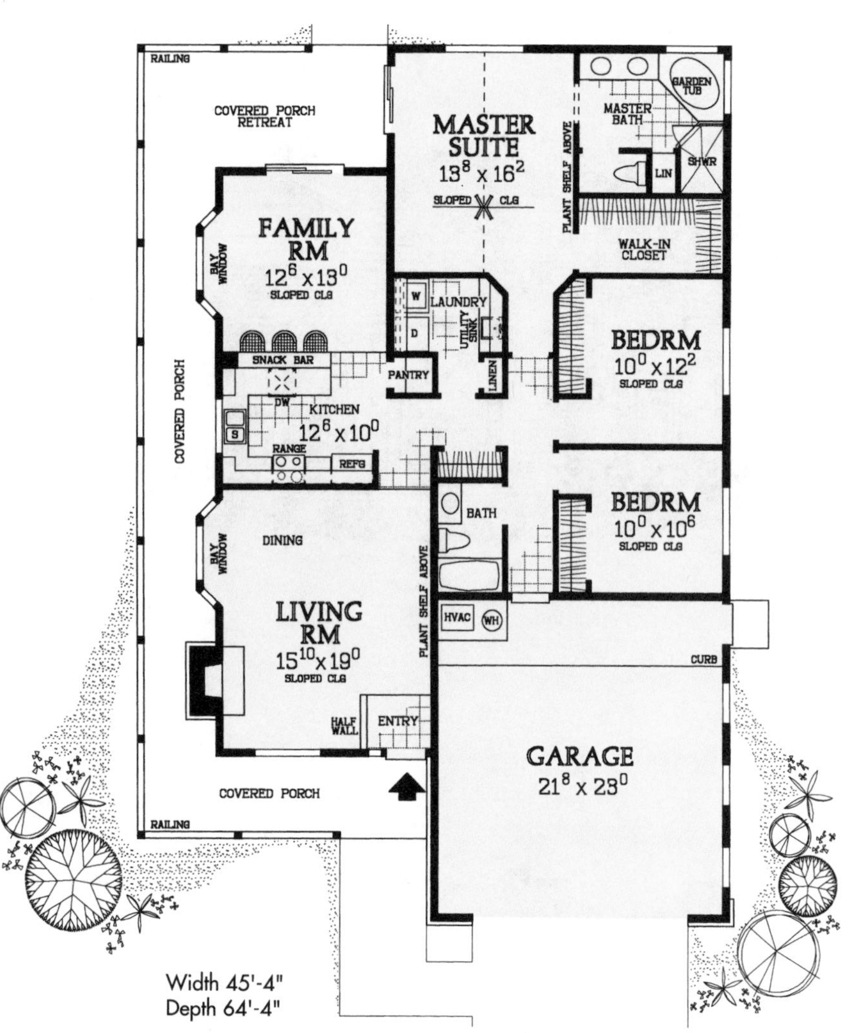
RAILING
COVERED PORCH RETREAT
MASTER SUITE
13^8 x 16^2
SLOPED CLG
GARDEN TUB
MASTER BATH
SHWR
LIN
PLANT SHELF ABOVE
WALK-IN CLOSET
FAMILY RM
12^6 x 13^0
SLOPED CLG
BAY WINDOW
W
D
LAUNDRY
UTILITY SINK
LINEN
SNACK BAR
PANTRY
BEDRM
10^0 x 12^2
SLOPED CLG
COVERED PORCH
DW
KITCHEN
12^6 x 10^0
S
RANGE
REFG
BATH
BEDRM
10^0 x 10^6
SLOPED CLG
DINING
BAY WINDOW
LIVING RM
15^{10} x 19^0
SLOPED CLG
PLANT SHELF ABOVE
HVAC
WH
CURB
HALF WALL
ENTRY
GARAGE
21^8 x 23^0
COVERED PORCH
RAILING
Width 45'-4"
Depth 64'-4"

Design 5508

Square Footage: 1,676

This cozy one-story home would make a nice addition to corner lots in any neighborhood. The covered front porch provides entrance into a combination living room and dining room that features a fireplace with a tiled hearth and a bay window. The central kitchen includes a large pantry and a snack bar to the family room with its bay window and rear porch access. The two-car garage is built to shield the family bedrooms from street noise. While the secondary bedrooms share a full bath, the master bedroom includes its own bath, complete with a separate tub, shower and toilet, dual sinks and a large walk-in closet. A handy utility room is conveniently located near all the bedrooms.

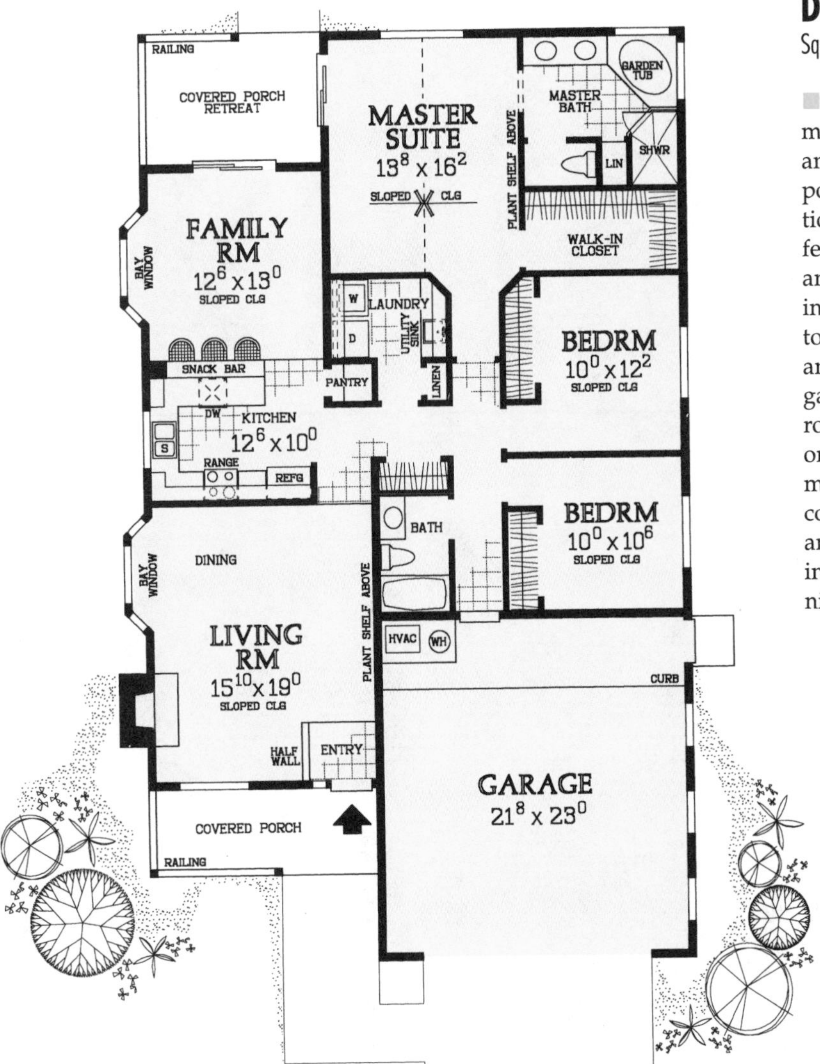
RAILING
COVERED PORCH RETREAT
MASTER SUITE
13⁸ x 16²
SLOPED CLG
PLANT SHELF ABOVE
GARDEN TUB
MASTER BATH
LIN
SHWR
WALK-IN CLOSET
FAMILY RM
12⁶ x 13⁰
SLOPED CLG
BAY WINDOW
W
D
LAUNDRY
UTILITY SINK
SNACK BAR
PANTRY
LINEN
BEDRM
10⁰ x 12²
SLOPED CLG
DW
KITCHEN
12⁶ x 10⁰
S
RANGE
REFG
BATH
BEDRM
10⁰ x 10⁶
SLOPED CLG
DINING
BAY WINDOW
PLANT SHELF ABOVE
LIVING RM
15¹⁰ x 19⁰
SLOPED CLG
HVAC
WH
CURB
HALF WALL
ENTRY
GARAGE
21⁸ x 23⁰
COVERED PORCH
RAILING

QUOTE ONE®

Cost to build? See page 516 to order complete cost estimate to build this house in your area!

Width 41'-0"
Depth 64'-0"

Design by
Home Planners

Design Q369

Square Footage: 1,760

This brick one-story offers a covered, rail porch that provides a weather-protected entry to the home. The vaulted foyer carries its ceiling detail into the living room where there is a fireplace and double-door access to the rear patio. The dining room has a tray ceiling and is found to the right of the entry. A screened porch decorates the breakfast room and allows for protected casual outdoor dining. The kitchen is U-shaped with a center work island and large pantry. A nearby laundry room has access to the two-car garage. Look no further than the master bedroom for true luxury. It boasts a tray ceiling and full bath with whirlpool spa, separate shower and double vanity. Family bedrooms have wall closets and share a full bath that separates them. An open rail stairway leads to a basement that could be expanded in the future. Plans include details for both a basement and a crawlspace foundation.

Design by
Select Home Designs

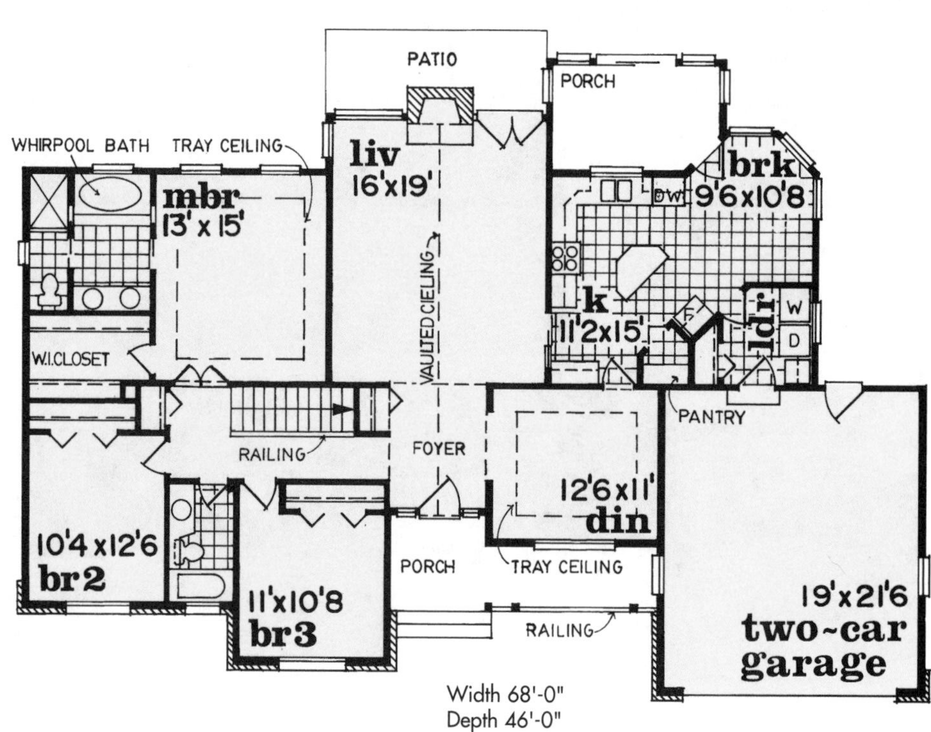
PATIO
PORCH
WHIRPOOL BATH
TRAY CEILING
liv
16'x19'
brk
9'6x10'8
mbr
13' x 15'
DW
VAULTED CEILING
k
11'2x15'
ldr
W
D
W.I.CLOSET
PANTRY
RAILING
FOYER
12'6x11'
din
10'4x12'6
br2
PORCH
TRAY CEILING
11'x10'8
br3
RAILING
19'x21'6
two-car
garage
Width 68'-0"
Depth 46'-0"

Rear Elevation

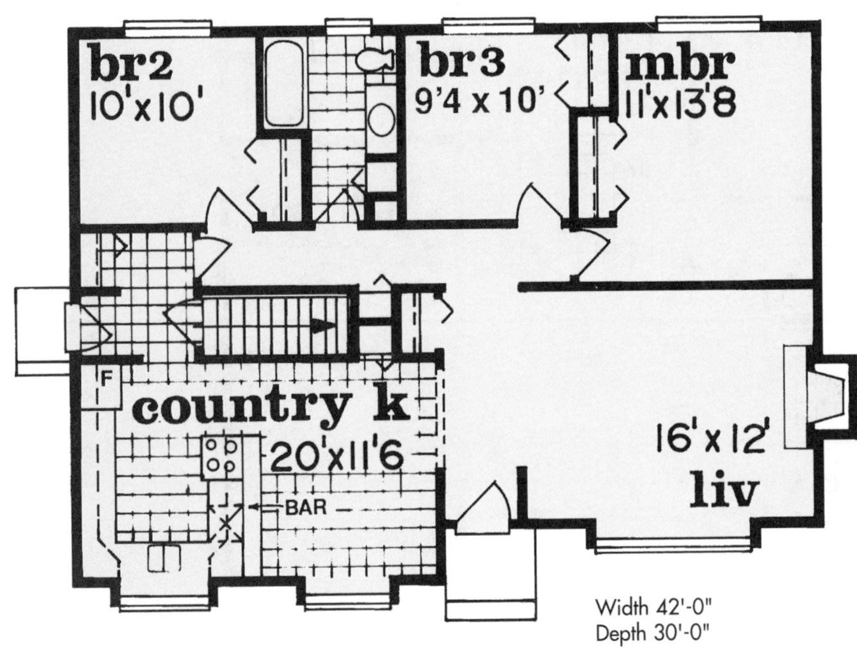
br2
10'x10'
br3
9'4 x 10'
mbr
11'x13'8
F
country k
20'x11'6
BAR
16'x12'
liv
Width 42'-0"
Depth 30'-0"

Design Q344

Square Footage: 1,197

This compact, three-bedroom design is ideal as a starter or retirement home. Its siding and brick combination and lovely bumped-out windows give it a cozy, rustic feeling. The bedrooms are positioned along the rear of the home for maximum privacy. Each bedroom has a large window overlooking the rear yard; the master bedroom is especially spacious. The entry opens directly onto a large living area with box-bay window and fireplace. The country kitchen contains long, roomy counters, a convenient serving bar and a breakfast nook with box-bay window. The side door provides quick, easy access to the kitchen and to the basement. If needed, the basement may be finished for additional living space or bedrooms.

Design by
Select Home Designs

Design by
Select Home Designs

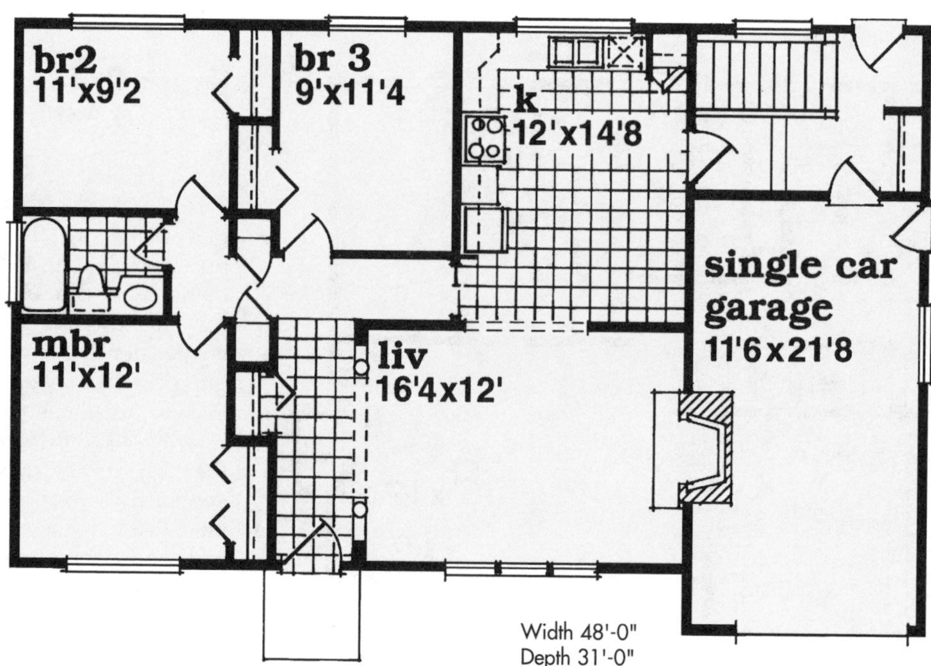
br2
11'x9'2
br 3
9'x11'4
k
12'x14'8
single car
garage
11'6x21'8
mbr
11'x12'
liv
16'4x12'
Width 48'-0"
Depth 31'-0"

Design Q229

Square Footage: 1,114

For a starter home, this three-bedroom retains plenty of style. Horizontal wood siding and shuttered windows bring a look of tradition to its facade. Inside, it holds a livable floor plan. The living room is introduced by columns and also has a fireplace and pocket doors that separate it from the large eat-in kitchen. A U-shaped work area in the kitchen is handy and efficient. Access in the kitchen leads to a service area with a door into the single-car garage and stairs to the full basement—perfect for future expansion. Use all three bedrooms for sleeping space, or turn one bedroom into a home office or den. All three bedrooms have wall closets and share the use of a full bath.

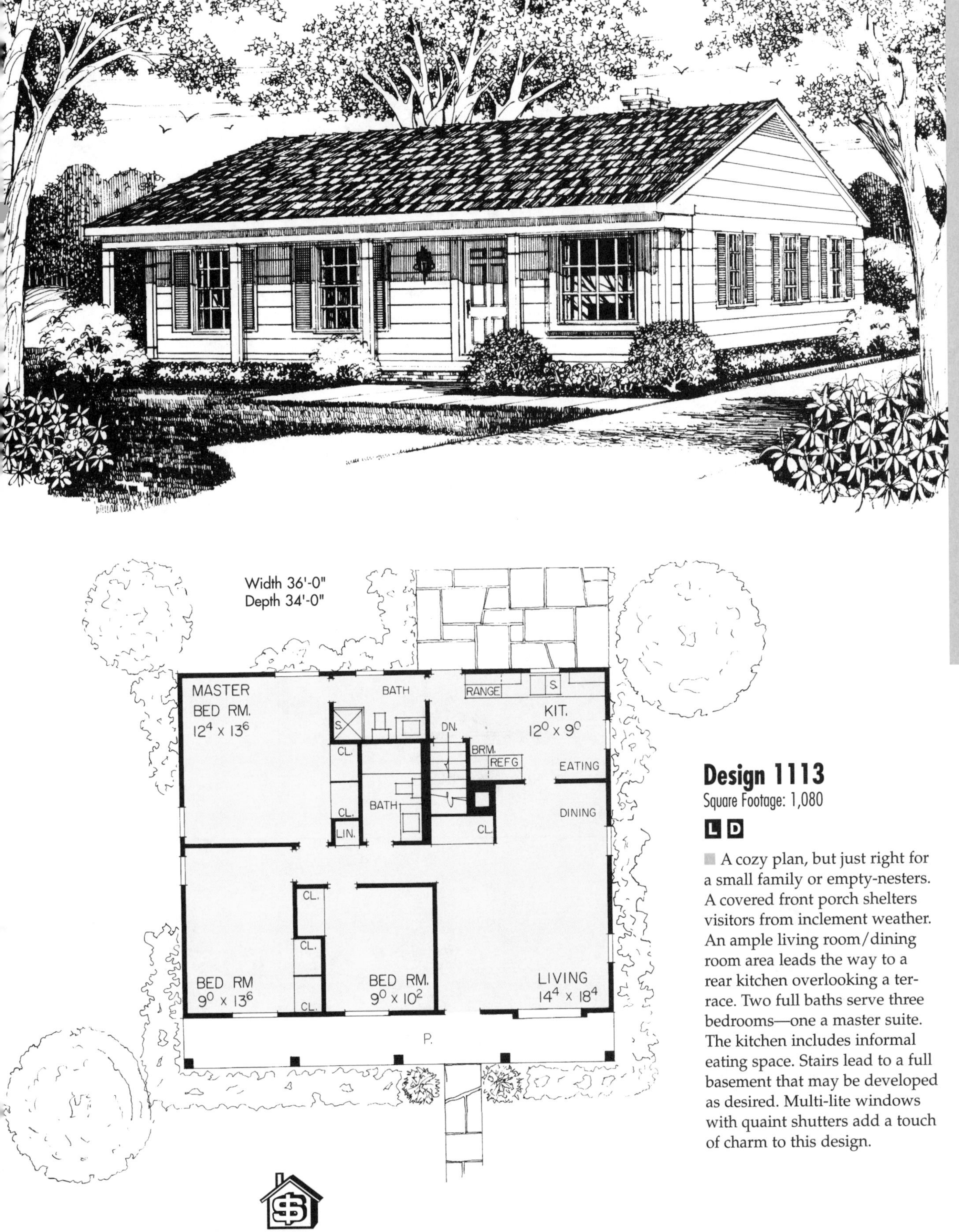
Width 36'-0"
Depth 34'-0"
MASTER BED RM. $12^4 \times 13^6$
BATH
RANGE
S.
KIT. $12^0 \times 9^0$
S.
DN.
CL.
BRM.
REFG
EATING
BATH
CL.
LIN.
CL.
DINING
CL.
CL.
CL.
BED RM $9^0 \times 13^6$
BED RM. $9^0 \times 10^2$
LIVING $14^4 \times 18^4$
P.

Design 1113

Square Footage: 1,080

L D

A cozy plan, but just right for a small family or empty-nesters. A covered front porch shelters visitors from inclement weather. An ample living room/dining room area leads the way to a rear kitchen overlooking a terrace. Two full baths serve three bedrooms—one a master suite. The kitchen includes informal eating space. Stairs lead to a full basement that may be developed as desired. Multi-lite windows with quaint shutters add a touch of charm to this design.

QUOTE ONE®

Cost to build? See page 516 to order complete cost estimate to build this house in your area!

Design by
Home Planners

Design Q237

Square Footage: 1,054

This cottage is not only affordable, it offers a choice of two charming exteriors: a traditional brick or a wood-sided version. Details for both are included in the blueprints. The interior holds many amenities unusual for a plan of its size. The front porch protects the entry which opens directly to a large living room with masonry fireplace. It is complemented by a formal dining room open to the galley kitchen. Sliding doors open to a rear patio. A service entrance leads to the single-car garage (optional). Bedrooms share a full hall bath and have wall closets of ample size. The hallway is also graced by a storage closet with folding doors. If you choose, Bedroom 3 could double as a den or home office.

© Copyright Select Home Designs. All rights reserved

Alternate Elevation

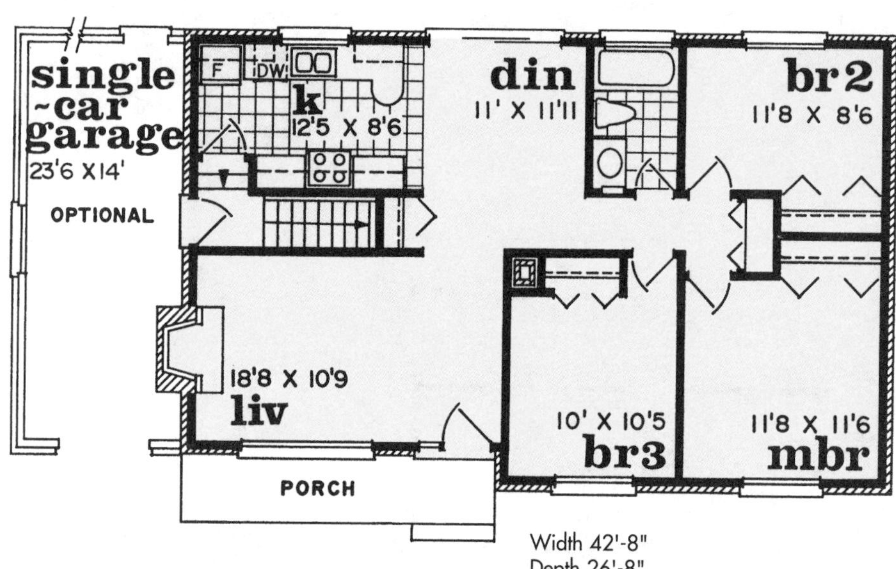
single
-car
garage
23'6 X14'
OPTIONAL
F
DW
k
12'5 X 8'6
din
11' X 11'11
br2
11'8 X 8'6
18'8 X 10'9
liv
10' X 10'5
br3
11'8 X 11'6
mbr
PORCH

Width 42'-8"
Depth 26'-8"

Design by
Select Home Designs

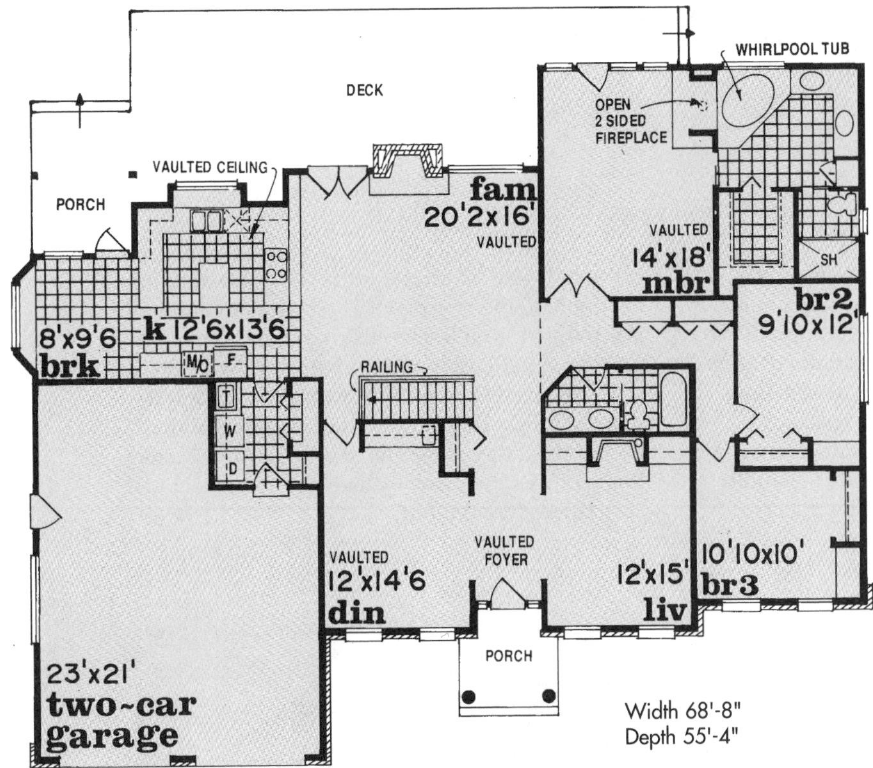
DECK
WHIRLPOOL TUB
OPEN 2 SIDED FIREPLACE
VAULTED CEILING
PORCH
fam 20'2x16'
VAULTED
VAULTED
14'x18'
mbr
SH
br2
9'10x12'
8'x9'6
brk
k 12'6x13'6
M/O
F
RAILING
W
D
VAULTED
12'x14'6
din
VAULTED FOYER
12'x15'
liv
10'10x10'
br3
PORCH
23'x21'
two-car garage

Width 68'-8"
Depth 55'-4"

Design Q391

Square Footage: 2,211

■ A high roofline on the exterior of this home allows for a vaulted ceiling extending from the foyer to the family room on the inside. Formal living and dining rooms open to either side of the foyer. The fireplace in the living room is flanked by shelves, while the fireplace in the family room has a door on one side that leads to the rear deck. A wet bar in the dining room allows easy entertaining. Abundant windows and high vaulted ceilings create a bright and spacious atmosphere in the bayed breakfast room and kitchen. The kitchen is U-shaped and has a center preparation island. At the opposite end of the plan, the master bedroom features a private access to the deck and a cozy two-sided fireplace. The bath in this suite offers His and Hers basins, a whirlpool tub and a large shower. Two family bedrooms share a full hall bath with dual sinks. Plans include details for both a basement and a crawlspace foundation.

Rear Elevation

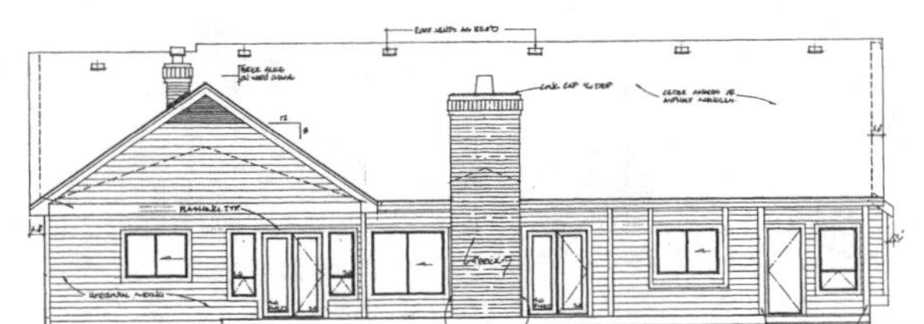

Design by
Select Home Designs

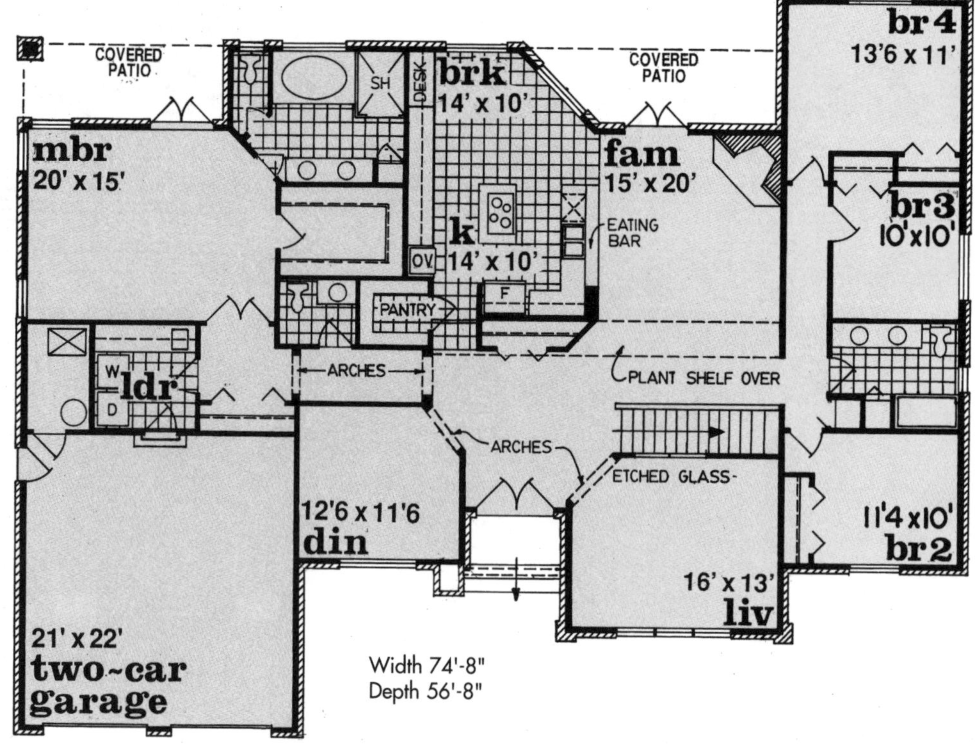
COVERED PATIO
SH
DESK
brk
14' x 10'
COVERED PATIO
br4
13'6 x 11'
mbr
20' x 15'
fam
15' x 20'
EATING BAR
br3
10'x10'
k
14' x 10'
OV
PANTRY
F
ARCHES
PLANT SHELF OVER
W
D
ldr
ARCHES
ETCHED GLASS
12'6 x 11'6
din
11'4 x10'
br2
16' x 13'
liv
21' x 22'
two-car garage
Width 74'-8"
Depth 56'-8"

Design by
Select Home Designs

Design Q408

Square Footage: 2,547

■ A brick exterior, with traditional arch details and elegant rooflines, defines this stately ranch home. Formal dining and living rooms open through arches from the front entry foyer. Additional arches define the center hall leading to the master suite. Chefs can utilize their talents in the spacious kitchen with center cooktop, abundant counter space and light-filled breakfast nook. The family room is separated from the kitchen by a snack counter. It also features a corner fireplace and double doors to the rear patio. The private master suite is separated from family bedrooms and offers a walk-in closet and luxurious bath with whirlpool spa, oversized shower, twin vanity and compartmented toilet. Three additional bedrooms allow design flexibility—use one as a guest room, den or home office. The plans include both basement and crawlspace foundations.

© Copyright 1990 Select Home Designs All rights reserved

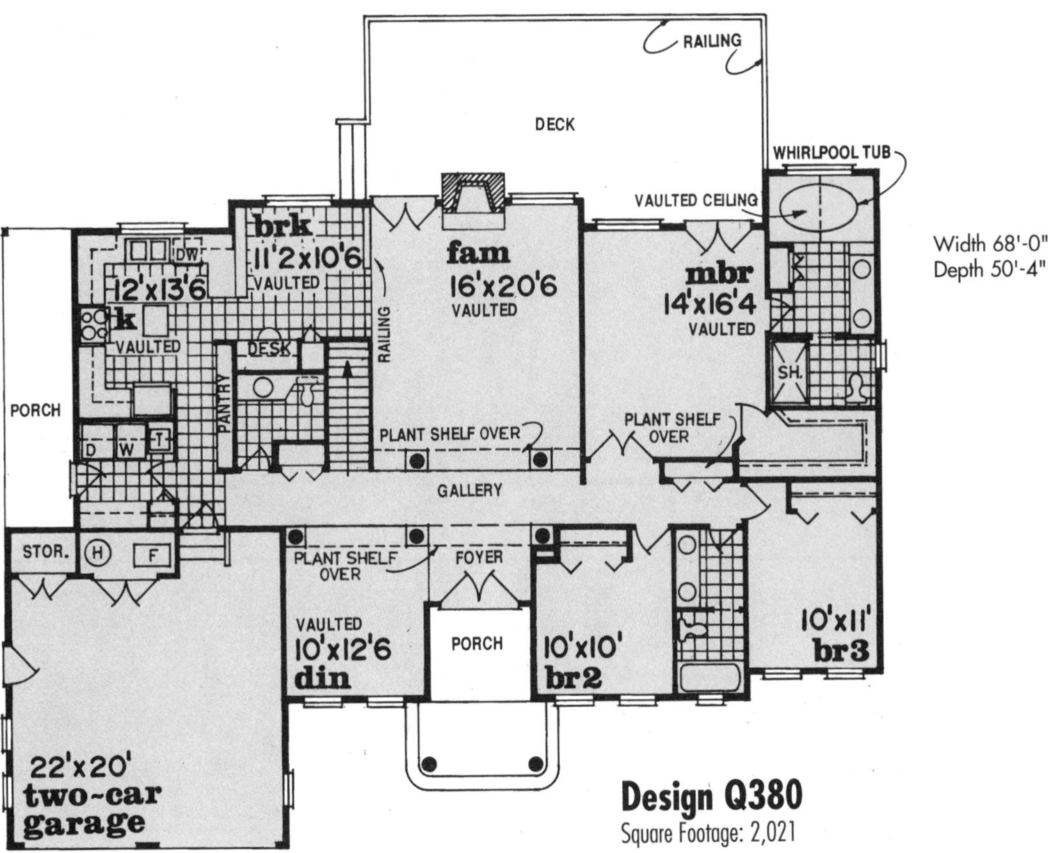
RAILING
DECK
WHIRLPOOL TUB
VAULTED CEILING
brk
11'2x10'6
VAULTED
fam
16'x20'6
VAULTED
mbr
14'x16'4
VAULTED
12'x13'6
k
VAULTED
DW
DESK
RAILING
PANTRY
SH.
PORCH
D
W
T
PLANT SHELF OVER
PLANT SHELF OVER
GALLERY
STOR.
H
F
PLANT SHELF OVER
FOYER
VAULTED
10'x12'6
din
PORCH
10'x10'
br2
10'x11'
br3
22'x20'
two-car
garage

Width 68'-0"
Depth 50'-4"

Design Q380

Square Footage: 2,021

■ This beautiful design is enhanced by brick siding and decorative wood columns at the entry. Plant ledges, which encompass the colonnaded foyer, and high vaulted ceilings throughout adorn the interior. Directly in view of the foyer is a vaulted family room which opens to a large railed deck beyond. The fireplace in the family room also warms the breakfast nook as the two are separated only by a low railing. A gourmet kitchen offers a center preparation island, a long pantry and a built-in desk. A formal dining room is also defined by columns and sits just across the hall from the family room. The master suite has double doors opening to the rear deck, a large walk-in closet, a whirlpool spa, His and Hers vanities and a separate shower. Family bedrooms share the use of a main bath in the hall. Plans include details for both a basement and a crawlspace foundation.

Design by
Select Home Designs

Design by
Home Planners

Design 3600

Square Footage: 2,258

L

■ This unique one-story plan seems tailor-made for empty-nesters or for a small family. A grand, tiled foyer opens to formal and informal living areas: to the left, an elegant formal dining room with raised ceiling and bay window, and to the right, a living room with sloped ceiling and view to the front property through triple windows. Ahead, the foyer leads to an open living area: a family room with vaulted ceiling, centered fireplace with tiled hearth, and access to the rear deck. The morning room bay adjoins a roomy well-equipped kitchen with a food preparation island, and offers separate access to the wood deck. The master suite is secluded to the rear of the plan and offers a sumptuous bath with a whirlpool tub, dual lavatories, a separate shower and walk-in closet. An adjoining office/den boasts a private porch. One family bedroom or guest room with a private, full bath is positioned for privacy on the opposite side of the plan.

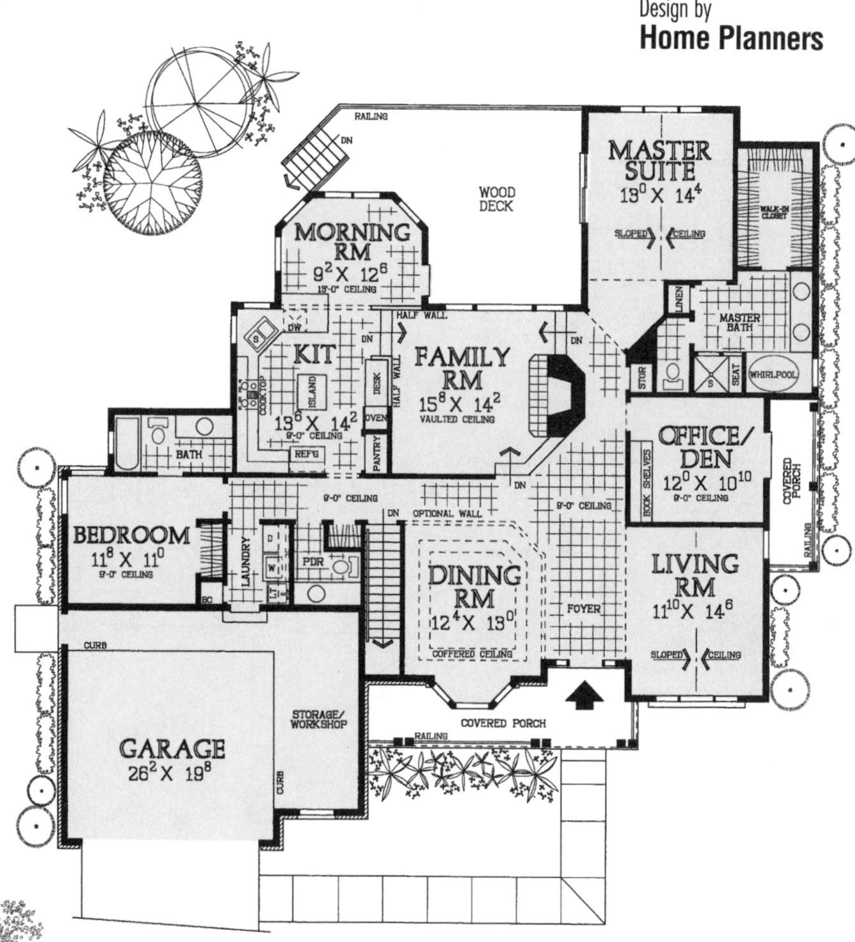
RAILING
WOOD DECK
MASTER SUITE
13⁰ X 14⁴
MORNING RM
9² X 12⁶
15'-0" CEILING
KIT
13⁶ X 14²
9'-0" CEILING
FAMILY RM
15⁸ X 14²
VAULTED CEILING
MASTER BATH
WHIRLPOOL
OFFICE/ DEN
12⁰ X 10¹⁰
9'-0" CEILING
BATH
BEDROOM
11⁸ X 11⁰
9'-0" CEILING
LAUNDRY
PDR
DINING RM
12⁴ X 13⁰
COFFERED CEILING
FOYER
LIVING RM
11¹⁰ X 14⁶
COVERED PORCH
GARAGE
26² X 19⁸
STORAGE/ WORKSHOP

Width 68'-0"
Depth 64'-0"

Rear Elevation

QUOTE ONE®

Cost to build? See page 516
to order complete cost estimate
to build this house in your area!

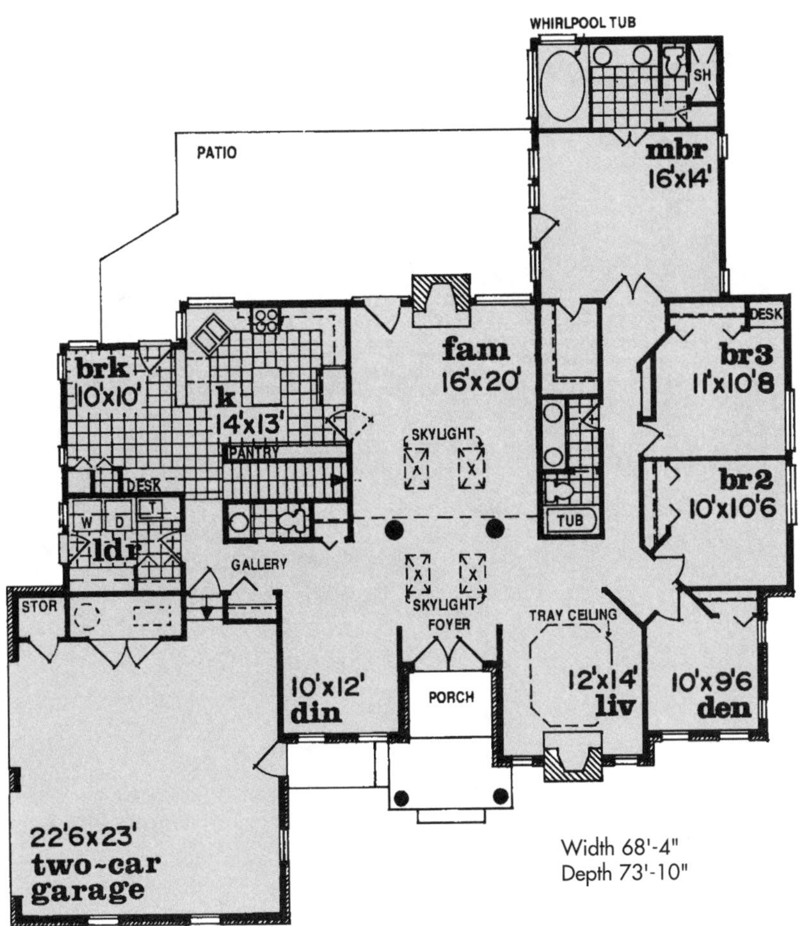
WHIRLPOOL TUB
SH
PATIO
mbr
16'x14'
DESK
br3
11'x10'8
fam
16'x20'
brk
10'x10'
k
14'x13'
PANTRY
DESK
SKYLIGHT
br2
10'x10'6
W D
T
ldr
TUB
GALLERY
SKYLIGHT
FOYER
TRAY CEILING
STOR
10'x12'
din
PORCH
12'x14'
liv
10'x9'6
den
22'6x23'
two-car
garage

Width 68'-4"
Depth 73'-10"

Design Q404

Square Footage: 2,404

■ Low-maintenance brick finish, shuttered windows and a covered porch surrounded by decorative pillars provide a fine welcoming exterior for this three-bedroom ranch design. Directly in view of the skylit foyer is a spacious family room with matching twin skylights. A plant shelf and decorative columns visually zone the entry and family room. The living room with tray ceiling and fireplace sits to the right of the foyer while the dining room sits to the left. A gourmet kitchen features a center prep island, long pantry, breakfast room and built-in desk. The spacious rear deck allows space for outdoor relaxation and extends the indoor living spaces. Bedrooms are positioned away from the living areas for privacy. The master bedroom boasts a walk-in closet, access to the rear deck and a lavish bath with His and Hers vanities and whirlpool spa. Plans include details for both a basement and a crawlspace foundation.

Design by
Select Home Designs

Design 3332

Square Footage: 2,203

L

■ Nothing completes a traditional-style home quite as well as a country kitchen with a fireplace and built-in wood box. Notice also the second fireplace (with raised hearth) and the sloped ceiling in the living room. The nearby dining room has an attached porch and separate dining terrace. Besides two family bedrooms with a shared full bath, there is also a marvelous master suite with rear terrace access, walk-in closet, whirlpool tub and double vanities. A handy washroom is near the laundry, just off the two-car garage.

QUOTE ONE®

Cost to build? See page 516 to order complete cost estimate to build this house in your area!

Design by
Home Planners

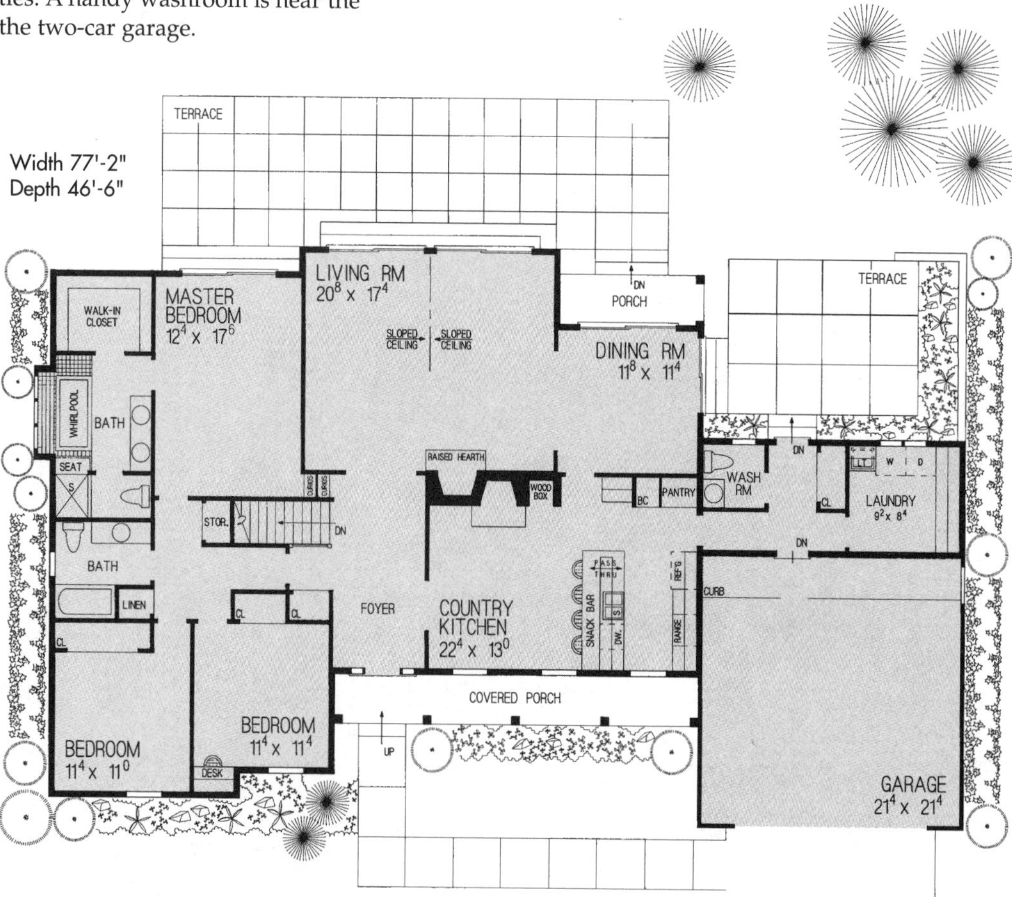

TERRACE
Width 77'-2"
Depth 46'-6"
LIVING RM
20⁸ x 17⁴
SLOPED CEILING
SLOPED CEILING
DN
PORCH
TERRACE
WALK-IN CLOSET
MASTER BEDROOM
12⁴ x 17⁶
DINING RM
11⁸ x 11⁴
WHIRLPOOL
BATH
SEAT
S
RAISED HEARTH
WOOD BOX
BC
PANTRY
WASH RM
DN
CL
W D
LAUNDRY
9² x 8⁴
STOR.
DN
BATH
LINEN
CL
CL
CL
FOYER
COUNTRY KITCHEN
22⁴ x 13⁰
PASS THRU
SNACK BAR
DW
S
REF'G
RANGE
CURB
DN
COVERED PORCH
UP
BEDROOM
11⁴ x 11⁰
BEDROOM
11⁴ x 11⁴
DESK
GARAGE
21⁴ x 21⁴

Design by
Home Planners

Design 3348

Square Footage: 2,549

L

QUOTE ONE®

Cost to build? See page 516 to order complete cost estimate to build this house in your area!

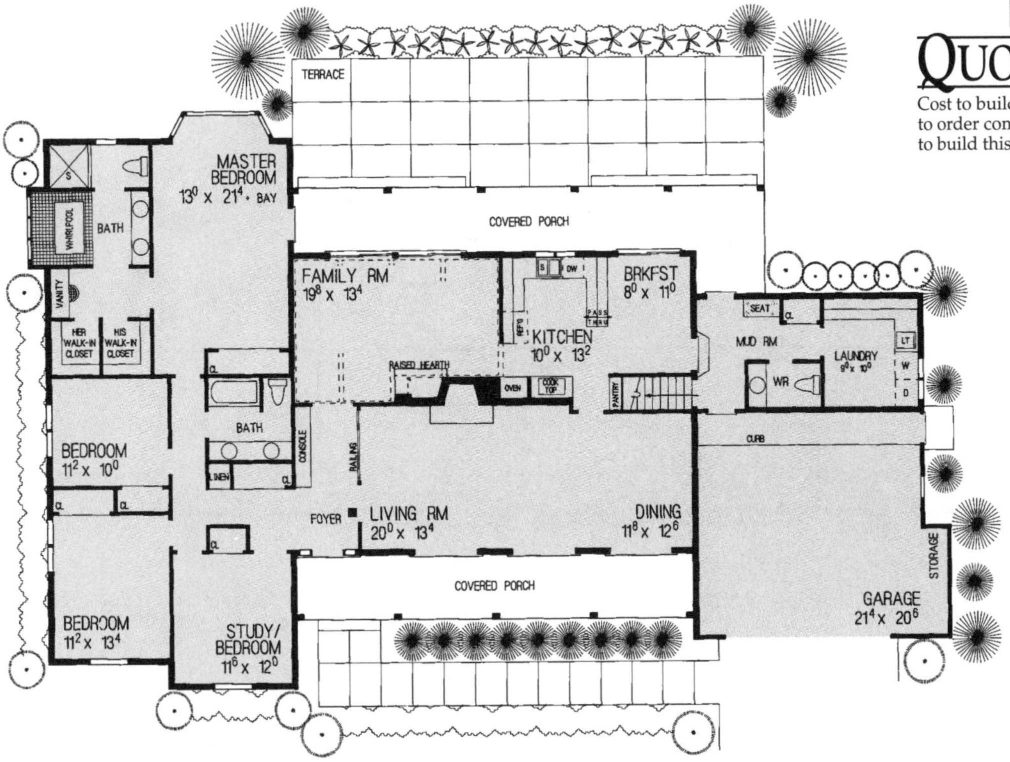

Width 88'-8"
Depth 53'-6"

■ Covered porches—front and rear—will be the envy of the neighborhood when this house is built. The interior plan meets family needs perfectly with well-zoned areas: a sleeping wing with four bedrooms, a living zone with formal and informal gathering space, and a work zone with U-shaped kitchen, breakfast room and laundry with washroom. Both the family room and living room sport fireplaces. The master bedroom has a bay window and private bath with whirlpool tub and His and Hers walk-in closets. If you choose, one of the family bedrooms could become a den or home office. Note the sliding glass doors in the breakfast room and the family room that lead to the rear covered porch. The two-car garage has a large storage area.

Design 2888

Square Footage: 3,018

L

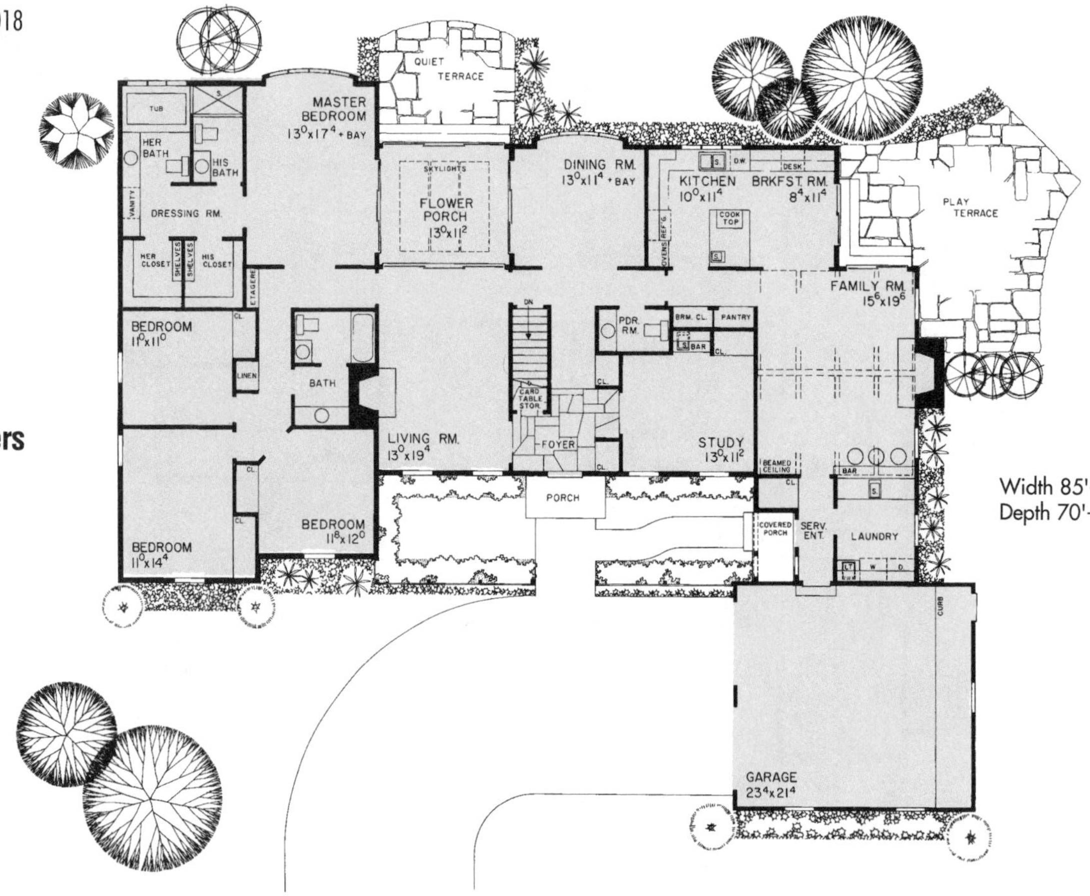

Design by
Home Planners

Width 85'-8"
Depth 70'-0"

■ This is an outstanding Early American adaptation which includes such exterior features as narrow clapboards, multi-paned windows and a cupola—reminiscent of historic design. Interior planning is strictly up-to-date. A formal living room, an informal family room, plus a study comprise the living spaces. Both the family room and living room have fireplaces. The L-shaped kitchen has a breakfast room and is near the formal dining room with bow window. At the opposite side of the plan are the bedrooms—four in all including a grand master suite. Note the bowed window, separate tub and shower, dressing area and walk-in closet. Family bedrooms share a full bath. The two-car garage rounds out the plan. It is reached through a service entry at the laundry room.

QUOTE ONE®

Cost to build? See page 516 to order complete cost estimate to build this house in your area!

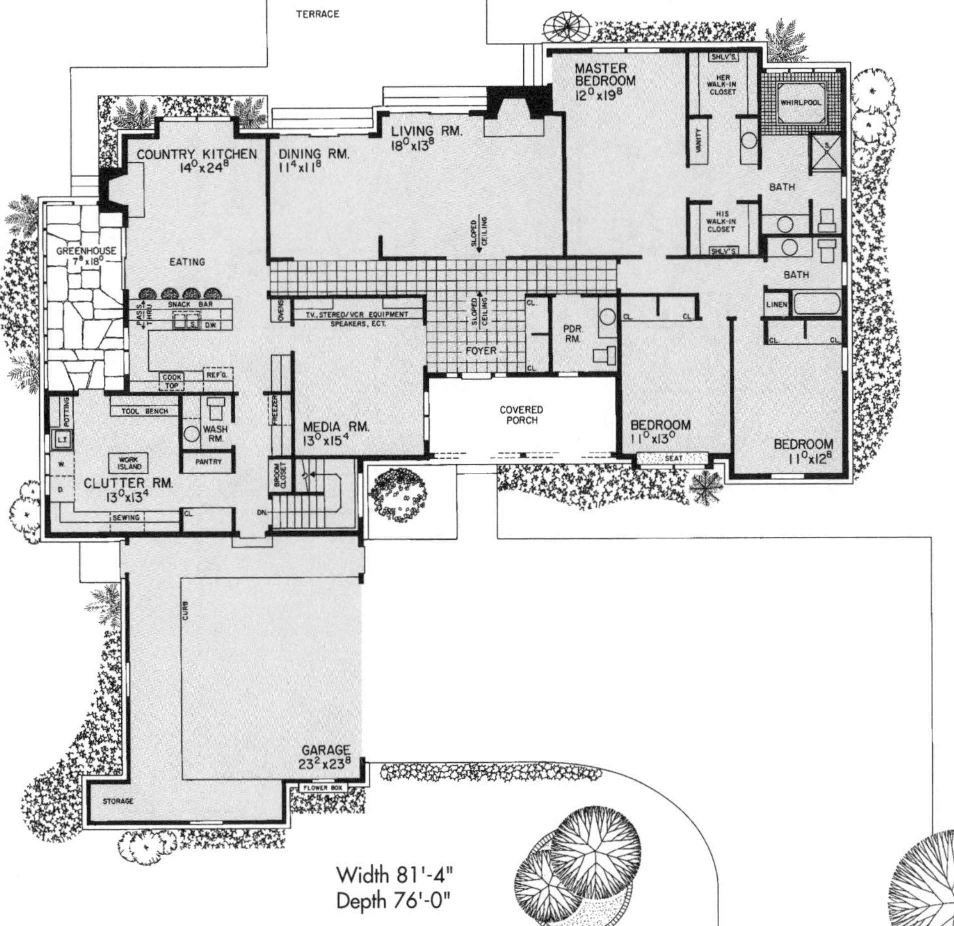
TERRACE
MASTER BEDROOM $12^0 \times 19^8$
SHLV'S.
HER WALK-IN CLOSET
WHIRLPOOL
VANITY
BATH
HIS WALK-IN CLOSET
BATH
LINEN
COUNTRY KITCHEN $14^0 \times 24^8$
DINING RM. $11^4 \times 11^8$
LIVING RM. $18^0 \times 13^8$
SLOPED CEILING
GREENHOUSE $7^8 \times 18^0$
EATING
SNACK BAR
PASS THRU
COOK TOP
REF'G.
TV, STEREO/VCR EQUIPMENT SPEAKERS, ECT.
FOYER
PDR. RM.
CL.
TOOL BENCH
WASH RM.
PANTRY
WORK ISLAND
CLUTTER RM. $13^0 \times 13^4$
SEWING
MEDIA RM. $13^0 \times 15^4$
BROOM CLOSET
COVERED PORCH
BEDROOM $11^0 \times 13^0$
SEAT
BEDROOM $11^0 \times 12^8$
CURB
GARAGE $23^2 \times 23^8$
FLOWER BOX
STORAGE

Width 81'-4"
Depth 76'-0"

Design 2880

Square Footage: 2,758

Greenhouse: 149 square feet

L D

■ This comfortable traditional home offers plenty of modern livability. A clutter room off the two-car garage is an ideal space for a workbench, sewing or hobbies. Across the hall one finds a media room, the perfect place for stereo, video and more. A spacious country kitchen to the right of the greenhouse (great for fresh herbs) is a cozy gathering place for family and friends, as well as a convenient work area. Both the formal living room, with its friendly fireplace, and the dining room provide access to the rear grounds. A spacious, amenity-filled master suite features His and Hers walk-in closets, a relaxing whirlpool tub and access to the rear terrace. Two large secondary bedrooms share a full bath.

Design by
Home Planners

Design 2931

Square Footage: 2,032

■ Little details make the difference in this charming showplace: picket-fenced courtyard, carriage lamp, window boxes, shutters, muntined windows, multi-gabled roof, cornice returns, vertical and horizontal siding with corner board, front door with glass side lites, etc. Inside this appealing exterior there is a truly outstanding floor plan for the small family or empty-nesters. The master bedroom suite is long on luxury with a separate dressing room, private vanities and whirlpool bath. An adjacent study is just the right retreat. There's room to move and what a warm touch! It has its own fireplace. Other attractions: roomy kitchen and breakfast area, spacious gathering room, rear and side terraces and an attached two-car garage with storage.

TERRACE
STUDY $12^6 \times 16^0$
GATHERING RM. $16^6 \times 16^0$
MASTER BEDROOM $14^0 \times 16^0$
DINING RM. $11^8 \times 10^8$
TERRACE
BRKFST. RM. $11^8 \times 10^8$
SLOPED CEILING
LINEN
BAR
DRESSING RM.
WALK-IN CLOSET
BATH
VANITY
BATH
WHIRLPOOL
SEAT
FOYER
CURIOS
RAILING
DN.
DESK
KITCHEN $11^8 \times 10^0$
OVENS
LAUND.
REF'G
COOK TOP
PASS THRU
DW
COVERED PORCH
BEDROOM $12^4 \times 12^6$
COURTYARD
GARAGE $21^4 \times 21^4$
CURB
STORAGE

Width 63'-0"
Depth 64'-4"

Design by
Home Planners

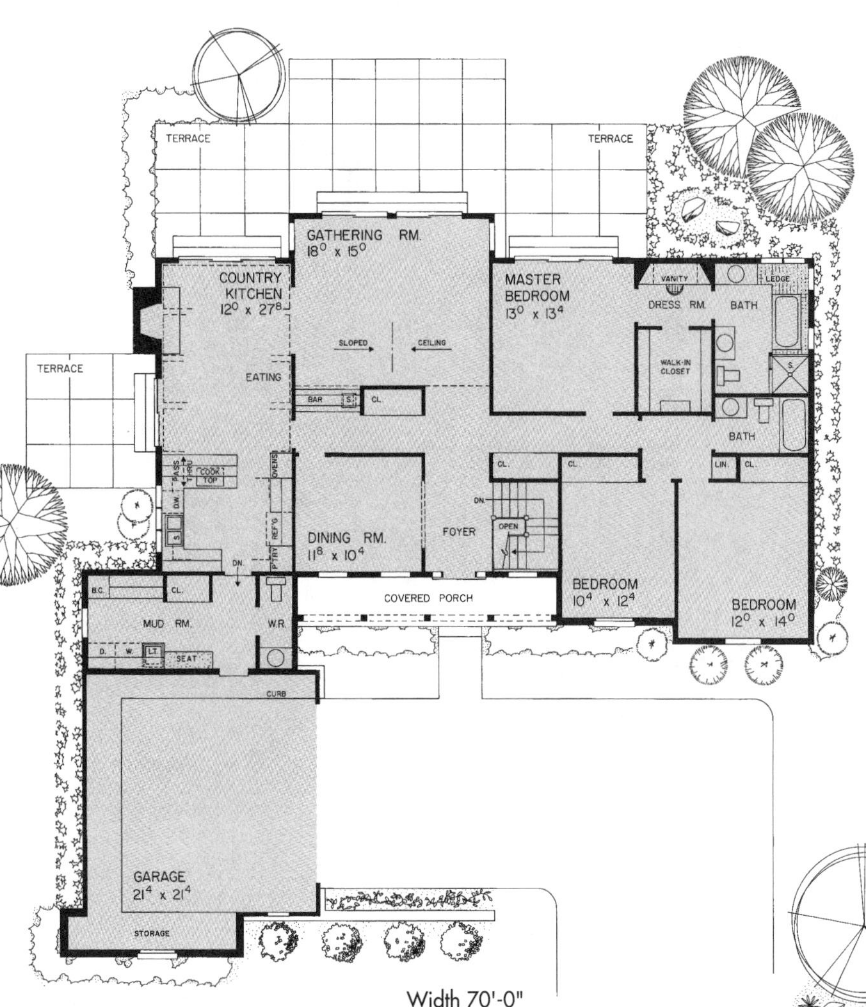
TERRACE
TERRACE
TERRACE
GATHERING RM.
18⁰ x 15⁰
COUNTRY
KITCHEN
12⁰ x 27⁸
EATING
SLOPED
CEILING
MASTER
BEDROOM
13⁰ x 13⁴
VANITY
LEDGE
DRESS. RM.
BATH
WALK-IN CLOSET
BATH
BAR
CL.
LIN.
DINING RM.
11⁸ x 10⁴
FOYER
DN.
OPEN
BEDROOM
10⁴ x 12⁴
BEDROOM
12⁰ x 14⁰
COVERED PORCH
MUD RM.
W.R.
SEAT
CURB
GARAGE
21⁴ x 21⁴
STORAGE
Width 70'-0"
Depth 66'-8"

Design 2916

Square Footage: 2,129

L

■ Pride of ownership will be forever yours as the occupant of this Early American home. The covered front porch provides a shelter for the inviting paneled front door with its flanking side lites. Designed for fine family living, this three-bedroom home offers wonderful formal and informal living patterns. The 27' country kitchen features a beam ceiling, a fireplace and an efficient U-shaped work center. It is but a step from the mud room area with its laundry equipment, closets, cupboards, counter space and washroom. There are two dining areas—an informal eating space and a formal, separate dining room. The more formal gathering room is spacious with a sloping ceiling and two sets of sliding glass doors to the rear terrace.

QUOTE ONE®

Cost to build? See page 516 to order complete cost estimate to build this house in your area!

Design by
Home Planners

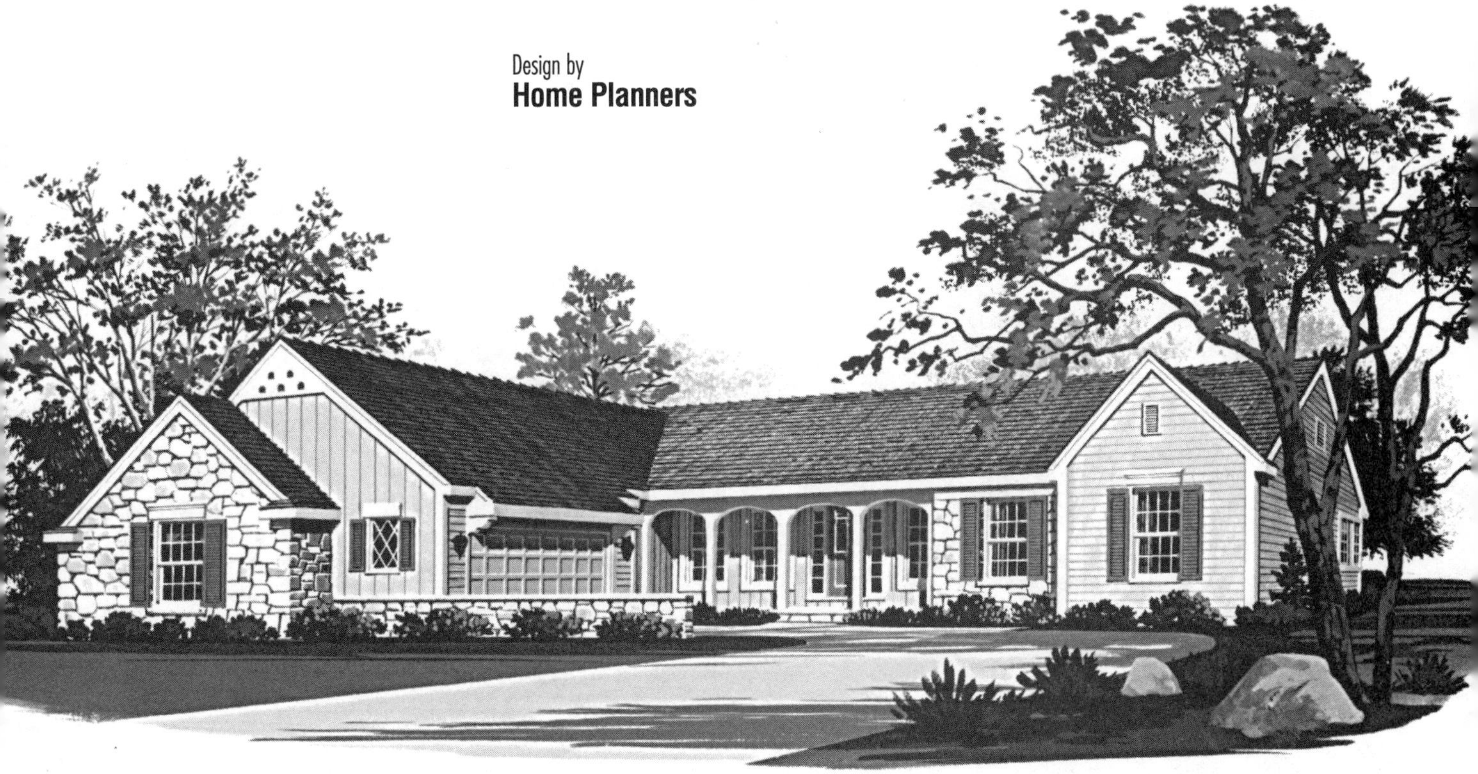

Design 2768

Square Footage: 3,436

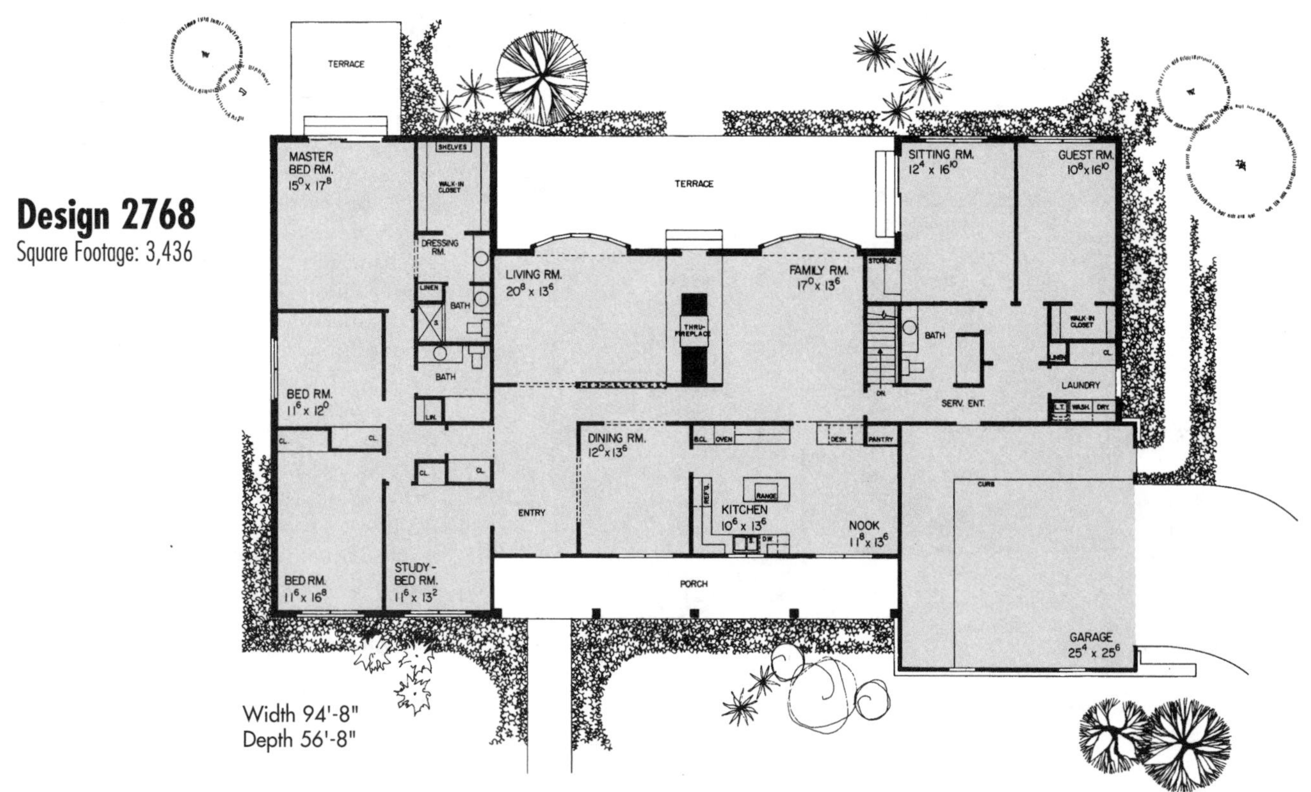

TERRACE
MASTER BED RM. 15^{0} x 17^{8}
DRESSING RM.
LINEN
BATH
TERRACE
LIVING RM. 20^{8} x 13^{6}
THRU-FIREPLACE
FAMILY RM. 17^{0} x 13^{6}
STORAGE
SITTING RM. 12^{4} x 16^{10}
GUEST RM. 10^{8} x 16^{10}
BATH
WALK-IN CLOSET
LAUNDRY
SERV. ENT.
BED RM. 11^{6} x 12^{0}
CL.
CL.
LIN.
CL.
CL.
DINING RM. 12^{0} x 13^{6}
KITCHEN 10^{6} x 13^{6}
RANGE
DESK
PANTRY
NOOK 11^{8} x 13^{6}
ENTRY
CURB
BED RM. 11^{6} x 16^{8}
STUDY-BED RM. 11^{6} x 13^{2}
PORCH
GARAGE 25^{4} x 25^{6}
Width 94'-8"
Depth 56'-8"

Besides its elegant traditionally styled exterior, with long covered front porch, this home has an exceptionally livable interior. There is an outstanding four-bedroom, two-bath sleeping wing. The efficient kitchen with island range is flanked by the formal dining room and the informal breakfast nook. Separated by a through-fireplace, the formal living room and the family room both overlook the rear terrace. A guest suite—or in-law suite—sits behind the garage and includes a sitting room, full bath and bedroom with walk-in closet. The master bedroom has a private terrace and a bath with walk-in closet, dressing room and double sinks. One of three family bedrooms could be used as a study.

Design by
Home Planners

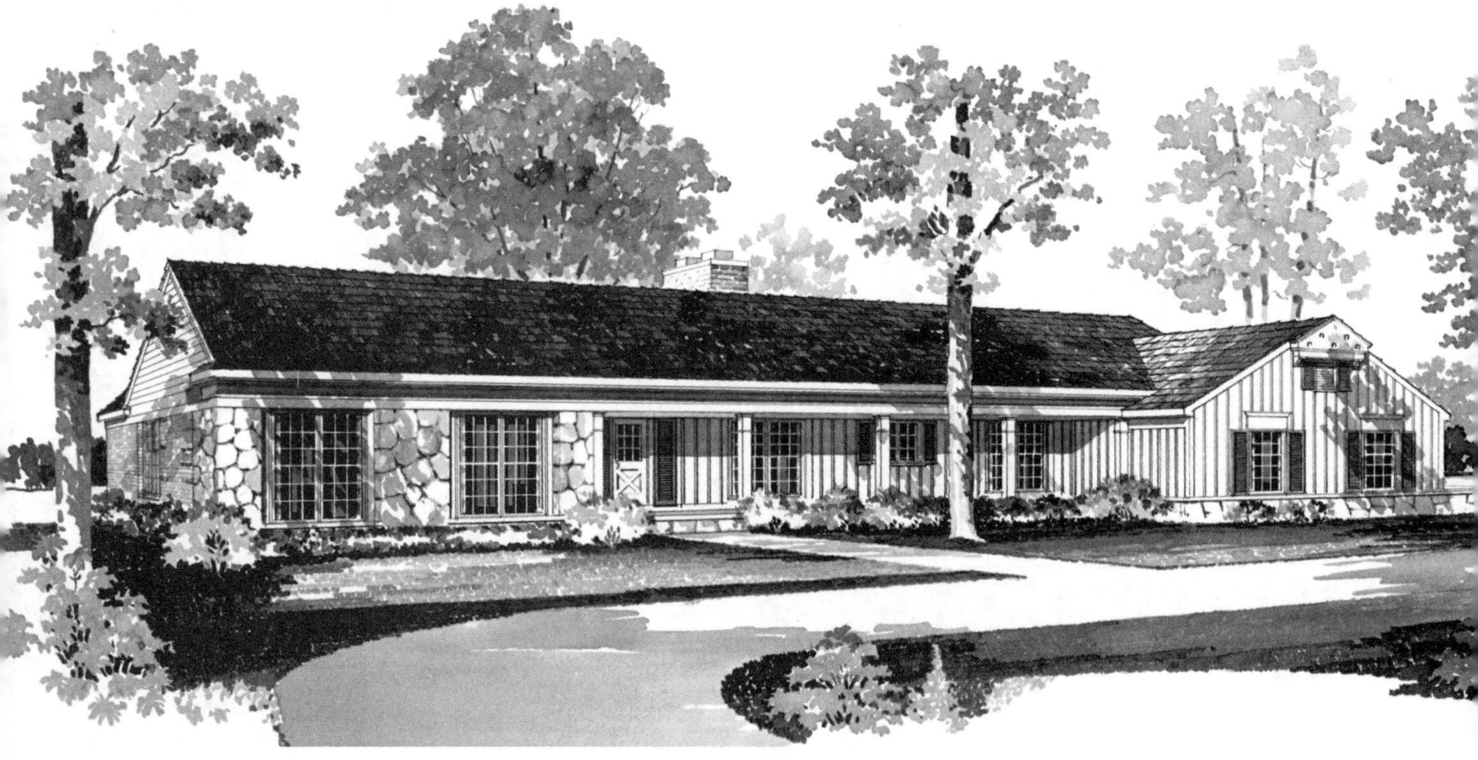

Design 2544

Square Footage: 2,527

D

Design by
Home Planners

A blend of exterior materials enhance the beauty of this fine home. Here, the masonry material used is fieldstone to contrast effectively with the horizontal siding. You may substitute brick or quarried stone if you wish. Adding appeal are the various projections and their roof planes, the window treatment and the recessed front entrance. Two large living areas highlight the interior. Each has a fireplace. The homemaking effort will be easily and enjoyably dispatched with such features as the efficient kitchen, the walk-in pantry, the handy storage areas, the first-floor laundry and extra bedrooms, two baths with vanities and good closet accommodations. There's a basement for additional storage and recreation activities.

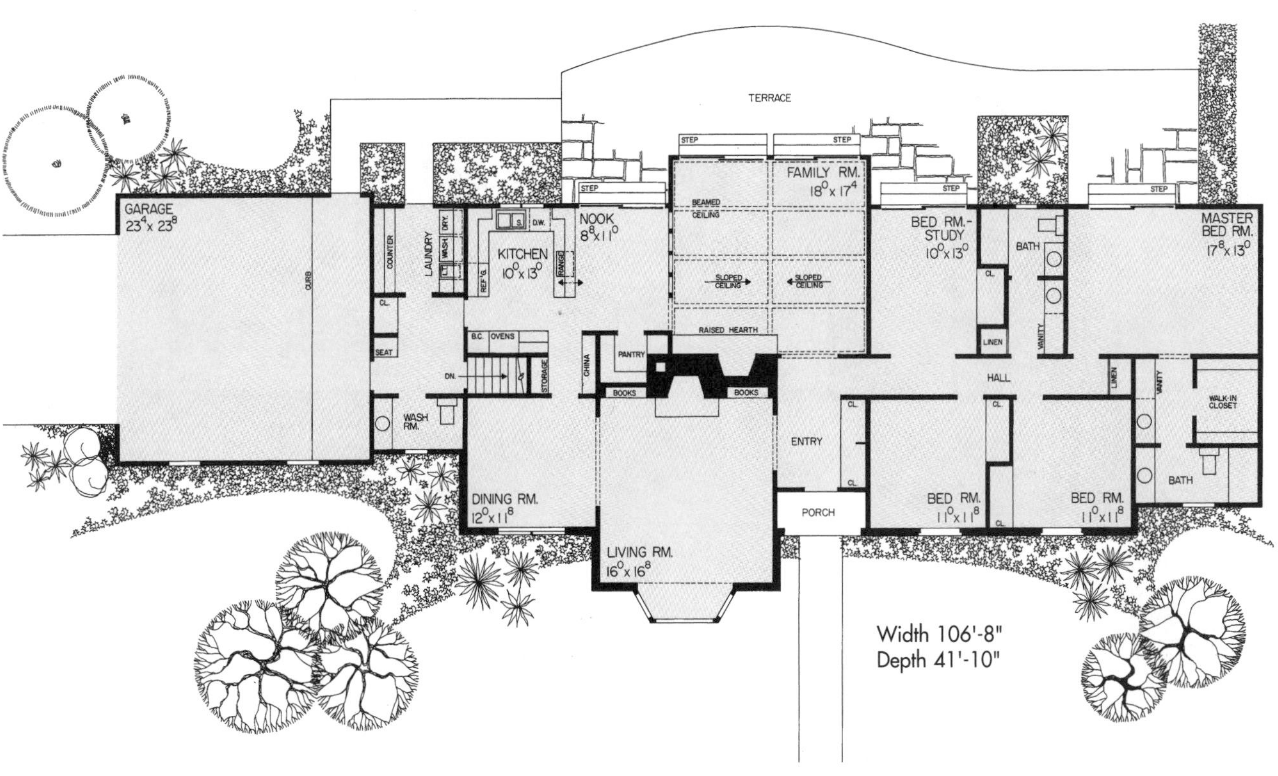
TERRACE
GARAGE 23⁴x 23⁸
LAUNDRY
KITCHEN 10⁰x 13⁰
NOOK 8⁸x 11⁰
FAMILY RM. 18⁰x 17⁴
BEAMED CEILING
SLOPED CEILING
RAISED HEARTH
PANTRY
BOOKS
WASH RM.
DINING RM. 12⁰x 11⁸
LIVING RM. 16⁰x 16⁸
ENTRY
PORCH
BED RM.-STUDY 10⁰x 13⁰
BATH
HALL
MASTER BED RM. 17⁸x 13⁰
WALK-IN CLOSET
BED RM. 11⁰x 11⁸
BED RM. 11⁰x 11⁸
Width 106'-8"
Depth 41'-10"

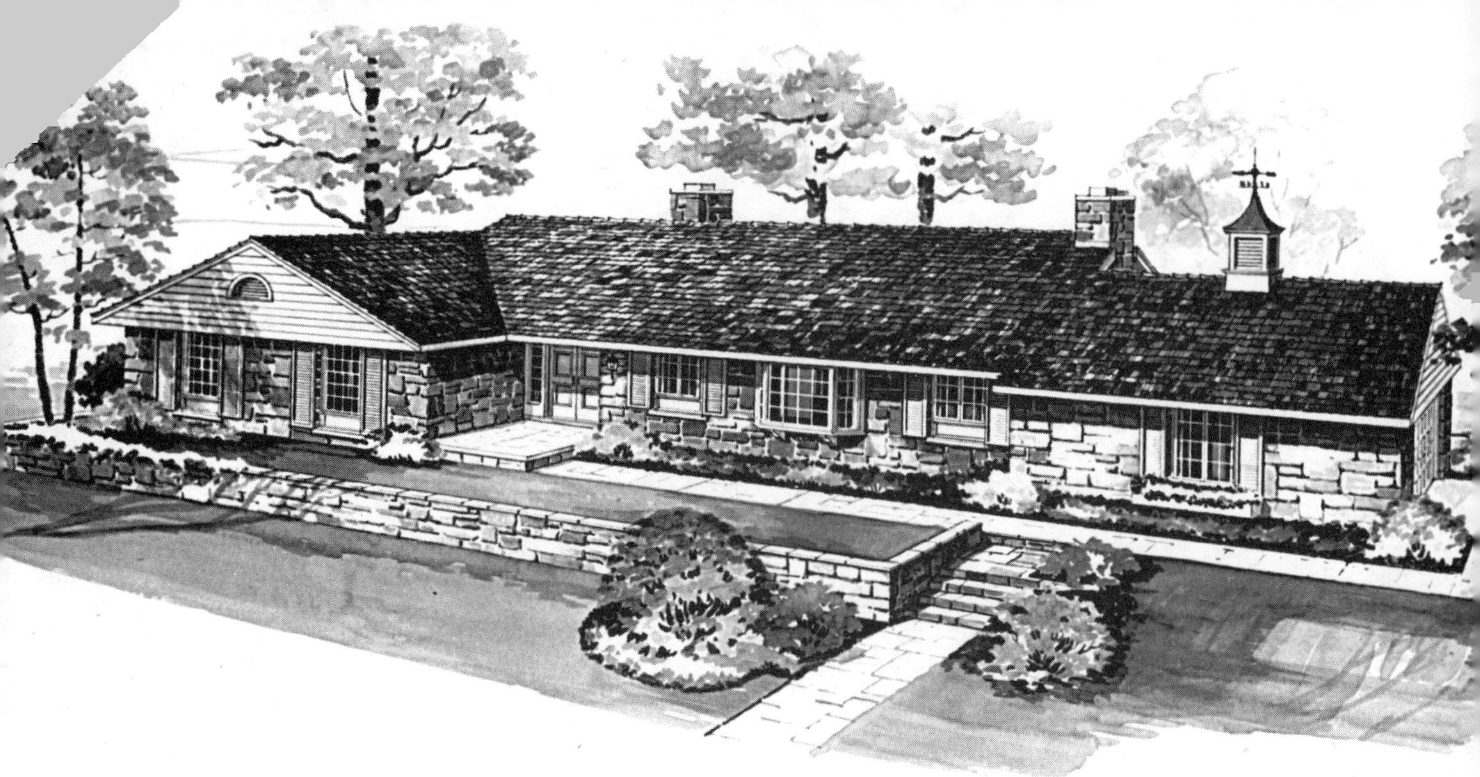

Design 2181

Square Footage: 2,612

L D

Design by
Home Planners

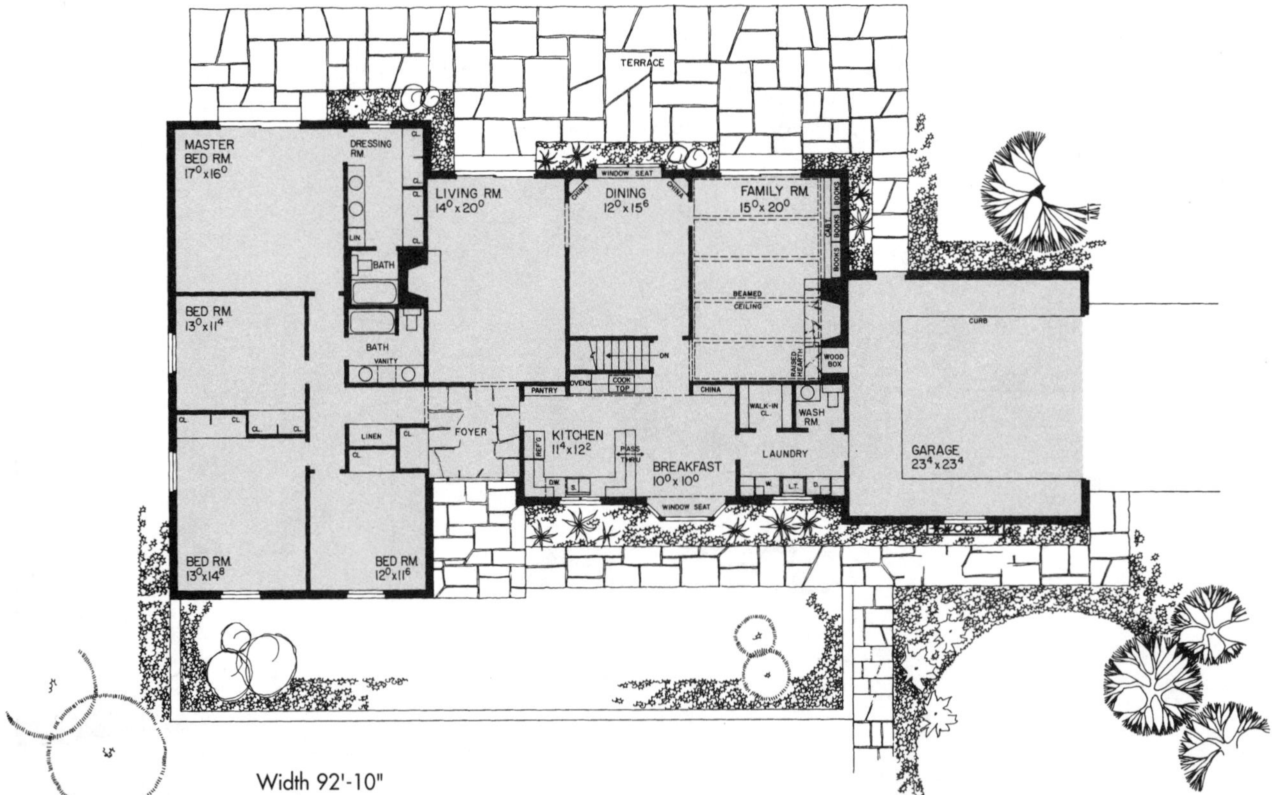

TERRACE

MASTER BED RM. 17⁰x16⁰

DRESSING RM

LIVING RM. 14⁰x20⁰

DINING 12⁰x15⁶

FAMILY RM. 15⁰x20⁰

BED RM. 13⁰x11⁴

BATH

KITCHEN 11⁴x12²

BREAKFAST 10⁰x10⁰

FOYER

LAUNDRY

GARAGE 23⁴x23⁴

BED RM. 13⁰x14⁸

BED RM. 12⁰x11⁶

Width 92'-10"
Depth 46'-10"

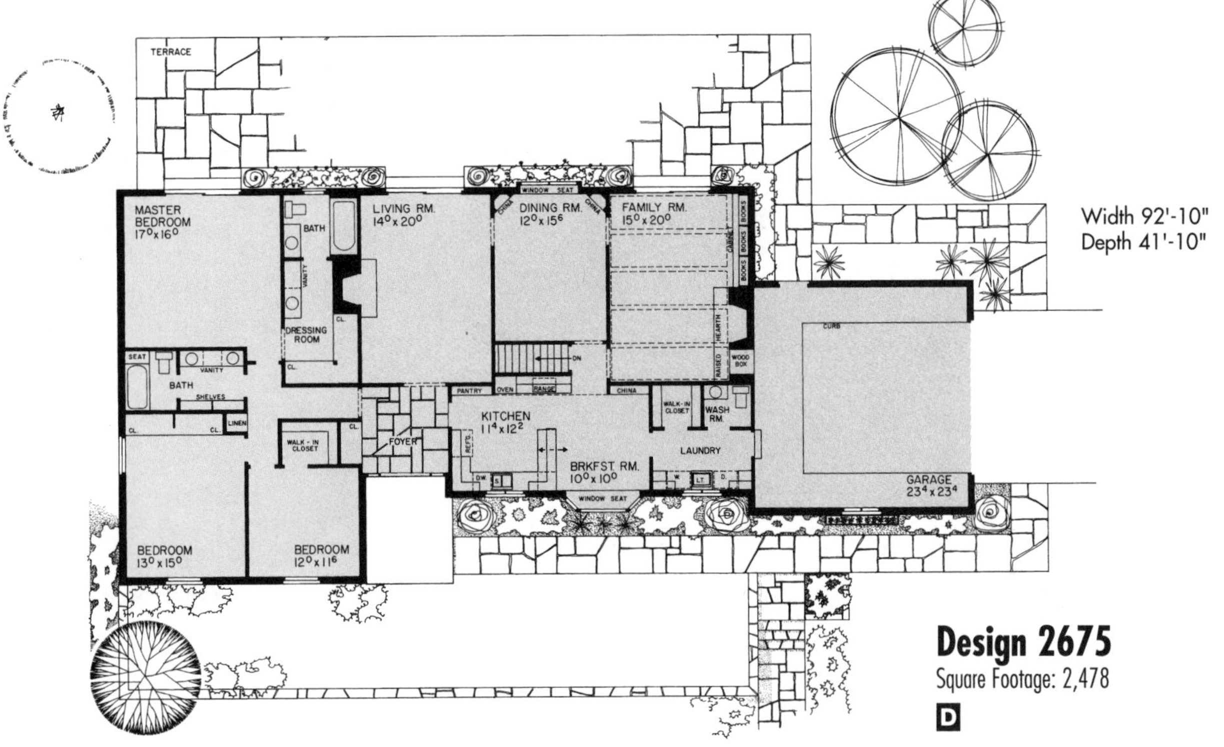
TERRACE
MASTER BEDROOM 17⁰x16⁰
BATH
DRESSING ROOM
LIVING RM. 14⁰x20⁰
DINING RM. 12⁰x15⁶
WINDOW SEAT
FAMILY RM. 15⁰x20⁰
BOOKS
RAISED HEARTH
WOOD BOX
BATH
VANITY
SHELVES
LINEN
WALK-IN CLOSET
FOYER
PANTRY
OVEN
RANGE
KITCHEN 11⁴x12²
CHINA
WALK-IN CLOSET
WASH RM.
LAUNDRY
BRKFST RM. 10⁰x10⁰
WINDOW SEAT
GARAGE 23⁴x23⁴
CURB
BEDROOM 13⁰x15⁰
BEDROOM 12⁰x11⁶

Width 92'-10"
Depth 41'-10"

Design 2675

Square Footage: 2,478

D

Design by
Home Planners

■ The stone facade of this home may be changed to siding or even brick, if this is what you would prefer. Inside, the floor plan caters to pampered living. The foyer centers traffic to the rear and right side of the home where there are both formal and informal areas. The living room has a fireplace and sliding glass doors to the rear terrace. The family room also has a fireplace and rear terrace access, but also offers a wood box and built-ins. In between the two is the formal dining room with corner china cabinets and a window seat. The U-shaped kitchen lies to the front of the plan and is complemented by a breakfast room with bayed window seat. The bedrooms are to the left of the plan and include two family bedrooms and a master suite with private bath, dressing room and terrace access. If you prefer a four-bedroom version, order Design 2181 on opposite page.

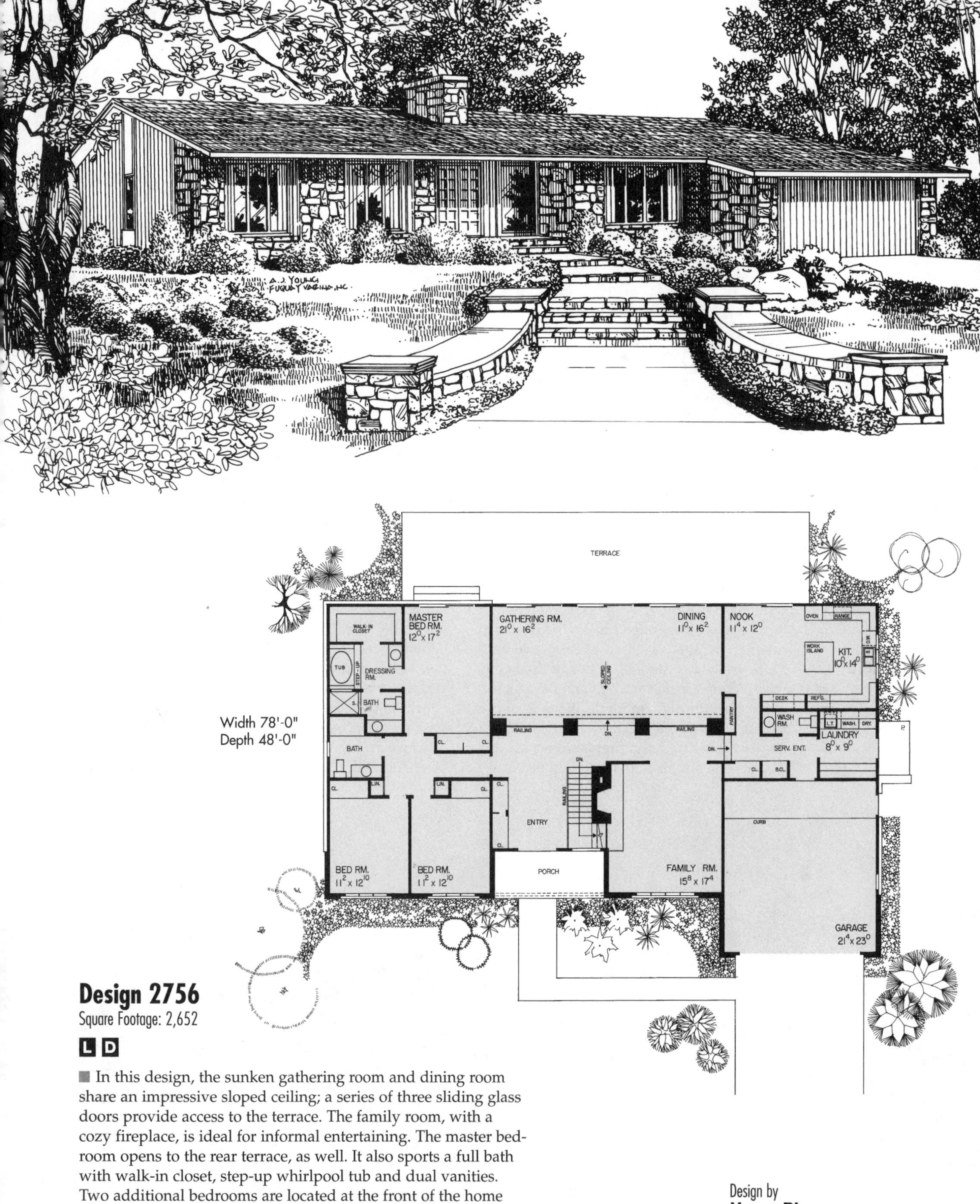

TERRACE
MASTER BED RM. 12^{0} x 17^{2}
WALK-IN CLOSET
TUB
STEP-UP
DRESSING RM.
S.
BATH
GATHERING RM. 21^{0} x 16^{2}
SLOPED CEILING
DINING 11^{0} x 16^{2}
NOOK 11^{4} x 12^{0}
OVEN
RANGE
WORK ISLAND
KIT. 10^{8} x 14^{0}
D/W
DESK
REF'G.
PANTRY
WASH RM.
L.T.
WASH
DRY
LAUNDRY 8^{0} x 9^{0}
SERV. ENT.
DN.
RAILING
CL.
B.CL.
BATH
LIN.
ENTRY
PORCH
BED RM. 11^{2} x 12^{10}
BED RM. 11^{2} x 12^{10}
FAMILY RM. 15^{8} x 17^{4}
CURB
GARAGE 21^{4} x 23^{0}
Width 78'-0"
Depth 48'-0"

Design 2756

Square Footage: 2,652

L D

In this design, the sunken gathering room and dining room share an impressive sloped ceiling; a series of three sliding glass doors provide access to the terrace. The family room, with a cozy fireplace, is ideal for informal entertaining. The master bedroom opens to the rear terrace, as well. It also sports a full bath with walk-in closet, step-up whirlpool tub and dual vanities. Two additional bedrooms are located at the front of the home and share a full bath. A service entrance has access to the two-car garage and to the side yard. It holds a wash room and laundry room with loads of counter space. Don't miss the U-shaped kitchen with island work center and attached nook with sliding glass doors to the rear terrace.

Design by
Home Planners

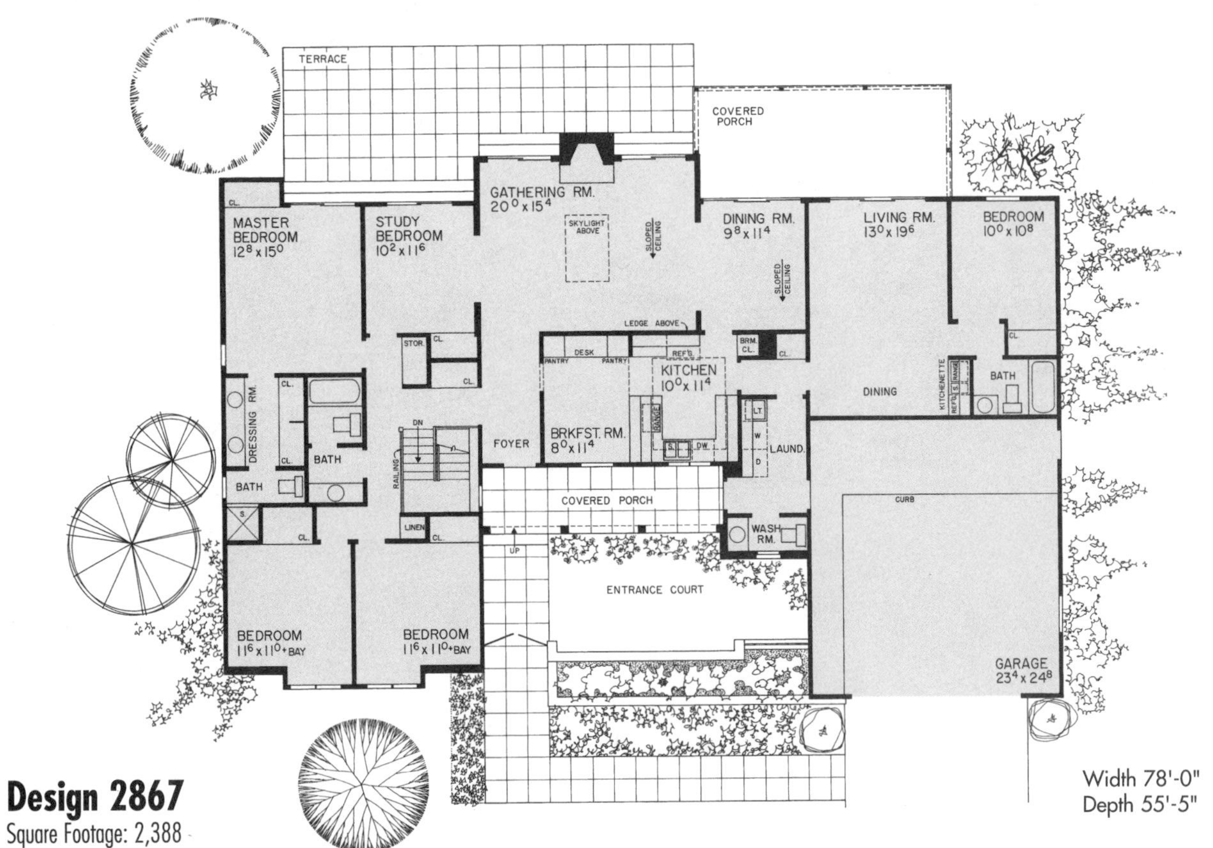
TERRACE
COVERED PORCH
GATHERING RM.
20^{0} x 15^{4}
SKYLIGHT ABOVE
SLOPED CEILING
DINING RM.
9^{8} x 11^{4}
SLOPED CEILING
LIVING RM.
13^{0} x 19^{6}
BEDROOM
10^{0} x 10^{8}
MASTER BEDROOM
12^{8} x 15^{0}
STUDY BEDROOM
10^{2} x 11^{6}
LEDGE ABOVE
STOR.
CL.
DESK
PANTRY
REFG.
KITCHEN
10^{0} x 11^{4}
BRM. CL.
DINING
KITCHENETTE
BATH
DRESSING RM.
BATH
FOYER
BRKFST. RM.
8^{0} x 11^{4}
RANGE
DW.
LT
W
D
LAUND.
DN
RAILING
BATH
COVERED PORCH
CURB
LINEN
UP
WASH RM.
ENTRANCE COURT
BEDROOM
11^{6} x 11^{0} + BAY
BEDROOM
11^{6} x 11^{0} + BAY
GARAGE
23^{4} x 24^{8}
Width 78'-0"
Depth 55'-5"

Design 2867

Square Footage: 2,388

L

■ A live-in relative would be very comfortable in this home. It features a self-contained suite (473 square feet) consisting of a bedroom, a bath, a living room and a kitchenette with dining room. This suite is nestled behind the garage away from the main areas of the house. The remainder of the home, faced with fieldstone and vertical wood siding, is also very comfortable. One whole wing houses the four family bedrooms and baths. The center of the plan has a front, U-shaped kitchen and breakfast room with planning desk. A formal dining room and the large gathering room have access to outdoor spaces. Notice that one of the family bedrooms opens to the gathering room and would make a perfect study.

Design by
Home Planners

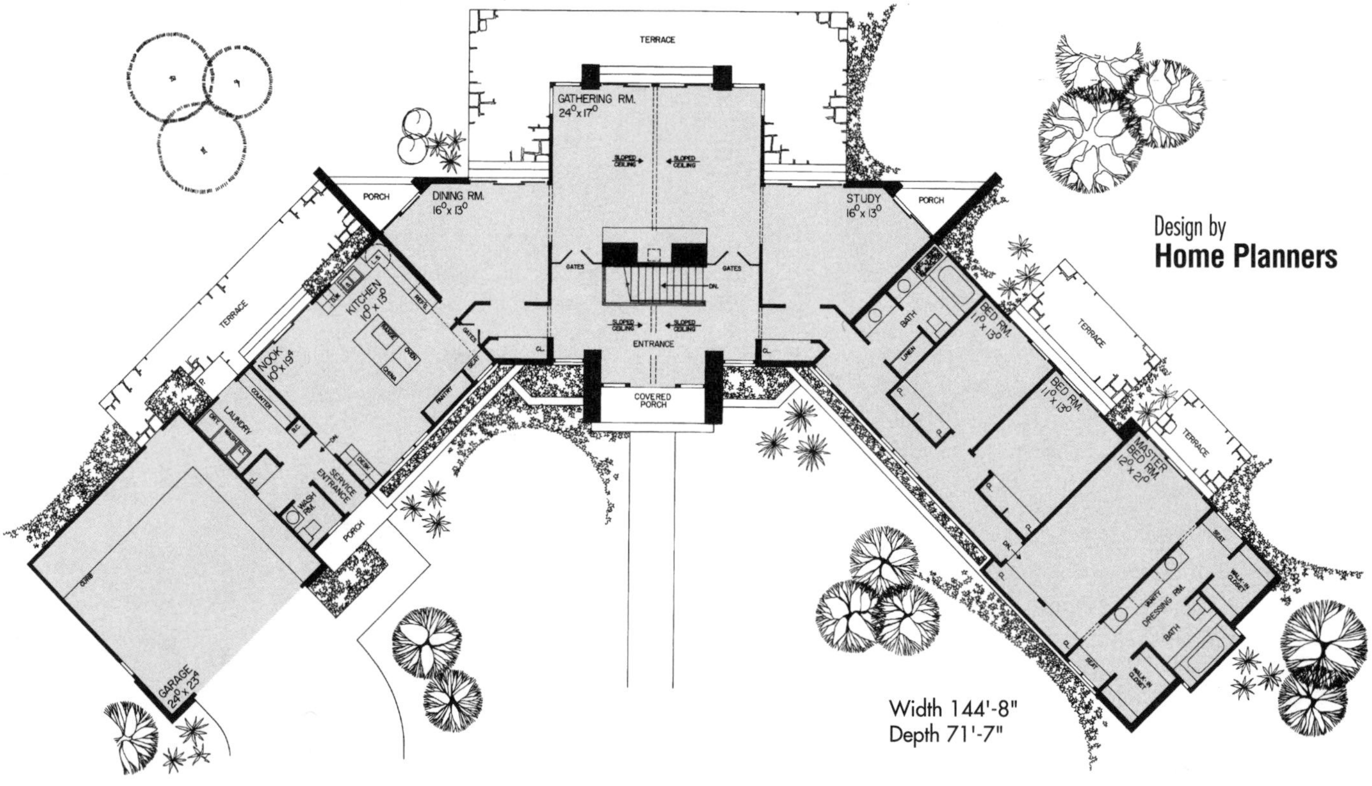

Design by
Home Planners

Width 144'-8"
Depth 71'-7"

Design 2534

Square Footage: 3,262

■ Using the best of Western design with in-line floor planning, this grand ranch house is made for open spaces. The wings effectively balance a truly dramatic front entrance. Massive masonry walls support the wide overhanging roof with its exposed beams. The patterned double front doors are surrounded by a delightful expanse of glass. The raised planter and the masses of quarried stone (or brick if you prefer) enhance the exterior appeal. Inside, a distinctive and practical floor plan emerges. The entry is impressive and leads through gates to the grand gathering room. The right wing holds the three bedrooms, each of which has terrace access. The master has three closets (two are walk-in!) and a dressing area in the bath. The left wing holds the kitchen, dining room and service areas. Be sure to notice the many terraces and porches.

QUOTE ONE®

Cost to build? See page 516 to order complete cost estimate to build this house in your area!

UPPER FAMILY ROOM
RAILING
SLOPED CEILING
DN
LOUNGE 23⁶x12⁰
RAILING
UPPER FOYER

Design 2879

First Floor: 3,173 square feet
Lounge: 267 square feet
Total: 3,440 square feet

■ This lavish modern design has it all, including an upper lounge, family room and foyer. A centrally located atrium with skylight provides focal interest downstairs. A large, efficient kitchen with snack bar service to the breakfast room enjoys its own greenhouse window. The spacious family room shares a warming fireplace and a view of the rear covered terrace. To the front, a living room with fireplace delights in a view of the garden court as well as the atrium. The deluxe master suite features a relaxing whirlpool, dressing area and an abundance of walk-in closets. Three secondary bedrooms, two with window seats, share a full bath.

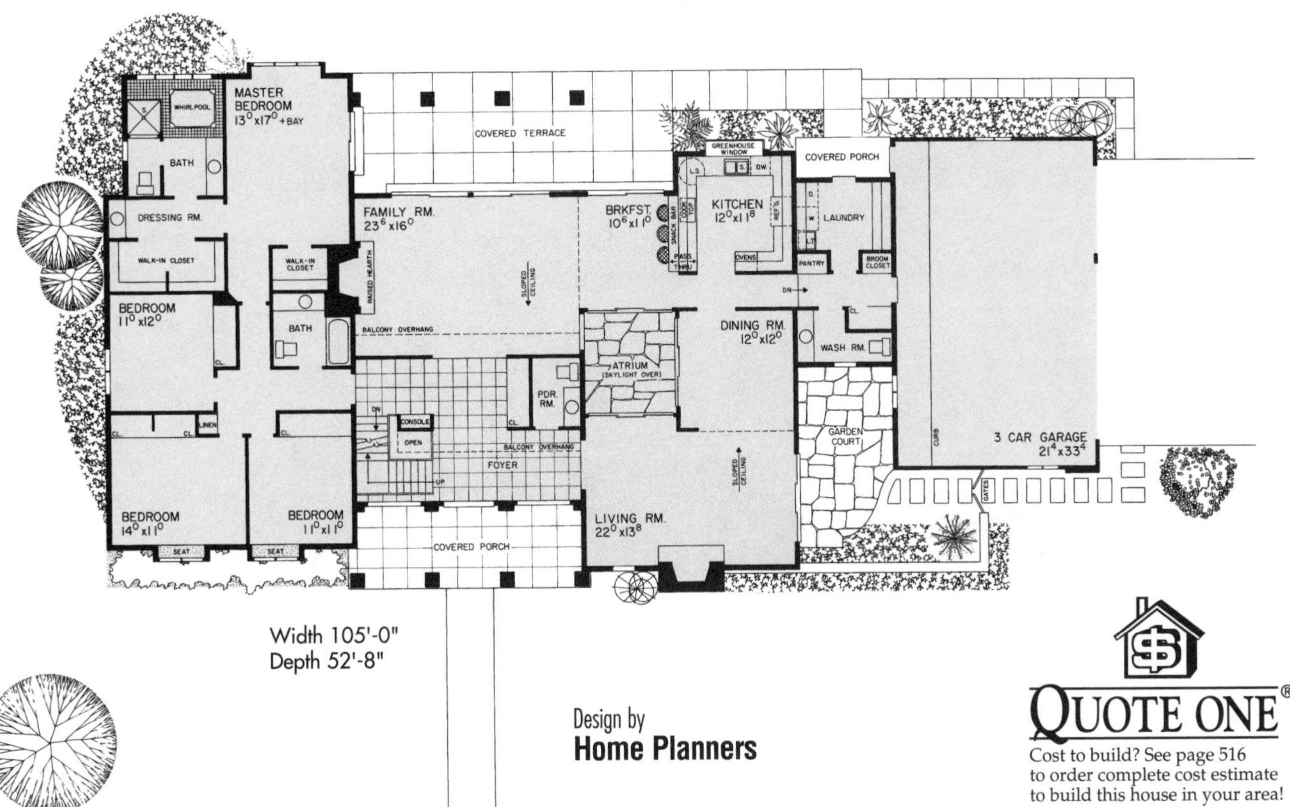
MASTER BEDROOM 13⁰x17⁰+BAY
WHIRLPOOL
BATH
DRESSING RM.
WALK-IN CLOSET
COVERED TERRACE
FAMILY RM. 23⁶x16⁰
RAISED HEARTH
SLOPED CEILING
BALCONY OVERHANG
BRKFST. 10⁶x11⁰
SNACK BAR
PASS THRU
GREENHOUSE WINDOW
KITCHEN 12⁰x11⁸
OVENS
PANTRY
COVERED PORCH
LAUNDRY
BROOM CLOSET
DN
CL.
WASH RM.
BEDROOM 11⁰x12⁰
BATH
CL.
LINEN
ATRIUM (SKYLIGHT OVER)
DINING RM. 12⁰x12⁰
PDR. RM.
CONSOLE
OPEN
UP
FOYER
GARDEN COURT
3 CAR GARAGE 21⁴x33⁴
CURB
GATES
BEDROOM 14⁰x11⁰
BEDROOM 11⁰x11⁰
SEAT
COVERED PORCH
LIVING RM. 22⁰x13⁸

Width 105'-0"
Depth 52'-8"

Design by
Home Planners

QUOTE ONE®
Cost to build? See page 516 to order complete cost estimate to build this house in your area!

Design Q303

Square Footage: 2,959

■ Large proportions and grand details mark this home as a mini-estate. The brick facade, two-story windows with circle-head tops and the double-door entry combine to good effect. The interior is no less elegant. Begin with a barrel-vaulted ceiling in the foyer, which opens directly to the sunken living and dining areas—separated from them only by decorative columns and planters. The living room is made for grand entertaining with a window seat, vaulted ceiling and through-fireplace to the dining room. The dining room is adorned with a tray ceiling. The family room is just across the hall and is also sunken and warmed by a fireplace. Sliding glass doors to the sundeck and hot tub outside make this room special. A kitchen with octagonal breakfast nook is nearby. A cozy den can be accessed either from the hall or from the master bedroom. Details in the master suite include a gas fireplace, a light-filled sitting room, a walk-in closet and a wonderful bath. Three additional bedrooms share a full bath with double vanity. Plans include details for both a basement and a crawlspace foundation.

Rear Elevation

Design by
Select Home Designs

HOT TUB
SUNDECK
SITTING
COFFERED CEILING
GAS F.P.
mbr 14'x18'
WHIRLPOOL TUB
SH.
brk 10'x9'6
SUNKEN
13'8x13'8
k
18'x13'8
fam
BOOKS
9'x11'
den
br2 13'8x10'
SEWING
ldr
W
D
DECORATIVE COLUMN
PLANTER
BARREL VAULT CEILING
RAILING
13'8x13'
din
14'x17'
liv
PLANTER
SUNKEN
14'x10'
br4
13'8x12'6
br3
TRAY CEILING
SEAT
DECORATIVE COLUMN
PLANTER
BARREL VAULT CEILING
23'1 x21'3
two-car garage

Width 99'-0"
Depth 72'-0"

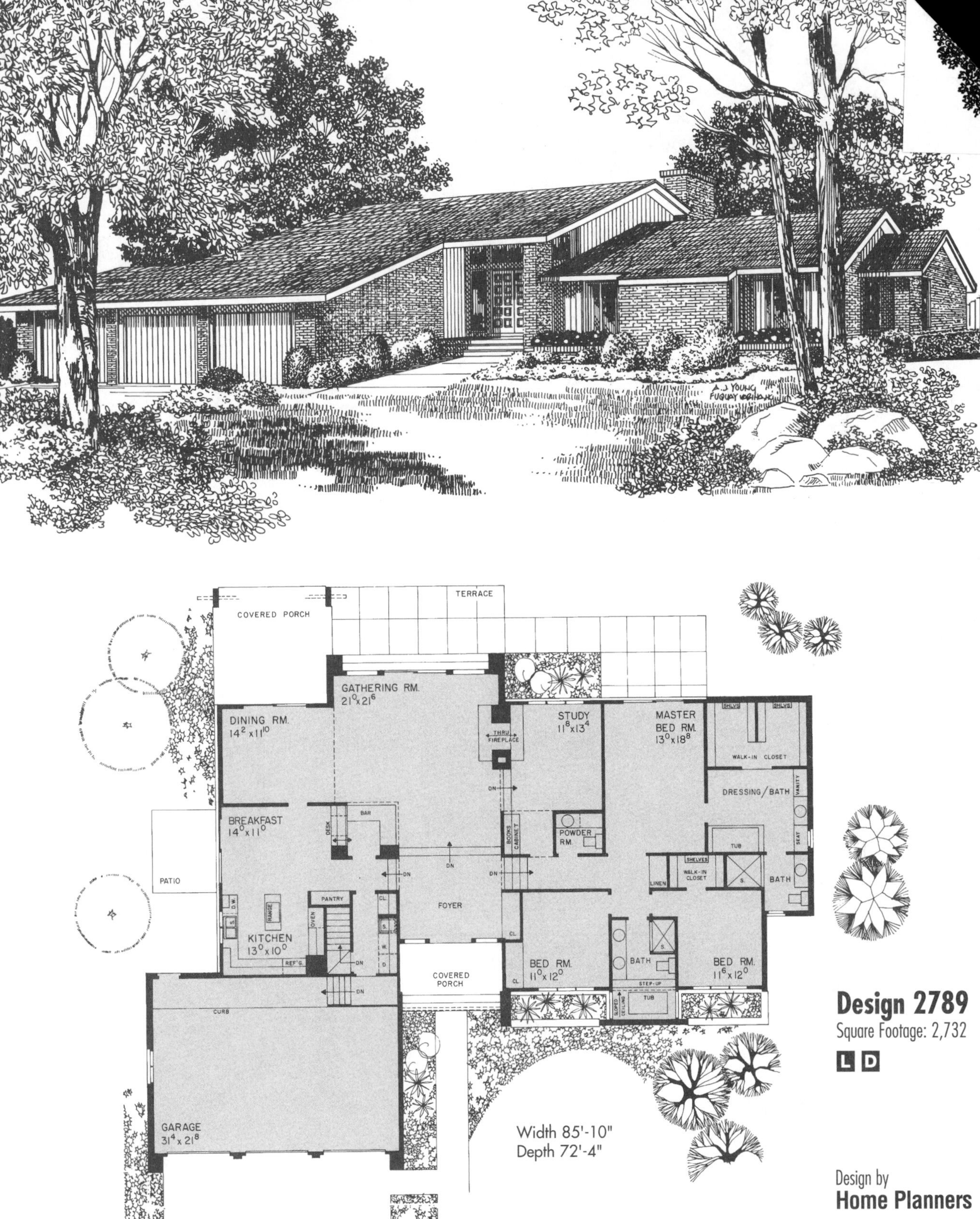
A.J. YOUNG
FUQUAY VARINA, NC
TERRACE
COVERED PORCH
GATHERING RM.
21⁰x21⁶
DINING RM.
14²x11¹⁰
STUDY
11⁸x13⁴
MASTER
BED RM.
13⁰x18⁸
WALK-IN CLOSET
DRESSING/BATH
THRU FIREPLACE
BREAKFAST
14⁰x11⁰
BAR
DESK
BOOKS
CABINET
POWDER RM.
TUB
SHELVES
WALK-IN CLOSET
LINEN
BATH
PATIO
PANTRY
FOYER
KITCHEN
13⁰x10⁰
RANGE
OVEN
REF'G.
COVERED PORCH
BED RM.
11⁰x12⁰
BATH
STEP-UP
TUB
BED RM.
11⁶x12⁰
CURB
GARAGE
31⁴x21⁸
Width 85'-10"
Depth 72'-4"

Design 2789

Square Footage: 2,732

L D

Design by
Home Planners

■ Besides an attached, three-car garage, this home has many features that make it fantastic. Up the steps at the entry and through the double doors, a large entry leads to each of three areas, each down a few steps. The living area has a large gathering room with a fireplace through to the cozy study. Look for built-ins in the study and a powder room just outside it. A dining room sits on the other side of the gathering room. Both the gathering room and dining room have sliding glass doors to the rear terrace (or a covered porch at the dining room). The work center has an efficient kitchen with an island range and planning desk, a breakfast room, a laundry and a bar. Two secondary bedrooms share a full bath with a raised tub and double-bowl vanity. The master suite has sliding glass doors to the rear terrace and a lavish bath featuring a walk-in closet, spa tub, window seat and two sinks.

Design 3636

Square Footage: 2,626

L

■ This adaptation reflects Frank Lloyd Wright's purest Prairie style. Note the access provided to the central, open courtyard from the family room/great room, country kitchen, bedroom, master suite and guest suite. Open planning combines the country kitchen with a snack bar and a formal dining room. Amenities that enhance the master suite include a sitting area, a walk-in closet and a luxurious master bath. The left wing of Design 3636 contains the sleeping quarters and an office/den. The large version, Design 3637, offers split planning with family bedrooms, a guest suite and a formal living room located on the left and the master suite on the right. Plans for a detached garage that has an optional guest suite with kitchenette and full bath are included with the blueprints for 3637. Note the plant shelf area with transom windows that is open above the entry/art gallery.

Width 75'-10"
Depth 69'-4"

MASTER SUITE $24^{2} \times 12^{0}$
SITTING AREA
COVERED PERGOLA
GARAGE $24^{2} \times 24^{2}$
MASTER BATH
WALK-IN CLOSET
LINEN
BATH
OPEN COURTYARD
BEDRM $10^{4} \times 11^{10}$
UTILITY SINK
LAUNDRY ROOM
REFG
ISLAND SNACK BAR
BEDRM $10^{4} \times 11^{6}$
FAMILY-GREAT RM $25^{10} \times 13^{10}$
COVERED PORCH
KIT $16^{8} \times 17^{2}$
COVERED PORCH
PANTRY
RAISED HEARTH
PLANT SHELF ABV
PLANT SHELF ABV
OFFICE-DEN $9^{6} \times 11^{6}$
POWDER ROOM
ENTRY ART GALLERY
DINING RM $16^{8} \times 11^{6}$
COVERED PORCH

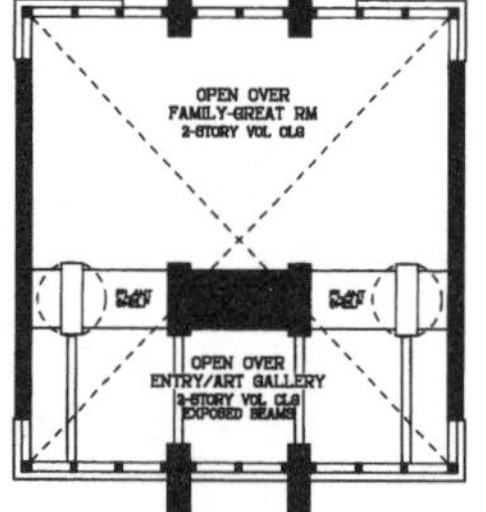
OPEN OVER FAMILY-GREAT RM 2-STORY VOL CLG
OPEN OVER ENTRY/ART GALLERY 2-STORY VOL CLG EXPOSED BEAMS

Design by
Home Planners

QUOTE ONE®

Cost to build? See page 516 to order complete cost estimate to build this house in your area!

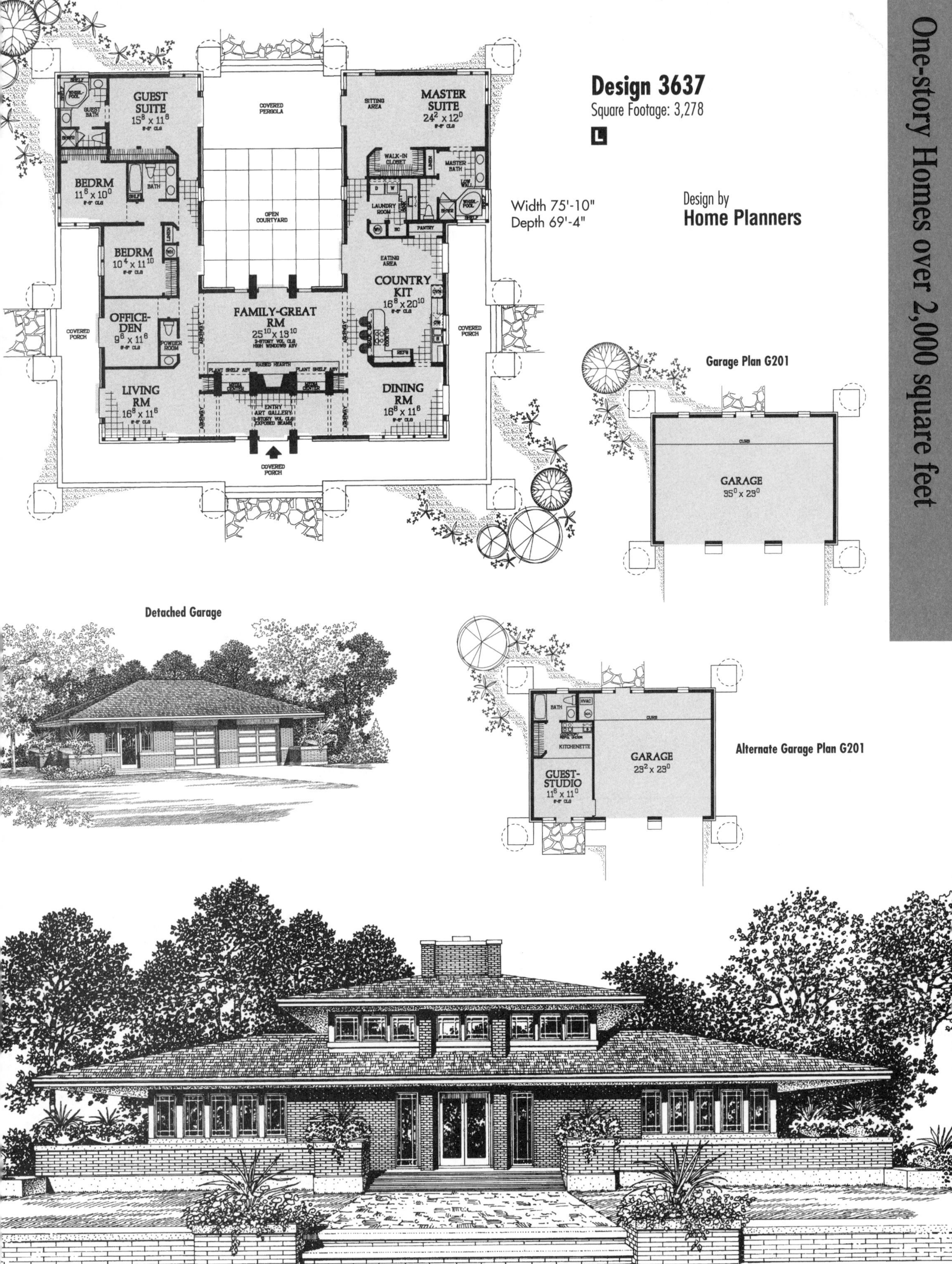
One-story Homes over 2,000 square feet
Design 3637
Square Footage: 3,278
L
Design by
Home Planners
Width 75'-10"
Depth 69'-4"
GUEST SUITE
MASTER SUITE
SITTING AREA
COVERED PERGOLA
WALK-IN CLOSET
MASTER BATH
BEDRM
BATH
OPEN COURTYARD
LAUNDRY ROOM
PANTRY
EATING AREA
COUNTRY KIT
FAMILY-GREAT RM
OFFICE-DEN
POWDER ROOM
COVERED PORCH
RAISED HEARTH
PLANT SHELF ABV
LIVING RM
ENTRY ART GALLERY
DINING RM
Garage Plan G201
GARAGE
Detached Garage
BATH
HVAC
KITCHENETTE
GUEST-STUDIO
Alternate Garage Plan G201

Design 2915

Square Footage: 2,758
Greenhouse: 149 square feet

L D

■ This grand plan excels in many ways. Start with the 340-square-foot country kitchen, which sports a fireplace, a snack bar and an a adjoining greenhouse. A nearby clutter room allows space for hobbies. Across the hall, the media room contains a wall of built-ins. The combination living room/dining area features a sloped ceiling, raised-hearth fireplace and doors leading to the back terrace. The king-sized master suite offers all the extras with a pair of walk-in closets, a whirlpool made for two, and loads of extra storage space. Family bedrooms share a full bath. Note the large, two-car garage with storage space and built-in storage locker.

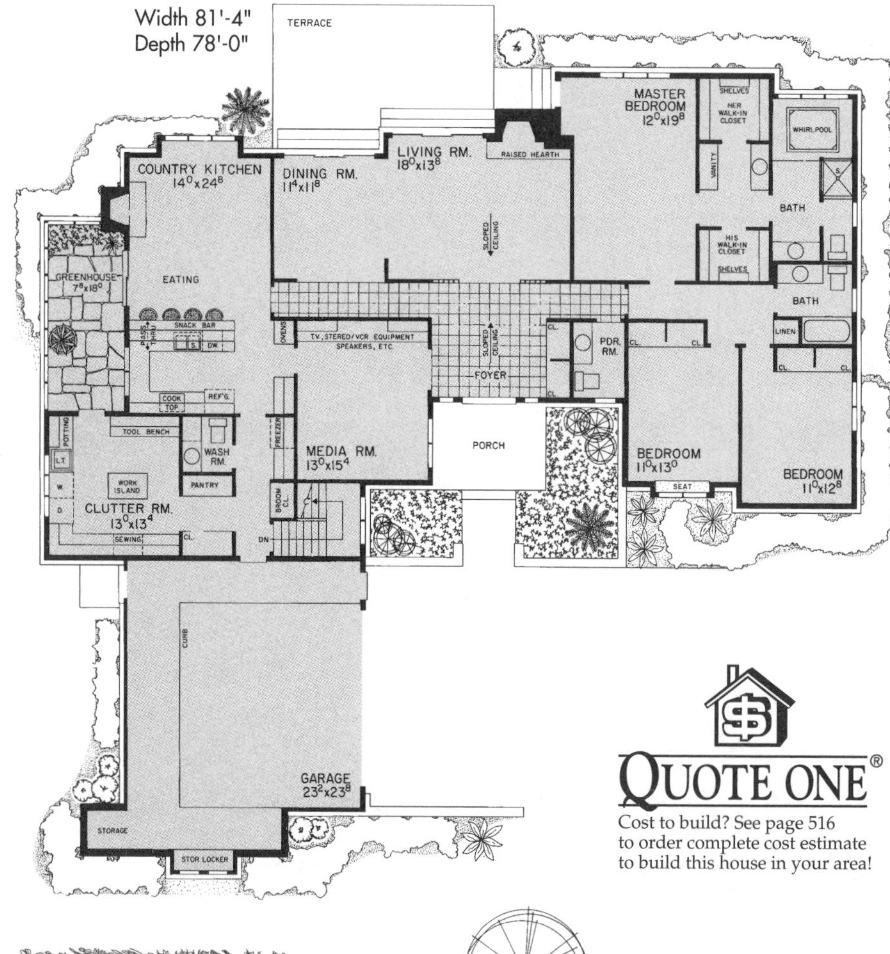

Width 81'-4"
Depth 78'-0"
TERRACE
COUNTRY KITCHEN
14⁰x24⁸
DINING RM.
11⁴x11⁸
LIVING RM.
18⁰x13⁸
RAISED HEARTH
MASTER BEDROOM
12⁰x19⁸
SHELVES
HER WALK-IN CLOSET
WHIRLPOOL
VANITY
BATH
HIS WALK-IN CLOSET
SHELVES
BATH
GREENHOUSE
7⁶x18⁰
EATING
SNACK BAR
DW
OVENS
T.V., STEREO/VCR EQUIPMENT SPEAKERS, ETC.
SLOPED CEILING
FOYER
CL.
PDR. RM.
CL.
LINEN
COOK TOP
REF'G.
TOOL BENCH
WASH RM.
PANTRY
FREEZER
MEDIA RM.
13⁰x15⁴
PORCH
BEDROOM
11⁰x13⁰
SEAT
BEDROOM
11⁰x12⁸
WORK ISLAND
CLUTTER RM.
13⁰x13⁴
SEWING
CL.
BROOM CL.
DN
CURB
GARAGE
23²x23⁸
STORAGE
STOR LOCKER

QUOTE ONE®
Cost to build? See page 516 to order complete cost estimate to build this house in your area!

Rear Elevation

Design by
Home Planners

Design 2832

Square Footage: 2,805 (excluding atrium)

D

■ The advantage of passive solar heating is a significant factor in this contemporary design. The huge skylight over the atrium shelters it during inclement weather, while permitting light to enter down below. The stone floor of this area absorbs an abundance of heat from the sun during the day and permits the circulation of warm air to other areas at night. Sloped ceilings highlight each of the major rooms: three bedrooms, formal living and dining rooms and the study. Broad expanses of roof can accommodate solar panels, if desired, to complement this design. Note the terraces at the side and rear and the sunken conversation area with through-fireplace to the living room.

Width 69'-8"
Depth 70'-4"

Design by
Home Planners

Rear Elevation

Design by
Home Planners

Design 2858

Square Footage: 2,231

■ This sun-oriented design was created to face the south so that it has minimal northern exposure. It has been designed primarily for more temperate US latitudes using 2x6 wall construction. The morning sun will brighten the living and dining rooms along with the adjacent terrace. Sun enters the garden room by way of the glass roof and walls. In the winter, the solar heat gain from the garden room should provide relief from high energy bills. Solar shades allow you to adjust the amount of light you want to enter in the warmer months. Interior planning includes a kitchen with snack bar on the garden side and a serving counter to the dining room. The breakfast room with attached laundry area is convenient to the kitchen. Three bedrooms are on the northern wall. The master suite has a large tub and separate shower with a four-foot-square skylight above. Don't miss the private terrace outside the master bedroom.

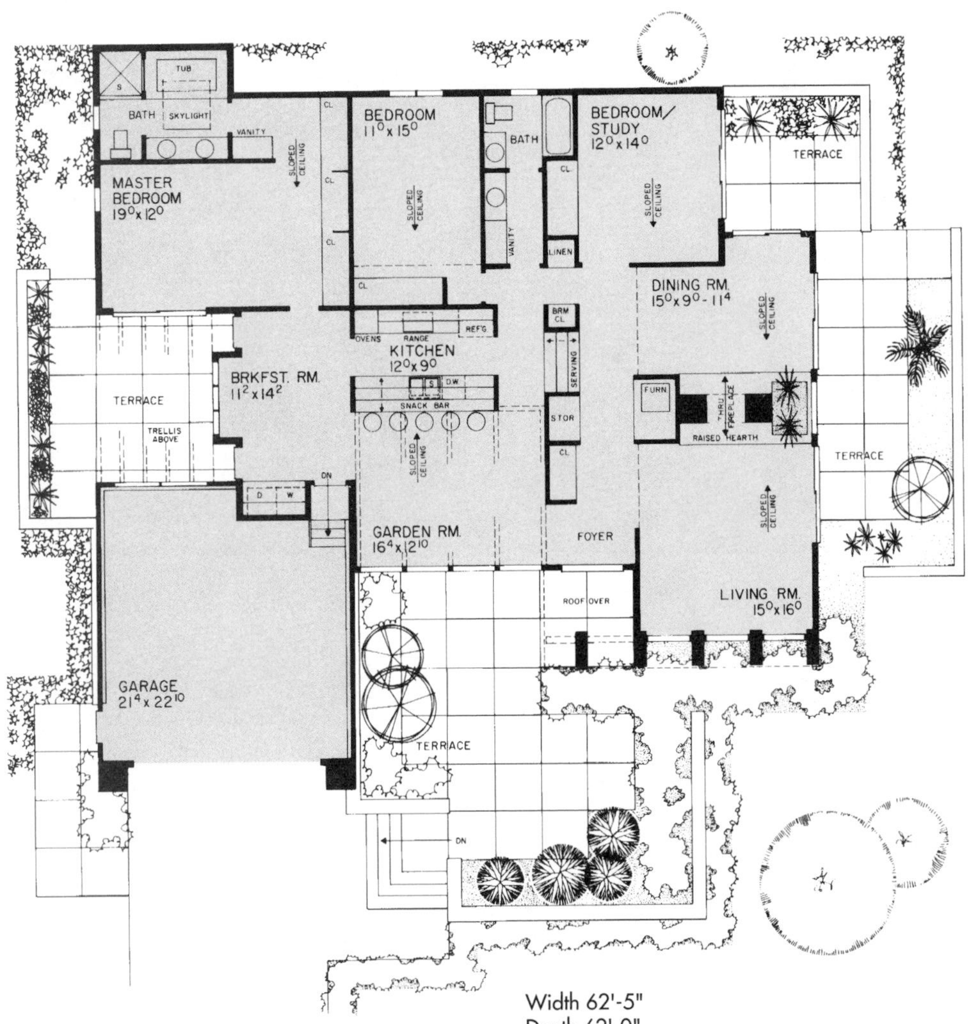
TUB
BATH
SKYLIGHT
VANITY
MASTER BEDROOM
19⁰x12⁰
SLOPED CEILING
CL
BEDROOM
11⁰x15⁰
BATH
VANITY
LINEN
BEDROOM/ STUDY
12⁰x14⁰
TERRACE
DINING RM.
15⁰x9⁰-11⁴
BRM CL
OVENS
RANGE
REF'G
KITCHEN
12⁰x9⁰
SERVING
BRKFST. RM.
11²x14²
TERRACE
TRELLIS ABOVE
SNACK BAR
D.W.
STOR
FURN
THRU FIREPLACE
RAISED HEARTH
TERRACE
DN
GARDEN RM.
16⁴x12¹⁰
FOYER
ROOF OVER
LIVING RM.
15⁰x16⁰
GARAGE
21⁴x22¹⁰
TERRACE

Width 62'-5"
Depth 62'-0"

Design 3559

Square Footage: 2,916

L D

■ Intricate details make the most of this lovely one-story. The floor plan caters to comfortable living. Besides the living room/dining room area to the rear, there is a large conversation area with fireplace and plenty of windows. The kitchen is separated from living areas by an angled snack-bar counter. A media room to the front of the plan provides space for more private activities. Three bedrooms grace the right side of the plan. The master suite features a tray vaulted ceiling and sliding glass doors to the rear terrace. The dressing area is graced by His and Hers walk-in closets, double-bowl lavatory and a compartmented commode.

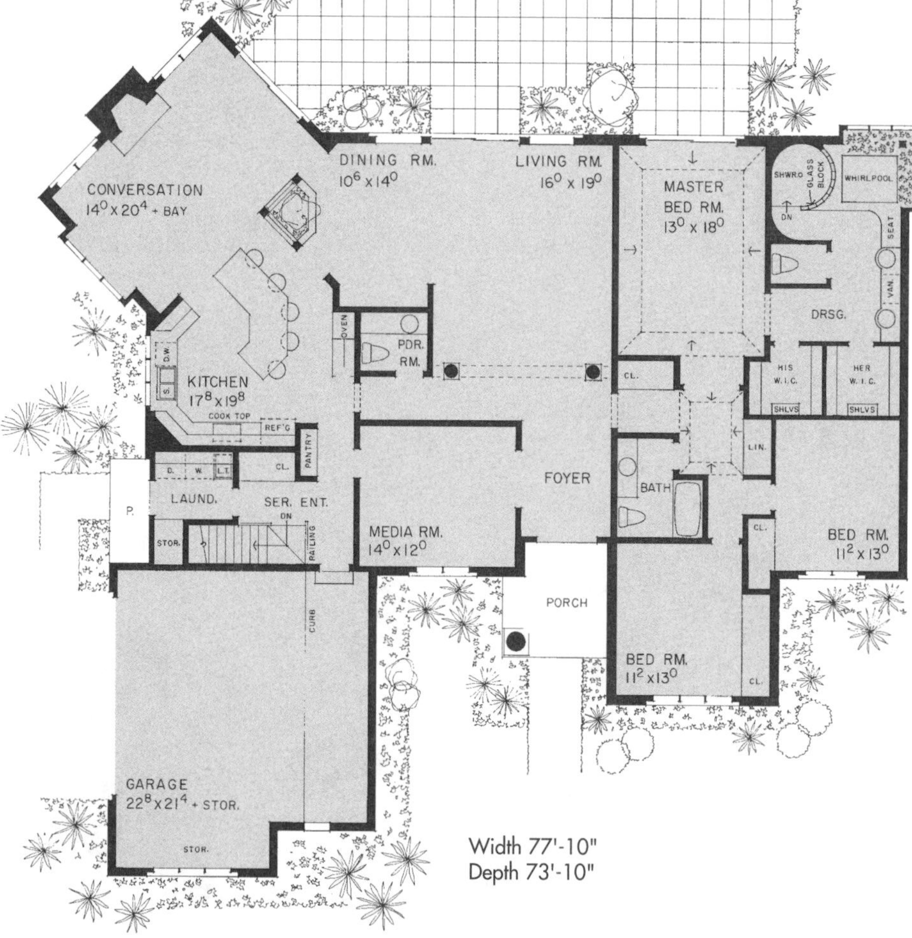

CONVERSATION
14⁰ x 20⁴ + BAY
DINING RM.
10⁶ x 14⁰
LIVING RM.
16⁰ x 19⁰
MASTER
BED RM.
13⁰ x 18⁰
SHWR.
GLASS BLOCK
WHIRLPOOL
SEAT
VAN.
DRSG.
HIS W.I.C.
HER W.I.C.
SHLVS
OVEN
PDR. RM.
KITCHEN
17⁸ x 19⁸
COOK TOP
REF'G
PANTRY
D.W.
CL.
LAUND.
SER. ENT.
STOR.
RAILING
MEDIA RM.
14⁰ x 12⁰
FOYER
BATH
LIN.
BED RM.
11² x 13⁰
PORCH
BED RM.
11² x 13⁰
CURB
GARAGE
22⁸ x 21⁴ + STOR.
STOR.

Width 77'-10"
Depth 73'-10"

QUOTE ONE®

Cost to build? See page 516 to order complete cost estimate to build this house in your area!

Design by
Home Planners

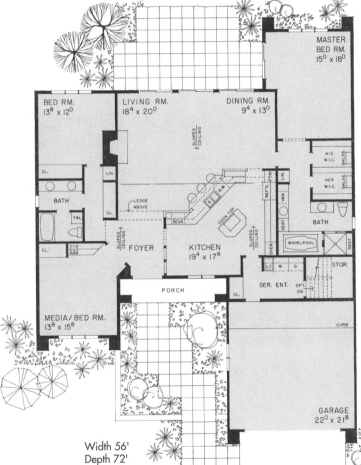

MASTER BED RM. 15^{0} x 18^{0}

BED RM. 13^{8} x 12^{0}

LIVING RM. 18^{4} x 20^{0}

DINING RM. 9^{4} x 13^{0}

HIS W.I.C. SHLVS.

HER W.I.C. SHLVS.

CL. LIN. BATH TWL. CL. LEDGE ABOVE SLOPED CEILING DESK COOK TOP S. D.W. PTRY REF'G. LIN. VAN. SEAT BATH WHIRLPOOL SEAT OVEN SLOPED CEILING

FOYER

KITCHEN 19^{4} x 17^{8}

L.T. W. D. STOR.

SER. ENT. OPT. DN

PORCH CL.

MEDIA/BED RM. 13^{8} x 15^{8}

CURB

GARAGE 22^{0} x 21^{8}

Width 56'
Depth 72'

Design by
Home Planners

Design 3560

Square Footage: 2,189

L

■ Simplicity is the key to the stylish good looks of this home's facade. A walled garden entry and large window areas appeal to outdoor enthusiasts. Inside, the kitchen forms the hub of the plan. It opens directly off the foyer and contains an island cooktop and a work counter with eating space on the living area side. A sloped ceiling, a fireplace and sliding glass doors to a rear terrace are highlights in the living area. The master bedroom also sports sliding glass doors to the terrace. Its dressing area is enhanced with double walk-in closets, a whirlpool tub and a seated shower. Two family bedrooms are found on the opposite side of the house. They share a full bath with twin vanities.

QUOTE ONE®
Cost to build? See page 516 to order complete cost estimate to build this house in your area!

Rear Elevation

Design Q387

Square Footage: 2,094

■ A bold arched entry with decorative columns and a half-round transom window opens to a skylit foyer. Directly ahead, a long plant shelf stretching from the dining room to the family room zones the hallway and enhances the vaulted ceilings. A quiet den sits immediately to the right of the foyer. A sunken living room with fireplace and a vaulted dining room with skylit patio beyond are ideal for formal entertaining. The gourmet kitchen, with pantry storage area, breakfast room and counter bar, is open to the family room (note the fireplace and twin skylights in the family room). The master bedroom is split from the two family bedrooms for privacy and contains a walk-in closet and bath with whirlpool tub and separate shower. The service area leads through a laundry room to the two-car garage with storage. Plans include details for both a basement and a crawlspace foundation.

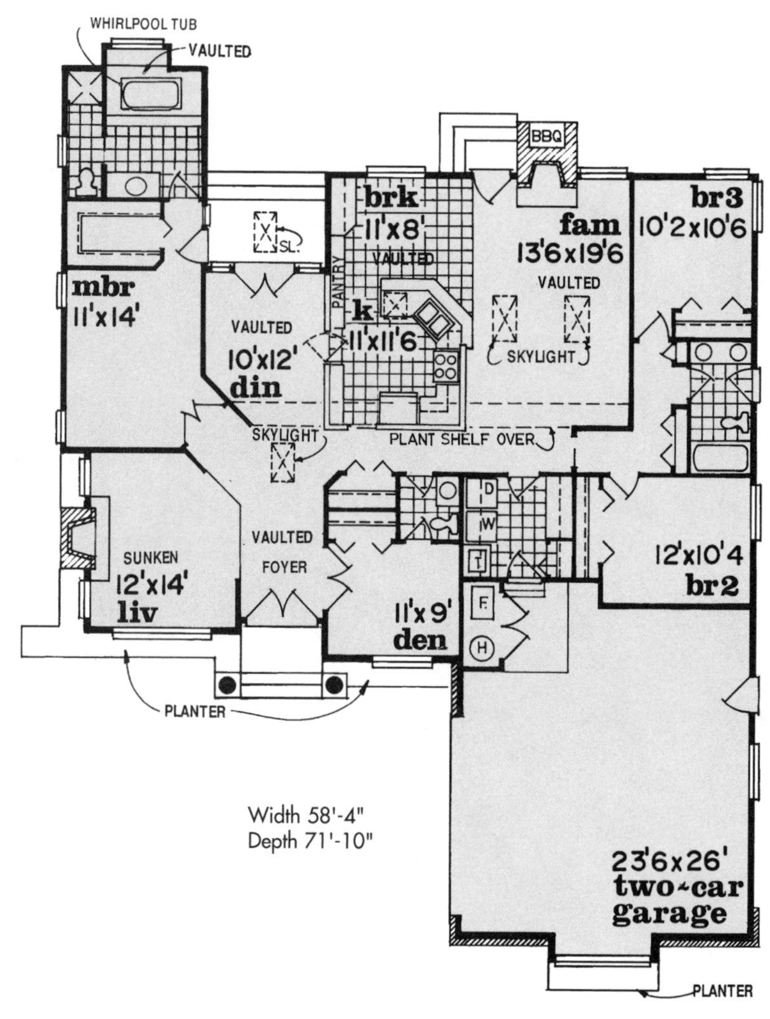

WHIRLPOOL TUB
VAULTED
BBQ
brk
11'x8'
VAULTED
PANTRY
k
11'x11'6
fam
13'6x19'6
VAULTED
SKYLIGHT
br3
10'2x10'6
SL.
mbr
11'x14'
VAULTED
10'x12'
din
SKYLIGHT
PLANT SHELF OVER
D
W
F
H
VAULTED
FOYER
SUNKEN
12'x14'
liv
11'x9'
den
12'x10'4
br2
PLANTER
23'6x26'
two-car
garage
PLANTER

Width 58'-4"
Depth 71'-10"

Design by
Select Home Designs

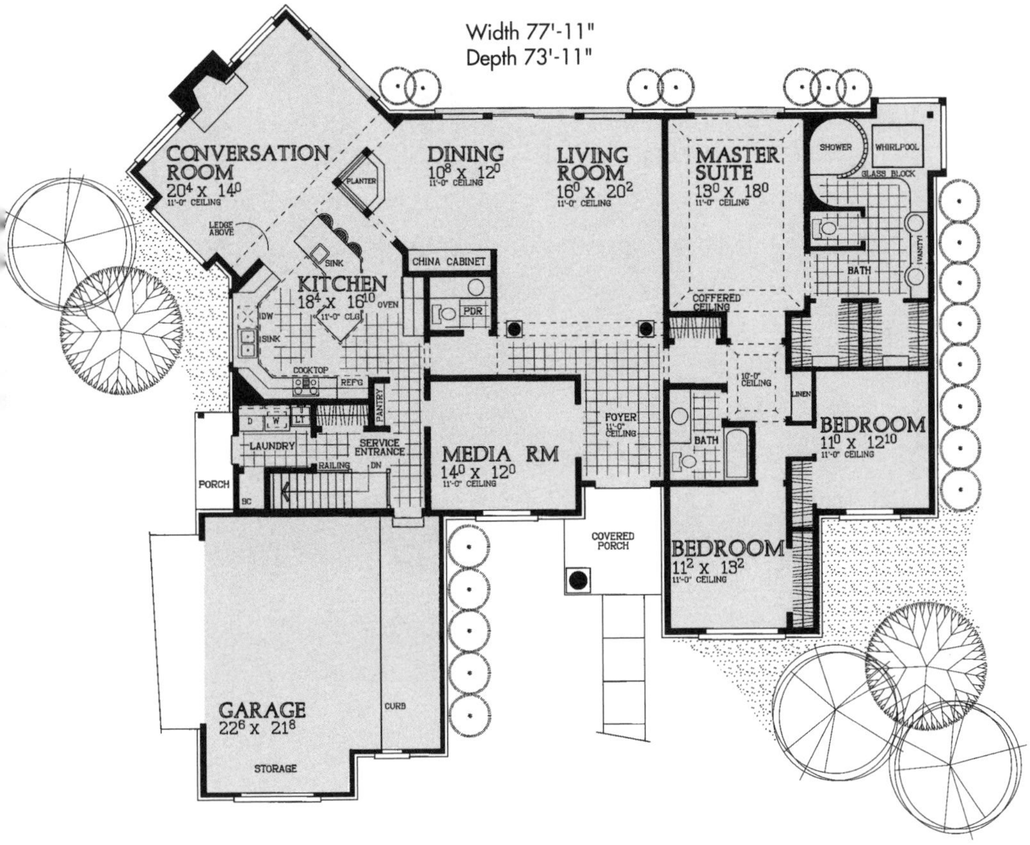

Width 77'-11"
Depth 73'-11"

Design 3327

Square Footage: 2,881

L D

QUOTE ONE®

Cost to build? See page 516 to order complete cost estimate to build this house in your area!

Design by
Home Planners

■ The high, massive hip roof of this home creates an imposing facade while varying roof planes and projecting gables enhance appeal. A central, high-ceilinged foyer routes traffic efficiently to the sleeping, formal and informal zones of the house. Note the sliding glass doors that provide access to outdoor living facilities. The built-in china cabinet and planter unit are fine features. In the angular kitchen, a high ceiling and efficient work patterning set the pace. The conversation room may act as a multi-purpose room. For TV time, a media room caters to audio-visual activities. Sleeping quarters include a spacious master bedroom; here you'll find a tray ceiling and sliding doors to the rear yard. An abundance of wall space for effective and flexible furniture arrangement further characterizes the room. Two sizable bedrooms serve the children.

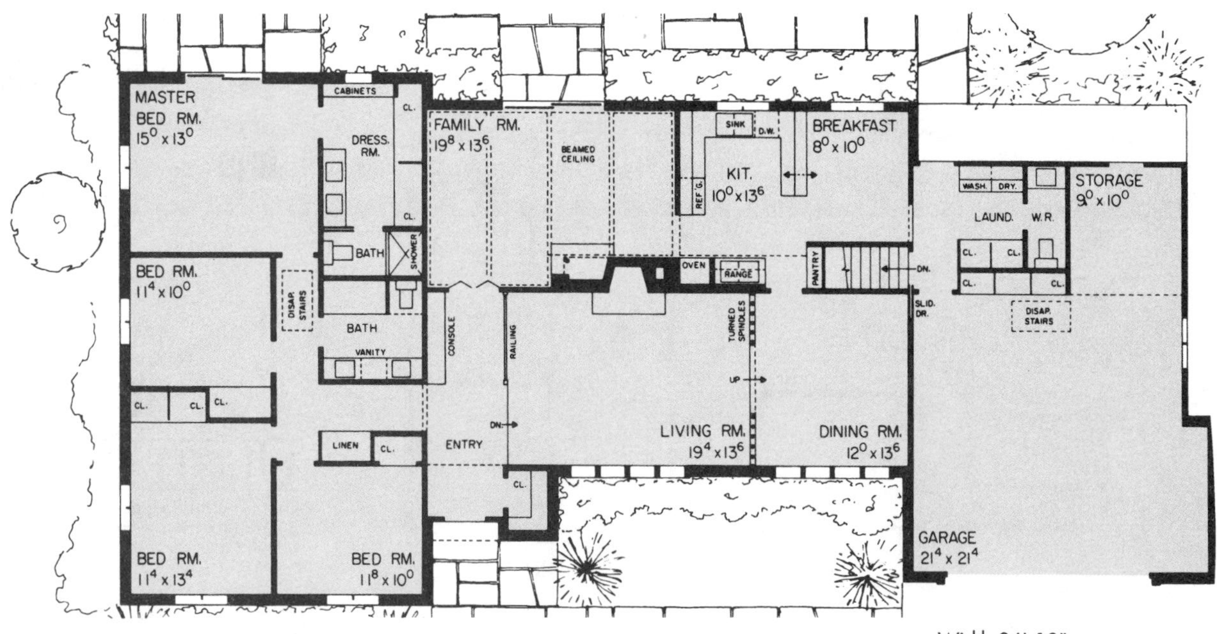

MASTER BED RM. 15⁰ x 13⁰
CABINETS
DRESS. RM.
CL.
BATH
SHOWER
FAMILY RM. 19⁸ x 13⁶
BEAMED CEILING
SINK
D.W.
BREAKFAST 8⁰ x 10⁰
KIT. 10⁰ x 13⁶
REF'G.
OVEN
RANGE
PANTRY
DN.
WASH.
DRY.
STORAGE 9⁰ x 10⁰
LAUND.
W.R.
SLID. DR.
DISAP. STAIRS
BED RM. 11⁴ x 10⁰
DISAP. STAIRS
BATH
VANITY
CONSOLE
RAILING
TURNED SPINDLES
UP
LIVING RM. 19⁴ x 13⁶
DINING RM. 12⁰ x 13⁶
LINEN
ENTRY
GARAGE 21⁴ x 21⁴
BED RM. 11⁴ x 13⁴
BED RM. 11⁸ x 10⁰

Width 86'-10"
Depth 40'-10"

Design 1989

Square Footage: 2,282

Design by
Home Planners

L D

■ High style abounds in this picturesque, ground-hugging design. The plan calls for a sunken living room with fireplace and a separate formal dining room. Overlooking the rear yard is a family room with beamed ceiling and corner hearth. The U-shaped kitchen serves a breakfast room with snack bar counter. Four bedrooms mean plenty of space for everyone in the family. The master suite has a private terrace, a bath with dressing room, built-in cabinets and double sinks. Family bedrooms share a full bath. The service entrance holds a laundry room and a washroom and allows access to the two-car garage. A large storage area in the garage could be used as a workshop.

TERRACE
MASTER BEDROOM 13⁰ X 19⁸
CL
MASTER BATH
WALK-IN CLOSET
WHIRLPOOL
VANITY
BATH
LIVING RM 18⁰ X 13⁸
RAISED HEARTH
SLOPED CEILING
LEDGE ABOVE
DINING RM 11⁰ X 11⁸
COUNTRY KITCHEN 14⁰ X 24⁸
EATING
GREEN HOUSE
SNACK BAR
LS
DW
OVEN
COOK TOP
REF'G
STORAGE
LINEN
LIN
PDR RM
FOYER
PORCH
MEDIA RM/ STUDY 13⁰ X 15⁴
FREEZER
CLUTTER RM 14⁴ X 13⁴
WORK ISLAND
WASH RM
PANTRY/ STORAGE
SEWING
BC
DN
CURB
BEDROOM 11⁰ X 15⁰
BEDROOM 11⁰ X 15⁰
GARAGE 23⁶ X 23⁸

Width 82'-8"
Depth 74'-0"

Design by
Home Planners

Design 3357

Square Footage: 2,913
Greenhouse: 147 square feet

L **D**

■ One-story living never had it so good! From the formal living and dining rooms to a private media room, this house is designed to be enjoyed. The greenhouse off the kitchen adds 147 square feet to the plan. It offers access to the clutter room where gardening or hobby activities can take place. At the opposite end of the house are a master bedroom with a generous bath and two family bedrooms. The master has rear-yard access, a walk-in closet and private bath with whirlpool tub, make-up vanity and separate shower. A media room, or study, opens offer the foyer and also into the U-shaped kitchen. A fireplace warms the country kitchen and there are sliding glass doors to the greenhouse here. Notice the wealth of built-ins throughout the house.

Design 3346

Square Footage: 2,032

L

■ This home boasts a delightful Tudor exterior with a terrific interior floor plan. Though compact, there's plenty of living space: a large study with a fireplace, a gathering room, a formal dining room and a breakfast room. The master bedroom is enhanced with His and Hers walk-in closets and a relaxing, private bath with a soothing whirlpool tub. An additional bedroom with a full bath nearby completes the sleeping quarters.

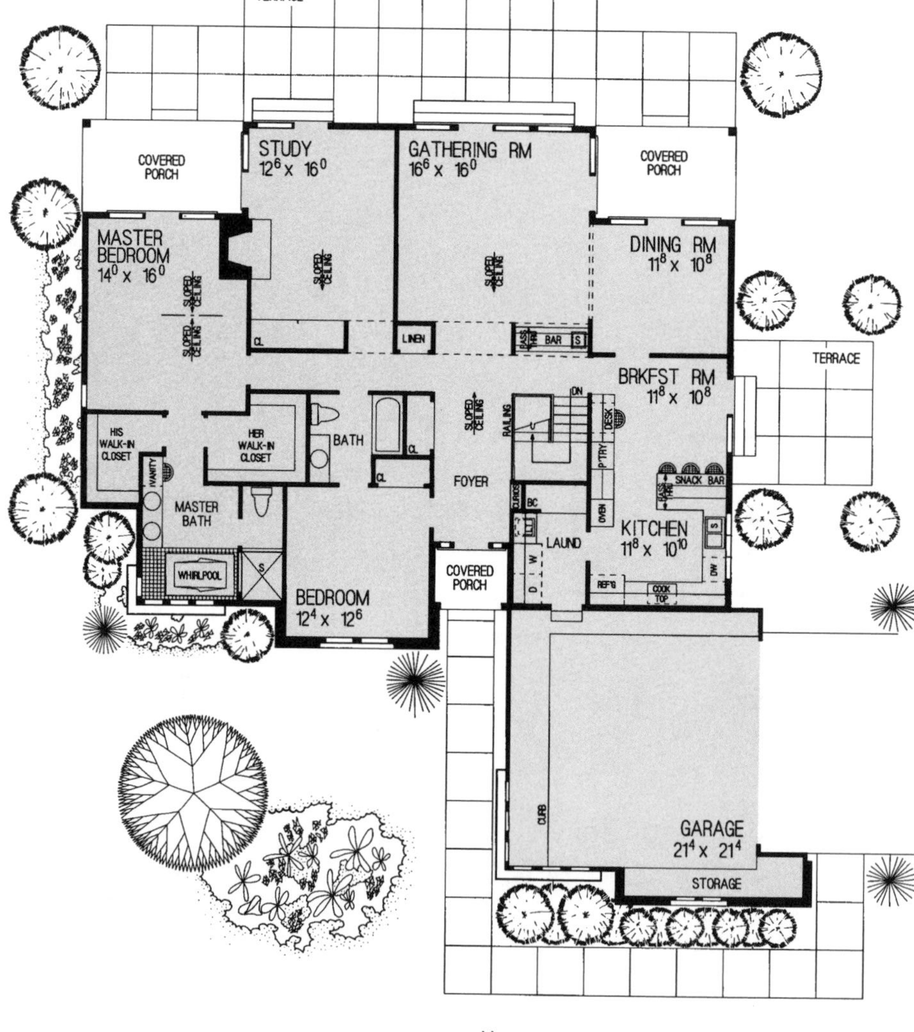
TERRACE
COVERED PORCH
STUDY
12^6 x 16^0
GATHERING RM
16^6 x 16^0
COVERED PORCH
MASTER BEDROOM
14^0 x 16^0
SLOPED CEILING
DINING RM
11^8 x 10^8
CL
LINEN
BAR
TERRACE
BRKFST RM
11^8 x 10^8
HIS WALK-IN CLOSET
HER WALK-IN CLOSET
BATH
FOYER
RAILING
DN
DESK
PTRY
SNACK BAR
MASTER BATH
VANITY
OVEN
KITCHEN
11^8 x 10^{10}
LAUND
BC
WHIRLPOOL
COVERED PORCH
REF'G
COOK TOP
DW
BEDROOM
12^4 x 12^6
CURB
GARAGE
21^4 x 21^4
STORAGE

QUOTE ONE®

Cost to build? See page 516 to order complete cost estimate to build this house in your area!

Design by
Home Planners

Width 63'-5"
Depth 64'-9"

Design 2962

Square Footage: 2,112

■ This home's English Tudor exterior houses a contemporary, well-planned interior. Each of the three main living areas—sleeping, living and working—are but a couple of steps from the foyer. Open planning, a sloped ceiling and plenty of glass create a nice environment for the living-dining area. Its appeal is further enhanced by the open staircase to the lower level recreation/hobby area. The L-shaped kitchen with its island range and work surface opens onto the large, sunny breakfast room. Nearby is the step-saving laundry room. The sleeping area has the flexibility of functioning as a two- or three-bedroom plan.

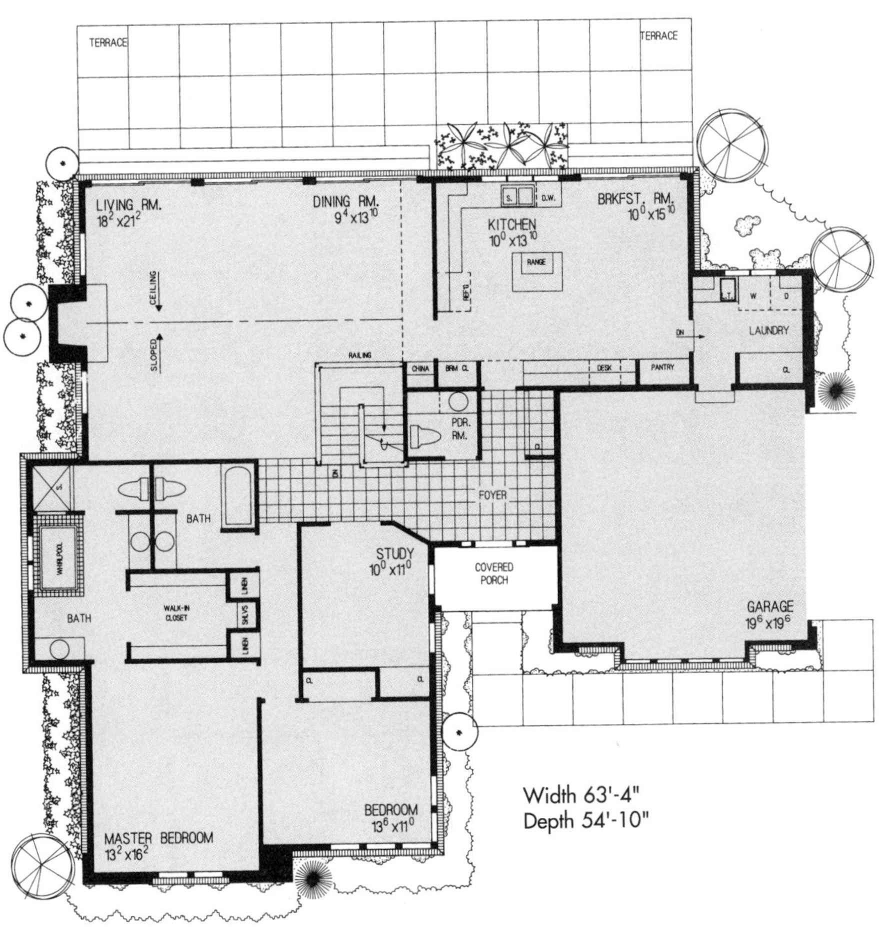
TERRACE
TERRACE
LIVING RM.
18^{2} x21^{2}
DINING RM.
9^{4} x13^{10}
KITCHEN
10^{0} x13^{10}
BRKFST. RM.
10^{0} x15^{10}
LAUNDRY
SLOPED CEILING
RAILING
CHINA
BRM CL
DESK
PANTRY
PDR. RM.
FOYER
BATH
STUDY
10^{0} x11^{0}
COVERED PORCH
BATH
WALK-IN CLOSET
GARAGE
19^{6} x19^{6}
MASTER BEDROOM
13^{2} x16^{2}
BEDROOM
13^{6} x11^{0}

Width 63'-4"
Depth 54'-10"

QUOTE ONE®

Cost to build? See page 516 to order complete cost estimate to build this house in your area!

Design by
Home Planners

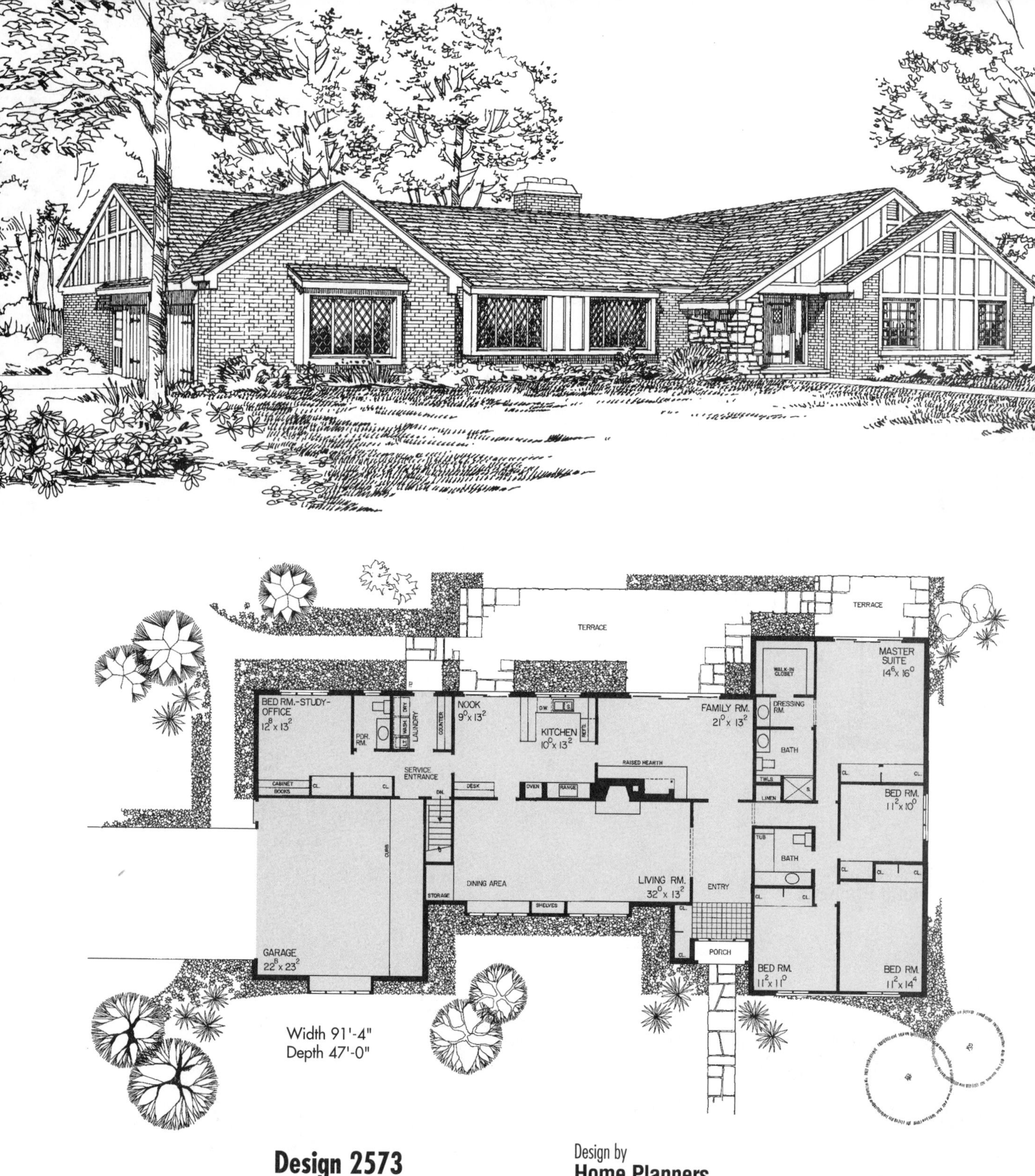

TERRACE
TERRACE
BED RM.-STUDY-OFFICE 12^8 x 13^2
POR. RM.
WASH
DRY
LAUNDRY
COUNTER
NOOK 9^0 x 13^2
D.W.
KITCHEN 10^0 x 13^2
FAMILY RM. 21^0 x 13^2
MASTER SUITE 14^6 x 16^0
WALK-IN CLOSET
DRESSING RM.
BATH
RAISED HEARTH
CABINET BOOKS
CL.
SERVICE ENTRANCE
DN.
DESK
OVEN
RANGE
TWLS
LINEN
BED RM. 11^2 x 10^6
CURB
TUB
BATH
DINING AREA
LIVING RM. 32^0 x 13^2
ENTRY
STORAGE
SHELVES
PORCH
GARAGE 22^8 x 23^2
BED RM. 11^2 x 11^0
BED RM. 11^2 x 14^4
Width 91'-4"
Depth 47'-0"

Design 2573

Square Footage: 2,747

L **D**

Design by
Home Planners

■ A dapper Tudor ranch, this plan combines wood, brick and stucco to create an elegantly appealing exterior. Inside is a thoroughly contemporary floor plan. The open living room and dining area, with more than 410 square feet, features a fireplace, a wall of built-in shelves and a clear view to the outside through diagonally shaped windows. Other highlights include a family room with a raised-hearth fireplace, a U-shaped kitchen and adjacent breakfast nook, an optional bedroom, a study or office and a four-bedroom sleeping wing including a master suite with access to a private terrace. The master suite also has a walk-in closet, two wall closets and a full bath with dressing room and double vanities.

Width 82'-8"
Depth 76'-0"

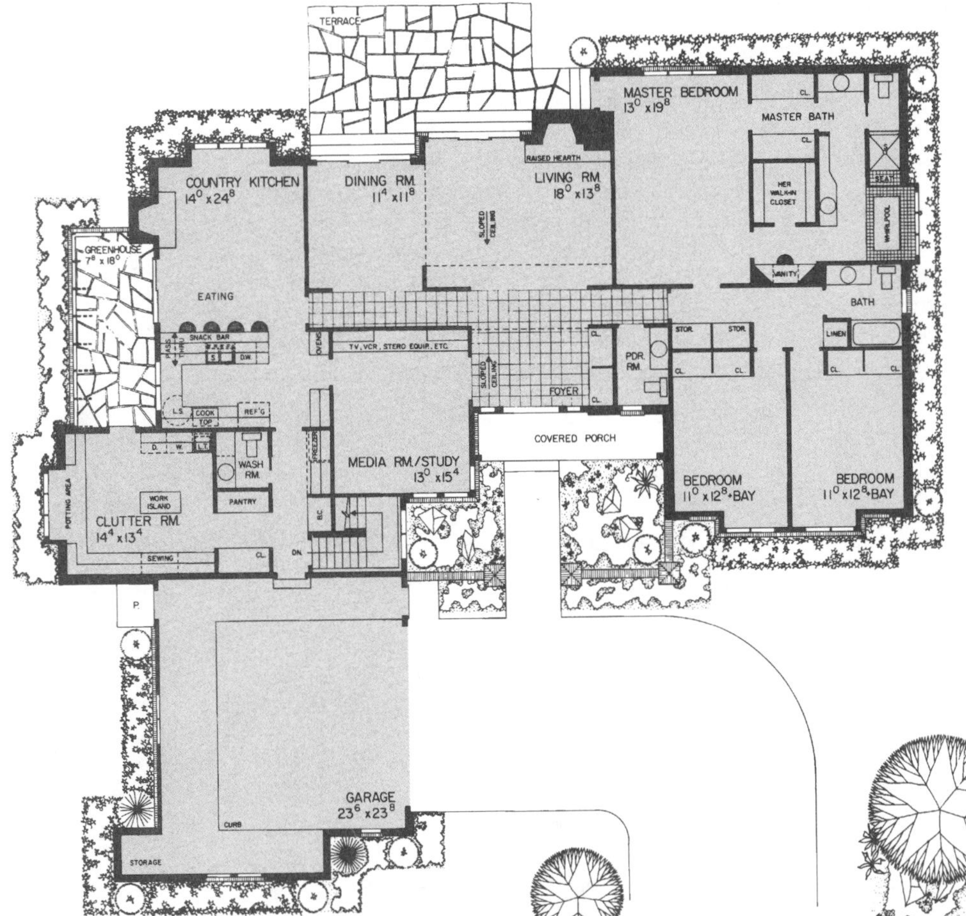
TERRACE
MASTER BEDROOM
13^0 x 19^8
MASTER BATH
COUNTRY KITCHEN
14^0 x 24^8
DINING RM.
11^4 x 11^8
RAISED HEARTH
LIVING RM.
18^0 x 13^8
SLOPED CEILING
GREENHOUSE
7^8 x 18^0
EATING
SNACK BAR
VANITY
BATH
LINEN
TV, VCR, STERO EQUIP., ETC.
PDR. RM.
FOYER
COVERED PORCH
MEDIA RM./STUDY
13^0 x 15^4
WASH RM.
PANTRY
WORK ISLAND
CLUTTER RM.
14^4 x 13^4
SEWING
BEDROOM
11^0 x 12^8+BAY
BEDROOM
11^0 x 12^8+BAY
GARAGE
23^6 x 23^8
STORAGE

Design 2961

Square Footage: 2,919

■ Cornice detailing and a brick exterior with stucco accents and beam work give this Tudor-style home its fashionable appeal. A brick wall forms the front courtyard. Inside, the spacious foyer with slate floor routes traffic to the living areas in the left wing or the sleeping zone in the right wing. Highlights include a media room, clutter room, country kitchen and 29-foot formal living/dining room area. Fireplaces warm both the country kitchen and the living room. A terrace in the back can be reached through sliding glass doors in the living room and dining room and a single door in the master bedroom. The large master bedroom has a luxurious private bath. An added feature is the walled greenhouse located between the kitchen and clutter room.

Design by
Home Planners

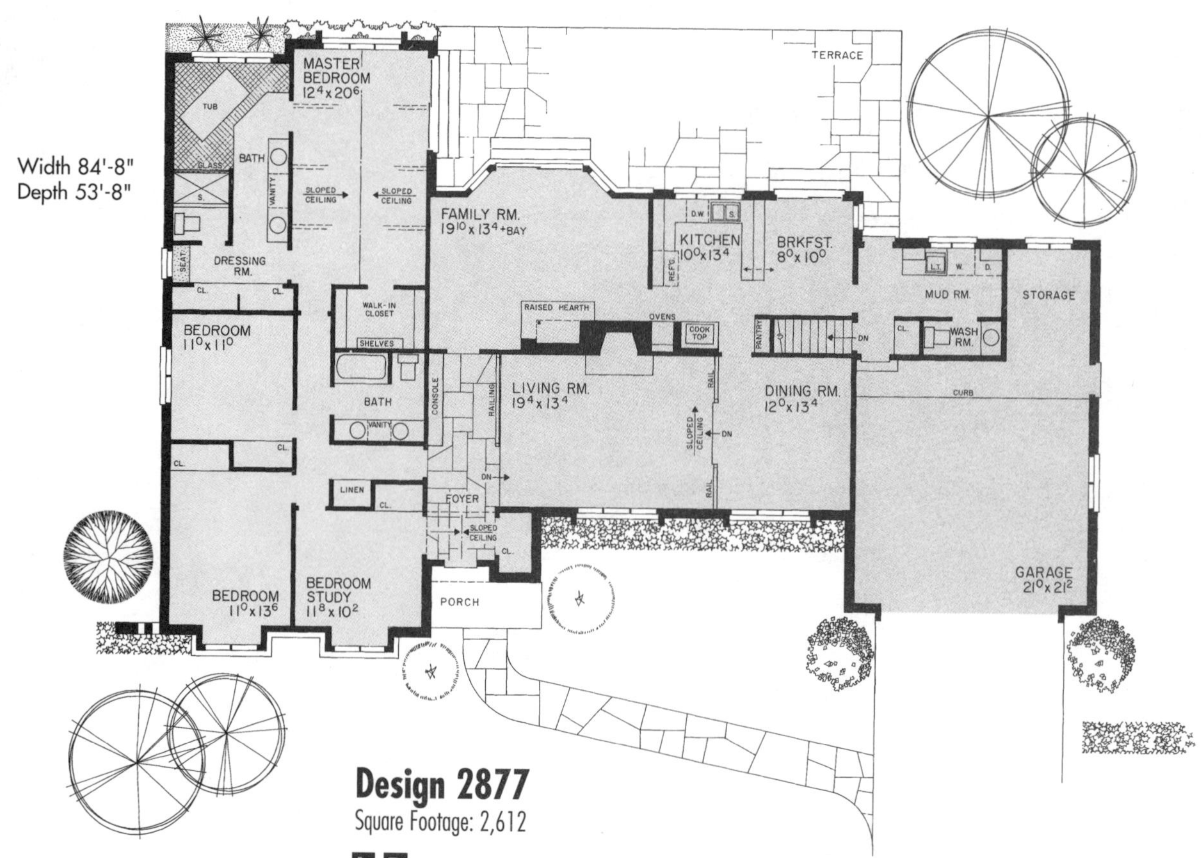

Width 84'-8"
Depth 53'-8"
MASTER BEDROOM $12^{4} \times 20^{6}$
TUB
BATH
GLASS
VANITY
SLOPED CEILING
SLOPED CEILING
DRESSING RM.
SEAT
CL.
CL.
WALK-IN CLOSET
SHELVES
BEDROOM $11^{0} \times 11^{0}$
BATH
VANITY
CONSOLE
RAILING
CL.
CL.
LINEN
CL.
FOYER
SLOPED CEILING
CL.
BEDROOM $11^{0} \times 13^{6}$
BEDROOM STUDY $11^{8} \times 10^{2}$
PORCH
TERRACE
FAMILY RM. $19^{10} \times 13^{4}$ +BAY
RAISED HEARTH
OVENS
COOK TOP
KITCHEN $10^{0} \times 13^{4}$
REFG.
D.W.
BRKFST. $8^{0} \times 10^{0}$
PANTRY
DN
LIVING RM. $19^{4} \times 13^{4}$
SLOPED CEILING
RAIL
DN
DINING RM. $12^{0} \times 13^{4}$
MUD RM.
W.
D.
CL.
WASH RM.
STORAGE
CURB
GARAGE $21^{0} \times 21^{2}$

Design 2877

Square Footage: 2,612

L **D**

■ This dramatic Post-Modern exterior has a popular floor plan with an outstanding master bedroom suite. The bedroom itself is spacious with a sloped ceiling, a walk-in closet and sliding glass doors to the terrace. There are also three family bedrooms sharing a full bath. The living area of the plan has formal areas to the front and informal areas to the rear. The formal living room features a sloped ceiling and a fireplace, plus is sunken a step from the foyer and dining room. The family room also has a fireplace and a bay window with terrace access. The U-shaped kitchen features an attached breakfast room with snack counter and terrace access. The roomy, two-car garage has a large storage area.

Design by
Home Planners

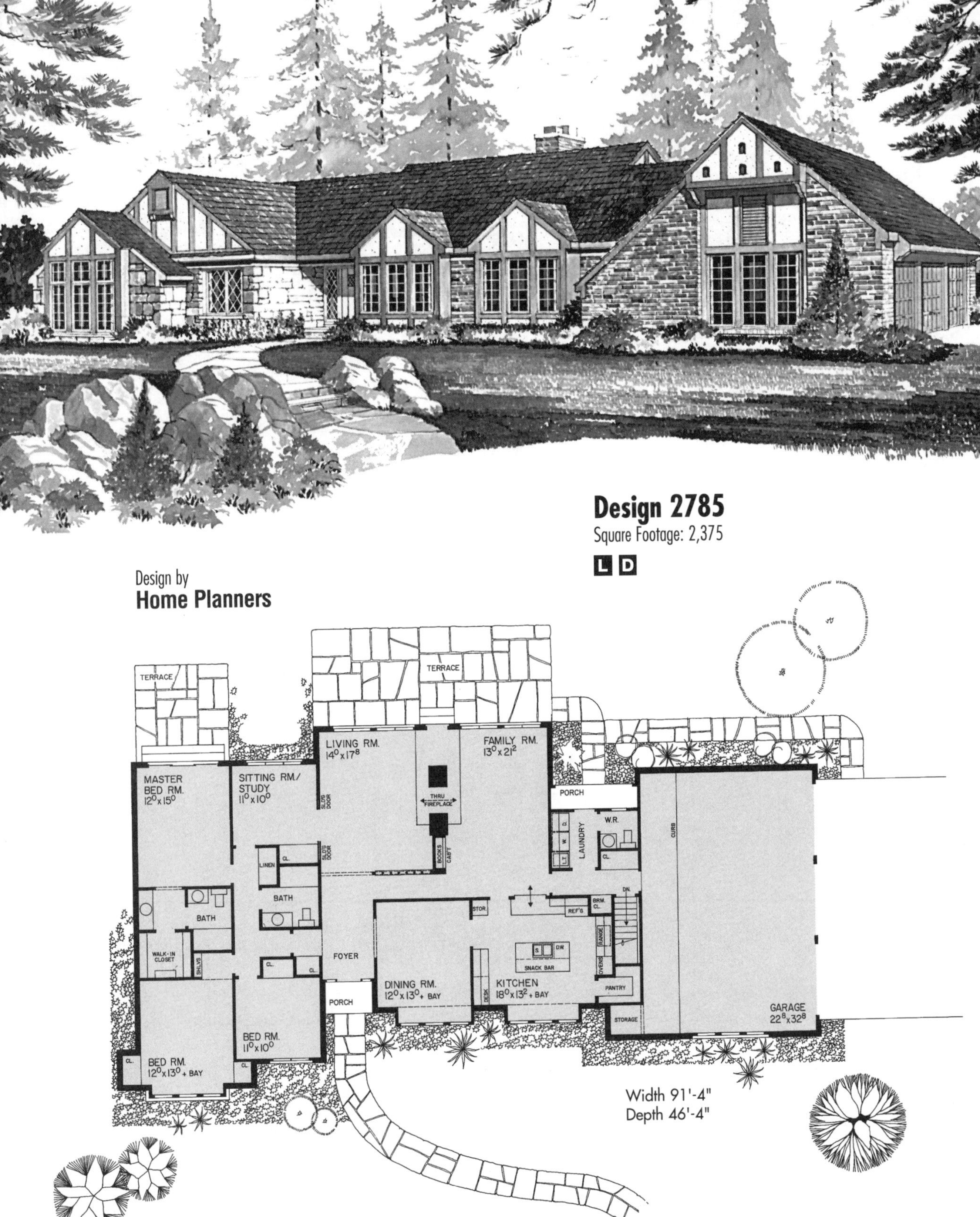
TERRACE
TERRACE
LIVING RM.
14⁰ x 17⁸
FAMILY RM.
13⁰ x 21²
MASTER BED RM.
12⁰ x 15⁰
SITTING RM./ STUDY
11⁰ x 10⁰
THRU FIREPLACE
PORCH
W.R.
LAUNDRY
LINEN
CL.
BATH
BATH
WALK-IN CLOSET
SHLVS.
FOYER
STOR.
REF'G
BRM. CL.
DN.
SNACK BAR
RANGE
OVENS
PANTRY
DINING RM.
12⁰ x 13⁰ + BAY
KITCHEN
18⁰ x 13² + BAY
DESK
PORCH
STORAGE
GARAGE
22⁸ x 32⁸
CURB
BED RM.
11⁰ x 10⁰
BED RM.
12⁰ x 13⁰ + BAY
CL.
Width 91'-4"
Depth 46'-4"

Design 2785

Square Footage: 2,375

L D

Design by
Home Planners

■ With exceptional Tudor details, this home bows to tradition with an updated floor plan. The layout speaks for itself in convenience and efficiency. The central foyer leads to a hallway connecting the dining room, living room and kitchen, but keeps traffic away from the quiet bedroom wing. The dining room also has an entry directly into the island kitchen for serving. The far end of the hall ends at a service area with laundry, washroom and connection to the three-car garage. There are three bedrooms in the plan including the grand master suite. It has a sitting room or study separated from the living room by a pocket door, a bath with double sinks, and a great walk-in closet. Two additional bedrooms share a full bath.

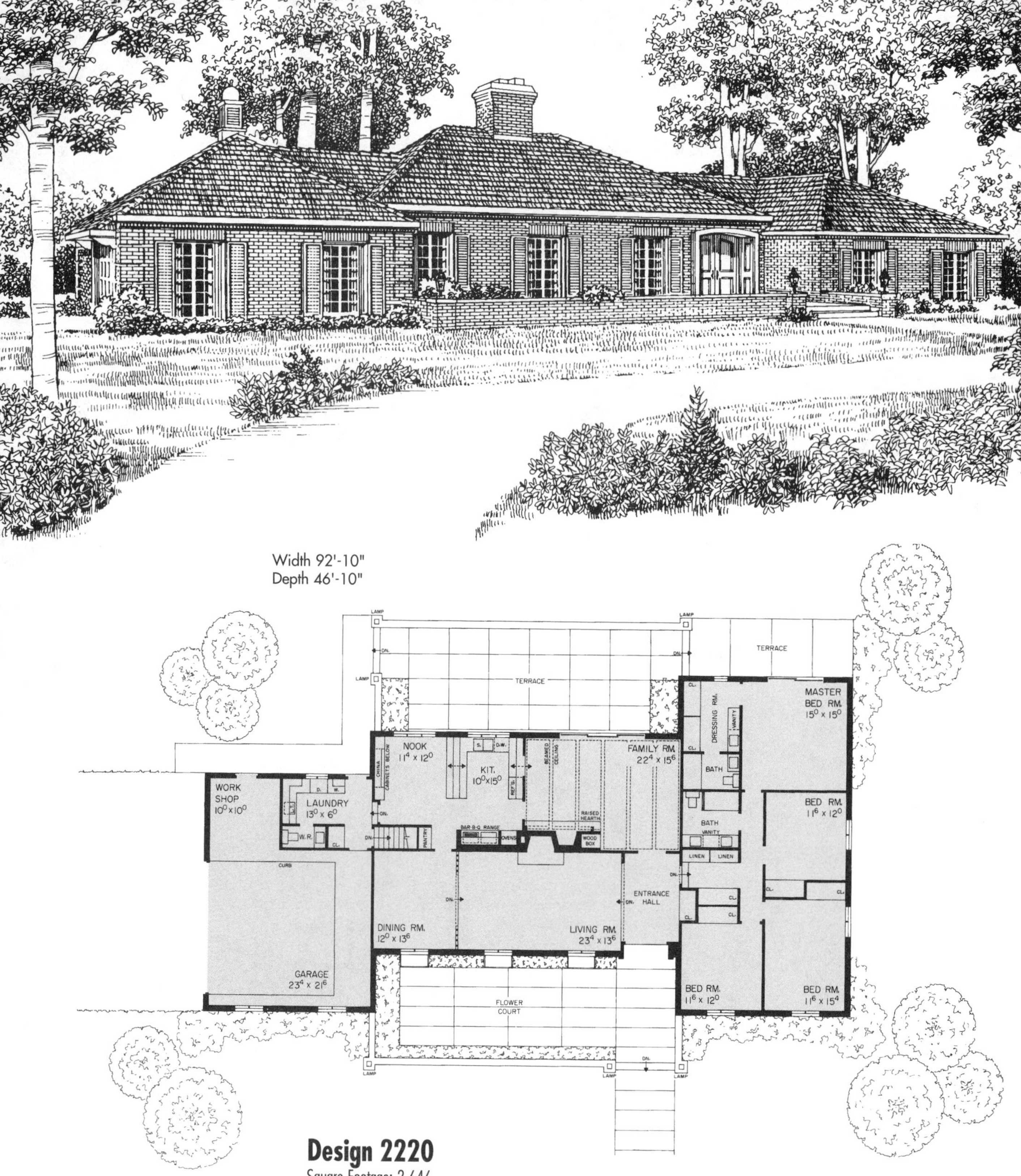
Width 92'-10"
Depth 46'-10"
TERRACE
TERRACE
LAMP
DN.
MASTER BED RM. $15^0 \times 15^0$
DRESSING RM.
VANITY
BATH
NOOK $11^4 \times 12^0$
CHINA CABINETS BELOW
KIT. $10^0 \times 15^0$
BEAMED CEILING
FAMILY RM. $22^4 \times 15^6$
WORK SHOP $10^0 \times 10^0$
LAUNDRY $13^0 \times 6^0$
W.R.
CL.
PANTRY
BAR-B-Q RANGE
OVENS
RAISED HEARTH
WOOD BOX
BED RM. $11^6 \times 12^0$
BATH
VANITY
LINEN
LINEN
CURB
ENTRANCE HALL
DINING RM. $12^0 \times 13^6$
LIVING RM. $23^4 \times 13^6$
GARAGE $23^4 \times 21^6$
BED RM. $11^6 \times 12^0$
BED RM. $11^6 \times 15^4$
FLOWER COURT

Design 2220

Square Footage: 2,646

L **D**

Design by
Home Planners

■ The gracious formality of this home is reminiscent of popular French styling. The hip roof, the brick quoins, the cornice details, the arched window heads, the distinctive shutters, the recessed double front doors, the massive center chimney and the delightful flower court are all features which set the dramatic appeal of this home. This floor plan is a favorite of many. The four-bedroom, two-bath sleeping wing is a zone by itself. Further, the formal living and dining rooms are ideally located—they function well together for entertaining and they look out upon the pleasant flower court. Overlooking the raised living terrace at the rear are the family and breakfast rooms and work center. Don't miss the laundry, extra wash room and workshop in garage.

Design 3368

Square Footage: 2,722

L **D**

QUOTE ONE®

Cost to build? See page 516 to order complete cost estimate to build this house in your area!

■ Rooflines are the key to the interesting exterior of this design. Their configuration allows for sloped ceilings in the gathering room and large foyer. Both the gathering room and the dining room offer access to the rear terrace via sliding glass doors. The master bedroom suite has a huge walk-in closet, garden whirlpool and separate shower. Two family bedrooms share a full bath. One of these bedrooms could be used as a media room with pass-through wet bar. Note the large kitchen with conversation bay and the wide terrace to the rear.

Design by
Home Planners

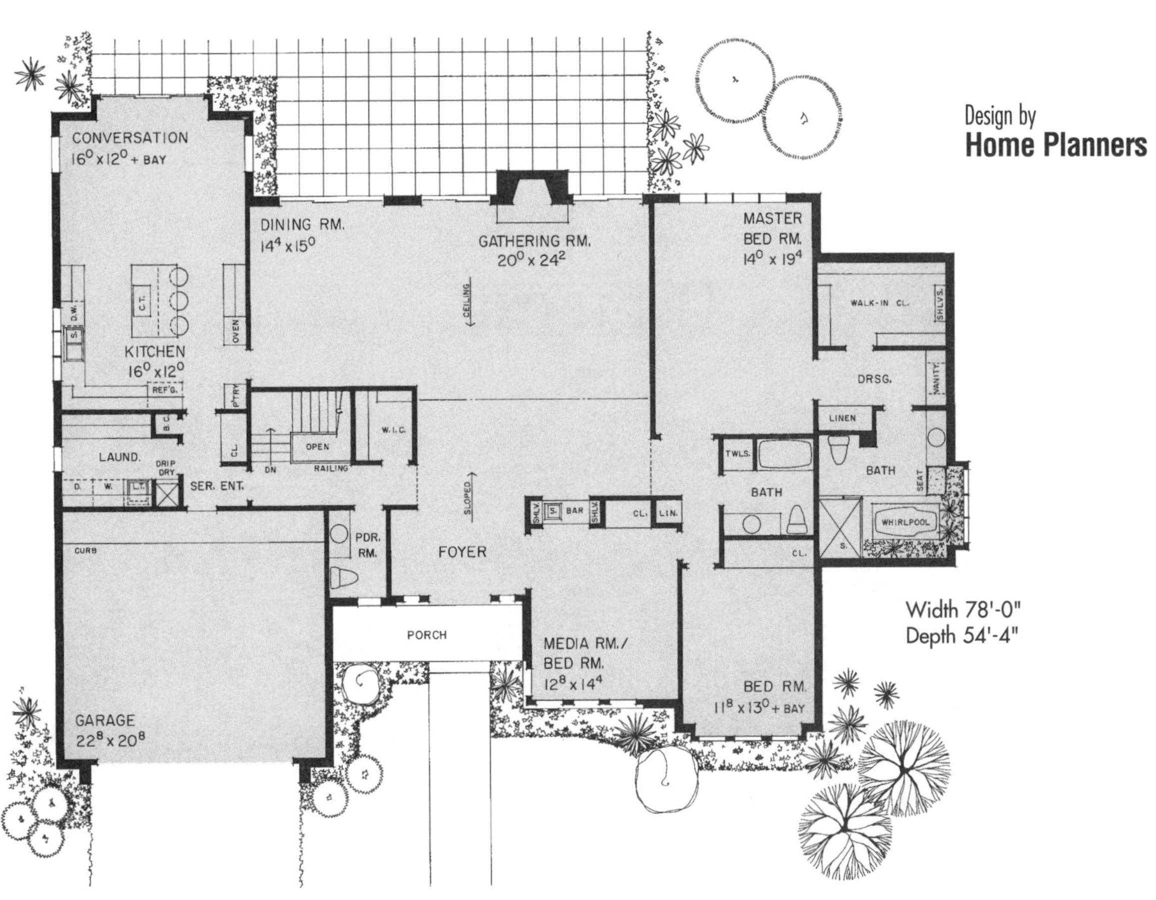
CONVERSATION
16^0 x 12^0 + BAY
D.W.
S.
C.T.
OVEN
KITCHEN
16^0 x 12^0
REF'G.
PTRY
DINING RM.
14^4 x 15^0
GATHERING RM.
20^0 x 24^2
CEILING
MASTER
BED RM.
14^0 x 19^4
WALK-IN CL.
SHLVS.
DRSG.
VANITY
LINEN
TWLS.
BATH
SEAT
WHIRLPOOL
S.
CL.
BATH
LAUND.
DRIP DRY
D.
W.
L.T.
CL.
OPEN
W.I.C.
DN
RAILING
SER. ENT.
SLOPED
SHLV.
BAR
CL.
LIN.
PDR.
RM.
FOYER
CURB
PORCH
MEDIA RM./
BED RM.
12^8 x 14^4
BED RM.
11^8 x 13^0 + BAY
GARAGE
22^8 x 20^8

Width 78'-0"
Depth 54'-4"

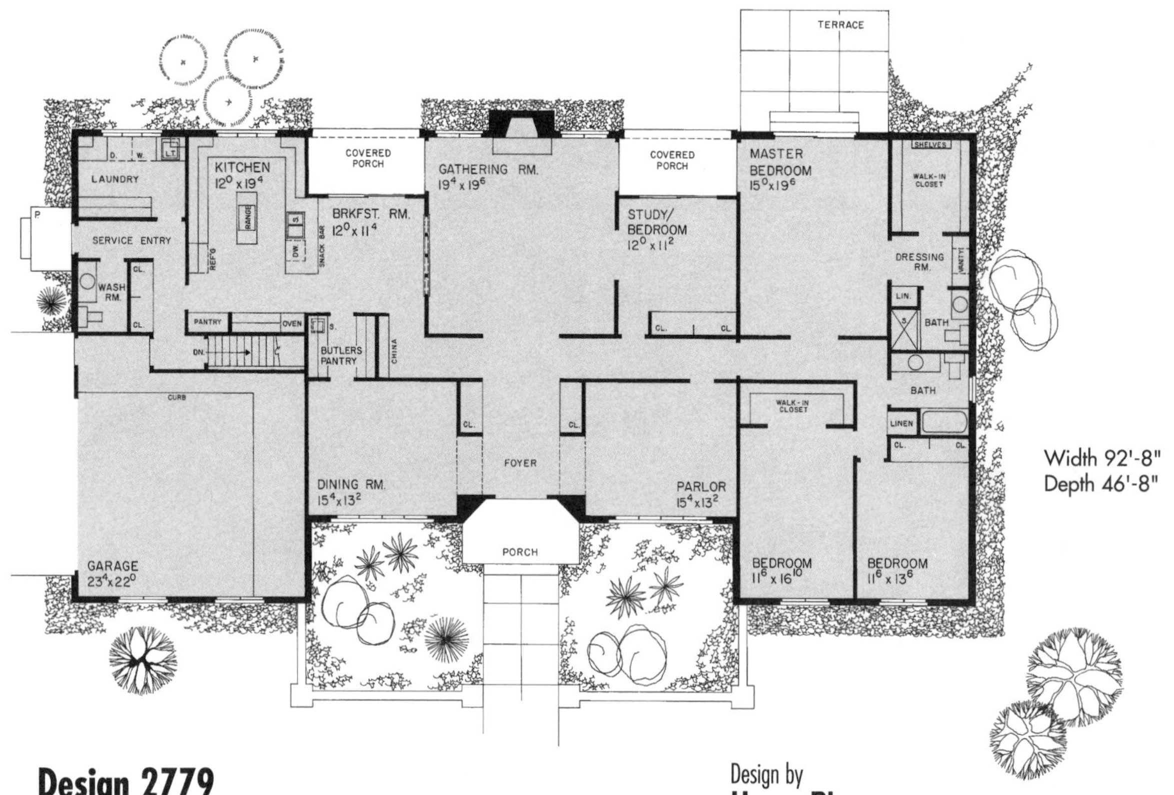

TERRACE
COVERED PORCH
COVERED PORCH
LAUNDRY
KITCHEN
$12^0 \times 19^4$
BRKFST. RM.
$12^0 \times 11^4$
GATHERING RM.
$19^4 \times 19^6$
STUDY/ BEDROOM
$12^0 \times 11^2$
MASTER BEDROOM
$15^0 \times 19^6$
WALK-IN CLOSET
DRESSING RM.
BATH
BATH
LINEN
WALK-IN CLOSET
SERVICE ENTRY
WASH RM.
PANTRY
OVEN
BUTLERS PANTRY
CHINA
SNACK BAR
RANGE
REF'G
DN
CURB
FOYER
DINING RM.
$15^4 \times 13^2$
PARLOR
$15^4 \times 13^2$
PORCH
GARAGE
$23^4 \times 22^0$
BEDROOM
$11^6 \times 16^{10}$
BEDROOM
$11^6 \times 13^6$
Width 92'-8"
Depth 46'-8"

Design 2779

Square Footage: 3,225

L **D**

Design by
Home Planners

■ This French design carries impressive exterior details. Its highlights are a hip roof, multi-paned windows a brick privacy wall and double front doors. The inside is just as appealing. Note the unique placement of rooms and features: formal dining room with butler's pantry, sizable parlor, gathering room with fireplace and sliding glass doors, and an adjacent study. The U-shaped kitchen has an island range, a snack bar, a breakfast nook and a pantry. Bedrooms are in the right wing of the home. They include two family bedrooms and a large master suite. The master suite is made special by sliding glass doors to a private terrace, a walk-in closet and a bath with dressing area. Note the placement of one of the bedrooms—with entry from the gathering room—making it a perfect study if needed.

QUOTE ONE®

Cost to build? See page 516 to order complete cost estimate to build this house in your area!

© Copyright 1987 Select Home Designs All rights reserved

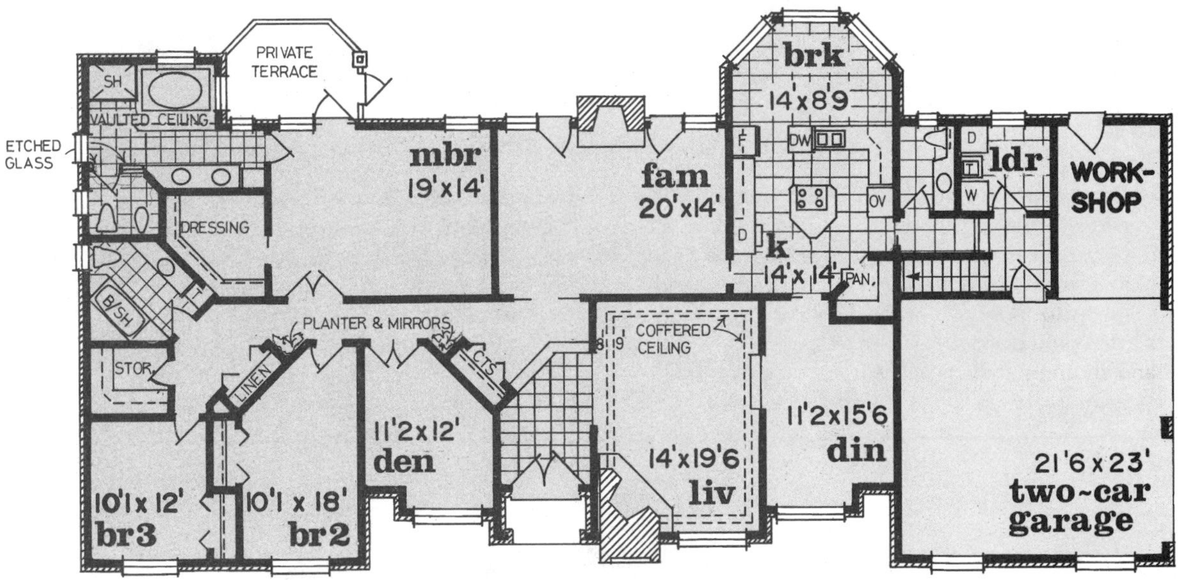
PRIVATE TERRACE
brk
14'x8'9
ETCHED GLASS
SH
VAULTED CEILING
mbr
19'x14'
fam
20'x14'
DW
OV
ldr
WORK-SHOP
DRESSING
k
14'x14'
PAN.
PLANTER & MIRRORS
COFFERED CEILING
B/SH
STOR
LINEN
CTS
11'2x12'
den
14'x19'6
liv
11'2x15'6
din
21'6 x 23'
two-car garage
10'1 x 12'
br3
10'1 x 18'
br2

Width 94'-2"
Depth 46'-5"

Design Q278

Square Footage: 2,796

■ This sprawling ranch has a brick exterior with quoins and sweeping roof accents. Double doors open to a sunken foyer which opens on the right to a coffered living room with corner fireplace. The dining room is nearby and features a pocket door to the convenient kitchen with cooktop island, walk-in pantry and bayed breakfast nook. The large family room has a masonry fireplace flanked by French doors to the rear yard. A private den has double-door access and a lovely box-bay window. Three bedrooms include two family bedrooms and the master suite. Nothing is left to chance in the master bedroom. It features a dressing room and private terrace, plus a vaulted bath with spa, twin vanity and shower. The two-car garage is made even more useful with a workshop area that has direct access to the yard. Plans include details for both a basement and a crawlspace foundation.

Design by
Select Home Designs

Design Q244

Square Footage: 2,419

Design by
Select Home Designs

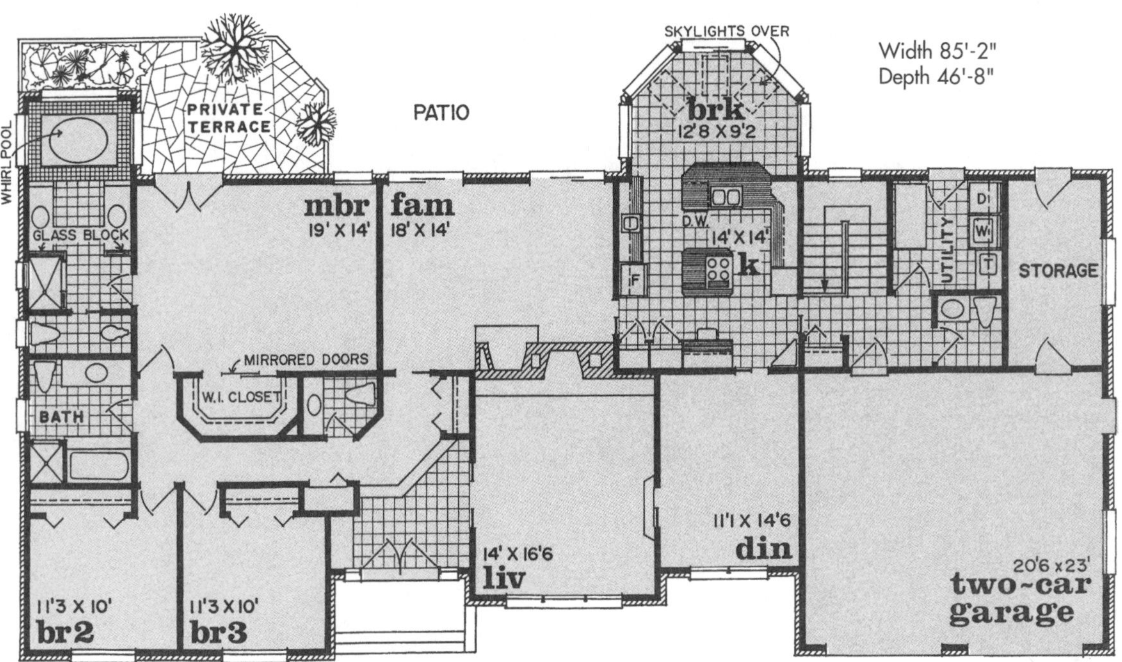

SKYLIGHTS OVER
Width 85'-2"
Depth 46'-8"
PRIVATE TERRACE
PATIO
WHIRLPOOL
GLASS BLOCK
mbr
19' X 14'
fam
18' X 14'
brk
12'8 X 9'2
D.W.
14' X 14'
k
F
UTILITY
D
W
T
STORAGE
MIRRORED DOORS
W.I. CLOSET
BATH
11'1 X 14'6
din
14' X 16'6
liv
20'6 x 23'
two-car garage
11'3 X 10'
br2
11'3 X 10'
br3

■ Long and low, with brick siding and multi-paned shuttered windows, this ranch home is the picture of elegance. Enter through double doors to a sunken foyer and sunken living room with fireplace. The dining room is beyond the living room and a step up. It also accesses the kitchen. The family room is to the rear of the plan and features a fireplace and sliding glass doors to the rear patio. The island kitchen has counter and cabinet space to suit any gourmet. Its attached breakfast nook is sunny due to skylights above. The master bedroom is huge and has a private terrace and bath with double sinks, whirlpool tub and separate shower. Family bedrooms are to the front of the plan. Plans include details for both a basement and a crawlspace foundation.

© Copyright 1985 Select Home Designs All rights reserved

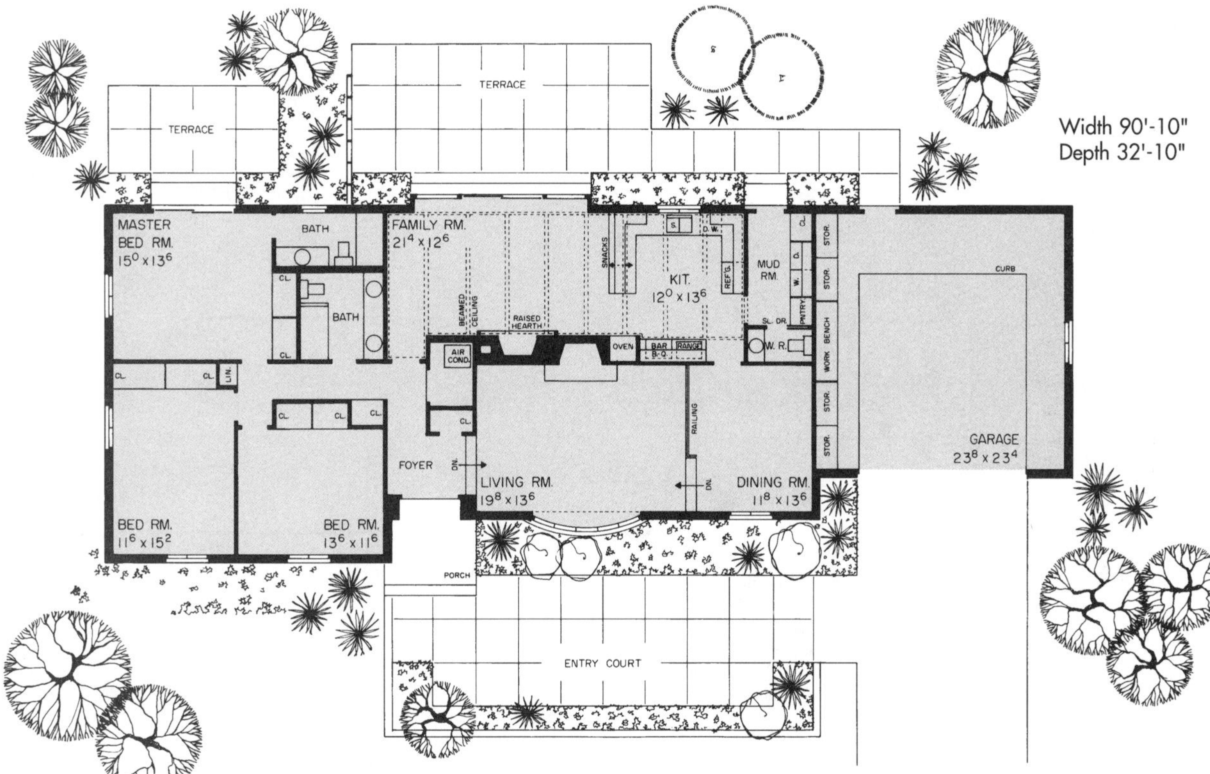

Width 90'-10"
Depth 32'-10"

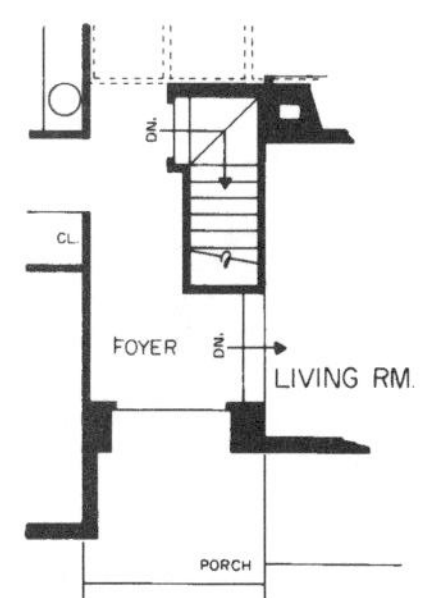
CL.
FOYER
LIVING RM.
PORCH

Optional Basement

Design 1892

Square Footage: 2,036

Design by
Home Planners

L D

■ The romance of a French Provincial is captured here by the hip roofs, the charm of the window detailing, the brick quoins at the corners, the delicate dentil work at the cornices, the massive centered chimney and the recessed double front doors. The slightly raised entry court completes the picture. The basic floor plan is a favorite of many. And little wonder, for all the areas work well together, while still maintaining a fine degree of separation of functions. The highlight of the interior, perhaps, will be the sunken living room. The family room, with its beam ceiling, will not be far behind in popularity. The separate dining room, mud room and efficient kitchen complete the livability.

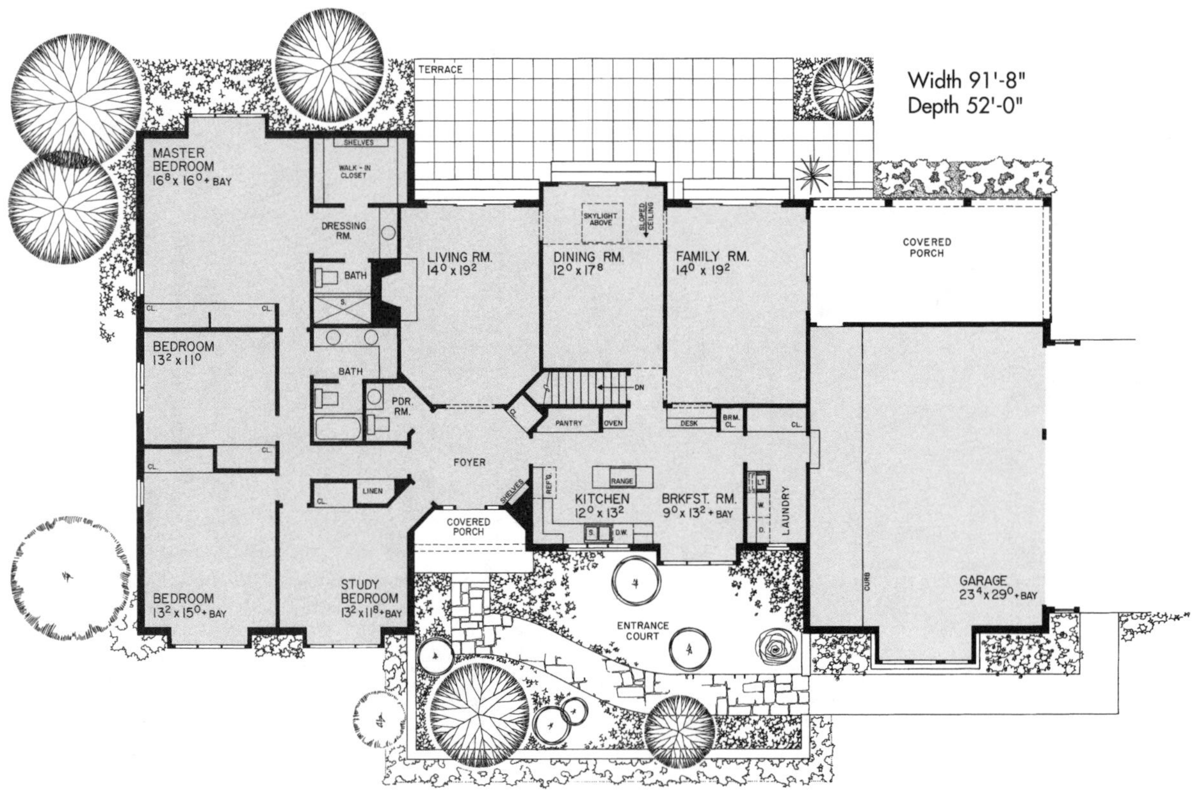

TERRACE
Width 91'-8"
Depth 52'-0"
MASTER BEDROOM
16^8 x 16^0 + BAY
SHELVES
WALK-IN CLOSET
DRESSING RM.
BATH
LIVING RM.
14^0 x 19^2
SKYLIGHT ABOVE
SLOPED CEILING
DINING RM.
12^0 x 17^8
FAMILY RM.
14^0 x 19^2
COVERED PORCH
CL.
CL.
BEDROOM
13^2 x 11^0
BATH
PDR. RM.
DN
PANTRY
OVEN
DESK
BRM. CL.
CL.
CL.
CL.
FOYER
LINEN
CL.
SHELVES
REF'G
RANGE
KITCHEN
12^0 x 13^2
BRKFST. RM.
9^0 x 13^2 + BAY
LAUNDRY
S.
D.W.
COVERED PORCH
BEDROOM
13^2 x 15^0 + BAY
STUDY BEDROOM
13^2 x 11^8 + BAY
ENTRANCE COURT
CURB
GARAGE
23^4 x 29^0 + BAY

Design 2851

Square Footage: 2,739

L

Design by
Home Planners

■ This spacious one-story home has a classic Country French hip roof. Beyond the covered porch is an octagonal foyer. All of the living areas overlook the rear yard. Features include a fireplace in the living room, a skylight in the dining room and a second set of sliding glass doors in the family room leading to a covered porch. An island cooktop and other-built-ins are featured in the roomy kitchen. Adjacent is the breakfast room which can be used for informal dining. The four bedrooms and the baths are clustered in one wing. Bay windows brighten the master bedroom, the breakfast room and the three-car garage.

QUOTE ONE®

Cost to build? See page 516 to order complete cost estimate to build this house in your area!

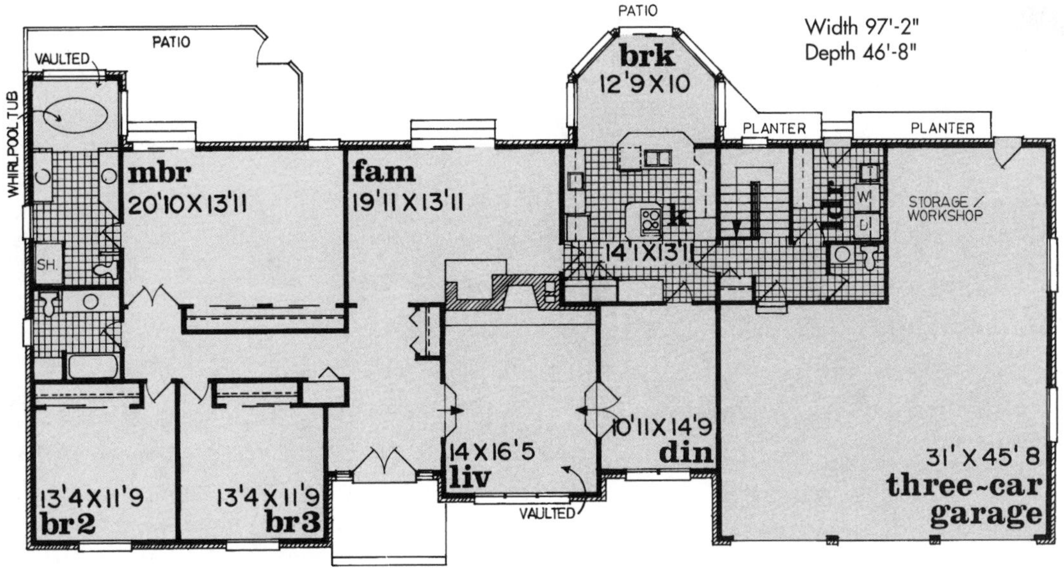
PATIO
VAULTED
WHIRLPOOL TUB
SH.
mbr
20'10X13'11
fam
19'11X13'11
PATIO
brk
12'9X10
PLANTER
PLANTER
k
14'1X13'11
ldr
W
D
STORAGE / WORKSHOP
10'11X14'9
din
14X16'5
liv
VAULTED
13'4X11'9
br2
13'4X11'9
br3
31' X45' 8
three-car garage

Width 97'-2"
Depth 46'-8"

Design Q288

Square Footage 2,559

Design by
Select Home Designs

■ A low profile, accented with brick cladding, quoins and shuttered windows, enhances the front exterior of this one-story plan. The weather-protected entry opens to a sunken living room with vaulted ceiling and fireplace. Double doors open to the formal dining room which also has direct access to the island kitchen. An octagonal breakfast bay overlooks the rear patio. The family room also has a warming fireplace and sliding glass doors to the patio. The master bedroom is a true retreat with a private patio, long wall closet and bath with vaulted ceiling over a whirlpool tub. The family bedrooms share a full hall bath. A three-car garage is reached through a door in the service area which also holds a washroom, stairs to the basement and the laundry. Note the large workshop or storage area in the garage. Plans include details for both a basement and a crawlspace foundation.

Rear Elevation

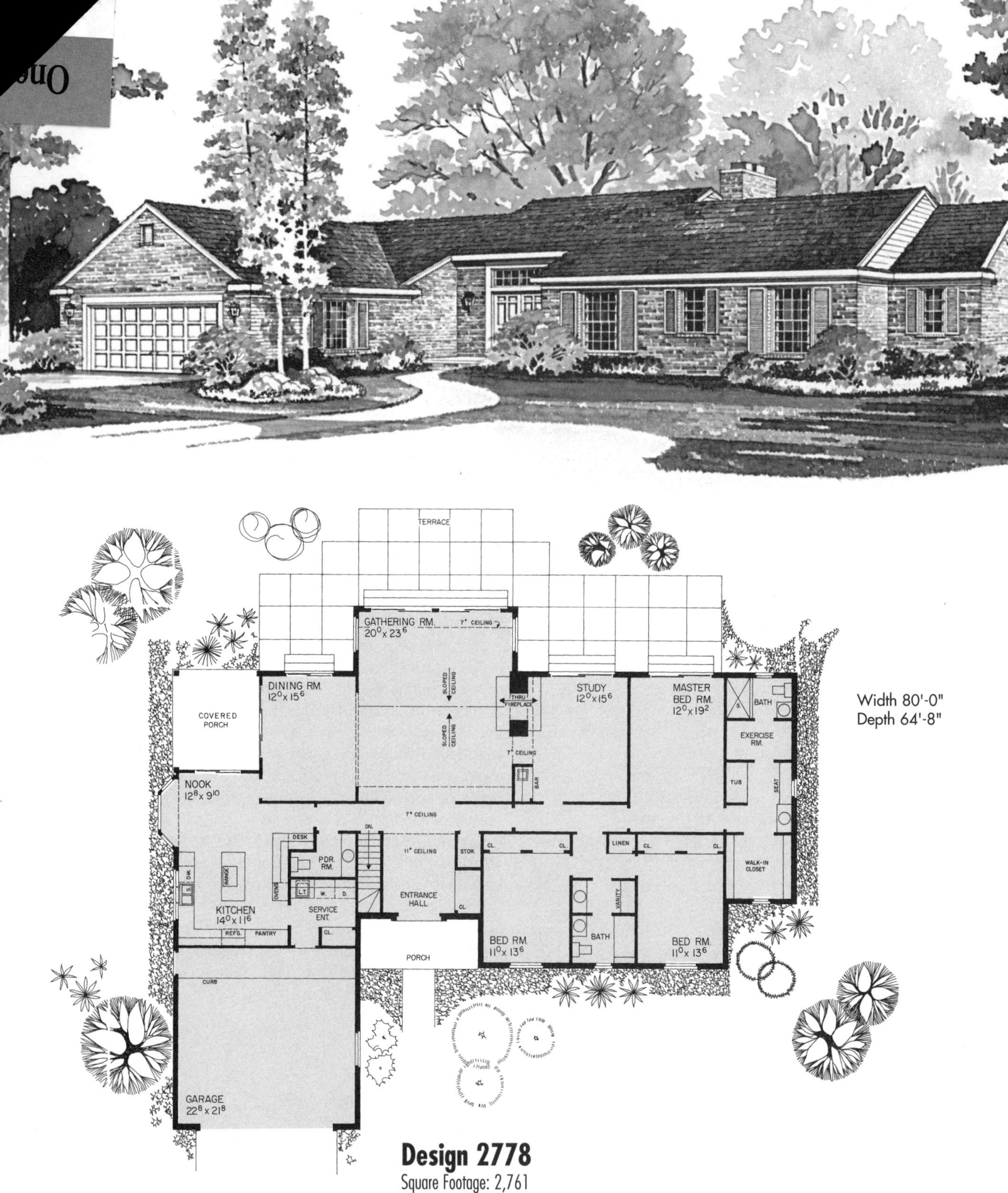
TERRACE
GATHERING RM.
20⁰ x 23⁶
7' CEILING
SLOPED CEILING
THRU FIREPLACE
BAR
DINING RM.
12⁰ x 15⁶
COVERED PORCH
STUDY
12⁰ x 15⁶
MASTER BED RM.
12⁰ x 19²
BATH
EXERCISE RM.
TUB
SEAT
WALK-IN CLOSET
NOOK
12⁸ x 9¹⁰
7' CEILING
11' CEILING
DESK
PDR. RM.
DN.
STOR.
CL.
LINEN
KITCHEN
14⁰ x 11⁶
RANGE
OVENS
REFG.
PANTRY
SERVICE ENT.
ENTRANCE HALL
VANITY
BED RM.
11⁰ x 13⁶
BATH
BED RM.
11⁰ x 13⁶
PORCH
CURB
GARAGE
22⁸ x 21⁸
Width 80'-0"
Depth 64'-8"

Design 2778

Square Footage: 2,761

D

■ No matter what the occasion, family and friends alike will enjoy the sizable gathering room in this home. This room has a through-fireplace to the study and two sets of sliding glass doors to the large rear terrace. Indoor/outdoor living can also be enjoyed in the dining room, study and master bedroom. There is also covered porch access through sliding glass doors in the dining room and breakfast nook. Three bedrooms include two family suites sharing a full bath. The master suite has a thoughtfully appointed bath with exercise room, double sinks, separate tub and shower and walk-in closet. A service entrance holds the laundry area and access to the two-car garage. Note the eleven-foot ceiling in the entrance hall and the central hall.

Design by
Home Planners

Design 2926

Main Level: 1,570 square feet
Upper Level: 598 square feet
Lower Level: 1,080 square feet
Total: 3,248 square feet

■ An incredible combination of curving lines and circles in this ultramodern design makes for an interesting floor plan. The dramatic use of balconies and overlooks highlights a first-floor gathering room with a fireplace open to the study, a formal dining room and a kitchen with a circular breakfast room. A goblet-shaped bedroom on this floor has a balcony and a full bath. Reached by a curved stair, the upper level is dominated by the master suite. A lower-level activities room with a bar and a fireplace, and an exercise room with an attached sauna, a hot tub and a bath overlook the lower terrace. Take special note of the generous use of skylights throughout.

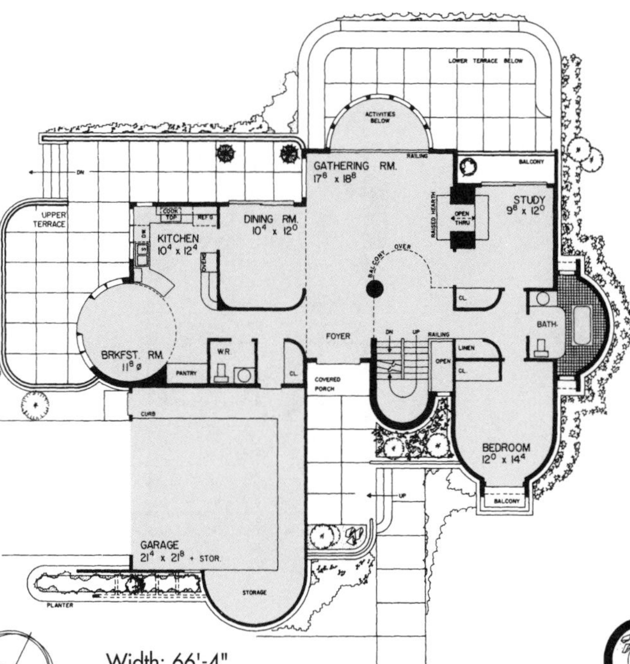

GATHERING RM.
17^{8} x 18^{8}
STUDY
9^{8} x 12^{0}
DINING RM.
10^{4} x 12^{0}
KITCHEN
10^{4} x 12^{4}
UPPER TERRACE
BRKFST. RM.
11^{8} ø
FOYER
BATH
BEDROOM
12^{0} x 14^{4}
GARAGE
21^{4} x 21^{8} + STOR.

Width: 66'-4"
Depth: 63'-8"

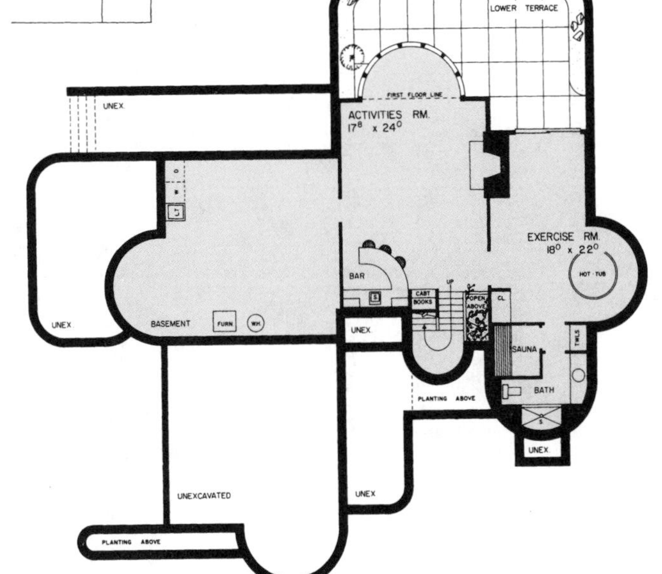

LOWER TERRACE
ACTIVITIES RM.
17^{8} x 24^{0}
EXERCISE RM.
18^{0} x 22^{0}
BAR
BASEMENT
SAUNA
BATH
UNEX
UNEXCAVATED

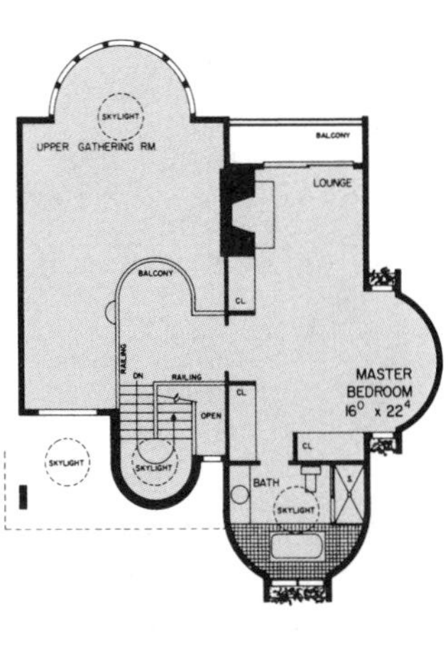

UPPER GATHERING RM.
LOUNGE
MASTER
BEDROOM
16^{0} x 22^{4}
BATH

Design by
Home Planners

Design 2850

Main Level: 1,530 square feet
Upper Level: 984 square feet
Lower Level: 951 square feet
Total: 3,465 square feet

L **D**

■ Enter this impressive Spanish design through a courtyard with pool and garden area. The entry is offset to the right and opens to a foyer with the formal living room on the left and the giant-sized family room to the rear. The family room has a sloped ceiling, raised-hearth fireplace and sliding glass doors to a rear terrace. A formal dining room connects to the living room and also to the L-shaped island kitchen with attached breakfast room. A mud room leads to the three-car garage and features a laundry area and wash room. To the right of the foyer, and down a few steps is a teen activities room, a bedroom with bath and a study. On the upper level are three more bedrooms, including the master suite. Here you'll find a private balcony, a walk-in closet and a bath with dressing room and make-up vanity.

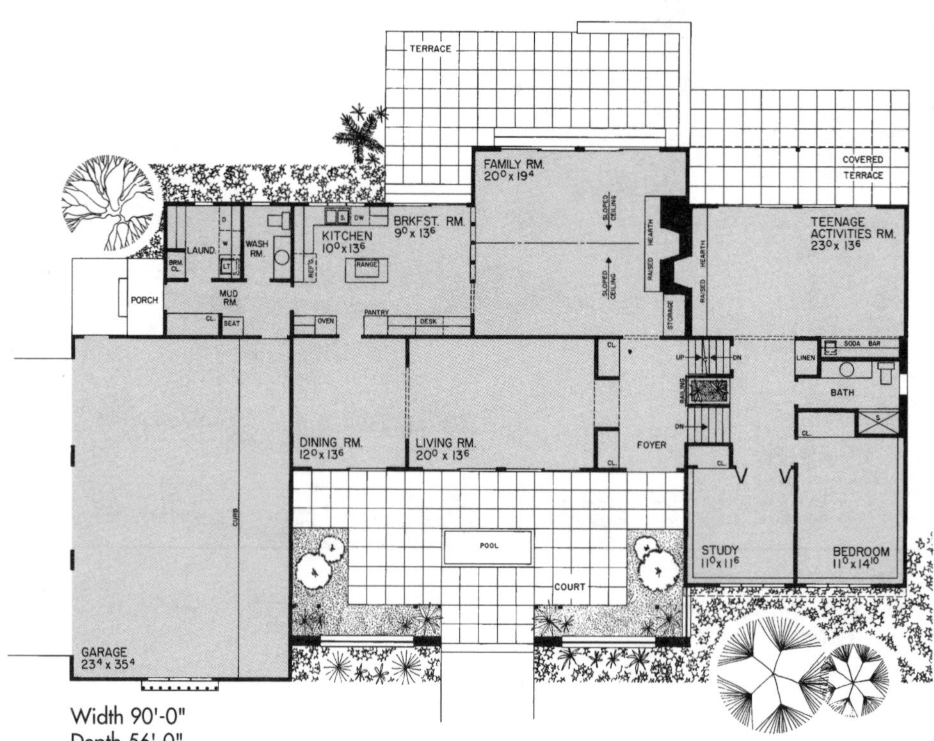
TERRACE
FAMILY RM. 20^{0} x 19^{4}
COVERED TERRACE
TEENAGE ACTIVITIES RM. 23^{0} x 13^{6}
BRKFST. RM. 9^{0} x 13^{6}
KITCHEN 10^{0} x 13^{6}
RANGE
LAUND.
WASH RM.
MUD RM.
PORCH
SEAT
OVEN
PANTRY
DESK
SLOPED CEILING
RAISED HEARTH
STORAGE
SODA BAR
LINEN
BATH
FOYER
RAILING
DINING RM. 12^{0} x 13^{6}
LIVING RM. 20^{0} x 13^{6}
STUDY 11^{0} x 11^{6}
BEDROOM 11^{0} x 14^{10}
POOL
COURT
CURB
GARAGE 23^{4} x 35^{4}
Width 90'-0"
Depth 56'-0"

Design by
Home Planners

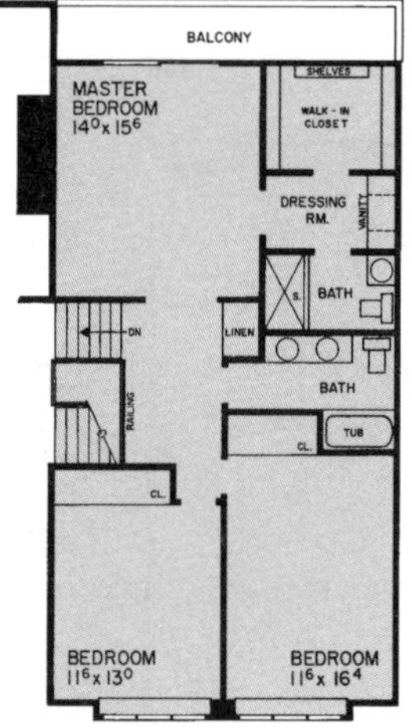
BALCONY
MASTER BEDROOM 14^{0} x 15^{6}
SHELVES
WALK-IN CLOSET
DRESSING RM.
VANITY
BATH
LINEN
BATH
TUB
DN
RAILING
CL.
BEDROOM 11^{6} x 13^{0}
BEDROOM 11^{6} x 16^{4}

QUOTE ONE®
Cost to build? See page 516
to order complete cost estimate
to build this house in your area!

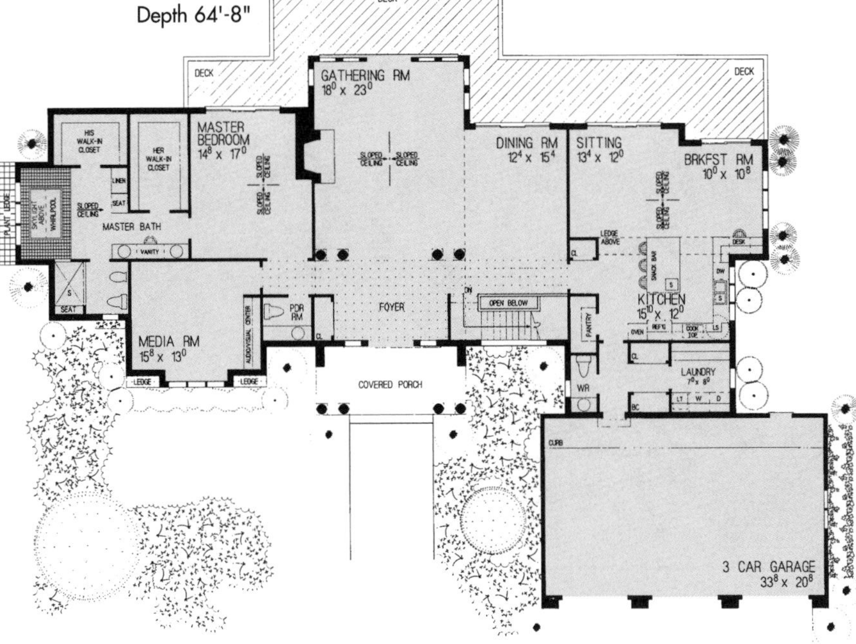
Width 98'-0"
Depth 64'-8"
DECK
GATHERING RM
18^0 x 23^0
MASTER BEDROOM
14^8 x 17^0
DINING RM
12^4 x 15^4
SITTING
13^4 x 12^0
BRKFST RM
10^0 x 10^8
MASTER BATH
FOYER
KITCHEN
15^{10} x 12^0
MEDIA RM
15^8 x 13^0
COVERED PORCH
LAUNDRY
3 CAR GARAGE
33^8 x 20^8

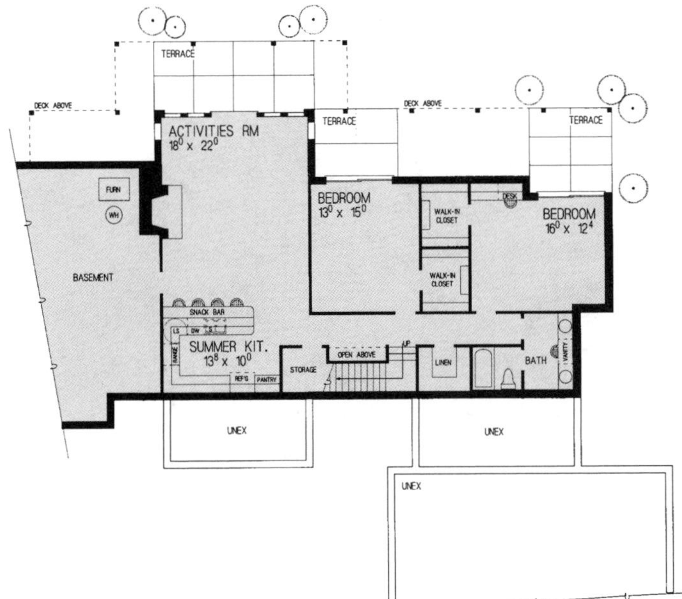
TERRACE
DECK ABOVE
ACTIVITIES RM
18^0 x 22^0
BEDROOM
13^0 x 15^0
BEDROOM
16^0 x 12^4
BASEMENT
SUMMER KIT.
13^8 x 10^0
BATH
UNEX

Design by
Home Planners

Design 3311

Main Level: 2,662 square feet
Lower Level: 1,548 square feet
Total: 4,210 square feet

L D

■ Here's a hillside haven for family living with plenty of room to entertain in style. Enter the main level from a dramatic columned portico that leads to a large entry hall. The gathering room, graced by a fireplace and sliding glass doors to the rear deck, is straight back and adjoins a formal dining area. A true gourmet kitchen with plenty of room for casual eating and conversation is nearby. The abundantly appointed master suite on this level is complemented by a luxurious bath. Note the media room to the front of the house. On the lower level are two more bedrooms—each with access to the rear terrace, a full bath, a large activity area with fireplace and a convenient summer kitchen.

QUOTE ONE®
Cost to build? See page 516 to order complete cost estimate to build this house in your area!

Design Q223

Square Footage: 1,530
Unfinished Basement: 1,440 square feet

■ Rustic in nature, this hillside home offers a surrounding deck and upper-level balcony on the exterior to complement its horizontal siding and stone detailing. The entry opens to a staircase leading up to the main level or down to finish-later space in the basement. The kitchen is at the heart of the home and has miles of counter space and a pass-through bar to the dining room. Both the living and dining rooms have sliding glass doors to the deck. A corner fireplace warms and lights both areas. One large bedroom sits to the right of the plan and has a private bath and deck access. Two additional bedrooms with a shared bath sit to the left of the plan. One of these bedrooms has deck access. Unfinished lower-level space adds 1,440 square feet to the total for future development.

Rear Elevation

Design by
Select Home Designs

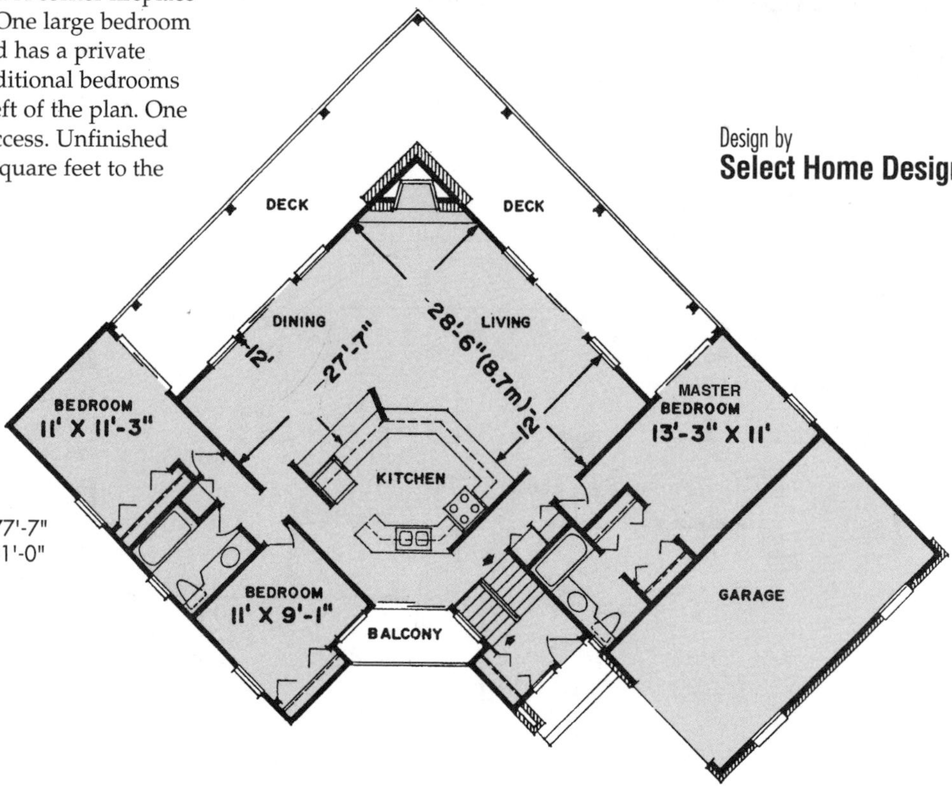

DECK
DECK
DINING
LIVING
12'
27'-7"
28'-6"(8.7m)
12'
BEDROOM
11' X 11'-3"
MASTER BEDROOM
13'-3" X 11'
KITCHEN
GARAGE
BEDROOM
11' X 9'-1"
BALCONY

Width 77'-7"
Depth 61'-0"

Design by
Home Planners

Design 4308

Main Level: 1,494 square feet
Upper Level: 597 square feet
Lower Level: 1,035 square feet
Total: 3,126 square feet

L

■ You can't help but feel spoiled by this design. Downstairs from the entry is a large living room with sloped ceiling and fireplace. Nearby is the U-shaped kitchen with a pass-through to the dining room. Also on this level, the master suite boasts a fireplace and a sliding glass door onto the deck, plus a walk-in closet and private bath. The living and dining rooms also feature deck access. Upstairs are two bedrooms with a shared bath. A balcony sitting area overlooks the living room. Finish the lower level when your budget and space needs allow. It includes a play room with a fireplace, a half-bath, a large bar and sliding glass doors onto the patio. Note the great storage space here.

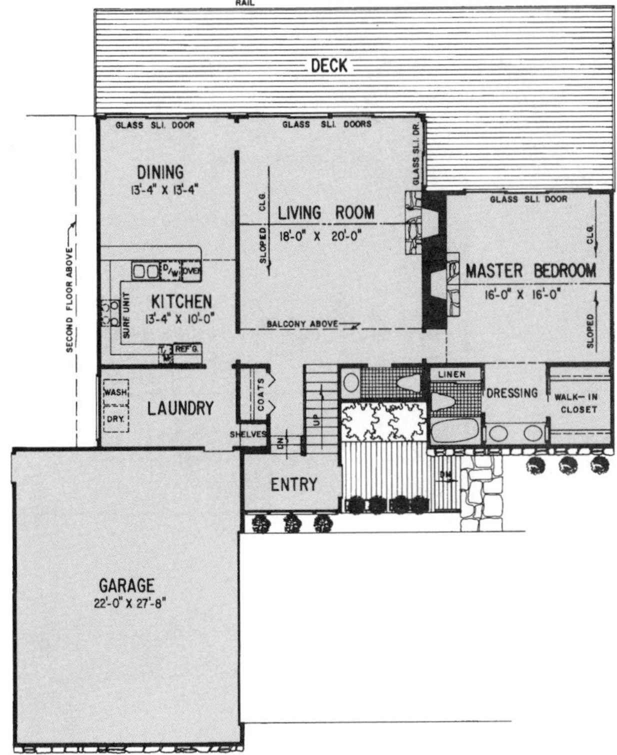
RAIL
DECK
GLASS SLI. DOOR
GLASS SLI. DOORS
DINING
13'-4" X 13'-4"
LIVING ROOM
18'-0" X 20'-0"
SLOPED CLG.
GLASS SLI. DOOR
MASTER BEDROOM
16'-0" X 16'-0"
KITCHEN
13'-4" X 10'-0"
BALCONY ABOVE
SECOND FLOOR ABOVE
LINEN
DRESSING
WALK-IN CLOSET
WASH
DRY
LAUNDRY
COATS
SHELVES
UP
DN
ENTRY
GARAGE
22'-0" X 27'-8"

Width 59'-0"
Depth 69'-8"

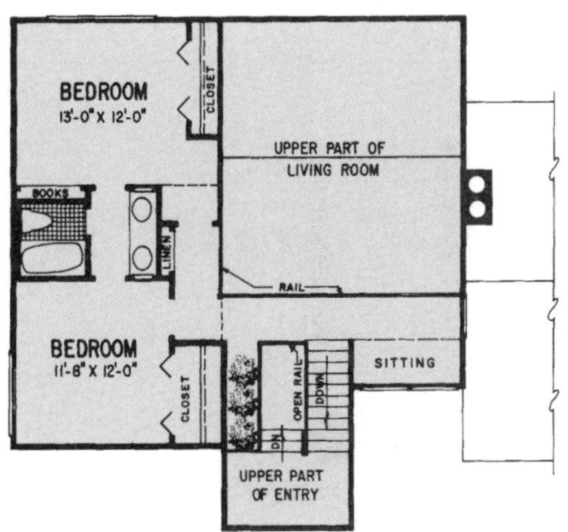
BEDROOM
13'-0" X 12'-0"
CLOSET
UPPER PART OF
LIVING ROOM
BOOKS
LINEN
RAIL
BEDROOM
11'-8" X 12'-0"
CLOSET
OPEN RAIL
DOWN
SITTING
UPPER PART
OF ENTRY

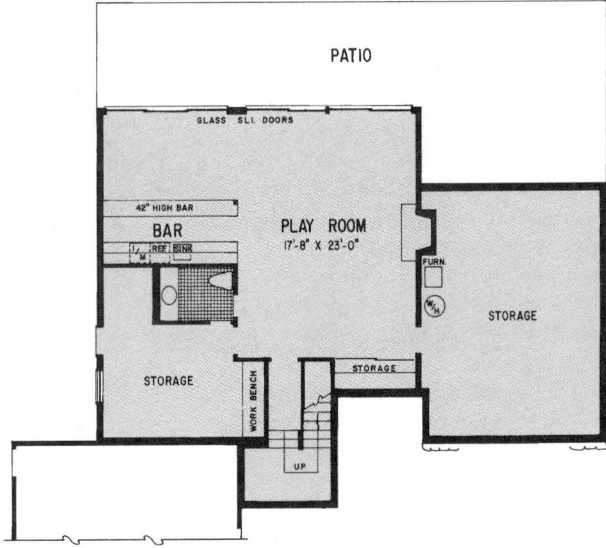
PATIO
GLASS SLI. DOORS
42" HIGH BAR
BAR
PLAY ROOM
17'-8" X 23'-0"
FURN.
STORAGE
STORAGE
WORK BENCH
STORAGE
UP

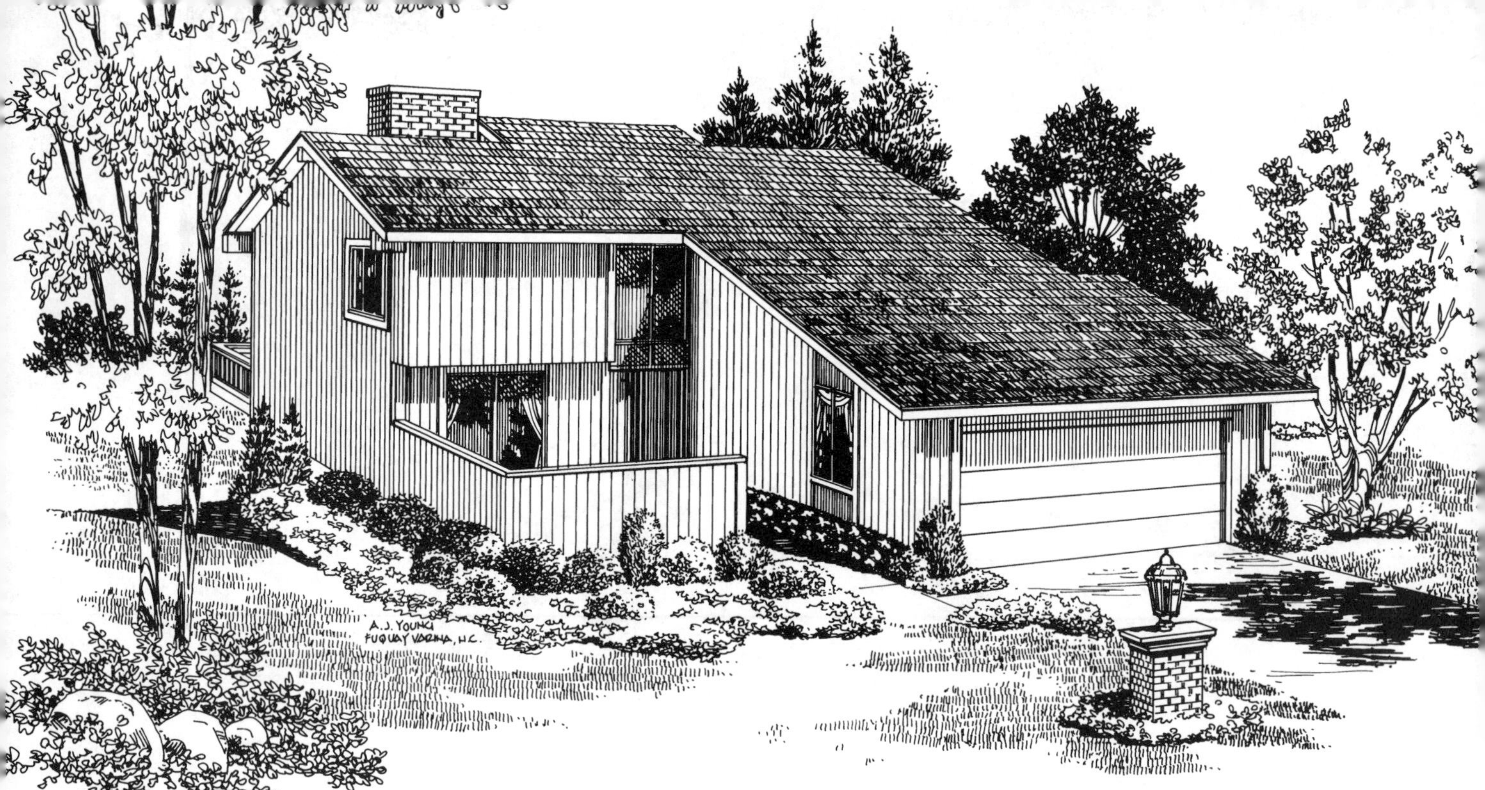

Design by
Home Planners

Design 2716

Main Level: 1,013 square feet
Upper Level: 885 square feet
Lower Level: 1,074 square feet
Total: 2,972 square feet

L

■ A genuinely luxurious master suite! It overlooks the gathering room through shuttered windows and includes a private balcony, a sitting/dressing room and a full bath. An additional bedroom and full bath are also found on this level. Below, on the main level, the two-story gathering room with a raised-hearth fireplace, sloped ceiling and sliding glass doors to the main balcony opens to the dining area. The through-fireplace is shared with the study. The kitchen is U-shaped and has an attached breakfast room with sliding glass doors to the balcony. The lower level offers a family room, with a second raised-hearth fireplace, and a guest room. A two-car garage opens through a service entrance in the main house.

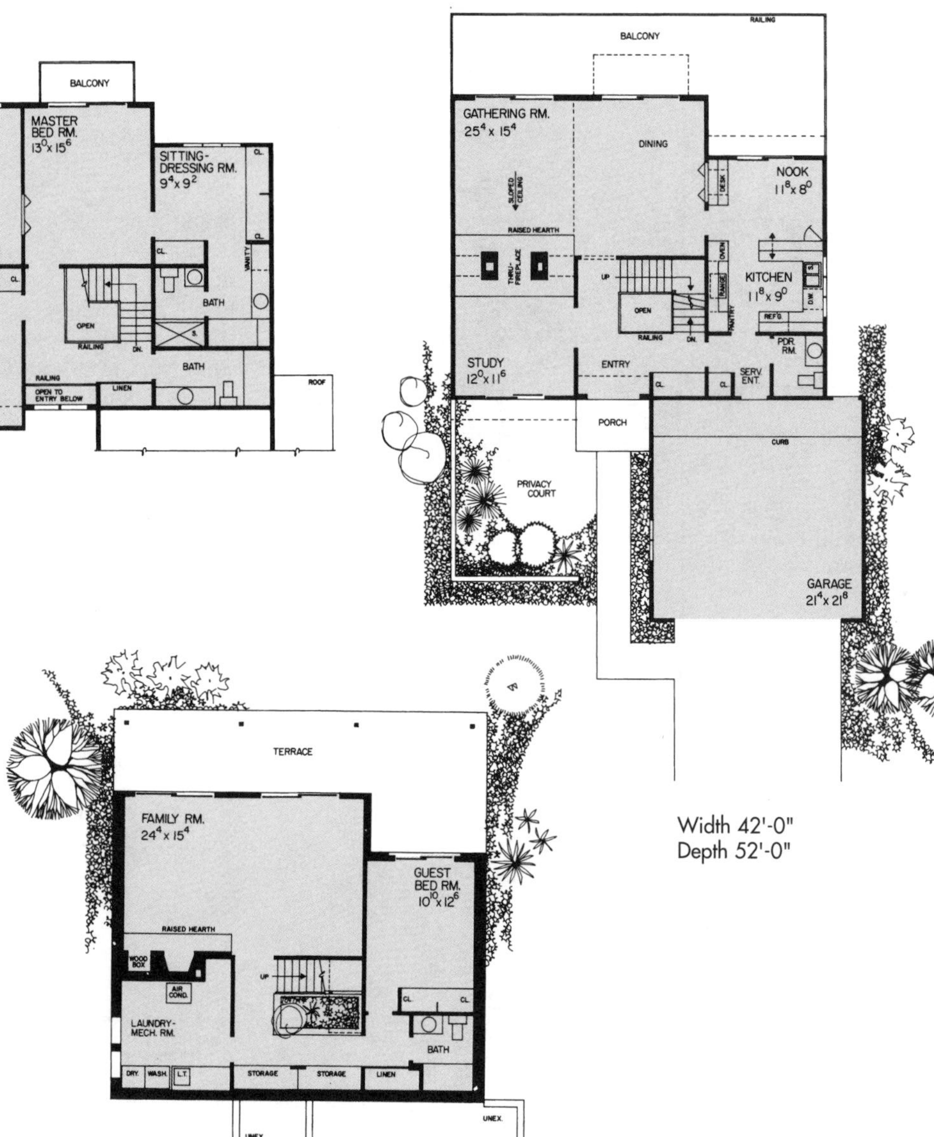

BALCONY
MASTER BED RM. 13⁰x 15⁶
SITTING-DRESSING RM. 9⁴x 9²
OPEN TO GATHERING RM. BELOW
BED RM. 12⁰x 13²
BATH
OPEN
RAILING
OPEN TO ENTRY BELOW
LINEN
ROOF
GATHERING RM. 25⁴x 15⁴
DINING
NOOK 11⁸x 8⁰
KITCHEN 11⁸x 9⁰
RAISED HEARTH
STUDY 12⁰x 11⁶
ENTRY
PORCH
PDR RM.
SERV. ENT.
PRIVACY COURT
GARAGE 21⁴x 21⁶
TERRACE
FAMILY RM. 24⁴x 15⁴
GUEST BED RM. 10¹⁰x 12⁶
LAUNDRY-MECH. RM.
STORAGE
STORAGE
LINEN
BATH
UNEX.

Width 42'-0"
Depth 52'-0"

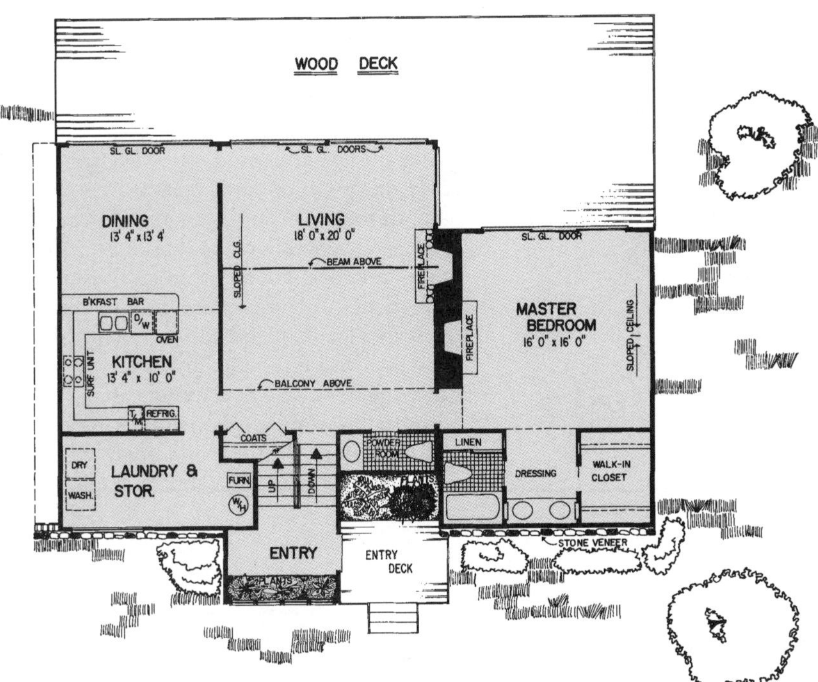
WOOD DECK
SL. GL. DOOR
SL. GL. DOORS
DINING
13' 4" x 13' 4'
LIVING
18' 0" x 20' 0"
SLOPED CLG.
BEAM ABOVE
FIREPLACE
SL. GL. DOOR
MASTER BEDROOM
16' 0" x 16' 0"
SLOPED CEILING
B'KFAST BAR
D/W
OVEN
KITCHEN
13' 4" x 10' 0"
SURF. UNIT
REFRIG.
BALCONY ABOVE
COATS
LINEN
POWDER ROOM
PLANTS
DRESSING
WALK-IN CLOSET
LAUNDRY & STOR.
DRY
WASH.
FURN.
UP
DOWN
ENTRY
ENTRY DECK
STONE VENEER
PLANTS

Width 50'-8"
Depth 47'-8"

Design 4115

Main Level: 1,494 square feet
Upper Level: 597 square feet
Total: 2,091 square feet

■ Interior spaces in this home are dramatically proportioned because of the long and varied rooflines on the exterior. The two-story living area has a sloped ceiling, as does the master bedroom and two upper-level bedrooms. The master bedroom is a fine retreat with a walk-in closet and private bath. Upper-level bedrooms are joined by a sitting room that overlooks the foyer below. Two fireplaces, a huge wooden deck, a small upstairs sitting room and a liberal number of windows make this a most comfortable residence. The U-shaped kitchen has a breakfast bar open to the dining room. Note the large convenient laundry room nearby.

Design by
Home Planners

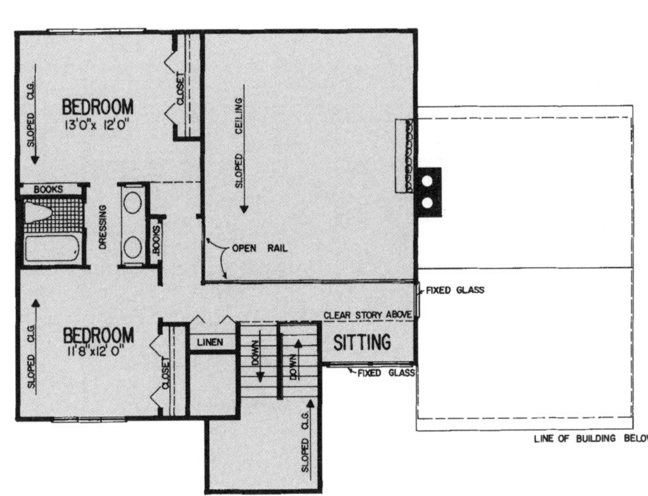
BEDROOM
13'0" x 12'0"
SLOPED CLG.
CLOSET
SLOPED CEILING
BOOKS
DRESSING
OPEN RAIL
FIXED GLASS
CLEAR STORY ABOVE
BEDROOM
11'8" x 12'0"
LINEN
DOWN
SITTING
FIXED GLASS
LINE OF BUILDING BELOW

Design by
Home Planners

Design 2511

Main Level: 1,043 square feet
Upper Level: 703 square feet
Lower Level: 794 square feet
Total: 2,540 square feet

L D

■ This outstanding multi-level home comes complete with outdoor deck and balconies. The entry level provides full living space: gathering room with fireplace, study (or optional bedroom) with bath, dining room and U-shaped kitchen. A huge deck area wraps around the gathering room and dining room for outdoor enjoyment. A bedroom and bunkroom on the upper level are joined by a wide balcony area and full bath. Lower-level space includes a large activities room with fireplace, an additional bunk room and a full bath. Built-ins and open window areas abound throughout the plan.

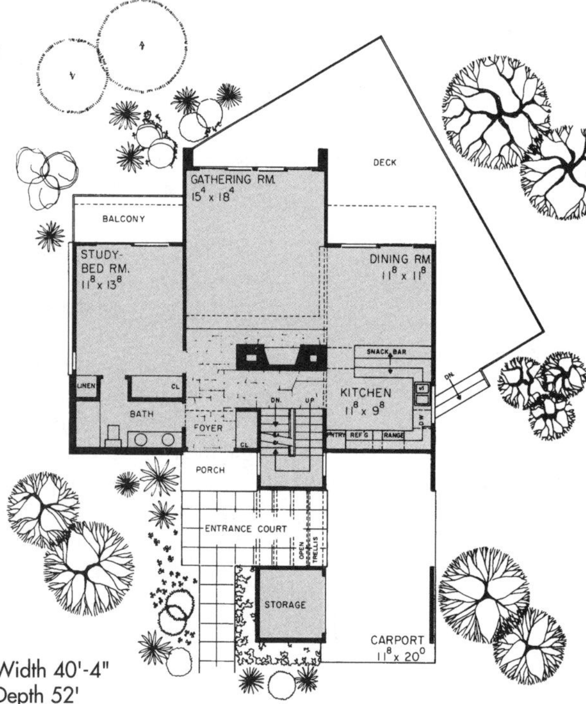

DECK
GATHERING RM.
15^4 x 18^4
BALCONY
STUDY-BED RM.
11^8 x 13^8
DINING RM.
11^8 x 11^8
SNACK BAR
KITCHEN
11^8 x 9^8
LINEN
CL
BATH
FOYER
DN.
UP
PNTRY
REF'G
RANGE
PORCH
ENTRANCE COURT
OPEN TRELLIS
STORAGE
CARPORT
11^8 x 20^0

Width 40'-4"
Depth 52'

QUOTE ONE®

Cost to build? See page 516 to order complete cost estimate to build this house in your area!

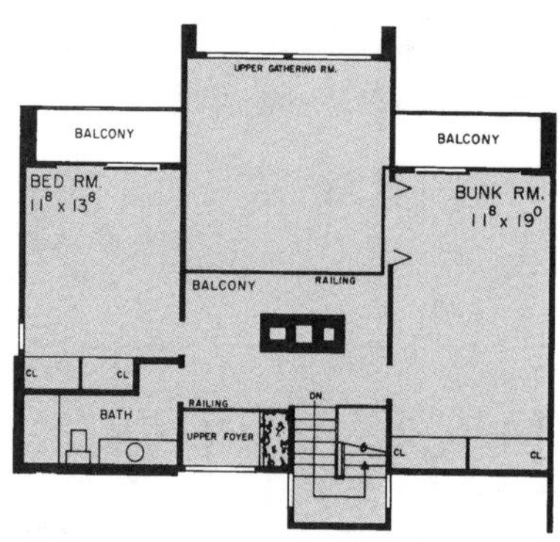

UPPER GATHERING RM.
BALCONY
BALCONY
BED RM.
11^8 x 13^8
BUNK RM.
11^8 x 19^0
BALCONY
RAILING
CL
CL
BATH
RAILING
UPPER FOYER
DN
CL
CL

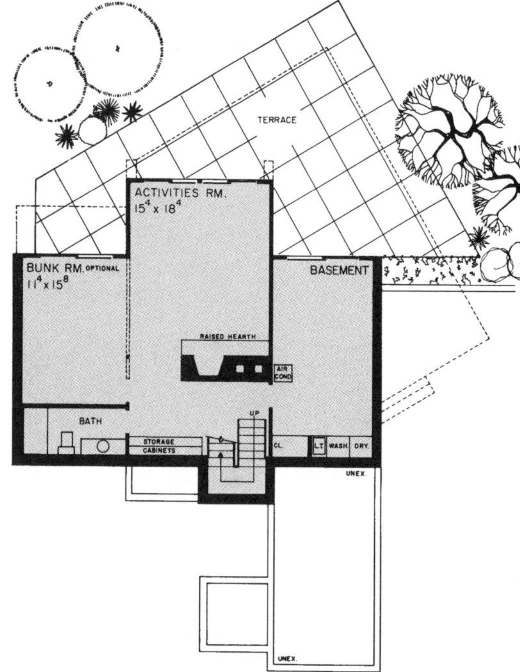

TERRACE
ACTIVITIES RM.
15^4 x 18^4
BUNK RM. OPTIONAL
11^4 x 15^8
BASEMENT
RAISED HEARTH
AIR COND
BATH
STORAGE CABINETS
UP
CL.
L.T.
WASH
DRY.
UNEX.
UNEX.

Design 2937

Main Level: 1,096 square feet
Upper Level: 1,115 square feet
Lower Level: 1,104 square feet
Total: 3,315 square feet

Design by
Home Planners

L

■ A splendidly symmetrical plan, this clean-lined, open-planned contemporary is a great place for the outdoor minded. A gathering room (with fireplace), dining room and breakfast room all lead out to a deck off the main level. Similarly, the lower-level activity room (another fireplace), hobby room and guest bedroom contain separate doors to the backyard terrace. Upstairs are three bedrooms, including a suite with through-fireplace, private balcony, walk-in closet, dressing room and whirlpool.

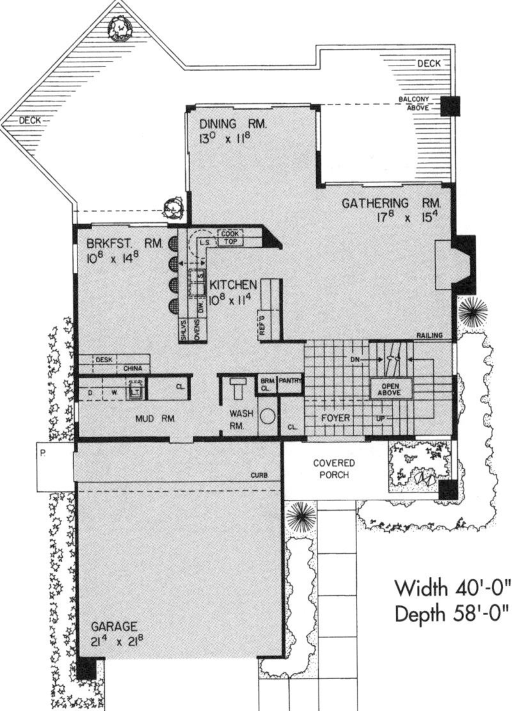
DECK
DECK
BALCONY ABOVE
DINING RM.
13⁰ x 11⁸
GATHERING RM.
17⁸ x 15⁴
BRKFST. RM.
10⁸ x 14⁸
KITCHEN
10⁸ x 11⁴
RAILING
DESK
CHINA
MUD RM.
WASH RM.
PANTRY
FOYER
OPEN ABOVE
DN
UP
CL.
COVERED PORCH
CURB
GARAGE
21⁴ x 21⁸
Width 40'-0"
Depth 58'-0"

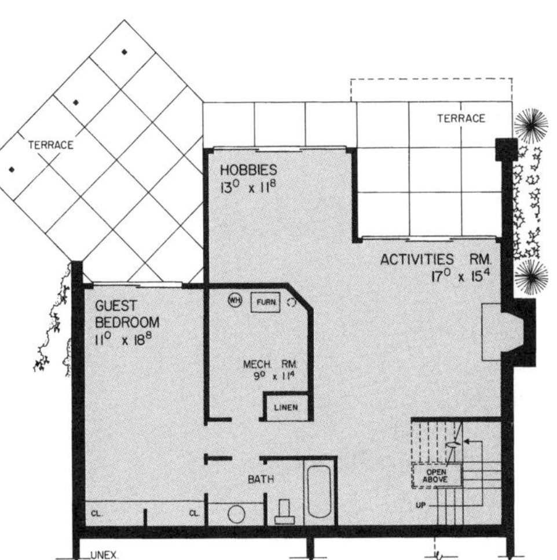
TERRACE
TERRACE
HOBBIES
13⁰ x 11⁸
ACTIVITIES RM.
17⁰ x 15⁴
GUEST
BEDROOM
11⁰ x 18⁸
FURN.
MECH. RM.
9⁰ x 11⁴
LINEN
BATH
OPEN ABOVE
UP
CL.
CL.
UNEX.

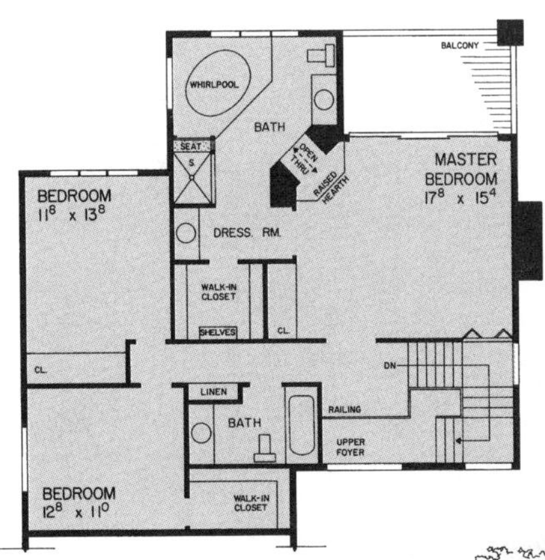
BALCONY
WHIRLPOOL
BATH
SEAT
MASTER
BEDROOM
17⁸ x 15⁴
RAISED HEARTH
BEDROOM
11⁸ x 13⁸
DRESS. RM.
WALK-IN CLOSET
SHELVES
CL.
CL.
DN
LINEN
BATH
RAILING
UPPER FOYER
BEDROOM
12⁸ x 11⁰
WALK-IN CLOSET

QUOTE ONE®

Cost to build? See page 516
to order complete cost estimate
to build this house in your area!

Design 2901

Main Level: 1,449 square feet
Upper Level: 665 square feet
Master Bedroom Level: 448 square feet
Activities Room Level: 419 square feet
Total: 2,981 square feet

L

■ This luxurious three-bedroom home offers comfort on many levels. Its modern design incorporates a rear garden room and conversation pit off a living and dining room plus skylights in an adjacent family room with high sloped ceiling. Other features include an entrance court, an activities room, a convenient kitchen, an upper lounge and a master bedroom.

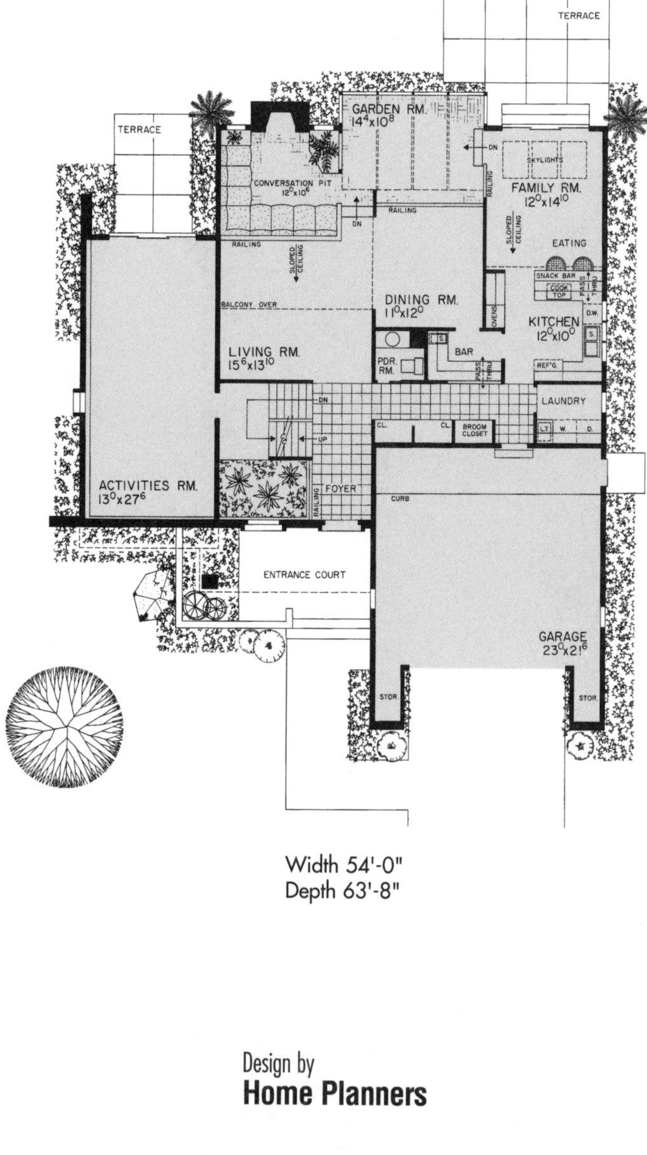
TERRACE
TERRACE
GARDEN RM.
14⁴x10⁸
CONVERSATION PIT
12⁰x10⁶
SKYLIGHTS
FAMILY RM.
12⁰x14¹⁰
EATING
SNACK BAR
COOK TOP
DINING RM.
11⁰x12⁰
KITCHEN
12⁰x10⁰
BALCONY OVER
LIVING RM.
15⁶x13¹⁰
PDR. RM.
BAR
LAUNDRY
BROOM CLOSET
ACTIVITIES RM.
13⁰x27⁶
FOYER
ENTRANCE COURT
GARAGE
23⁰x21⁶
STOR.
STOR.

ROOF
SKYLIGHTS
ROOF
BALCONY
UPPER LIVING RM.
BEDROOM
10¹⁰x14⁴
UPPER FAMILY RM.
MASTER BEDROOM
13⁶x18⁰
SKYLIGHTS
WALK-IN CLOSET
LOUNGE
RAILING
BATH
BEDROOM
12⁰x14⁰
BATH
SKYLIGHT
FOYER
WALK-IN CLOSET
TUB
ROOF

Width 54'-0"
Depth 63'-8"

Design by
Home Planners

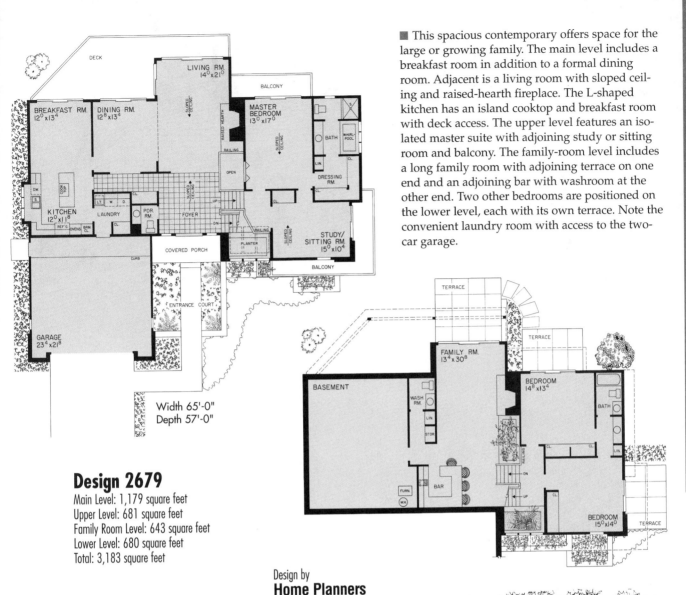

■ This spacious contemporary offers space for the large or growing family. The main level includes a breakfast room in addition to a formal dining room. Adjacent is a living room with sloped ceiling and raised-hearth fireplace. The L-shaped kitchen has an island cooktop and breakfast room with deck access. The upper level features an isolated master suite with adjoining study or sitting room and balcony. The family-room level includes a long family room with adjoining terrace on one end and an adjoining bar with washroom at the other end. Two other bedrooms are positioned on the lower level, each with its own terrace. Note the convenient laundry room with access to the two-car garage.

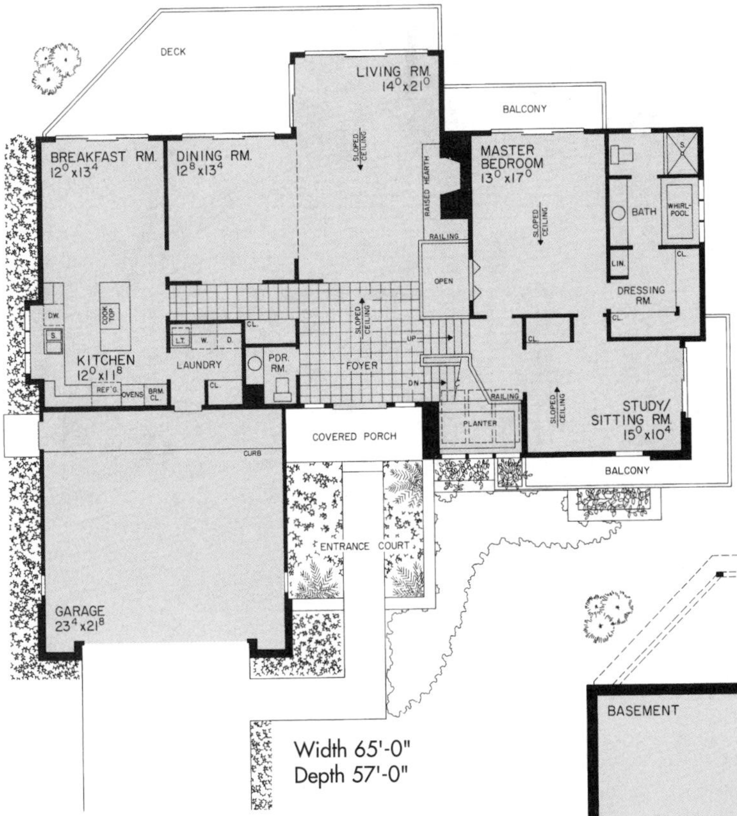

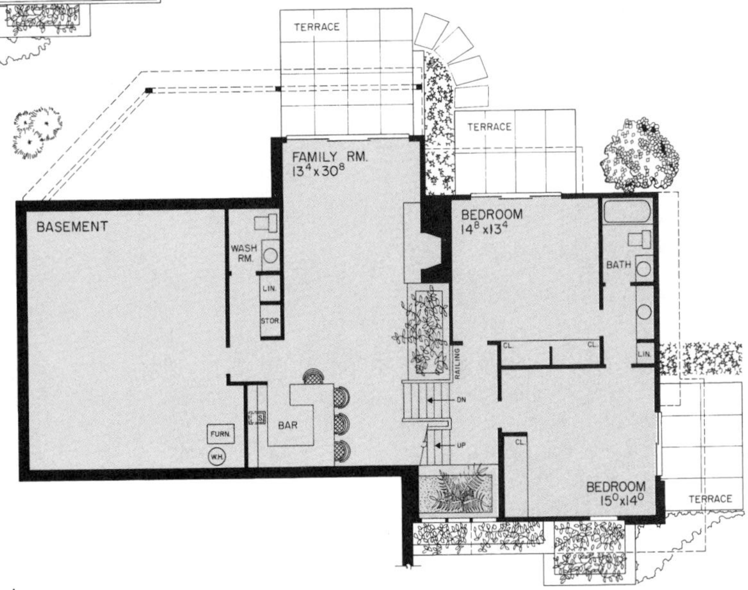

Width 65'-0"
Depth 57'-0"

Design 2679

Main Level: 1,179 square feet
Upper Level: 681 square feet
Family Room Level: 643 square feet
Lower Level: 680 square feet
Total: 3,183 square feet

Design by
Home Planners

Design 3366

Main Floor: 1,638 square feet
Upper Floor: 650 square feet
Lower Floor: 934 square feet
Total: 3,222 square feet

L

■ There is much more to this design than meets the eye. While it may look like a 1½-story plan, bonus recreation and hobby space in the walk-out basement adds almost 1,000 square feet. The first floor holds living and dining areas as well as the deluxe master bedroom suite. Two family bedrooms share a full bath on the second floor and are connected by a balcony that overlooks the gathering room below. Notice the covered porch beyond the breakfast and dining rooms.

QUOTE ONE®

Cost to build? See page 516 to order complete cost estimate to build this house in your area!

Width 57'-0"
Depth 51'-8"

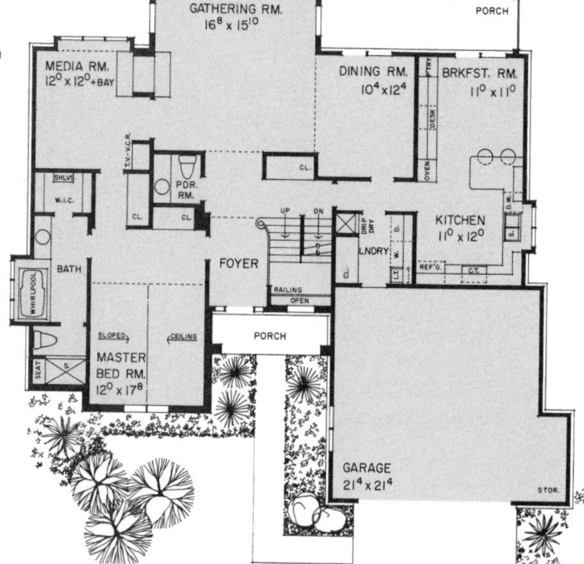
GATHERING RM.
16⁸ x 15¹⁰
PORCH
MEDIA RM.
12⁰ x 12⁰+BAY
DINING RM.
10⁴x12⁴
BRKFST. RM.
11⁰ x 11⁰
KITCHEN
11⁰ x 12⁰
FOYER
BATH
WHIRLPOOL
MASTER
BED RM.
12⁰ x 17⁸
PORCH
GARAGE
21⁴ x 21⁴

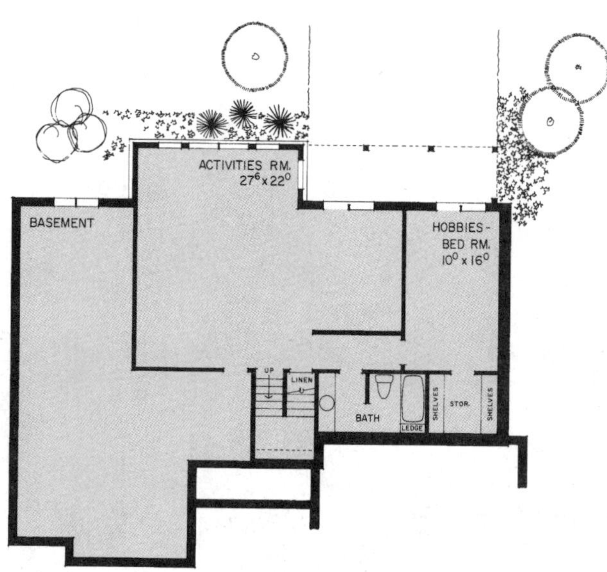
ACTIVITIES RM.
27⁶x22⁰
BASEMENT
HOBBIES-
BED RM.
10⁰ x 16⁰
BATH

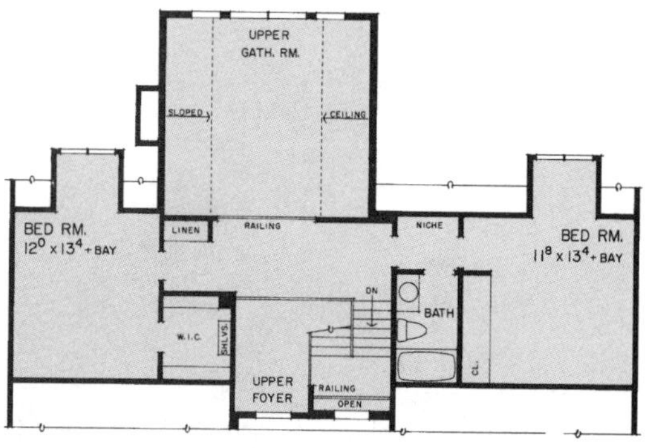
UPPER
GATH. RM.
BED RM.
12⁰ x 13⁴+BAY
BED RM.
11⁸ x 13⁴+BAY
BATH
UPPER
FOYER

Rear Elevation

Design by
Home Planners

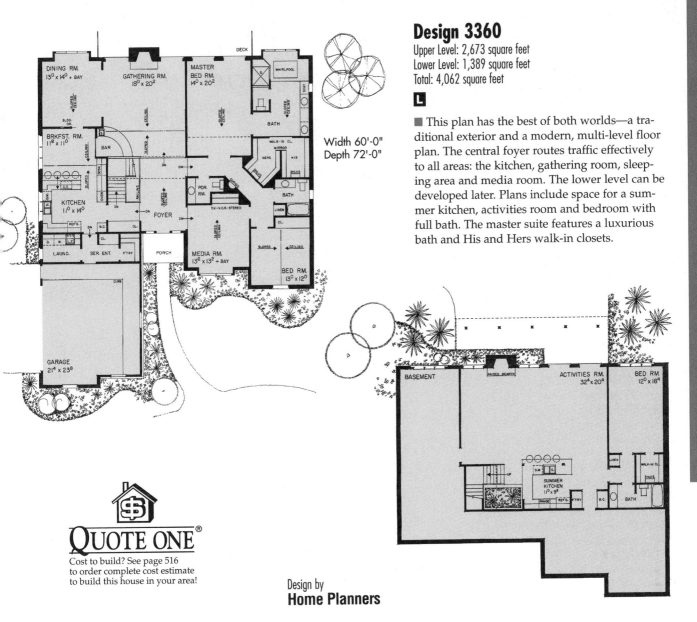

Design 3360

Upper Level: 2,673 square feet
Lower Level: 1,389 square feet
Total: 4,062 square feet

L

■ This plan has the best of both worlds—a traditional exterior and a modern, multi-level floor plan. The central foyer routes traffic effectively to all areas: the kitchen, gathering room, sleeping area and media room. The lower level can be developed later. Plans include space for a summer kitchen, activities room and bedroom with full bath. The master suite features a luxurious bath and His and Hers walk-in closets.

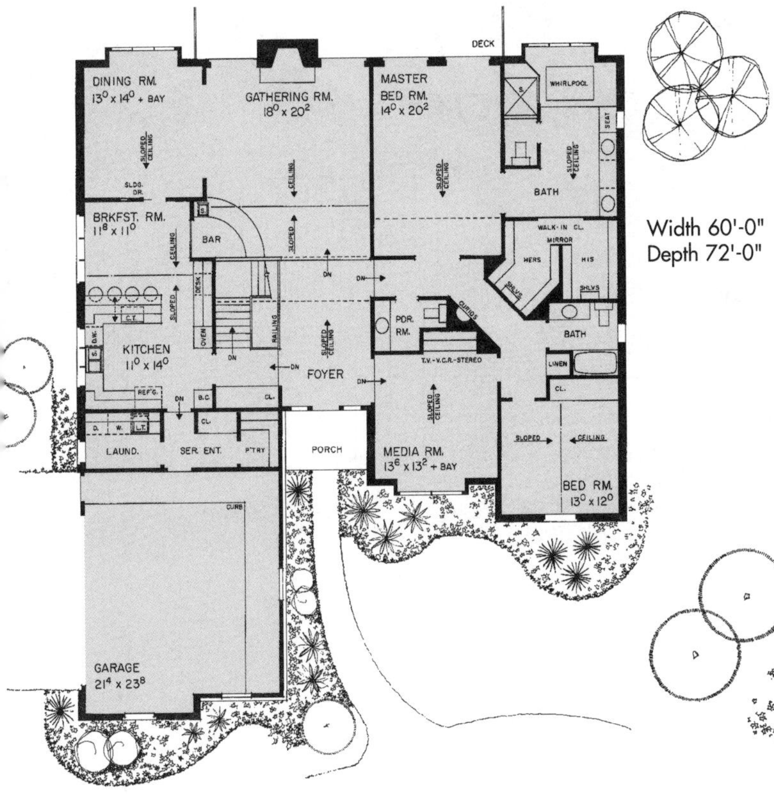

Width 60'-0"
Depth 72'-0"

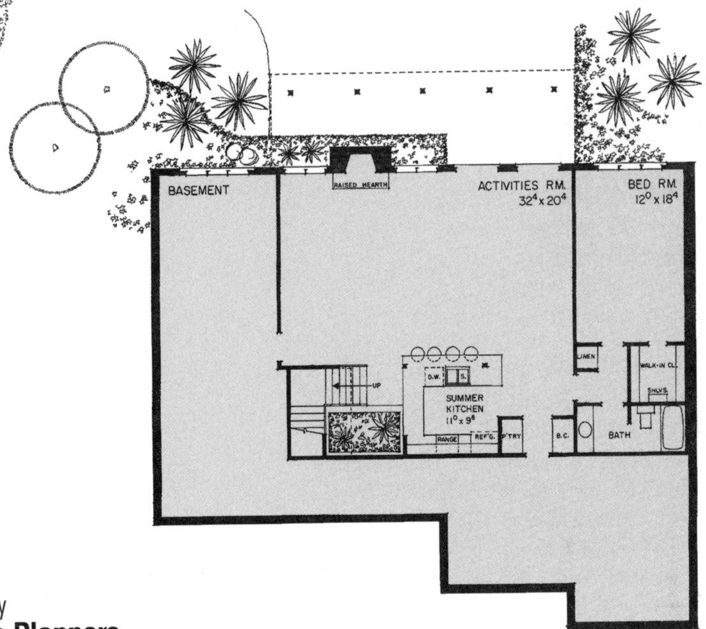

QUOTE ONE®
Cost to build? See page 516 to order complete cost estimate to build this house in your area!

Design by
Home Planners

Design 2608

Main Level: 728 square feet
Upper Level: 874 square feet
Lower Level: 310 square feet
Total: 1,912 square feet

L D

■ Tri-level living could hardly ask for more than this rustic design has to offer. Not only can you enjoy the three levels but there is also a fourth basement level for bulk storage and, perhaps, a shop area. The interior livability is outstanding. The main level has an L-shaped formal living/dining area with a fireplace in the living room, sliding glass doors in the dining room leading to the upper terrace, a U-shaped kitchen and an informal eating area. Down a few steps to the lower level is the family room with another fireplace and sliding doors to the lower terrace, a washroom and a laundry room. The upper level houses all of the sleeping facilities including three bedrooms, a bath and the master suite.

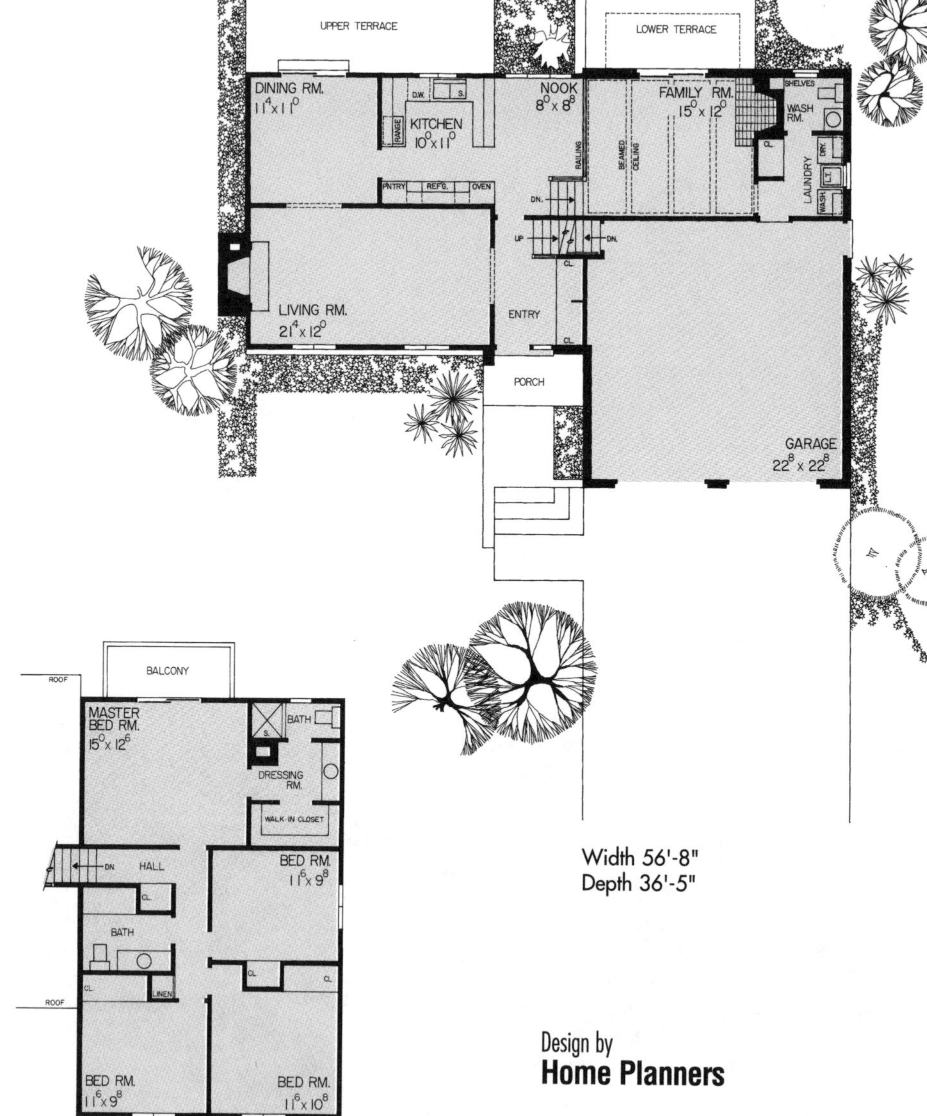

UPPER TERRACE
LOWER TERRACE
DINING RM. 11⁴x11⁰
KITCHEN 10⁰x11⁰
NOOK 8⁰x8⁸
FAMILY RM. 15⁰x12⁰
WASH RM.
LAUNDRY
LIVING RM. 21⁴x12⁰
ENTRY
PORCH
GARAGE 22⁸x22⁸
BALCONY
MASTER BED RM. 15⁰x12⁶
BATH
DRESSING RM.
WALK-IN CLOSET
HALL
BED RM. 11⁶x9⁸
BATH
BED RM. 11⁶x9⁸
BED RM. 11⁶x10⁸

Width 56'-8"
Depth 36'-5"

Design by
Home Planners

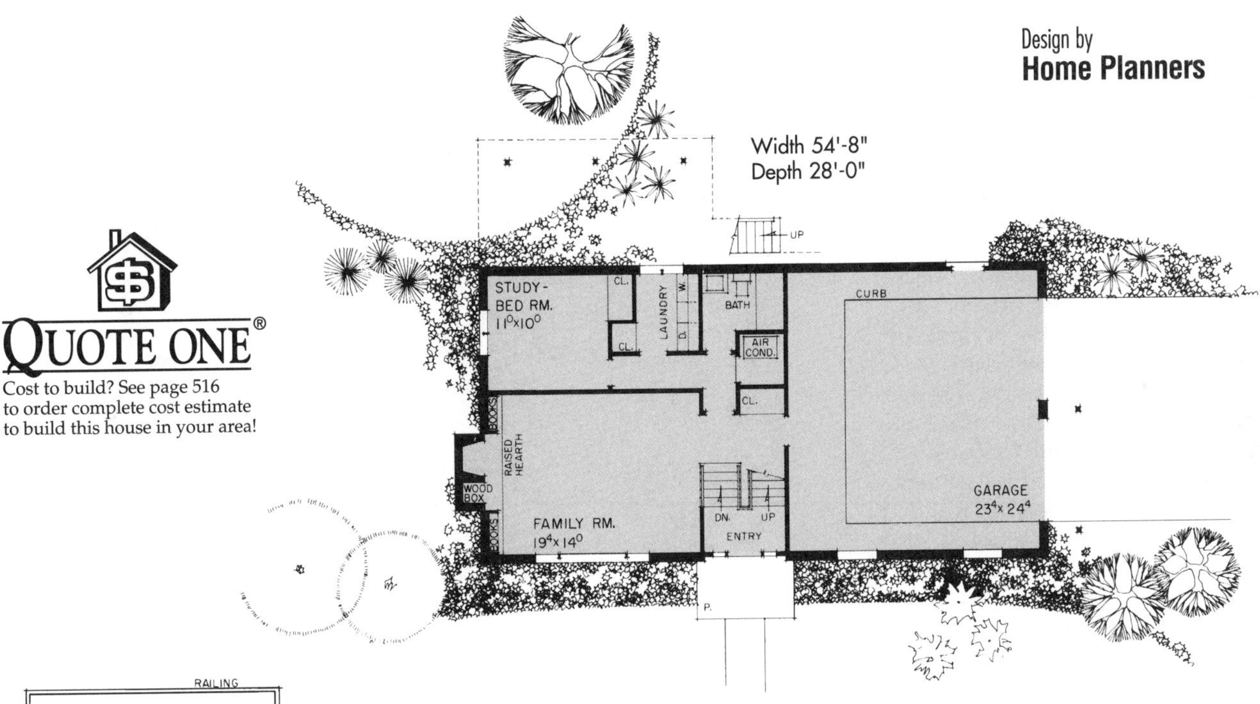
Design by
Home Planners
Width 54'-8"
Depth 28'-0"
QUOTE ONE®
Cost to build? See page 516
to order complete cost estimate
to build this house in your area!
UP
STUDY-
BED RM.
11^0x10^0
CL.
CL.
LAUNDRY
W.
D.
BATH
AIR COND.
CL.
CURB
WOOD BOX
RAISED HEARTH
BOOKS
BOOKS
FAMILY RM.
19^4x14^0
DN.
UP
ENTRY
GARAGE
23^4x24^4
P.

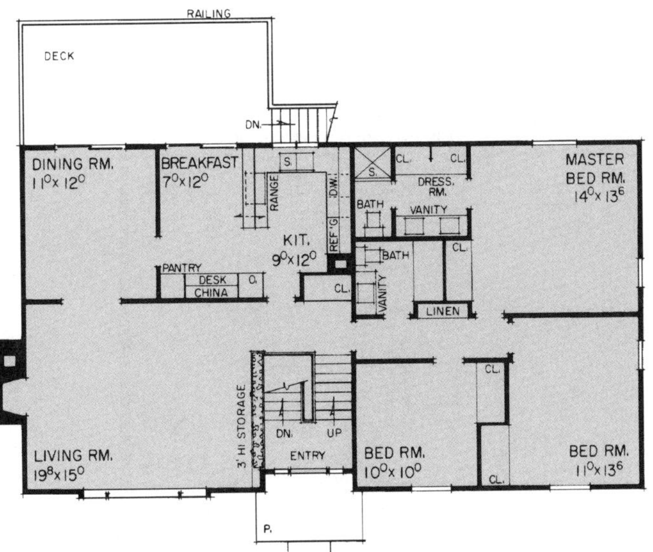
RAILING
DECK
DN.
DINING RM.
11^0x12^0
BREAKFAST
7^0x12^0
S.
RANGE
D.W.
REF'G.
KIT.
9^0x12^0
PANTRY
DESK
CHINA
C.
CL.
S.
CL.
CL.
DRESS. RM.
BATH
VANITY
BATH
VANITY
CL.
LINEN
MASTER
BED RM.
14^0x13^6
3' HI STORAGE
DN.
UP
ENTRY
LIVING RM.
19^8x15^0
BED RM.
10^0x10^0
CL.
CL.
BED RM.
11^0x13^6
P.

Design 1850

Main Level: 1,456 square feet
Lower Level: 728 square feet
Total: 2,184 square feet

■ A perfect rectangle, this split-level is comparatively inexpensive to build and very appealing to live in. It features a large upper-level living room with a fireplace, a formal dining room, three bedrooms (with two full baths nearby) and an outdoor deck. Another fireplace warms the family room on the lower level, which also has a full bath and room for a study or a fourth bedroom.

Design Q268

Square Footage: 1,282
Lower Level: 1,122 square feet

■ Bold horizontal siding and clean lines make a pleasing exterior for this hillside home. The living room and dining room flow together for a spacious entertaining area. The living room is warmed by a hearth; the dining room has buffet space. The country kitchen is an ideal gathering spot and allows access to a rear deck. The master bedroom is tucked into a window bay and features a private bath. Two additional bedrooms share a full bath. The suggested lower level holds laundry space, plus two additional bedrooms, a den and a large family room with fireplace—an additional 1,122 square feet—when finished. A warm sundeck graces the lower level.

Design by
Select Home Designs

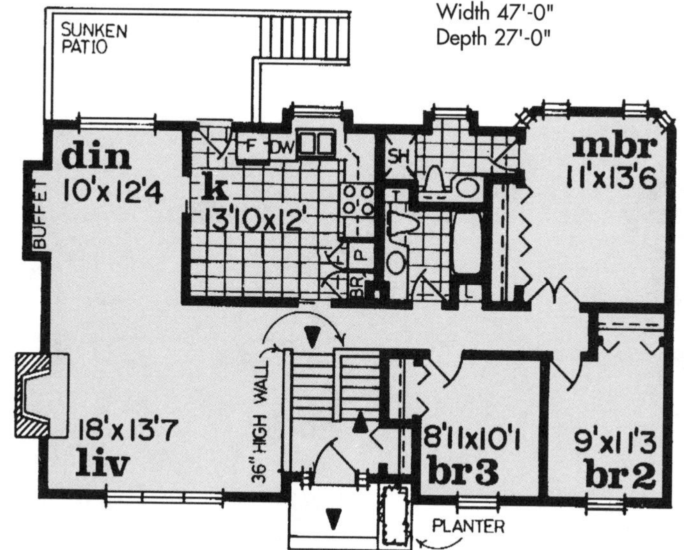
Width 47'-0"
Depth 27'-0"
SUNKEN PATIO
din
10'x12'4
BUFFET
k
13'10x12'
F
DW
SH
mbr
11'x13'6
36" HIGH WALL
18'x13'7
liv
8'11x10'1
br3
9'x11'3
br2
PLANTER

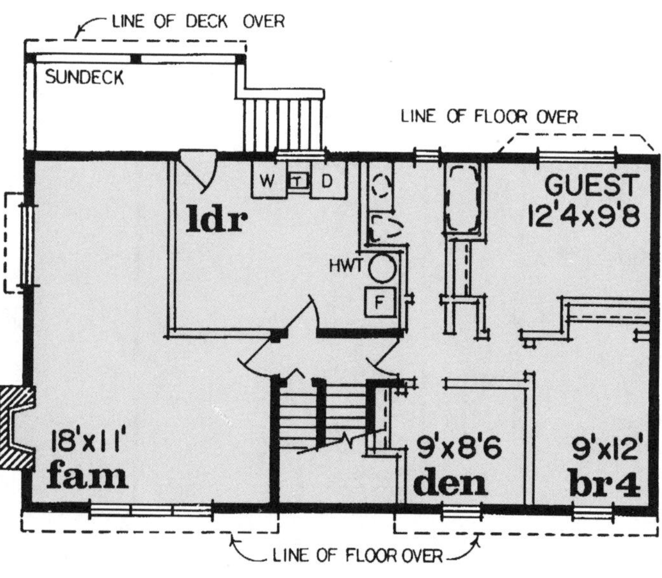
LINE OF DECK OVER
SUNDECK
LINE OF FLOOR OVER
W
D
ldr
HWT
F
GUEST
12'4x9'8
18'x11'
fam
9'x8'6
den
9'x12'
br4
LINE OF FLOOR OVER

Design Q265

Square Footage: 1,197
Lower Level: 522 square feet

■ Perfect for a hillside lot, this design combines brick and horizontal siding to lovely effect. Double doors with a transom over create a fine entry. A few steps up is the main home, with a living/dining room combination. The living room has a fireplace, while the dining room has sliding glass doors to the rear deck. The kitchen and attached breakfast room are nearby and also open to the deck. Three bedrooms are found on the left side of the plan. The master suite has a private bath with garden sink and corner shower. Family bedrooms share a full bath. If you choose to develop the lower level, you'll gain 522 square feet and a family room with fireplace, plus a full bath. The laundry and garage with storage space sit on the lower level.

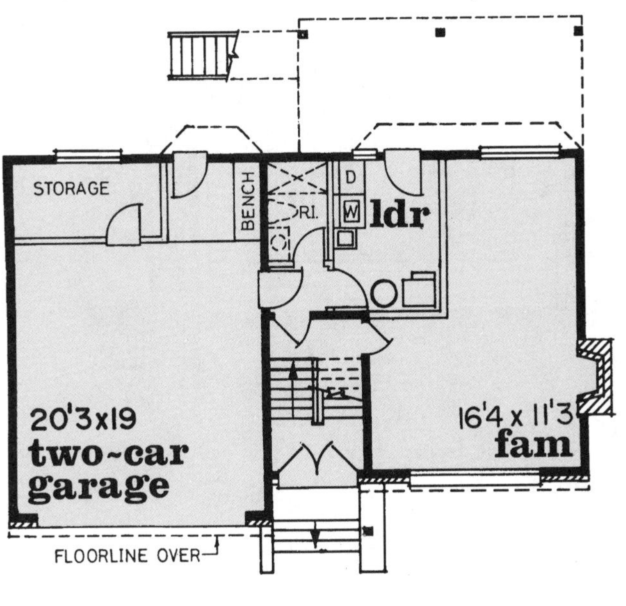
STORAGE
BENCH
D
W
ldr
20'3x19
two~car
garage
16'4 x 11'3
fam
FLOORLINE OVER

Width 44'-0"
Depth 30'-0"

DECK
din
9'3 x 10'5
mbr
11'6 x 11'
brk
k
14' x 8' & 10'
16'3 x 15'6
liv
9'3x10'10
br2
9'3x9'8
br3

Design by
Select Home Designs

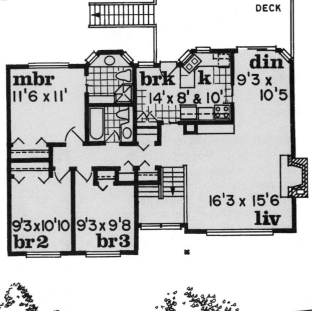

Design Q264

Square Footage: 1,194
Lower Level: 1,052 square feet

■ This traditional design offers not only a great exterior, but plenty of room for expansion in the future. The main level contains an open living room and dining room, warmed by a fireplace and open to the rear deck through sliding glass doors. The kitchen and breakfast room are reached easily from either the living room or dining room and also have access to the deck. The master bedroom and two family bedrooms are on the left side of the plan. The master has its own bath, while family bedrooms share a full bath. The lower level offers 1,052 square feet of unfinished space for two additional bedrooms, a den, a full bath and a family room with fireplace. The laundry room is also on this level.

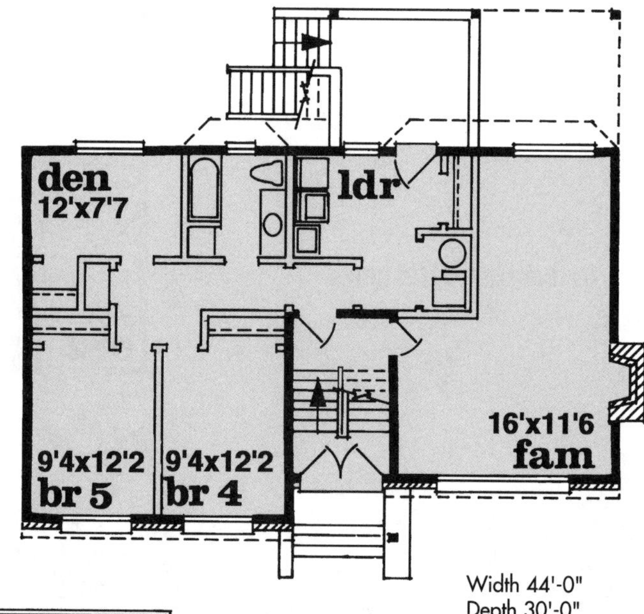

den
12'x7'7
ldr
16'x11'6
fam
9'4x12'2
br 5
9'4x12'2
br 4

Width 44'-0"
Depth 30'-0"

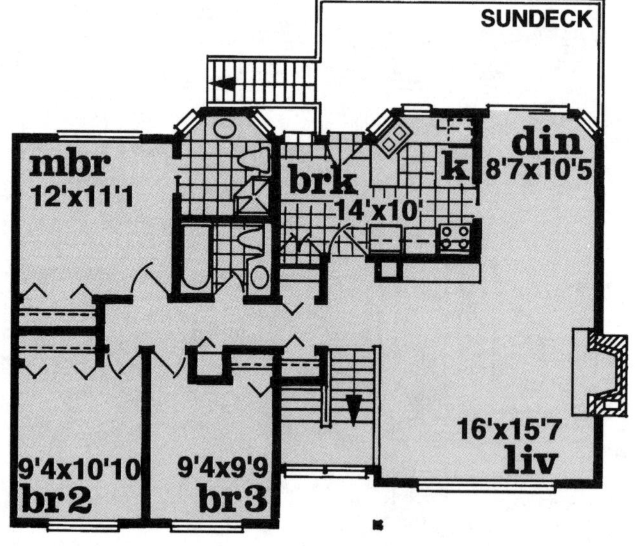

SUNDECK
mbr
12'x11'1
brk
14'x10'
k
din
8'7x10'5
16'x15'7
liv
9'4x10'10
br2
9'4x9'9
br3

Design by
Select Home Designs

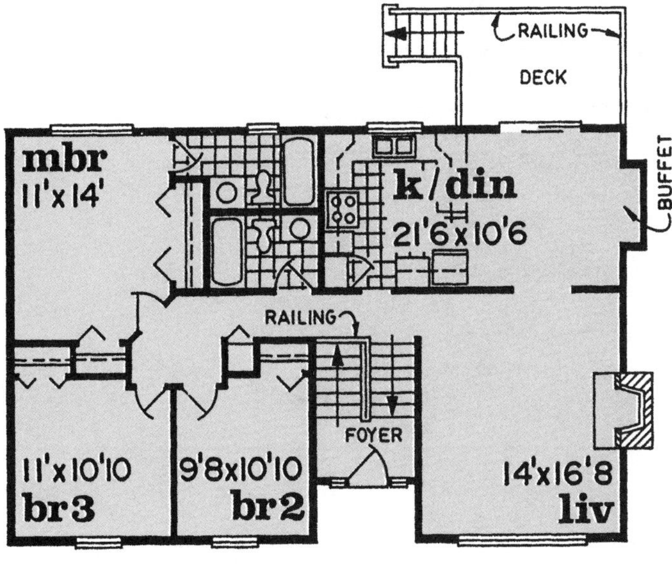
RAILING
DECK
mbr
11'x14'
k/din
21'6x10'6
BUFFET
RAILING
FOYER
11'x10'10
br3
9'8x10'10
br2
14'x16'8
liv

Width 44'-0"
Depth 28'-6"

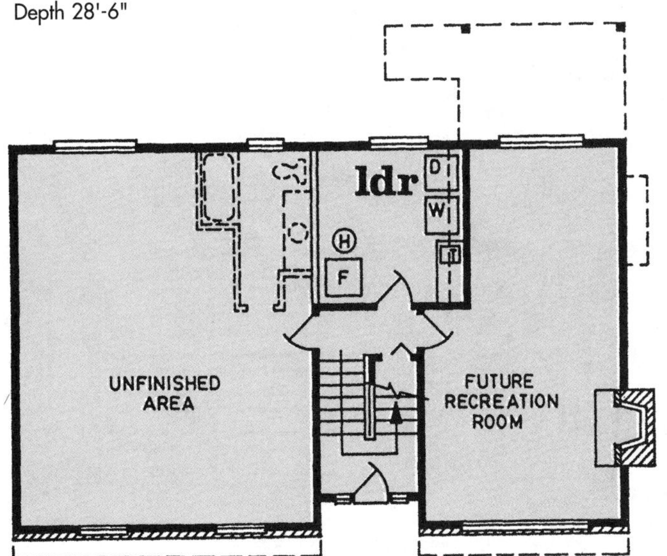
ldr
UNFINISHED AREA
FUTURE RECREATION ROOM

Design Q312

Square Footage: 1,235
Lower Level: 1,161 square feet

■ Horizontal siding and brick lead to an entry that boasts a half-round window over its door. A cathedral ceiling is found in the foyer, leading upstairs to the main living level. Amenities include a living room with masonry fireplace, a dining room with buffet space and sliding glass doors to the rear terrace, and a U-shaped kitchen open to the dinette. The master bedroom features a large wall closet and private bath. Family bedrooms sit to the front and share a bath. The lower level has 1,161 square feet of unfinished space for a recreation room with fireplace, additional bedrooms, a full bath or even a home office. The laundry is also found here.

Design by
Select Home Designs

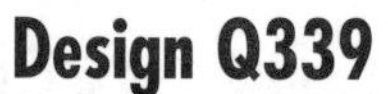

Design Q339

Square Footage: 1,007
Lower Level: 1,007 square feet

■ To accommodate a very narrow lot, this plan can be built without the deck and the garage, though the plan includes the options for both. The lower level can be finished later into a family room and additional bedrooms and a bath, if you choose. The cathedral entry offers steps up to the main living areas. The living room has a fireplace and leads to the L-shaped kitchen. Here you'll find abundant counter and cupboard space and room for a breakfast table. Sliding glass doors open to the optional deck. Bedrooms include a master suite with wall closet and two family bedrooms. All three share the use of a full hall bath. A laundry room is tucked away in the lower level.

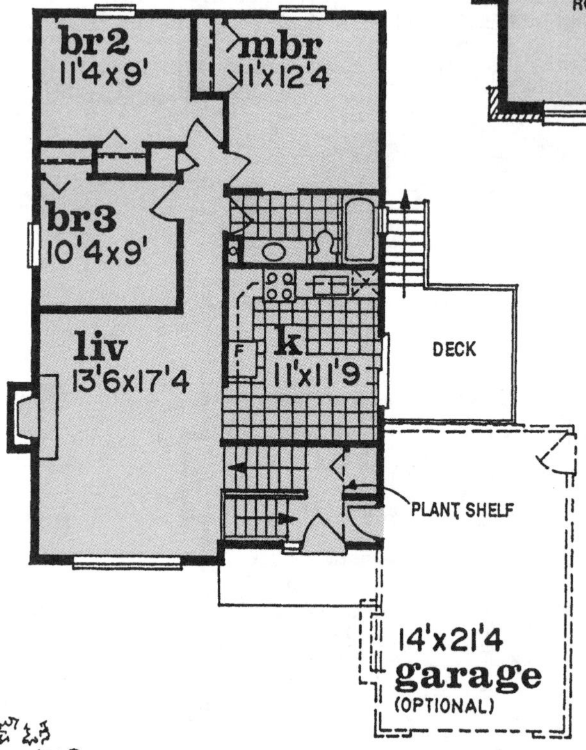

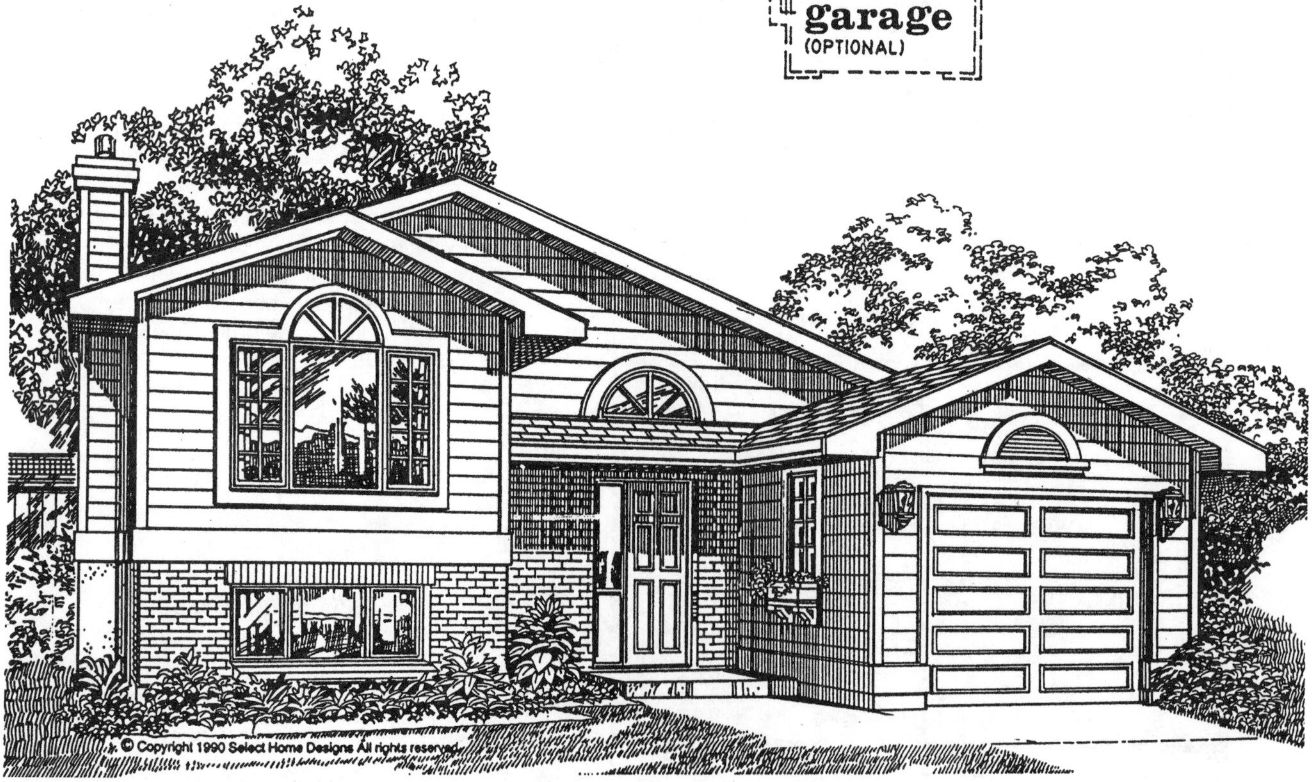

Width 26'-0" (40'-0" with garage)
Depth 39'-4" (51'-0" with garage)

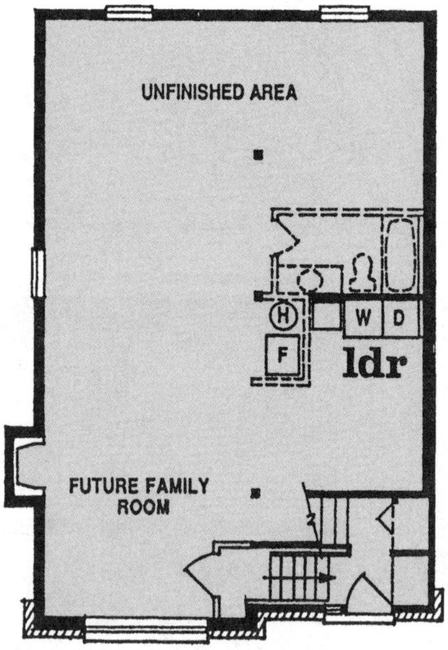

UNFINISHED AREA
H
W
D
F
ldr
FUTURE FAMILY ROOM

br2
11'4x9'
mbr
11'x12'4
br3
10'4x9'
liv
13'6x17'4
k
11'x11'9
F
DECK
PLANT SHELF
14'x21'4
garage
(OPTIONAL)

Design by
Select Home Designs

© Copyright 1990 Select Home Designs All rights reserved

© Copyright 1990 Select Home Designs. All rights reserved.

Design Q360

Square Footage: 1,449
Lower Level: 1,222 square feet

■ This lovely split-level home offers full livability on one floor with the possibility of expanding to the lower level at a future time. The main living level includes a large living room with optional bay window and a fireplace. The connecting dining room has access directly to the L-shaped kitchen (note that there is space for a breakfast table in the kitchen). Bedrooms are to the rear of the plan and include a master suite with private bath and two family bedrooms sharing a full bath. All three bedrooms have ample wall closets. The laundry is at the entry level, where there are stairs to the lower level, as well. When developed, the lower level will include a family room with fireplace, additional bedrooms and a full bath.

br2 12'1x11'
mbr 11'8x13'6
PATIO
br3 9'6x10'10
k 11'8x10'10
FOYER
19'x23' two-car garage
12'10x20'6 liv
11'8x11'4 din
OPTIONAL BAY

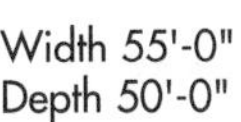
Width 55'-0"
Depth 50'-0"

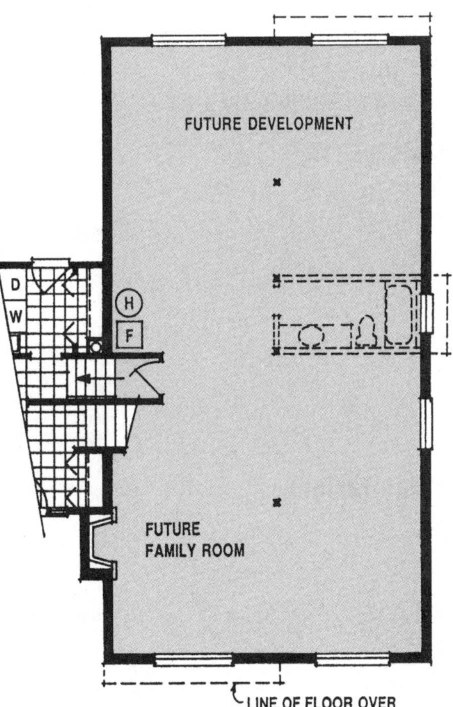
FUTURE DEVELOPMENT
D
W
H
F
FUTURE FAMILY ROOM
LINE OF FLOOR OVER

Design by
Select Home Designs

Design Q216

Square Footage: 1,033
Lower Level: 939 square feet

■ Build this home with full livability on one level, with the option of expanding to the lower level in the future. Double doors open to the entry where a few steps lead up to the main level. The living room overlooks the cathedral entry and also sports a fireplace. An L-shaped country kitchen has space for a breakfast table and is open to the family room. A single entrance leads to a small deck in back. The right side of the plan is reserved for bedrooms—two family bedrooms and a master bedroom. All have adequate wall closets and share a full bath. Space on the lower level can accommodate a den or family room, home office and bedrooms—providing an additional 939 square feet of living space. A handy carport protects the family vehicle.

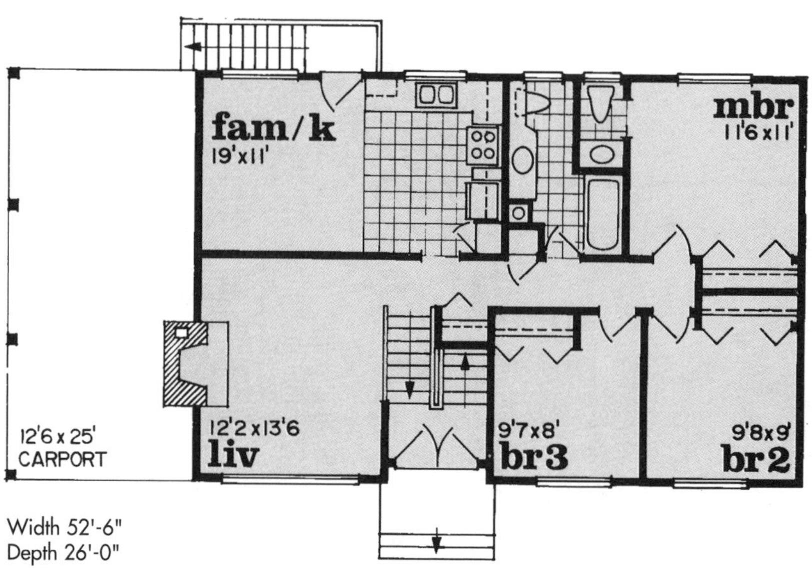

fam/k
19'x11'
mbr
11'6x11'
12'6 x 25'
CARPORT
12'2 x13'6
liv
9'7x8'
br3
9'8x9'
br2

Width 52'-6"
Depth 26'-0"

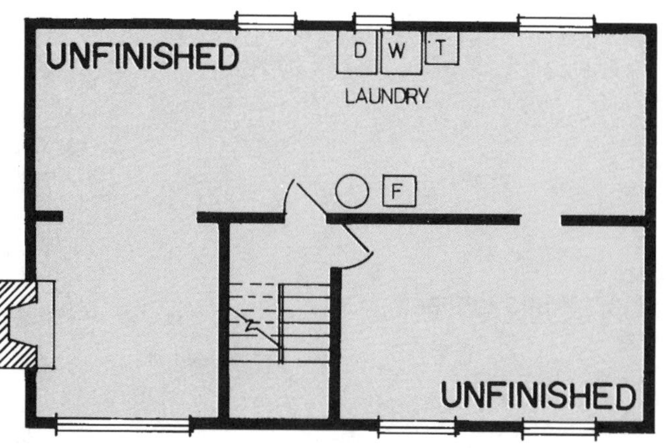

UNFINISHED
D
W
T
LAUNDRY
F
UNFINISHED

Design by
Select Home Designs

© Copyright 1988 Select Home Design All rights reserved

Design Q289

Square Footage: 1,299
Lower Level: 514 square feet

■ This elegant split-level home is made even more so with columns at the front entry, further adorned by a half-circular transom window. Railings in the living room overlook the cathedral entry. The living room connects to a formal dining room and is warmed by a fireplace. Look for handy buffet space in the dining room. Sliding glass doors lead out to a deck in the dining room and the breakfast room. The kitchen is U-shaped and holds abundant counter space. Two family bedrooms with box-bay windows join a master suite on the left side of the plan. The master has a private bath, while family bedrooms share a full bath. Space on the lower level—514 square feet—can be developed into a family room with fireplace and sliding glass doors to a covered patio. The laundry is also found on this level and includes a full bath. Note the great storage area in the two-car garage.

RAILING
DECK
brk 11'x7'
mbr 12'10x12'
SH
k 11'x10'
din 9'x10'
BUFFET
RAILING
10'x11' br2
10'x10' br3
13'2x19' liv
DECORATIVE COLUMNS

Width 42'-0"
Depth 40'-0"

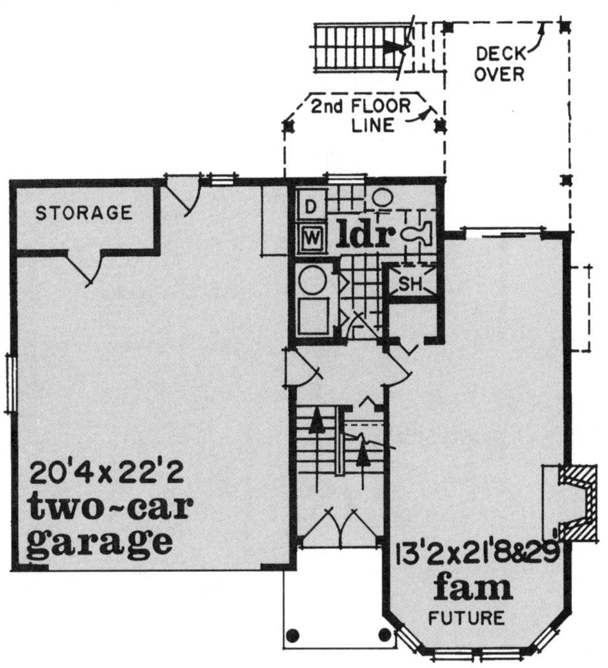
DECK OVER
2nd FLOOR LINE
STORAGE
D
W
ldr
SH
20'4x22'2
two-car garage
13'2x21'8&29'
fam
FUTURE

Design by
Select Home Designs

Design Q230

Square Footage: 1,211
Lower Level: 346 square feet

■ Adorned with horizontal siding and brick, the exterior of this home sports details for a rustic, country appeal. The entry is deep-set for weather protection and opens directly to the open living and dining room area of the home. A fireplace and box-bay window here are added features. The kitchen is also at this level. Its L-shaped configuration is made for convenience and allows space for a breakfast table. Up a few steps are the bedrooms—two family bedrooms and a master suite with full bath. One family bedroom boasts a walk-in closet. Space on the lower level can be developed into a family room with double-door access to a rear patio, a den or recreation room with fireplace and bedrooms, if you choose. Rough-in plumbing is included for a half-bath and the laundry room.

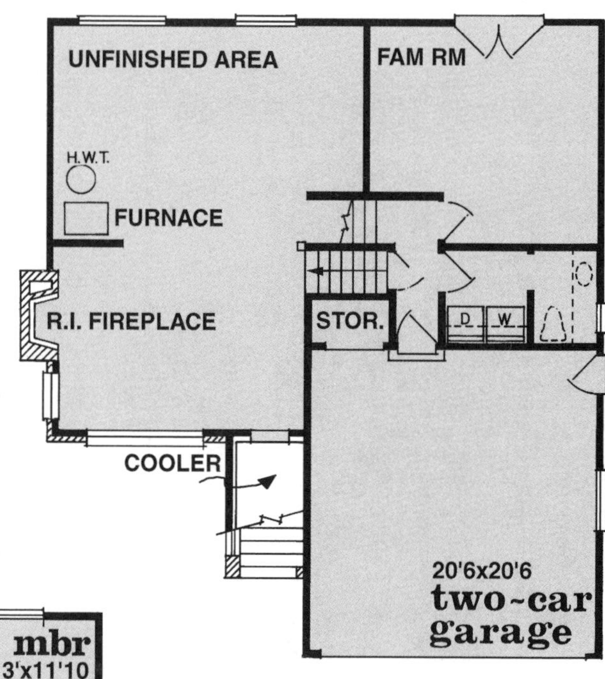
PATIO
UNFINISHED AREA
FAM RM
H.W.T.
FURNACE
R.I. FIREPLACE
STOR.
D
W
COOLER
20'6x20'6
two-car garage

Width 38'-0"
Depth 42'-5"

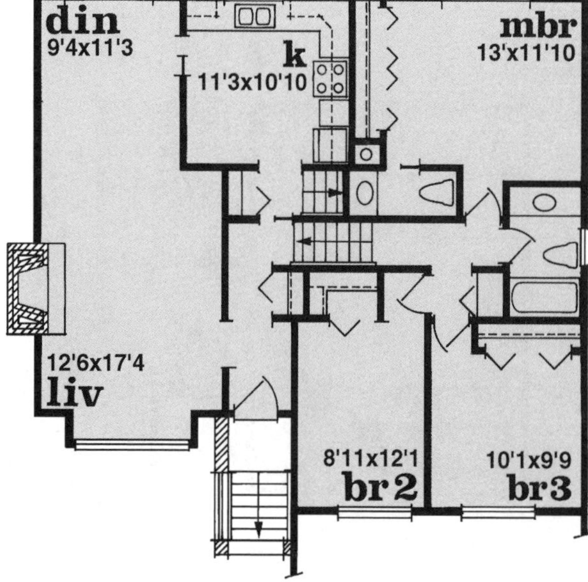
din
9'4x11'3
k
11'3x10'10
mbr
13'x11'10
12'6x17'4
liv
8'11x12'1
br2
10'1x9'9
br3

Design by
Select Home Designs

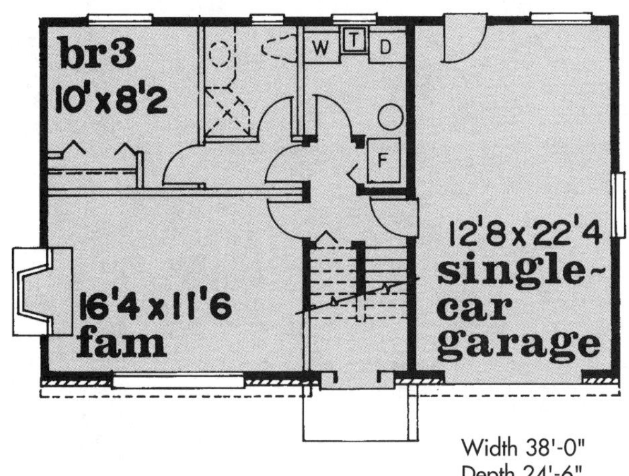
br3
10'x8'2
W
T
D
F
12'8x22'4
single-car garage
16'4x11'6
fam

Width 38'-0"
Depth 24'-6"

Design Q262

Square Footage: 924
Lower Level: 646 square feet

■ This home comes with a choice of two elevations—one has a single-car garage. Finish both with horizontal wood siding and brick for a comfortable, traditional look. The entry opens to a cathedral entry with half-wall separating it from the living room. A fireplace warms this living space. The dining room is attached and has sliding glass doors to a sundeck. The kitchen features a box window over the sink and a U-shaped work area. Two bedrooms sit at the right side of the plan. They share a full bath. If you choose to finish the lower level, you'll gain 646 square feet with the garage or 736 without the garage. One option allows for a bedroom, full bath and family room with fireplace. The other adds another bedroom and a workshop.

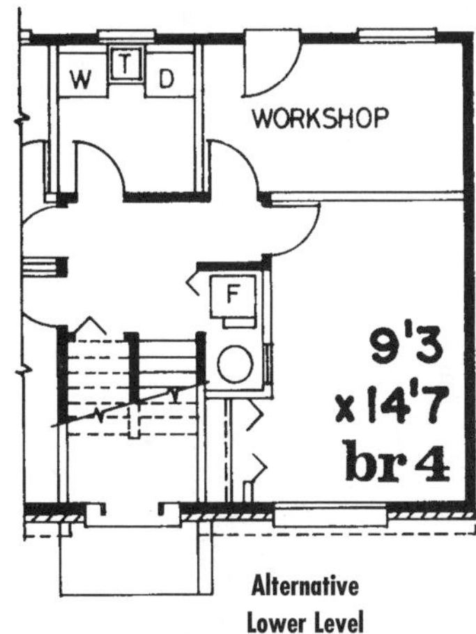
W
T
D
WORKSHOP
F
9'3
x14'7
br4

Alternative Lower Level

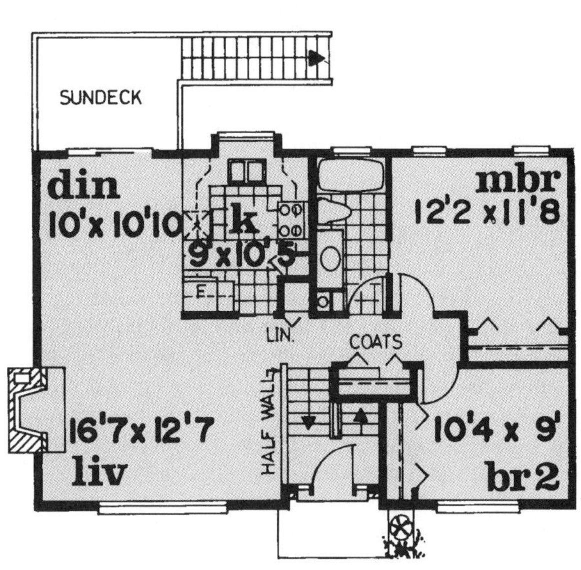
SUNDECK
din
10'x 10'10
k
9x10'5
mbr
12'2 x11'8
LIN.
COATS
HALF WALL
16'7x12'7
liv
10'4 x 9'
br2

Design by
Select Home Designs

Design Q225

Square Footage: 1,161
Lower Level: 891 square feet

■ This spacious split-level home is well-suited to a medium to narrow frontage lot. Steps lead up to a covered front porch at the entry with a single door into the foyer and double doors into the living room. The living room and dining room are part of one large open area, warmed by a fireplace. The kitchen is L-shaped and saves room for a breakfast table. The kitchen can be isolated by pocket doors at each entrance. The master bedroom sits to the back and features a walk-in closet and half-bath. Family bedrooms sit to the front and share a full bath. The stairway to the lower level is found in the center of the plan. Unfinished space provides 891 square feet for future development that might include a family room with fireplace and an additional bedroom with half-bath. The two-car garage offers storage and work-bench space.

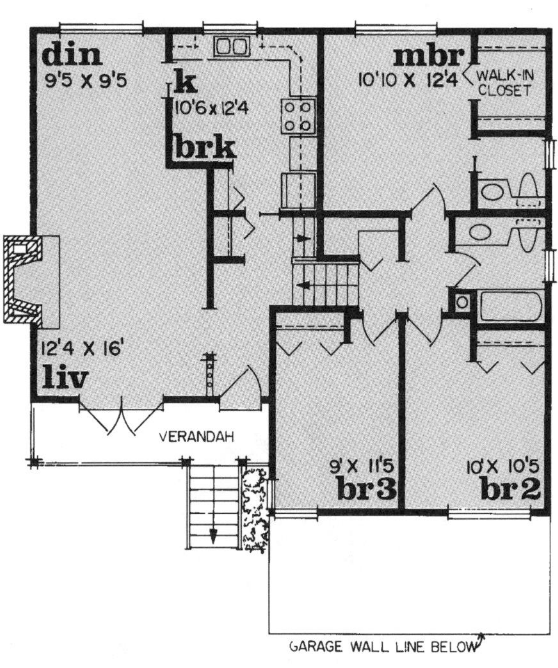
din
9'5 X 9'5
k
10'6 x 12'4
brk
mbr
10'10 X 12'4
WALK-IN CLOSET
12'4 X 16'
liv
VERANDAH
9' X 11'5
br3
10' X 10'5
br2
GARAGE WALL LINE BELOW

Width 38'-0"
Depth 42'-5"

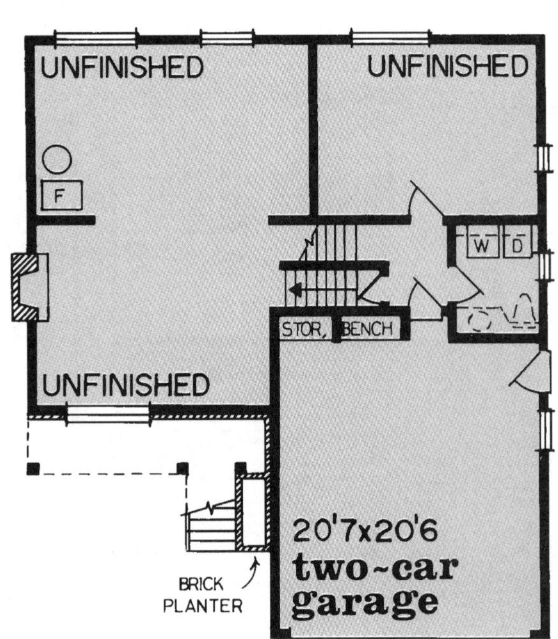
UNFINISHED
UNFINISHED
F
W
D
STOR, BENCH
UNFINISHED
20'7x20'6
two-car garage
BRICK PLANTER

Design by
Select Home Designs

Design by
Select Home Designs

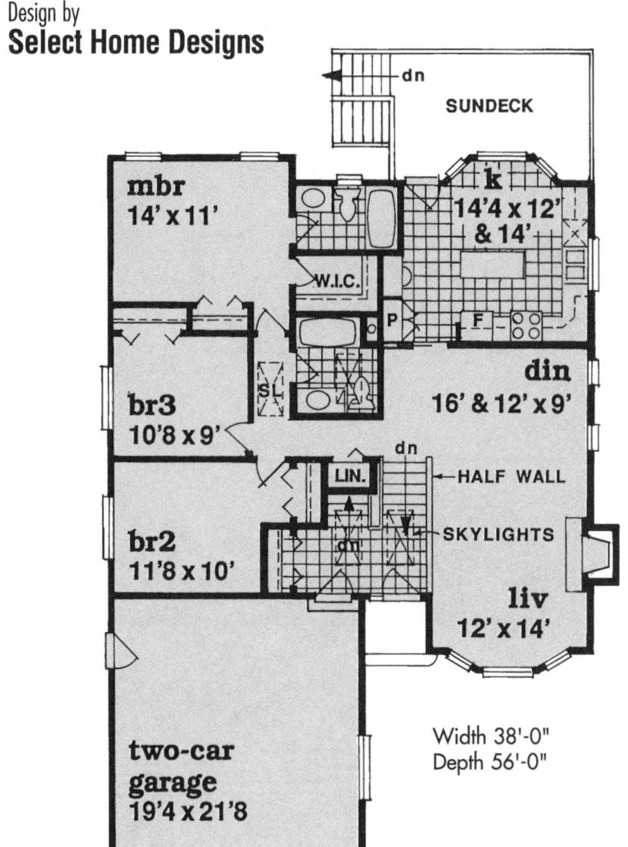

dn
SUNDECK
mbr
14' x 11'
k
14'4 x 12'
& 14'
W.I.C.
P
F
din
16' & 12' x 9'
br3
10'8 x 9'
SL
dn
LIN.
HALF WALL
SKYLIGHTS
br2
11'8 x 10'
dn
liv
12' x 14'
two-car
garage
19'4 x 21'8
Width 38'-0"
Depth 56'-0"

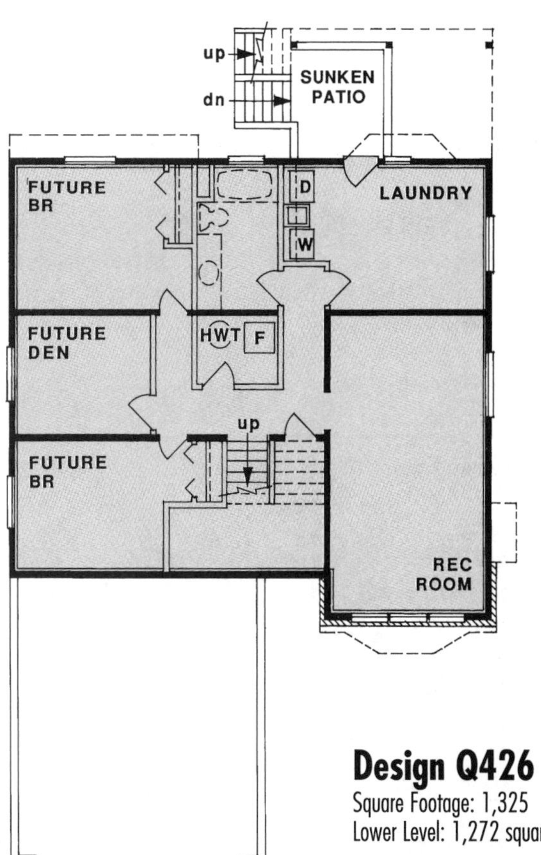

up
dn
SUNKEN
PATIO
FUTURE
BR
D
W
LAUNDRY
FUTURE
DEN
HWT
F
up
FUTURE
BR
REC
ROOM

Design Q426

Square Footage: 1,325
Lower Level: 1,272 square feet

■ A lovely bay window and a recessed entry, complemented by vertical wood siding, enhance the exterior of this split level. Skylights brighten the entry foyer and staircase to the main level. A half-wall separates the staircase and the living room—note the fireplace in the living room. The dining area connects to an L-shaped kitchen with breakfast bay and access to the rear sundeck. Three bedrooms line the left side of the plan. The master suite has a full bath and walk-in closet. Family bedrooms share a full bath just off a skylit hall. The lower level contains 1,272 square feet of unfinished space that can be developed into two additional bedrooms, a full bath, a den and a recreation room. The laundry is also on this level and offers access to a sunken patio.

Design Q341

Square Footage: 1,120
Lower Level: 1,056 square feet

■ This economical three-bedroom split level offers an efficient floor plan that can be expanded. Brick veneer and siding grace the outside, further enhanced by two box-bay windows and a bay window. The living and dining rooms are on the left side of the plan and offer a fireplace and buffet alcove. The U-shaped kitchen has loads of cupboards and counter space and connects directly to the dining room. Bedrooms are on the right side and are comprised of a master suite with half-bath and two family bedrooms sharing a full bath. The lower level is reached via a staircase at the rear. It includes space for a family room with fireplace, one or two bedrooms and a full bath. The laundry is also located here.

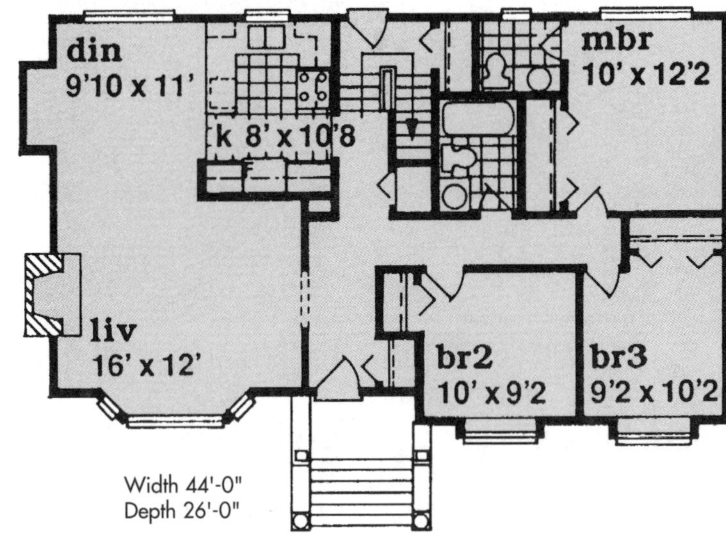
din
9'10 x 11'
k 8' x 10'8
mbr
10' x 12'2
liv
16' x 12'
br2
10' x 9'2
br3
9'2 x 10'2
Width 44'-0"
Depth 26'-0"

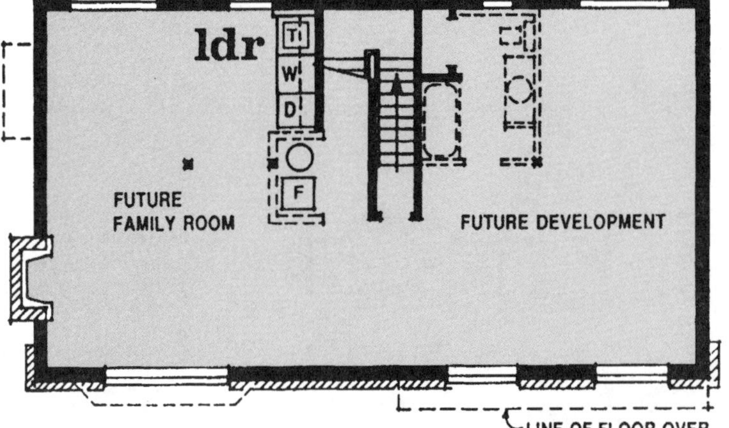
ldr
W
D
F
FUTURE
FAMILY ROOM
FUTURE DEVELOPMENT
LINE OF FLOOR OVER

Design by
Select Home Designs

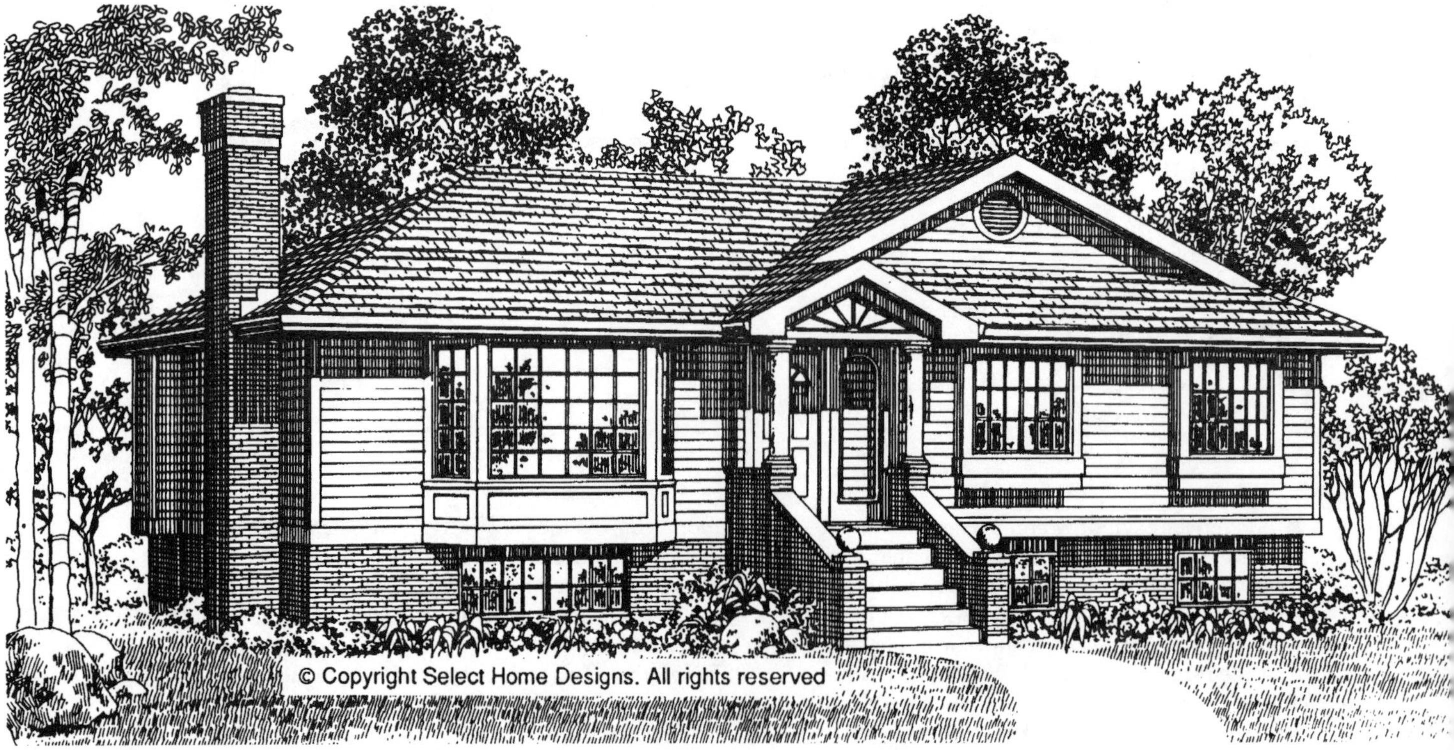

© Copyright Select Home Designs. All rights reserved.

Design Q478

Upper Level: 1,128 square feet
Lower Level: 1,092 square feet
Total: 2,220 square feet

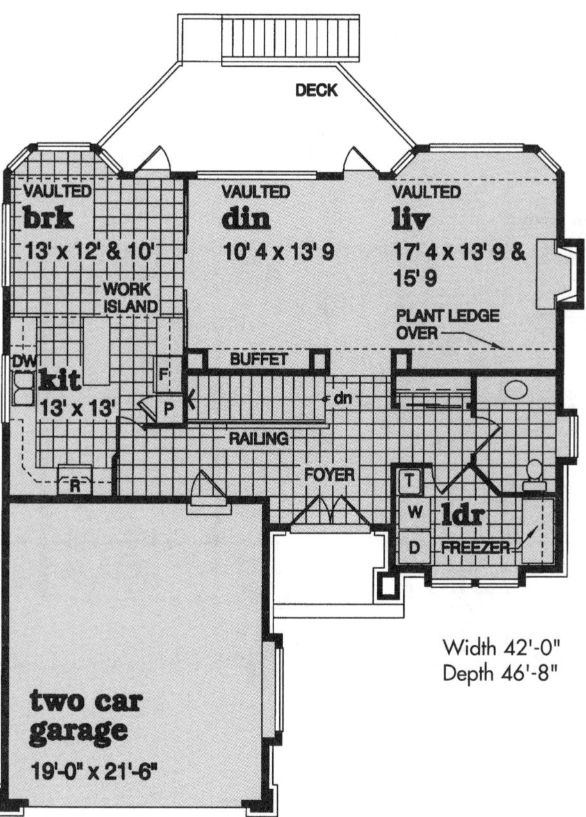
DECK
VAULTED
brk
13' x 12' & 10'
VAULTED
din
10' 4 x 13' 9
VAULTED
liv
17' 4 x 13' 9 &
15' 9
WORK ISLAND
PLANT LEDGE OVER
BUFFET
DW
kit
13' x 13'
F
P
dn
RAILING
FOYER
R
T
W
D
ldr
FREEZER
two car garage
19'-0" x 21'-6"

Width 42'-0"
Depth 46'-8"

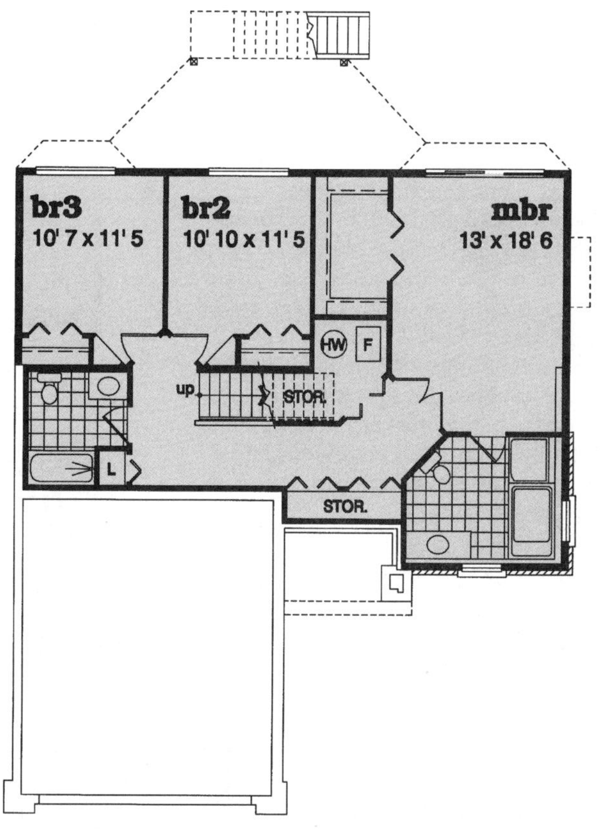
br3
10' 7 x 11' 5
br2
10' 10 x 11' 5
mbr
13' x 18' 6
HW
F
up
STOR.
L
STOR.

■ Beautiful craftsman accents are evident in this design, perfect for a sloping lot. A double-door entry opens off a covered porch to an impressive vaulted foyer. Living areas are to the back and manifest in vaulted living and dining rooms. The living room boasts a bay window and fireplace. Access to the deck sits between the living and dining rooms. The L-shaped kitchen features an island work space and vaulted breakfast bay with deck access. The laundry area is to the front of the house and contains a half bath. Stairs to the lower level are found in the foyer. Sleeping quarters are found below—two family bedrooms and a master suite. The master suite has a walk-in closet and bath with separate tub and shower. Family bedrooms share a full bath.

Design by
Select Home Designs

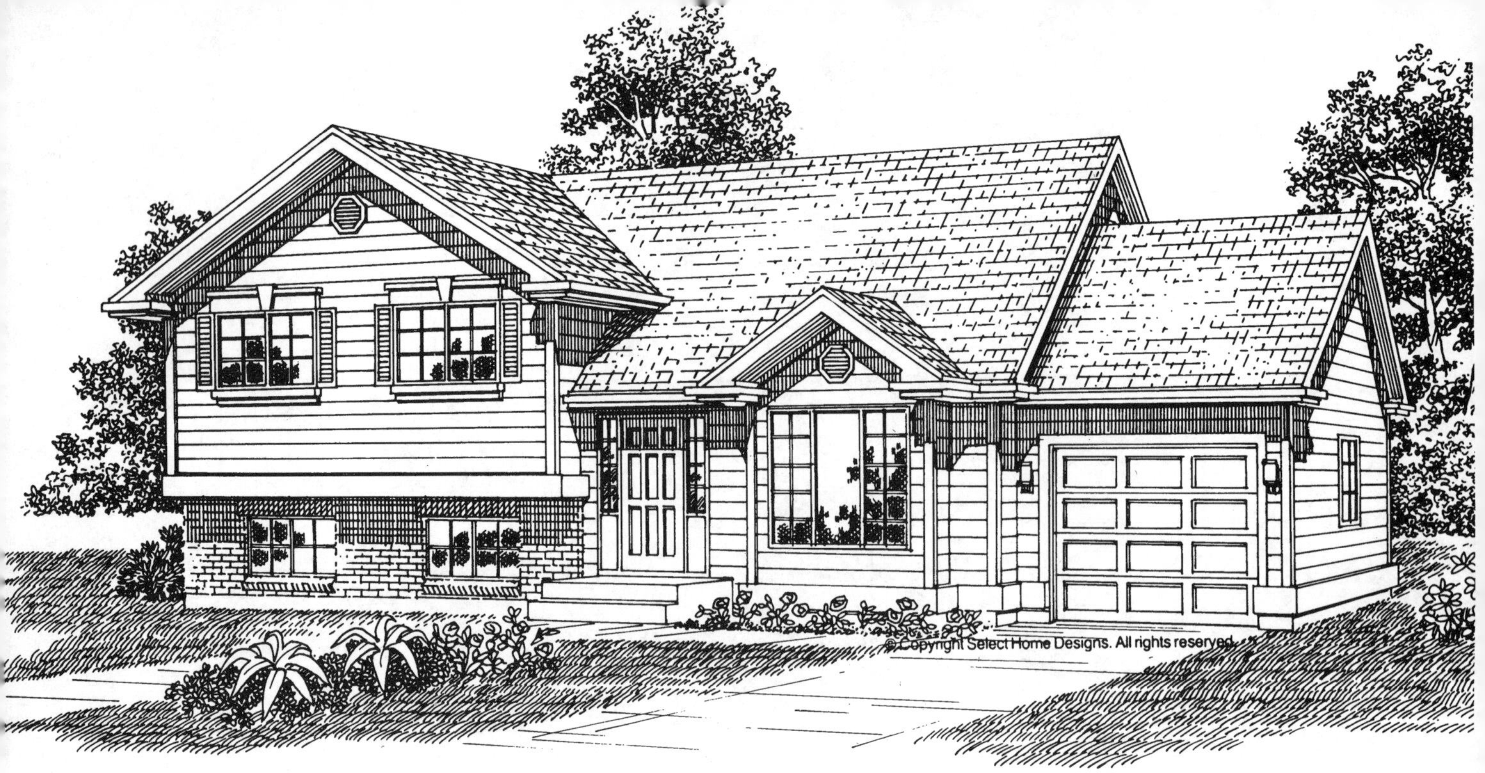

Design Q423

Square Footage: 1,200
Lower Level: 858 square feet

■ This well-planned split level leaves room for expansion in the future. The foyer opens to steps leading both up and down—up to the main level, down to expansion space. The main level holds a living room with window seat and railing that separates it from the dining room. Reach the sundeck through sliding glass doors in the dining room. The L-shaped kitchen is nearby and has an island workspace. Three bedrooms include a master suite with full bath and walk-in closet and two family bedrooms with shared bath. The lower level has 858 square feet of unfinished space that may be developed into a family room, a full bath, a den and a bedroom. The laundry is also found on this level.

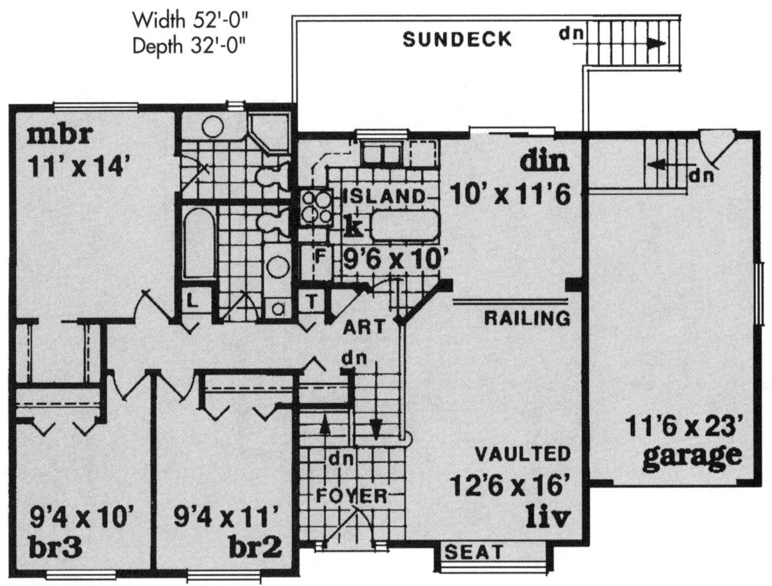
Width 52'-0"
Depth 32'-0"
SUNDECK
dn
mbr
11' x 14'
din
10' x 11'6
ISLAND
k
9'6 x 10'
F
L
T
ART
RAILING
dn
dn
11'6 x 23'
garage
VAULTED
12'6 x 16'
liv
dn
FOYER
9'4 x 10'
br3
9'4 x 11'
br2
SEAT

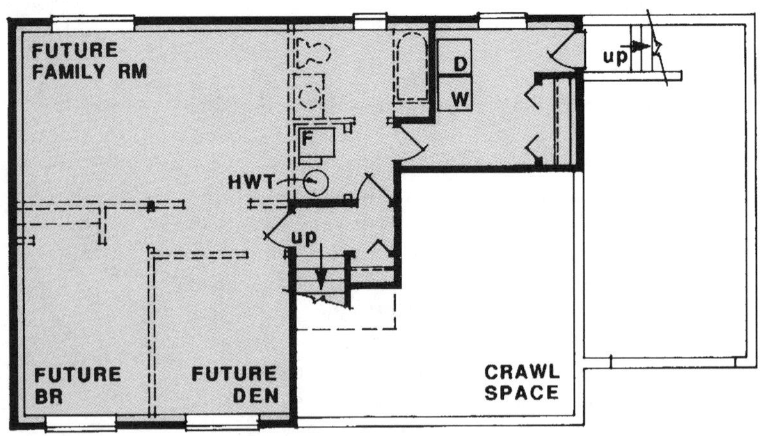
FUTURE
FAMILY RM
D
W
up
F
HWT
up
FUTURE
BR
FUTURE
DEN
CRAWL
SPACE

Design by
Select Home Designs

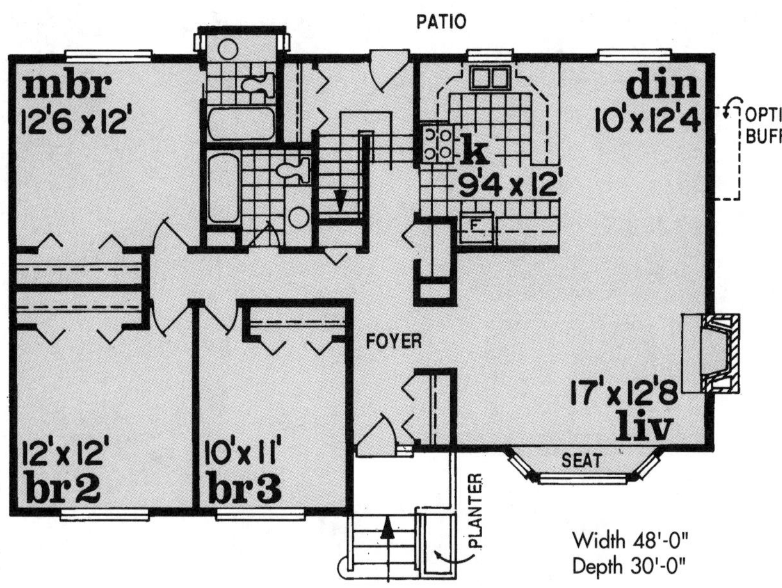
PATIO
mbr
12'6 x 12'
din
10'x12'4
OPTIONAL
BUFFET
k
9'4 x 12'
F
FOYER
17'x12'8
liv
SEAT
12'x12'
br2
10'x11'
br3
PLANTER
Width 48'-0"
Depth 30'-0"

Design Q355

Square Footage: 1,352
Lower Level: 1,341 square feet

■ This compact plan begins with a wood sided exterior, accented with brick and shuttered windows. The entry is up a few steps and opens to a foyer with the living and dining rooms on the right and bedrooms on the left. The living room features a window seat in a bay window and a fireplace. The dining room has an optional buffet alcove. The U-shaped kitchen is nearby. Three bedrooms include two family bedrooms and a full bath, plus the master suite with private bath. The lower level includes space for a recreation room with fireplace, a den, two bedrooms and a full bath. Note the laundry room on the lower level and the large wall closets found in each bedroom.

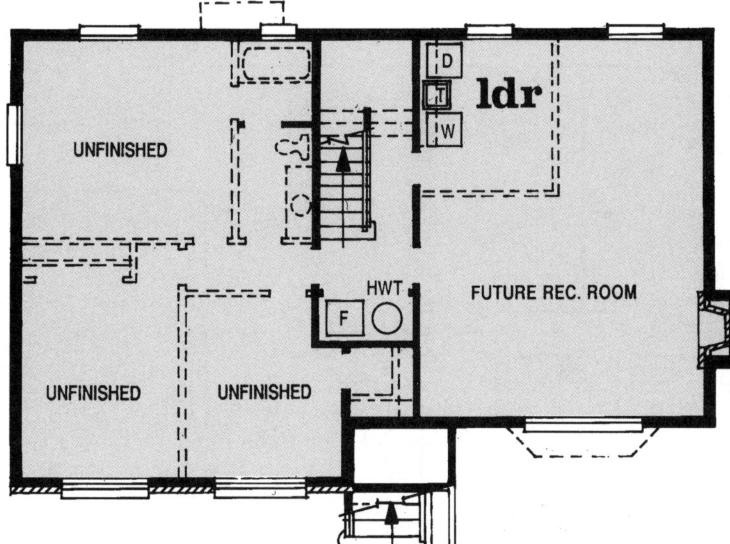
D
W
ldr
UNFINISHED
HWT
F
FUTURE REC. ROOM
UNFINISHED
UNFINISHED

Design by
Select Home Designs

Design 1974

Main Level: 1,680 square feet
Lower Level: 1,344 square feet
Total: 3,024 square feet

■ You would never guess from looking at the front of this traditional design that it possessed such a strikingly different rear. From the front, it looks as though all the livability is on one floor. If you choose, you can build the home without finishing the lower level immediately then adding it as your need for space increases. The main level includes grand livability on its own: a living and dining room, kitchen with breakfast room and three bedrooms with two full baths. The finished lower level would add a family room, a game room, a laundry and hobby room, a bedroom or study and another full bath.

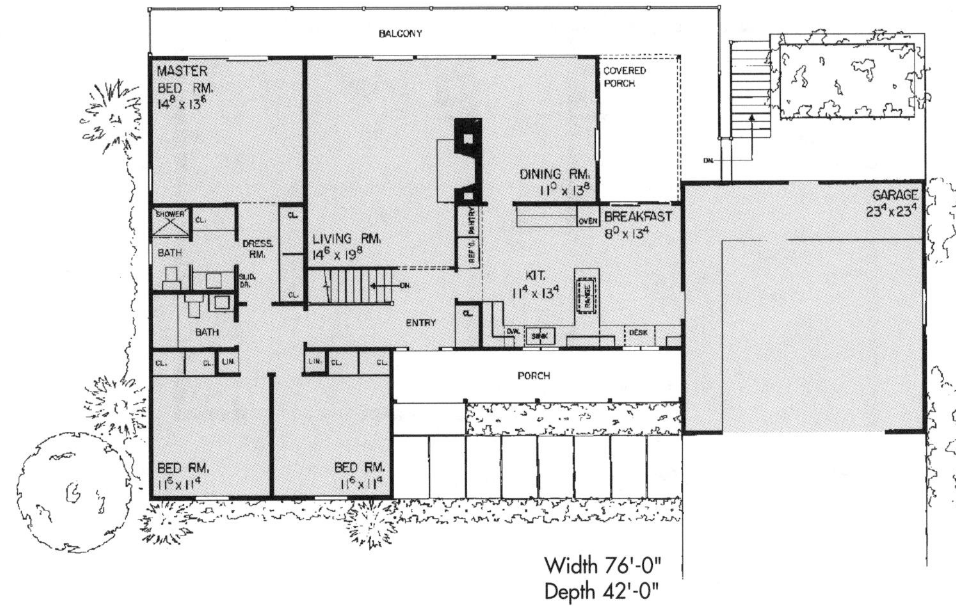
BALCONY
MASTER BED RM. 14^{8} x 13^{6}
COVERED PORCH
DINING RM. 11^{0} x 13^{8}
GARAGE 23^{4} x 23^{4}
SHOWER
CL.
BATH
DRESS. RM.
LIVING RM. 14^{6} x 19^{8}
PANTRY
REF'G.
OVEN
BREAKFAST 8^{0} x 13^{4}
KIT. 11^{4} x 13^{4}
RANGE
DN.
ENTRY
SINK
DESK
BATH
LIN.
PORCH
BED RM. 11^{6} x 11^{4}
BED RM. 11^{6} x 11^{4}

Width 76'-0"
Depth 42'-0"

Design by
Home Planners

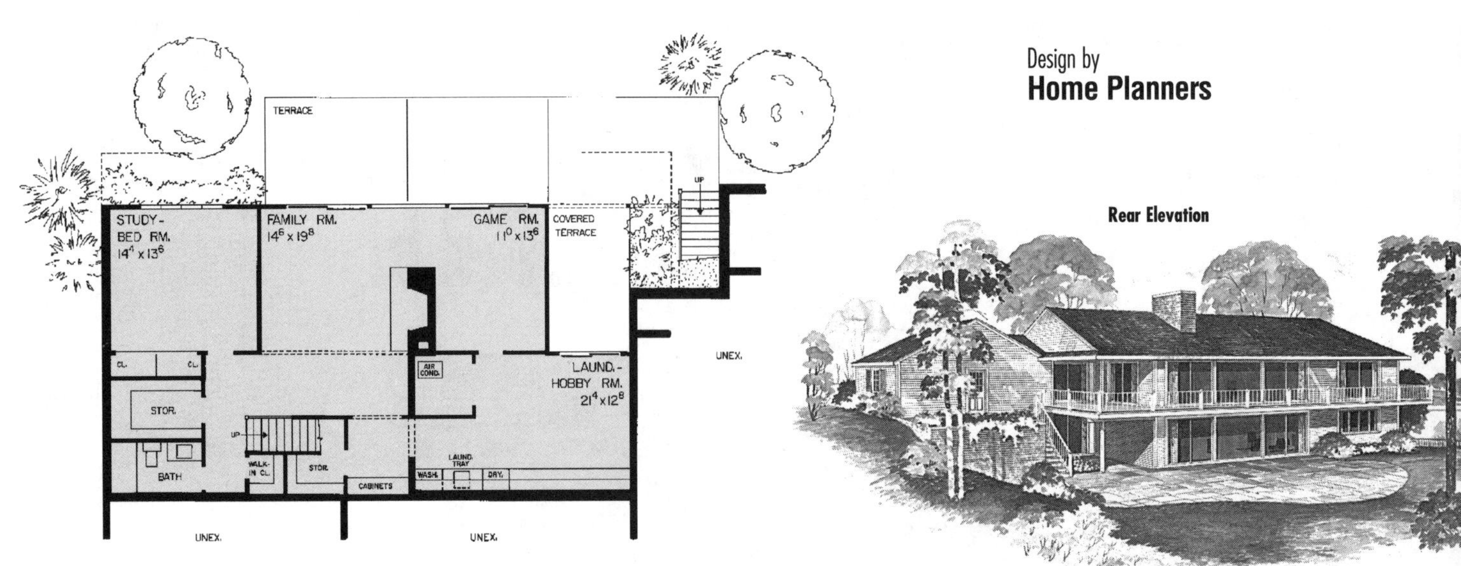
TERRACE
UP
STUDY-BED RM. 14^{4} x 13^{6}
FAMILY RM. 14^{6} x 19^{8}
GAME RM. 11^{0} x 13^{6}
COVERED TERRACE
UNEX.
CL.
AIR COND.
LAUND.-HOBBY RM. 21^{4} x 12^{8}
STOR.
BATH
WALK-IN CL.
STOR.
CABINETS
WASH.
LAUND. TRAY
DRY.
UNEX.
UNEX.
Rear Elevation

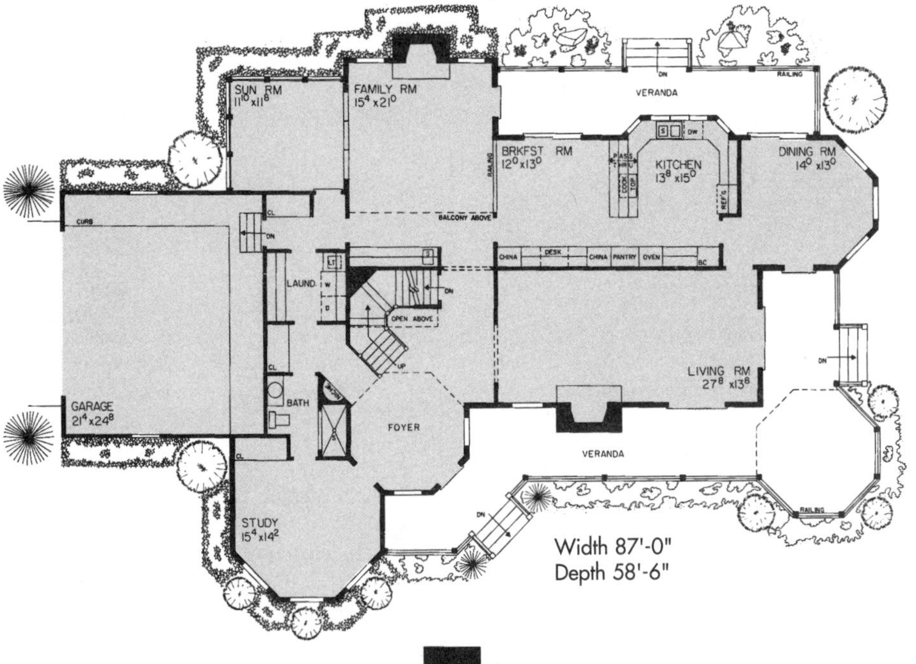

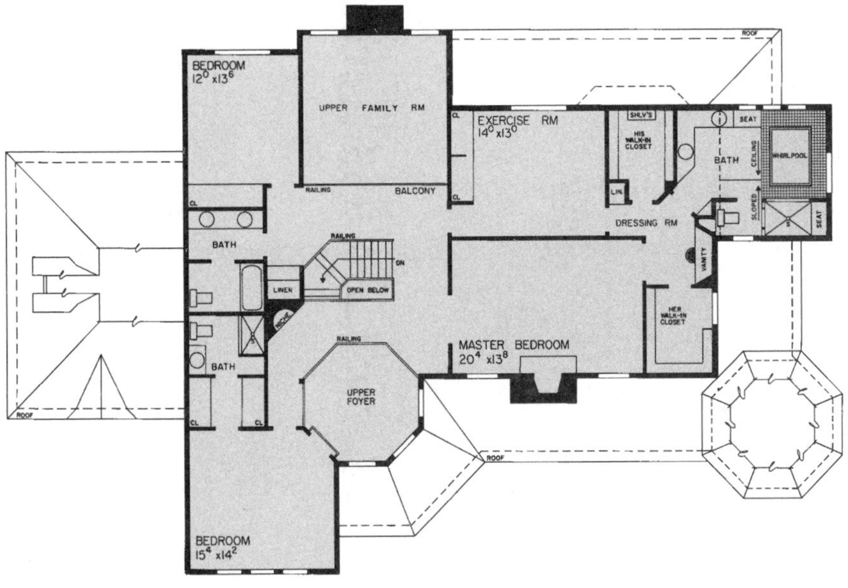

Design by
Home Planners

Design 3304

First Floor: 2,102 square feet
Second Floor: 1,971 square feet
Total: 4,073 square feet

L

■ Say hello to the return of the Golden Era. From front and rear verandas to stately turrets and impressive chimney stack, Victorian style is exquisitely displayed. Besides the grand living room, formal dining room and study, there's a two-story family room. A gourmet kitchen with built-ins has a pass-through counter to the breakfast room. The master suite, located on the second floor, includes a romantic fireplace. Space for a ballet barre or an entire aerobics class is available in the exercise room. After a tough workout, head for the master bath's relaxing whirlpool spa. Two walk-in closets round out the suite. Two additional bedrooms, each with a full bath, are contained on the second floor.

Width 87'-0"
Depth 58'-6"

QUOTE ONE®

Cost to build? See page 516 to order complete cost estimate to build this house in your area!

Design by
Home Planners

Design 2954

First Floor: 3,079 square feet
Second Floor: 1,461 square feet
Total: 4,540 square feet

L

■ This enchanting manor displays architectural elements typical of the Victorian Style: asymmetrical facade, decorative shingles and gables, and a covered porch. The two-story living room with fireplace and wet bar opens to the glass-enclosed rear porch with skylights. A spacious kitchen is filled with amenities including an island cooktop, built-in desk, and butler's pantry connecting to the dining room. The master suite, adjacent to the study, opens to the rear deck; a cozy fireplace keeps the room warm on chilly evenings. Separate His and Hers dressing rooms are outfitted with vanities and walk-in closets, and a luxurious whirlpool tub connects the baths. The second floor opens to a large lounge with built-in cabinets and bookshelves. Three bedrooms and two full baths complete the second-floor livability. The three-car garage contains disappearing stairs to an attic storage area.

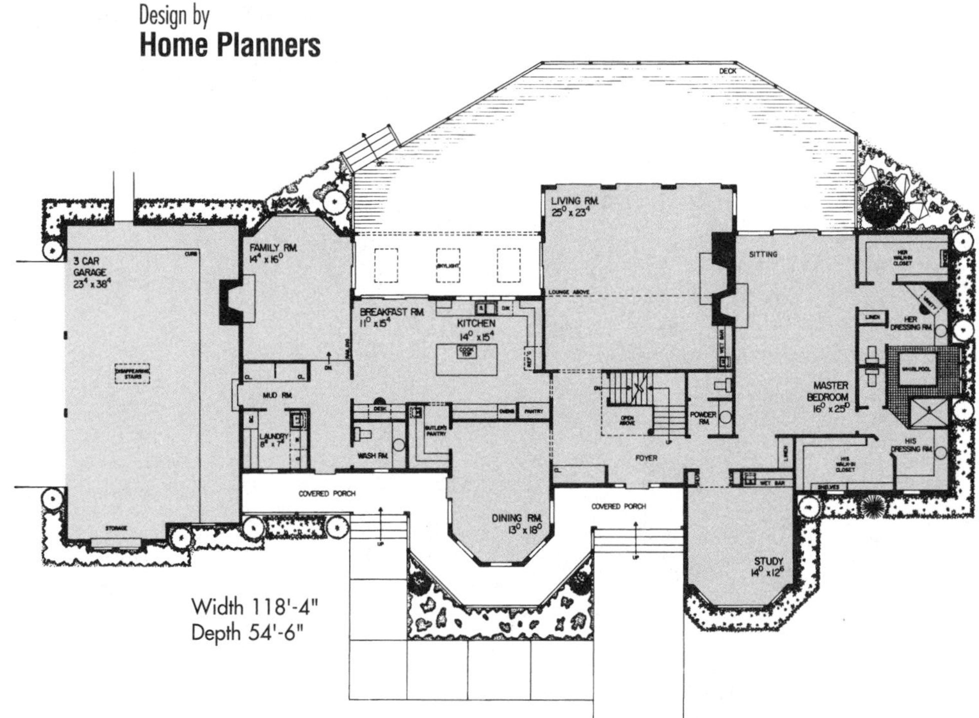
DECK
LIVING RM.
3 CAR GARAGE
FAMILY RM.
SITTING
BREAKFAST RM.
KITCHEN
MUD RM.
LAUNDRY
WASH RM.
FOYER
POWDER RM.
MASTER BEDROOM
COVERED PORCH
DINING RM.
COVERED PORCH
STUDY
Width 118'-4"
Depth 54'-6"

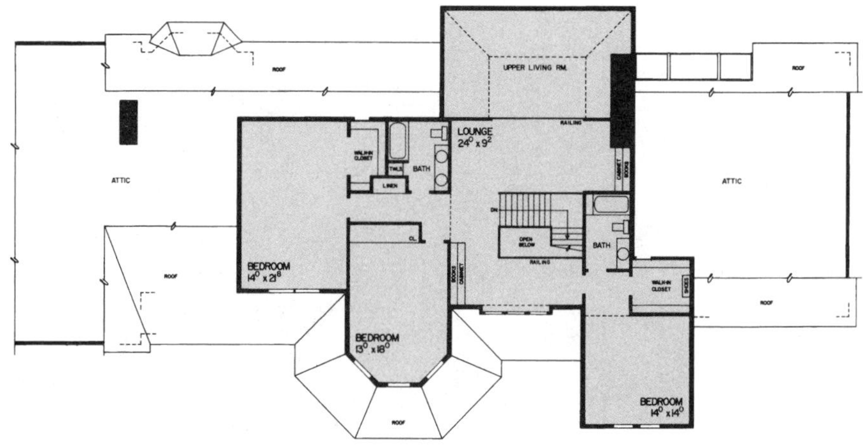
UPPER LIVING RM.
LOUNGE
ATTIC
BATH
BEDROOM
BEDROOM
BATH
ATTIC
ROOF
BEDROOM

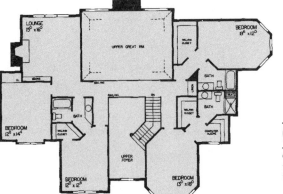

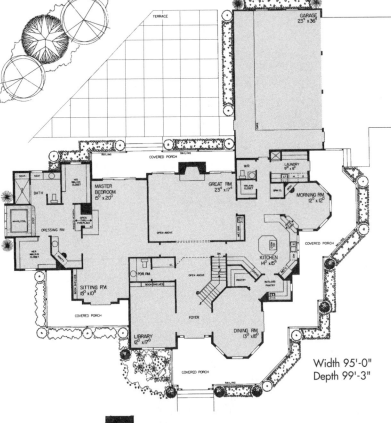

Design 2953

First Floor: 2,995 square feet
Second Floor: 1,831 square feet
Total: 4,826 square feet

L D

■ A magnificent, finely wrought covered porch wraps around this impressive Victorian estate home. The gracious two-story foyer provides a direct view past the stylish bannister and into the great room with a large central fireplace. To the left of the foyer is a bookshelf-lined library and to the right is a dramatic, octagonal-shaped dining room. The island cooktop completes a convenient work triangle in the kitchen and a pass-through connects this room with the Victorian-style morning room. A butler's pantry, a walk-in closet and a broom closet offer plenty of storage space. A luxurious master suite is located on the first floor and opens to the rear covered porch. A through-fireplace warms the bedroom, sitting room and dressing room, which includes His and Hers walk-in closets. The step-up whirlpool tub is an elegant focal point to the master bath. Four uniquely designed bedrooms, three full baths, and a restful lounge with fireplace are located on the second floor.

Width 95'-0"
Depth 99'-3"

QUOTE ONE®
Cost to build? See page 516 to order complete cost estimate to build this house in your area!

Design by
Home Planners

2968

,736 square feet
: 2,264 square feet
Total: 6,000 square feet

L

■The distinctive covered entry to this stunning manor, flanked by twin turrets, leads to a gracious foyer with impressive fan lights. The plan opens from the foyer to a formal dining room, master study and step-down gathering room. The spacious kitchen has numerous amenities including an island work station and a built-in desk. The adjacent morning room and gathering room with a wet bar and a raised-hearth fireplace are bathed in light and open to the terrace for outdoor entertaining. The luxurious master suite has a wealth of amenities as well. The second floor features four bedrooms and an oversized activities room with a fireplace and a balcony. Unfinished attic space can be completed to your specifications.

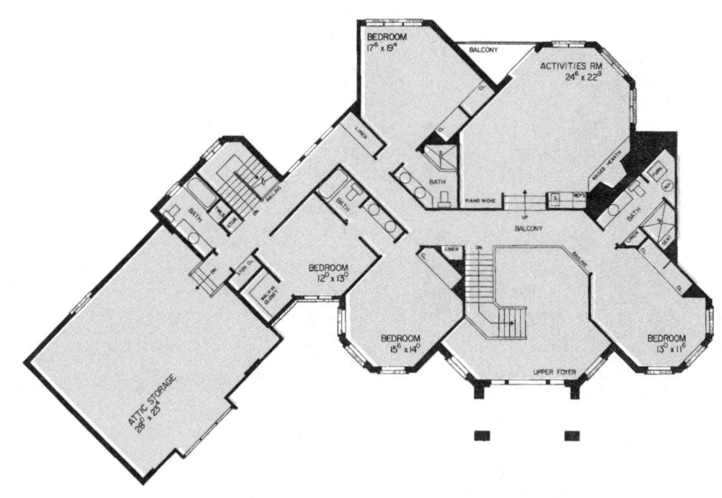

BEDROOM
BALCONY
ACTIVITIES RM
BATH
BEDROOM
BEDROOM
BEDROOM
UPPER FOYER
ATTIC STORAGE

Design by
Home Planners

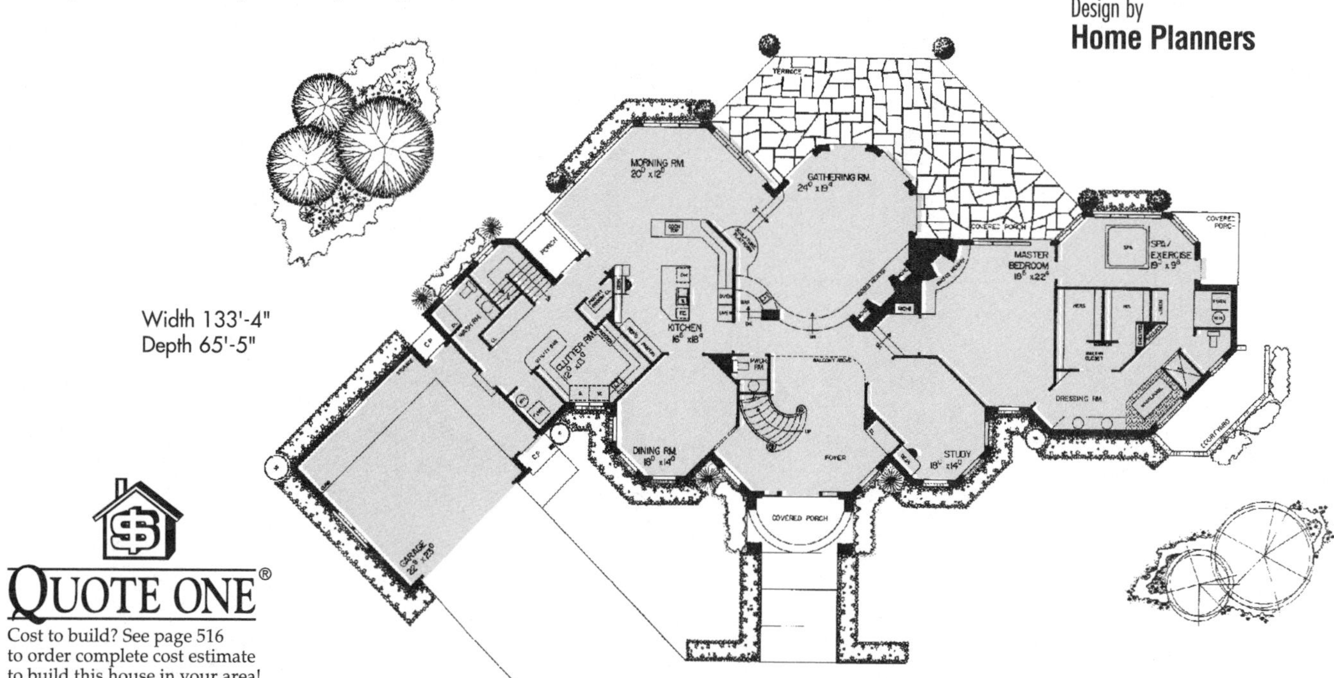

TERRACE
MORNING RM.
GATHERING RM.
MASTER BEDROOM
SPA/ EXERCISE
KITCHEN
DRESSING RM
DINING RM.
FOYER
STUDY
COVERED PORCH
GARAGE

Width 133'-4"
Depth 65'-5"

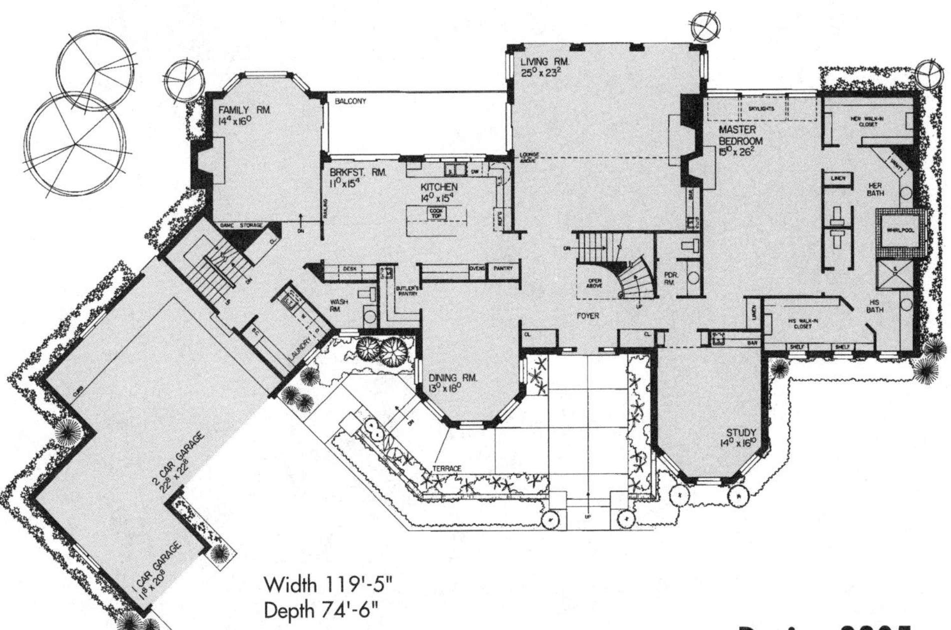

LIVING RM.
FAMILY RM.
BALCONY
MASTER BEDROOM
BRKFST. RM.
KITCHEN
FOYER
DINING RM.
STUDY
TERRACE
2 CAR GARAGE
1 CAR GARAGE
Width 119'-5"
Depth 74'-6"

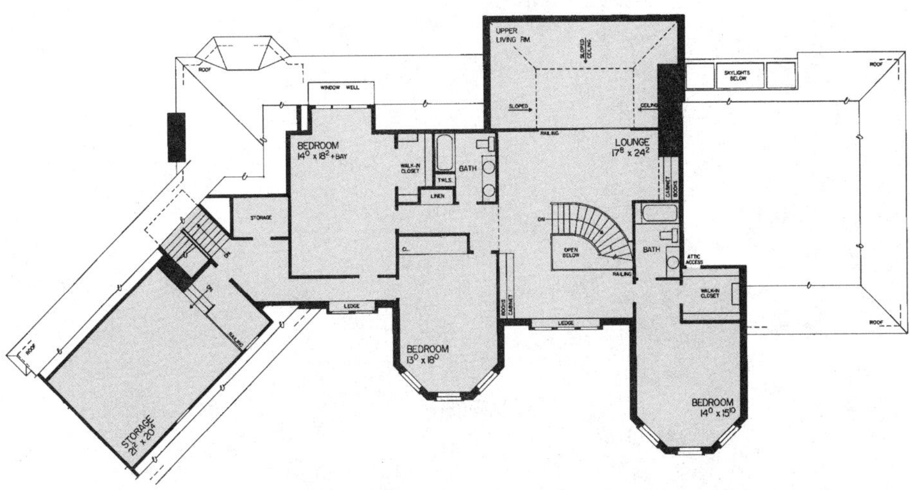

UPPER LIVING RM.
LOUNGE
BEDROOM
BATH
BEDROOM
BEDROOM
STORAGE

Design 3305

First Floor: 3,644 square feet
Second Floor: 2,005 square feet
Total: 5,649 square feet

■ A steeply pitched roof, a generous supply of multi-paned windows and fanlights and glass side panels accenting the front entry signal the grand design of this home. Highlights include an elegant first-floor master suite, two-story foyer and living room, a study with wet bar, a bayed formal dining room and bonus storage over the garage. Note the three fireplaces, plenty of outdoor access and the three-car garage. A lounge on the second floor has built-in space for books and other sundries. Two sets of stairs lead to the second floor; one set has downstairs access also.

Design by
Home Planners

Design 2952

First Floor: 2,870 square feet
Second Floor: 2,222 square feet
Total: 5,092 square feet

L

■ Semi-circular arches complement the strong linear rooflines and balconies of this exciting contemporary. The first floor is filled with well-planned amenities for entertaining and relaxing. The foyer opens to a step-down living room with a dramatic sloped ceiling, a fireplace and three sliding glass doors that access the front courtyard and terrace. A tavern with built-in wine rack and an adjacent butler's pantry are ideal for entertaining. The family room features a fireplace, sliding glass door and a handy snack bar. The kitchen allows meal preparation, cooking and storage within a step of the central work island. Three second-floor bedrooms, each with a private bath and balcony, are reached by either of two staircases. The master suite, with His and Hers baths and walk-in closets, whirlpool and fireplace, adds the finishing touch to this memorable home.

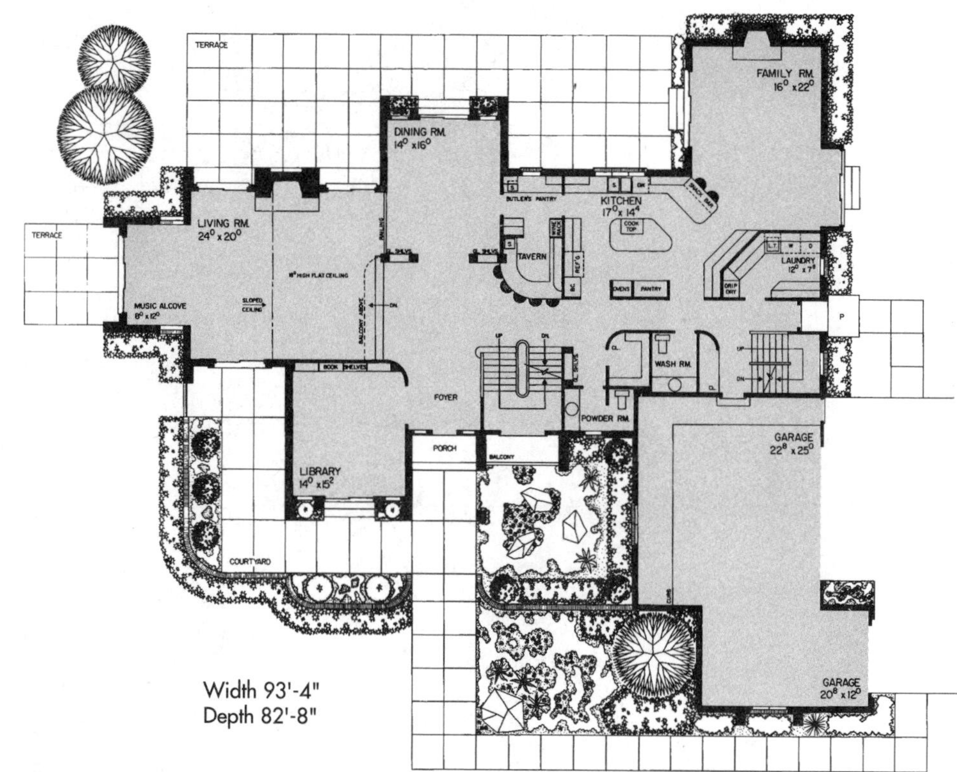
TERRACE
DINING RM. 14^{0} x 16^{0}
FAMILY RM. 16^{0} x 22^{0}
LIVING RM. 24^{0} x 20^{0}
KITCHEN 17^{0} x 14^{4}
TAVERN
LAUNDRY 12^{0} x 7^{4}
MUSIC ALCOVE 8^{0} x 12^{0}
WASH RM.
FOYER
POWDER RM.
GARAGE 22^{8} x 25^{0}
LIBRARY 14^{0} x 15^{2}
PORCH
BALCONY
COURTYARD
GARAGE 20^{8} x 12^{0}
Width 93'-4"
Depth 82'-8"

Design by
Home Planners

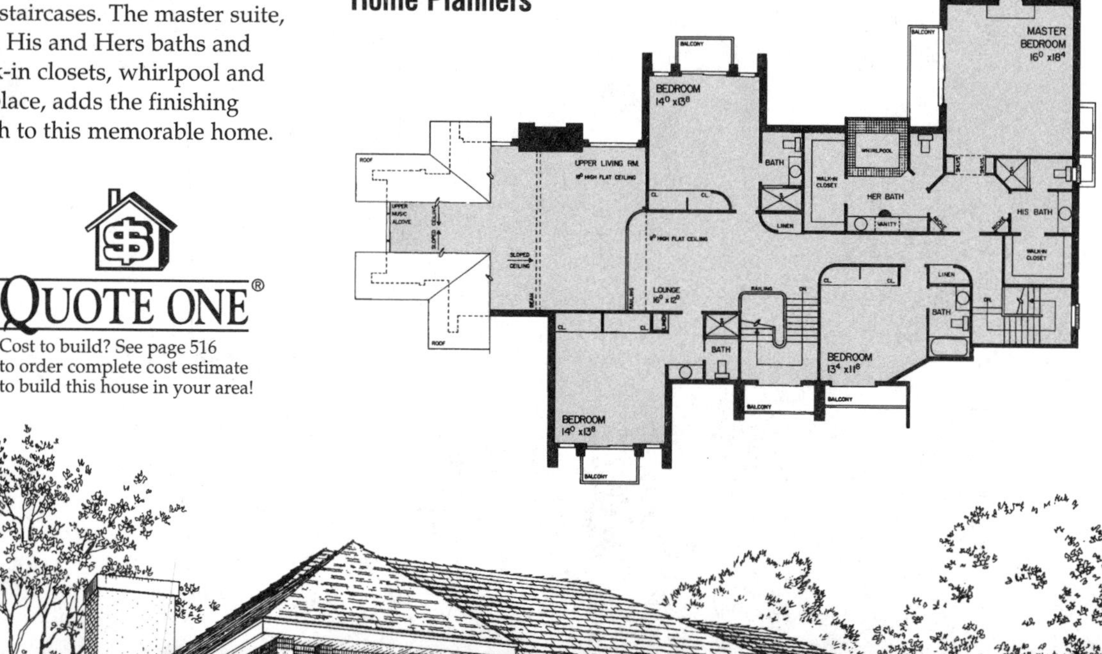
MASTER BEDROOM 16^{0} x 18^{4}
BEDROOM 14^{0} x 13^{8}
UPPER LIVING RM.
WHIRLPOOL
HER BATH
HIS BATH
LOUNGE 16^{0} x 12^{0}
BATH
BEDROOM 13^{4} x 11^{8}
BEDROOM 14^{0} x 13^{8}
BALCONY

QUOTE ONE®
Cost to build? See page 516 to order complete cost estimate to build this house in your area!

UPPER GATHERING RM.
BED RM. 14⁰ x 12⁴
BED RM. 13⁸ x 12⁴
BALCONY
RAILING
BATH
BATH
UPPER FOYER
LEDGE
BED RM. 14⁰ x 12⁰
BED RM. 14⁰ x 12⁰

Design 3380

First Floor: 3,350 square feet
Second Floor: 1,298 square feet
Total: 4,648 square feet

■ Reminiscent of a Mediterranean villa, this grand manor is a show-stopper on the outside and a comfortable residence on the inside. An elegant receiving hall boasts a double staircase and is flanked by the formal dining room and the library. A huge gathering room is found to the back and is graced by a fireplace and a wall of sliding glass doors to the rear terrace. The master bedroom is found on the first floor for privacy. With a lavish bath to pamper you, and His and Hers walk-in closets, this suite will be a delight to retire to each evening. Upstairs are four additional bedrooms with ample storage space, a large balcony overlooking the gathering room and two full baths.

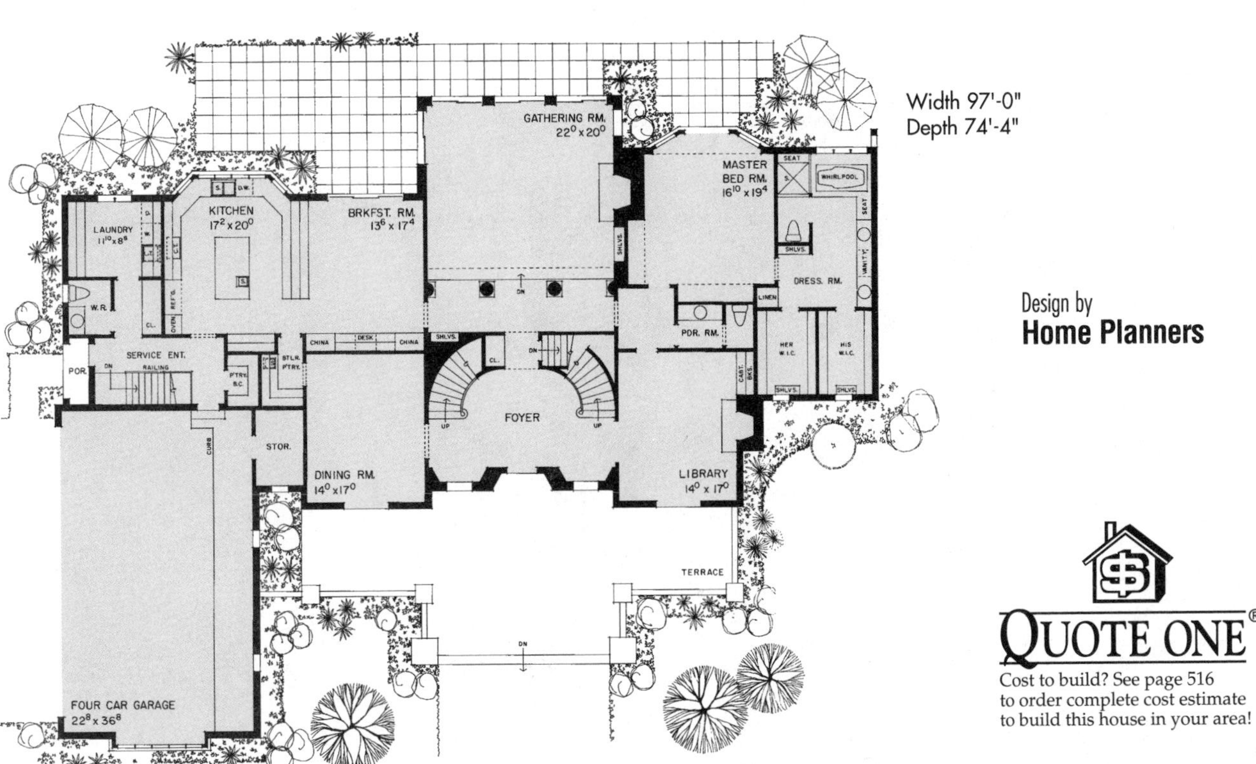
GATHERING RM. 22⁰ x 20⁰
MASTER BED RM. 16¹⁰ x 19⁴
WHIRLPOOL
DRESS. RM.
HER W.I.C.
HIS W.I.C.
PDR. RM.
KITCHEN 17² x 20⁰
BRKFST. RM. 13⁶ x 17⁴
LAUNDRY 11¹⁰ x 8⁸
SERVICE ENT.
FOYER
DINING RM. 14⁰ x 17⁰
LIBRARY 14⁰ x 17⁰
STOR.
TERRACE
FOUR CAR GARAGE 22⁸ x 36⁸

Width 97'-0"
Depth 74'-4"

Design by
Home Planners

QUOTE ONE®
Cost to build? See page 516 to order complete cost estimate to build this house in your area!

Design by
Home Planners

Design 2940

First Floor: 4,786 square feet
Second Floor: 1,842 square feet
Total: 6,628 square feet

L D

■ Graceful window arches soften the massive chimneys and steeply gabled roof of this grand Norman manor. A two-story gathering room is two steps down from the adjacent lounge with impressive wet bar and semi-circular music alcove. The highly efficient galley-style kitchen overlooks the family room fireplace and spectacular windowed breakfast room. The master suite is a private retreat with a fireplace and a wood box tucked into the corner of its sitting room. Separate His and Hers baths and dressing rooms guarantee plenty of space and privacy. A large, built-in whirlpool tub adds the final touch. Upstairs, a second-floor balcony overlooks the gathering room below. There are also four additional bedrooms, each with a private bath.

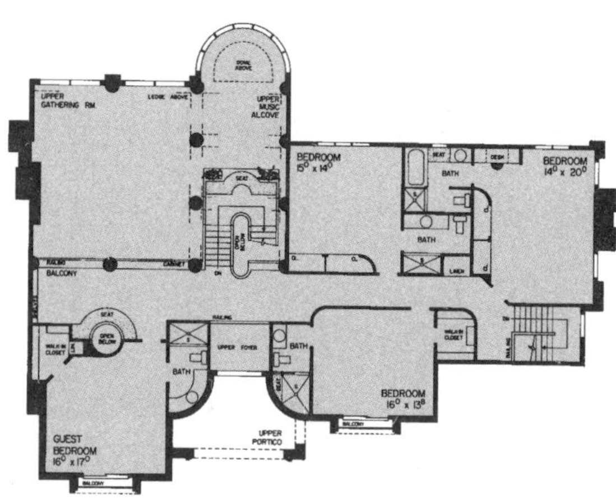
UPPER GATHERING RM.
UPPER MUSIC ALCOVE
BEDROOM
BEDROOM
BALCONY
BATH
UPPER FOYER
BEDROOM
GUEST BEDROOM
UPPER PORTICO

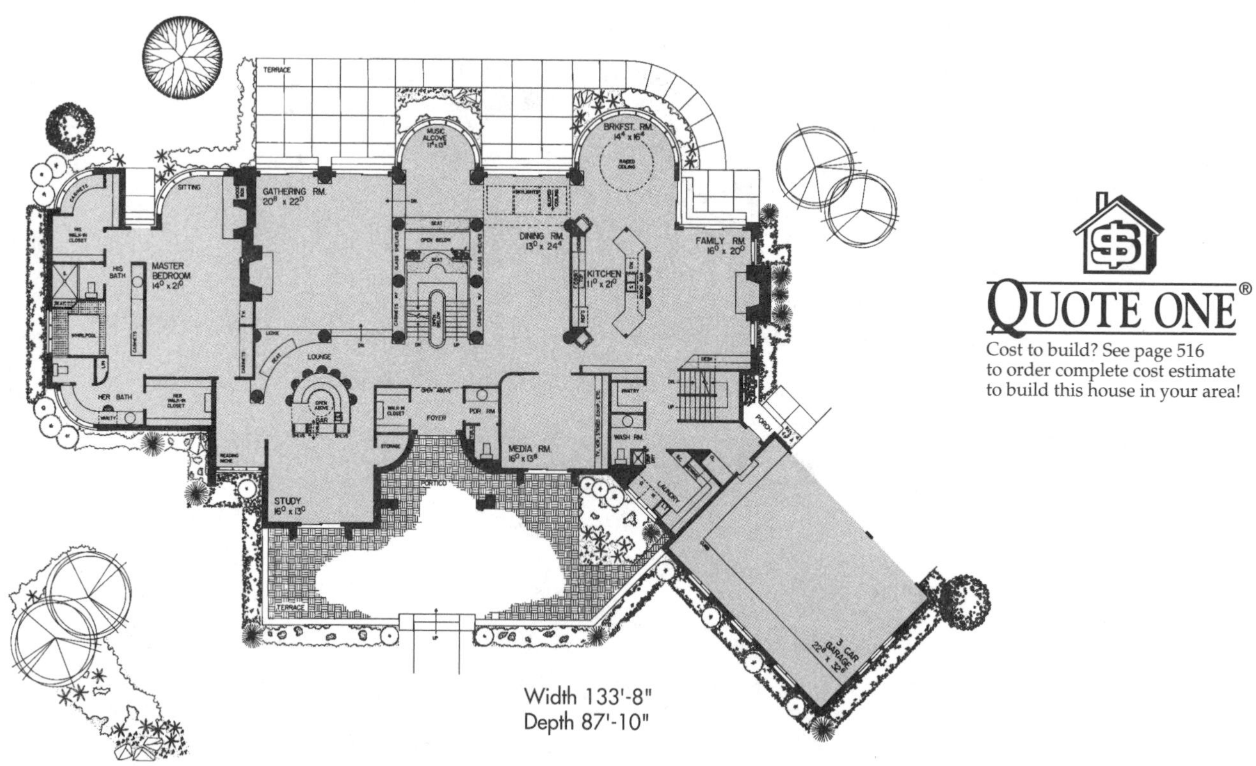
TERRACE
MUSIC ALCOVE
BRKFST. RM.
GATHERING RM.
SITTING
DINING RM.
FAMILY RM.
MASTER BEDROOM
HIS BATH
KITCHEN
LOUNGE
HER BATH
FOYER
MEDIA RM.
STUDY
PORTICO
LAUNDRY
PORCH
TERRACE
3 CAR GARAGE
Width 133'-8"
Depth 87'-10"

QUOTE ONE®
Cost to build? See page 516 to order complete cost estimate to build this house in your area!

Design 2543

First Floor: 2,345 square feet
Second Floor: 1,687 square feet
Total: 4,032 square feet

L D

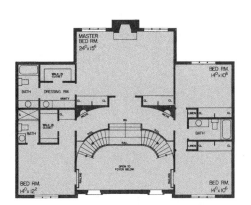

Design by
Home Planners

■ This bestselling French adaptation is highlighted by effective window treatment, delicate cornice detailing, appealing brick quoins and excellent proportion. Inside, a large, two-story foyer leads under the arch of a dual staircase to a gathering room graced by a central fireplace and access to the rear terrace. The formal living and dining rooms flank the foyer and work well together for entertaining. The gourmet kitchen offers a work island and has an attached breakfast room with access to the terrace and offers a huge walk-in pantry. Upstairs, a deluxe master bedroom suite is lavish in its efforts to pamper you. Three secondary bedrooms share this level, one with its own bath and a walk-in closet while two others share a full hall bath.

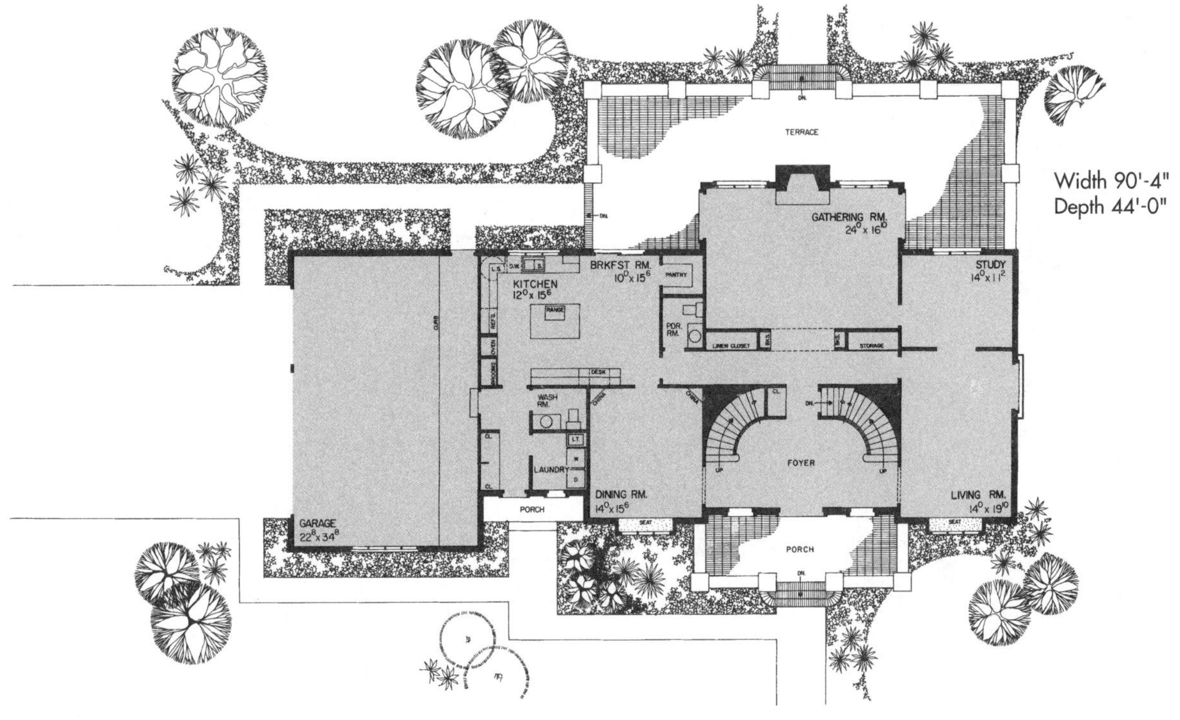
TERRACE
GATHERING RM.
BRKFST RM.
PANTRY
KITCHEN
STUDY
PDR RM.
LINEN CLOSET
STORAGE
WASH RM.
LAUNDRY
FOYER
DINING RM.
LIVING RM.
PORCH
GARAGE

Width 90'-4"
Depth 44'-0"

Design 2957

First Floor: 2,557 square feet
Second Floor: 1,939 square feet
Total: 4,496 square feet

L **D**

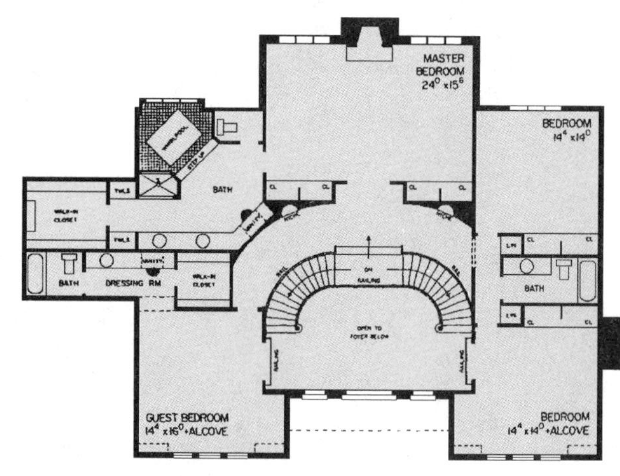
MASTER BEDROOM $24^{0} \times 15^{6}$
BEDROOM $14^{4} \times 14^{0}$
BATH
DRESSING RM
BATH
GUEST BEDROOM $14^{4} \times 16^{0}$+ALCOVE
BEDROOM $14^{4} \times 14^{0}$+ALCOVE

■ The decorative half-timbers and stone wall-cladding on this manor are stately examples of Tudor architecture. A grand double staircase is the highlight of the elegant, two-story foyer that opens to each of the main living areas. The living and gathering rooms are anchored by impressive central fireplaces. Filled with amenities, the island kitchen has a nearby breakfast room for casual meals. Functioning with both the kitchen and the formal dining room is the butler's pantry. Accessible from both the gathering and living rooms is the quiet study. The outstanding master suite features a cozy bedroom fireplace, a picturesque whirlpool bath and a convenient walk-in closet. Three additional second-floor bedrooms include a guest suite with a dressing room and a walk-in closet.

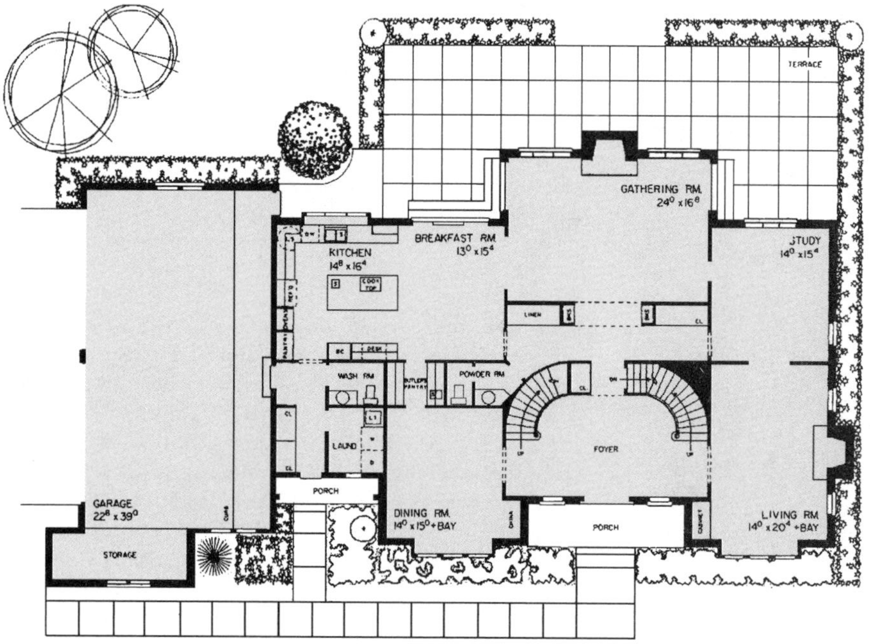

Width 97'-4"
Depth 53'-0"

Design by
Home Planners

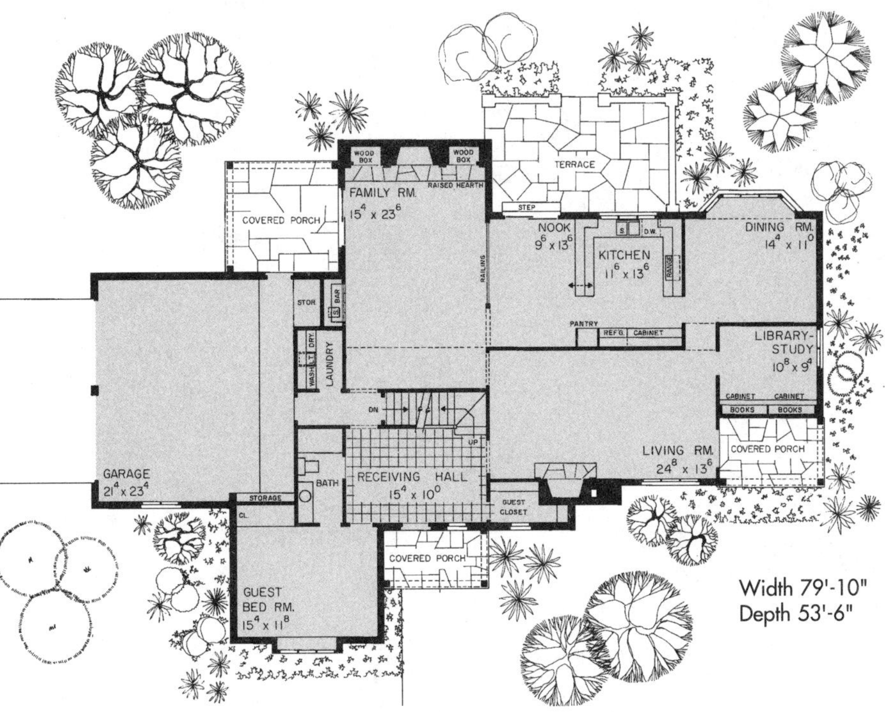

WOOD BOX
WOOD BOX
TERRACE
RAISED HEARTH
FAMILY RM. $15^4 \times 23^6$
COVERED PORCH
STEP
NOOK $9^6 \times 13^6$
KITCHEN $11^6 \times 13^6$
D.W.
DINING RM. $14^4 \times 11^0$
RAILING
STOR
BAR
WASH
DRY
LAUNDRY
PANTRY
REFG.
CABINET
LIBRARY-STUDY $10^8 \times 9^4$
CABINET
CABINET
BOOKS
BOOKS
DN
UP
GARAGE $21^4 \times 23^4$
BATH
RECEIVING HALL $15^4 \times 10^0$
LIVING RM. $24^8 \times 13^6$
COVERED PORCH
STORAGE
CL.
GUEST CLOSET
COVERED PORCH
GUEST BED RM. $15^4 \times 11^8$

Width 79'-10"
Depth 53'-6"

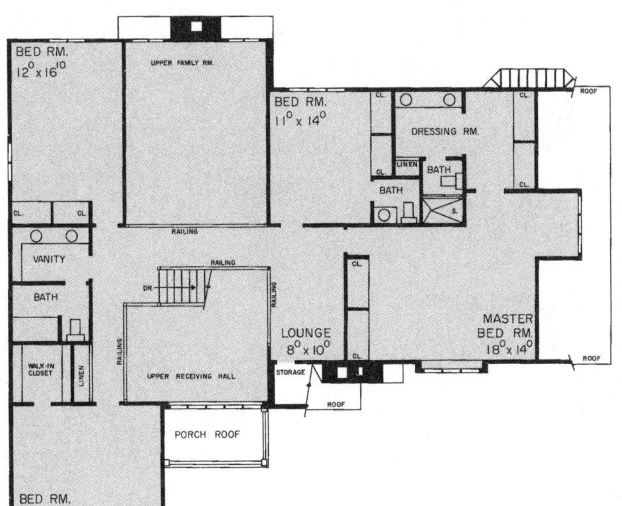

BED RM. $12^0 \times 16^{10}$
UPPER FAMILY RM.
BED RM. $11^0 \times 14^0$
CL.
DRESSING RM.
ROOF
LINEN
BATH
BATH
CL.
CL.
CL.
RAILING
VANITY
RAILING
BATH
DN
RAILING
MASTER BED RM. $18^0 \times 14^0$
LOUNGE $8^0 \times 10^0$
CL.
WALK-IN CLOSET
LINEN
RAILING
UPPER RECEIVING HALL
STORAGE
ROOF
ROOF
PORCH ROOF
BED RM. $16^2 \times 13^0$

Design 2356

First Floor: 1,969 square feet
Second Floor: 1,702 square feet
Total: 3,671 square feet

L D

■ Here is truly an exquisite Tudor adaptation. The exterior, with its interesting rooflines, window treatment, stately chimney and its appealing use of brick and stucco, could hardly be more dramatic. Inside, the delightfully large receiving hall has a two-story ceiling and controls the flexible traffic patterns. The living and dining rooms, with the library nearby, will cater to formal living pursuits. The guest room offers another haven for the enjoyment of peace and quiet. Observe the adjacent full bath. For the family's informal activities there are the interactions of the family room—covered porch—nook—kitchen zone. Notice the raised-hearth fireplace, the wood boxes, the sliding glass doors, built-in bar and the kitchen pass-through. Adding to the charm of the family room is its high ceiling. The second floor offers three family bedrooms, a lounge and a deluxe master suite.

Design by
Home Planners

Design 2955

First Floor: 3,840 square feet
Second Floor: 3,435 square feet
Total: 7,275 square feet

■ Cross gables, decorative half-timbers and three massive chimneys mark the exterior of this magnificent baronial Tudor. A circular staircase housed in the turret makes an impressive opening statement in the two-story foyer. A powder room and telephone center are located off the foyer for easy use by guests. Two steps down lead to the elegant living room with a music alcove or the sumptuous library with a wet bar. The kitchen is a chef's delight with a work island, a full cooking counter and a butler's pantry leading to the formal dining room. The second floor features four bedrooms, two with fireplaces and each with a private bath and abundant closet space. The master suite contains an additional fireplace, His and Hers walk-in closets, a whirlpool bath and a private sitting room in a windowed alcove. Adjacent to the master suite is a nursery that would also make an ideal exercise room.

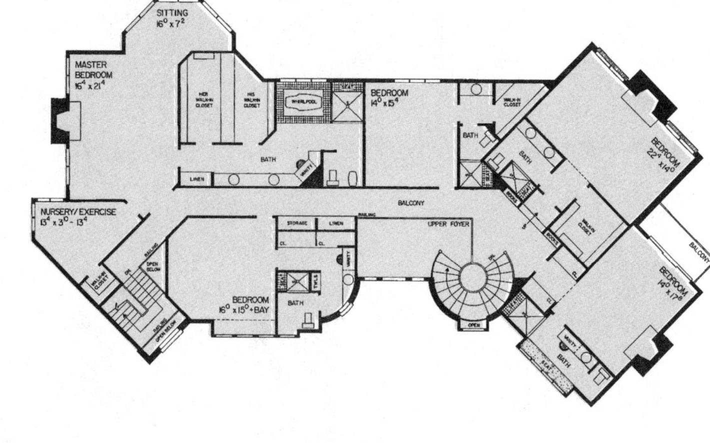

SITTING
MASTER BEDROOM
BEDROOM
BATH
BALCONY
UPPER FOYER
NURSERY/EXERCISE
BEDROOM
BEDROOM
BEDROOM

Design by
Home Planners

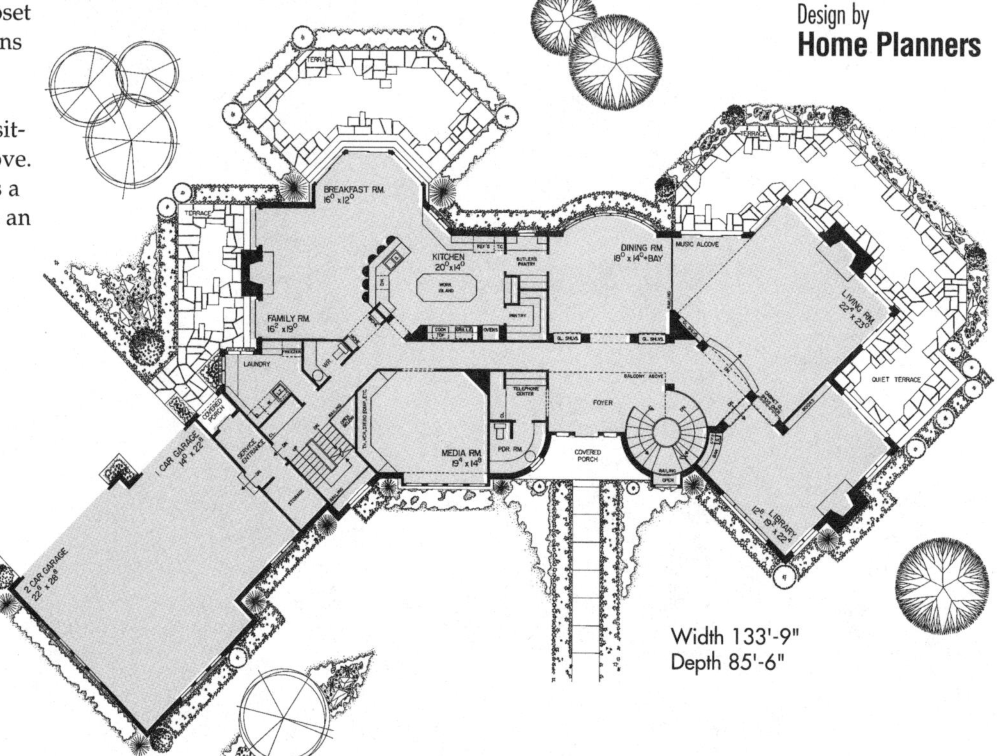

TERRACE
BREAKFAST RM.
KITCHEN
DINING RM.
MUSIC ALCOVE
LIVING RM.
FAMILY RM.
LAUNDRY
FOYER
MEDIA RM.
QUIET TERRACE
LIBRARY
COVERED PORCH
1 CAR GARAGE
2 CAR GARAGE

Width 133'-9"
Depth 85'-6"

QUOTE ONE®
Cost to build? See page 516 to order complete cost estimate to build this house in your area!

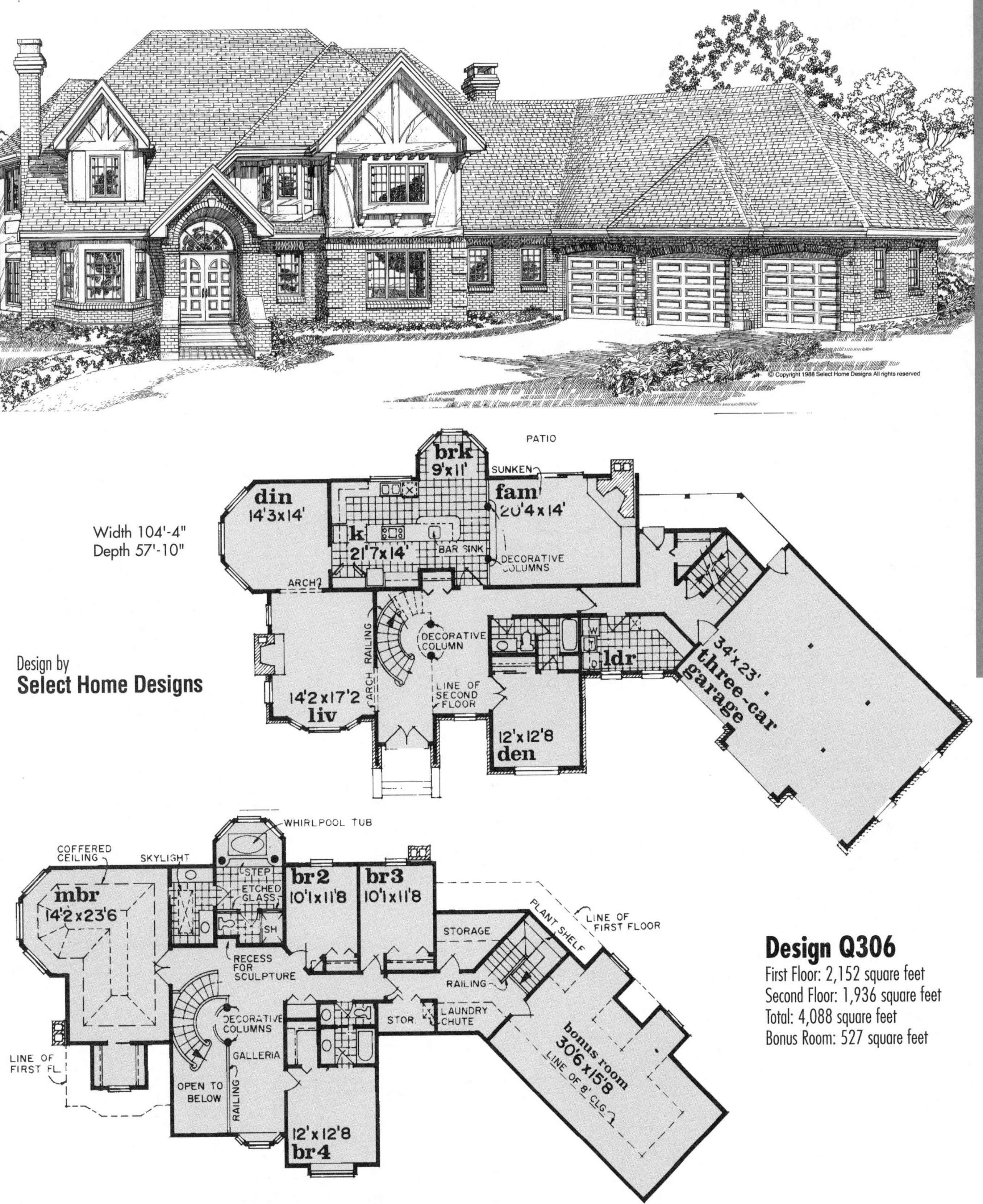
© Copyright 1988 Select Home Designs All rights reserved
PATIO
brk 9'x11'
SUNKEN
din 14'3x14'
fam 20'4x14'
k 21'7x14'
BAR SINK
DECORATIVE COLUMNS
ARCH
RAILING
DECORATIVE COLUMN
ARCH
LINE OF SECOND FLOOR
ldr
34'x23' three-car garage
14'2x17'2 liv
12'x12'8 den
WHIRLPOOL TUB
COFFERED CEILING
SKYLIGHT
STEP
ETCHED GLASS
SH
mbr 14'2x23'6
br2 10'1x11'8
br3 10'1x11'8
STORAGE
PLANT SHELF
LINE OF FIRST FLOOR
RECESS FOR SCULPTURE
RAILING
DECORATIVE COLUMNS
STOR.
LAUNDRY CHUTE
GALLERIA
LINE OF FIRST FL.
OPEN TO BELOW
RAILING
bonus room 30'6x15'8
LINE OF 8' CLG.
12'x12'8 br4

Width 104'-4"
Depth 57'-10"

Design by
Select Home Designs

Design Q306

First Floor: 2,152 square feet
Second Floor: 1,936 square feet
Total: 4,088 square feet
Bonus Room: 527 square feet

■ In elegant Tudor style, this estate home has all of the best of luxury living. The vaulted foyer has a circular staircase and galleria above. The living room with bay window and fireplace is on the left; a cozy den with double-door access on the right. The dining room is defined by an arched opening and has a bay window, also. The U-shaped kitchen features a bar sink and bayed breakfast nook. Enter the sunken family room through decorative columns. You'll find a corner fireplace and sliding glass doors to the rear yard. The second floor holds four bedrooms—one of which is a master suite with coffered ceiling and private bath. Family bedrooms share a full bath.
A bonus room allows for 527 square feet of finish-later space. Plans include details for both a basement and a crawlspace foundation.

Design 2951

First Floor: 4,195 square feet
Second Floor: 2,094 square feet
Total: 6,289 square feet

■ A single prominent turret with two-story divided windows draws attention to this stately Tudor home. The open foyer allows an uninterrupted view into the impressive, two-story great room with wet bar, where a fireplace with raised hearth runs the entire length of one wall. The expansive kitchen, conveniently located near the service entrance, has a U-shaped work area and a snack bar that opens to the morning room. The adjacent sloped-ceiling family room has an additional fireplace and a comfortable window seat. A Victorian-inspired, octagon-shaped sitting room is tucked into the corner of the unique master bedroom. His and Hers baths and walk-in closets complete the impressive first-floor suite. Two bedrooms, a study and a guest suite with private sitting room are located on the second floor. A magnificent second-floor bridge overlooks the foyer and gathering room and provides extraordinary views to guests on the way to their bedroom.

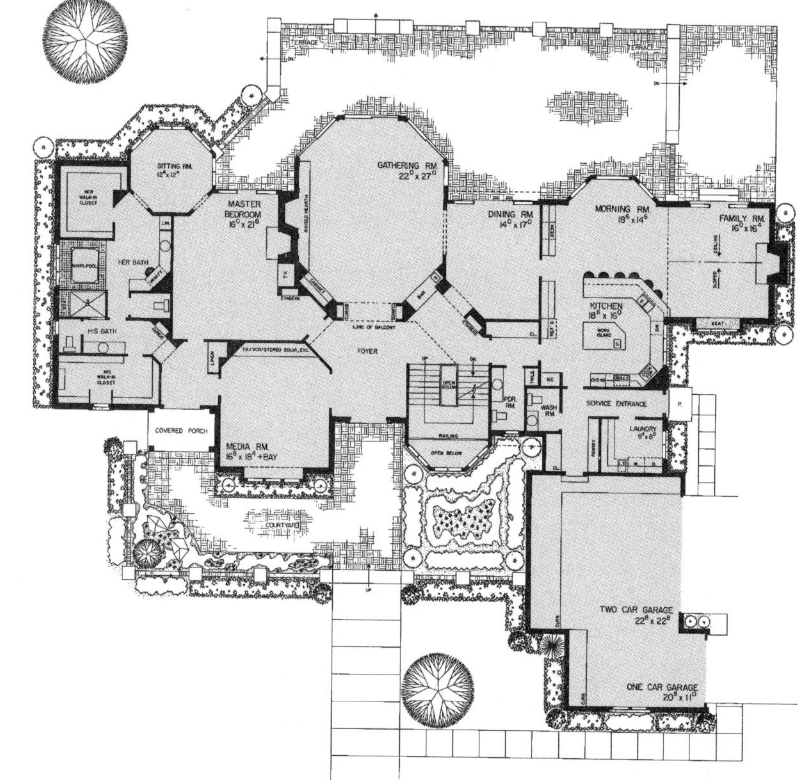

SITTING RM. $12^4 \times 12^4$
GATHERING RM. $22^0 \times 27^0$
MASTER BEDROOM $16^0 \times 21^8$
HER BATH
HIS BATH
DINING RM. $14^0 \times 17^0$
MORNING RM. $18^6 \times 14^6$
FAMILY RM. $16^0 \times 16^4$
KITCHEN $18^8 \times 16^0$
FOYER
SERVICE ENTRANCE
LAUNDRY
COVERED PORCH
MEDIA RM. $16^8 \times 16^4$ +BAY
TWO CAR GARAGE $22^8 \times 22^8$
ONE CAR GARAGE $20^8 \times 11^0$

Width 111'-4"
Depth 87'-6"

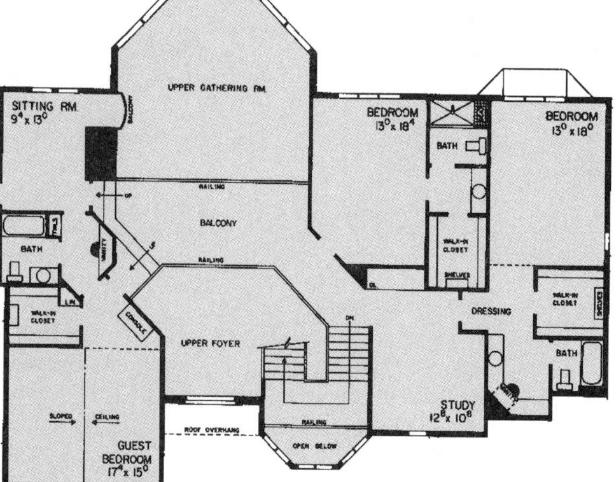

UPPER GATHERING RM.
SITTING RM. $9^4 \times 13^0$
BEDROOM $13^0 \times 18^4$
BEDROOM $13^0 \times 18^0$
BATH
BALCONY
RAILING
WALK-IN CLOSET
DRESSING
UPPER FOYER
ROOF OVERHANG
OPEN BELOW
STUDY $12^8 \times 10^8$
GUEST BEDROOM $17^4 \times 15^0$

Design by
Home Planners

Design by
Home Planners

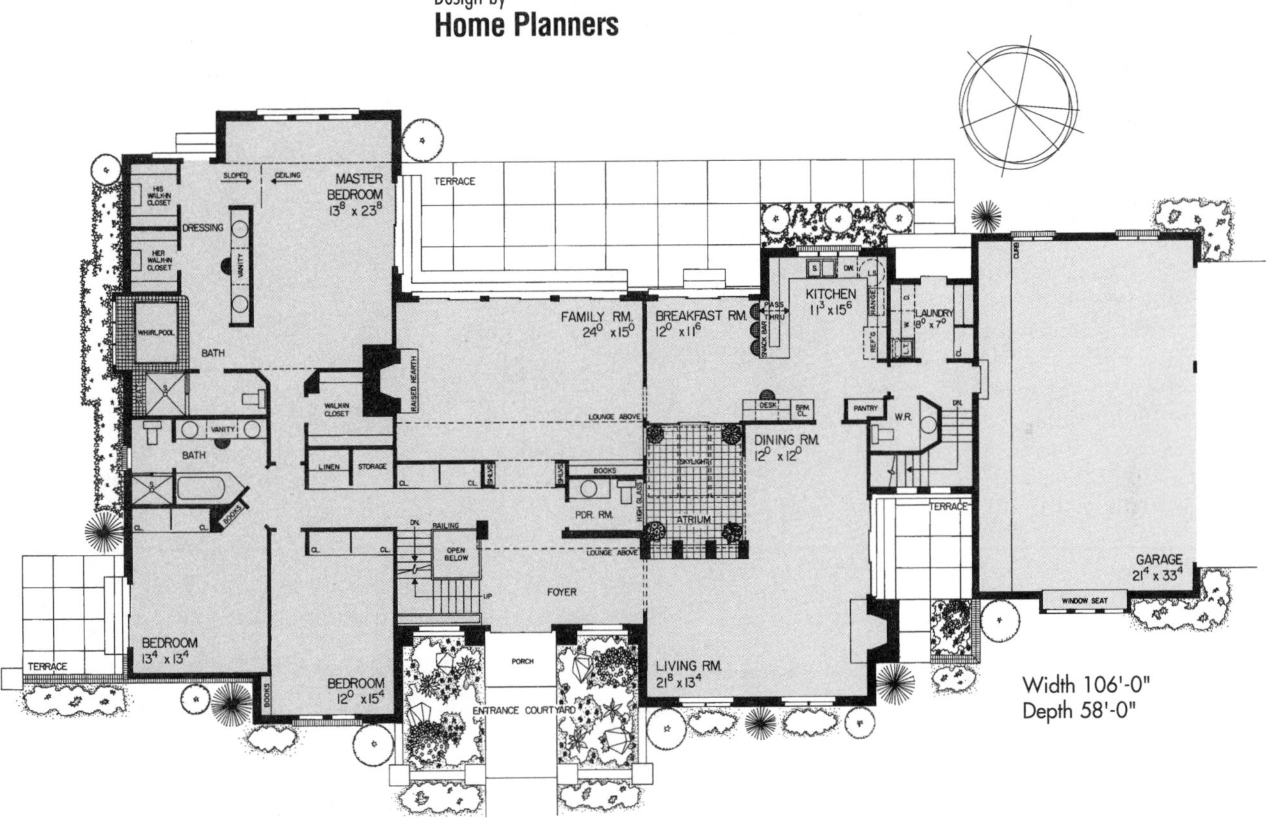

TERRACE
MASTER BEDROOM 13⁸ x 23⁸
SLOPED CEILING
HIS WALK-IN CLOSET
DRESSING
HER WALK-IN CLOSET
VANITY
WHIRLPOOL
BATH
WALK-IN CLOSET
RAISED HEARTH
FAMILY RM. 24⁰ x 15⁰
BREAKFAST RM. 12⁰ x 11⁶
KITCHEN 11³ x 15⁶
LAUNDRY 8⁰ x 7⁰
PANTRY
W.R.
DESK
LOUNGE ABOVE
VANITY
BATH
LINEN
STORAGE
BOOKS
SKYLIGHT
DINING RM. 12⁰ x 12⁰
PDR. RM.
HIGH GLASS
ATRIUM
TERRACE
OPEN BELOW
RAILING
FOYER
GARAGE 21⁴ x 33⁴
WINDOW SEAT
BEDROOM 13⁴ x 13⁴
TERRACE
PORCH
BEDROOM 12⁰ x 15⁴
ENTRANCE COURTYARD
LIVING RM. 21⁸ x 13⁴
Width 106'-0"
Depth 58'-0"

Design 2966

Square Footage: 3,403
Lounge: 284 square feet

■ This Tudor adaptation is as dramatic inside as it is outside. From the front courtyard to the rear terrace, up-to-date amenities like the courtyard atrium that adjoins the formal rooms invite entertaining and offer relaxation for busy lifestyles. A spacious foyer features a sloped ceiling and leads to open living space, which offers a raised-hearth fireplace and spacious views of the rear grounds. The secluded master suite boasts a lavish bath with a tiled-rim spa tub, two walk-in closets and twin lavatories with a knee-space vanity. A gallery hall leads to two additional bedrooms and a hall bath with its own vanity. A second-story lounge adds 284 square feet to the total.

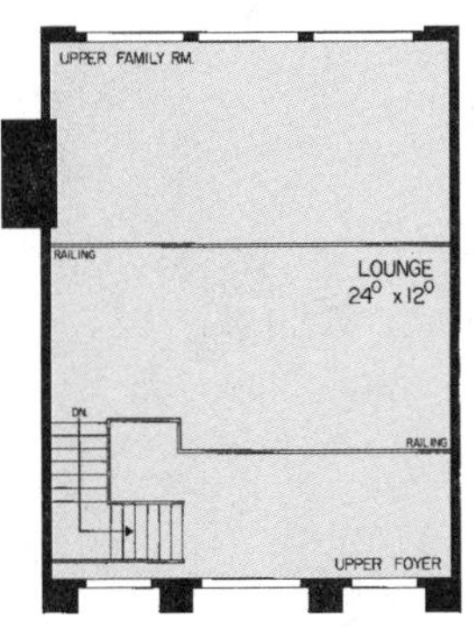

UPPER FAMILY RM.
RAILING
LOUNGE 24⁰ x 12⁰
DN.
RAILING
UPPER FOYER

Design 1228

First Floor: 2,583 square feet
Second Floor: 697 square feet
Total: 3,280 square feet

L **D**

■ This beautiful house has a wealth of detail taken from the rich traditions of French Regency design. The roof itself is a study in pleasant dormers and the hips and valleys add interest. A close examination of the plan shows the careful arrangement of space for privacy as well as livability. The spacious formal entrance hall sets the stage for formal entertaining in the living and dining rooms. The family room features a beam ceiling and pass-through to the U-shaped island kitchen. An attached breakfast room gains access to the rear terrace. Three family bedrooms are found on the first floor and share a full bath. The master suite is by itself on the second floor and has double walk-in closets and a private bath.

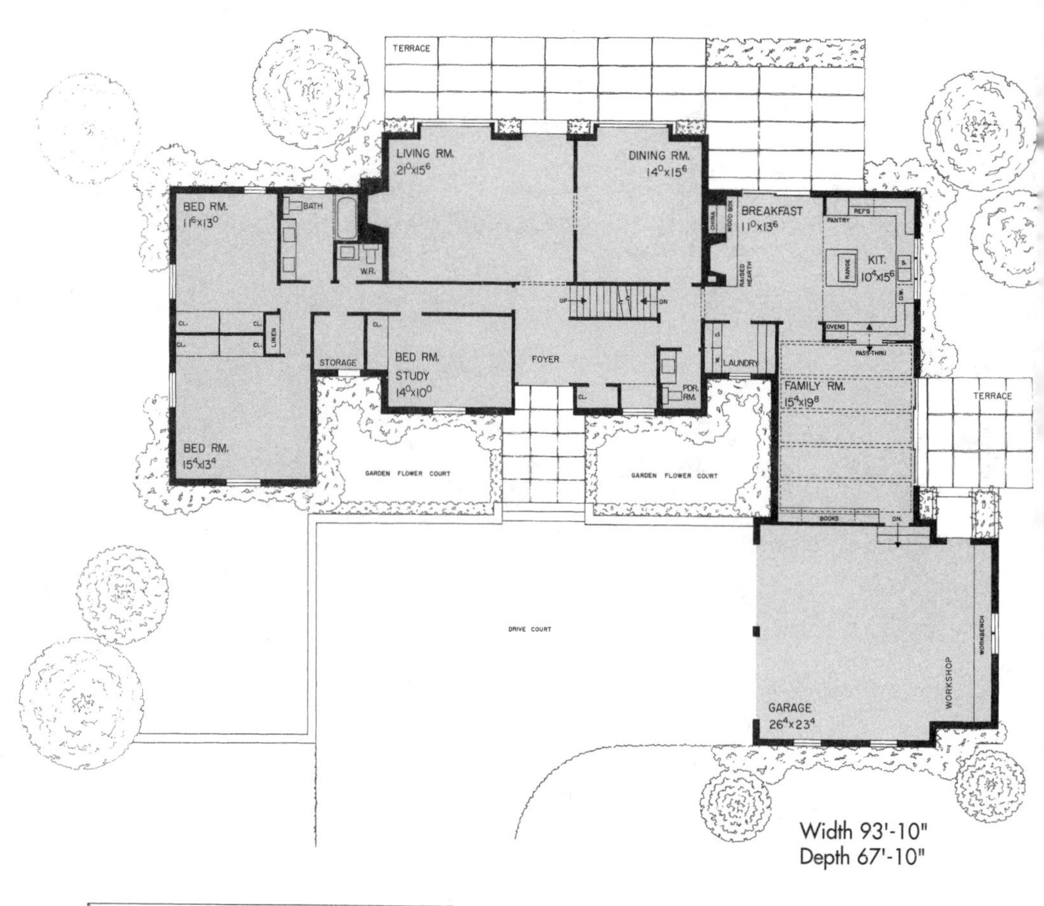

TERRACE
LIVING RM.
$21^{0} \times 15^{6}$
DINING RM.
$14^{0} \times 15^{6}$
BED RM.
$11^{6} \times 13^{0}$
BATH
W.R.
BREAKFAST
$11^{0} \times 13^{6}$
PANTRY
KIT.
$10^{4} \times 15^{6}$
OVENS
PASS-THRU
STORAGE
BED RM.
STUDY
$14^{0} \times 10^{0}$
FOYER
LAUNDRY
PDR. RM.
FAMILY RM.
$15^{4} \times 19^{8}$
TERRACE
BED RM.
$15^{4} \times 13^{4}$
GARDEN FLOWER COURT
GARDEN FLOWER COURT
BOOKS
DRIVE COURT
WORKSHOP
GARAGE
$26^{4} \times 23^{4}$

Width 93'-10"
Depth 67'-10"

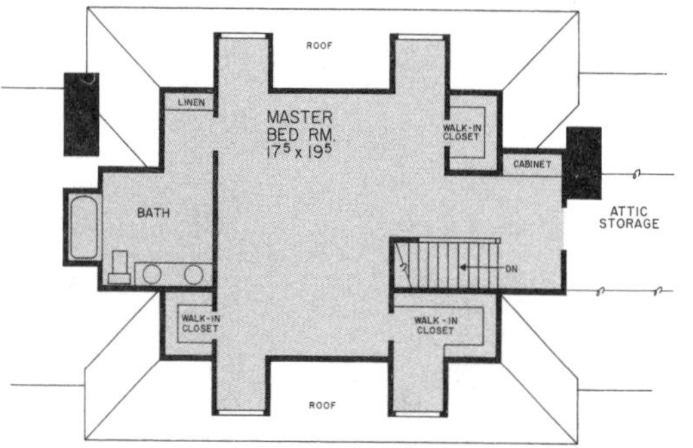

ROOF
LINEN
MASTER
BED RM.
$17^{5} \times 19^{5}$
WALK-IN CLOSET
CABINET
BATH
ATTIC STORAGE
DN
WALK-IN CLOSET
WALK-IN CLOSET
ROOF

Design by
Home Planners

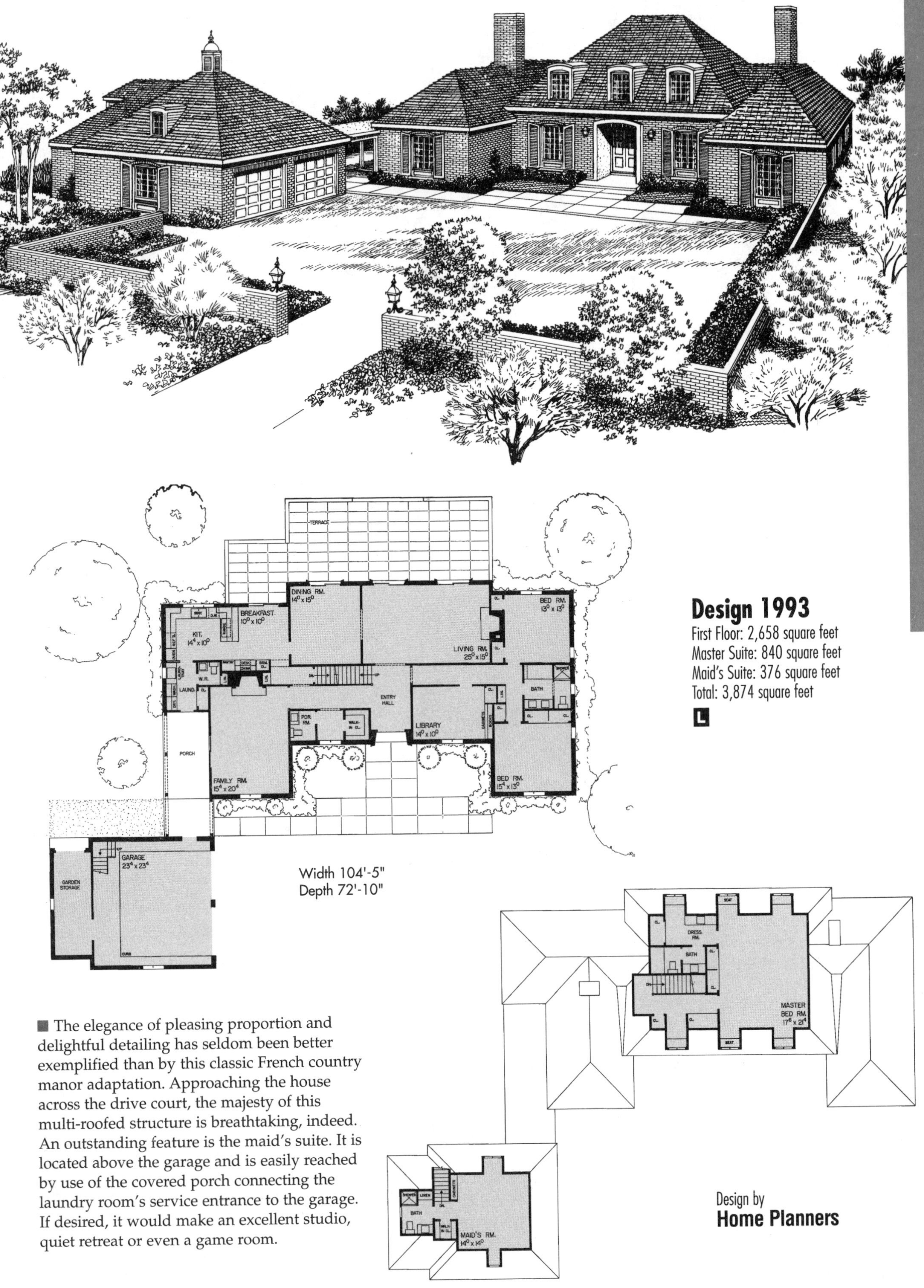
TERRACE
DINING RM. 14⁰ x 15⁰
BREAKFAST 10⁰ x 10⁰
KIT. 14⁴ x 10⁰
LIVING RM. 25⁰ x 15⁰
BED RM. 13⁰ x 13⁰
LAUND.
W.R.
ENTRY HALL
BATH
POR. RM.
LIBRARY 14⁰ x 10⁰
PORCH
FAMILY RM. 15⁴ x 20⁴
BED RM. 15⁴ x 13⁰
GARAGE 23⁴ x 23⁴
GARDEN STORAGE
Width 104'-5"
Depth 72'-10"
DRESS. RM.
BATH
MASTER BED RM. 17⁶ x 21⁴
BATH
MAID'S RM. 14⁰ x 14⁰

Design 1993

First Floor: 2,658 square feet
Master Suite: 840 square feet
Maid's Suite: 376 square feet
Total: 3,874 square feet

L

■ The elegance of pleasing proportion and delightful detailing has seldom been better exemplified than by this classic French country manor adaptation. Approaching the house across the drive court, the majesty of this multi-roofed structure is breathtaking, indeed. An outstanding feature is the maid's suite. It is located above the garage and is easily reached by use of the covered porch connecting the laundry room's service entrance to the garage. If desired, it would make an excellent studio, quiet retreat or even a game room.

Design by
Home Planners

Design 2615

First Floor: 2,563 square feet
Second Floor: 552 square feet
Total: 3,115 square feet

L **D**

■ It's easy to imagine this lovely New England home in a Norman Rockwell painting. Two arched entryways form covered porches, while the center front door conveys a special welcome. A warming fireplace greets you in the formal living room, providing passage to a solarium. The kitchen is situated to serve both formal and informal areas well, and the family room, featuring a corner bar, allows plenty of space for activities. The master bedroom, at the rear of the first floor, offers walk-in closets and a private bath. The second floor holds two family bedrooms, a full bath, dual linen storage and a built-in desk/vanity.

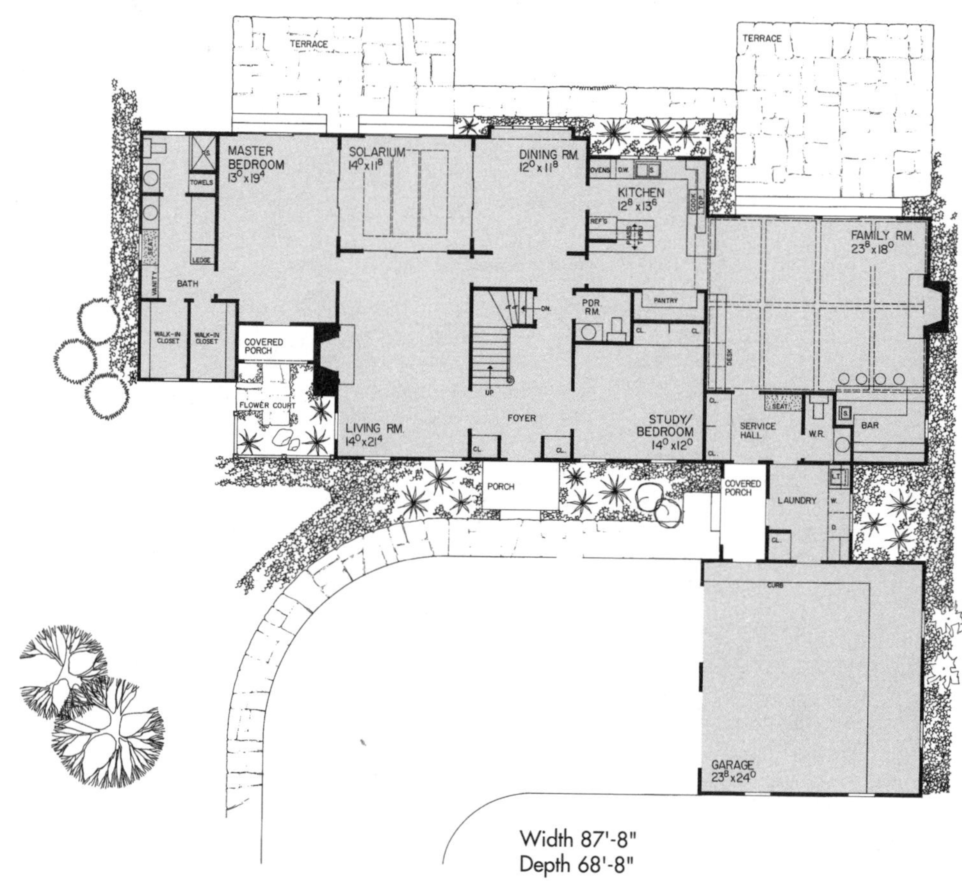

TERRACE
TERRACE
MASTER BEDROOM 13⁰x19⁴
SOLARIUM 14⁰x11⁸
DINING RM. 12⁰x11⁸
KITCHEN 12⁸x13⁶
FAMILY RM. 23⁸x18⁰
BATH
WALK-IN CLOSET
WALK-IN CLOSET
COVERED PORCH
FLOWER COURT
LIVING RM. 14⁰x21⁴
FOYER
PDR. RM.
PANTRY
STUDY/ BEDROOM 14⁰x12⁰
SERVICE HALL
W.R.
BAR
PORCH
COVERED PORCH
LAUNDRY
GARAGE 23⁸x24⁰

Width 87'-8"
Depth 68'-8"

QUOTE ONE®

Cost to build? See page 516 to order complete cost estimate to build this house in your area!

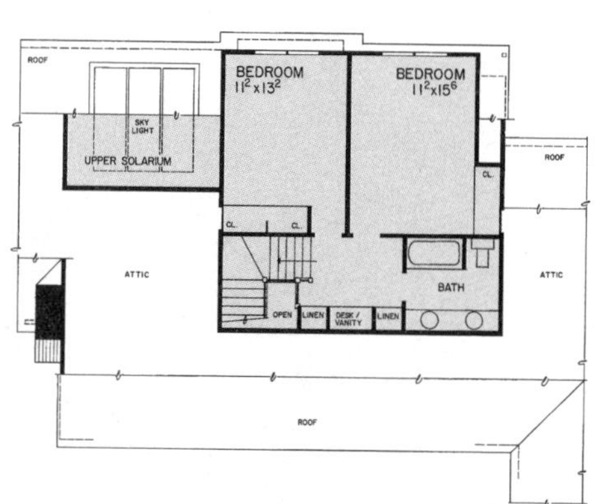

ROOF
BEDROOM 11²x13²
BEDROOM 11²x15⁶
UPPER SOLARIUM
ATTIC
BATH
ATTIC
ROOF

Design by
Home Planners

Width 106'-8"
Depth 32'-0"

Design by
Home Planners

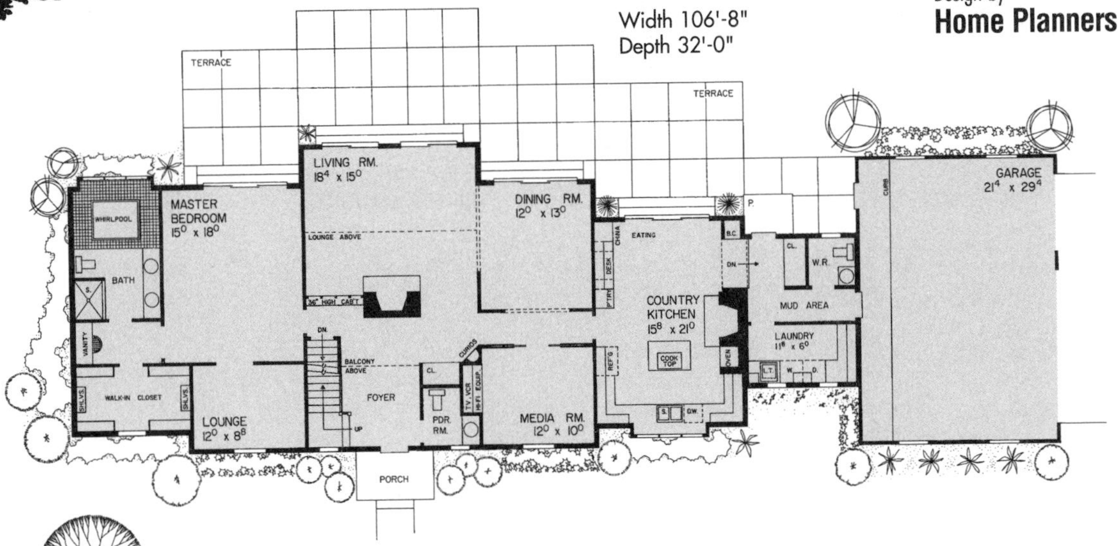

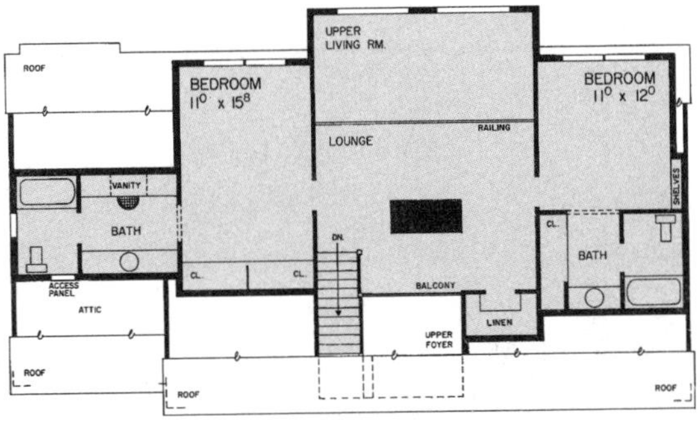

TERRACE
LIVING RM. 18⁴ x 15⁰
DINING RM. 12⁰ x 13⁰
MASTER BEDROOM 15⁰ x 18⁰
WHIRLPOOL
BATH
WALK-IN CLOSET
LOUNGE 12⁰ x 8⁸
FOYER
PDR. RM.
MEDIA RM. 12⁰ x 10⁰
COUNTRY KITCHEN 15⁸ x 21⁰
EATING
MUD AREA
LAUNDRY 11⁸ x 6⁰
W.R.
GARAGE 21⁴ x 29⁴
PORCH

UPPER LIVING RM.
BEDROOM 11⁰ x 15⁸
BEDROOM 11⁰ x 12⁰
LOUNGE
BATH
BALCONY
LINEN
UPPER FOYER
ATTIC
ROOF

Design 2699

First Floor: 2,188 square feet
Second Floor: 858 square feet
Total: 3,046 square feet

L

QUOTE ONE®
Cost to build? See page 516 to order complete cost estimate to build this house in your area!

This handsome Cape Cod offers lots of room for the family to grow. To the left of the foyer, a spacious master suite invites relaxation with its pampering master bath and an adjacent lounge which could easily convert into a study. A large living room with access to the rear terrace is warmed by a cheerful fireplace. The right side of the plan is comprised of a media room, a dining room and a country kitchen that is a cook's delight. A conveniently located mud room and laundry room complete the first floor. The second floor contains two secondary bedrooms, each with its own full bath, and a spacious lounge.

Rear Elevation

Design 3612

Square Footage: 2,946

L

Width 94'-1"
Depth 67'-4"

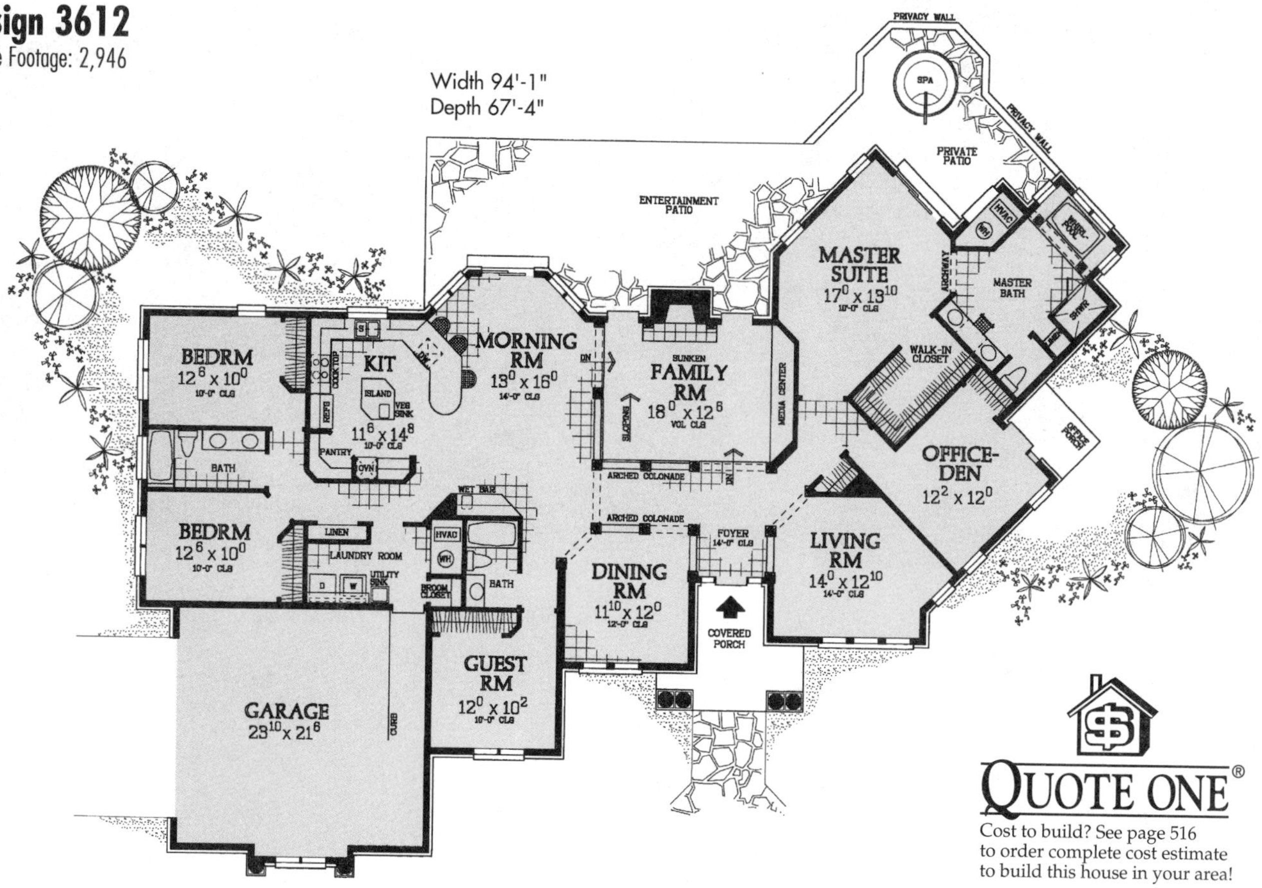

QUOTE ONE®

Cost to build? See page 516 to order complete cost estimate to build this house in your area!

■ Varying hip roof planes complement a glass-paneled entry and divided-light transoms that reflect a well-articulated style and make a bold statement. The tiled foyer opens to formal and casual living areas, defined by arched colonnades and set off by an extended-hearth fireplace in the family room. The gourmet kitchen boasts a food preparation island, an angled snack bar and a walk-in pantry. A guest suite, or study, resides just off the living area. The secluded master suite enjoys a private patio with a spa, as well as a spacious bath with a box-bay whirlpool tub, twin lavatories and a knee-space vanity. A home office or den with a separate entry and porch, and two family bedrooms with a full bath complete the plan.

Design by
Home Planners

Design by
Home Planners

QUOTE ONE®

Cost to build? See page 516 to order complete cost estimate to build this house in your area!

Width 132'-0"
Depth 53'-6"

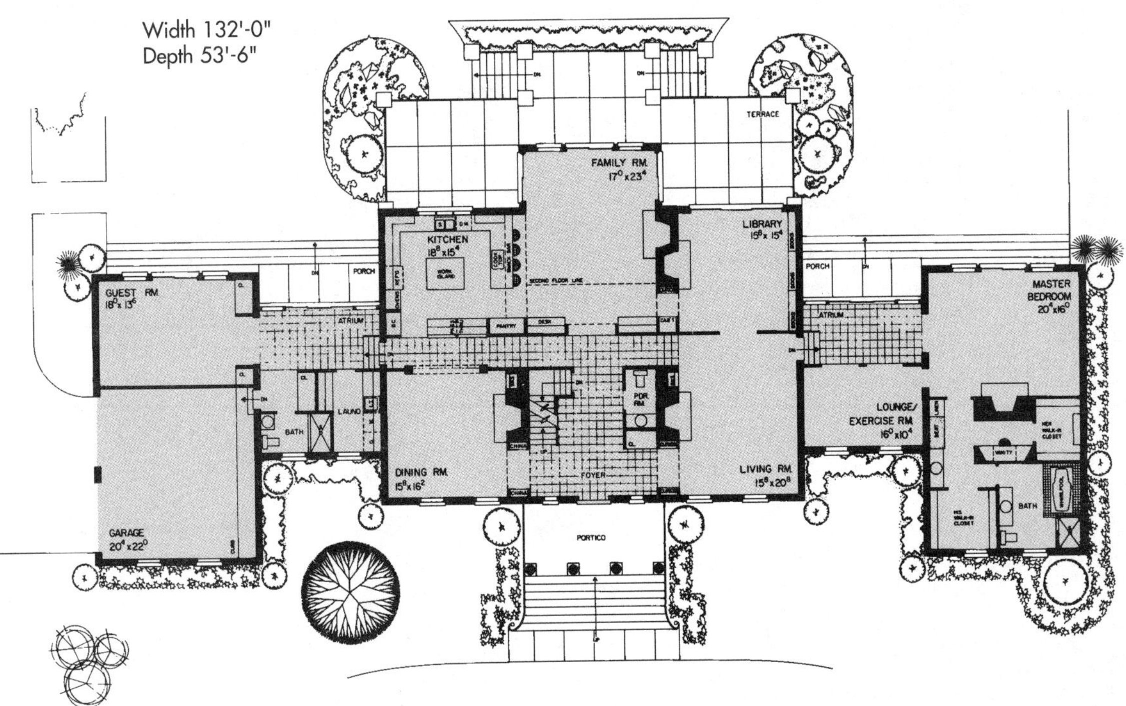

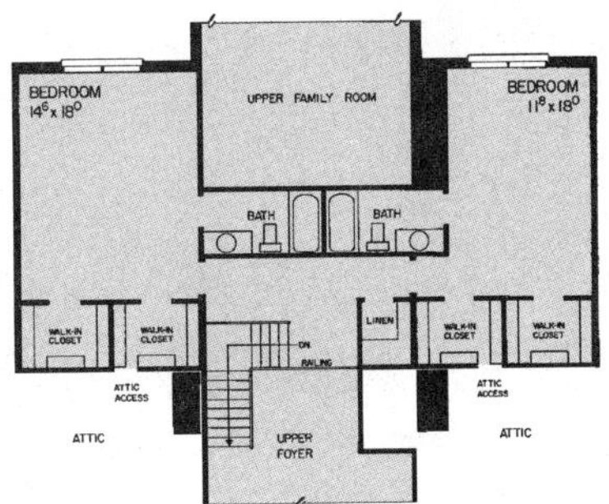

Design 2977

First Floor: 4,104 square feet
Second Floor: 979 square feet
Total: 5,083 square feet

L

■ Both front and rear facades of this elegant brick manor depict classic Georgian symmetry. A columned, Greek entry opens to an impressive two-story foyer. Fireplaces, built-in shelves and cabinets highlight each of the four main gathering areas, living room, dining room, family room and library. The master bedroom is situated in its own wing and is complete with a fireplace, lavish bath and outdoor access.

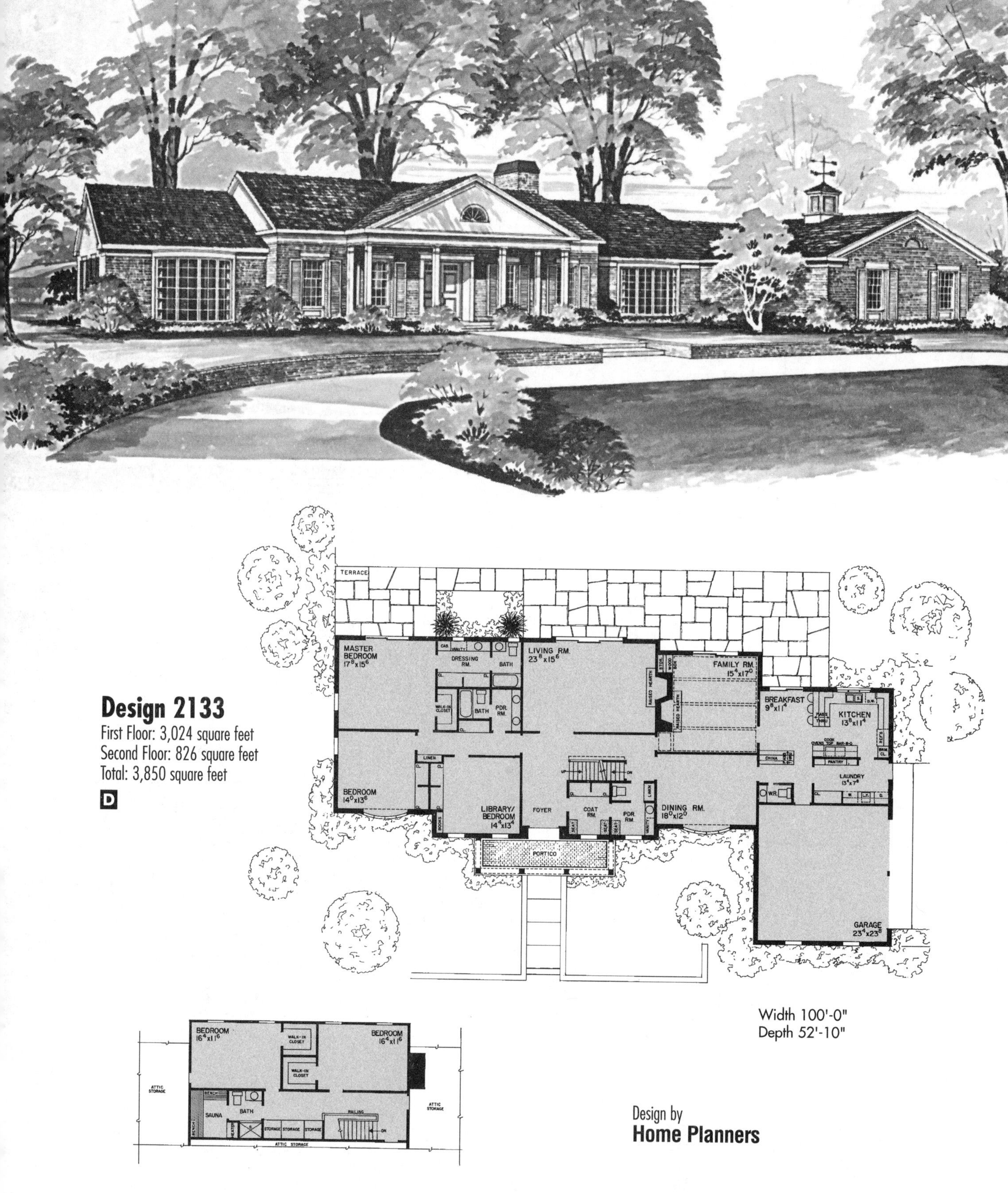
TERRACE
MASTER BEDROOM 17⁸x15⁶
DRESSING RM.
BATH
WALK-IN CLOSET
PDR. RM.
LIVING RM. 23⁸x15⁶
RAISED HEARTH
FAMILY RM. 15⁴x17⁰
BREAKFAST 9⁸x11⁴
KITCHEN 13⁸x11⁴
PANTRY
CHINA
LAUNDRY 13⁴x7⁴
LINEN
BEDROOM 14⁰x13⁶
LIBRARY/ BEDROOM 14⁴x13⁴
FOYER
COAT RM.
DINING RM. 18⁰x12⁰
PORTICO
GARAGE 23⁴x23⁸
BEDROOM 16⁴x11⁶
WALK-IN CLOSET
BEDROOM 16⁴x11⁶
ATTIC STORAGE
SAUNA
BATH
RAILING
STORAGE STORAGE STORAGE
ATTIC STORAGE

Design 2133

First Floor: 3,024 square feet
Second Floor: 826 square feet
Total: 3,850 square feet

D

Width 100'-0"
Depth 52'-10"

Design by
Home Planners

■ The projecting pediment gable of this country-estate home is supported by finely proportioned columns that lend elegance to the exterior. The window treatment, front-door detailing, capped chimney, traditional cupola, brick veneer and varying roof planes complete the characterization of an impressive home. Inside, there are 3,024 square feet on the first floor. In addition, there is an optional two-bedroom second floor. However, whether functioning as one or 1½ stories, this design will provide a lifetime of gracious living. Special amenities include compartmented baths, a large library, a coat room with powder room, a beamed-ceiling family room, two fireplaces and a pass-through from the kitchen to the breakfast room.

Rear Elevation

Design 2693

Square Footage: 3,462

■ A stunning example of Georgian symmetry, this one-story house features two wings surrounding a central living area that boasts four fireplaces (in the country kitchen, library, dining room and living room) and a central foyer with a powder room. Built-ins include bookshelves in the library, a desk in the kitchen, china cabinets in the dining room and curio shelves in the living room. The combination bedroom/sewing room is adjacent to a full bath and near the clutter room with space for a workshop, gardening and laundry. All three bedrooms feature walk-in closets and the master bath sports a step-up whirlpool.

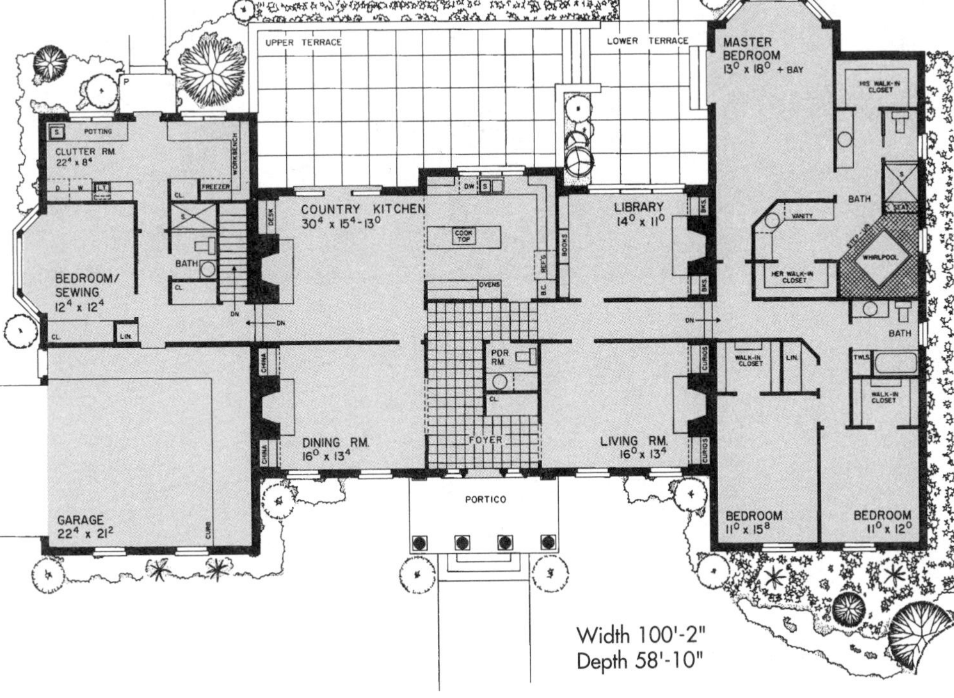
UPPER TERRACE
LOWER TERRACE
MASTER BEDROOM 13⁰ x 18⁰ + BAY
HIS WALK-IN CLOSET
BATH
VANITY
WHIRLPOOL
HER WALK-IN CLOSET
POTTING
CLUTTER RM. 22⁴ x 8⁴
WORKBENCH
FREEZER
BEDROOM/ SEWING 12⁴ x 12⁴
BATH
COUNTRY KITCHEN 30⁴ x 15⁴-13⁰
DESK
COOK TOP
OVENS
BOOKS
LIBRARY 14⁰ x 11⁰
BKS.
BATH
WALK-IN CLOSET
LIN.
WALK-IN CLOSET
PDR RM.
CHINA
DINING RM. 16⁰ x 13⁴
FOYER
LIVING RM. 16⁰ x 13⁴
CURIOS
GARAGE 22⁴ x 21²
PORTICO
BEDROOM 11⁰ x 15⁸
BEDROOM 11⁰ x 12⁰

Width 100'-2"
Depth 58'-10"

Design by
Home Planners

Design 2192

First Floor: 1,884 square feet
Second Floor: 1,521 square feet
Total: 3,405 square feet
Third-floor Bonus: 808 square feet

L D

■ This is surely a fine adaptation from the 18th-Century, when formality and elegance were bywords. The authentic detailing of this design centers around the fine proportions, the dentils, the window symmetry, the front door and entranceway, the massive chimneys and the masonry work. The rear elevation retains all the grandeur exemplary of exquisite architecture. Inside, the formal living room features a corner fireplace. A second fireplace is found in the family room. Built-in amenities include a wall of bookshelves and cabinets in the library, corner china cabinets in the formal dining room, cabinets in both passages to the family room and a china cabinet in the breakfast room. Two family bedrooms share a hall bath on the second floor while the master bedroom offers a private bath. A bonus area on the third floor may be developed into studio and playroom space.

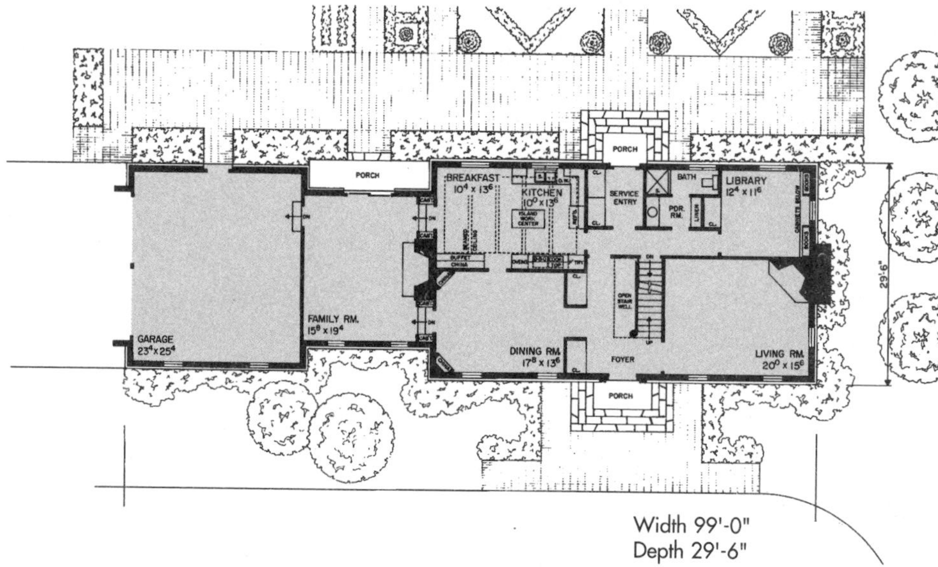
PORCH
BREAKFAST 10⁴ x 13⁶
KITCHEN 10⁰ x 13⁶
SERVICE ENTRY
BATH
PDR RM.
LIBRARY 12⁴ x 11⁶
FAMILY RM. 15⁸ x 19⁴
GARAGE 23⁴ x 25⁴
DINING RM. 17⁸ x 13⁶
FOYER
LIVING RM. 20⁰ x 15⁶
29'-6"
Width 99'-0"
Depth 29'-6"

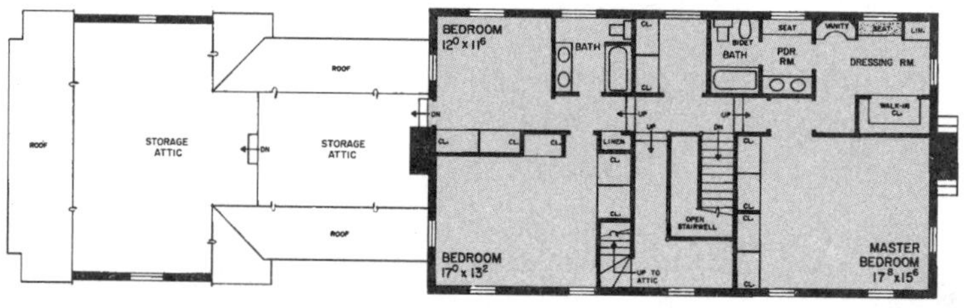
BEDROOM 12⁰ x 11⁶
BATH
PDR RM
DRESSING RM.
ROOF
STORAGE ATTIC
STORAGE ATTIC
ROOF
BEDROOM 17⁰ x 13²
MASTER BEDROOM 17⁸ x 15⁶

Design by
Home Planners

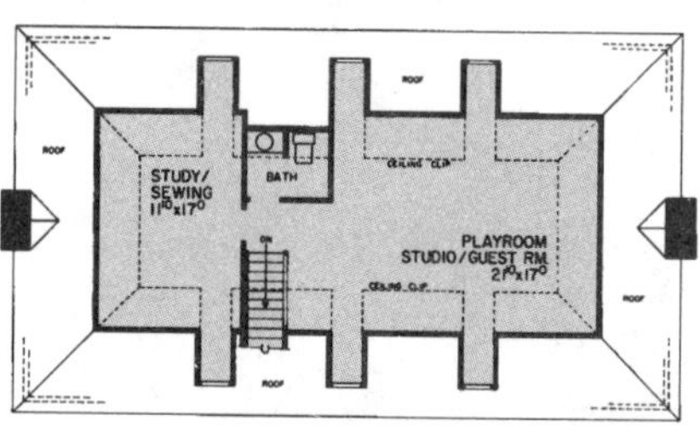
STUDY/ SEWING 11⁶ x 17⁰
BATH
PLAYROOM STUDIO/GUEST RM. 21⁰ x 17⁰

Design 2662

First Floor: 1,735 square feet
Second Floor: 1,075 square feet
Third Floor: 746 square feet
Total: 3,556 square feet

L

■ Three floors of livability are available in this stately brick Federal design. From the two chimney stacks to the five dormer windows, the appeal is pure Americana. First-floor features include fireplaces in the gathering room, the breakfast room and the study, as well as a built-in barbecue in the gourmet kitchen. A handy mud room with a powder room connects the kitchen to the laundry and to the garage beyond. The second floor is dominated by a sumptuous master suite and two family bedrooms that share a full bath. A third floor holds two additional bedrooms that might serve well as guest rooms or as a studio or study space. A full bath with a double vanity finishes this floor.

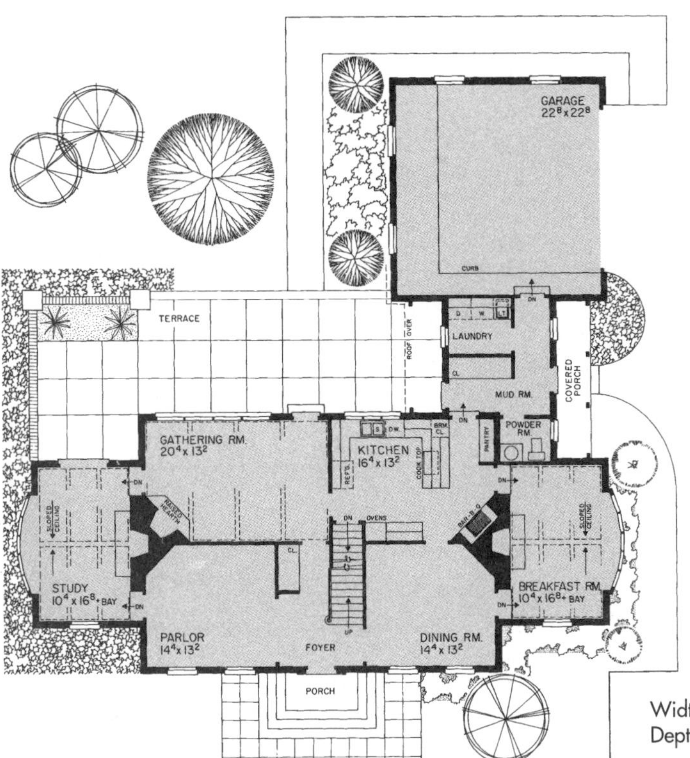
GARAGE $22^8 \times 22^8$
TERRACE
LAUNDRY
ROOF OVER
COVERED PORCH
MUD RM.
POWDER RM.
PANTRY
GATHERING RM. $20^4 \times 13^2$
KITCHEN $16^4 \times 13^2$
SLOPED CEILING
STUDY $10^4 \times 16^8$ + BAY
BREAKFAST RM. $10^4 \times 16^8$ + BAY
PARLOR $14^4 \times 13^2$
FOYER
DINING RM. $14^4 \times 13^2$
PORCH

Width 64'-0"
Depth 64'-0"

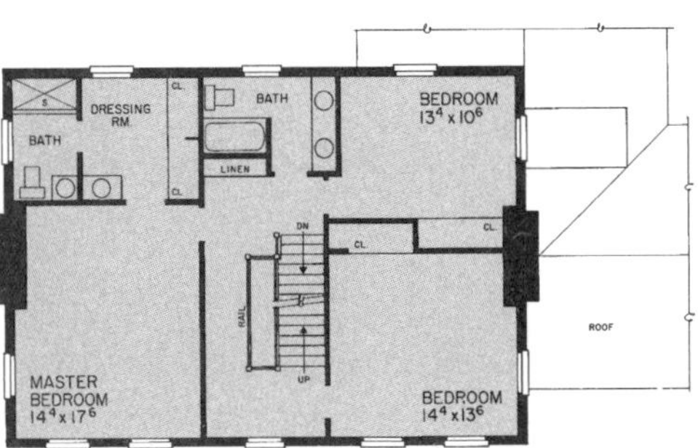
DRESSING RM.
BATH
BATH
LINEN
BEDROOM $13^4 \times 10^6$
MASTER BEDROOM $14^4 \times 17^6$
BEDROOM $14^4 \times 13^6$
ROOF

QUOTE ONE®

Cost to build? See page 516 to order complete cost estimate to build this house in your area!

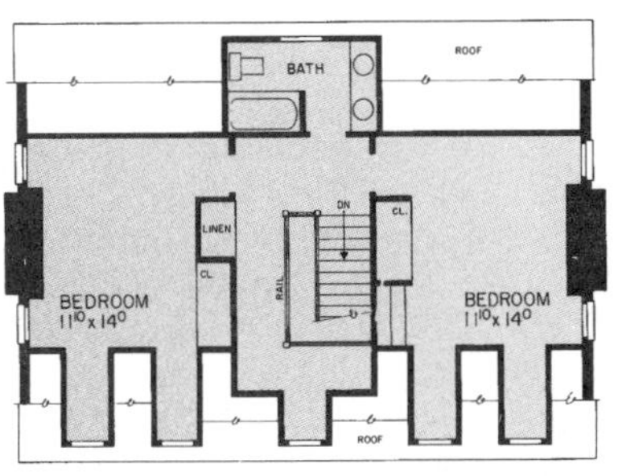
BATH
ROOF
LINEN
BEDROOM $11^{10} \times 14^0$
BEDROOM $11^{10} \times 14^0$

Design by
Home Planners

Design 2633

First Floor: 1,338 square feet
Second Floor: 1,200 square feet
Third Floor: 506 square feet
Total: 3,044 square feet

■ This pleasing Georgian home has a facade that features a front porch with a roof supported by 12" diameter wooden columns. The garage wing has a sheltered service entry and brick facing which complements the design. Formal living and dining areas are complemented by a beamed-ceiling family room. Both the living room and family room have corner fireplaces. A cozy study provides private space. Sliding glass doors link the terrace and family room, providing an indoor/outdoor area for entertaining. The stairway in the foyer leads to four second-floor bedrooms. The master suite features two walk-in closets and a private bath. The third floor is windowed and can be used as a studio and study.

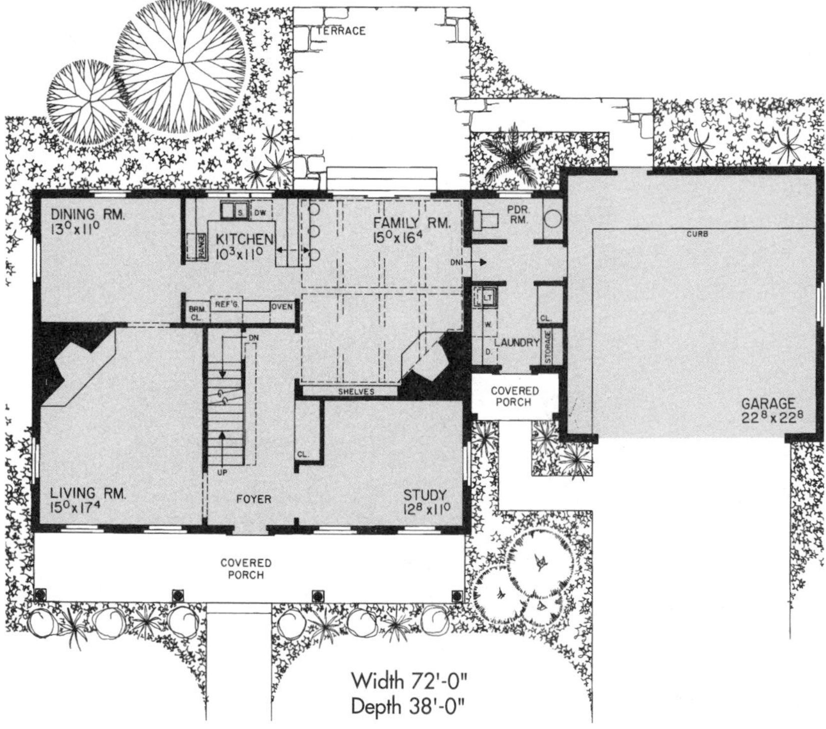
TERRACE
DINING RM.
13^0 x 11^0
KITCHEN
10^3 x 11^0
FAMILY RM.
15^0 x 16^4
PDR. RM.
CURB
LAUNDRY
STORAGE
COVERED PORCH
GARAGE
22^8 x 22^8
SHELVES
LIVING RM.
15^0 x 17^4
FOYER
STUDY
12^8 x 11^0
COVERED PORCH
Width 72'-0"
Depth 38'-0"

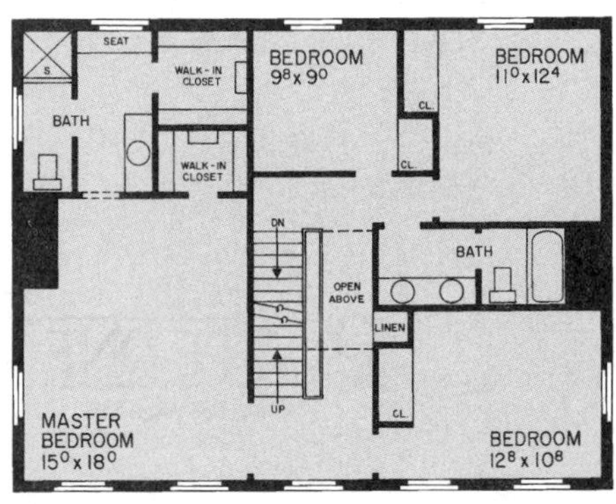
SEAT
WALK-IN CLOSET
BEDROOM
9^8 x 9^0
BEDROOM
11^0 x 12^4
BATH
WALK-IN CLOSET
OPEN ABOVE
BATH
LINEN
MASTER BEDROOM
15^0 x 18^0
BEDROOM
12^8 x 10^8

Design by
Home Planners

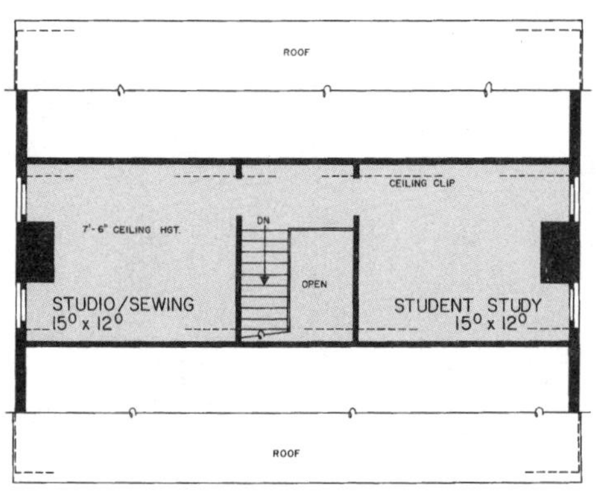
ROOF
CEILING CLIP
7'-6" CEILING HGT.
OPEN
STUDIO/SEWING
15^0 x 12^0
STUDENT STUDY
15^0 x 12^0
ROOF

Design 2683

First Floor: 2,126 square feet
Second Floor: 1,882 square feet
Total: 4,008 square feet

L D

■ This historical Georgian home has its roots in the 18th-Century. The full two-story center section is delightfully complemented by the 1½-story wings. An elegant gathering room, three steps down from the rest of the house, has ample space for entertaining on a grand scale. Guests and family alike will enjoy the two rooms flanking the foyer, the study and the formal dining room. Each of these rooms has a fireplace as its highlight. The breakfast room, the kitchen, the powder room and the laundry are arranged for maximum efficiency. The second floor houses the family bedrooms. Take special note of the spacious master bedroom suite. It has a deluxe bath, a fireplace and a sunken lounge with a dressing room and a walk-in closet.

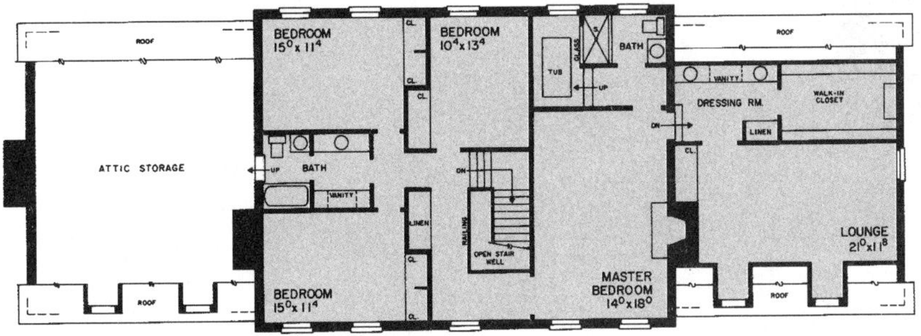
ROOF
BEDROOM $15^0 \times 11^4$
BEDROOM $10^4 \times 13^4$
BATH
TUB
DRESSING RM.
WALK-IN CLOSET
VANITY
LINEN
ATTIC STORAGE
BATH
VANITY
OPEN STAIR WELL
RAILING
LOUNGE $21^0 \times 11^6$
MASTER BEDROOM $14^0 \times 18^0$
BEDROOM $15^0 \times 11^4$

Design by
Home Planners

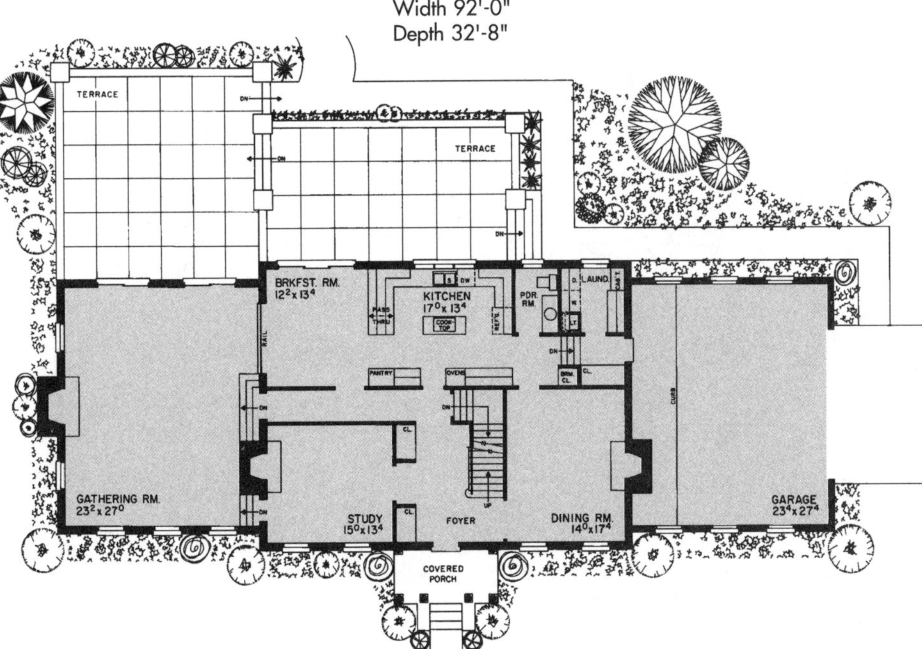
Width 92'-0"
Depth 32'-8"
TERRACE
TERRACE
BRKFST. RM. $12^2 \times 13^4$
KITCHEN $17^0 \times 13^4$
COOK-TOP
PDR. RM.
LAUND.
PANTRY
OVENS
GATHERING RM. $23^2 \times 27^0$
STUDY $15^0 \times 13^4$
FOYER
DINING RM. $14^0 \times 17^4$
GARAGE $23^4 \times 27^4$
COVERED PORCH

QUOTE ONE®
Cost to build? See page 516
to order complete cost estimate
to build this house in your area!

Design 2889

First Floor: 2,348 square feet
Second Floor: 1,872 square feet
Total: 4,220 square feet

L D

■This classic Georgian design offers outstanding features, inside and out: a pediment gable with cornice work and dentils, quoins and Doric columns. The interior steps out in contemporary style with spacious formal areas off the two-story receiving hall. The gathering room with a raised-hearth fireplace framed by floor-to-ceiling windows offers a place to spread out—or throw a bash on the entertainment terrace. A nearby study allows private access to the outdoors. Upstairs, an extension over the garage permits an oversized walk-in closet in the master suite, which also includes an angled bath with a corner windowed tub and twin vanities.

Width 90'-4"
Depth 44'-8"

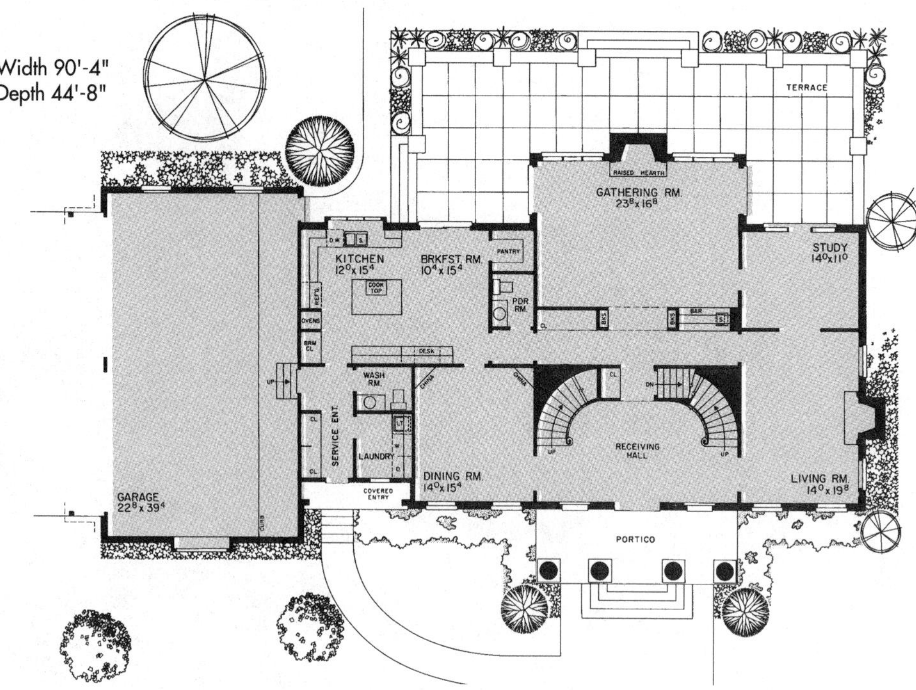

TERRACE
RAISED HEARTH
GATHERING RM.
KITCHEN
BRKFST. RM.
PANTRY
STUDY
PDR RM.
WASH RM.
SERVICE ENT.
LAUNDRY
RECEIVING HALL
DINING RM.
LIVING RM.
GARAGE
COVERED ENTRY
PORTICO

Design by
Home Planners

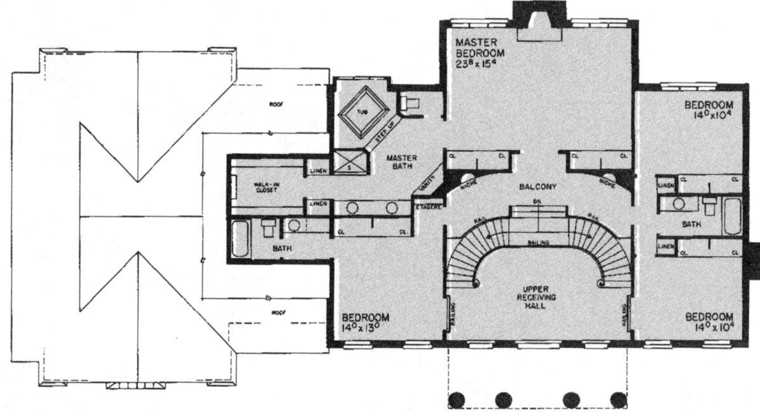

MASTER BEDROOM
BEDROOM
MASTER BATH
BALCONY
BATH
UPPER RECEIVING HALL
BEDROOM
BEDROOM
ROOF

QUOTE ONE®

Cost to build? See page 516 to order complete cost estimate to build this house in your area!

This home, as shown in the photograph, may differ from the actual blueprints. For more detailed information, please check the floor plans carefully.

Photo by Andrew D. Lautman

Design by
Home Planners

Design 2984

First Floor: 3,116 square feet
Second Floor: 1,997 square feet
Total: 5,113 square feet

L

An echo of Whitehall, built in 1765 in Anne Arundel County, Maryland, resounds in this home. Its classic symmetry and columned facade herald a grand interior. There's no lack of space whether entertaining formally or just enjoying a family get-together, and all are kept cozy with fireplaces in the gathering room, study and family room. An island kitchen with attached breakfast room handily serves the nearby dining room. Four second-floor bedrooms include a large master suite with another fireplace, a whirlpool tub and His and Hers closets in the bath. Three more full baths are found on this floor.

TERRACE
TERRACE
BREAKFAST RM. 14^4 x 11^8
FAMILY RM. 14^0 x 21^8
STUDY 14^4 x 20^8
KITCHEN 17^0 x 13^8
LAUNDRY
COVERED PORCH
PANTRY
GALLERY 17^0 x 9^4
FOYER
PDR RM.
WALK-IN CLOSET
DINING RM. 16^8 x 16^4
GATHERING RM. 22^4 x 36^4
GARAGE 22^4 x 36^4
PORTICO

Width 104'-0"
Depth 54'-8"

MASTER BEDROOM 14^8 x 19^4
SLOPED CEILING
HIS WALK-IN CLOSET
HER WALK-IN CLOSET
BATH
WHIRLPOOL
DRESSING RM.
VANITY
SEAT
BEDROOM 14^0 x 12^0
BATH
OPEN BELOW
RAILING
BEDROOM 16^8 x 12^0
BATH
BATH
BEDROOM 16^8 x 14^0

Rear Elevation

QUOTE ONE®

Cost to build? See page 516
to order complete cost estimate
to build this house in your area!

Design 3337

First Floor: 2,167 square feet
Second Floor: 1,992 square feet
Total: 4,159 square feet

L

■ The elegant facade of this design with its columned portico, fanlights and dormers houses an amenity-filled interior. The gathering room, study and dining room, each with a fireplace, provide plenty of room for relaxing and entertaining. A large work area contains a kitchen with a breakfast room, a snack bar, a laundry room and a pantry. The four-bedroom upstairs includes a master suite with a sumptuous bath and an exercise room.

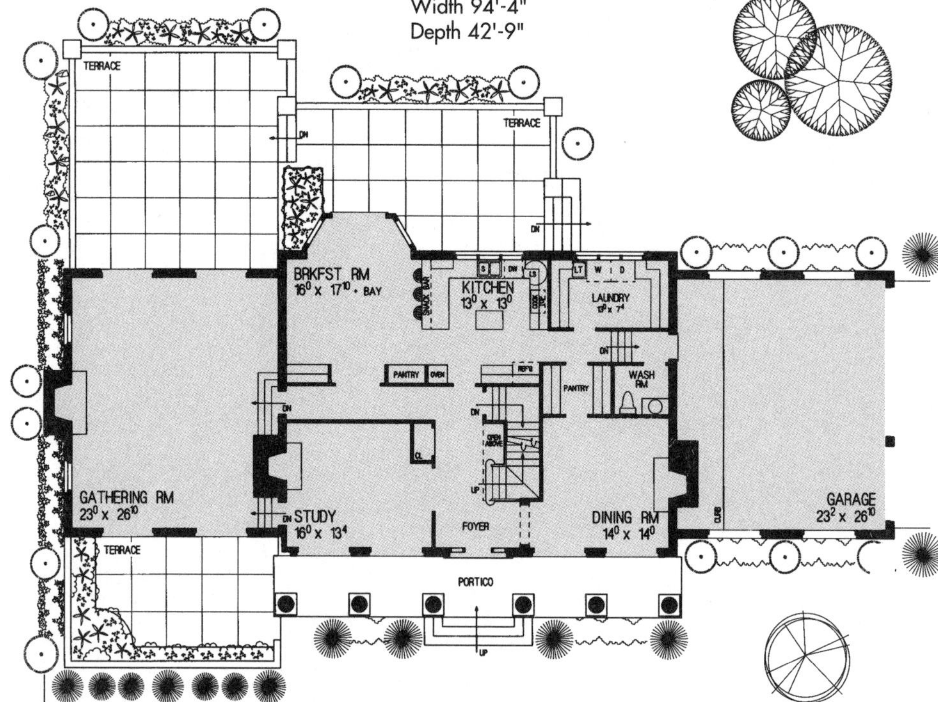

Width 94'-4"
Depth 42'-9"
TERRACE
TERRACE
BRKFST RM
16⁰ x 17¹⁰ + BAY
KITCHEN
13⁰ x 13⁰
LAUNDRY
WASH RM
PANTRY
GATHERING RM
23⁰ x 26¹⁰
STUDY
16⁰ x 13⁴
FOYER
DINING RM
14⁰ x 14⁰
GARAGE
23² x 26¹⁰
TERRACE
PORTICO

Design by
Home Planners

QUOTE ONE®

Cost to build? See page 516 to order complete cost estimate to build this house in your area!

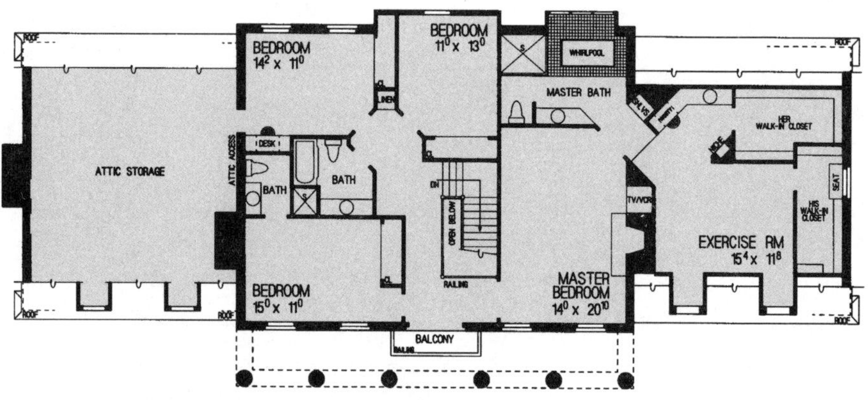

BEDROOM
14² x 11⁰
BEDROOM
11⁰ x 13⁰
WHIRLPOOL
MASTER BATH
HER WALK-IN CLOSET
ATTIC STORAGE
BATH
BATH
EXERCISE RM
15⁴ x 11⁸
BEDROOM
15⁰ x 11⁰
MASTER BEDROOM
14⁰ x 20¹⁰
BALCONY

Design 3349

First Floor: 2,807 square feet
Second Floor: 1,363 square feet
Total: 4,170 square feet

L D

■ Grand traditional design comes to the forefront in this elegant two story. From the dramatic front entry with curving double stairs to the less formal gathering room with a fireplace and terrace access, this plan accommodates family lifestyles. Notice the split-bedroom plan with the master suite, complete with a separate study, His and Hers walk-in closets and a lavish bath on the first floor, and four family bedrooms, sharing two full baths, upstairs. A four-car garage handles the largest of family fleets.

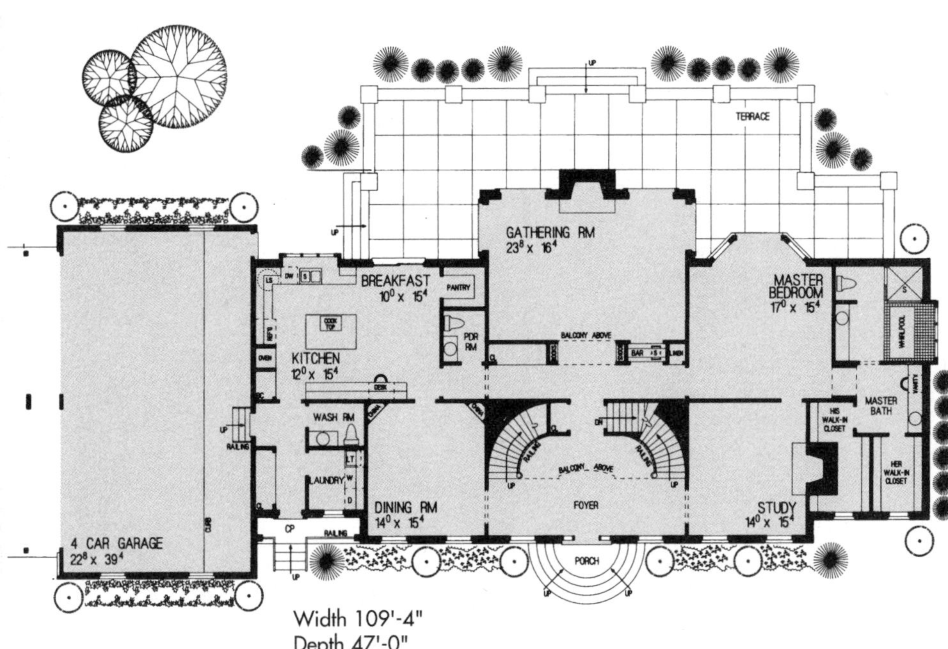
TERRACE
GATHERING RM 23⁸ x 16⁴
BREAKFAST 10⁰ x 15⁴
PANTRY
MASTER BEDROOM 17⁰ x 15⁴
KITCHEN 12⁰ x 15⁴
PDR RM
BALCONY ABOVE
WASH RM
MASTER BATH
HIS WALK-IN CLOSET
HER WALK-IN CLOSET
LAUNDRY
DINING RM 14⁰ x 15⁴
FOYER
STUDY 14⁰ x 15⁴
4 CAR GARAGE 22⁸ x 39⁴
PORCH
Width 109'-4"
Depth 47'-0"

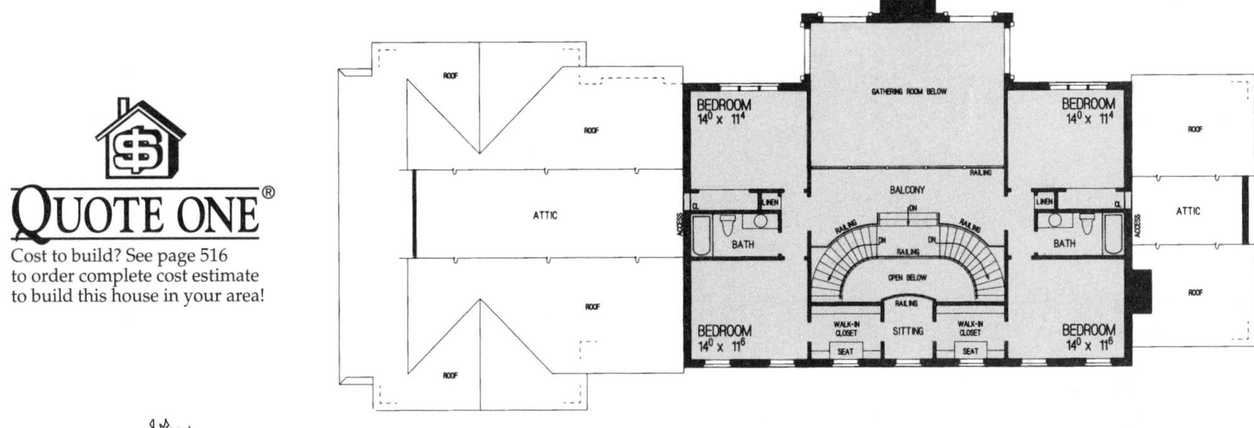
ROOF
ATTIC
BEDROOM 14⁰ x 11⁴
GATHERING ROOM BELOW
BEDROOM 14⁰ x 11⁴
BALCONY
BATH
BATH
OPEN BELOW
BEDROOM 14⁰ x 11⁶
WALK-IN CLOSET
SITTING
WALK-IN CLOSET
BEDROOM 14⁰ x 11⁶
SEAT
SEAT

QUOTE ONE®

Cost to build? See page 516 to order complete cost estimate to build this house in your area!

Design by
Home Planners

Design 3303

First Floor: 2,563 square feet
Second Floor: 1,496 square feet
Total: 4,059 square feet

L

■ With its stately columns and one-story wings, this home is a fine adaptation of 18th-Century designs. A formal living room with a cozy fireplace and a dining room with a built-in china cabinet flank the entry foyer. More casual living dominates the back section, where a family room and combination kitchen and breakfast room feature access to the rear terrace. The left-wing garage is connected to the main structure by a service entrance. The right wing contains the private master suite with a whirlpool tub in the bath and twin dressing rooms. Four second-floor bedrooms share two full baths. Each has its own walk-in closet.

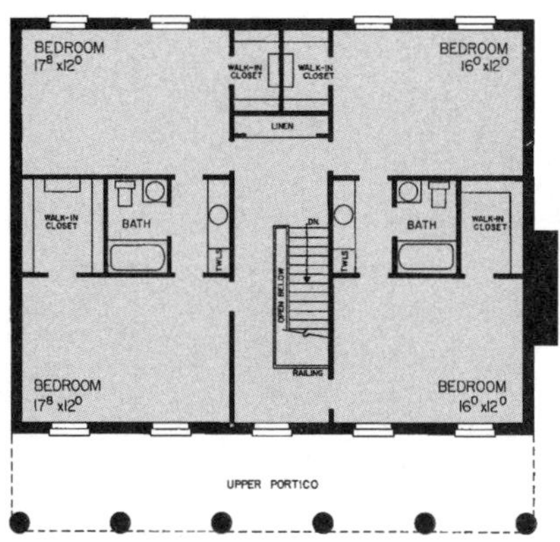

BEDROOM 17^8 x 12^0
BEDROOM 16^0 x 12^0
WALK-IN CLOSET
WALK-IN CLOSET
LINEN
WALK-IN CLOSET
BATH
BATH
WALK-IN CLOSET
OPEN BELOW
RAILING
BEDROOM 17^8 x 12^0
BEDROOM 16^0 x 12^0
UPPER PORTICO

Design by
Home Planners

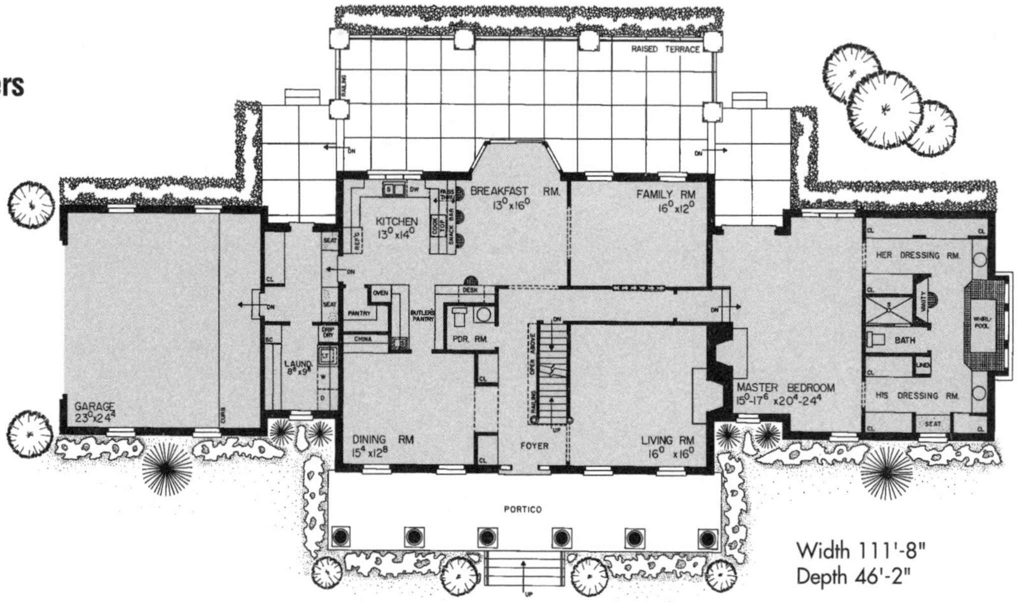

RAISED TERRACE
BREAKFAST RM. 13^0 x 16^0
KITCHEN 13^0 x 14^0
FAMILY RM 16^0 x 12^0
HER DRESSING RM.
WHIRLPOOL
BATH
HIS DRESSING RM.
MASTER BEDROOM 15^0-17^6 x 20^4-24^4
PANTRY
BUTLERS PANTRY
CHINA
DESK
PDR. RM.
LAUND. 8^0 x 9^8
GARAGE 23^0 x 24^4
DINING RM 15^4 x 12^8
FOYER
LIVING RM 16^0 x 16^0
PORTICO

Width 111'-8"
Depth 46'-2"

QUOTE ONE®

Cost to build? See page 516 to order complete cost estimate to build this house in your area!

Design Q402

First Floor: 1,783 square feet
Second Floor: 768 square feet
Total: 2,551 square feet
Bonus Room: 456 square feet

■ Spindles and wood detailing add to the exterior of this Victorian home. A wrapping veranda introduces the entry and opens to a vaulted foyer lit by a transom window. The living room has a tray ceiling and is just across the hall from the dining room with box-bay window. An arched entry leads to the spacious family room. Note the fireplace and French-door access to the veranda. A gourmet kitchen, with adjoining bayed breakfast nook, includes a walk-in pantry, built-in desk and center cooking island with breakfast bar. The master bedroom also has a tray ceiling and includes private access to the veranda, a walk-in closet and lavish bath with whirlpool tub. Family bedrooms are on the second floor along with a bonus room of 456 square feet. Plans include details for both a basement and a crawlspace foundation

VERANDAH
FRENCH DOORS
fam 16'8 x 14'
HALF WALL
brk 9' x 10'
9'6 x 18'4 k
BREAKFAST BAR
FRENCH DOORS
mbr 16' x 15'2
WHIRLPOOL
SH.
OV.
DESK
PAN.
F
TRAY CEILING
TRAY CEILING
ARCH
FLOORLINE OVER
FOYER
D
W
12' x 15'8 liv
10'2 x 12' din
VERANDAH
20' x 21' two~car garage

Width 64'-6"
Depth 50'-0"

Design by
Select Home Designs

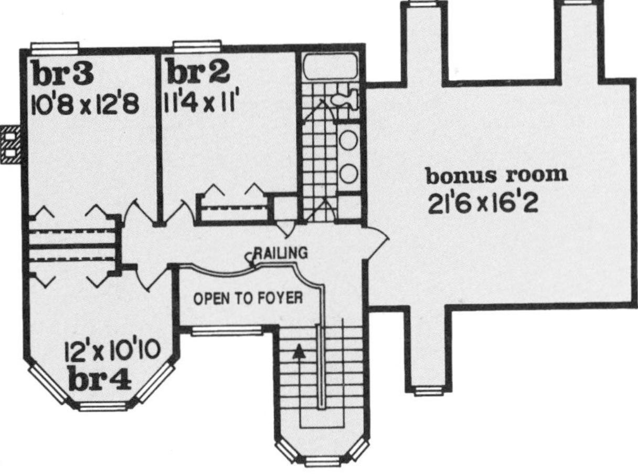
br3
10'8 x 12'8
br2
11'4 x 11'
bonus room
21'6 x 16'2
RAILING
OPEN TO FOYER
12' x 10'10
br4

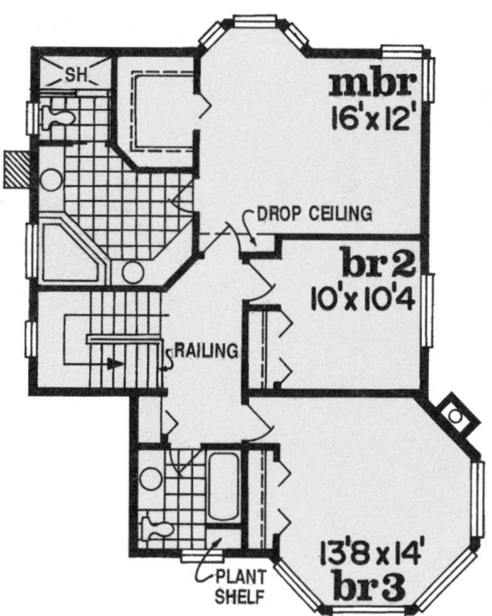

SH
mbr
16'x12'
DROP CEILING
br2
10'x10'4
RAILING
PLANT SHELF
13'8x14'
br3

Design by
Select Home Designs

Width 46'-6"
Depth 54'-6"

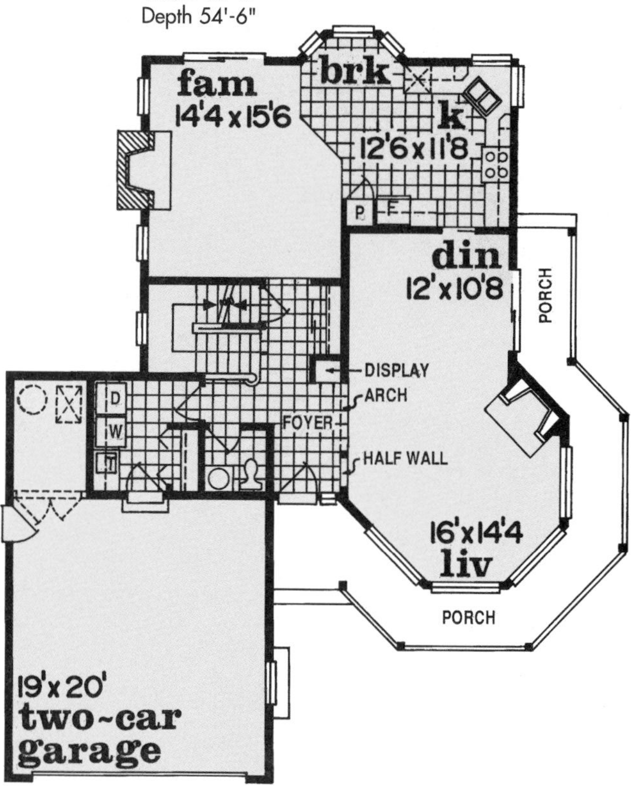

fam
14'4x15'6
brk
k
12'6x11'8
P
F
din
12'x10'8
PORCH
DISPLAY
ARCH
FOYER
HALF WALL
D
W
16'x14'4
liv
PORCH
19'x20'
two-car
garage

Design Q381

First Floor: 1,056 square feet
Second Floor: 987 square feet
Total: 2,043 square feet

■ Victorian detailing and a wraparound covered porch grace this three-bedroom farmhouse. An archway introduces the octagonal living room and its adjoining dining room. Sliding glass doors in the dining room lead to the porch; the living room enjoys a fireplace. A pocket door separates the kitchen and bayed breakfast nook from the dining room. Workspace in the kitchen is L-shaped for convenience. The family room is open to this area and features sliding glass doors to the rear yard and a fireplace. Reach the two-car garage through a service entrance near the laundry. Bedrooms are upstairs. The master suite has a bay window, walk-in closet and private bath with corner whirlpool and double vanity. Two family bedrooms include one nestled in a windowed bay. Plans include details for both a basement and a crawlspace foundation.

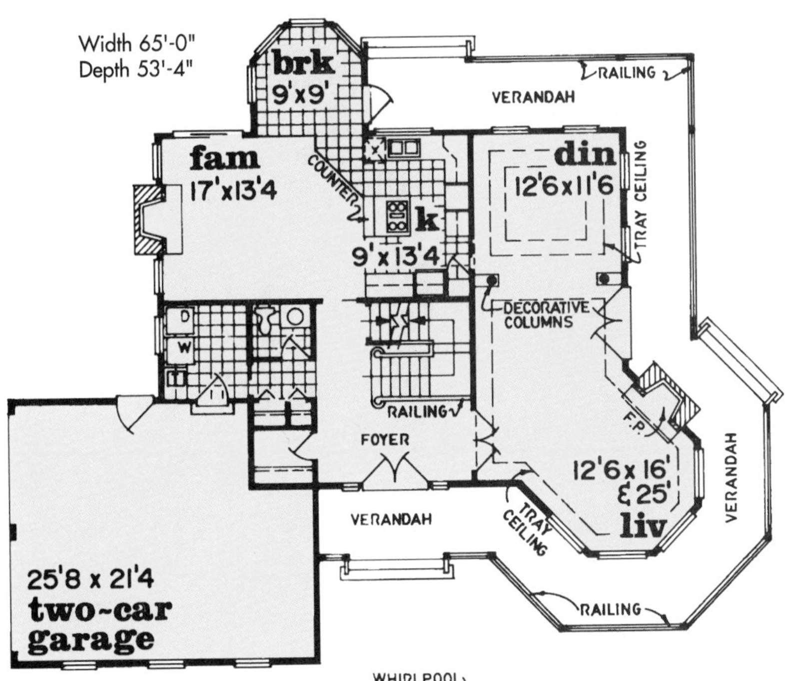
Width 65'-0"
Depth 53'-4"
brk
9'x9'
RAILING
VERANDAH
fam
17'x13'4
COUNTER
k
9'x13'4
din
12'6x11'6
TRAY CEILING
DECORATIVE COLUMNS
D
W
RAILING
F.P.
FOYER
12'6x16'
& 25'
liv
VERANDAH
VERANDAH
TRAY CEILING
RAILING
25'8 x 21'4
two-car
garage

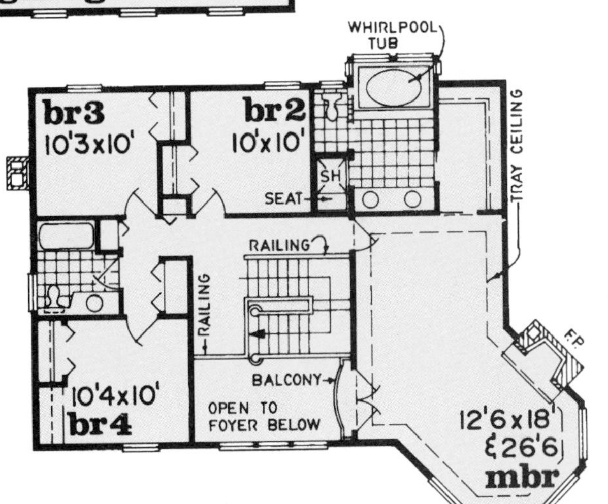
WHIRLPOOL TUB
br3
10'3x10'
br2
10'x10'
TRAY CEILING
SH
SEAT
RAILING
RAILING
F.P.
BALCONY
10'4x10'
br4
OPEN TO FOYER BELOW
12'6x18'
& 26'6
mbr

Design Q333

First Floor: 1,290 square feet
Second Floor: 1,270 square feet
Total: 2,560 square feet

■ With both farmhouse flavor and Victorian details, this plan features a wraparound veranda and a large bayed area on the first and second floors. The living room is nestled in one of these bays and has a tray ceiling, a masonry fireplace and French-door access to the veranda. A pair of columns separates the living and dining rooms. Note the tray ceiling in the dining room. The kitchen has a handy center work island and is open to the both the breakfast bay and the family room. A fireplace is enjoyed from all angles. The master suite is tucked into the bay on the second floor. Its amenities include a fireplace, a walk-in closet and a private bath with whirlpool tub. Three family bedrooms share a full bath. Plans include details for both a basement and a crawlspace foundation.

Design by
Select Home Designs

Rear Elevation

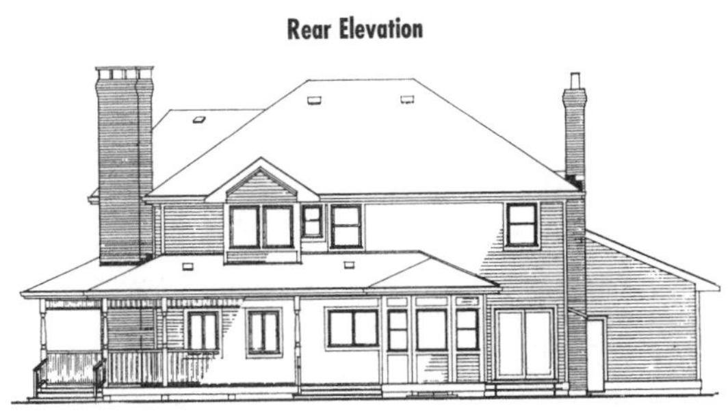

Design Q392

First Floor: 1,128 square feet
Second Floor: 1,130 square feet
Total: 2,258 square feet

■ A gazebo porch, topped with a turret roof, and nostalgic wood detailing grace this four-bedroom Victorian design. Double front doors open to a spacious living room and adjoining dining room. The living room has a warming fireplace. The kitchen, with center prep island and raised eating bar, serves a sunny breakfast bay and the family room. A door leads out to a rear patio. The family room is graced by its own hearth. All four bedrooms are on the second floor. The master suite has a bayed window area, a walk-in closet and bath with corner whirlpool adorned by columns. Family bedrooms share a full bath. A small study area is located at the top of the stairs. Plans include details for both a basement and a crawlspace foundation.

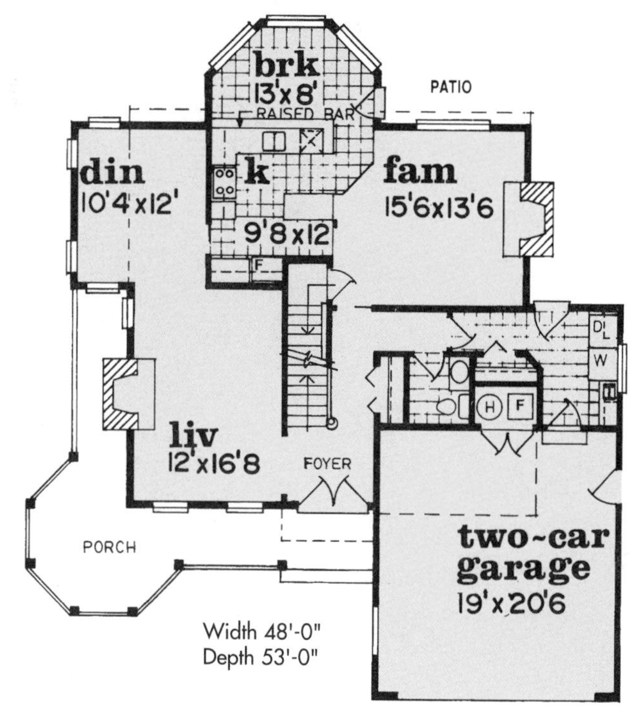
brk
13'x8'
RAISED BAR
PATIO
din
10'4x12'
k
9'8x12'
fam
15'6x13'6
liv
12'x16'8
FOYER
PORCH
two-car garage
19'x20'6
Width 48'-0"
Depth 53'-0"

Rear Elevation

Design by
Select Home Designs

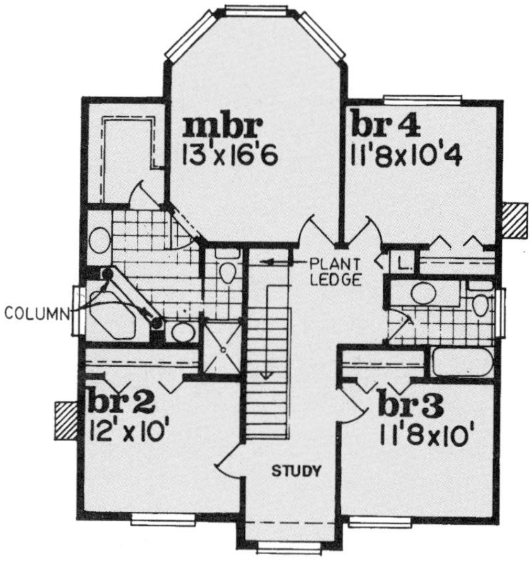

mbr 13'x16'6
br 4 11'8x10'4
PLANT LEDGE
COLUMN
br 2 12'x10'
br 3 11'8x10'
STUDY

Design 2971

First Floor: 1,766 square feet
Second Floor: 1,519 square feet
Total: 3,285 square feet

L

Design by
Home Planners

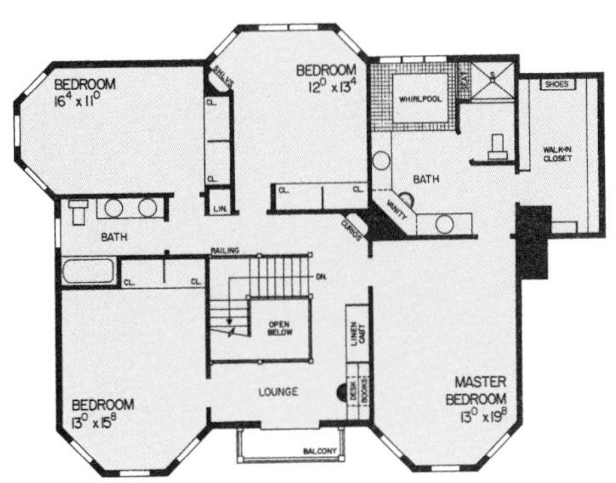

BEDROOM 16^4 x 11^0
BEDROOM 12^0 x 13^4
WHIRLPOOL
SHOES
WALK-IN CLOSET
BATH
CL.
LIN.
VANITY
BATH
RAILING
DN.
OPEN BELOW
LINEN CAB'T
LOUNGE
BOOKS
DESK
MASTER BEDROOM 13^0 x 19^8
BEDROOM 13^0 x 15^8
BALCONY

■ The stately proportions and exquisite Victorian detailing of this home are exciting. Like so many of this style, interesting rooflines set the character of this design. The delightful mixture of gable roof, hip roof and dramatic turret provide a pleasant combination. The delicate detailing of the windows, railings, cornices and front entry provides added appeal. Inside, the kitchen features a center island with a cooktop and shares a wide counter for casual dining with the adjoining family room. A dining room with access to the rear porch is available for more formal occasions. Upstairs, each of the four bedrooms features a bay area and plenty of closet space.

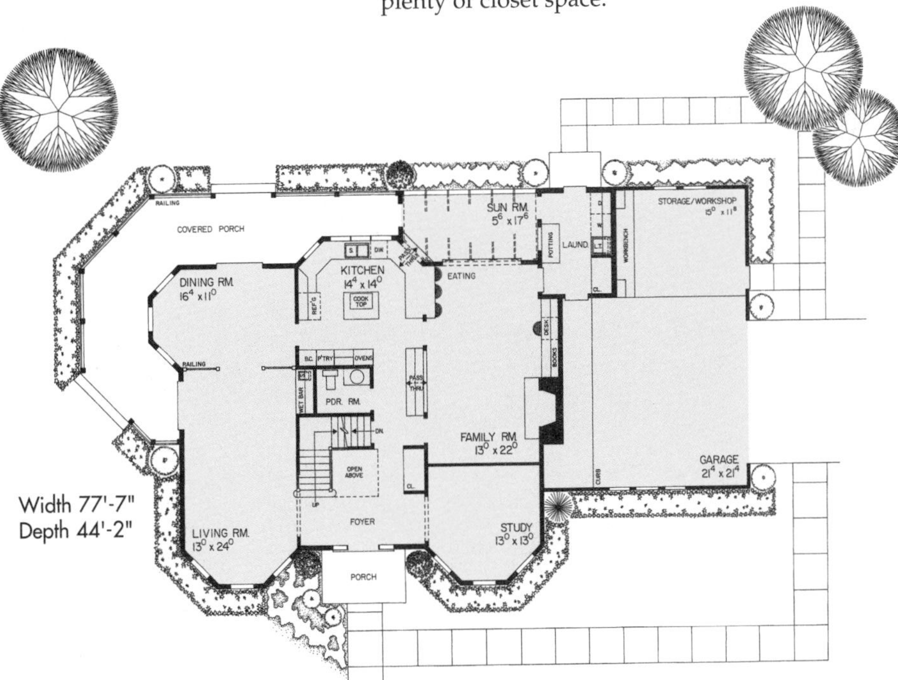

RAILING
COVERED PORCH
SUN RM. 5^6 x 17^6
POTTING
LAUND.
WORKBENCH
STORAGE/WORKSHOP 10^0 x 11^8
DINING RM. 16^4 x 11^0
KITCHEN 14^4 x 14^0
COOK TOP
EATING
RAILING
PDR. RM.
FAMILY RM. 13^0 x 22^0
DESK
BOOKS
OPEN ABOVE
DN.
UP
FOYER
GARAGE 21^4 x 21^4
LIVING RM. 13^0 x 24^0
STUDY 13^0 x 13^0
PORCH

Width 77'-7"
Depth 44'-2"

QUOTE ONE®

Cost to build? See page 516 to order complete cost estimate to build this house in your area!

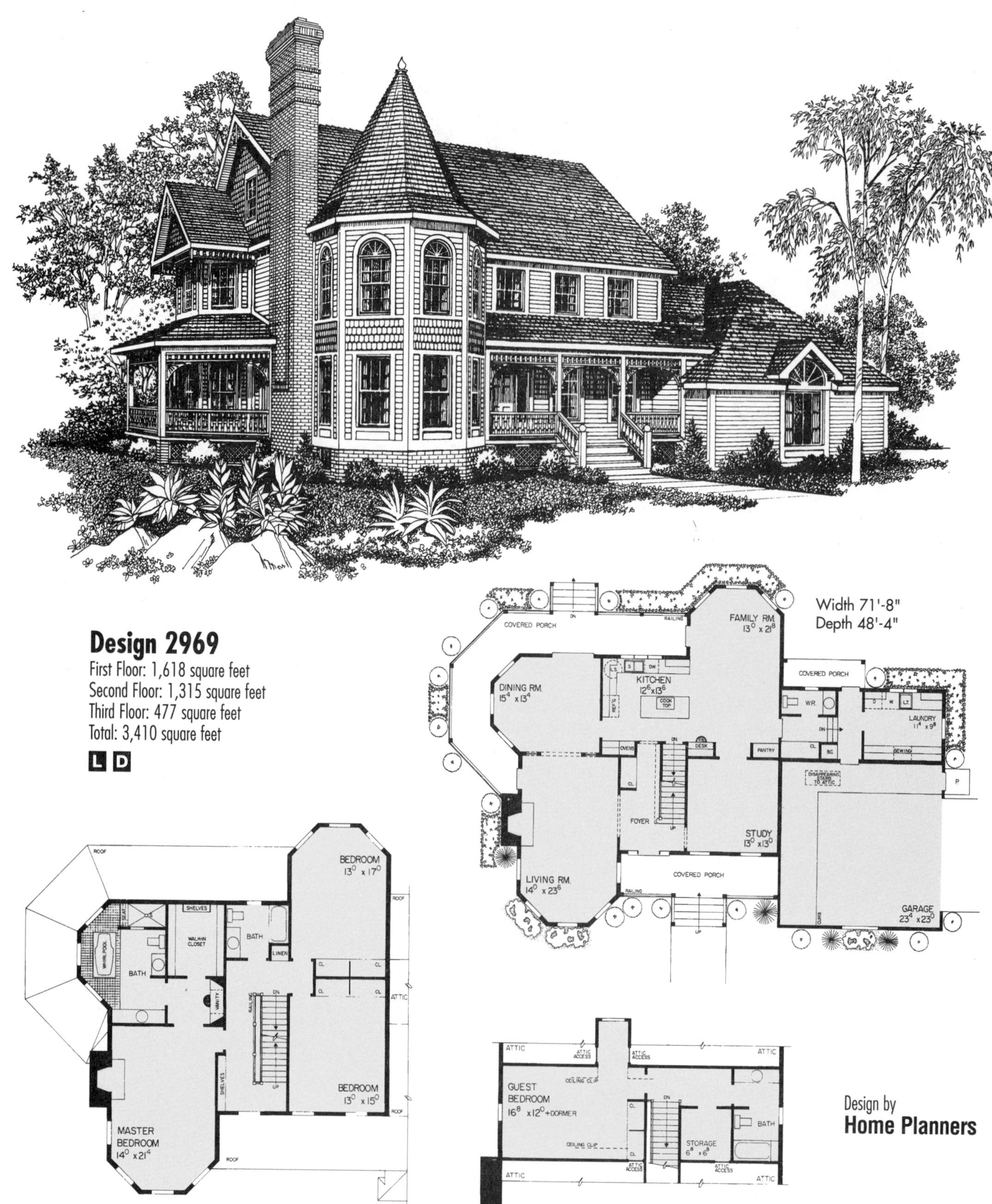
COVERED PORCH
RAILING
FAMILY RM.
13⁰ x 21⁸
Width 71'-8"
Depth 48'-4"
DINING RM.
15⁴ x 13⁴
KITCHEN
12⁶x13⁶
COOK TOP
COVERED PORCH
W.R.
LAUNDRY
11⁴ x 9⁸
SEWING
OVENS
DESK
PANTRY
DISAPPEARING STAIRS TO ATTIC
FOYER
STUDY
13⁰ x13⁰
COVERED PORCH
LIVING RM.
14⁰ x 23⁶
GARAGE
23⁴ x23⁰
ROOF
BEDROOM
13⁰ x 17⁰
SHELVES
WHIRLPOOL
BATH
WALK-IN CLOSET
BATH
LINEN
VANITY
RAILING
ATTIC
SHELVES
BEDROOM
13⁰ x 15⁰
MASTER BEDROOM
14⁰ x21⁴
ATTIC
ATTIC ACCESS
GUEST BEDROOM
16⁸ x12⁰+DORMER
CEILING CLIP
STORAGE
6⁸ x6⁸
BATH

Design 2969

First Floor: 1,618 square feet
Second Floor: 1,315 square feet
Third Floor: 477 square feet
Total: 3,410 square feet

L D

Design by
Home Planners

What could beat the charm of a turreted Victorian with covered porches to the front, side and rear? This delicately detailed exterior houses an outstanding family-oriented floor plan. Projecting bays make their contribution to the exterior styling. In addition, they provide an extra measure of livability to the living, dining and family rooms, plus two of the bedrooms. The efficient kitchen, with its island cooking station, functions well with the dining and family rooms. A study provides a quiet first-floor haven for the family's less active pursuits. Upstairs, there are three big bedrooms and a fine master bath. The third floor provides a guest suite and huge bulk storage area (make it a cedar closet if you wish). This house has a basement for the development of further recreational and storage facilities. Note the two fireplaces, large laundry and attached two-car garage.

Design 2970

First Floor: 1,538 square feet
Second Floor: 1,526 square feet
Third Floor: 658 square feet
Total: 3,722 square feet

L

This charming Victorian features a covered outdoor living area on all four sides! It even ends at a screened porch which features a sundeck above. This interesting plan offers three floors of livability. And what livability it is! Plenty of formal and informal living facilities to go along with the potential of five bedrooms. The master suite is just fantastic. It is adjacent to a wonderful sitting room and offers a sundeck and lavish bath/personal care facilities. The third floor will make a wonderful haven for the family's student members.

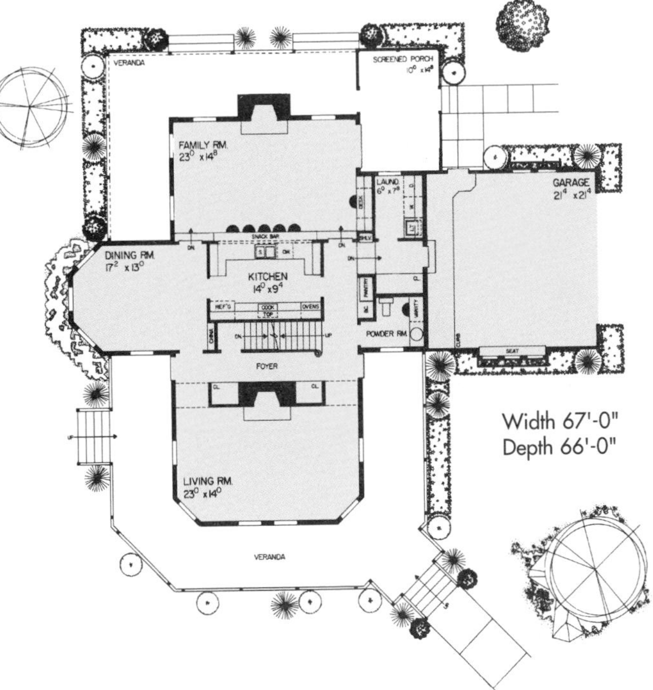
VERANDA
SCREENED PORCH
FAMILY RM. 23^0 x 14^8
LAUND.
GARAGE 21^4 x 21^4
DINING RM. 17^2 x 13^0
KITCHEN 14^0 x 9^4
POWDER RM.
FOYER
LIVING RM. 23^0 x 14^0
VERANDA

Width 67'-0"
Depth 66'-0"

Design by
Home Planners

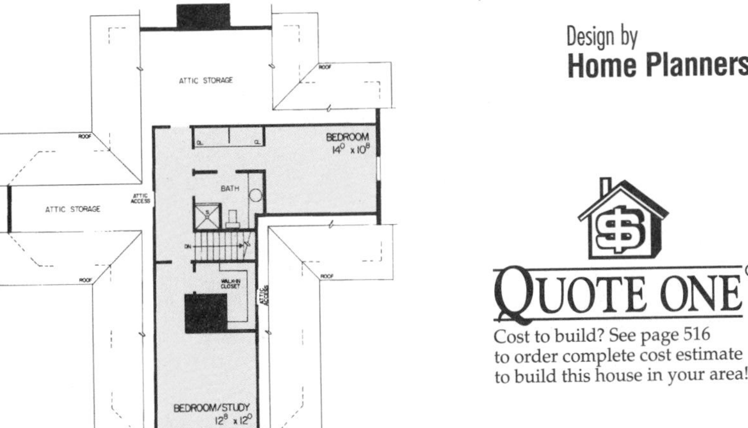
ATTIC STORAGE
BEDROOM 14^0 x 10^8
BATH
ATTIC STORAGE
BEDROOM/STUDY 12^8 x 12^0

QUOTE ONE®
Cost to build? See page 516 to order complete cost estimate to build this house in your area!

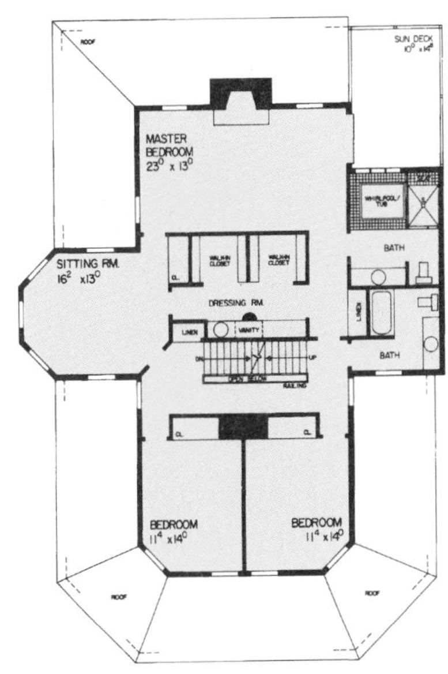
SUN DECK
MASTER BEDROOM 23^0 x 13^0
SITTING RM. 16^2 x 13^0
DRESSING RM.
BATH
BATH
BEDROOM 11^4 x 14^0
BEDROOM 11^4 x 14^0

Design Q398

First Floor: 1,180 square feet
Second Floor: 1,121 square feet
Total: 2,301 square feet
Three-bedroom Layout: 2,154 square feet

■ A turret roof, prominent bay window and a wraparound veranda sign this four-bedroom design as classic Victorian. The plans include two second-level layouts—one with four bedrooms or one with three bedrooms and a vaulted ceiling over the family room. Both include a lavish master suite with octagonal tray ceiling in the sitting room, a walk-in closet and private bath with columned whirlpool spa and separate shower. The first floor holds a formal living room with windows overlooking the veranda, a formal dining room and a family room with fireplace. The kitchen is U-shaped and has an octagonal breakfast bay. A half-bath and a laundry room are found in the service area that also leads to the two-car garage. Plans include details for both a basement and a crawlspace foundation.

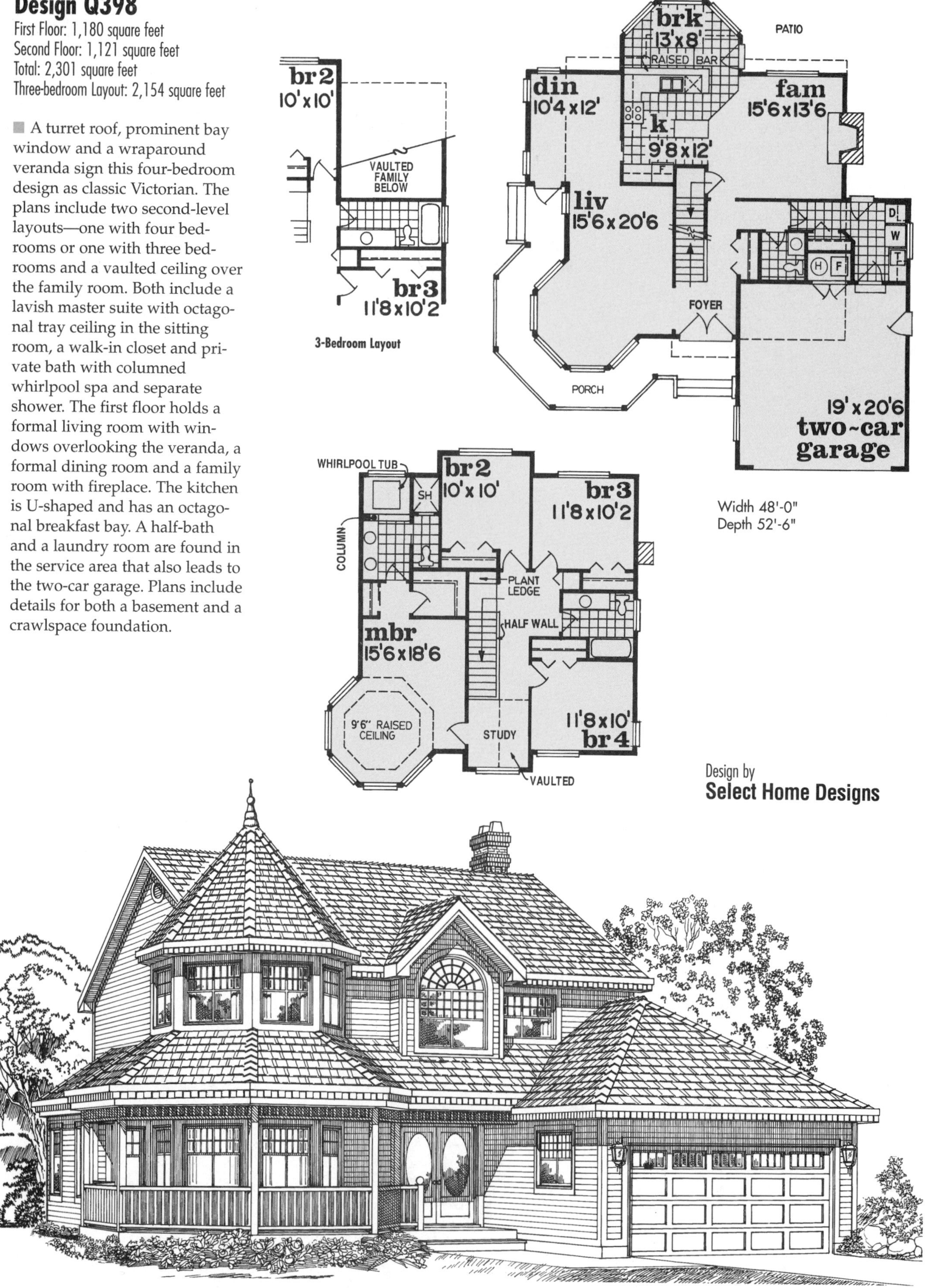

br2
10'x10'
VAULTED FAMILY BELOW
br3
11'8x10'2
3-Bedroom Layout
brk
13'x8'
RAISED BAR
PATIO
din
10'4x12'
k
9'8x12'
fam
15'6x13'6
liv
15'6x20'6
D
W
T
H
F
FOYER
PORCH
19'x20'6
two-car garage
Width 48'-0"
Depth 52'-6"
WHIRLPOOL TUB
SH
br2
10'x10'
br3
11'8x10'2
COLUMN
PLANT LEDGE
HALF WALL
mbr
15'6x18'6
9'6" RAISED CEILING
STUDY
11'8x10'
br4
VAULTED
Design by
Select Home Designs

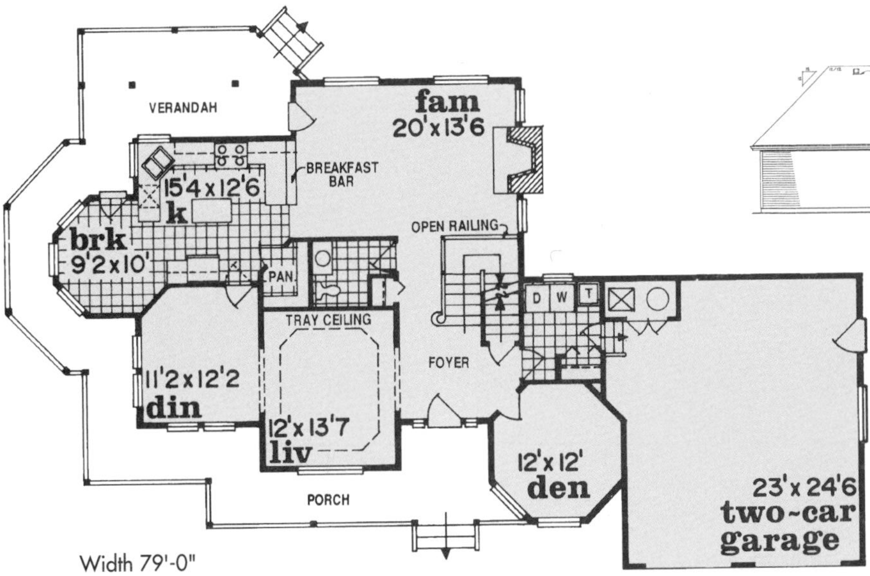

VERANDAH
fam 20'x13'6
BREAKFAST BAR
15'4x12'6 k
brk 9'2x10'
PAN.
OPEN RAILING
TRAY CEILING
11'2x12'2 din
12'x13'7 liv
FOYER
D W T
12'x12' den
23'x24'6 two-car garage
PORCH

Width 79'-0"
Depth 44'-0"

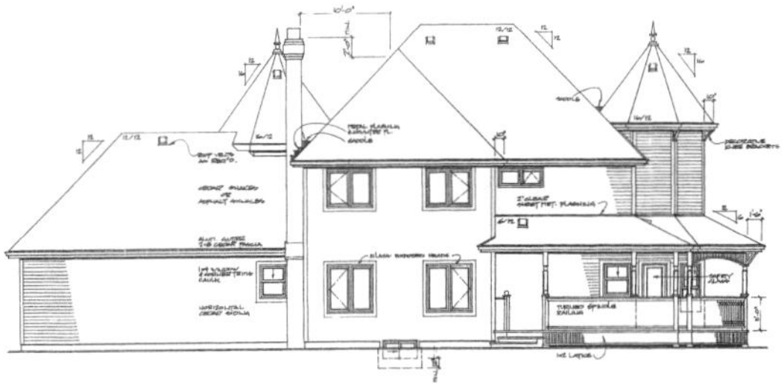

Rear Elevation

Design by
Select Home Designs

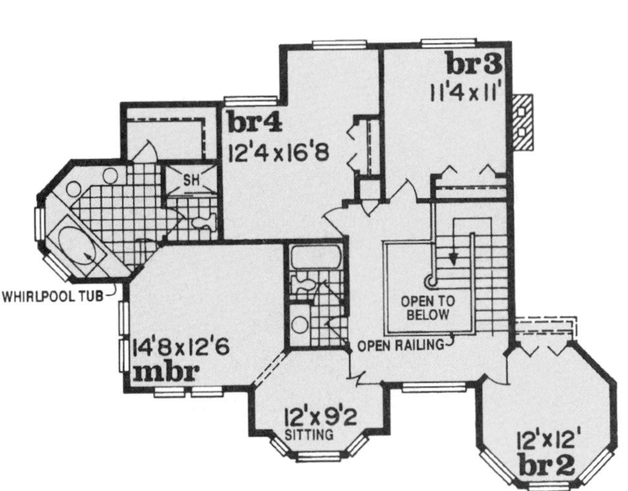
br3
11'4x11'
br4
12'4x16'8
SH
WHIRLPOOL TUB
OPEN TO BELOW
OPEN RAILING
14'8x12'6
mbr
12'x9'2
SITTING
12'x12'
br2

Design Q416

First Floor: 1,362 square feet
Second Floor: 1,270 square feet
Total: 2,632 square feet

■ Filled with Victorian details—scalloped shingles, intricate wood detailing, a wraparound veranda and turrets—this home is a classic beauty with a modern floor plan. Archways open into the distinctive living room with tray ceiling and also to the dining room beyond. An octagonal den across the foyer is a private spot for reading or studying. The U-shaped island kitchen holds an octagonal breakfast bay and a pass-through breakfast bar to the family room. A doorway from the family room accesses the veranda; a fireplace warms this casual space inside. Four bedrooms reside on the second floor: a master suite and three family bedrooms. The master suite is appointed with a private bath, a sitting room and a walk-in closet. Plans include details for both a basement and a crawlspace foundation.

Design 2973

First Floor: 1,269 square feet
Second Floor: 1,227 square feet
Total: 2,496 square feet

L

Design by
Home Planners

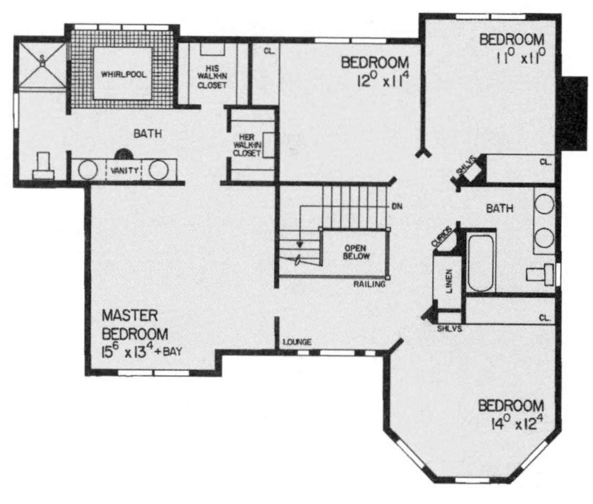

WHIRLPOOL
HIS WALKIN CLOSET
CL.
BEDROOM $12^{0} \times 11^{4}$
BEDROOM $11^{0} \times 11^{0}$
BATH
HER WALKIN CLOSET
VANITY
DN
OPEN BELOW
RAILING
SHLVS
CL.
BATH
LINEN
CL.
MASTER BEDROOM $15^{6} \times 13^{4}$ + BAY
LOUNGE
SHLVS
BEDROOM $14^{0} \times 12^{4}$

■ Sunbursts, simple balusters and a stylish turret set off this Victorian exterior, complete with two finely detailed covered porches. An unrestrained floor plan offers bays and nooks, open spaces and cozy niches—a proper combination for an active family. Formal living and dining areas invite gatherings, whether large or small, planned or casual—but the heart of the home is the family area. A wide bay window and a fireplace with an extended hearth warm up both the family room and the breakfast area, while the nearby kitchen offers a snack counter for easy meals. The second floor includes three family bedrooms and a lavish master suite with an oversized whirlpool spa and twin walk-in closets.

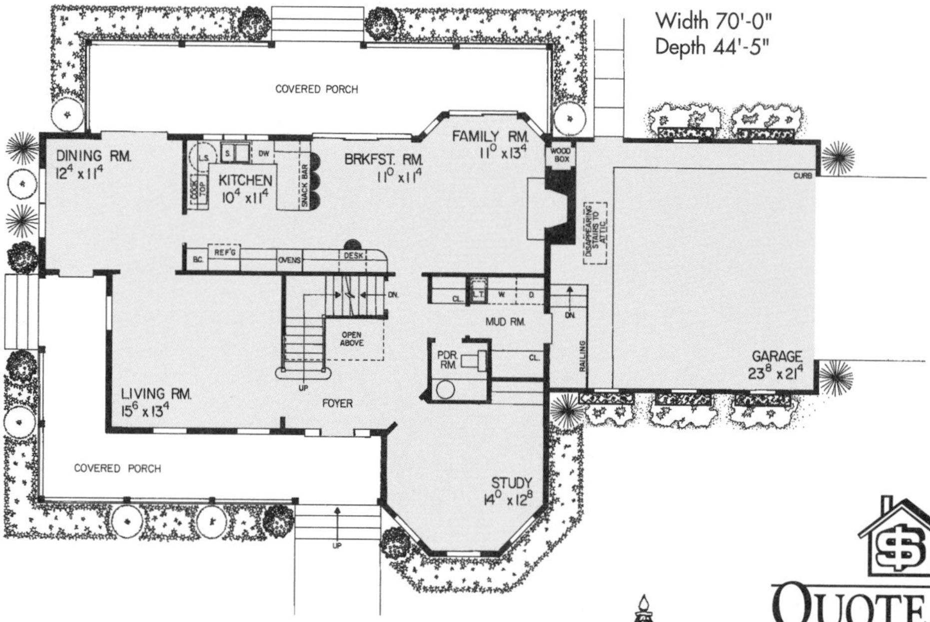

Width 70'-0"
Depth 44'-5"

COVERED PORCH
DINING RM. $12^{4} \times 11^{4}$
KITCHEN $10^{4} \times 11^{4}$
BRKFST. RM. $11^{0} \times 11^{4}$
FAMILY RM. $11^{0} \times 13^{4}$
MUD RM.
GARAGE $23^{8} \times 21^{4}$
LIVING RM. $15^{6} \times 13^{4}$
FOYER
PDR. RM.
COVERED PORCH
STUDY $14^{0} \times 12^{8}$

QUOTE ONE®
Cost to build? See page 516 to order complete cost estimate to build this house in your area!

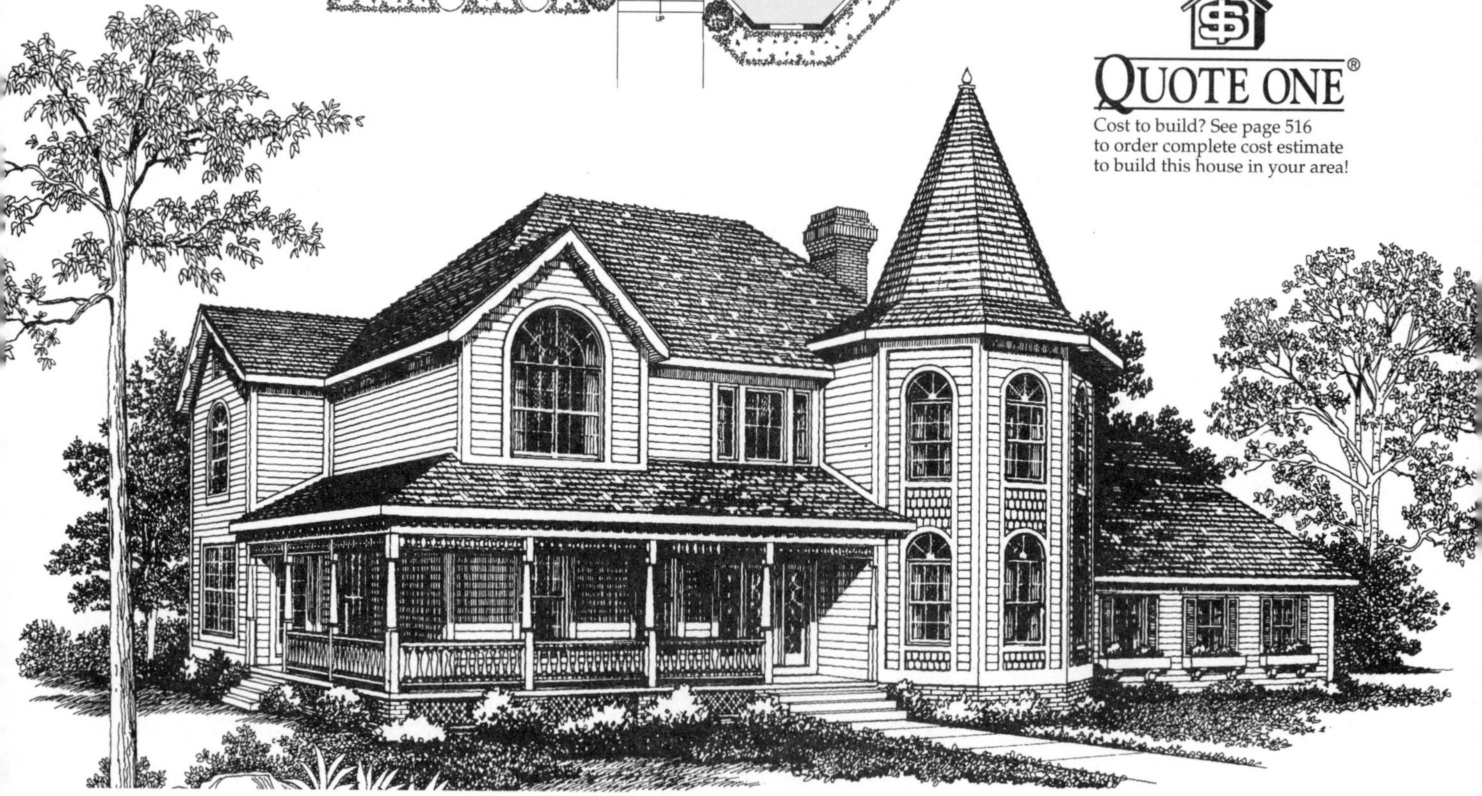

Design by
Select Home Designs

Design Q412

First Floor: 1,324 square feet
Second Floor: 1,192 square feet
Total: 2,516 square feet

■ A turret, wood detailing and a wraparound veranda signal Victorian design for this home. The double-door entry opens to a foyer with curved staircase and leads into the living and dining rooms on the right and the den on the left. All three rooms have tray ceilings; the living room has a fireplace; the dining room, a buffet alcove. Sliding glass doors in the dining room open to the veranda. The family room sits on the other side of the kitchen and breakfast nook. It has a fireplace and sliding glass door access to the rear yard. A laundry room holds access to the two-car garage. Four bedrooms are on the second floor. The master suite has a tray ceiling, walk-in closet and private bath. Bedroom 2 has a cozy window seat. Plans include details for both a basement and a crawlspace foundation.

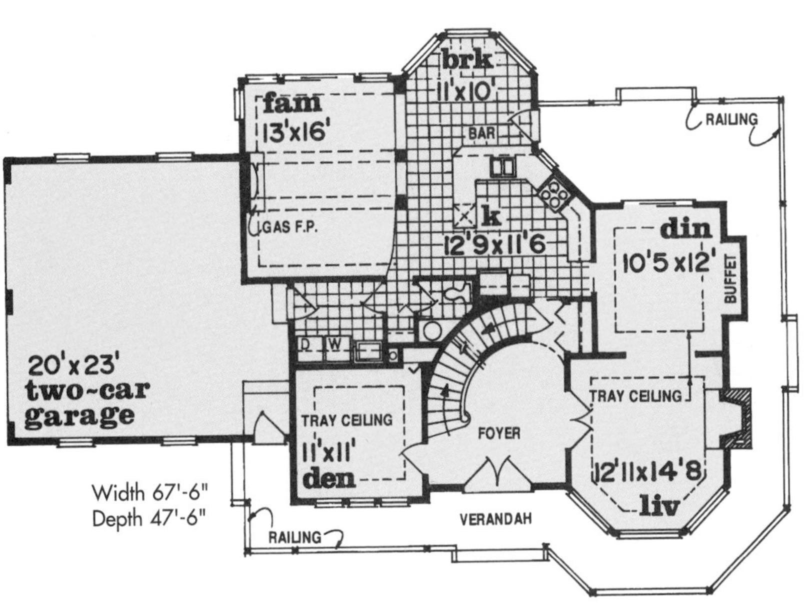
WHIRLPOOL TUB
SITTING
mbr
13'2x18'
TRAY CEILING
SH.
SEAT
br2
13'3x11'5
W.I. CLOSET
VAULTED
br3
11'x10'
OPEN TO
FOYER BELOW
PLANT LEDGE
12'11x12'
br4
brk
11'x10'
fam
13'x16'
BAR
RAILING
k
12'9x11'6
din
10'5 x12'
BUFFET
GAS F.P.
20'x23'
two-car
garage
D W
TRAY CEILING
11'x11'
den
FOYER
TRAY CEILING
12'11x14'8
liv
VERANDAH
RAILING

Width 67'-6"
Depth 47'-6"

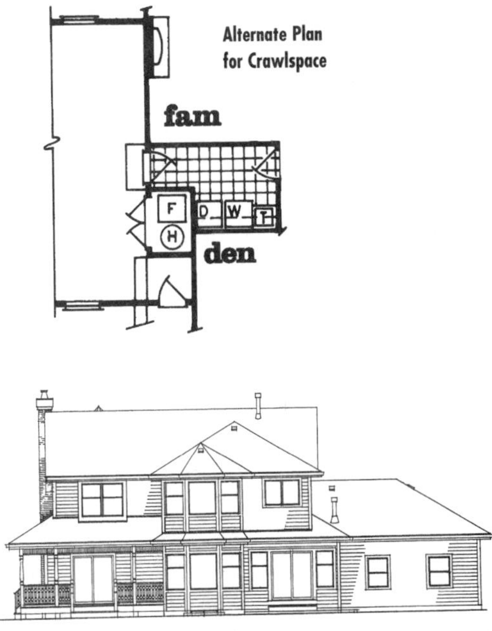
Alternate Plan
for Crawlspace
fam
F
H
D W
den
Rear Elevation

Design 3382

First Floor: 1,366 square feet
Second Floor: 837 square feet
Third Floor: 363 square feet
Total: 2,566 square feet

L **D**

QUOTE ONE®
Cost to build? See page 516 to order complete cost estimate to build this house in your area!

A simple but charming Queen Anne Victorian, this enchanting three-story home includes a living room with fireplace, large family kitchen with snack bar and a second fireplace, and a dining room with nearby wet bar. The second floor holds two bedrooms, one a master suite with grand bath. A tucked-away guest suite on the third floor has a private bath.

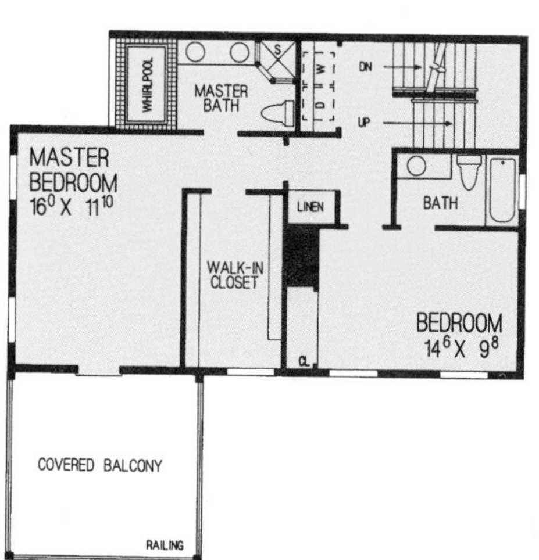

WHIRLPOOL
MASTER BATH
DN
UP
MASTER BEDROOM 16^{0} X 11^{10}
LINEN
BATH
WALK-IN CLOSET
CL
BEDROOM 14^{6} X 9^{8}
COVERED BALCONY
RAILING

RAILING
DN
RAILING
GAZEBO
VERANDA
EATING
RAISED HEARTH
FAMILY KITCHEN 29^{6} X 14^{8}
COOK TOP SNACK BAR
OVENS
REF'G
PANTRY
BC
PDR RM
CL
WET BAR
RAILING
DN
UP
FOYER
BENCH
DINING RM 12^{0} x 16^{2}
ENTRY
LIVING RM 14^{6} X 15^{0}+ BAY
VERANDA
RAILING
UP
Width 50'-2"
Depth 69'-3"
BATH
RAILING
LINEN
CEILING CLIP
GUEST BEDROOM 11^{6}X 15^{2}
CL
ROOF

Design by
Home Planners

VERANDA
SCREENED PORCH 11^2 x 11^6
LIVING RM. 13^4 x 17^0
DINING RM. 11^8 x 11^0
KITCHEN 12^0 x 9^4
SNACK BAR
FOYER
PDR RM.
BRKFST. RM. 12^0 x 8^4 + BAY
LAUND.
STORAGE
WORKBENCH
GARAGE 11^8 x 23^4
COVERED PORCH

Width 38'-0"
Depth 52'-0"

Design 2974

First Floor: 911 square feet
Second Floor: 861 square feet
Total: 1,772 square feet

L

Victorian houses are well known for their orientation on narrow building sites. At only 38 feet wide, this home is still highly livable. From the covered front porch, the foyer directs traffic all the way to the back of the plan where the open living and dining rooms reside. The U-shaped kitchen conveniently serves both the dining room and the front breakfast room. The veranda and the screen porch, both at the rear of the home, extend an invitation to enjoy the outdoors. Three bedrooms, including the master bedroom, and two baths fill the second floor. The attic provides ample storage space.

Design by
Home Planners

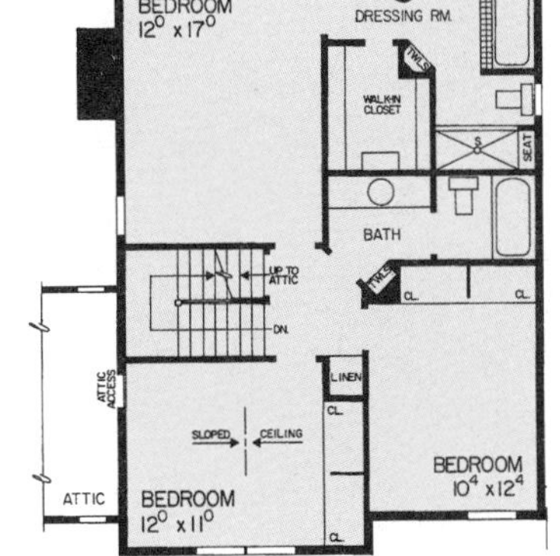
MASTER BEDROOM 12^0 x 17^0
DRESSING RM.
WALK-IN CLOSET
BATH
UP TO ATTIC
DN.
LINEN
SLOPED CEILING
ATTIC
BEDROOM 12^0 x 11^0
BEDROOM 10^4 x 12^4

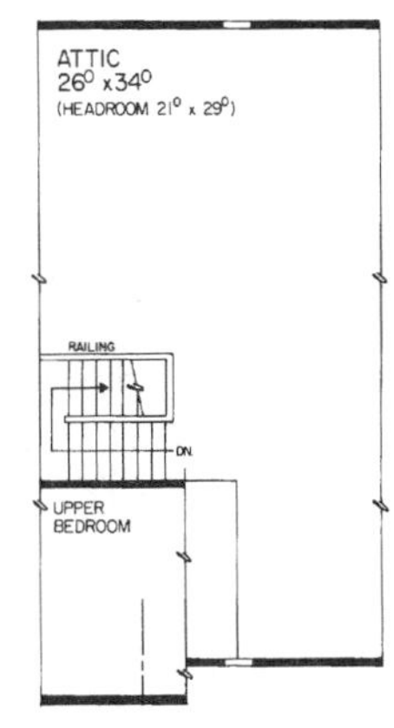
ATTIC 26^0 x 34^0
(HEADROOM 21^0 x 29^0)
RAILING
DN.
UPPER BEDROOM

Design Q373

First Floor: 967 square feet
Second Floor: 853 square feet
Total: 1,820 square feet
Alternate First Floor: 1,090 square feet

This charming, smaller home is decorated in quaint Victorian detail—a covered porch with turned wood spindles, unique window treatment and decorative wood trim. The two-story foyer is brightened by a half-round window and open to the gallery above. A large living/dining room area sits to the left; the living room sports a fireplace. A nearby country kitchen offers a walk-in pantry, U-shaped work counter, breakfast bar, a fireplace and sunny eating area. A covered porch offers casual alfresco dining. If you choose the alternate first floor, the family room is open to the breakfast and has another fireplace and sliding glass doors to the rear yard. Bedrooms on the second floor include a master suite with bay window and full bath with garden whirlpool. Family bedrooms share a full bath. Plans include details for both a basement and a crawlspace foundation.

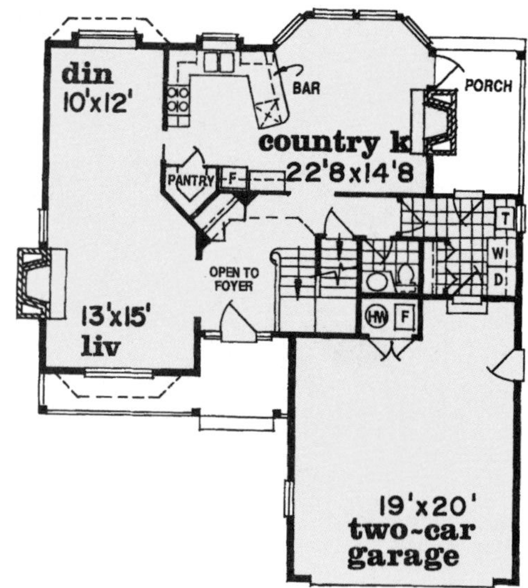

din
10'x12'
BAR
PORCH
country k
22'8x14'8
PANTRY
F
OPEN TO FOYER
13'x15'
liv
W
D
T
HW
F
19'x20'
two-car
garage

Width 42'-0"
Depth 48'-0"

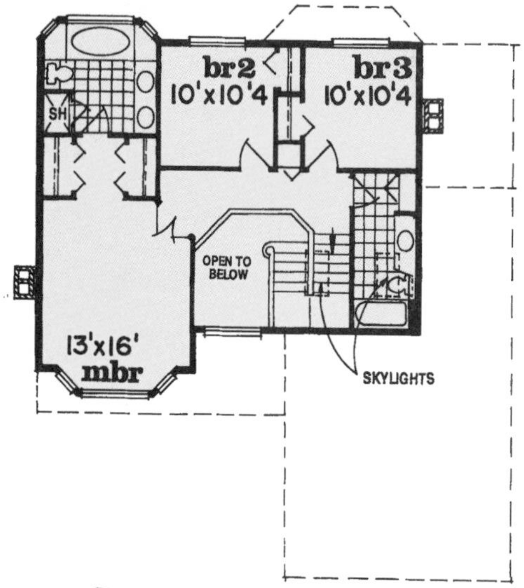

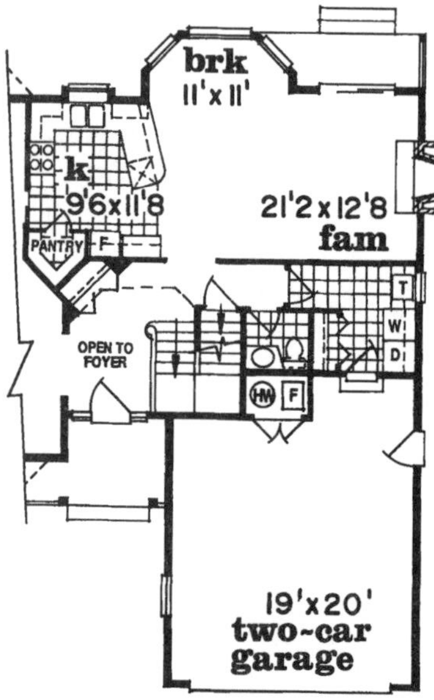

Alternate First Floor

Design by
Select Home Designs

© Copyright 1990 Select Home Designs All rights reserved

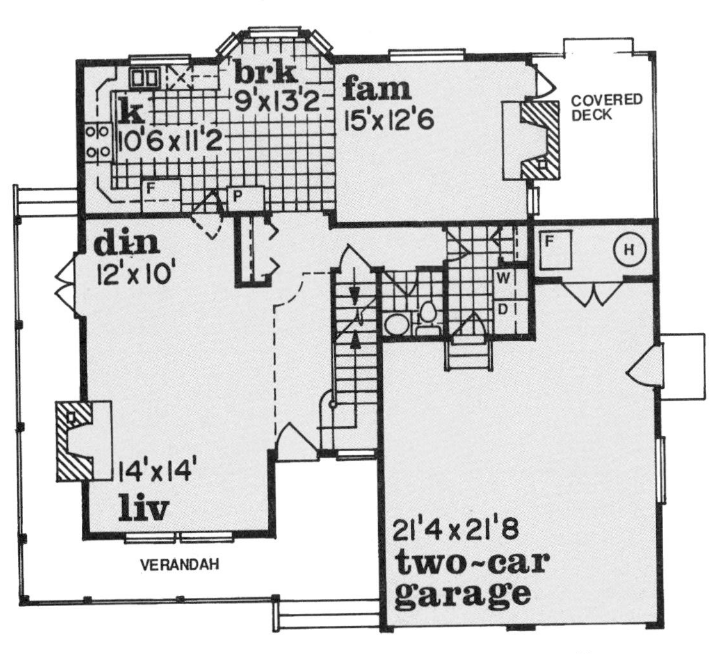
brk
9'x13'2
k
10'6x11'2
fam
15'x12'6
COVERED DECK
F
P
din
12'x10'
F
H
W
D
14'x14'
liv
VERANDAH
21'4x21'8
two-car garage

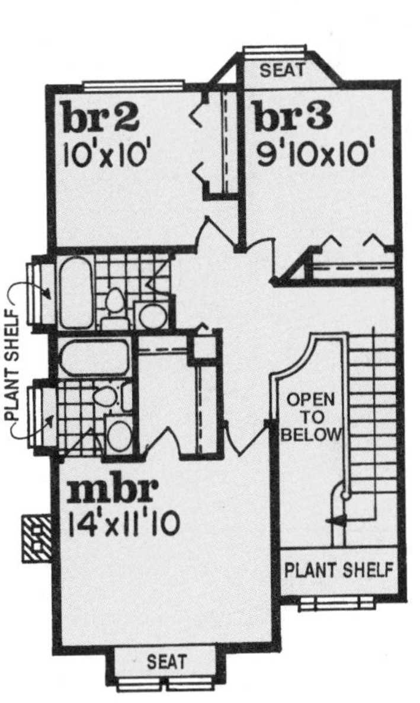
SEAT
br2
10'x10'
br3
9'10x10'
PLANT SHELF
OPEN TO BELOW
mbr
14'x11'10
PLANT SHELF
SEAT

Width 50'-0"
Depth 46'-0"

Design Q374

First Floor: 1,092 square feet
Second Floor: 757 square feet
Total: 1,849 square feet

Design by
Select Home Designs

■ A covered veranda protects the entry of this charming home, and then wraps around to the left side where the spacious living room and dining room are found. The dining room features French-door access to the veranda; the living room is warmed by a fireplace. The open kitchen offers casual comfort for family gatherings, from the breakfast bay to the family-room area warmed by another fireplace. A covered porch sits beyond the family room. The master bedroom is on the second floor and has an intimate window seat, walk-in closet and private bath. Bedroom 3 also has a window seat. A hall bath with soaking tub serves the two family bedrooms. Plans include details for both basement and crawlspace foundations.

Design 3385

First Floor: 1,096 square feet
Second Floor: 900 square feet
Total: 1,996 square feet

L **D**

■ Covered porches front and rear are the first signal that this is a fine example of Folk Victorian styling. Complementing the exterior is a grand plan for family living. A formal living room and attached dining room provide space for entertaining guests. The large family room with fireplace is a gathering room for everyday. Both areas have access to outdoor spaces. Four bedrooms occupy the second floor. The master suite features two lavatories, a window seat and three closets. One of the family bedrooms has its own private balcony and could be used as a study. Note the open staircase and linen storage.

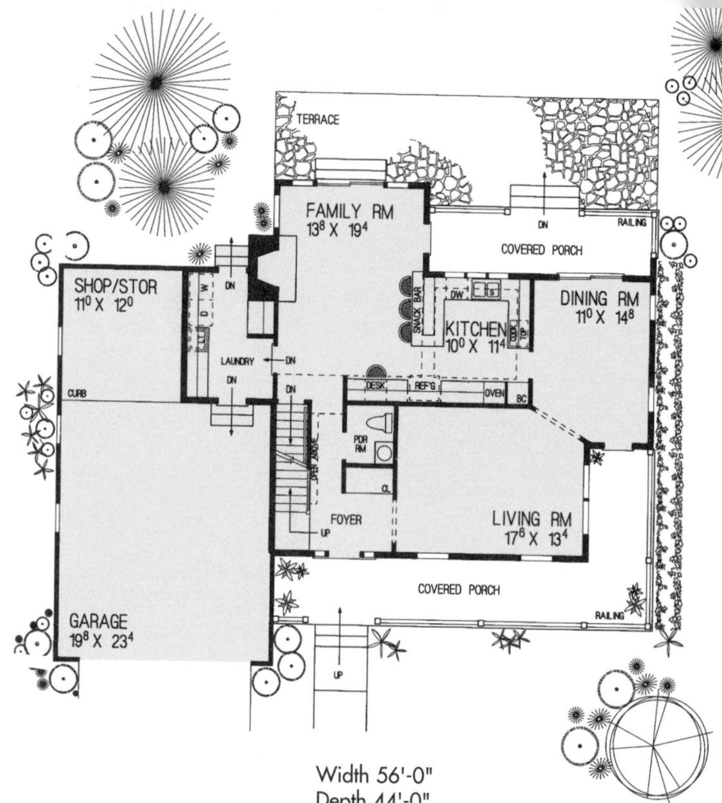
TERRACE
FAMILY RM
13^{8} X 19^{4}
COVERED PORCH
DN
RAILING
SHOP/STOR
11^{0} X 12^{0}
DINING RM
11^{0} X 14^{8}
KITCHEN
10^{0} X 11^{4}
SNACK BAR
DW
LAUNDRY
DESK
REF'G
OVEN
BC
CURB
PDR RM
CL
FOYER
UP
LIVING RM
17^{6} X 13^{4}
COVERED PORCH
RAILING
GARAGE
19^{8} X 23^{4}
UP

Width 56'-0"
Depth 44'-0"

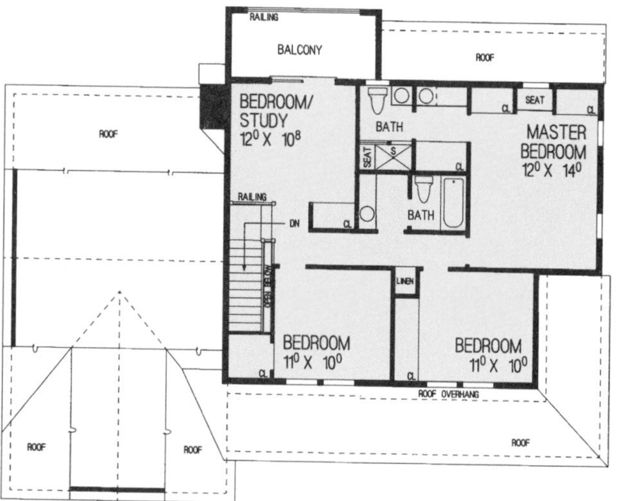
RAILING
BALCONY
ROOF
BEDROOM/
STUDY
12^{0} X 10^{8}
BATH
SEAT
CL
MASTER
BEDROOM
12^{0} X 14^{0}
RAILING
DN
BATH
LINEN
BEDROOM
11^{0} X 10^{0}
BEDROOM
11^{0} X 10^{0}
ROOF OVERHANG
ROOF

Design by
Home Planners

QUOTE ONE®

Cost to build? See page 516 to order complete cost estimate to build this house in your area!

© Copyright 1990 Select Home Designs. All rights reserved.

Design Q378

First Floor: 1,026 square feet
Second Floor: 912 square feet
Total: 1,938 square feet

■ Distinguishing the exterior of this classy Victorian are a covered porch with spindles, a distinctive bay window and wood detailing. The interior is exquisite in its own right. The foyer opens to a living room with bay window and an adjoining dining room. A fireplace warms the living room, while the dining room has optional buffet space. The kitchen features a long, angled counter to serve the sunny breakfast bay and the family room. Note an additional fireplace in the family room, plus double doors to the rear yard. The service area contains a laundry and access to the two-car garage and a door to a cute side porch. The master suite has a partially vaulted sitting bay, a walk-in closet and private bath with whirlpool tub. Two family bedrooms with a shared bath join the master suite on the second floor. Plans include details for both a basement and a crawlspace foundation.

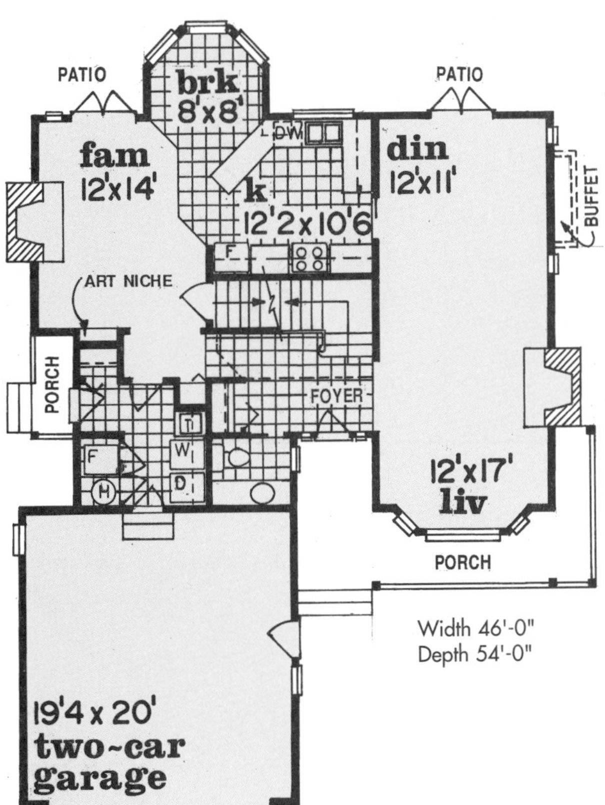
PATIO
brk
8'x8'
PATIO
DW
fam
12'x14'
din
12'x11'
k
12'2x10'6
BUFFET
F
ART NICHE
PORCH
FOYER
T
W
F
D
H
12'x17'
liv
PORCH
19'4 x 20'
two-car
garage

Width 46'-0"
Depth 54'-0"

Design by
Select Home Designs

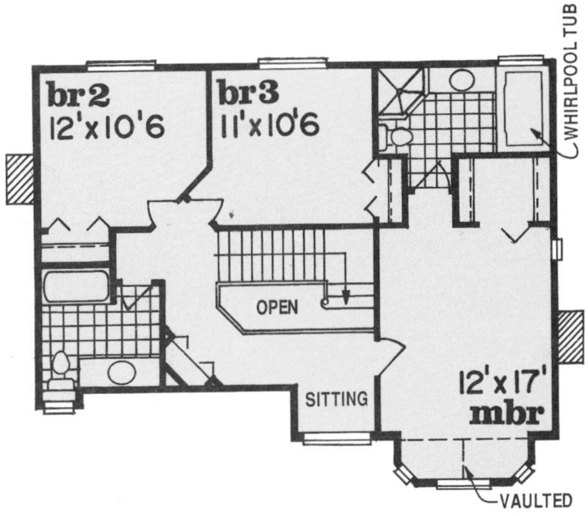
br2
12'x10'6
br3
11'x10'6
WHIRLPOOL TUB
OPEN
SITTING
12'x17'
mbr
VAULTED

Design Q388

First Floor: 1,360 square feet
Second Floor: 734 square feet
Total: 2,094 square feet
Bonus Room: 378 square feet

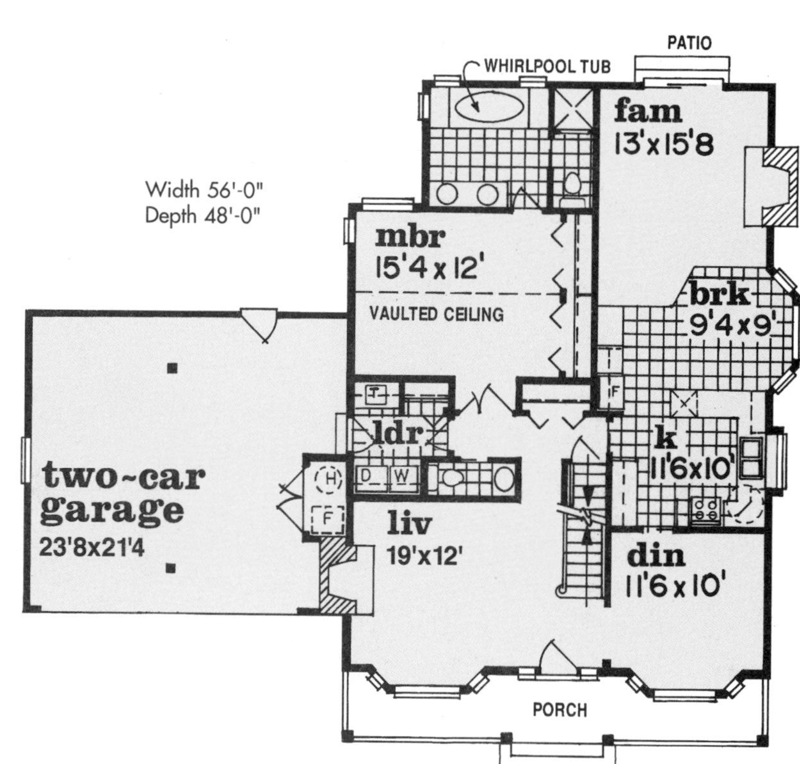

PATIO
WHIRLPOOL TUB
fam
13'x15'8
Width 56'-0"
Depth 48'-0"
mbr
15'4 x 12'
VAULTED CEILING
brk
9'4x9'
ldr
k
11'6x10'
two~car
garage
23'8x21'4
liv
19'x12'
din
11'6 x 10'
PORCH

■ Traditional accents and a covered porch lend charm to the exterior of this Victorian home. The entry opens directly to a living room with fireplace on the left and a dining room on the right. Both areas have bay windows. The U-shaped kitchen has an attached breakfast bay, which is open to the family room. A fireplace and sliding glass doors to the rear yard are highlights of the family room. The master bedroom is split from family bedrooms by being situated on the first floor. It is appointed with a vaulted ceiling and a private bath with whirlpool tub. Three secondary bedrooms on the second floor share a full bath. Bonus space of 393 square feet can be developed later into an additional bedroom or as a media center or game room. Plans include details for both a basement and a crawlspace foundation.

Design by
Select Home Designs

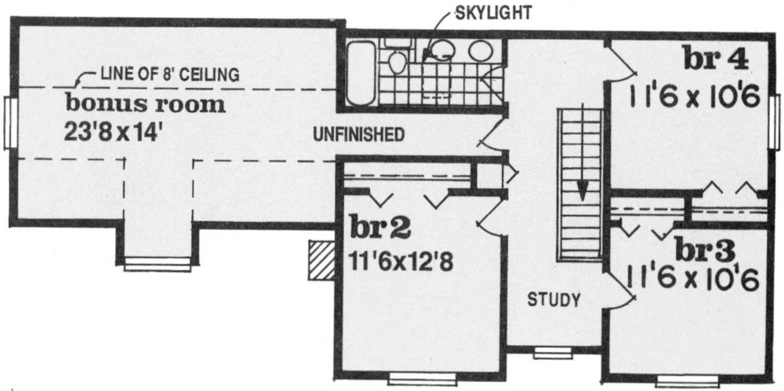

SKYLIGHT
LINE OF 8' CEILING
bonus room
23'8x14'
UNFINISHED
br 4
11'6 x 10'6
br2
11'6x12'8
br3
11'6 x 10'6
STUDY

Design Q501

First Floor: 1,620 square feet
Second Floor: 642 square feet
Total: 2,262 square feet

■ A wraparound veranda and extensive screened porch bring outdoor enjoyment to the owners of this fine design. A vaulted foyer introduces the interior and leads across a gallery to a vaulted living room. Special details here include a fireplace, double doors to the porch and an overlook from the upstairs gallery. A country kitchen with skylit dining area has abundant counter space and is warmed in cold months by a cozy hearth. The master bedroom resides on the first floor for privacy. It holds a skylight, access to a private deck, access to the screened porch, a walk-in closet and its own bath. Two second-floor bedrooms share a full bath and are adorned with dormer windows. Plans include details for both a basement and a crawlspace foundation.

COVERED PORCH
liv 17x22'
din 14'x17'
mbr 14'x16'10
DECK
SKYLIGHT
GALLERY
k 14'x12'
FOYER
VERANDAH

Width 60'-0"
Depth 54'-0"

Design by
Select Home Designs

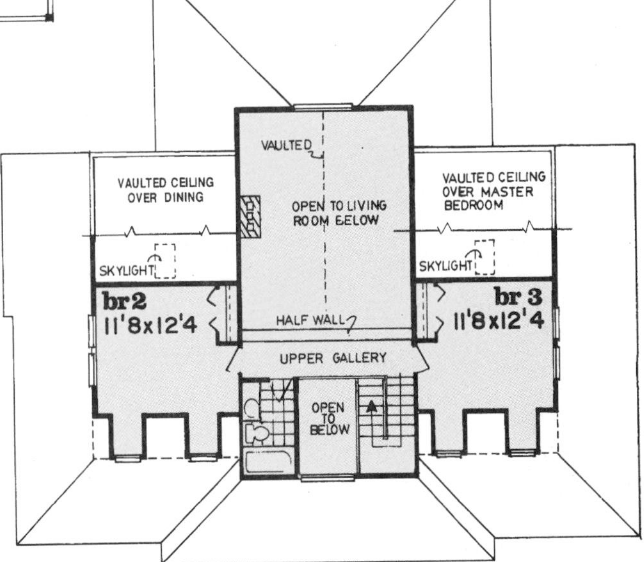
VAULTED
VAULTED CEILING OVER DINING
OPEN TO LIVING ROOM BELOW
VAULTED CEILING OVER MASTER BEDROOM
SKYLIGHT
SKYLIGHT
br2 11'8x12'4
br 3 11'8x12'4
HALF WALL
UPPER GALLERY
OPEN TO BELOW

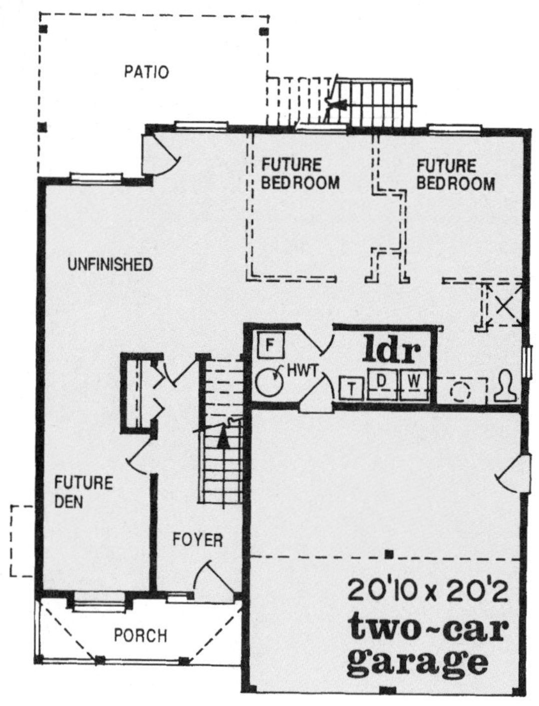
PATIO
FUTURE BEDROOM
FUTURE BEDROOM
UNFINISHED
ldr
F
HWT
T
D
W
FUTURE DEN
FOYER
20'10 x 20'2
two-car garage
PORCH

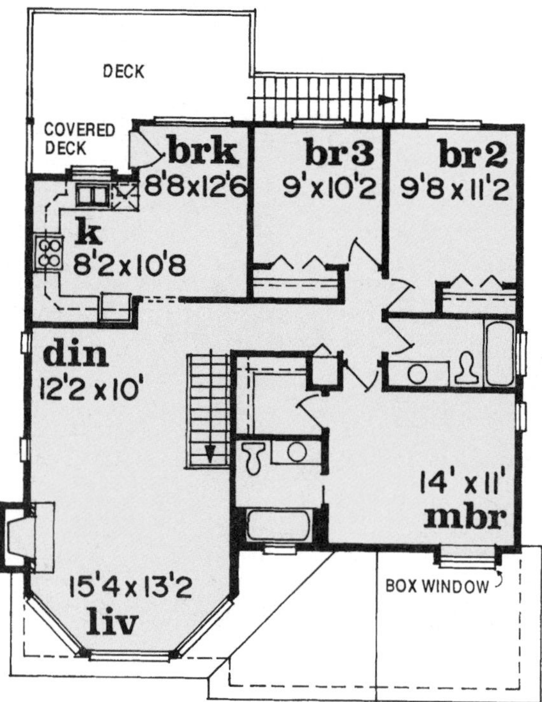
DECK
COVERED DECK
brk 8'8x12'6
br3 9'x10'2
br2 9'8 x 11'2
k 8'2x10'8
din 12'2 x 10'
14' x 11' mbr
15'4x13'2 liv
BOX WINDOW

Width 37'-0"
Depth 41'-0"

Design Q347

First Floor: 136 square feet
Second Floor: 1,221 square feet
Total: 1,357 square feet

■ The main living level of this home is on the second floor. You can save development of the lower level for a future time, if you choose. The foyer occupies 136 square feet of finished space and leads up a staircase to a living and dining area with fireplace. The nearby, U-shaped kitchen has a breakfast room with access to a covered deck in the back. The bedrooms sit on the right side of the plan and include a master and two family bedrooms. The master has a box window, a walk-in closet and private bath. Family bedrooms share the use of a full hall bath. When finished, the lower level will yield two additional bedrooms, a future den and a full bath. The laundry room and two-car garage are also at this level.

Design by
Select Home Designs

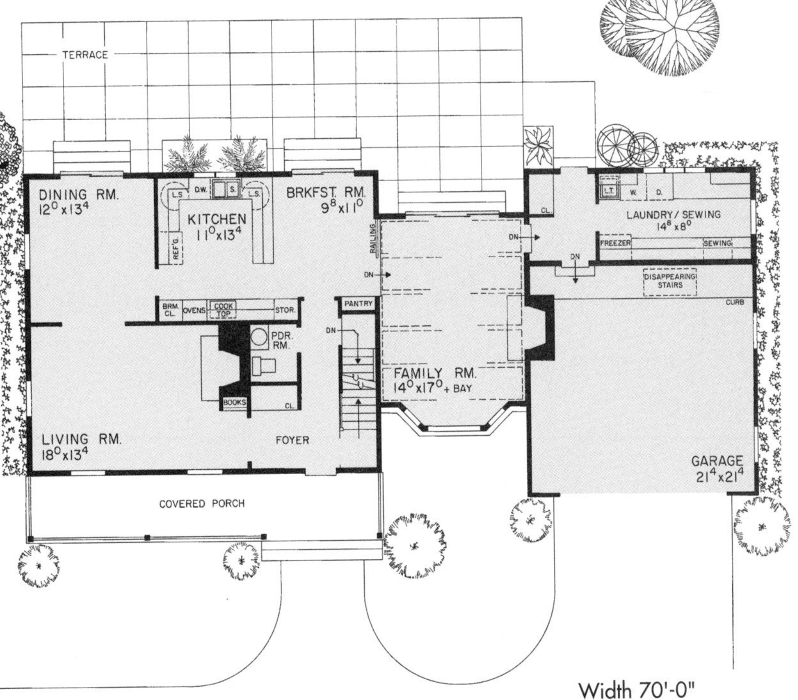
TERRACE
DINING RM.
12^{0}x13^4
KITCHEN
11^{0}x13^4
BRKFST RM.
9^{8}x11^0
LAUNDRY / SEWING
14^{8}x8^0
FREEZER
SEWING
DISAPPEARING STAIRS
PANTRY
PDR. RM.
BOOKS
FAMILY RM.
14^{0}x17^0+ BAY
LIVING RM.
18^{0}x13^4
FOYER
GARAGE
21^{4}x21^4
COVERED PORCH
Width 70'-0"
Depth 34'-0"

Design 2908

First Floor: 1,427 square feet
Second Floor: 1,153 square feet
Total: 2,580 square feet

L D

■ This Early American offers plenty of modern comfort with its covered front porch with pillars and rails, double chimneys, spacious rooms and large country kitchen with breakfast room. A step-down family room features a fireplace, as does the formal living room. Upstairs, three family bedrooms share a full hall bath. The master suite is complete with a dual vanity and a compartmented bath with dressing room. Special features of this home include a laundry/sewing room with freezer and washer/dryer space, a large rear terrace and an entry-hall powder room.

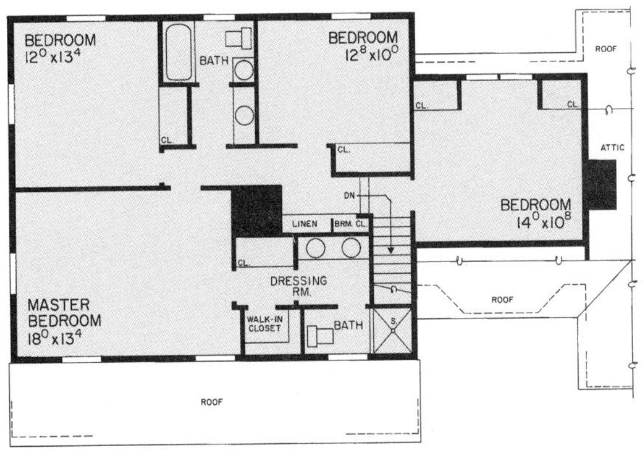
BEDROOM
12^{0}x13^4
BATH
BEDROOM
12^{8}x10^0
ROOF
ATTIC
BEDROOM
14^{0}x10^8
LINEN
DRESSING RM.
MASTER BEDROOM
18^{0}x13^4
WALK-IN CLOSET
BATH
ROOF

QUOTE ONE®

Cost to build? See page 516 to order complete cost estimate to build this house in your area!

Design by
Home Planners

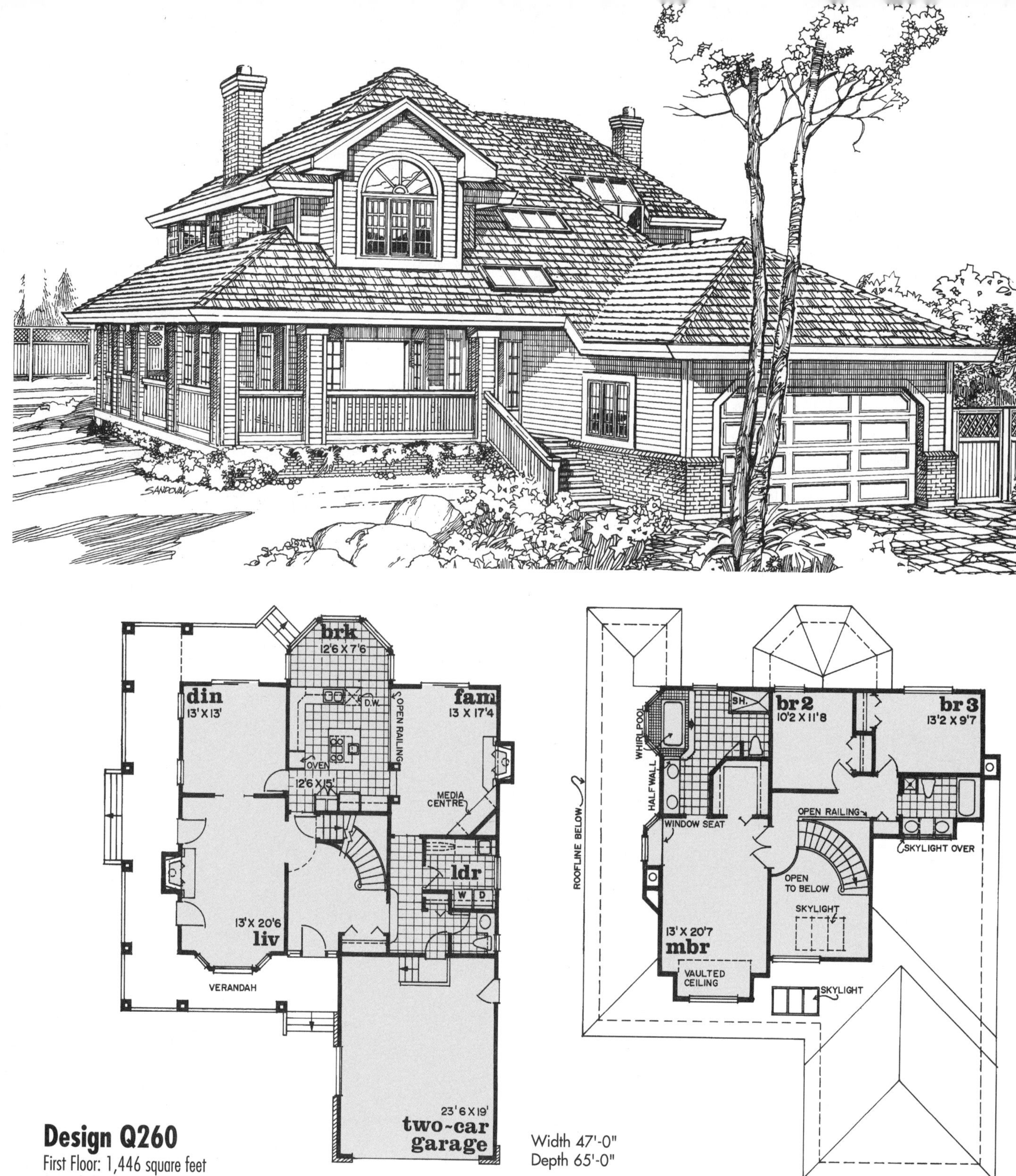

brk
12'6 X 7'6
din
13'X 13'
D.W.
OPEN RAILING
fam
13 X 17'4
OVEN
12'6 X 15'
MEDIA CENTRE
ldr
W D
13'X 20'6
liv
VERANDAH
23'6 X 19'
two-car garage
SH.
WHIRLPOOL
HALFWALL
br 2
10'2 X 11'8
br 3
13'2 X 9'7
WINDOW SEAT
OPEN RAILING
SKYLIGHT OVER
OPEN TO BELOW
SKYLIGHT
13' X 20'7
mbr
VAULTED CEILING
SKYLIGHT
ROOFLINE BELOW
ROOFLINE BELOW

Design Q260

First Floor: 1,446 square feet
Second Floor: 1,047 square feet
Total: 2,493 square feet

Width 47'-0"
Depth 65'-0"

■ This unique design is bedecked with a veranda that wraps around two sides of the design. The foyer is skylit and contains a curved staircase to the second floor. On the left are the living room with fireplace and bay window and dining room with sliding glass doors to the veranda. The living room has double doors to access the veranda. A family room is at the other end of the plan and holds a corner media center and a fireplace. Sliding glass doors open to the rear yard. In between is an island kitchen with breakfast bay. The bedrooms are upstairs and include a master suite with walk-in closet, vaulted alcove and private bath with whirlpool tub. Family bedrooms share a full bath with double vanity.

Design by
Select Home Designs

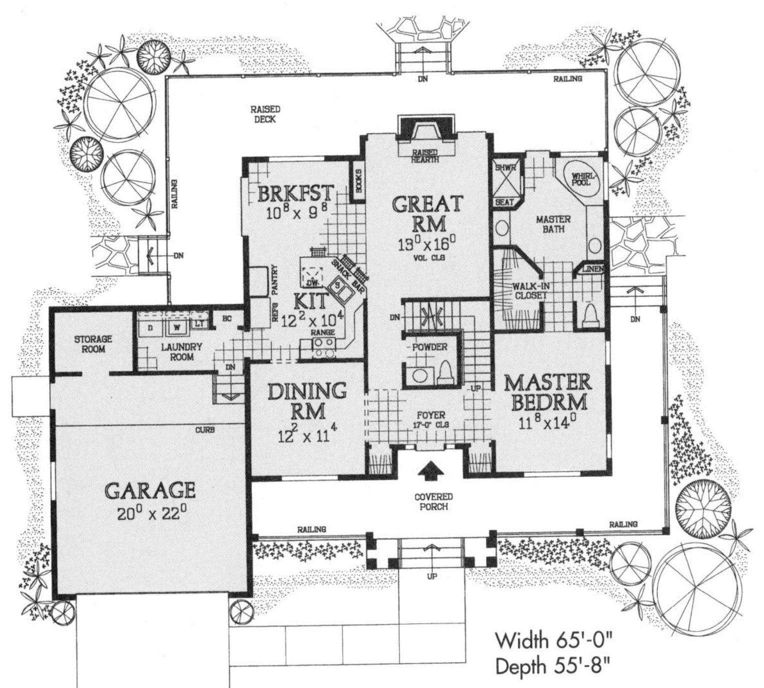
RAISED DECK
RAILING
DN
BRKFST
10^8 x 9^8
BOOKS
RAISED HEARTH
GREAT RM
13^0 x 16^0
VOL CLG
SHWR
SEAT
WHIRL POOL
MASTER BATH
PANTRY
KIT
12^2 x 10^4
RANGE
SNACK BAR
WALK-IN CLOSET
LINEN
STORAGE ROOM
LAUNDRY ROOM
POWDER
DINING RM
12^2 x 11^4
FOYER
17'-0" CLG
MASTER BEDRM
11^8 x 14^0
CURB
GARAGE
20^0 x 22^0
COVERED PORCH
UP
Width 65'-0"
Depth 55'-8"

Design 3615

First Floor: 1,355 square feet
Second Floor: 582 square feet
Total: 1,937 square feet

L

A portico makes a strong architectural statement and provides shelter for this home's front entrance. The central foyer with its two-story ceiling and dramatic glass area routes traffic directly to all zones. To the left of the foyer is the formal dining room which is but a step from the angular kitchen. The great room has a high volume ceiling. Its raised-hearth fireplace is flanked by doors to the deck. To the right of the foyer is the master suite. The master bath is compartmented and includes separate vanities, a walk-in closet, a whirlpool, a stall shower with seat, linen storage and access to the rear deck. Upstairs are two family bedrooms, a full hall bath and a balcony overlooking the great room below.

Design by
Home Planners

QUOTE ONE®
Cost to build? See page 516
to order complete cost estimate
to build this house in your area!

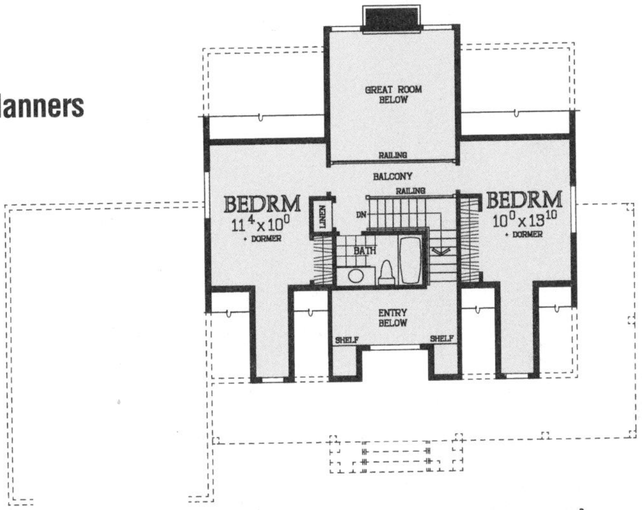

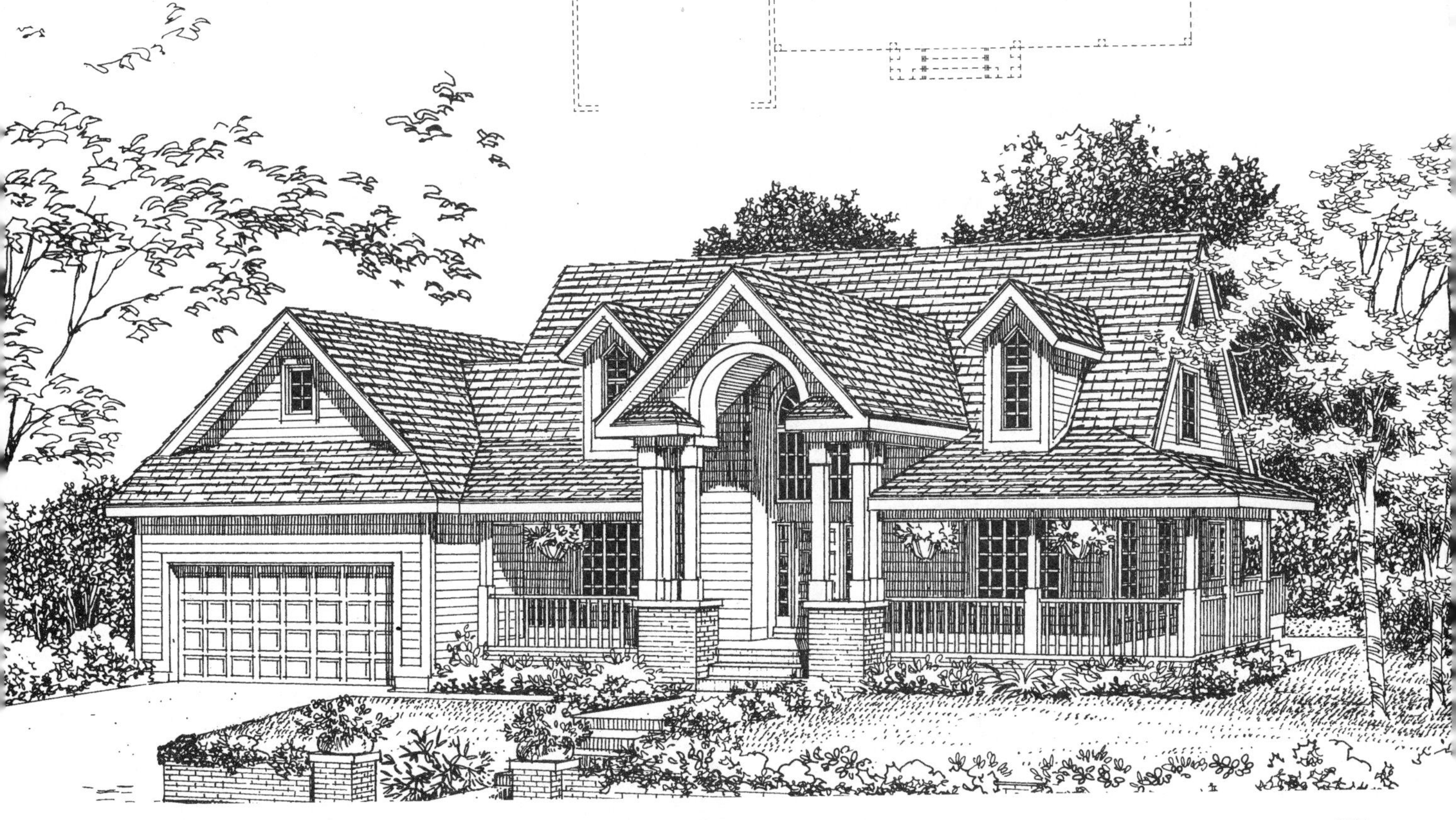

Design 5552

First Floor: 720 square feet
Second Floor: 1,263 square feet
Total: 1,983 square feet

QUOTE ONE®

Cost to build? See page 516 to order complete cost estimate to build this house in your area!

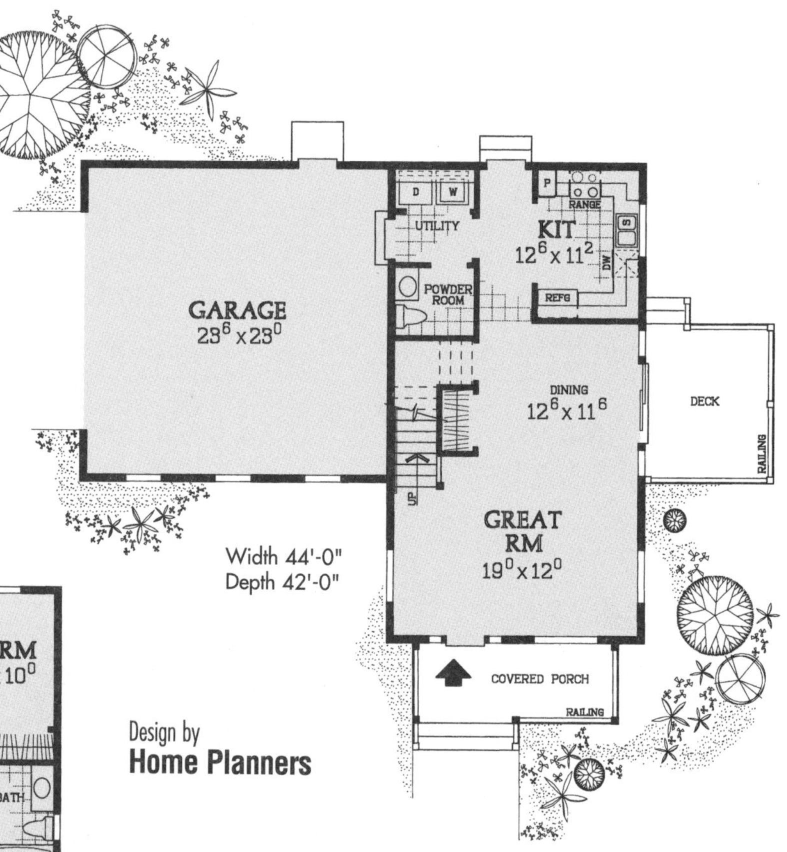

D
W
UTILITY
P
RANGE
KIT
12⁶ x 11²
S
DW
POWDER ROOM
REFG
GARAGE
23⁶ x 23⁰
DINING
12⁶ x 11⁶
DECK
RAILING
UP
GREAT RM
19⁰ x 12⁰
COVERED PORCH
RAILING
Width 44'-0"
Depth 42'-0"

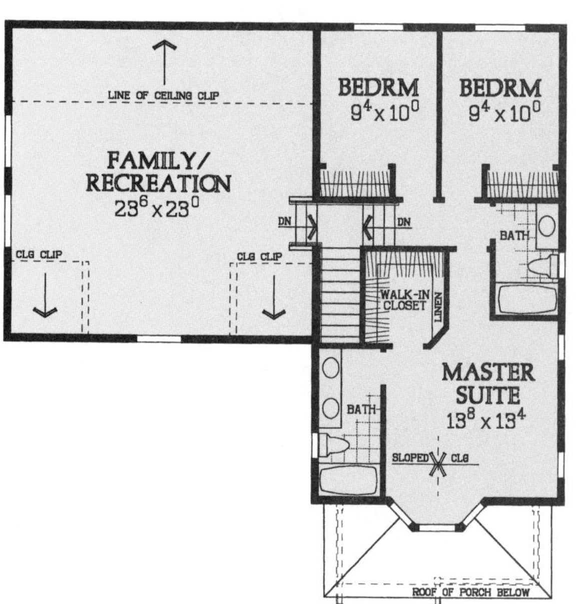

LINE OF CEILING CLIP
FAMILY/ RECREATION
23⁶ x 23⁰
CLG CLIP
CLG CLIP
DN
DN
BEDRM
9⁴ x 10⁰
BEDRM
9⁴ x 10⁰
BATH
WALK-IN CLOSET
LINEN
BATH
MASTER SUITE
13⁸ x 13⁴
SLOPED CLG
ROOF OF PORCH BELOW

Design by
Home Planners

■ This narrow-lot design utilizes every square foot to provide a comfortable, yet roomy design. The great room provides ample room for entertaining, both inside or outside via the side deck. The efficient U-shaped kitchen serves this main room with ease and is conveniently located near the utility area, with a powder room, and the two-car garage. Upstairs, two family bedrooms share a full hall bath, while the master bedroom features a private bath, a walk-in closet and a bayed sitting area. The spacious family room, also located on the second floor, will become a favorite spot at day's end to share the day's events while watching TV or playing a competitive game of pool.

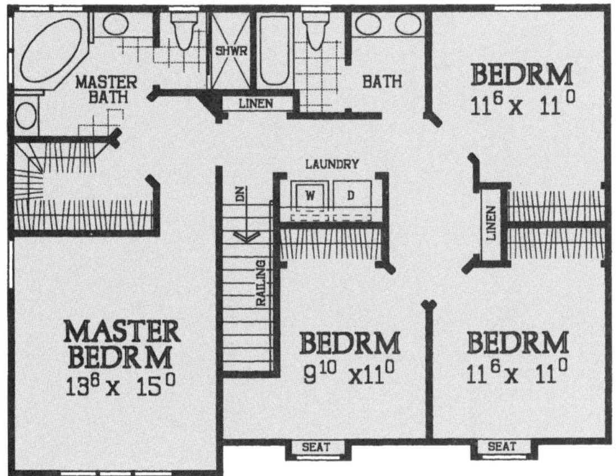
MASTER BATH
SHWR
LINEN
BATH
BEDRM
11^6 x 11^0
LAUNDRY
W
D
DN
LINEN
RAILING
MASTER BEDRM
13^6 x 15^0
BEDRM
9^{10} x11^0
BEDRM
11^6x 11^0
SEAT
SEAT

Design 5542

First Floor: 1,179 square feet
Second Floor: 1,120 square feet
Total: 2,299 square feet

■ A comfortable covered porch bids welcome to this two-story home. Inside, the open floor plan on the first floor allows you to move from room to room with ease. The large great room features excellent opportunities for entertaining. The U-shaped kitchen offers plenty of counter space and access to the breakfast nook and to the rear yard or to the garage. A corner media room can also be used for a quiet den. Upstairs, the master bedroom features a walk-in closet and a master bath with a satisfying corner whirlpool. Three additional bedrooms share a full hall bath that provides a separate sink area. The washer and dryer are conveniently located on the second floor near the family bedrooms with an alternative location in the garage.

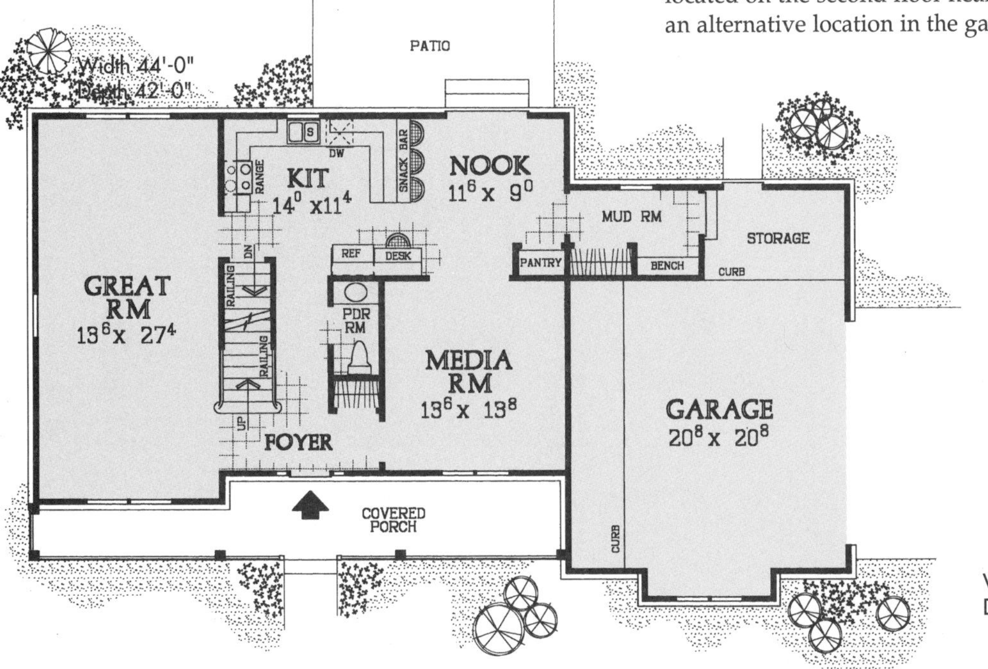
PATIO
Width 44'-0"
Depth 42'-0"
S
DW
SNACK BAR
RANGE
KIT
14^0 x11^4
NOOK
11^6 x 9^0
MUD RM
STORAGE
REF
DESK
DN
PANTRY
BENCH
CURB
GREAT RM
13^6x 27^4
RAILING
PDR RM
MEDIA RM
13^6 x 13^8
GARAGE
20^8 x 20^8
UP
FOYER
COVERED PORCH
CURB

Design by
Home Planners

QUOTE ONE®
Cost to build? See page 516
to order complete cost estimate
to build this house in your area!

Width 61'-8"
Depth 35'-8"

© Copyright 1990 Select Home Designs. All rights reserved.

Design Q419

First Floor: 1,639 square feet
Second Floor: 1,158 square feet
Total: 2,797 square feet

■ This grand farmhouse design is anything but ordinary. Its lovely details—a Palladian window, a covered veranda and shutters—put it a cut above the rest. The interior features classic floor planning with a vaulted center-hall foyer and staircase to the second floor. Formal living areas—a living room and a dining room—are on the right, while a cozy den and the large family room are on the left. A full bath sits near the den so that it can double as guest space. Both the living room and the family room have fireplaces. The family room features access to the veranda in the front, while the dining room has double-door access to it in the back. The island kitchen and breakfast room are near the dining room in the back. Bedrooms are on the second floor—a master suite and three family bedrooms. The master suite has a private bath. Plans include details for both a basement and a crawlspace foundation.

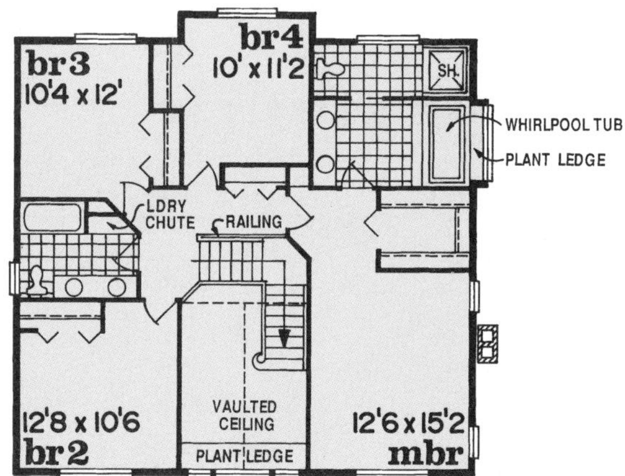
br3
10'4 x 12'
br4
10' x 11'2
SH.
WHIRLPOOL TUB
PLANT LEDGE
LDRY CHUTE
RAILING
12'8 x 10'6
br2
VAULTED CEILING
PLANT LEDGE
12'6 x 15'2
mbr

Design by
Select Home Designs

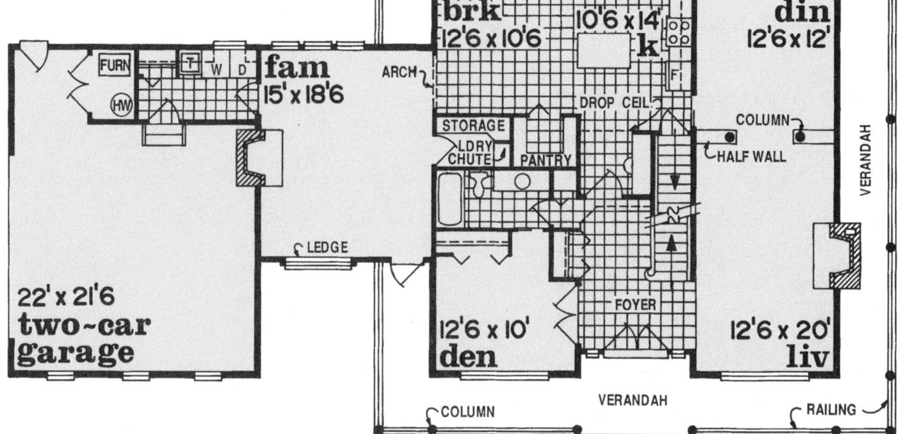
COLUMN
VERANDAH
RAILING
brk
12'6 x 10'6
10'6 x 14'
k
din
12'6 x 12'
FURN
HW
W
D
fam
15' x 18'6
ARCH
DROP CEIL.
STORAGE
LDRY CHUTE
PANTRY
COLUMN
HALF WALL
VERANDAH
LEDGE
22' x 21'6
two-car
garage
12'6 x 10'
den
FOYER
12'6 x 20'
liv
COLUMN
VERANDAH
RAILING

Rear Elevation

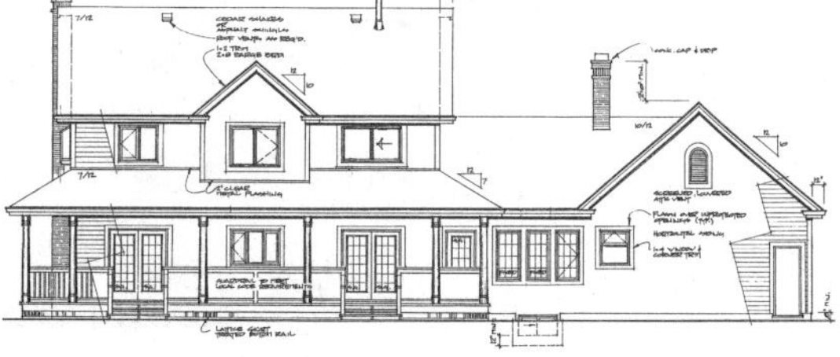

Width 80'-0"
Depth 44'-0"

Design 2981

First Floor: 2,104 square feet
Second Floor: 2,015 square feet
Total: 4,119 square feet

This formal two-story recalls a Louisiana plantation house, Land's End, built in 1857. The Ionic columns of the front porch and the pediment gable echo the Greek Revival style. Highlighting the interior is the bright and cheerful spaciousness of the informal family-room area. It features a wall of glass stretching to the second-story, sloping ceiling. Enhancing the drama of this area is the adjacent glass area of the breakfast room. Note the His and Hers areas of the master bedroom.

Design by
Home Planners

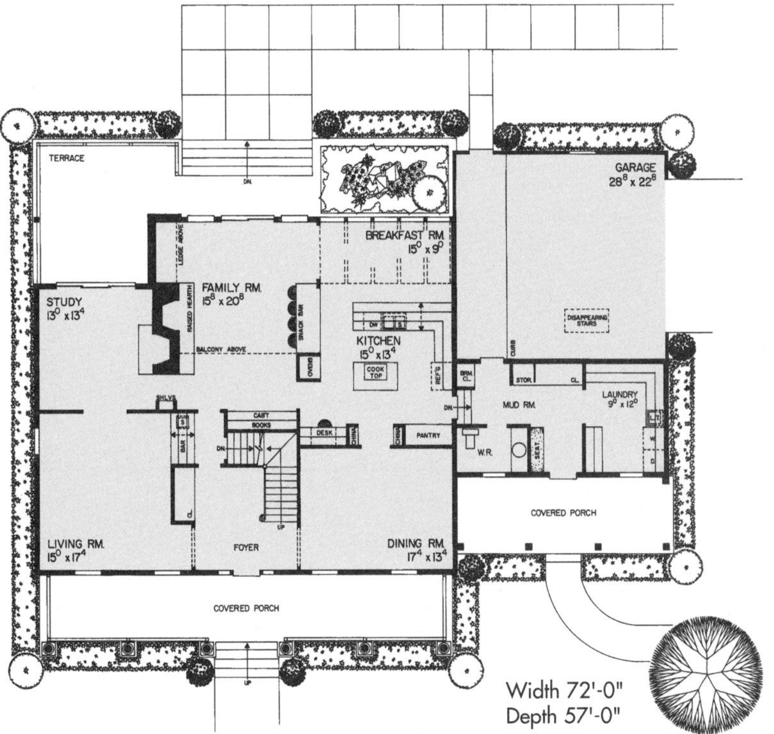
TERRACE
GARAGE
BREAKFAST RM.
FAMILY RM.
STUDY
KITCHEN
MUD RM.
LAUNDRY
COVERED PORCH
LIVING RM.
FOYER
DINING RM.
COVERED PORCH

Width 72'-0"
Depth 57'-0"

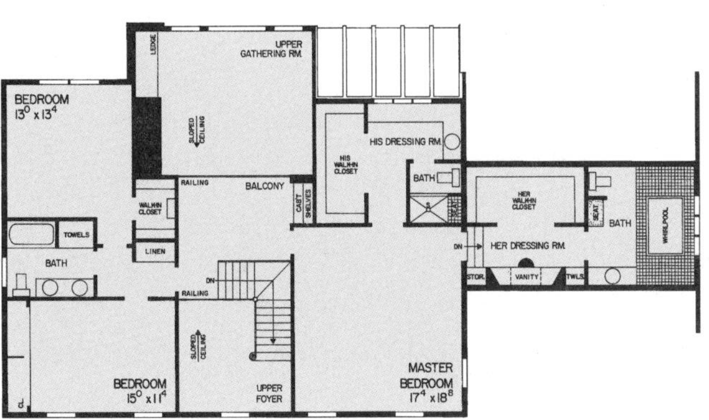
UPPER GATHERING RM.
BEDROOM
HIS DRESSING RM.
BALCONY
BATH
HER DRESSING RM.
BEDROOM
UPPER FOYER
MASTER BEDROOM

Rear Elevation

Design 2694

First Floor: 2,026 square feet
Second Floor: 1,386 square feet
Total: 3,412 square feet

L

■ This two-story design faithfully recalls the 18th-Century homestead of Secretary of Foreign Affairs John Jay. Classic siding and shutters work to create a classic exterior which will blend beautifully into pedigree neighborhoods, Arcadian farmland or casual countryside. A discreet library offers a place for books and curios. The living room features a grand fireplace, a music alcove and an expansive back porch—perfect for outdoor entertaining. The formal dining room offers a bay bathed in sunlight, with great views of the rear grounds. Upstairs, a plush master suite with a two-vanity bath shares a balcony hall with two sizable family bedrooms and a bath.

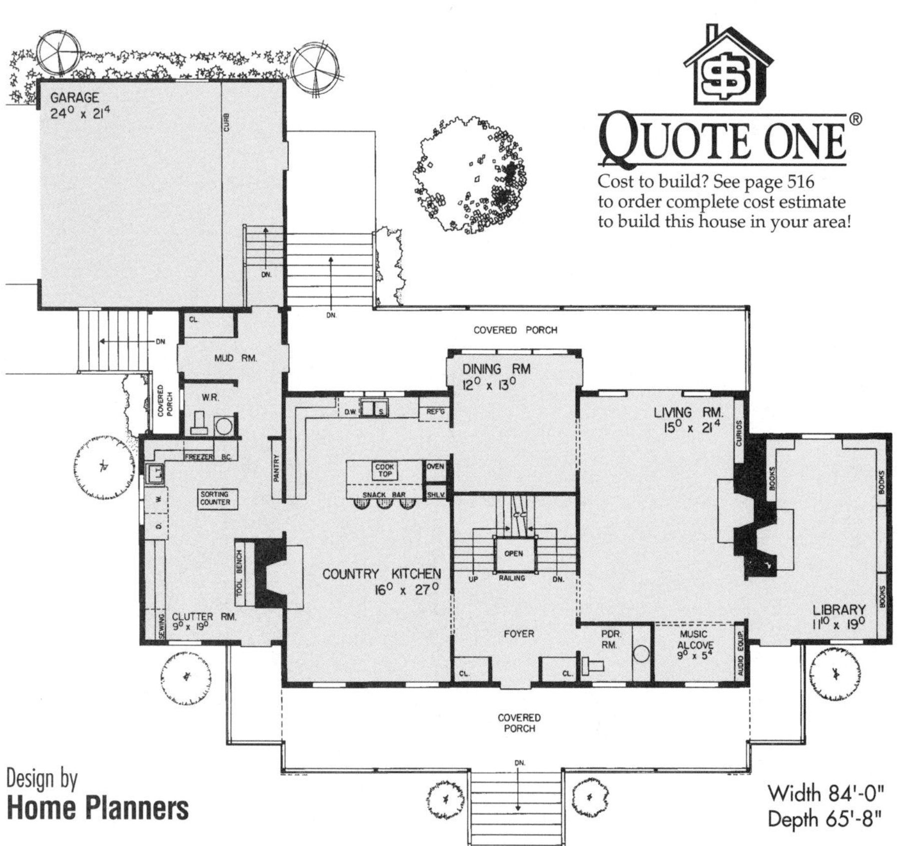

GARAGE
24⁰ x 21⁴
CURB
DN.
CL.
MUD RM.
COVERED PORCH
W.R.
FREEZER
PANTRY
SORTING COUNTER
TOOL BENCH
CLUTTER RM.
9⁰ x 19⁰
COVERED PORCH
DINING RM
12⁰ x 13⁰
D.W.
REF'G
COOK TOP
OVEN
SNACK BAR
SHLV.
COUNTRY KITCHEN
16⁰ x 27⁰
UP
OPEN
RAILING
DN.
FOYER
PDR. RM.
LIVING RM.
15⁰ x 21⁴
CURIOS
BOOKS
MUSIC ALCOVE
9⁶ x 5⁴
AUDIO EQUIP.
LIBRARY
11¹⁰ x 19⁰
COVERED PORCH

QUOTE ONE®

Cost to build? See page 516 to order complete cost estimate to build this house in your area!

Design by
Home Planners

Width 84'-0"
Depth 65'-8"

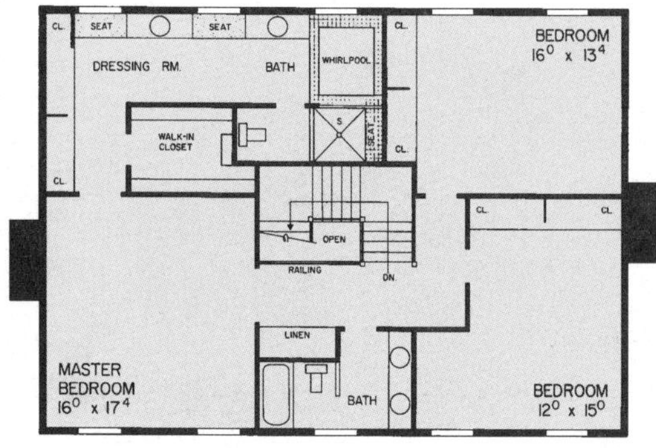

SEAT
DRESSING RM.
BATH
WHIRLPOOL
WALK-IN CLOSET
CL.
OPEN
RAILING
DN.
BEDROOM
16⁰ x 13⁴
LINEN
MASTER BEDROOM
16⁰ x 17⁴
BATH
BEDROOM
12⁰ x 15⁰

Rear Elevation

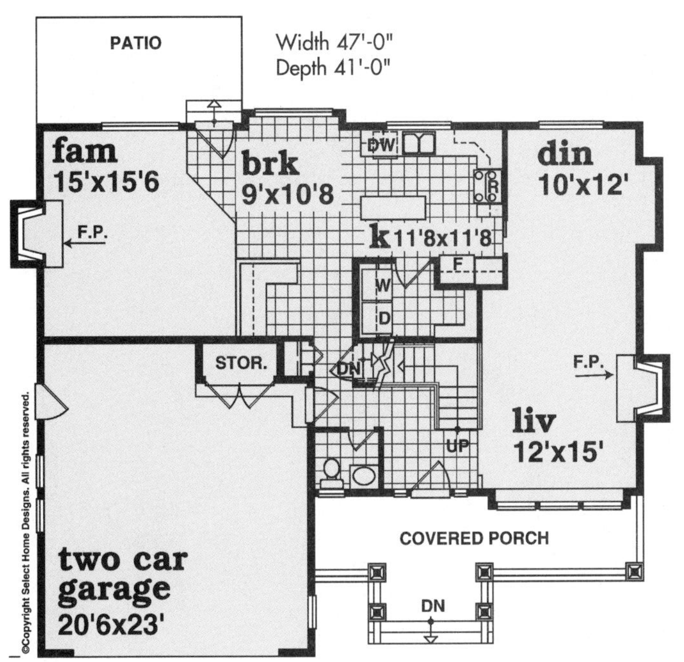
PATIO
Width 47'-0"
Depth 41'-0"
fam
15'x15'6
F.P.
brk
9'x10'8
DW
R
k 11'8x11'8
F
W
D
din
10'x12'
STOR.
DN
UP
F.P.
liv
12'x15'
COVERED PORCH
two car
garage
20'6x23'
DN
©Copyright Select Home Designs. All rights reserved.

Rear Elevation

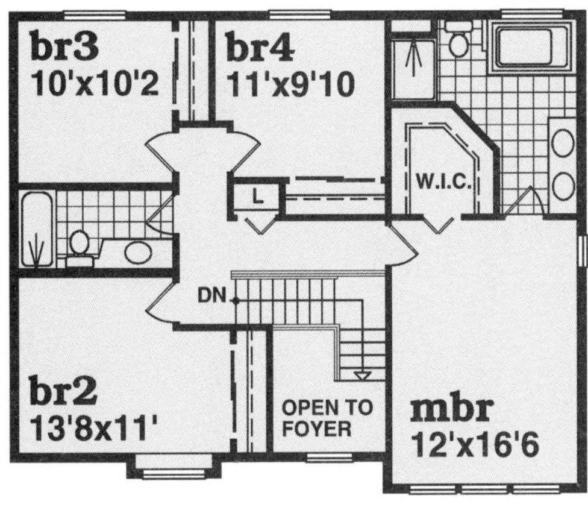
br3
10'x10'2
br4
11'x9'10
W.I.C.
L
DN
br2
13'8x11'
OPEN TO
FOYER
mbr
12'x16'6

Design Q481

First Floor: 1,100 square feet
Second Floor: 1,016 square feet
Total: 2,116 square feet

■ With stylish details borrowed from craftsman, Victorian and farmhouse styles, this design is elegant without being pretentious. The entry opens to a two-story foyer which holds a half-bath, coat closet and stairs to the second floor. The living and dining rooms are on the right. The dining room has a buffet alcove. A family room is in the opposite corner and features patio access. Both the family room and the living room have fireplaces. In between the living spaces is an island kitchen with sunny breakfast room attached. Three family bedrooms and their shared bath, plus the master bedroom are on the second floor. The master bedroom has a private bath with double vanities and separate shower and tub. The two-car garage features great storage space. Plans include details for both a basement and a crawlspace foundation.

Design by
Select Home Designs

©Copyright Select Home Designs. All rights reserved.

Design 5543

First Floor: 1,211 square feet
Second Floor: 1,120 square feet
Total: 2,331 square feet

■ A brick facade and twin bay windows offer a noble exterior to this two-story traditional home. Inside, the sunny bays add just the right touch to both the family media room and the great room. The U-shaped kitchen includes a windowed sink area and a snack bar pass-through to the breakfast nook with its access to both the rear yard and the two-car garage. Upstairs, three family bedrooms share a full hall bath with dual sinks and close proximity to the washer and dryer. The large master bedroom features a walk-in closet and a luxurious bath with a corner whirlpool tub, individual sinks and a separate toilet and shower area. If you prefer, the mud room at the garage may be converted to a laundry room.

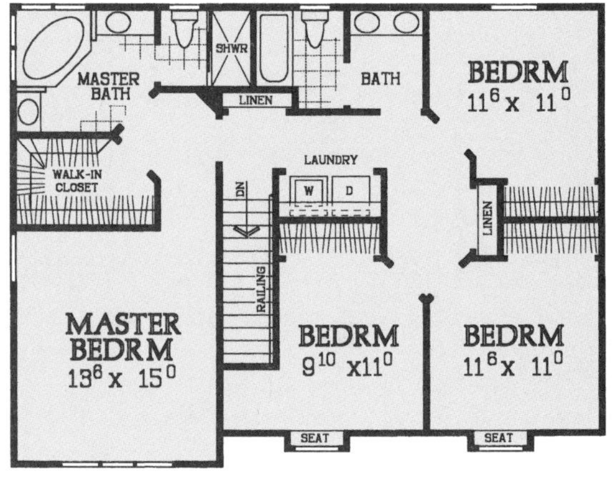
MASTER BATH
SHWR
LINEN
BATH
BEDRM 11^6 x 11^0
WALK-IN CLOSET
LAUNDRY
W D
DN
LINEN
RAILING
MASTER BEDRM 13^6 x 15^0
BEDRM 9^{10} x11^0
BEDRM 11^6x 11^0
SEAT
SEAT

Design by
Home Planners

QUOTE ONE®
Cost to build? See page 516 to order complete cost estimate to build this house in your area!

Width 61'-8"
Depth 35'-8"

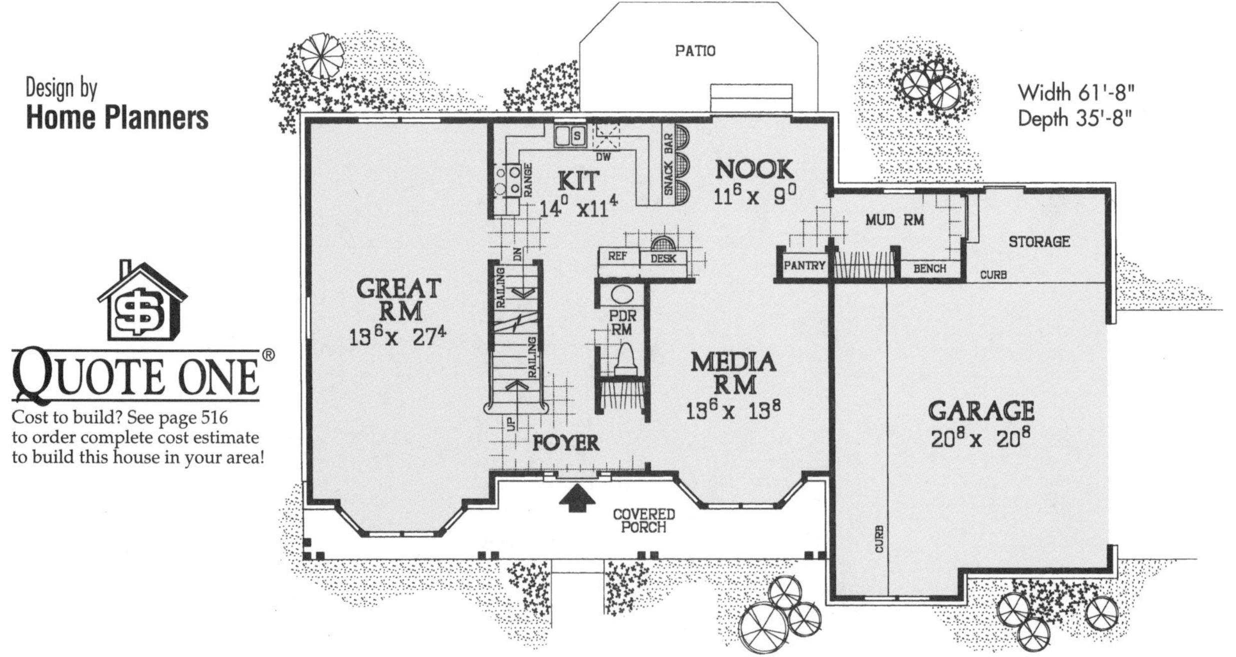
PATIO
KIT 14^0 x11^4
DW
SNACK BAR
RANGE
NOOK 11^6x 9^0
MUD RM
STORAGE
PANTRY
BENCH
CURB
REF
DESK
GREAT RM 13^6x 27^4
PDR RM
MEDIA RM 13^6 x 13^8
GARAGE 20^8 x 20^8
RAILING
DN
UP
FOYER
COVERED PORCH
CURB

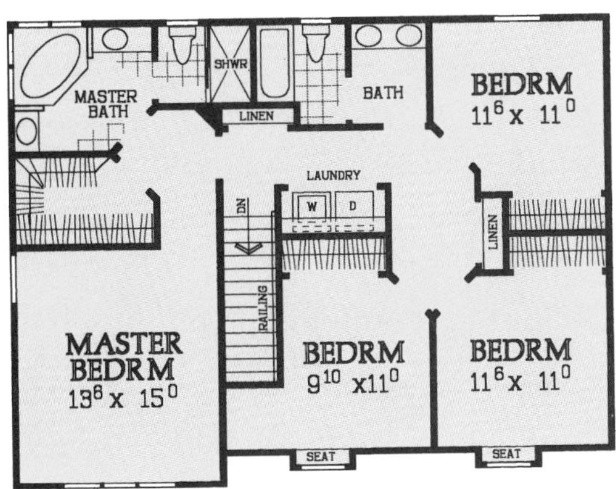
MASTER BATH
SHWR
LINEN
BATH
BEDRM
11^6 x 11^0
LAUNDRY
W
D
DN
LINEN
RAILING
MASTER BEDRM
13^8 x 15^0
BEDRM
9^{10} x11^0
BEDRM
11^6x 11^0
SEAT
SEAT

Design 5541

First Floor: 1,179 square feet
Second Floor: 1,120 square feet
Total: 2,299 square feet

■ A flowing floor plan and easy access make this an ideal design for the family who likes to entertain. From the covered porch, the foyer provides access to all areas of the home. To the right is a cozy media room—perfect for viewing the latest movie or for relaxing by the TV, or with a good book. To the left is the spacious great room. Straight ahead is the open U-shaped kitchen and a breakfast nook with access to the rear yard, the mud room and the garage. Upstairs, three family bedrooms share a full bath with dual sinks. The master bedroom features a luxury bath with a corner whirlpool tub, separate sinks, a separate shower and a walk-in closet. The washer and dryer is located upstairs for convenience. If you prefer a first-floor laundry room, space is available in the mud room.

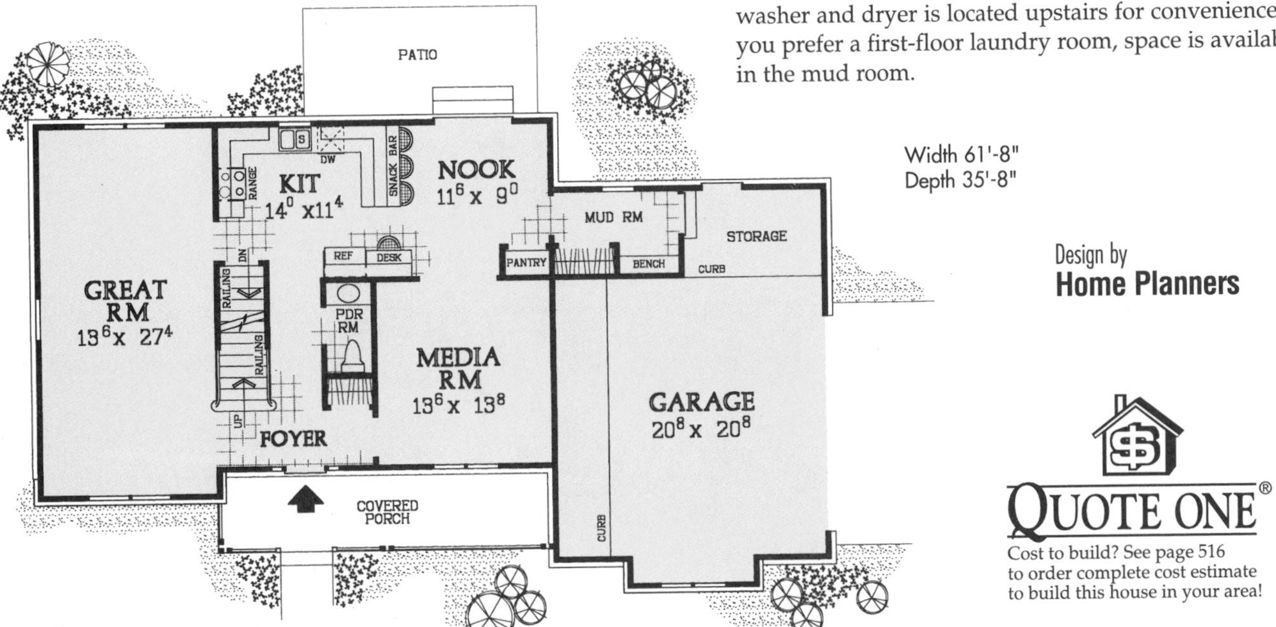
PATIO
DW
SNACK BAR
RANGE
KIT
14^0 x11^4
NOOK
11^6 x 9^0
MUD RM
STORAGE
PANTRY
BENCH
CURB
REF
DESK
DN
RAILING
GREAT RM
13^6x 27^4
PDR RM
MEDIA RM
13^6 x 13^8
GARAGE
20^8 x 20^8
UP
FOYER
COVERED PORCH
CURB

Width 61'-8"
Depth 35'-8"

Design by
Home Planners

QUOTE ONE®

Cost to build? See page 516 to order complete cost estimate to build this house in your area!

Design Q235

First Floor: 1,132 square feet
Second Floor: 864 square feet
Total: 1,996 square feet

■ This traditional farmhouse has great outdoor livability in a covered veranda and a rear sundeck. The foyer leads to a sunken living room with fireplace and the adjoining dining room. A U-shaped kitchen features a sunshine ceiling and a pass-through snack bar to the breakfast room. The family room is also sunken and has a fireplace and double-door access to the rear yard. Bedrooms on the second floor include a master suite with private bath and three family bedrooms sharing a full bath. Two of the family bedrooms have walk-in closets, as does the master bedroom. To accommodate narrow lots, this design may be easily adapted to 32 feet wide by building without the family room, utility room and garage.

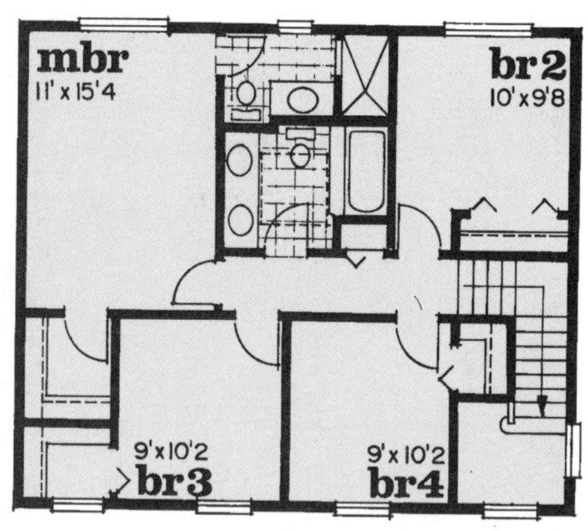
mbr
11'x15'4
br2
10'x9'8
9'x10'2
br3
9'x10'2
br4

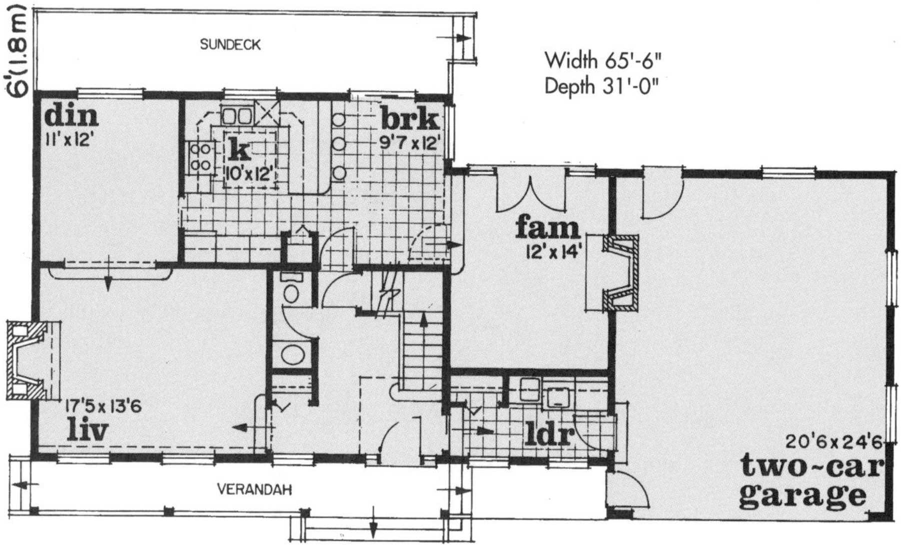

SUNDECK
6'(1.8m)
din
11'x12'
k
10'x12'
brk
9'7x12'
fam
12'x14'
17'5x13'6
liv
ldr
20'6x24'6
two-car garage
VERANDAH

Width 65'-6"
Depth 31'-0"

Design by
Select Home Designs

ENTERTAINMENT TERRACE
LINE OF WALL ABOVE
RAISED HEARTH
FAMILY RM
21^0 x 14^{10}
RAILING
DN
MORNING RM
14^0 x 12^{10}
EXPOSED BEAM CEILING
PASS THRU
KIT
ISLAND
COOK TOP
14^0 x 12^{10}
BAY WINDOW
DINING RM
12^{10} x 13^0
DESK
PANTRY
OVN
REFR
LAUNDRY ROOM
LT
D
W
BC
DN
STORAGE
DN
PDR
LIVING RM
19^8 x 14^0
COVERED PORCH
RAILING
UP
FOYER
CURB
GARAGE
21^0 x 21^6
COVERED PORCH
RAILING
RAILING
RAILING
RAILING
Width 63'-6"
Depth 48'-0"

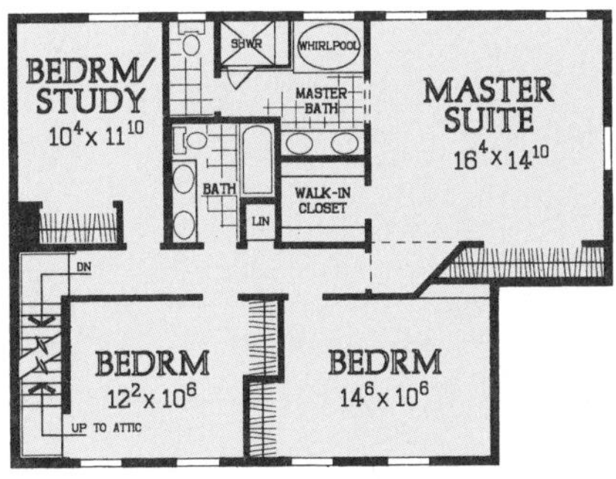
BEDRM/ STUDY
10^4 x 11^{10}
SHWR
WHIRLPOOL
MASTER BATH
MASTER SUITE
16^4 x 14^{10}
BATH
LIN
WALK-IN CLOSET
DN
BEDRM
12^2 x 10^6
UP TO ATTIC
BEDRM
14^6 x 10^6

QUOTE ONE®

Cost to build? See page 516 to order complete cost estimate to build this house in your area!

Design 3325

First Floor: 1,595 square feet
Second Floor:1,112 square feet
Total:2,707 square feet

L D

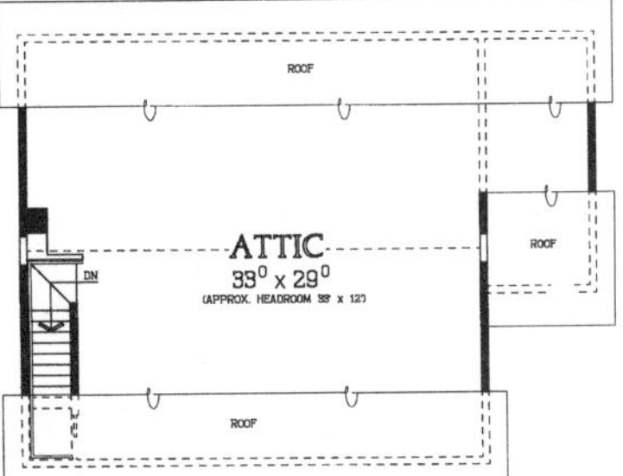
ROOF
ATTIC
33^0 x 29^0
(APPROX. HEADROOM 33' x 12')
DN
ROOF
ROOF

Design by
Home Planners

■ Horizontal clapboard siding, varying roof planes and finely detailed window treatments set a delightful tone for this farmhouse favorite. A tiled foyer leads past a convenient powder room to a spacious central morning room with an exposed beam ceiling and a wide door to the entertainment terrace. The U-shaped island kitchen offers service to the formal dining room, which enjoys a bay window and leads to an expansive living room. Upstairs, a gallery hall connects three family bedrooms and a hall bath.

Design 3462

First Floor: 1,395 square feet
Second Floor: 813 square feet
Total: 2,208 square feet

L

■ Horizontal siding with corner boards, muntin windows and a raised veranda enhance the appeal of this country home. Twin carriage lamps flank the sheltered entrance. Inside, the central foyer delights with its two sets of columns at the openings to the formal living and dining rooms. In the L-shaped kitchen, an adjacent snack bar offers everyday ease. Open to the kitchen, the great room boasts a centered fireplace, a high ceiling and access to the veranda. Sleeping accommodations start off with the master bedroom; a connecting bath will be a favorite spot. Upstairs, the bedrooms share a full bath with twin lavatories.

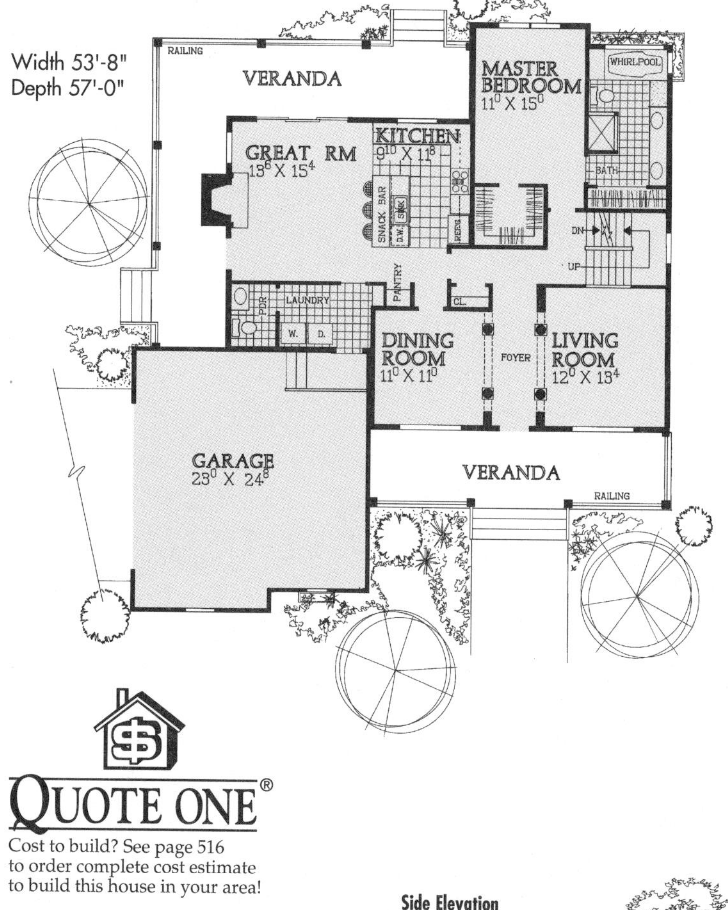

Width 53'-8"
Depth 57'-0"
RAILING
VERANDA
MASTER BEDROOM
11^0 X 15^0
WHIRLPOOL
BATH
KITCHEN
9^{10} X 11^8
GREAT RM
13^6 X 15^4
SNACK BAR
D.W.
REFG
DN
UP
PANTRY
LAUNDRY
PDR
W.
D.
CL.
DINING ROOM
11^0 X 11^0
FOYER
LIVING ROOM
12^0 X 13^4
GARAGE
23^0 X 24^8
VERANDA
RAILING

BEDROOM
11^0 X 13^0
OPEN BELOW
STORAGE
BATH
DN
LINEN
BEDROOM
12^8 X 12^0
DESK
BEDROOM
12^0 X 14^4

QUOTE ONE®

Cost to build? See page 516 to order complete cost estimate to build this house in your area!

Side Elevation

Design by
Home Planners

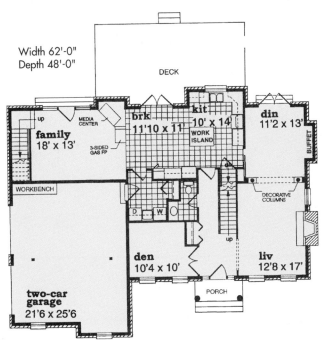

Width 62'-0"
Depth 48'-0"

DECK
family 18' x 13'
up
MEDIA CENTER
3-SIDED GAS FP
brk 11'10 x 11'
kit 10' x 14'
WORK ISLAND
din 11'2 x 13'
BUFFET
WORKBENCH
D W
DECORATIVE COLUMNS
up
den 10'4 x 10'
liv 12'8 x 17'
PORCH
two-car garage 21'6 x 25'6

Design Q452

First Floor: 1,452 square feet
Second Floor: 1,100 square feet
Total: 2,552 square feet
Bonus Room: 687 square feet

■ Build this home as a wood-sided farmhouse with wrapping veranda, or as a stately brick traditional. Plans include details for both facades. Enter the foyer and you'll be greeted by double doors opening to the den on the left and a spacious living room with fireplace on the right. The dining room is separated from the living room by a plant bridge and pair of columns. It has double-door access to the rear yard. The kitchen includes entertainment-sized space with a center work island and an abundance of counter space. The sunny breakfast room has double doors to the rear deck. The full-sized family room features a three-sided fireplace and a corner media center, plus access to the rear yard. A staircase from the family room leads to bonus space over the garage totaling an additional 687 square feet of unfinished space. Four bedrooms on the second floor cluster around a center hall. The master suite and one family bedroom have walk-in closets. Plans include details for both a basement and a crawlspace foundation.

Design by
Select Home Designs

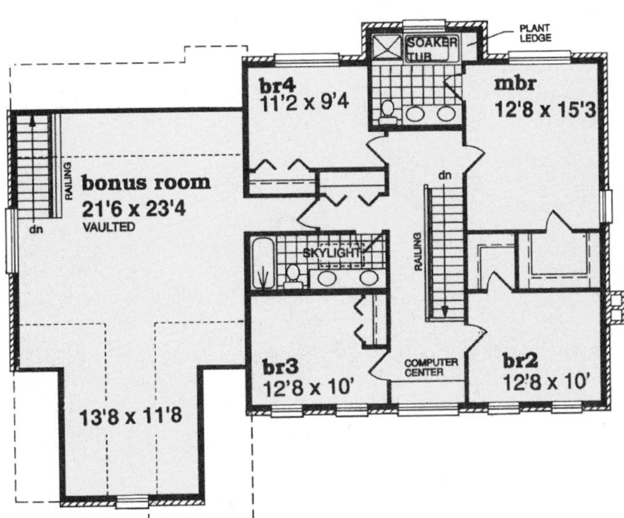
PLANT LEDGE
SOAKER TUB
br4 11'2 x 9'4
mbr 12'8 x 15'3
bonus room 21'6 x 23'4
VAULTED
RAILING
dn
dn
SKYLIGHT
RAILING
br3 12'8 x 10'
COMPUTER CENTER
br2 12'8 x 10'
13'8 x 11'8

Alternate Elevation

Design 5521

First Floor: 1,378 square feet
Second Floor: 912 square feet
Total: 2,290 square feet

■ A beautiful country facade with a wrapping porch is just the beginning of what this design has to offer. Inside, the two-story foyer includes a large coat closet and decorative entry to the formal living room. The foyer also leads, through a hall with a convenient half-bath, to the formal dining room and family room with its three-sided fireplace. The family room opens to a gourmet kitchen which features a snack bar, a walk-in pantry and access to a two-car garage with a workshop/storage area. The master bedroom is located on the first floor for privacy and features a French door to the wrapping porch and a luxurious master bath. The second floor includes three large bedrooms, a full bath, a multi-media loft and an amenity-filled laundry room.

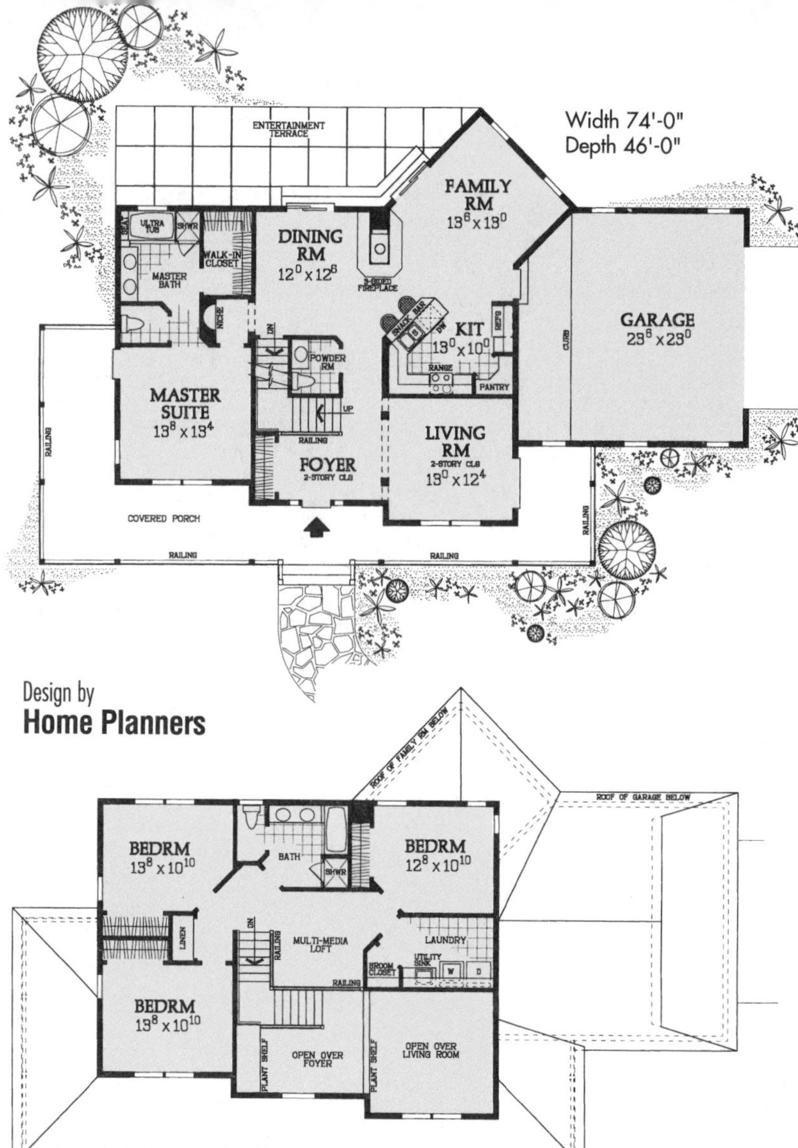

Width 74'-0"
Depth 46'-0"
ENTERTAINMENT TERRACE
FAMILY RM $13^6 \times 13^0$
DINING RM $12^0 \times 12^6$
MASTER BATH
WALK-IN CLOSET
GARAGE $23^6 \times 23^0$
KIT $13^0 \times 10^0$
POWDER RM
PANTRY
MASTER SUITE $13^8 \times 13^4$
LIVING RM 2-STORY CLG $13^0 \times 12^4$
FOYER 2-STORY CLG
COVERED PORCH
RAILING
Design by
Home Planners
ROOF OF FAMILY RM BELOW
ROOF OF GARAGE BELOW
BEDRM $13^8 \times 10^{10}$
BATH
BEDRM $12^8 \times 10^{10}$
MULTI-MEDIA LOFT
LAUNDRY
BEDRM $13^8 \times 10^{10}$
OPEN OVER FOYER
OPEN OVER LIVING ROOM
ROOF OF PORCH BELOW

QUOTE ONE®
Cost to build? See page 516
to order complete cost estimate
to build this house in your area!

© Copyright Select Home Designs. All rights reserved.

Design Q454

First Floor: 1,439 square feet
Second Floor: 1,419 square feet
Total: 2,858 square feet
Optional Space: 241 square feet

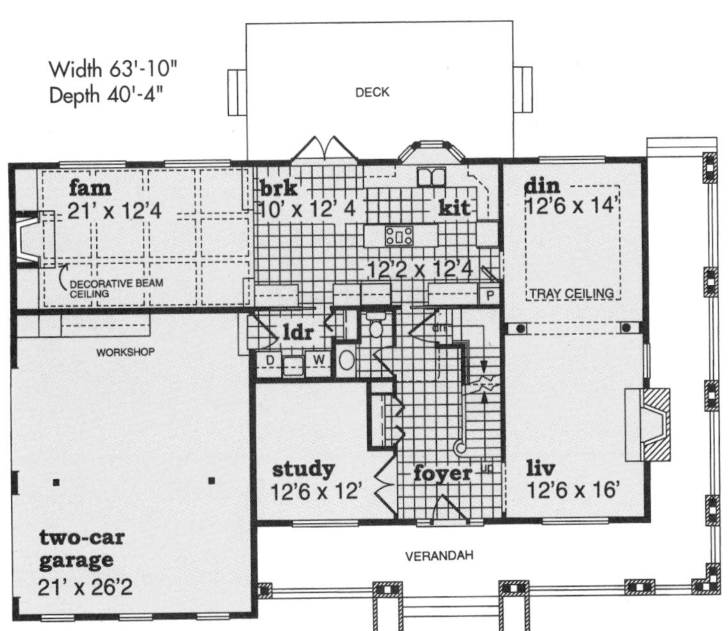
Width 63'-10"
Depth 40'-4"
DECK
fam
21' x 12'4
DECORATIVE BEAM CEILING
brk
10' x 12' 4
kit
12'2 x 12'4
din
12'6 x 14'
TRAY CEILING
ldr
D
W
WORKSHOP
study
12'6 x 12'
foyer
liv
12'6 x 16'
two-car garage
21' x 26'2
VERANDAH

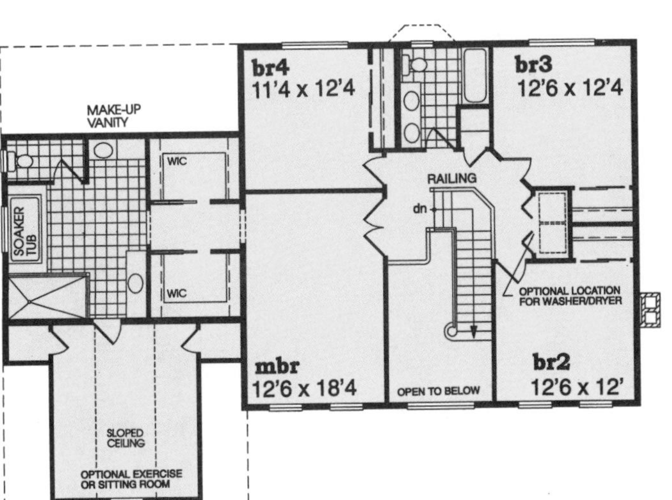
MAKE-UP VANITY
WIC
SOAKER TUB
WIC
br4
11'4 x 12'4
br3
12'6 x 12'4
RAILING
dn
OPTIONAL LOCATION FOR WASHER/DRYER
mbr
12'6 x 18'4
OPEN TO BELOW
br2
12'6 x 12'
SLOPED CEILING
OPTIONAL EXERCISE OR SITTING ROOM

■ Choose from one of two exteriors for this grand design—a lovely wood-sided farmhouse or a stately brick traditional. Plans include details for both facades. Special mouldings and trim add interest to the nine-foot ceilings on the first floor. The dining room features a tray ceiling and is separated from the hearth-warmed living room by decorative columns. A study is secluded behind double doors just off the entry. The centrally located kitchen features a large cooking island, pantry, telephone desk and ample cupboard and counter space. The family room has a decorative beam ceiling and fireplace. The private master bedroom has a most exquisite bath with His and Hers walk-in closets, a soaking tub, separate shower and make-up vanity. An optional exercise/sitting room adds 241 square feet to the total. Family bedrooms share a full bath. If you choose, situate the washer and dryer in an alcove on the second floor. Plans include details for both a basement and a crawlspace foundation.

Design by
Select Home Designs

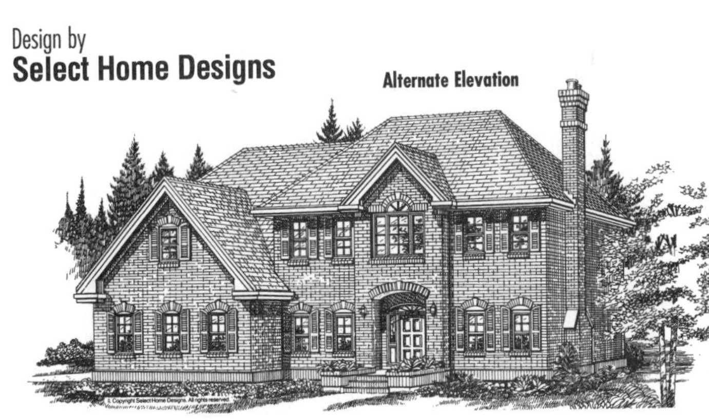
Alternate Elevation

Design Q389

First Floor: 1,132 square feet
Second Floor: 1,004 square feet
Total: 2,136 square feet

■ Double front doors open off a covered veranda to a vaulted foyer with plant shelf above. The living room is on the left and features a window seat, while the dining room, on the right, has a wet bar or serving counter. The kitchen, with generous counter space and pantry, adjoins the breakfast room and then the family room beyond. Look for yard access and a fireplace in the family room. The second level has a railed hallway that shows a view of the foyer and staircase below. The master bedroom offers an optional fireplace, a large walk-in closet and bath with His and Hers vanity, a whirlpool tub and shower. Three family bedrooms share a main bath with double vanity. Plans include details for both a basement and a crawlspace foundation.

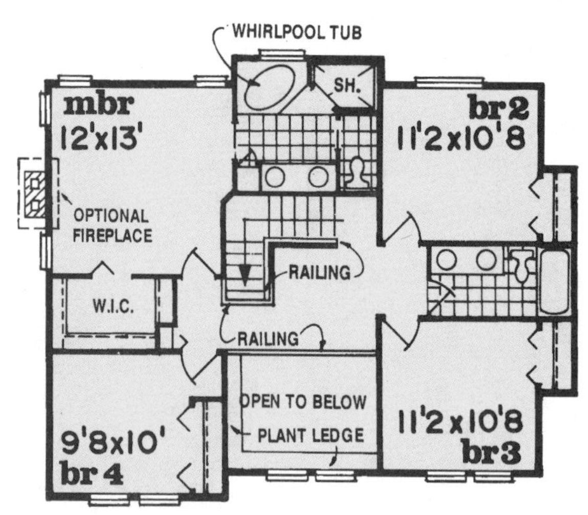
WHIRLPOOL TUB
SH.
mbr
12'x13'
br2
11'2x10'8
OPTIONAL
FIREPLACE
RAILING
W.I.C.
RAILING
OPEN TO BELOW
PLANT LEDGE
9'8x10'
br 4
11'2x10'8
br3

Design by
Select Home Designs

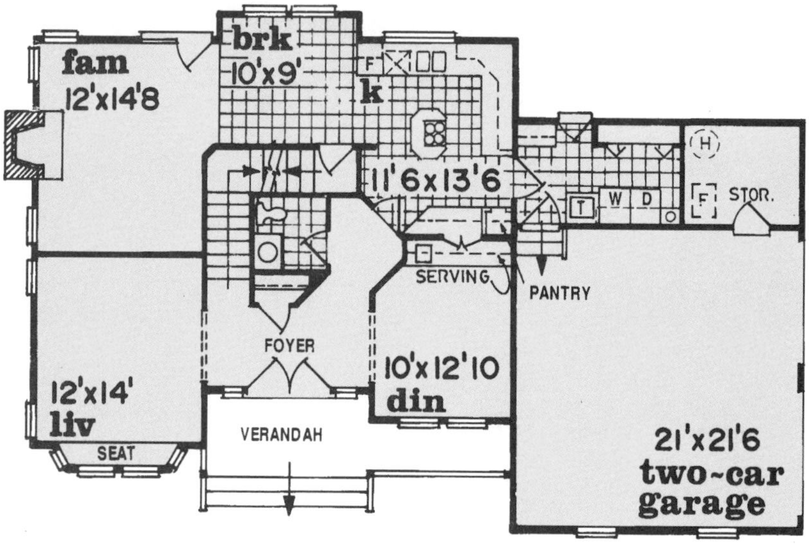

fam
12'x14'8
brk
10'x9'
k
11'6x13'6
F
H
W D
T
F STOR.
SERVING
PANTRY
FOYER
10'x12'10
din
12'x14'
liv
SEAT
VERANDAH
21'x21'6
two-car
garage

Rear Elevation

Width 57'-6"
Depth 38'-0"

© Copyright 1990 Select Home Designs All rights reserved

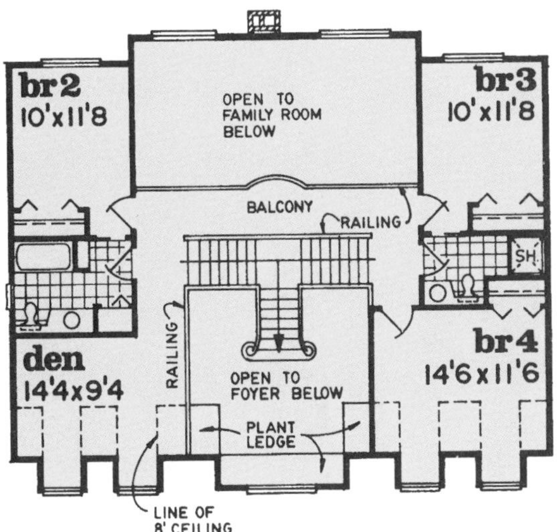
br2
10'x11'8
OPEN TO FAMILY ROOM BELOW
br3
10'x11'8
BALCONY
RAILING
SH.
den
14'4x9'4
RAILING
OPEN TO FOYER BELOW
br4
14'6x11'6
PLANT LEDGE
LINE OF 8' CEILING

Design Q335

First Floor: 2,042 square feet
Second Floor: 1,099 square feet
Total: 3,141 square feet

■ A wide, wrapping veranda graces the front of this design and is accessed from the living room and the dining room, as well as double doors at the entry. Both the living and dining rooms have tray ceilings. The family room is vaulted and has a cozy fireplace as its focal point. To either side of the fireplace are double doors to the rear yard. The kitchen has a center cooking island, spacious counters and a pass-through to the dining room. The breakfast room serves for casual occasions. The main-floor master suite features a lavish master bath with roomy walk-in closet, whirlpool spa and twin vanity. A den or media center is found on the second floor with three family bedrooms and two full baths. Plans include details for both a basement and a crawlspace foundation.

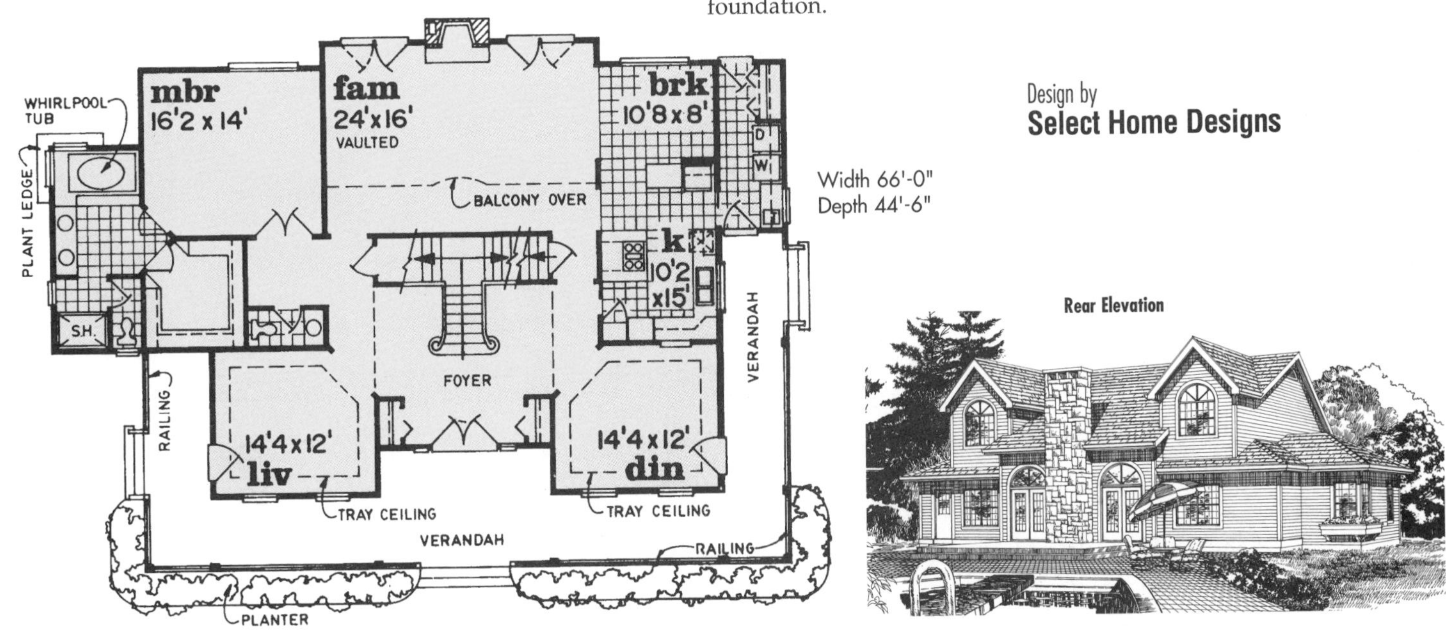
WHIRLPOOL TUB
PLANT LEDGE
mbr
16'2 x 14'
fam
24'x16'
VAULTED
brk
10'8x8'
D
W
BALCONY OVER
k
10'2
x15'
SH.
VERANDAH
RAILING
FOYER
14'4x12'
liv
14'4x12'
din
TRAY CEILING
TRAY CEILING
VERANDAH
RAILING
PLANTER
Rear Elevation

Design by
Select Home Designs

Width 66'-0"
Depth 44'-6"

Design 5553

First Floor: 720 square feet
Second Floor: 1,267 square feet
Total: 1,987 square feet

■ A wraparound porch gives this two-story home a special flair that will set it apart from its neighbors. Inside, the open floor plan welcomes entertaining and comfortable family living. The great room and dining area includes access to the side porch and deck. The U-shaped kitchen features a windowed sink and is located near the utility room and a powder room. A massive family/recreation room is found upstairs. It can be used for a games room, a kid's play room or an office. While two family bedrooms share a full hall bath, the master bedroom includes its own private bath as well as a walk-in closet and a box-bay window.

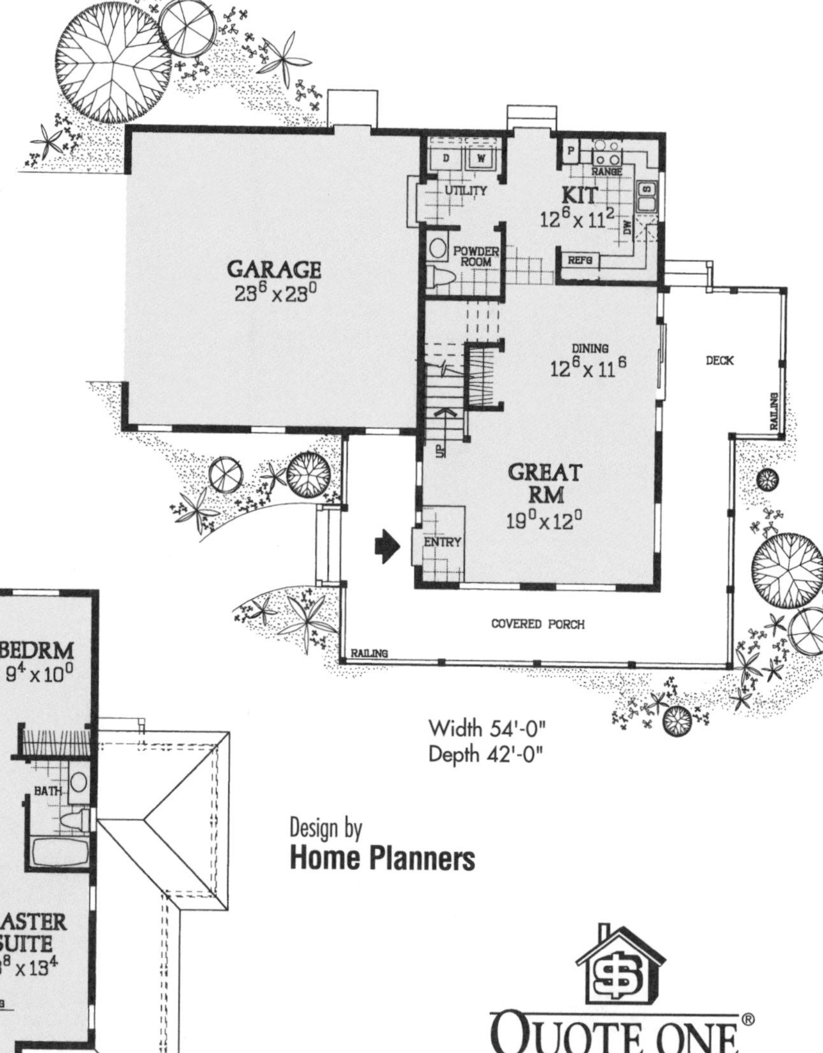
GARAGE
23^6 x 23^0
UTILITY
KIT
12^6 x 11^2
RANGE
POWDER ROOM
REFG
DINING
12^6 x 11^6
DECK
RAILING
GREAT RM
19^0 x 12^0
ENTRY
UP
COVERED PORCH
RAILING

Width 54'-0"
Depth 42'-0"

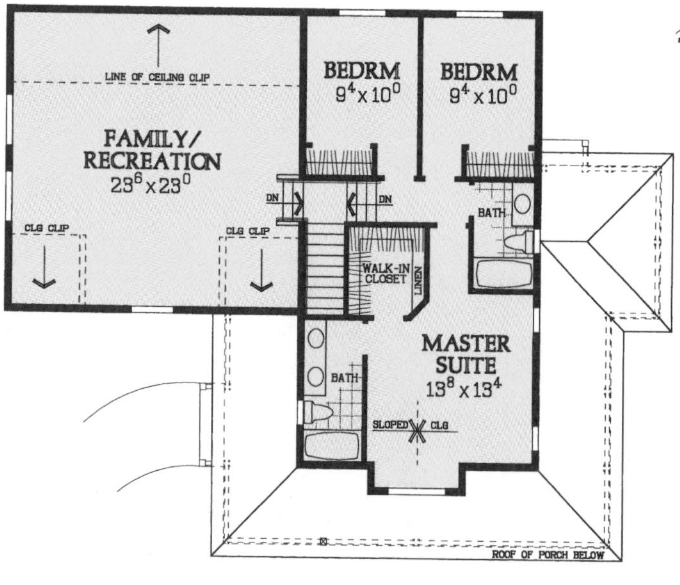

Design by
Home Planners

QUOTE ONE®
Cost to build? See page 516 to order complete cost estimate to build this house in your area!

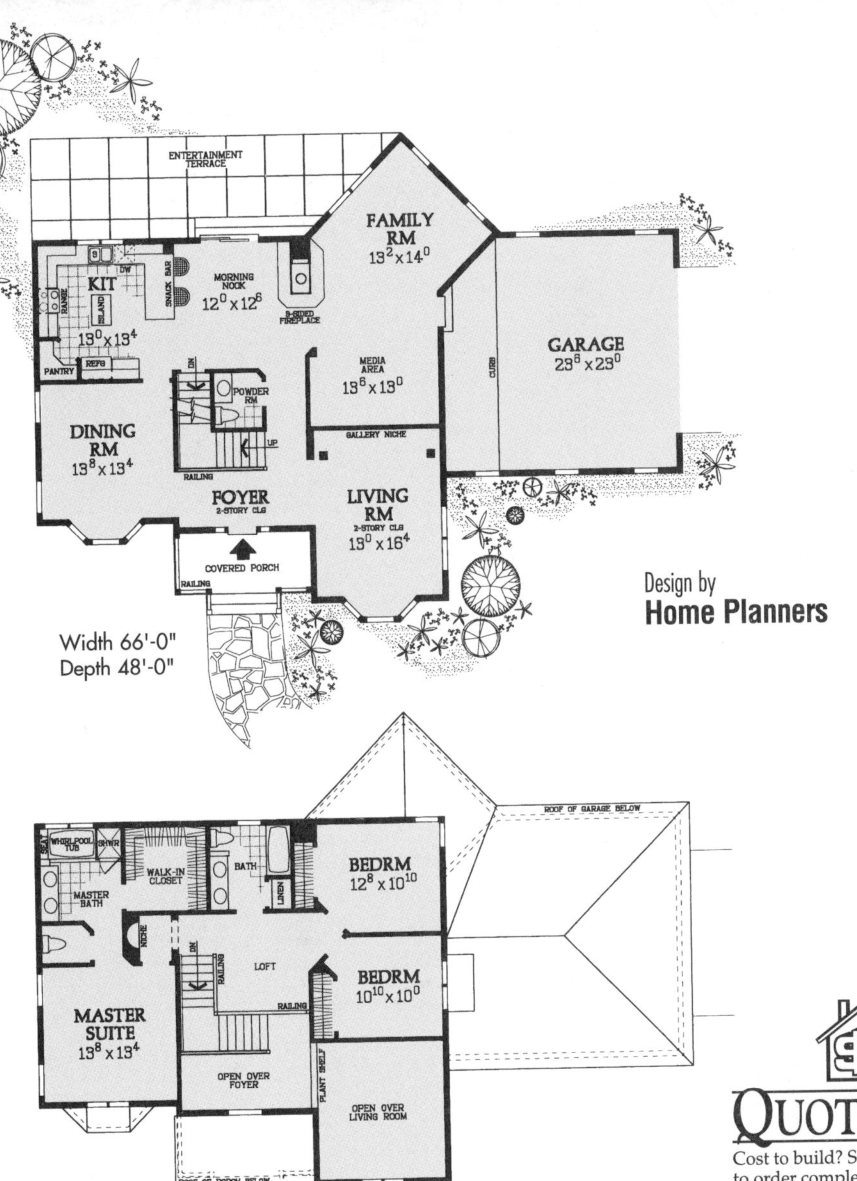
ENTERTAINMENT TERRACE
FAMILY RM 13²x14⁰
KIT 13⁰x13⁴
MORNING NOOK 12⁰x12⁶
3-SIDED FIREPLACE
MEDIA AREA 13⁶x13⁰
GARAGE 23⁶x23⁰
PANTRY
POWDER RM
DINING RM 13⁸x13⁴
GALLERY NICHE
FOYER 2-STORY CLG
LIVING RM 2-STORY CLG 13⁰x16⁴
COVERED PORCH
RAILING
Width 66'-0"
Depth 48'-0"
ROOF OF GARAGE BELOW
WHIRLPOOL TUB
WALK-IN CLOSET
BATH
BEDRM 12⁸x10¹⁰
MASTER BATH
LOFT
BEDRM 10¹⁰x10⁰
MASTER SUITE 13⁸x13⁴
OPEN OVER FOYER
OPEN OVER LIVING ROOM
ROOF OF PORCH BELOW

Design by
Home Planners

Design 5534

First Floor: 1,444 square feet
Second Floor: 952 square feet
Total: 2,396 square feet

The asymmetrical front facade of this three-bedroom traditional-style home gives offers great curb appeal. Inside, the open floor plan is a study in luxury and comfort. The two-story foyer provides access to all rooms, including the formal living room and dining room. Both feature a bay window, while the living room also includes a gallery wall for your family portraits or prized artwork. The large, U-shaped kitchen features a walk-in pantry, an island worktop and a snack bar to the morning nook with its terrace access. The family room is complete with a three-sided fireplace and a tiled hearth, a sitting area, a separate media area and access to the two-car garage with space for storage or a workshop. Upstairs, the master bedroom features a large bath with a walk-in closet and a special whirlpool tub with a seat. Two family bedrooms share a full hall bath and a multi-media loft area.

QUOTE ONE®

Cost to build? See page 516 to order complete cost estimate to build this house in your area!

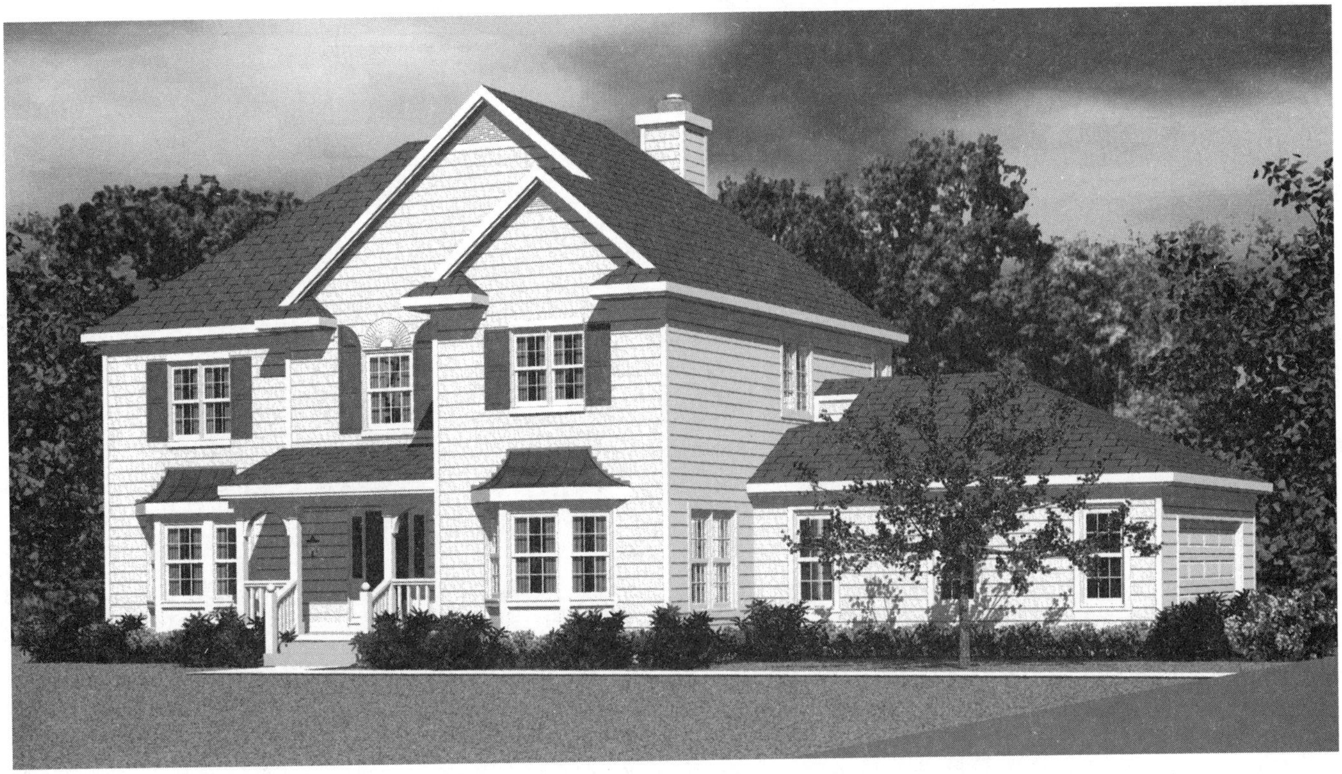

Design Q384

First Floor: 1,290 square feet
Second Floor: 796 square feet
Total: 2,086 square feet

Simplicity in design makes this farmhouse such an appealing choice. A covered porch shelters an entry that opens to a central, vaulted foyer with the living and dining rooms immediately on the right. A fireplace warms the living room; the dining room has a box-bay window. A country kitchen offers a center preparation island, a pantry, a fireplace and access to a rear covered porch. There is space enough here for casual gatherings and dining. The main-level master suite has a walk-in closet, a private access to the porch and a bath with His and Hers vanities, whirlpool tub and separate shower. On the second floor, a railed gallery with dormer window makes the perfect study, library or media center. Family bedrooms share this second-floor space, as well as a full bath. Plans include details for both a basement and a crawlspace foundation.

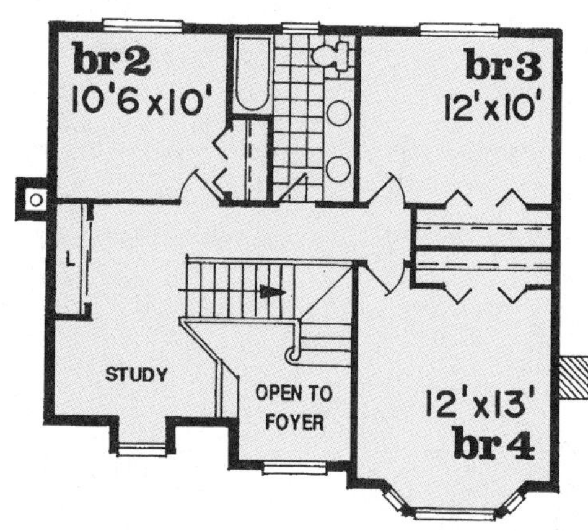
br2
10'6x10'
br3
12'x10'
STUDY
OPEN TO FOYER
12'x13'
br4

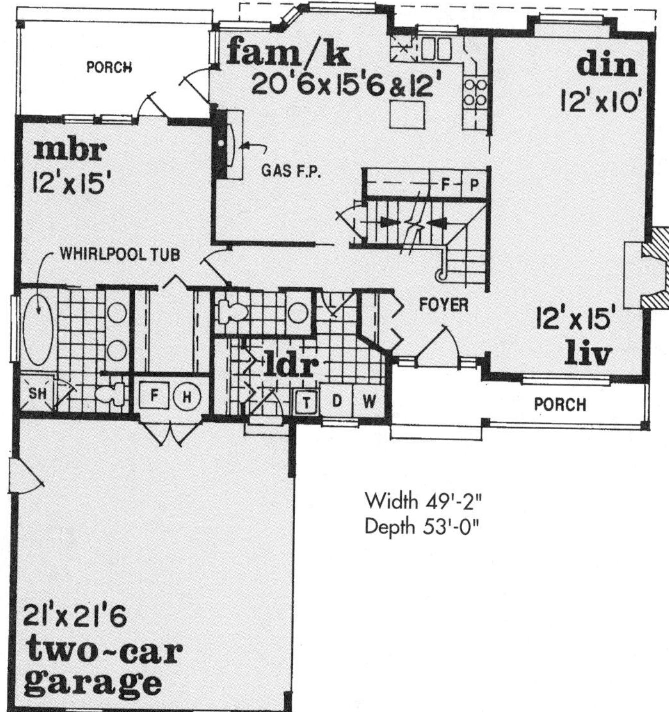
PORCH
fam/k
20'6x15'6 & 12'
din
12'x10'
mbr
12'x15'
GAS F.P.
F
P
WHIRLPOOL TUB
FOYER
12'x15'
liv
ldr
SH
F
H
T
D
W
PORCH
21'x21'6
two-car garage

Design by
Select Home Designs

Width 49'-2"
Depth 53'-0"

Design Q407

First Floor: 1,261 square feet
Second Floor: 1,185 square feet
Total: 2,446 square feet

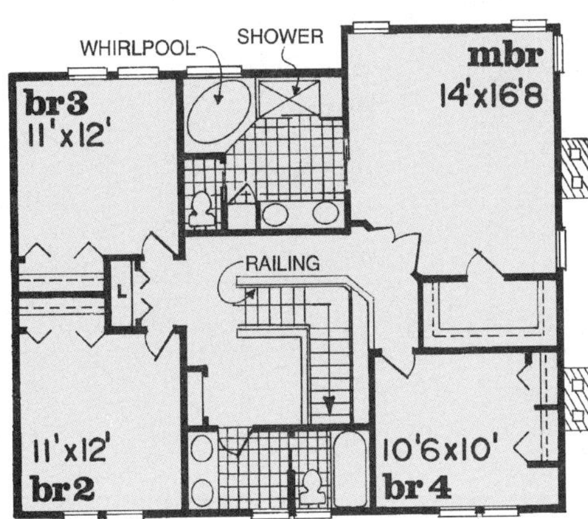
WHIRLPOOL
SHOWER
mbr
14'x16'8
br3
11'x12'
L
RAILING
11'x12'
br2
10'6x10'
br4

■ Covered porches front and rear make this a very comfortable farmhouse. Double doors open to the foyer, flanked by the formal dining room and sunken living room. A butler's pantry, complete with wet bar, separates the dining room and L-shaped island kitchen. A sunny breakfast room adjoins the kitchen on one side and the family room with fireplace is just beyond. Double doors open to the rear porch. The master suite is on the second level and offers a walk-in closet and full bath with corner whirlpool, separate shower and double vanity. Three family bedrooms share a full bath with vanity dressing room. The two-car garage connects to the main house via a service area with laundry room.

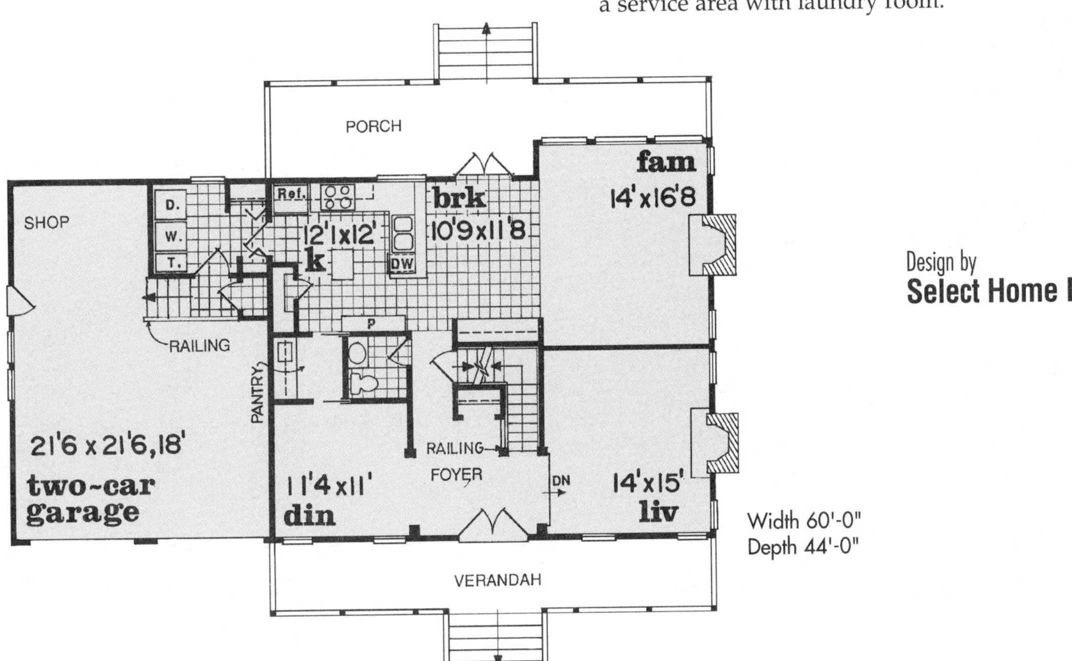
PORCH
fam
14'x16'8
SHOP
D.
W.
T.
Ref.
12'1x12'
k
brk
10'9x11'8
DW
P
RAILING
PANTRY
21'6 x 21'6,18'
two-car
garage
RAILING
11'4x11'
din
FOYER
DN
14'x15'
liv
VERANDAH
Width 60'-0"
Depth 44'-0"

Design by
Select Home Designs

Design Q393

First Floor: 1,187 square feet
Second Floor: 1,084 square feet
Total: 2,271 square feet
Bonus Room: 740 square feet

Multi-paned, shuttered windows and a covered porch provide a country character for this four- bedroom home. The vaulted foyer, brightened by second-story windows, spills into the sunken living room where a window seat is nestled in a bay window. The dining room is to the right of the foyer, just across the hall from the U-shaped kitchen with angled counter and corner sink under a window. A breakfast bar separates the kitchen from the breakfast room, where a cozy window seat resides. The family room is also sunken and holds a fireplace and access to the rear yard. Use the service entrance to reach the two-car garage with workshop. The laundry is found in the service area. Bedrooms upstairs include a master suite with walk-in closet and full bath and three family bedrooms. Bedroom 4 has a window seat. A large bonus room is reached via stairs in the garage and holds an additional 740 square feet of unfinished space. Plans include details for both a basement and a crawlspace foundation.

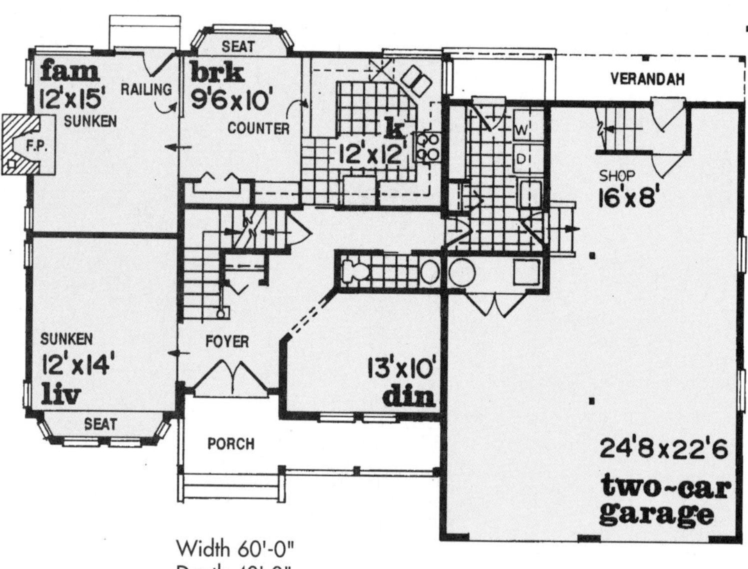

SEAT
fam
12'x15'
RAILING
SUNKEN
F.P.
brk
9'6x10'
COUNTER
k
12'x12'
VERANDAH
W
D
SHOP
16'x8'
SUNKEN
12'x14'
liv
SEAT
FOYER
13'x10'
din
PORCH
24'8x22'6
two-car
garage

Width 60'-0"
Depth 40'-0"

Rear Elevation

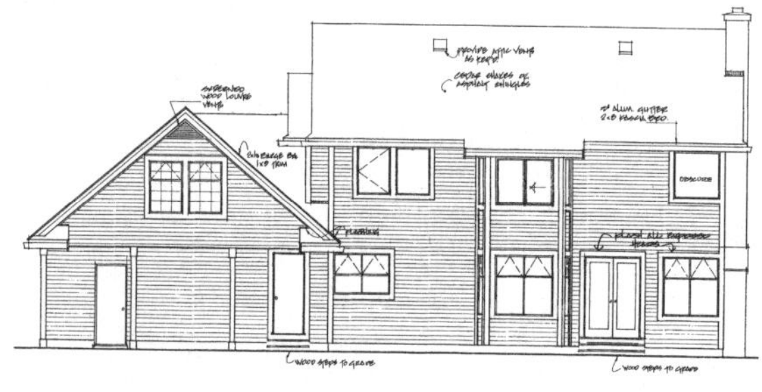

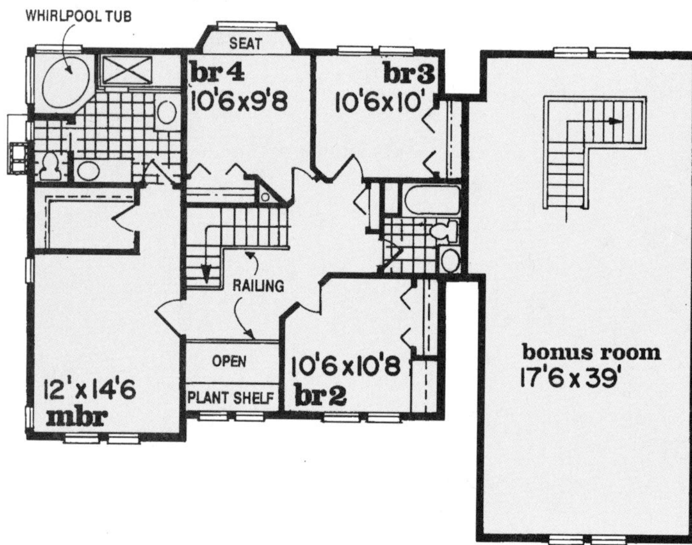

WHIRLPOOL TUB
SEAT
br4
10'6x9'8
br3
10'6x10'
RAILING
OPEN
PLANT SHELF
12'x14'6
mbr
10'6x10'8
br2
bonus room
17'6x39'

Design by
Select Home Designs

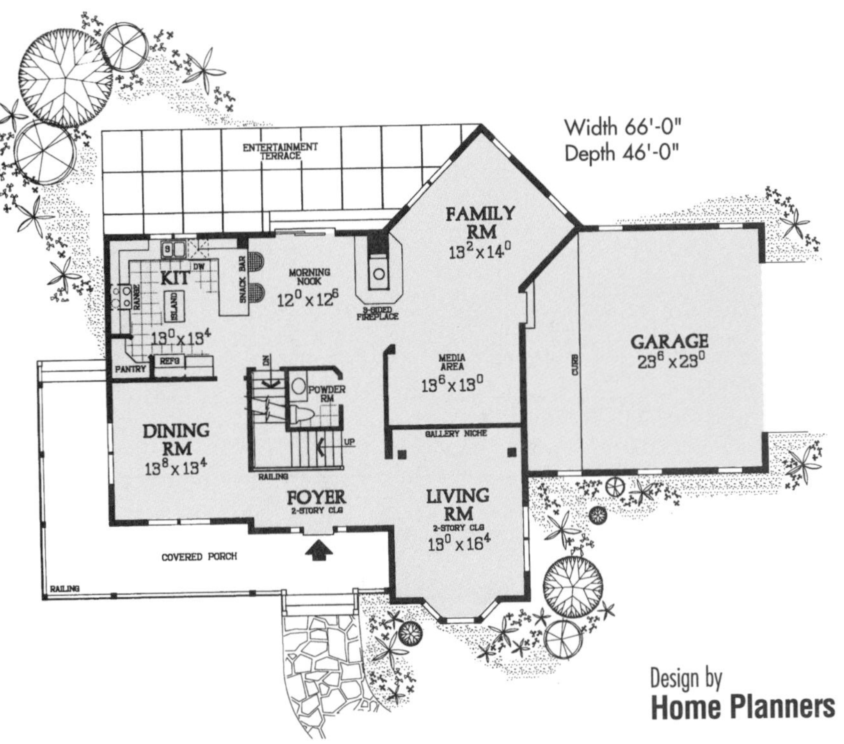

Width 66'-0"
Depth 46'-0"
ENTERTAINMENT TERRACE
FAMILY RM
$13^2 \times 14^0$
KIT
$13^0 \times 13^4$
MORNING NOOK
$12^0 \times 12^6$
SNACK BAR
ISLAND
RANGE
DW
PANTRY
REFG
3-SIDED FIREPLACE
MEDIA AREA
$13^6 \times 13^0$
GARAGE
$23^6 \times 23^0$
CURB
POWDER RM
DN
UP
DINING RM
$13^8 \times 13^4$
RAILING
FOYER
2-STORY CLG
GALLERY NICHE
LIVING RM
2-STORY CLG
$13^0 \times 16^4$
COVERED PORCH
RAILING

■ Rain or shine, the large wrapping porch at the front and side of this three-bedroom home will become a favorite spot with which to take in the sights and scents of life around you. To the left of the two-story foyer is the formal dining room. The two-story living room, to the right of the foyer, includes a bay window and a gallery wall for treasured pictures and artwork. The U-shaped kitchen includes a walk-in pantry and a snack bar, allowing the cook to converse with friends and family members in the morning room. The angular family room features a three-sided fireplace and a separate media area for your audio/visual equipment. The upstairs sleeping zone includes two family bedrooms that share a full hall bath and a multi-media loft, and a private master bedroom that features a large master bath with a whirlpool tub, dual sinks and a spacious walk-in closet.

Design by
Home Planners

Design 5535

First Floor: 1,432 square feet
Second Floor: 952 square feet
Total: 2,384 square feet

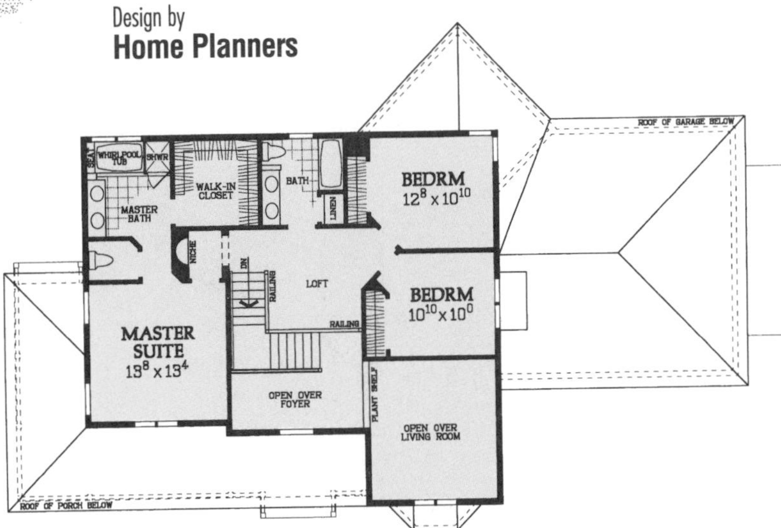

ROOF OF GARAGE BELOW
WHIRLPOOL TUB
SHWR
WALK-IN CLOSET
BATH
LINEN
BEDRM
$12^8 \times 10^{10}$
MASTER BATH
NICHE
DN
RAILING
LOFT
BEDRM
$10^{10} \times 10^0$
RAILING
MASTER SUITE
$13^8 \times 13^4$
OPEN OVER FOYER
PLANT SHELF
OPEN OVER LIVING ROOM
ROOF OF PORCH BELOW

QUOTE ONE®

Cost to build? See page 516 to order complete cost estimate to build this house in your area!

Design 3397

First Floor: 1,855 square feet
Second Floor: 1,241 square feet
Total: 3,096 square feet

L D

■ Five second-story dormers and a covered front porch add to the country charm of this farmhouse design. Inside, the entry foyer opens to the left to a formal living room and attached dining room. To the right is a private study. The back of the plan is dominated by a country kitchen featuring an island cook top. Both the country kitchen and the living room feature warm fireplaces. On this floor is the master suite with covered porch access and a bath with a whirlpool tub, separate shower, dual lavatories and a large walk-in closet. The second floor holds three bedrooms with two full baths. If you choose, the middle bedroom could be used as a sitting room or study—it features a built-in desk.

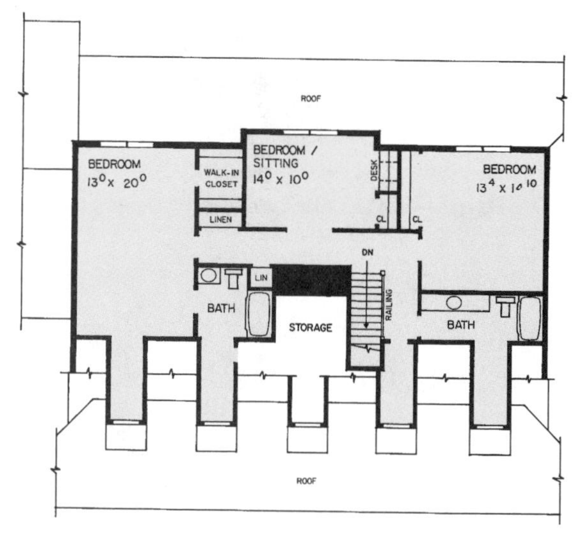

ROOF
BEDROOM
13⁰ x 20⁰
WALK-IN CLOSET
LINEN
BEDROOM / SITTING
14⁰ x 10⁰
DESK
CL
CL
BEDROOM
13⁴ x 16¹⁰
DN
LIN
BATH
STORAGE
RAILING
BATH
ROOF

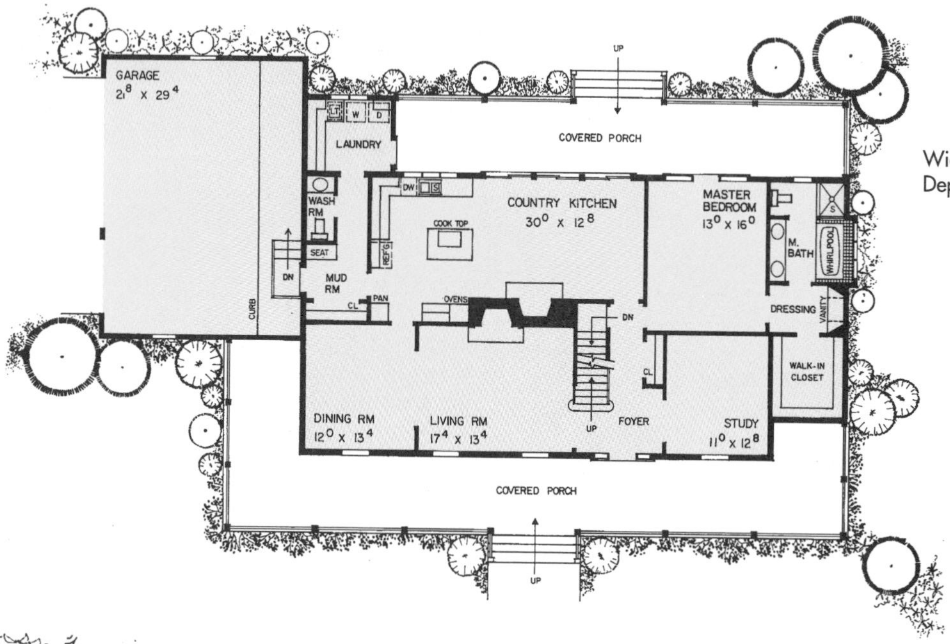

Design by
Home Planners

Width 82'-0"
Depth 50'-0"

QUOTE ONE®

Cost to build? See page 516 to order complete cost estimate to build this house in your area!

Design 5511

First Floor: 1,160 square feet
Second Floor: 1,135 square feet
Total: 2,295 square feet

■ Amenities fill this two-story country home, beginning with a full wraparound porch that offers access to each room on the first floor. Formal living and dining rooms border the central foyer, each with French-door access to the covered porch. At the rear of the first floor is an open family area with a U-shaped kitchen, a bayed breakfast or morning area and a large family room with a fireplace and access to the rear porch. Upstairs, three family bedrooms share a centrally located utility room and a full hall bath with dual sinks. The master bedroom features a box-bay window seat and a master bath with separate sinks and a walk-in closet. An additional half-bath on the first floor completes this exquisite design.

RAILING
WRAP-AROUND COVERED PORCH
KIT $13^0 \times 11^8$
BREAKFAST-MORNING $13^0 \times 11^8$
SNACK BAR
FAMILY RM $13^0 \times 15^0$
DW
COOK TOP
REFG
PANTRY
OVN
DN
POWDER RM
DINING RM $12^8 \times 11^8$
RAILING
UP
FOYER
LIVING RM $12^8 \times 11^8$
WRAP-AROUND COVERED PORCH
RAILING

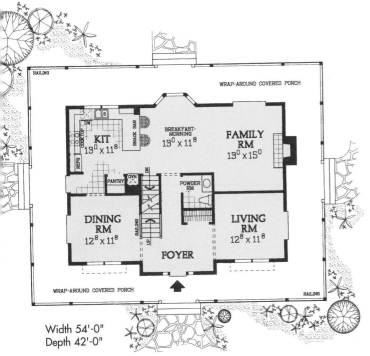

Width 54'-0"
Depth 42'-0"

Design by
Home Planners

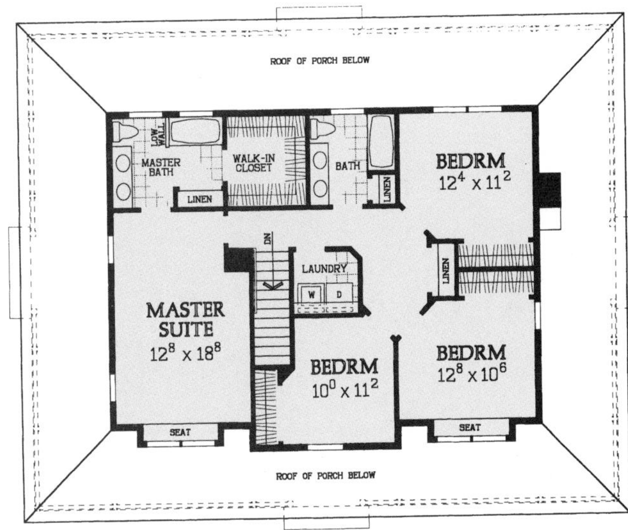
ROOF OF PORCH BELOW
LOW WALL
MASTER BATH
LINEN
WALK-IN CLOSET
BATH
LINEN
BEDRM $12^4 \times 11^2$
DN
LAUNDRY
W
D
LINEN
MASTER SUITE $12^8 \times 18^8$
BEDRM $10^0 \times 11^2$
BEDRM $12^8 \times 10^6$
SEAT
SEAT
ROOF OF PORCH BELOW

QUOTE ONE®

Cost to build? See page 516 to order complete cost estimate to build this house in your area!

Design Q219

First Floor: 1,026 square feet
Second Floor: 994 square feet
Total: 2,020 square feet
Bonus Room: 377 square feet

This inviting country home is enhanced by a full-width covered front porch, a fieldstone exterior and a trio of dormers on the second floor. Double doors open to a foyer flanked by a living room on the right and dining room on the left. The living room extends the full depth of the house and has a fireplace and sliding glass doors to the rear patio. A U-shaped kitchen adjoins a breakfast room with sliding glass doors to the patio, also. A laundry and half-bath connect the home to a two-car garage. Second-floor space includes two family bedrooms with shared bath and a master suite with full bath and walk-in closet. A large bonus room adds 377 square feet of living space on the second floor.

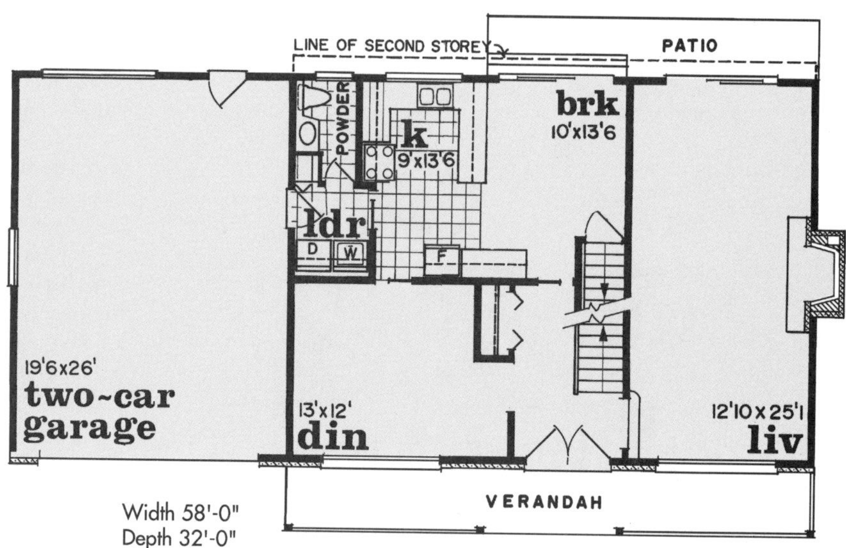
LINE OF SECOND STOREY
PATIO
POWDER
k
9'x13'6
brk
10'x13'6
ldr
D
W
F
19'6x26'
two~car garage
13'x12'
din
12'10x25'1
liv
VERANDAH

Width 58'-0"
Depth 32'-0"

Design by
Select Home Designs

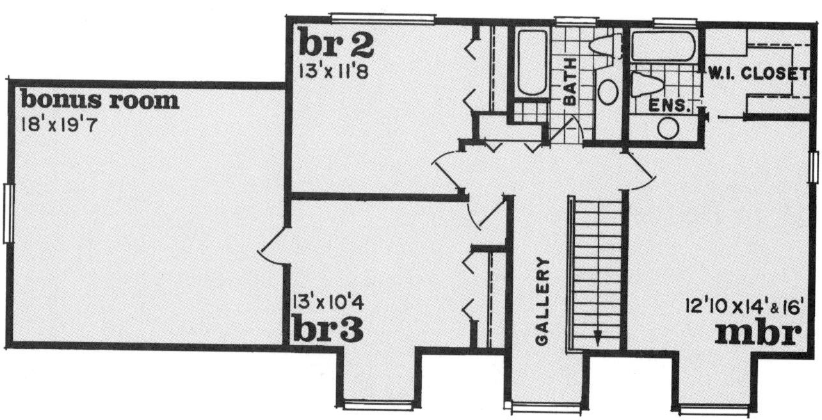
br 2
13'x 11'8
BATH
W.I. CLOSET
ENS.
bonus room
18'x19'7
GALLERY
13'x10'4
br3
12'10 x14' & 16'
mbr

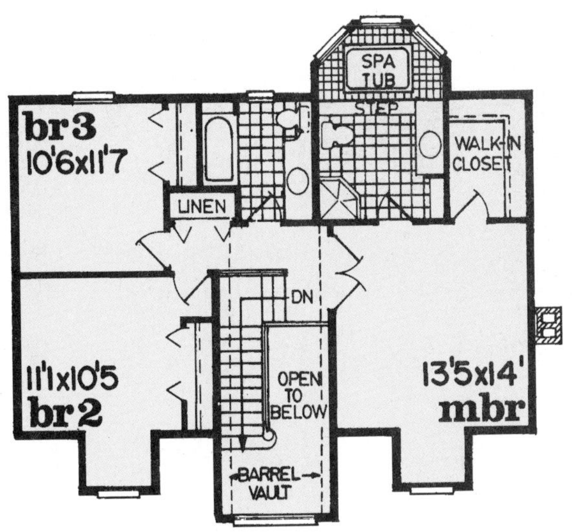
SPA TUB
STEP
br3
10'6x11'7
WALK-IN CLOSET
LINEN
DN
11'1x10'5
br2
OPEN TO BELOW
13'5x14'
mbr
BARREL VAULT

Design Q277

First Floor: 1,371 square feet
Second Floor: 1,018 square feet
Total: 2,389 square feet

A full-width covered porch and three dormer windows add charming touches to this country home. The foyer has a barrel vault and leads to a living room on the left side of the plan and a family room with wood stove on the right. The formal dining room sits between the living room and the U-shaped kitchen for convenience. A bayed breakfast room enhances the kitchen and allows space for casual dining. A half-bath and laundry room lead to the two-car garage. Rounding out the first floor is a den, which easily doubles as a guest room. The second floor brings three bedrooms—two family bedrooms and a master suite. The master suite has a walk-in closet and private bath with spa tub. Family bedrooms share a full hall bath with linen closet. Plans include details for both a basement and a crawlspace foundation.

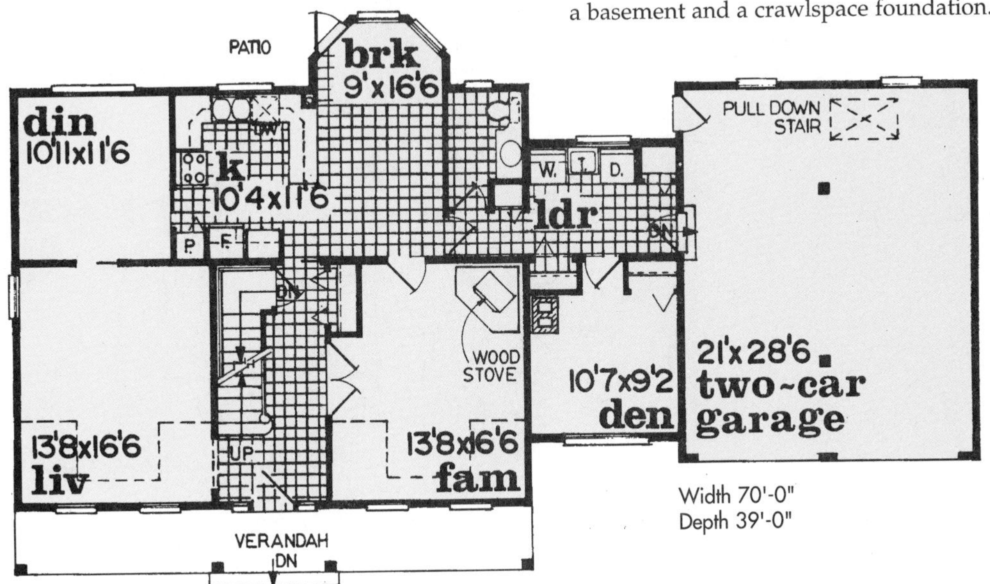
PATIO
brk
9'x16'6
din
10'11x11'6
k
10'4x11'6
DW
P
F
W.
D.
ldr
DN
PULL DOWN STAIR
WOOD STOVE
13'8x16'6
liv
UP
13'8x16'6
fam
10'7x9'2
den
21'x28'6
two-car garage
VERANDAH
DN

Width 70'-0"
Depth 39'-0"

Design by
Select Home Designs

Design Q233

First Floor: 1,140 square feet
Second Floor: 1,096 square feet
Total: 2,236 square feet
Bonus Room: 414 square feet

■ With charm-plus, this country home is as roomy as it is attractive. A classic floor plan features a double-door entry to a center hall, flanked by living areas. The sunken living room is on the left and boasts a fireplace; the den is on the right and has double-door access. A dining room sits between the living room and the U-shaped kitchen. Note the pass-through counter separating the kitchen and the breakfast bay. Sliding glass doors open from the breakfast bay to the rear yard. A laundry with half-bath is found in the service entrance to the two-car garage. Four bedrooms and a large bonus room (414 square feet) are on the second floor. The master bedroom has a walk-in closet with extra storage space and a full bath. Family bedrooms share a full hall bath. Plans include details for both a basement and a crawlspace foundation.

Design by
Select Home Designs

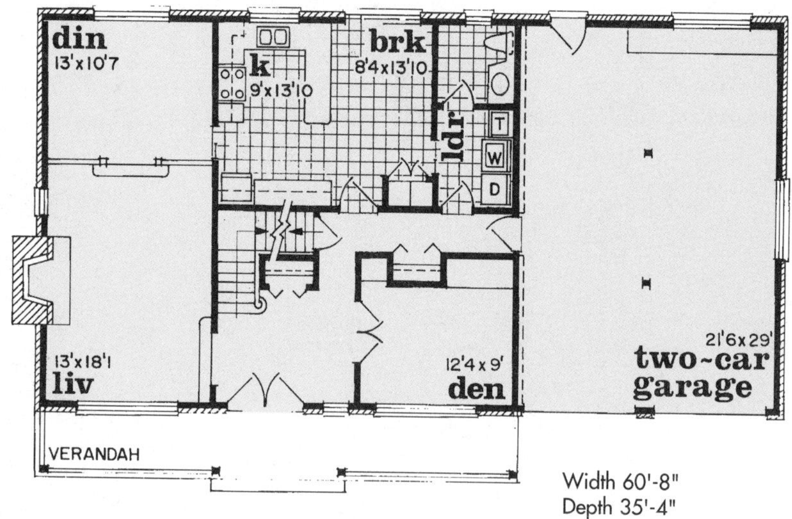
din
13'x10'7
k
9'x13'10
brk
8'4x13'10
ldr
T
W
D
13'x18'1
liv
12'4 x 9'
den
21'6x29'
two-car
garage
VERANDAH
Width 60'-8"
Depth 35'-4"

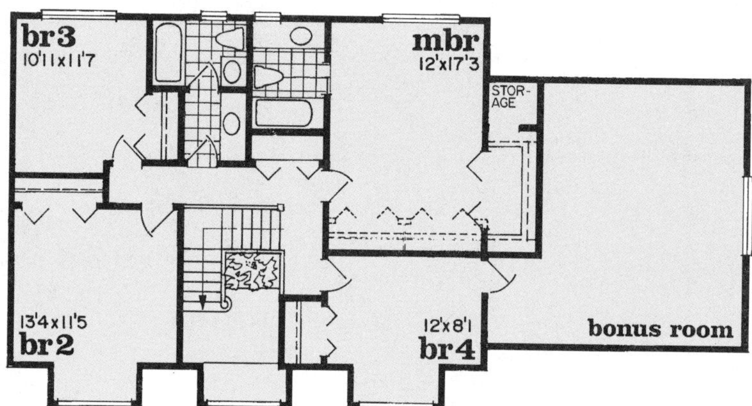
br3
10'11x11'7
mbr
12'x17'3
STOR-
AGE
13'4x11'5
br2
12'x8'1
br4
bonus room

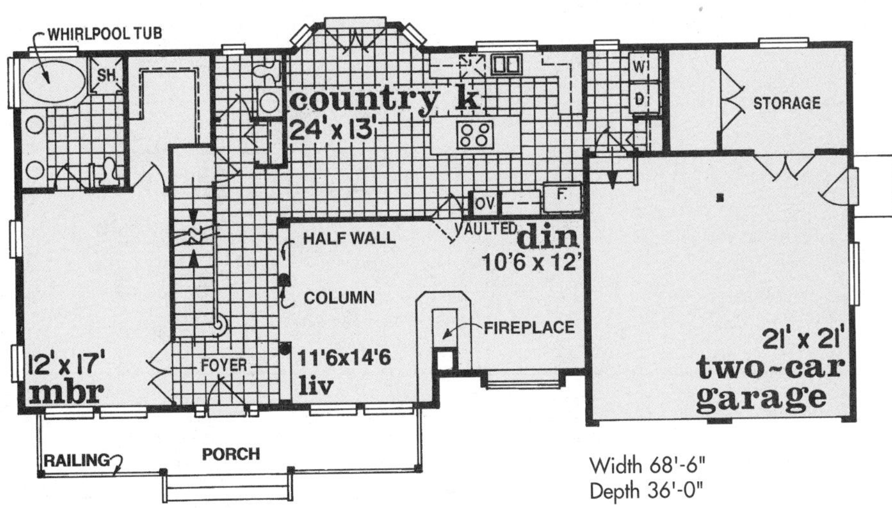
WHIRLPOOL TUB
SH.
country k
24'x 13'
W
D
STORAGE
OV
F.
HALF WALL
VAULTED din
10'6 x 12'
COLUMN
FIREPLACE
21' x 21'
two-car
garage
12'x 17'
mbr
FOYER
11'6x14'6
liv
RAILING
PORCH
Width 68'-6"
Depth 36'-0"

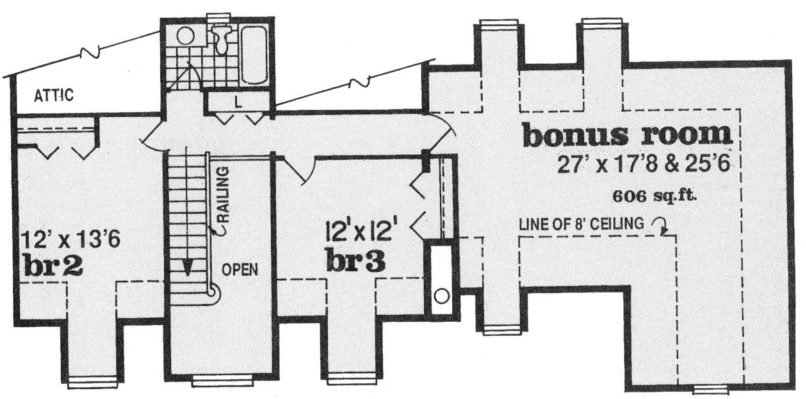
ATTIC
L
bonus room
27' x 17'8 & 25'6
606 sq.ft.
RAILING
OPEN
LINE OF 8' CEILING
12' x 13'6
br2
12'x12'
br3

Design Q386

First Floor: 1,404 square feet
Second Floor: 640 square feet
Total: 2,044 square feet
Bonus Room: 695 square feet

A rustic plan, with just the right classic touches, this home is made for country living. The covered porch shelters an entry that opens to a two-story foyer flanked by the master bedroom and the living room. The living room shares a three-sided fireplace with the dining room and features columns and a half-wall at its entry. The master suite opens through double doors and has a walk-in closet and full bath with whirlpool tub. Across the back of the plan is the country kitchen with island cooktop, L-shaped work center and bayed eating area. The second floor has two family bedrooms, plus a full bath and a large bonus space of 695 square feet that can be finished later into additional bedrooms or hobby space.

Design by
Select Home Designs

© Copyright Select Home Designs. All rights reserved.

Design Q472

First Floor: 1,099 square feet
Second Floor: 535 square feet
Total: 1,634 square feet
Optional Loft 83 square feet

■ This design offers several different options to make the floor plan exactly as you like it. The exterior is graced by a wrapping veranda, round columns, stone facing with cedar shingled accents and a trio of dormers. Inside, the open plan includes a vaulted great room with fireplace, a vaulted dining room, a vaulted kitchen and three bedrooms. The kitchen has a pass-through to the dining room and large pantry. The master bedroom is found on the first floor for privacy. It contains a walk-in closet with dressing room, sitting area and full skylit bath. Family bedrooms are on the second floor and share a full bath. An optional loft is also available on the second floor. If you choose, you can reconfigure the master bath to allow for a half-bath in the laundry. Plans include details for both a basement and a crawlspace foundation.

Width 44'-8"
Depth 41'-4"

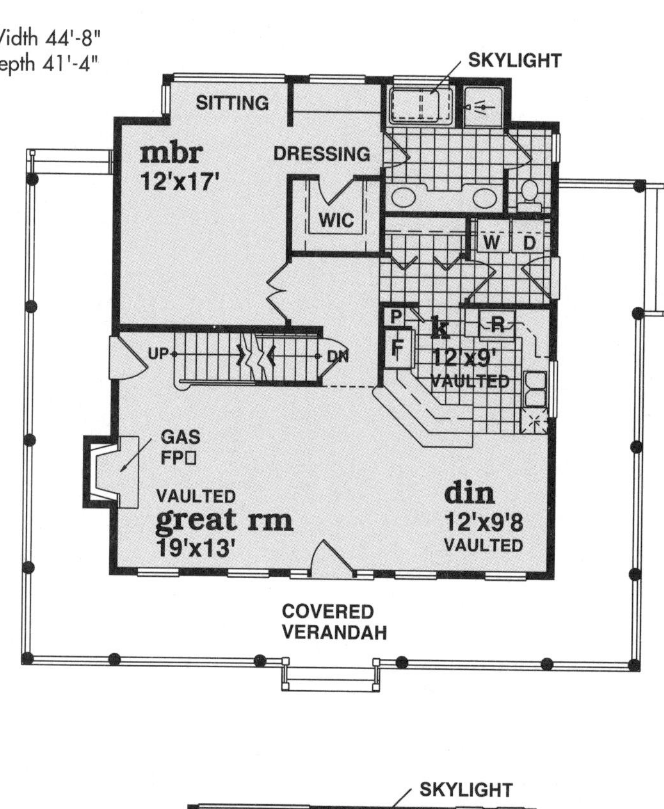
SKYLIGHT
SITTING
mbr
12'x17'
DRESSING
WIC
W
D
P
F
R
k
12'x9'
VAULTED
UP
DN
GAS
FP
VAULTED
great rm
19'x13'
din
12'x9'8
VAULTED
COVERED
VERANDAH

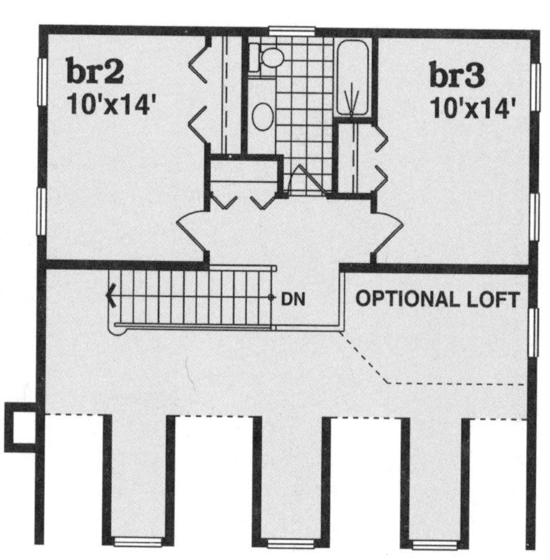
br2
10'x14'
br3
10'x14'
DN
OPTIONAL LOFT

Design by·
Select Home Designs

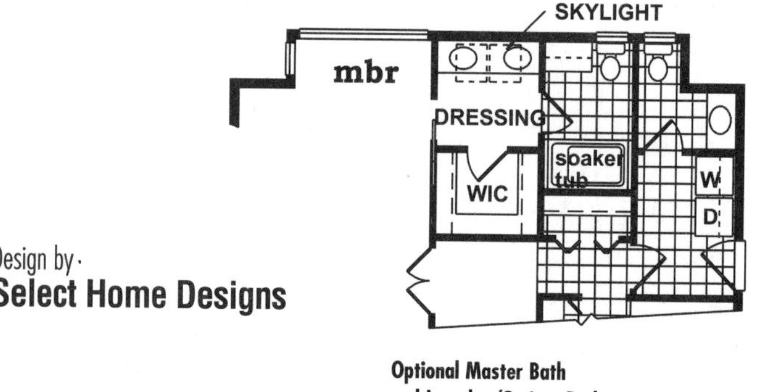
SKYLIGHT
mbr
DRESSING
soaker
tub
WIC
W
D

Optional Master Bath and Laundry/2 piece Bath

Design Q451

First Floor: 1,292 square feet
Second Floor: 1,189 square feet
Total: 2,481 square feet
Bonus Room: 343 square feet

■ This country home retains just enough classic details to make it elegant, yet still a country-style design. The covered front porch, with round columns, and the five dormer windows add touches of grace. The entry foyer is lit by a second-story dormer and leads to a living room with fireplace on the left and a study on the right. The family room at the back is graced by a decorative beam ceiling and shares a fireplace with the hearth room where a French door leads out to the deck. The U-shaped kitchen features a center island. All four bedrooms are on the second floor, along with a bonus room of 343 square feet to finish as you choose. The master suite has a private bath, while family bedrooms share a full bath. A built-in desk in the center serves family students. Plans include details for both a basement and a crawlspace foundation.

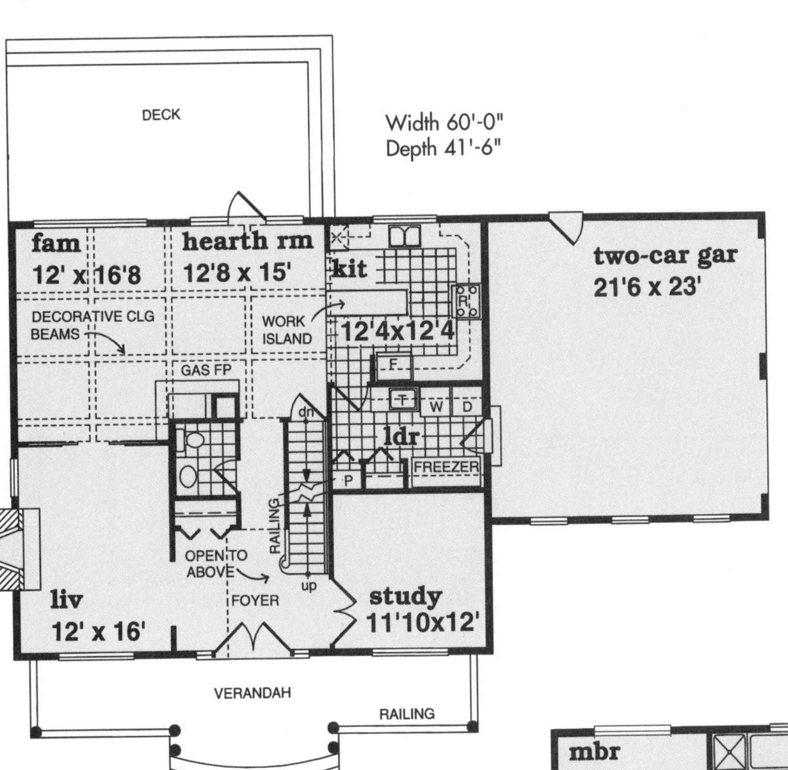
DECK
Width 60'-0"
Depth 41'-6"
fam
12' x 16'8
hearth rm
12'8 x 15'
kit
12'4x12'4
two-car gar
21'6 x 23'
DECORATIVE CLG BEAMS
WORK ISLAND
GAS FP
R
F
W
D
ldr
P
FREEZER
dn
RAILING
up
OPEN TO ABOVE
FOYER
liv
12' x 16'
study
11'10x12'
VERANDAH
RAILING

Design by
Select Home Designs

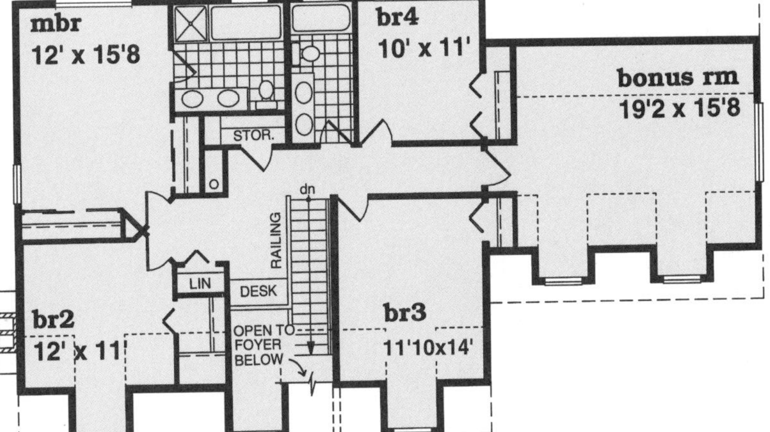
mbr
12' x 15'8
br4
10' x 11'
bonus rm
19'2 x 15'8
STOR.
dn
RAILING
LIN
DESK
OPEN TO FOYER BELOW
br2
12' x 11
br3
11'10x14'

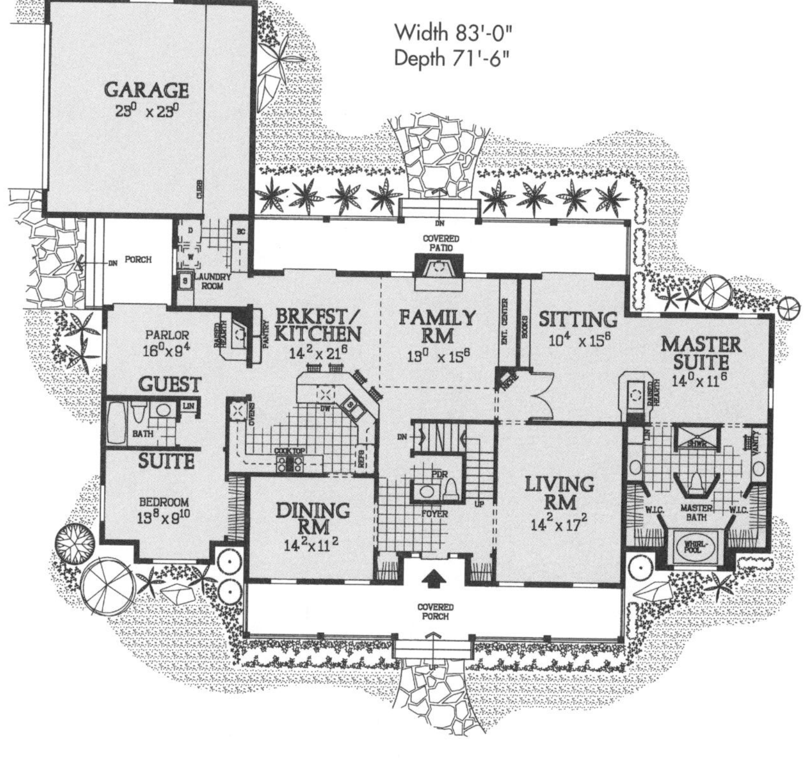

Width 83'-0"
Depth 71'-6"
GARAGE
$23^0 \times 23^0$
PORCH
LAUNDRY ROOM
COVERED PATIO
PARLOR
$16^0 \times 9^4$
GUEST
BATH
SUITE
BEDROOM
$13^8 \times 9^{10}$
BRKFST/ KITCHEN
$14^2 \times 21^6$
PANTRY
OVENS
COOK TOP
FAMILY RM
$13^0 \times 15^6$
ENT. CENTER
BOOKS
SITTING
$10^4 \times 15^6$
MASTER SUITE
$14^0 \times 11^6$
DINING RM
$14^2 \times 11^2$
PDR
FOYER
LIVING RM
$14^2 \times 17^2$
W.I.C.
MASTER BATH
W.I.C.
WHIRL-POOL
COVERED PORCH

Design 3614

First Floor: 2,300 square feet
Second Floor: 812 square feet
Total: 3,112 square feet

L **D**

If you're looking for the real McCoy—lightly influenced by classic style—you need look no further. A circle-top window and proportional balustrades provide the refined appearance on this charming farmhouse. Inside, the foyer opens to a formal living room on the right and a formal dining room on the left. The kitchen—bordered by a snack bar—unites the breakfast room with the family room, which features an entertainment center and a fireplace. The first-floor master suite is filled with amenities that include a raised-hearth fireplace, a sitting room, a wall of bookshelves and a unique master bath with a relaxing whirlpool tub. Tucked behind the kitchen is a guest suite. A private bath and a parlor with a raised-hearth fireplace will make visiting family and guests feel like royalty. The second floor contains two family bedrooms and a full bath.

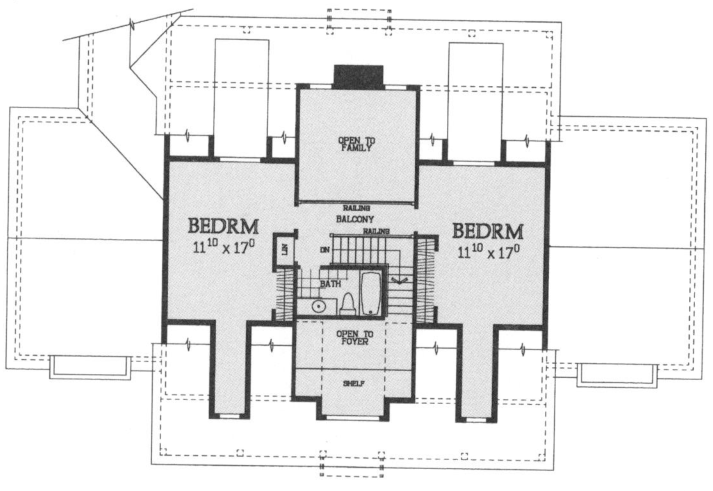

OPEN TO FAMILY
RAILING
BALCONY
RAILING
BEDRM
$11^{10} \times 17^0$
BEDRM
$11^{10} \times 17^0$
BATH
OPEN TO FOYER
SHELF

Design by
Home Planners

QUOTE ONE®

Cost to build? See page 516 to order complete cost estimate to build this house in your area!

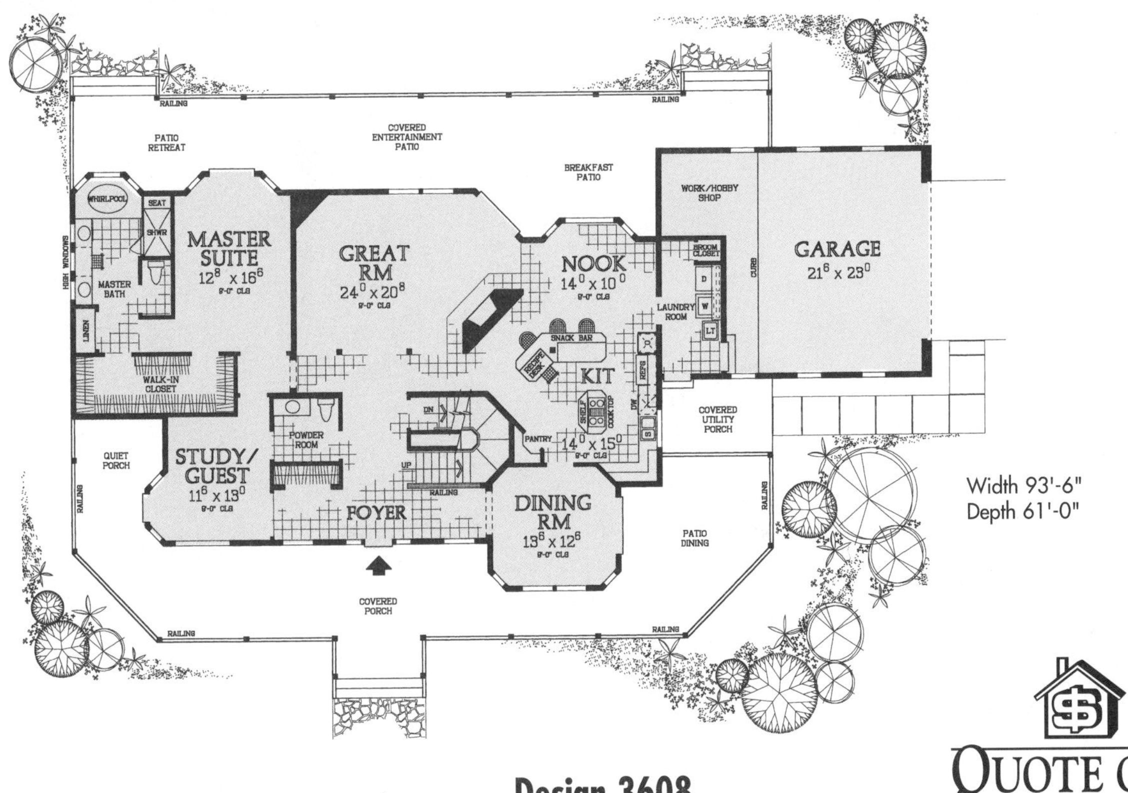
PATIO RETREAT
COVERED ENTERTAINMENT PATIO
BREAKFAST PATIO
WORK/HOBBY SHOP
WHIRLPOOL
MASTER SUITE
12⁸ x 16⁶
MASTER BATH
WALK-IN CLOSET
GREAT RM
24⁰ x 20⁸
NOOK
14⁰ x 10⁰
LAUNDRY ROOM
GARAGE
21⁶ x 23⁰
KIT
14⁰ x 15⁰
PANTRY
COVERED UTILITY PORCH
QUIET PORCH
STUDY/ GUEST
11⁶ x 13⁰
POWDER ROOM
FOYER
DINING RM
13⁶ x 12⁶
PATIO DINING
COVERED PORCH
RAILING

Width 93'-6"
Depth 61'-0"

QUOTE ONE®
Cost to build? See page 516 to order complete cost estimate to build this house in your area!

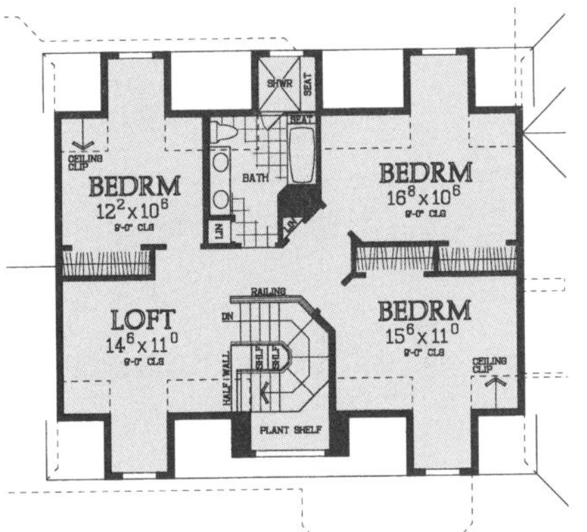
BEDRM
12²x10⁸
BATH
BEDRM
18⁸x10⁶
LOFT
14⁶x11⁰
BEDRM
15⁶x11⁰
PLANT SHELF

Design 3608

First Floor: 2,347 square feet
Second Floor: 1,087 square feet
Total: 3,434 square feet

Varied rooflines and sunburst trim provide an extra measure of style with this new farmhouse. The sunburst is repeated on a clerestory window, which lets sunlight into the foyer. Traditional elegance is splashed with contemporary style in the formal dining room. A centered hearth warms casual living and dining areas, which open to an outdoor entertainment patio. A secluded master suite offers a bumped-out bay with wide views to the rear property, and private access to the patio. Each of the three second-floor bedrooms, as well as the loft, has a dormer window. A full bath with twin vanities and a separate shower with a seat complete the plan.

Design by
Home Planners

Design 5545

First Floor: 720 square feet
Second Floor: 686 square feet
Total: 1,406 square feet

■ As a starter home or vacation home, this design offers a vast array of amenities. An engaging wrap-around covered porch with a side deck is just the beginning of a plan filled with charm and comfort. The open entry leads to a spacious great room that encompasses the majority of the first floor and includes side-deck access. A U-shaped kitchen with plenty of counter space and a utility and powder room are found nearby. On the second floor, the master bedroom features a box-bay window—perfect for relaxing with a good book or with stationary and pen. A walk-in closet and a private bath with dual sinks complete this private retreat. Two additional bedrooms share a full bath.

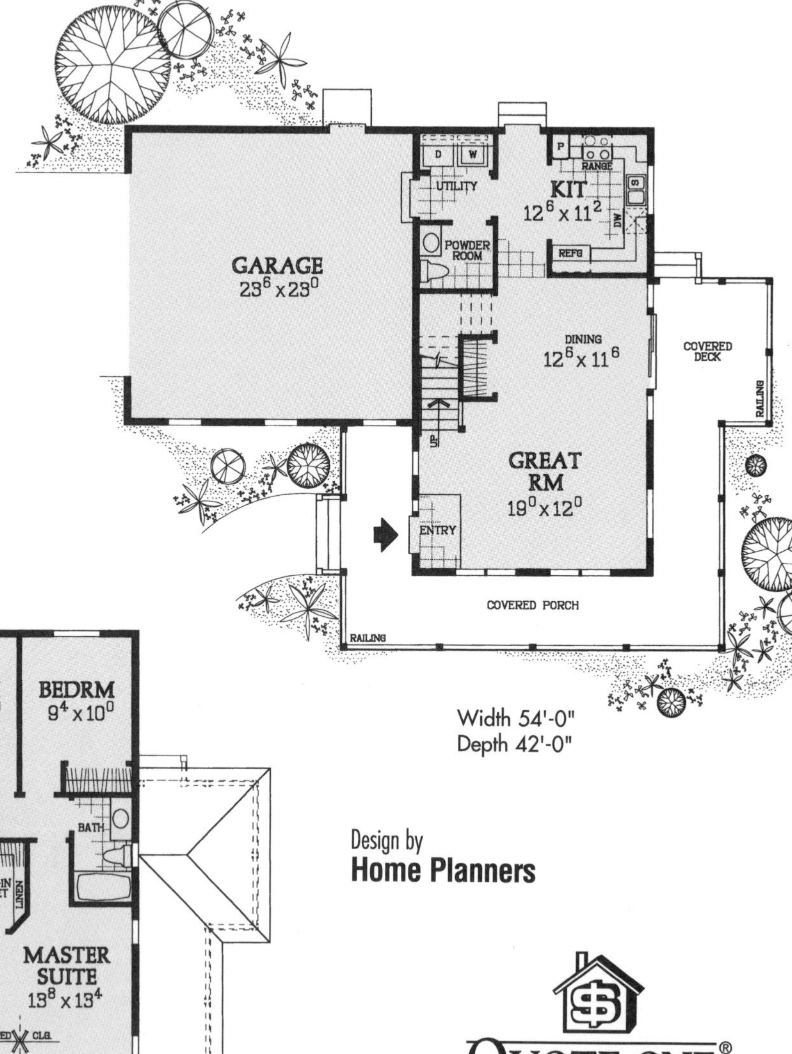

GARAGE
23⁶ x 23⁰
UTILITY
D
W
POWDER ROOM
KIT
12⁶ x 11²
RANGE
REFG
DW
P
DINING
12⁶ x 11⁶
COVERED DECK
RAILING
GREAT RM
19⁰ x 12⁰
ENTRY
UP
COVERED PORCH
RAILING
ROOF OF GARAGE BELOW
BEDRM
9⁴ x 10⁰
BEDRM
9⁴ x 10⁰
DN
BATH
WALK-IN CLOSET
LINEN
MASTER SUITE
13⁸ x 13⁴
BATH
SLOPED CLG.
ROOF OF PORCH BELOW

Width 54'-0"
Depth 42'-0"

Design by
Home Planners

QUOTE ONE®

Cost to build? See page 516 to order complete cost estimate to build this house in your area!

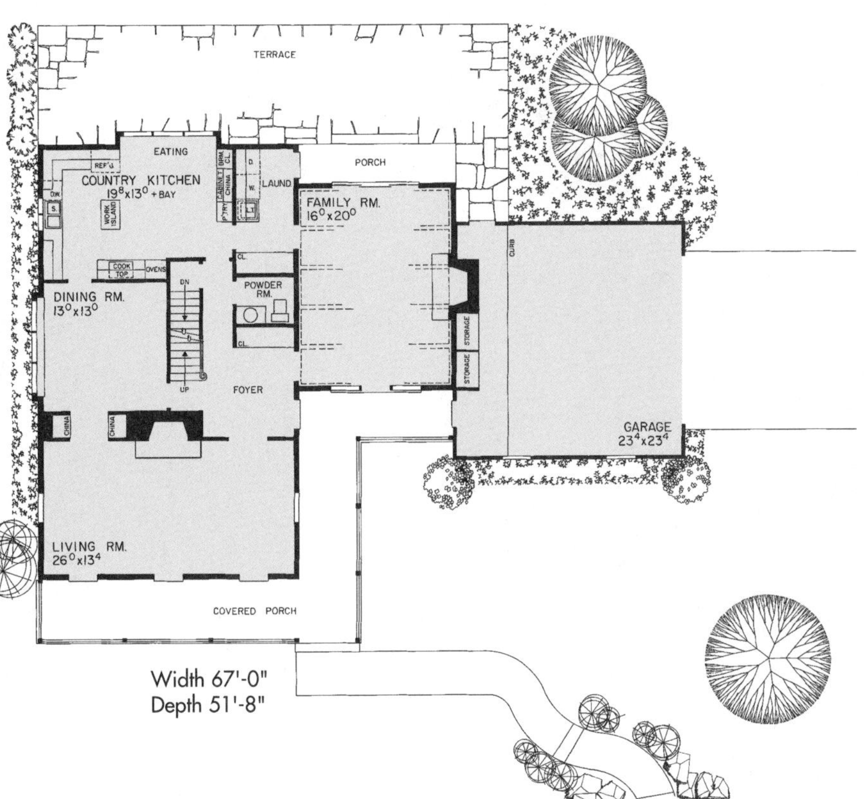
TERRACE
EATING
PORCH
COUNTRY KITCHEN
19⁸x13⁰ + BAY
LAUND.
FAMILY RM.
16⁰x20⁰
DINING RM.
13⁰x13⁰
POWDER RM.
FOYER
GARAGE
23⁴x23⁴
LIVING RM.
26⁰x13⁴
COVERED PORCH

Width 67'-0"
Depth 51'-8"

Design 2907

First Floor: 1,546 square feet
Second Floor: 1,144 square feet
Total: 2,690 square feet

L

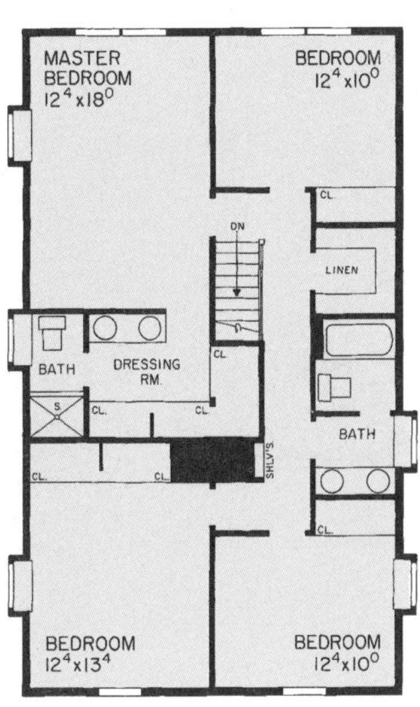
MASTER BEDROOM
12⁴x18⁰
BEDROOM
12⁴x10⁰
LINEN
BATH
DRESSING RM.
BATH
BEDROOM
12⁴x13⁴
BEDROOM
12⁴x10⁰

This traditional, L-shaped farmhouse is charming, indeed, with its gambrel roof, dormer windows and covered porch supported by slender columns and side rails. A spacious country kitchen with a bay provides a cozy gathering place for family and friends, as well as a convenient place for food preparation with its central work island and size. There's a formal dining room also adjacent to the kitchen. A rear family room features its own fireplace, as does a large living room in the front. All four bedrooms are isolated upstairs, away from other household activity and noise. Included is a large master bedroom suite with its own bath, dressing room and abundant closet space.

Design by
Home Planners

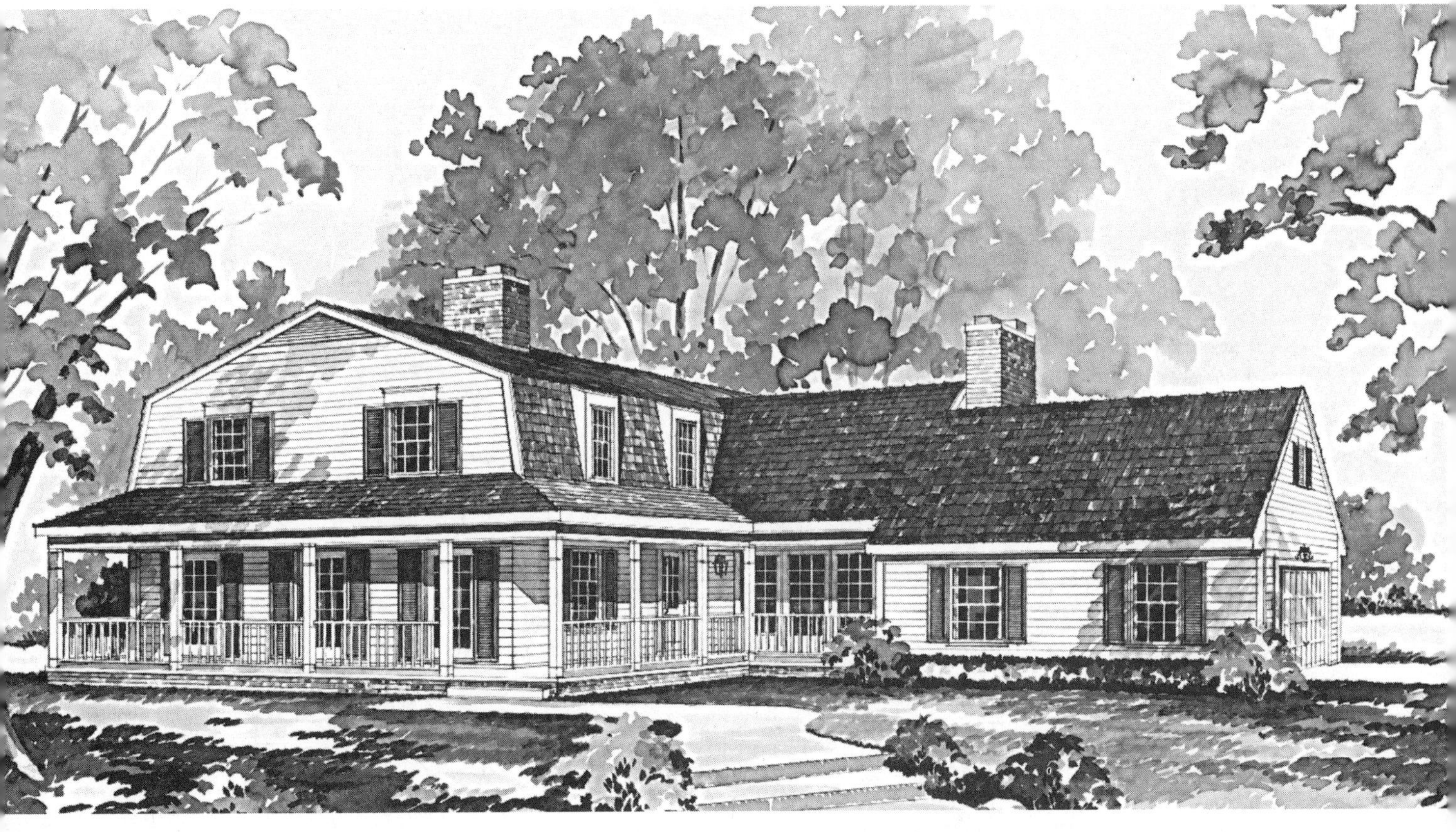

Design Q226

First Floor: 836 square feet
Second Floor: 581 square feet
Total: 1,417 square feet
Bonus Room: 228 square feet

■ Charming details add to the rustic appeal of this smaller farmhouse design. The covered porch shelters an entry that opens to a center hall with the living and dining rooms on one side and a cozy den on the other. The living/dining room space is warmed by a fireplace. The den has access to a full bath and can double as a guest room. An L-shaped kitchen is both step-saving and convenient; just beyond is a laundry room and service entrance to the single-car garage. Two bedrooms are on the upper level: a master bedroom with wall closet and a family bedroom. Both share a full bath. Bonus space equal to 228 square feet also is found on the second floor and can be made into another bedroom or a hobby room when needed. Plans include details for both a basement and a crawl-space foundation.

Design by
Select Home Designs

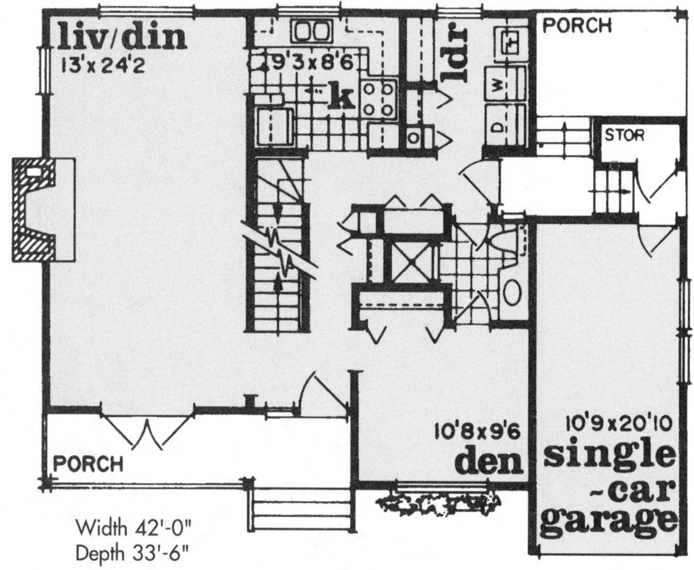

liv/din
13'x 24'2
9'3 x 8'6
k
ldr
PORCH
STOR
PORCH
10'8 x 9'6
den
10'9 x 20'10
single
-car
garage
Width 42'-0"
Depth 33'-6"

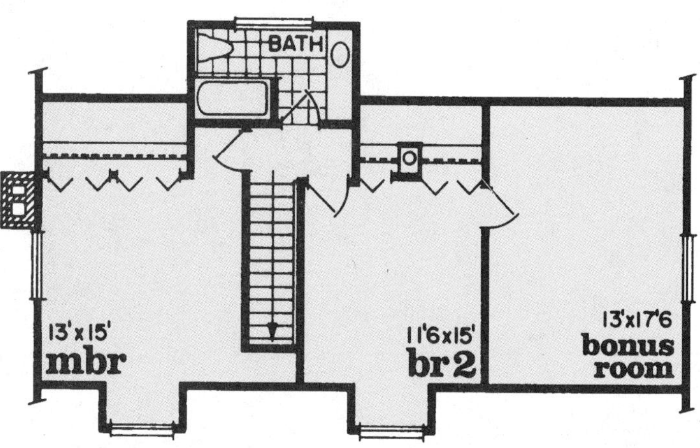

BATH
13'x 15'
mbr
11'6 x 15'
br 2
13'x 17'6
bonus
room

Design 2776

First Floor: 1,134 square feet
Second Floor: 874 square feet
Total: 2,008 square feet

L D

■ This board-and-batten farmhouse design has all of the country charm of New England. The large covered front porch surely will be appreciated during the beautiful warm weather months. Immediately off the front entrance is the delightful corner living room. The dining room with a bay window will be easily served by the U-shaped kitchen. Informal family living enjoyment will be obtained in the family room which features a raised-hearth fireplace, sliding glass doors to the rear terrace and easy access to the work center. The second floor houses all of the sleeping facilities. There is a master bedroom with a private bath and a walk-in closet. Two secondary bedrooms share a full bath.

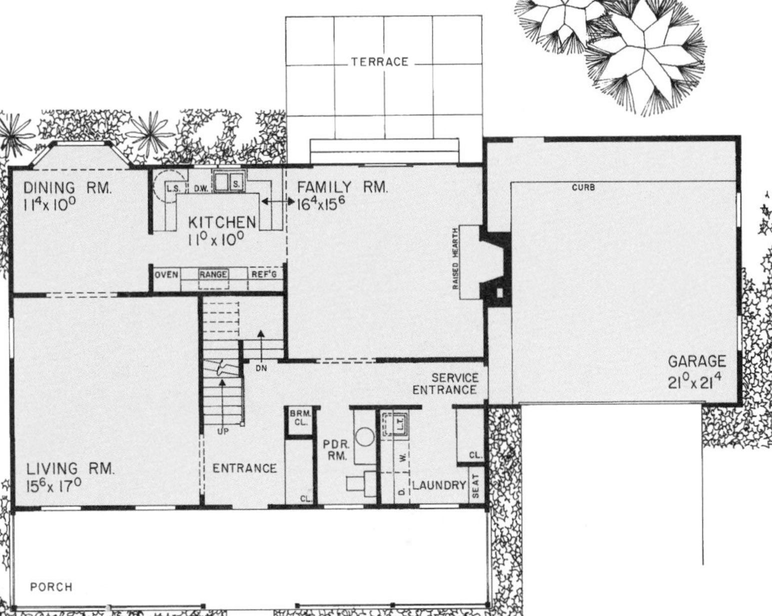
TERRACE
DINING RM. 11^4x10^0
KITCHEN 11^0x10^0
L.S.
DW.
S.
OVEN
RANGE
REF'G
FAMILY RM. 16^4x15^6
RAISED HEARTH
CURB
GARAGE 21^0x21^4
SERVICE ENTRANCE
DN
UP
BRM. CL.
PDR. RM.
W.
D.
LAUNDRY
CL.
SEAT
LIVING RM. 15^6x 17^0
ENTRANCE
CL.
PORCH

Width 61'-4"
Depth 38'-0"

QUOTE ONE®

Cost to build? See page 516 to order complete cost estimate to build this house in your area!

Design by
Home Planners

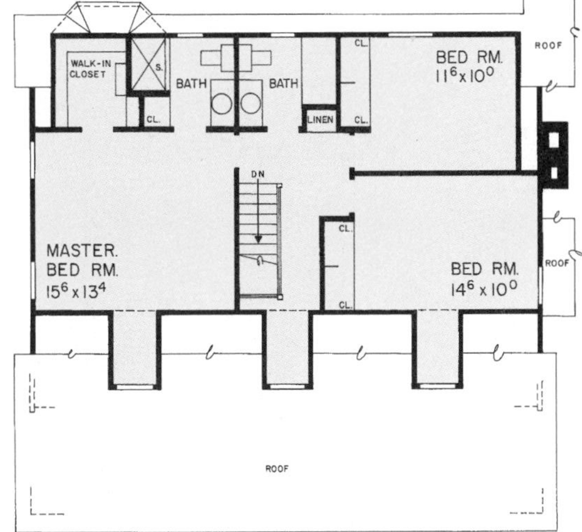
WALK-IN CLOSET
S.
BATH
BATH
CL.
LINEN
CL.
CL.
BED RM. 11^6x10^0
ROOF
DN
MASTER BED RM. 15^6x13^4
CL.
CL.
BED RM. 14^6x10^0
ROOF
ROOF

Design 3461

First Floor: 1,391 square feet
Second Floor: 611 square feet
Total: 2,002 square feet

L

■ Muntin windows, shutters and flower boxes add charm to this well-designed family farmhouse. The impressive foyer boasts a high ceiling and opens through decorative columns to the living room. Casual living takes off in the family room, with its own fireplace, and the open gourmet kitchen, which offers space for gathering. The first-floor master bedroom provides a sunny bay window, while the master bath offers a large walk-in closet, a knee-space vanity and a tiled-rim whirlpool tub. Three family bedrooms share an ample full bath upstairs.

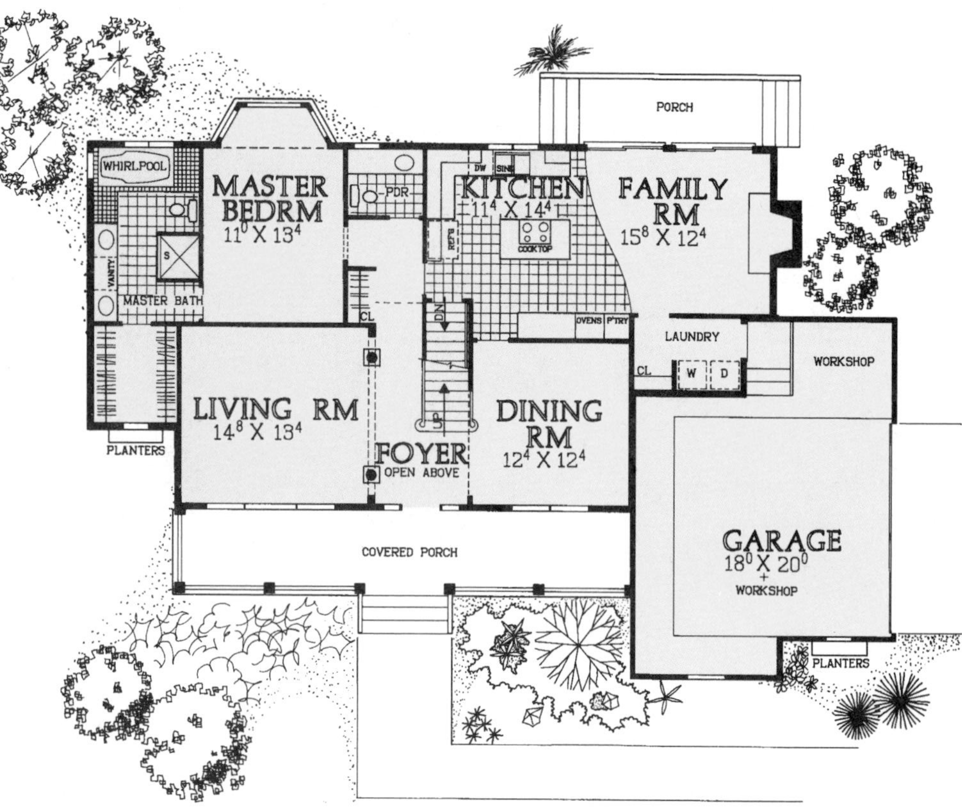

PORCH
WHIRLPOOL
VANITY
MASTER BATH
MASTER BEDRM
11⁰ X 13⁴
PDR
CL
KITCHEN
11⁴ X 14⁴
DW
SINK
REF'G
COOKTOP
OVENS
P'TRY
FAMILY RM
15⁸ X 12⁴
LAUNDRY
CL.
W
D
WORKSHOP
LIVING RM
14⁸ X 13⁴
FOYER
OPEN ABOVE
DINING RM
12⁴ X 12⁴
DN
UP
PLANTERS
COVERED PORCH
GARAGE
18⁰ X 20⁰
+
WORKSHOP
PLANTERS

Width 64'-0"
Depth 44'-0"

QUOTE ONE®

Cost to build? See page 516 to order complete cost estimate to build this house in your area!

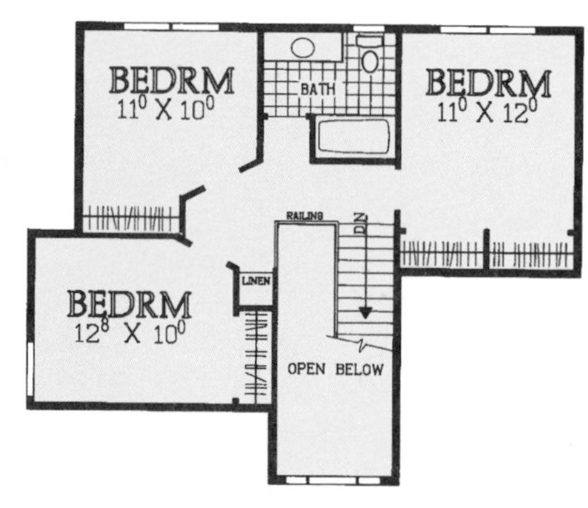

BEDRM
11⁰ X 10⁰
BATH
BEDRM
11⁰ X 12⁰
RAILING
DN
LINEN
BEDRM
12⁸ X 10⁰
OPEN BELOW

Design by
Home Planners

Design 3328

First Floor: 2,300 square feet
Second Floor: 812 square feet
Total: 3,112 square feet

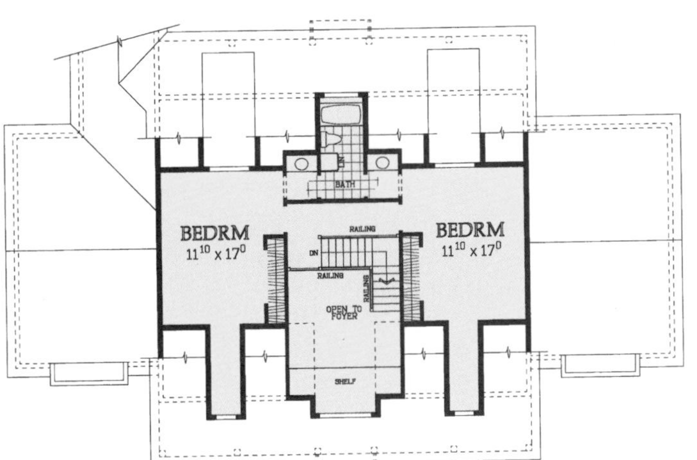
BATH
BEDRM
$11^{10} \times 17^{0}$
RAILING
DN
BEDRM
$11^{10} \times 17^{0}$
RAILING
RAILING
OPEN TO FOYER
SHELF

■ Dormered windows, a covered porch and symmetrical balustrades provide a warm country welcome. Formal living and dining rooms flank the foyer. To the left of the dining room is a spacious family room which contains a raised-hearth fireplace. It is conveniently located near the breakfast/kitchen area which features an island cooktop, a pantry and a planning desk. Just past the study, or optional guest room, is the master suite's sitting area which provides access to the covered patio and the master bedroom. A three-sided fireplace warms both the sitting room and master bedroom. A lavish master bath is complete with a whirlpool tub and separate His and Hers dressing areas. The second floor contains two family bedrooms and a full bath.

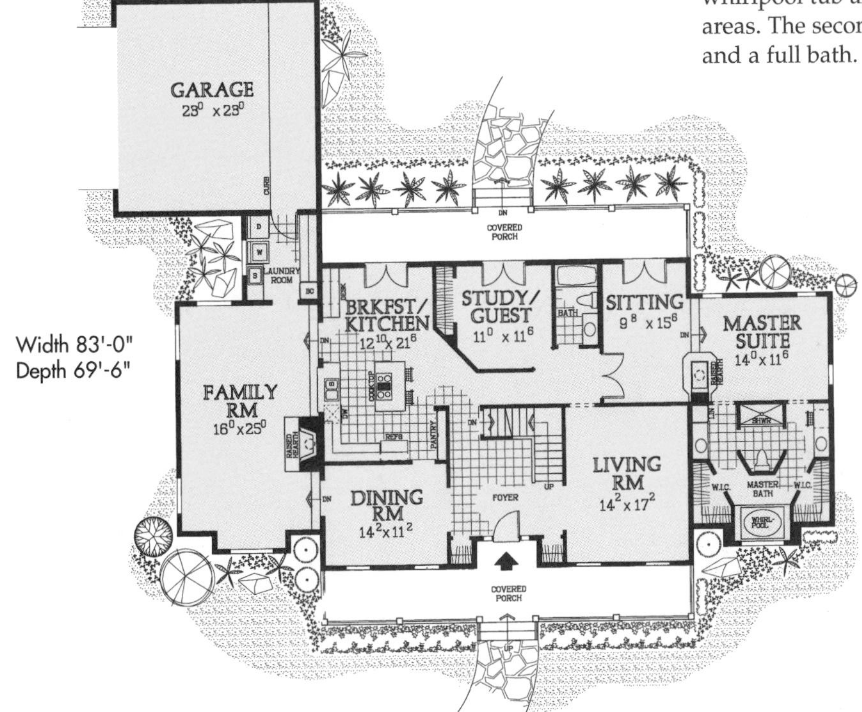
GARAGE
$23^{0} \times 23^{0}$
COVERED PORCH
LAUNDRY ROOM
BRKFST/ KITCHEN
$12^{10} \times 21^{6}$
STUDY/ GUEST
$11^{0} \times 11^{6}$
BATH
SITTING
$9^{8} \times 15^{6}$
MASTER SUITE
$14^{0} \times 11^{6}$
Width 83'-0"
Depth 69'-6"
FAMILY RM
$16^{0} \times 25^{0}$
PANTRY
FOYER
UP
LIVING RM
$14^{2} \times 17^{2}$
DINING RM
$14^{2} \times 11^{2}$
W.I.C.
MASTER BATH
W.I.C.
COVERED PORCH

Design by
Home Planners

QUOTE ONE®

Cost to build? See page 516
to order complete cost estimate
to build this house in your area!

Design 3466

Square Footage: 1,800

L D

Small but inviting, this one-story ranch-style farmhouse is the perfect choice for empty-nesters—and it's loaded with amenities to please the most particular homeowner. Step into a spectacular foyer, bathed in sunlight streaming through dual clerestories, front and rear. The foyer opens to formal living areas on the left and right and leads to split sleeping quarters toward the rear of the plan. Guests and family alike will enjoy the spacious living room, complete with sloped ceiling, warming fireplace, entertainment center and decorative plant shelves. The formal dining room offers a wet bar, sloped ceiling, built-in shelves and natural light from windows to the front and rear of the plan. A sumptuous master suite boasts a warming fireplace, sloped ceiling, whirlpool bath and separate shower. A family bedroom or guest suite offers a full bath on the opposite side of the plan. The kitchen is replete with popular amenities and shares light with a sunny breakfast nook with access to the entertainment terrace.

Width 89'-0"
Depth 46'-2"

BEDRM $15^0 \times 13^0$ 9'-0" CLG.

MASTER BATH
WALK-IN CLOSET
SHWR
LINEN
PLANT SHELF ABOVE
MSTR BEDRM $19^0 \times 12^0$ SLOPED CEILING

RAILING
COVERED PATIO

WH HVAC D W LINEN BC BATH LAUNDRY

GARAGE $21^6 \times 21^0$
CURB

P REFG
KIT $20^6 \times 10^0$ 9'-0" CLG. SINK DW
BREAKFAST NOOK
STORAGE

WET BAR
PLANT SHELF ABOVE
SHLVS
DINING RM $10^2 \times 13^6$ SLOPED CLG
FOYER CLERESTORIES ABOVE

ENTERTAINMENT CENTER
TILE
PLANT SHELF ABOVE
LIVING RM $18^4 \times 13^6$ SLOPED CLG
COVERED PORCH

B-BQ GRILL
ENTERTAINMENT TERRACE

RAILING
COVERED PORCH
RAILING

QUOTE ONE®

Cost to build? See page 516 to order complete cost estimate to build this house in your area!

Design by
Home Planners

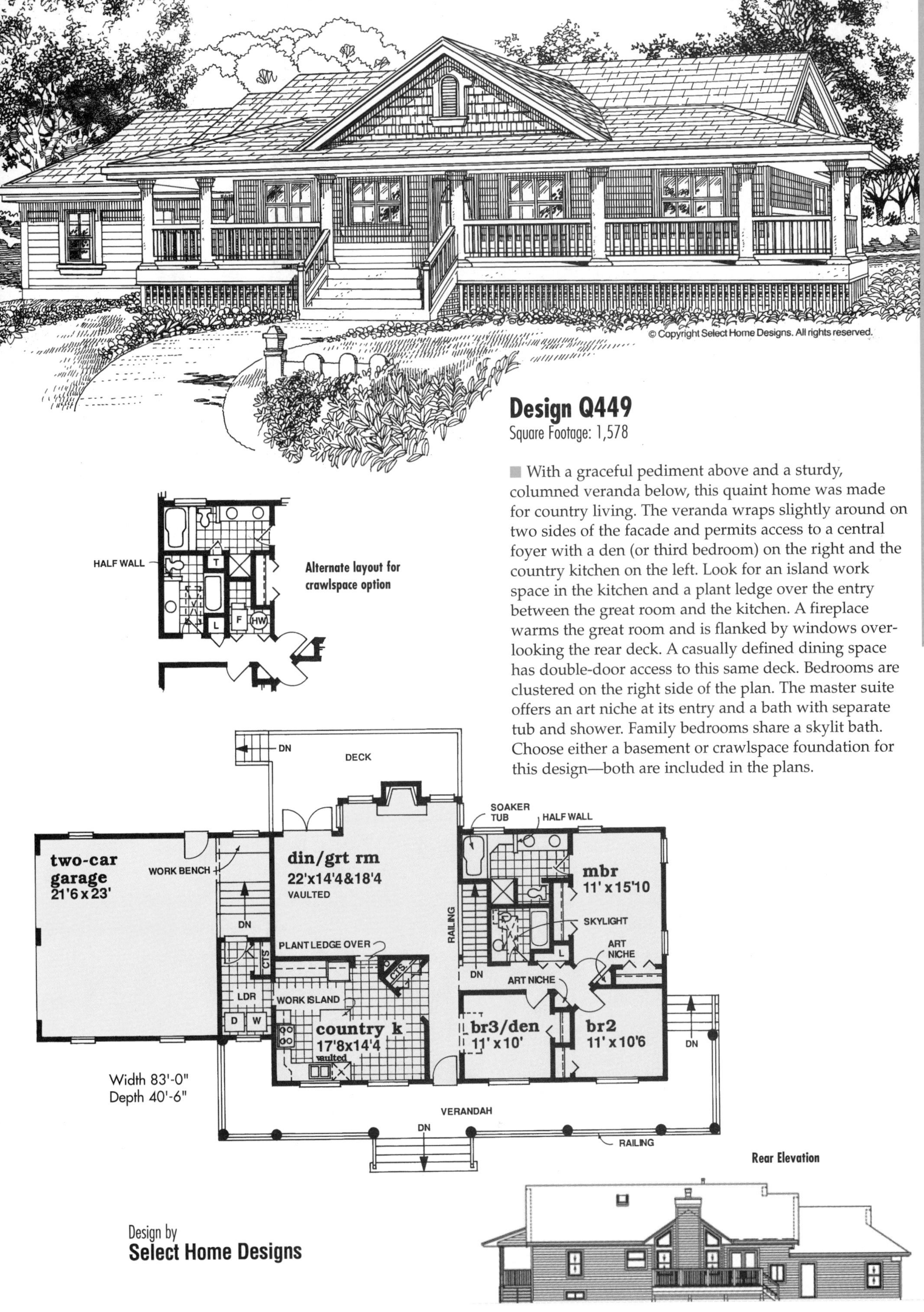

HALF WALL
T
L
F
HW
Alternate layout for crawlspace option
DN
DECK
SOAKER TUB
HALF WALL
two-car garage
21'6 x 23'
WORK BENCH
din/grt rm
22'x14'4&18'4
VAULTED
mbr
11' x 15'10
DN
RAILING
SKYLIGHT
PLANT LEDGE OVER
CTS
ART NICHE
LDR
WORK ISLAND
D
W
country k
17'8x14'4
vaulted
br3/den
11' x 10'
br2
11' x 10'6
DN
VERANDAH
DN
RAILING
Width 83'-0"
Depth 40'-6"
Rear Elevation

Design Q449

Square Footage: 1,578

With a graceful pediment above and a sturdy, columned veranda below, this quaint home was made for country living. The veranda wraps slightly around on two sides of the facade and permits access to a central foyer with a den (or third bedroom) on the right and the country kitchen on the left. Look for an island work space in the kitchen and a plant ledge over the entry between the great room and the kitchen. A fireplace warms the great room and is flanked by windows overlooking the rear deck. A casually defined dining space has double-door access to this same deck. Bedrooms are clustered on the right side of the plan. The master suite offers an art niche at its entry and a bath with separate tub and shower. Family bedrooms share a skylit bath. Choose either a basement or crawlspace foundation for this design—both are included in the plans.

Design by
Select Home Designs

Design Q446

Square Footage: 1,408

Country details make the most of this delightful one-story home. Horizontal wood siding, shuttered windows and a covered veranda enhanced by turned spindles lend their magic. The entry opens into a vaulted great room, warmed by a focal-point fireplace. A charming pot ledge is found over the coat closet at the entry. The country kitchen is also vaulted and features a work island, walk-in pantry, open railing on the stairway to the basement and sliding glass doors to the rear deck. A service entrance connects the kitchen with the two-car garage and handy workshop and features space for a laundry. Bedrooms are to the right of the plan and include two family bedrooms that share a skylit main bath. The master bedroom is graced by two wall closets and a private bath with double vanity and soaking tub in a box-bay window. Plans for a basement or crawlspace foundation are included.

Design by
Select Home Designs

Rear Elevation

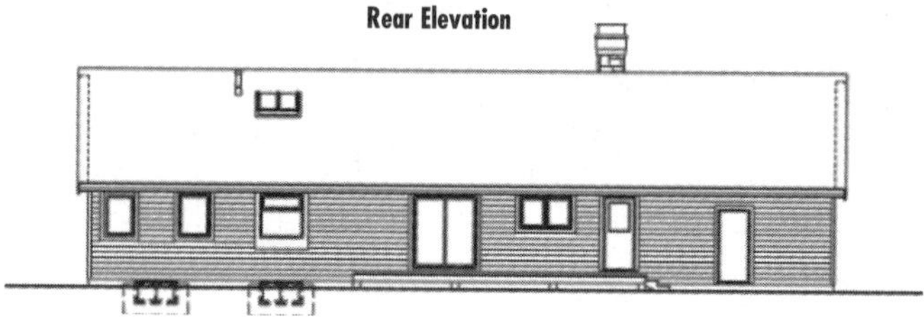

F
HW

Alternate layout for crawlspace option

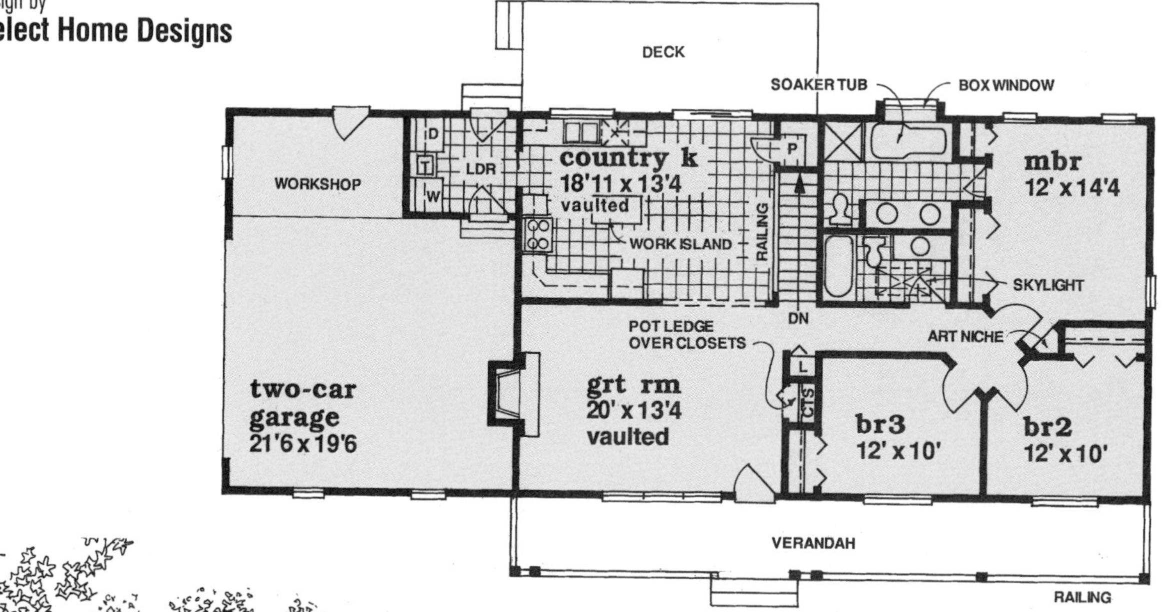
DECK
SOAKER TUB
BOX WINDOW
WORKSHOP
D
T
W
LDR
country k
18'11 x 13'4
vaulted
P
WORK ISLAND
RAILING
mbr
12' x 14'4
SKYLIGHT
DN
POT LEDGE OVER CLOSETS
ART NICHE
L
CTS
two-car garage
21'6 x 19'6
grt rm
20' x 13'4
vaulted
br3
12' x 10'
br2
12' x 10'
VERANDAH
RAILING

Width 70'-0"
Depth 34'-0"

© Copyright Select Home Designs. All rights reserved.

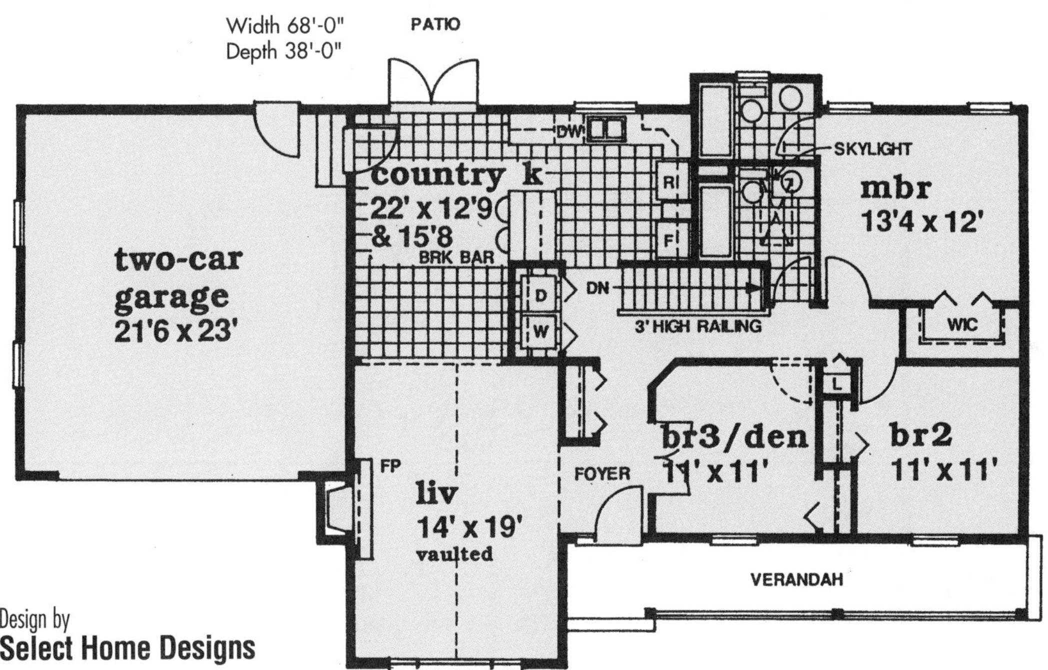
Width 68'-0"
Depth 38'-0"
PATIO
DW
country k
22' x 12'9
& 15'8
BRK BAR
RI
F
SKYLIGHT
mbr
13'4 x 12'
two-car
garage
21'6 x 23'
D
W
DN
3' HIGH RAILING
WIC
L
br3/den
11' x 11'
br2
11' x 11'
FP
FOYER
liv
14' x 19'
vaulted
VERANDAH
Design by
Select Home Designs

Design Q447

Square Footage: 1,428

■ This clever one-story ranch features a covered veranda at the front to enhance outdoor livability. The entry opens to a foyer that leads into a vaulted living room with fireplace on the left and a den or third bedroom on the right. The country kitchen is found to the back and is highlighted by a breakfast bar and sliding glass door to the rear patio. The hallway contains an open-railed stairway to the basement and a laundry alcove, plus coat closet. Bedrooms are large and have ample closet space. The master bedroom features a walk-in closet and a full, private bath. Family bedrooms share the use of a skylit main bath. A two-car garage handles the family vehicles and faces front for convenience. Plans include details for both a basement and a crawlspace foundation.

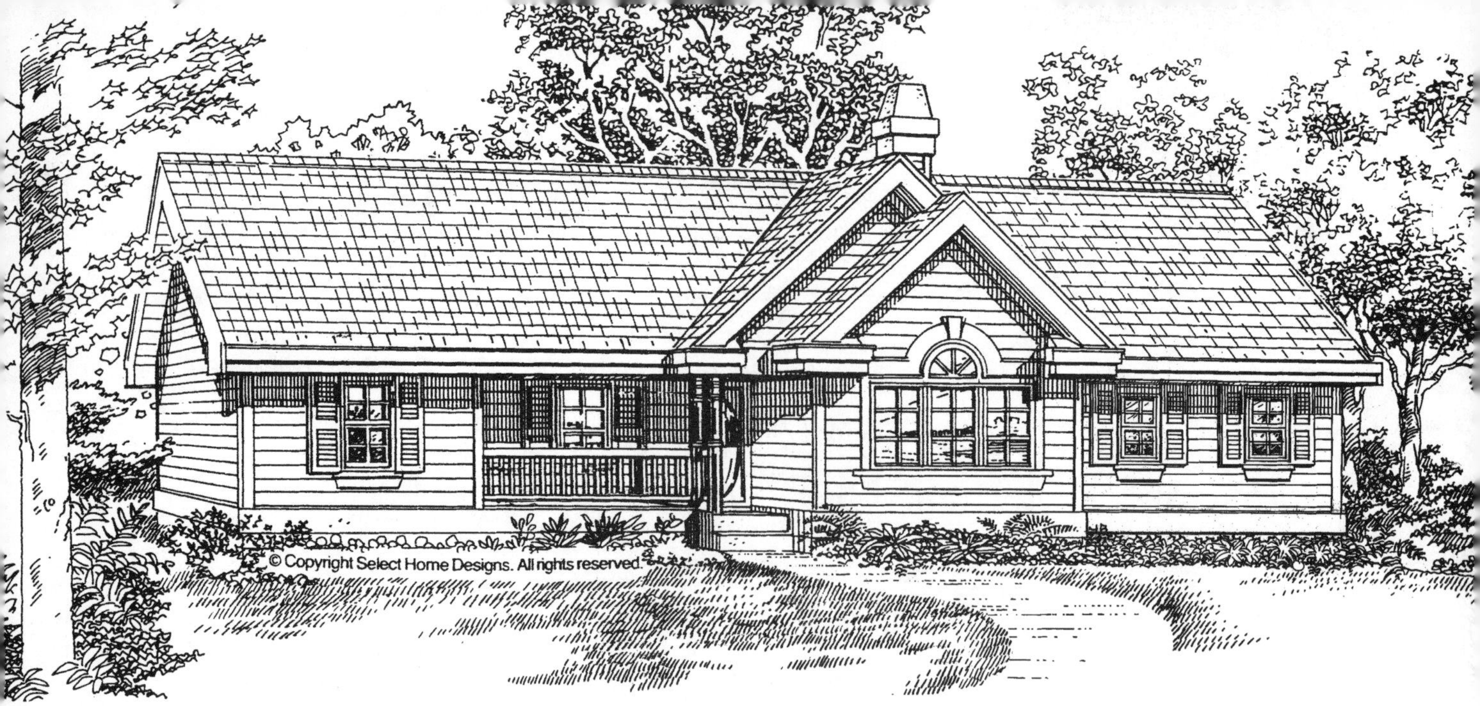

Design by
Select Home Designs

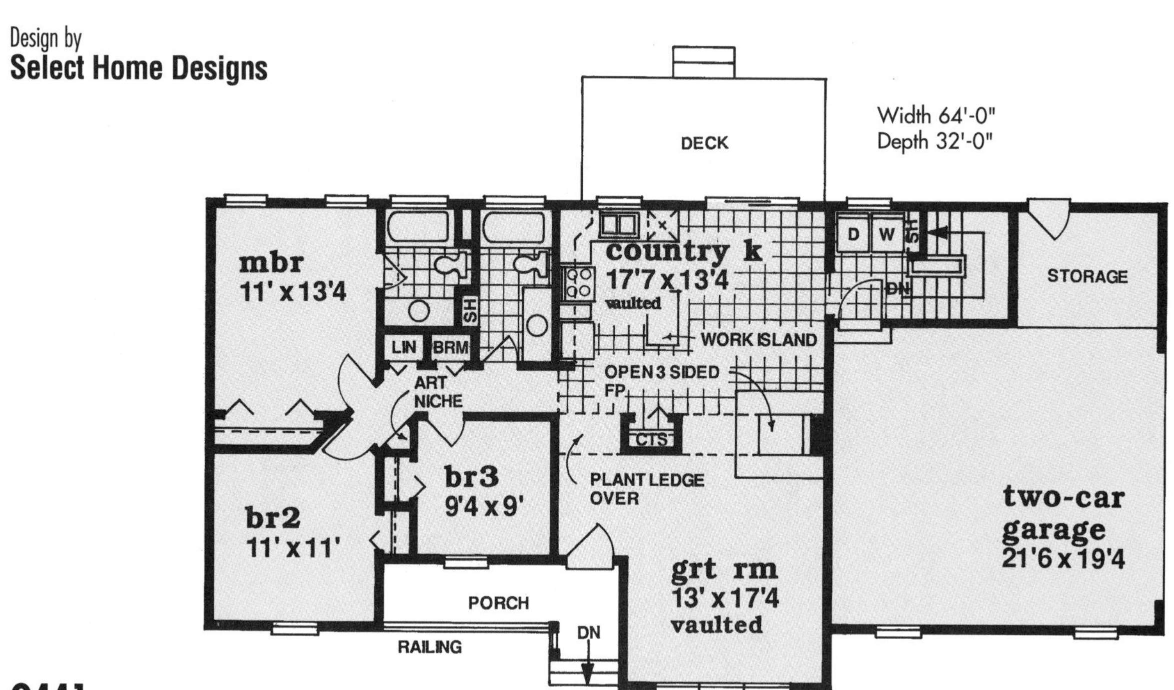

Width 64'-0"
Depth 32'-0"
DECK
mbr
11' x 13'4
country k
17'7 x 13'4
vaulted
D
W
SH
DN
STORAGE
SH
LIN
BRM
WORK ISLAND
OPEN 3 SIDED FP
ART NICHE
CTS
br3
9'4 x 9'
PLANT LEDGE OVER
br2
11' x 11'
two-car garage
21'6 x 19'4
grt rm
13' x 17'4
vaulted
PORCH
RAILING
DN

Design Q441

Square Footage: 1,265

■ This compact, country home is perfect as a starter design or for empty-nesters. Detailing on the outside includes a covered porch, shuttered windows and a Palladian-style window at the great room. The front entry opens directly into the great room, which is vaulted and features a three-sided fireplace which it shares with the country kitchen. A deck just beyond the kitchen will serve as an outdoor dining spot, accessed easily through sliding glass doors. The kitchen itself is L-shaped and has a handy work island. A nearby laundry area holds the stairway to the basement and access to the two-car garage with storage space. Three bedrooms include two family bedrooms and a full bath, plus a master bedroom with private bath. Plans include details for both a basement and a crawlspace foundation.

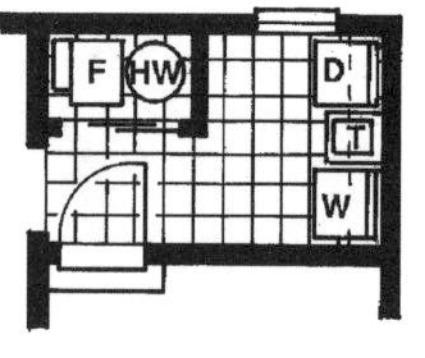

F
HW
D
T
W

Alternate layout for crawlspace option

Design Q443

Square Footage: 1,298

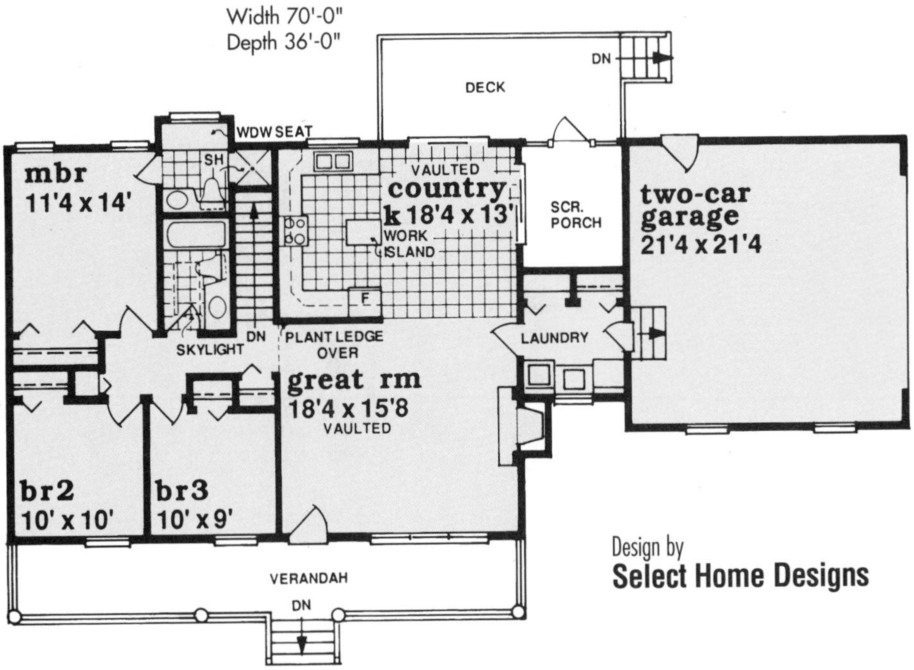

Width 70'-0"
Depth 36'-0"

DECK
DN
WDW SEAT
SH
mbr 11'4 x 14'
VAULTED
country k 18'4 x 13'
WORK ISLAND
F
SCR. PORCH
two-car garage 21'4 x 21'4
SKYLIGHT
DN
PLANT LEDGE OVER
LAUNDRY
great rm 18'4 x 15'8
VAULTED
br2 10' x 10'
br3 10' x 9'
VERANDAH
DN

Design by
Select Home Designs

■ A front veranda, cedar lattice and solid stone chimney enhance the appeal of this one-story country-style home. The open plan begins with the great room which has a fireplace and a plant ledge over the wall separating the living space from the country kitchen. The kitchen is U-shaped and has an island work counter and sliding glass doors to the rear deck and a screened porch. Vaulted ceilings in both the kitchen and great room add spaciousness. Look for three bedrooms, clustered together at the left of the plan. Family bedrooms feature wall closets and share the use of a skylit main bath. The master suite also has a wall closet and a private bath with window seat. The two-car garage is reached via the service entrance where there is a convenient laundry with utility closets. Plans for both a basement and a crawlspace foundation are included.

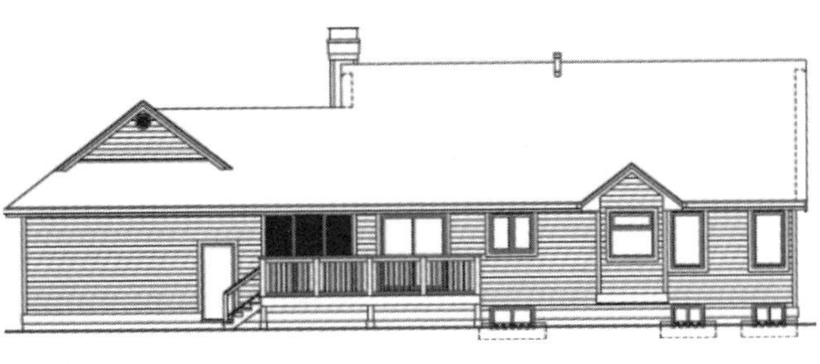

Rear Elevation

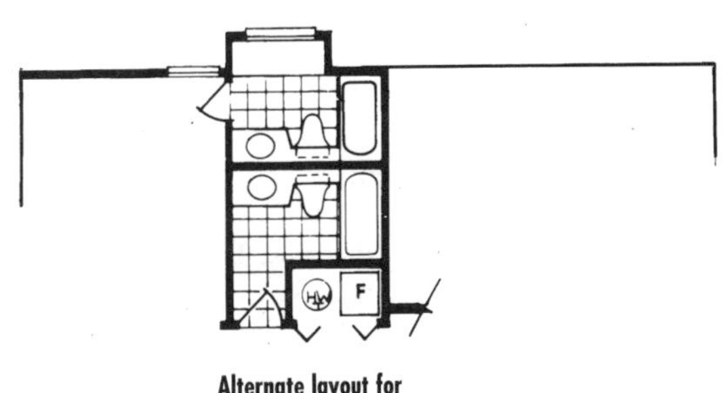

Alternate layout for crawlspace option

Design 3460

Square Footage: 1,389

L

■ A double dose of charm, this special farmhouse plan offers two elevations in its blueprint package. Though rooflines and porch options are different, the floor plan is basically the same and very livable. A formal living room has a warming fireplace and a delightful bay window. The kitchen separates this area from the more casual family room. Three bedrooms include two family bedrooms served by a full, shared bath and a lovely master suite with its own private bath. Each room has a vaulted ceiling and large windows to let the outdoors in beautifully.

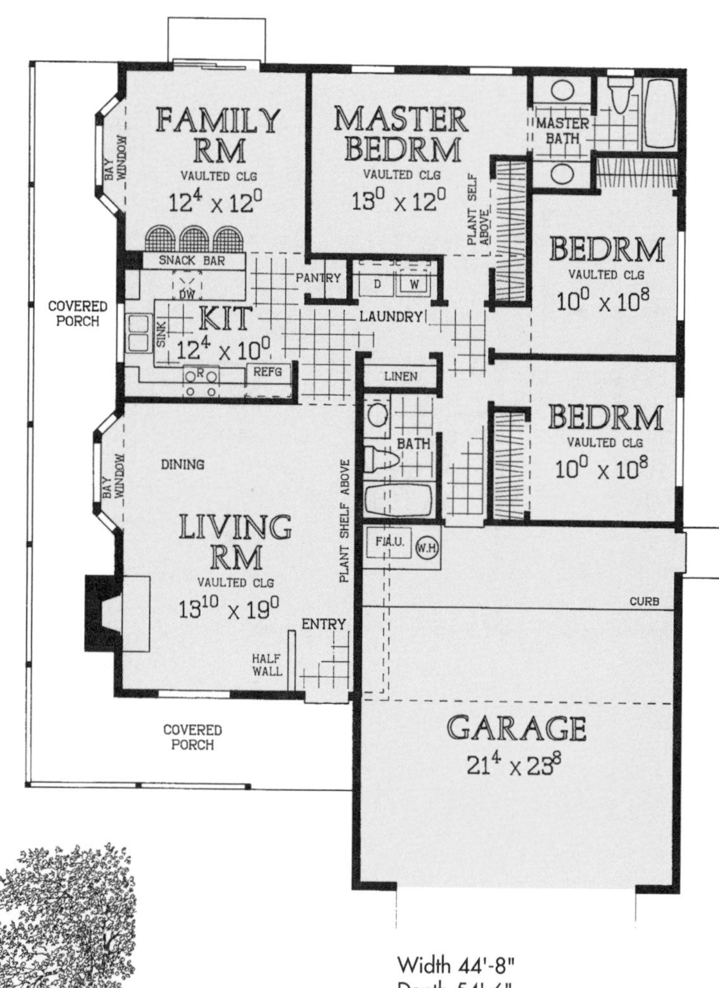

FAMILY RM
VAULTED CLG
$12^{4} \times 12^{0}$
BAY WINDOW
MASTER BEDRM
VAULTED CLG
$13^{0} \times 12^{0}$
PLANT SELF ABOVE
MASTER BATH
BEDRM
VAULTED CLG
$10^{0} \times 10^{8}$
SNACK BAR
PANTRY
D
W
DW
COVERED PORCH
KIT
$12^{4} \times 10^{0}$
SINK
R
REFG
LAUNDRY
LINEN
BATH
BEDRM
VAULTED CLG
$10^{0} \times 10^{8}$
DINING
BAY WINDOW
LIVING RM
VAULTED CLG
$13^{10} \times 19^{0}$
PLANT SHELF ABOVE
F.A.U.
W.H.
CURB
ENTRY
HALF WALL
COVERED PORCH
GARAGE
$21^{4} \times 23^{8}$

Width 44'-8"
Depth 54'-6"

Alternate Elevation

Design by
Home Planners

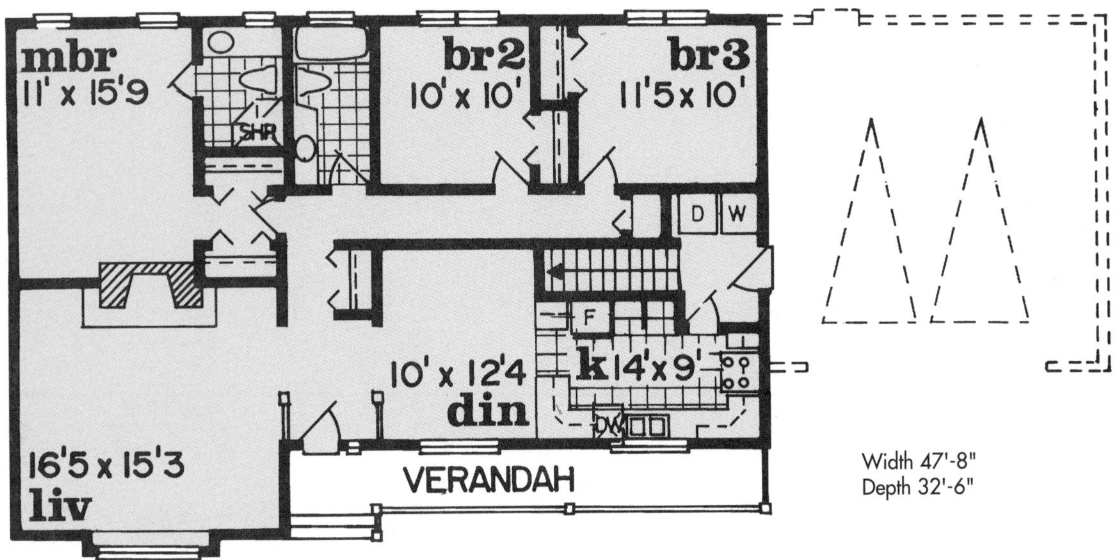
mbr
11' x 15'9
SHR
br2
10' x 10'
br3
11'5 x 10'
D
W
F
k 14' x 9'
10' x 12'4
din
DW
16'5 x 15'3
liv
VERANDAH
Width 47'-8"
Depth 32'-6"

Design Q273

Square Footage: 1,383

Enhanced by farmhouse details—turned spindles on a covered porch and gable trim—this compact home is as pleasing as it is affordable. The entry opens to a center hall with a living room on one side and dining room on the other. The living room features a box-bay window and warming fireplace. The dining room attaches to the U-shaped kitchen. A handy laundry area with access to the two-car garage (optional) is nearby. The three bedrooms stretch out along the rear width of the home. The master suite has a private bath and wall closet. Two family bedrooms also have wall closets and share the use of a full bath. The basement may be finished later for additional living or sleeping space.

Design by
Select Home Designs

Design Q445

Square Footage: 1,360

Smaller in size, but big on livability, this one-story home has amenities and options usually found only in larger homes. Begin with the covered veranda and its entry to a central foyer. On the right is a vaulted living room with central fireplace. On the left, a bedroom—or make it a den. A hall closet holds coats and other outdoor gear. The country kitchen lives up to its name. It features an open-railed stair to the basement, an L-shaped work counter, a breakfast snack island and a bayed breakfast nook with double-door access to the backyard. The two family bedrooms share a full main bath, while the master bedroom has a private bath. A two-car garage sits to the side of the plan. Plans include details for both a basement and a crawlspace foundation.

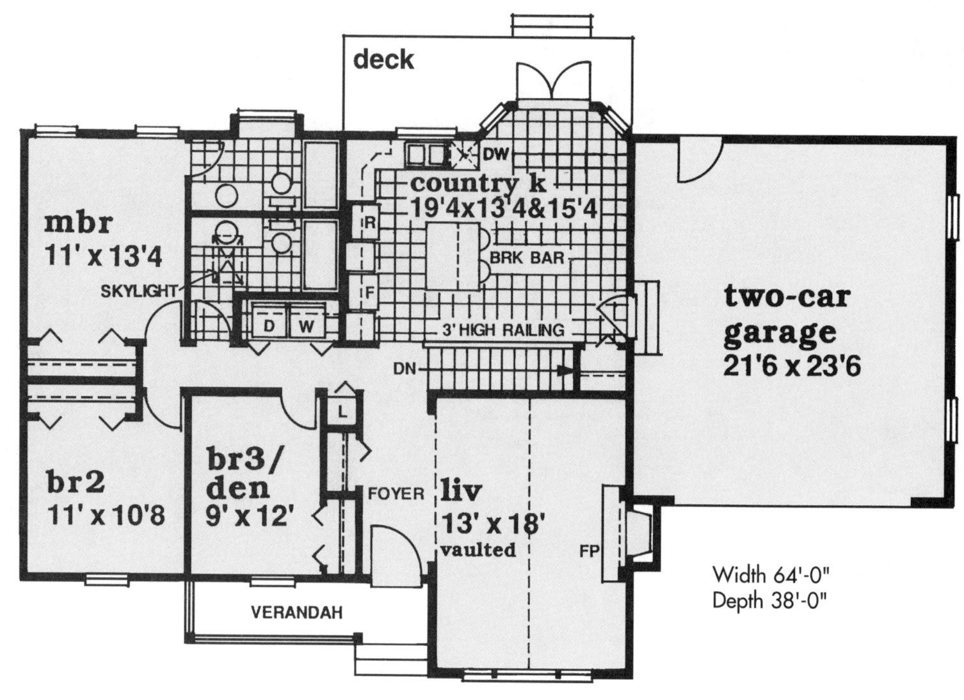
deck
DW
country k
19'4x13'4&15'4
R
F
BRK BAR
3' HIGH RAILING
mbr
11' x 13'4
SKYLIGHT
D
W
two-car
garage
21'6 x 23'6
DN
L
br2
11' x 10'8
br3/
den
9' x 12'
FOYER
liv
13' x 18'
vaulted
FP
VERANDAH
Width 64'-0"
Depth 38'-0"

Design by
Select Home Designs

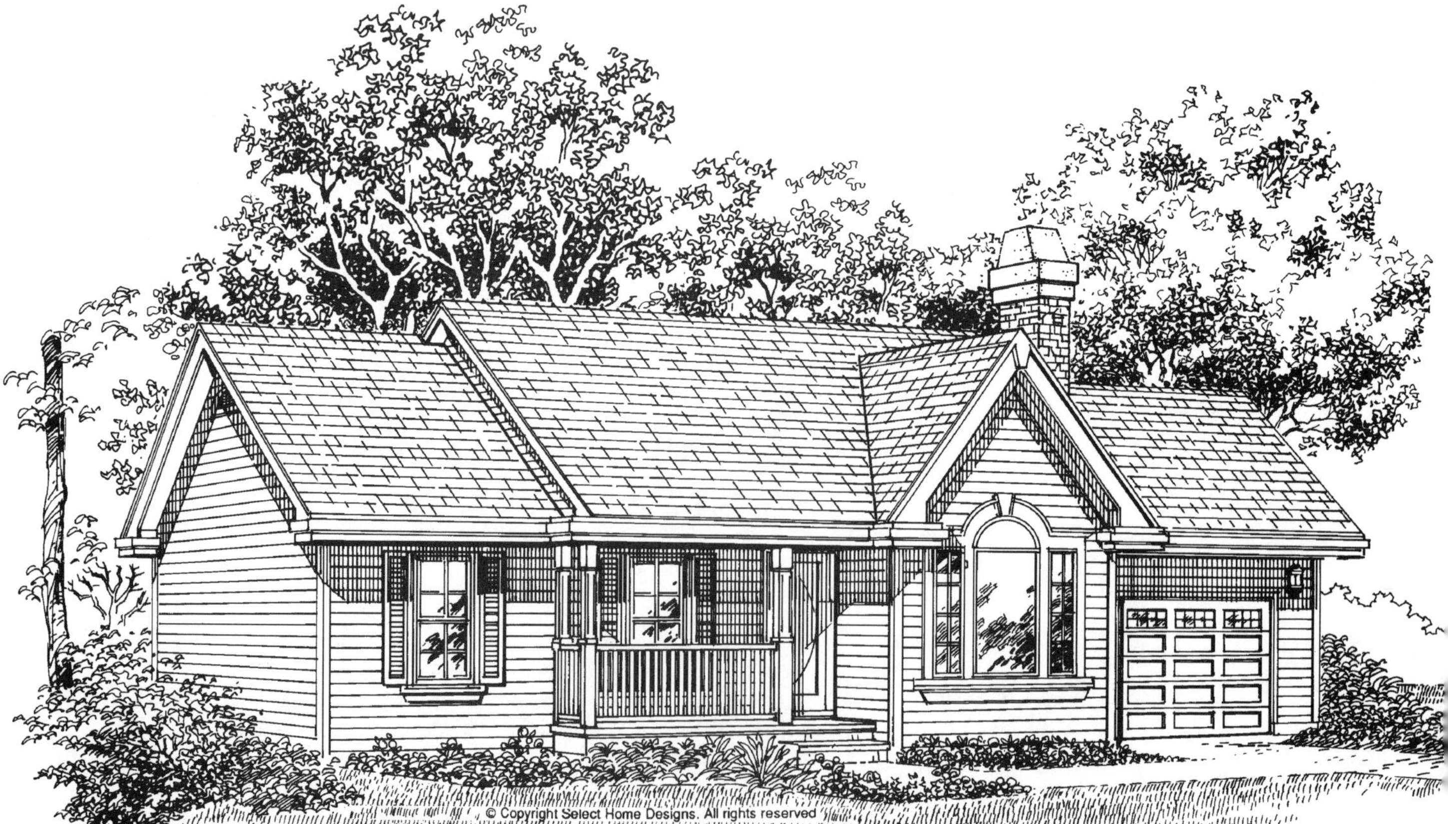

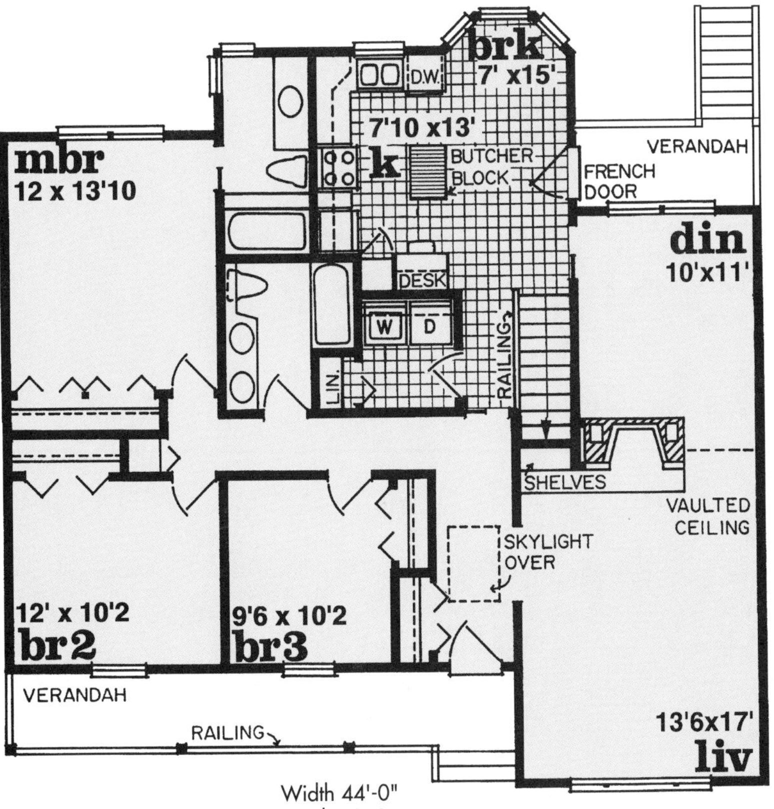
brk
7' x15'
D.W.
7'10 x13'
k
BUTCHER BLOCK
VERANDAH
FRENCH DOOR
mbr
12 x 13'10
din
10'x11'
DESK
W
D
RAILING
LIN.
SHELVES
VAULTED CEILING
SKYLIGHT OVER
12' x 10'2
br2
9'6 x 10'2
br3
VERANDAH
RAILING
13'6x17'
liv

Width 44'-0"
Depth 43'-0"

Design Q252

Square Footage: 1,475

A railed veranda, turned posts, and filigree in the corner and at the gable points complement a lovely Palladian window on the exterior of this home. The interior opens with a skylit foyer and living and dining rooms to the right. The living room is vaulted and features a fireplace and built-in bookshelves. The dining room overlooks a covered veranda accessed through a door in the breakfast room (note the bayed eating area). The kitchen takes advantage of this veranda access, as well. It is further enhanced by an L-shaped work area and butcher-block island. The bedrooms are clustered to the left of the plan. They include a master suite with full bath and two family bedrooms sharing a full bath with double vanity. Plans include details for both a basement and a crawlspace foundation.

Design by
Select Home Designs

Rear Elevation

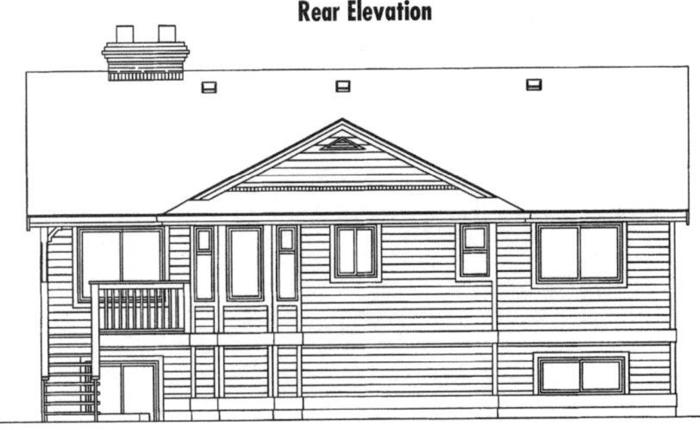

Design Q250

Square Footage: 1,399

Classic floor planning dominates this ideal one-story starter home, but the exterior is worthy of consideration as well. It features a Palladian window, a covered veranda and multi-paned windows. The entry opens to a central foyer flanked by a living room with fireplace on the left and formal dining room on the right. Across the hall is the U-shaped kitchen and breakfast room with sliding glass doors to the rear terrace. A laundry area has access to the two-car garage and to the rear yard. There are three bedrooms and two full baths. The master bedroom has a large wall closet and private bath. Family bedrooms share a full bath. A full basement can be developed at a later time, if needed. Or, choose a crawlspace foundation—plans include details for both.

Design by
Select Home Designs

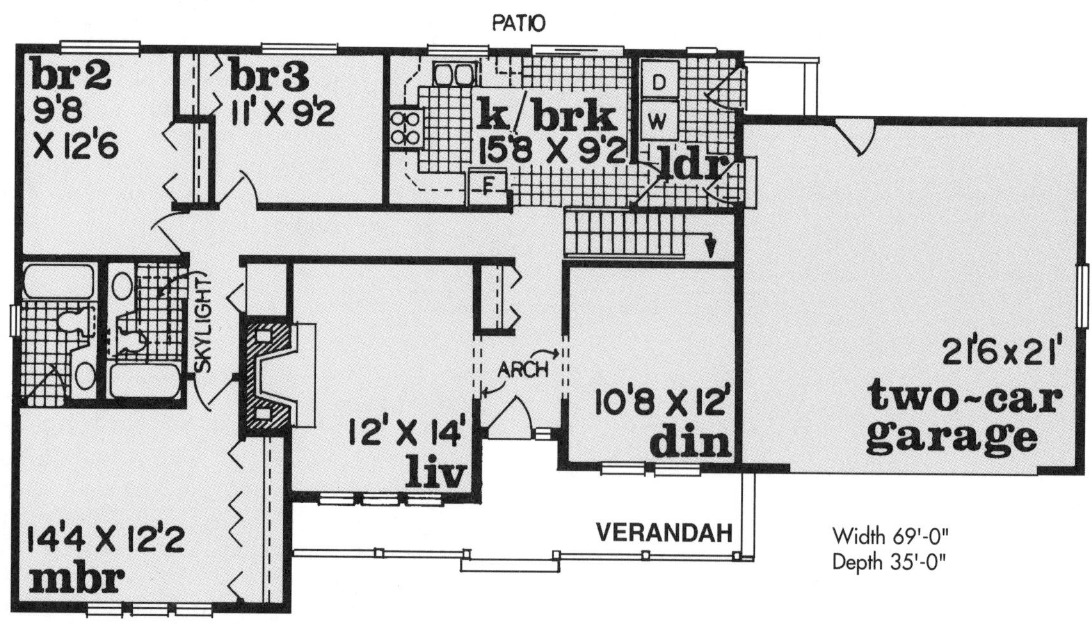
PATIO
br2
9'8
X 12'6
br3
11' X 9'2
k/brk
15'8 X 9'2
D
W
ldr
F
SKYLIGHT
ARCH
12' X 14'
liv
10'8 X 12'
din
21'6 x 21'
two-car
garage
14'4 X 12'2
mbr
VERANDAH

Width 69'-0"
Depth 35'-0"

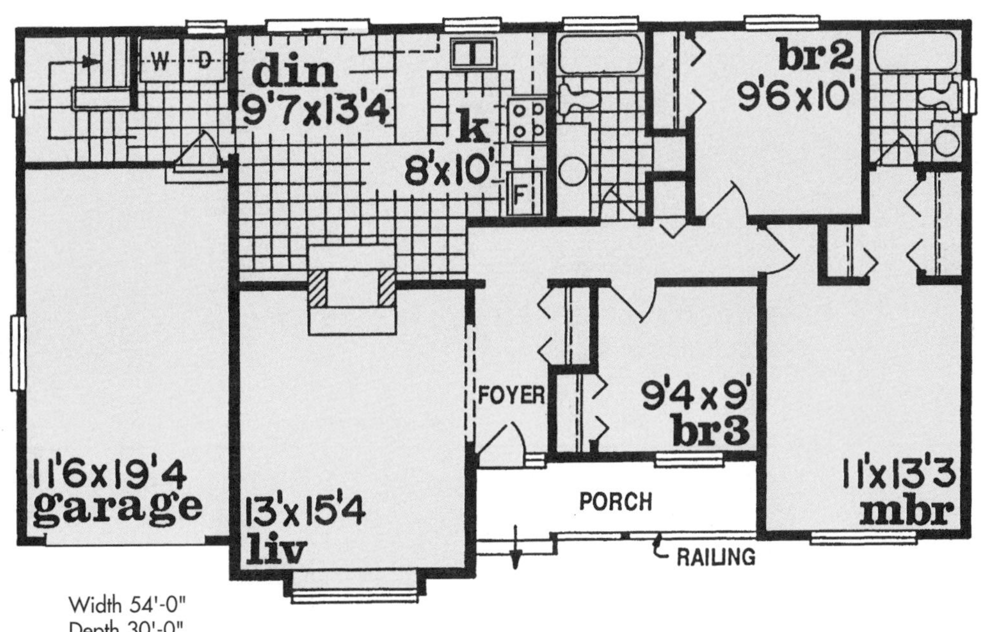
W
D
din
9'7x13'4
k
8'x10'
F
br2
9'6x10'
FOYER
9'4x9'
br3
11'6x19'4
garage
13'x15'4
liv
PORCH
RAILING
11'x13'3
mbr

Width 54'-0"
Depth 30'-0"

Design Q346

Square Footage: 1,233

A covered railed veranda, shuttered windows, siding and wood detailing and a Palladian window all lend their charm to this one-story ranch. The living room shares a through-fireplace with the dining area and also has a box-bay at the front. A U-shaped kitchen is efficient and pleasant with a window to the backyard over the sink. Garage access is through the laundry room, where you will also find stairs to the basement. The three bedrooms are on the right side of the plan. The master has two wall closets and a private bath. Family bedrooms share a full hall bath. A single-car garage sits to the side for convenience. If you choose, the basement can be developed later for additional space.

Design by
Select Home Designs

Design Q222

Square Footage: 1,356

Charmingly compact, this easy-to-build design is ideal for first-time homeowners. The exterior is appealing with a brick facade, horizontal wood siding on the sides, a large brick chimney and a full-width covered veranda. The living room/dining room combination is warmed by a masonry fireplace and includes an optional spindle screen wall at the entry. A country kitchen has ample counter space, a U-shaped work area and dining space. Outdoor access can also be found here. Three bedrooms include a master suite with private bath and two family bedrooms sharing a full hall bath. Each bedroom has a roomy wall closet. Stairs to the basement are located in the kitchen area. Or choose the crawlspace foundation—plans include details for both.

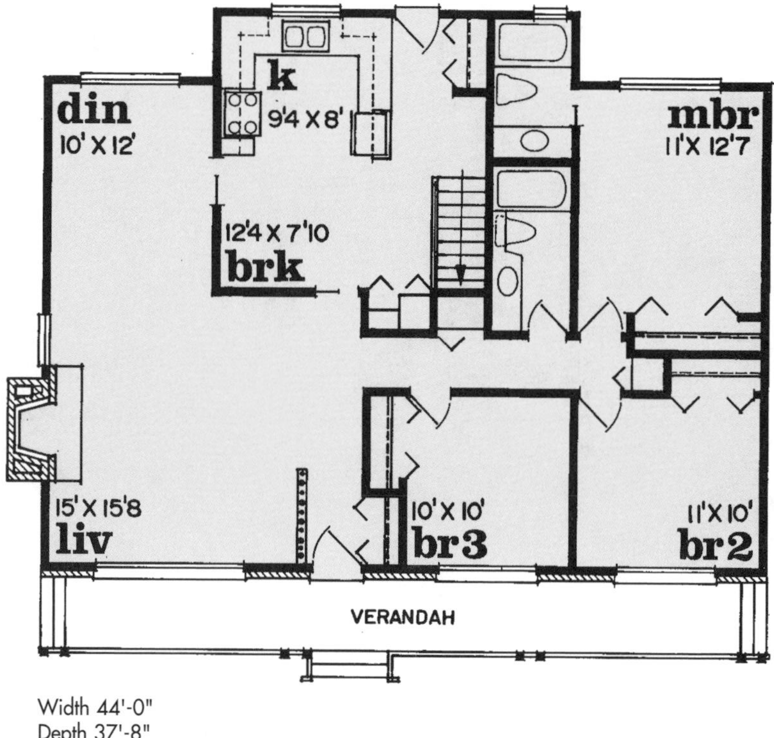
k
9'4 X 8'
din
10' X 12'
mbr
11'X 12'7
12'4 X 7'10
brk
15' X 15'8
liv
10' X 10'
br3
11'X 10'
br2
VERANDAH

Width 44'-0"
Depth 37'-8"

Design by
Select Home Designs

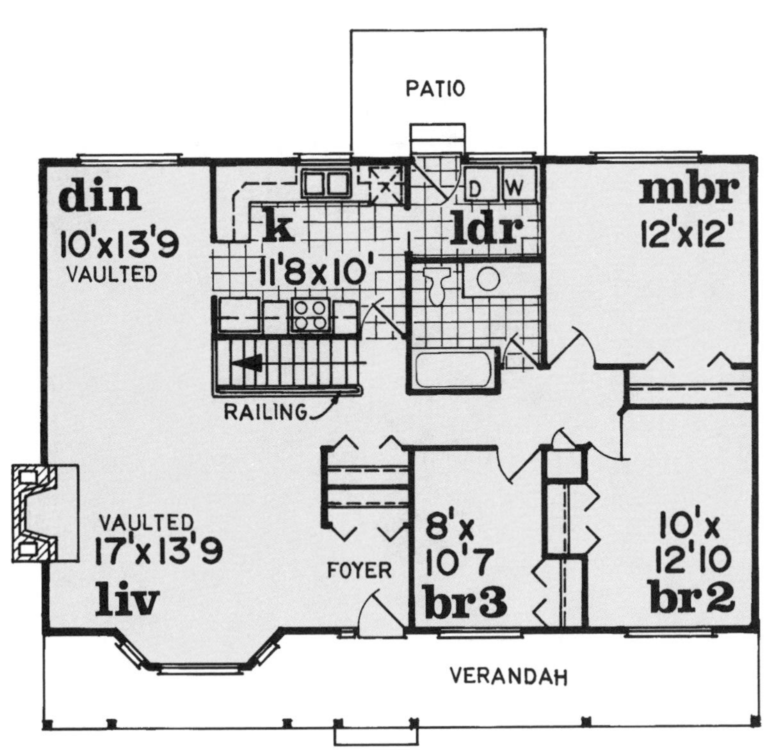
PATIO
din
10'x13'9
VAULTED
k
11'8x10'
ldr
D
W
mbr
12'x12'
RAILING
VAULTED
17'x13'9
liv
FOYER
8'x
10'7
br3
10'x
12'10
br2
VERANDAH

Width 44'-0"
Depth 34'-0"

Design Q313

Square Footage: 1,254

■ Simple details make this starter home quite appealing. A posted front porch, with corner detail, a bay window and shuttered windows all lend a traditional flavor. The central foyer has a coat closet and opens on the left to a vaulted living room with fireplace. The dining room is also vaulted, but overlooks the backyard. An L-shaped kitchen and attached laundry share access to the back patio through a door between them. An additional hall closet sits at the beginning of its stretch to three bedrooms. Each of the bedrooms has a wall closet; two family bedrooms overlook the veranda. All three share the use of a full hall bath. Choose either a basement or crawlspace foundation—plans include details for both.

Design by
Select Home Designs

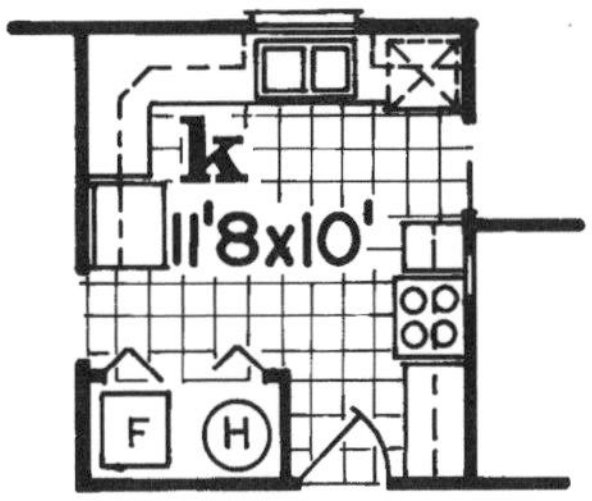

Alternate Layout for Crawlspace

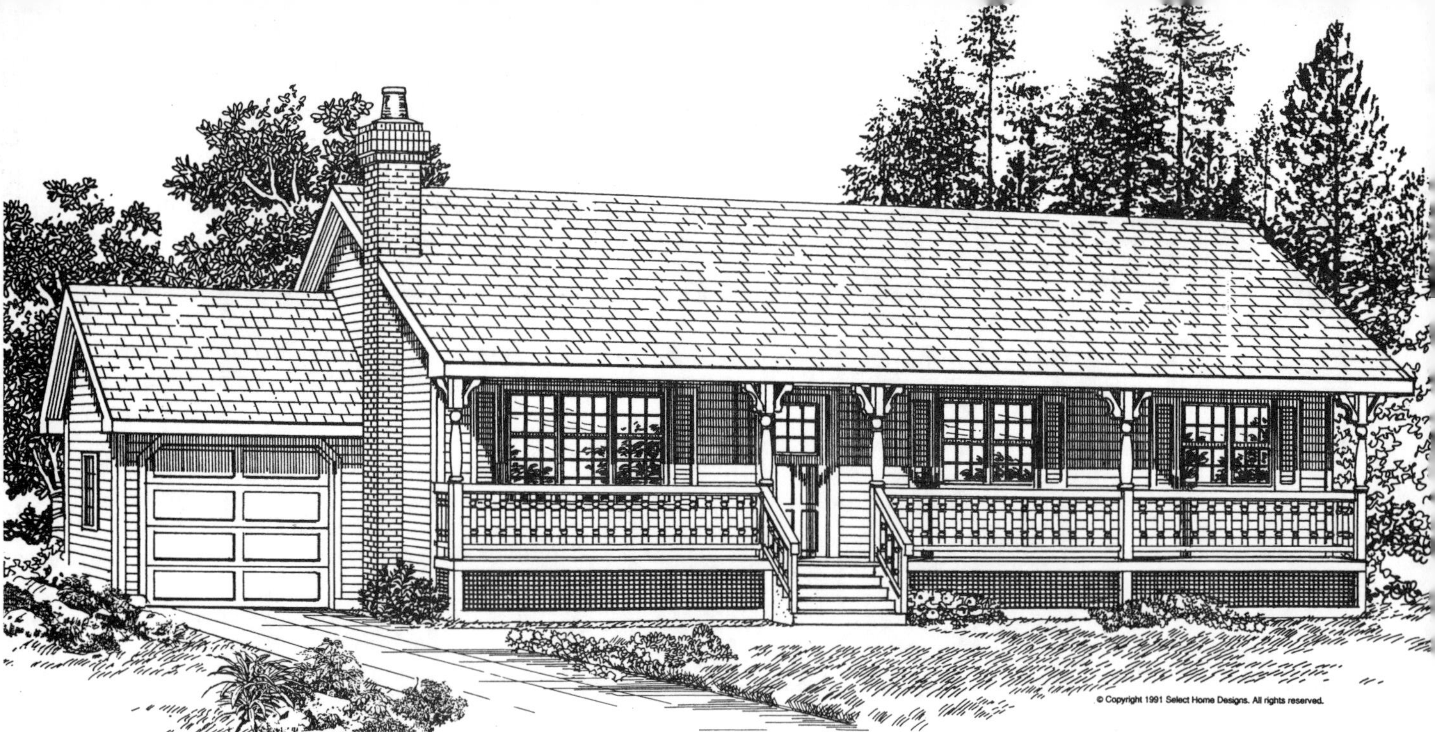

Width 56'-0"
Depth 41'-0"

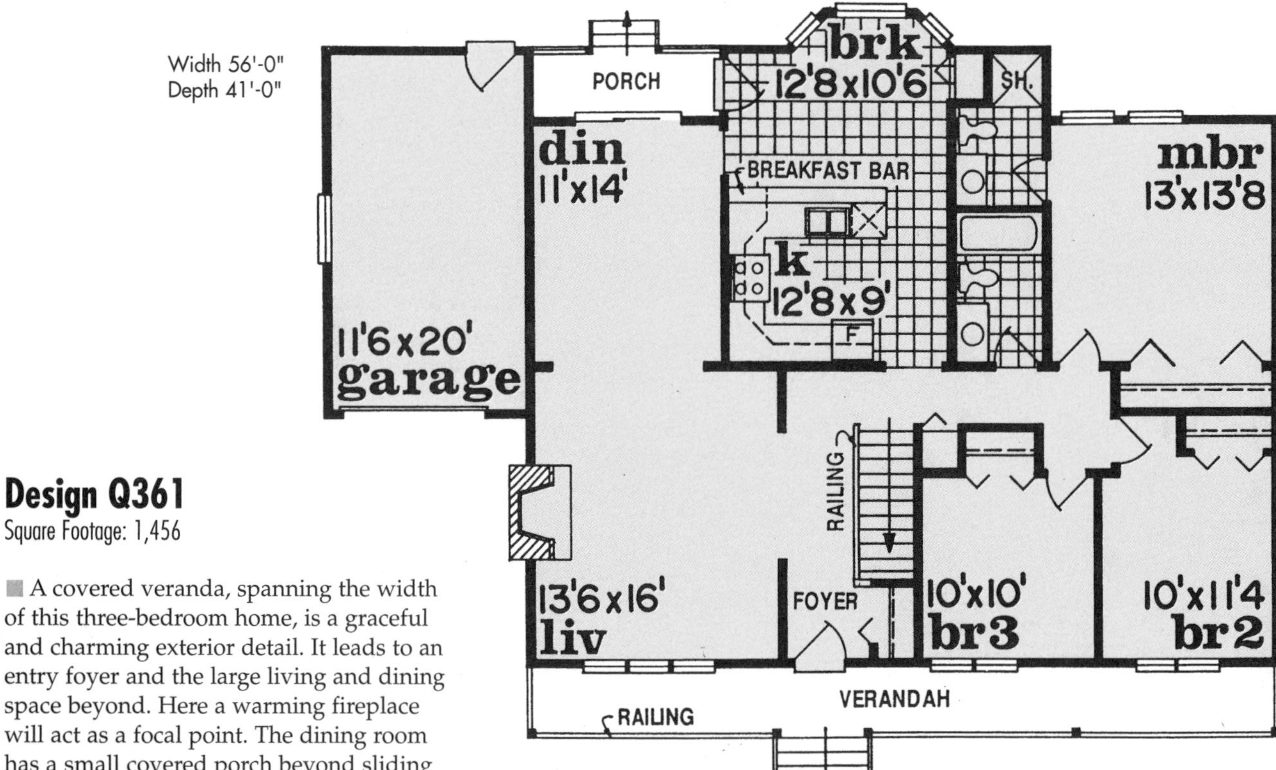
PORCH
brk
12'8x10'6
SH.
din
11'x14'
BREAKFAST BAR
mbr
13'x13'8
k
12'8x9'
F
11'6x20'
garage
RAILING
13'6x16'
liv
FOYER
10'x10'
br3
10'x11'4
br2
VERANDAH
RAILING

Design Q361

Square Footage: 1,456

■ A covered veranda, spanning the width of this three-bedroom home, is a graceful and charming exterior detail. It leads to an entry foyer and the large living and dining space beyond. Here a warming fireplace will act as a focal point. The dining room has a small covered porch beyond sliding glass doors. The U-shaped kitchen has a breakfast bar and serves the dining room and sunny breakfast bay easily. The master bedroom is one of three at the right of the plan and features a wall closet and full bath with shower. Two family bedrooms share use of a full hall bath. A full basement, with open-rail staircase, allows for future expansion. The single-car garage has rear-yard access.

Design by
Select Home Designs

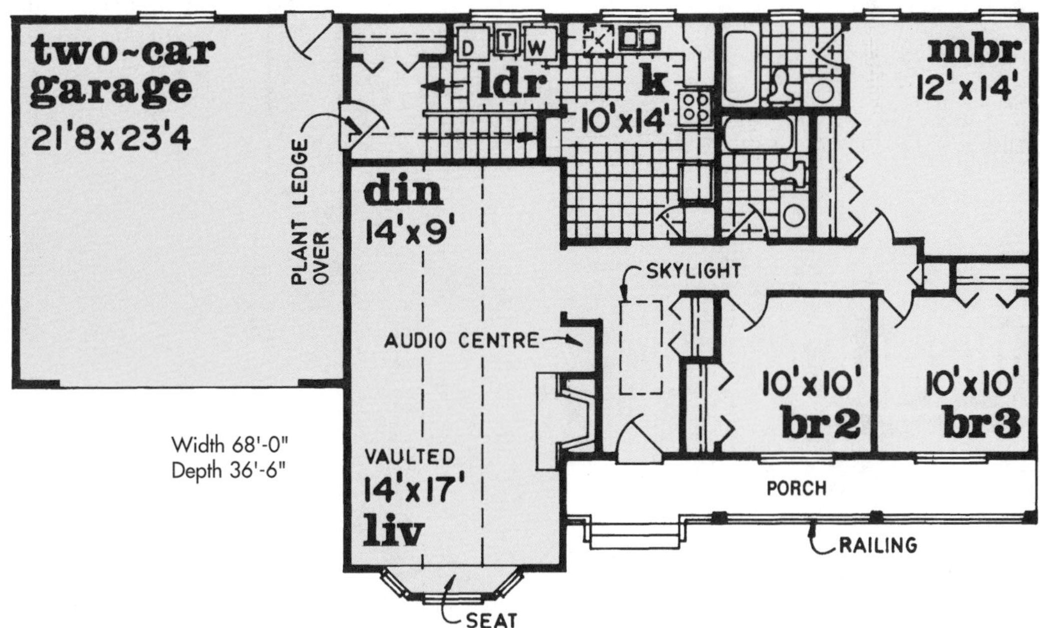
two~car garage
21'8x23'4
PLANT LEDGE OVER
D T W
ldr
k
10'x14'
mbr
12'x14'
din
14'x9'
SKYLIGHT
AUDIO CENTRE
10'x10'
br2
10'x10'
br3
Width 68'-0"
Depth 36'-6"
VAULTED
14'x17'
liv
PORCH
RAILING
SEAT

Design Q318

Square Footage: 1,452

■ This compact three-bedroom home is as economical to build as it beautiful to behold. Its appeal begins right on the outside with a bay window, a half-circle window over the bay and a railed front porch. The entry foyer is skylit and leads to a hallway connecting the living areas with the sleeping quarters. The living room is vaulted and has a fireplace, a built-in audio-visual center and a window seat in the bay window. The open dining room shares the vaulted ceiling. The kitchen, with ample work counters, has plenty of room for a breakfast table. It attaches to a laundry/mud room with storage closet and access to the two-car garage. Stairs to the basement are also found here. Use all three bedrooms or convert Bedroom 2 to a handy den or home office. The master bedroom has a private bath. Plans include details for both a basement and a crawlspace foundation.

Design by
Select Home Designs

Design Q275

Square Footage: 1,525

■ This charming country home is sized right for economy, but leaves out nothing in the way of livability. A bay window, front and rear verandas and a sweeping roof all enrich its heritage design. The front veranda opens to the center hall which leads to the large living and dining areas. A corner fireplace in the living room warms the space in cold winter months. The kitchen and bayed breakfast nook sit to the rear and open to another veranda through double doors. Two family bedrooms are at the back of the plan and share a full hall bath. The master bedroom has a bay window, walk-in closet and private bath. Plans include a single-car option, so you can add on if you choose.

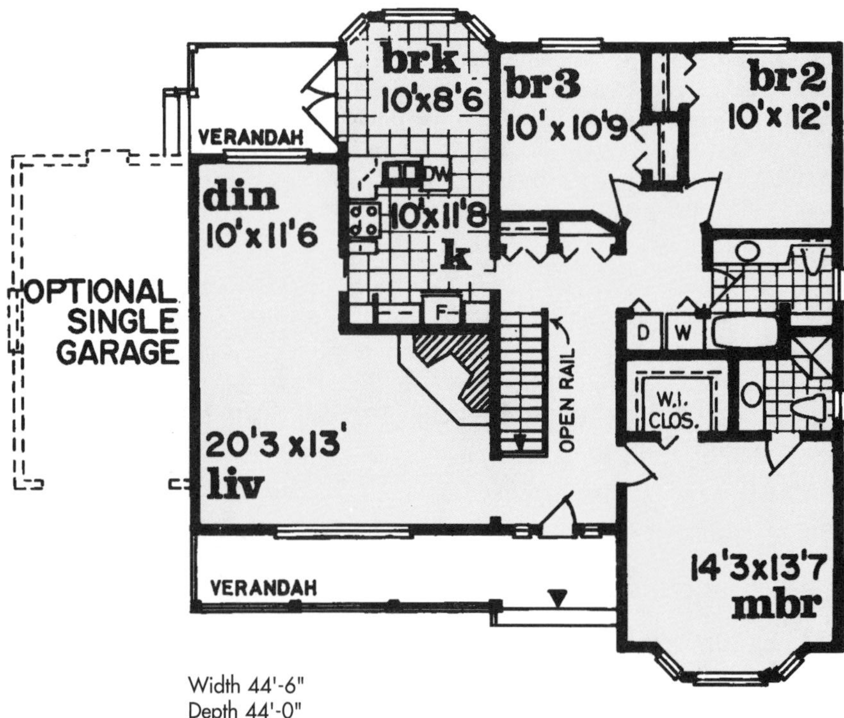

brk
10'x8'6
br3
10' x 10'9
br2
10' x 12'
VERANDAH
DW
din
10' x 11'6
10'x11'8
k
F
OPTIONAL
SINGLE
GARAGE
D
W
W.I.
CLOS.
OPEN RAIL
20'3 x 13'
liv
VERANDAH
14'3x13'7
mbr

Width 44'-6"
Depth 44'-0"

Design by
Select Home Designs

©1990 Select Home Designs. All rights reserved.

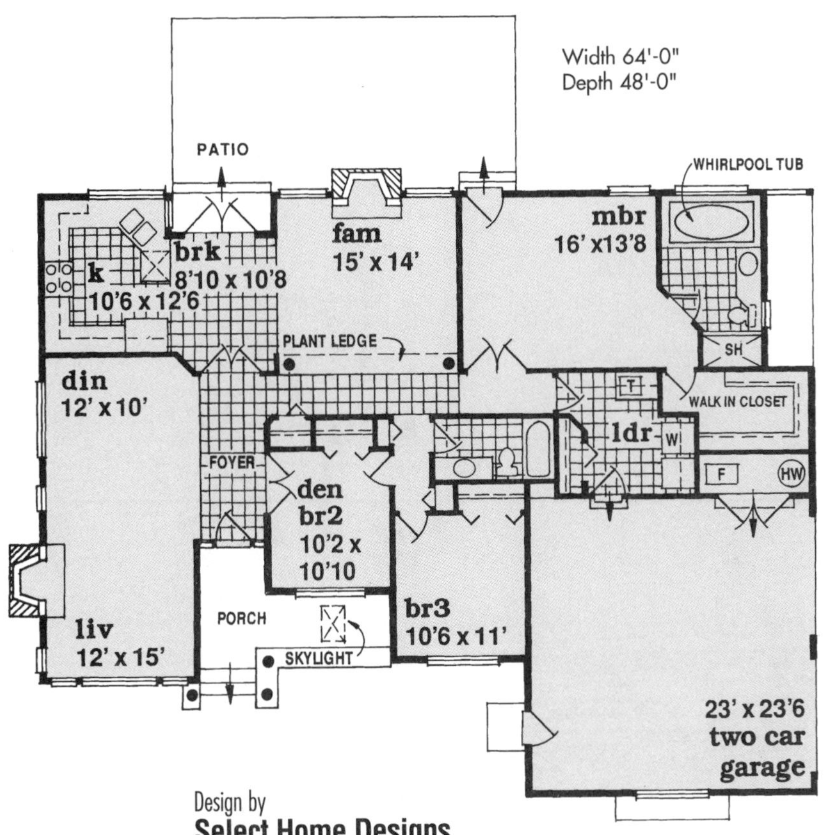
Width 64'-0"
Depth 48'-0"
PATIO
WHIRLPOOL TUB
brk
8'10 x 10'8
k
10'6 x 12'6
fam
15' x 14'
mbr
16' x13'8
PLANT LEDGE
SH
din
12' x 10'
WALK IN CLOSET
ldr
FOYER
den
br2
10'2 x
10'10
F
HW
liv
12' x 15'
PORCH
SKYLIGHT
br3
10'6 x 11'
23' x 23'6
two car
garage

Design by
Select Home Designs

Design Q372

Square Footage: 1,883

■ Finish this home in either California stucco or horizontal siding, with the garage opening to the front or the side of the home. Rooflines vary depending on your choice. The interior retains the same great floor plan. From a skylit, covered porch, the plan begins with a large entry opening to the living room with fireplace and den—or Bedroom 2—which can be accessed through double doors in the entry or a single door in the hall. Decorative columns line the hall and define the family-room space. A fireplace, flanked by windows, is a focal point in this casual living area. The nearby breakfast room opens to the patio and connects the family room to the U-shaped kitchen. The master bedroom is huge—and amenity filled. It also has patio access and features a bath with whirlpool tub, and separate shower. An additional bedroom is served by a full bath. Plans include details for both a basement and a crawlspace foundation.

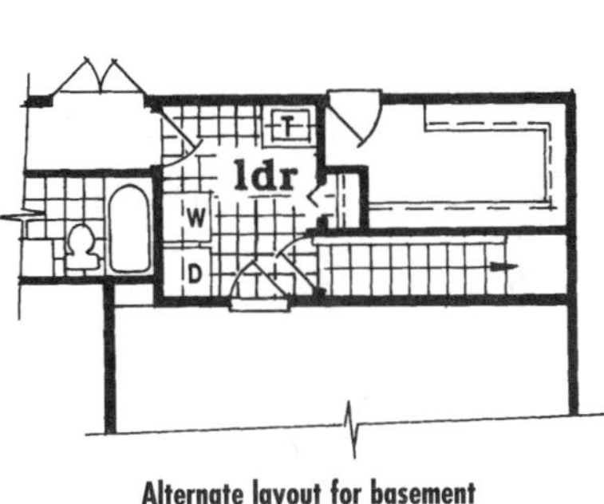
ldr
W
D

Alternate layout for basement

Alternate Front Elevation

Design Q319

Square Footage: 1,501

■ Choose either the California stucco option or the version with horizontal siding and brick for the facade of this home. Details for both are included in the plans. An interesting floor plan awaits inside. A kitchen and breakfast room reside just beyond the entry and are open to a long living room/dining room combination. This area has a vaulted ceiling, a fireplace and access to the rear patio. A plant ledge decorates the hall entry and is lit by a centered skylight. Three bedrooms line the right side of the plan. Family bedrooms share a full hall bath. The master suite is to the rear and has an plant ledge at its entry, a vaulted ceiling and a bath with whirlpool tub. A door to the rear yard brightens the master bedroom. A laundry alcove sits in a service entrance to the two-car garage. If you choose, you may build this plan with a basement that can be expanded at a later time. Or choose the crawlspace foundation—plans include details for both.

Design by
Select Home Designs

Width 39'-0"
Depth 59'-0"

Alternate Elevation

Basement Stair Location

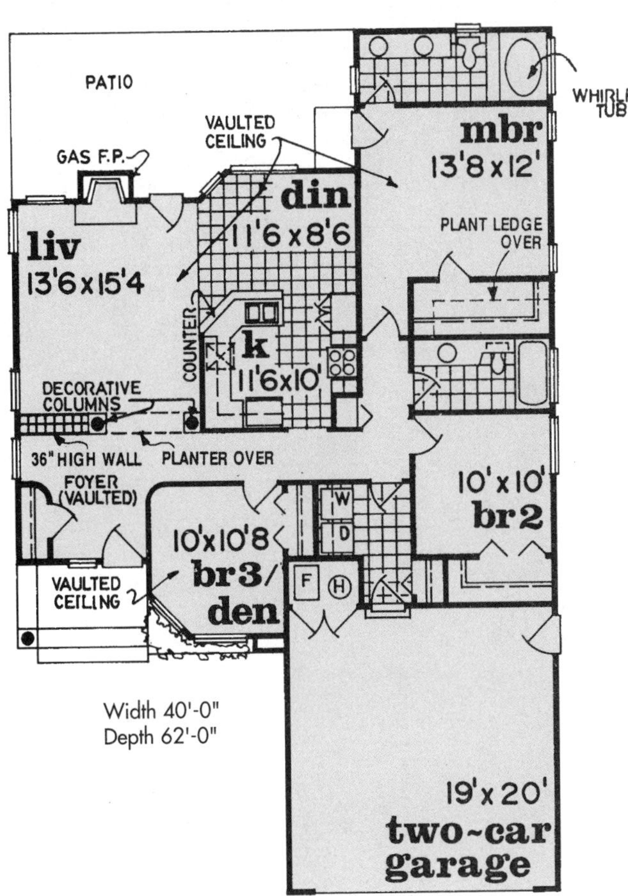
PATIO
VAULTED CEILING
GAS F.P.
WHIRLPOOL TUB
mbr
13'8 x 12'
din
11'6 x 8'6
liv
13'6 x 15'4
PLANT LEDGE OVER
COUNTER
k
11'6 x 10'
DECORATIVE COLUMNS
36" HIGH WALL
PLANTER OVER
FOYER (VAULTED)
10' x 10'
br2
10'x 10'8
br3/
den
VAULTED CEILING
W
D
F
H
19' x 20'
two-car
garage

Width 40'-0"
Depth 62'-0"

Design Q314

Square Footage: 1,365

■ This design offers the option of a traditional wood-sided plan or a cool, stucco version. Details for both facades are included in the plans. The interior offers a very comfortable floor plan in a smaller footprint. The off-set entry is covered and opens to a vaulted foyer with coat closet. Decorative columns and a three-foot high wall mark the boundary of the living room, which is vaulted and warmed by a gas fireplace. The dining area is nearby and connects to a U-shaped kitchen with peninsular counter. Both have cathedral ceilings. A den in the hall might be used as a third bedroom, if you choose. An additional family bedroom has a walk-in closet and full bath nearby. A vaulted ceiling highlights the master bedroom. Additional features here include a walk-in closet and a fully appointed bath. A two-car garage remains in the front of the plan and acts as a shield for the bedrooms. Plans include details for both a basement and a crawlspace foundation.

Design by
Select Home Designs

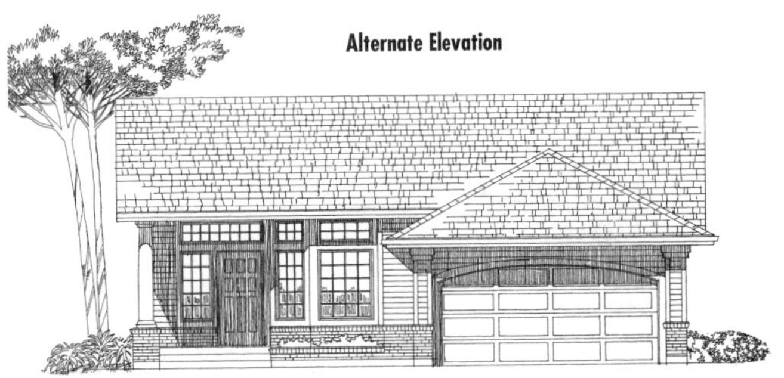
Alternate Elevation

Design 3423

Square Footage: 2,577

■ This spacious Southwestern home will be a pleasure to come home to. Immediately off the foyer are the dining room and step-down living room with bay window. The highlight of the four-bedroom sleeping area is the master suite with porch access and a whirlpool for soaking away the day's worries. The informal living area features an enormous family room with fireplace and bay-windowed kitchen and breakfast room. Notice the snack bar pass-through to the family room.

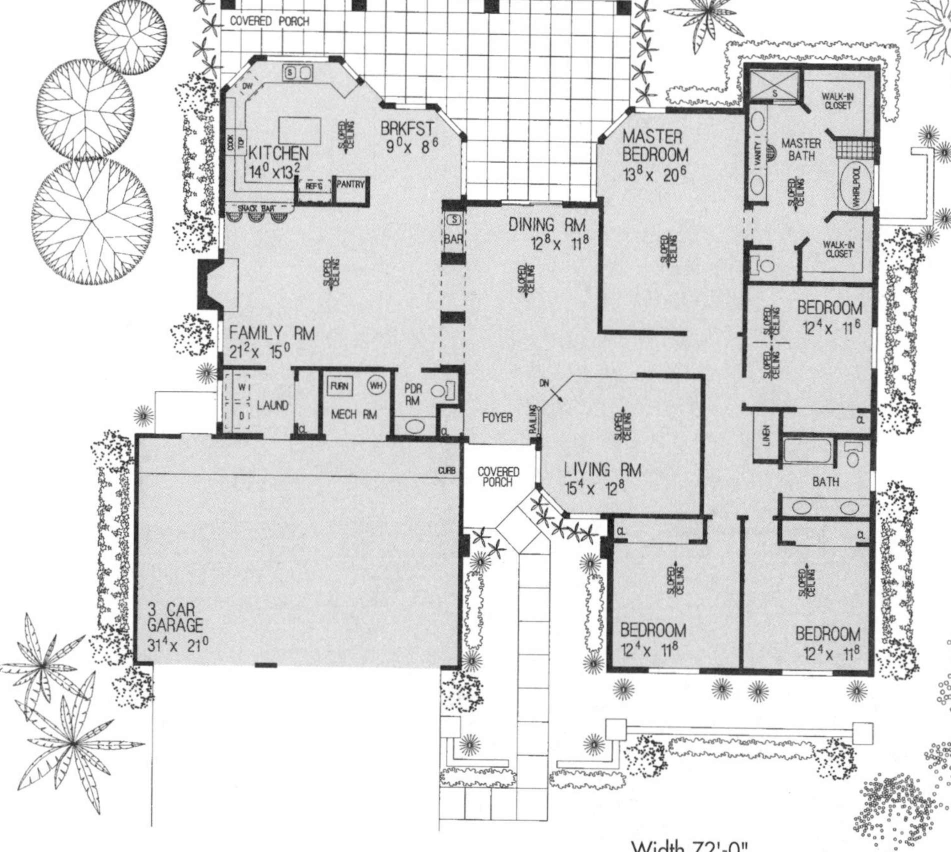

COVERED PORCH
KITCHEN 14^0 x 13^2
BRKFST 9^0 x 8^6
PANTRY
SNACK BAR
BAR
FAMILY RM 21^2 x 15^0
DINING RM 12^8 x 11^8
MASTER BEDROOM 13^8 x 20^6
WALK-IN CLOSET
MASTER BATH
WHIRLPOOL
VANITY
BEDROOM 12^4 x 11^6
LAUND
MECH RM
FURN
WH
PDR RM
FOYER
RAILING
COVERED PORCH
LIVING RM 15^4 x 12^8
LINEN
BATH
CURB
3 CAR GARAGE 31^4 x 21^0
BEDROOM 12^4 x 11^8
BEDROOM 12^4 x 11^8
SLOPED CEILING

Width 72'-0"
Depth 57'-4"

QUOTE ONE®

Cost to build? See page 516 to order complete cost estimate to build this house in your area!

Design by
Home Planners

Design 3413

Square Footage: 2,517

L

■ Though distinctly Southwestern in design, this home has some features that are universally appealing. Note, for instance, the central gallery, perpendicular to the raised entry hall, and running almost the entire width of the house. An L-shaped, angled kitchen serves the breakfast room and family room in equal fashion. Sleeping areas are found in four bedrooms including an optional study and an exquisite master suite.

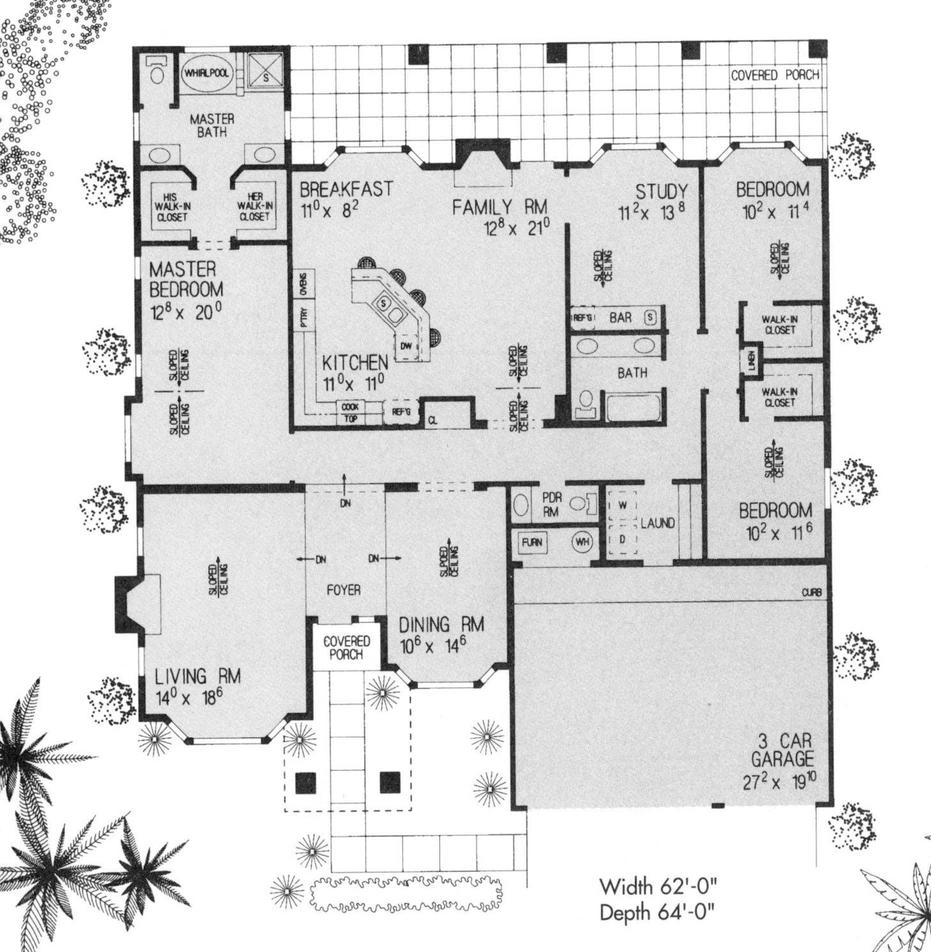

WHIRLPOOL
MASTER BATH
HIS WALK-IN CLOSET
HER WALK-IN CLOSET
COVERED PORCH
BREAKFAST 11^0 x 8^2
FAMILY RM 12^8 x 21^0
STUDY 11^2x 13^8
BEDROOM 10^2 x 11^4
MASTER BEDROOM 12^8 x 20^0
SLOPED CEILING
OVENS
PTRY
KITCHEN 11^0x 11^0
DW
COOK TOP
REF'G
CL
REF'G
BAR
BATH
WALK-IN CLOSET
LINEN
WALK-IN CLOSET
BEDROOM 10^2 x 11^6
DN
PDR RM
FURN
WH
W
D
LAUND
FOYER
DINING RM 10^6 x 14^6
COVERED PORCH
LIVING RM 14^0 x 18^6
CURB
3 CAR GARAGE 27^2 x 19^{10}

Width 62'-0"
Depth 64'-0"

QUOTE ONE®

Cost to build? See page 516 to order complete cost estimate to build this house in your area!

Design by
Home Planners

Design Q334

Square Footage: 2,966

■ Wrapping around a patio courtyard, this three- or four-bedroom home works perfectly in sunny climes. Decorative quoins adorn the exterior, including a wide entry with double doors opening to the foyer. Columns introduce the living room and separate the dining room from the central hall. The living room is further enhanced by skylights, a vaulted ceiling, a fireplace and French doors to the patio beyond. An island kitchen features a peninsular counter overlooking the breakfast room and a roomy pantry. The breakfast room also has double doors to the patio. A nearby family room sports built-ins, another fireplace and more patio access. Bedrooms are split with the family bedrooms—each with its own bath—on the right and the master suite on the left. The master bedroom has a tray ceiling, walk-in closet, patio access and a through-fireplace to the master bath. Look for a spa tub and separate shower here. A cozy den opens through double doors in the master suite entry. The two-car garage is accessed through the service entrance. Plans include details for both a basement and a crawlspace foundation. Details for two elevations are also included.

POOL
SPA
ETCHED GLASS
SH
WHIRLPOOL TUB
SKYLIGHT
FIREPLACE
ENTERTAINMENT CENTER
PATIO
BOOKS
fam 13'x19'10
Width 67'-6"
Depth 81'-0"
mbr 13'9x23'4
brk 10'x8'6
k 13'4x12'6
br2 14'x12'
TRAY CEILING
liv 20'x16'
SKYLIGHTS
VAULTED CEILING
SKYLIGHT
VAN
DECORATIVE COLUMNS
PLANTER OVER
ETCHED GLASS
WALK-IN CLOSET
12'x11'9 den
12'x11'9 din
14'x12' br3
23'6x 20'9 two-car garage
(THREE CAR GARAGE OPTIONAL)

Design by
Select Home Designs

Rear Elevation

Design 3569

Square Footage: 1,981

L D

■ An impressive arched entry graces this transitional one-story design. An elegant foyer introduces an open gathering room/dining room combination. A front-facing study with sloped ceiling could easily be converted to a guest room with a full bath accessible from the rear of the room. In the kitchen, such features as an island cooktop and a built-in desk add style and convenience. A corner bedroom offers front and side views, and the nearby master suite sports a whirlpool bath and walk-in closet, and offers access to the rear terrace. Other special features of the plan include multi-pane windows, a warming fireplace, a cozy covered dining porch and a two-car garage. Note the handy storage closet in the laundry area.

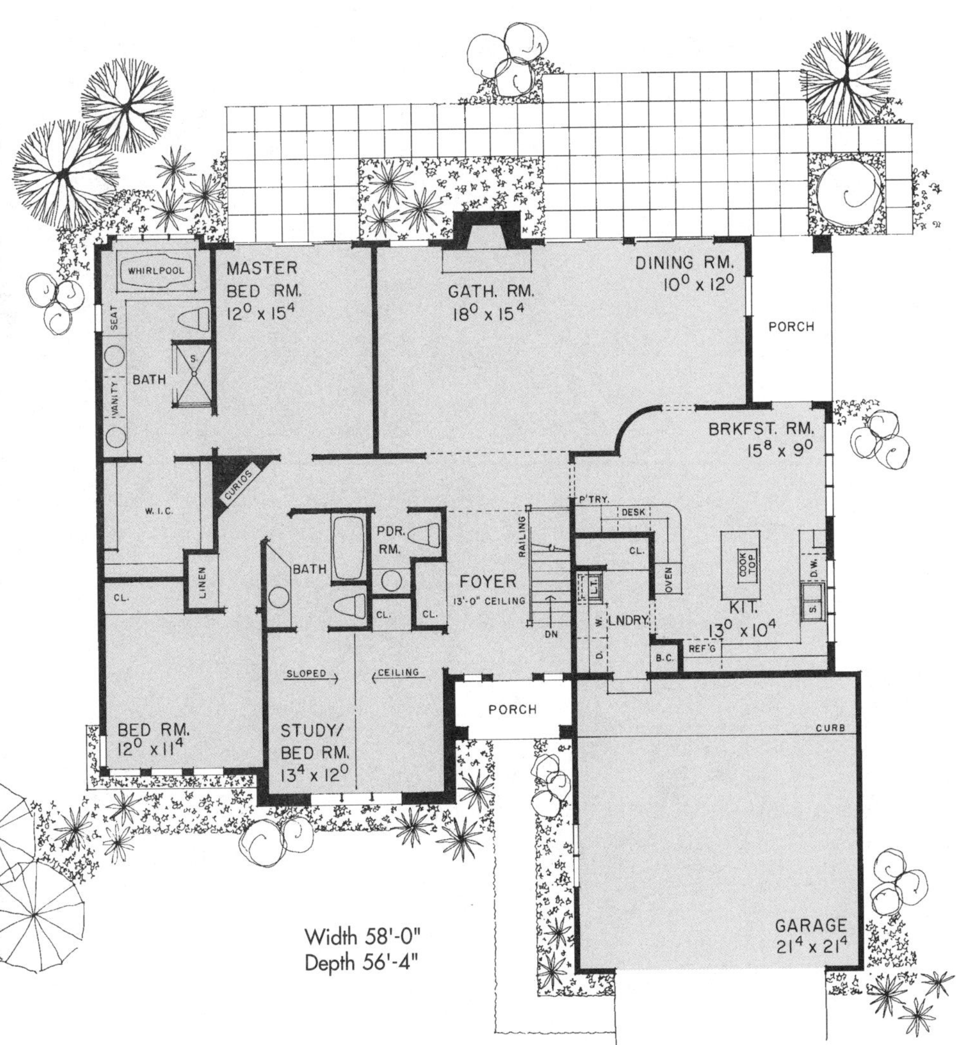
WHIRLPOOL
MASTER BED RM. 12^{0} x 15^{4}
GATH. RM. 18^{0} x 15^{4}
DINING RM. 10^{0} x 12^{0}
PORCH
SEAT
BATH
VANITY
BRKFST. RM. 15^{8} x 9^{0}
W. I. C.
CURIOS
P'TRY.
DESK
PDR. RM.
RAILING
CL.
COOK TOP
BATH
FOYER
13'-0" CEILING
OVEN
D.W.
LINEN
CL.
CL.
CL.
L.T.
W.
LNDRY.
KIT. 13^{0} x 10^{4}
S.
DN
D.
B.C.
REF'G
SLOPED
CEILING
PORCH
CURB
BED RM. 12^{0} x 11^{4}
STUDY/ BED RM. 13^{4} x 12^{0}
GARAGE 21^{4} x 21^{4}
Width 58'-0"
Depth 56'-4"

QUOTE ONE®

Cost to build? See page 516 to order complete cost estimate to build this house in your area!

Design by
Home Planners

Design Q418

Square Footage: 2,761

■ Dramatic rooflines dominate this three-bedroom sun-country design. Interior space begins with a double-door entrance leading directly through the vaulted foyer to a sunken living room with vaulted ceiling and fireplace. A fully glazed wall at one end of the living room allows views to the covered, skylit lanai. A built-in barbecue adds to the fun on the lanai. Decorative columns separate the living room, dining room and Bedroom 3 from the foyer. If you choose, Bedroom 3 could be used as a den. The dining room reaches to the kitchen through a butler's pantry. In the kitchen are snack counters and an attached breakfast room with bay window. A sunken family room is just beyond. It is warmed by a fireplace and has double-door access to a rear patio. Bedrooms include a master suite with hearth-warmed sitting room, lanai access and bath with walk-in closet and whirlpool tub. Plans include details for both a basement and a crawlspace foundation.

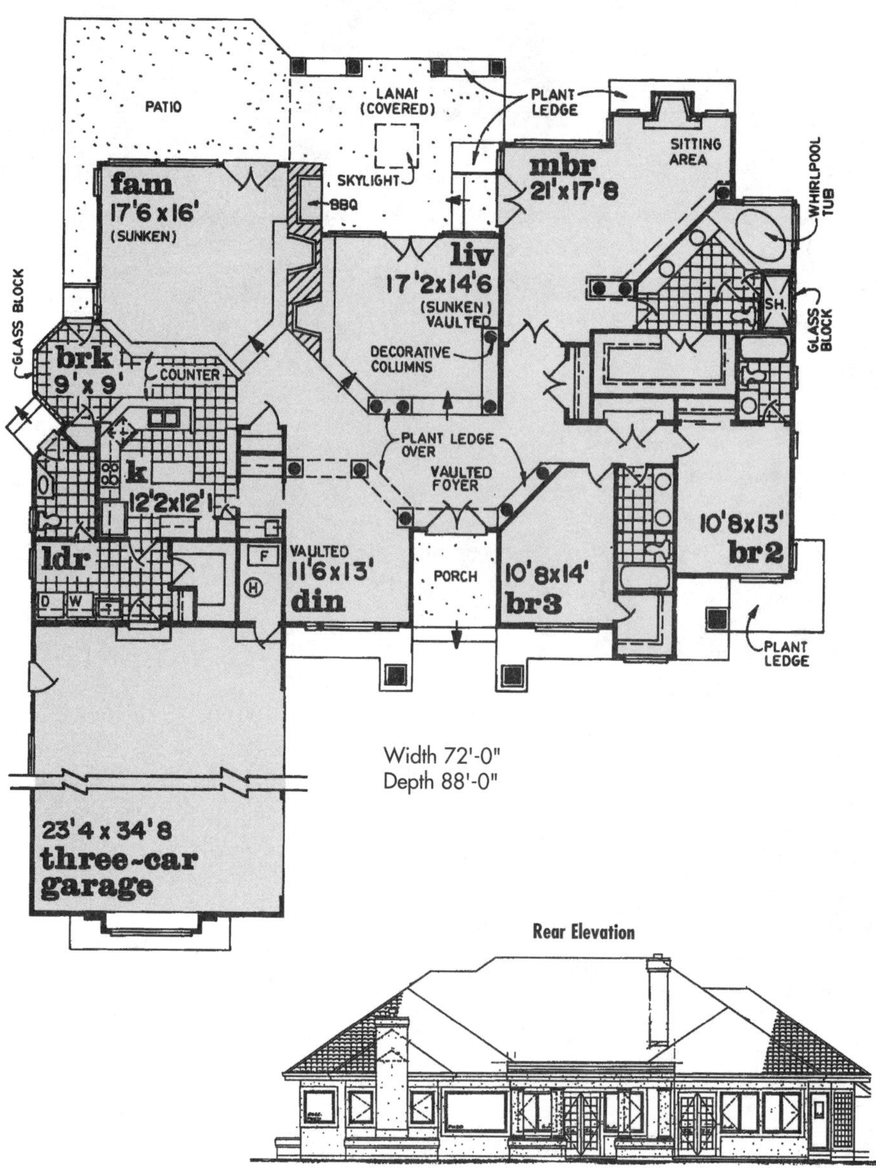

PATIO
LANAI (COVERED)
PLANT LEDGE
SITTING AREA
WHIRLPOOL TUB
fam
17'6 x 16'
(SUNKEN)
SKYLIGHT
BBQ
mbr
21'x17'8
liv
17'2x14'6
(SUNKEN) VAULTED
GLASS BLOCK
SH.
GLASS BLOCK
brk
9'x 9'
COUNTER
DECORATIVE COLUMNS
k
12'2x12'1
PLANT LEDGE OVER
VAULTED FOYER
10'8x13'
br2
ldr
F
D W
H
VAULTED
11'6x13'
din
PORCH
10'8x14'
br3
PLANT LEDGE
Width 72'-0"
Depth 88'-0"
23'4 x 34'8
three-car garage
Rear Elevation

Design by
Select Home Designs

Design Q420

Square Footage: 3,018

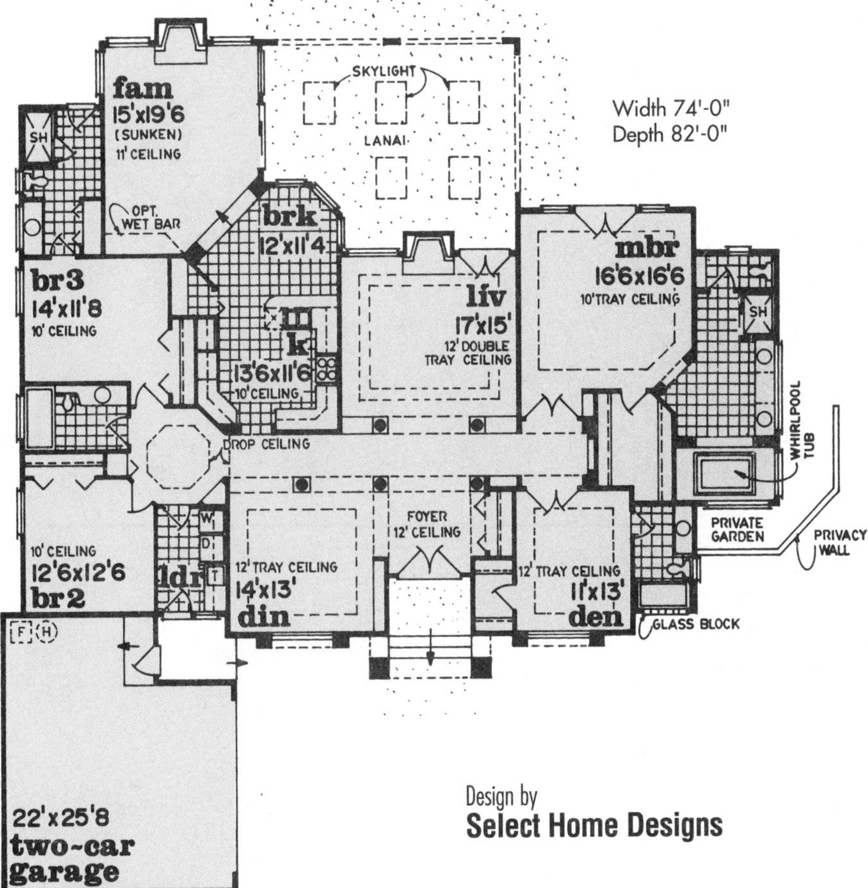

SKYLIGHT
LANAI
Width 74'-0"
Depth 82'-0"
fam
15'x19'6
(SUNKEN)
11' CEILING
SH
OPT. WET BAR
brk
12'x11'4
mbr
16'6x16'6
10' TRAY CEILING
SH
br3
14'x11'8
10' CEILING
liv
17'x15'
12' DOUBLE TRAY CEILING
k
13'6x11'6
10' CEILING
WHIRLPOOL TUB
DROP CEILING
FOYER
12' CEILING
PRIVATE GARDEN
PRIVACY WALL
10' CEILING
12'6x12'6
br2
ldr
12' TRAY CEILING
14'x13'
din
12' TRAY CEILING
11'x13'
den
GLASS BLOCK
22'x25'8
two-car garage

Design by
Select Home Designs

■ Two distinct exteriors can be built from the details for this plan—both are perfect as sun-country designs. The entry is grand and allows for a twelve-foot ceiling in the entry foyer. Open planning calls for columns to separate the formal living room and the formal dining room from the foyer and central hall. Both rooms have tray ceilings, the living room has a fireplace and double-door access to the skylit lanai. The modified U-shaped kitchen has an attached breakfast room and steps down to the family room with fireplace and optional wet bar. A lovely octagonal foyer introduces family bedrooms and their private baths. A den with tray ceiling and full bath sits to the right of the foyer and doubles as guest room space when needed. The master suite is separated from family bedrooms. It has double-door access to the rear yard, a walk-in closet and a full bath with whirlpool tub, double vanity, compartmented toilet and separate shower. Plans include details for both a basement and a crawlspace foundation.

Alternate Elevation

Rear Elevation

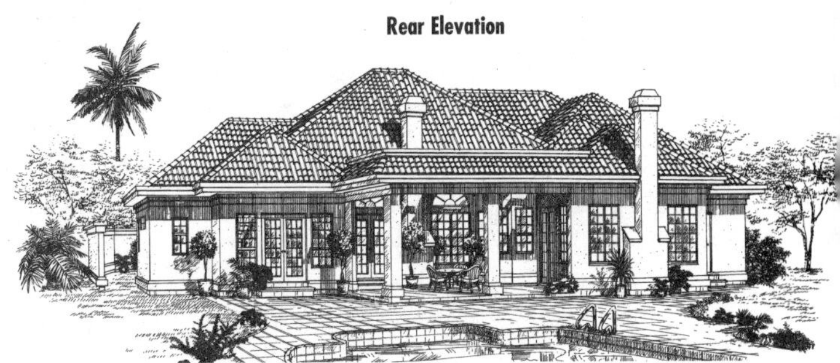

Design Q302

First Floor: 1,920 square feet
Second Floor: 932 square feet
Total: 2,852 square feet

Design by
Select Home Designs

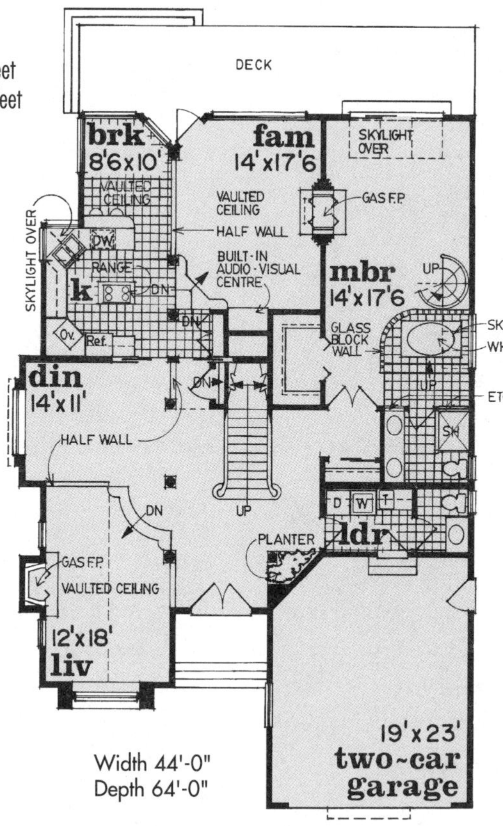

DECK
brk
8'6x10'
VAULTED CEILING
fam
14'x17'6
SKYLIGHT OVER
VAULTED CEILING
GAS F.P.
HALF WALL
BUILT-IN AUDIO-VISUAL CENTRE
SKYLIGHT OVER
DW
RANGE
k
DN
Ov.
Ref.
mbr
14'x17'6
UP
GLASS BLOCK WALL
SKYLIGHT OVER
WHIRLPOOL TUB
ETCHED GLASS
din
14'x11'
DN
HALF WALL
SH
UP
D
W
T
DN
ldr
PLANTER
GAS F.P.
VAULTED CEILING
12'x18'
liv
19'x23'
two-car garage
Width 44'-0"
Depth 64'-0"

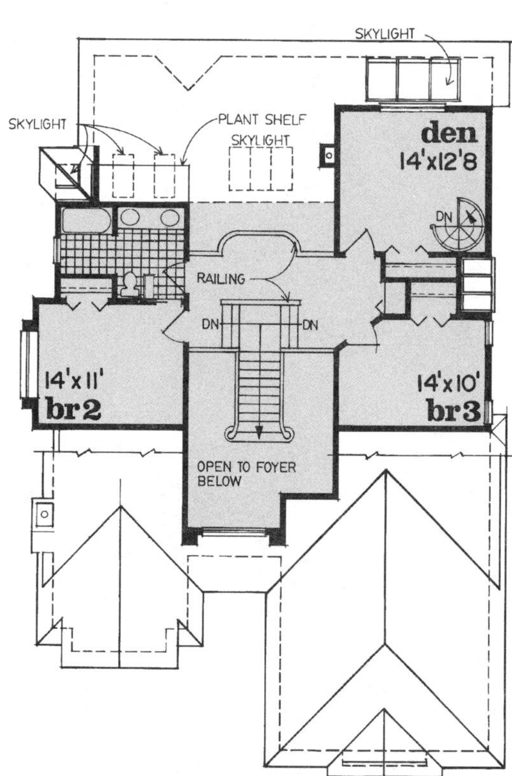

SKYLIGHT
SKYLIGHT
PLANT SHELF
SKYLIGHT
den
14'x12'8
DN
RAILING
DN
DN
14'x11'
br2
14'x10'
br3
OPEN TO FOYER BELOW

■ Complete in California stucco, this handsome design features large windows for capturing light and views. The sunken living room boasts a vaulted ceiling and gas fireplace and is separated from the hall by decorative columns that also adorn the dining room. The skylit, U-shaped kitchen with attached breakfast room separates the dining room and the family room. Special features in the family room include deck access, a through-fireplace to the master bedroom and a built-in audio-visual center. The master suite is truly lavish. It has a skylit sitting area with sliding glass doors to the deck, a spiral stair to the den on the second floor and a bath with skylit whirlpool and double vanities. Besides the den, the second floor also holds two family bedrooms and a full bath. Choose a basement or crawlspace foundation—plans included for both.

Rear Elevation

Design Q330

First Floor: 1,520 square feet
Second Floor: 929 square feet
Total: 2,449 square feet

■ A recessed entry with double doors introduces this lovely plan. Vaulted ceilings throughout the foyer, living room, dining room and kitchen add a sense of spaciousness and allow for plant ledges. A peninsula fireplace separates the dining room and living room. The family room has another fireplace, flanked by shelves to serve as an entertainment center. A private den sits just beyond the family room. Note the deck that sits outside the dining room and breakfast room. Bedrooms are on the second floor: a master suite and two family bedrooms. The master bedroom has a walk-in closet and private bath with raised whirlpool tub. Family bedrooms share a full hall bath and a built-in desk on the landing. Plans include details for both a basement and a crawlspace foundation.

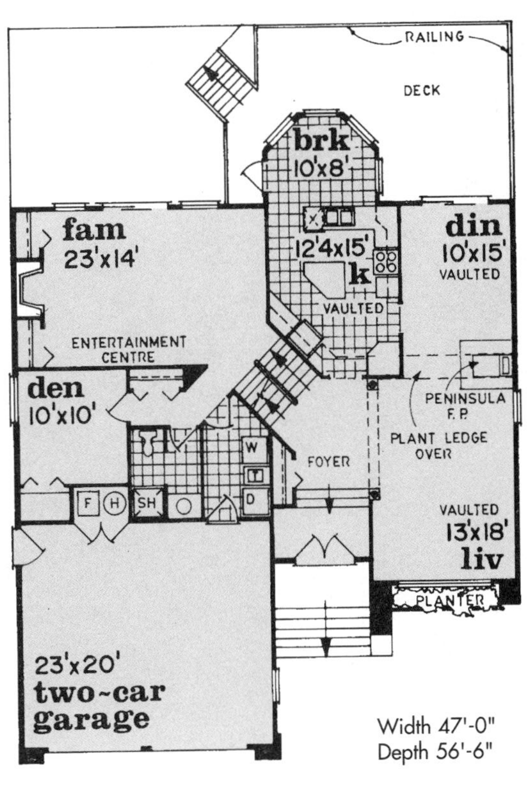
RAILING
DECK
brk
10'x8'
fam
23'x14'
12'4x15'
k
VAULTED
din
10'x15'
VAULTED
ENTERTAINMENT CENTRE
den
10'x10'
PENINSULA F.P.
PLANT LEDGE OVER
FOYER
W
D
F
H
SH
VAULTED
13'x18'
liv
PLANTER
23'x20'
two-car garage
Width 47'-0"
Depth 56'-6"

Design by
Select Home Designs

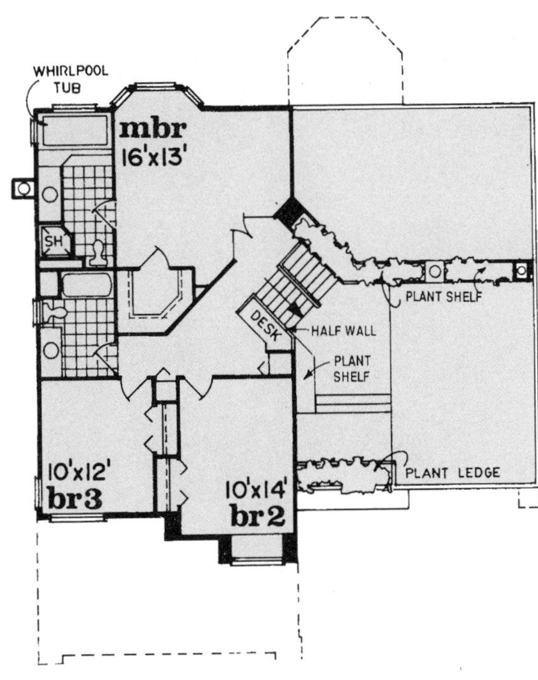
WHIRLPOOL TUB
mbr
16'x13'
SH
PLANT SHELF
DESK
HALF WALL
PLANT SHELF
10'x12'
br3
10'x14'
br2
PLANT LEDGE

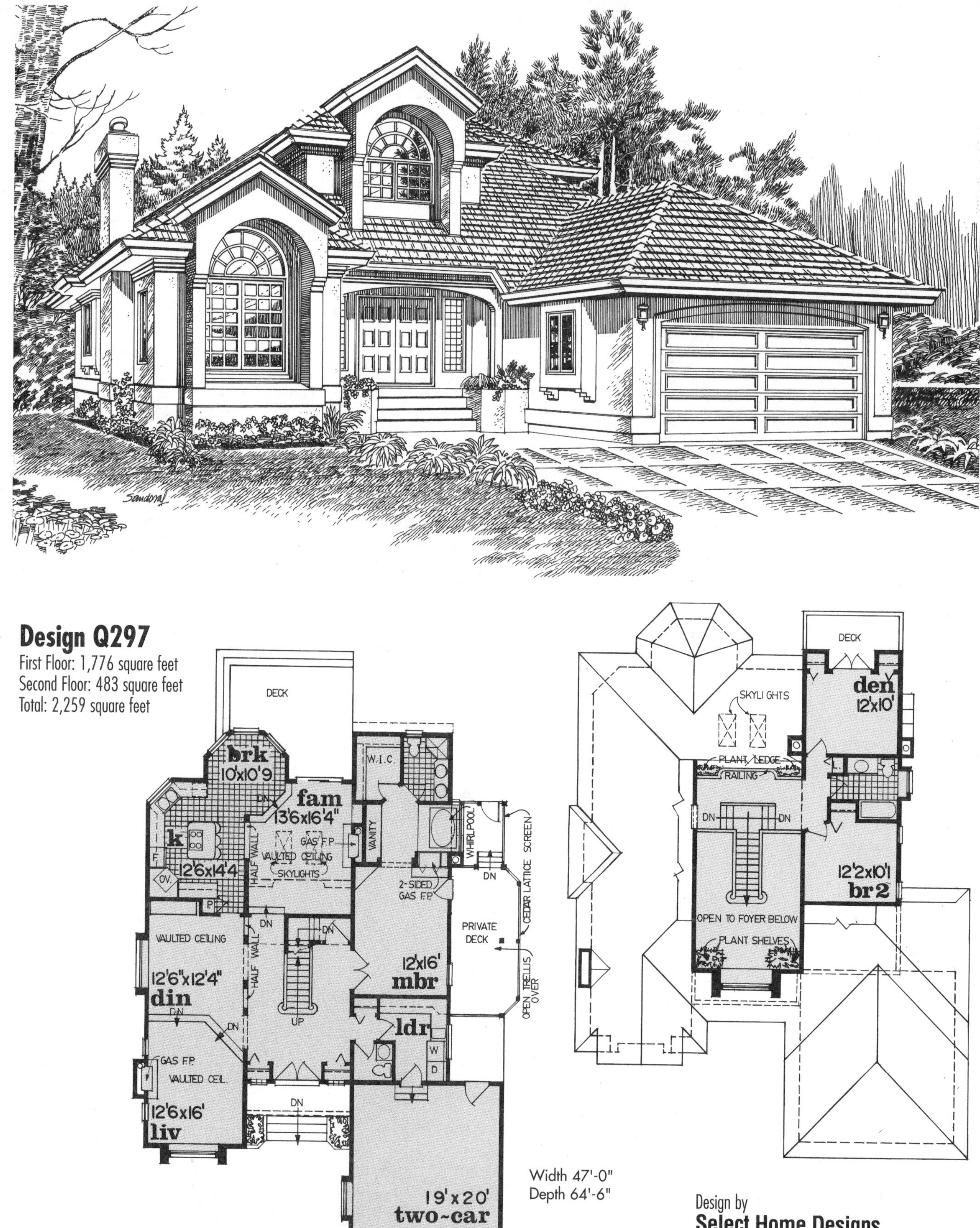

DECK
brk
10'x10'9
fam
13'6x16'4"
k
12'6x14'4
W.I.C.
VANITY
WHIRLPOOL
HALF WALL
GAS F.P.
VAULTED CEILING
SKYLIGHTS
2-SIDED GAS F.P.
CEDAR LATTICE SCREEN
PRIVATE DECK
VAULTED CEILING
12'6"x12'4"
din
12'x16'
mbr
OPEN TRELLIS OVER
UP
DN
ldr
W
D
GAS F.P.
VAULTED CEIL.
12'6x16'
liv
19'x20'
two-car garage
SKYLIGHTS
PLANT LEDGE
RAILING
OPEN TO FOYER BELOW
PLANT SHELVES
den
12'x10'
12'2x10'1
br2
Width 47'-0"
Depth 64'-6"

Design Q297

First Floor: 1,776 square feet
Second Floor: 483 square feet
Total: 2,259 square feet

Design by
Select Home Designs

■ Two circle-top windows—one over the entry and one in the living room—echo the gentle arch over the recessed entry of this home. Double doors open to a center hall with staircase to the second floor. Formal living and dining rooms are on the left. The living room is sunken and boasts a gas fireplace. Both have vaulted ceilings. The family room also has a vaulted ceiling and a gas fireplace and is brightened by skylights. In between sits the island kitchen with attached breakfast bay. The master bedroom is on the first floor for privacy. It holds a private deck, a through-fireplace to its well-appointed bath and a walk-in closet. An additional bedroom with full bath and a den with private deck are found on the second floor. Plans include details for both a basement and a crawlspace foundation.

Design 3425

First Floor: 1,776 square feet
Second Floor: 1,035 square feet
Total: 2,811 square feet

■ Here's a two-story Spanish design with an appealing, angled exterior. Inside is an interesting floor plan containing rooms with a variety of shapes. Formal areas are to the right of the entry tower: a sunken living room with a fireplace and a large dining room with access to the rear porch. The kitchen has loads of counter space and is complemented by a bumped-out breakfast room. Note the second fireplace in the family room and the first-floor bedroom which could also be a guest suite. Three second-floor bedrooms radiate around the upper foyer, including the deluxe master suite. Among its many amenities; a private balcony, a walk-in closet and a sumptuous bath.

BALCONY
RAILING
MASTER BEDROOM 14¹⁰ x 14⁸
UPPER DINING
WHIRLPOOL
WALK-IN CLOSET
MASTER BATH
LINEN
SLOPED CEILING
FURN
MECH RM
OPEN TO FIRST FLOOR
BEDROOM 11⁸ x 11⁸
DN
BATH
BEDROOM 15⁰ x 10⁰
UPPER FOYER
UPPER LIVING RM
ROOF
COVERED PORCH
BRKFST RM 10⁹ x 10⁹
PORCH
STORAGE
FAMILY RM 17⁶ x 13⁴
DINING 12⁴ x 12⁶
KITCHEN 16⁶ x 10⁰
PTRY
OVEN
COOK TOP
REF'G
BOOKS
BEDROOM 12⁰ x 11²
LAUNDRY
LIVING RM 14⁰ x 18⁶
RAILING
LEDGE
UP
BATH
FURN
WH
WALK-IN CLOSET
FOYER
CURB
COVERED PORCH
GARAGE 32² x 20⁶
Width 52'-0"
Depth 64'-4"

QUOTE ONE®
Cost to build? See page 516 to order complete cost estimate to build this house in your area!

Design by
Home Planners

© Copyright 1990 Select Home Designs All rights reserved

Design Q329

First Floor: 1,199 square feet
Second Floor: 921 square feet
Total: 2,120 square feet

■ An angled entry gives a new slant to this cool California design. The two-story foyer is lighted by a multi-paned window and leads down two steps to a sunken foyer. A pair of decorative columns separates the living room and formal dining room. A U-shaped kitchen, with walk-in pantry, serves the breakfast room. Just beyond is the family room with fireplace and rear-yard access. A den is tucked in between the laundry room and two-car garage (note storage). On the second floor, the master suite has a walk-in closet and private bath with corner whirlpool and separate shower. Two additional bedrooms share a full bath. A laundry chute in the hall sends clothes to the laundry room for washing. Plans include details for both a basement and a crawlspace foundation.

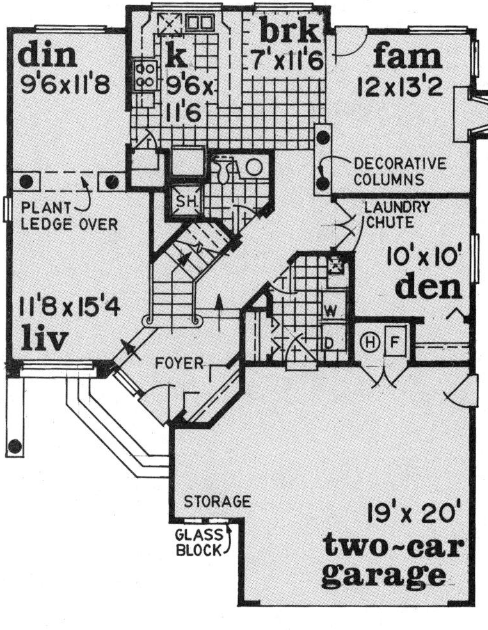
din
9'6x11'8
k
9'6x
11'6
brk
7'x11'6
fam
12x13'2
DECORATIVE COLUMNS
PLANT LEDGE OVER
LAUNDRY CHUTE
10'x10'
den
11'8x15'4
liv
FOYER
W
D
H
F
STORAGE
GLASS BLOCK
19'x 20'
two-car garage

Width 40'-0"
Depth 50'-6"

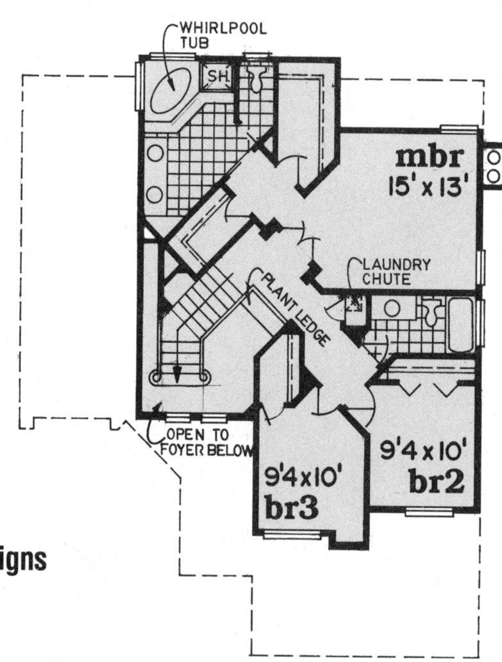
WHIRLPOOL TUB
SH
mbr
15' x 13'
LAUNDRY CHUTE
PLANT LEDGE
OPEN TO FOYER BELOW
9'4x10'
br3
9'4x10'
br2

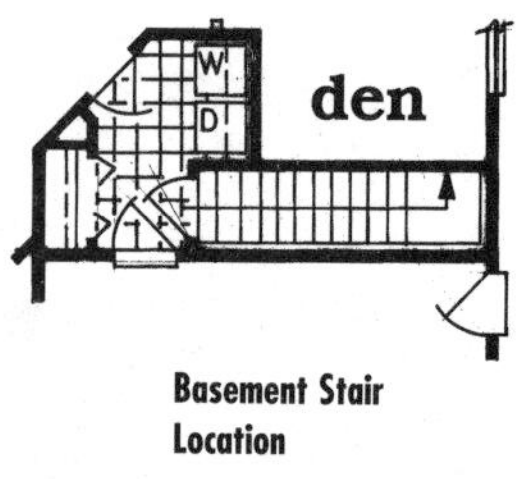
W
D
den

Basement Stair Location

Design by
Select Home Designs

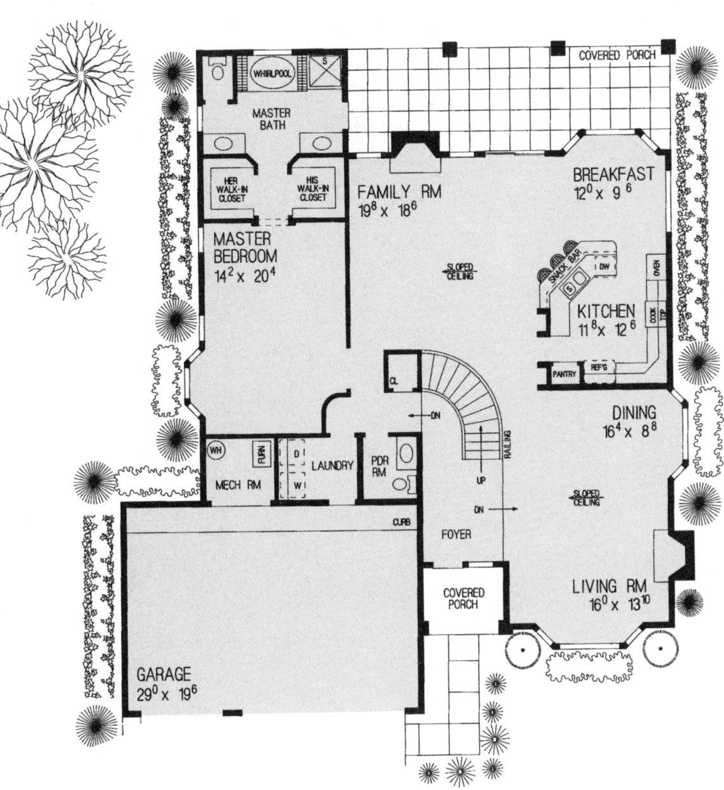

COVERED PORCH
WHIRLPOOL
MASTER BATH
HER WALK-IN CLOSET
HIS WALK-IN CLOSET
FAMILY RM
19^{8} x 18^{6}
BREAKFAST
12^{0} x 9^{6}
MASTER BEDROOM
14^{2} x 20^{4}
SLOPED CEILING
SNACK BAR
KITCHEN
11^{8} x 12^{6}
PANTRY
REF'G
DINING
16^{4} x 8^{8}
MECH RM
LAUNDRY
PDR RM
FOYER
CURB
COVERED PORCH
LIVING RM
16^{0} x 13^{10}
GARAGE
29^{0} x 19^{6}

Width 57'-0"
Depth 64'-0"

QUOTE ONE®

Cost to build? See page 516 to order complete cost estimate to build this house in your area!

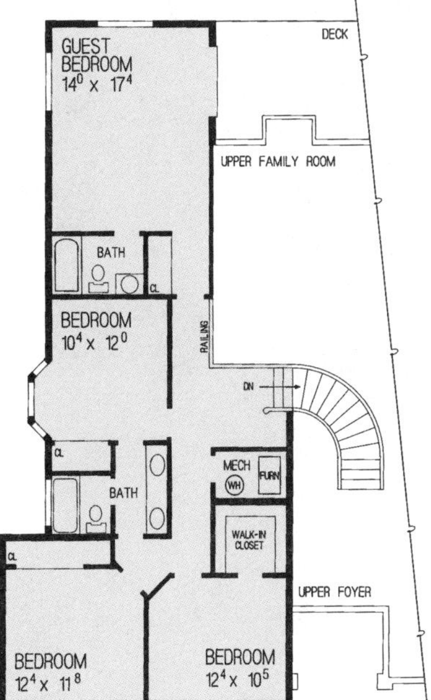

DECK
GUEST BEDROOM
14^{0} x 17^{4}
UPPER FAMILY ROOM
BATH
BEDROOM
10^{4} x 12^{0}
RAILING
MECH
BATH
WALK-IN CLOSET
UPPER FOYER
BEDROOM
12^{4} x 11^{8}
BEDROOM
12^{4} x 10^{5}

Design 3414

First Floor: 2,024 square feet
Second Floor: 1,144 square feet
Total: 3,168 square feet

L

Design by
Home Planners

■ Though seemingly compact from the exterior, this home gives a definite feeling of spaciousness inside. The two-story entry connects directly to a formal living/dining area, a fitting complement to the more casual family room and cozy, bayed breakfast room. Located on the first floor for privacy, the master suite is luxury defined. A bayed sitting area, His and Hers walk-in closets, a whirlpool tub and twin vanities all combine to provide a lavish retreat. Upstairs, three family bedrooms share a full hall bath, while a large guest room waits to pamper with its private bath and access to its own deck. A three-car garage will protect both the family fleet and visitor's vehicles.

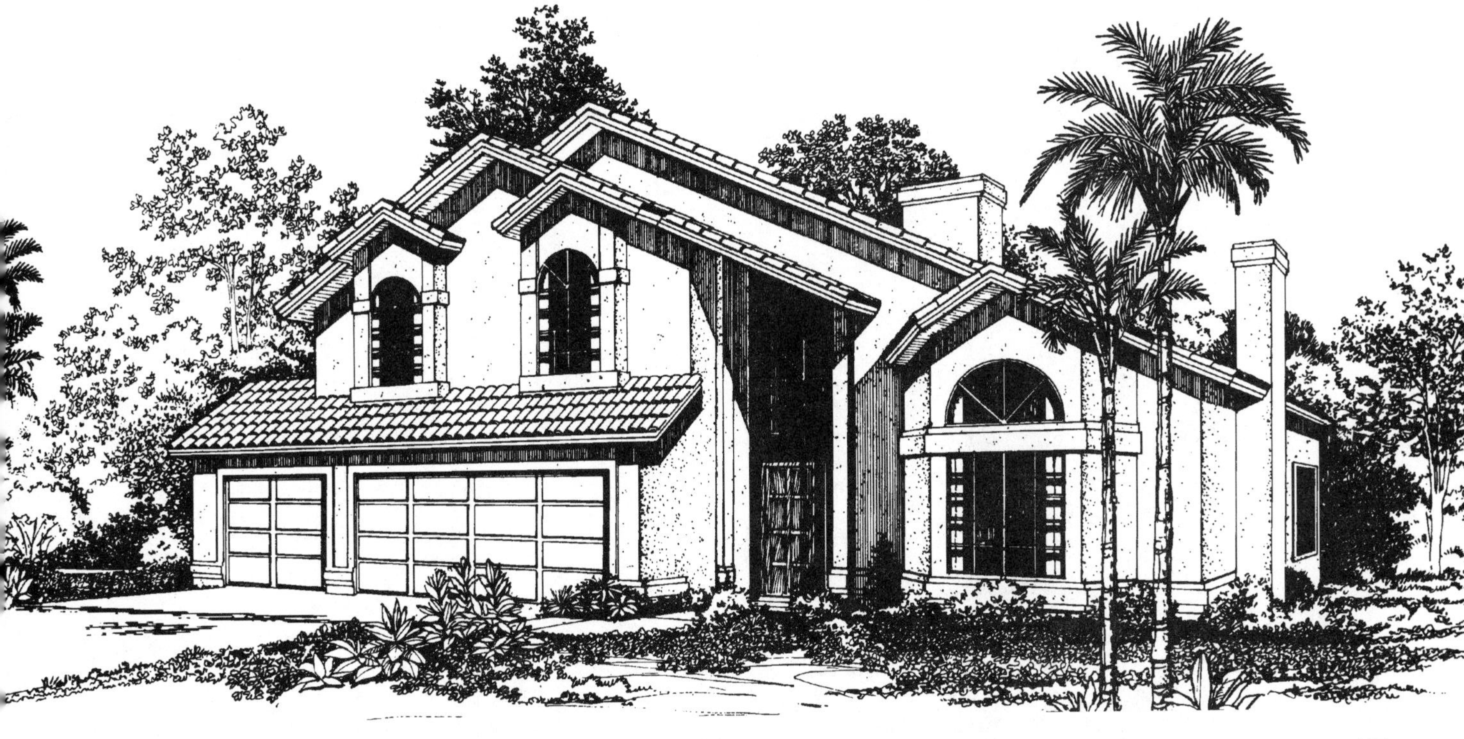

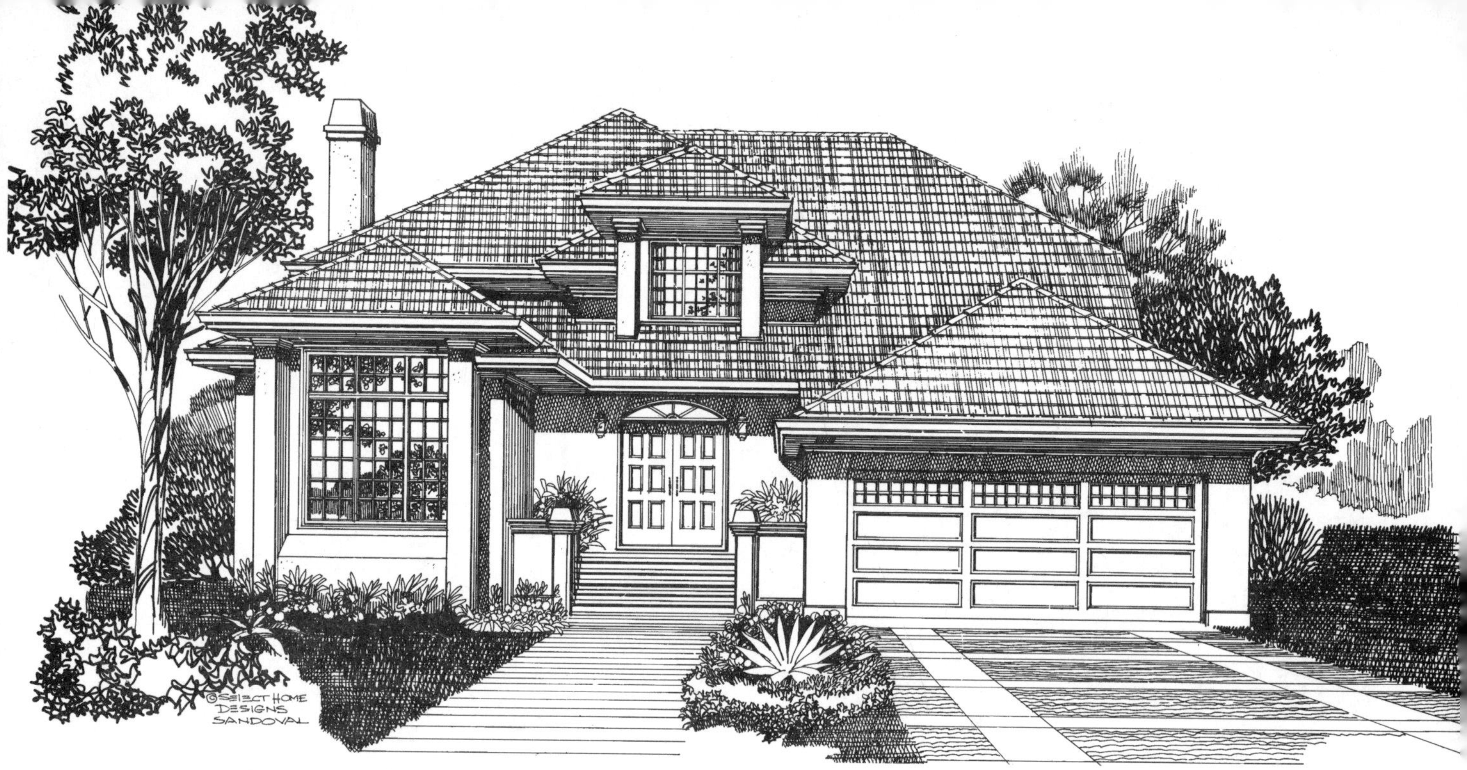

Design Q287

First Floor: 1,462 square feet
Second Floor: 1,076 square feet
Total: 2,538 square feet

■ With a courtyard entry, this design has the lovely look of California design. Double doors open onto a two-story foyer with angled staircase. Living and dining rooms sit on the left and share a fireplace. The family room is sunken and graced by a fireplace and double doors to a den and to a covered deck. A laundry and half-bath sit in a service area leading to the two-car garage. Upstairs there are three bedrooms—a master suite and two family bedrooms. The master bedroom features a coffered ceiling, a walk-in closet and a private bath with spa tub and double vanities. Family bedrooms share a full bath. Plans include details for both a basement and a crawlspace foundation.

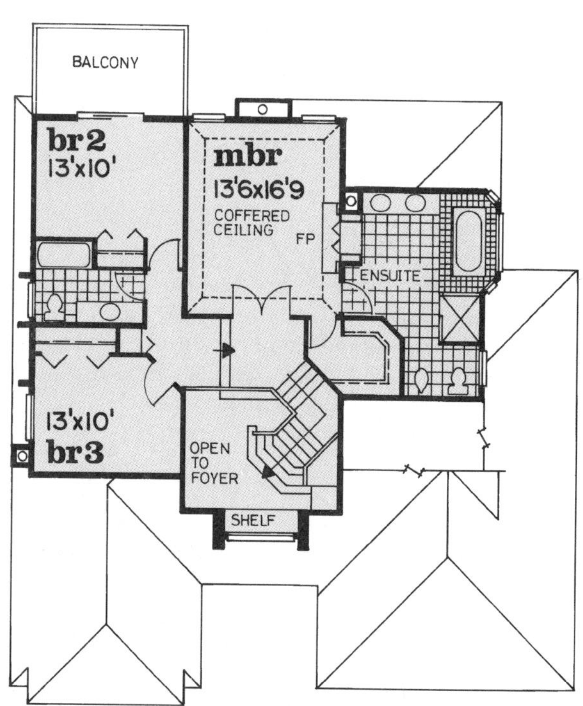

BALCONY
br2
13'x10'
mbr
13'6x16'9
COFFERED CEILING
FP
ENSUITE
13'x10'
br3
OPEN TO FOYER
SHELF

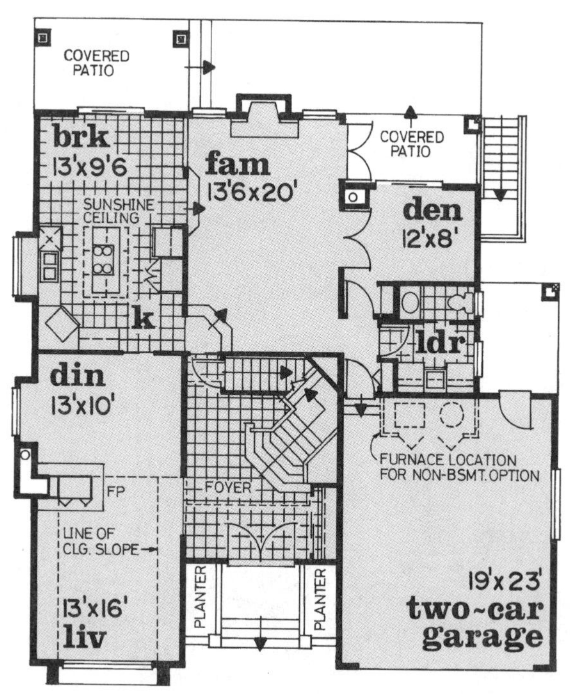

COVERED PATIO
brk
13'x9'6
SUNSHINE CEILING
fam
13'6x20'
COVERED PATIO
den
12'x8'
k
ldr
din
13'x10'
FP
FOYER
FURNACE LOCATION FOR NON-BSMT. OPTION
LINE OF CLG. SLOPE
13'x16'
liv
PLANTER
PLANTER
19'x23'
two-car garage

Width 47'-6"
Depth 49'-6"

Design by
Select Home Designs

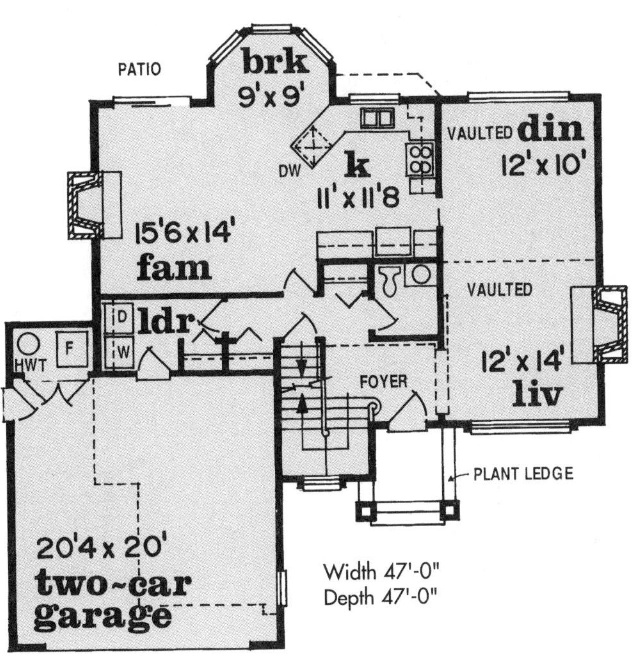
PATIO
brk
9'x9'
VAULTED din
12'x10'
DW
k
11'x11'8
15'6x14'
fam
VAULTED
ldr
D
W
HWT
F
FOYER
12'x14'
liv
PLANT LEDGE
20'4 x 20'
two~car
garage
Width 47'-0"
Depth 47'-0"

Design Q377

First Floor: 1,023 square feet
Second Floor: 837 square feet
Total: 1,860 square feet

■ Plans for this design include both a contemporary stucco exterior and a traditional brick and siding version. Both feature a grand and livable floor plan. From the two-story foyer, go right to a vaulted living room with fireplace and vaulted dining room. The peninsula kitchen blends into a bayed breakfast room and the open family room, which features a fireplace and sliding glass doors to the patio. The upper level contains three bedrooms. The master suite features a private bath with arched access, whirlpool tub, separate shower and double vanity. Family bedrooms share a full bath with linen closet. Plans include details for both a basement and a crawlspace foundation.

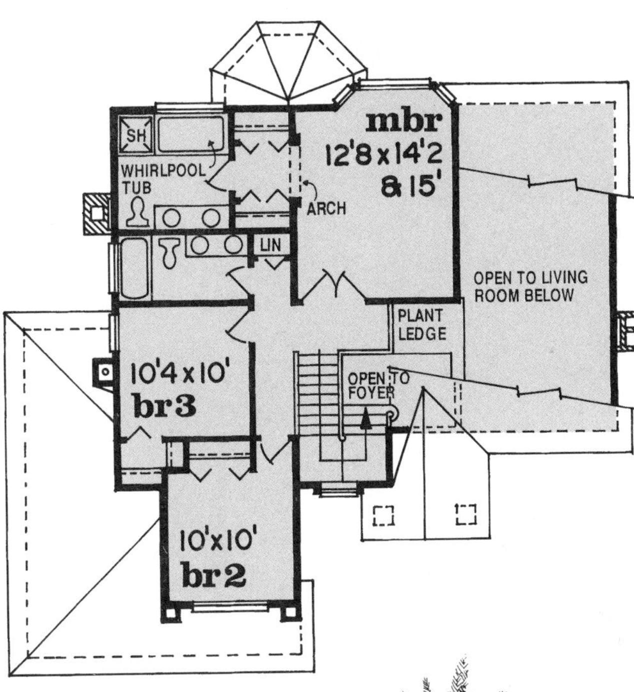
SH
WHIRLPOOL
TUB
mbr
12'8 x 14'2
& 15'
ARCH
LIN
OPEN TO LIVING
ROOM BELOW
PLANT
LEDGE
10'4 x 10'
br3
OPEN TO
FOYER
10'x10'
br2

Design by
Select Home Designs

Alternate Elevation

Design 3421

Square Footage: 2,145

L

■ Split-bedroom planning makes the most of a one-story design. In this case the master suite is on the opposite side of the house from two family bedrooms. It is graced by a walk-in closet, sloped ceiling and bath with whirlpool and separate shower. Gourmets can rejoice at the abundant work space in the U-shaped kitchen and will appreciate the natural light afforded by the large bay window in the breakfast room. The family room is separated from the kitchen by a snack bar. The rear covered porch can be reached through sliding glass doors in the family room. A formal sunken living room has a sunken conversation area with a cozy fireplace as its focus and opens directly from the foyer.

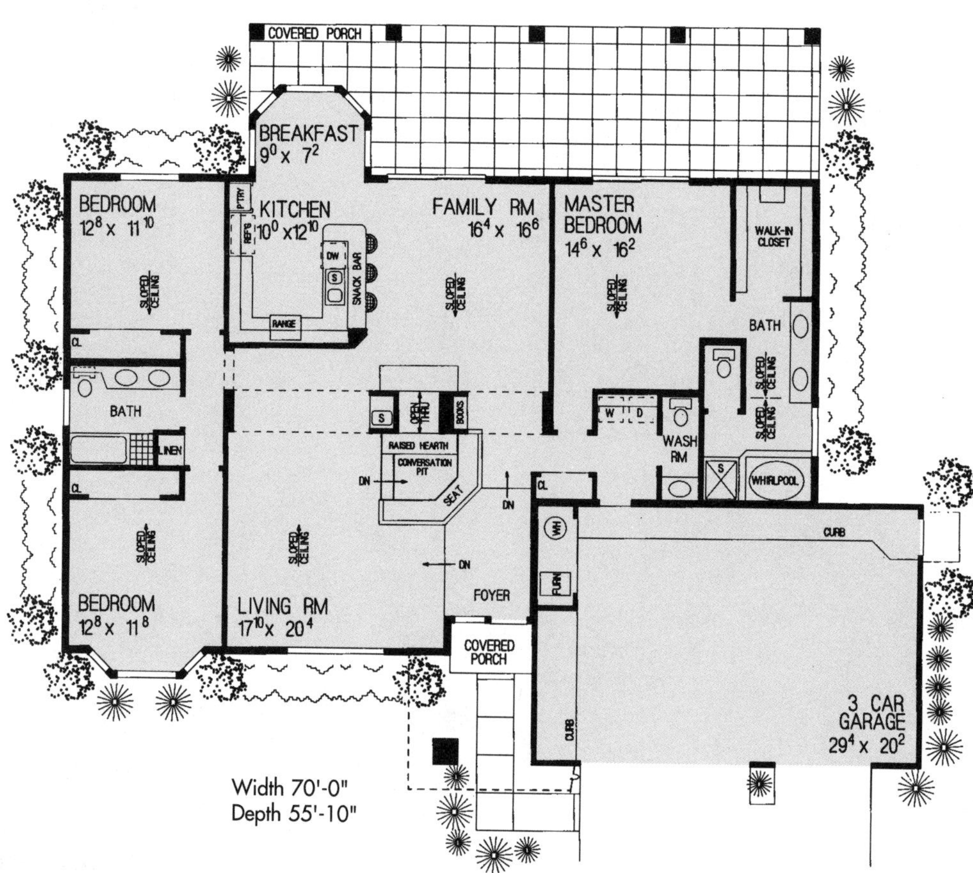
COVERED PORCH
BREAKFAST
9^{0} x 7^{2}
BEDROOM
12^{8} x 11^{10}
KITCHEN
10^{0} x 12^{10}
FAMILY RM
16^{4} x 16^{6}
MASTER BEDROOM
14^{6} x 16^{2}
WALK-IN CLOSET
BATH
SNACK BAR
RANGE
SLOPED CEILING
CL
BATH
LINEN
RAISED HEARTH
CONVERSATION PIT
SEAT
BOOKS
W
D
WASH RM
WHIRLPOOL
DN
FOYER
CURB
BEDROOM
12^{8} x 11^{8}
LIVING RM
17^{10} x 20^{4}
COVERED PORCH
3 CAR GARAGE
29^{4} x 20^{2}
Width 70'-0"
Depth 55'-10"

QUOTE ONE®

Cost to build? See page 516 to order complete cost estimate to build this house in your area!

Design by
Home Planners

Design Q354

Square Footage: 1,336

■ This compact plan may be built with a Floridian facade in stucco, or a more traditional siding-and-brick facade. Details for both exteriors are included in the plans. You also have the option of two or three bedrooms. One of the bedrooms could be used as a family room. A half-wall separates the foyer from the living room, which is highlighted by a window seat in its box window, a fireplace and an attached dining room. A U-shaped kitchen features abundant counter space, an angled sink under a corner plant shelf and a sunny breakfast area with access to the rear patio. The family room—or third bedroom—has a bright window seat, also. The master bedroom has no rival for luxury. It has a bay-window seating area, large wall closet and private bath. Access the two-car garage through the service entrance at the laundry alcove. Plans include optional basement foundation details.

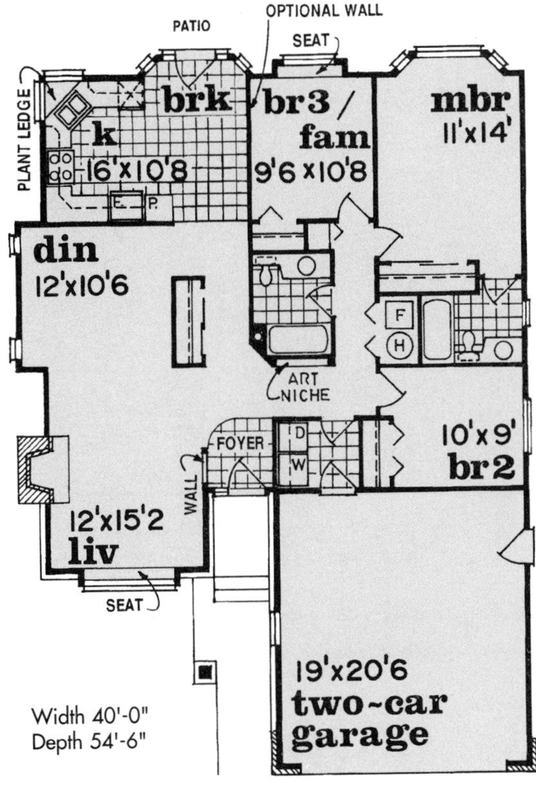

OPTIONAL WALL
PATIO
SEAT
PLANT LEDGE
brk
k
16'x10'8
E. P.
br3 / fam
9'6 x 10'8
mbr
11'x14'
din
12'x10'6
F
H
ART NICHE
FOYER
D
W
10'x9'
br2
WALL
12'x15'2
liv
SEAT
19'x20'6
two-car garage

Width 40'-0"
Depth 54'-6"

Design by
Select Home Designs

Alternate Elevation

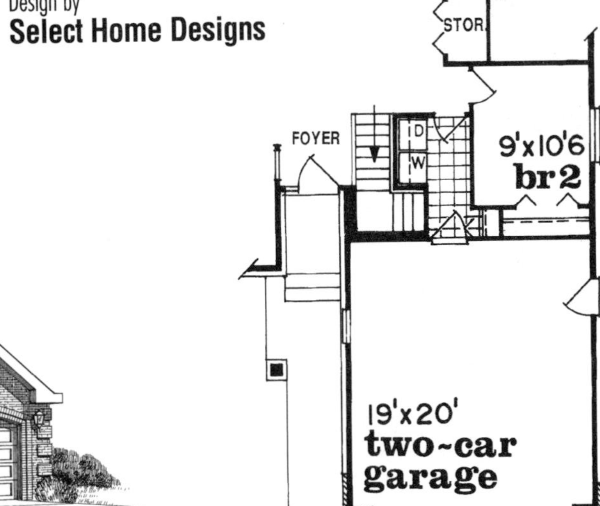

STOR
FOYER
D
W
9'x10'6
br2
19'x20'
two-car garage

Basement Stair Location

Design 3440

Square Footage: 2,290

L

■ There's plenty of room for everyone in this three- or optional four-bedroom home. The expansive gathering room welcomes family and guests with a through-fireplace in the dining room, an audio/visual center and a door to the outside. The kitchen includes a wide pantry, an island cooktop, a snack bar and a separate eating area. Included in the master suite: two walk-in closets, a shower, a whirlpool tub and seat, dual vanities and linen storage. Two family rooms share a full bath. If you choose, the study/den can become an additional bedroom. Note the three-car garage and the half-bath in the foyer.

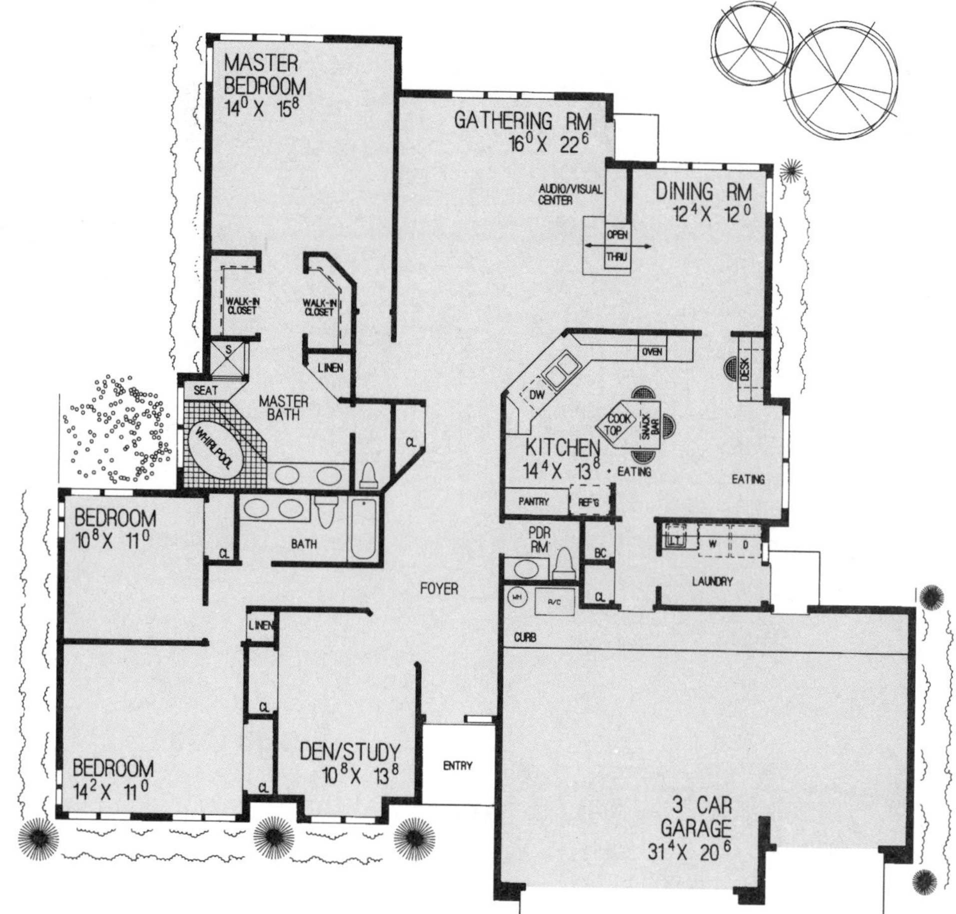

MASTER BEDROOM 14^0 X 15^8
GATHERING RM 16^0 X 22^6
AUDIO/VISUAL CENTER
OPEN THRU
DINING RM 12^4 X 12^0
WALK-IN CLOSET
WALK-IN CLOSET
LINEN
OVEN
DESK
SEAT
MASTER BATH
WHIRLPOOL
CL
DW
COOK TOP
SNACK BAR
KITCHEN 14^4 X 13^8
EATING
EATING
PANTRY
REF'G
BEDROOM 10^8 X 11^0
BATH
CL
PDR RM
BC
FOYER
LAUNDRY
CL
LINEN
CURB
CL
ENTRY
DEN/STUDY 10^8 X 13^8
BEDROOM 14^2 X 11^0
CL
3 CAR GARAGE 31^4 X 20^6

Width 66'-6"
Depth 64'-0"

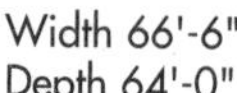

QUOTE ONE®

Cost to build? See page 516 to order complete cost estimate to build this house in your area!

Design by
Home Planners

© Copyright Select Home Designs. All rights reserved.

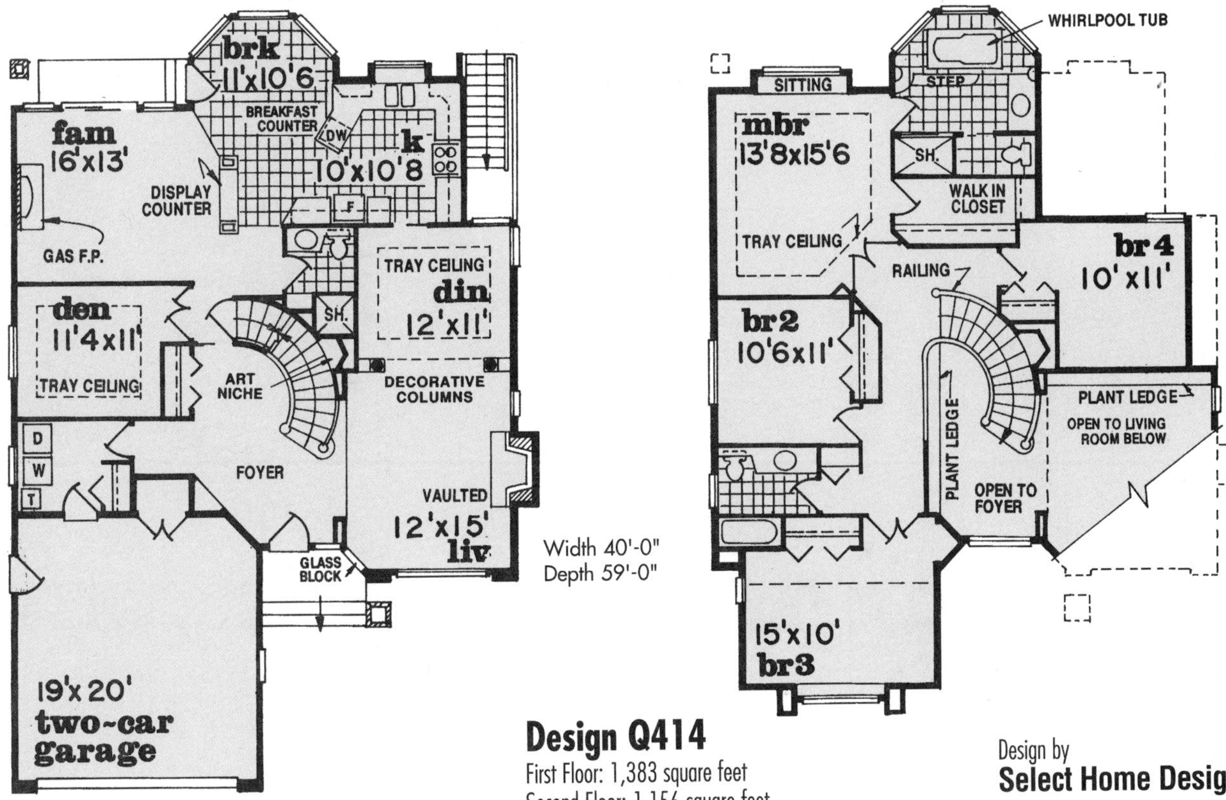
brk
11'x10'6
BREAKFAST COUNTER
DW
k
10'x10'8
fam
16'x13'
DISPLAY COUNTER
GAS F.P.
F
TRAY CEILING
din
12'x11'
den
11'4x11'
TRAY CEILING
SH.
ART NICHE
DECORATIVE COLUMNS
D
W
T
FOYER
VAULTED
12'x15'
liv
GLASS BLOCK
19'x20'
two-car garage
Width 40'-0"
Depth 59'-0"
WHIRLPOOL TUB
SITTING
STEP
mbr
13'8x15'6
SH.
WALK IN CLOSET
TRAY CEILING
RAILING
br4
10'x11'
br2
10'6x11'
PLANT LEDGE
OPEN TO LIVING ROOM BELOW
PLANT LEDGE
OPEN TO FOYER
15'x10'
br3

Design Q414

First Floor: 1,383 square feet
Second Floor: 1,156 square feet
Total: 2,539 square feet

Design by
Select Home Designs

Alternate Elevation

■ This well-planned stucco (or brick and siding) home is suited for a narrow lot. Its interior begins with a two-story foyer with a sweeping, curved staircase, an art niche and crowned with a plant ledge. Columns separate the living and dining rooms; the dining room has a tray ceiling. The step-saving kitchen is adjacent to a carousel breakfast room with a French door to the rear yard. A gas fireplace warms the family room, which features a room-dividing display counter and sliding glass doors. A den with tray ceiling rounds out the first floor. The master bedroom also has a tray ceiling and a window seat. Three family bedrooms share a full bath. Plans include details for both a basement and a crawlspace foundation.

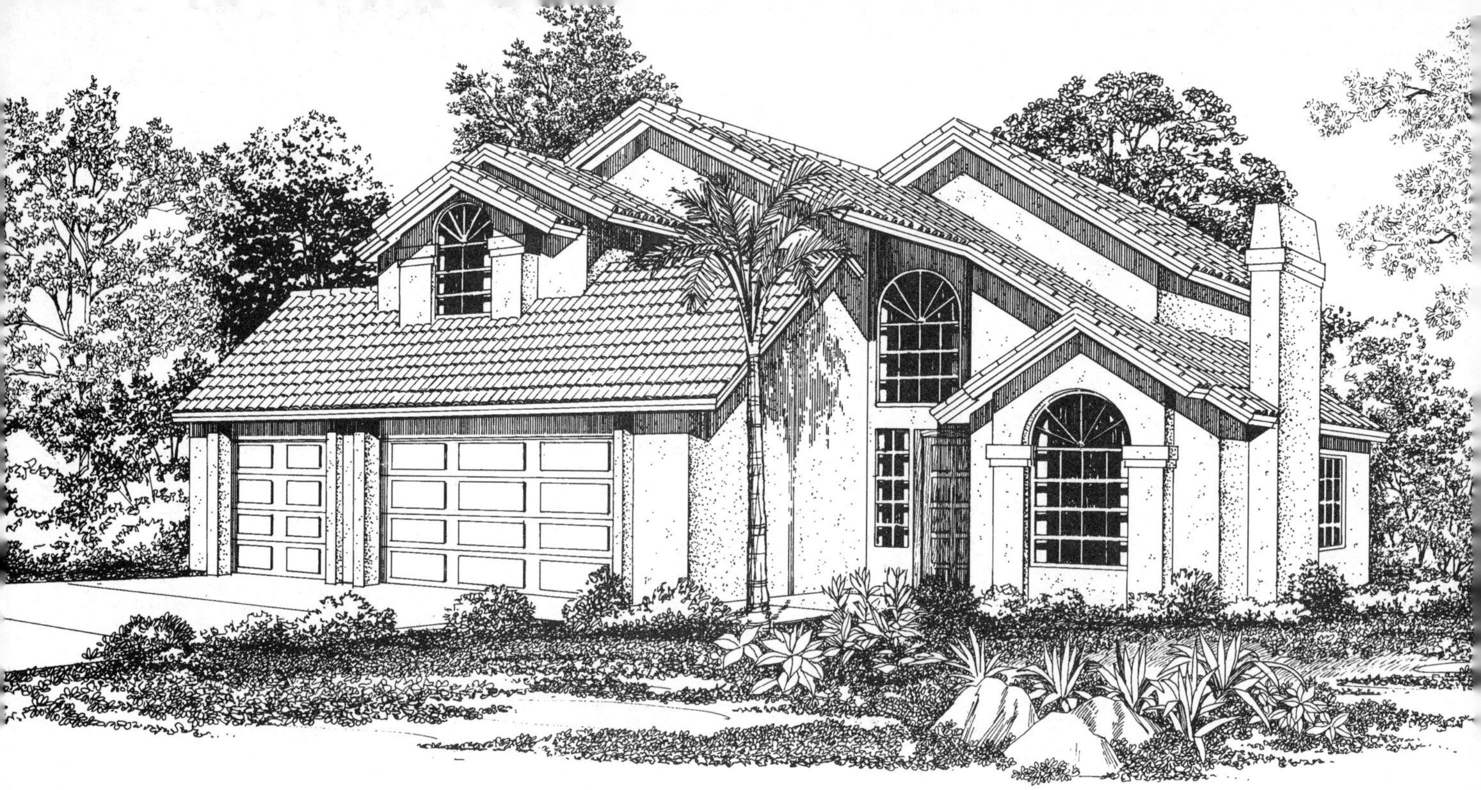

Design 3429

First Floor: 1,739 square feet
Second Floor: 1,376 square feet
Total: 3,115 square feet

Design by
Home Planners

Width 57'-4"
Depth 63'-6"

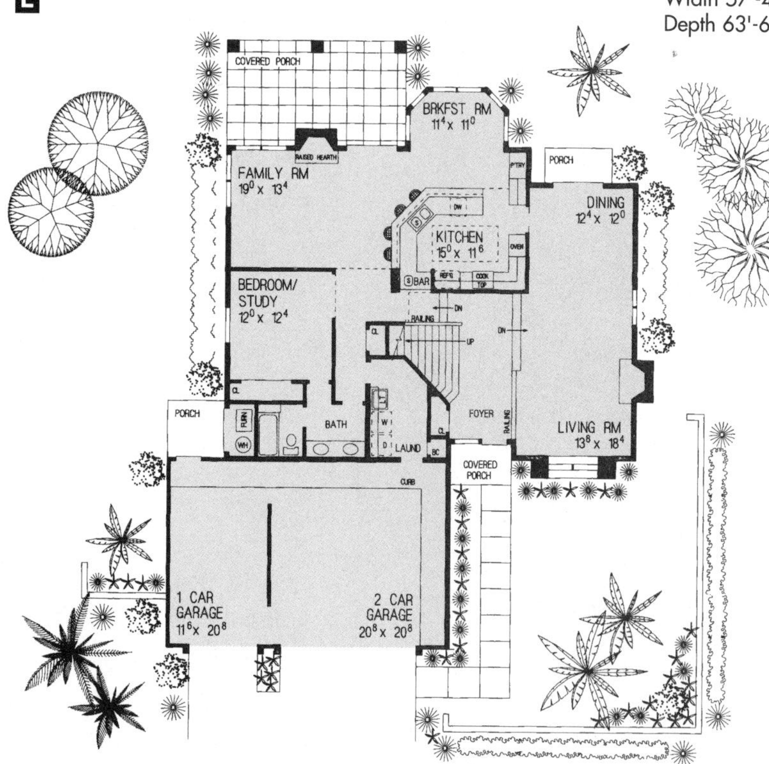

COVERED PORCH
BRKFST RM
$11^4 \times 11^0$
FAMILY RM
$19^0 \times 13^4$
RAISED HEARTH
PORCH
DINING
$12^4 \times 12^0$
KITCHEN
$15^0 \times 11^6$
BAR
BEDROOM/
STUDY
$12^0 \times 12^4$
FOYER
LIVING RM
$13^8 \times 18^4$
PORCH
BATH
LAUND
COVERED PORCH
1 CAR
GARAGE
$11^6 \times 20^8$
2 CAR
GARAGE
$20^8 \times 20^8$

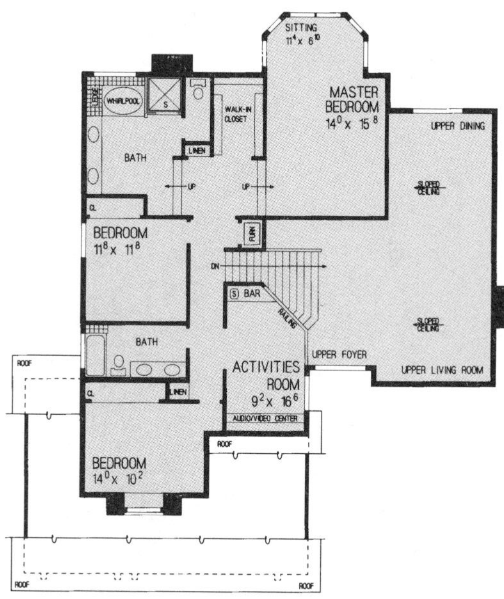

SITTING
$11^4 \times 6^0$
MASTER
BEDROOM
$14^0 \times 15^8$
WALK-IN CLOSET
BATH
UPPER DINING
BEDROOM
$11^8 \times 11^8$
BAR
BATH
ACTIVITIES
ROOM
$9^2 \times 16^6$
AUDIO/VIDEO CENTER
UPPER FOYER
UPPER LIVING ROOM
BEDROOM
$14^0 \times 10^2$
ROOF

QUOTE ONE®

Cost to build? See page 516 to order complete cost estimate to build this house in your area!

■ From the dramatic open entry to the covered back porch, this home delivers a full measure of livability in Spanish design. Formal living areas (living room and dining room) are balanced by a family room and a glassed-in breakfast room. Both the living room and the family room have fireplaces. The kitchen is a hub for both areas and holds a snack bar counter and bayed breakfast area. The first-floor study, with an adjacent bath, doubles nicely as a guest room. On the second floor, the activities room serves two family bedrooms and a grand master suite and has a handy wet bar and audio-visual center. The master bath is enhanced with dual lavatories and a whirlpool tub. Family bedrooms share a full bath.

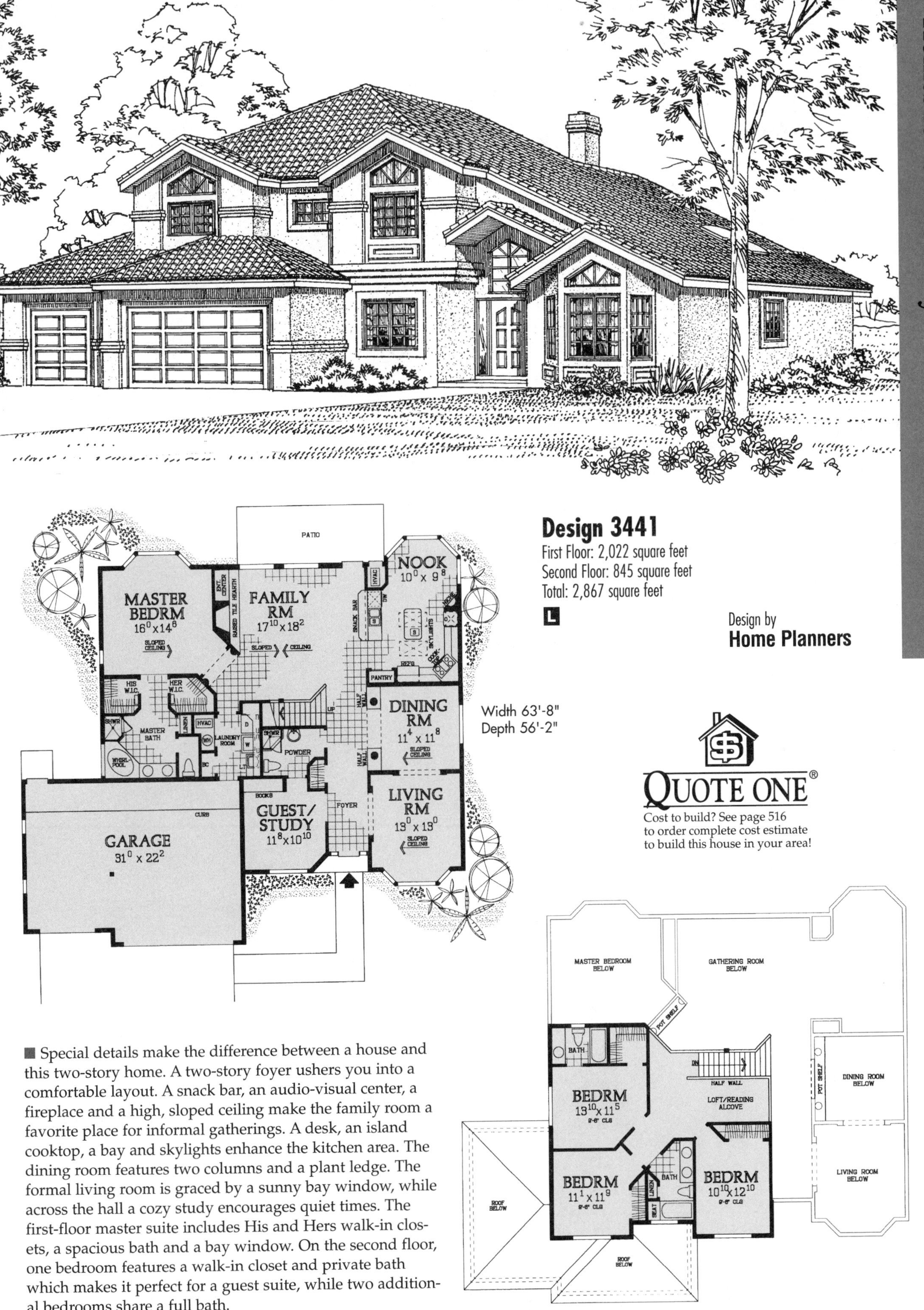
PATIO
NOOK
$10^0 \times 9^8$
MASTER BEDRM
$16^0 \times 14^6$
SLOPED CEILING
FAMILY RM
$17^{10} \times 18^2$
SLOPED CEILING
ENT. CENTER
RAISED TILE HEARTH
SNACK BAR
SKYLIGHTS
PANTRY
REFG
HIS W.I.C.
HER W.I.C.
MASTER BATH
WHIRLPOOL
SHWR
LINEN
HVAC
LAUNDRY ROOM
POWDER
UP
HALF WALL
DINING RM
$11^4 \times 11^8$
SLOPED CEILING
BOOKS
GUEST/ STUDY
$11^8 \times 10^{10}$
FOYER
LIVING RM
$13^0 \times 13^0$
SLOPED CEILING
GARAGE
$31^0 \times 22^2$
CURB
MASTER BEDROOM BELOW
GATHERING ROOM BELOW
POT SHELF
BATH
DN
HALF WALL
LOFT/READING ALCOVE
BEDRM
$13^{10} \times 11^5$
DINING ROOM BELOW
BEDRM
$11^1 \times 11^9$
BATH
LINEN
SEAT
BEDRM
$10^{10} \times 12^{10}$
LIVING ROOM BELOW
ROOF BELOW
ROOF BELOW

Design 3441

First Floor: 2,022 square feet
Second Floor: 845 square feet
Total: 2,867 square feet

L

Design by
Home Planners

Width 63'-8"
Depth 56'-2"

QUOTE ONE®
Cost to build? See page 516 to order complete cost estimate to build this house in your area!

■ Special details make the difference between a house and this two-story home. A two-story foyer ushers you into a comfortable layout. A snack bar, an audio-visual center, a fireplace and a high, sloped ceiling make the family room a favorite place for informal gatherings. A desk, an island cooktop, a bay and skylights enhance the kitchen area. The dining room features two columns and a plant ledge. The formal living room is graced by a sunny bay window, while across the hall a cozy study encourages quiet times. The first-floor master suite includes His and Hers walk-in closets, a spacious bath and a bay window. On the second floor, one bedroom features a walk-in closet and private bath which makes it perfect for a guest suite, while two additional bedrooms share a full bath.

Design Q326

First Floor: 1,237 square feet
Second Floor: 794 square feet
Total: 2,031 square feet

■ A weather-protected entry with decorative columns introduces this innovative design. The foyer spills into an open-plan living and dining room. A pair of columns and planter bridge visually zone the two rooms. The family room has a fireplace and sliding glass doors to the rear patio. It is separated from formal living and dining areas by the island kitchen and light-filled breakfast room. A cozy den opens through double doors just off the foyer. The master bedroom is on the second floor with two family bedrooms. It features a walk-in closet and bath with whirlpool tub and separate shower. The family bedrooms share a full bath with soaking tub. Plans include details for both a basement and a crawlspace foundation.

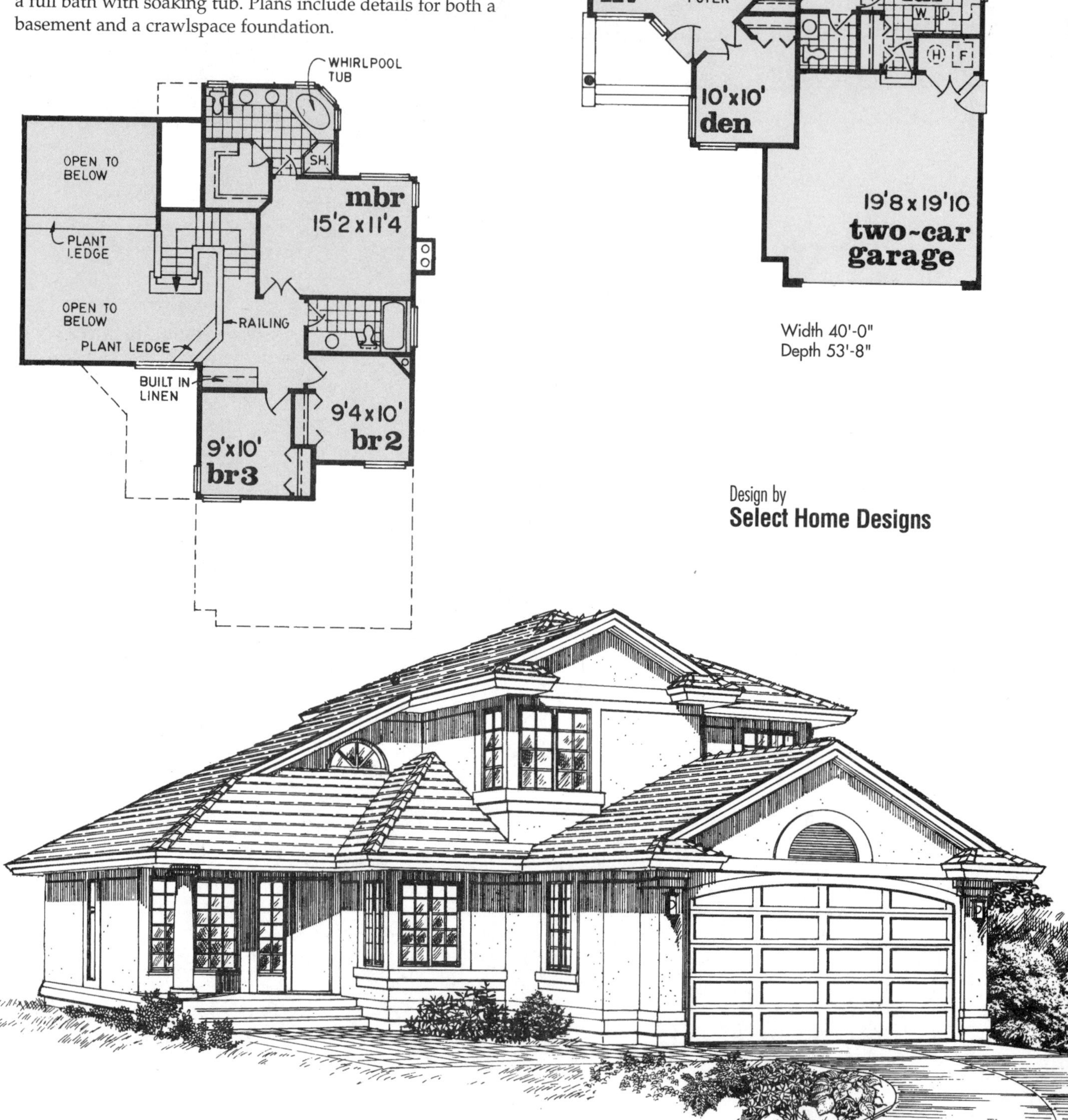

brk
7'6 x 8'
PATIO
din
13'2 x 10'
10' x 12'
fam
15'2 x 13'10
DECORATIVE COLUMNS
13'2 x 13'4
liv
FOYER
ldr
10' x 10'
den
19'8 x 19'10
two-car garage
WHIRLPOOL TUB
OPEN TO BELOW
SH.
mbr
15'2 x 11'4
PLANT LEDGE
OPEN TO BELOW
RAILING
PLANT LEDGE
BUILT IN LINEN
9'4 x 10'
br2
9' x 10'
br3

Width 40'-0"
Depth 53'-8"

Design by
Select Home Designs

Design 3558

First Floor: 2,328 square feet
Second Floor: 603 square feet
Total: 2,931 square feet

L D

■ This contemporary home wraps traditional formality with an avant-garde spirit to create the perfect blend of old elegance and new style. The foyer opens to the formal living room, which offers broad views of the rear property, and to a gallery hall that leads to casual family areas. The first-floor master suite offers a sumptuous bath with a corner whirlpool tub. A coffered ceiling highlights the master bedroom, which leads out to a private patio. Two family bedrooms share a full bath on the second floor.

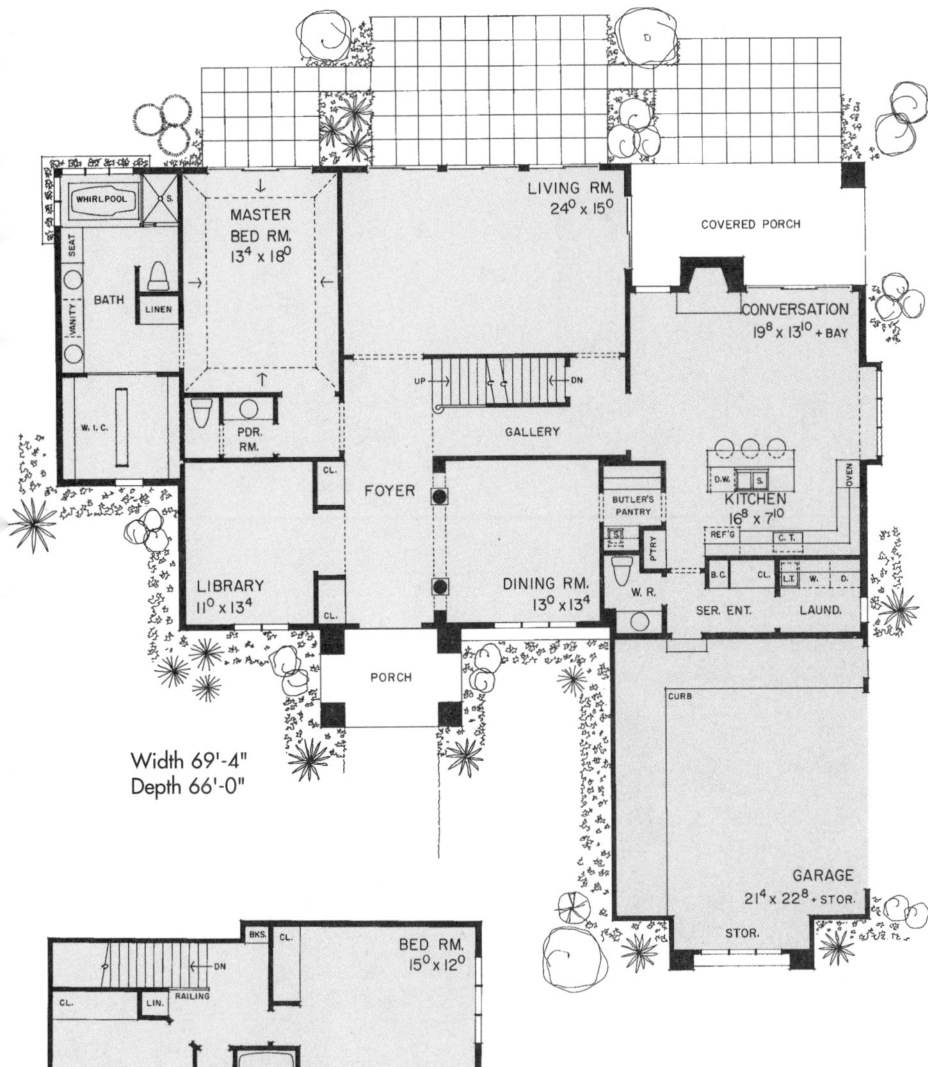
WHIRLPOOL
MASTER BED RM. 13⁴ x 18⁰
LIVING RM. 24⁰ x 15⁰
COVERED PORCH
SEAT
VANITY
BATH
LINEN
CONVERSATION 19⁸ x 13¹⁰ + BAY
UP
DN
W. I. C.
PDR. RM.
GALLERY
CL.
FOYER
BUTLER'S PANTRY
D.W.
S.
KITCHEN 16⁸ x 7¹⁰
OVEN
REF'G
C. T.
PTRY
LIBRARY 11⁰ x 13⁴
DINING RM. 13⁰ x 13⁴
W. R.
B.C.
L.T.
W.
D.
SER. ENT.
LAUND.
PORCH
CURB
GARAGE 21⁴ x 22⁸ + STOR.
STOR.
BKS.
BED RM. 15⁰ x 12⁰
RAILING
LIN.
BATH
BED RM. 12⁰ x 15⁴

Width 69'-4"
Depth 66'-0"

Design by
Home Planners

QUOTE ONE®

Cost to build? See page 516 to order complete cost estimate to build this house in your area!

Design 3463

First Floor: 1,163 square feet
Second Floor: 1,077 square feet
Total: 2,240 square feet

L

■ With a perfect floor plan for family living, this grand two-story is beautiful as well as practical. The tiled foyer leads to a stately living room with sliding glass doors to the back terrace. Columns separate it from the dining room. For casual living, the family room/breakfast room combination works well. On the second floor, the master bedroom draws attention with a fireplace, access to a deck and a super bath. The study niche in the hallway shares the outside deck. Two family bedrooms are also on the second floor—they share the use of a full bath. The two-car garage sits to the front of the plan and connects directly to the kitchen through the laundry area.

Design by
Home Planners

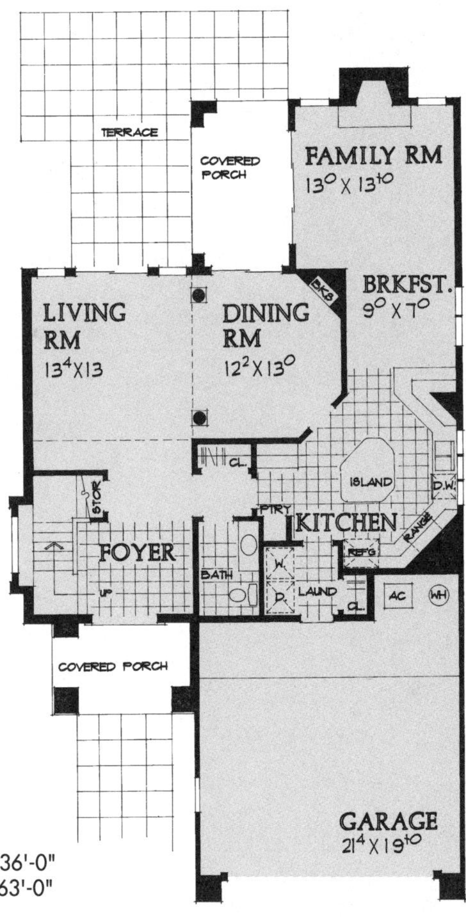

TERRACE
COVERED PORCH
FAMILY RM
$13^{0} \times 13^{+0}$
BRKFST.
$9^{0} \times 7^{0}$
LIVING RM
$13^{4} \times 13$
DINING RM
$12^{2} \times 13^{0}$
ISLAND
KITCHEN
FOYER
BATH
LAUND
COVERED PORCH
GARAGE
$21^{4} \times 19^{+0}$

Width 36'-0"
Depth 63'-0"

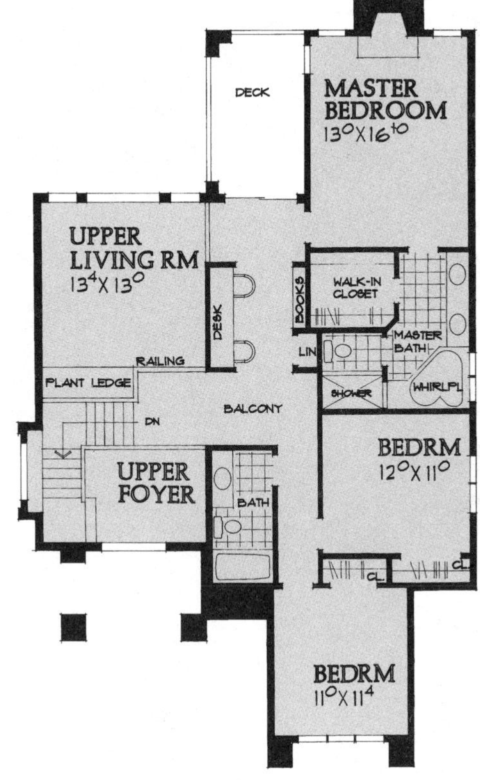

DECK
MASTER BEDROOM
$13^{0} \times 16^{+0}$
UPPER LIVING RM
$13^{4} \times 13^{0}$
DESK
BOOKS
WALK-IN CLOSET
MASTER BATH
WHIRLPL
SHOWER
RAILING
PLANT LEDGE
BALCONY
DN
UPPER FOYER
BATH
BEDRM
$12^{0} \times 11^{0}$
BEDRM
$11^{0} \times 11^{4}$

QUOTE ONE®

Cost to build? See page 516 to order complete cost estimate to build this house in your area!

Design 3457

First Floor: 1,252 square feet
Second Floor: 972 square feet
Total: 2,224 square feet

L

■ For family living, this delightful three-bedroom plan scores big. The family room focuses on a fireplace and enjoys direct access to a covered porch. The breakfast room allows plenty of space for friendly meals—the island kitchen remains open to this room thus providing ease in serving meals and, of course, conversations with the cook. From the two-car garage, a utility area opens to the main-floor living areas. Upstairs, the master suite affords a quiet retreat with its private bath; here you'll find a whirlpool tub set in a sunny nook. A balcony further enhances this bedroom. The two secondary bedrooms share a hall bath with a double-bowl vanity.

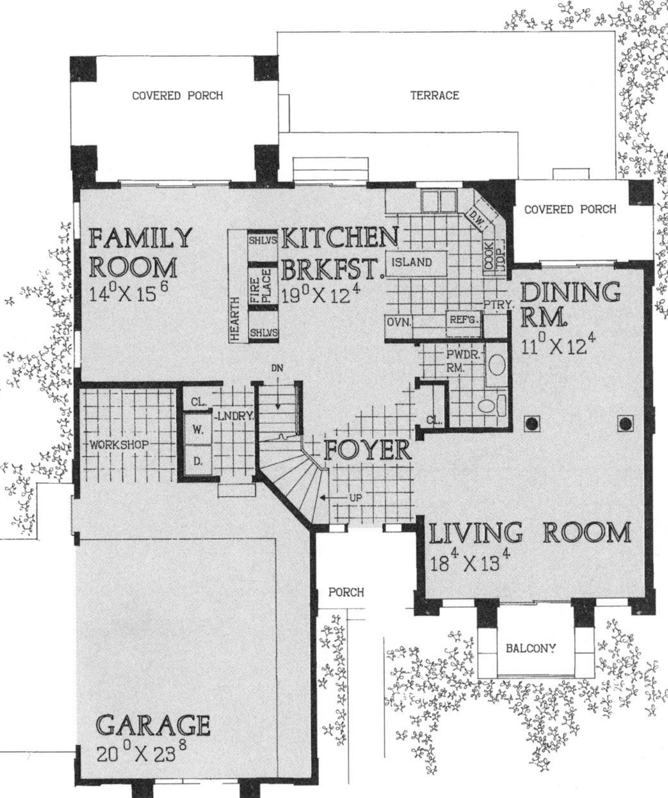
COVERED PORCH
TERRACE
COVERED PORCH
FAMILY ROOM
14^0X15^6
KITCHEN BRKFST.
19^0X12^4
ISLAND
DINING RM.
11^0X12^4
PWDR. RM.
LNDRY.
WORKSHOP
FOYER
LIVING ROOM
18^4X13^4
PORCH
BALCONY
GARAGE
20^0X23^8

Width 48'-0"
Depth 58'-0"

BALCONY
MASTER BEDROOM
16^0X 9^{10}
BEDRM.
12^0X11^0
BALCONY
BEDRM.
11^0X12^8
WHIRL POOL
MASTER BATH
SHOWER
WALK-IN CL.
RAILING
UPPER FOYER
WALK-IN CLOSET
UPPER LIVING RM.

QUOTE ONE®

Cost to build? See page 516 to order complete cost estimate to build this house in your area!

Design by
Home Planners

Design 3480

Square Footage: 1,845

L **D**

■ The inviting facade of this sun-country home introduces a most livable floor plan. Beyond the grand entry, a comfortable gathering room, with a central fireplace, shares sweeping, open spaces with the dining room. An efficiently patterned kitchen makes use of a large, walk-in pantry and a breakfast room. Nearby, a full laundry room rounds out this utilitarian area. Away from the hustle and bustle of the day, three bedrooms provide ample sleeping accommodations for the whole family. Two secondary bedrooms each enjoy full proportions and the convenience of a nearby bath. In the master bedroom, look for double closets and a pampering bath with double lavs, a vanity and a whirlpool bath.

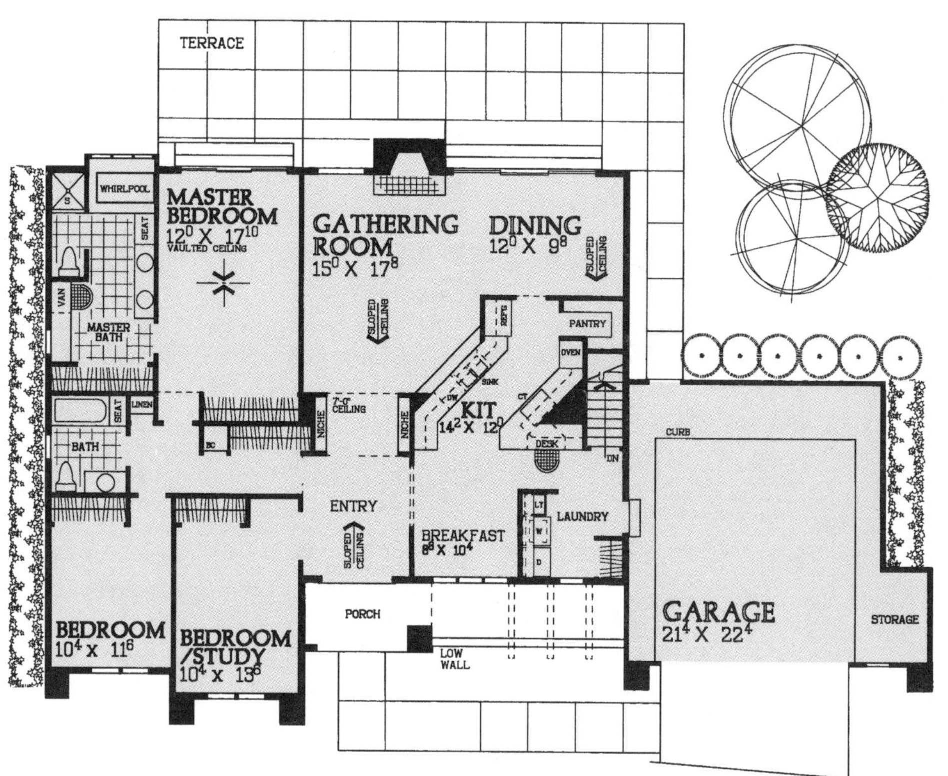
TERRACE
WHIRLPOOL
MASTER BEDROOM
12^{0} X 17^{10}
VAULTED CEILING
GATHERING ROOM
15^{0} X 17^{8}
DINING
12^{0} X 9^{8}
SLOPED CEILING
SEAT
VAN
MASTER BATH
PANTRY
REF'G
OVEN
SINK
DW
CT
LINEN
SEAT
BATH
NICHE
7'-0" CEILING
NICHE
KIT
14^{2} X 12^{0}
DESK
DN
CURB
ENTRY
LAUNDRY
BREAKFAST
8^{8} X 10^{4}
PORCH
BEDROOM
10^{4} X 11^{6}
BEDROOM /STUDY
10^{4} X 13^{6}
LOW WALL
GARAGE
21^{4} X 22^{4}
STORAGE

Width 75'-0"
Depth 47'-5"

QUOTE ONE®

Cost to build? See page 516
to order complete cost estimate
to build this house in your area!

Design by
Home Planners

Design 3322

First Floor: 1,860 square feet
Second Floor: 935 square feet
Total: 2,795 square feet

L D

■ This cleverly designed Southwestern-style home takes its cue from the California craftsman and bungalow styles that are so popular today. Nonetheless, it is suited to just about any climate. Its convenient floor plans include living and working areas on the first floor in addition to a master suite. Both the master bedroom and the gathering room sport fireplaces; the kitchen has a cooktop island. The second floor holds two family bedrooms and a guest bedroom. Note the abundance of window area to the rear of the plan.

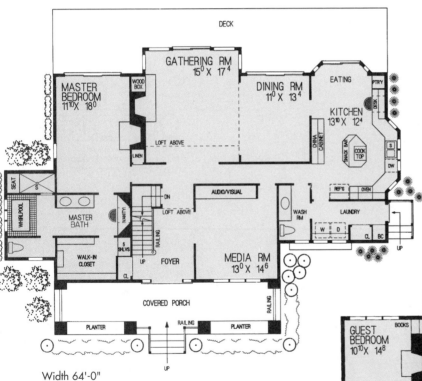

DECK
GATHERING RM 15⁰ X 17⁴
MASTER BEDROOM 11¹⁰X 18⁰
WOOD BOX
DINING RM 11⁰ X 13⁴
EATING
KITCHEN 13¹⁰ X 12⁴
PTRY
DESK
CHINA CABINET
SNACK BAR
COOK TOP
LOFT ABOVE
LINEN
S
DW
SEAT
WHIRLPOOL
MASTER BATH
VANITY
DN
LOFT ABOVE
AUDIO/VISUAL
REF'G
OVEN
WASH RM
LAUNDRY
W D
CL BC
UP
5 SHLVS
RAILING
WALK-IN CLOSET
CL
UP
FOYER
MEDIA RM 13⁰ X 14⁶
COVERED PORCH
RAILING
PLANTER
RAILING
PLANTER
UP

Width 64'-0"
Depth 44'-6"

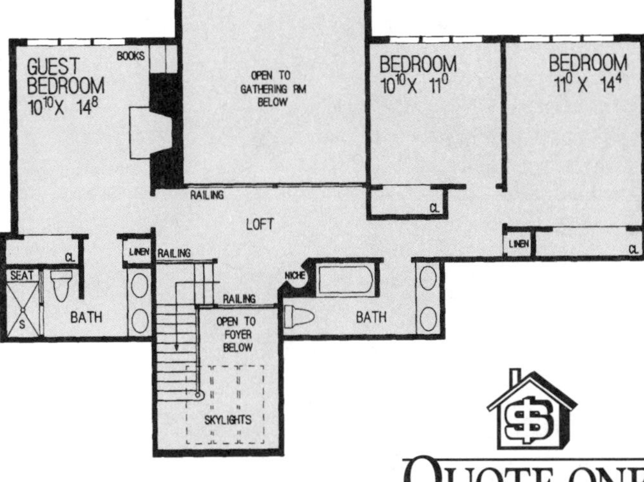
GUEST BEDROOM 10¹⁰X 14⁸
BOOKS
OPEN TO GATHERING RM BELOW
BEDROOM 10¹⁰X 11⁰
BEDROOM 11⁰ X 14⁴
RAILING
LOFT
CL
LINEN
CL
CL
LINEN RAILING
SEAT
NICHE
S
BATH
RAILING
OPEN TO FOYER BELOW
BATH
SKYLIGHTS

Rear Elevation

Design by
Home Planners

Width 75'-0"
Depth 43'-5"

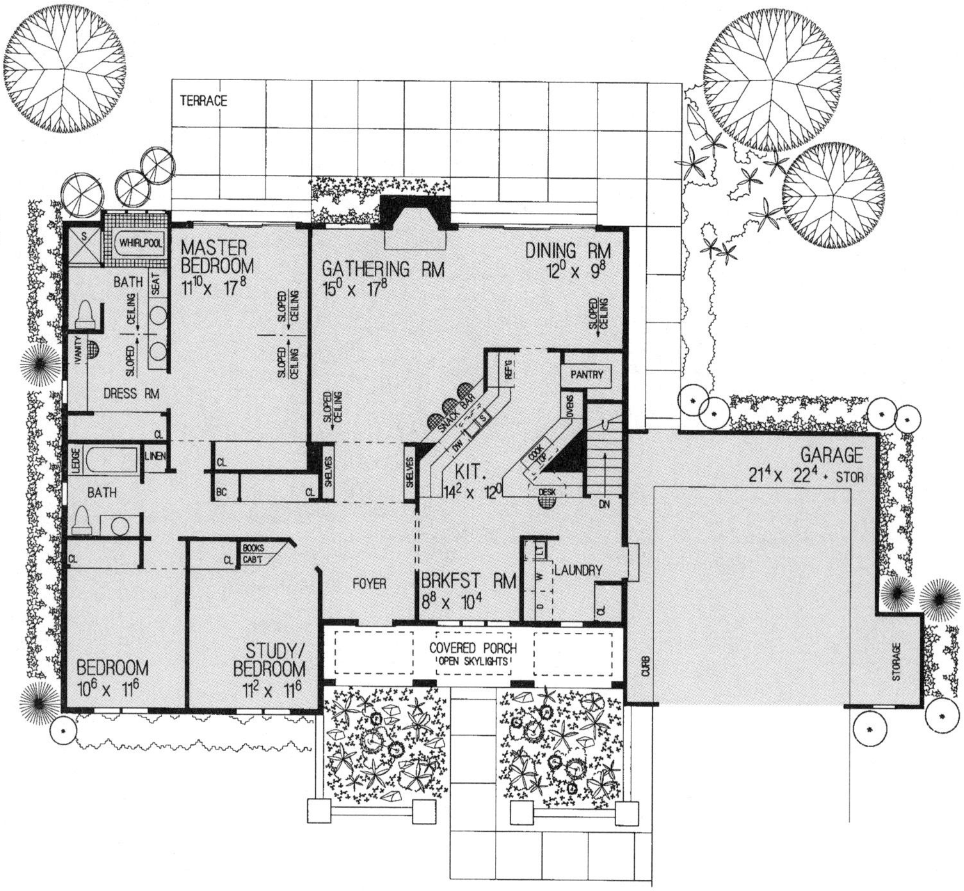

Design by
Home Planners

Design 2948

Square Footage: 1,830

■ Originally styled for Southwest living, this home is a good choice in any region where casual elegance is desired. Easy living is the focus of the large gathering room, apparent in its open relationship to the dining room and kitchen via a snack bar. The long galley kitchen is designed for work efficiency and has a planning desk, service entrance and a beautiful breakfast room framed with windows. The master bedroom and bath have a dramatic sloped ceiling and are joined by a traditional dressing room. Two secondary bedrooms—the front facing one would make a nice study—share a hall bath.

QUOTE ONE®

Cost to build? See page 516 to order complete cost estimate to build this house in your area!

Design by
Home Planners

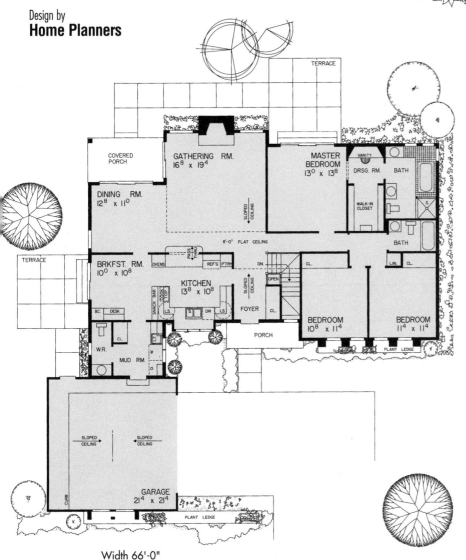

Design 2912

Square Footage: 1,864

■ This contemporary design with smart Spanish styling incorporates careful zoning by room functions with lifestyle comfort. All three bedrooms, including a master bedroom suite with a large dressing area and lavish bath, are isolated at one end of the home. Entry to a breakfast room and kitchen is possible through a mud room off the garage. That's good news for carrying groceries from car to kitchen or slipping off muddy shoes. The efficient kitchen includes a snack bar and a convenient cooktop with easy service to the breakfast room, dining room and gathering room. A large rear gathering room features a sloped ceiling and a fireplace. A covered porch just off the dining room furthers living potential.

Width 66'-0"
Depth 62'-0"

QUOTE ONE®

Cost to build? See page 516 to order complete cost estimate to build this house in your area!

Design 2950

Square Footage: 2,559

■ A natural desert dweller, this stucco, tile-roofed beauty is equally comfortable in any clime. Inside, there's a well-planned design. Common living areas—gathering room, formal dining room and breakfast room—are offset by a quiet study that could be used as a bedroom or guest room. A master suite features two walk-in closets, a double vanity and whirlpool spa. The two-car garage provides a service entrance; close by is an adequate laundry area and a pantry. A lovely hearth warms the gathering room and complements the snack bar area.

Design by
Home Planners

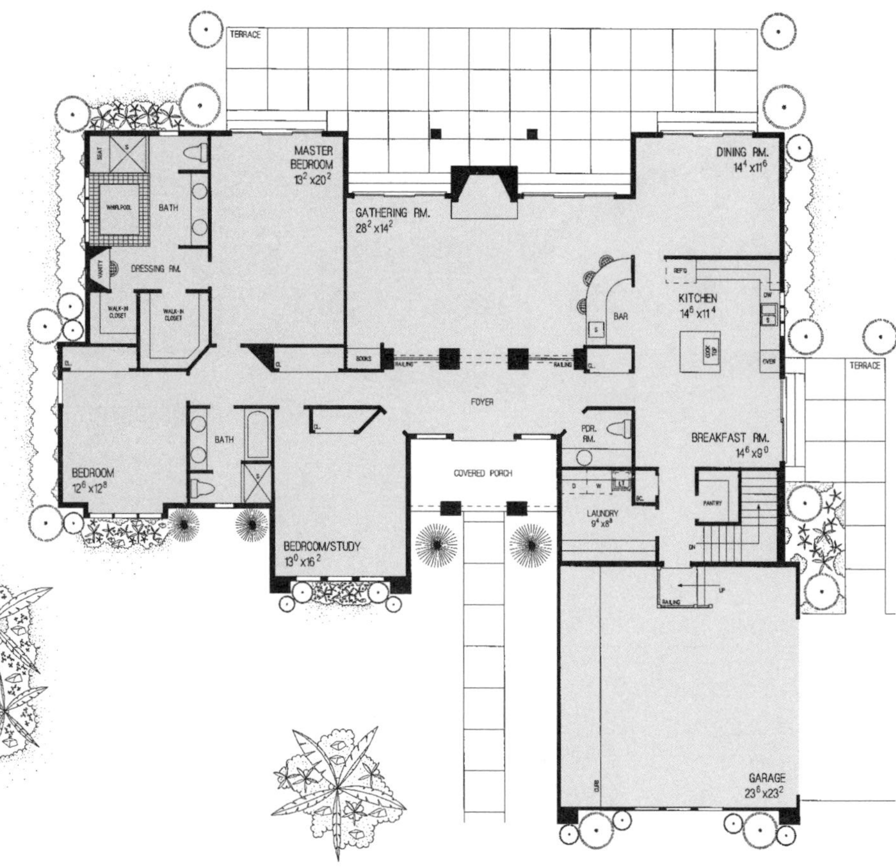

TERRACE
MASTER BEDROOM $13^2 \times 20^2$
BATH
WHIRLPOOL
DRESSING RM.
WALK-IN CLOSET
WALK-IN CLOSET
GATHERING RM. $28^2 \times 14^2$
DINING RM. $14^4 \times 11^6$
KITCHEN $14^6 \times 11^4$
BAR
FOYER
BATH
BEDROOM $12^6 \times 12^8$
PDR. RM.
BREAKFAST RM. $14^6 \times 9^0$
COVERED PORCH
LAUNDRY $9^4 \times 8^8$
PANTRY
BEDROOM/STUDY $13^0 \times 16^2$
TERRACE
GARAGE $23^6 \times 23^2$

Width 74'-0"
Depth 66'-10"

QUOTE ONE®
Cost to build? See page 516
to order complete cost estimate
to build this house in your area!

Design 2875

Square Footage: 1,913

L D

Design by
Home Planners

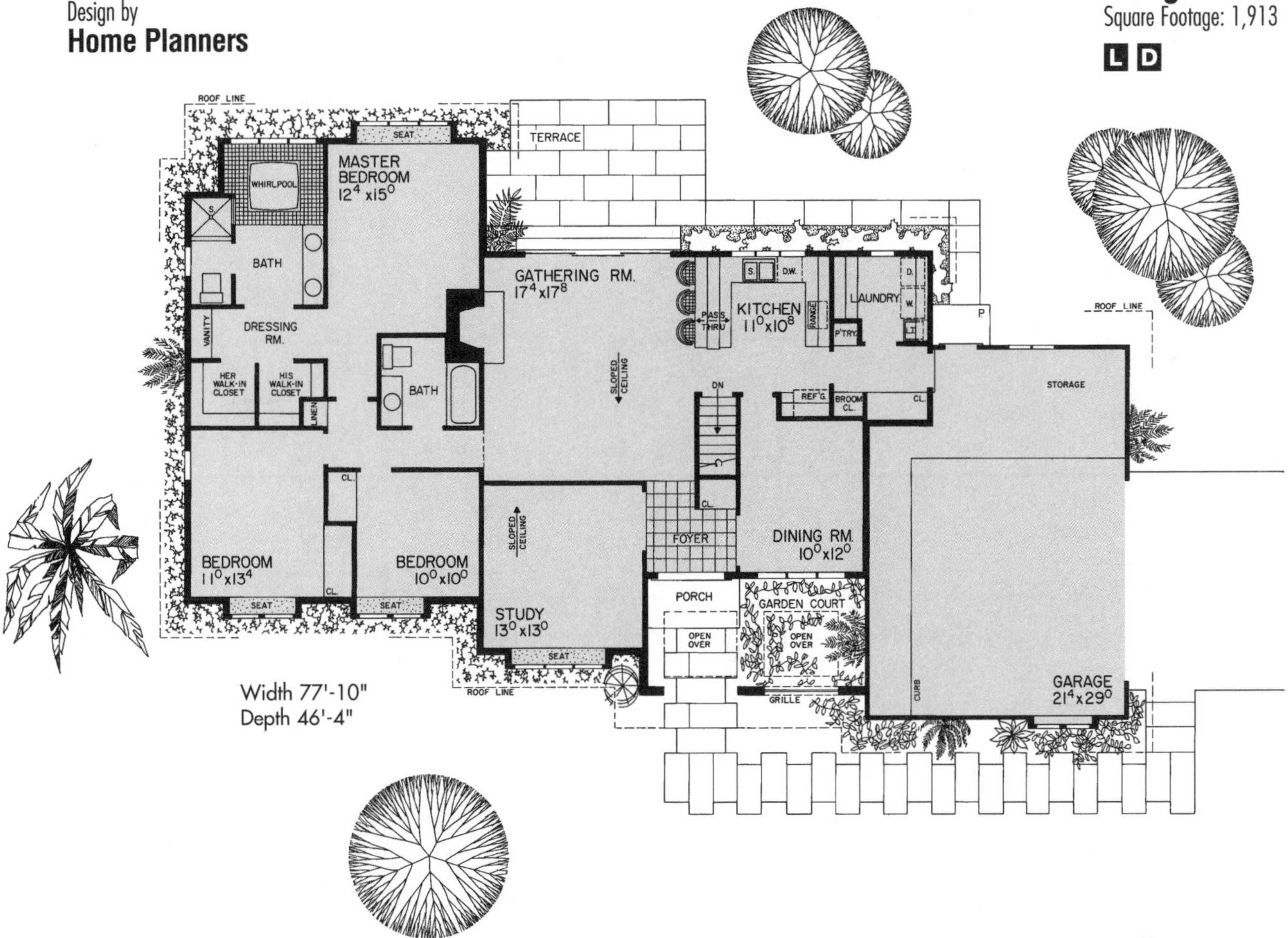

Width 77'-10"
Depth 46'-4"

■ This elegant Spanish design incorporates excellent indoor/outdoor living relationships for families who enjoy the sun. Note the overhead openings for rain and sun to fall upon a front garden, while a twin-arched entry leads to the front porch and foyer. Inside, the floor plan features a modern kitchen with pass-through to a large gathering room with fireplace. Other features include a dining room, laundry room, a study off the foyer, plus three bedrooms including a master bedroom with its own whirlpool tub.

QUOTE ONE®

Cost to build? See page 516
to order complete cost estimate
to build this house in your area!

Design 3632

Square Footage: 2,539

L

■ Exposed rafter tails, arched porch detailing, massive paneled front doors and stucco exterior walls enhance the western character of this U-shaped ranch house. Double doors open to a spacious, slope-ceilinged art gallery. The quiet sleeping zone is comprised of an entire wing. The extra room at the front of this wing may be used for a den or an office. The family dining and kitchen activities are located at the opposite end of the plan. Indoor-outdoor living relationships are outstanding. The large open courtyard is akin to the fabled Greek atrium. It is accessible from each of the zones and functions with a covered arbor which looks out over the rear landscape. The master suite has a generous sitting area, a walk-in closet, twin lavatories and a whirlpool plus a stall shower.

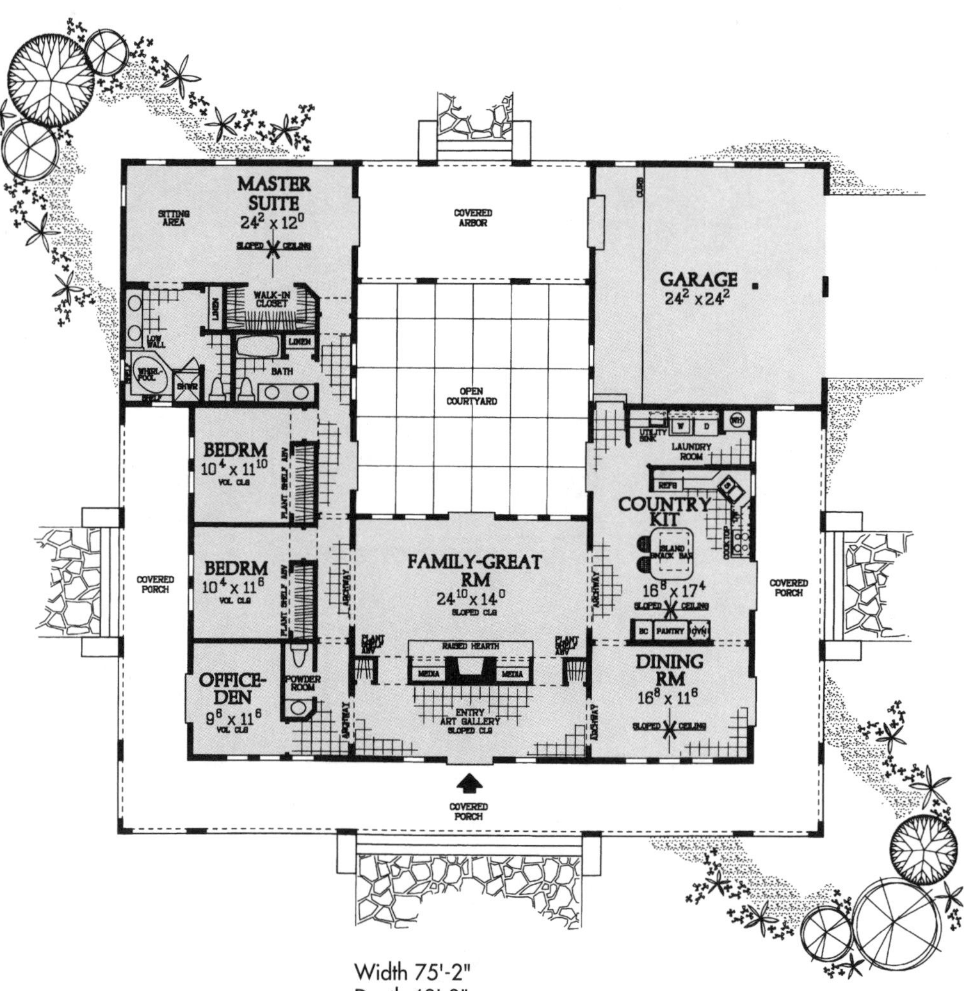

MASTER SUITE
24² x 12⁰
SITTING AREA
SLOPED CEILING
WALK-IN CLOSET
LINEN
BATH
COVERED ARBOR
GARAGE
24² x 24²
OPEN COURTYARD
LAUNDRY ROOM
COUNTRY KIT
16⁸ x 17⁴
BEDRM
10⁴ x 11¹⁰
BEDRM
10⁴ x 11⁶
COVERED PORCH
FAMILY-GREAT RM
24¹⁰ x 14⁰
SLOPED CLG
RAISED HEARTH
MEDIA
OFFICE-DEN
9⁶ x 11⁶
POWDER ROOM
ENTRY ART GALLERY SLOPED CLG
DINING RM
16⁸ x 11⁶
SLOPED CEILING
COVERED PORCH

Width 75'-2"
Depth 68'-8"

QUOTE ONE®

Cost to build? See page 516 to order complete cost estimate to build this house in your area!

Design by
Home Planners

Design 3630

Square Footage: 3,034

L

QUOTE ONE®

Cost to build? See page 516 to order complete cost estimate to build this house in your area!

■ A grand entry enhances the exterior of this elegant stucco home. The foyer leads to an open formal area that will invite planned occasions. The corner kitchen with bayed breakfast area serves casual meals with a snack-bar counter, and more traditional and festive events with the formal dining room, defined by a decorative half-wall. The private master suite boasts an indoor retreat by a cozy fireplace, as well as access to a private patio with a spa, secluded by a privacy wall. Two family bedrooms on the opposite side of the plan share a full bath and a gallery hall that leads to the casual living area and to a media room.

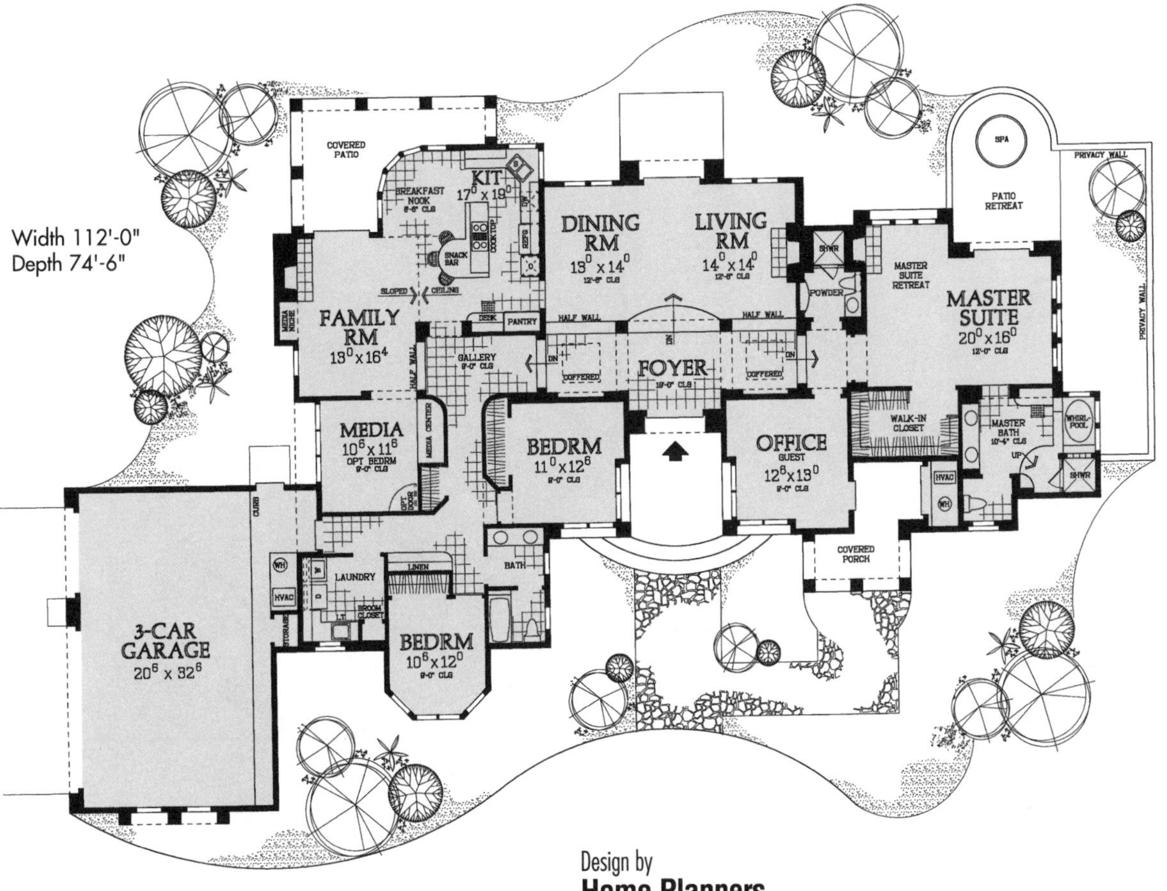
Width 112'-0"
Depth 74'-6"
COVERED PATIO
BREAKFAST NOOK
KIT
17⁰ x 19⁰
DINING RM
13⁰ x 14⁰
LIVING RM
14⁰ x 14⁰
SPA
PATIO RETREAT
PRIVACY WALL
MASTER SUITE RETREAT
MASTER SUITE
20⁰ x 16⁰
FAMILY RM
13⁰ x 16⁴
GALLERY
FOYER
HALF WALL
POWDER
WALK-IN CLOSET
MASTER BATH
MEDIA
10⁶ x 11⁶
OPT. BEDRM
BEDRM
11⁰ x 12⁶
OFFICE
GUEST
12⁶ x 13⁰
COVERED PORCH
LAUNDRY
LINEN
BATH
3-CAR GARAGE
20⁶ x 32⁶
BEDRM
10⁶ x 12⁰

Design by
Home Planners

Design by
Home Planners

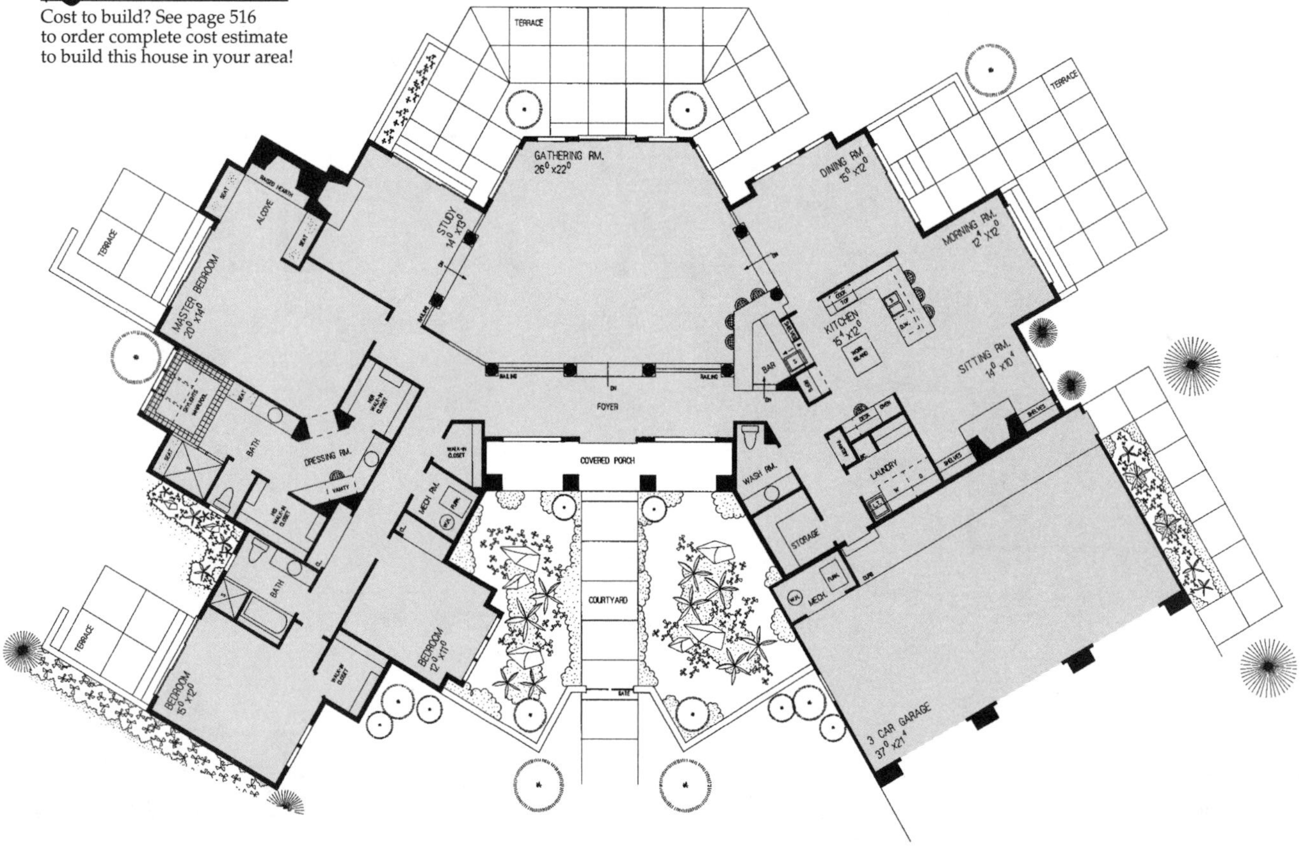

Width 110'-7"
Depth 66'-11"

Design 2922

Square Footage: 3,505

■ Loaded with custom features, this plan seems to have everything imaginable. It's the perfect home for entertaining—there's an enormous sunken gathering room and cozy study. A full-sized bar is fashioned to serve the gathering room. The country-style kitchen contains an efficient work area, as well as space for relaxing in the morning room and fireside chats in the sitting room. Two nice-sized bedrooms share a hall bath. The luxurious master suite has a fireplace alcove, and an amenity-rich bath complete with twin walk-in closets, a dressing area and spa style tub.

Design by
Home Planners

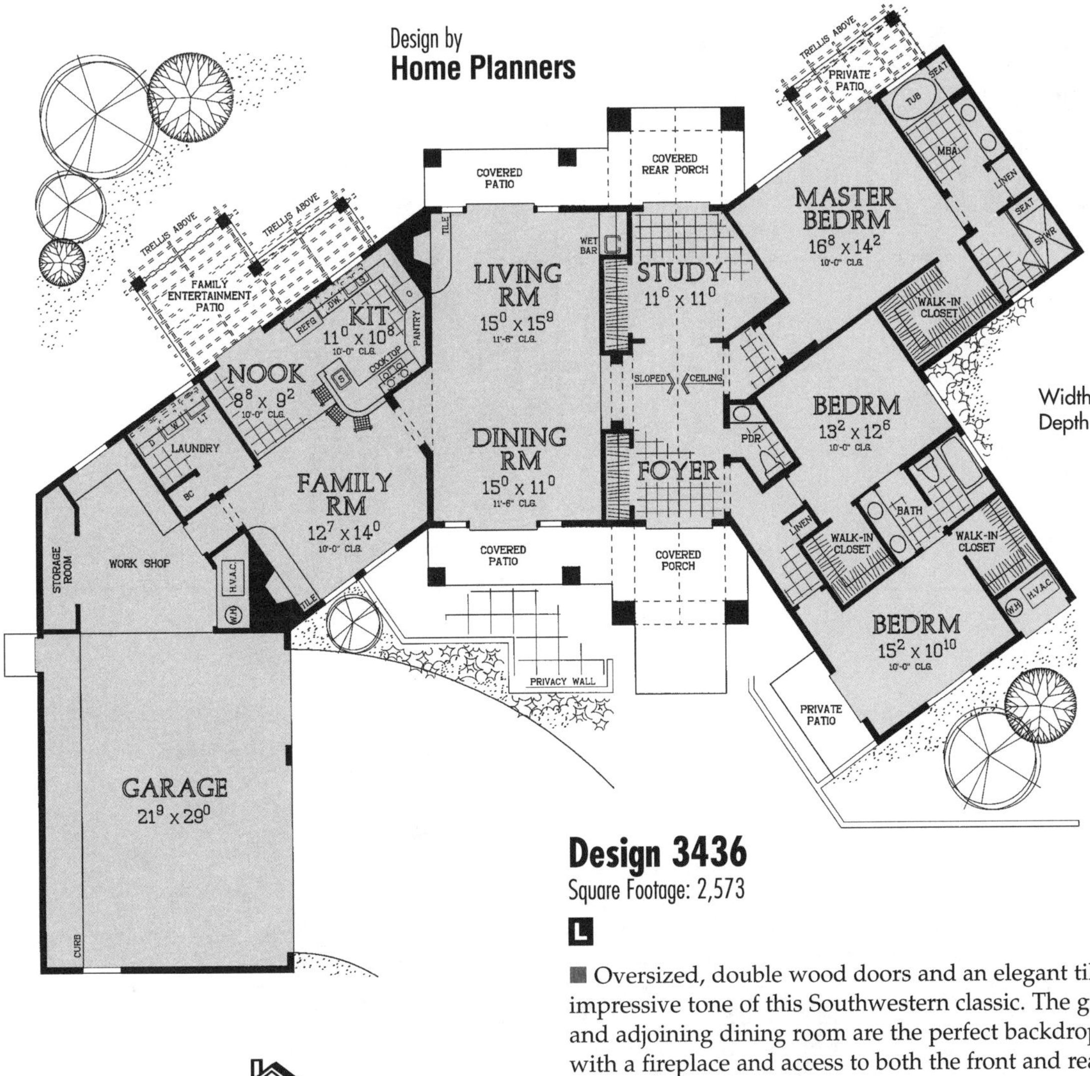

Width 94'-6"
Depth 79'-11"

Design 3436

Square Footage: 2,573

L

■ Oversized, double wood doors and an elegant tile foyer set the impressive tone of this Southwestern classic. The grand living room and adjoining dining room are the perfect backdrop for entertaining, with a fireplace and access to both the front and rear covered patios. Casual living is just as inviting in the family room with a snack bar and its own fireplace with an extended bench. The large, gourmet kitchen has a breakfast nook that opens onto the family entertainment patio. The sleeping zone features two family bedrooms with walk-in closets and private entrances to the compartmented bath. The master suite has a private patio, huge walk-in closet and a master bath with luxe appointments such as a spa tub, dual vanity and an oversized, walk-in shower.

QUOTE ONE®

Cost to build? See page 516
to order complete cost estimate
to build this house in your area!

Design 3344

Square Footage: 3,054

L

■ This home features interior planning for today's active family. Informal areas include a living room with a fireplace, a family room with fireplace and a study with a wet bar. Convenient to the kitchen is the formal dining room with an attractive bay window overlooking the backyard. The four-bedroom sleeping area contains a sumptuous master suite. Its bath includes His and Hers areas, His and Hers walk-in closets and a dressing room with double vanity. Notice the cheerful flower porch with access from the master suite, living room and dining room. The two-car garage connects to the main house via a service entrance near the laundry room.

Width 85'-8"
Depth 70'-2"

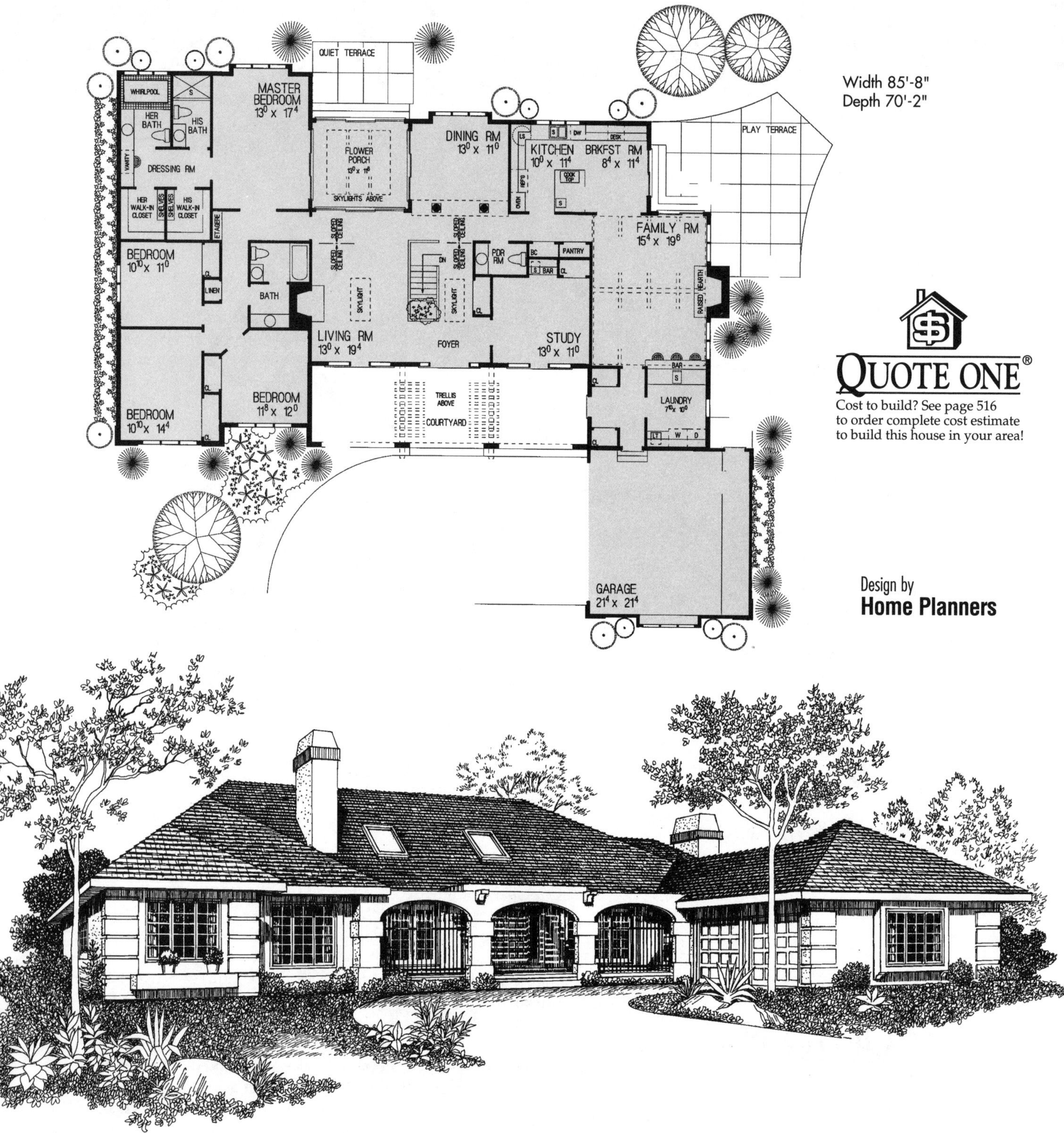

QUIET TERRACE
PLAY TERRACE
MASTER BEDROOM $13^0 \times 17^4$
HER BATH
HIS BATH
DRESSING RM
FLOWER PORCH
DINING RM $13^0 \times 11^0$
KITCHEN $10^0 \times 11^4$
BRKFST RM $8^4 \times 11^4$
FAMILY RM $15^4 \times 19^6$
BEDROOM $10^{10} \times 11^0$
BATH
LIVING RM $13^0 \times 19^4$
FOYER
STUDY $13^0 \times 11^0$
LAUNDRY
BEDROOM $10^{10} \times 14^4$
BEDROOM $11^8 \times 12^0$
COURTYARD
GARAGE $21^4 \times 21^4$

QUOTE ONE®

Cost to build? See page 516 to order complete cost estimate to build this house in your area!

Design by
Home Planners

QUOTE ONE®

Cost to build? See page 516 to order complete cost estimate to build this house in your area!

Design 2670

Square Footage: 3,058
Lounge: 279 square feet

L

■ Sunny climates demand lots of light-gathering areas and outdoor spaces. This home delivers with a covered entry foyer, enclosed atrium, long rear terrace and plenty of windows. The atrium has a built-in seat and will bring light to the adjacent living room, dining room and breakfast room. Beyond the foyer, down a step, is the tiled reception hall that includes a powder room. This area leads to the sleeping wing and up one step to the family room with a raised-hearth fireplace and sliding glass doors to the rear terrace. Overlooking the family room is a railed lounge which can be used for a variety of activities. The sleeping area includes a master suite and three family bedrooms. The master features a sloped ceiling, a dressing room with a vanity sink, a separate tub and shower, and terrace access. Family bedrooms share a full bath.

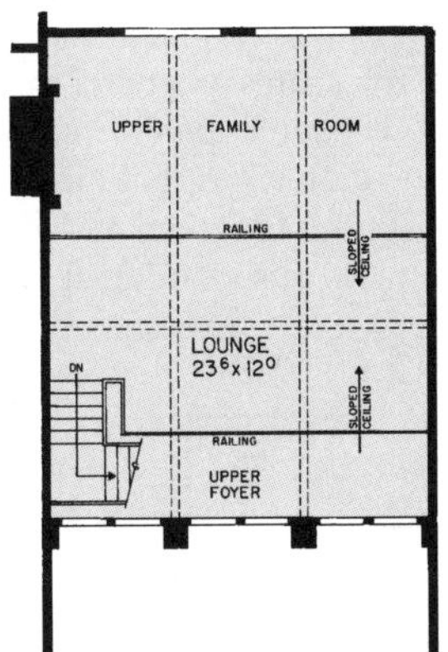

UPPER FAMILY ROOM
RAILING
SLOPED CEILING
LOUNGE
23⁶x 12⁰
DN
RAILING
UPPER FOYER

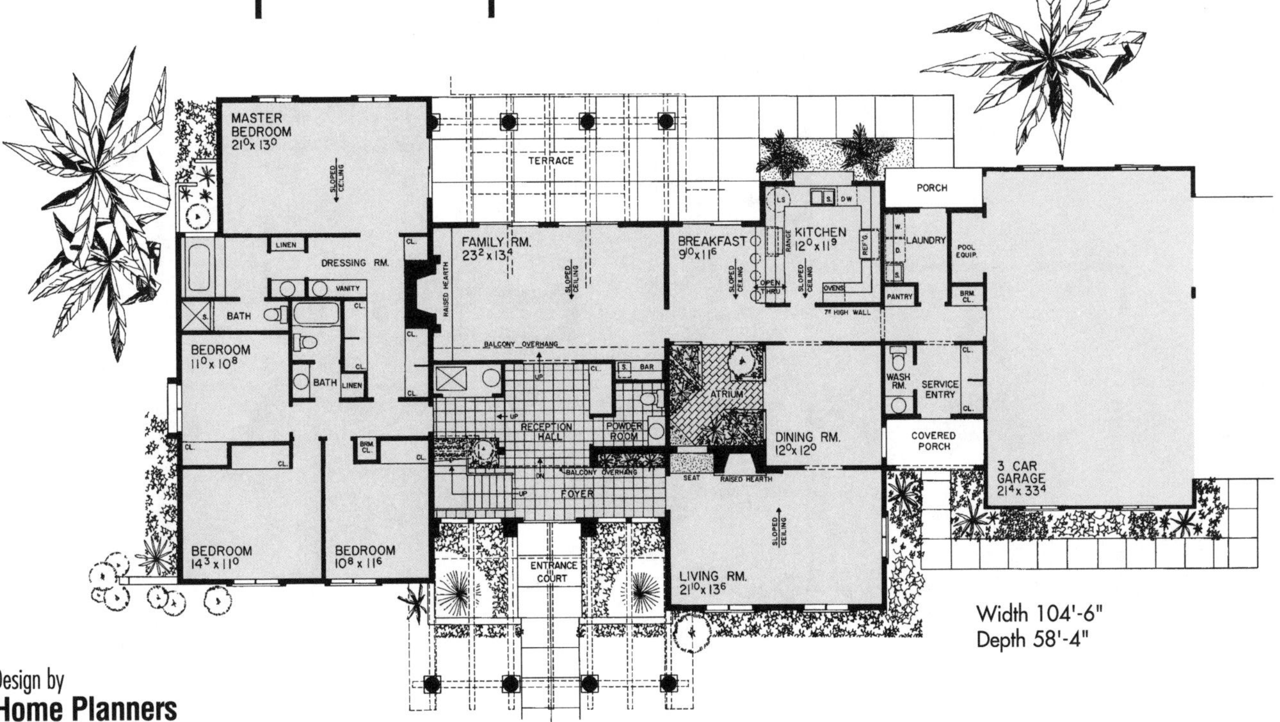

MASTER BEDROOM
21⁰x 13⁰
TERRACE
PORCH
LINEN
DRESSING RM.
VANITY
FAMILY RM.
23²x 13⁴
BREAKFAST
9⁰x 11⁶
KITCHEN
12⁰x 11⁹
LAUNDRY
POOL EQUIP.
PANTRY
BATH
BEDROOM
11⁰x 10⁸
BATH
BALCONY OVERHANG
ATRIUM
WASH RM.
SERVICE ENTRY
RECEPTION HALL
POWDER ROOM
DINING RM.
12⁰x 12⁰
COVERED PORCH
FOYER
RAISED HEARTH
3 CAR GARAGE
21⁴x 33⁴
BEDROOM
14³x 11⁰
BEDROOM
10⁸x 11⁶
ENTRANCE COURT
LIVING RM.
21¹⁰x 13⁶

Width 104'-6"
Depth 58'-4"

Design by
Home Planners

Design by
Home Planners

Design 3486

Square Footage: 2,000

This classic stucco design provides a cool retreat in any climate. From the covered porch, enter the skylit foyer to find an arched ceiling leading to the central gathering room with its raised-hearth fireplace and terrace access. A connecting corner dining room is conveniently located near the amenity-filled kitchen that features an abundant pantry, a snack bar and a separate breakfast area. The large master bedroom includes terrace access and a master bath with a whirlpool tub, a separate shower and plenty of closet space. A second bedroom and a study that can be converted to a bedroom complete this wonderful plan.

QUOTE ONE®

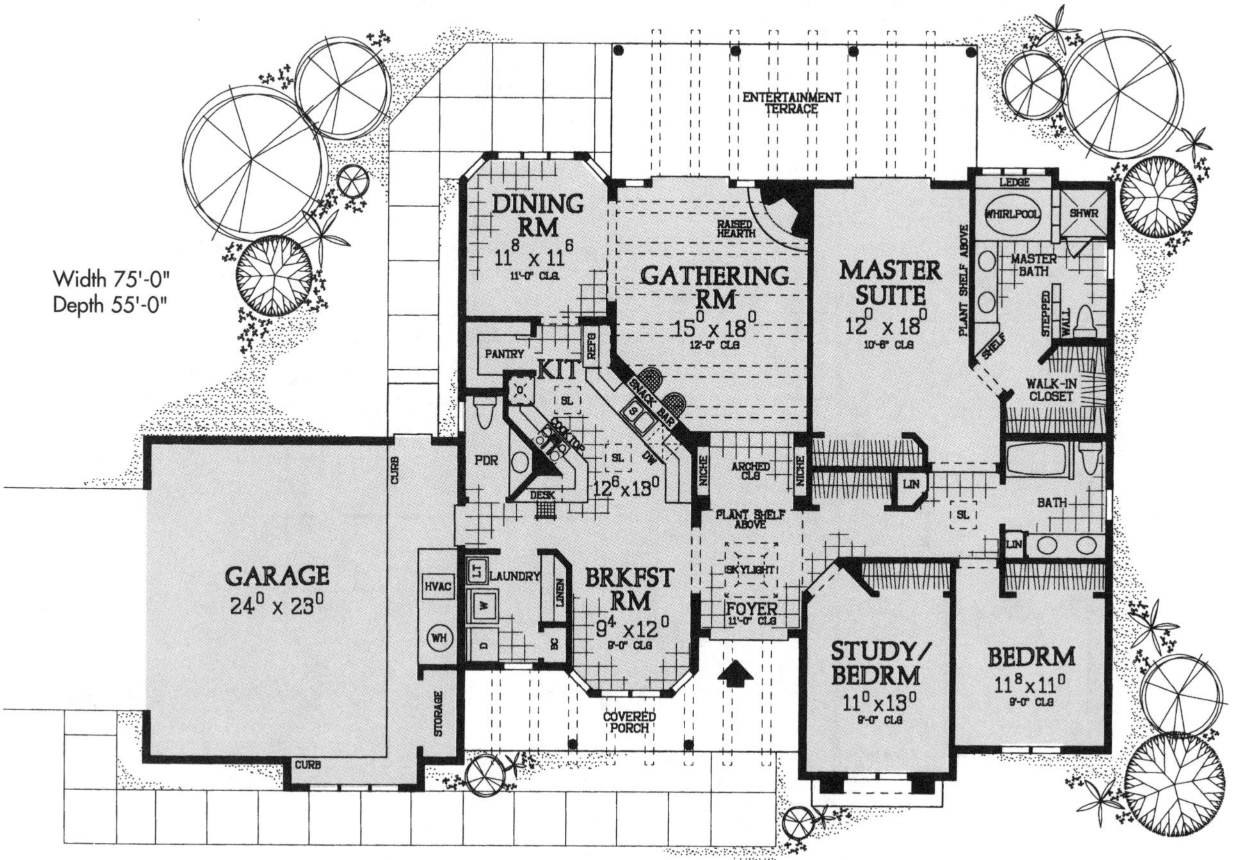

Cost to build? See page 516 to order complete cost estimate to build this house in your area!

Width 75'-0"
Depth 55'-0"

Width 61'-6"
Depth 67'-4"

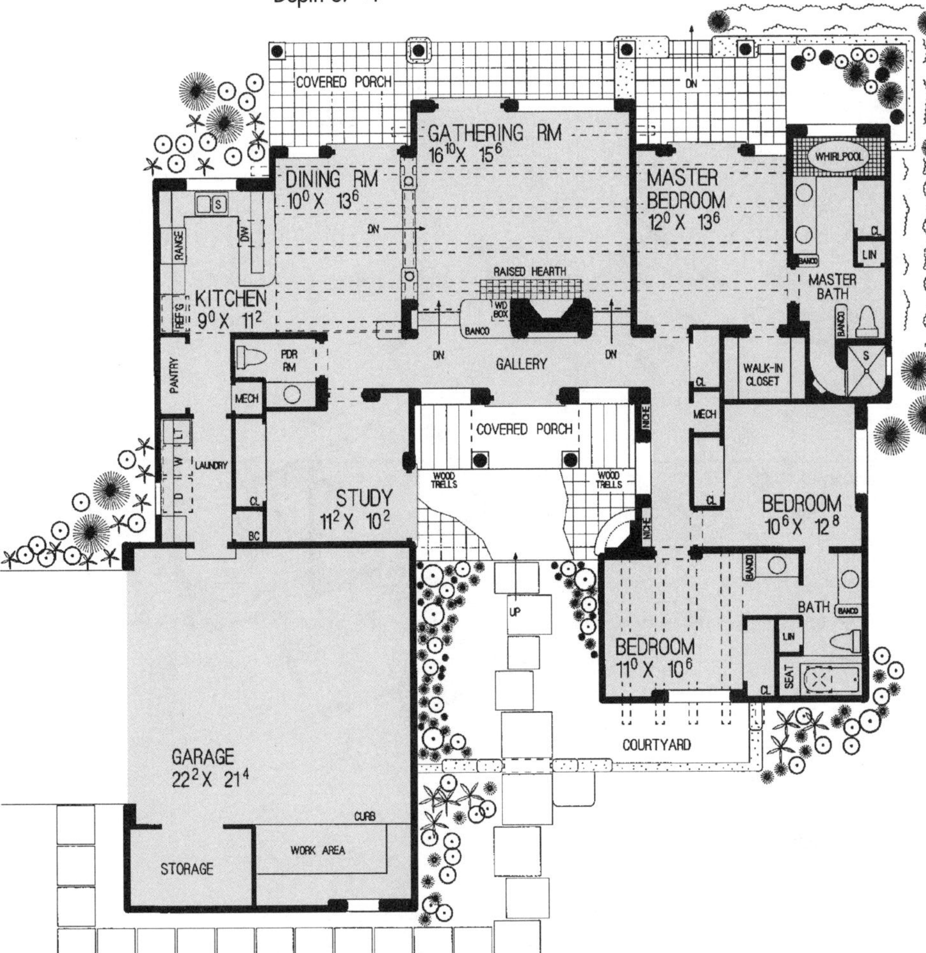
COVERED PORCH
DN
GATHERING RM
16^{10} X 15^{6}
DINING RM
10^{0} X 13^{6}
MASTER BEDROOM
12^{0} X 13^{6}
WHIRLPOOL
CL
LIN
MASTER BATH
RAISED HEARTH
WD BOX
BANCO
RANGE
DW
KITCHEN
9^{0} X 11^{2}
REF'G
PANTRY
PDR RM
MECH
GALLERY
WALK-IN CLOSET
CL
MECH
COVERED PORCH
NICHE
WOOD TRELLS
LAUNDRY
STUDY
11^{2} X 10^{2}
BC
BEDROOM
10^{6} X 12^{8}
BATH
BEDROOM
11^{0} X 10^{6}
LIN
SEAT
UP
COURTYARD
GARAGE
22^{2} X 21^{4}
CURB
WORK AREA
STORAGE

QUOTE ONE®

Cost to build? See page 516 to order complete cost estimate to build this house in your area!

Design 3431

Square Footage: 1,907

■ Graceful curves welcome you into the courtyard of this Santa Fe home. Inside, a gallery directs traffic to the work zone on the left or the sleeping zone on the right. Straight ahead lies a sunken gathering room with a beam ceiling and a raised-hearth fireplace. A large pantry offers extra storage space for kitchen items. The covered rear porch is accessible from the dining room, gathering room and secluded master bedroom. The master bath has a whirlpool tub, a separate shower, a double vanity and lots of closet space. Two family bedrooms share a compartmented bath.

Design by
Home Planners

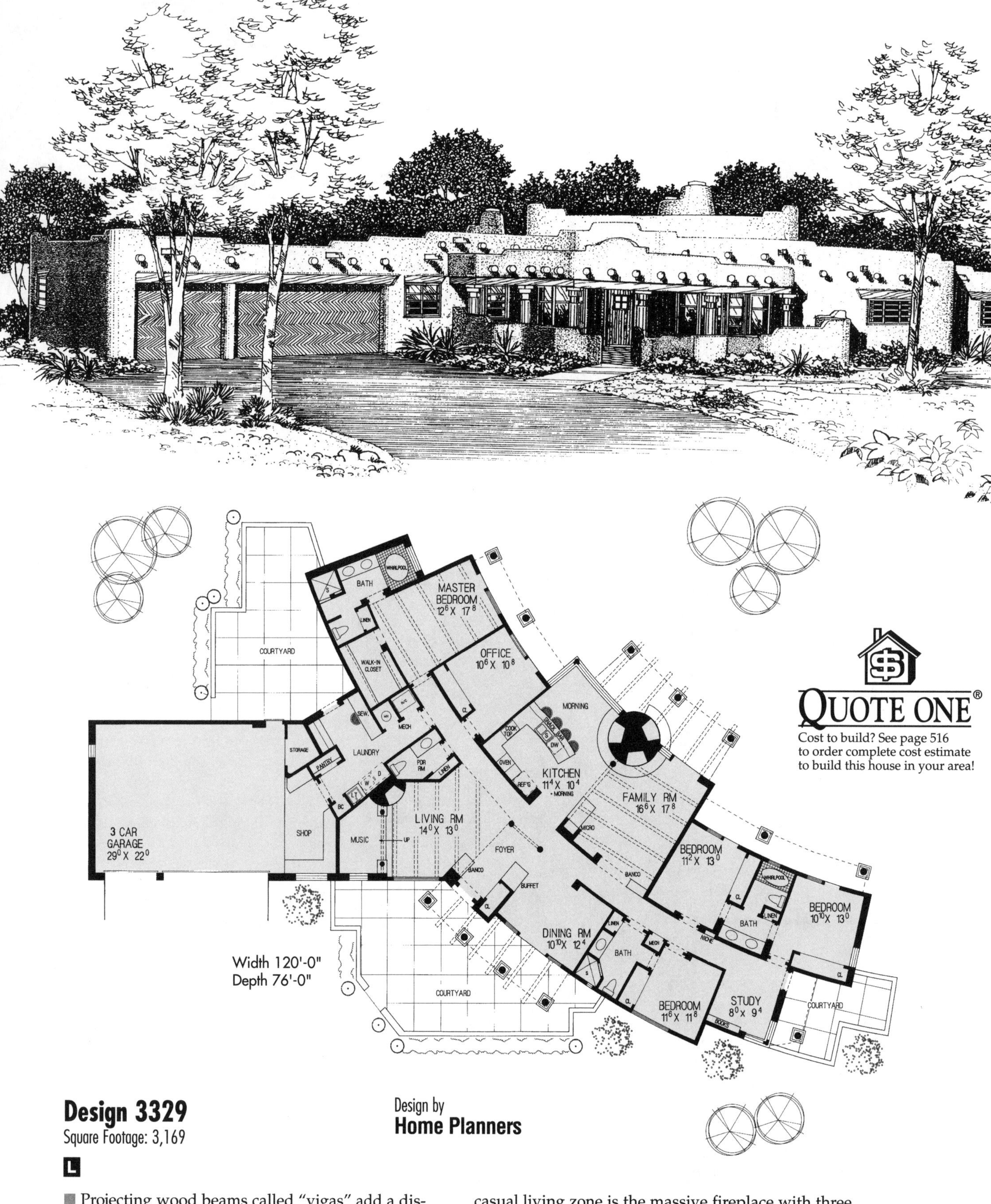
BATH
WHIRLPOOL
MASTER BEDROOM 12^6 X 17^8
LINEN
WALK-IN CLOSET
COURTYARD
OFFICE 10^6 X 10^8
MORNING
SEW.
MECH
STORAGE
PANTRY
LAUNDRY
PDR RM
LINEN
COOK TOP
SNACK BAR
DW
OVEN
REF'G
KITCHEN 11^4 X 10^4 + MORNING
FAMILY RM 16^6 X 17^8
MICRO
3 CAR GARAGE 29^0 X 22^0
SHOP
MUSIC
UP
LIVING RM 14^0 X 13^0
FOYER
BANCO
BUFFET
CL
BANCO
BEDROOM 11^2 X 13^0
WHIRLPOOL
BATH
LINEN
BEDROOM 10^{10} X 13^0
NICHE
DINING RM 10^{10} X 12^4
LINEN
BATH
MECH
Width 120'-0"
Depth 76'-0"
COURTYARD
BEDROOM 11^6 X 11^8
STUDY 8^0 X 9^4
BOOKS
COURTYARD
QUOTE ONE®
Cost to build? See page 516
to order complete cost estimate
to build this house in your area!

Design 3329

Square Footage: 3,169

L

Design by
Home Planners

■ Projecting wood beams called "vigas" add a distinctive touch to this Santa Fe exterior. A private courtyard leads to the entryway of this radially planned home. To the left of the foyer rests a living room with a wood-beamed ceiling, music alcove and fireplace. Past the formal dining room on the right is the family room and large country kitchen with snack bar and morning room. The focal point of this casual living zone is the massive fireplace with three separate fire boxes—the center of the plan's radius. Three family bedrooms, two full baths and an open study with adjoining courtyard round out the right wing. Wood-beams and an oversized, spa-style bath give the master suite a posh attitude. Completing this wing is an office, powder room, laundry/utility room and a three-car garage with work room.

Design 3434

Square Footage: 3,428

L

QUOTE ONE®

Cost to build? See page 516 to order complete cost estimate to build this house in your area!

■ A low, walled courtyard and exposed viga beams add Southwestern flair to this extraordinary Santa Fe pueblo home. Formal living and dining rooms are complemented by a large casual area containing a family room, morning room and kitchen. These are warmed by a circular hearth that extends outside to the patio. Three family bedrooms are found on the right side of the plan, as is a bonus room—perfect for hobbies, games or an additional bedroom. Two family bedrooms share a private bath with whirlpool tub, with the other bedroom having private access to a hall bath. The master suite, with lush bath and huge walk-in closet, is on the left side of the plan, adjacent to a handy home office. A covered patio extends the entire length of the home—a welcome invitation to outdoor living.

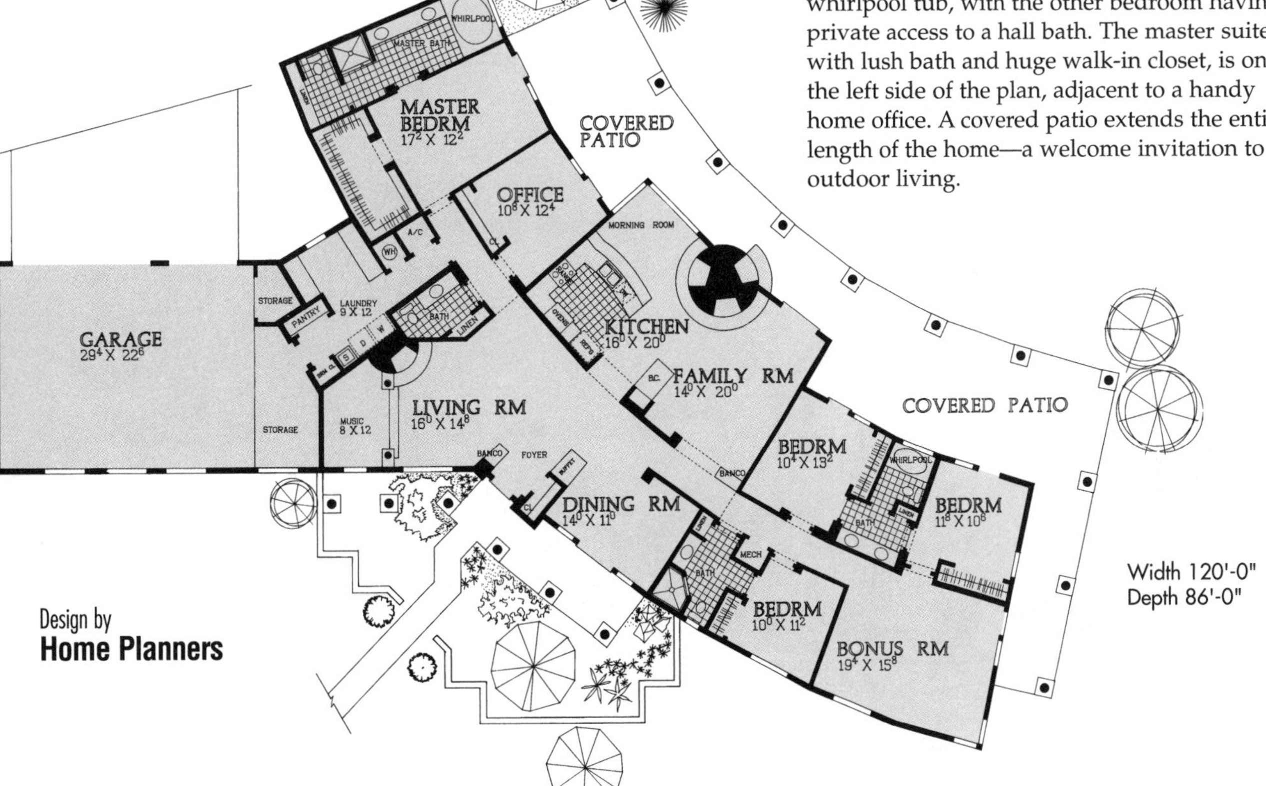
WHIRLPOOL
MASTER BATH
MASTER BEDRM 17^2 X 12^2
COVERED PATIO
OFFICE 10^8 X 12^4
A/C
WH
MORNING ROOM
KITCHEN 16^0 X 20^0
OVENS
REFR
B.C.
FAMILY RM 14^0 X 20^0
GARAGE 29^4 X 22^6
STORAGE
PANTRY
LAUNDRY 9 X 12
BATH
LINEN
LIVING RM 16^0 X 14^8
MUSIC 8 X 12
STORAGE
BANCO
FOYER
BUFFET
DINING RM 14^0 X 11^0
BANCO
COVERED PATIO
BEDRM 10^4 X 13^2
WHIRLPOOL
BEDRM 11^8 X 10^8
BATH
LINEN
MECH
BATH
BEDRM 10^0 X 11^2
BONUS RM 19^4 X 15^8

Width 120'-0"
Depth 86'-0"

Design by
Home Planners

Design 2949

Square Footage: 2,922

■ This one-story matches traditional Southwestern design elements such as stucco, tile and exposed rafters (called vigas) with an up-to-date floor plan. The 43-foot gathering room provides a dramatic multi-purpose living area. Interesting angles highlight the kitchen, which offers plenty of counter and cabinet space, a planning desk, a snack bar pass-through into the gathering room and a morning room with a bumped-out bay. A media room could serve as a third bedroom. The luxurious master bedroom contains a walk-in closet and an amenity-filled bath with a whirlpool tub. A three-car garage easily serves the family fleet.

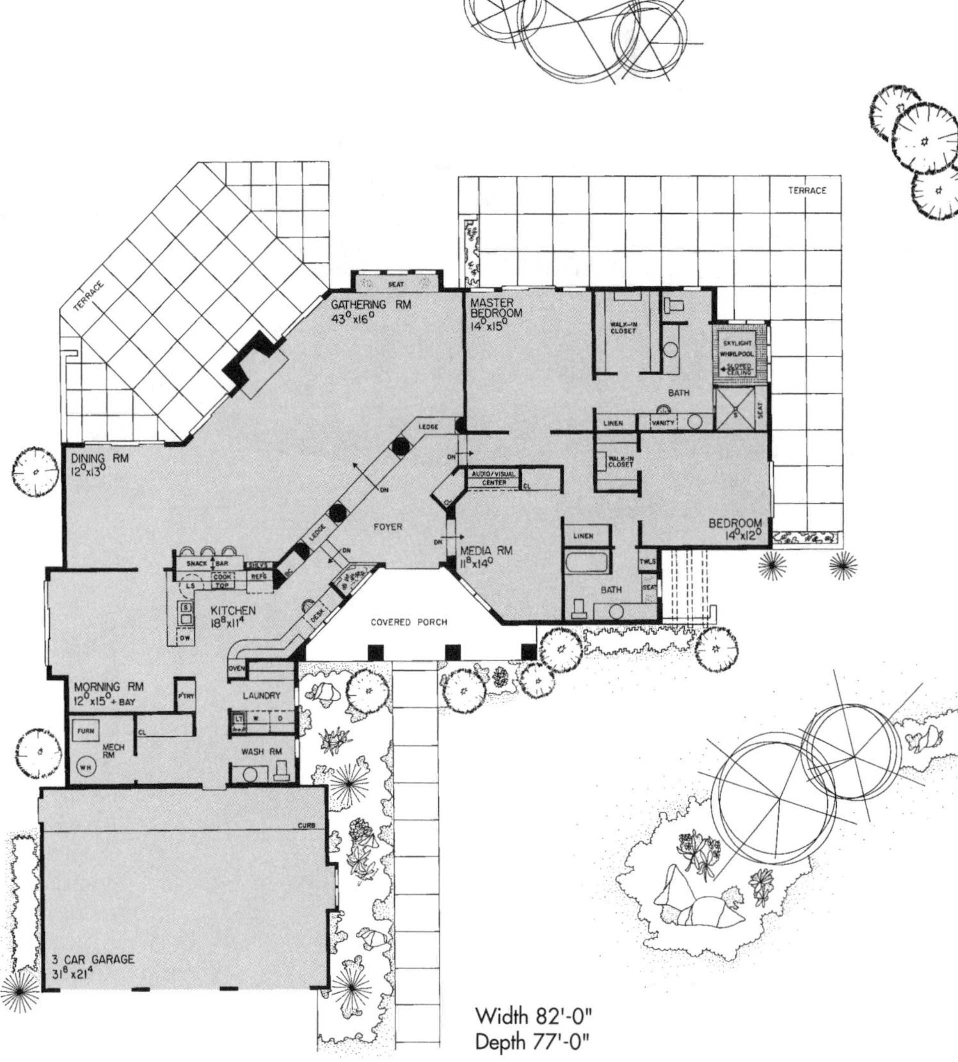
TERRACE
TERRACE
GATHERING RM
MASTER BEDROOM
DINING RM
FOYER
MEDIA RM
BEDROOM
KITCHEN
COVERED PORCH
MORNING RM
LAUNDRY
WASH RM
MECH RM
3 CAR GARAGE
BATH
BATH
Width 82'-0"
Depth 77'-0"

QUOTE ONE®

Cost to build? See page 516 to order complete cost estimate to build this house in your area!

Design by
Home Planners

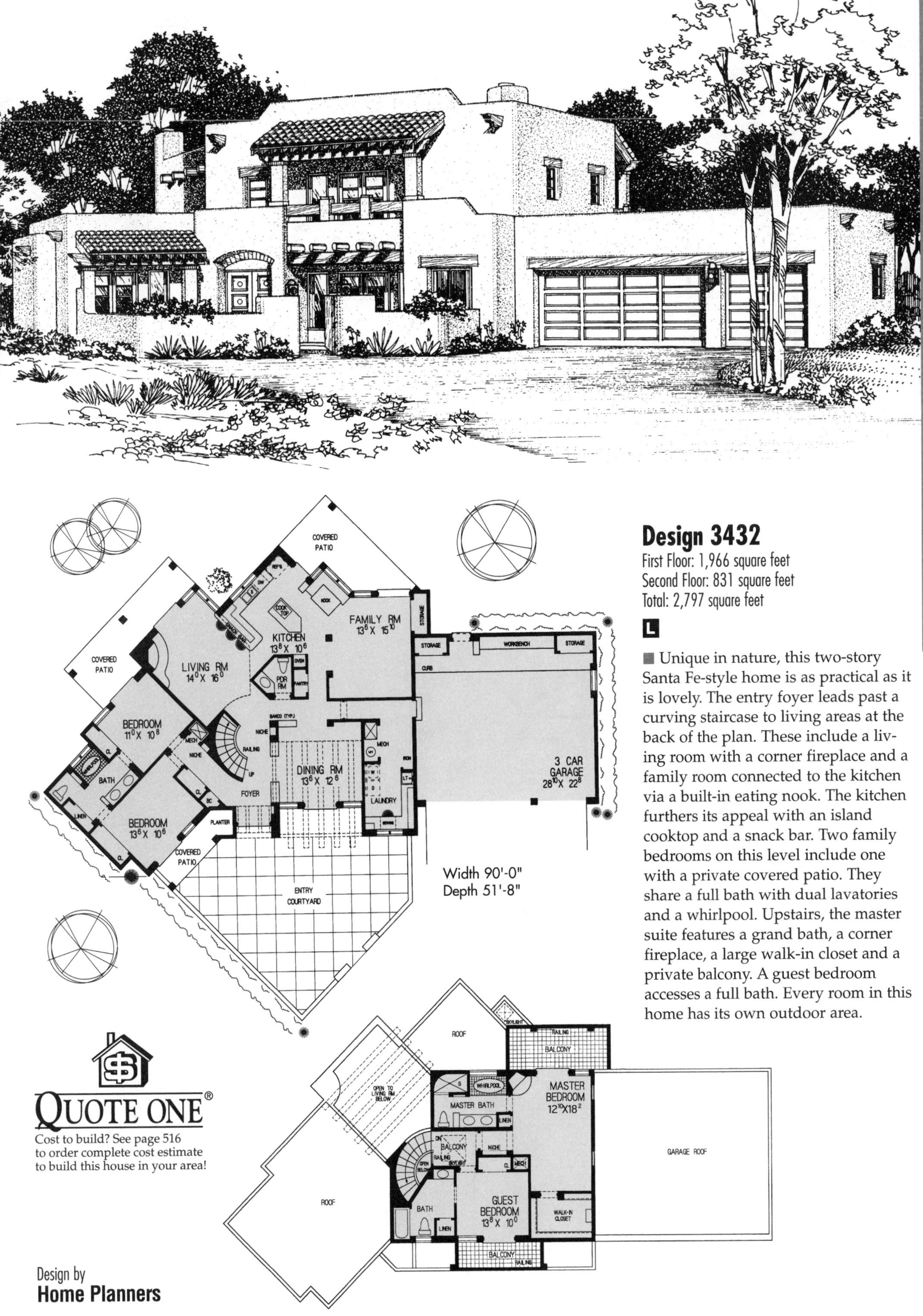
COVERED PATIO
COVERED PATIO
REF'R
DW
COOK TOP
NOOK
SNACK BAR
KITCHEN
13⁸ X 10⁶
FAMILY RM
13⁶ X 15¹⁰
STORAGE
LIVING RM
14⁰ X 16⁰
OVEN
PDR RM
PANTRY
STORAGE
WORKBENCH
STORAGE
CURB
BEDROOM
11⁰ X 10⁸
BANCO (TYP.)
NICHE
MECH
NICHE
RAILING
UP
DINING RM
13⁶ X 12⁶
MECH
IRON
3 CAR GARAGE
28¹⁰ X 22⁸
BATH
CL
FOYER
CL
BC
LAUNDRY
LINEN
BEDROOM
13⁶ X 10⁶
PLANTER
COVERED PATIO
CL
ENTRY COURTYARD
Width 90'-0"
Depth 51'-8"
ROOF
SKYLIGHT
RAILING
BALCONY
OPEN TO LIVING RM BELOW
WHIRLPOOL
MASTER BEDROOM
12¹⁰X18²
MASTER BATH
LINEN
BALCONY
NICHE
GARAGE ROOF
RAILING
SKYLIGHT
OPEN BELOW
CL
MECH
ROOF
BATH
LINEN
GUEST BEDROOM
13⁸ X 10⁰
WALK-IN CLOSET
BALCONY
RAILING

Design 3432

First Floor: 1,966 square feet
Second Floor: 831 square feet
Total: 2,797 square feet

L

■ Unique in nature, this two-story Santa Fe-style home is as practical as it is lovely. The entry foyer leads past a curving staircase to living areas at the back of the plan. These include a living room with a corner fireplace and a family room connected to the kitchen via a built-in eating nook. The kitchen furthers its appeal with an island cooktop and a snack bar. Two family bedrooms on this level include one with a private covered patio. They share a full bath with dual lavatories and a whirlpool. Upstairs, the master suite features a grand bath, a corner fireplace, a large walk-in closet and a private balcony. A guest bedroom accesses a full bath. Every room in this home has its own outdoor area.

QUOTE ONE®

Cost to build? See page 516 to order complete cost estimate to build this house in your area!

Design by
Home Planners

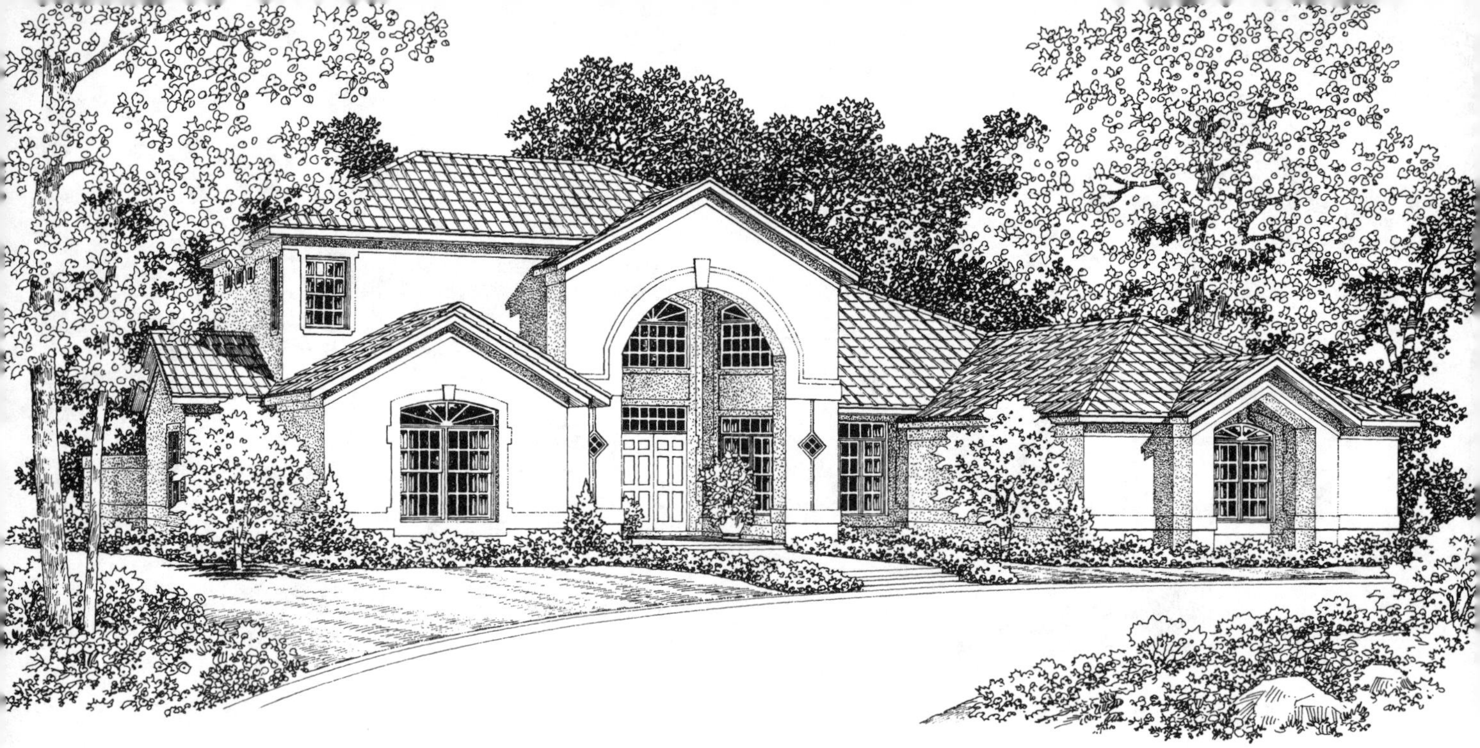

QUOTE ONE®

Cost to build? See page 516 to order complete cost estimate to build this house in your area!

Design by
Home Planners

ROOF BELOW
BEDRM
10^0 x 13^{10}
HIGH WINDOWS
LIVING ROOM BELOW
BATH
HALF WALL
LOFT/READING ALCOVE
BEDRM
11^4 x 10^0
LINEN
COVERED PORCH BELOW
SEAT
ROOF BELOW
ROOF BELOW
ROOF BELOW

Design 3639

First Floor: 2,137 square feet
Second Floor: 671 square feet
Total: 2,808 square feet

L

■ If first impressions really make the most important statements—this home makes it in grand style. The two-story entryway and double doors to the reception foyer make a first impression that can't be beat. Inside, formal living areas grab your attention with a dining room and an elegant living room that opens to a covered entertainment area outside. The family room—with a fireplace—features open views to the kitchen and breakfast nook. The nearby "recipe corner" includes a built-in desk. The laundry room is fully functional with a laundry tub and a broom closet. On the left side of the plan, the master bedroom suite has a full, private bath and a lanai perfect for a spa. A large den could easily double as a study. Two bedrooms and a full bath are located upstairs.

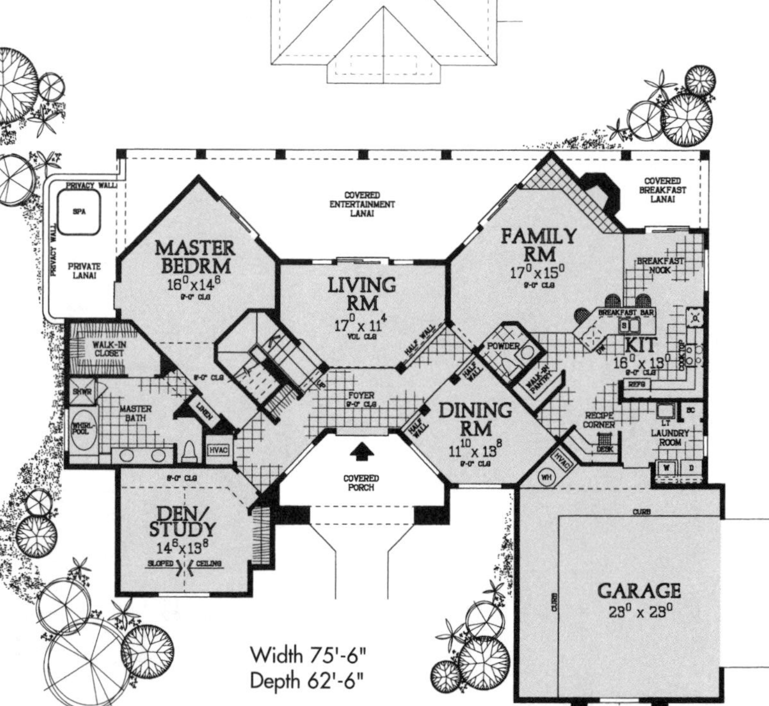
PRIVACY WALL
SPA
PRIVATE LANAI
COVERED ENTERTAINMENT LANAI
COVERED BREAKFAST LANAI
MASTER BEDRM
16^0 x 14^6
LIVING RM
17^0 x 11^4
FAMILY RM
17^0 x 15^0
BREAKFAST NOOK
BREAKFAST BAR
WALK-IN CLOSET
POWDER
KIT
16^0 x 13^0
MASTER BATH
FOYER
DINING RM
11^{10} x 13^8
RECIPE CORNER
DESK
LAUNDRY ROOM
COVERED PORCH
DEN/ STUDY
14^6 x 13^8
SLOPED CEILING
GARAGE
23^0 x 23^0
Width 75'-6"
Depth 62'-6"

GUEST BEDROOM 10⁰ x 11⁰
BEDROOM 10⁶ x 11⁰
BATH
BALCONY
RAILING
OPEN TO BELOW
OPEN TO GATHERING RM BELOW
BEDROOM 11² x 10⁴

Design 3437

First Floor: 1,522 square feet
Second Floor: 800 square feet
Total: 2,322 square feet

L

■ This two-story Spanish Mission-style home has character inside and out. The first-floor master suite features a fireplace and gracious bath with walk-in closet, whirlpool, shower, dual vanities and linen storage. A second fireplace serves both the gathering room and media room or library. The kitchen with island cooktop includes a snack bar and an adjoining breakfast nook. Three bedrooms and two full baths occupy the second floor.

Design by
Home Planners

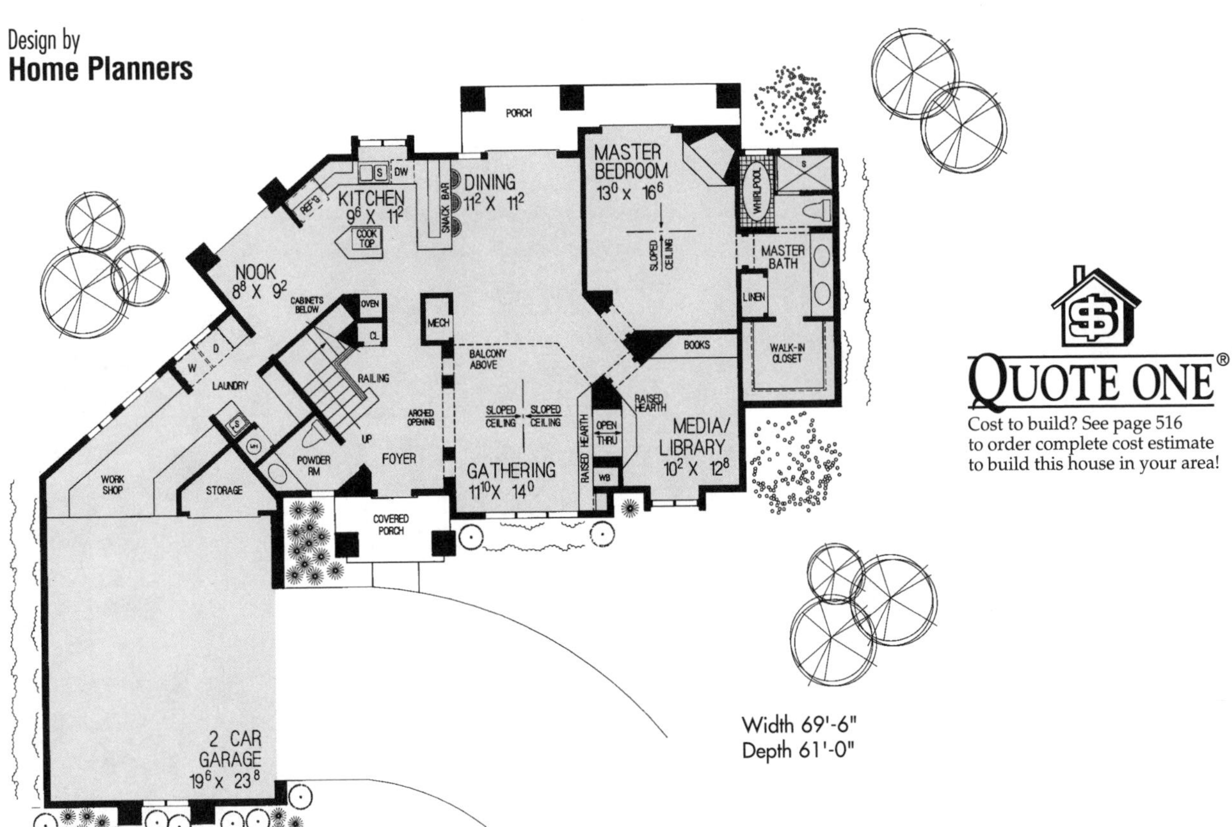
PORCH
MASTER BEDROOM 13⁰ x 16⁶
KITCHEN 9⁶ X 11²
DINING 11² X 11²
NOOK 8⁸ X 9²
MASTER BATH
WALK-IN CLOSET
BALCONY ABOVE
LAUNDRY
FOYER
GATHERING 11¹⁰X 14⁰
MEDIA/ LIBRARY 10² X 12⁸
WORK SHOP
STORAGE
POWDER RM
COVERED PORCH
2 CAR GARAGE 19⁶ x 23⁸
Width 69'-6"
Depth 61'-0"

QUOTE ONE®
Cost to build? See page 516 to order complete cost estimate to build this house in your area!

Design 2843

Upper Level: 1,861 square feet
Lower Level: 1,181 square feet
Total: 3,042 square feet

L

■ A Spanish-style bi-level? Why not? This one has lots going for it upstairs and down. Up top, note the living room and formal dining room; they share a fireplace, and each leads to a comfy deck out back. In addition, the kitchen and breakfast area are centers of attention; the latter has a wonderful, oversized pantry. Zoned to the left of the entry are three bedrooms (two if you make one a study). Down below is a potpourri of space: family room, lounge with raised-hearth fireplace, large laundry room (note the bay window), another bedroom, full bath and plenty of storage in the garage.

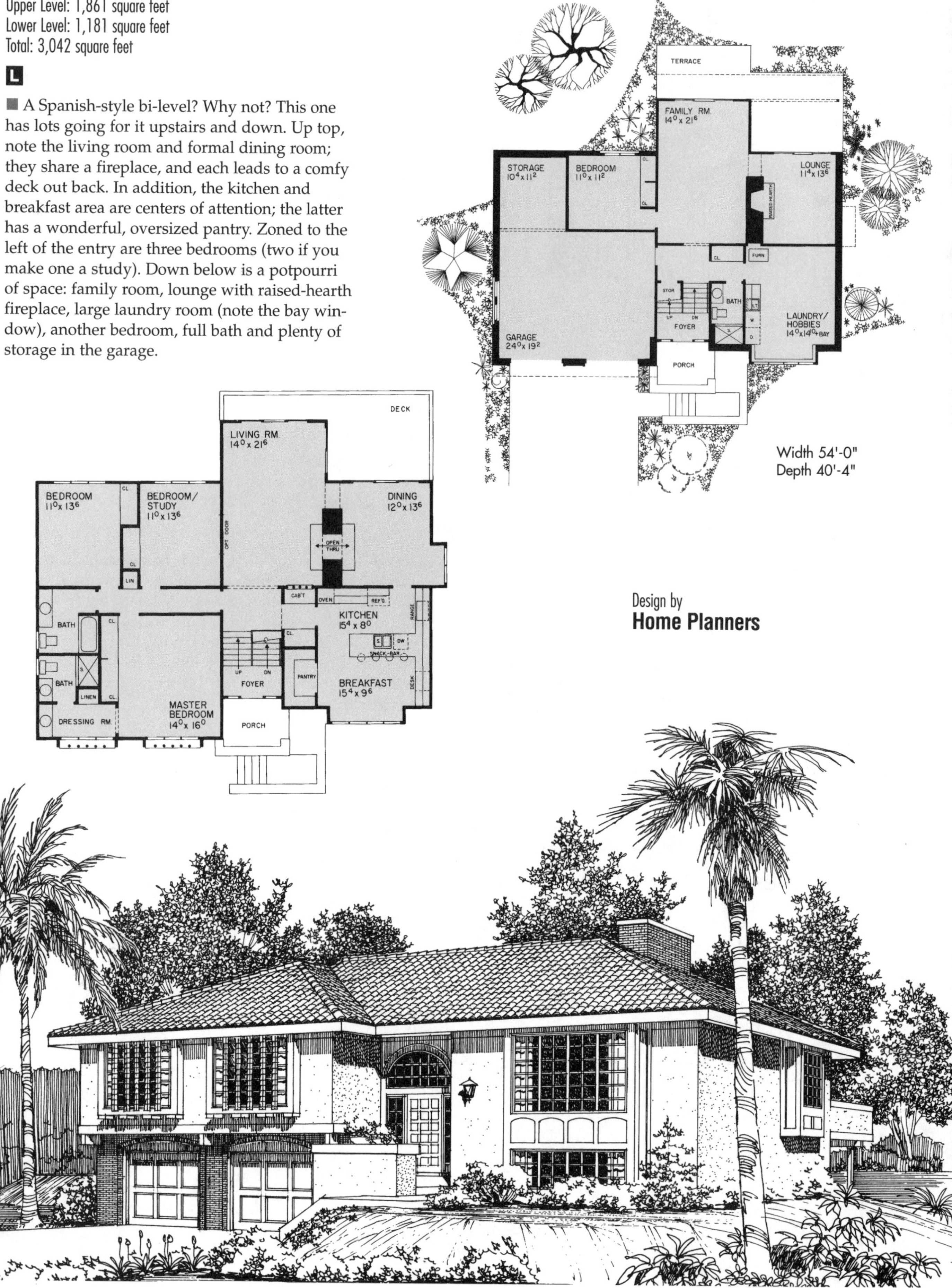
TERRACE
FAMILY RM. 14^0 x 21^6
STORAGE 10^4 x 11^2
BEDROOM 11^0 x 11^2
CL
LOUNGE 11^4 x 13^6
RAISED HEARTH
CL
FURN
STOR
BATH
UP DN
FOYER
GARAGE 24^0 x 19^2
LAUNDRY/ HOBBIES 14^0 x 14^{10} + BAY
PORCH
Width 54'-0"
Depth 40'-4"
DECK
LIVING RM. 14^0 x 21^6
BEDROOM 11^0 x 13^6
BEDROOM/ STUDY 11^0 x 13^6
DINING 12^0 x 13^6
OPT. DOOR
OPEN THRU
CL
LIN
CAB'T
OVEN
REF'G
KITCHEN 15^4 x 8^0
RANGE
BATH
CL
S
DW
SNACK-BAR
BATH
UP DN
FOYER
PANTRY
BREAKFAST 15^4 x 9^6
DESK
LINEN
DRESSING RM.
MASTER BEDROOM 14^0 x 16^0
PORCH
Design by
Home Planners

Design 4061

First Floor: 1,036 square feet
Second Floor: 273 square feet
Total: 1,309 square feet

D

This charming farmhouse design will be economical to build and a pleasure to occupy. Like most vacation homes, this design features an open plan. The large living area includes a living room, a dining room and a massive stone fireplace. A partition separates the kitchen from the living room. The first floor also holds a bedroom, a full bath and a laundry room. Upstairs is a spacious sleeping loft overlooking the living room. Don't miss the large front porch—this will be a favorite spot for relaxing.

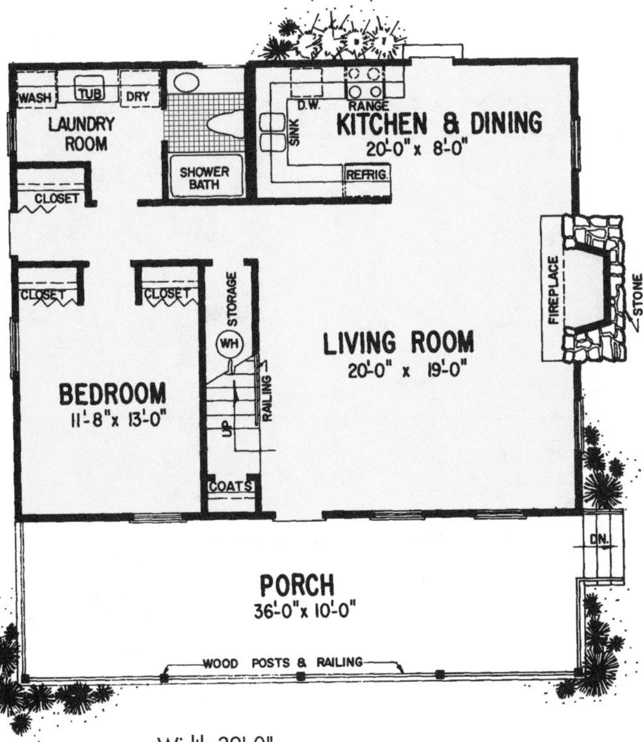

WASH
TUB
DRY
LAUNDRY ROOM
CLOSET
SHOWER BATH
D.W.
RANGE
SINK
KITCHEN & DINING
20'-0" x 8'-0"
REFRIG.
FIREPLACE
STONE
CLOSET
CLOSET
STORAGE
WH
UP
RAILING
LIVING ROOM
20'-0" x 19'-0"
BEDROOM
11'-8" x 13'-0"
COATS
DN.
PORCH
36'-0" x 10'-0"
WOOD POSTS & RAILING

Width 39'-0"
Depth 38'-0"

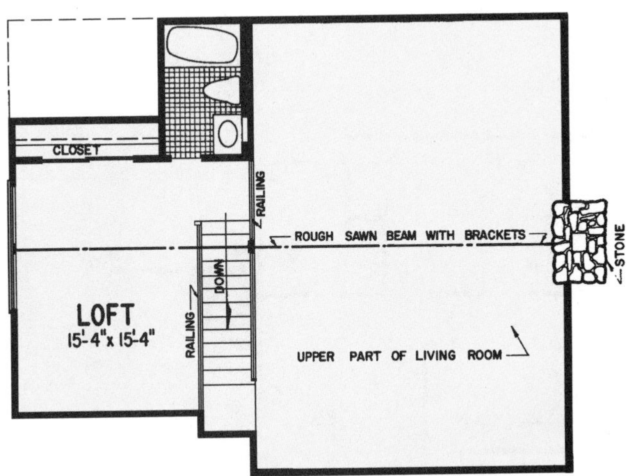

CLOSET
RAILING
ROUGH SAWN BEAM WITH BRACKETS
STONE
DOWN
LOFT
15'-4" x 15'-4"
RAILING
UPPER PART OF LIVING ROOM

QUOTE ONE®

Cost to build? See page 516 to order complete cost estimate to build this house in your area!

Design by
Home Planners

Design 2488

First Floor: 1,113 square feet
Second Floor: 543 square feet
Total: 1,656 square feet

D

For a lakeside retreat or as a retirement haven, this charming design offers the best in livability. The gathering room has an oversized corner fireplace and a dramatic, full length wall of windows. The space-saving, U-shaped kitchen has a snack bar for meals on the go and an attached dining room with doors to the lovely deck. The first-floor master suite is completed with a compartmented bath. Two bedrooms with a full bath and a balcony lounge upstairs complement the design and provide sleeping accommodations for family and guests.

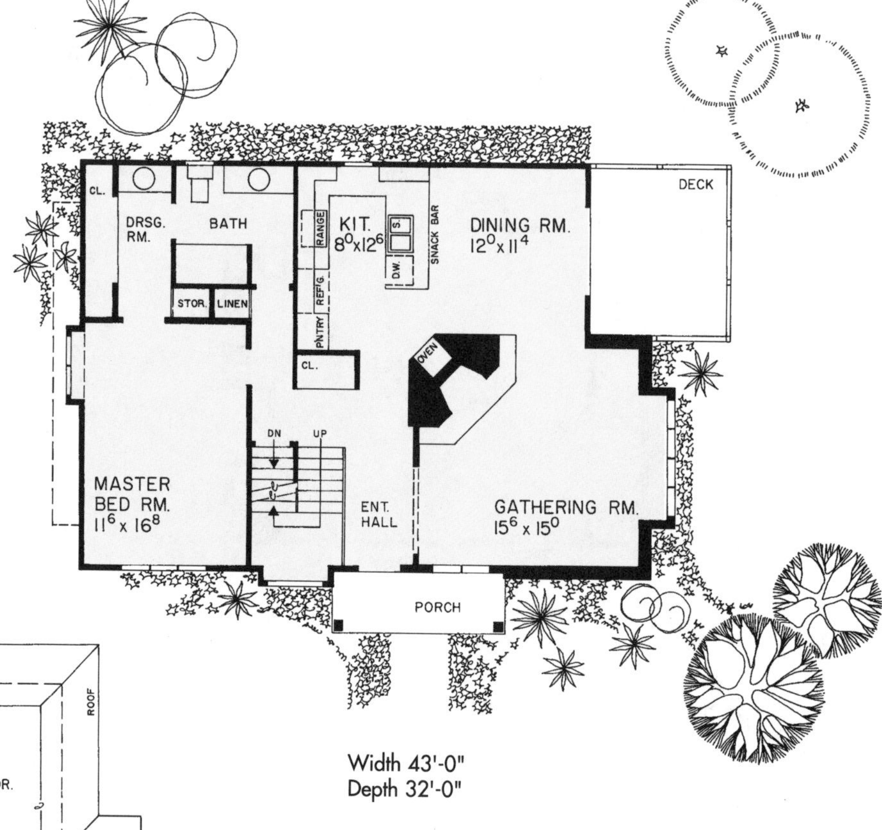

CL.
DRSG. RM.
BATH
STOR.
LINEN
RANGE
REFIG
PNTRY
KIT. $8^0 \times 12^6$
S
D.W.
SNACK BAR
DINING RM. $12^0 \times 11^4$
DECK
CL.
OVEN
DN
UP
MASTER BED RM. $11^6 \times 16^8$
ENT. HALL
GATHERING RM. $15^6 \times 15^0$
PORCH

Width 43'-0"
Depth 32'-0"

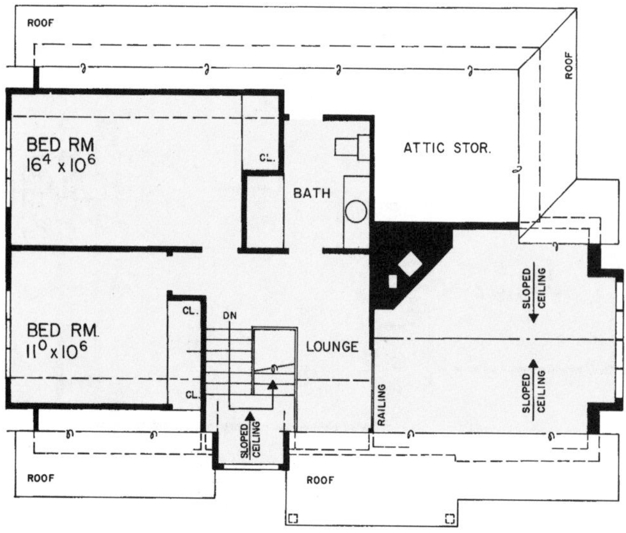

ROOF
ROOF
BED RM $16^4 \times 10^6$
CL.
BATH
ATTIC STOR.
BED RM. $11^0 \times 10^6$
CL.
DN
LOUNGE
CL.
SLOPED CEILING
SLOPED CEILING
RAILING
SLOPED CEILING
ROOF
ROOF

Design by
Home Planners

QUOTE ONE®

Cost to build? See page 516 to order complete cost estimate to build this house in your area!

Design Q490

First Floor: 843 square feet
Second Floor: 370 square feet
Total: 1,213 square feet
Bonus Room: 227 square feet

■ This country-style vacation home is economical to build and offers additional space for future development. A bonus room of 227 square feet may be used as an extra bedroom, a play room or a media center. The front veranda opens to a living room with wood stove and vaulted ceiling. The kitchen and breakfast room are nearby; the kitchen has an L-shaped work counter. The master bedroom is on the first floor for privacy and has its own deck, accessed through sliding glass doors, and private bath. Note the storage room just beyond the carport. Family bedrooms are on the second floor as is the bonus room.

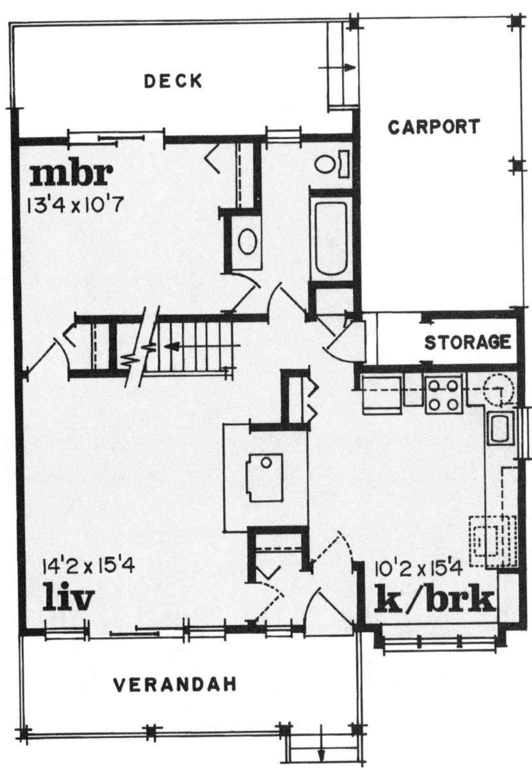
DECK
CARPORT
mbr
13'4 x 10'7
STORAGE
14'2 x 15'4
liv
10'2 x 15'4
k/brk
VERANDAH

Width 32'-4"
Depth 44'-1"

Design by
Select Home Designs

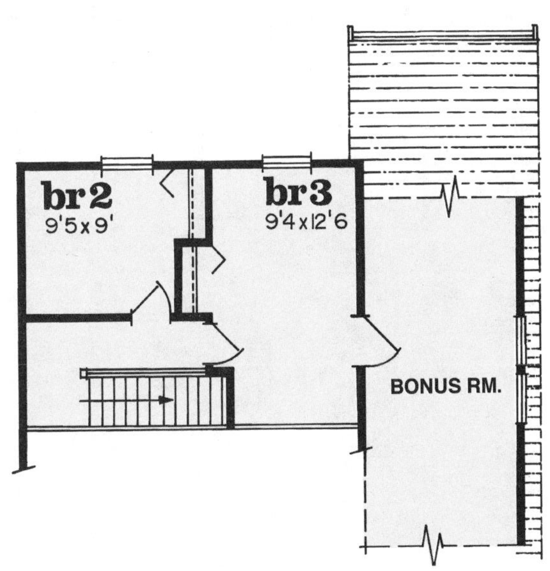
br2
9'5 x 9'
br3
9'4 x 12'6
BONUS RM.

Design 4027

Square Footage: 1,320
Optional Basement: 1,320 square feet

Good things come in small packages! The size and shape of this design will help hold down construction costs without sacrificing livability. The enormous great room is a multi-purpose living space with room for a dining area and several seating areas. Also notice the sloped ceilings. Sliding glass doors provide access to the wraparound deck and sweeping views of the outdoors. The well-equipped kitchen includes a pass-through and pantry. Two bedrooms, each with sloped ceilings and compartmented bath, round out the plan. Develop space in the basement at a later time, if you wish.

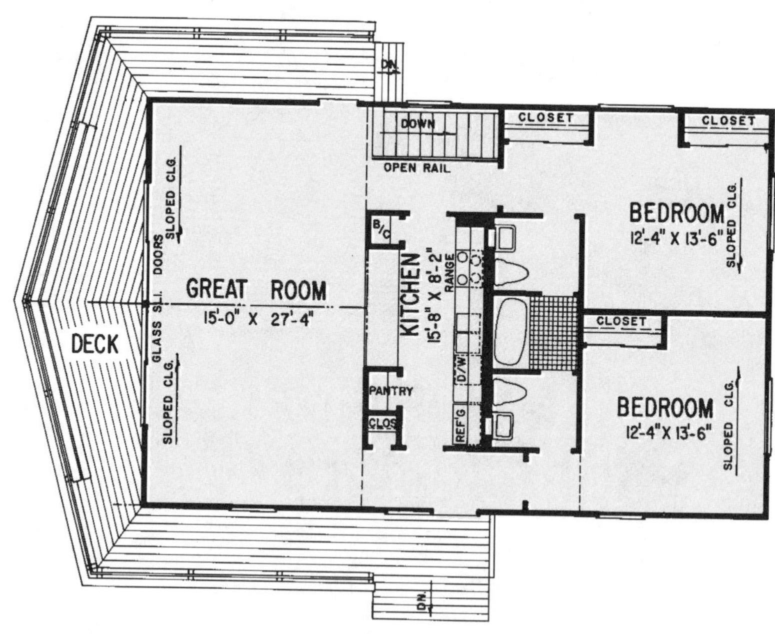

DN
DOWN
OPEN RAIL
CLOSET
CLOSET
BEDROOM
12'-4" X 13'-6"
SLOPED CLG.
SLOPED CLG.
GLASS SLI. DOORS
GREAT ROOM
15'-0" X 27'-4"
DECK
SLOPED CLG.
B/C
KITCHEN
15'-8" X 8'-2"
RANGE
D/W
PANTRY
CLOS
REF'G
CLOSET
BEDROOM
12'-4" X 13'-6"
SLOPED CLG.
DN

Width 52'-0"
Depth 36'-0"

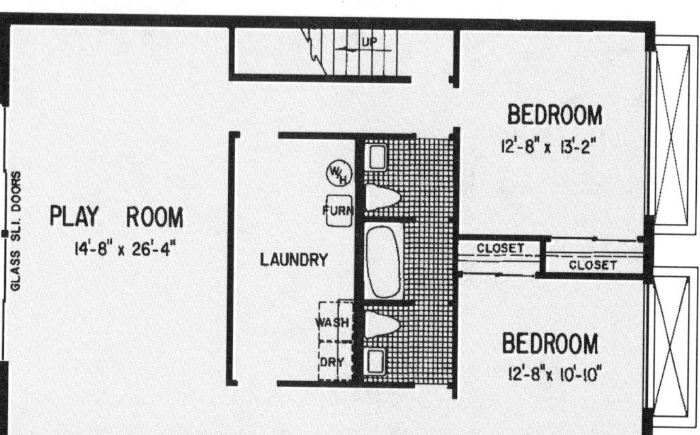

UP
BEDROOM
12'-8" x 13'-2"
W/H
FURN
GLASS SLI. DOORS
PLAY ROOM
14'-8" x 26'-4"
LAUNDRY
CLOSET
CLOSET
WASH
DRY
BEDROOM
12'-8" x 10'-10"

QUOTE ONE®

Cost to build? See page 516 to order complete cost estimate to build this house in your area!

Design by
Home Planners

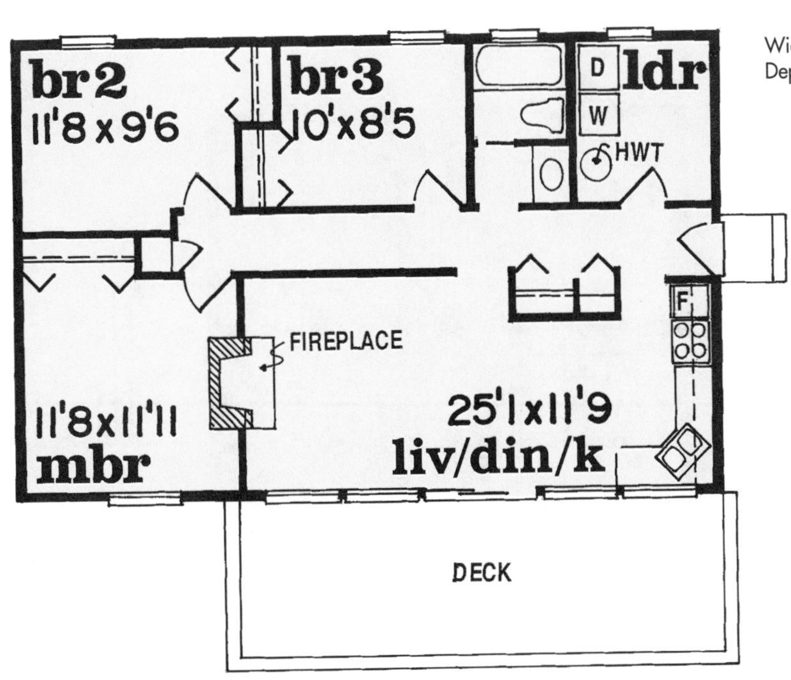
br2
11'8 x 9'6
br3
10'x8'5
ldr
D
W
HWT
FIREPLACE
11'8x11'11
mbr
25'1x11'9
liv/din/k
F
DECK

Width 38'-0"
Depth 25'-0"

Design Q210

Square Footage: 950

This open-plan cottage is perfect for family living—or as a getaway for relaxing vacations. The living area is totally open to act as living room/dining room and corner kitchen. A fireplace at one end adds a warm glow on chilly evenings. Sliding glass doors here open to a wide deck for outdoor enjoyment or alfresco dining. Three bedrooms allow plenty of sleeping space. The master bedroom overlooks views beyond the deck. All three bedrooms share a full bath with soaking tub and separate vanity area. The laundry is large enough to hold a washer and dryer and also to serve as a mud room. There is a side door here.

Design by
Select Home Designs

© Copyright Select Home Designs. All rights reserved
© Copyright Select Home Designs. All rights reserved.

Design Q421

Square Footage: 817

This compact, economical cottage is perfect as a getaway retreat or for a cozy retirement home. Abundant windows overlook the sundeck and capture the views beyond for panoramic enjoyment. Vaulted ceilings and an open floor plan throughout the living and dining rooms enhance the feeling of spaciousness on the inside. For colder months, there is a wood stove in the living room. The kitchen is also vaulted and features a U-shaped workspace and countertop open to the dining area. Two bedrooms are to the rear; each has a wall closet. They share a full bath with linen closet.

Design by
Select Home Designs

br1
11'4 x 10'

br2
9' x 10'

L

H

ST

k
8' x 9'
VAULTED

WOOD STOVE

F

liv
11'9 x 15'
VAULTED

din
11'3x 9'6
VAULTED

SUNDECK

Width 24'-0"
Depth 36'-0"

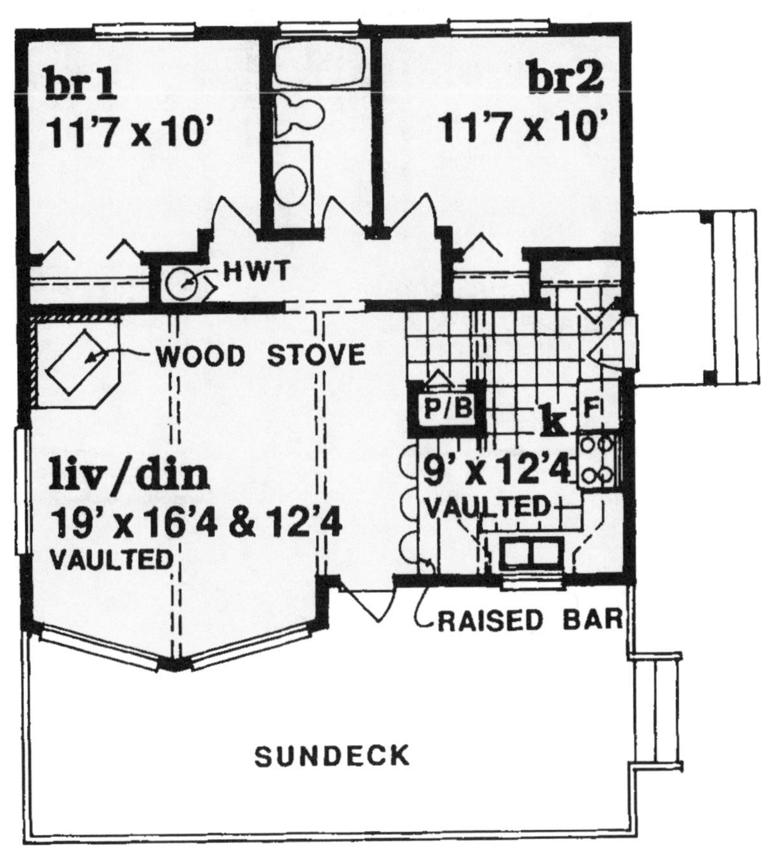
br1
11'7 x 10'
br2
11'7 x 10'
HWT
WOOD STOVE
P/B
k
F
liv/din
19' x 16'4 & 12'4
VAULTED
9' x 12'4
VAULTED
RAISED BAR
SUNDECK

Width 30'-0"
Depth 30'-0"

Design Q422

Square Footage: 825

Compact and economical to build, this vacation home is nonetheless quite comfortable. It will fit easily into just about any vacation setting, from seaside to mountainside. A sundeck to the front stretches the width of the home and opens to a vaulted living room/dining room area with corner wood stove and full-height window wall. The kitchen has a raised bar with seating space open to the living area and also features a U-shaped work-space, a window over the sink and a large pantry or broom closet. Two bedrooms are to the back. They have wall closets and share a full bath with soaking tub.

Design by
Select Home Designs

Design 4153

First Floor: 893 square feet
Second Floor: 549 square feet
Total: 1,442 square feet

L D

The rectangular shape of this design will make it an economical and easy-to-build choice for those wary of high construction costs. The first floor benefits from the informality of open planning: the living room and dining room combine to make one large living space. The partitioned kitchen is conveniently adjacent yet keeps the cooking process out of the living area. Also downstairs is the master bedroom and bath. The second floor houses two large bedrooms, a full bath and a balcony over the living room.

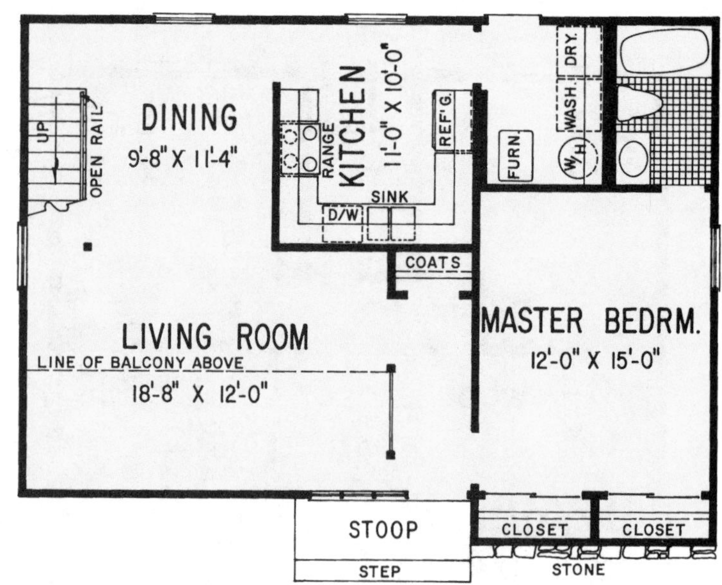

UP
OPEN RAIL
DINING
9'-8" X 11'-4"
RANGE
KITCHEN
11'-0" X 10'-0"
REF'G.
SINK
D/W
FURN.
W/H
WASH.
DRY.
COATS
LIVING ROOM
LINE OF BALCONY ABOVE
18'-8" X 12'-0"
MASTER BEDRM.
12'-0" X 15'-0"
STOOP
STEP
CLOSET
CLOSET
STONE

Width 36'-0"
Depth 26'-4"

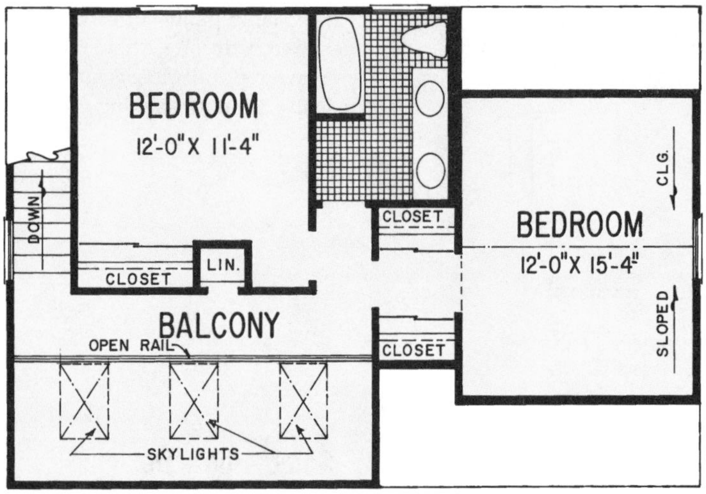

BEDROOM
12'-0" X 11'-4"
DOWN
CLOSET
LIN.
CLOSET
BEDROOM
12'-0" X 15'-4"
CLG.
SLOPED
BALCONY
OPEN RAIL
CLOSET
SKYLIGHTS

Design by
Home Planners

Design Q204

First Floor: 1,022 square feet
Second Floor: 551 square feet
Total: 1,573 square feet

■ This quaint cottage works equally well in the mountains or at a lake shore. Its entry is sliding glass and opens to a vaulted living room with fireplace tucked into a large windowed bay. The dining room has sliding glass access to the deck. The skylit kitchen features a greenhouse window over the sink and is just across from a handy laundry room. The master bedroom captures views through sliding glass doors and a triangular feature window. It has the use of a full bath. The second floor holds another bedroom and full bath and a loft area that could be used as a bedroom, if you choose.

k 11'9 x 8'5
ldr
din
16'2
13'6
11'6
liv
12' x 17'3 & 23'3
mbr
DECK
DECK

Width 39'-0"
Depth 32'-0"

Design by
Select Home Designs

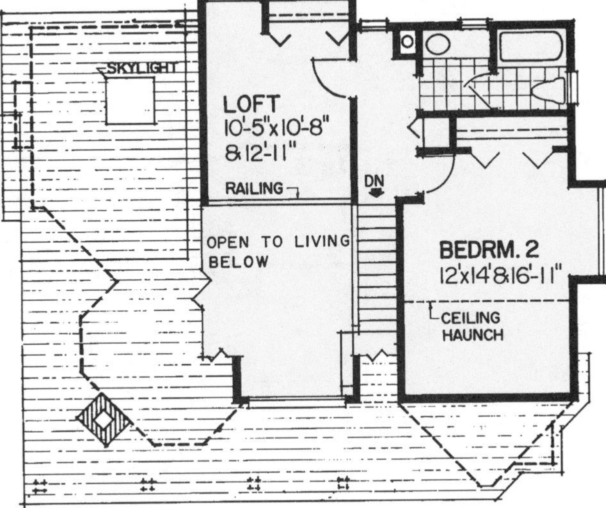
SKYLIGHT
LOFT
10'-5"x10'-8"
& 12'-11"
RAILING
DN
OPEN TO LIVING
BELOW
BEDRM. 2
12'x14'8&16'-11"
CEILING
HAUNCH

Design Q205

First Floor: 1,185 square feet
Second Floor: 497 square feet
Total: 1,682 square feet

■ A full-length multi-paned window wall adorns the living room of this cottage and is covered on the exterior by a gabled roof. The living room is vaulted and has a masonry fireplace and wood storage bin. Double doors open to the covered patio. The kitchen is open to the dining room and has an L-shaped work area. The rear covered veranda opens to a storage room and the laundry room. The first-floor master bedroom features a walk-through closet to a private bath with corner tub and separate shower. Second-floor bedrooms are separated by a gallery and share a full bath. Plans include details for both a basement and a crawlspace foundation.

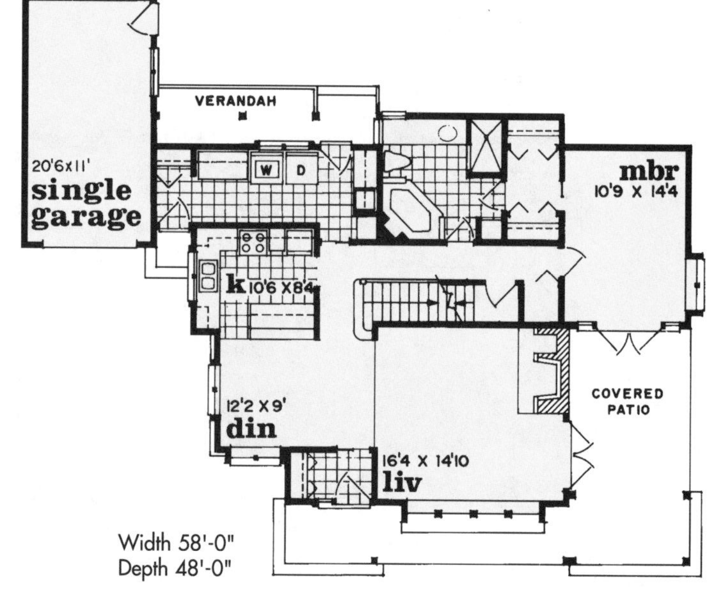
VERANDAH
20'6X11'
single garage
W
D
mbr
10'9 X 14'4
k 10'6 X 8'4
COVERED PATIO
12'2 X 9'
din
16'4 X 14'10
liv

Width 58'-0"
Depth 48'-0"

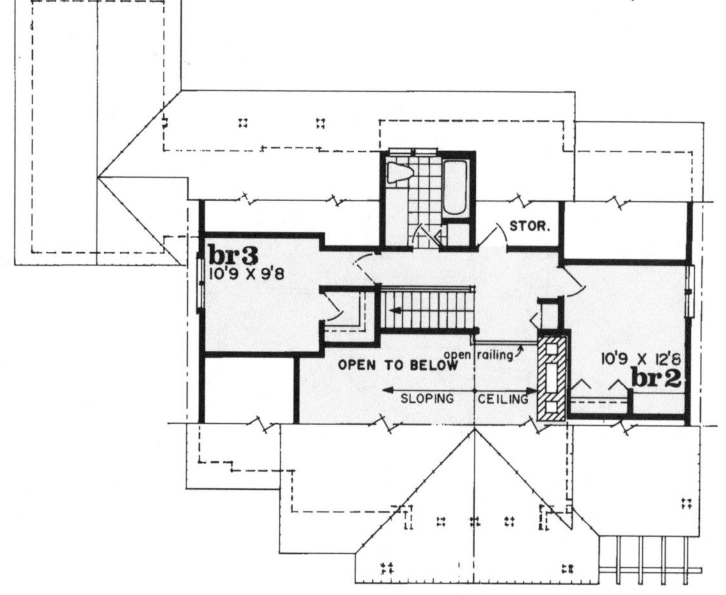
STOR.
br3
10'9 X 9'8
OPEN TO BELOW
open railing
SLOPING CEILING
10'9 X 12'8
br2

Design by
Select Home Designs

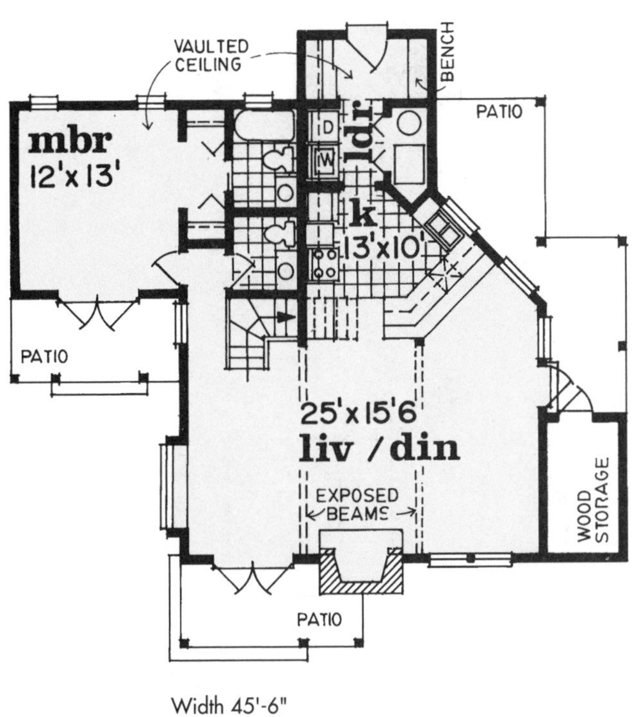
VAULTED CEILING
BENCH
PATIO
mbr
12'x13'
D
W
ldr.
k
13'x10'
PATIO
25'x15'6
liv / din
EXPOSED BEAMS
WOOD STORAGE
PATIO

Width 45'-6"
Depth 44'-0"

Design Q292

First Floor: 1,036 square feet
Second Floor: 630 square feet
Total: 1,666 square feet

Stone and siding work in complement for this cozy design, with chalet features. The vaulted living and dining rooms, with exposed beam ceilings, are open to the loft above. A spacious wood storage area is found off the living room to feed the warm hearth inside. The kitchen features a pass-through counter to the dining area and leads to a laundry room with work bench. The master suite is on the first floor and has a private patio and bath. An additional half-bath is located in the main hall. The second floor holds a family room with desk and two family bedrooms with shared bath.

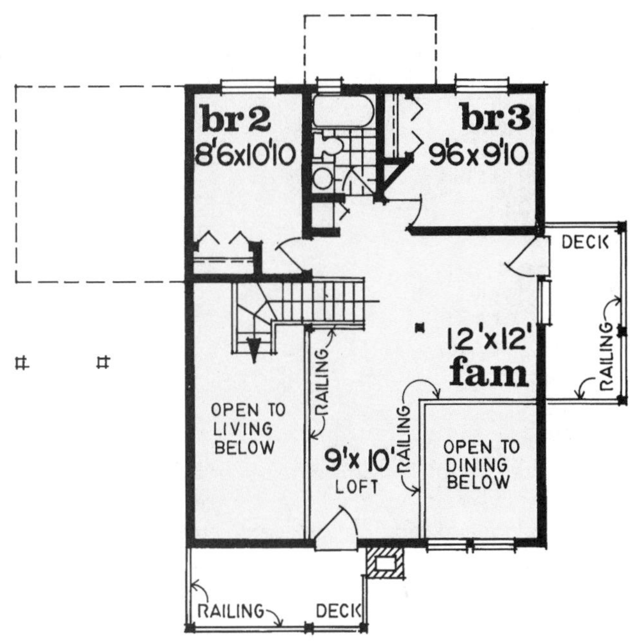
br2
8'6x10'10
br3
9'6x9'10
DECK
12'x12'
fam
RAILING
RAILING
OPEN TO LIVING BELOW
9'x 10'
LOFT
RAILING
OPEN TO DINING BELOW
RAILING
DECK

Design by
Select Home Designs

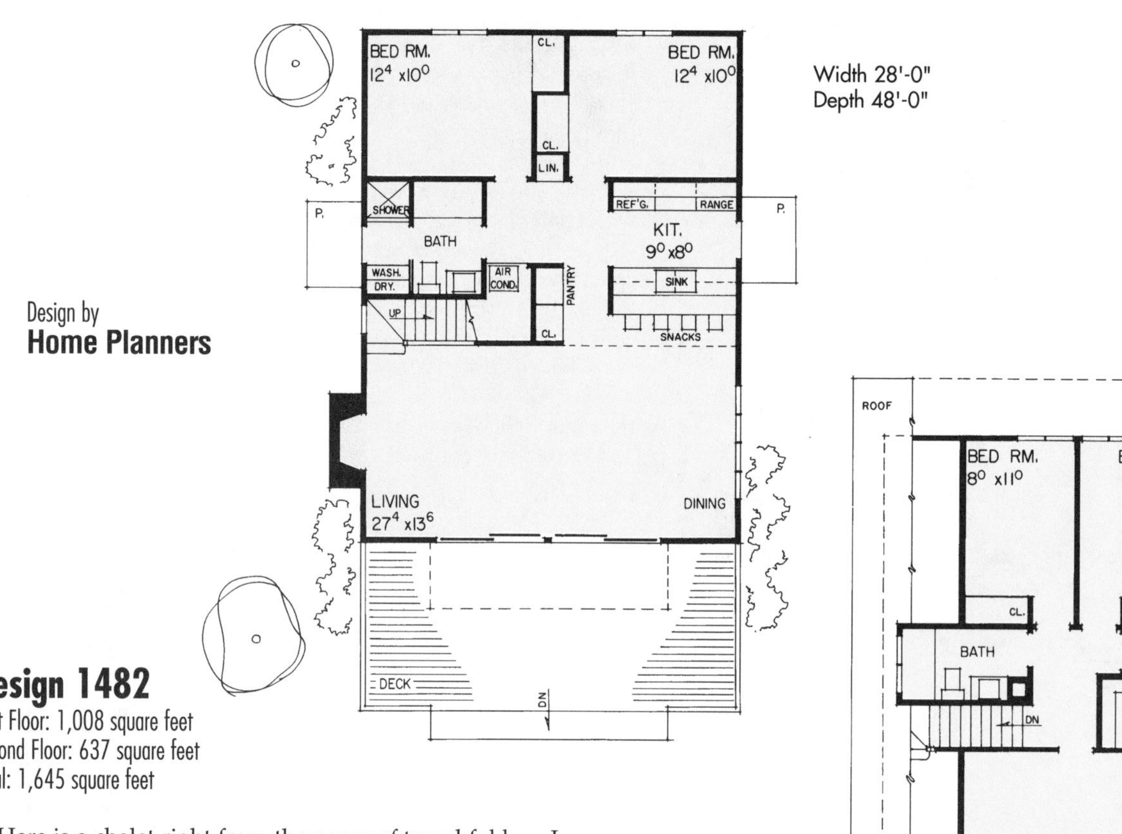

BED RM.
12^4 x10^0
CL.
BED RM.
12^4 x10^0
CL.
LIN.
SHOWER
REF'G.
RANGE
P.
P.
BATH
KIT.
9^0 x8^0
WASH. DRY.
AIR COND.
PANTRY
SINK
UP
CL.
SNACKS
LIVING
27^4 x13^6
DINING
DECK
DN

Width 28'-0"
Depth 48'-0"

Design by
Home Planners

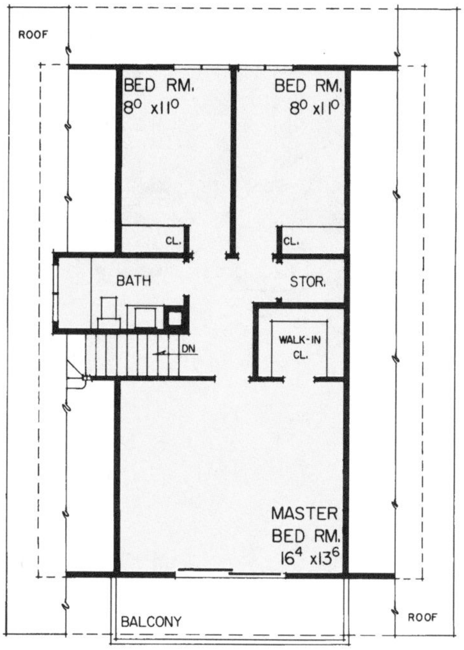

Design 1482

First Floor: 1,008 square feet
Second Floor: 637 square feet
Total: 1,645 square feet

ROOF
BED RM.
8^0 x11^0
BED RM.
8^0 x11^0
CL.
CL.
BATH
STOR.
WALK-IN CL.
DN
MASTER BED RM.
16^4 x13^6
BALCONY
ROOF

Here is a chalet right from the pages of travel folders. In addition to the big bedrooms on the first floor, there are three more and a storage area upstairs. The large master bedroom has a balcony which overlooks the lower wood deck and a walk-in closet. There are two full baths. The first-floor bath is directly accessible from the outdoors. The large living and dining area features a fireplace and sliding glass doors to the wide deck outside. Note the snack bar and the pantry in the galley-style kitchen. A laundry area is adjacent to the side door. There is even space for a washer and dryer at the side entrance.

Design 2427

First Floor: 840 square feet
Second Floor: 508 square feet
Total: 1,348 square feet

Make your vacation dreams a reality with this fabulous chalet. The most carefree characteristic is the second-floor master bedroom balcony which looks down onto the wood deck. Also on the second floor is the three-bunk dormitory. Panels through the knee walls give access to an abundant storage area—perfect for all of your seasonal storage needs. Downstairs, the kitchen utilizes a dining area and an efficient layout and has direct access to the outside. A large living room offers a grand view to a fantastic deck and has a warming fireplace. A first-floor bedroom enjoys the use of a full hall bath.

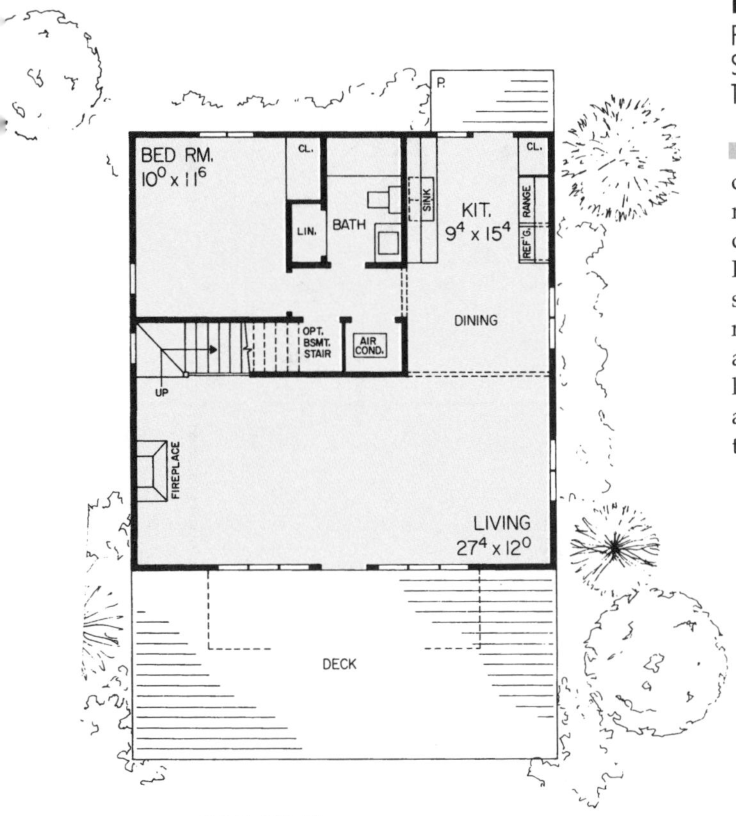

Width 30'-0"
Depth 28'-0"

Design by
Home Planners

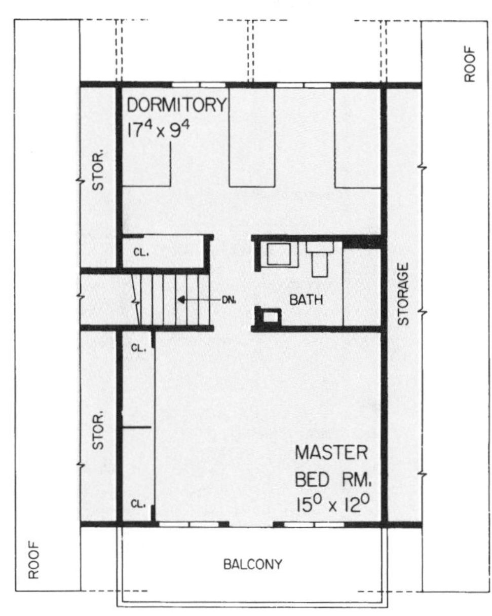
DORMITORY
17⁴ x 9⁴
STOR.
ROOF
CL.
DN.
BATH
STORAGE
CL.
STOR.
MASTER
BED RM.
15⁰ x 12⁰
CL.
ROOF
BALCONY

Design Q212

First Floor: 725 square feet
Second Floor: 561 square feet
Total: 1,286 square feet

■ This cozy chalet design begins with a railed veranda opening to a living room with warm fireplace and a dining room with snack-bar counter through to the kitchen. The kitchen itself is U-shaped and has a sink with window over. A full bath and large storage area sit just beyond the kitchen. One bedroom with roomy wall closet is on the first floor. The second floor holds two additional bedrooms—one a master suite with private balcony—and a full bath. Additional storage is found on the second floor, as well.

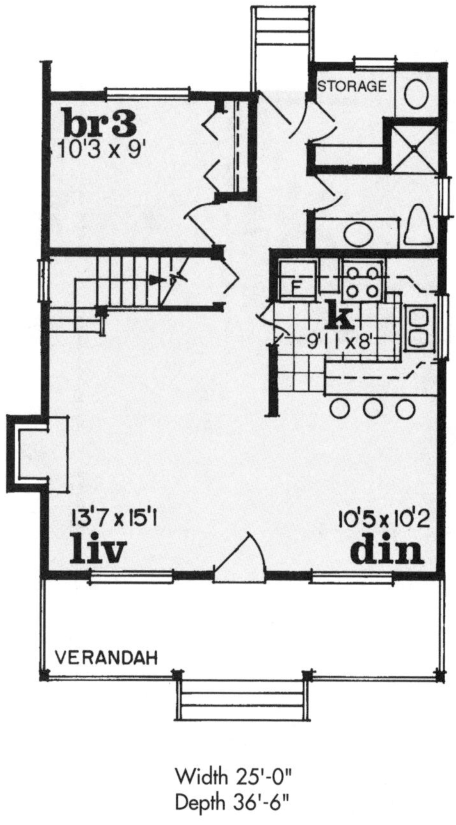
STORAGE
br3
10'3 x 9'
F
k
9'11 x8'
13'7 x 15'1
liv
10'5 x 10'2
din
VERANDAH

Width 25'-0"
Depth 36'-6"

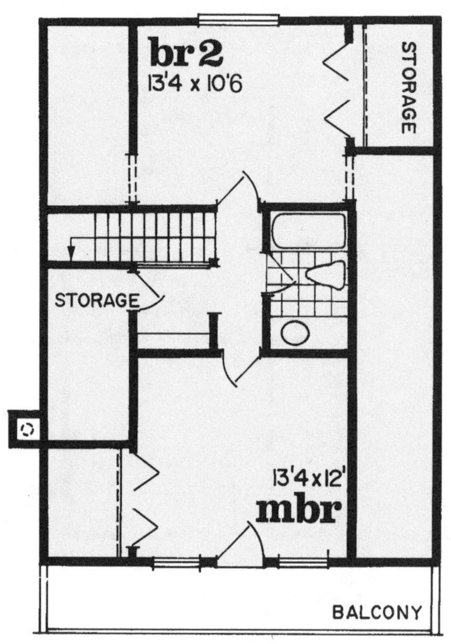
br2
13'4 x 10'6
STORAGE
STORAGE
13'4x12'
mbr
BALCONY

Design by
Select Home Designs

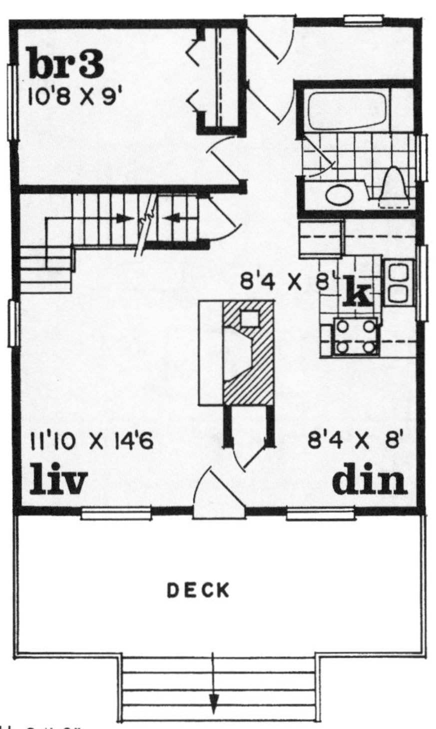
br3
10'8 X 9'
8'4 X 8'
k
11'10 X 14'6
liv
8'4 X 8'
din
DECK

Width 24'-0"
Depth 36'-0"

Design Q207

First Floor: 672 square feet
Second Floor: 401 square feet
Total: 1,073 square feet

Design by
Select Home Designs

This chalet plan is enhanced by a steep gable roof, scalloped fascia boards and fieldstone chimney detail. The front facing deck and covered balcony add to outdoor living spaces. The fireplace is the main focus in the living room. It separates it from the dining room, which is near the U-shaped kitchen. One bedroom is found on the first floor. It has the use of a full hall bath. A storage/mudroom is at the back for keeping skis and boots. Two additional bedrooms and a full bath are upstairs. The master bedroom has a full bath and walk-in closet. Three large storage areas are also found on the second floor. Plans include details for both a basement and a crawlspace foundation.

Rear Elevation

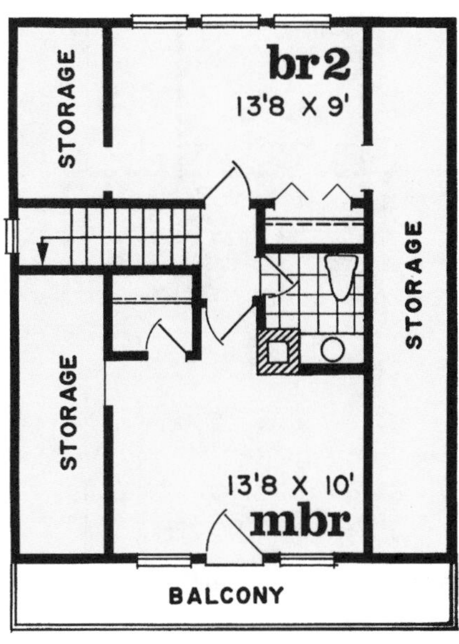
STORAGE
br2
13'8 X 9'
STORAGE
STORAGE
13'8 X 10'
mbr
BALCONY

Design 2431

First Floor: 1,057 square feet
Second Floor: 406 square feet
Total: 1,463 square feet

A favorite for mountain lots or lakeside retreats, this A-frame features beautiful detailing. The living room sports a high ceiling which slopes and has exposed beams. The kitchen is galley-style and has a side entrance to a small deck. A powder room sits in the middle of the plan. The second-floor master suite has a private balcony, a private bath and a lounge. Two first-floor bedrooms share a full bath. The living area is warmed by a raised-hearth fireplace and overlooks a sunny deck.

Width 28'-0"
Depth 60'-0"

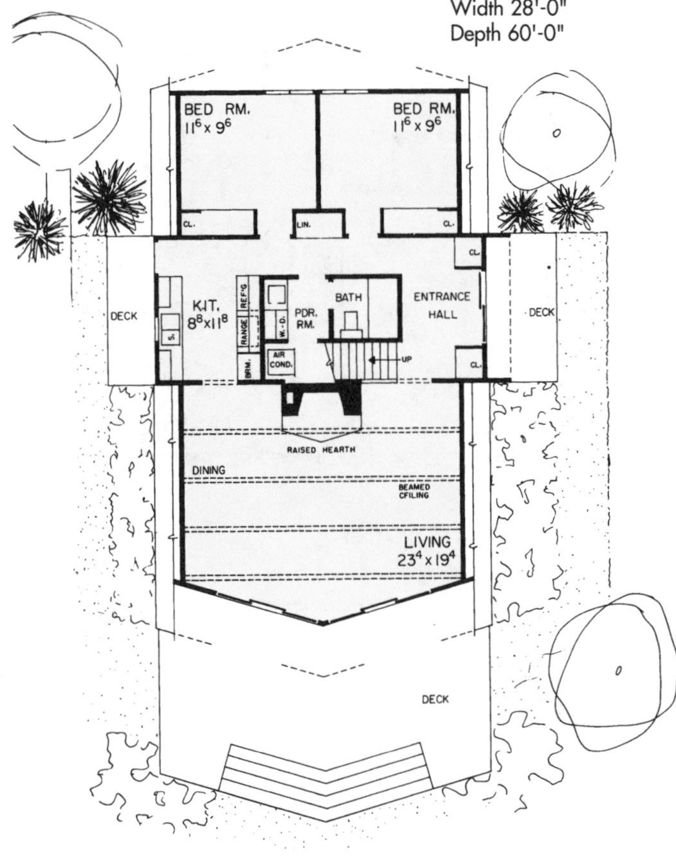
BED RM.
$11^6 \times 9^6$
BED RM.
$11^6 \times 9^6$
CL.
LIN.
CL.
CL.
DECK
KIT.
$8^8 \times 11^8$
REF'G
RANGE
W.-D.
PDR. RM.
BATH
ENTRANCE HALL
DECK
BRM.
AIR COND.
UP
CL.
RAISED HEARTH
DINING
BEAMED CEILING
LIVING
$23^4 \times 19^4$
DECK

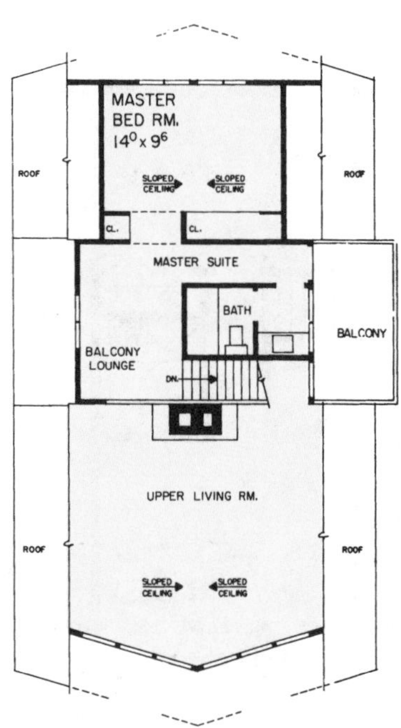
MASTER BED RM.
$14^0 \times 9^6$
SLOPED CEILING
SLOPED CEILING
ROOF
ROOF
CL.
CL.
MASTER SUITE
BATH
BALCONY
BALCONY LOUNGE
DN.
UPPER LIVING RM.
ROOF
ROOF
SLOPED CEILING
SLOPED CEILING

Design by
Home Planners

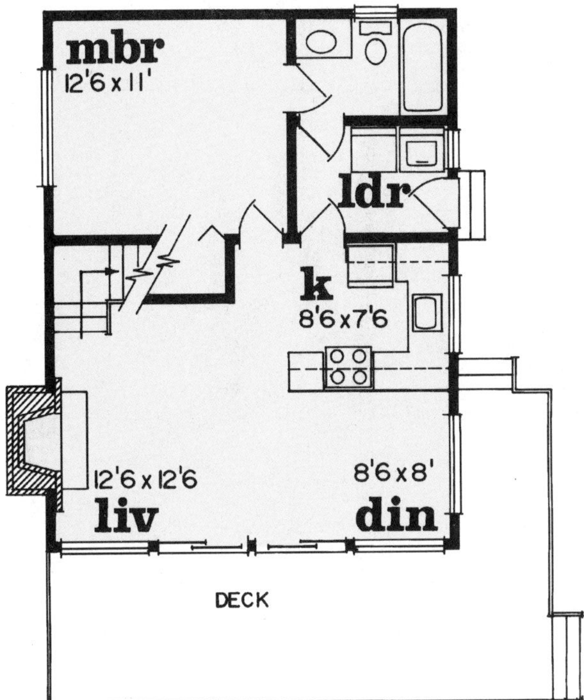
mbr
12'6 x 11'
ldr
k
8'6x7'6
12'6 x 12'6
liv
8'6 x 8'
din
DECK

Width 22'-0"
Depth 28'-0"

Design Q211

First Floor: 616 square feet
Second Floor: 300 square feet
Total: 916 square feet

■ Rustic details such as a stone fireplace work well for a country cottage such as this. A floor-to-ceiling window wall accents the living and dining rooms and provides an expansive view past a wide deck on this design. Twin sliding glass doors access the deck from the living space. The U-shaped kitchen offers roomy counters and is open to the dining room. Behind it is a laundry room and then a full bath serving the master bedroom. An additional bedroom sits on the second floor and may be used as a studio, if you wish.

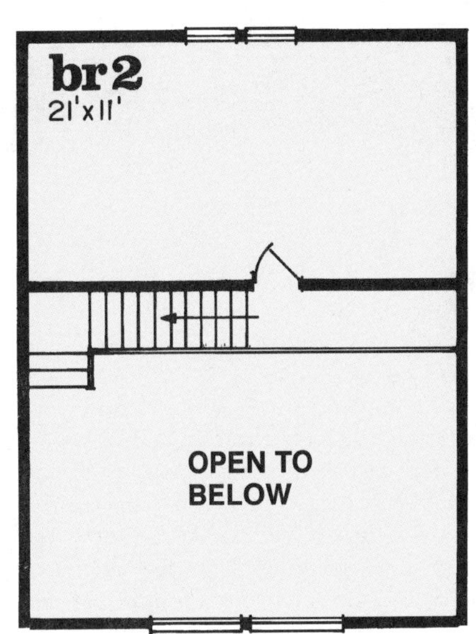
br2
21'x11'
OPEN TO
BELOW

Design by
Select Home Designs

Design Q437

First Floor: 1,084 square feet
Second Floor: 343 square feet
Total: 1,427 square feet

Vertical siding and a wide deck grace the exterior of this plan. Inside, the floor plan features a secluded second-floor master suite with private bath and walk-in closet. Extra-high vaulted ceilings and a wall of windows make the living/dining room a comfortable gathering area. It is warmed by a fireplace and open to the U-shaped kitchen. A laundry room is just beyond. The back entrance has a closet and opens to a rear deck. Two family bedrooms are on the first floor and share a full bath.

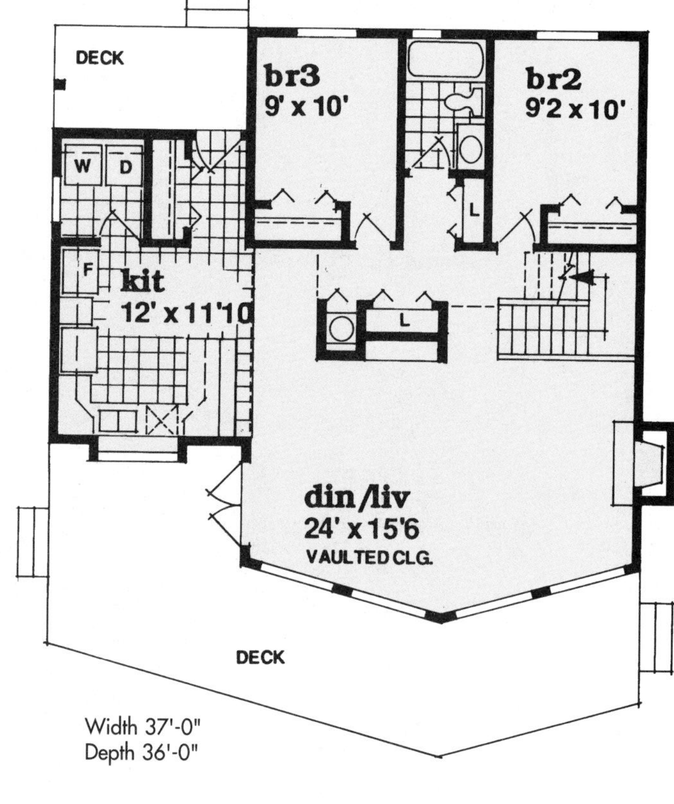
DECK
br3
9' x 10'
br2
9'2 x 10'
W
D
F
kit
12' x 11'10
L
L
din/liv
24' x 15'6
VAULTED CLG.
DECK
Width 37'-0"
Depth 36'-0"

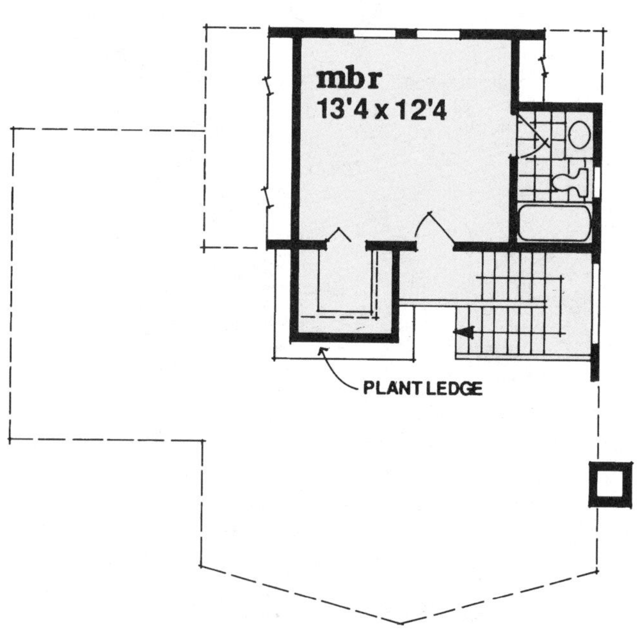
mbr
13'4 x 12'4
PLANT LEDGE

Design by
Select Home Designs

© Copyright Select Home Designs. All rights reserved.

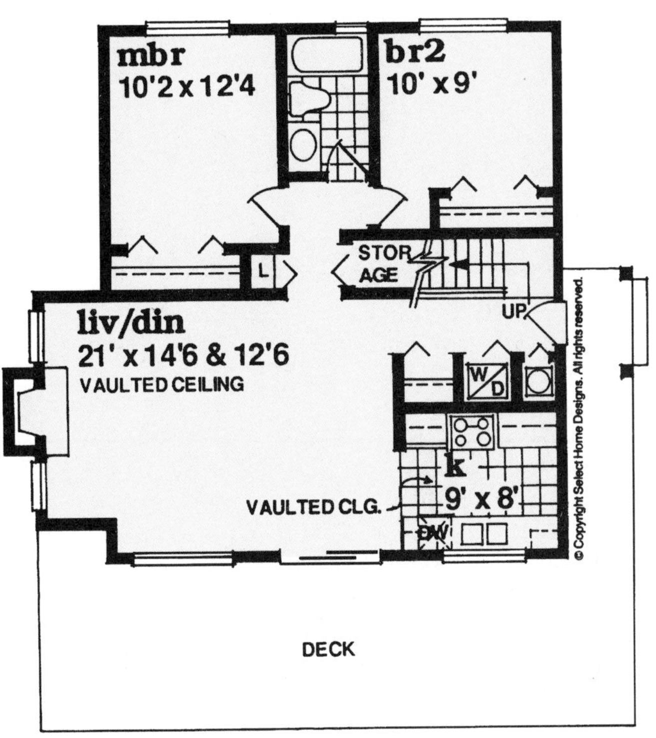
mbr
10'2 x 12'4
br2
10' x 9'
STOR AGE
L
UP
liv/din
21' x 14'6 & 12'6
VAULTED CEILING
W D
k
9' x 8'
VAULTED CLG.
DW
DECK
© Copyright Select Home Designs. All rights reserved.

Width 35'-0"
Depth 30'-6"

Design Q428

First Floor: 878 square feet
Second Floor: 262 square feet
Total: 1,140 square feet

■ Windows galore and sliding glass doors take advantage of views in this vacation home. A full deck wraps around to the side to a covered side entry. Vaulted ceilings throughout the living and dining rooms and the large upstairs bedroom give a feeling of spaciousness to the plan and allow for tall, bright windows. The kitchen is open to the dining room and is galley-style. Two bedrooms line the rear of the plan—a master bedroom and a secondary bedroom. They share the full bath, along with Bedroom 3. Convenient storage is found under the stairs.

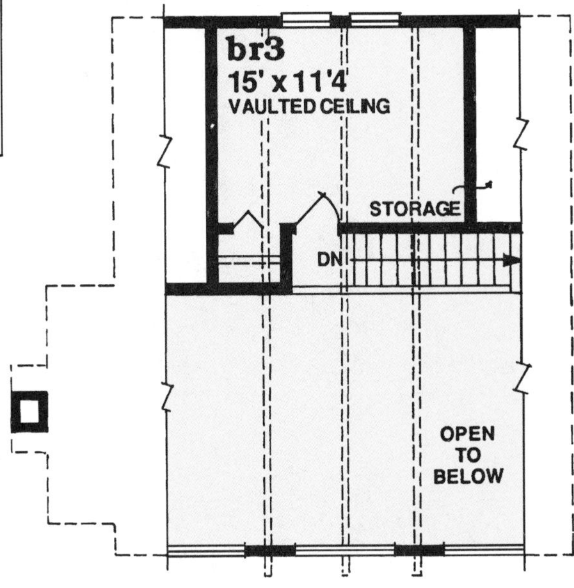
br3
15' x 11'4
VAULTED CEILING
STORAGE
DN
OPEN
TO
BELOW

Design by
Select Home Designs

Design Q424

First Floor: 898 square feet
Second Floor: 358 square feet
Total: 1,256 square feet

A surrounding sundeck and expansive window wall capitalize on vacation-home views in this design. The full-height windows flood the living and dining rooms with abundant natural light and bring attention to the high vaulted ceilings. A wood stove in the living area warms cold winter nights. The efficient U-shaped kitchen has ample counter and cupboard space. Behind it is a laundry room and rear entrance. The master bedroom sits on this floor and has a large wall closet and full bath. Two family bedrooms are on the second floor and have use of a half-bath.

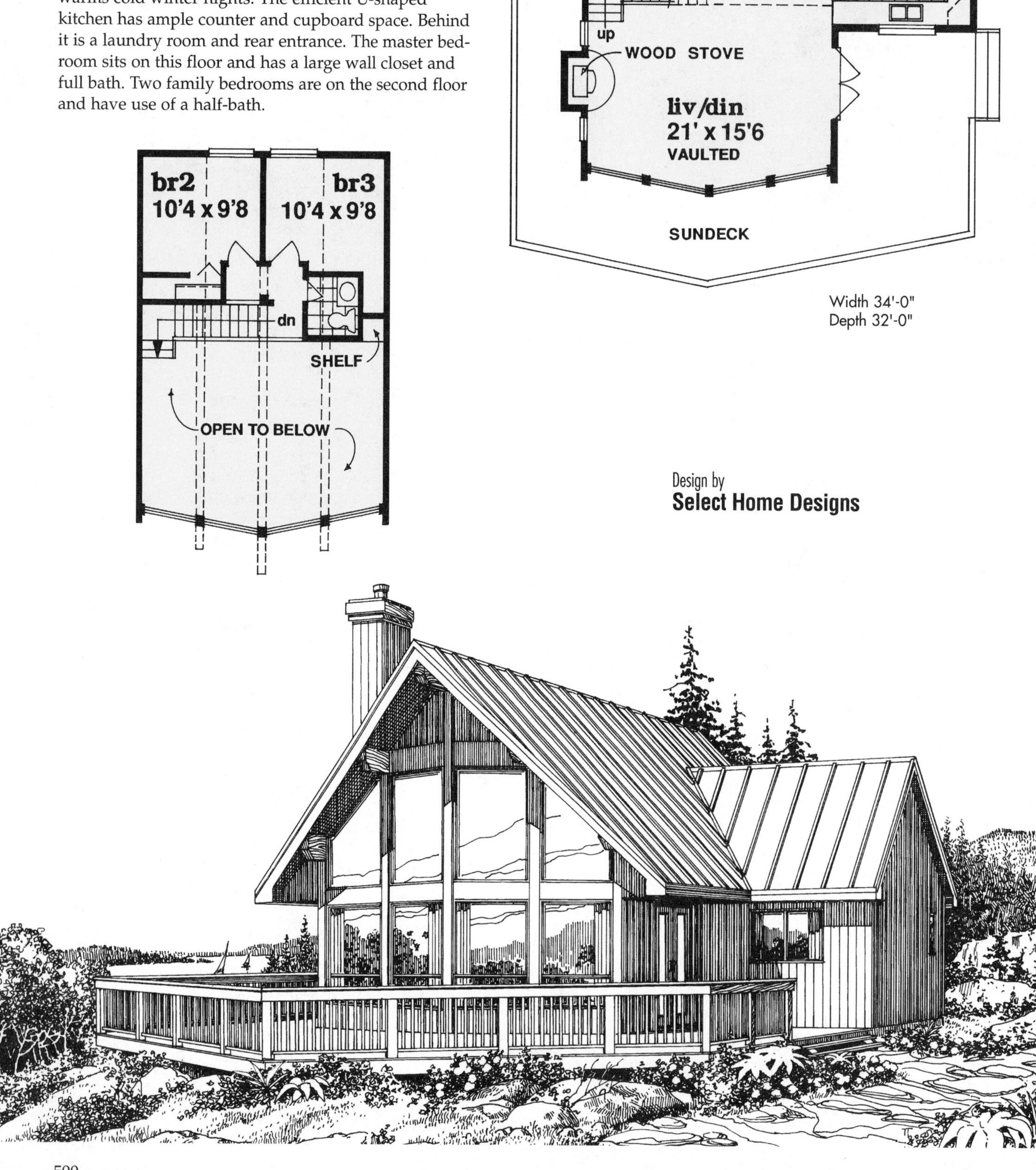

mbr
13'6 x 12'
W
D
F
k
12' x 8'10
up
WOOD STOVE
liv/din
21' x 15'6
VAULTED
SUNDECK
br2
10'4 x 9'8
br3
10'4 x 9'8
dn
SHELF
OPEN TO BELOW

Width 34'-0"
Depth 32'-0"

Design by
Select Home Designs

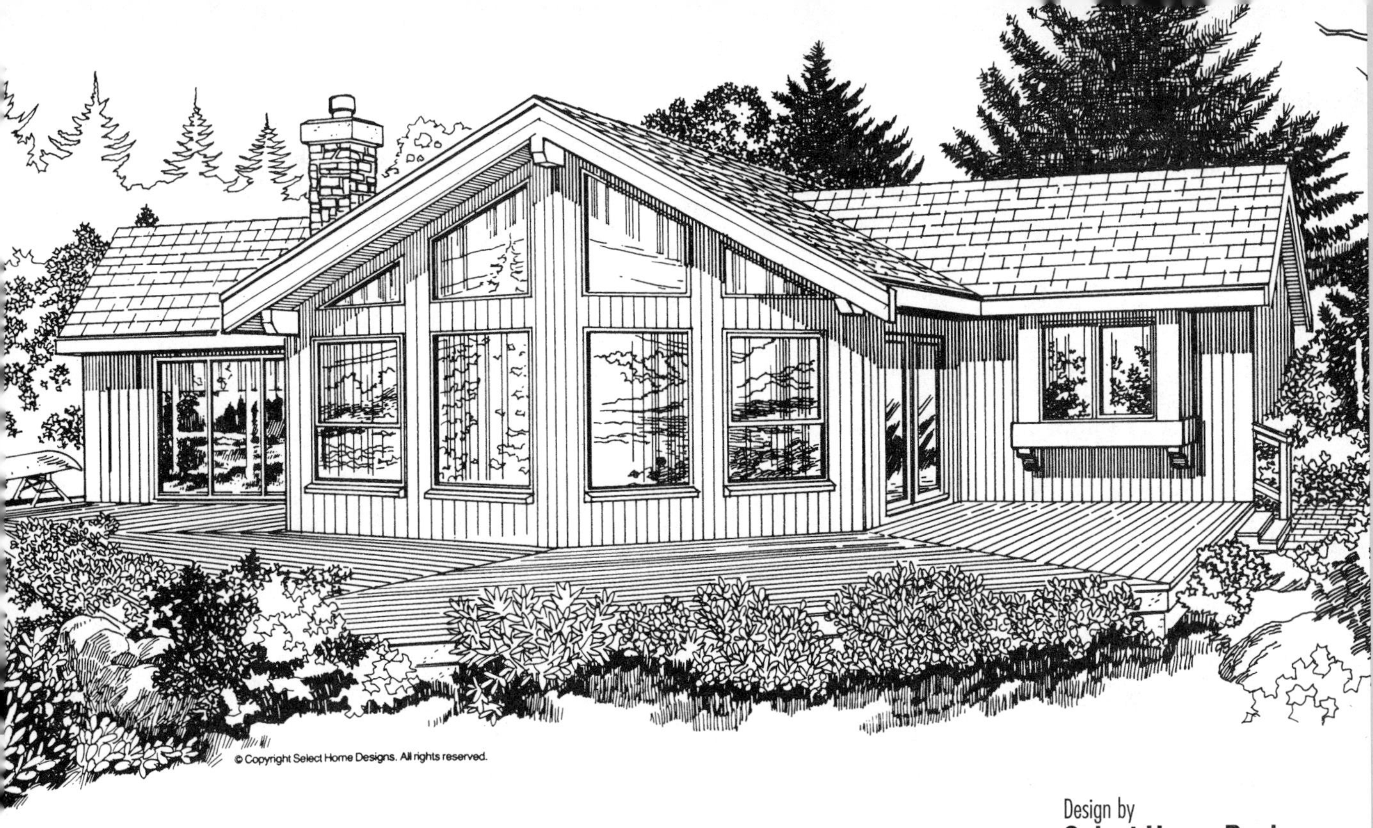

Design by
Select Home Designs

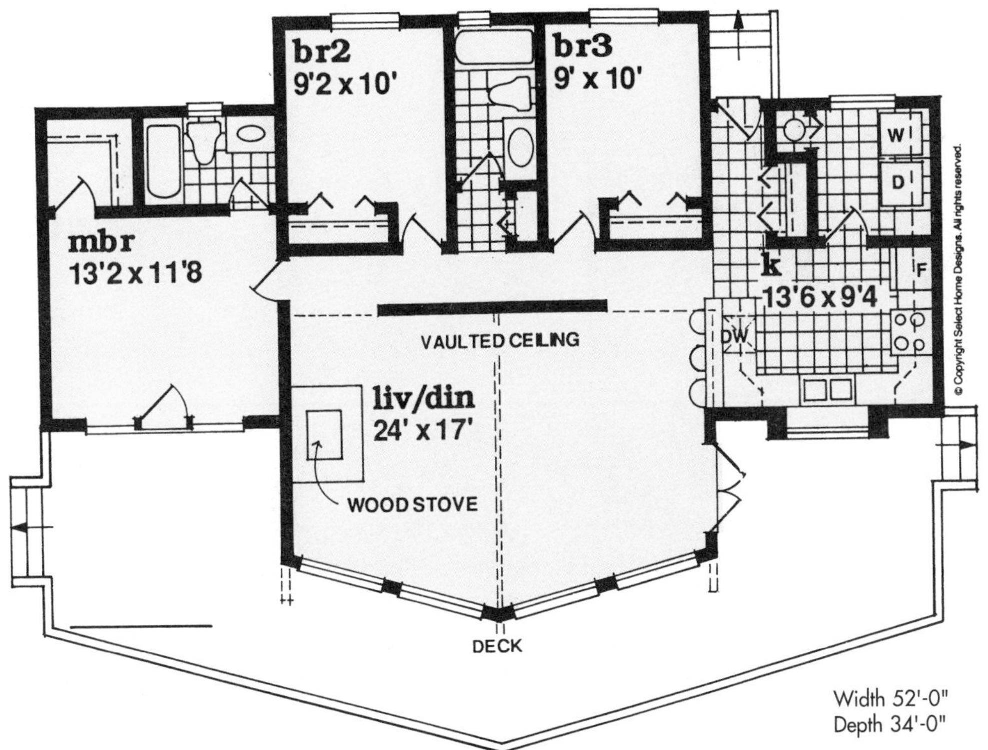
br2
9'2 x 10'
br3
9' x 10'
mbr
13'2 x 11'8
k
13'6 x 9'4
W
D
F
DW
VAULTED CEILING
liv/din
24' x 17'
WOOD STOVE
DECK
© Copyright Select Home Designs. All rights reserved.

Width 52'-0"
Depth 34'-0"

Design Q436

Square Footage: 1,292

This three-bedroom cottage is cozy and comfortable, yet roomy enough for the whole family. Its vertical wood siding and massive chimney stack grace the facade. Inside, a wall of windows in the living area allows for wonderful views; a vaulted ceiling and a wood stove further enhance its appeal. Double glass doors lead to a full-width deck that surrounds the living/dining area. The U-shaped kitchen features a box-bay window over the double sink and a pass-through counter to the dining area. Just beyond is the laundry. The master bedroom leaves nothing to chance, with deck access, a walk-in closet and full private bath. Family bedrooms share a full bath that separates them.

Design Q491

First Floor: 1,197 square feet
Second Floor: 497 square feet
Total: 1,694 square feet

A fieldstone fireplace and wrapping deck add much to the rustic beauty of this design. An expansive window wall highlights the living and dining room's vaulted ceiling and fills the area with natural light. An oversized masonry fireplace is flanked by a set of sliding glass doors opening to the deck. The U-shaped kitchen has great counter and shelf space. Pocket doors seclude it from the dining room and the laundry room at the back. Behind the laundry room is a bedroom with wall closet. It shares a bath with the master bedroom, which has a walk-in closet. A vaulted loft can serve as additional sleeping space. Plans include details for both a basement and a crawlspace foundation.

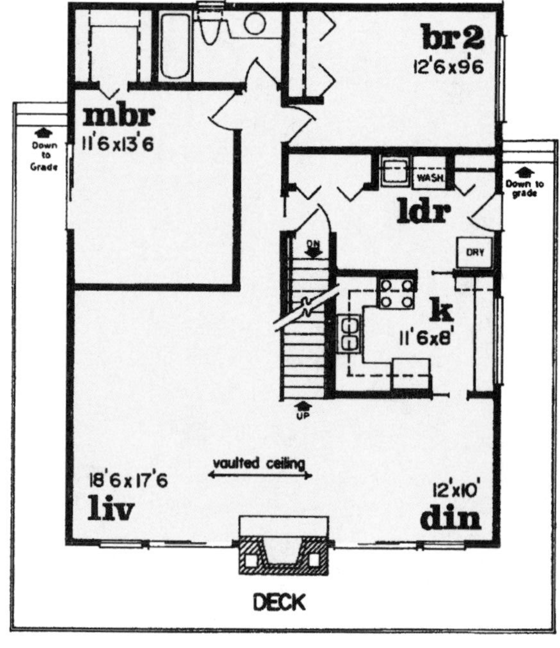
br2
12'6x9'6
mbr
11'6x13'6
Down to Grade
WASH
Down to grade
ldr
DN
DRY
k
11'6x8'
UP
vaulted ceiling
18'6x17'6
liv
12'x10'
din
DECK

VAULTED
LOFT
railing
OPEN TO LIVING-DINING BELOW

Width 31'-6"
Depth 38'-0"

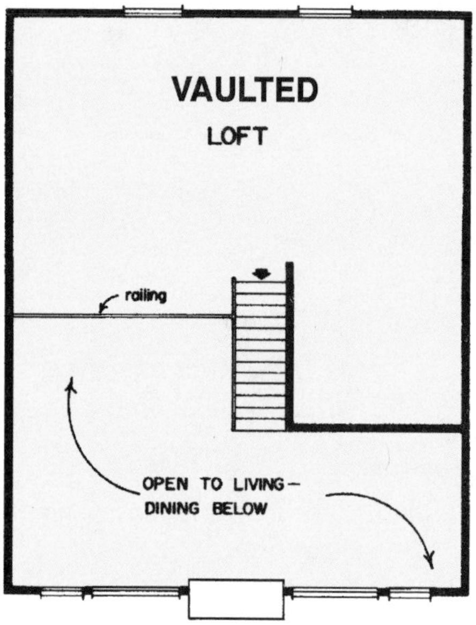

Design by
Select Home Designs

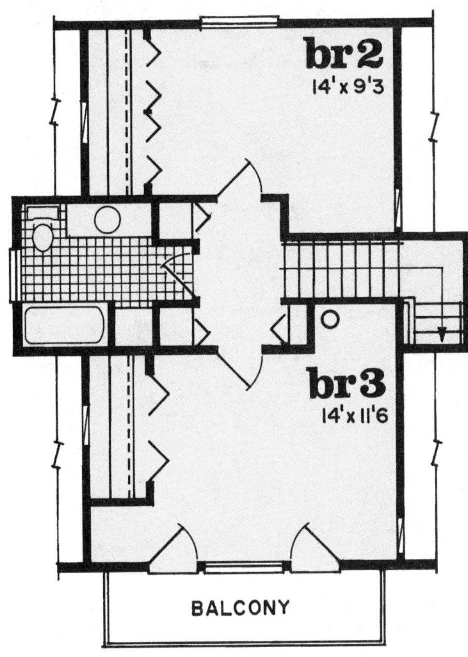
br2
14'x9'3
br3
14'x11'6
BALCONY

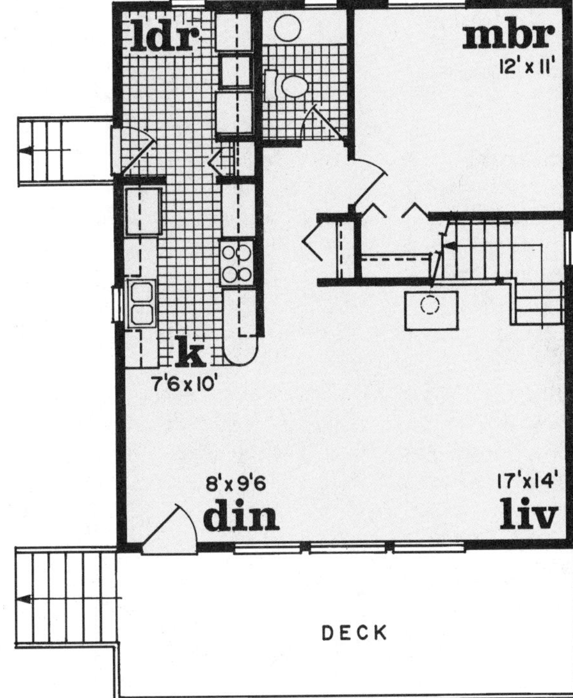
ldr
mbr
12'x11'
k
7'6x10'
8'x9'6
din
17'x14'
liv
DECK

Design Q208

First Floor: 780 square feet
Second Floor: 601 square feet
Total: 1,381 square feet

Width 26'-0"
Depth 30'-0"

■ This A-frame cottages takes advantage of a front view from a deck and a balcony. The side entrance has direct access to the laundry/mudroom, which connects directly into the galley kitchen. The open living and dining rooms are warmed by a wood stove and stretch out to enjoy the deck. The master bedroom is to the rear and has a walk-in closet and a bath nearby. Two bedrooms upstairs have large wall closets and share a full bath. Bedroom 3 has double doors to the balcony.

Design by
Select Home Designs

Design Q499

First Floor: 1,157 square feet
Second Floor: 638 square feet
Total: 1,795 square feet

This leisure home is perfect for outdoor living with French doors opening to a large sundeck and sunken spa. The open-beam, vaulted ceiling and high window wall provide views for the living and dining rooms, which are decorated with wood columns and warmed by a fireplace. The step-saving U-shaped kitchen has ample counter space and a bar counter to the dining room. The master bedroom on the first floor features a walk-in closet and bath with twin vanity, shower and soaking tub. A convenient mudroom with adjoining laundry accesses a rear deck. Two bedrooms are on the second floor and share a full bath. Plans include details for both a basement and a crawlspace foundation.

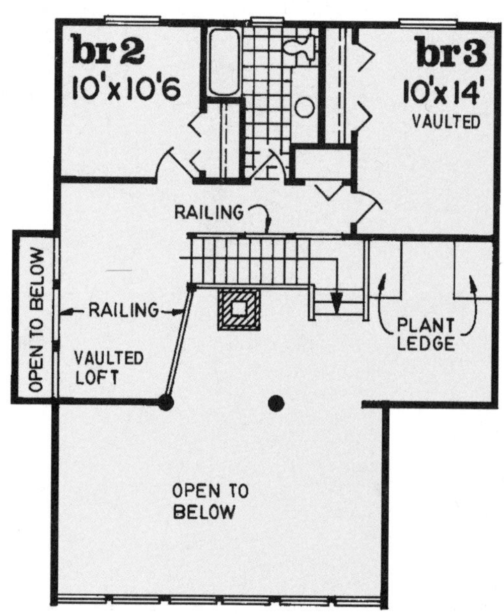
br2
10'x10'6
br3
10'x14'
VAULTED
RAILING
OPEN TO BELOW
RAILING
VAULTED
LOFT
PLANT
LEDGE
OPEN TO
BELOW

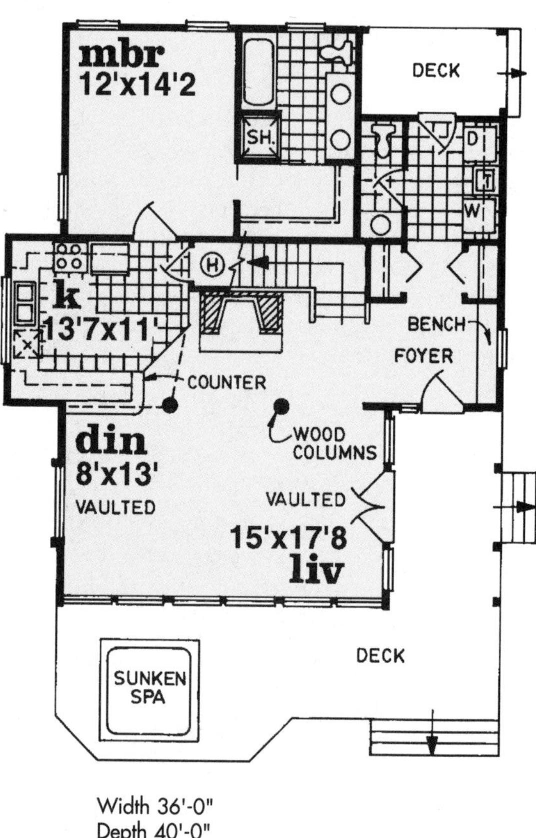
mbr
12'x14'2
SH.
DECK
D
T
W
H
k
13'7x11'
BENCH
FOYER
COUNTER
din
8'x13'
VAULTED
WOOD
COLUMNS
VAULTED
15'x17'8
liv
DECK
SUNKEN
SPA

Width 36'-0"
Depth 40'-0"

Design by
Select Home Designs

© Copyright Select Home Designs. All rights reserved.

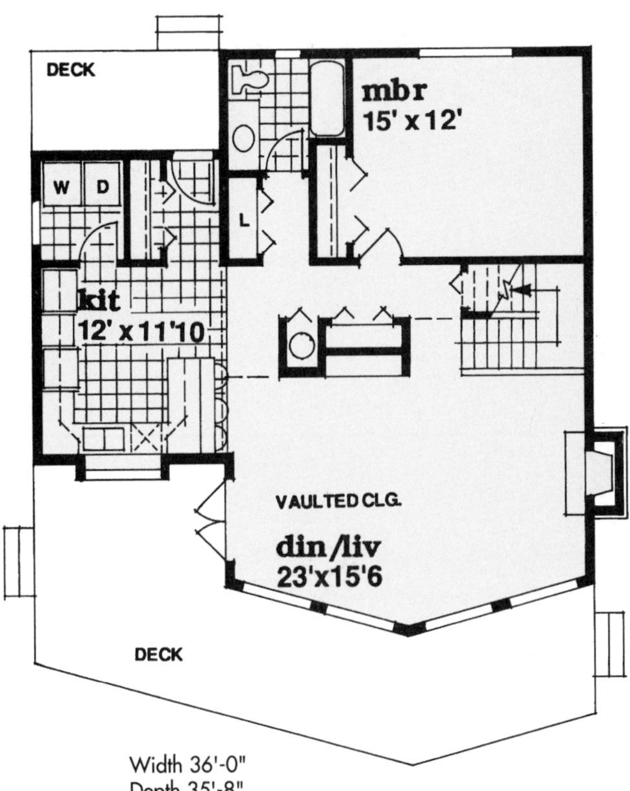
DECK
mbr
15' x 12'
W
D
L
kit
12' x 11'10
VAULTED CLG.
din/liv
23'x15'6
DECK
Width 36'-0"
Depth 35'-8"

Design Q439

First Floor: 1,042 square feet
Second Floor: 456 square feet
Total: 1,498 square feet

■ With a deck to the front, this vacation can't miss out on any outdoor fun. The living and dining rooms are dominated by a window wall to take advantage of the view. A high vaulted ceiling and wood-burning fireplace create a warm atmosphere. The U-shaped kitchen, with adjoining laundry room, is open to the dining room with a pass-through counter. Note the deck beyond the kitchen and full wall closet. The master bedroom is to the rear and has the use of a full bath with large linen closet. Two family bedrooms are upstairs and share a full bath with skylight. Plans include details for both a basement and a crawlspace foundation.

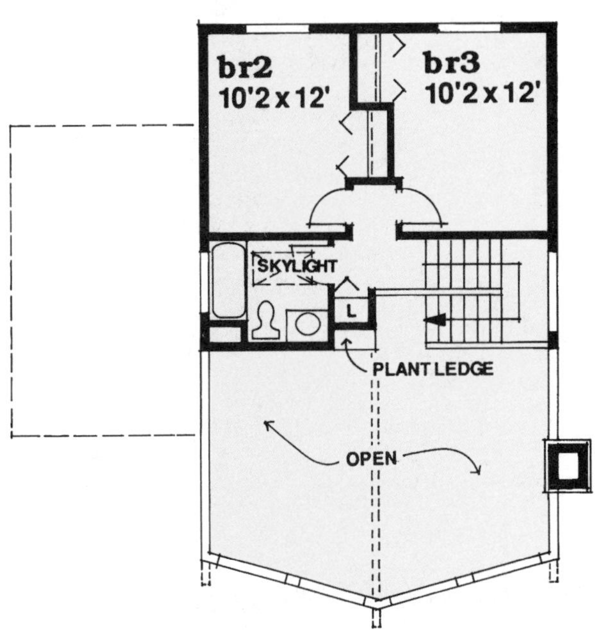
br2
10'2 x 12'
br3
10'2 x 12'
SKYLIGHT
L
PLANT LEDGE
OPEN

Design by
Select Home Designs

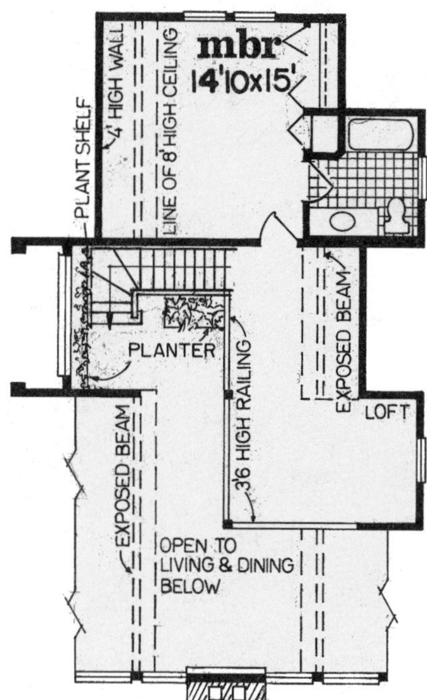
mbr
14'10x15'
4' HIGH WALL
LINE OF 8' HIGH CEILING
PLANT SHELF
PLANTER
3'6 HIGH RAILING
EXPOSED BEAM
LOFT
EXPOSED BEAM
OPEN TO
LIVING & DINING
BELOW

Design by
Select Home Designs

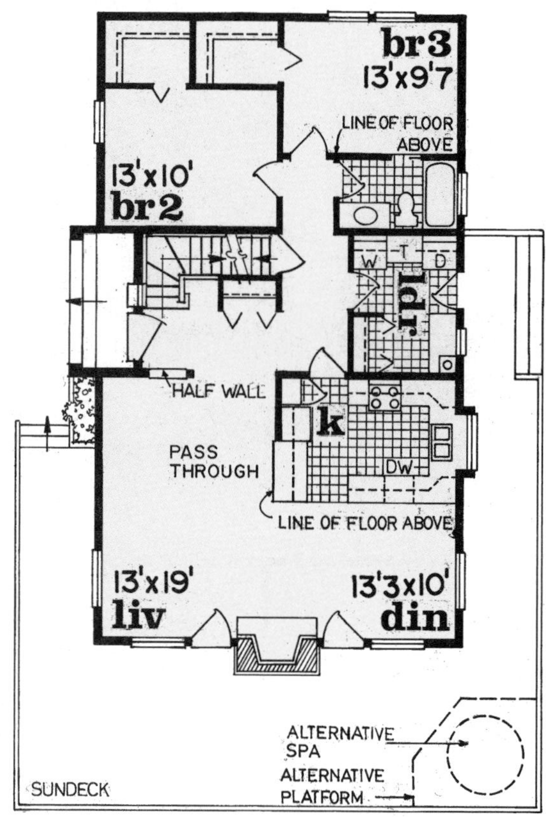
br3
13'x9'7
LINE OF FLOOR
ABOVE
13'x10'
br2
ldr.
W
T
D
HALF WALL
k
PASS
THROUGH
DW
LINE OF FLOOR ABOVE
13'x19'
liv
13'3x10'
din
ALTERNATIVE
SPA
ALTERNATIVE
PLATFORM
SUNDECK

Design Q295

First Floor: 1,235 square feet
Second Floor: 543 square feet
Total: 1,778 square feet

An expansive sundeck with optional spa wraps around this design to highlight outdoor living. Tall windows accent the living and dining rooms' vaulted ceiling. Both areas are warmed by a central fireplace flanked by doors to the deck. A U-shaped kitchen is open to the dining room. Two bedrooms with walk-in closets sit to the back of the first floor. They share the use of a full bath. The master suite dominates the upper level and has a full bath and large wall closet. Note the laundry room and side entries.

Width 27'-6"
Depth 46'-0"

Design Q430

First Floor: 1,061 square feet
Second Floor: 482 square feet
Total: 1,543 square feet

■ A sundeck makes this design so popular, but it is enhanced by views through an expansive wall of glass in the living and dining rooms. They are warmed by a wood stove and enjoy vaulted ceilings, as well. The kitchen is also vaulted and has a prep island and breakfast bar. Behind the kitchen is a laundry room with side access. Two bedrooms and a full bath are found on the first floor. A skylit staircase leads up to the master bedroom and its walk-in closet and private bath on the second floor.

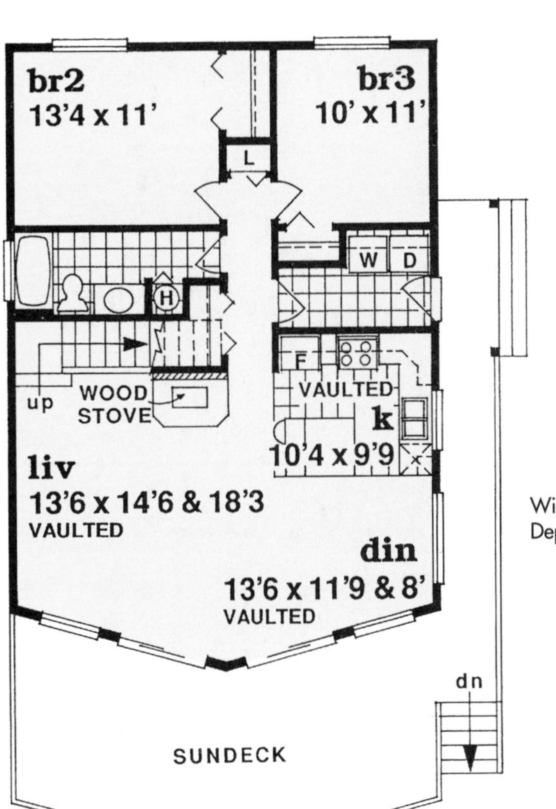
br2
13'4 x 11'
br3
10' x 11'
L
W
D
H
F
up
WOOD STOVE
VAULTED
k
10'4 x 9'9
liv
13'6 x 14'6 & 18'3
VAULTED
din
13'6 x 11'9 & 8'
VAULTED
dn
SUNDECK

Width 28'-0"
Depth 39'-9"

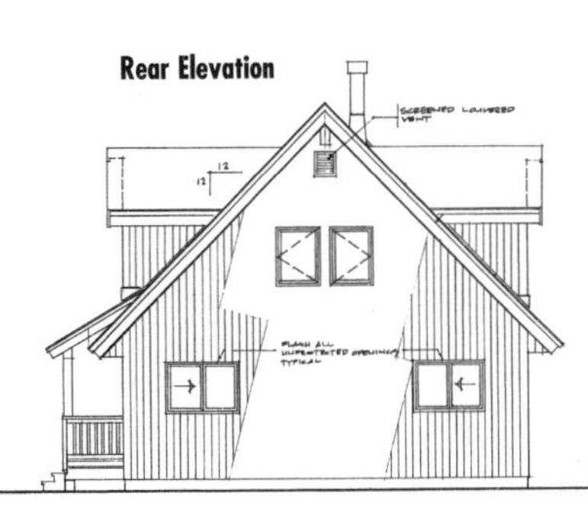
Rear Elevation

Design by
Select Home Designs

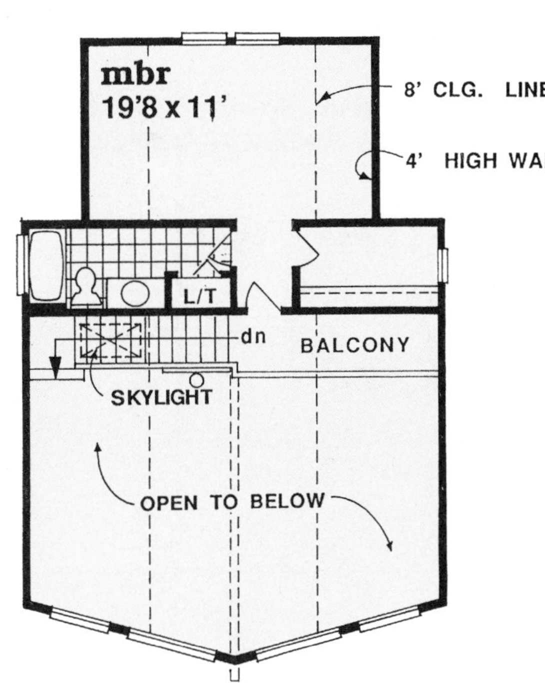
mbr
19'8 x 11'
8' CLG. LINE
4' HIGH WALL
L/T
dn
BALCONY
SKYLIGHT
OPEN TO BELOW

Design 3658

First Floor: 784 square feet
Second Floor: 275 square feet
Total: 1,059 square feet

L **D**

This chalet-type vacation home with its steep, overhanging roof, will catch the eye of even the most casual onlooker. It is designed to be completely livable whether the season be for swimming or skiing. The dormitory on the upper level will sleep many vacationers, while the two bedrooms on the first floor provide the more convenient and conventional sleeping facilities. The upper level overlooks the beam-ceilinged living and dining area. With a wraparound terrace and plenty of storage space, what more could you ask for?

Design by
Home Planners

QUOTE ONE®
Cost to build? See page 516
to order complete cost estimate
to build this house in your area!

Width 32'-0"
Depth 30'-0"

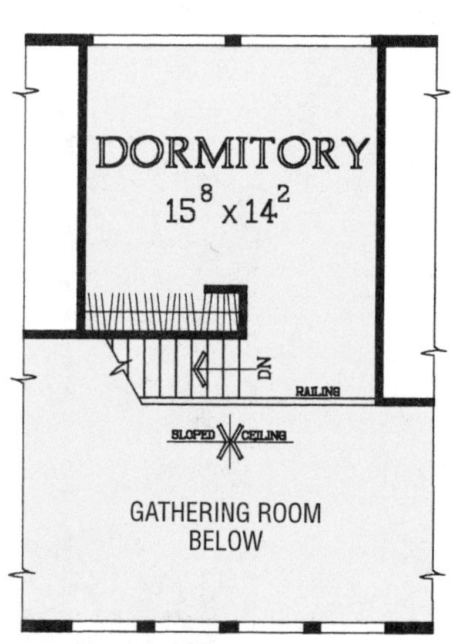

DORMITORY
15⁸ x 14²
DN
RAILING
SLOPED CEILING
GATHERING ROOM
BELOW

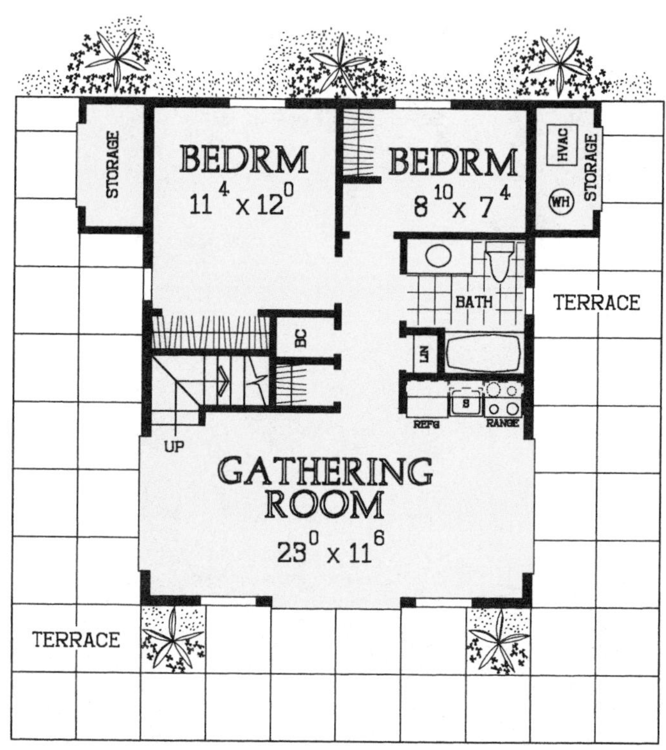

STORAGE
BEDRM
11⁴ x 12⁰
BEDRM
8¹⁰ x 7⁴
HVAC
WH
STORAGE
BATH
TERRACE
BC
LIN
REFG
RANGE
UP
GATHERING
ROOM
23⁰ x 11⁶
TERRACE

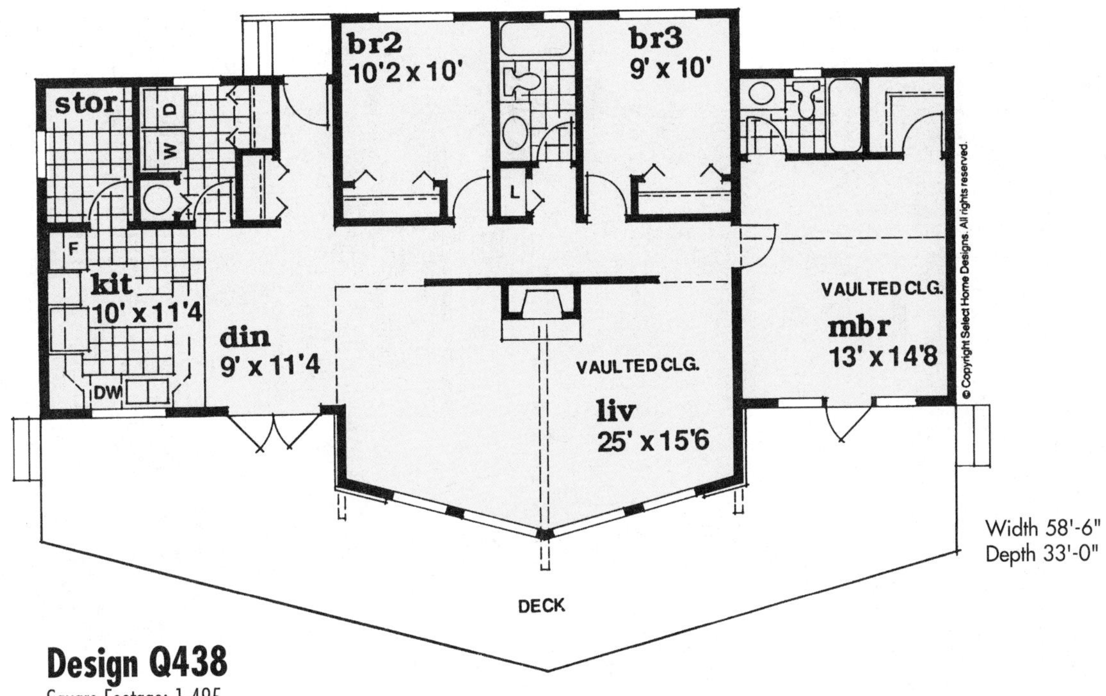
br2
10'2 x 10'
br3
9' x 10'
stor
D
W
F
L
kit
10' x 11'4
DW
din
9' x 11'4
VAULTED CLG.
liv
25' x 15'6
VAULTED CLG.
mbr
13' x 14'8
© Copyright Select Home Designs. All rights reserved.
Width 58'-6"
Depth 33'-0"
DECK

Design Q438

Square Footage: 1,495

This three-bedroom cottage has just the right rustic mix of vertical wood siding and stone accents. Inside, the living is pure resort-style comfort. High vaulted ceilings are featured throughout the living room and master bedroom. The living room also has a fireplace and full-height windows overlooking the deck. The dining room has double door access to the deck; the master bedroom has a single door that opens to the deck. A convenient kitchen has a U-shaped work area with a large storage space beyond. A laundry room with closet is also nearby. Two family bedrooms share a bath that is situated between them. The master suite features a walk-in closet and private bath.

Design by
Select Home Designs

Design by
Select Home Designs

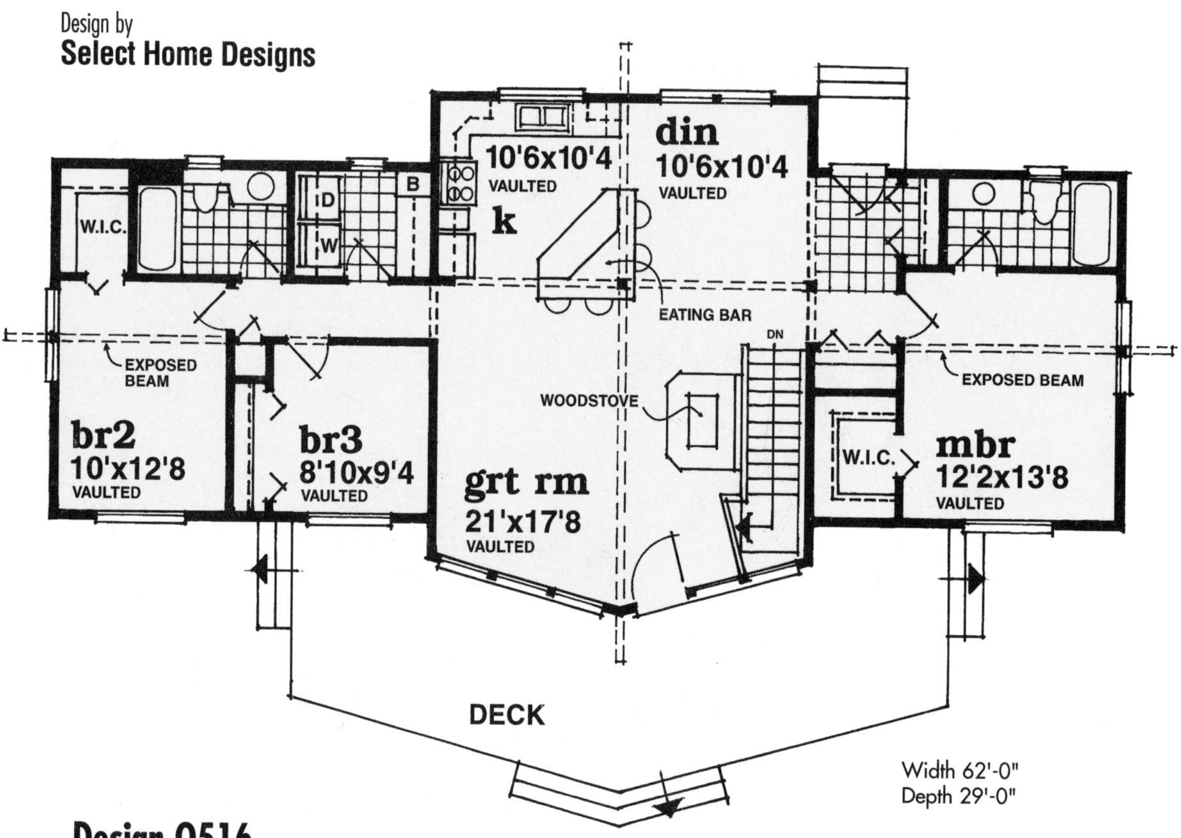

din
10'6x10'4
VAULTED
10'6x10'4
VAULTED
k
W.I.C.
D
W
B
EATING BAR
DN
EXPOSED BEAM
EXPOSED BEAM
WOODSTOVE
br2
10'x12'8
VAULTED
br3
8'10x9'4
VAULTED
grt rm
21'x17'8
VAULTED
W.I.C.
mbr
12'2x13'8
VAULTED
DECK

Width 62'-0"
Depth 29'-0"

Design Q516

Square Footage: 1,405

This three-bedroom leisure home is perfect for the family that spends casual time out of doors. An expansive wall of glass gives a spectacular view to the great room and accentuates the high vaulted ceilings throughout the design. The great room is also warmed by a hearth and is open to the dining room and L-shaped kitchen. A triangular snack bar graces the kitchen and provides space for casual meals. Bedrooms are split, with the master bedroom on the right side of the plan and family bedrooms on the left. The master has exposed beams in the ceiling, a walk-in closet and a full bath with soaking tub. Family bedrooms share a full bath. Plans include details for both a basement and a crawlspace foundation.

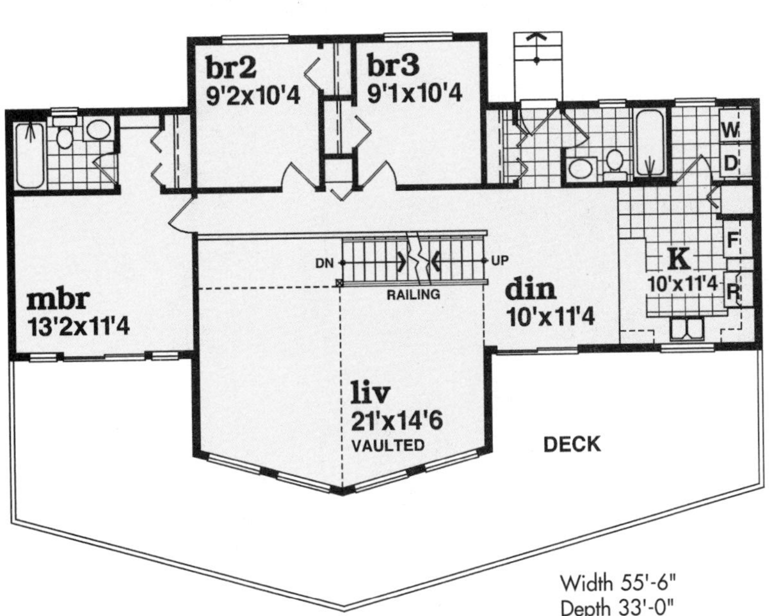
br2
9'2x10'4
br3
9'1x10'4
W
D
F
R
K
10'x11'4
DN
UP
RAILING
mbr
13'2x11'4
din
10'x11'4
liv
21'x14'6
VAULTED
DECK
Width 55'-6"
Depth 33'-0"

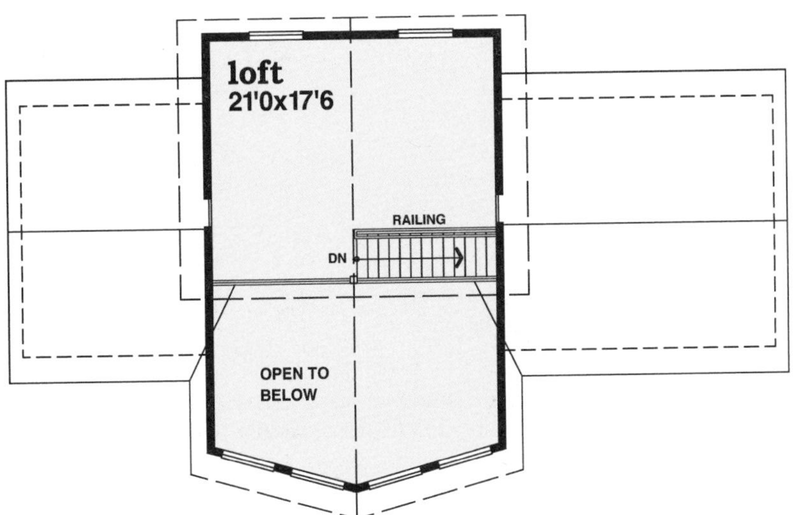
loft
21'0x17'6
RAILING
DN
OPEN TO
BELOW

Design Q508

First Floor: 1,296 square feet
Second Floor: 396 square feet
Total: 1,692 square feet

If your lot slopes to the front and enjoys a view in that direction, this may be the perfect plan for you. The prow front features a wall of windows extending a full two stories, to ensure a view from both the loft and the living room. The huge deck can be accessed from the dining room or the master bedroom and also shelters the lower-level entry. The master bedroom is on the main living level along with two family bedrooms. The master has a private bath, while the family bedrooms share a full bath. A loft area provides additional sleeping space if you need it. The plan calls for the lower-level foyer to be finished, with a complete unfinished basement available for future growth.

Design by
Select Home Designs

Design 2485

Main Level: 1,108 square feet
Lower Level: 983 square feet
Total: 2,091 square feet

■ This hillside vacation home contains lots of livability. Notice the projecting deck and how it shelters the terrace. Each of the generous glassed areas is protected from the summer sun by overhangs and extended walls. The gathering room has a warming fireplace and sloped ceiling and is open to the dining room. The U-shaped kitchen easily serves an adjacent nook as well as the formal dining room. The master bedroom sits on the main level and has a private bath and walk-in closet. A bunk room, second bedroom, full bath and activities room with fireplace sit on the lower level.

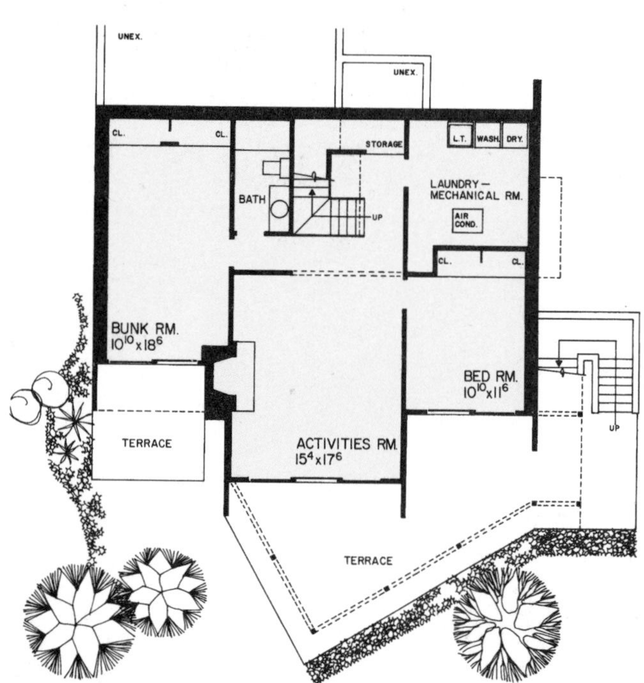
UNEX.
UNEX.
CL.
CL.
BATH
STORAGE
L.T.
WASH
DRY
LAUNDRY—
MECHANICAL RM.
AIR COND.
UP
CL.
CL.
BUNK RM.
$10^{10} \times 18^{6}$
BED RM.
$10^{10} \times 11^{6}$
ACTIVITIES RM.
$15^{4} \times 17^{6}$
TERRACE
TERRACE
UP

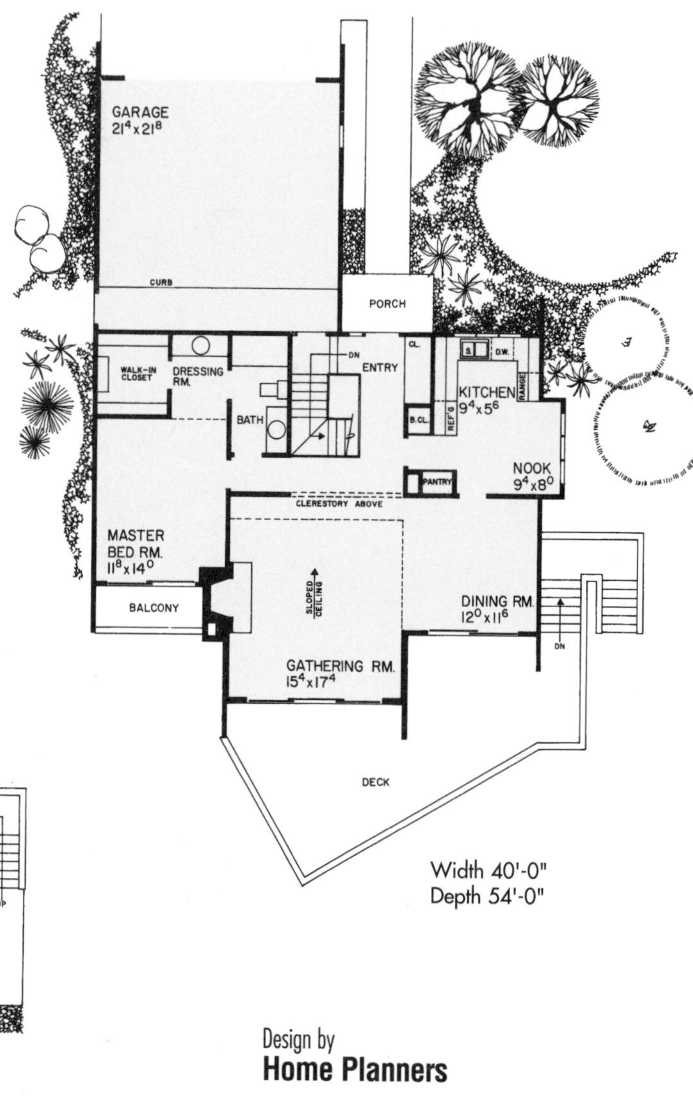
GARAGE
$21^{4} \times 21^{8}$
CURB
PORCH
WALK-IN CLOSET
DRESSING RM.
DN
ENTRY
CL.
S.
D.W.
KITCHEN
$9^{4} \times 5^{6}$
RANGE
REF'G
B.CL.
BATH
PANTRY
NOOK
$9^{4} \times 8^{0}$
CLERESTORY ABOVE
MASTER BED RM.
$11^{8} \times 14^{0}$
BALCONY
SLOPED CEILING
DINING RM.
$12^{0} \times 11^{6}$
GATHERING RM.
$15^{4} \times 17^{4}$
DN
DECK

Width 40'-0"
Depth 54'-0"

Design by
Home Planners

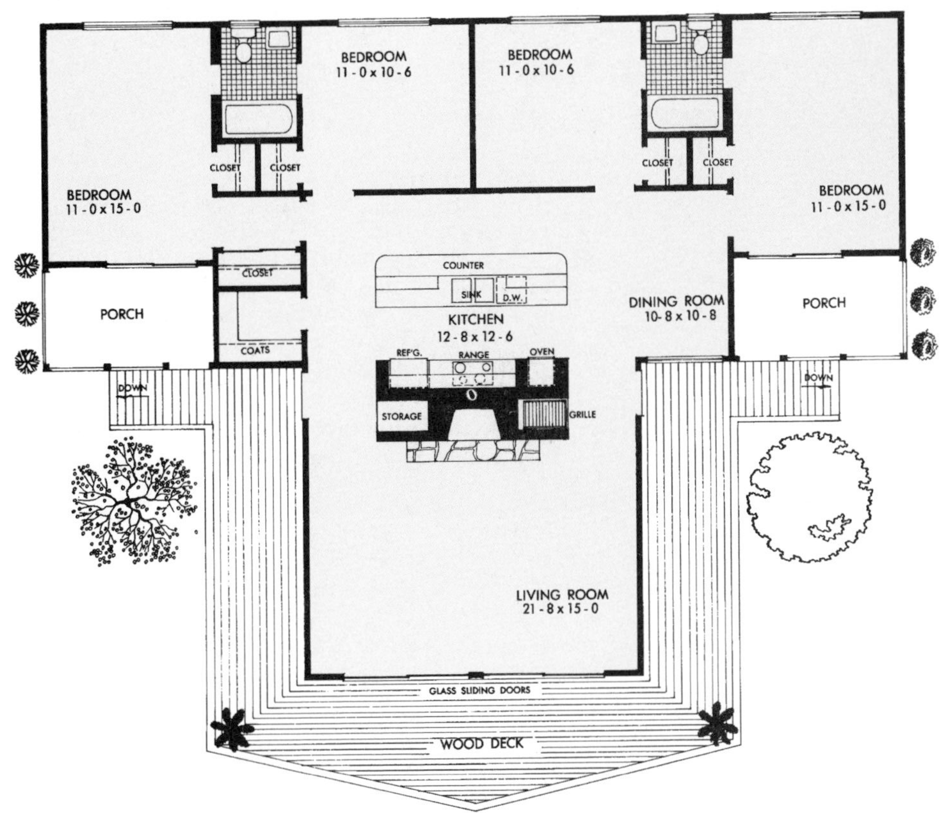
BEDROOM
11-0 x 10-6
BEDROOM
11-0 x 10-6
CLOSET
CLOSET
CLOSET
CLOSET
BEDROOM
11-0 x 15-0
BEDROOM
11-0 x 15-0
CLOSET
PORCH
COATS
COUNTER
SINK
D.W.
KITCHEN
12-8 x 12-6
REF'G.
RANGE
OVEN
DINING ROOM
10-8 x 10-8
PORCH
DOWN
DOWN
STORAGE
GRILLE
LIVING ROOM
21-8 x 15-0
GLASS SLIDING DOORS
WOOD DECK

Width 57'-0"
Depth 50'-8"

Design 4015

Square Footage: 1,420

The perfect vacation home combines open, informal living spaces with lots of sleeping space. The spacious living room has a warming fireplace and sliding glass doors onto the deck. Convenient to the dining room, the efficient kitchen is carefully placed so as not to interfere with the living room. Notice the four spacious bedrooms—there's plenty of room for accommodating guests. Two of the bedrooms boast private porches.

Design by
Home Planners

When You're Ready To Order . . .

Let Us Show You Our Home Blueprint Package.

Building a home? Planning a home? Our Blueprint Package has nearly everything you need to get the job done right, whether you're working on your own or with help from an architect, designer, builder or subcontractors. Each Blueprint Package is the result of many hours of work by licensed architects or professional designers.

QUALITY

Hundreds of hours of painstaking effort have gone into the development of your blueprint set. Each home has been quality-checked by professionals to insure accuracy and buildability.

VALUE

Because we sell in volume, you can buy professional-quality blueprints at a fraction of their development cost. With our plans, your dream home design costs only a few hundred dollars, not the thousands of dollars that custom architects charge.

SERVICE

Once you've chosen your favorite home plan, you'll receive fast, efficient service whether you choose to mail or fax your order to us or call us toll free at 1-800-521-6797. For customer service, call toll free 1-888-690-1116.

SATISFACTION

Over 50 years of service to satisfied home plan buyers provide us unparalleled experience and knowledge in producing quality blueprints. What this means to you is satisfaction with our product and performance.

ORDER TOLL FREE 1-800-521-6797

After you've looked over our Blueprint Package and Important Extras on the following pages, simply mail the order form on page 525 or call toll free on our Blueprint Hotline: 1-800-521-6797. We're ready and eager to serve you. For customer service, call toll free 1-888-690-1116.

Each set of blueprints is an interrelated collection of detail sheets which includes components such as floor plans, interior and exterior elevations, dimensions, cross-sections, diagrams and notations. These sheets show exactly how your house is to be built.

Among the sheets included may be:

Frontal Sheet
This artist's sketch of the exterior of the house gives you an idea of how the house will look when built and landscaped. Large ink-line floor plans show all levels of the house and provide an overview of your new home's livability, as well as a handy reference for deciding on furniture placement.

Foundation Plan
This sheet shows the foundation layout

SAMPLE PACKAGE

including support walls, excavated and unexcavated areas, if any, and foundation notes. If slab construction rather than basement, the plan shows footings and details for a monolithic slab. This page, or another in the set, may include a sample plot plan for locating your house on a building site.

Detailed Floor Plans

These plans show the layout of each floor of the house. Rooms and interior spaces are carefully dimensioned and keys are given for cross-section details provided later in the plans. The positions of electrical outlets and switches are shown.

House Cross-Sections

Large-scale views show sections or cut-aways of the foundation, interior walls, exterior walls, floors, stairways and roof details. Additional cross-sections may show important changes in floor, ceiling or roof heights or the relationship of one level to another. Extremely valuable for construction, these sections show exactly how the various parts of the house fit together.

Interior Elevations

Many of our drawings show the design and placement of kitchen and bathroom cabinets, laundry areas, fireplaces, bookcases and other built-ins. Little "extras," such as mantelpiece and wainscoting drawings, plus moulding sections, provide details that give your home that custom touch.

Exterior Elevations

These drawings show the front, rear and sides of your house and give necessary notes on exterior materials and finishes. Particular attention is given to cornice detail, brick and stone accents or other finish items that make your home unique.

Note: Because of the diversity of local building codes, our blueprints may not include Electrical, Plumbing or Mechanical plans or layouts.

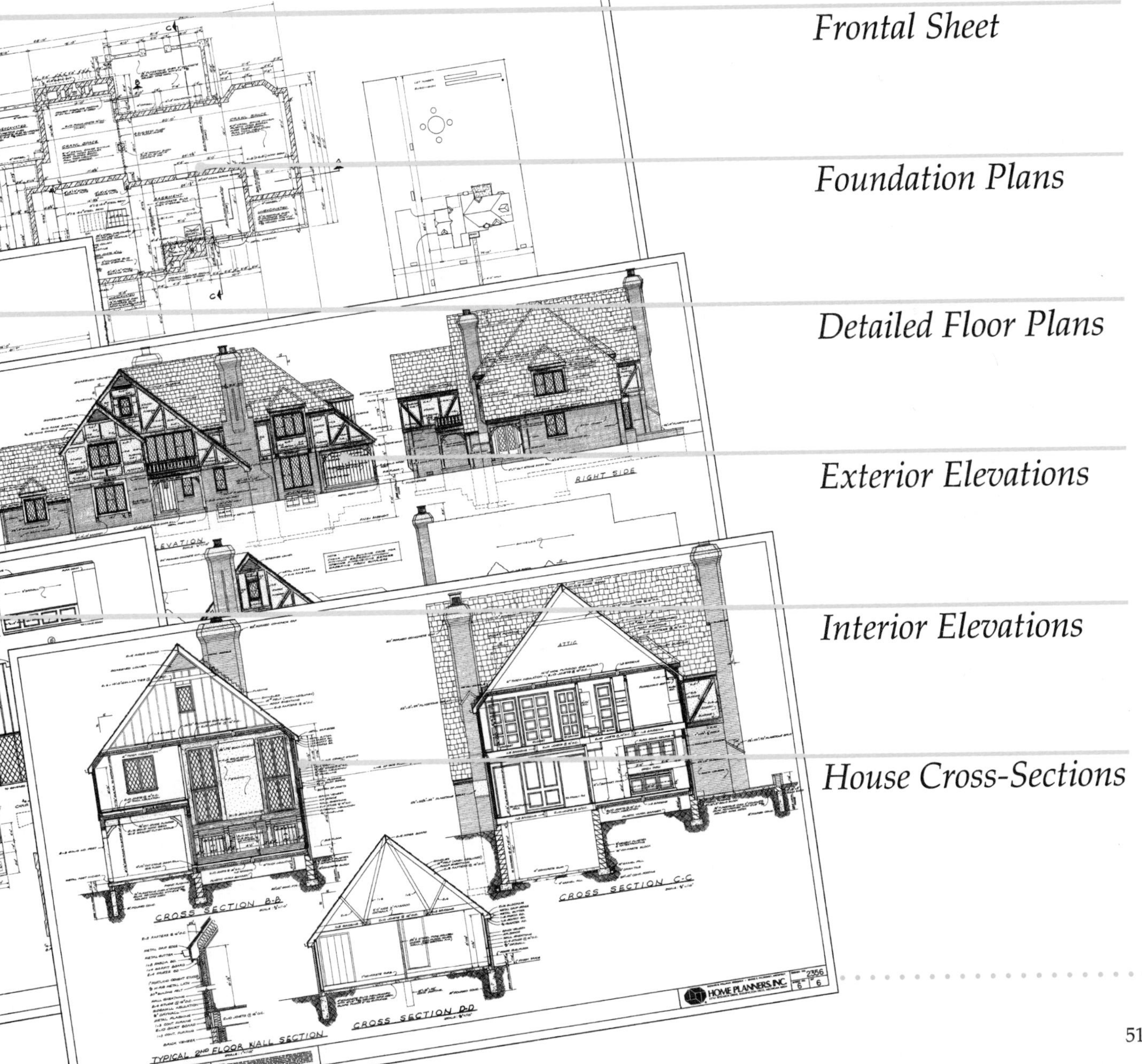
Frontal Sheet
Foundation Plans
Detailed Floor Plans
Exterior Elevations
Interior Elevations
House Cross-Sections
RIGHT SIDE
CROSS SECTION B-B
CROSS SECTION C-C
CROSS SECTION D-D
TYPICAL 2ND FLOOR WALL SECTION
ATTIC
HOME PLANNERS, INC
2356

Important Extras To Do The Job Right!

Introducing eight important planning and construction aids developed by our professionals to help you succeed in your home-building project.

MATERIALS LIST

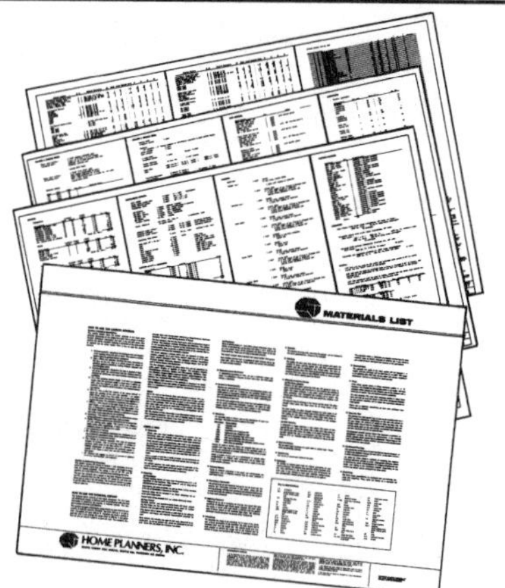

(Note: Because of the diversity of local building codes, our Materials List does not include mechanical materials.)

For many of the designs in our portfolio, we offer a customized materials take-off that is invaluable in planning and estimating the cost of your new home. This Materials List outlines the quantity, type and size of materials needed to build your house (with the exception of mechanical system items). Included are framing lumber, windows and doors, kitchen and bath cabinetry, rough and finish hardware, and much more. This handy list helps you or your builder cost out materials and serves as a reference sheet when you're compiling bids. A Materials List cannot be ordered before blueprints are ordered.

SPECIFICATION OUTLINE

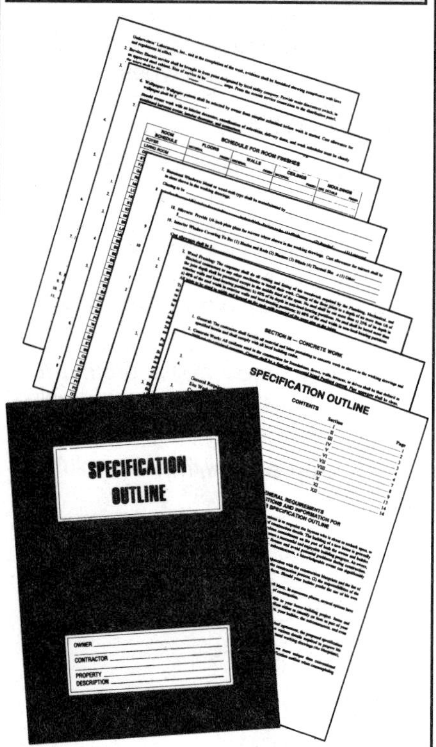

This valuable 16-page document is critical to building your house correctly. Designed to be filled in by you or your builder, this book lists 166 stages or items crucial to the building process. It provides a comprehensive review of the construction process and helps in choosing materials. When combined with the blueprints, a signed contract, and a schedule, it becomes a legal document and record for the building of your home.

QUOTE ONE®

Summary Cost Report / Materials Cost Report

A new service for estimating the cost of building select designs, the Quote One® system is available in two separate stages: The Summary Cost Report and the Materials Cost Report.

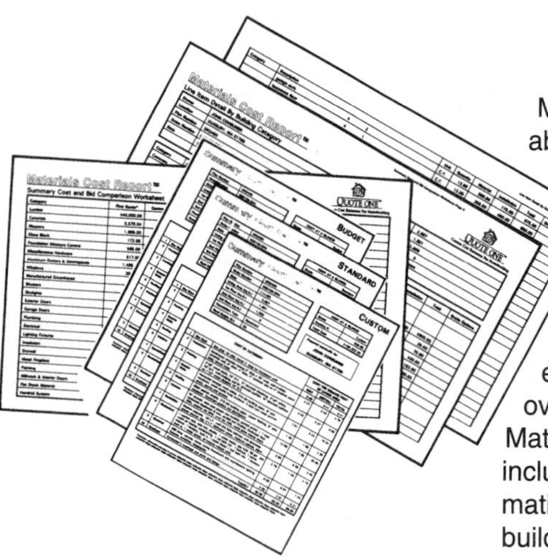

The Summary Cost report is the first stage in the package and shows the total cost per square foot for your chosen home in your zip-code area and then breaks that cost down into various categories showing the costs for building materials, labor and installation. The total cost for the report (which includes three grades: Budget, Standard and Custom) is just $29.95 for one home, and additionals are only $14.95. These reports allow you to evaluate your building budget and compare the costs of building a variety of homes in your area.

Make even more informed decisions about your home-building project with the second phase of our package, our Materials Cost Report. This tool is invaluable in planning and estimating the cost of your new home. The material and installation (labor and equipment) cost is shown for each of over 1,000 line items provided in the Materials List (Standard grade), which is included when you purchase this estimating tool. It allows you to determine building costs for your specific zip-code area and for your chosen home design. Space is allowed for additional estimates from contractors and subcontractors. This invaluable tool is available for a price of $120 ($130 for a Schedule C4-L4 plan), which includes a Materials List. A Materials Cost Report cannot be ordered before blueprints are ordered.

The Quote One® program is continually updated with new plans. If you are interested in a plan that is not indicated as Quote One®, please call and ask our sales reps. They will be happy to verify the status for you. To order these invaluable reports, use the order form on page 525 or call 1-800-521-6797.

Construction Information

If you want to know more about techniques—and deal more confidently with subcontractors—we offer these useful sheets. Each set is an excellent tool that will add to your understanding of these technical subjects.

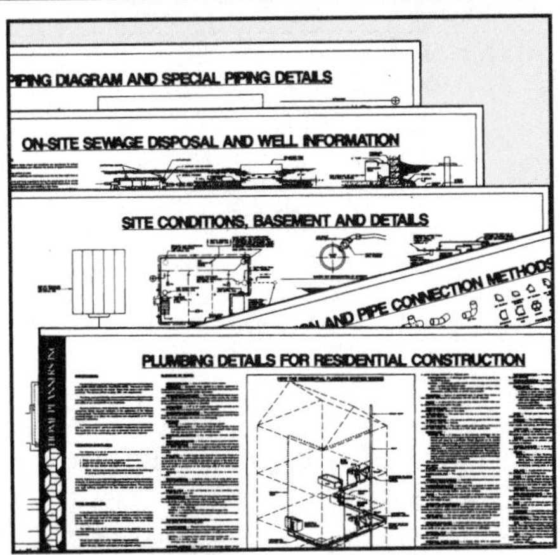
PIPING DIAGRAM AND SPECIAL PIPING DETAILS
ON-SITE SEWAGE DISPOSAL AND WELL INFORMATION
SITE CONDITIONS, BASEMENT AND DETAILS
PLUMBING DETAILS FOR RESIDENTIAL CONSTRUCTION

Plumbing

The Blueprint Package includes locations for all the plumbing fixtures in your new house, including sinks, lavatories, tubs, showers, toilets, laundry trays and water heaters. However, if you want to know more about the complete plumbing system, these 24x36-inch detail sheets will prove very useful. Prepared to meet requirements of the National Plumbing Code, these six fact-filled sheets give general information on pipe schedules, fittings, sump-pump details, water-softener hookups, septic system details and much more. Color-coded sheets include a glossary of terms.

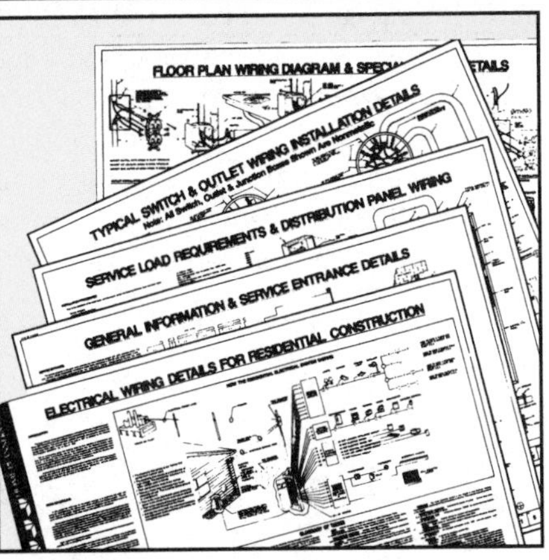
TYPICAL SWITCH & OUTLET WIRING INSTALLATION DETAILS
SERVICE LOAD REQUIREMENTS & DISTRIBUTION PANEL WIRING
GENERAL INFORMATION & SERVICE ENTRANCE DETAILS
ELECTRICAL WIRING DETAILS FOR RESIDENTIAL CONSTRUCTION

Electrical

The locations for every electrical switch, plug and outlet are shown in your Blueprint Package. However, these Electrical Details go further to take the mystery out of household electrical systems. Prepared to meet requirements of the National Electrical Code, these comprehensive 24x36-inch drawings come packed with helpful information, including wire sizing, switch-installation schematics, cable-routing details, appliance wattage, door-bell hookups, typical service panel circuitry and much more. Six sheets are bound together and color-coded for easy reference. A glossary of terms is also included.

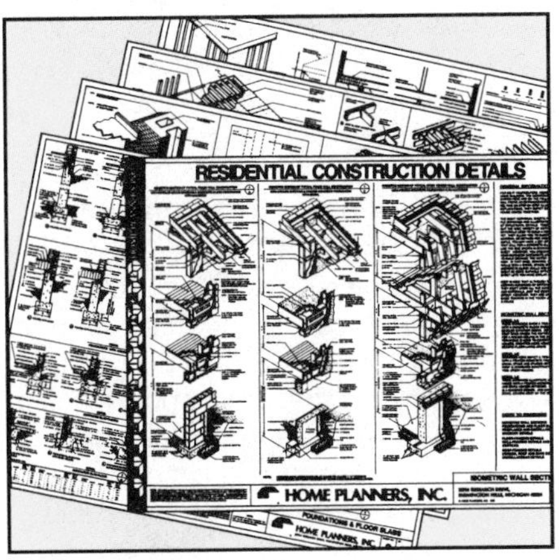
RESIDENTIAL CONSTRUCTION DETAILS
HOME PLANNERS, INC.

Construction

The Blueprint Package contains everything an experienced builder needs to construct a particular house. However, it doesn't show all the ways that houses can be built, nor does it explain alternate construction methods. To help you understand how your house will be built—and offer additional techniques—this set of drawings depicts the materials and methods used to build foundations, fireplaces, walls, floors and roofs. Where appropriate, the drawings show acceptable alternatives. These six sheets will answer questions for the advanced do-it-yourselfer or home planner.

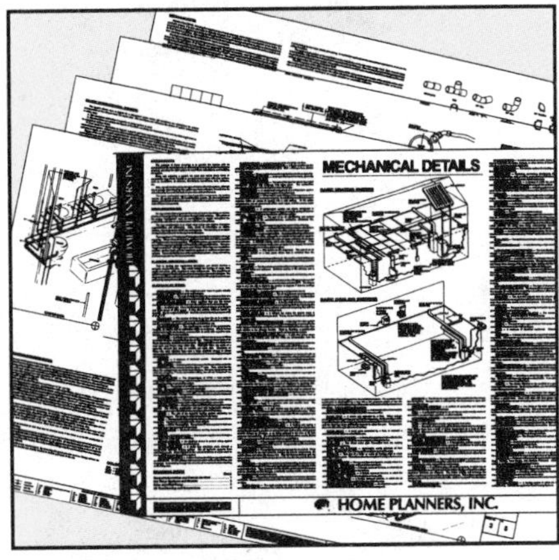
MECHANICAL DETAILS
HOME PLANNERS, INC.

Mechanical

This package contains fundamental principles and useful data that will help you make informed decisions and communicate with subcontractors about heating and cooling systems. The 24x36-inch drawings contain instructions and samples that allow you to make simple load calculations and preliminary sizing and costing analysis. Covered are today's most commonly used systems from heat pumps to solar fuel systems. The package is packed full of illustrations and diagrams to help you visualize components and how they relate to one another.

Plan-A-Home®

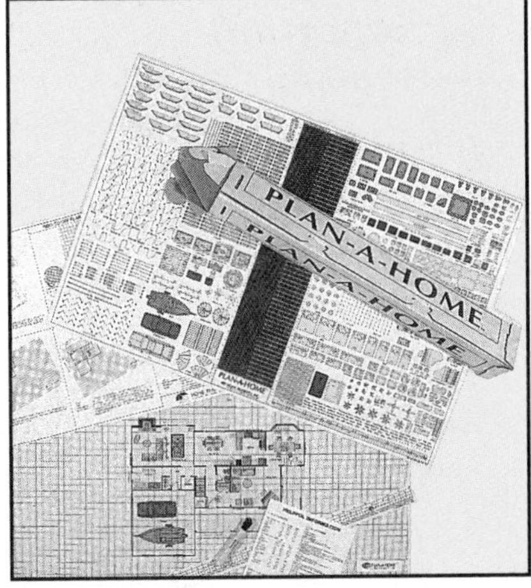
PLAN-A-HOME

Plan-A-Home® is an easy-to-use tool that helps you design a new home, arrange furniture in a new or existing home, or plan a remodeling project. Each package contains:

- **More than 700 reusable peel-off planning symbols** on a self-stick vinyl sheet including walls, windows, doors, all types of furniture, kitchen components, bath fixtures and many more.
- **A reusable, transparent, 1/4-inch scale planning grid** that matches the scale of actual working drawings (1/4-inch equals one foot). This grid provides the basis for house layouts of up to 140x92 feet.
- **Tracing paper** and a protective sheet for copying or transferring your completed plan.
- **A felt-tip pen,** with water-soluble ink that wipes away quickly.

Plan-A-Home® lets you lay out areas as large as a 7,500 square foot, six-bedroom, seven-bath house.

To Order, Call Toll Free 1-800-521-6797

To add these important extras to your Blueprint Package, simply indicate your choices on the order form on page 525 or call us Toll Free 1-800-521-6797 and we'll tell you more about these exciting products.
For customer service, call toll free 1-888-690-1116.

D The Deck Blueprint Package

Many of the homes in this book can be enhanced with a professionally designed Home Planners Deck Plan. Those home plans highlighted with a D have a matching or corresponding deck plan available which includes a Deck Plan Frontal Sheet, Deck Framing and Floor Plans, Deck Elevations and a Deck Materials List. A Standard Deck Details Package, also available, provides all the how-to information necessary for building *any* deck. Our Complete Deck Building Package contains one set of Custom Deck Plans of your choice, plus one set of Standard Deck Building Details all for one low price. Our plans and details are carefully prepared in an easy-to-understand format that will guide you through every stage of your deck-building project. This page contains a sampling of 12 of the 25 different Deck layouts to match your favorite house. See page 520 for prices and ordering information.

SPLIT-LEVEL SUN DECK
Deck Plan D100

BI-LEVEL DECK WITH COVERED DINING
Deck Plan D101

WRAPAROUND FAMILY DECK
Deck Plan D104

DECK FOR DINING AND VIEWS
Deck Plan D107

TREND SETTER DECK
Deck Plan D110

TURN-OF-THE-CENTURY DECK
Deck Plan D111

WEEKEND ENTERTAINER DECK
Deck Plan D112

CENTER-VIEW DECK
Deck Plan D114

KITCHEN-EXTENDER DECK
Deck Plan D115

SPLIT-LEVEL ACTIVITY DECK
Deck Plan D117

TRI-LEVEL DECK WITH GRILL
Deck Plan D119

CONTEMPORARY LEISURE DECK
Deck Plan D120

The Landscape Blueprint Package

For the homes marked with an L in this book, Home Planners has created a front-yard landscape plan that matches or is complementary in design to the house plan. These comprehensive blueprint packages include a Frontal Sheet, Plan View, Regionalized Plant & Materials List, a sheet on Planting and Maintaining Your Landscape, Zone Maps and Plant Size and Description Guide. These plans will help you achieve professional results, adding value and enjoyment to your property for years to come. Each set of blueprints is a full 18″ x 24″ in size with clear, complete instructions and easy-to-read type. Six of the forty front-yard Landscape Plans to match your favorite house are shown below.

Regional Order Map

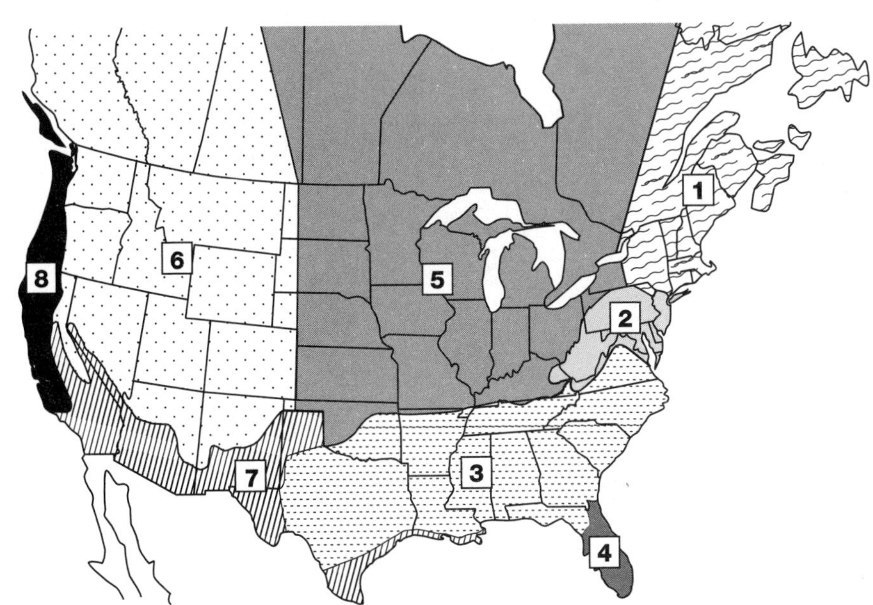

1
2
3
4
5
6
7
8

Most of the Landscape Plans shown on these pages are available with a Plant & Materials List adapted by horticultural experts to 8 different regions of the country. Please specify Geographic Region when ordering your plan. See page 520 for prices, ordering information and regional availability.

Region	1	Northeast
Region	2	Mid-Atlantic
Region	3	Deep South
Region	4	Florida & Gulf Coast
Region	5	Midwest
Region	6	Rocky Mountains
Region	7	Southern California & Desert Southwest
Region	8	Northern California & Pacific Northwest

CAPE COD COTTAGE
Landscape Plan L202

GAMBREL-ROOF COLONIAL
Landscape Plan L203

CENTER-HALL COLONIAL
Landscape Plan L204

CLASSIC NEW ENGLAND COLONIAL
Landscape Plan L205

COUNTRY-STYLE FARMHOUSE
Landscape Plan L207

TRADITIONAL SPLIT-LEVEL
Landscape Plan L228

Price Schedule & Plans Index

Blueprint Price Schedule (Prices guaranteed through December 31, 2000)					
Tiers	1-set Study Package	4-set Building Package	8-set Building Package	1-set Reproducible Sepias	Home Customizer® Package
P1	$20	$50	$90	N/A	N/A
P2	$40	$70	$110	N/A	N/A
P3	$60	$90	$130	N/A	N/A
P4	$80	$110	$150	N/A	N/A
P5	$100	$130	$170	N/A	N/A
P6	$120	$150	$190	N/A	N/A
A1	$400	$440	$500	$600	$650
A2	$440	$480	$540	$660	$710
A3	$480	$520	$580	$720	$770
A4	$520	$560	$620	$780	$830
C1	$560	$600	$660	$840	$890
C2	$600	$640	$700	$900	$950
C3	$650	$690	$750	$950	$1000
C4	$700	$740	$800	$1000	$1050
L1	$750	$790	$850	$1050	$1100
L2	$800	$840	$900	$1100	$1150
L3	$900	$940	$1000	$1200	$1250
L4	$1000	$1040	$1100	$1300	$1350

Options for plans in Tiers A1-L4

Additional Identical Blueprints in same order for "A1-L4" price plans ....$50 per set

Reverse Blueprints (mirror image) with 4- or 8-set order for "A1-L4" price plans ....$50 fee per order

Specification Outlines ....$10 each

Materials Lists for "A1-C3" price plans ....$60 each

Materials Lists for "C4-L4" price plans ....$70 each

Options for plans in Tiers P1-P6

Additional Identical Blueprints in same order for "P1-P6" price plans ....$10 per set

Reverse Blueprints (mirror image) for "P1-P6" price plans ....$10 per set

1 Set of Deck Construction Details ....$14.95 each

Deck Construction Package ....add $10 to Building Package price

(1 set of "P1-P6" price plans, plus 1 set Standard Deck Construction Details)

1 Set of Gazebo Construction Details..........$14.95 each

Gazebo Construction Package ......add $10 to Building Package price

(1 set of "P1-P6" price plans, plus 1 set Standard Gazebo Construction Details)

IMPORTANT NOTES

The 1-set study package is marked "not for construction." Prices for 4- or 8-set Building Packages honored only at time of original order.

Index

To use the Index below, refer to the design number listed in numerical order (a helpful page reference is also given). Note the price index letter and refer to the House Blueprint Price Schedule above for the cost of one, four or eight sets of blueprints or the cost of a reproducible sepia. Additional prices are shown for identical and reverse blueprint sets, as well as other very useful products for many of the plans. Also note in the Index below those plans that have matching or complementary Deck Plans or Landscape Plans. Refer to the schedules above for prices of these plans. All Home Planners plans can be customized with Home Planners Home Customizer® Package. These plans are indicated below with this symbol: ☗. See page 525 for information. Some plans are also part of our Quote One® estimating service and are indicated by this symbol: ⌂. See page 516 for more information.

To Order: Fill in and send the order form on page 525—or call toll free 1-800-521-6797 or 520-297-8200. Fax: 1-800-224-6699 or 520-544-3086.

DESIGN	PRICE	PAGE	MATERIALS LIST	CUSTOMIZABLE	QUOTE ONE®	DECK	DECK PRICE	LANDSCAPE	LANDSCAPE PRICE	REGIONS
1113	A3	239	✓	☗	⌂	D113	P2	L202	P3	1-3, 5,6,8
1228	C2	336	✓	☗		D124	P3	L217	P3	1-8
1305	A2	206	✓	☗		D106	P3			
1323	A3	165	✓	☗	⌂	D117	P3	L225	P3	1-3, 5,6,8
1325	A4	204	✓	☗		D106	P3	L225	P3	1-3, 5,6,8
1482	A4	492	✓	☗						
1718	C1	157	✓	☗		D114	P2	L210	P3	1-3,5,6,8
1719	A3	76	✓	☗		D105	P2	L203	P3	1-3, 5,6,8
1791	A4	148	✓	☗	⌂	D114	P2	L205	P3	1-3, 5,6,8
1829	A4	168	✓	☗		D113	P2	L226	P3	1-8
1850	C1	303	✓	☗	⌂					
1858	L1	66	✓	☗		D101	P2			
1890	A3	205	✓	☗						
1892	A4	285	✓	☗		D106	P3	L225	P3	1-3, 5,6,8
1896	A3	207	✓	☗						
1920	A4	164	✓	☗	⌂			L225	P3	1-3, 5,6,8
1956	A3	82	✓	☗	⌂	D117	P3			
1957	A4	46	✓	☗	⌂	D100	P2	L228	P3	1-8
1974	C2	320	✓	☗						
1989	A4	272	✓	☗		D100	P2	L220	P3	1-3, 5,6,8
1993	C3	337	✓	☗	⌂			L213	P4	1-8
2133	C3	342	✓	☗		D106	P3			
2145	A3	152	✓	☗	⌂			L209	P3	1-6, 8
2146	A3	154	✓	☗		D114	P2	L203	P3	1-3, 5,6,8
2170	A3	193	✓	☗				L221	P3	1-3, 5,6,8
2181	C1	254	✓	☗		D100	P2	L226	P3	1-8
2192	C2	344	✓	☗		D117	P3	L218	P4	1-6, 8
2206	A3	194	✓	☗	⌂			L220	P3	1-3, 5,6,8
2211	A4	85	✓	☗		D117	P3	L201	P3	1-3, 5,6,8
2220	C1	280	✓	☗		D114	P2	L217	P3	1-8
2283	C1	84	✓	☗		D114	P2	L206	P4	1-6, 8
2356	C3	331	✓	☗		D119	P3	L219	P4	1-3, 5,6,8
2427	A3	493	✓	☗						
2431	A3	496	✓	☗						
2485	A4	512	✓	☗						
2488	A4	482	✓	☗	⌂	D102	P2			
2490	C2	127	✓	☗	⌂					
2505	A2	216	✓	☗	⌂	D113	P2	L226	P3	1-8
2511	C1	296	✓	☗	⌂	D108	P2	L229	P3	1-8
2534	C2	258	✓	☗	⌂			L227	P4	1-8
2538	C1	88	✓	☗		D113	P2	L201	P3	1-3, 5,6,8
2540	C1	68	✓	☗		D113	P2	L205	P3	1-3, 5,6,8

DESIGN	PRICE	PAGE	MATERIALS LIST	CUSTOMIZABLE	QUOTE ONE®	DECK	DECK PRICE	LANDSCAPE	LANDSCAPE PRICE	REGIONS
2543	L1	329	✓	✓		D107	P3	L218	P4	1-6, 8
2544	C1	253	✓	✓		D124	P3			
2559	A4	144	✓	✓		D112	P2			
2563	C1	155	✓	✓	✓	D114	P2	L201	P3	1-3 ,5,6,8
2565	A3	186	✓	✓	✓	D101	P2	L225	P3	1-3, 5,6,8
2573	C1	276	✓	✓		D114	P2	L220	P3	1-3, 5,6,8
2596	A4	153	✓	✓		D114	P2	L201	P3	1-3, 5,6,8
2597	A3	171	✓	✓	✓	D114	P2	L226	P3	1-8
2603	A4	203	✓	✓	✓	D106	P3	L220	P3	1-3, 5,6,8
2606	A3	189	✓	✓	✓			L221	P3	1-3, 5,6,8
2607	A2	195	✓	✓				L220	P3	1-3, 5,6,8
2608	A4	302	✓	✓	✓	D112	P2	L228	P3	1-8
2610	C2	89	✓	✓	✓	D114	P2	L204	P3	1-3, 5,6,8
2615	C2	338	✓	✓	✓	D106	P3	L211	P3	1-8
2622	A3	73	✓	✓	✓	D103	P2	L200	P3	1-3, 5,6,8
2633	C2	346	✓	✓						
2657	A4	150	✓	✓	✓			L200	P3	1-3, 5,6,8
2659	C2	71	✓	✓	✓	D113	P2	L205	P3	1-3, 5,6,8
2661	A4	149	✓	✓	✓	D113	P2	L202	P3	1-3, 5,6,8
2662	C3	345	✓	✓	✓			L216	P3	1-3, 5,6,8
2665	C3	64	✓	✓						
2667	C2	67	✓	✓				L216	P3	1-3, 5,6,8
2668	C1	60	✓	✓	✓			L214	P4	1-3, 5,6,8
2670	C2	471	✓	✓	✓			L236	P4	3,4,7
2671	A4	210	✓	✓	✓	D114	P2	L234	P3	1-8
2672	A3	169	✓	✓	✓	D112	P2	L226	P3	1-8
2675	A4	255	✓	✓		D106	P3			
2678	A3	197	✓	✓		D117	P3	L220	P3	1-3, 5,6,8
2679	C3	299	✓	✓						
2682	A4	146	✓	✓	✓	D115	P2	L200	P3	1-3, 5,6,8
2683	L1	347	✓	✓	✓	D101	P2	L214	P4	1-3, 5,6,8
2684	C2	145	✓	✓		D114	P2	L204	P3	1-3, 5,6,8
2693	C3	343	✓	✓						
2694	C3	380	✓	✓	✓			L209	P3	1-6, 8
2699	C3	339	✓	✓	✓			L211	P3	1-8
2707	A3	198	✓	✓	✓	D117	P3	L226	P3	1-8
2711	A4	126	✓	✓	✓	D105	P2	L229	P3	1-8
2716	C1	294	✓	✓				L229	P3	1-8
2728	A3	192	✓	✓		D112	P2	L221	P3	1-3, 5,6,8
2729	C1	123	✓	✓				L234	P3	1-8
2731	A4	70	✓	✓		D114	P2	L205	P3	1-3, 5,6,8
2733	A4	72	✓	✓	✓	D100	P2	L205	P3	1-3, 5,6,8
2737	A3	191	✓	✓				L220	P3	1-3, 5,6,8
2756	C2	256	✓	✓		D101	P2	L234	P3	1-8
2768	C2	252	✓	✓						
2774	C1	19	✓	✓	✓	D100	P2	L207	P4	1-6, 8
2776	A4	413	✓	✓	✓	D113	P2	L207	P4	1-6, 8
2778	C1	288	✓	✓		D120	P2			
2779	C3	282	✓	✓		D100	P2	L217	P3	1-8
2781	C3	125	✓	✓	✓	D121	P3	L230	P4	1-8
2785	A4	279	✓	✓		D100	P2	L220	P3	1-3, 5,6,8
2789	C1	261	✓	✓		D117	P3	L228	P3	1-8
2800	A3	79	✓	✓	✓	D113	P2	L220	P3	1-3, 5,6,8
2802	A3	188	✓	✓	✓	D118	P2	L220	P3	1-3, 5,6,8
2805	A4	199	✓	✓	✓	D113	P2	L220	P3	1-3, 5,6,8
2806	A3	199	✓	✓		D113	P2	L220	P3	1-3, 5,6,8
2810	A4	202	✓	✓	✓	D112	P2	L204	P3	1-3, 5,6,8
2818	A3	212	✓	✓	✓	D101	P2	L234	P3	1-8
2822	A3	120	✓	✓	✓			L229	P3	1-8
2826	A4	112	✓	✓	✓	D116	P2			
2832	C1	265	✓	✓		D113	P2			
2843	C2	480	✓	✓				L228	P3	1-8
2850	C3	290	✓	✓	✓	D122	P3	L236	P4	3,4,7
2851	C2	286	✓	✓	✓			L217	P3	1-8
2854	C1	139	✓	✓	✓	D112	P2	L220	P3	1-3, 5,6,8
2855	C2	77	✓	✓	✓	D103	P2	L219	P4	1-3, 5,6,8
2858	A4	266	✓	✓						
2864	A3	214	✓	✓	✓	D100	P2	L225	P3	1-3, 5,6,8
2867	A4	257	✓	✓				L220	P3	1-3, 5,6,8
2871	A4	208	✓	✓	✓	D117	P3			
2875	A4	465	✓	✓	✓	D113	P2	L236	P4	3,4,7
2877	C1	278	✓	✓		D114	P2	L200	P3	1-3, 5,6,8
2878	A4	222	✓	✓	✓	D112	P2	L200	P3	1-3, 5,6,8
2879	C3	259	✓	✓	✓					
2880	C2	249	✓	✓	✓	D114	P2	L212	P4	1-8
2888	C2	248	✓	✓				L211	P3	1-8
2889	L1	348	✓	✓	✓	D107	P3	L215	P4	1-6,8
2901	C1	298	✓	✓				L229	P3	1-8
2902	A4	182	✓	✓	✓			L234	P3	1-8
2905	A4	118	✓	✓	✓	D121	P3	L229	P3	1-8
2907	C1	411	✓	✓				L224	P3	1-3, 5,6,8
2908	C2	373	✓	✓	✓	D117	P3	L205	P3	1-3, 5,6,8
2911	A2	184	✓	✓						
2912	A4	463	✓	✓	✓					
2913	A4	213	✓	✓		D124	P3			
2915	C2	264		✓	✓	D114	P2	L212	P4	1-8
2916	A4	251		✓	✓			L221	P3	1-3, 5,6,8
2920	C4	128		✓	✓	D104	P3	L212	P4	1-8
2921	C4	159		✓	✓	D104	P3	L212	P4	1-8
2922	C4	468		✓	✓					
2925	A3	124		✓						
2926	C3	289		✓						
2927	C1	119		✓	✓	D100	P2			
2929	A3	190		✓						
2931	A4	250		✓						
2937	C3	297		✓	✓			L229	P3	1-8
2940	L3	328		✓	✓	D114	P2	L230	P4	1-8
2941	A3	185		✓		D112	P2			
2945	C1	381		✓	✓					
2946	C2	18		✓	✓	D114	P2	L207	P4	1-6,8
2947	A4	161		✓	✓	D112	P2	L200	P3	1-3, 5,6,8
2948	A4	462		✓	✓					
2949	C1	476		✓	✓					
2950	C2	464		✓	✓					
2951	L2	334		✓						
2952	L1	326		✓	✓			L235	P4	1-3, 5,6,8
2953	C4	323		✓	✓	D111	P3	L223	P4	1-3, 5,6,8
2954	C4	322		✓				L223	P4	1-3, 5,6,8
2955	L3	332		✓	✓					
2957	C4	330		✓		D107	P3	L218	P4	1-6,8
2959	A4	78		✓	✓					
2961	C1	277		✓						
2962	C1	275		✓	✓					
2964	A4	138		✓	✓					
2966	C3	335		✓						
2967	A4	136		✓	✓			L217	P3	1-8
2968	L2	324		✓	✓			L227	P4	1-8
2969	C2	358		✓		D110	P2	L223	P4	1-3, 5,6,8
2970	C3	359		✓	✓			L223	P4	1-3, 5,6,8
2971	C2	357		✓	✓			L223	P4	1-3, 5,6,8
2973	A4	362		✓	✓			L223	P4	1-3, 5,6,8
2974	A4	365		✓	✓			L223	P4	1-3, 5,6,8
2977	L1	341		✓	✓			L214	P4	1-3, 5,6,8
2979	C1	61		✓						
2981	L1	379		✓				L224	P3	1-3, 5,6,8
2984	L2	349		✓	✓			L214	P4	1-3, 5,6,8
2995	C3	158		✓	✓	D106	P3	L217	P3	1-8
3126	A3	156		✓		D114	P2	L203	P3	1-3, 5,6,8
3303	C4	352		✓	✓			L215	P4	1-6, 8
3304	C4	321		✓	✓			L209	P3	1-6, 8
3305	L1	325		✓						
3309	C1	21		✓	✓			L209	P3	1-6, 8
3310	C1	107		✓	✓	D111	P3	L227	P4	1-8
3311	C4	291		✓	✓	D109	P3	L220	P3	1-3, 5,6,8
3314	A4	224		✓	✓			L200	P3	1-3, 5,6,8
3316	A3	142		✓	✓			L202	P3	1-3, 5,6,8
3318	A4	143		✓	✓	D111	P3	L202	P3	1-3, 5,6,8
3322	C3	461		✓	✓	D118	P2	L234	P3	1-8
3325	C2	387		✓	✓	D100	P2	L238	P3	3,4,7,8
3327	C1	271		✓	✓	D110	P2	L217	P3	1-8
3328	C2	415		✓	✓					
3329	C2	474		✓	✓			L233	P3	3,4,7
3331	A3	140		✓	✓			L203	P3	1-3, 5,6,8
3332	C1	246		✓	✓			L200	P3	1-3, 5,6,8
3333	C1	62		✓	✓			L204	P3	1-3, 5,6,8
3337	C4	350		✓	✓			L214	P4	1-3, 5,6,8
3340	A4	201		✓	✓			L224	P3	1-3, 5,6,8
3342	A4	135		✓	✓			L217	P3	1-8
3344	C2	470		✓	✓			L211	P3	1-8
3345	A3	200		✓	✓			L220	P3	1-3, 5,6,8
3346	A4	274		✓	✓			L204	P3	1-3, 5,6,8
3348	C2	247		✓	✓			L200	P3	1-3, 5,6,8

DESIGN	PRICE	PAGE	MATERIALS LIST	CUSTOMIZABLE	QUOTE ONE®	DECK	DECK PRICE	LANDSCAPE	LANDSCAPE PRICE	REGIONS
3349	C4	351	✓	✓	✓	D107	P3	L216	P3	1-3, 5,6,8
3351	C1	137	✓	✓	✓	D115	P2	L209	P3	1-6, 8
3355	A2	223	✓	✓	✓	D117	P3	L220	P3	1-3, 5,6,8
3357	C1	273	✓	✓	✓	D115	P2	L211	P3	1-8
3360	L1	301	✓	✓	✓			L207	P4	1-6,8
3366	C2	300	✓	✓	✓			L220	P3	1-3, 5,6,8
3368	C1	281	✓	✓	✓	D104	P3	L220	P3	1-3, 5,6,8
3376	A3	209	✓	✓	✓	D114	P2	L205	P3	1-3, 5,6,8
3380	L1	327	✓	✓	✓					
3382	C1	364	✓	✓	✓	D110	P2	L202	P3	1-3, 5,6,8
3385	A3	368	✓	✓	✓	D100	P2	L207	P4	1-6,8
3397	C2	400	✓	✓	✓	D110	P2	L209	P3	1-6,8
3403	C3	113	✓	✓	✓			L237	P3	7
3405	C3	28	✓	✓	✓			L236	P4	3,4,7
3413	C1	437	✓	✓	✓			L238	P3	3,4,7,8
3414	C3	447	✓	✓	✓			L233	P3	3,4,7
3421	A4	450	✓	✓	✓			L328	P3	3,4,7,8
3423	C1	436	✓	✓	✓					
3425	C2	445	✓	✓	✓					
3429	C2	454	✓	✓	✓			L233	P3	3,4,7
3431	A4	473	✓	✓	✓					
3432	C2	477	✓	✓	✓			L233	P3	3,4,7
3433	C1	29	✓	✓	✓			L213	P4	1-8
3434	C2	475	✓	✓	✓			L233	P3	3,4,7
3436	C1	469	✓	✓	✓			L227	P4	1-8
3437	A4	479	✓	✓	✓			L212	P4	1-8
3440	A4	452	✓	✓	✓			L233	P3	3,4,7
3441	C1	455	✓	✓	✓			L239	P4	1-8
3442	A3	174	✓	✓	✓	D115	P2	L200	P3	1-3, 5,6,8
3454	A3	176	✓	✓	✓	D110	P2	L220	P3	1-3, 5,6,8
3456	A4	114	✓	✓	✓			L238	P3	3,4,7,8
3457	A4	459	✓	✓	✓			L217	P3	1-8
3458	C1	134	✓	✓	✓	D105	P2	L222	P3	1-3, 5,6,8
3460	A3	422	✓	✓				L200	P3	1-3, 5,6,8
3461	C1	414	✓	✓	✓			L204	P3	1-3, 5,6,8
3462	A4	388	✓	✓	✓			L207	P4	1-6, 8
3463	A4	458	✓		✓			L238	P3	3,4,7,8
3465	A2	225	✓	✓	✓			L205	P3	1-3, 5,6,8
3466	A3	416	✓	✓	✓	D110	P2	L207	P4	1-6, 8
3471	L1	23	✓	✓	✓			L236	P4	3,4,7
3480	C1	460	✓	✓	✓	D112	P2	L238	P3	3,4,7,8
3484	A4	111	✓	✓	✓	D105	P2	L200	P3	1-3, 5,6,8
3486	A3	472	✓	✓	✓					
3487	A4	183	✓	✓	✓			L209	P3	1-6, 8
3508	C3	63	✓	✓	✓			L206	P4	1-6,8
3558	C2	457	✓	✓	✓	D105	P2	L203	P3	1-3, 5,6,8
3559	C2	268	✓	✓	✓	D111	P3	L217	P3	1-8
3560	C1	269	✓	✓	✓			L234	P3	1-8
3562	A4	116	✓	✓	✓	D110	P2	L238	P3	3,4,7,8
3563	A3	117	✓	✓	✓	D115	P2	L233	P3	3,4,7
3569	A3	439	✓	✓	✓	D105	P2	L238	P3	3,4,7,8
3600	A4	244	✓	✓	✓			L200	P3	1-3, 5,6,8
3606	C2	160	✓	✓	✓	D110	P2	L224	P3	1-3, 5,6,8
3608	C3	409	✓	✓	✓			L223	P4	1-3, 5,6,8
3612	C2	340	✓	✓	✓			L206	P4	1-6, 8
3614	C2	408	✓	✓	✓	D111	P3	L209	P3	1-6, 8
3615	A3	375	✓	✓	✓			L200	P3	1-3, 5,6,8
3630	C3	467	✓	✓	✓			L209	P3	1-6, 8
3632	C2	466	✓	✓	✓			L237	P3	7
3636	C2	262	✓	✓	✓			L238	P3	3,4,7,8
3637	C3	263	✓	✓	✓			L235	P4	1-3, 5,6,8
3639	C2	478	✓	✓	✓			L217	P3	1-8
3658	A3	508	✓	✓	✓	D102	P2	L202	P3	1-3, 5,6,8
3700	A3	162	✓	✓						
3701	A3	226	✓	✓						
3704	A3	227	✓	✓						
3715	A4	151	✓	✓						
4015	A3	513	✓							
4027	A3	484	✓		✓					
4061	A3	481	✓	✓	✓	D115	P2			
4115	A4	295								
4153	A3	488	✓			D115	P2	L202	P3	1-3, 5,6,8
4287	A4	115	✓			D111	P3	L230	P4	1-8
4308	C2	293	✓					L231	P4	1-8
5501	C1	80	✓	✓	✓					
5502	C1	81	✓	✓	✓					
5503	C1	59	✓	✓	✓					
5504	C1	54	✓	✓	✓					
5505	C1	101	✓	✓	✓					
5506	C1	98	✓	✓	✓					
5507	A4	228	✓	✓	✓					
5508	A4	235	✓	✓	✓					
5509	A4	234	✓	✓	✓					
5511	C1	401	✓	✓	✓					
5512	C1	69	✓	✓	✓					
5513	C1	92	✓	✓	✓					
5514	A3	44	✓	✓	✓					
5515	A3	74	✓	✓	✓					
5516	A3	45	✓	✓	✓					
5517	C1	96	✓	✓	✓					
5518	C1	104	✓	✓	✓					
5519	C1	94	✓	✓	✓					
5521	C1	390	✓	✓	✓					
5522	C1	57	✓	✓	✓					
5523	C1	53	✓	✓	✓					
5524	C1	103	✓	✓	✓					
5525	A4	106	✓	✓	✓					
5526	C1	99	✓	✓	✓					
5527	C2	100	✓	✓	✓					
5528	C2	58	✓	✓	✓					
5529	C2	102	✓	✓	✓					
5531	A4	232	✓	✓	✓					
5532	A4	229	✓	✓	✓					
5533	A4	233	✓	✓	✓					
5534	C1	395	✓	✓	✓					
5535	C1	399	✓	✓	✓					
5536	C1	83	✓	✓	✓					
5537	A3	75	✓	✓	✓					
5538	A2	51	✓	✓	✓					
5539	A4	105	✓	✓	✓					
5541	C1	385	✓	✓	✓					
5542	C1	377	✓	✓	✓					
5543	C1	384	✓	✓	✓					
5544	A3	110	✓	✓	✓					
5545	A3	410	✓	✓	✓					
5546	A3	108	✓	✓	✓					
5547	C1	49	✓	✓	✓					
5548	C1	50	✓	✓	✓					
5549	C1	55	✓	✓	✓					
5551	A4	109	✓	✓	✓					
5552	A4	376	✓	✓	✓					
5553	A4	394	✓	✓	✓					
5554	C2	9	✓	✓	✓					
5555	C2	91	✓	✓	✓					
5556	C2	13	✓	✓	✓					
C120	A4	5								
Q202	A2	30	✓							
Q204	A3	489	✓							
Q205	A4	490	✓							
Q207	C1	495	✓							
Q208	C1	503	✓							
Q210	A4	485								
Q211	A4	497	✓							
Q212	C1	494								
Q216	A4	310	✓							
Q219	A4	402	✓							
Q221	A2	163	✓							
Q222	C1	428	✓							
Q223	C1	292	✓							
Q225	C1	314	✓							
Q226	C1	412	✓							
Q229	A2	238	✓							
Q230	C1	312	✓							
Q231	A4	86	✓							
Q233	C1	404	✓							
Q234	C1	39	✓							
Q235	C1	386								
Q237	C1	240	✓							
Q240	A4	215	✓							
Q241	A4	122	✓							
Q244	C3	284	✓							
Q246	A2	42	✓							
Q250	C1	426	✓							
Q251	A4	170	✓							
Q252	C1	425	✓							
Q253	A4	38	✓							

DESIGN	PRICE	PAGE	MATERIALS LIST	CUSTOMIZABLE	QUOTE ONE®	DECK	DECK PRICE	LANDSCAPE	LANDSCAPE PRICE	REGIONS
Q258	C1	34	✓							
Q259	C1	35	✓							
Q260	C1	374	✓							
Q262	A4	313	✓							
Q264	C1	306	✓							
Q265	C1	305	✓							
Q267	A2	36	✓							
Q268	C1	304	✓							
Q273	C1	423	✓							
Q275	A4	432	✓							
Q276	C1	56	✓							
Q277	C1	403	✓							
Q278	C1	283								
Q279	C1	90	✓							
Q282	C1	24	✓							
Q287	C1	448	✓							
Q288	C1	287	✓							
Q289	A2	311	✓							
Q290	C1	22	✓							
Q292	A4	491	✓							
Q295	C1	506	✓							
Q296	C1	175	✓							
Q297	C3	444	✓							
Q299	C3	17	✓							
Q300	C3	15	✓							
Q301	C1	93	✓							
Q302	C1	442	✓							
Q303	C4	260	✓							
Q304	C3	12	✓							
Q305	C3	4								
Q306	C4	333								
Q312	C1	307								
Q313	A2	429								
Q314	C1	435	✓							
Q318	A4	431	✓							
Q319	A4	434								
Q320	A4	167								
Q321	A4	166								
Q322	A4	130								
Q323	C1	181								
Q326	C1	456								
Q328	C3	16	✓							
Q329	C1	446	✓							
Q330	C1	443	✓							
Q332	C1	40	✓							
Q333	C1	355	✓							
Q334	C3	438	✓							
Q335	C3	393	✓							
Q338	A2	25	✓							
Q339	C1	308	✓							
Q341	C1	316	✓							
Q343	C1	173	✓							
Q344	A2	237	✓							
Q345	C1	179	✓							
Q346	C1	427	✓							
Q347	A2	372	✓							
Q352	A2	230	✓							
Q354	C1	451	✓							
Q355	C1	319	✓							
Q357	A3	48	✓							
Q360	C1	309	✓							
Q361	A4	430	✓							
Q362	A4	219	✓							
Q364	C1	220	✓							
Q365	C1	178	✓							
Q366	A4	218	✓							
Q367	A4	172	✓							
Q369	C1	236	✓							
Q371	C1	180	✓							
Q372	A4	433	✓							
Q373	A4	366	✓							
Q374	A4	367	✓							
Q375	A4	37	✓							
Q376	C1	10	✓							
Q377	C1	449	✓							
Q378	C1	369	✓							
Q380	C1	243	✓							
Q381	C1	354	✓							
Q384	C1	396	✓							
Q385	C3	133	✓							
Q386	C3	405	✓							
Q387	C1	270	✓							
Q388	C1	370	✓							
Q389	C3	392	✓							
Q390	C1	132	✓							
Q391	C1	241	✓							
Q392	C1	356	✓							
Q393	C1	398	✓							
Q395	C1	141	✓							
Q396	C1	129	✓							
Q397	C1	87	✓							
Q398	C1	360	✓							
Q400	C3	11	✓							
Q402	C1	353	✓							
Q404	C1	245	✓							
Q406	A4	20	✓							
Q407	A4	397	✓							
Q408	C3	242	✓							
Q409	C1	43	✓							
Q410	A4	95	✓							
Q411	C1	33	✓							
Q412	C3	363	✓							
Q413	C3	97	✓							
Q414	C3	453	✓							
Q416	C3	361	✓							
Q418	C1	440	✓							
Q419	C3	378	✓							
Q420	C3	441	✓							
Q421	A4	486	✓							
Q422	A4	487	✓							
Q423	C1	318	✓							
Q424	C1	500	✓							
Q426	C1	315	✓							
Q427	C1	177	✓							
Q428	C1	499	✓							
Q429	C1	31	✓							
Q430	C1	507	✓							
Q435	L1	32	✓							
Q436	C1	501	✓							
Q437	C1	498	✓							
Q438	C1	509	✓							
Q439	C1	505	✓							
Q440	C1	26	✓							
Q441	C1	420	✓							
Q443	C1	421	✓							
Q445	A2	424	✓							
Q446	C1	418	✓							
Q447	C1	419	✓							
Q448	A4	196	✓							
Q449	C1	417	✓							
Q451	C3	407	✓							
Q452	C3	389	✓							
Q454	C3	391	✓							
Q457	L1	7	✓							
Q467	C1	6	✓							
Q470	A2	27	✓							
Q472	C1	406	✓							
Q473	A4	14	✓							
Q477	C3	382	✓							
Q478	C1	317	✓							
Q479	C3	8	✓							
Q481	C1	383	✓							
Q482	C1	52	✓							
Q488	A2	121	✓							
Q490	A2	483	✓							
Q491	A2	502	✓							
Q495	C1	211	✓							
Q499	C1	504	✓							
Q501	C1	371	✓							
Q505	A2	221	✓							
Q508	A4	511	✓							
Q510	C1	41	✓							
Q513	A4	231	✓							
Q516	A4	510	✓							

Before You Order . . .

Before filling out the coupon at right or calling us on our Toll-Free Blueprint Hotline, you may want to learn more about our services and products. Here's some information you will find helpful.

Quick Turnaround

We process and ship every blueprint order from our office within two business days. Because of this quick turnaround, we won't send a formal notice acknowledging receipt of your order.

Our Exchange Policy

Since blueprints are printed in response to your order, we cannot honor requests for refunds. However, we will exchange your entire first order for an equal number of blueprints at a price of $50 for the first set and $10 for each additional set; $70 total exchange fee for 4 sets; $100 total exchange fee for 8 sets . . . *plus* the difference in cost if exchanging for a design in a higher price bracket or *less* the difference in cost if exchanging for a design in lower price bracket. One exchange is allowed within a year of purchase date. **(Sepias and reproducibles are not refundable, returnable or exchangeable.)** All sets from the first order must be returned before the exchange can take place. Please add $18 for postage and handling via Regular Service; $30 via Priority Service; $40 via Express Service. Returns and cancellations are subject to a 20% restocking fee, shipping and handling charges are not refundable.

About Reverse Blueprints

If you want to build in reverse of the plan as shown, we will include an extra set of reverse blueprints (mirror image) for an additional fee of $50. Although lettering and dimensions will appear backward, reverses will be a useful aid if you decide to flop the plan.

Revising, Modifying and Customizing Plans

The wide variety of designs available in this publication allows you to select ideas and concepts for a home to fit your building site and match your family's needs, wants and budget. Like many homeowners who buy these plans, you and your builder, architect or engineer may want to make changes to them. Some minor changes may be made by your builder, but we recommend that most changes be made by a licensed architect or engineer. If you need to make alterations to a design that is customizable, you need only order our Home Customizer® Package to get you started. As set forth below, we cannot assume any responsibility for blueprints which have been changed, whether by you, your builder or by professionals selected by you or referred to you by us, because such individuals are outside our supervision and control.

Architectural and Engineering Seals

Some cities and states are now requiring that a licensed architect or engineer review and "seal" a blueprint, or officially approve it, prior to construction due to concerns over energy costs, safety and other factors. Prior to application for a building permit or the start of actual construction, we strongly advise that you consult your local building official who can tell you if such a review is required.

About the Designers

The architects and designers whose work appears in this publication are among America's leading residential designers. Each plan was designed to meet the requirements of a nationally recognized model building code in effect at the time and place the plan was drawn. Because national building codes change from time to time, plans may not comply with any such code at the time they are sold to a customer. In addition, building officials may not accept these plans as final construction documents of record as the plans may need to be modified and additional drawings and details added to suit local conditions and requirements. We strongly advise that purchasers consult a licensed architect or engineer, and their local building official, before starting any construction related to these plans.

Local Building Codes and Zoning Requirements

At the time of creation, our plans are drawn to specifications published by the Building Officials and Code Administrators (BOCA) International, Inc.; the Southern Building Code Congress (SBCCI) International, Inc.; the International Conference of Building Officials; or the Council of American Building Officials (CABO). Our plans are designed to meet or exceed national building standards. Because of the great differences in geography and climate throughout the United States and Canada, each state, county and municipality has its own building codes, zone requirements, ordinances and building regulations. Your plan may need to be modified to comply with local requirements regarding snow loads, energy codes, soil and seismic conditions and a wide range of other matters. In addition, you may need to obtain permits or inspections from local governments before and in the course of construction. Prior to using blueprints ordered from us, we strongly advise that you consult a licensed architect or engineer—and speak with your local building official—before applying for any permit or beginning construction. We authorize the use of our blueprints on the express condition that you strictly comply with all local building codes, zoning requirements and other applicable laws, regulations, ordinances and requirements. **Notice:** Plans for homes to be built in Nevada must be redrawn by a Nevada-registered professional. Consult your building official for more information on this subject.

Foundation and Exterior Wall Changes

Most of our plans are drawn with either a full or partial basement foundation. Depending on your specific climate or regional building practices, you may wish to change this basement to a slab or crawlspace. Most professional contractors and builders can easily adapt your plans to alternate foundation types. Likewise, most can easily change 2x4 wall construction to 2x6, or vice versa.

Disclaimer

We and the designers we work with have put substantial care and effort into the creation of our blueprints. However, because we cannot provide on-site consultation, supervision and control over actual construction, and because of the great variance in local building requirements, building practices and soil, seismic, weather and other conditions, WE CANNOT MAKE ANY WARRANTY, EXPRESS OR IMPLIED, WITH RESPECT TO THE CONTENT OR USE OF OUR BLUEPRINTS, INCLUDING BUT NOT LIMITED TO ANY WARRANTY OF MERCHANTABILITY OR OF FITNESS FOR A PARTICULAR PURPOSE.

Terms and Conditions

These designs are protected under the terms of United States Copyright Law and may not be copied or reproduced in any way, by any means, unless you have purchased Sepias or Reproducibles which clearly indicate your right to copy or reproduce. We authorize the use of your chosen design as an aid in the construction of one single family home only. You may not use this design to build a second or multiple dwellings without purchasing another blueprint or blueprints or paying additional design fees.

How Many Blueprints Do You Need?

A single set of blueprints is sufficient to study a home in greater detail. However, if you are planning to obtain cost estimates from a contractor or subcontractors—or if you are planning to build immediately—you will need more sets. Because additional sets are cheaper when ordered in quantity with the original order, make sure you order enough blueprints to satisfy all requirements. The following checklist will help you determine how many you need:

___ Owner

___ Builder (generally requires at least three sets; one as a legal document, one to use during inspections, and at least one to give to subcontractors)

___ Local Building Department (often requires two sets)

___ Mortgage Lender (usually one set for a conventional loan; three sets for FHA or VA loans)

___ TOTAL NUMBER OF SETS

Toll Free 1-800-521-6797

Regular Office Hours:
8:00 a.m. to 8:00 p.m. Eastern Time, Monday through Friday
Our staff will gladly answer any questions during regular office hours. Our answering service can place orders after hours or on weekends.

If we receive your order by 4:00 p.m. Eastern Time, Monday through Friday, we'll process it and ship within two business days. When ordering by phone, please have your credit card ready. We'll also ask you for the Order Form Key Number at the bottom of the coupon.

By FAX: Copy the Order Form on the next page and send it on our FAX line: 1-800-224-6699 or 1-520-544-3086.

Canadian Customers
Order Toll-Free 1-877-223-6389

For faster service and plans that are modified for building in Canada, customers may now call in orders directly to our Canadian supplier of plans and charge the purchase to a credit card. Or, you may complete the order form at right, adding 40% to all prices and mail in Canadian funds to:

Home Planners Canada 301-611 Alexander Street
c/o Select Home Designs Vancouver, B.C., Canada
V6A 1E1

OR: Copy the Order Form and send it via our FAX line: 1-800-224-6699.

Have You Seen Our Newest Designs?

Home Planners is one of the country's most active home design firms, creating nearly 100 new plans each year. At least 50 of our latest creations are featured in each edition of our New Design Portfolio. You may have received a copy with your latest purchase by mail. If not, or if you purchased this book from a local retailer, just return the coupon below for your FREE copy. Make sure you consider the very latest of what Home Planners has to offer.

Yes! Please send my FREE copy of your latest New Design Portfolio.

Offer good to U.S. shipping address only.

Name ____________________

Address ____________________

City__________ State______ Zip ______

Order Form Key: TB59

HOME PLANNERS, LLC
Wholly owned by Hanley-Wood, Inc.
3275 WEST INA ROAD, SUITE 110
TUCSON, ARIZONA 85741

The Home Customizer® 

"This house is perfect...if only the family room were two feet wider." Sound familiar? In response to the numerous requests for this type of modification, Home Planners has developed **The Home Customizer® Package**. This exclusive package offers our top-of-the-line materials to make it easy for anyone, anywhere to customize any Home Planners design to fit their needs. Check the index on pages 520-523 for those plans which are customizable.

Some of the changes you can make to any of our plans include:

- exterior elevation changes
- kitchen and bath modifications
- roof, wall and foundation changes
- room additions and more!

The Home Customizer® Package includes everything you'll need to make the necessary changes to your favorite Home Planners design. The package includes:

- instruction book with examples
- architectural scale and clear work film
- erasable red marker and removable correction tape
- 1/4"-scale furniture cutouts
- 1 set reproducible, erasable Sepias
- 1 set study blueprints for communicating changes to your design professional
- a copyright release letter so you can make copies as you need them
- referral letter with the name, address and telephone number of the professional in your region who is trained in modifying Home Planners designs efficiently and inexpensively.

The price of the **Home Customizer® Package** ranges from $650 to $1350, depending on the price schedule of the design you have chosen. **The Home Customizer® Package** will not only save you 25% to 75% of the cost of drawing the plans from scratch with a custom architect or engineer, it will also give you the flexibility to have your changes and modifications made by our referral network or by the professional of your choice. Now it's even easier and more affordable to have the custom home you've always wanted.

ORDER TOLL FREE!
For information about any of our services or to order call 1-800-521-6797 or 520-297-8200
Browse our website: www.homeplanners.com

BLUEPRINTS ARE NOT REFUNDABLE
EXCHANGES ONLY

For Customer Service, call toll free 1-888-690-1116.

ORDER FORM

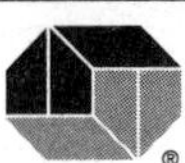

HOME PLANNERS, LLC
Wholly owned by Hanley-Wood, Inc.
3275 WEST INA ROAD, SUITE 110
TUCSON, ARIZONA 85741

THE BASIC BLUEPRINT PACKAGE
Rush me the following (please refer to the Plans Index and Price Schedule in this section):

_____ Set(s) of blueprints for plan number(s) __________. $_______
_____ Set(s) of sepias for plan number(s) __________. $_______
_____ Home Customizer® Package for plan(s)__________. $_______
_____ Additional identical blueprints in same order @ $50 per set. $_______
_____ Reverse blueprints @ $50 per set. $_______

IMPORTANT EXTRAS
Rush me the following:

_____ Materials List: $50 (Must be purchased with Blueprint set.) $75 Design Basics.Add $10 for a Schedule C4-L4 plan. $_______
_____ **Quote One®** Summary Cost Report @ $29.95 for 1, $14.95 for each additional, for plans __________ $_______
Building location: City __________ Zip Code __________
_____ **Quote One®** Materials Cost Report @ $120 Schedule P1-C3; $130 Schedules C4-L4 for plan__________ $_______
(Must be purchased with Blueprints set.)
Building location: City __________ Zip Code __________
_____ Specification Outlines @ $10 each. $_______
_____ Detail Sets @ $14.95 each; any two for $22.95; any three for $29.95; all four for $39.95 (save $19.85). $_______
❑ Plumbing ❑ Electrical ❑ Construction ❑ Mechanical
(These helpful details provide general construction advice and are not specific to any single plan.)
_____ Plan-A-Home® @ $29.95 each. $_______

DECK BLUEPRINTS

_____ Set(s) of Deck Plan __________. $_______
_____ Additional identical blueprints in same order @ $10 per set. $_______
_____ Reverse blueprints @ $10 per set. $_______
_____ Set of Standard Deck Details @ $14.95 per set. $_______
_____ Set of Complete Building Package (Best Buy!) Includes Custom Deck Plan __________. (See Index and Price Schedule) Plus Standard Deck Details $_______

LANDSCAPE BLUEPRINTS

_____ Set(s) of Landscape Plan __________. $_______
_____ Additional identical blueprints in same order @ $10 per set. $_______
_____ Reverse blueprints @ $10 per set. $_______

Please indicate the appropriate region of the country for Plant & Material List. (See Map on page 519): Region _______

POSTAGE AND HANDLING	1–3 sets	4+ sets
Signature is required for all deliveries.		
DELIVERY NO CODS (Requires street address–No P.O. Boxes)		
•Regular Service (Allow 7–10 business days delivery)	❑ $15.00	❑ $18.00
•Priority (Allow 4–5 business days delivery)	❑ $20.00	❑ $30.00
•Express (Allow 3 business days delivery)	❑ $30.00	❑ $40.00
CERTIFIED MAIL	❑ $20.00	❑ $30.00
If no street address available. (Allow 7–10 days delivery)		
OVERSEAS DELIVERY Note: All delivery times are from date Blueprint Package is shipped.	fax, phone or mail for quote	

POSTAGE (From box above) $_______
SUBTOTAL $_______
SALES TAX (AZ, MI, & WA residents, please add appropriate state and local sales tax.) $_______
TOTAL (Subtotal and tax) $_______

YOUR ADDRESS (please print)
Name __________
Street __________
City __________ State __________ Zip __________
Daytime telephone number (_____) __________

FOR CREDIT CARD ORDERS ONLY
Please fill in the information below:
Credit card number __________
Exp. Date: Month/Year __________
Check one ❑ Visa ❑ MasterCard ❑ Discover Card ❑ American Express

Signature __________

Please check appropriate box: ❑ Licensed Builder-Contractor ❑ Homeowner

ORDER TOLL FREE!
1-800-521-6797 or 520-297-8200

Order Form Key
TB59

Helpful Books & Software

Home Planners wants your building experience to be as pleasant and trouble-free as possible. That's why we've expanded our library of Do-It-Yourself titles to help you along. In addition to our beautiful plans books, we've added books to guide you through specific projects as well as the construction process. In fact, these are titles that will be as useful after your dream home is built as they are right now.

ONE-STORY

ONE-STORY HOMES

1 448 designs for all lifestyles. 860 to 5,400 square feet.
384 pages $9.95

TWO-STORY

TWO-STORY HOMES

2 460 designs for one-and-a-half and two stories. 1,245 to 7,275 square feet.
384 pages $9.95

VACATION

VACATION & SECOND HOMES

3 345 designs for recreation, retirement and leisure.
312 pages $8.95

MULTI-LEVEL

HILLSIDE HOMES

4 214 designs for split-levels, bi-levels, multi-levels and walkouts.
224 pages $8.95

COUNTRY

200 FARMHOUSE & COUNTRY HOME PLANS

5 200 country designs from classic to contemporary by 7 winning designers.
224 pages $8.95

MOVE-UP

200 MOVE-UP

6 200 stylish designs for today's growing families from 9 hot designers.
224 pages $8.95

NARROW-LOT

200 NARROW-LOT HOME PLANS

7 200 unique homes less than 60' wide from 7 designers. Up to 3,000 square feet.
224 pages $8.95

SMALL HOUSE

SMALL HOUSE PLANS

8 200 beautiful designs chosen for versatility and affordability.
224 pages $8.95

BUDGET-SMART

200 BUDGET-SMART HOME PLANS

9 200 efficient plans from 7 top designers, that you can really afford to build!
224 pages $8.95

EXPANDABLES

200 EXPANDABLE HOME PLANS

10 200 flexible plans that expand with your needs from 7 top designers.
240 pages $8.95

ENCYCLOPEDIA

ENCYCLOPEDIA OF HOME DESIGNS
500 House Plans
New Revised Edition!

11 500 exceptional plans for all styles and budgets—the best book of its kind!
352 pages $9.95

AFFORDABLE

AFFORDABLE HOME PLANS
300 HOME DESIGNS FOR MODEST & MEDIUM BUDGETS

12 Completely revised and updated, featuring 300 designs for modest budgets.
256 pages $9.95

ENCYCLOPEDIA 2

ENCYCLOPEDIA OF HOME DESIGNS VOLUME II

13 500 completely new plans. Spacious and stylish designs for every budget and taste.
352 pages $9.95

VICTORIAN

Victorian DREAM HOMES

14 160 striking Victorian and Farmhouse designs from three leading designers.
192 pages $12.95

ESTATE

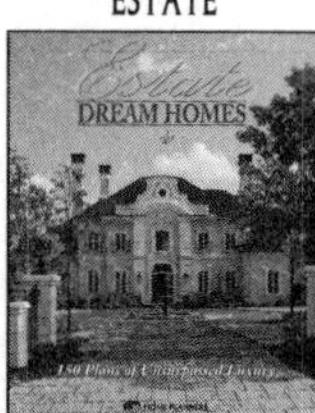
Estate DREAM HOMES

15 Dream big! Twenty-one designers showcase their biggest and best plans.
208 pages. $15.95

LUXURY

Luxury DREAM HOMES

16 154 fine luxury plans—loaded with luscious amenities!
192 pages $14.95

COTTAGES

Cottages
The Sater Design Collection

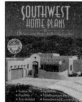

17 25 fresh new designs that are as warm as a tropical breeze. A blend of the best aspects of many coastal styles.
64 pages. $19.95

BEST SELLERS

HOME PLANNERS Gold

18 Our 50th Anniversary book with 200 of our very best designs in full color!
224 pages $12.95

SPECIAL COLLECTION

THE DESIGNS OF WILLIAM E. POOLE

19 70 romantic house plans that capture the classic tradition of home design.
160 pages $17.95

COUNTRY HOUSES

Country Houses

20 208 unique home plans that combine traditional style and modern livability.
224 pages $9.95

CLASSIC

CLASSIC HOME PLANS

21 Timeless, elegant designs that always feel like home. Gorgeous plans that are as flexible and up-to-date as their occupants.
240 pages. $9.95

CONTEMPORARY

CONTEMPORARY Home Plans

22 The most complete and imaginative collection of contemporary designs available anywhere.
240 pages. $9.95

EASY-LIVING

EASY-LIVING HOMES
200

23 200 efficient and sophisticated plans that are small in size, but big on livability.
224 pages $8.95

SOUTHERN

SOUTHERN Home Plans

24 207 homes rich in Southern styling and comfort.
240 pages $8.95

SUNBELT

25 215 designs that capture the spirit of the Southwest.
208 pages $10.95

WESTERN

26 215 designs that capture the spirit and diversity of the Western lifestyle.
208 pages $9.95

ENERGY GUIDE

RESIDENTIAL ENERGY

27 The most comprehensive energy efficiency and conservation guide available.
280 pages $35.00

Design Software

BOOK & CD ROM

HOME PLANNERS Gold

28 Both the Home Planners Gold book and matching Windows™ CD ROM with 3D floorplans.
$24.95

3D DESIGN SUITE

PLANIX HOME Design Suite 3D

29 Home design made easy! View designs in 3D, take a virtual reality tour, add decorating details and more. $59.95

Outdoor Projects

OUTDOOR

YARD & GARDEN STRUCTURES

30 42 unique outdoor projects. Gazebos, strombellas, bridges, sheds, playsets and more!
96 pages $7.95

GARAGES & MORE

GREAT GARAGES
Sheds & Outdoor Buildings

31 101 multi-use garages and outdoor structures to enhance any home.
96 pages $7.95

DECKS

DECK PLANNER

32 25 outstanding single-, double- and multi-level decks you can build.
112 pages $7.95

Landscape Designs

EASY CARE

EASY-CARE LANDSCAPE PLANS

33 41 special landscapes designed for beauty and low maintenance.
160 pages $14.95

FRONT & BACK

THE HOME LANDSCAPER

34 The first book of do-it-yourself landscapes. 40 front, 15 backyards.
208 pages $14.95

BACKYARDS

THE BACKYARD LANDSCAPER
40 Professional Designs For Do-It-Yourselfers

35 40 designs focused solely on creating your own specially themed backyard oasis.
160 pages $14.95

BEDS & BORDERS

Beds & Borders
40 PROFESSIONAL DESIGNS FOR DO-IT-YOURSELFERS

36 Practical advice and maintenance techniques for a wide variety of yard projects.
160 pages. $14.95

BATHROOMS

CREATIVE HOMEOWNER PRESS
DESIGNING AND PLANNING BATHROOMS

37 An innovative guide to organizing, remodeling and decorating your bathroom.
96 pages $10.95

KITCHENS

CREATIVE HOMEOWNER PRESS
KITCHENS
Design • Remodel • Build

38 An imaginative guide to designing the perfect kitchen. Chock full of bright ideas to make your job easier. 176 pages $14 .95

HOUSE CONTRACTING

3rd Edition
Be Your Own HOUSE CONTRACTOR
Save 25% without Lifting a Hammer
CARL HELDMANN

39 Everything you need to know to act as your own general contractor...and save up to 25% off building costs.
134 pages $14.95

WINDOWS & DOORS

CREATIVE HOMEOWNER PRESS
QUICK GUIDE
WINDOWS & DOORS

40 Installation techniques and tips that make your project easier and more professional looking. 80 pages $7.95

ROOFING

CREATIVE HOMEOWNER PRESS
QUICK GUIDE
ROOFING

41 Information on the latest tools, materials and techniques for roof installation or repair.
80 pages $7.95

FRAMING

RESIDENTIAL FRAMING
A HOMEBUILDER'S CONSTRUCTION GUIDE
William P. Spence

42 For those who want to take a more-hands on approach to their dream.
319 pages $19.95

VISUAL HANDBOOK

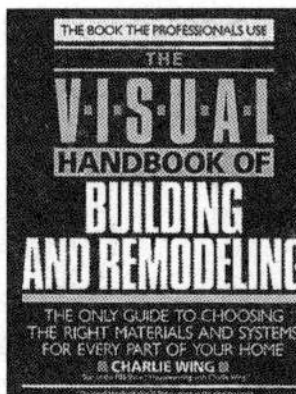
THE BOOK THE PROFESSIONALS USE
THE VISUAL HANDBOOK OF BUILDING AND REMODELING
THE ONLY GUIDE TO CHOOSING THE RIGHT MATERIALS AND SYSTEMS FOR EVERY PART OF YOUR HOME
CHARLIE WING

43 A plain-talk guide to the construction process; financing to final walk-through, this book covers it all. 498 pages $19.95

BASIC WIRING

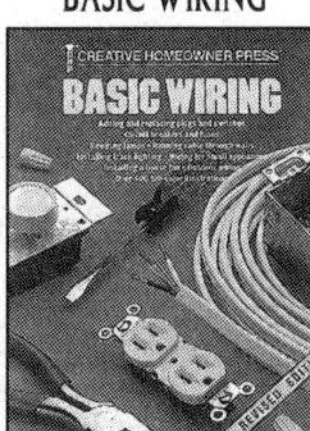
CREATIVE HOMEOWNER PRESS
BASIC WIRING

44 A straight forward guide to one of the most misunderstood systems in the home.
160 pages $12.95

PATIOS & WALKS

CREATIVE HOMEOWNER PRESS
QUICK GUIDE
PATIOS & WALKS

45 Clear step-by-step instructions take you from the basic design stages to the finished project.
80 pages $7.95

TILE

Working with TILE

46 Every kind of tile for every kind of application. Includes tips on use installation and repair.
176 pages $12.95

TRIM & MOLDING

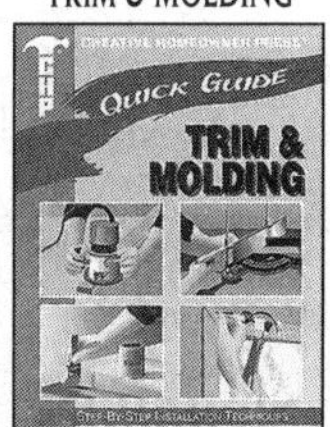
CREATIVE HOMEOWNER PRESS
QUICK GUIDE
TRIM & MOLDING

47 Step-by-step instructions for installing baseboards, window and door casings and more. 80 pages $7.95

Additional Books Order Form

To order your books, just check the box of the book numbered below and complete the coupon. We will process your order and ship it from our office within 48 hours. Send coupon and check (in U.S. funds).

YES! Please send me the books I've indicated:

☐ 1:VO	$9.95	☐ 25:SW	$10.95
☐ 2:VT	$9.95	☐ 26:WH	$9.95
☐ 3:VH	$8.95	☐ 27:RES	$35.00
☐ 4:VS	$8.95	☐ 28:HPGC	$24.95
☐ 5:FH	$8.95	☐ 29:PLANSUITE	$59.95
☐ 6:MU	$8.95	☐ 30:YG	$7.95
☐ 7:NL	$8.95	☐ 31:GG	$7.95
☐ 8:SM	$8.95	☐ 32:DP	$7.95
☐ 9:BS	$8.95	☐ 33:ECL	$14.95
☐ 10:EX	$8.95	☐ 34:HL	$14.95
☐ 11:EN	$9.95	☐ 35:BYL	$14.95
☐ 12:AF	$9.95	☐ 36:BB	$14.95
☐ 13:E2	$9.95	☐ 37:CDB	$10.95
☐ 14:VDH	$12.95	☐ 38:CKI	$14.95
☐ 15:EDH	$15.95	☐ 39:SBC	$14.95
☐ 16:LD2	$14.95	☐ 40:CGD	$7.95
☐ 17:CTG	$19.95	☐ 41:CGR	$7.95
☐ 18:HPG	$12.95	☐ 42:SRF	$19.95
☐ 19:WEP	$17.95	☐ 43:RVH	$19.95
☐ 20:CN	$9.95	☐ 44:CBW	$12.95
☐ 21:CS	$9.95	☐ 45:CGW	$7.95
☐ 22:CM	$9.95	☐ 46:CWT	$12.95
☐ 23:EL	$8.95	☐ 47:CGT	$7.95
☐ 24:SH	$8.95		

Canadian Customers
Order Toll-Free 1-877-223-6389

Additional Books Subtotal $______
ADD Postage and Handling $ 4.00
Sales Tax: (AZ, MI, & WA residents, please add appropriate state and local sales tax.) $______
YOUR TOTAL (Subtotal, Postage/Handling, Tax) $______

YOUR ADDRESS (Please print)

Name ______________________________

Street ______________________________

City ______________ State ________ Zip ____________

Phone (______) ____________ — ____________

YOUR PAYMENT
Check one: ☐ Check ☐ Visa ☐ MasterCard ☐ Discover Card ☐ American Express
Required credit card information:
Credit Card Number ______________________________

Expiration Date (Month/Year) __________/__________

Signature Required ______________________________

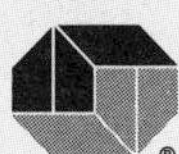

Home Planners, LLC
Wholly owned by Hanley-Wood, Inc.
3275 W. Ina Road, Suite 110, Dept. BK, Tucson, AZ 85741

TB59

Design 3608, page 409

OVER 3 MILLION BLUEPRINTS SOLD

"We instructed our builder to follow the plans including all of the many details which make this house so elegant…Our home is a fine example of the results one can achieve by purchasing and following the plans which you offer…Everyone who has seen it has assured us that it belongs in 'a picture book.' I truly mean it when I say that my home 'is a DREAM HOUSE.' "

S.P.
Anderson, SC

"We have had a steady stream of visitors, many of whom tell us this is the most beautiful home they've seen. Everyone is amazed at the layout and remarks on how unique it is. Our real estate attorney, who is a Chicago dweller and who deals with highly valued properties, told me this is the only suburban home he has seen that he would want to live in."

W. & P.S.
Flossmoor, IL

"Your blueprints saved us a great deal of money. I acted as the general contractor and we did a lot of the work ourselves. We probably built it for half the cost! We are thinking about more plans for another home. I purchased a competitor's book but my husband wants only your plans!"

K.M.
Grovetown, GA

"We are very happy with the product of our efforts. The neighbors and passersby appreciate what we have created. We have had many people stop by to discuss our house and kindly praise it as being the nicest house in our area of new construction. We have even had one person stop and make us an unsolicited offer to buy the house for much more than we have invested in it."

K. & L.S.
Bolingbrook, IL

"The traffic going past our house is unbelievable. On several occasions, we have heard that it is the 'prettiest house in Batavia.' Also, when meeting someone new and mentioning what street we live on, quite often we're told, 'Oh, you're the one in the yellow house with the wrap-around porch! I love it!' "

A.W.
Batavia, NY

"I have been involved in the building trades my entire life…Since building our home we have built two other homes for other families. Their plans from local professional architects were not nearly as good as yours. For that reason we are ordering additional plan books from you."

T.F.
Kingston, WA

"The blueprints we received from you were of excellent quality and provided us with exactly what we needed to get our successful home-building project underway. We appreciate your invaluable role in our home-building effort."

T.A.
Concord, TN